Organization Development and Change

SEVENTH EDITION

Organization Development and Change

SEVENTH EDITION

Thomas G. Cummings
University of Southern California

Christopher G. Worley
Pepperdine University

South-Western College Publishing
Thomson Learning™

Australia • Canada • Mexico • Singapore • Spain • United Kingdom • United States

Organization Development & Change, 7e,
by Thomas G. Cummings & Christopher G. Worley

Vice President/Publisher: Jack W. Calhoun
Executive Editor: John Szilagyi
Marketing Manager: Rob Bloom
Developmental Editor: Denise Simon
Production Editor: Elizabeth A. Shipp
Media Production Editor: Kristen Meere
Manufacturing Coordinator: Sandee Milewski
Internal Design: Jennifer Martin Lambert
Cover Design: Jennifer Martin Lambert
Cover Illustration: ©1999, PhotoDisc, Inc.
Production House: UpperCase Publication Services, Ltd.
Printer: Westgroup

Printed in the United States of America
 2 3 4 5 03 02

For more information contact South-Western College Publishing
5191 Natorp Road, Mason, Ohio, 45040
or find us on the Internet at http://www.swcollege.com

For permission to use material from this text or product, contact us by
- **telephone: 1-800-730-2214**
- **fax: 1-800-730-2215**
- **Web: http://www.thomsonrights.com**

Library of Congress Cataloging-in-Publication Data

This book is printed on acid-free paper.

To the ones who mentored us:

Will McWhinney, Eric Trist, and Warren Bennis

Jon Atzet, Walter Ross, Pat Williams, and Tom Cummings

Brief Contents

Contents

Part 3
HUMAN PROCESS INTERVENTIONS   215

Part 4

TECHNOSTRUCTURAL INTERVENTIONS   279

Part 5
HUMAN RESOURCES MANAGEMENT INTERVENTIONS   379

Part 6
STRATEGIC INTERVENTIONS   469

Part 7
SPECIAL APPLICATIONS OF ORGANIZATION DEVELOPMENT   553

Preface

This is the seventh edition of a text about organization development (OD). OD is the application of behavioral science knowledge to improve organization performance and organization functioning. The distinction between performance and functioning never has been more important. OD's behavioral science orientation traditionally resulted in more attention to functioning than to performance. Armed with a set of humanistic values and concerned with the unintended negative social consequences of bureaucratic organizations, OD offered a *process* for making the organization more hospitable to people. But it usually stopped short of trying to improve performance; it was enough to say that the organization had become more human.

OD, in that context, is increasingly challenged as irrelevant. It often helps people see the situation more clearly or makes people feel better, but questions linger regarding its ability to influence organization effectiveness and performance. Moreover, the prevalence of fast-paced Internet companies and the emergence of a global, knowledge-based economy have led to pronouncements that leading-edge organizations are the ones creating change. People who profess the ability to manage change are part of the crowd to be left in the dust. OD, therefore, stands at a crossroads. Will it cling to its humanistic traditions and focus on functioning or increase its relevance by integrating more performance-related values? How will it incorporate values related to globalization, cultural integration, the concentration of wealth, and environmental sustainability? Can it afford not to address the issues that threaten an organization's survival? These are heady questions for a field barely fifty years old.

The original edition of this text, authored by OD pioneer Edgar Huse in 1975, became a market leader because it faced the relevance issue. It took an objective, research perspective and placed OD practice on stronger theoretical footing. Ed showed that, in some cases, OD did produce meaningful results but that additional work was still needed. Sadly, Ed passed away following publication of the second edition. His wife Mary Huse and West Publishing (now South-Western/Thomson Learning) asked Tom Cummings to revise the book for subsequent editions. With the fifth edition, Tom asked Chris Worley to work with him in writing the text.

The most recent editions have had an important influence on the perception of OD. While maintaining the book's strengths of even treatment and unbiased reporting, the newer editions made even larger strides in placing OD on a strong theoretical foundation. The third and fourth editions broadened the scope and increased the relevance of OD by including interventions that had a *content* component, including work design, employee involvement, and organization structure. The fifth and sixth editions took another step toward relevance and suggested that OD had begun to incorporate a strategic perspective. This strategic orientation proposed that OD could be as concerned with performance issues as it was with human potential. Effective OD, from this newer perspective, relied as much on knowledge about organization theory and economics as it did on the behavioral sciences. It is our greatest hope that the current edition continues this tradition of rigor and relevance.

REVISIONS IN THE SEVENTH EDITION

Our goal in the seventh edition is to update the field once again. Although we have retained several features of the original text, we have made some important changes.

Organizing as a Competitive Advantage

The concept of organization design remains an important feature of strategy implementation and competitive advantage. In line with this trend, we have revised and emphasized organization-level issues throughout the text. In Part 2, the Process of Organization Development, a chapter is devoted to diagnosing strategy and organization design. In Part 3, coverage of large-group interventions that focus on organizationwide problems and issues has been given a major overhaul and infused with a strategic perspective. In Part 4, Chapter 14, Restructuring Organizations, briefly describes traditional structures and more thoroughly covers network structures and team-based or process-based organizations. In response to feedback from users, the chapter also describes downsizing and reengineering interventions. The entire chapter is written with a strategic emphasis. Descriptions of other technostructural interventions, such as parallel structures, high-involvement organizations, total quality management, and self-managing teams, have been thoroughly updated. In Part 6, a new section on OD in mergers and acquisitions has been added to the chapter on organization and environment relationships, and the chapter on organization transformation has received an important overhaul. There is a new section on organization learning and knowledge management.

An Emphasis on OD in Different Settings

Several reviewers of the fifth and sixth editions commented on the growing influence of OD in international and nonprofit settings. We responded to those comments in several ways. First, we revised the chapter on international OD. Although much continues to be written about OD in cross-cultural settings, the primary emphasis in the literature is on the diffusion of OD techniques to a particular country. There remains a dearth of research describing *how* OD is practiced in different cultures. We distilled the available literature into a state-of-the-art description of OD's application in three different contexts: in different countries and cultures, in organizations that operate on a worldwide basis, and in global social change organizations. Second, as each intervention is discussed in the main body of the text, we have referred the reader to relevant international and nonprofit applications or research. Third, we revised the chapter about OD in nonprofit settings. The section describing OD in the government and the public sector is new, and the section about OD in health care has been updated.

The Early Phases of OD

In this edition, we revised earlier chapters to integrate more thoroughly the history of OD and make the intervention chapters more efficient. First, the introductory chapter has been modified by integrating background material, previously discussed in the intervention chapters, into the history of OD. Second, the chapter on theories of planned change has been thoroughly revised and placed immediately after the introductory chapter so that students get an immediate introduction to the process of change. In addition, the chapter has been updated to reflect the important work on social constructionism and the more positive and participatory processes of change. Third, the chapters in Part 2, the Process of Organization Development, now describe a complete cycle of change, from entry and contracting to evaluation and institutionalization. These changes have made the chapters focusing on interventions more content driven.

The Future of OD

We have added a new chapter to the end of the book. Chapter 23, Future Directions in Organization Development, examines the emerging context of OD and the potential influence of several trends on OD practice. The interrelated changes in the economy, technology, the workforce, and organizations provide an important crossroads for the content, process, and values of the field.

DISTINGUISHING PEDAGOGICAL FEATURES

The text is designed to facilitate the learning of organization development theory and interventions. We kept the chapter sequence from the previous edition. Based on feedback from reviewers, this format more closely matches the OD process. Professors can teach the process and then link OD practice to the interventions.

Organization

The seventh edition is organized into seven parts. Following an introductory chapter, Part 2 provides an overview of organization development. It discusses the fundamental theories that underlie planned change (Chapter 2) and describes the people who practice it (Chapter 3). Part 3 is an eight-chapter description of the process of planned change. It describes how OD practitioners enter and contract with client systems (Chapter 4); diagnose organizations, groups, and jobs (Chapters 5 and 6); collect, analyze, and feed back diagnostic data (Chapters 7 and 8); design interventions (Chapter 9); lead and manage change (Chapter 10); and evaluate and institutionalize change (Chapter 11). In this manner, professors can focus on the OD process without distraction. Parts 3, 4, 5, and 6 then cover the major OD interventions used today according to the same classification scheme used in previous editions of the text. Part 3 covers human process interventions; Part 4 describes technostructural approaches; Part 5 presents interventions in human resources management; and Part 6 addresses strategic change interventions. In the final section, Part 7, we cover special applications of OD, including international OD (Chapter 21); OD in health care, schools, and the public sector (Chapter 22); and the future of OD (Chapter 23). We believe this ordering provides professors with more flexibility in teaching OD.

Applications

Within each chapter, we describe actual situations in which different OD techniques or interventions were used. These applications provide students with a chance to see how OD is actually practiced in organizations. In the sixth edition, more than 60 percent of the applications were new. In the seventh edition, more than 40 percent of the applications are new and many others have been updated to maintain the text's relevance. In response to feedback from reviewers, almost all of the new applications describe a real situation in a real organization (although sometimes we felt it necessary to use disguised names). Each situation is one in which we or our practicing students have been involved, or one that has been described in the popular or research literature. In many cases, the organizations are large and readily recognizable public companies.

Cases

At the end of each major part in the book, we have included cases to permit a more in-depth discussion of the OD process. Three of the fifteen cases are new to the seventh edition. We have kept those cases that have been favorites over the years, as well as several of the favorably received cases introduced in the last edition. Also in response to feedback from users of the text, we have endeavored to provide cases that vary in levels of detail, complexity, and sophistication to offer professors some flexibility in teaching the material to either undergraduate or graduate students.

Internet Resources

Throughout the book we have provided references to the World Wide Web and to sites related to the organizations discussed. Although these sites are often updated, moved, or abandoned altogether (so we can't guarantee that the links will be maintained as cited), these give students an opportunity to explore the information available on the Internet.

Audience

This book can be used in a number of different ways and by a variety of people. First, it serves as a primary textbook in organization development for students at both the graduate and undergraduate levels. Second, the book can serve as an independent study guide for people wishing to learn more about how organization development can improve productivity and human satisfaction. Third, the book is valuable to OD professionals, managers, and administrators, specialists in such fields as personnel, training, occupational stress, and human resources management, and anyone interested in the complex process known as organization development.

EDUCATIONAL AIDS AND SUPPLEMENTS

Instructor's Manual with Test Bank (ISBN: 0-324-01988-2)

An instructor's manual is available to assist instructors in the delivery of a course on organization development. The instructor's manual has been revised thoroughly in response to feedback from users. The manual contains important material that can improve the student's appreciation of OD and improve the professor's effectiveness in the classroom.

Chapter Objectives and Lecture Notes

For each chapter, summary learning objectives provide a quick orientation to the chapter's material. The material in the chapter is outlined and comments are made concerning important pedagogical points, such as crucial assumptions that should be noted for students, important aspects of practical application, and alternative points of view that might be used to enliven class discussion.

Exam Questions

A variety of multiple choice, true/false, and essay questions are suggested for each chapter. Instructors can use these questions directly with their students, or they may find that the questions suggest additional questions that reflect the professor's own style.

Case Notes

For each case in the text, teaching notes have been developed to assist instructors in preparing for case discussions. The notes provide an outline of the case, suggestions about where to place the case during the course, discussion questions to focus student attention, and analysis of the case situation. In combination with the professor's own insights, the notes can help to enliven the case discussion or role playing.

Audiovisual Materials

Finally, a list is included comprising films, videos, and other materials that can be used to supplement different parts of the text, along with the addresses and phone numbers of vendors who supply the materials.

Video (ISBN: 0-324-06784-4)

A new video library is available to users of the seventh edition to show how organizations and leaders apply organization development to the real world. A tape of Video Examples examines a range of issues. Critical thinking questions appear at appropriate intervals in the ten- to fifteen-minute-long segments.

PowerPoint™ Presentation Slides (ISBN: 0-324-01989-0)

The PowerPoint presentation package consists of tables and figures used in the book. These colorful slides can greatly aid the integration of text material during lectures and discussions.

Web Site

A rich Web site at http://cummings.swcollege.com complements the text, providing many extras for the student.

ACKNOWLEDGMENTS

At the risk of being arrogant (which, to our friends and colleagues, is no risk at all because they know we are), we are proud of this book. Every few years we get the chance to think about a field we believe has relevance and communicate to others what the field is about. That's a lot of fun. This is our third collaboration on the text and although our relationship continues to evolve, one thing has remained constant over time: Clear and concise writing is our passion. We argue over the right word in the right place; we can often finish each other's sentences; we agreed with the criticism that our paragraphs consisted of short, declarative sentences and thought we were being complimented (with a nod to Strunk and White's *Elements of Style*); and we are all too familiar with the admonishment that "there's no such thing as good writing, only good rewriting." But all of the discussions, editing, proofing, and researching do take their toll. We're glad to be done again.

Although it's rewarding to be finished, we would be remiss if we did not acknowledge those who assisted us along the way. To recognize everyone by name is impossible, but we are deeply grateful to and for our families: Nancy, Sarah, and Seth, and Debbie, Sarah, Hannah, and Samuel. We would like to thank our colleagues and students at the University of Southern California and Pepperdine University for their comments on the previous edition and for helping us try out new ideas and perspectives. A particular word of thanks goes to Gordon Brooks and Peggy Sue Sherman, who took on additional tasks to help us prepare the manuscript, collect data, and generally protect us so we could write. Xochitl Boehm and Christine Mattos graciously performed the task of tracking down recent research and wrote several applications. As well, the following people reviewed the text and influenced our thinking with their honest and constructive feedback:

Jim Eubanks   *Central Washington University*
Charles E. List   *Metropolitan State University–Minnesota*
Craig C. Lundberg   *Cornell University*
Rodney Lowman   *California School of Professional Psychology, San Diego*
Ken Murrell   *University of West Florida*
Saroj Parasuraman   *Drexel University*
James F. Pickens   *Tulsa Community College/University of Oklahoma*
Anne H. Reilly   *Loyola University–Chicago*
Deborah Rupp   *University of West Florida*

We also would like to express our appreciation to members of the staff at South-Western/Thomson Learning for their aid and encouragement. Special thanks go to John Szilagyi and Denise Simon for their help and guidance throughout the development of this revision. Libby Shipp and Christine Cotting patiently took on the task of editing and producing this book.

Thomas G. Cummings   Christopher G. Worley
Palos Verdes Estates, California   San Juan Capistrano, California
Winter 2000

1. General Introduction to Organization Development

This is a book about *organization development* (OD)—a process that applies behavioral science knowledge and practices to help organizations achieve greater effectiveness, including increased financial performance and improved quality of work life. Organization development differs from other planned change efforts, such as technological innovation, training and development, or new product development, because the focus is on building the organization's ability to assess its current functioning and to achieve its goals. Moreover, OD is oriented to improving the total system—the organization and its parts in the context of the larger environment that affects them.

This book reviews the broad background of OD and examines assumptions, strategies and models, intervention techniques, and other aspects of OD. This chapter provides an introduction to OD, describing first the concept of OD itself. Second, it explains why OD has expanded rapidly in the past fifty years, both in terms of people's needs to work with and through others in organizations and in terms of organizations' needs to adapt in a complex and changing world. Third, it reviews briefly the history of OD, and fourth, it describes the evolution of OD into its current state. This introduction to OD is followed by an overview of the rest of the book.

ORGANIZATION DEVELOPMENT DEFINED

Organization development is both a professional field of social action and an area of scientific inquiry. The practice of OD covers a wide spectrum of activities, with seemingly endless variations upon them. Team building with top corporate management, structural change in a municipality, and job enrichment in a manufacturing firm are all examples of OD. Similarly, the study of OD addresses a broad range of topics, including the effects of change, the methods of organizational change, and the factors influencing OD success.

A number of definitions of OD exist and are presented in Table 1.1. Each definition has a slightly different emphasis. For example, Burke's description focuses attention on culture as the target of change; French's definition is concerned with OD's long-term interest and the use of consultants; and Beckhard's and Beer's definitions address the process of OD. The following definition incorporates most of these views and is used in this book: *organization development is a systemwide application of behavioral science knowledge to the planned development, improvement, and reinforcement of the strategies, structures, and processes that lead to organization effectiveness.*

This definition emphasizes several features that differentiate OD from other approaches to organizational change and improvement, such as management consulting, technological innovation, operations management, and training and development. The definition also helps to distinguish OD from two related subjects, change management and organization change, that also are addressed in this book.

First, OD applies to the strategy, structure, and processes of an entire system, such as an organization, a single plant of a multiplant firm, or a department or

Table 1•1	Definitions of Organizational Development

- Organization development is a planned process of change in an organization's culture through the utilization of behavioral science technology, research, and theory. (Warner Burke)[1]
- Organization development refers to a long-range effort to improve an organization's problem-solving capabilities and its ability to cope with changes in its external environment with the help of external or internal behavioral-scientist consultants, or *change agents,* as they are sometimes called. (Wendell French)[2]
- Organization development is an effort (1) planned, (2) organization-wide, and (3) managed from the top, to (4) increase organization effectiveness and health through (5) planned interventions in the organization's "processes," using behavioral science knowledge. (Richard Beckhard)[3]
- Organization development is a systemwide process of data collection, diagnosis, action planning, intervention, and evaluation aimed at (1) enhancing congruence among organizational structure, process, strategy, people, and culture; (2) developing new and creative organizational solutions; and (3) developing the organization's self-renewing capacity. It occurs through the collaboration of organizational members working with a change agent using behavioral science theory, research, and technology. (Michael Beer)[4]

work group. A change program aimed at modifying an organization's strategy, for example, might focus on how the organization relates to a wider environment and on how those relationships can be improved. It might include changes both in the grouping of people to perform tasks (structure) and in methods of communicating and solving problems (process) to support the changes in strategy. Similarly, an OD program directed at helping a top-management team become more effective might focus on interactions and problem-solving processes within the group. This focus might result in the improved ability of top management to solve company problems in strategy and structure. This contrasts with approaches focusing on one or only a few aspects of a system, such as training and development, technological innovation, or operations management. In these approaches, attention is narrowed to individuals within a system, to improvement of particular products or processes, or to development of production or service delivery functions.

Second, OD is based on behavioral science knowledge and practice, including microconcepts such as leadership, group dynamics, and work design, and macroapproaches such as strategy, organization design, and international relations. These subjects distinguish OD from such applications as management consulting, technological innovation, or operations management that emphasize the economic, financial, and technical aspects of organizations. These approaches tend to neglect the personal and social characteristics of a system.

Third, OD is concerned with managing planned change, but not in the formal sense typically associated with management consulting or technological innovation, which tend to be programmatic and expert-driven approaches to change. Rather, OD is more an adaptive process for planning and implementing change than a blueprint for how things should be done. It involves planning to diagnose and solve organizational problems, but such plans are flexible and often revised as new information is gathered about the progress of the change program. If, for example, there was concern about the performance of a set of international subsidiaries, a reorganization process might begin with plans to assess the current relationships between the international divisions and the corporate headquarters and to redesign them if necessary. These plans would be modified if the assessment discovered that most of the senior management teams were not given adequate cross-cultural training prior to their international assignments.

Fourth, OD involves both the creation and the subsequent reinforcement of change. It moves beyond the initial efforts to implement a change program to a longer-term concern for stabilizing and institutionalizing new activities within the organization. For example, the implementating of self-managed work teams might focus on ways in which supervisors could give workers more control over work methods. After workers had more control, attention would shift to ensuring that supervisors continued to provide that freedom. That assurance might include rewarding supervisors for managing in a participative style. This attention to reinforcement is similar to training and development approaches that address maintenance of new skills or behaviors, but it differs from other change perspectives that do not address how a change can be institutionalized.

Finally, OD is oriented to improving organizational effectiveness. This involves two major assumptions. First, an effective organization is able to solve its own problems and focus its attention and resources on achieving key goals. OD helps organization members gain the skills and knowledge necessary to conduct these activities by involving them in the process. Second, an effective organization has both high performance, including financial returns, quality products and services, high productivity, and continuous improvement, and a high quality of work life. The organization's performance responds to the needs of external groups, such as stockholders, customers, suppliers, and government agencies, that provide the organization with resources and legitimacy. Moreover, it is able to attract and motivate effective employees, who then perform at high levels. Other forms of organization change clearly differ from OD in their focus. Management consulting, for example, is almost solely concerned with financial performance, whereas training and development addresses individual effectiveness.

This definition also helps to distinguish OD from two other related subjects of interest in this book: change management and organization change. OD and change management both address the effective implementation of planned change. They are concerned with the sequence of activities, processes, and leadership issues that produce organization improvements. They differ, however, in their underlying value orientation. OD's behavioral science foundation supports values of human potential, participation, and development, whereas change management is more focused on values of economic potential and the creation of competitive advantage.[5] As a result, OD's distinguishing feature is its concern with the transfer of knowledge and skill such that the system is more able to manage change in the future. Change management does not necessarily require the transfer of these skills. In short, all OD involves change management, but change management may not involve OD.

Similarly, organization change is a broader concept than OD. As discussed above, organization development can be applied to managing organizational change. However, it is primarily concerned with managing change in such a way that knowledge and skills are transferred to build the organization's capability to achieve goals and solve problems. It is intended to change the organization in a particular direction, toward improved problem solving, responsiveness, quality of work life, and effectiveness. Organization change, in contrast, is more broadly focused and can apply to *any* kind of change, including technical and managerial innovations, organization decline, or the evolution of a system over time. These changes may or may not be directed at making the organization more developed in the sense implied by OD.

The behavioral sciences have developed useful concepts and methods for helping organizations to deal with changing environments, competitor initiatives, technological innovation, globalization, or restructuring. They help managers and administrators to manage the change process. Many of these concepts and techniques are described in this book, particularly in relation to managing change.

THE GROWTH AND RELEVANCE OF ORGANIZATION DEVELOPMENT

In each of the previous editions of this book, we argued that organizations must adapt to increasingly complex and uncertain technological, economic, political, and cultural changes. We also argued that OD could help an organization to create effective responses to these changes and, in many cases, to proactively influence the strategic direction of the firm. The rapidly changing conditions of the past few years confirm our arguments and accentuate their relevance. According to several observers, organizations are in the midst of unprecedented uncertainty and chaos, and nothing short of a management revolution will save them.[6] Three major trends are shaping change in organizations: globalization, information technology, and managerial innovation.[7]

First, *globalization* is changing the markets and environments in which organizations operate as well as the way they function. New governments, new leadership, new markets, and new countries are emerging and creating a new global economy. The toppling of the Berlin Wall symbolized and energized the reunification of Germany; entrepreneurs appeared in Russia, the Balkans, and Siberia as the former Soviet Union evolves, in fits and starts, into separate, market-oriented states; and China emerged as an open market and as the governance mechanism over Hong Kong to represent a powerful shift in global economic influence. The establishment of the European Economic Community and the far-reaching impact of the Asian financial crisis clearly demonstrate the interconnectedness of the global economy.

Second, *information technology* is redefining the traditional business model by changing how work is performed, how knowledge is used, and how the cost of doing business is calculated. The way an organization collects, stores, manipulates, uses, and transmits information can lower costs or increase the value and quality of products and services. Information technology, for example, is at the heart of emerging e-commerce strategies and organizations. Amazon.com, E-TRADE, and eBay are among many recent entrants to the information economy, and the amount of business being conducted on the Internet is projected to grow at double-digit rates for well over ten years. Moreover, the underlying rate of innovation is not expected to decline. Electronic data interchange, a state-of-the-art technology application a few years ago, is now considered routine business practice. The ability to move information easily and inexpensively throughout and among organizations has fueled the downsizing, delayering, and restructuring of firms. The Internet and the World Wide Web have enabled a new form of work known as telecommuting; organization members can work from their homes or cars without ever going to the office. Finally, information technology is changing how knowledge is used. Information that is widely shared reduces the concentration of power at the top of the organization. Organization members now share the same key information that senior managers once used to control decision making. Ultimately, information technology will generate new business models in which communication and information sharing is nearly free.

Third, *managerial innovation* has responded to the globalization and information technology trends and has accelerated their impact on organizations. New organizational forms, such as networks, strategic alliances, and virtual corporations, provide organizations with new ways of thinking about how to manufacture goods and deliver services. The strategic alliance, for example, has emerged as one of the indispensable tools in strategy implementation. No single organization, not even IBM, Mitsubishi, or General Electric, can control the environmental and market uncertainty it faces. Sun Microsystems' network is so complex that some products it sells are never touched by a Sun employee. In addition, new methods of change, such as downsizing and reengineering, have radically reduced the size of organizations and increased their flexibility, and new large-group interventions, such as the search conference and open space, have increased the speed with which organizational change can take place.[8] Managers, OD practitioners, and researchers argue that these forces not only are powerful in their own right but are interrelated. Their interaction makes for a highly uncertain and chaotic environment for all kinds of organizations, including manufacturing and service firms and those in the public and private sectors. There is no question that these forces are profoundly affecting organizations.

Fortunately, a growing number of organizations are undertaking the kinds of organizational changes needed to survive and prosper in today's environment. They are making themselves more streamlined and nimble and more responsive to external demands. They are involving employees in key decisions and paying for performance rather than for time. They are taking the initiative in innovating and managing change, rather than simply responding to what has already happened.

Organization development is playing an increasingly key role in helping organizations change themselves. It is helping organizations assess themselves and their environments, and revitalize and rebuild their strategies, structures, and processes. OD is helping organization members go beyond surface changes to transform the underlying assumptions and values governing their behaviors. The different concepts and methods discussed in this book increasingly are finding their way into government agencies, manufacturing firms, multinational corporations, service industries, educational institutions, and not-for-profit organizations. Perhaps at no other time has OD been more responsive and practically relevant to organizations' needs to operate effectively in a highly complex and changing world.

OD is obviously important to those who plan a professional career in the field, either as an internal consultant employed by an organization or as an external consultant practicing in many organizations. A career in OD can be highly rewarding, providing challenging and interesting assignments working with managers and employees to improve their organizations and their work lives. In today's environment, the demand for OD professionals is rising rapidly. For example, the large accounting firms not only have added significant "management" consulting practices; they also are moving aggressively to add "change management" to their service offerings. Career opportunities in OD should continue to expand in the United States and abroad.

Organization development also is important to those who have no aspirations to become professional practitioners. All managers and administrators are responsible for supervising and developing subordinates and for improving their departments' performance. Similarly, all staff specialists, such as accountants, financial analysts, engineers, information technologists, personnel specialists, or market researchers, are responsible for offering advice and counsel to managers and for introducing new methods and practices. Finally, OD is important to general managers and other senior executives because OD can help the whole organization be more flexible, adaptable, and effective.

Organization development can help managers and staff personnel perform their tasks more effectively. It can provide the skills and knowledge necessary for establishing effective interpersonal and helping relationships. It can show personnel how to work effectively with others in diagnosing complex problems and in devising appropriate solutions. It can help others become committed to the solutions, thereby increasing chances for their successful implementation. In short, OD is highly relevant to anyone having to work with and through others in organizations.

A SHORT HISTORY OF ORGANIZATION DEVELOPMENT

A brief history of OD will help to clarify the evolution of the term as well as some of the problems and confusion that have surrounded it. As currently practiced, OD emerged from five major backgrounds or stems, as shown in Figure 1.1. The first was the growth of the National Training Laboratories (NTL) and the development of training groups, otherwise known as sensitivity training or T-groups. The second stem of OD was the classic work on action research conducted by social scientists interested in applying research to managing change. An important feature of action research was a technique known as survey feedback. Kurt Lewin, a prolific theorist, researcher, and practitioner in group dynamics and social change, was instrumental in the development of T-groups, survey feedback, and action research. His work led to the creation of OD and still serves as a major source of its concepts and methods. The third stem reflects the work of Rensis Likert and represents the application of

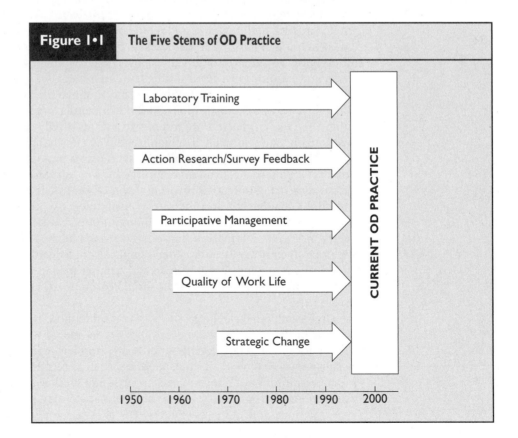

Figure 1•1   The Five Stems of OD Practice

Laboratory Training

Action Research/Survey Feedback

Participative Management

Quality of Work Life

Strategic Change

CURRENT OD PRACTICE

1950   1960   1970   1980   1990   2000

participative management to organization structure and design. The fourth background is the approach focusing on productivity and the quality of work life. The fifth stem of OD, and the most recent influence on current practice, involves strategic change and organization transformation.

Laboratory Training Background

This stem of OD pioneered laboratory training, or the T-group—a small, unstructured group in which participants learn from their own interactions and evolving dynamics about such issues as interpersonal relations, personal growth, leadership, and group dynamics. Essentially, laboratory training began in the summer of 1946, when Kurt Lewin and his staff at the Research Center for Group Dynamics at the Massachusetts Institute of Technology (MIT) were asked by the Connecticut Interracial Commission and the Committee on Community Interrelations of the American Jewish Congress for help in research on training community leaders. A workshop was developed, and the community leaders were brought together to learn about leadership and to discuss problems. At the end of each day, the researchers discussed privately what behaviors and group dynamics they had observed. The community leaders asked permission to sit in on these feedback sessions. Reluctant at first, the researchers finally agreed. Thus, the first T-group was formed in which people reacted to data about their own behavior. The researchers drew two conclusions about this first T-group experiment: (1) feedback about group interaction was a rich learning experience, and (2) the process of "group building" had potential for learning that could be transferred to "back-home" situations.[9]

As a result of this experience, the Office of Naval Research and the National Education Association provided financial backing to form the National Training Laboratories, and Gould Academy in Bethel, Maine, was selected as a site for further work (since then, Bethel has played an important part in NTL). The first Basic Skill Groups were offered in the summer of 1947. The program was so successful that the Carnegie Foundation provided support for programs in 1948 and 1949. This led to a permanent program for NTL within the National Education Association.

A new phenomenon arose in 1950. An attempt was made to have T-groups in the morning and cognitive-skill groups (A-groups) in the afternoon. However, the staff found that the high level of carry-over from the morning sessions turned the afternoon A-groups into T-groups, despite the resistance of the afternoon staff members, who were committed to cognitive-skill development. This was the beginning of a decade of learning experimentation and frustration, especially in the attempt to transfer skills learned in the T-group setting to the "back-home" situation.

In the 1950s, three trends emerged: (1) the emergence of regional laboratories, (2) the expansion of summer program sessions to year-round sessions, and (3) the expansion of the T-group into business and industry, with NTL members becoming increasingly involved with industry programs. Notable among these industry efforts was the pioneering work of Douglas McGregor at Union Carbide, of Herbert Shepard and Robert Blake at Esso Standard Oil (now Exxon), and of McGregor and Richard Beckhard at General Mills. Applications of T-group methods at these three companies spawned the term "organization development" and, equally important, led corporate personnel and industrial relations specialists to expand their roles to offer internal consulting services to managers.[10]

Applying T-group techniques to organizations gradually became known as *team building*—a process for helping work groups become more effective in accomplishing tasks and satisfying member needs.

Action Research and Survey Feedback Background

Kurt Lewin also was involved in the second movement that led to OD's emergence as a practical field of social science. This second background refers to the processes of action research and survey feedback. The action research contribution began in the 1940s with studies conducted by social scientists John Collier, Kurt Lewin, and William Whyte. They discovered that research needed to be closely linked to action if organization members were to use it to manage change. A collaborative effort was initiated between organization members and social scientists to collect research data about an organization's functioning, to analyze it for causes of problems, and to devise and implement solutions. After implementation, further data were collected to assess the results, and the cycle of data collection and action often continued. The results of action research were twofold: members of organizations were able to use research on themselves to guide action and change, and social scientists were able to study that process to derive new knowledge that could be used elsewhere.

Among the pioneering action research studies was the work of Lewin and his students at the Harwood Manufacturing Company[11] and the classic research by Lester Coch and John French on overcoming resistance to change.[12] The latter study led to the development of participative management as a means of getting employees involved in planning and managing change. Other notable action research contributions included Whyte and Edith Hamilton's famous study of Chicago's Tremont Hotel[13] and Collier's efforts to apply action research techniques to improving race relations when he was commissioner of Indian affairs from 1933 to 1945.[14] These studies did much to establish action research as integral to organization change. Today, it is the backbone of most OD applications.

A key component of most action research studies was the systematic collection of survey data that was fed back to the client organization. Following Lewin's death in 1947, his Research Center for Group Dynamics at MIT moved to Michigan and joined with the Survey Research Center as part of the Institute for Social Research. The institute was headed by Rensis Likert, a pioneer in developing scientific approaches to attitude surveys. Likert's doctoral dissertation at Columbia University, "A Technique for the Measurement of Attitudes," was the classic study in which he developed the widely used, five-point "Likert Scale."[15]

In an early study by the institute, Likert and Floyd Mann administered a companywide survey of management and employee attitudes at Detroit Edison.[16] Over a two-year period beginning in 1948, three sets of data were developed: (1) the viewpoints of eight thousand nonsupervisory employees about their supervisors, promotion opportunities, and work satisfaction with fellow employees; (2) similar reactions from first- and second-line supervisors; and (3) information from higher levels of management.

The feedback process that evolved was an "interlocking chain of conferences." The major findings of the survey were first reported to the top management and then transmitted throughout the organization. The feedback sessions were conducted in task groups, with supervisors and their immediate subordinates discussing the data together. Although there was little substantial research evidence, the researchers intuitively felt that this was a powerful process for change.

In 1950, eight accounting departments asked for a repeat of the survey, thus generating a new cycle of feedback meetings. In four departments, feedback approaches were used, but the method varied, with two of the remaining departments receiving feedback only at the departmental level. Because of changes in key personnel, nothing was done in two departments.

A third follow-up study indicated that more significant and positive changes, such as job satisfaction, had occurred in the departments receiving feedback than in the two departments that did not participate. From those findings, Likert and Mann derived several conclusions about the effects of survey feedback on organization change. This led to extensive applications of survey-feedback methods in a variety of settings. The common pattern of data collection, data feedback, action planning, implementation, and follow-up data collection in both action research and survey feedback can be seen in these examples.

Participative Management Background

The intellectual and practical advances from the laboratory training stem and the action research/survey-feedback stem were followed closely by the belief that a human relations approach represented a one-best-way to manage organizations. This belief was exemplified in research that associated Likert's Participative Management (System 4) style with organizational effectiveness.[17] This framework characterized organizations as having one of four types of management systems:[18]

- *Exploitive authoritative* systems (System 1) exhibit an autocratic, top-down approach to leadership. Employee motivation is based on punishment and occasional rewards. Communication is primarily downward, and there is little lateral interaction or teamwork. Decision making and control reside primarily at the top of the organization. System 1 results in mediocre performance.

- *Benevolent authoritative* systems (System 2) are similar to System 1, except that management is more paternalistic. Employees are allowed a little more interaction, communication, and decision making but within boundaries defined by management.

- *Consultative* systems (System 3) increase employee interaction, communication, and decision making. Although employees are consulted about problems and decisions, management still makes the final decisions. Productivity is good, and employees are moderately satisfied with the organization.

- *Participative group* systems (System 4) are almost the opposite of System 1. Designed around group methods of decision making and supervision, this system fosters high degrees of member involvement and participation. Work groups are highly involved in setting goals, making decisions, improving methods, and appraising results. Communication occurs both laterally and vertically, and decisions are linked throughout the organization by overlapping group membership. System 4 achieves high levels of productivity, quality, and member satisfaction.

Likert applied System 4 management to organizations using a survey-feedback process. The intervention generally started with organization members completing the *Profile of Organizational Characteristics*.[19] The survey asked members for their opinions about both the present and ideal conditions of six organizational features: leadership, motivation, communication, decisions, goals, and control. In the second stage, the data were fed back to different work groups within the organization. Group members examined the discrepancy between their present situation and their ideal, generally using System 4 as the ideal benchmark, and generated action plans to move the organization toward System 4 conditions.

Productivity and Quality-of-Work-Life Background

The contribution of the productivity and quality-of-work-life (QWL) background to OD can be described in two phases. The first phase is described by the original projects developed in Europe in the 1950s and their emergence in the United States during the 1960s. Based on the research of Eric Trist and his colleagues at the Tavistock Institute of Human Relations in London, early practitioners in Great Britain, Ireland, Norway, and Sweden developed work designs aimed at better integrating technology and people.[20] These QWL programs generally involved joint participation by unions and management in the design of work and resulted in work designs giving employees high levels of discretion, task variety, and feedback about results. Perhaps the most distinguishing characteristic of these QWL programs was the development of self-managing work groups as a new form of work design. These groups were composed of multiskilled workers who were given the necessary autonomy and information to design and manage their own task performances.

As these programs migrated to America, a variety of concepts and techniques were adopted and the approach tended to be more mixed than in European practice. For example, two definitions of QWL emerged during its initial development.[21] QWL was first defined in terms of people's reaction to work, particularly individual outcomes related to job satisfaction and mental health. Using this definition, QWL focused primarily on the personal consequences of the work experience and how to improve work to satisfy personal needs.

A second definition of QWL defined it as an approach or method.[22] People defined QWL in terms of specific techniques and approaches used for improving work.[23] It was viewed as synonymous with methods such as job enrichment, self-managed teams, and labor–management committees. This technique orientation derived mainly from the growing publicity surrounding QWL projects, such as the General Motors–United Auto Workers project at Tarrytown and the Gaines Pet Food plant project. These pioneering projects drew attention to specific approaches for improving work.

The excitement and popularity of this first phase of QWL in the United States lasted until the mid-1970s, when other, more pressing issues, such as inflation and energy costs, diverted national attention. However, starting in 1979, a second phase of QWL activity emerged. A major factor contributing to the resurgence of QWL was growing international competition faced by the United States in markets at home and abroad. It became increasingly clear that the relatively low cost and high quality of foreign-made goods resulted partially from the management practices used abroad, especially in Japan. Books extolling the virtues of Japanese management, such as Ouchi's *Theory Z*,[24] made bestseller lists.

As a result, QWL programs expanded beyond their initial focus on work design to include other features of the workplace that can affect employee productivity and satisfaction, such as reward systems, work flows, management styles, and the physical work environment. This expanded focus resulted in larger-scale and longer-term projects than had the early job enrichment programs and shifted attention beyond the individual worker to work groups and the larger work context. Equally important, it added the critical dimension of organizational efficiency to what had been up to that time a primary concern for the human dimension.

At one point, the productivity and QWL approach became so popular that it was called an ideological movement. This was particularly evident in the spread of quality circles within many companies. Popularized in Japan, *quality circles* are groups of employees trained in problem-solving methods who meet regularly to resolve work-environment, productivity, and quality-control concerns and to develop more efficient ways of working. At the same time, many of the QWL programs started in the early 1970s were achieving success. Highly visible corporations, such as General Motors, Ford, and Honeywell, and unions, such as the United Automobile Workers, the Oil, Chemical, and Atomic Workers, the Communications Workers of America, and the Steelworkers, were more willing to publicize their QWL efforts. In 1980, for example, more than eighteen hundred people attended an international QWL conference in Toronto, Canada. Unlike previous conferences, which were dominated by academics, the presenters at Toronto were mainly managers, workers, and unionists from private and public corporations.

Today, this second phase of QWL activity continues primarily under the banner of "employee involvement," rather than of QWL. For many OD practitioners, the term "EI" signifies, more than the name QWL, the growing emphasis on how employees can contribute more to running the organization so it can be more flexible, productive, and competitive. Recently, the term "employee empowerment" has been used interchangeably with the term EI, the former suggesting the power inherent in moving decision making downward in the organization.[25] "Employee empowerment" may be too restrictive, however. Because it draws attention to the power aspects of these interventions, it may lead practitioners to neglect other important elements needed for success, such as information, skills, and rewards. Consequently, EI seems a broader and less restrictive banner than does employee empowerment for these approaches to organizational improvement.

Finally, the productivity and QWL approach has gained new momentum by joining forces with the total quality movement advocated by W. Edwards Deming[26] and Joseph Juran.[27] In this approach, the organization is viewed as a set of processes that can be linked to the quality of products and services, modeled through statistical techniques and improved continuously.[28] Quality efforts at Ford, Motorola, and Xerox, along with federal government support through the establishment of the Malcolm Baldrige National Quality Award, have popularized this strategy of organization development.

Strategic Change Background

The strategic change background is a recent influence on OD's evolution. As organizations and their technological, political, and social environments have become more complex and more uncertain, the scale and intricacies of organizational change have increased. This trend has produced the need for a strategic perspective from OD and encouraged planned change processes at the organization level.[29]

Strategic change involves improving the alignment among an organization's environment, strategy, and organization design.[30] Strategic change interventions include efforts to improve both the organization's relationship to its environment and the fit between its technical, political, and cultural systems.[31] The need for strategic change is usually triggered by some major disruption to the organization, such as the lifting of regulatory requirements, a technological breakthrough, or a new chief executive officer coming in from outside the organization.[32]

One of the first applications of strategic change was Richard Beckhard's use of *open systems planning*.[33] He proposed that an organization's environment and its strategy could be described and analyzed. Based on the organization's core mission, the differences between what the environment demanded and how the organization responded could be reduced and performance improved. Since then, change agents have proposed a variety of large-scale or strategic change models,[34] each of which recognizes that strategic change involves multiple levels of the organization and a change in its culture, is often driven from the top by powerful executives, and has important effects on performance.

The strategic change background has significantly influenced OD practice. For example, implementing strategic change requires OD practitioners to be familiar with competitive strategy, finance, and marketing, as well as team building, action research, and survey feedback. Together, these skills have improved OD's relevance to organizations and their managers.

EVOLUTION IN ORGANIZATION DEVELOPMENT

Current practice in organization development is strongly influenced by those five backgrounds as well as by the trends shaping change in organizations. The laboratory training, action research and survey feedback, and participative management roots of OD are evident in the strong value focus that underlies its practice. The more recent influences, the quality-of-work-life and strategic change backgrounds, have greatly improved the relevance and rigor of OD practice. They have added financial and economic indicators of effectiveness to OD's traditional measures of work satisfaction and personal growth.

Today, the field is being influenced by the globalization and information technology trends described earlier. OD is being carried out in many more countries and in many more organizations operating on a worldwide basis. This is generating a whole new set of interventions as well as adaptations to traditional OD practice.[35] In addition, OD must adapt its methods to the technologies being used in organizations. As information technology continues to influence organization environments, strategies, and structures, OD will need to manage change processes in cyberspace as well as face-to-face. The diversity of this evolving discipline has led to tremendous growth in the number of professional practitioners, in the kinds of organizations involved with OD, and in the range of countries within which OD is practiced.

The expansion of the OD Network (http://www.odnet.org), which began in 1964, is one indication of this growth. It has grown from two hundred members in 1970 to more than thirty-seven hundred OD practitioners today. At the same time, Division 14 of the American Psychological Association, formerly known as the Division of Industrial Psychology, has changed its title to the Division of Industrial and Organizational Psychology. In 1968, the American Society of Training and Development set up an OD division, which currently has more than two thousand members. In 1971, the Academy of Management established a Division of Organization Development and Change, which currently has more than two thousand members. Pepperdine University (http://bschool.pepperdine.edu), Bowling Green State University (http://www.bgsu.edu), and Case Western Reserve University (http://www.cwru.edu) offered the first master's degree programs in OD in 1975, and Case Western Reserve University began the first doctoral program in OD. Organization development now is being taught at the graduate and undergraduate levels in a large number of universities.[36]

In addition to the growth of professional societies and educational programs in OD, the field continues to develop new theorists, researchers, and practitioners who are building on the work of the early pioneers and extending it to contemporary issues and conditions. Included among the first generation of contributors are Chris Argyris, who has developed a learning and action-science approach to OD;[37] Warren Bennis, who has tied executive leadership to strategic change;[38] Edgar Schein, who continues to develop process approaches to OD, including the key role of organizational culture in change management;[39] Richard Beckhard, who focused attention on the importance of managing transitions;[40] and Robert Tannenbaum, who continues to sensitize OD to the personal dimension of participants' lives.[41]

Among the second generation of contributors are Warner Burke, whose work has done much to make OD a professional field;[42] Larry Greiner, who has brought the ideas of power and evolution into the mainstream of OD;[43] Edward Lawler III, who has extended OD to reward systems and employee involvement;[44] Anthony Raia and Newton Margulies, who together have kept our attention on the values underlying OD and what those mean for contemporary practice;[45] and Peter Vaill and Craig Lundberg, who continue to develop OD as a practical science.[46]

Included among the newest generation of OD contributors are Dave Brown, whose work on action research and developmental organizations has extended OD into community and societal change;[47] Thomas Cummings, whose work on sociotechnical systems, self-designing organizations, and transorganizational development has led OD beyond the boundaries of single organizations to groups of organizations and their environments;[48] Max Elden, whose international work in industrial democracy draws attention to the political aspects of OD;[49] William Pasmore and Jerry Porras, who have done much to put OD on a sound research and conceptual base;[50] and Peter Block, who has focused attention on consulting skills, empowerment processes, and reclaiming our individuality.[51] Others making important contributions to the field include Ken Murrell and Joanne Preston, who have focused attention on the internationalization of OD;[52] Sue Mohrman and Gerry Ledford, who have focused on team-based organizations and compensation;[53] and David Cooperrider, who has turned our attention toward the positive aspects of organizations.[54] These academic contributors are joined by a large number of internal OD practitioners and external consultants who lead organizational change.

Many different organizations have undertaken a wide variety of OD efforts. In many cases, organizations have been at the forefront of innovating new change techniques and methods as well as new organizational forms. Larger corporations that have engaged in organization development include General Electric, Boeing, Texas Instruments, American Airlines, Du Pont, Intel, Hewlett-Packard, GTE, John Hancock Mutual Life Insurance, Polaroid, Ralston Purina, General Foods, Procter & Gamble, IBM, TRW Systems, Bank of America, and Cummins Engine. Traditionally, much of the work was considered confidential and was not publicized. Today, however, organizations increasingly have gone public with their OD efforts, sharing the lessons with others.

OD work also is being done in schools, communities, and local, state, and federal governments. A recent review of OD projects is directed primarily at OD in public administration.[55] Extensive OD work was done in the armed services, including the army, navy, air force, and Coast Guard, although OD activity and research have declined significantly with the reduction in the size of the military. Public schools began using both group training and survey feedback relatively early in the history of OD.[56] Usually, the projects took place in suburban middle-class schools, where stresses and strains of an urban environment were not prominent and ethnic and socioeconomic differences between consultants and clients were not high. In more recent years, OD methods have been extended to urban schools and to colleges and universities.

Organization development is increasingly international. It has been applied in Canada, Sweden, Norway, Germany, Japan, Australia, Israel, South Africa, Mexico, Venezuela, the Philippines, China, Hong Kong, Russia, New Zealand, and The Netherlands. These efforts have involved such organizations as Saab (Sweden),

Norsk Hydro (Norway), Imperial Chemical Industries (England), Shell Oil Company, Orfors (Sweden), and AkzoNobel (The Netherlands).

Although it is evident that OD has expanded vastly in recent years, relatively few of the total number of organizations in the United States are actively involved in formal OD programs. However, many organizations are applying OD approaches and techniques without knowing that such a term exists.

OVERVIEW OF THE BOOK

This book presents the process and practice of organization development in a logical flow, as shown in Figure 1.2. Part 1 provides an overview of OD that describes the process of planned change and those who perform the work. It consists of two chapters. Chapter 2 discusses the nature of planned change and presents some models describing the change process. Planned change is viewed as an ongoing cycle of four activities: entering and contracting, diagnosing, planning and implementing, and evaluating and institutionalizing. Chapter 3 describes the OD practitioner and provides insight into the knowledge and skills needed to practice OD and the kinds of career issues that can be expected.

Part 2 is composed of eight chapters that describe the process of organization development. Chapter 4 characterizes the first activity in this process—entering an organizational system and contracting with it for organization development work. Chapters 5, 6, 7, and 8 present the steps associated with the next major activity of the OD process: diagnosing. This involves helping the organization understand its current functioning and discover areas for improvement. Chapters 5 and 6 present an open systems model to guide diagnosis at three levels of analysis: the total organization, the group or department, and the individual job or position. Chapters 7 and 8 review methods for collecting, analyzing, and feeding back diagnostic data. Chapters 9 and 10 address issues concerned with the third activity: planning and implementing change. Chapter 9 presents an overview of the intervention design process. Major kinds of interventions are identified, and the specific approaches that make up the next four parts of the book are introduced. Chapter 10 discusses the process of managing change and identifies key factors contributing to the successful implementation of change programs. Chapter 11 describes the final activity of the planned change process—evaluating OD interventions and stabilizing or institutionalizing them as a permanent part of organizational functioning.

Parts 3 through 6 present the major interventions used in OD today. Part 3 (Chapters 12 and 13) is concerned with human process interventions aimed at the social processes occurring within organizations. These are the oldest and most traditional interventions in OD. Chapter 12 describes interpersonal and group process approaches, such as T-groups, process consultation, and team building. Chapter 13 presents more systemwide process approaches, such as organizational confrontation meetings, intergroup relations, and large-group interventions.

Part 4 (Chapters 14, 15, and 16) reviews technostructural interventions that are aimed at organization structure and at better integrating people and technology. Chapter 14 is about restructuring organizations; it describes the alternative methods of organizing work activities as well as processes for downsizing and reengineering the organization. Chapter 15 presents interventions for improving employee involvement. These change programs increase employee knowledge, power, information, and rewards through parallel structures, high-involvement organizations, and total quality management. Chapter 16 describes change programs directed at work design, both of individual jobs and of work groups, for greater employee satisfaction and productivity.

Part 5 (Chapters 17 and 18) presents human resource management interventions that are directed at integrating people into the organization. These interventions are

Figure 1•2	Overview of the Book

Part 1: Overview of Organization Development

The Nature of Planned Change
(Chapter 2)

The Organization Development Practitioner
(Chapter 3)

Part 2: The Process of Organization Development

Entering and Contracting (Chapter 4)	Diagnosing Organizations (Chapter 5)	Diagnosing Groups and Jobs (Chapter 6)	Collecting and Analyzing Diagnostic Information (Chapter 7)
Feeding Back Diagnostic Information (Chapter 8)	Designing Interventions (Chapter 9)	Managing Change (Chapter 10)	Evaluating and Institutionalizing Interventions (Chapter 11)

Part 3: Human Process Interventions	**Part 4: Technostructural Interventions**	**Part 5: Human Resources Management Interventions**	**Part 6: Strategic Interventions**
Interpersonal and Group Process Approaches (Chapter 12)	Restructuring Organizations (Chapter 14)	Performance Management (Chapter 17)	Organization and Environment Relationships (Chapter 19)
Organization Process Approaches (Chapter 13)	Employee Involvement (Chapter 15)	Developing and Assisting Members (Chapter 18)	Organization Transformation (Chapter 20)
	Work Design (Chapter 16)		

Part 7: Special Applications of Organization Development

Organization Development in Global Settings (Chapter 21)	Organization Development in Health Care, School Systems, and the Public Sector (Chapter 22)	Future Directions in Organization Development (Chapter 23)

associated traditionally with the personnel function in the organization and increasingly have become a part of OD activities. Chapter 17 concerns the process of performance management. This is a cycle of activities that helps groups and individuals to set goals, appraise work, and reward performance. Chapter 18 discusses three interventions—career planning and development, workforce diversity, and employee wellness—that develop and assist organization members.

Part 6 (Chapters 19 and 20) concerns strategic interventions that focus on organizing the firm's resources to gain a competitive advantage in the environment. These change programs generally are managed from the top of the organization and take considerable time, effort, and resources. Chapter 19 presents three interventions having to do with organization and environment relationships: integrated strategic change, transorganizational development, and mergers and acquisitions. Integrated strategic change infuses strategy formulation and implementation with the OD perspective to improve organization performance. Transorganizational development helps organizations form partnerships with other organizations to perform tasks that are too complex and costly for organizations to undertake alone. Merger and acquisition processes are key strategic change efforts, the success of which depends on the integration of strategies, structures, systems, and cultures. Chapter 20 describes three interventions for radically transforming organizations: culture change, self-designing organizations, and organization learning. Culture change is directed at changing the values, beliefs, and norms shared by organization members. Self-designing organization interventions are concerned with helping organizations gain the internal capacity to alter themselves fundamentally. Finally, organization learning is a change process aimed at helping organizations develop and use knowledge to change and improve themselves continually.

Part 7 (Chapters 21, 22, and 23) is concerned with special topics in OD. Chapter 21 describes the practice of OD in international settings. OD in organizations operating outside of the United States requires modification of the interventions to fit the country's cultural context. Organization development in worldwide organizations is aimed at improving the internal alignment of strategy, structure, and process to achieve global objectives. Finally, the practice of OD in global social change organizations promotes sustainable development and improving human potential in emerging countries. Chapter 22 presents broad applications of OD in different kinds of organizations, including educational, government, and health-care agencies. Finally, Chapter 23 examines the future of organization development, including the trends affecting the field and the prospects for its influence on organization effectiveness.

■ SUMMARY

This chapter introduced OD as a planned change discipline concerned with applying behavioral science knowledge and practice to help organizations achieve greater effectiveness. Managers and staff specialists must work with and through people to perform their jobs, and OD can help them form effective relationships with others. Organizations are faced with rapidly accelerating change, and OD can help them cope with the consequences of change. The concept of OD has multiple meanings. The definition provided here resolved some of the problems with earlier definitions. The history of OD reveals its five roots: laboratory training, action research and survey feedback, participative management, productivity and quality of work life, and strategic change. The current practice of OD goes far beyond its humanistic origins by incorporating concepts from organization strategy and structure that complement the early emphasis on social processes. The continued growth in the number and diversity of OD approaches, practitioners, and involved organizations attests to the health of the discipline and offers a favorable prospect for the future.

■ NOTES

1. W. Burke, *Organization Development: Principles and Practices* (Boston: Little, Brown, 1982).

2. W. French, "Organization Development: Objectives, Assumptions, and Strategies," *California Management Review* 12, 2 (1969): 23–34.

3. R. Beckhard, *Organization Development: Strategies and Models* (Reading, Mass.: Addison-Wesley, 1969).

4. M. Beer, *Organization Change and Development: A Systems View* (Santa Monica, Calif.: Goodyear Publishing, 1980).

5. R. Marshak, "Reclaiming the Heart of OD: Putting People Back into Organizations," (keynote address to the National OD Network Conference, Orlando, Fl., 6 October 1996).

6. T. Peters, *Liberation Management: Necessary Disorganization for the Nanosecond Nineties* (New York: Alfred A. Knopf, 1992); J. Kotter, *Leading Change* (Boston: Harvard Business School Press, 1996); S. Brown and K. Eisenhardt, *Competing on the Edge* (Boston: Harvard Business School Press, 1998); M. Wheatley, *Leadership and the New Science* (San Francisco: Berrett-Koehler, 1999); W. Joyce, *Megachange* (New York: Free Press, 1999).

7. T. Stewart, "Welcome to the Revolution," *Fortune,* 13 December 1993, 66–80; C. Farrell, "The New Economic Era," *Business Week* (18 November 1994).

8. M. Anderson, ed., *Fast Cycle Organization Development* (Cincinnati: South-Western College Publishing, 2000).

9. L. Bradford, "Biography of an Institution," *Journal of Applied Behavioral Science* 3 (1967): 127; A. Marrow, "Events Leading to the Establishment of the National Training Laboratories," *Journal of Applied Behavioral Science* 3 (1967): 145–50.

10. W. French, "The Emergence and Early History of Organization Development with Reference to Influences upon and Interactions among Some of the Key Actors," in *Contemporary Organization Development: Current Thinking and Applications,* ed. D. Warrick (Glenview, Ill.: Scott, Foresman, 1985): 12–27.

11. A. Marrow, D. Bowers, and S. Seashore, *Management by Participation* (New York: Harper & Row, 1967).

12. L. Coch and J. French, "Overcoming Resistance to Change," *Human Relations* 1 (1948): 512–32.

13. W. Whyte and E. Hamilton, *Action Research for Management* (Homewood, Ill.: Irwin-Dorsey, 1964).

14. J. Collier, "United States Indian Administration as a Laboratory of Ethnic Relations," *Social Research* 12 (May 1945): 275–76.

15. French, "Emergence and Early History," 19–20.

16. F. Mann, "Studying and Creating Change," in *The Planning of Change: Readings in the Applied Behavioral Sciences,* eds. W. Bennis, K. Benne, and R. Chin (New York: Holt, Rinehart, & Winston, 1962): 605–15.

17. R. Likert, *The Human Organization* (New York: McGraw-Hill, 1967); S. Seashore and D. Bowers, "Durability of Organizational Change," *American Psychologist* 25 (1970): 227–33; D. Mosley, "System Four Revisited: Some New Insights," *Organization Development Journal* 5 (Spring 1987): 19–24.

18. Likert, *Human Organization.*

19. Ibid.

20. A. Rice, *Productivity and Social Organization: The Ahmedabad Experiment* (London: Tavistock Publications, 1958); E. Trist and K. Bamforth, "Some Social and Psychological Consequences of the Longwall Method of Coal-Getting," *Human Relations* 4 (January 1951): 1–38; P. Gyllenhamer, *People at Work* (Reading, Mass.: Addison-Wesley, 1977); E. Thorsrud, B. Sorensen, and B. Gustavsen, "Sociotechnical Approach to Industrial Democracy in Norway," in *Handbook of Work Organization and Society,* ed. R. Dubin (Chicago: Rand McNally, 1976): 648–87; *Work in America: Report of a Special Task Force to the Secretary of Health, Education, and Welfare* (Cambridge: MIT Press, 1973); L. Davis and A. Cherns, eds., *The Quality of Working Life,* 2 vols. (New York: Free Press, 1975).

21. D. Nadler and E. Lawler III, "Quality of Work Life: Perspectives and Directions" (working paper, Center for Effective Organizations, University of Southern California, Los Angeles, 1982); L. Davis, "Enhancing the Quality of Work Life: Developments in the United States," *International*

Labour Review 116 (July-August 1977): 53–65; L. Davis, "Job Design and Productivity: A New Approach," *Personnel* 33 (1957): 418–30.

22. Ibid.

23. R. Ford, "Job Enrichment Lessons from AT&T," *Harvard Business Review* 51 (January-February 1973): 96–106; J. Taylor, J. Landy, M. Levine, and D. Kamath, *Quality of Working Life: An Annotated Bibliography, 1957–1972* (Center for Organizational Studies, Graduate School of Management, University of California at Los Angeles, 1972); J. Taylor, "Experiments in Work System Design: Economic and Human Results," *Personnel Review* 6 (1977): 28–37; J. Taylor, "Job Satisfaction and Quality of Working Life: A Reassessment," *Journal of Occupational Psychology* 50 (December 1977): 243–52.

24. W. Ouchi, *Theory Z* (Reading, Mass.: Addison-Wesley, 1981).

25. J. Vogt and K. Murrell, *Empowerment in Organizations* (San Diego: University Associates, 1990).

26. M. Walton, *The Deming Management Method* (New York: Dodd, Mead, 1986).

27. J. Juran, *Juran on Leadership for Quality: An Executive Handbook* (New York: Free Press, 1989).

28. "The Quality Imperative," *Business Week,* Special Issue (25 October 1991).

29. M. Jelinek and J. Litterer. "Why OD Must Become Strategic," in *Research in Organizational Change and Development,* vol. 2, eds. W. Pasmore and R. Woodman (Greenwich, Conn.: JAI Press, 1988): 135–62; P. Buller, "For Successful Strategic Change: Blend OD Practices with Strategic Management," *Organizational Dynamics* (Winter 1988): 42–55; C. Worley, D. Hitchin, and W. Ross, *Integrated Strategic Change* (Reading, Mass.: Addison-Wesley, 1996).

30. Worley, Hitchin, and Ross, *Integrated Strategic Change;* N. Rajagopalan and G. Spreitzer, "Toward a Theory of Strategic Change: A Multi-Lens Perspective and Integrative Framework," *Academy of Management Review* 22 (1997): 48–79.

31. R. Beckhard and R. Harris, *Organizational Transitions: Managing Complex Change,* 2d ed. (Reading, Mass.: Addison-Wesley, 1987); N. Tichy, *Managing Strategic Change* (New York: John Wiley & Sons, 1983); E. Schein, *Organizational Culture and Leadership* (San Francisco: Jossey-Bass, 1985); C. Lundberg, "Working with Culture," *Journal of Organization Change Management* 1 (1988): 38–47.

32. D. Miller and P. Freisen, "Momentum and Revolution in Organization Adaptation," *Academy of Management Journal* 23 (1980): 591–614; M. Tushman and E. Romanelli, "Organizational Evolution: A Metamorphosis Model of Convergence and Reorientation," in *Research in Organizational Behavior,* vol. 7, eds. L. Cummings and B. Staw (Greenwich, Conn.: JAI Press, 1985): 171–222.

33. Beckhard and Harris, *Organizational Transitions.*

34. T. Covin and R. Kilmann, "Critical Issues in Large-Scale Organization Change," *Journal of Organization Change Management* 1 (1988): 59–72; A. Mohrman, S. Mohrman, G. Ledford Jr., T. Cummings, and E. Lawler, eds., *Large-Scale Organization Change* (San Francisco: Jossey-Bass, 1989); W. Torbert, "Leading Organizational Transformation," in *Research in Organizational Change and Development,* vol. 3, eds. R. Woodman and W. Pasmore (Greenwich, Conn.: JAI Press, 1989): 83–116; J. Bartunek and M. Louis, "The Interplay of Organization Development and Organization Transformation," in *Research in Organizational Change and Development,* vol. 2, eds. W. Pasmore and R. Woodman (Greenwich, Conn.: JAI Press, 1988): 97–134; A. Levy and U. Merry, *Organizational Transformation: Approaches, Strategies, Theories* (New York: Praeger, 1986).

35. A. Jaeger, "Organization Development and National Culture: Where's the Fit?" *Academy of Management Review* 11 (1986): 178; G. Hofstede, *Culture's Consequences: International Differences in Work-Related Values* (London: Sage, 1980); P. Sorensen Jr., T. Head, N. Mathys, J. Preston, and D. Cooperrider, *Global and International Organization Development* (Champaign, Ill.: Stipes, 1995); A. Chin (with C. Chin), *Internationalizing OD: Cross-Cultural Experiences of NTL Members* (Alexandria, Va.: NTL Institute, 1997).

36. G. Varney and A. Darrow, "Market Position of Master-Level Graduate Programs in OD," *OD Practitioner* 27 (1995): 39–43; OD Institute, *International Registry of O.D. Professionals and O.D. Handbook* (Cleveland: OD Institute, 1995); G. Varney and A. Darrow, "Name Recognition of Master's Level Graduate Programs in Organization Development and Change," *OD Practitioner* 30 (1998).

37. C. Argyris and D. Schon, *Organizational Learning II* (Reading, Mass.: Addison-Wesley, 1996); C. Argyris, R. Putnam, and D. Smith, *Action Science* (San Francisco: Jossey-Bass, 1985).

38. W. Bennis, *Managing People Is Like Herding Cats: Warren Bennis on Leadership* (New York: Executive Excellence, 1997); W. Bennis and B. Nanus, *Leaders* (New York: Harper & Row, 1985).

39. E. Schein, *Process Consultation Revisited: Creating the Helping Relationship* (Reading, Mass.: Addison-Wesley, 1999); E. Schein, *Process Consultation: Its Role in Organization*

Development (Reading, Mass.: Addison-Wesley, 1969); E. Schein, *Process Consultation Volume II: Lessons for Managers and Consultants* (Reading, Mass.: Addison-Wesley, 1987); E. Schein, *Organizational Culture and Leadership,* 2d ed., (San Francisco: Jossey-Bass, 1997).

40. Beckhard and Harris, *Organizational Transitions;* R. Beckhard and W. Pritchard, *Changing the Essence* (San Francisco: Jossey-Bass, 1992); R. Beckhard, *Agent of Change* (San Francisco: Jossey-Bass, 1997).

41. R. Tannenbaum and R. Hanna, "Holding On, Letting Go, and Moving On: Understanding a Neglected Perspective on Change," in *Human Systems Development*, eds. R. Tannenbaum, N. Margulies, and F. Massarik (San Francisco: Jossey-Bass, 1985): 95–121.

42. W. Burke, *Organization Development: Principles and Practices* (Boston: Little, Brown, 1982); W. Burke, *Organization Development: A Normative View* (Reading, Mass.: Addison-Wesley, 1987); W. Burke, "Organization Development: Then, Now, and Tomorrow," *OD Practitioner* 27 (1995): 5–13.

43. L. Greiner and V. Schein, *Power and Organizational Development: Mobilizing Power to Implement Change* (Reading, Mass.: Addison-Wesley, 1988).

44. E. Lawler III, *Pay and Organization Development* (Reading, Mass.: Addison-Wesley, 1981); E. Lawler III, *High-Involvement Management* (San Francisco: Jossey-Bass, 1986); E. Lawler III, *From the Ground Up* (San Francisco: Jossey-Bass, 1996).

45. A. Raia and N. Margulies, "Organization Development: Issues, Trends, and Prospects," in *Human Systems Development*, eds. R. Tannenbaum, N. Margulies, and F. Massarik (San Francisco: Jossey-Bass, 1985): 246–72; N. Margulies and A. Raia, "Some Reflections on the Values of Organizational Development," *Academy of Management OD Newsletter* (Winter 1988): 1, 9–11.

46. P. Vaill, "OD as a Scientific Revolution," in *Contemporary Organization Development: Current Thinking and Applications* (Glenview, Ill.: Scott, Foresman, 1985): 28–41; C. Lundberg, "On Organization Development Interventions: A General Systems-Cybernetic Perspective," in *Systems Theory for Organizational Development*, ed. T. Cummings (Chichester, England: John Wiley & Sons, 1980): 247–71; P. Frost, L. Moore, M. Louis, C. Lundberg, *Reframing Organizational Culture* (Newbury Park, Calif.: Sage Publications, 1991).

47. L. D. Brown and J. Covey, "Development Organizations and Organization Development: Toward an Expanded Paradigm for Organization Development," in *Research*

in Organizational Change and Development, vol. 1, eds. R. Woodman and W. Pasmore (Greenwich, Conn.: JAI Press, 1987): 59–87.

48. T. Cummings and S. Srivastva, *Management of Work: A Socio-Technical Systems Approach* (San Diego: University Associates, 1977); T. Cummings, "Transorganizational Development," in *Research in Organizational Behavior*, vol. 6, eds. B. Staw and L. Cummings (Greenwich, Conn.: JAI Press, 1984): 367–422; T. Cummings and S. Mohrman, "Self-Designing Organizations: Towards Implementing Quality-of-Work-Life Innovations," in *Research in Organizational Change and Development*, vol. 1, eds. R. Woodman and W. Pasmore (Greenwich, Conn.: JAI Press, 1987): 275–310.

49. M. Elden, "Sociotechnical Systems Ideas as Public Policy in Norway: Empowering Participation through Worker Managed Change," *Journal of Applied Behavioral Science* 22 (1986): 239–55.

50. W. Pasmore, C. Haldeman, and A. Shani, "Sociotechnical Systems: A North American Reflection on Empirical Studies in North America," *Human Relations* 32 (1982): 1179–1204; W. Pasmore and J. Sherwood, *Sociotechnical Systems: A Source Book* (San Diego: University Associates, 1978); J. Porras, *Stream Analysis: A Powerful Way to Diagnose and Manage Organizational Change* (Reading, Mass.: Addison-Wesley, 1987); J. Porras, P. Robertson, and L. Goldman, "Organization Development: Theory, Practice, and Research," in *Handbook of Industrial and Organizational Psychology*, 2d ed., ed. M. Dunnette (Chicago: Rand McNally, 1990); J. Collins and J. Porras, *Built to Last: Successful Habits of Visionary Companies* (New York: Harper Business, 1997).

51. P. Block, *Flawless Consulting* (Austin, Tex.: Learning Concepts, 1981); P. Block, *The Empowered Manager: Positive Political Skills at Work* (San Francisco: Jossey-Bass, 1987); P. Block, *Stewardship* (San Francisco: Berrett-Koehler, 1994).

52. K. Murrell, "Organization Development Experiences and Lessons in the United Nations Development Program," *Organization Development Journal* 12 (1994): 1–16; J. Vogt and K. Murrell, *Empowerment in Organizations* (San Diego: Pfeiffer, 1990); J. Preston and L. DuToit, "Endemic Violence in South Africa: An OD Solution Applied to Two Educational Settings," *International Journal of Public Administration* 16 (1993): 1767–91; J. Preston, L. DuToit, and I. Barber, "A Potential Model of Transformational Change Applied to South Africa," in *Research in Organizational Change and Development*, vol. 9 (Greenwich, Conn.: JAI Press, 1998).

53. S. Mohrman, S. Cohen, and A. Mohrman, *Designing Team-Based Organizations* (San Francisco: Jossey-Bass,

1995); S. Cohen and G. Ledford Jr., "The Effectiveness of Self-Managing Teams: A Quasi-Experiment," *Human Relations* 47 (1994): 13–43; G. Ledford and E. Lawler, "Research on Employee Participation: Beating a Dead Horse?" *Academy of Management Review* 19 (1994): 633–36; G. Ledford, E. Lawler, and S. Mohrman, "The Quality Circle and Its Variations," in *Productivity in Organizations: New Perspectives from Industrial and Organizational Psychology,* eds. J. Campbell, R. Campbell, and Associates (San Francisco: Jossey-Bass, 1988); Mohrman, Ledford, Mohrman, et al., *Large-Scale Organization Change.*

54. D. Cooperrider and T. Thachankary, "Building the Global Civic Culture: Making Our Lives Count," in *Global and International Organization Development,* eds. Sorensen, Head, Mathys, et al., 282–306; D. Cooperrider, "Positive Image, Positive Action: The Affirmative Basis for Organizing," in *Appreciative Management and Leadership,* eds. S. Srivastva, D. Cooperrider, and Associates (San Francisco: Jossey-Bass, 1990); D. Cooperrider and S. Srivastva, "Appreciative Inquiry in Organizational Life," in *Organization-*

al Change and Development, vol. 1, eds. R. Woodman and W. Pasmore (Greenwich, Conn.: JAI Press, 1987): 129–70.

55. R. Golembiewski, C. Proehl, and D. Sink, "Success of OD Applications in the Public Sector, Toting Up the Score for a Decade, More or Less," *Public Administration Review* 41 (1981): 679–82; R. Golembiewski, *Humanizing Public Organizations* (Mt. Airy, Md.: Lomond, 1985); P. Robertson and S. Seneviratne, "Outcomes of Planned Organization Change in the Public Sector: A Meta-Analytic Comparison to the Private," *Public Administration Review* 55 (1995): 547–61.

56. R. Shmuck and M. Miles, *Organizational Development in Schools* (Palo Alto, Calif.: National Press Books, 1971); R. Havelock, *The Change Agent's Guide to Innovation in Education* (Englewood Cliffs, N.J.: Educational Technology, 1973); R. Schmuck and P. Runkel, "Organization Development in Schools," *Consultation* 4 (Fall 1985): 236–57; S. Mohrman and E. Lawler, "Motivation for School Reform," (working paper, Center for Effective Organizations, University of Southern California, Los Angeles, 1995).

Overview of Organization Development

1

2

The Nature of Planned Change

The pace of global, economic, and technological development makes change an inevitable feature of organizational life. However, change that happens to an organization can be distinguished from change that is planned by its members. In this book, the term *change* will refer to planned change. Organization development is directed at bringing about planned change to increase an organization's effectiveness. It is generally initiated and implemented by managers, often with the help of an OD practitioner either from inside or outside of the organization. Organizations can use planned change to solve problems, to learn from experience, to reframe shared perceptions, to adapt to external environmental changes, to improve performance, and to influence future changes.

All approaches to OD rely on some theory about planned change. The theories describe the different stages through which planned change may be effected in organizations and explain the temporal process of applying OD methods to help organization members manage change. In this chapter, we first describe and compare three major theories of organization change that have received considerable attention in the field: Lewin's change model, the action research model, and contemporary adaptations of action research. Next we present a general model of planned change that integrates the earlier models and incorporates recent conceptual advances in OD. The general model has broad applicability to many types of planned change efforts and serves to organize the chapters in this book. We then discuss different types of change and how the process can vary depending on the change situation. Finally, we present several critiques of planned change.

THEORIES OF PLANNED CHANGE

Conceptions of planned change have tended to focus on how change can be implemented in organizations.[1] Called "theories of changing," these frameworks describe the activities that must take place to initiate and carry out successful organizational change. In this section, we describe and compare three theories of changing: Lewin's change model, the action research model, and contemporary approaches to change. These frameworks have received widespread attention in OD and serve as the primary basis for a general model of planned change.

Lewin's Change Model

One of the early fundamental models of planned change was provided by Kurt Lewin.[2] He conceived of change as modification of those forces keeping a system's behavior stable. Specifically, a particular set of behaviors at any moment in time is the result of two groups of forces—those striving to maintain the status quo and those pushing for change. When both sets of forces are about equal, current behaviors are maintained in what Lewin termed a state of "quasi-stationary equilibrium." To change that state, one can increase those forces pushing for change, decrease those forces maintaining the current state, or apply some combination of both. For example, the level of performance of a work group might be stable because group norms maintaining that level are equivalent to the supervisor's pressures for change to higher levels. This level can be increased either by changing the group norms to support higher levels of performance or by increasing supervisor pressures to produce at higher levels. Lewin suggested that modifying those forces maintaining the status quo produces less tension and resistance than increasing forces for change and consequently is a more effective change strategy.

Lewin viewed this change process as consisting of the following three steps, which are shown in Figure 2.1(A):

1. *Unfreezing.* This step usually involves reducing those forces maintaining the organization's behavior at its present level. Unfreezing is sometimes accomplished through a process of "psychological disconfirmation." By introducing information that shows discrepancies between behaviors desired by organization members and those behaviors currently exhibited, members can be motivated to engage in change activities.[3]
2. *Moving.* This step shifts the behavior of the organization, department, or individual to a new level. It involves intervening in the system to develop new behaviors, values, and attitudes through changes in organizational structures and processes.
3. *Refreezing.* This step stabilizes the organization at a new state of equilibrium. It is frequently accomplished through the use of supporting mechanisms that reinforce the new organizational state, such as organizational culture, norms, policies, and structures.

Lewin's model provides a general framework for understanding organizational change. Because the three steps of change are relatively broad, considerable effort has gone into elaborating them. For example, the planning model, developed by Lippitt, Watson, and Westley, arranges Lewin's model into seven steps: scouting, entry, diagnosis (unfreezing), planning, action (movement), stabilization and evaluation, and termination (refreezing).[4] Lewin's model remains closely identified with the field of OD, however, and is used to illustrate how other types of change can be implemented. For example, Lewin's three-step model has been used to explain how information technologies can be implemented more effectively.[5]

Action Research Model

The action research model focuses on planned change as a cyclical process in which initial research about the organization provides information to guide subsequent action. Then the results of the action are assessed to provide further information to guide further action, and so on. This iterative cycle of research and action involves considerable collaboration among organization members and OD practitioners. It places heavy emphasis on data gathering and diagnosis prior to action planning and implementation, as well as careful evaluation of results after action is taken.

Action research is traditionally aimed both at helping specific organizations to implement planned change and at developing more general knowledge that can be applied to other settings.[6] Although action research was originally developed to have this dual focus on change and knowledge, it has been adapted to OD efforts in which the major emphasis is on planned change.[7] Figure 2.1(B) shows the cyclical phases of planned change as defined by the original action research model. There are eight main steps.

1. ***Problem identification.*** This stage usually begins when a key executive in the organization or someone with power and influence senses that the organization has one or more problems that might be solved with the help of an OD practitioner.
2. ***Consultation with a behavioral science expert.*** During the initial contact, the OD practitioner and the client carefully assess each other. The practitioner has

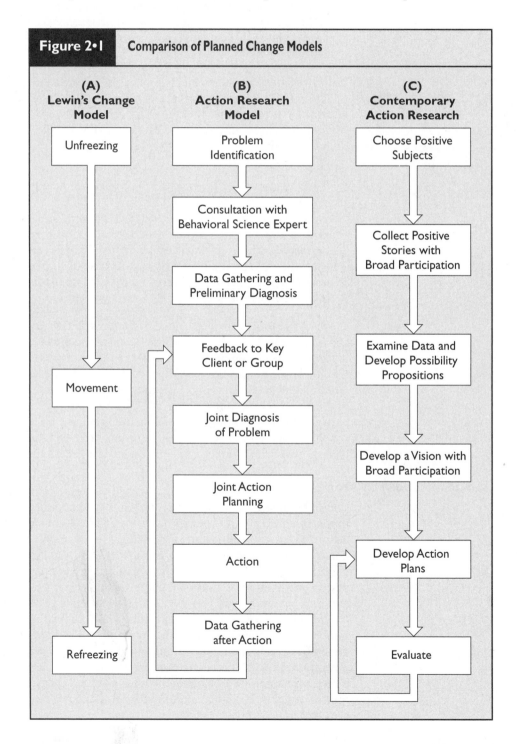

Figure 2•1   Comparison of Planned Change Models

(A) Lewin's Change Model	(B) Action Research Model	(C) Contemporary Action Research
Unfreezing	Problem Identification	Choose Positive Subjects
	Consultation with Behavioral Science Expert	Collect Positive Stories with Broad Participation
	Data Gathering and Preliminary Diagnosis	Examine Data and Develop Possibility Propositions
Movement	Feedback to Key Client or Group	Develop a Vision with Broad Participation
	Joint Diagnosis of Problem	Develop Action Plans
	Joint Action Planning	
	Action	
Refreezing	Data Gathering after Action	Evaluate

his or her own normative, developmental theory or frame of reference and must be conscious of those assumptions and values.[8] Sharing them with the client from the beginning establishes an open and collaborative atmosphere.

3. *Data gathering and preliminary diagnosis.* This step is usually completed by the OD practitioner, often in conjunction with organization members. It involves gathering appropriate information and analyzing it to determine the underlying causes of organizational problems. The four basic methods of gathering data are interviews, process observation, questionnaires, and organizational performance data (unfortunately, often overlooked). One approach to diagnosis begins with observation, proceeds to a semistructured interview, and concludes with a questionnaire to measure precisely the problems identified by the earlier steps.[9] When gathering diagnostic information, OD practitioners may influence members from whom they are collecting data. In OD, "every action on the part of the . . . consultant constitutes an intervention" that will have some effect on the organization.[10]

4. *Feedback to a key client or group.* Because action research is a collaborative activity, the diagnostic data are fed back to the client, usually in a group or work-team meeting. The feedback step, in which members are given the information gathered by the OD practitioner, helps them determine the strengths and weaknesses of the organization or the department under study. The consultant provides the client with all relevant and useful data. Obviously, the practitioner will protect confidential sources of information and, at times, may even withhold data. Defining what is relevant and useful involves consideration of privacy and ethics as well as judgment about whether the group is ready for the information or if the information would make the client overly defensive.

5. *Joint diagnosis of the problem.* At this point, members discuss the feedback and explore with the OD practitioner whether they want to work on identified problems. A close interrelationship exists among data gathering, feedback, and diagnosis because the consultant summarizes the basic data from the client members and presents the data to them for validation and further diagnosis. An important point to remember, as Schein suggests, is that the action research process is very different from the doctor–patient model, in which the consultant comes in, makes a diagnosis, and prescribes a solution. Schein notes that the failure to establish a common frame of reference in the client–consultant relationship may lead to a faulty diagnosis or to a communications gap whereby the client is sometimes "unwilling to believe the diagnosis or accept the prescription." He believes "most companies have drawers full of reports by consultants, each loaded with diagnoses and recommendations which are either not understood or not accepted by the 'patient.'"[11]

6. *Joint action planning.* Next, the OD practitioner and the client members jointly agree on further actions to be taken. This is the beginning of the moving process (described in Lewin's change model), as the organization decides how best to reach a different quasi-stationary equilibrium. At this stage, the specific action to be taken depends on the culture, technology, and environment of the organization; the diagnosis of the problem; and the time and expense of the intervention.

7. *Action.* This stage involves the actual change from one organizational state to another. It may include installing new methods and procedures, reorganizing structures and work designs, and reinforcing new behaviors. Such actions typically cannot be implemented immediately but require a transition period as the organization moves from the present to a desired future state.[12]

8. *Data gathering after action.* Because action research is a cyclical process, data must also be gathered after the action has been taken to measure and determine the effects of the action and to feed the results back to the organization. This, in turn, may lead to rediagnosis and new action.

Contemporary Adaptations of Action Research

The action research model underlies most current approaches to planned change and is often identified with the practice of OD. Recently, action research has been extended to new settings and applications, and consequently researchers and practitioners have made requisite adaptations of its basic framework.[13] The adaptations are depicted in Figure 2.1(C).

Trends in the application of action research include movement from smaller subunits of organizations to total systems and communities.[14] In those larger contexts, action research is more complex and political than in smaller settings. Therefore, the action research cycle is coordinated across multiple change processes and includes a diversity of stakeholders who have an interest in the organization. (We describe these applications more thoroughly in Chapters 19 and 20.)

Action research also is applied increasingly in international settings, particularly in developing nations in the southern hemisphere.[15] Embedded within the action research model, however, are "northern-hemisphere" assumptions about change. For example, action research traditionally views change more linearly than do Eastern cultures, and it treats the change process more collaboratively than do Latin American and African countries.[16] To achieve success in those settings, action research is tailored to fit cultural assumptions. (See "Different Types of Planned Change" below and Chapter 21.)

Finally, action research is applied increasingly to promote social change and innovation,[17] as demonstrated most clearly in community development and global social change projects.[18] Those applications are heavily value laden and seek to redress imbalances in power and resource allocations across different groups. Action researchers tend to play an activist role in the change process, which is often chaotic and conflictual. (Chapter 21 reviews global social change processes.)

In light of these general trends, action research has undergone two key adaptations. First, contemporary applications have increased substantially the degree of member involvement in the change process. That contrasts with traditional approaches to planned change, whereby consultants carried out most of the change activities, with the agreement and collaboration of management.[19] Although consultant-dominated change still persists in OD, there is a growing tendency to involve organization members in learning about their organization and about how to change it. Referred to as "participatory action research,"[20] "action learning,"[21] "action science,"[22] "self-design,"[23] or "appreciative inquiry,"[24] this approach to planned change emphasizes the need for organization members to learn firsthand about planned change if they are to gain the knowledge and skills needed to change the organization. In today's complex and changing environment, some argue that OD must go beyond solving particular problems to helping members gain the competence needed to change and improve the organization continually.[25]

In this modification of action research, the role of OD consultants is to work with members to facilitate the learning process. Both parties are "co-learners" in diagnosing the organization, designing changes, and implementing and assessing them.[26] Neither party dominates the change process. Rather, each participant brings unique information and expertise to the situation, and they combine their resources to learn how to change the organization. Consultants, for example, know how to design diagnostic instruments and OD interventions, and organization members have local knowledge about the organization and how it functions. Each participant learns from the change process. Organization members learn how to change their organization and how to refine and improve it. OD consultants learn how to facilitate complex organizational change and learning.

The second adaptation to action research is the integration of an "interpretive" or "social constructionist" approach to planned change.[27] Called "appreciative inquiry," this model proposes that words and conversations determine what is important and meaningful in organizational life. Take, for example, the work group whose daily conversations are dominated by management feedback that its costs are too high. Even if the group performs well on quality and customer satisfaction, the focus on cost problems can lead group members to believe that the group is a poor performer. Accordingly, this approach to change involves starting new conversations that drive new shared meanings of key goals, processes, and achievements. Proponents of appreciative inquiry point out that most organizational conversations are focused on poor financial results or on how the organization could be better, on the gap between where the organization is and where it wants to be, and on the problems it faces. Metaphorically, organizations are like problems to be solved and the conversations among members dwell on the organization's faults.[28]

Appreciative inquiry challenges that assumption. It suggests that the most important change an organization can make is to begin conversations about what the organization is doing right.[29] Appreciative inquiry helps organization members to understand and describe their organization when it is working at its best. That knowledge is then applied to creating a powerful and guiding image of what the organization could be. Broad involvement of organization members in creating the vision starts a new conversation about the organization's potential and creates a new focus and positive expectation. Considerable research on expectation effects supports this positive approach to planned change.[30] It suggests that people tend to act in ways that make their expectations occur: a positive vision of the organization's future energizes and directs behavior to make that expectation come about.

Planned change emphasizes member involvement and starts with which organization features to examine. For example, members can choose to look for successful male–female collaboration (as opposed to sexual discrimination), instances of customer satisfaction (as opposed to customer dissatisfaction), particularly effective work teams, or product development processes that brought new ideas to market especially fast. If the focus of inquiry is real and vital to organization members, the change process itself will take on these positive attributes. The second step involves gathering data about the "best of what is" in the organization. A broad array of organization members are involved in developing data-gathering instruments, collecting information, and analyzing it. In the third step, members examine the data to find stories, however small, that present a truly exciting and possible picture of the future. From those stories, members develop "possibility propositions"—statements that bridge the organization's current best practices with ideal possibilities for future organizing.[31] That effort redirects attention from "what is" to "what might be." In step four, relevant stakeholders are brought together to construct a vision of the future and to devise action plans for moving in that direction. The vision becomes a statement of "what should be." Finally, implementation of those plans proceeds similarly to the action and assessment phases of action research described previously. Members make changes, assess the results, make necessary adjustments, and so on as they move the organization toward the vision.

Comparisons of Change Models

All three models—Lewin's change model, the action research model, and contemporary adaptations to the action research model—describe the phases by which planned change occurs in organizations. As shown in Figure 2.1, the models overlap in that their emphasis on action to implement organizational change is preceded by a preliminary stage (unfreezing, diagnosis, or examining positive aspects of the organization) and is followed by a closing stage (refreezing or evaluation). Moreover, all three approaches emphasize the application of behavioral science knowledge, involve organization members in the change process to varying degrees, and recognize that any interaction between a consultant and an organization constitutes an intervention that may affect the organization. However, Lewin's change model differs from the other two in that it focuses on the general process of planned change, rather than on specific OD activities.

Lewin's model and the action research model differ from contemporary approaches in terms of the level of involvement of the participants and the focus of change. The first two models emphasize the role of the consultant with limited member involvement in the change process. Contemporary applications, on the other hand, treat both consultants and participants as co-learners who are heavily involved in planned change. In addition, Lewin's model and action research are more concerned with fixing problems than with focusing on what the organization does well and leveraging those strengths. That difference in focus derives from differences in defining reality as objective or socially constructed.[32]

GENERAL MODEL OF PLANNED CHANGE

The three theories of planned change in organizations described above—Lewin's change model, the action research model, and contemporary adaptations to the action research model—suggest a general framework for planned change, as shown in Figure 2.2. The framework describes the four basic activities that practitioners and organization members jointly carry out in organization development. The arrows connecting the different activities in the model show the typical sequence of events, from entering and contracting, to diagnosing, to planning and implementing change, to evaluating and institutionalizing change. The lines connecting the activities emphasize that organizational change is not a straightforward, linear process but involves considerable overlap and feedback among the activities. Because the

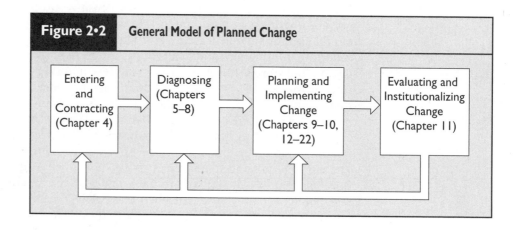

Figure 2•2   General Model of Planned Change

| Entering and Contracting (Chapter 4) | Diagnosing (Chapters 5–8) | Planning and Implementing Change (Chapters 9–10, 12–22) | Evaluating and Institutionalizing Change (Chapter 11) |

model serves to organize the remaining parts of this book, Figure 2.2 also shows which specific chapters apply to the four major change activities.

Entering and Contracting

The first set of activities in planned change concerns entering and contracting (events described in Chapter 4). Those events help managers decide whether they want to engage further in a planned change program and to commit resources to such a process. Entering an organization involves gathering initial data to understand the problems facing the organization or the positive opportunities for inquiry. Once this information is collected, the problems or opportunities are discussed with managers and other organization members to develop a contract or agreement to engage in planned change. The contract spells out future change activities, the resources that will be committed to the process, and how OD practitioners and organization members will be involved. In many cases, organizations do not get beyond this early stage of planned change because disagreements about the need for change surface, resource constraints are encountered, or other methods for change appear more feasible. When OD is used in nontraditional and international settings, the entering and contracting process must be sensitive to the context in which the change is taking place.

Diagnosing

In this stage of planned change, the client system is carefully studied. Diagnosis can focus on understanding organizational problems, including their causes and consequences, or on identifying the organization's positive attributes. The diagnostic process is one of the most important activities in OD. It includes choosing an appropriate model for understanding the organization and gathering, analyzing, and feeding back information to managers and organization members about the problems or opportunities that exist.

Diagnostic models for analyzing problems (described in Chapters 5 and 6) explore three levels of activities. Organization issues represent the most complex level of analysis and involve the total system. Group-level issues are associated with department and group effectiveness. Individual-level issues involve the way jobs are designed.

Gathering, analyzing, and feeding back data are the central change activities in diagnosis. Chapter 7 describes how data can be gathered through interviews, observations, survey instruments, or such archival sources as meeting minutes and organization charts. It also explains how data can be reviewed and analyzed. In Chapter 8, we describe the process of feeding back diagnostic data. Organization members, often in collaboration with an OD practitioner, jointly discuss the data and their implications for change.

Planning and Implementing Change

In this stage, organization members and practitioners jointly plan and implement OD interventions. They design interventions to achieve the organization's vision or goals and make action plans to implement them. There are several criteria for designing interventions, including the organization's readiness for change, its current change capability, its culture and power distributions, and the change agent's skills and abilities (discussed in Chapter 9). Depending on the outcomes of diagnosis, there are four major types of interventions in OD:

1. Human process interventions at the individual, group, and total system levels (Chapters 12 and 13)

2. Interventions that modify an organization's structure and technology (Chapters 14, 15, and 16)

3. Human resource interventions that seek to improve member performance and wellness (Chapters 17 and 18)

4. Strategic interventions that involve managing the organization's relationship to its external environment and the internal structure and process necessary to support a business strategy (Chapters 19 and 20).

Chapters 21 and 22 present specialized information for carrying out OD in international settings and in such nontraditional organizations as schools, health-care institutions, and the public sector.

Implementing interventions is concerned with managing the change process. As discussed in Chapter 10, it includes motivating change, creating a desired future vision of the organization, developing political support, managing the transition toward the vision, and sustaining momentum for change.

Evaluating and Institutionalizing Change

The final stage in planned change involves evaluating the effects of the intervention and managing the institutionalization of successful change programs. (Those two activities are described in Chapter 11.) Feedback to organization members about the intervention's results provides information about whether the changes should be continued, modified, or suspended. Institutionalizing successful changes involves reinforcing them through feedback, rewards, and training.

Application 2.1 describes how the different phases of planned change were applied at the Comstock Michigan Fruit Division of Curtice Burns Foods, Inc.[33] It demonstrates how traditional planned change activities, such as entry and contracting, survey feedback, and change planning, can be combined with contemporary methods, such as large-group interventions and high levels of participation.

DIFFERENT TYPES OF PLANNED CHANGE

The general model of planned change describes how the OD process typically unfolds in organizations. In actual practice, the different phases are not nearly as orderly as the model implies. OD practitioners tend to modify or adjust the stages to fit the needs of the situation. Steps in planned change may be implemented in a variety of ways, depending on the client's needs and goals, the change agent's skills and values, and the organization's context. Thus, planned change can vary enormously from one situation to another.

To understand the differences better, planned change can be contrasted across situations on three key dimensions: the magnitude of organizational change, the degree to which the client system is organized, and whether the setting is domestic or international.

Magnitude of Change

Planned change efforts can be characterized as falling along a continuum ranging from incremental changes that involve fine-tuning the organization to quantum changes that entail fundamentally altering how it operates.[34] Incremental changes tend to involve limited dimensions and levels of the organization, such as the

APPLICATION 2•1   Planned Change at Curtice Burns Foods

Comstock Michigan Fruit is the largest of six divisions in Curtice Burns Foods, Inc., a privately held cooperative with annual sales in excess of $750 million. Comstock is the largest processor and distributor of vegetables and fruit fillings in the United States. It competes in the grocery trade under its own brand names, like Comstock, Thank You, and Wilderness, as well as private-label brands. Comstock also sells products to restaurants and public institutions. It employs about sixteen hundred employees and has annual sales of approximately $370 million.

In the early 1990s, as competitive pressures rose to unprecedented levels in the food industry, Comstock sought to make substantial improvements in product quality and cost management. To achieve those goals, the company relied heavily on its traditional "command-and-control" culture, which emphasized top-down decision making and employee compliance with management directives. Although the culture had served Comstock well in the past, it quickly became a liability in the more competitive environment. The directive culture underutilized employees' knowledge and talents; it failed to apply their competence to making significant improvements in costs and quality. These problems were particularly evident in the company's manufacturing plants, where most of the improvements had to occur.

At two of the plants, managers became sufficiently frustrated with the status quo to seek ways to change it. They felt that a more participative culture that promoted employee involvement in problem solving and change would enable the firm to respond quickly to rapidly changing competitive conditions. Consequently, they contacted Comstock's vice president for organization development to explore how to get employees more involved in the improvement efforts. After several conversations, the managers concluded that continuous improvements in costs and quality would require a high-involvement culture where employees were empowered to make decisions and were rewarded for their contributions. Moreover, to create a high-involvement culture, the change process itself would need to be highly involving; it would need to model how employees could participate more in the daily operation and improvement of the plants.

Based on these early discussions, the vice president for organization development agreed to provide internal OD consultants to help the plant managers and their employees design and implement a high-involvement culture. The change process would rely heavily on survey feedback methods and large-group interventions. Members from the plants would review previous survey data to diagnose the culture of their own work units. They would also learn about customers' requirements, propose specific improvements in costs and quality, and make decisions about particular action items. The consultants would provide design and facilitation expertise and coach the participants throughout the change process.

Initially, the OD consultants worked with representatives from each of the two plants to design a two-day meeting where all plant members could learn about the competitive situation, diagnose their current organizations, and devise action plans for improvement. That design activity was highly intense and reflected in many ways how employees in both plants would react to the forthcoming meeting and the subsequent change process. At first, the plant representatives voiced frustration about the company's problems and skepticism about the prospects for positive change. Such disclosure enabled members to vent their negative emotions so they could then focus more positively on designing the two-day meeting.

Next, members at the two plants were informed about the upcoming meeting. The purpose of the change program and the agenda for the meeting were communicated both orally and in writing throughout the plants. Shortly thereafter, the plants were closed for two days so that all members could attend the meeting. Although each plant held a separate meeting, both facilities followed the same meeting design.

The first day of the meeting can best be described as "getting collectively smart." Key members of Comstock presented important information about customers, competitors, and the industry. Plant managers supplied data about costs and quality and the challenges of managing $20–30-million budgets and all of the tradeoffs required. Comstock's president and CEO described the competitive environment and expectations for improvement. Employees were encouraged to ask questions and to share their own views about the challenges facing the firm.

The first day of the meeting was also designed to make everyone in the organization think like a manager. Employees were given information about how the business operated and the challenges that lay ahead. Because such information had never been shared with employees, many were surprised at the candor of the speakers. Specific knowledge about the business and the competitive situation was essential if members were to become actively involved in operating the plants and improving them.

The second day of the meeting began with a brief overview of an organizational climate survey that had been conducted throughout Comstock several months earlier. It measured various aspects of leadership, problem solving, communication, and quality management. The consultants summarized the survey data by major topic for each plant. Then participants worked in small groups to review and react to the results. They were encouraged to share surprises and disappointments and to discuss what they were pleased with and what they thought was on target. Next, based on brainstorming in the subgroups, all plant members came together to identify the greatest barriers and enablers to plant success. This issue was discussed in the context of everything that they had learned the previous day about plant performance and the challenges facing the business overall.

The final part of the meeting addressed action planning. Once again, the entire group brainstormed possible action items and voted on priorities. Before leaving the meeting, employees were given the opportunity to join committees to address the issues that most concerned them.

The evaluations from both of these sessions were very positive. There was also a healthy dose of skepticism as employees wondered if anything would come of all of the work. Less than a year later, a number of positive changes were reported. For example, one plant worked out a flexible hours and maximum consecutive workdays schedule for the busy summer season. This resulted in more time off than was possible in the past. In another plant, the employees became very involved in designing their own work schedules and defining a process for awarding overtime. The maintenance group in one plant became more involved in the quality of the product produced, attended quality meetings, and took greater responsi-

bility for the operation of the plant. As a result, the quality of cut green beans greatly improved over the year because of better equipment and more attention by the employees. A self-directed team developed operating procedures on one production line with the goal of learning how an organization can push decision making down to the lowest possible levels. A pay-for-performance team was established in one plant and developed guidelines and procedures for evaluating performance. Those procedures were introduced during the winter of 1995 and organization members have reported an improvement in how performance is evaluated. Their next step is to revise the pay structure to link rewards with clearly identified skills and to clarify what is required for people to advance.

And finally, both facilities have increased the amount of management training. Greater effort is being made to gather the input from key stakeholders before making decisions. One facility reorganized to give maintenance personnel more responsibility for slowing production when there are problems. This is no longer the sole responsibility of management. Both facilities have made progress in creating the kind of environment that encourages shared responsibility for business success. More needs to be done, but there is a critical mass of people who are committed to making the changes. Developing that critical mass was the greatest challenge to managing change. ■

decision-making processes of work groups. They occur within the context of the organization's existing business strategy, structure, and culture and are aimed at improving the status quo. Quantum changes, on the other hand, are directed at significantly altering how the organization operates. They tend to involve several organizational dimensions, including structure, culture, reward systems, information processes, and work design. They also involve changing multiple levels of the organization, from top-level management through departments and work groups to individual jobs.

Planned change traditionally has been applied in situations involving incremental change. Organizations in the 1960s and 1970s were concerned mainly with fine-tuning their bureaucratic structures by resolving many of the social problems that emerged with increasing size and complexity. In those situations, planned change involves a relatively bounded set of problem-solving activities. OD practitioners are typically contracted by managers to help solve specific problems in particular organizational systems, such as poor communication among members of a work team or low customer satisfaction scores in a department store. Diagnostic and change activities tend to be limited to the defined issues, although additional problems may be uncovered and may need to be addressed. Similarly, the change process tends to focus on those organizational systems having specific problems, and it generally terminates when the problems are resolved. Of course, the change agent may contract to help solve additional problems.

In recent years, OD has been concerned increasingly with quantum change. As described in Chapter 1, the greater competitiveness and uncertainty of today's environment have led a growing number of organizations to alter drastically the way in which they operate. In such situations, planned change is more complex, extensive, and long term than when applied to incremental change.[35] Because quantum change involves most features and levels of the organization, it is typically driven from the top, where corporate strategy and values are set. Change agents help senior managers create a vision of a desired future organization and energize movement in that direction. They also help executives develop structures for managing the transition from the present to the future organization and may include, for example, a variety of overlapping steering committees and redesign teams. Staff experts also may redesign many features of the firm, such as performance measures, rewards, planning processes, work designs, and information systems.

Because of the complexity and extensiveness of quantum change, OD professionals often work in teams comprising members with different yet complementary areas of expertise. The consulting relationship persists over relatively long time periods and includes a great deal of renegotiation and experimentation among consultants and managers. The boundaries of the change effort are more uncertain and diffuse than in incremental change, thus making diagnosis and change seem more like discovery than like problem solving. (We describe complex strategic and transformational types of change in more detail in Chapters 19 and 20.)

It is important to emphasize that quantum change may or may not be developmental in nature. Organizations may drastically alter their strategic direction and way of operating without significantly developing their capacity to solve problems and to achieve both high performance and quality of work life. For example, firms may simply change their marketing mix, dropping or adding products, services, or customers; they may drastically downsize by cutting out marginal businesses and laying off managers and workers; or they may tighten managerial and financial controls and attempt to squeeze more out of the labor force. On the other hand, organizations may undertake quantum change from a developmental perspective. They may seek to make themselves more competitive by developing their human resources; by getting managers and employees more involved in problem solving and innovation; and by promoting flexibility and direct, open communication. That OD approach to quantum change is particularly relevant in today's rapidly changing and competitive environment. To succeed in this setting, firms such as General Electric, Kimberly-Clark, ABB, Hewlett-Packard, and Motorola are transforming themselves from control-oriented bureaucracies to high-involvement organizations capable of changing and improving themselves continually.

Degree of Organization

Planned change efforts also can vary depending on the degree to which the organization or client system is organized. In overorganized situations, such as in highly mechanistic, bureaucratic organizations, various dimensions such as leadership styles, job designs, organization structure, and policies and procedures are too rigid and overly defined for effective task performance. Communication between management and employees is typically suppressed, conflicts are avoided, and employees are apathetic. In underorganized organizations, on the other hand, there is too little constraint or regulation for effective task performance. Leadership, structure, job design, and policy are poorly defined and fail to control task behaviors effectively. Communication is fragmented, job responsibilities are ambiguous, and employees' energies are dissipated because they lack direction. Underorganized situations are typically found in such areas as product development, project management, and community development, where relationships among diverse groups and participants must be coordinated around complex, uncertain tasks.

In overorganized situations, where much of OD practice has historically taken place, planned change is generally aimed at loosening constraints on behavior. Changes in leadership, job design, structure, and other features are designed to liberate suppressed energy, to increase the flow of relevant information between employees and managers, and to promote effective conflict resolution. The typical steps of planned change—entry, diagnosis, intervention, and evaluation—are intended to penetrate a relatively closed organization or department and make it increasingly open to self-diagnosis and revitalization. The relationship between the OD practitioner and the management team attempts to model this loosening process. The consultant shares leadership of the change process with management, encourages open communications and confrontation of conflict, and maintains flexibility in relating to the organization.

When applied to organizations facing problems in being underorganized, planned change is aimed at increasing organization by clarifying leadership roles, structuring communication between managers and employees, and specifying job and departmental responsibilities. These activities require a modification of the traditional phases of planned change and include the following four steps:[36]

1. *Identification.* This step identifies the relevant people or groups who need to be involved in the change program. In many underorganized situations, people and departments can be so disconnected that there is ambiguity about who should be included in the problem-solving process. For example, when managers of different departments have only limited interaction with each other, they may disagree or be confused about which departments should be involved in developing a new product or service.

2. *Convention.* In this step the relevant people or departments in the company are brought together to begin organizing for task performance. For example, department managers might be asked to attend a series of organizing meetings to discuss the division of labor and the coordination required to introduce a new product.

3. *Organization.* Different organizing mechanisms are created to structure the newly required interactions among people and departments. This might include creating new leadership positions, establishing communication channels, and specifying appropriate plans and policies.

4. *Evaluation.* In this final step the outcomes of the organization step are assessed. The evaluation might signal the need for adjustments in the organizing process or for further identification, convention, and organization activities.

In carrying out these four steps of planned change in underorganized situations, the relationship between the OD practitioner and the client system attempts to reinforce the organizing process. The consultant develops a well-defined leadership role, which might be autocratic during the early stages of the change program. Similarly, the consulting relationship is clearly defined and tightly specified. In effect, the interaction between the consultant and the client system supports the larger process of bringing order to the situation.

Application 2.2 is an example of planned change in an underorganized situation. In this case, the change agent is a person from industry who identifies a multifaceted problem: university research that should be helpful to manufacturing

APPLICATION 2•2   Planned Change in an Underorganized System

The Institute for Manufacturing and Automation Research (IMAR) was founded in 1987 in Los Angeles by a group of manufacturing industry members. In its earliest stages of development, one person who had a clear picture of the obstacles to manufacturing excellence was Dale Hartman, IMAR's executive director and former director for manufacturing at Hughes Aircraft Company. He and several other industry associates pinpointed the predominant reasons for flagging competitiveness: needless duplication of effort among manufacturing innovators; difficulties in transferring technological breakthroughs from university to industry; frequent irrelevance of university research to the needs of industry; and the inability of individual industry members to commit the time and funds to research projects needed for continued technological advances.

Hartman and his colleagues determined that organizations should create a pool of funds for research and concluded that the research would most efficiently be carried out in existing university facilities. They worked through at least several plans before they arrived at the idea of the IMAR consortium. The United States Navy had been interested in joint efforts for innovations in artificial intelligence, but its constraints and interests were judged to be too narrow to address the problems that Hartman and the others identified.

Networking with other industry members—TRW, Hughes, Northrup, and Rockwell—and two universities with which Hughes had been engaging in ongoing research—the University of Southern California (USC) and University of California, Los Angeles (UCLA)—this original group formed a steering committee to investigate the viability of a joint research and development consortium. Each of the six early planners contributed $5,000 as seed money for basic expenses. The steering committee, based on experience in cooperative research, determined that a full-time person was needed to assume leadership of the consortium. Members of the committee persuaded Dale Hartman to retire early from Hughes and take on IMAR's leadership full time. Hartman brought with him a wealth of knowledge about barriers to innovation and technology transfer, and a solid reputation in both industry and academia that was crucial for the success of multiple-sector partnerships. As a former Hughes networker, he knew how to lobby state and federal government sources for funds and legislation that promoted industry innovation. He also knew a host of talented people in southern California whom he would persuade to become IMAR members.

In his thirty years in manufacturing, Hartman found that university-driven research had not produced a respectable yield of usable information. University research was frequently irrelevant to industry needs and seldom provided for transfer of usable innovation to the plant floor. Industry was only

tangentially involved in what the university was doing and saw little opportunity for the two sectors to benefit from a partnership. Therefore, it was determined that IMAR would be user-driven. Industry would set the agenda by choosing projects from among university proposals that promised to be of generic use to industry members, and it would benefit by influencing the direction of research and receiving early information about research results.

In the next several months, the steering committee and Hartman met regularly to define common research needs and locate funding sources. They sought industry sponsors from high-technology companies with an understanding of the problems in manufacturing research and a desire to do more than merely supply money. They wanted members who would be willing to get involved in IMAR's programs. Furthermore, they wanted all members to be able to use the results of IMAR's generic research while not competing directly with each other. Finally, they decided that they wanted a relatively small membership. If the membership grew too large, it might become unwieldy and thus obstruct efforts to get things done.

IMAR's industrial advisory board was formed with six industrial organizations represented—Xerox, Hughes, TRW, Northrup, IBM, and Rockwell—in addition to USC and UCLA. Members were to pay $100,000 each and make a three-year commitment to IMAR. With initial objectives in place and a committed membership, Hartman was already searching for additional funding sources. He was successful in getting a bill introduced in California's state legislature, later signed by the governor, that authorized the state department of commerce to fund IMAR $200,000. Moreover, IMAR was able to tie into the Industry–University Cooperative Research Center Program (IUCRCP) of the National Science Foundation (NSF) by forming an industry–university consortium called the Center for Manufacturing and Automation Research (CMAR). NSF funded CMAR with a $2-million grant and a five-year commitment. NSF funding in particular was sought because of the instant credibility that NSF sponsorship gives to such an institute.

NSF requested that several more universities be added to the consortium. In addition, an NSF evaluator was to be present at all IMAR meetings and conduct ongoing evaluation of CMAR's progress. IMAR already had UCLA and USC among its members and now added four university affiliates to work on research projects: the University of California, Irvine; University of California, Santa Barbara; Caltech; and Arizona State University. The IMAR steering committee then voted to fund research projects at an affiliated university only if it involved cooperation with either USC or UCLA. Each of the four university affiliates was paired with either USC or

UCLA. Each affiliate university was selected because it provided expertise in an area of interest to IMAR's industrial membership. Arizona State, for example, had expertise in knowledge-based simulation systems in industrial engineering, a field of special concern to IMAR's membership.

Currently, IMAR has funded nine projects: four are joint with the affiliated universities, one is joint between investigators at USC and UCLA, and two each are conducted separately at USC and UCLA. Figure 2.3 shows IMAR's structure.

CMAR operates under the auspices of IMAR with the same board of directors serving both consortia. There are two co-directors of CMAR: Dr. George Bekey, chairman of the Computer Science Department at USC, and Dr. Michel Melkanoff, director of UCLA's Center for Integrated Manufacturing. As co-directors they have an indirect reporting rela-

tionship to Dale Hartman. Their responsibilities are to distribute the research funds and to serve as the focal point on their respective campuses. Questions from project team members are directed to one or the other co-director, depending on the project. Each of the co-directors takes responsibility for managing project team members and providing rewards, such as reduced course loads, to research professors wherever possible.

The co-directors further work to encourage informal ties with industry members. For example, Dr. Bekey has initiated efforts to have IMAR representatives regularly visit others' facilities to encourage them to cooperate and share ideas. That practice further deepens each industrial member's commitment to IMAR because the representatives are associating with one another and other colleagues in the workplace. In

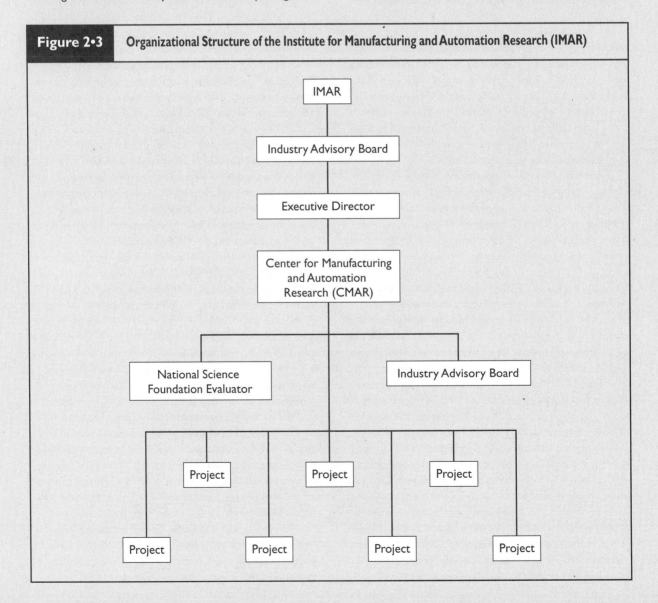

Figure 2•3　Organizational Structure of the Institute for Manufacturing and Automation Research (IMAR)

the event that an industry or university representative leaves, an associate is more likely to be there to take his or her place. Further, Bekey notes that the association between industry and university helps industry to overcome its short-term orientation and helps university people appreciate applied problems and manufacturing needs.

IMAR's board of directors sets the research agenda at annual reviews in which it makes recommendations for topics to be funded. IMAR takes these recommendations and translates them into "requests for proposals" to be circulated among the participating university members. CMAR's co-directors then solicit proposals from the university membership. Researchers' proposals are evaluated and ranked by industry representatives and then passed back to the industry advisory board, which finally determines which projects should be funded.

Not only is IMAR engaged in nine research projects in such technologies as microelectronics, digital computers, lasers, and fiber optics; it is further working to resolve critical problems for manufacturing innovation research. One area of study is technology transfer. IMAR is trying to establish a pilot production facility that Hartman has called "a halfway house for manufacturing." The facility would permit basic research to be brought to maturity and would be capable of producing deliverable parts. The facility would also engage in systems-level research in such areas as management and systems software. Such a facility would provide an excellent training ground for students.

Yet another function that Hartman believes IMAR must assume is graduate and continuing education. Graduate education is fostered through the various projects; continuing education for industrial members is provided through affiliation with state-of-the-art research being done by university researchers. Furthermore, USC and UCLA faculty are available to assist IMAR in presenting seminars.

Another strength of IMAR is its affiliation with an NSF evaluator who is appointed to follow the progress of the industry–university cooperative research centers. Dr. Ann Marczak is IMAR's NSF evaluator. NSF conducts a regular audit of the thirty-nine IUCRCPs it sponsors and makes information available about survey results, others' reports of what works,

and so forth. Dr. Marczak serves a valuable function to IMAR as an objective source of feedback. After her first evaluation, for example, Marczak recommended that a project team be formed to conduct ongoing progress assessment for each of the nine research projects IMAR is sponsoring. The evaluator's findings also serve as NSF's means of determining how well each of the funded centers is performing. A center is judged successful if after five years it can exist without NSF funds. NSF also evaluates each center in terms of how much industry money its projects generated, how much additional money the center generated in research projects, the number of patents granted, products produced, and the satisfaction of faculty and industry participants.

Although it is too soon to assess IMAR's success in meeting its objectives, it is well positioned to take advantage of the full range of benefits offered by joint industry–university research. After only one year of operation, IMAR has dealt with many of the problems that so frequently plague collaborative research and development efforts among organizations. It has a well-defined purpose that is strongly supported by its members. It is well structured and has a good balance of resources and needs among its membership. Formal and informal communication networks have been established. It has strong leadership. Members of IMAR respect Hartman for his technological expertise and skills as a networker. Hartman has a strong sense of IMAR's mission. After a discussion with him, one gets the sense that there is not an obstacle he will not overcome. His vision further instills commitment among the IMAR membership. As one member put it, "You end up wanting to see what you can do for the cause."

Not only does IMAR have the commitment of a full-time leader and strong feedback from its NSF evaluator, but it involves user-driven research. Although the research is basic, it is chosen by the users themselves to benefit all members of the consortium. If the research had been applied, it would have been more difficult for members to find projects yielding information that all of them could use. The involvement of multiple universities further provides the talent of top researchers in diverse areas of technological expertise. Finally, NSF is furnishing a large proportion of the funding for the first five years as well as regular evaluations. ■

organizations is not being shaped, coordinated, or transferred. In response, he forms an organization to tighten up the relationships between the two parties.[37]

Domestic vs. International Settings

Planned change efforts traditionally have been applied in North American and European settings but increasingly are used outside of those cultures. Developed in western societies, the action research model reflects the underlying values and assumptions of these geographic settings, including equality, involvement, and short-term time horizons. Under such conditions, the action research model works quite well. In other societies, however, a very different set of cultural values and assumptions may operate and make the application of OD problematic. For example, the cultures of most Asian countries are more hierarchical and status conscious, are less open to discussing personal issues, more concerned with saving "face," and have a longer time horizon for results. Even when the consultant is aware of the cultural norms and values that permeate the society, those cultural differences make the traditional action research steps more difficult for a North American or European consultant to implement.

The cultural values that guide OD practice in the United States, for example, include a tolerance for ambiguity, equality among people, individuality, and achievement motives. An OD process that encourages openness among individuals, high levels of participation, and actions that promote increased effectiveness are viewed favorably. The OD practitioner is also assumed to hold those values and to model them in the conduct of planned change. Most reported cases of OD involve western-based organizations using practitioners trained in the traditional model and raised and experienced in western society.

When OD is applied outside of the North American or European context (and sometimes even within those settings), the action research process must be adapted to fit the cultural context. For example, the diagnostic phase, which is aimed at understanding the current drivers of organization effectiveness, can be modified in a variety of ways. Diagnosis can involve many organization members or include only senior managers; be directed from the top, conducted by an outside consultant, or performed by internal consultants; or involve face-to-face interviews or organization documents. Each step in the general model of planned change must be carefully mapped against the cultural context.

Conducting OD in international settings is highly stressful on OD practitioners. To be successful, they must develop a keen awareness of their own cultural biases, be open to seeing a variety of issues from another perspective, be fluent in the values and assumptions of the host country, and understand the economic and political context of business there. Most OD practitioners are not able to meet all of those criteria and adopt a "cultural guide," often a member of the organization, to help navigate the cultural, operational, and political nuances of change in that society.

CRITIQUE OF PLANNED CHANGE

Despite their continued refinement, the models and practice of planned change are still in a formative stage of development, and there is considerable room for improvement. Critics of OD have pointed out several problems with the way planned change has been conceptualized and practiced.

Conceptualization of Planned Change

Planned change has typically been characterized as involving a series of activities for carrying out effective organization development. Although current models outline a general set of steps to be followed, considerably more information is needed to guide how those steps should be performed in specific situations. In an extensive review and critique of planned change theory, Porras and Robertson argued that planned change activities should be guided by information about (1) the organizational features that can be changed, (2) the intended outcomes from making those changes, (3) the causal mechanisms by which those outcomes are achieved, and

(4) the contingencies upon which successful change depends.[38] In particular, they noted that the key to organizational change is change in the behavior of each member and that the information available about the causal mechanisms that produce individual change is lacking. Overall, Porras and Robertson concluded that the necessary information to guide change is only partially available and that a good deal more research and thinking are needed to fill the gaps. Chapters 12 through 20 on OD interventions review what is currently known about change features, outcomes, causal mechanisms, and contingencies.

A related area where current thinking about planned change is deficient is knowledge about how the stages of planned change differ across situations. Most models specify a general set of steps that are intended to be applicable to most change efforts. The previous section of this chapter showed, however, how change activities can vary depending on such factors as the magnitude of change, the degree to which the client system is organized, and whether change is being conducted in a domestic or an international setting. Considerably more effort needs to be expended identifying situational factors that may require modifying the general stages of planned change. That would likely lead to a rich array of planned change models, each geared to a specific set of situational conditions. Such contingency thinking is sorely needed in planned change.

Planned change also tends to be described as a rationally controlled, orderly process. Critics have argued that although this view may be comforting, it is seriously misleading.[39] They point out that planned change has a more chaotic quality, often involving shifting goals, discontinuous activities, surprising events, and unexpected combinations of changes. For example, managers often initiate changes without clear plans that clarify their strategies and goals. As change unfolds, new stakeholders may emerge and demand modifications reflecting previously unknown or unvoiced needs. Those emergent conditions make planned change a far more disorderly and dynamic process than is customarily portrayed, and conceptions need to capture that reality.

Finally, the relationship between planned change and organizational performance and effectiveness is not well understood. OD traditionally has had problems assessing whether interventions are producing observed results. The complexity of the change situation, the lack of sophisticated analyses, and the long time periods for producing results have contributed to weak evaluation of OD efforts. Moreover, managers have often accounted for OD efforts with post hoc testimonials, reports of possible future benefits, and calls to support OD as the right thing to do. In the absence of rigorous assessment and measurement, it is difficult to make resource allocation decisions about change programs and to know which interventions are most effective in certain situations.

Practice of Planned Change

Critics have suggested several problems with the way planned change is carried out.[40] Their concerns are not with the planned change model itself but with how change takes place and with the qualifications and activities of OD practitioners.

A growing number of OD practitioners have acquired skills in a specific technique, such as team building, total quality management, large-group interventions, or gain sharing and have chosen to specialize in that method. Although such specialization may be necessary, it can lead to a certain myopia given the complex array of techniques that make up modern OD. Some OD practitioners favor particular techniques and ignore other strategies that might be more appropriate, tending to interpret organizational problems as requiring the favored technique. Thus, for example, it is not unusual to see consultants pushing such methods as diversity training, reengineering, organization learning, or self-managing work teams as solutions to most organizational problems.

Effective change depends on a careful diagnosis of how the organization is functioning. Diagnosis identifies the underlying causes of organizational problems, such as poor product quality and employee dissatisfaction. It requires both time and money, and some organizations are not willing to make the necessary investment. Rather, they rely on preconceptions about what the problem is and hire consultants with skills appropriate to solve that problem. Managers may think, for example, that work design is the problem, so they hire an expert in job enrichment to implement a change program. The problem may be caused by other factors such as poor reward practices, however, and job enrichment would be inappropriate. Careful diagnosis can help to avoid such mistakes.

In situations requiring complex organizational changes, planned change is a long-term process involving considerable innovation and learning on site. It requires a good deal of time and commitment and a willingness to modify and refine changes as the circumstances require. Some organizations demand more rapid solutions to their problems and seek quick fixes from experts. Unfortunately, some OD consultants are more than willing to provide quick solutions.[41] They sell prepackaged programs for organizations to adopt. Those programs appeal to managers because they typically include an explicit recipe to be followed, standard training materials, and clear time and cost boundaries. The quick fixes have trouble gaining wide organizational support and commitment, however, and they seldom produce the positive results that have been advertised.

Other organizations have not recognized the systemic nature of change. Too often they believe that intervention into one aspect or subpart of the organization will be sufficient to ameliorate the problems, and are unprepared for the other changes that may be necessary to support a particular intervention. For example, at GTE of California, the positive benefits of an employee involvement program did not begin to appear until after the organization redesigned its reward system to support the cross-functional collaboration necessary to solve highly complex problems. Changing any one part or feature of an organization often requires adjustments in the other parts to maintain an appropriate alignment. Thus, although quick fixes and change programs that focus on only one part or aspect of the organization may resolve some specific problems, they generally do not lead to complex organizational change or increase members' capacity to carry out change.[42]

■ SUMMARY

Theories of planned change describe the activities necessary to modify strategies, structures, and processes to increase an organization's effectiveness. Lewin's change model, the action research model, and more recent adaptations of action research offer different views of the phases through which planned change occurs in organizations. Lewin's change model views planned change as a three-step process of unfreezing, movement, and refreezing. It provides a general description of the process of planned change. The action research model focuses on planned change as a cyclical process involving joint activities between organization members and OD practitioners. It involves eight sequential steps that overlap and interact in practice: problem identification, consultation with a behavioral science expert, data gathering and preliminary diagnosis, feedback to a key client or group, joint diagnosis of the problem, joint action planning, action, and data gathering after action. The action research model places heavy emphasis on data gathering and diagnosis prior to action planning and implementation, and on assessment of results after action is taken. In addition, change strategies often are modified on the basis of continued diagnosis, and termination of one OD program may lead to further work in other areas of the firm. Recent trends in action research include movement from smaller to larger systems, from domestic to international applications, and from organizational issues to social change. Those trends have led to two key adaptations of action research: increased involvement of participants in the change process and a more appreciative approach to organizational change.

Planned change theories can be integrated into a general model. Four sets of activities—entering and contracting, diagnosing, planning and implementing, and evaluating and institutionalizing—can be used to describe how change is accomplished in organizations. These four sets of activities also describe the general structure of the chapters in this book. The general model has broad applicability to planned change. It identifies the steps an organization typically moves through to implement change and specifies the OD activities needed to effect change. Although the planned change models describe general stages of how the OD process unfolds, there are different types of change depending on the situation. Planned change efforts can vary in terms of the magnitude of the change and the degree to which the client system is organized. When situations differ on those dimensions, planned change can vary greatly. Critics of OD have pointed out several problems with the way planned change has been conceptualized and practiced, and specific areas where planned change can be improved.

■ NOTES

1. W. Bennis, *Changing Organizations* (New York: McGraw-Hill, 1966); J. Porras and P. Robertson, "Organization Development Theory: A Typology and Evaluation," in *Research in Organizational Change and Development*, vol. 1, eds. R. Woodman and W. Pasmore (Greenwich, Conn.: JAI Press, 1987): 1–57.

2. K. Lewin, *Field Theory in Social Science* (New York: Harper & Row, 1951).

3. E. Schein, *Process Consultation*, vols. 1 and 2 (Reading, Mass.: Addison-Wesley, 1987).

4. R. Lippitt, J. Watson, and B. Westley, *The Dynamics of Planned Change* (New York: Harcourt, Brace and World, 1958).

5. R. Benjamin and E. Levinson, "A Framework for Managing IT-Enabled Change," *Sloan Management Review* (Summer 1993): 23–33.

6. A. Shani and G. Bushe, "Visionary Action Research: A Consultation Process Perspective," *Consultation* 6 (Spring 1987): 3–19; G. Sussman and R. Evered, "An Assessment of the Scientific Merit of Action Research," *Administrative Science Quarterly* 12 (1978): 582–603.

7. W. French, "Organization Development: Objectives, Assumptions, and Strategies," *California Management Review* 12 (1969): 23–34; A. Frohman, M. Sashkin, and M. Kavanagh, "Action Research as Applied to Organization Development," *Organization and Administrative Sciences* 7 (1976): 129–42; E. Schein, *Organizational Psychology*, 3d ed. (Englewood Cliffs, N.J.: Prentice Hall, 1980).

8. N. Tichy, "Agents of Planned Change: Congruence of Values, Cognitions, and Actions," *Administrative Science Quarterly* 19 (1974): 163–82.

9. M. Beer, "The Technology of Organization Development," in *Handbook of Industrial and Organizational Psychology*, ed. M. Dunnette (Chicago: Rand McNally, 1976): 945.

10. E. Schein, *Process Consultation: Its Role in Organization Development* (Reading, Mass.: Addison-Wesley, 1969): 98.

11. Ibid, 6.

12. R. Beckhard and R. Harris, *Organizational Transitions*, 2d ed. (Reading, Mass.: Addison-Wesley, 1987).

13. M. Elden and R. Chisholm, "Emerging Varieties of Action Research: Introduction to the Special Issue," *Human Relations* 46, 2 (1993): 121–42.

14. G. Ledford and S. Mohrman, "Self-Design for High In-volvement," *Human Relations* 46 (1993): 143–68; B. B. Bunker and B. Alban, "The Large Group Intervention—A New Social Innovation?" *Journal of Applied Behavioral Science* 28, 4 (1992): 473–80.

15. R. Marshak, "Lewin Meets Confucius: A Re-view of the OD Model of Change," *Journal of Applied Behavioral Science* 29, 4 (1993): 393–415; K. Murrell, "Evaluation as Action Research: The Case of the Management Develop-ment Institute in Gambia, West Africa," *International Jour-nal of Public Administration* 16, 3 (1993): 341–56; J. Preston and L. DuToit, "Endemic Violence in South Africa: An OD Solution Applied to Two Educational Settings," *Interna-tional Journal of Public Administration* 16 (1993): 1767–91.

16. D. Brown, "Participatory Action Research for Social Change: Collective Reflections with Asian Nongovern-mental Development Organizations," *Human Relations* 46, 2 (1993): 208–27.

17. D. Cooperrider and S. Srivastva, "Appreciative Inquiry in Organizational Life," in *Research in Organizational Change and Development*, vol. 1, eds. R. Woodman and W. Pasmore (Greenwich, Conn.: JAI Press, 1987): 129–70.

18. D. Cooperrider and W. Pasmore, "Global Social Change: A New Agenda for Social Science?" *Human Rela-tions* 44, 10 (1991): 1037–55.

19. W. Burke, *Organization Development: A Normative View* (Reading, Mass.: Addison-Wesley, 1987).

20. D. Greenwood, W. Whyte, and I. Harkavy, "Participa-tory Action Research as Process and as Goal," *Human Rela-tions* 46, 2 (1993): 175–92.

21. G. Morgan and R. Ramirez, "Action Learning: A Holo-graphic Metaphor for Guiding Social Change," *Human Re-lations* 37 (1984): 1–28.

22. C. Argyris, R. Putnam, and D. Smith, *Action Science* (San Francisco: Jossey-Bass, 1985).

23. S. Mohrman and T. Cummings, *Self-Designing Organi-zations: Learning How to Create High Performance* (Reading, Mass.: Addison-Wesley, 1989).

24. Cooperrider and Srivastva, "Appreciative Inquiry"; S. Hammond and C. Royal, *Lessons from the Field: Applying Appreciative Inquiry* (Plano, Tex.: Practical Press).

25. P. Senge, *The Fifth Discipline* (New York: Doubleday, 1990).

26. M. Weisbord, *Productive Workplaces* (San Francisco: Jossey-Bass, 1987).

27. K. Gergen, "The Social Constructionist Movement in Modern Psychology," *American Psychologist* 40 (1985): 266–75; L. Isabella, "Evolving Interpretations as Change Unfolds: How Managers Construe Key Organizational Events," *Academy of Management Journal* 33 (1990): 7–41; D. Cooperrider, "Positive Image, Positive Action: The Af-firmative Basis for Organizing," in *Appreciative Management and Leadership*, eds. S. Srivastva, D. Cooperrider, and Asso-ciates (San Francisco: Jossey-Bass, 1990); D. Cooperrider (lecture notes, presentation to the MSOD Chi Class, Mon-terey, Calif., October 1995); F. Barrett, G. Thomas, and S. Hocevar, "The Central Role of Discourse in Large-Scale Change: A Social Constructionist Perspective," *Journal of Applied Behavioral Science* 31 (1995): 352–72; D. Cooper-rider, F. Barrett, and S. Srivastva, "Social Construction and Appreciative Inquiry: A Journey in Organization Theory," in *Management and Organization: Relational Alter-natives to Individualism*, eds. D. Hosking, P. Dachler, and K. Gergen (Aldershot, U.K.: Avebury Press, 1995).

28. F. Barrett and D. Cooperrider, "Generative Metaphor Intervention: A New Approach for Working with Systems Divided by Conflict and Caught in Defensive Perception," *Journal of Applied Behavioral Science* 26 (1990): 219–39.

29. Cooperrider and Srivastva, "Appreciative Inquiry."

30. D. Eden, "Creating Expectation Effects in OD: Apply-ing Self-Fulfilling Prophecy," in *Research in Organizational Change and Development*, vol. 2, eds. W. Pasmore and R. Woodman (Greenwich, Conn.: JAI Press, 1988); D. Eden, "OD and Self-Fulfilling Prophesy: Boosting Productivity by Raising Expectations," *Journal of Applied Behavioral Sci-ence* 22 (1986): 1–13; Cooperrider, "Positive Image."

31. Barrett and Cooperrider, "Generative Metaphor Inter-vention."

32. Gergen, "Social Constructionist Movement."

33. This application was submitted by Bill Fitzgerald, the internal consultant at Comstock Michigan Fruit Division, who designed the planned change effort described here.

34. D. Nadler, "Organizational Frame-Bending: Types of Change in the Complex Organization," in *Corporate Trans-formation*, eds. R. Kilmann and T. Covin (San Francisco: Jossey-Bass, 1988): 66–83; P. Watzlawick, J. Weakland, and R. Fisch, *Change* (New York: W. W. Norton, 1974); R. Golembiewski, K. Billingsley, and S. Yeager, "Measuring Change and Persistence in Human Affairs: Types of Change Generated by OD Designs," *Journal of Applied Behavioral Science* 12 (1975): 133–57; A. Meyer, G. Brooks, and J. Goes, "Environmental Jolts and Industry Revolutions:

Organizational Responses to Discontinuous Change," *Strategic Management Journal* 11 (1990): 93–110.

35. A. Mohrman, G. Ledford Jr., S. Mohrman, E. Lawler III, and T. Cummings, *Large-Scale Organization Change* (San Francisco: Jossey-Bass, 1989).

36. L. D. Brown, "Planned Change in Underorganized Systems," in *Systems Theory for Organization Development*, ed. T. Cummings (Chichester, England: John Wiley & Sons, 1980): 181–203.

37. T. Cummings and M. Nathan, "Fostering New University–Industry Relationships" in *Making Organizations Competitive*, ed. R. Kilman (San Francisco: Jossey-Bass, 1991).

38. Porras and Robertson, "Organization Development Theory"; J. Porras and P. Robertson, "Organization Development: Theory, Practice, and Research," in *Handbook of Industrial and Organizational Psychology*, 2d ed., vol. 3, eds. M. Dunnette and M. Hough (Palo Alto, Calif: Consulting Psychologists Press, 1992).

39. T. Cummings, S. Mohrman, A. Mohrman, and G. Ledford, "Organization Design for the Future: A Collaborative Research Approach," in *Doing Research That Is Useful for Theory and Practice,* eds. E. Lawler III, A. Mohrman, S. Mohrman, G. Ledford, and T. Cummings (San Francisco: Jossey-Bass, 1985): 275–305.

40. Frohman, Sashkin, and Kavanagh, "Action Research"; Mohrman and Cummings, Self-Designing Organizations; M. Beer, R. Eisenstat, and B. Spector, "Why Change Programs Don't Produce Change," *Harvard Business Review* 6 (November-December 1990): 158–66.

41. C. Worley and R. Patchett, "Myth and Hope Meet Reality: The Fallacy of and Opportunities for Reducing Cycle Time in Strategic Change," in *Fast Cycle Organization Development,* ed. M. Anderson (Cincinnati: South-Western College Publishing, 2000).

42. Beer, Eisenstat, and Spector, "Change Programs."

3

The Organization Development Practitioner

Chapters 1 and 2 provided an overview of the field of organization development and a description of the nature of planned change. This chapter extends that introduction by examining the people who perform OD. A closer look at OD practitioners can provide a more personal perspective on the field and can help us understand the essential character of OD as a helping profession, involving personal relationships between practitioners and organization members.

Much of the literature about OD practitioners views them as internal or external consultants providing professional services—diagnosing problems, developing solutions, and helping to implement them. More recent perspectives expand the practice scope to include professionals in related disciplines, such as industrial psychology and organization theory, as well as line managers who have learned how to carry out OD to change and develop their departments.

A great deal of opinion and some research studies have focused on the necessary skills and knowledge of an effective OD practitioner. Studies of the profession provide a comprehensive list of basic skills and knowledge that all effective OD practitioners must possess.

Most of the relevant literature focuses on people specializing in OD as a profession and addresses their roles and careers. The OD role can be described in relation to the position of practitioners: internal to the organization, external to it, or in a team comprising both internal and external consultants. The OD role also can be examined in terms of its marginality in organizations, of the emotional demands made on the practitioner, and of where it fits along a continuum from client-centered to consultant-centered functioning. Finally, organization development is an emerging profession providing alternative opportunities for gaining competence and developing a career. The stressful nature of helping professions, however, suggests that OD practitioners must cope with the possibility of professional burnout.

As in other helping professions, such as medicine and law, values and ethics play an important role in guiding OD practice and in minimizing the chances that clients will be neglected or abused.

WHO IS THE ORGANIZATION DEVELOPMENT PRACTITIONER?

Throughout this text, the term *organization development practitioner* refers to at least three sets of people. The most obvious group of OD practitioners are those people specializing in OD as a profession. They may be internal or external consultants who offer professional services to organization clients, including top managers, functional department heads, and staff groups. OD professionals traditionally have shared a common set of humanistic values promoting open communications, employee involvement, and personal growth and development. They tend to have common training, skills, and experience in the social processes of organizations (for example, group dynamics, decision making, and communications). In recent years,

OD professionals have expanded those traditional values and skill sets to include more concern for organizational effectiveness, competitiveness, and bottom-line results, and greater attention to the technical, structural, and strategic parts of organizations. That expansion, mainly in response to the highly competitive demands facing modern organizations, has resulted in a more diverse set of OD professionals geared to helping organizations cope with those pressures.[1]

Second, the term OD practitioner applies to people specializing in fields related to OD, such as reward systems, organization design, total quality, information technology, and business strategy. These content-oriented fields increasingly are becoming integrated with OD's process orientation, particularly as OD projects have become more comprehensive, involving multiple features and varying parts of organizations. The integrated strategic change intervention described in Chapter 19, for example, is the result of marrying OD with business strategy.[2] A growing number of professionals in these related fields are gaining experience and competence in OD, mainly through working with OD professionals on large-scale projects and through attending OD training sessions. For example, most of the large accounting firms have diversified into management consulting and change management.[3] In most cases, professionals in these related fields do not subscribe fully to traditional OD values, nor do they have extensive OD training and experience. Rather, they have formal training and experience in their respective specialties, such as industrial relations, management consulting, information systems, health care, and work design. They are OD practitioners in the sense that they apply their special competence within an OD-like process, typically by engaging OD professionals and managers to design and implement change programs. They also practice OD when they apply their OD competence to their own specialties, thus spreading an OD perspective into such areas as compensation practices, work design, labor relations, and planning and strategy.

Third, the term OD practitioner applies to the increasing number of managers and administrators who have gained competence in OD and who apply it to their own work areas. Studies and recent articles argue that OD applied by managers rather than OD professionals is growing rapidly.[4] They suggest that the faster pace of change affecting organizations today is highlighting the centrality of the manager in managing change. Consequently, OD must become a general management skill. Along those lines, Kanter studied a growing number of firms, such as General Electric, Hewlett-Packard, and 3M, where managers and employees have become "change masters."[5] They have gained the expertise to introduce change and innovation into the organization.

Managers tend to gain competence in OD through interacting with OD professionals in actual change programs. This on-the-job training frequently is supplemented with more formal OD training, such as the variety of workshops offered by the National Training Laboratories, the Center for Creative Leadership, the Gestalt Institute, UCLA's Extension Service, University Associates, and others. Line managers increasingly are attending such external programs. Moreover, a growing number of organizations, including Texas Instruments, Motorola, and General Electric, have instituted in-house training programs for managers to learn how to develop and change their work units. As managers gain OD competence, they become its most basic practitioners.

In practice, the distinctions among the three sets of OD practitioners are blurring. A growing number of managers have transferred, either temporarily or permanently, into the OD profession. For example, companies such as Procter & Gamble have trained and rotated managers into full-time OD roles so that they can gain skills and experience needed for higher-level management positions. Also, it is increasingly common to find managers using their experience in OD to become external consultants. More OD practitioners are gaining professional competence in related specialties, such as business process reengineering, reward systems, and organization design. Conversely, many specialists in those related areas are achieving professional competence in OD. Cross-training and integration are producing a more comprehensive and complex kind of OD practitioner, one with a greater diversity of values, skills, and experience than a traditional practitioner.

COMPETENCIES OF AN EFFECTIVE ORGANIZATION DEVELOPMENT PRACTITIONER

Much of the literature about the competencies of an effective OD practitioner reveals a mixture of personality traits, experiences, knowledge, and skills presumed to lead to effective practice. For example, research on the characteristics of successful change practitioners yields the following list of attributes and abilities: diagnostic ability, basic knowledge of behavioral science techniques, empathy, knowledge of the theories and methods within the consultant's own discipline, goal-setting ability, problem-solving ability, ability to perform self-assessment, ability to see things objectively, imagination, flexibility, honesty, consistency, and trust.[6] Although these qualities and skills are laudable, there has been relatively little consensus about their importance to effective OD practice.

Two ongoing projects are attempting to define and categorize the skills and knowledge required of OD practitioners. In the first effort, fifty well-known practitioners and researchers annually update a list of professional competencies. The most recent list has grown to 187 statements in nine areas of OD practice, including entry, start-up, assessment and feedback, action planning, intervention, evaluation, adoption, separation, and general competencies.[7] The statements range from "staying centered in the present, focusing on the ongoing process" and "understanding and explaining how diversity will affect the diagnosis of the culture" to "basing change on business strategy and business needs" and "being comfortable with quantum leaps, radical shifts, and paradigm changes." The discussion is currently considering additional items related to international OD, large-group interventions, and transorganization skills.

The second project, sponsored by the Organization Development and Change Division of the Academy of Management,[8] seeks to develop a list of competencies to guide curriculum development in graduate OD programs. So far, more than forty OD practitioners have worked to develop the two competency lists shown in Table 3.1. First, foundation competencies are oriented toward descriptions of an existing system. They include knowledge from organization behavior, psychology, group dynamics, management and organization theory, research methods, and business practices. Second, core competencies are aimed at how systems change over time. They include knowledge of organization design, organization research, system dynamics, OD history, and theories and models for change; they also involve the skills needed to manage the consulting process, to analyze and diagnose systems, to design and choose interventions, to facilitate processes, to develop clients' capability to manage their own change, and to evaluate organization change.

The information in Table 3.1 applies primarily to people specializing in OD as a profession. For them, possessing the listed knowledge and skills seems reasonable, especially in light of the growing diversity and complexity of interventions in OD.

Table 3•1	Knowledge and Skill Requirements of OD Practitioners

	FOUNDATION COMPETENCIES	**CORE COMPETENCIES**

Knowledge	1. Organization behavior
	   A. Organization culture
	   B. Work design
	   C. Interpersonal relations
	   D. Power and politics
	   E. Leadership
	   F. Goal setting
	   G. Conflict
	   H. Ethics
	
	2. Individual psychology
	   A. Learning theory
	   B. Motivation theory
	   C. Perception theory
	
	3. Group dynamics
	   A. Roles
	   B. Communication processes
	   C. Decision-making process
	   D. Stages of group development
	   E. Leadership
	
	4. Management and organization theory
	   A. Planning, organizing, leading, and controlling
	   B. Problem solving and decision making
	   C. Systems theory
	   D. Contingency theory
	   E. Organization structure
	   F. Characteristics of environment and technology
	   G. Models of organization and system
	
	5. Research methods/statistics
	   A. Measures of central tendency
	   B. Measures of dispersion
	   C. Basic sampling theory
	   D. Basic experimental design
	   E. Sample inferential statistics
	
	6. Comparative cultural perspectives
	   A. Dimensions of natural culture
	   B. Dimensions of industry culture
	   C. Systems implications
	
	7. Functional knowledge of business
	   A. Interpersonal communication (listening, feedback, and articulation)
	   B. Collaboration/working together
	   C. Problem solving
	   D. Using new technology
	   E. Conceptualizing
	   F. Project management
	   G. Present/education/coach
		1. Organization design: the decision process associated with formulating and aligning the elements of an organizational system, including but not limited to structural systems, human resource systems, information systems, reward systems, work design, political systems, and organization culture.
		   A. The concept of fit and alignment.
		   B. Diagnostic and design model for various subsystems that make up an organization at any level of analysis, including the structure of work, human resources, information systems, reward systems, work design, political systems, and so on.
		   C. Key thought leaders in organization design.
		
		2. Organization research: field research methods; interviewing; content analysis; design of questionnaires and interview protocol; designing change evaluation processes; longitudinal data collection and analysis; understanding and detecting alpha, beta, and gamma change; and a host of quantitative and qualitative methods.
		
		3. System dynamics: the description and understanding of how systems evolve and develop over time, how systems respond to exogenous and endogenous disruption as well as planned interventions (e.g., evolution and revolution, punctuated equilibrium theory, chaos theory, catastrophe theory, incremental vs. quantum change, transformation theory and so on).
		
		4. History of organization development and change: an understanding of the social, political, economic, and personal forces that led to the emergence and development of organization development and change, including the key thought leaders, the values underlying their writings and actions, the key events and writings, and related documentation.
		   A. Human relations movement
		   B. NTL/T-groups/sensitivity training
		   C. Survey research
		   D. Quality of work life
		   E. Tavistock Institute
		   F. Key thought leaders
		   G. Humanistic values
		   H. Statement of ethics
		
		5. Theories and models for change: the basic action research model, participatory action research model, planning model, change typologies (e.g., fast, slow, incremental, quantum, revolutionary), Lewin's model, transition models, and so on.

Continued on page 48

Table 3•1	Knowledge and Skill Requirements of OD Practitioners, *continued*

FOUNDATION COMPETENCIES	CORE COMPETENCIES
Skills	1. Managing the consulting process: the ability to enter, contract, diagnose, design appropriate interventions, implement those interventions, manage unprogrammed events, and evaluate change process.
	2. Analysis/diagnosis: the abilities to conduct an inquiry into a system's effectiveness, to see the root cause(s) of a system's current level of effectiveness; the core skill is interpreted to include all systems—individual, group, organization, and multiorganization—as well as the ability to understand and inquire into one's self.
	3. Designing/choosing appropriate, relevant interventions: understanding how to select, modify, or design effective interventions that will move the organization from its current state to its desired future state.
	4. Facilitation and process consultation: the ability to assist an individual or group toward a goal; the ability to conduct an inquiry into individual and group processes such that the client system maintains ownership of the issue, increases its capacity for reflection on the consequences of its behaviors and actions, and develops a sense of increased control and ability.
	5. Developing client capability: the ability to conduct a change process in such a way that the client is more able to plan and implement a successful change process in the future, using technologies of planned change in a values-based and ethical manner.
	6. Evaluating organization change: the ability to design and implement a process to evaluate the impact and effects of change intervention, including control of alternative explanations and interpretation of performance outcomes.

Gaining competence in those areas may take considerable time and effort, and it is questionable whether the other two types of OD practitioners—managers and specialists in related fields—also need that full range of skills and knowledge. It seems more reasonable to suggest that some subset of the items listed in Table 3.1 should apply to all OD practitioners, whether they are OD professionals, managers, or related specialists. Those items would constitute the practitioner's basic skills and knowledge. Beyond that background, the three types of OD practitioners likely would differ in areas of concentration. OD professionals would extend their breadth of skills across the remaining categories in Table 3.1; managers would focus on the functional knowledge of business areas; and related specialists would concentrate on skills in their respective areas.

Based on the data in Table 3.1 and the other studies available, all OD practitioners should have the following basic skills and knowledge to be effective:

1. *Intrapersonal skills.* Despite the growing knowledge base and sophistication of the field, organization development is still a human craft. As the primary instrument of diagnosis and change, practitioners often must process complex, ambiguous information and make informed judgments about its relevance to organizational issues.

   The core competency of analysis and diagnosis listed in Table 3.1 includes the ability to inquire into one's self, and it remains one of the cornerstone skills in OD. Practitioners must have the personal centering to know their own values, feelings, and purposes as well as the integrity to behave responsibly in a helping relationship with others. Bob Tannenbaum, one of the founders of OD, argues that self-knowledge is the most central ingredient in OD practice and suggests that practitioners are becoming too enamored with skills and techniques.[9] There are data to support his view. A study of 416 OD practitioners found that 47 percent agreed with the statement, "Many of the new entrants into the field have little understanding of or appreciation for the history or values underlying the field."[10] Because OD is a highly uncertain process requiring constant adjustment and innovation, practitioners must have active learning skills and a reasonable balance between their rational and emotional sides. Finally, OD practice can be highly stressful and can lead to early burnout, so practitioners need to know how to manage their own stress.

2. *Interpersonal skills.* Practitioners must create and maintain effective relationships with individuals and groups within the organization and help them gain the competence necessary to solve their own problems. Table 3.1 identifies group dynamics, comparative cultural perspectives, and business functions as foundation knowledge, and managing the consulting process and facilitation as core skills. All of these interpersonal competencies promote effective helping relationships. Such relationships start with a grasp of the organization's perspective and require listening to members' perceptions and feelings to understand how they see themselves and the organization. This understanding provides a starting point for joint diagnosis and problem solving. Practitioners must establish trust and rapport with organization members so that they can share pertinent information and work effectively together. This requires being able to converse in members' own language and to give and receive feedback about how the relationship is progressing.

   To help members learn new skills and behaviors, practitioners must serve as concrete role models of what is expected. They must act in ways that are credible to organization members and provide them with the counseling and coaching necessary to develop and change. Because the helping relationship is jointly determined, practitioners need to be able to negotiate an acceptable role and to manage changing expectations and demands.

3. *General consultation skills.* Table 3.1 identifies the ability to manage the consulting process and the ability to design interventions as core competencies that all OD practitioners should possess. OD starts with diagnosing an organization or department to understand its current functioning and to discover areas for further development. OD practitioners need to know how to carry out an effective diagnosis, at least at a rudimentary level. They should know how to engage organization members in diagnosis, how to help them ask the right questions, and how to collect and analyze information. A manager, for example, should be able to work with subordinates to determine jointly the organization's or department's strengths or problems. The manager should know basic diagnostic

questions (see Chapters 5 and 6), some methods for gathering information, such as interviews or surveys, and some techniques for analyzing it, such as force-field analysis or statistical means and distributions (see Chapters 7 and 8).

In addition to diagnosis, OD practitioners should know how to design and execute an intervention. They need to be able to define an action plan and to gain commitment to the program. They also need to know how to tailor the intervention to the situation, using information about how the change is progressing to guide implementation (see Chapter 11). For example, managers should be able to develop action steps for an intervention with subordinates. They should be able to gain their commitment to the program (usually through participation), sit down with them and assess how it is progressing, and make modifications if necessary.

4. *Organization development theory.* The last basic tool OD practitioners should have is a general knowledge of organization development, such as is presented in this book. They should have some appreciation for planned change, the action research model, and contemporary approaches to managing change. They should be familiar with the range of available interventions and the need for evaluating and institutionalizing change programs. Perhaps most important is that OD practitioners should understand their own role in the emerging field of organization development, whether it is as an OD professional, a manager, or a specialist in a related area.

THE PROFESSIONAL ORGANIZATION DEVELOPMENT PRACTITIONER

Most of the literature about OD practitioners has focused on people specializing in OD as a profession. In this section, we discuss the role and typical career paths of OD professionals.

Role of Organization Development Professionals

Position

Organization development professionals have positions that are either internal or external to the organization. *Internal consultants* are members of the organization and often are located in the human resources department. They may perform the OD role exclusively, or they may combine it with other tasks, such as compensation practices, training, or labor relations.[11] Many large organizations, such as Intel, Merck, Abitibi Consolidated, BHP, Philip Morris, Levi Strauss, Procter & Gamble, Weyerhaeuser, GTE, and Citigroup, have created specialized OD consulting groups. These internal consultants typically have a variety of clients within the organization, serving both line and staff departments.

External consultants are not members of the client organization; they typically work for a consulting firm, a university, or themselves. Organizations generally hire external consultants to provide a particular expertise that is unavailable internally and to bring a different and potentially more objective perspective into the organization development process. Table 3.2 describes the differences between these two roles at each stage of the action research process.[12]

During the entry process, internal consultants have clear advantages. They have ready access to and relationships with clients, know the language of the organization, and have insights about the root cause of many of its problems. This allows internal consultants to save time in identifying the organization's culture, informal practices, and sources of power. They have access to a variety of information, including rumors, company reports, and direct observations. In addition, entry is more efficient and congenial, and their pay is not at risk. External consultants, however, have the advantage of being able to select the clients they want to work with according to their own criteria. The contracting phase is less formal for internal consultants and there is less worry about expenses, but there is less choice about whether to complete the assignment. Both types of consultants must address issues of confidentiality, risk project termination (and other negative consequences) by the client, and fill a third-party role.

Table 3•2	The Differences Between External and Internal Consulting	
STAGE OF CHANGE	**EXTERNAL CONSULTANTS**	**INTERNAL CONSULTANTS**
Entering	• Source clients • Build relationships • Learn company jargon • "Presenting problem" challenge • Time consuming • Stressful phase • Select project/client according to own criteria • Unpredictable outcome	• Ready access to clients • Ready relationships • Knows company jargon • Understands root causes • Time efficient • Congenial phase • Obligated to work with everyone • Steady pay
Contracting	• Formal documents • Can terminate project at will • Guard against out-of-pocket expenses • Information confidential • Loss of contract at stake • Maintain third-party role	• Informal agreements • Must complete projects assigned • No out-of-pocket expenses • Information can be open or confidential • Risk of client retaliation and loss of job at stake • Act as third party, driver (on behalf of client), or pair of hands
Diagnosing	• Meet most organization members for the first time • Prestige from being external • Build trust quickly • Confidential data can increase political sensitivities	• Has relationships with many organization members • Prestige determined by job rank and client stature • Sustain reputation as trustworthy over time • Data openly shared can reduce political intrigue
Intervening	• Insist on valid information, free and informed choice, and internal commitment • Confine activities within boundaries of client organization	• Insist on valid information, free and informed choice, and internal commitment • Run interference for client across organizational lines to align support
Evaluating	• Rely on repeat business and customer referral as key measures of project success • Seldom see long-term results	• Rely on repeat business, pay raise, and promotion as key measures of success • Can see change become institutionalized • Little recognition for job well done

SOURCE: M. Lacey, "Internal Consulting: Perspectives on the Process of Planned Change," *Journal of Organizational Change Management* 8 (1995): 76.

During the diagnosis process, internal consultants already know most organization members and enjoy a basic level of rapport and trust. But external consultants often have higher status than internal consultants, which allows them to probe difficult issues and assess the organization more objectively. In the intervention phase, both types of consultants must rely on valid information, free and informed choice, and internal commitment for their success.[13] However, an internal consultant's strong ties to the organization may make him or her overly cautious, particularly when powerful others can affect a career. Internal consultants also may lack certain skills and experience in facilitating organizational change. Insiders may have some small advantages in being able to move around the system and cross key organizational boundaries. Finally, the measures of success and reward differ from those of the external practitioner in the evaluation process.

A promising approach to having the advantages of both internal and external OD consultants is to include them both as members of an internal–external consulting team.[14] External consultants can combine their special expertise and objectivity with the inside knowledge and acceptance of internal consultants. The two parties can use complementary consulting skills while sharing the workload and possibly accomplishing more than either would by operating alone. Internal consultants, for example, can provide almost continuous contact with the client, and their external counterparts can provide specialized services periodically, such as two or three days each month. External consultants also can help train their organization partners, thus transferring OD skills and knowledge to the organization.

Although little has been written on internal–external consulting teams, recent studies suggest that the effectiveness of such teams depends on members developing strong, supportive, collegial relationships. They need to take time to develop the consulting team, confronting individual differences and establishing appropriate roles and exchanges. Members need to provide each other with continuous feedback and make a commitment to learning from each other. In the absence of these team-building and learning activities, internal–external consulting teams can be more troublesome and less effective than consultants working alone.

Application 3.1 provides a personal account of the internal and external consulting positions as well as interactions between them.[15]

Marginality

A promising line of research on the professional OD role centers on the issue of marginality.[16] The marginal person is one who successfully straddles the boundary between two or more groups with differing goals, value systems, and behavior patterns. Whereas in the past, the marginal role always was seen as dysfunctional, marginality now is seen in a more positive light. There are many examples of marginal roles in organizations: the salesperson, the buyer, the first-line supervisor, the integrator, and the project manager.

Evidence is mounting that some people are better at taking marginal roles than are others. Those who are good at it seem to have personal qualities of low dogmatism, neutrality, open-mindedness, objectivity, flexibility, and adaptable information-processing ability. Rather than being upset by conflict, ambiguity, and stress, they thrive on it. Individuals with marginal orientations are more likely than others to develop integrative decisions that bring together and reconcile viewpoints among opposing organizational groups and are more likely to remain neutral in controversial situations. Thus, the research suggests that the marginal role can have positive effects when it is filled by a person with a marginal orientation. Such a person can be more objective and better able to perform successfully in linking, integrative, or conflict-laden roles.[17]

APPLICATION 3•1   Personal Views of the Internal and External Consulting Positions

The Internal Consultant's View

An instrument of change—that's what I am. I live in the organization, trying to work with two levels of concern at the same time: those on the surface and those that lurk just below.

I try to use my mind and body to sense the existing data, to diagnose problems, and to develop strategies for change. I absorb all that I encounter: the excitement of a new project, the struggle to get it started, and the reactions of the organization. Some reactions are positive; many are not. The fear, anger, and frustration are around, even if they aren't directed toward me.

Of course, I understand these reactions. They mean that change is occurring. The system is unfreezing. I'm patient, working with the process, helping it along, working through the stuck places, working with people who are critical to the project's success, working with groups to help them adapt, and the like.

Sometimes my body aches and I feel depressed. I know how to take care of myself—deep breathing, meditation, exercise. Gradually, I become adept at analyzing the situation, building models to explain behavior, and learning to cope personally. But still the emotions of others regarding the changes bombard me. I seal my body off fairly well. I don't feel as much or as intensely as before, but I do feel. On the other hand, I sometimes get so excited about all the possibilities, the risks I see people taking, their commitment to a difficult change effort—the adrenaline flows and I feel fulfilled.

I feel isolated, even from my staff. But that's what an internal feels—never quite in or like anyone else in the organization, a little apart but still showing loyalty and commitment. But I know how to manage it: call on the friendly external consultant. Over the years, I have called on many of them. I needed them for training events, team building, design work, and strategizing. However, underneath each piece of work, I needed them for professional and personal support. I educated them all about my organization and its idiosyncrasies. The smart ones listened, did the job they were hired to do, and in some way managed to meet my unspoken request for support. Through them, I learned the valuable lessons necessary to develop an effective internal–external consulting team. Eventually, I even learned to ask for personal support directly,

not always couched in terms such as, "what is good for the organization."

The External Consultant's View

I am an agent of change. I spend most of my time helping internal consultants and managers initiate and manage changes they have stimulated. In that process I, too, am the recipient of others' feelings. Fortunately, most of those feelings are positive. I am appreciated for my assistance, applauded for my knowledge, and liked for my interpersonal skills. Finally, I am rewarded handsomely for my time and effort. Thus, for the most part, I feel pleased and rewarded for my work as a consultant.

In my role, I may leave an organization while the time-consuming and important work of nursing a change along is being done. So, althoughI experience the risk and excitement at the beginning of a change, I do not always experience the difficult day-to-day maintenance that the internal person experiences. When I tire of a particular person or project (or they tire of me), I have several others to provide my emotional and financial sustenance. However, there are still times when I feel exhausted. The work has taken its toll, and no amount of positive support takes away the weariness. I rest, play tennis, and practice better health habits—knowing that in a few days I will be working with another client on another problem.

I am asked by clients to perform a wide variety of tasks ranging from being a content expert to listening to them as a therapist might. Regardless of the request, however, I am usually aware of an unspoken need on the part of the internal consultant to have me support his or her project, position, or person. When the request is to support a project, it is usually clear. When the request is to support a position, it is less clear but is often made in the selection of me as the consultant. However, when the request is to support the individual personally, the request is almost never overt.

Often comments such as, "You seem very concerned about this situation" or "You must feel pretty unsupported right now" go unanswered. Perhaps the relationship isn't at a point where we can discuss personal needs. Maybe that wouldn't be professional. Perhaps we are still maintaining "face" for each other. ■

A study of 89 external OD practitioners and 246 internal ones (response rates of 59 percent and 54 percent, respectively) showed that external professionals were more comfortable with the marginal role than were internal professionals. Internal consultants with more years of experience were more marginally oriented than were those with less experience.[18] These findings, combined with other research on marginal roles, suggest the importance of maintaining the OD practitioner's marginality, with its flexibility, independence, and boundary-spanning characteristics.

Emotional Demands

The OD practitioner role is emotionally demanding. Research and practice support the importance of understanding emotions and their impact on the practitioner's effectiveness. The research on emotional intelligence in organizations suggests a set of abilities that can aid OD practitioners in conducting successful change efforts.[19] *Emotional intelligence* refers to the ability to recognize and express emotions appropriately, to use emotions in thought and decisions, and to regulate emotion in oneself and in others.[20] It is, therefore, a different kind of intelligence from problem-solving ability, engineering aptitude, or the knowledge of concepts. In tandem with traditional knowledge and skill, emotional intelligence affects and supplements rational thought; emotions help prioritize thinking by directing attention to important information not addressed in models and theories. In that sense, some researchers argue that emotional intelligence is as important as cognitive intelligence.[21]

Reports from OD practitioners support the importance of emotional intelligence in practice. At each stage of planned change, they must relate to and help organization members adapt to resistance, commitment, and ambiguity. Facing those important and difficult issues raises emotions such as the fear of failure or rejection.[22] As the client and others encounter these kinds of emotions, OD practitioners must have a clear sense of emotional effects, including their own internal emotions. Ambiguity or denial of emotions can lead to inaccurate and untimely interventions. For example, a practitioner who is uncomfortable with conflict may intervene to diffuse conflict because of the discomfort he or she feels, not because the conflict is destructive. In such a case, the practitioner is acting to address a personal need rather than intervening to improve the system's effectiveness.

Evidence suggests that emotional intelligence increases with age and experience.[23] In addition, it can be developed through personal growth processes such as sensitivity training, counseling, and therapy. It seems reasonable to suggest that professional OD practitioners dedicate themselves to a long-term regimen of development that includes acquiring both cognitive learning and emotional intelligence.

Use of Knowledge and Experience

The professional OD role has been described in terms of a continuum ranging from client-centered (using the client's knowledge and experience) to consultant-centered (using the consultant's knowledge and experience), as shown in Figure 3.1. Traditionally, OD consultants have worked at the client-centered end of the continuum. Organization development professionals, relying mainly on sensitivity training, process consultation, and team building (see Chapter 12), have been expected to remain neutral, refusing to offer expert advice on organizational problems. Rather than contracting to solve specific problems, the consultant has tended to work with organization members to identify problems and potential solutions, to help them study what they are doing now and consider alternative behaviors and solutions, and to help them discover whether, in fact, the consultant and they can learn to do things better. In doing that, the OD professional has generally listened and reflected upon members' perceptions and ideas and helped clarify and interpret their communications and behaviors.

With the recent proliferation of OD interventions in the structural, human resource management, and strategy areas, that limited definition of the professional OD role has expanded to include the consultant-centered end of the continuum. In many of the newer approaches, the consultant may have to take on a modified role

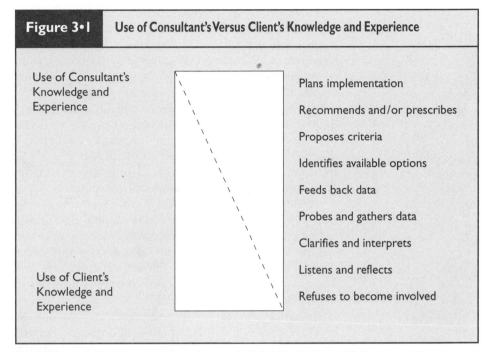

Figure 3•1   **Use of Consultant's Versus Client's Knowledge and Experience**

Use of Consultant's
Knowledge and
Experience

Plans implementation

Recommends and/or prescribes

Proposes criteria

Identifies available options

Feeds back data

Probes and gathers data

Clarifies and interprets

Use of Client's
Knowledge and
Experience

Listens and reflects

Refuses to become involved

SOURCE: Adapted by permission of the authors from W. Schmidt and A. Johnson, "A Continuum of Consultancy Styles" (unpublished manuscript, July 1970), p. 1.

of expert, with the consent and collaboration of organization members. For example, if a consultant and managers were to try to bring about a major structural re-design (see Chapter 14), managers may not have the appropriate knowledge and expertise to create and manage the change. The consultant's role might be to present the basic concepts and ideas and then to struggle jointly with the managers to select an approach that might be useful to the organization and to decide how it might best be implemented. In this situation, the OD professional recommends or prescribes particular changes and is active in planning how to implement them. This expertise, however, is always shared rather than imposed.

With the development of new and varied intervention approaches, the OD professional's role needs to be seen as falling along the entire continuum from client-centered to consultant-centered. At times, the consultant will rely mainly on organization members' knowledge and experiences to identify and solve problems. At other times, it will be more appropriate to take on the role of expert, withdrawing from that role as managers gain more knowledge and experience.

Careers of Organization Development Professionals

In contrast to such long-standing occupations as medicine and law, organization development is an emerging practice, still developing the characteristics of an established profession: a common body of knowledge, educational requirements, accrediting procedures, a recognized code of ethics, and rules and methods for governing conduct. People enter professional OD careers from a variety of educational and work backgrounds. Because they do not have to follow an established career path, they have some choice about when to enter or leave an OD career and whether to be an internal or external consultant.[24]

Despite the looseness or flexibility of the field, most professionals have had specific training in OD. That training can include relatively short courses (one day to two weeks), programs, and workshops conducted within organizations or at outside institutions (such as NTL, University Associates, Columbia University, the University of Michigan, Stanford University, and UCLA). OD training also can be more formal and lengthy, including master's programs (for example, at American University, Bowling Green State University, Brigham Young University, Case Western Reserve University, Eastern Michigan University, the Fielding Institute, and Pepperdine University) and doctoral training (for example, at Benedictine University, Case Western Reserve University, Columbia University Teachers College, the Fielding Institute, George Washington University, the University of Michigan, UCLA, Pepperdine University, and Stanford University).

As might be expected, career choices widen as people gain training and experience in OD. Those with rudimentary training tend to be internal consultants, often taking on OD roles as temporary assignments on the way to higher managerial or staff positions. Holders of master's degrees generally are evenly split between internal and external consultants. Those with doctorates may join a university faculty and do consulting part-time, join a consulting firm, or seek a position as a relatively high-level internal consultant.

External consultants tend to be older, to have more managerial experience, and to spend more of their time in OD than do internal practitioners. However, a recent study suggested there were no differences between internal and external consultants in pay or years of consulting experience.[25] Perhaps the most common career path is to begin as an internal consultant, gain experience and visibility through successful interventions or publishing, and then become an external consultant. A field study found that internal consultants acquired greater competence by working with external consultants who purposely helped develop them. This development took place through a tutorial arrangement of joint diagnosis and intervention in the organization, which gave the internal consultants a chance to observe and learn from the model furnished by the external consultants.[26]

There is increasing evidence that an OD career can be stressful, sometimes leading to burnout.[27] Burnout comes from taking on too many jobs, becoming overcommitted and generally working too hard. The number-one complaint of OD practitioners is constant traveling.[28] OD work often requires six-day work weeks, with some days running as long as fourteen hours. Consultants may spend a week working with one organization or department and then spend the weekend preparing for the next client. They may spend 50 to 75 percent of their time on the road, living in planes, cars, hotels, meetings, and restaurants. Indeed, one practitioner has suggested that the majority of OD consultants would repeat the phrase "quality of work life for consultants" this way: "Quality of work life? For consultants?"[29]

OD professionals increasingly are taking steps to cope with burnout. They may shift jobs, moving from external to internal roles to gain more predictable hours or avoid travel. They may learn to pace themselves better and to avoid taking on too much work. Many are engaging in fitness and health programs and are using stress-management techniques, such as those described in Chapter 18.

PROFESSIONAL VALUES

Values have played an important role in organization development from its beginning. Traditionally, OD professionals have promoted a set of values under a humanistic framework, including a concern for inquiry and science, democracy, and being helpful.[30] They have sought to build trust and collaboration; to create an open, problem-solving climate; and to increase the self-control of organization members. More recently, OD practitioners have extended those humanistic values to include a concern for improving organizational effectiveness (for example, to increase productivity or to reduce turnover) and performance (for example, to increase profitability). They have shown an increasing desire to optimize both human benefits and production objectives.[31]

The joint values of humanizing organizations and improving their effectiveness have received widespread support in the OD profession as well as increasing encouragement from managers, employees, and union officials. Indeed, it would be difficult not to support those joint concerns. But in practice OD professionals face serious challenges in simultaneously pursuing greater humanism and organizational effectiveness.[32] More practitioners are experiencing situations in which there is conflict between employees' needs for greater meaning and the organization's need for more effective and efficient use of its resources. For example, expensive capital equipment may run most efficiently if it is highly programmed and routinized, but people may not derive satisfaction from working with such technology. Should efficiency be maximized at the expense of people's satisfaction? Can technology be changed to make it more humanly satisfying while remaining efficient? What compromises are possible? How do these tradeoffs shift when they are applied in different social cultures? These are the value dilemmas often faced when we try to optimize both human benefits and organizational effectiveness.

In addition to value issues within organizations, OD practitioners are dealing more and more with value conflicts with powerful outside groups. Organizations are open systems and exist within increasingly turbulent environments. For example, hospitals are facing complex and changing task environments. This has led to a proliferation of external stakeholders with interests in the organization's functioning, including patients, suppliers, medical groups, insurance companies, employers, the government, stockholders, unions, the press, and various interest groups. Those external groups often have different and competing values for judging the organization's effectiveness. For example, stockholders may judge the firm in terms of earnings per share, the government in terms of compliance with equal employment opportunity legislation, patients in terms of quality of care, and ecology groups in terms of hazardous waste disposal. Because organizations must rely on these external groups for resources and legitimacy, they cannot simply ignore these competing values. They must somehow respond to them and try to reconcile the different interests.

Recent attempts to help firms manage external relationships suggest the need for new interventions and competence in OD.[33] Practitioners must have not only social skills like those proposed in Table 3.1 but also political skills. They must understand the distribution of power, conflicts of interest, and value dilemmas inherent in managing external relationships and be able to manage their own role and values with respect to those dynamics. Interventions promoting collaboration and system maintenance may be ineffective in this larger arena, especially when there are power and dominance relationships among organizations and competition for scarce resources. Under those conditions, OD practitioners may need more power-oriented interventions, such as bargaining, coalition forming, and pressure tactics.

For example, firms in the tobacco industry have waged an aggressive campaign against the efforts of external groups, such as the U.S. surgeon general, the American Lung Association, and local governments, to limit or ban the smoking of tobacco products. They have formed a powerful industry coalition to lobby against antismoking legislation; they have spent enormous sums of money advertising tobacco products, conducting public relations campaigns, and refuting research purportedly showing the dangers of smoking. Such power-oriented strategies are intended to manage an increasingly hostile environment and may be necessary for the industry's survival.

People practicing OD in such settings may need to help organizations implement such strategies if organizations are to manage their environments effectively. That effort will require political skills and greater attention to how the OD practitioner's own values fit with those of the organization.

PROFESSIONAL ETHICS

Ethical issues in OD are concerned with how practitioners perform their helping relationship with organization members. Inherent in any helping relationship is the potential for misconduct and client abuse. OD practitioners can let personal values stand in the way of good practice or use the power inherent in their professional role to abuse (often unintentionally) organization members.

Ethical Guidelines

To its credit, the field of OD always has shown concern for the ethical conduct of its practitioners. There have been several articles and symposia about ethics in OD.[34] In addition, statements of ethics governing OD practice have been sponsored by the Organization Development Institute (http://members.aol.com/ODInst),[35] the American Society for Training & Development (http://www.astd.org),[36] and a consortium of professional associations in OD. The consortium has jointly sponsored an ethical code derived from a large-scale project conducted at the Center for the Study of Ethics in the Professions at the Illinois Institute of Technology. The project's purposes included preparing critical incidents describing ethical dilemmas and using that material for preprofessional and continuing education in OD, providing an empirical basis for a statement of values and ethics for OD professionals, and initiating a process for making the ethics of OD practice explicit on a continuing basis.[37] The ethical guidelines from that project appear in the appendix to this chapter.

Ethical Dilemmas

Although adherence to statements of ethics helps prevent the occurrence of ethical problems, OD practitioners still can encounter ethical dilemmas. Figure 3.2 is a process model that explains how ethical dilemmas can occur in OD. The antecedent conditions include an OD practitioner and a client system with different goals, values, needs, skills, and abilities. During the entry and contracting phase these differences may or may not be addressed and clarified. If the contracting process is incomplete, the subsequent intervention process or role episode is subject to role conflict and role ambiguity. Neither the client nor the OD practitioner is clear about respective responsibilities. Each party is pursuing different goals, and each is using different skills and values to achieve those goals. The role conflict and ambiguity may produce five types of ethical dilemmas: misrepresentation, misuse of data, coercion, value and goal conflict, and technical ineptness.

Misrepresentation

Misrepresentation occurs when OD practitioners claim that an intervention will produce results that are unreasonable for the change program or the situation. The

Figure 3•2	A Role Episodic Model of Ethical Dilemmas

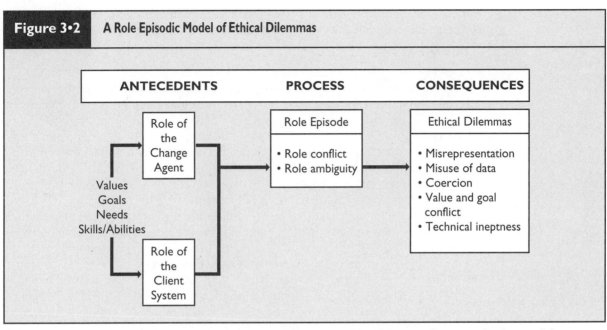

SOURCE: Kluwer Academic Publishers, *Journal of Business Ethics*, 11 (1992), page 665, "Ethical Dilemmas in Organization Development: A Cross-Cultural Analysis," L. White and M. Rhodeback, Figure 1. © 1992, Kluwer. With kind permission from Kluwer Academic Publishers.

client can contribute to the problem by portraying inaccurate goals and needs. In either case, one or both parties is operating under false pretenses and an ethical dilemma exists. For example, in an infamous case called "The Undercover Change Agent," an attempt was made to use laboratory training in an organization whose top management did not understand it and was not ready for it. The OD consultant sold T-groups as the intervention that would solve the problems facing the organization. After the president of the firm made a surprise visit to the site where the training was being held, the consultant was fired because the nature and style of the T-group was in direct contradiction to the president's concepts about leadership.[38] Misrepresentation is likely to occur in the entering and contracting phases of planned change when the initial consulting relationship is being established. To prevent misrepresentation, OD practitioners need to gain clarity about the goals of the change effort and to explore openly with the client its expected effects, its relevance to the client system, and the practitioner's competence in executing the intervention.

Misuse of Data

Misuse of data occurs when information gathered during the OD process is used punitively. Large amounts of information are invariably obtained during the entry and diagnostic phases of OD. Although most OD practitioners value openness and trust, it is important that they be aware of how such data are going to be used. It is a human tendency to use data to enhance a power position. Openness is one thing, but leaking inappropriate information can be harmful to individuals and to the organization. It is easy for a consultant, under the guise of obtaining information, to gather data about whether a particular manager is good or bad. When, how, or if this information can be used is an ethical dilemma not easily resolved. To minimize misuse of data, practitioners should reach agreement up front with organization members about how data collected during the change process will be used. This agreement should be reviewed periodically in light of changing circumstances.

Coercion

Coercion occurs when organization members are forced to participate in an OD intervention. People should have the freedom to choose whether to participate in a change program if they are to gain self-reliance to solve their own problems. In team building, for example, team members should have the option of deciding not to become involved in the intervention. Management should not decide unilaterally that team building is good for members. However, freedom to make a choice requires knowledge about OD. Many organization members have little information about OD interventions, what they involve, and the nature and consequences of becoming involved with them. This makes it imperative for OD practitioners to educate clients about interventions before choices are made for implementing them.

Coercion also can pose ethical dilemmas for the helping relationship between OD practitioners and organization members. Inherent in any helping relationship are possibilities for excessive manipulation and dependency, two facets of coercion. Kelman pointed out that behavior change "inevitably involves some degree of manipulation and control, and at least an implicit imposition of the change agent's values on the client or the person he [or she] is influencing."[39] This places the practitioner on two horns of a dilemma: (1) any attempt to change is in itself a change and thereby a manipulation, no matter how slight, and (2) there exists no formula or method to structure a change situation so that such manipulation can be totally absent. To attack the first aspect of the dilemma, Kelman stressed freedom of choice, seeing any action that limits freedom of choice as being ethically ambiguous or worse. To address the second aspect, Kelman argued that the OD practitioner must remain keenly aware of her or his own value system and alert to the possibility that those values are being imposed on a client. In other words, an effective way to resolve this dilemma is to make the change effort as open as possible, with the free consent and knowledge of the individuals involved.

The second facet of coercion that can pose ethical dilemmas for the helping relationship involves dependency. Helping relationships invariably create dependency between those who need help and those who provide it.[40] A major goal in OD is to lessen clients' dependency on consultants by helping clients gain the knowledge and skills to address organizational problems and manage change themselves. In some cases, however, achieving independence from OD practitioners can result in clients being either counterdependent or overdependent, especially in the early stages of the relationship. To resolve dependency issues, consultants can openly and explicitly discuss with the client how to handle the dependency problem, especially what the client and consultant expect of one another. Another approach is to focus on problem finding. Usually, the client is looking for a solution to a perceived problem. The consultant can redirect the energy to improved joint diagnosis so that both are working on problem identification and problem solving. Such action moves the energy of the client away from dependency. Finally, dependency can be reduced by changing the client's expectation from being helped or controlled by the practitioner to a greater focus on the need to manage the problem. Such a refocusing can reinforce the understanding that the consultant is working for the client and offering assistance that is at the client's discretion.

Value and Goal Conflict

This ethical conflict occurs when the purpose of the change effort is not clear or when the client and the practitioner disagree over how to achieve the goals. The important practical issue for OD consultants is whether it is justifiable to withhold services unilaterally from an organization that does not agree with their values or methods. OD pioneer Gordon Lippitt suggested that the real question is the following: assuming that some kind of change is going to occur anyway, doesn't the consultant have a responsibility to try to guide the change in the most constructive fashion possible?[41] That question may be of greater importance and relevance to an internal consultant or to a consultant who already has an ongoing relationship with the client.

Argyris takes an even stronger stand, maintaining that the responsibilities of professional OD practitioners to clients are comparable to those of lawyers or physicians, who, in principle, may not refuse to perform their services. He suggests that the very least the consultant can do is to provide "first aid" to the organization, as long as the assistance does not compromise the consultant's values. Argyris suggests that if the Ku Klux Klan asked for assistance and the consultant could at least determine whether the KKK was genuinely interested in assessing itself and willing to commit itself to all that a valid assessment would entail concerning both itself and other groups, the consultant should be willing to help. If later the Klan's objectives proved to be less than honestly stated, the consultant would be free to withdraw without being compromised.[42]

Technical Ineptness

This final ethical dilemma occurs when OD practitioners try to implement interventions for which they are not skilled or when the client attempts a change for which it is not ready. Critical to the success of any OD program is the selection of an appropriate intervention, which depends, in turn, on careful diagnosis of the organization. Selecting an intervention is closely related to the practitioner's own values, skills, and abilities. In solving organizational problems, many OD consultants emphasize a favorite intervention or technique, such as team building, total quality management, or self-managed teams. They let their own values and beliefs dictate the change method.[43] Technical ineptness dilemmas also can occur when interventions do not align with the ability of the organization to implement them. Again, careful diagnosis can reveal the extent to which the organization is ready to make a change and possesses the skills and knowledge to implement it.

Application 3.2 presents an ethical dilemma that arises frequently in OD consulting.[44] What points in the process represent practical opportunities to intervene? Do you agree with Kindred's resolution to the problem? What other options did she have?

■ SUMMARY

This chapter has examined the role of the organization development practitioner. That term applies to three sets of people: individuals specializing in OD as a profession, people from related fields who have gained some competence in OD, and managers having the OD skills necessary to change and develop their organizations or departments. Comprehensive lists enumerate core and advanced skills and knowledge that an effective OD specialist should possess, but a smaller set of basic skills and knowledge is applicable for all practitioners at all levels. These include four kinds of background: intrapersonal skills, interpersonal skills, general consultation skills, and knowledge of OD theory.

The professional OD role can apply to internal consultants who belong to the organization undergoing change, to external consultants who are members of universities and consulting firms or are self-employed, and to members of internal–

APPLICATION 3·2   Kindred Todd and the Ethics of OD

Kindred Todd had just finished her master's degree in organization development and had landed her first consulting position with a small consulting company in Edmonton, Alberta, Canada. The president, Larry Stepchuck, convinced Kindred that his growing organization offered her a great opportunity to learn the business. He had a large number of contacts, an impressive executive career, and several years of consulting experience behind him.

In fact, the firm was growing, adding new clients and projects as fast as Larry could hire consultants. A few weeks after Kindred was hired, Larry assigned her to a new client, a small oil and gas company. "I've met with the client for several hours," he told her. "They are an important and potentially large opportunity for our firm. They're looking to us to help them address some long-range planning issues. From the way they talk, they could also use some continuous quality improvement work as well."

As Kindred prepared for her initial meeting with the client, she reviewed financial data from the firm's annual report, examined trends in the client's industry, and thought about the issues that young firms face. Larry indicated that Kindred would first meet with the president of the firm to discuss initial issues and next steps.

When Kindred walked into the president's office, she was greeted by the firm's entire senior management team. Team members expressed eagerness to get to work on the important issues of how to improve the organization's key business processes. They believed that an expert in continuous quality improvement (CQI), such as Kindred, was exactly the kind of help they needed to increase efficiency and cut costs in the core business. Members began to ask direct questions of Kindred about technical details of CQI, the likely timeframe within which they might expect results, how to map key processes, and how to form quality improvement teams to identify and implement process improvements.

Kindred was stunned and overwhelmed. Nothing that Larry had said about the issues facing this company was being discussed and, worse, it was clear that he had sold Kindred to the client as an "expert" in CQI. Her immediate response was to suggest that all of their questions were good ones, but that they needed to be answered in the context of the long-range goals and strategies of the firm. Kindred proposed that the best way to begin was for team members to provide her with some history about the organization. In doing so, she was able to avert disaster and embarrassment for herself and her company, and to appear to be doing all the things necessary to begin a CQI project. The meeting ended with Kindred and the management team agreeing to meet again the following week.

Immediately the next day, Kindred sought out Larry. She reported on the results of the meeting and her surprise at being sold to this client as an expert on CQI. Kindred suggested that her own competencies did not fit the needs of the client and requested that another consultant—one with expertise in CQI—be assigned to the project.

Larry responded to her concerns: "I've known these people for over ten years. They don't know exactly what they need. CQI is an important buzzword. It's the flavor of the month and if that's what they want, that's what we'll give them." He also told Kindred that there were no other consultants available for this project. "Besides," he said, "the president of the client firm had just called to say how much he had enjoyed meeting with you and was looking forward to getting started on the project right away."

Kindred felt that Larry's response to her concerns included a strong, inferred ultimatum: if you want to stay with this company, you had better take this job. "I knew I had to sink or swim with this job and this client," Kindred later reported.

As Kindred reflected on her options, she pondered the following questions:

- How can I be honest with this client and thus not jeopardize my values of openness and honesty?
- How can I be helpful to this client?
- How much do I know about quality improvement processes?
- How do I satisfy the requirements of my employer?
- What obligations do I have?
- Who's going to know if I do or don't have the credentials to perform this work?
- What if I fail?

After thinking about those issues, Kindred summarized her position in terms of three dilemmas: a dilemma of self (who is Kindred?), a dilemma of competence (what can I do?), and a dilemma of confidence (do I like who I work for?). Based on the issues, Kindred made the following tactical decisions. She spent two days at the library reading about and studying total quality management and continuous improvement. She also contacted several of her friends and former classmates who had experience with quality improvement efforts. Eventually, she contracted with one of them to be her "shadow" consultant—to work with her behind the scenes on formulating and implementing an intervention for the client.

Based on her preparation in the library and the discussions with her shadow consultant, Kindred was able to facilitate an appropriate and effective intervention for the client. Shortly after her assignment was completed, she resigned from the consulting organization. ∎

external consulting teams. The OD role may be described aptly in terms of marginality and emotional demands. People with a tolerance for marginal roles seem especially suited for OD practice because they are able to maintain neutrality and objectivity and to develop integrative solutions that reconcile viewpoints among opposing organizational departments. Similarly, the OD practitioner's emotional intelligence and awareness are keys to implementing their role successfully. Whereas in the past the OD role has been described as standing at the client end of the continuum from client-centered to consultant-centered functioning, the development of new and varied interventions has shifted the role of the OD professional to cover the entire range of that continuum.

Although OD is still an emerging profession, most practitioners have specific training in the field, training that ranges from short courses and workshops to graduate and doctoral education. No single career path exists, but internal consulting is often a stepping-stone to becoming an external consultant. Because of the hectic pace of OD practice, specialists should be prepared to cope with high levels of stress and the possibility of career burnout.

Values have played a key role in OD, and traditional values promoting trust, collaboration, and openness have been supplemented recently with concerns for improving organizational effectiveness and productivity. OD specialists may face value dilemmas in trying to jointly optimize human benefits and organization performance. They also may encounter value conflicts when dealing with powerful external stakeholders, such as the government, stockholders, and customers. Dealing with those outside groups may take political skills, as well as the more traditional social skills.

Ethical issues in OD involve how practitioners perform their helping role with clients. As a profession, OD always has shown a concern for the ethical conduct of its practitioners, and several ethical codes for OD practice have been developed by various professional associations. Ethical dilemmas in OD arise around misrepresentation, misuse of data, coercion, value and goal conflict, and technical ineptness.

■ NOTES

1. A. Church and W. Burke, "Practitioner Attitudes about the Field of Organization Development," in *Research in Organizational Change and Development*, eds. W. Pasmore and R. Woodman (Greenwich, Conn.: JAI Press, 1995).

2. C. Worley, D. Hitchin, and W. Ross, *Integrated Strategic Change* (Reading, Mass.: Addison-Wesley, 1996).

3. R. Henkoff, "Inside Anderson's Army of Advice," *Fortune* (4 October 1993).

4. M. Beer and E. Walton, "Organization Change and Development," *Annual Review of Psychology* 38 (1987): 229–72; S. Sherman, "Wanted: Company Change Agents," *Fortune* (11 December 1999): 197–98.

5. R. Kanter, *The Change Masters* (New York: Simon & Schuster, 1983).

6. B. Glickman, "Qualities of Change Agents" (unpublished manuscript, May 1974); R. Havelock, *The Change Agent's Guide to Innovation in Education* (Englewood Cliffs, N.J.: Educational Technology, 1973); R. Lippitt, "Dimensions of the Consultant's Job," in *The Planning of Change*, eds. W. Bennis, K. Benne, and R. Chin (New York: Holt, Rinehart, & Winston, 1961): 156–61; C. Rogers, *On Becoming a Person* (Boston: Houghton Mifflin, 1971); N. Paris, "Some Thoughts on the Qualifications for a Consultant" (unpublished manuscript, 1973); "OD Experts Reflect on the Major Skills Needed by Consultants: With Comments from Edgar Schein," *Academy of Management OD Newsletter* (Spring 1979): 1–4; K. Shepard and A. Raia, "The OD Training Challenge," *Training & Development Journal* 35 (April 1981): 90–96; J. Esper, "Core Competencies in Organization Development" (independent study conducted as partial fulfillment of the M.B.A. degree, Graduate School of Business Administration, University of Southern California, June 1987); E. Neilsen, *Becoming an OD Practitioner* (Englewood Cliffs, N.J.: Prentice Hall,

1984); S. Eisen, H. Steele, and J. Cherbeneau, "Developing OD Competence for the Future," in *Practicing Organization Development,* eds. W. Rothwell, R. Sullivan, and G. McLean (San Diego: Pfeiffer, 1995).

7. R. Sullivan and K. Quade, "Essential Competencies for Internal and External OD Consultants," in *Practicing Organization Development,* eds. W. Rothwell, R. Sullivan, and G. McLean (San Diego: Pfeiffer, 1995).

8. C. Worley and G. Varney, "A Search for a Common Body of Knowledge for Master's Level Organization Development and Change Programs—An Invitation to Join the Discussion," *Academy of Management ODC Newsletter* (Winter 1998): 1–4.

9. B. Tannenbaum, "Letter to the Editor," *Consulting Practice Communique,* Academy of Management Managerial Consultation Division 21, 3, (1993): 16–17; B. Tannenbaum, "Self-Awareness: An Essential Element Underlying Consultant Effectiveness," *Journal of Organizational Change Management* 8, 3 (1995): 85–86.

10. A. Church and W. Burke, "Practitioner Attitudes about the Field of Organization Development," in *Research in Organizational Change and Development,* eds. W. Pasmore and R. Woodman (Greenwich, Conn.: JAI Press, 1995).

11. M. Lacey, "Internal Consulting: Perspectives on the Process of Planned Change," *Journal of Organizational Change Management* 8, 3 (1995): 75–84.

12. Ibid.

13. C. Argyris, *Intervention Theory and Method* (Reading, Mass.: Addison-Wesley, 1973).

14. E. Kirkhart and T. Isgar, "Quality of Work Life for Consultants: The Internal–External Relationship," *Consultation* 5 (Spring 1986): 5–23; J. Thacker and N. Kulick, "The Use of Consultants in Joint Union/Management Quality of Work Life Efforts," *Consultation* 5 (Summer 1986): 116–26.

15. Reproduced by permission of the publisher from Kirkhart and Isgar, "Quality of Work Life for Consultants," 6–7.

16. R. Ziller, *The Social Self* (Elmsford, N.Y.: Pergamon, 1973).

17. R. Ziller, B. Stark, and H. Pruden, "Marginality and Integrative Management Positions," *Academy of Management Journal* 12 (December 1969): 487–95; H. Pruden and B. Stark, "Marginality Associated with Interorganizational Linking Process, Productivity and Satisfaction," *Academy of Management Journal* 14 (March 1971): 145–48; W. Liddell, "Marginality and Integrative Decisions," *Academy of Man-*

agement Journal 16 (March 1973): 154–56; P. Brown and C. Cotton, "Marginality, A Force for the OD Practitioner," *Training & Development Journal* 29 (April 1975): 14–18; H. Aldrich and D. Gerker, "Boundary Spanning Roles and Organizational Structure," *Academy of Management Review* 2 (April 1977): 217–30; C. Cotton, "Marginality—A Neglected Dimension in the Design of Work," *Academy of Management Review* 2 (January 1977): 133–38; N. Margulies, "Perspectives on the Marginality of the Consultant's Role," in *The Cutting Edge,* ed. W. Burke (La Jolla, Calif.: University Associates, 1978): 60–79.

18. P. Brown, C. Cotton, and R. Golembiewski, "Marginality and the OD Practitioner," *Journal of Applied Behavioral Science* 13 (1977): 493–506.

19. D. Goleman, *Emotional Intelligence* (New York: Bantam Books, 1995); R. Cooper and A. Sawaf, *Executive EQ: Emotional Intelligence in Leadership and Organizations* (New York: Grosset/Putnum, 1997); P. Salovey and D. Sluyter, eds., *Emotional Development and Emotional Intelligence* (New York: Basic Books, 1997).

20. J. Mayer and P. Salovey, "What Is Emotional Intelligence?" in Salovey and Sluyter, *Emotional Development.*

21. Goleman, *Emotional Intelligence.*

22. J. Sanford, *Fritz Kunkel: Selected Writings* (Mahwah, N.J.: Paulist Press, 1984).

23. J. Mayer, D. Caruso, and P. Salovey, "Emotional Intelligence Meets Traditional Standards for an Intelligence," *Intelligence* (in press).

24. D. Kegan, "Organization Development as OD Network Members See It," *Group and Organization Studies* 7 (March 1982): 5–11.

25. D. Griffin and P. Griffin, "The Consulting Survey," *Consulting Today,* Special Issue (Fall 1998): 1–11 (http://www.consultingtoday.com).

26. J. Lewis III, "Growth of Internal Change Agents in Organizations" (Ph.D. Diss., Case Western Reserve University, 1970).

27. G. Edelwich and A. Brodsky, *Burn-Out Stages of Disillusionment in the Helping Professions* (New York: Human Science, 1980); M. Weisbord, "The Wizard of OD: Or, What Have Magic Slippers to Do with Burnout, Evaluation, Resistance, Planned Change, and Action Research?" *OD Practitioner* 10 (Summer 1978): 1–14; M. Mitchell, "Consultant Burnout," in *The 1977 Annual Handbook for Group Facilitators,* eds. J. Jones and W. Pfeiffer (La Jolla, Calif: University Associates, 1977): 145–56.

28. Griffin and Griffin, "Consulting Survey."

29. T. Isgar, "Quality of Work Life of Consultants," *Academy of Management OD Newsletter* (Winter 1983): 2–4.

30. P. Hanson and B. Lubin, *Answers to Questions Most Frequently Asked about Organization Development* (Newbury Park, Calif.: Sage Publications, 1995).

31. Church and Burke, "Practitioner Attitudes."

32. D. Jamieson and B. Tannenbaum, *The Heart and Mind of the Practitioner: Enduring Values and Perspectives for the Practice of Change* (San Francisico: Jossey-Bass, in press).

33. J. Schermerhorn, "Interorganizational Development," *Journal of Management* 5 (1979): 21–38; T. Cummings, "Interorganization Theory and Organization Development," in *Systems Theory for Organization Development*, ed. T. Cummings (Chichester, England: John Wiley & Sons, 1980): 323–38.

34. D. Warrick and H. Kelman, "Ethical Issues in Social Intervention," in *Processes and Phenomena of Social Change*, ed. G. Zaltman (New York: John Wiley & Sons, 1973): 377–449; R. Walton, "Ethical Issues in the Practice of Organization Development" (working paper no. 1840, Harvard University Graduate School of Business Administration, 1973); D. Bowen, "Value Dilemmas in Organization Development," *Journal of Applied Behavioral Science* 13 (1977): 545–55; L. Greiner and R. Metzger, *Consulting to Management* (Englewood Cliffs, N.J.: Prentice Hall, 1983): 311–25; L. White and K. Wooten, "Ethical Dilemmas in Various Stages of Organization Development," *Academy of Management Review* 8 (1963): 690–97; K. Scalzo, "When Ethics and Consulting Collide" (unpublished Master's Thesis, Pepperdine University, Graziadio School of Business and Management, Culver City, Calif., 1994); L. White and M. Rhodeback, "Ethical Dilemmas in Organization Development: A Cross-Cultural Analysis," *Journal of Business Ethics* 11, 9 (1992): 663–70; S. DeVogel, R. Sullivan, G. McLean, and W. Rothwell, "Ethics in OD," in *Practicing Organization Development*, eds. W. Rothwell, R. Sullivan, and G. McLean (San Diego: Pfeiffer, 1995).

35. OD Institute, *International Registry of O.D. Professionals and O.D. Handbook* (Cleveland: OD Institute, 1992).

36. *Who's Who in Training and Development* (Alexandria, Va: American Society for Training & Development, 1992).

37. W. Gellerman, M. Frankel, and R. Ladenson, *Values and Ethics in Organization and Human System Development: Responding to Dilemmas in Professional Life* (San Francisco: Jossey-Bass, 1990).

38. W. Bennis, *Organization Development: Its Nature, Origins, and Prospects* (Reading, Mass.: Addison-Wesley, 1969).

39. H. Kelman, "Manipulation of Human Behavior: An Ethical Dilemma for the Social Scientist," in *The Planning of Change*, 2d ed., eds. W. Bennis, K. Benne, and R. Chin (New York: Holt, Rinehart, & Winston, 1969): 584.

40. E. Schein, Process Consultation Revisited (Reading, Mass.: Addison-Wesley, 1999); R. Beckhard, "The Dependency Dilemma," *Consultants' Communique* 6 (July-September 1978): 1–3.

41. G. Lippitt, *Organization Renewal* (Englewood Cliffs, N.J.: Prentice Hall, 1969).

42. C. Argyris, "Explorations in Consulting–Client Relationships," *Human Organizations* 20 (Fall 1961): 121–33.

43. J. Slocum Jr., "Does Cognitive Style Affect Diagnosis and Intervention Strategies?" *Group and Organization Studies* 3 (June 1978): 199–210.

44. This application was submitted by Kathy Scalzo and is based on an actual case from her interviews with OD consultants on how they resolve ethical dilemmas. The names and places have been changed to preserve anonymity.

■ APPENDIX

Ethical Guidelines for an Organization Development/Human Systems Development (OD/HSD) Professional

Sponsored by the Human Systems Development Consortium (HSDC), a significant integrative effort by Bill Gellermann has been under way to develop "A Statement of Values and Ethics for Professionals in Organization and Human System Development." HSDC is an informal collection of the leaders of most of the professional associations related to the application of the behavioral and social sciences. A series of drafts based on extensive contributions, comments, and discussions involving many professionals and organizations has led to the following version of this statement.

As an OD/HSD Professional, I commit to supporting and acting in accordance with the following guidelines:

I. Responsibility for Professional Development and Competence

A. Accept responsibility for the consequences of my acts and make every effort to ensure that my services are properly used.

B. Recognize the limits of my competence, culture, and experience in providing services and using techniques; neither seek nor accept assignments outside those limits without clear understanding by the client when exploration at the edge of my competence is reasonable; refer client to other professionals when appropriate.

C. Strive to attain and maintain a professional level of competence in the field, including

1. broad knowledge of theory and practice in

   a. applied behavioral science generally.
   b. management, administration, organizational behavior, and system behavior specifically.
   c. multicultural issues including issues of color and gender.
   d. other relevant fields of knowledge and practice.

2. ability to

   a. relate effectively with individuals and groups.
   b. relate effectively to the dynamics of large, complex systems.
   c. provide consultation using theory and methods of the applied behavioral sciences.
   d. articulate theory and direct its application, including creation of learning experiences for individuals, small and large groups, and for whole systems.

D. Strive continually for self-knowledge and personal growth; be aware that "what is in me" (my perceptions of myself in my world) and "what is outside me" (the realities that exist apart from me) are not the same; be aware that my values, beliefs, and aspirations can both limit and empower me and that they are primary determinants of my perceptions, my behavior, and my personal and professional effectiveness.

E. Recognize my own personal needs and desires and deal with them responsibly in the performance of my professional roles.

F. Obtain consultation from OD/HSD professionals who are native to and aware of the specific cultures within which I work when those cultures are different from my own.

II. Responsibility to Clients and Significant Others

A. Serve the short- and long-term welfare, interests, and development of the client system and all its stakeholders; maintain balance in the timing, pace, and magnitude of planned change so as to support a mutually beneficial relationship between the system and its environment.

B. Discuss candidly and fully goals, costs, risks, limitations, and anticipated outcomes of any program or other professional relationship under consideration; seek to avoid automatic confirmation of predetermined conclusions, either the client's or my own; seek optimum involvement by client system members in every step of the process, including managers and workers' representatives; fully inform client system members about my role, contribution, and strategy in working with them.

C. Fully inform participants in any activity or procedure as to its sponsorship, nature, purpose, implications, and any significant risk associated with it so that they can freely choose their participation in any activity initiated by me; acknowledge that their choice may be limited with activity initiated by recognized authorities; be particularly sensitive to implications and risks when I work with people from cultures other than my own.

D. Be aware of my own personal values, my values as an OD/HSD professional, the values of my native culture, the values of the people with whom I am working, and the values of their cultures; involve the client system in making relevant cultural differences explicit and exploring the possible implications of any OD/HSD intervention for all the stakeholders involved; be prepared to make explicit my assumptions, values, and standards as an OD/HSD professional.

E. Help all stakeholders while developing OD/HSD approaches, programs, and the like, if they wish such help; for example, this could include workers' representatives as well as managers in the case of work with a business organization.

F. Work collaboratively with other internal and external consultants serving the same client system and resolve conflicts in terms of the balanced best interests of the client system and all its stakeholders; make appropriate arrangements with other internal and external consultants about how responsibilities will be shared.

G. Encourage and enable my clients to provide for themselves the services I provide rather than foster continued reliance on me; encourage, foster, and support self-education and self-development by individuals, groups, and all other human systems.

H. Cease work with a client when it is clear that the client is not benefiting or the contract has been completed; do not accept an assignment if its scope is so limited that the client will not benefit or it would involve serious conflict with the values and ethics outlined in this statement.

I. Avoid conflicts of interest.

1. Fully inform the client of my opinion about serving similar or competing organizations; be clear with myself, my clients, and other concerned stakeholders about my loyalties and responsibilities when conflicts of interest arise; keep parties informed of these conflicts; cease work with the client if the conflicts cannot be adequately resolved.

2. Seek to act impartially when involved in conflicts between parties in the client system; help them resolve their conflicts themselves, without taking

sides; if necessary to change my role from serving as impartial consultant, do so explicitly; cease work with the client, if necessary.

3. Identify and respond to any major differences in professionally relevant values or ethics between myself and my clients with the understanding that conditions may require ceasing work with the client.

4. Accept differences in the expectations and interests of different stakeholders and realize that those differences cannot be reconciled all the time.

J. Seek consultation and feedback from neutral third parties in case of conflict between myself and my client.

K. Define and protect the confidentiality of my client–professional relationships.

1. Make limits of confidentiality clear to clients/participants.

2. Reveal information accepted in confidence only to appropriate or agreed-upon recipients or authorities.

3. Use information obtained during professional work in writings, lectures, or other public forums only with prior consent or when disguised so that it is impossible from my presentations alone to identify the individuals or systems with whom I have worked.

4. Make adequate provisions for maintaining confidentiality in the storage and disposal of records; make provisions for responsibly preserving records in the event of my retirement or disability.

L. Establish mutual agreement on a contract covering services and remuneration.

1. Ensure a clear understanding of and mutual agreement on the services to be performed; do not shift from that agreement without both a clearly defined professional rationale for making the shift and the informed consent of the clients/participants; withdraw from the agreement if circumstances beyond my control prevent proper fulfillment.

2. Ensure mutual understanding and agreement by putting the contract in writing to the extent feasible, yet recognize that

    a. the spirit of professional responsibility encompasses more than the letter of the contract.

    b. some contracts are necessarily incomplete because complete information is not available at the outset.

    c. putting the contract in writing may be neither necessary nor desirable.

3. Safeguard the best interests of the client, the profession, and the public by making sure that financial arrangements are fair and in keeping with appropriate statutes, regulations, and professional standards.

M. Provide for my own accountability by evaluating and assessing the effects of my work.

1. Make all reasonable efforts to determine if my activities have accomplished the agreed-upon goals and have not had other undesirable consequences; seek to undo any undesirable consequences, and do not attempt to cover up these situations.

2. Actively solicit and respond with an open mind to feedback regarding my work and seek to improve.

3. Develop, publish, and use assessment techniques that promote the welfare and best interests of clients/participants; guard against the misuse of assessment results.

N. Make public statements of all kinds accurately, including promotion and advertising, and give service as advertised.

    1. Base public statements providing professional opinions or information on scientifically acceptable findings and techniques as much as possible, with full recognition of the limits and uncertainties of such evidence.

    2. Seek to help people make informed choices when making statements as part of promotion or advertising.

    3. Deliver services as advertised and do not shift without a clear professional rationale and the informed consent of the participants/clients.

III. Responsibility to the Profession

A. Act with due regard for the needs, special competencies and obligations of my colleagues in OD/HSD and other professions; respect the prerogatives and obligations of the institutions or organizations with which these other colleagues are associated.

B. Be aware of the possible impact of my public behavior upon the ability of colleagues to perform their professional work; perform professional activity in a way that will bring credit to the profession.

C. Work actively for ethical practice by individuals and organizations engaged in OD/HSD activities and, in case of questionable practice, use appropriate channels for confronting it, including

    1. direct discussion when feasible.

    2. joint consultation and feedback, using other professionals as third parties.

    3. enforcement procedures of existing professional organizations.

    4. public confrontation.

D. Contribute to continuing professional development by

    1. supporting the development of other professionals, including mentoring with less experienced professionals.

    2. contributing ideas, methods, findings, and other useful information to the body of OD/HSD knowledge and skill.

E. Promote the sharing of OD/HSD knowledge and skill by various means including

    1. granting use of my copyrighted material as freely as possible, subject to a minimum of conditions, including a reasonable price defined on the basis of professional as well as commercial values.

    2. giving credit for the ideas and products of others.

IV. Social Responsibility

A. Strive for the preservation and protection of fundamental human rights and the promotion of social justice.

B. Be aware that I bear a heavy social responsibility because my recommendations and professional actions may alter the lives and well-being of individuals within my client systems, the systems themselves, and the larger systems of which they are subsystems.

C. Contribute knowledge, skill, and other resources in support of organizations, programs, and activities that seek to improve human welfare; be prepared to accept clients who do not have sufficient resources to pay my full fees at reduced fees or no charge.

D. Respect the cultures of the organization, community, country, or other human system within which I work (including the cultures' traditions, values, and moral and ethical expectations and their implications), yet recognize and constructively confront the counterproductive aspects of those cultures whenever feasible; be sensitive to cross-cultural differences and their implications; be aware of the cultural filters which bias my view of the world.

E. Recognize that accepting this statement as a guide for my behavior involves holding myself to a standard that may be more exacting than the laws of any country in which I practice.

F. Contribute to the quality of life in human society at large; work toward and support a culture based on mutual respect for each other's rights as human beings; encourage the development of love, trust, openness, mutual responsibility, authentic and harmonious relationships, empowerment, participation, and involvement in a spirit of freedom and self-discipline as elements of this culture.

G. Engage in self-generated or collaborative endeavor to develop means for helping across cultures.

H. Serve the welfare of all the people of Earth, all living things, and their environment.

The Process of Organization Development

2

4

Entering and Contracting

The planned change process described in Chapter 2 generally starts when one or more key managers or administrators somehow sense that their organization, department, or group could be improved or has problems that could be alleviated through organization development. The organization might be successful yet have room for improvement. It might be facing impending environmental conditions that necessitate a change in how it operates. The organization could be experiencing particular problems, such as poor product quality, high rates of absenteeism, or dysfunctional conflicts among departments. Conversely, the problems might appear more diffuse and consist simply of feelings that the organization should be "more innovative," "more competitive," or "more effective."

Entering and contracting are the initial steps in the OD process. They involve defining in a preliminary manner the organization's problems or opportunities for development and establishing a collaborative relationship between the OD practitioner and members of the client system about how to work on those issues. Entering and contracting set the initial parameters for carrying out the subsequent phases of OD: diagnosing the organization, planning and implementing changes, and evaluating and institutionalizing them. They help to define what issues will be addressed by those activities, who will carry them out, and how they will be accomplished.

Entering and contracting can vary in complexity and formality depending on the situation. In those cases where the manager of a work group or department serves as his or her own OD practitioner, entering and contracting typically involve the manager and group members meeting to discuss what issues to work on and how they will jointly accomplish that. Here, entering and contracting are relatively simple and informal. They involve all relevant members directly in the process without a great number of formal procedures. In situations where managers and administrators are considering the use of professional OD practitioners, either from inside or from outside the organization, entering and contracting tend to be more complex and formal.[1] OD practitioners may need to collect preliminary information to help define the problematic or development issues. They may need to meet with representatives of the client organization rather than with the total membership; they may need to formalize their respective roles and how the change process will unfold.

This chapter first discusses the activities and content-oriented issues involved in entering into and contracting for an OD initiative. Major attention here will be directed at complex processes involving OD professionals and client organizations. Similar entering and contracting issues, however, need to be addressed in even the simplest OD efforts where managers serve as OD practitioners for their own work units. Unless there is clarity and agreement about what issues to work on, who will address them, and how that will be accomplished, subsequent stages of the OD process are likely to be confusing and ineffective. The chapter concludes with a discussion of the interpersonal process issues involved in entering and contracting for OD work.

ENTERING INTO AN OD RELATIONSHIP

An OD process generally starts when a member of an organization or unit contacts an OD practitioner about potential help in addressing an organizational issue.[2] The organization member may be a manager, staff specialist, or some other key participant, and the practitioner may be an OD professional from inside or outside of the organization. Determining whether the two parties should enter into an OD relationship typically involves clarifying the nature of the organization's current functioning and the issue(s) to be addressed, the relevant client system for that issue, and the appropriateness of the particular OD practitioner.[3] In helping assess these issues, the OD practitioner may need to collect preliminary data about the organization. Similarly, the organization may need to gather information about the practitioner's competence and experience.[4] This knowledge will help both parties determine whether they should proceed to develop a contract for working together.

This section describes the following activities involved in entering an OD relationship: clarifying the organizational issue, determining the relevant client, and selecting the appropriate OD practitioner.

Clarifying the Organizational Issue

When seeking help from OD practitioners, organizations typically start with a *presenting problem*—the issue that has caused them to consider an OD process. It may be specific (decreased market share, increased absenteeism) or general ("we're growing too fast," "we need to prepare for rapid changes"). The presenting problem often has an implied or stated solution. For example, managers may believe that because members of their teams are in conflict, team building is the obvious answer. They may even state the presenting problem in the form of a solution: "We need some team building."

In many cases, however, the presenting problem is only a symptom of an underlying problem. For example, conflict among members of a team may result from several deeper causes, including ineffective reward systems, personality differences, inappropriate structure, and poor leadership. The issue facing the organization or department must be clarified early in the OD process so that subsequent diagnostic and intervention activities are focused correctly.[5]

Gaining a clearer perspective on the organizational issue may require collecting preliminary data.[6] OD practitioners often examine company records and interview a few key members to gain an introductory understanding of the organization, its context, and the nature of the presenting problem. Those data are gathered in a relatively short period of time, typically over a few hours to one or two days. They are intended to provide enough rudimentary knowledge of the organizational issue to enable the two parties to make informed choices about proceeding with the contracting process.

The diagnostic phase of OD involves a far more extensive assessment of the problematic or development issue than occurs during the entering and contracting stage. The diagnosis also might discover other issues that need to be addressed, or it might lead to redefining the initial issue that was identified during the entering and contracting stage. This is a prime example of the emergent nature of the OD process, where things may change as new information is gathered and new events occur.

Determining the Relevant Client

A second activity in entering an OD relationship is to define who is the relevant client for addressing the organizational issue.[7] Generally, the relevant client includes those organization members who can directly impact the change issue, whether it is solving a particular problem or improving an already successful organization or department. Unless these members are identified and included in the entering and contracting process, they may withhold their support for and commitment to the OD process. In trying to improve the productivity of a unionized manufacturing plant, for example, the relevant client may need to include union officials as well as managers and staff personnel. It is not unusual for an OD project to fail because the relevant client was inappropriately defined.

Determining the relevant client can vary in complexity depending on the situation. In those cases where the organizational issue can be addressed in a specific organization unit, client definition is relatively straightforward. Members of that unit constitute the relevant client. They or their representatives must be included in the entering and contracting process. For example, if a manager asked for help in improving the decision-making process of his or her team, the manager and team members would be the relevant client. Unless they are actively involved in choosing an OD practitioner and defining the subsequent change process, there is little likelihood that OD will improve team decision making.

Determining the relevant client is more complex when the organizational issue cannot readily be addressed in a single unit. Here, it may be necessary to expand the definition of the client to include members from multiple units, from different hierarchical levels, and even from outside of the organization. For example, the manager of a production department may seek help in resolving conflicts between his or her unit and other departments in the organization. The relevant client would extend beyond the boundaries of the production department because that department alone cannot resolve the issue. The client might include members from all departments involved in the conflict as well as the executive to whom all of the departments report. If that interdepartmental conflict also involved key suppliers and customers from outside of the firm, the relevant client might include members of those groups.

In such complex situations, OD practitioners need to gather additional information about the organization to determine the relevant client, generally as part of the preliminary data collection that typically occurs when clarifying the issue to be addressed. When examining company records or interviewing personnel, practitioners can seek to identify the key members and organizational units that need to be involved. For example, they can ask organization members such questions as Who can directly impact the organizational issue? Who has a vested interest in it? Who has the power to approve or reject the OD effort? Answers to those questions can help determine who is the relevant client for the entering and contracting stage, although the client may change during the later stages of the OD process as new data are gathered and changes occur. If so, participants may have to return to and modify this initial stage of the OD effort.

Selecting an OD Practitioner

The last activity involved in entering an OD relationship is selecting an OD practitioner who has the expertise and experience to work with members on the organizational issue. Unfortunately, little systematic advice is available on how to choose a competent OD professional, whether from inside or outside of the organization.

Perhaps the best criteria for selecting, evaluating, and developing OD practitioners are those suggested by the late Gordon Lippitt, a pioneering practitioner in the field.[8] Lippitt listed areas that managers should consider before selecting a practitioner, including the ability of the consultant to form sound interpersonal relationships, the degree of focus on the problem, the skills of the practitioner relative to the problem, the extent that the consultant clearly informs the client as to his or her role and contribution, and whether the practitioner belongs to a professional association. References from other clients are highly important. A client may not like the consultant's work, but it is critical to know the reasons for both pleasure and displeasure. One important consideration is whether the consultant approaches the organization with openness and an insistence on diagnosis or whether the practitioner appears to have a fixed program that is applicable to almost any organization.

Certainly, OD consulting is as much a *person* specialization as it is a *task* specialization. The OD professional needs not only a repertoire of technical skills but also the personality and interpersonal competence to use himself or herself as an instrument of change. Regardless of technical training, the consultant must be able to maintain a boundary position, coordinating among various units and departments and mixing disciplines, theories, technology, and research findings in an organic rather than a mechanical way. The practitioner is potentially the most important OD technology available.

Thus, in selecting an OD practitioner, perhaps the most important issue is the fundamental question, How effective has the person been in the past, with what kinds of organizations, using what kinds of techniques? In other words, references must be checked. Interpersonal relationships are tremendously important, but even con artists have excellent interpersonal relationships and skills.

The burden of choosing an effective OD practitioner should not rest entirely with the client organization.[9] Consultants also bear a heavy responsibility for seeking an appropriate match between their skills and knowledge and what the organization or department needs. Few managers are sophisticated enough to detect or to understand subtle differences in expertise among OD professionals, and they often do not understand the difference between intervention specialties. Thus, practitioners should help educate potential clients, being explicit about their strengths and weaknesses and about their range of competence. If OD professionals realize that a good match does not exist, they should inform managers and help them find more suitable help.

Application 4.1 describes the entering process at Charity Medical Center and highlights the importance of clarifying the organizational issue, identifying the relevant client, and helping the organization to choose an appropriate consultant.

DEVELOPING A CONTRACT

The activities of entering an OD relationship are a necessary prelude to developing an OD contract. They define the major focus for contracting, including the relevant parties. Contracting is a natural extension of the entering process and clarifies how the OD process will proceed. It typically establishes the expectations of the parties, the time and resources that will be expended, and the ground rules under which the parties will operate.

The goal of contracting is to make a good decision about how to carry out the OD process.[10] It can be relatively informal and involve only a verbal agreement between the client and OD practitioner. A team leader with OD skills, for example, may voice his or her concerns to members about how the team is functioning.

APPLICATION 4•1 Entering Charity Medical Center

Charity Medical Center (CMC), a five hundred-bed acute-care hospital, was part of the Jefferson Hospital Corporation (JHC). JHC, which operated several long-term and acute-care facilities and was sponsored by a large religious organization, had recently been formed and was trying to establish accounting and finance, materials management, and human resources systems to manage and coordinate the different facilities. Of particular concern to CMC, however, was a market share that had been declining steadily for six months. Senior management recognized that other hospitals in the area were newer, had better facilities, were more "user friendly," and had captured the interest of referring physicians. In the context of JHC's changes, CMC invited several consultants, including an external OD practitioner named John Murray, to make presentations on how a total quality management process might be implemented in the hospital.

John conducted an initial interview with CMC's vice president of patient-care services, Joan Grace. Joan noted that the hospital's primary advantage was its designation as a level-one trauma center. CMC offered people needing emergency care for major trauma their best chance for survival. "Unfortunately," Joan said, "the reputation of the hospital is that once we save a patient's life, we tend to forget they are here." Perceptions of patient-care quality were low and influenced by the age and decor of the physical plant. CMC had been one of the original facilities in the metropolitan area. Finally, Joan suggested that the hospital had lost a substantial amount of money last year and considerable pressure was coming from JHC to turn things around.

John thanked Joan for her time and asked for additional materials that might help him better understand the hospital. Joan provided a corporate mission statement, a recent strategic planning document, an organization chart, and an analysis of recent performance. John also sought permission to interview other members of the hospital and the corporate office to get as much information as possible for his presentation to the hospital's senior management. He interviewed the hospital president, observed one of the nursing units, and spoke with the human resources vice president from the corporate office.

The interviews and documents provided important information. First, the documents revealed that CMC was not one hospital but two. A small, 150-bed hospital located in the suburbs also reported to the president of CMC, and several members of the hospital's staff held managerial positions at both hospitals. Second, last year's strategic plan included a budget for initiating a patient-care quality improvement process. Budget responsibility for the project was assigned to Joan Grace's department. Third, the mission statement was a standard expression of values and was heavily influenced by the religious group's beliefs. Fourth, the performance reports confirmed both poor financial results and decreasing market share.

John's interviews and observations pointed out several additional pieces of information. First, the corporate organization, JHC, truly was in a state of flux. There were clear goals and objectives for each of the hospitals, but patient, physician, and employee satisfaction measures, human resources policies, financial practices, and material logistics were still being established. Second, the management and nursing staff heads at CMC were extremely busy—usually attending meetings for most of the day. In fact, Joan's secretary kept a notebook dedicated to tracking who was meeting where and when. Third, a large consulting firm had just been awarded a contract to do "job redesign" work in two departments of the hospital. And fourth, most of the nursing units operated under traditional and somewhat outdated nursing management principles.

In developing his presentation, John thought about several issues. For example, the relevant client would be difficult to identify. Joan Grace was clearly responsible for the project and its success, but the president, referring physicians, the suburban hospital, and the corporate office were important stakeholders in a TQM process and needed a voice if it was to succeed. In addition, the presenting problem was a decline in market share. The job redesign contract awarded to the other consulting firm seemed disconnected from the TQM effort, and both efforts seemed disconnected from the market share problem. John wondered how the hospital viewed the relationships among total quality management, job design, and market share. He also questioned whether he was the appropriate consultant for CMC. The firm doing the job redesign used a packaged approach to change that conflicted with John's OD-based philosophy.

Using the information gathered and his reflections on the project, John gave his presentation to senior management about implementing a total quality management process at CMC. His presentation included a history of the quality movement and how it had been applied to other health-care organizations. Several examples of the gains made in patient satisfaction, clinical outcomes (such as decreased infection rates), and physician satisfaction were incorporated. He noted that implementing a quality process was a major organizational change, requiring a thorough diagnosis of the hospital, a considerable commitment of resources, and a high level of involvement by senior management. Without such involvement, it was not reasonable to expect the kinds of results he had described. John also suggested that total quality management was capable of addressing certain problems but was not designed to address directly such broader performance issues as market share.

Finally, John described his track record at implementing quality improvement processes in health-care organizations. He shared several references with the group members and encouraged them to talk with former clients regarding his style and impact. John also noted that he had been referred to CMC by the religious organization that sponsored the hospital system and that it was aware of his work in another medical facility. ■

After some discussion, they might agree to devote one hour of future meeting time to diagnosing the team with the help of the leader. Here, entering and contracting are done together informally. In other cases, contracting can be more protracted and result in a formal document. That typically occurs when organizations employ outside OD practitioners. Government agencies, for example, generally have procurement regulations that apply to contracting with outside consultants.[11]

Regardless of the level of formality, all OD processes require some form of explicit contracting that results in either a verbal or a written agreement. Such contracting clarifies the client's and the practitioner's expectations about how the OD process will take place. Unless there is mutual understanding and agreement about the process, there is considerable risk that someone's expectations will be unfilled.[12] That can lead to reduced commitment and support, to misplaced action, or to premature termination of the process.

The contracting step in OD generally addresses three key areas:[13] what each party expects to gain from the OD process, the time and resources that will be devoted to it, and the ground rules for working together.

Mutual Expectations

This part of the contracting process focuses on the expectations of the client and the OD practitioner. The client states the services and outcomes to be provided by the OD practitioner and describes what the organization expects from the process and the consultant. Clients usually can describe the desired outcomes, such as decreased turnover or higher job satisfaction. Encouraging them to state their wants in the form of outcomes, working relationships, and personal accomplishments can facilitate the development of a good contract.[14]

The OD practitioner also should state what he or she expects to gain from the OD process. This can include opportunities to try new interventions, report the results to other potential clients, and receive appropriate compensation or recognition.

Time and Resources

To accomplish change, the organization and the OD practitioner must commit time and resources to the effort. Each must be clear about how much energy and how many resources will be dedicated to the change process. Failure to make explicit the necessary requirements of a change process can quickly ruin an OD effort. For example, a client may clearly state that the assignment involves diagnosing the causes of poor productivity in a work group. However, the client may expect the practitioner to complete the assignment without talking to the workers. Typically, clients want to know how much time will be necessary to complete the assignment, who needs to be involved, how much it will cost, and so on.

Block has suggested that resources can be divided into two parts.[15] *Essential requirements* are things that are absolutely necessary if the change process is to be successful. From the practitioner's perspective, they can include access to key people or information, enough time to do the job, and commitment from certain people. The organization's essential requirements might include a speedy diagnosis or assurances that the project will be conducted at the lowest price. Being clear about the constraints on carrying out the assignment will facilitate the contracting process and improve the chances for success. *Desirable requirements* are those things that would be nice to have but are not absolutely necessary, such as access to special resources and written rather than verbal reports.

Ground Rules

The final part of the contracting process involves specifying how the client and the OD practitioner will work together. The parameters established may include such issues as confidentiality, if and how the OD practitioner will become involved in personal or interpersonal issues, how to terminate the relationship, and whether the practitioner is supposed to make expert recommendations or help the manager make decisions. For internal consultants, organizational politics make it especially important to clarify issues of how to handle sensitive information and how to deliver "bad news."[16] Such process issues are as important as the needed substantive changes. Failure to address the concerns may mean that the client or the practitioner has inappropriate assumptions about how the process will unfold.

Application 4.2 describes the contracting meeting for the quality improvement process at Charity Medical Center.

PERSONAL PROCESS ISSUES IN ENTERING AND CONTRACTING

The prior discussion on entering and contracting addressed the activities and content-oriented issues associated with beginning an OD project. In this final section, we discuss the interpersonal issues an OD practitioner must be aware of to produce a successful agreement. In most cases, the client's expectations, resources, and working relationship requirements will not fit perfectly with the OD practitioner's essential and desirable requirements. Negotiating the differences to improve the likelihood of success can be intra- and interpersonally challenging.

Entering and contracting are the first exchanges between a client and an OD practitioner. Establishing a healthy relationship at the outset makes it more likely that the client's desired outcomes will be achieved and that the OD practitioner will be able to improve the organization's capacity to manage change in the future. In this initial stage, both parties are facing a considerable amount of uncertainty and ambiguity. On the one hand, the client is likely to feel exposed, inadequate, or vulnerable. The organization's current effectiveness and the request for help may seem to the client like an admission that they are incapable of solving the problem or providing the leadership necessary to achieve a set of results. Moreover, they are entering into a relationship where they may feel unable to control the activities of the OD practitioner. As a result, they feel vulnerable because of their dependency on the practitioner to provide assistance. Consciously or unconsciously, feelings of exposure, inadequacy, or vulnerability may lead the client to resist coming to closure on the contract. The OD practitioner must be alert to the signs of resistance, such as asking for extraordinary amounts of detail, and be able to address them skillfully.

On the other hand, the OD practitioner may have feelings of empathy, unworthiness, and dependency. The practitioner may overidentify with the client's issues and want to be so helpful that she or he agrees to unreasonable deadlines or inadequate resources. The practitioner's desire to be seen as competent and worthy may lead to an agreement on a project for which the practitioner has few skills or

APPLICATION 4•2   Contracting at Charity Medical Center

John Murray's presentation to the senior management team at CMC, based on the information outlined in Application 4.1, was well received, and patient-care vice president Joan Grace asked John to meet with her to discuss how the change process might go forward. At the meeting, John thanked Joan for the opportunity to work with CMC and suggested that the next year or two represented a challenging time for the hospital's management. He identified several knotty issues that needed to be discussed before work could begin. Most important, the hospital's rush to implement a total quality management process was admirable, but he was worried that it lacked an appropriate base of knowledge. Although performance and market share were the big issues facing the hospital, the relationship between those problems and a quality program was not clear. In addition, even if a TQM process made sense, managers and nursing heads were frustrated by their inability to influence change because of their busy meeting schedules. A quality improvement process might solve some of those problems but certainly not all of them.

Joan acknowledged that both performance and frustration with change were problems that needed to be addressed. She explained that the hospital wanted help to improve the quality of patient care and to increase patient, employee, and physician satisfaction with the hospital. Improvements in those areas were expected to produce important gains in hospital performance. Joan asked John if he could generate a proposal that addressed those issues as well as managerial frustration with the inability to make necessary changes.

John agreed to put a proposal in writing but suggested that it would be helpful to discuss first what should be included in it. John thought that discussing several issues now would improve the chances of getting started quickly. He outlined several issues that the proposal would cover. First, the hospital should thoroughly diagnose the reasons for market-share decline, the current level of patient-care quality, and managerial frustration with making changes. That diagnosis would require access to the corporate officers at JHC to discuss their relationships with CMC. In addition, several managers and employees of the hospital, as well as some physicians, needed to be interviewed. Second, the proposed job redesign effort being conducted by the other consulting firm should be postponed. Finally, CMC management should meet for two days to examine the information generated by the diagnosis and to make a joint decision about whether a total quality management process made sense.

Joan looked uncomfortable. John's requirements seemed unreasonable given that the hospital simply wanted to improve patient-care quality and stakeholder satisfaction. For example, getting the senior administrators to commit to two days away from the hospital would be difficult. Everyone was busy, and finding a time when they could all meet for that long was nearly impossible. In addition, there was a sense of urgency in the hospital to begin the process right away. Collecting information seemed like a waste of time. Finally, and perhaps most important, postponing the job redesign effort was a sensitive issue. The project had strong political support, and the other consultants had provided a clear ten-step process and timetable for the work design changes.

John told Joan that he appreciated her concerns and her willingness to confront these issues. He explained that his requests were necessary if the project was to be successful and that he had thought carefully about them. Collecting the diagnostic information was, in fact, the first step in any quality management process. The very basis of a TQM effort was data-based decision making. To begin a quality process without valid information violated fundamental principles of the approach. More important, to proceed without that information could very well mean that the wrong change would be implemented. John suggested, for instance, that the market share problem could result from the way CMC was treating the physicians. If that were true, a quality program would be inappropriate and costly. Instead, a program to improve the relationships with physicians might provide a better return on CMC's investment.

The two-day meeting was therefore very important. Once appropriate data were collected, the senior managers could decide, based on fact, what exactly should be done to address hospital performance; employee, patient, and physician satisfaction; and managerial frustration. John explained that a quality management process, if necessary, required attention to CMC's structure, measurement, and reward systems as well as its culture. The two-day meeting of the senior management team would permit a full explanation of the TQM process, a description of the necessary resources, and a discussion of the commitment necessary to implement it. Following that meeting, he could provide a more explicit outline of the change process.

Finally, John acknowledged that the politically sensitive nature of the job redesign program made resolving this issue more difficult. He explained his belief that any redesign effort that did not take into account a potential TQM process likely would have to be redone. He argued that to proceed blindly with a job redesign effort might result in money spent for nothing.

Joan believed that John could have access to the consulting firm doing job redesign but that there was little chance of postponing the program for very long. Again acknowledging the political support for the program, John offered to coordinate with the other consultants but strongly urged Joan to postpone initiating the project until after the two-day management meeting. Joan said she understood his concerns but stated that she could not make that decision without talking with the senior management team.

John accepted that and asked if his other requests now made better sense. Joan replied that a two-day meeting did seem important and worth the effort. In addition, access to the corporate officers, employees, managers, and physicians was a reasonable request and could be arranged. Responding to John's example of a physician relations program, Joan informed him that although CMC had such a program, it was not very effective because managers had become too busy to pay attention to it.

At this point, Joan had to go to another meeting. They adjourned with the understanding that Joan would speak with the other managers and get back to John. A week later, Joan called and agreed to John's requests. She asked him to submit a written proposal covering the issues discussed as soon as possible. A copy of his proposal is shown below.

John Murray and Associates
Organization Development Consultants
1234 Main Ave., Los Angeles, CA 00000

January 20, 200X

Ms. Joan Grace
Charity Medical Center
Metropolis, USA 00000

Dear Joan:

This letter is to propose consulting work with Charity Medical Center (CMC). It describes the activities, expectations, resources, and outcomes associated with diagnosing problem areas at CMC and determining the feasibility of a quality improvement process.

Statement of the Problem

Charity Medical Center is facing two interrelated problems: performance declines and managerial frustration with effecting change. The performance problems include recent declines in profitability and market share as well as in patient-care quality and employee, physician, and patient satisfaction. The managerial frustration reflects a feeling of not being able to address performance, patient, physician, and corporate concerns in a timely fashion.

Expected Outcomes of the Diagnosis

The diagnosis of CMC's operations is expected to produce two important outcomes: (1) a better understanding of the causes of poor performance and managerial frustration, and (2) the opportunity to make an informed decision about how to address those two issues. The diagnosis and resulting decision should provide hospital managers with a clearer sense of how to spend their time to resolve those problems.

Roles, Expectations, and Resources

First, a diagnosis of CMC's current operations will be made. This activity requires that

1. Jefferson Hospital Corporation (JHC) officers will be available to the consultant to discuss its operations and relationship with CMC.
2. The hospital will make available to the consultant information regarding the current structure and function of the physician relations program.
3. The senior management team, middle managers, and first-level supervisors as well as several hospital employees will be available to the consultant for interviews. These confidential interviews will focus on peoples' perceptions of hospital functioning and how it could be improved.

Second, a two-day meeting of the hospital's senior management team will review the diagnostic information collected and discuss the appropriate way to address the performance and frustration issues. The meeting will also include a discussion of the necessary commitment and resources required to implement an improvement program and a specification of the objectives and implementation plans that might make sense for CMC. Following the meeting, the consultant, in cooperation with management, will propose a more detailed outline of the implementation process.

The job redesign project should be postponed until after this two-day meeting. In the event that a change program is initiated, the consultant agrees to coordinate with the job redesign effort and the hospital agrees to provide access to the consultants for that effort.

The diagnostic process described above will take approximately six consulting days to complete. Two days will be required for interviews with managers, employees, and corporate officers. Two days will be needed to analyze the data and prepare for the two-day meeting. Consulting services are billed at $1,000 per day plus ordinary expenses.

I appreciate the opportunity to work with the Charity Medical Center. I will call you within the next few days to set up dates for diagnostic interviews and to establish the dates for the senior management meeting.

Sincerely,
John Murray
Consultant

experience. Finally, in response to reasonable client requests, the practitioner may challenge the client's motivation and become defensive.

Actually coming to agreement during the contracting phase can be difficult and intense. A number of complex emotional and psychological issues are in play, and OD practitioners must be mindful of their own as well as the client's perspectives. Attending to those issues as well as to the content of the contract will help increase the likelihood of success.

■ SUMMARY

The entering and contracting processes constitute the initial activities of the OD process. They set the parameters for the phases of planned change that follow: diagnosing, planning and implementing change, and evaluating and institutionalizing it. Organizational entry involves clarifying the organizational issue or presenting problem, determining the relevant client, and selecting an OD practitioner. Developing an OD contract focuses on making a good decision about whether to proceed and allows both the client and the OD practitioner to clarify expectations about how the change process will unfold. Contracting involves setting mutual expectations, negotiating time and resources, and developing ground rules for working together.

■ NOTES

1. M. Lacey, "Internal Consulting: Perspectives on the Process of Planned Change," *Journal of Organization Change Management* 8, 3 (1995): 75–84; J. Geirland and M. Maniker-Leiter, "Five Lessons for Internal Organization Development Consultants," *OD Practitioner* 27 (1995): 44–48.

2. P. Block, *Flawless Consulting: A Guide to Getting Your Expertise Used,* 2d ed. (San Francisco: Jossey-Bass, 1999); C. Margerison, "Consulting Activities in Organizational Change," *Journal of Organizational Change Management* 1 (1988): 60–67; R. Harrison, "Choosing the Depth of Organizational Intervention," *Journal of Applied Behavioral Science* 6 (1970): 182–202.

3. M. Beer, *Organization Change and Development: A Systems View* (Santa Monica, Calif.: Goodyear, 1980); G. Lippitt and R. Lippitt, *The Consulting Process in Action,* 2d ed. (San Diego: University Associates, 1986).

4. L. Greiner and R. Metzger, *Consulting to Management* (Englewood Cliffs, N.J.: Prentice Hall, 1983): 251–58; Beer, *Organization Change and Development,* 81–83.

5. Block, *Flawless Consulting.*

6. D. Jamieson, "Start-up," in *Practicing Organization Development,* eds. W. Rothwell, R. Sullivan, and G. McLean (San Diego: Pfeiffer, 1995); J. Fordyce and R. Weil, *Managing WITH People,* 2d ed. (Reading, Mass.: Addison-Wesley, 1979).

7. Beer, *Organization Change and Development;* Fordyce and Weil, *Managing WITH People.*

8. G. Lippitt, "Criteria for Selecting, Evaluating, and Developing Consultants," *Training and Development Journal* 28 (August 1972): 10–15.

9. Greiner and Metzger, *Consulting to Management.*

10. Block, *Flawless Consulting;* Beer, *Organization Change and Development.*

11. T. Cody, *Management Consulting: A Game Without Chips* (Fitzwilliam, N.H.: Kennedy and Kennedy, 1986): 108–16; H. Holtz, *How to Succeed as an Independent Consultant,* 2d ed. (New York: John Wiley & Sons, 1988): 145–61.

12. G. Bellman, *The Consultant's Calling* (San Francisco: Jossey-Bass, 1990).

13. M. Weisbord, "The Organization Development Contract," *Organization Development Practitioner* 5 (1973): 1–4; M. Weisbord, "The Organization Contract Revisited," *Consultation* 4 (Winter 1985): 305–15; D. Nadler, *Feedback and Organization Development: Using Data-Based Methods* (Reading, Mass.: Addison-Wesley, 1977): 110–14.

14. Block, *Flawless Consulting.*

15. Ibid.

16. Lacey, "Internal Consulting."

5
Diagnosing Organizations

Diagnosing organizations is the second major phase in the model of planned change described in Chapter 2 (Figure 2.2). It follows the entering and contracting stage (Chapter 4) and precedes the planning and implementation phase. When it is done well, diagnosis clearly points the organization and the OD practitioner toward a set of appropriate intervention activities that will improve organization effectiveness.

Diagnosis is the process of assessing the functioning of the organization, department, group, or job to discover the sources of problems and areas for improvement. It involves collecting pertinent information about current operations, analyzing those data, and drawing conclusions for potential change and improvement. Effective diagnosis provides the systematic understanding of the organization needed to design appropriate interventions. Thus, OD interventions derive from diagnosis and include specific actions intended to resolve problems and to improve organizational functioning. (Chapters 12 through 20 present the major interventions used in OD today.)

This chapter is the first of four chapters that describe different aspects of the diagnostic process. This chapter presents a general definition of diagnosis and discusses the need for diagnostic models in guiding the process. Diagnostic models derive from conceptions about how organizations function and tell OD practitioners what to look for in diagnosing organizations, departments, groups, or jobs. They represent a road map for discovering current functioning. A general, comprehensive diagnostic model is presented based on open systems theory. The chapter concludes with a description and application of an organization-level diagnostic model. Chapter 6 describes and applies diagnostic models at the group and job levels. Chapters 7 and 8 complete the diagnostic phase by discussing processes of data collection, analysis, and feedback.

WHAT IS DIAGNOSIS?

Diagnosis is the process of understanding how the organization is currently functioning, and it provides the information necessary to design change interventions. It generally follows from successful entry and contracting, which set the stage for successful diagnosis. They help OD practitioners and client members jointly determine organizational issues to focus on, how to collect and analyze data to understand them, and how to work together to develop action steps from the diagnosis.

Unfortunately, the term *diagnosis* can be misleading when applied to organizations. It suggests a model of organization change analogous to medicine: an organization (patient) experiencing problems seeks help from an OD practitioner (doctor); the practitioner examines the organization, finds the causes of the problems, and prescribes a solution. Diagnosis in organization development, however, is much more collaborative than such a medical perspective implies and does not accept the implicit assumption that something is wrong with the organization.

First, the values and ethical beliefs that underlie OD suggest that both organization members and change agents should be involved in discovering the determinants of current organizational effectiveness. Similarly, both should be involved actively in developing appropriate interventions and implementing them. For example, a manager might seek OD help to reduce absenteeism in his or her department. The manager and an OD consultant jointly might decide to diagnose the cause of the problem by examining company absenteeism records and by interviewing selected employees about possible reasons for absenteeism. Alternatively, they might examine employee loyalty and discover the organizational elements that encourage people to stay. Analysis of those data could uncover determinants of absenteeism or loyalty in the department, thus helping the manager and the practitioner to develop an appropriate intervention to address the issue. The choice about how to approach the issue of absenteeism and the decisions about how to address it are made jointly by the OD practitioner and the manager.

Second, the medical model of diagnosis also implies that something is wrong with the patient and that one needs to uncover the cause of the illness. In those cases where organizations do have specific problems, diagnosis can be problem oriented, seeking reasons for the problems. On the other hand, as suggested by the absenteeism example above, the practitioner and the client may choose to frame the issue positively. Additionally, the client and OD practitioner may be looking for ways to enhance the organization's existing functioning. Many managers involved with OD are not experiencing specific organizational problems. Here, diagnosis is development oriented. It assesses the current functioning of the organization to discover areas for future development. For example, a manager might be interested in using OD to improve a department that already seems to be functioning well. Diagnosis might include an overall assessment of both the task-performance capabilities of the department and the impact of the department on its individual members. This process seeks to uncover specific areas for future development of the department's effectiveness.

In organization development, diagnosis is used more broadly than a medical definition would suggest. *It is a collaborative process between organization members and the OD consultant to collect pertinent information, analyze it, and draw conclusions for action planning and intervention.* Diagnosis may be aimed at uncovering the causes of specific problems; be focused on understanding effective processes; or be directed at assessing the overall functioning of the organization or department to discover areas for future development. Diagnosis provides a systematic understanding of organizations so that appropriate interventions may be developed for solving problems and enhancing effectiveness.

THE NEED FOR DIAGNOSTIC MODELS

Entry and contracting processes can result in a need to understand a whole system or some part, process, or feature of the organization. To diagnose an organization, OD practitioners and organization members need to have an idea about what information to collect and analyze. Choices about what to look for invariably depend on how organizations are perceived. Such perceptions can vary from intuitive hunches to scientific explanations of how organizations function. Conceptual frameworks that people use to understand organizations are referred to as *diagnostic models*.[1] They describe the relationships among different features of the organization, its context, and its effectiveness. As a result, diagnostic models point out what areas to examine and what questions to ask in assessing how an organization is functioning.

However, all models represent simplifications of reality and therefore choose certain features as critical. Focusing attention on those features, often to the exclusion of others, can result in a biased diagnosis. For example, a diagnostic model that relates team effectiveness to the handling of interpersonal conflict would lead an OD practitioner to ask questions about relationships among members, decision-making processes, and conflict resolution methods. Although relevant, those questions ignore other group issues such as the composition of skills and knowledge, the complexity of the tasks performed by the group, and member interdependencies. Thus, diagnostic models must be chosen carefully to address the organization's presenting problems as well as to ensure comprehensiveness.

Potential diagnostic models are everywhere. Any collection of concepts and relationships that attempts to represent a system or explain its effectiveness can potentially qualify as a diagnostic model. Major sources of diagnostic models in OD are the thousands of articles and books that discuss, describe, and analyze how organizations function. They provide information about how and why certain organizational systems, processes, or functions are effective. The studies often concern a specific facet of organizational behavior, such as employee stress, leadership, motivation, problem solving, group dynamics, job design, and career development. They also can involve the larger organization and its context, including the environment, strategy, structure, and culture. Diagnostic models can be derived from that information by noting the dimensions or variables that are associated with organizational effectiveness.

Another source of diagnostic models is OD practitioners' experience in organizations. That field knowledge is a wealth of practical information about how organizations operate. Unfortunately, only a small part of that vast experience has been translated into diagnostic models that represent the professional judgments of people with years of experience in organizational diagnosis. The models generally link diagnosis with specific organizational processes, such as group problem solving, employee motivation, or communication between managers and employees. The models list specific questions for diagnosing such processes.

This chapter presents a general framework for diagnosing organizations rather than trying to cover the range of OD diagnostic models. The framework describes the systems perspective prevalent in OD today and integrates several of the more popular diagnostic models. The systems model provides a useful starting point for diagnosing organizations or departments. (Additional diagnostic models that are linked to specific OD interventions are presented in Chapters 12 through 20.)

OPEN-SYSTEMS MODEL

This section introduces systems theory, a set of concepts and relationships describing the properties and behaviors of things called *systems*—organizations, groups, and people, for example. Systems are viewed as unitary wholes composed of parts or subsystems; the system serves to integrate the parts into a functioning unit. For example, organization systems are composed of departments such as sales, operations, and finance. The organization serves to coordinate behaviors of its departments so that they function together in service of a goal or strategy. The general diagnostic model based on systems theory that underlies most of OD is called the *open-systems model.*

Organizations as Open Systems

Systems can vary in how open they are to their outside environments. *Open systems*, such as organizations and people, exchange information and resources with their environments. They cannot completely control their own behavior and are influenced in part by external forces. Organizations, for example, are affected by such environmental conditions as the availability of raw material, customer demands, and government regulations. Understanding how these external forces affect the organization can help explain some of its internal behavior.

Open systems display a hierarchical ordering. Each higher level of system comprises lower-level systems: systems at the level of society comprise organizations; organizations comprise groups (departments); and groups comprise individuals. Although systems at different levels vary in many ways—in size and complexity, for example—they have a number of common characteristics by virtue of being open systems, and those properties can be applied to systems at any level. The following key properties of open systems are described below: inputs, transformations, and outputs; boundaries; feedback; equifinality; and alignment.

Inputs, Transformations, and Outputs

Any organizational system is composed of three related parts: inputs, transformations, and outputs, as shown in Figure 5.1. *Inputs* consist of human or other resources, such as information, energy, and materials, coming into the system. Inputs are acquired from the system's external environment. For example, a manufacturing organization acquires raw materials from an outside supplier. Similarly, a hospital nursing unit acquires information concerning a patient's condition from the attending physician. In each case, the system (organization or nursing unit) obtains resources (raw materials or information) from its external environment.

Transformations are the processes of converting inputs into outputs. In organizations, a production or operations function composed of both social and technological components generally carries out transformations. The social component consists of people and their work relationships, whereas the technological component involves tools, techniques, and methods of production or service delivery. Organizations have developed elaborate mechanisms for transforming incoming resources into goods and services. Banks, for example, transform deposits into mortgage loans and interest income. Schools attempt to transform students into more educated

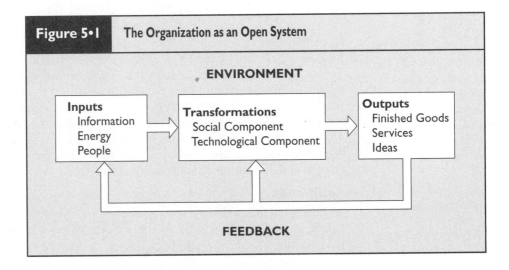

Figure 5•1   The Organization as an Open System

ENVIRONMENT

Inputs
Information
Energy
People

Transformations
Social Component
Technological Component

Outputs
Finished Goods
Services
Ideas

FEEDBACK

people. Transformation processes also can take place at the group and individual levels. For example, research and development departments can transform the latest scientific advances into new product ideas.

Outputs are the results of what is transformed by the system and sent to the environment. Thus, inputs that have been transformed represent outputs ready to leave the system. Group health insurance companies receive premiums, healthy and unhealthy individuals, and medical bills, transform them through physician visits and record keeping, and export treated patients and payments to hospitals and physicians.

Boundaries

The idea of boundaries helps to distinguish between systems and environments. Closed systems have relatively rigid and impenetrable boundaries, whereas open systems have far more permeable borders. Boundaries—the borders, or limits, of the system—are easily seen in many biological and mechanical systems. Defining the boundaries of social systems is more difficult because there is a continuous inflow and outflow through them. For example, where are the organizational boundaries in this case? When a fire alarm sounds in Malmo, Sweden, a firefighter puts the address of the fire into a computer terminal. A moment later, the terminal gives out a description of potential hazards at the address. The computer storing the information is in Cleveland, Ohio. The emergence of the information superhighway and worldwide information networks will continue to challenge the notion of boundaries in open systems.

The definition of a *boundary* is somewhat arbitrary because a social system has multiple subsystems and the boundary line for one subsystem may not be the same as that for a different subsystem. As with the system itself, arbitrary boundaries may have to be assigned to any social organization, depending on the variable to be stressed. The boundaries used for studying or analyzing leadership, for instance, may be quite different from those used to study intergroup dynamics.

Just as systems can be considered relatively open or closed, the permeability of boundaries also varies from fixed to diffuse. The boundaries of a community's police force are probably far more rigid and sharply defined than those of the community's political parties. Conflict over boundaries is always a potential problem within an organization, just as it is in the world outside the organization.

Feedback

As shown in Figure 5.1, *feedback* is information regarding the actual performance or the results of the system. Not all such information is feedback, however. Only information used to control the future functioning of the system is considered feedback. Feedback can be used to maintain the system in a steady state (for example, keeping an assembly line running at a certain speed) or to help the organization adapt to changing circumstances. McDonald's, for example, has strict feedback processes to ensure that a meal in one outlet is as similar as possible to a meal in any other outlet. On the other hand, a salesperson in the field may report that sales are not going well and may insist on some organizational change to improve sales. A market research study may lead the marketing department to recommend a change to the organization's advertising campaign.

Equifinality

In closed systems, a direct cause-and-effect relationship exists between the initial condition and the final state of the system: when a computer's "on" switch is pushed, the system powers up. Biological and social systems, however, operate quite differently. The idea of *equifinality* suggests that similar results may be achieved with different initial conditions and in many different ways. This concept suggests that a manager can use varying degrees of inputs into the organization and can transform them in a variety of ways to obtain satisfactory outputs. Thus, the function of management is not to seek a single rigid solution but rather to develop a variety of satisfactory options. Systems and contingency theories suggest that there is no universal best way to design an organization. Organizations and departments providing routine services, such as AT&T's and MCIWorldCom's long-distance phone services could be designed quite differently and still achieve the same result. Similarly, customer service functions at major retailers, software manufacturers, or airlines could be designed according to similar principles.

Alignment

A system's overall effectiveness is determined by the extent to which the different parts are aligned with each other. This alignment or fit concerns the relationships between inputs and transformations, between transformations and outputs, and among the subsystems of the transformation process. Diagnosticians who view the relationships among the various parts of a system as a whole are taking what is referred to as a *systemic* perspective.

Alignment refers to a characteristic of the relationship between two or more parts. It represents the extent to which the features, operations, and characteristics of one system support the effectiveness of another system. Just as the teeth in two wheels of a watch must mesh perfectly for the watch to keep time, so do the parts of an organization need to mesh for it to be effective. For example, General Electric attempts to achieve its goals through a strategy of diversification, and a divisional structure is used to support that strategy. A functional structure would not be a good fit with the strategy because it is more efficient for one division to focus on one product line than for one manufacturing department to try to make many different products. The systemic perspective suggests that diagnosis is the search for misfits among the various parts and subsystems of an organization.

Diagnosing Organizational Systems

When viewed as open systems, organizations can be diagnosed at three levels. The highest level is the overall organization and includes the design of the company's strategy, structure, and processes. Large organization units, such as divisions, subsidiaries, or strategic business units, also can be diagnosed at that level. The next-lowest level is the group or department, which includes group design and such devices for structuring interactions among members as norms and work schedules. The lowest level is the individual position or job. This includes ways in which jobs are designed to elicit required task behaviors.

Diagnosis can occur at all three organizational levels, or it may be limited to issues occurring at a particular level. The key to effective diagnosis is to know what to look for at each level as well as how the levels affect each other.[2] For example, diagnosing a work group requires knowledge of the variables important for group functioning and how the larger organization design affects the group. In fact, a basic understanding of organization-level issues is important in almost any diagnosis because they serve as critical inputs to understanding groups and individuals.

Figure 5.2 presents a comprehensive model for diagnosing these different organizational systems. For each level, it shows: (1) the inputs that the system has to work with, (2) the key design components of the transformation subsystem, and (3) the system's outputs.

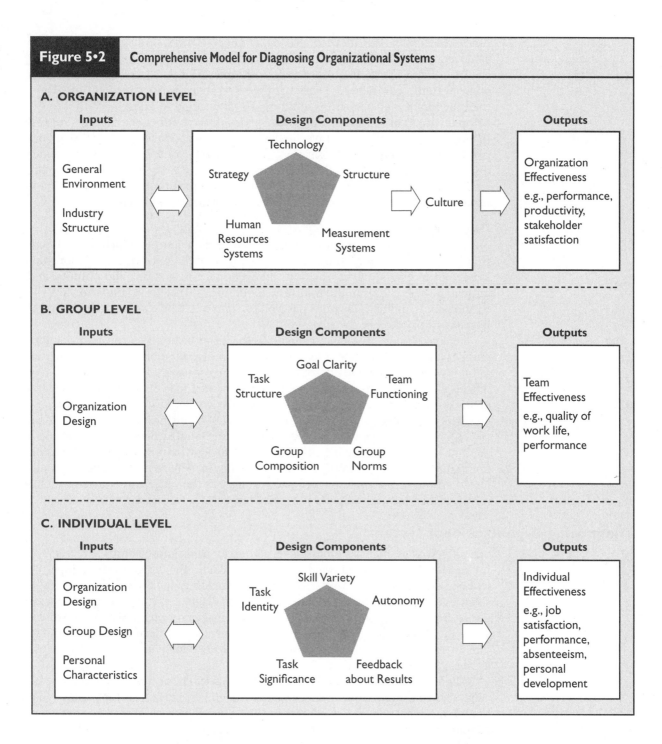

Figure 5•2   Comprehensive Model for Diagnosing Organizational Systems

The relationships shown in Figure 5.2 illustrate how each organization level affects the lower levels. The larger environment is an input to organization design. Organization design is an input to group design, which in turn serves as an input to job design. These cross-level relationships emphasize that organizational levels must fit with each other if the organization is to operate effectively. For example, organization structure must fit with and support group task design, which in turn must fit with individual job design.

The following discussion on organization-level diagnosis and the discussion in Chapter 6 on group- and job-level diagnosis provide a general overview of the dimensions (and their relationships) that need to be understood at each level. It is beyond the scope of this book to describe in detail the many variables and relationships reported in the extensive literature on organizations. However, specific diagnostic questions are identified and concrete examples are included as an introduction to this phase of the planned change process.

ORGANIZATION-LEVEL DIAGNOSIS

The organization level of analysis is the broadest systems perspective typically taken in diagnostic activities. The model shown in Figure 5.2(A) is similar to other popular organization-level diagnostic models. These include Weisbord's six-box model,[3] Nadler and Tushman's congruency model,[4] Galbraith's star model,[5] and Kotter's organization dynamics model.[6] Figure 5.2(A) proposes that an organization's transformation processes, or design components, represent the way the organization positions and organizes itself within an environment (inputs) to achieve specific outputs. The combination of design component elements is called a *strategic orientation*.[7]

Inputs

To understand how a total organization functions, it is necessary to examine particular inputs, design components, and the alignment of the two sets of dimensions. Figure 5.2 shows that two key inputs affect the way an organization designs its strategic orientation: the general environment and industry structure.

The *general environment* represents the external elements and forces that can affect the attainment of organization objectives.[8] It can be described in terms of the amount of uncertainty present in social, technological, economic, ecological, and political forces. The more uncertainty there is in how the environment will affect the organization, the more difficult it is to design an effective strategic orientation. For example, the technological environment in the watch industry has been highly uncertain over time. The Swiss, who build precision watches with highly skilled craftspeople, were caught off guard by the mass production and distribution technology of Timex in the 1960s. Similarly, many watch manufacturers were surprised by and failed to take advantage of digital technology. Similarly, the increased incidence of AIDS in the workplace (social environment) and the passage of the Americans with Disabilities Act (political environment) have forced changes in the strategic orientations of organizations.

An organization's *industry structure* or *task environment* is another important input into strategic orientation. As defined by Michael Porter, an organization's task environment consists of five forces: supplier power, buyer power, threats of substitutes, threats of entry, and rivalry among competitors.[9] First, strategic orientations must be sensitive to powerful suppliers who can increase prices (and therefore lower profits) or force the organization to pay more attention to the supplier's needs than to the organization's needs. For example, unions represent powerful suppliers of labor that can affect the costs of any organization within an industry. Second, strategic orientations must be sensitive to powerful buyers. Airplane purchasers, such as American Airlines or country governments, can force Airbus Industrie or Boeing to lower prices or appoint the planes in particular ways. Third, strategic orientations must be sensitive to the threat of new firms entering into competition. Profits in the restaurant business tend to be low because of the ease of starting a new restaurant. Fourth, strategic orientations must be sensitive to the threat of new products or services that can replace existing offerings. Ice cream producers must carefully monitor their costs and prices because it is easy for a consumer to purchase frozen yogurt or other types of desserts instead. Finally, strategic orientations must be sensitive to rivalry among existing competitors. If many organizations are competing for the same customers, for example, then the strategic orientation must monitor product offerings, costs, and structures carefully if the organization is to survive and prosper. Together, these forces play an important role in determining the success of an organization, whether it is a manufacturing or service firm, a nonprofit organization, or a government agency.

General environments and industry structures describe the input content. In addition to understanding what inputs are available, the inputs must be understood for their rate of change and complexity.[10] An organization's general environment or industry structure can be characterized along a *dynamic–static continuum*. Dynamic environments change rapidly and unpredictably and suggest that the organization adopt a flexible strategic orientation. Dynamic environments are relatively high in uncertainty. The *complexity* of the environment refers to the number of important elements in the general environment and industry structure. For example, software development organizations face dynamic and complex environments. Not only do technologies, regulations, customers, and suppliers change rapidly, but all of them are important to the firm's survival. On the other hand, manufacturers of glass jars face more stable and less complex environments.

Design Components

Figure 5.2(A) shows that a strategic orientation is composed of five major design components—strategy, technology, structure, measurement systems, and human resources systems—and an intermediate output—culture. Effective organizations align their design components to each other and to the environment.

A *strategy* represents the way an organization uses its resources (human, economic, or technical) to gain and sustain a competitive advantage.[11] It can be described by the organization's mission, goals and objectives, strategic intent, and functional policies. A mission statement describes the long-term purpose of the organization, the range of products or services offered, the markets to be served, and the social needs served by the organization's existence. Goals and objectives are statements that provide explicit direction, set organization priorities, provide guidelines for management decisions, and serve as the cornerstone for organizing activities, designing jobs, and setting standards of achievement. Goals and objectives should set a target of achievement (such as 50-percent gross margins, an average employee satisfaction score of four on a five-point scale, or some level of productivity); provide a means or system for measuring achievement; and provide a deadline or timeframe for accomplishment.[12] A strategic intent is a succinct label that describes how the organization intends to achieve its goals and objectives. For example, an organization can achieve goals through differentiation of its product or service, by achieving the lowest costs in the industry, or by growth. Finally, functional policies are the methods, procedures, rules, or administrative practices that guide decision making and convert plans into actions. In the semiconductor business, for example, Intel has a policy of allocating about 30 percent of revenues to research and development to maintain its lead in microprocessors production.[13]

Technology is concerned with the way an organization converts inputs into products and services. It represents the core of the transformation function and includes production methods, work flow, and equipment. Automobile companies have traditionally used an assembly-line technology to build cars and trucks. Two features of the technological core have been shown to influence other design components: interdependence and uncertainty.[14] *Technical interdependence* involves ways in which the different parts of a technological system are related. High interdependence requires considerable coordination among tasks, such as might occur when departments must work together to bring out a new product. *Technical uncertainty* refers to the amount of information processing and decision making required during task performance. Generally, when tasks require high amounts of information processing and decision making, they are difficult to plan and routinize. The technology of car manufacturing is relatively certain and moderately interdependent. As a result, automobile manufacturers can specify in advance the behaviors workers should perform and how their work should be coordinated.

The *structural system* describes how attention and resources are focused on task accomplishment. It represents the basic organizing mode chosen to (1) divide the overall work of an organization into subunits that can assign tasks to individuals or groups and (2) coordinate these subunits for completion of the overall work.[15] Structure, therefore, needs to be closely aligned with the organization's technology.

Two ways of determining how an organization divides work are to examine its formal structure or to examine its level of differentiation and integration. Formal structures divide work by function (accounting, sales, or production), by product or service (Chevrolet, Buick, or Pontiac), or by some combination of both (a matrix composed of functional departments and product groupings). These are described in more detail in Chapter 14. The second way to describe how work is divided is to specify the amount of differentiation and integration there is in a structure. Applied to the total organization, differentiation refers to the degree of similarity or difference in the design of two or more subunits or departments.[16] In a highly differentiated organization, there are major differences in design among the departments. Some departments are highly formalized with many rules and regulations, others have few rules and regulations, and still others are moderately formal or flexible.

The way an organization coordinates the work across subunits is called *integration*. Integration can be achieved in a variety of ways—for example, by using plans and schedules; using budgets; assigning special roles, such as project managers, liaison positions, or integrators; or creating cross-departmental task forces and teams. The amount of integration required in a structure is a function of (1) the amount of uncertainty in the environment, (2) the level of differentiation in the structure, and (3) the amount of interdependence among departments. As uncertainty, differentiation, and interdependence increase, more sophisticated integration devices are required.

Measurement systems are methods of gathering, assessing, and disseminating information on the activities of groups and individuals in organizations. Such data tell how well the organization is performing and are used to detect and control deviations from goals. Closely related to structural integration, measurement systems monitor organizational operations and feed data about work activities to managers and members so that they can better understand current performance and coordinate work. Effective information and control systems clearly are linked to strategic objectives; provide accurate, understandable, and timely information; are accepted as legitimate by organization members; and produce benefits in excess of their cost.

Human resources systems include mechanisms for selecting, developing, appraising, and rewarding organization members. These influence the mix of skills, personalities, and behaviors of organization members. The strategy and technology provide important information about the skills and knowledge required if the organization is to be successful. Appraisal processes identify whether those skills and knowledge are being applied to the work, and reward systems complete the cycle by recognizing performance that contributes to goal achievement. Reward systems may be tied to measurement systems so that rewards are allocated on the basis of measured results. (Specific human resources systems, such as rewards and career development, are discussed in Chapters 15 and 16.)

Organization culture is the final design component. It represents the basic assumptions, values, and norms shared by organization members.[17] Those cultural elements are generally taken for granted and serve to guide members' perceptions, thoughts, and actions. For example, McDonald's culture emphasizes efficiency, speed, and consistency. It orients employees to company goals and suggests the kinds of behaviors necessary for success. In Figure 5.2(A), culture is shown as an intermediate output from the five other design components because it represents both an outcome and a constraint. It is an outcome of the organization's history and environment[18] as well as of prior choices made about the strategy, technology, structure, measurement systems, and human resources systems. It is also a constraint in that it is more difficult to change than the other components. In that sense it can either hinder or facilitate change. In diagnosis, the interest is in understanding the current culture well enough to determine its alignment with the other design factors. Such information may partly explain current outcomes, such as performance or effectiveness. (Culture is discussed in more detail in Chapter 18.)

Outputs

The outputs of a strategic orientation can be classified into three components. First, organization performance refers to financial outputs such as profits, return on investment, and earnings per share. For nonprofit and government agencies, performance often refers to the extent to which costs were lowered or budgets met. Second, productivity concerns internal measurements of efficiency such as sales per employee, waste, error rates, quality, or units produced per hour. Third, stakeholder satisfaction reflects how well the organization has met the expectations of different groups. Customer satisfaction can be measured in terms of market share or focus-group data; employee satisfaction can be measured in terms of an opinion survey; investor satisfaction can be measured in terms of stock price.

Alignment

The effectiveness of an organization's current strategic orientation requires knowledge of the above information to determine the alignment among the different elements.

1. Does the organization's strategic orientation fit with the inputs?
2. Do the design components fit with each other?

For example, if the elements of the external environment (inputs) are fairly similar in their degree of certainty, then an effective organization structure (design factor) should have a low degree of differentiation. Its departments should be designed similarly because each faces similar environmental demands. On the other hand, if the environment is complex and each element presents different amounts of uncertainty, a more differentiated structure is warranted. Chevron Oil Company's regulatory, ecological, technological, and social environments differ greatly in their amount of uncertainty. The regulatory environment is relatively slow paced and detail oriented. Accordingly, the regulatory affairs function within Chevron is formal and bound by protocol. In the technological environment, on the other hand, new methods for discovering, refining, and distributing oil and oil products are changing at a rapid pace. Those departments are much more flexible and adaptive, very different from the regulatory affairs function.

Analysis

Application 5.1 describes the Nike organization and provides an opportunity to perform the following organization-level analysis.[19] Organization-level dimensions and relationships may be applied to diagnose this example. A useful starting point is to ask how well the organization is currently functioning. Examination of the organization's outputs yields measures of market share, financial performance, and stakeholder satisfaction. Nike's string of solid annual increases over six years was followed by real or predicted declines. Discovering the underlying causes of these problems begins with an assessment of the inputs and strategic orientation and then proceeds to an evaluation of the alignments among the different parts. In diagnosing the inputs, these two questions are important:

1. *What is the company's general environment?* Nike's environment is uncertain and complex. Technologically, Nike is dependent on the latest breakthroughs in shoe design and materials to keep its high-performance image. Socially and politically, Nike's international manufacturing and marketing operations require that it be aware of a variety of stakeholder demands from several countries, cultures, and governments, including the U.S. government, which might view Nike's foreign manufacturing strategy with some concern about U.S. jobs. Other stakeholders are pressuring Nike for changes to its human resources practices.

2. *What is the company's industry structure?* Nike's industry is highly competitive and places considerable pressure on profits. First, the threat of entry is high. It is not difficult or expensive to enter the athletic shoe market. Many shoe manufacturers could easily offer an athletic shoe if they wanted. The threat of substitute products is also high. Nike's image and franchise depend on people wanting to be athletic. If fitness trends were to change, then other footwear could easily fill the need. This possibility clearly exists because Nike's marketing has sensationalized professional athletes and sports, rather than emphasizing fitness for the average person. The bargaining power of suppliers, such as providers of labor, shoe materials, and manufacturing, is generally low because the resources are readily available and there are many sources. The bargaining power of buyers is moderate. At the high-performance end, buyers are willing to pay more for high quality, whereas at the casual end, price is important and the purchasing power of large accounts can bid down Nike's price. Finally, rivalry among firms is severe. A number of international and domestic competitors exist, such as Reebok, Adidas, New Balance, Puma, Converse, and Tiger. Many of them have adopted marketing and promotion tactics similar to Nike's and are competing for the same customers. Thus, the likelihood of new competition, the threat of new substitute products, and the rivalry among existing competitors are the primary forces creating uncertainty in the environment and squeezing profits in the athletic shoe industry.

The following questions are important in assessing Nike's strategic orientation:

1. *What is the company's strategy?* Nike's strategy is clear on some points and nebulous on others. First, although the company has no formal mission statement,

APPLICATION 5•1   Nike's Strategic Orientation

In 1993, Nike was the leader in domestic-brand athletic footwear with more than 30 percent market share. It also produced sports apparel, hiking boots, and upscale men's shoes. But after six years of solid growth, international sales were falling, sales of basketball shoes were down, and the firm's stock price had dropped 41 percent since November 1992. Analysts were projecting declines in both total revenues and profits for the next fiscal year. In addition, Nike had been the focus of attack from several stakeholder groups. Organized labor believed that Nike exploited foreign labor; the African-American sector noted the lack of diversity in Nike's workforce; and the general public was growing tired of sensationalizing athletes.

Nike's traditional strategy was built around high-performance, innovative athletic shoes, aggressive marketing, and low-cost manufacturing. Using input from athletes, Nike developed a strong competence in producing high-quality athletic shoes, first for running, then for basketball and other sports. By contracting with well-known and outspoken athletes to endorse its products, a Nike image of renegade excellence and high performance emerged. Other consumers who wanted to associate with the Nike image could do so by purchasing its shoes. Thus, a large market of "weekend warriors," people pursuing a more active lifestyle, serious runners, and anyone wanting to project a more athletic image became potential customers. Nike contracted with low-cost, foreign manufacturing plants to produce its shoes.

An athletic shoe retailer places orders with Nike representatives, who are not employees of Nike but contract with Nike to sell its shoes, for delivery in six to eight months. The Futures program, as it is called, offers the retailer 10 percent off the wholesale price for making these advanced orders. The orders are then compiled and production scheduled with one of Nike's Asian manufacturing partners. Nike doesn't actually make shoes. Instead, it develops contract relationships with Taiwanese, Korean, Japanese, and other low-cost sources. On-site Nike employees guarantee that the shoes meet the Nike standards of quality.

Nike's culture is distinctive. The organization, built by athletes for athletes, is very entrepreneurial, and the "Just Do It" marketing campaign aptly describes the way things are done at Nike. As one senior executive put it, "It's fine to develop structures and plans and policies, if they are viewed, and used, as tools. But it is so easy for them to become substitutes for good thinking, alibis for not taking responsibility, reasons to not become involved. And then we'd no longer be Nike."

What emerged, by the mid-1980s, was a way of working that involved setting direction, dividing up the work, pulling things together, and providing rewards.

Although Phil Knight, founder and chairman of Nike, sets the general direction for Nike, he rarely sets clear goals. For example, Knight views Nike as a growth company. The athletic drive pushes employees to achieve bigger sales and put more shoes on more feet than anyone else. Others are concerned that the decision to go public in the early 1980s has produced pressures for profitability that sometimes work against growth. Implementation of the general direction depends on people being tuned into the day-to-day operations. "You tune into what other people are doing, and if you're receptive, you start to see the need for something to be done," Knight says.

Nike changed from a functional organization in 1985 to a product division structure in 1987. In addition, 1993 brought additional structural change. The new president, Tom Clark, was busy implementing stronger communication and collaboration among manufacturing, marketing, and sales. This description, however, belies the informality of the organization. In essence, the aim of the Nike structure is to fit the pieces together in ways that best meet the needs of the product, the customers, and the market.

In pulling things together, Nike relies on meetings as the primary method for coordination. The word "meeting" connotes more formality than is intended. Meetings, which occur at all levels and all parts of the organization, range from an informal gathering in the hallway, to a three-day off-site event, to formal reviews of a product line. Membership in a meeting is equally fluid, with the people who need to be involved invited and those who don't, not invited. Although more formal systems have emerged over the years, their use is often localized to the people or groups who invented them and is met with resistance by others. Thus, with the exception of the Futures program, there is little in the way of formal information systems.

Finally, Knight favors an annual performance review system with annual pay increases tied to performance. In fact, the system is fairly unstructured; some managers take time to do the reviews well and others do not. Although no formal compensation policy exists, most employees and managers believe that Nike is a "great place to work." For the majority of people there, rewards come in the form of growth opportunities, autonomy, and responsibility. ■

it has a clear sense about its initial purpose in producing high-quality, high-performance athletic footwear. That focus has blurred somewhat as Nike has ventured into apparel, hiking boots, and casual shoes. Its goals also are nebulous because Phil Knight does not set specific goals, only general direction. The tension between growth and profits is a potential source of problems for the organization. On the other hand, its strategic intent is fairly clear. It is attempting to achieve its growth and profitability goals by offering a differentiated product—a high quality, high-performance shoe. Informal policies dominate the Nike organization.

2. ***What are the company's technology, structure, measurement systems, and human resources systems?*** First, the technology of Nike is moderately uncertain and interdependent. For example, developing high-quality, state-of-the-art shoes is uncertain, but there is no evidence that research and development is tightly linked to production. In addition, the Futures program creates low interdependence between manufacturing and distribution, both of which are fairly routine processes. Second, Nike's product division structure appears moderately differentiated, but the new president's emphasis on communication and coordination suggests that it is not highly integrated. Moreover, although Nike appears to have a divisional structure, its contract relationships with manufacturing plants and sales representatives give it a fluid, network-like structure. Third, human resources and measurement systems are underdeveloped. There is no compensation policy, for example, and formal control systems are generally resisted. The one exception to this is the Futures program that tracks orders (which are really advance revenues).

3. ***What is Nike's culture?*** Finally, Nike's culture is a dominant feature of the organization design. The organization appears driven by typical athletic norms of winning, competition, achievement, and performance.

Now that the organization inputs, design components, and outputs have been assessed, it is time to ask the crucial question about how well they fit together. The first concern is the fit between the inputs and the strategic orientation. The complex and uncertain environment fits well with Nike's focus on differentiation and a generally flexible organization design. That explains its incredible success during the 1970s, 1980s, and into the 1990s. The alignment between its strategic orientation and its environment appears sound.

The second concern is the alignment of the design components. With respect to strategy, the individual elements of Nike's strategy are not aligned. It clearly intends to differentiate its product by serving the high-end athlete with high-performance shoes. However, this small group of athletes may have trouble communicating its needs to a large, diversified organization. Growth goals and a diversified mission obviously do not align with Nike's differentiation intent. The market for higher priced and more specialized athletic shoes is much smaller than the market for low-priced tennis shoes and limits the growth potential of sales. That hypothesis is supported by the lack of clear goals in general and policies that support neither growth nor profitability. However, there appears to be a good fit between strategy and the other design components. The differentiated strategic intent requires technologies, structures, and systems that focus on creating new ideas in products, marketing, and manufacturing. The flexible structure, informal systems, and driving culture would seem well suited for that purpose.

The technology appears well supported and aligned with the structure. Product development, market development, and manufacturing development are inherently unprogrammable tasks that require flexibility and adaptability from the organization. Although a product structure overlays most of Nike's activities, the structure is not rigid, and there appears to be a willingness to create structure as necessary to complete a task. In addition, the Futures program is important for two reasons. First, it reduces uncertainty from the market by getting retailers to take the risk that a shoe will not do well. For the retailer, this risk is mitigated by Nike's tremendous reputation and marketing clout. Second, knowing in advance what will be ordered provides Nike with the ability to schedule production and distribution far in advance. This is a powerful device for integrating Nike's activities. Finally, the lack of a formal human resources system supports the fluid and flexible design, but it creates problems in that there is no direction for hiring and development, a point noted by the various stakeholders at the beginning of the application.

Obviously, any discussion of Nike's organization design has to recognize the powerful role its culture plays. More than any design component, the culture promotes coordination of a variety of tasks, serves as a method for socializing and developing people, and establishes methods for moving information around the organization. Clearly, any change effort at Nike will have to acknowledge this role and design an intervention accordingly. The strong culture will either sabotage or facilitate change depending on how the change process aligns with the culture's impact on individual behavior.

Based on this diagnosis of the Nike organization, at least two intervention possibilities are suggested. First, in collaboration with the client, the OD practitioner could suggest increasing Nike's clarity about its strategy. In this intervention, the practitioner would want to avoid talking about formalizing Nike's strategy because the culture would resist such an attempt. However, there are some clear advantages to be gained from a clearer sense of Nike's future, its businesses, and the relationships among them. Second, Nike could focus on increasing the integration and coordination of its structure, measurement systems, and human resources systems. Although the culture provides a considerable amount of social control, the lack of any human resources systems and the relatively underdeveloped integration mechanisms suggest that finding ways to coordinate activities without increasing formalization would be a value-added intervention.

■ SUMMARY

This chapter presented background information for diagnosing organizations, groups, and individual jobs. Diagnosis is a collaborative process, involving both managers and consultants in collecting pertinent data, analyzing them, and drawing conclusions for action planning and intervention. Diagnosis may be aimed at discovering the causes of specific problems, or it may be directed at assessing the organization or department to find areas for future development. Diagnosis provides the necessary practical understanding to devise interventions for solving problems and improving organization effectiveness.

Diagnosis is based on conceptual frameworks about how organizations function. Such diagnostic models serve as road maps by identifying areas to examine and questions to ask in determining how an organization or department is operating.

The comprehensive model presented here views organizations as open systems. The organization serves to coordinate the behaviors of its departments. It is open to exchanges with the larger environment and is influenced by external forces. As open systems, organizations are hierarchically ordered; that is, they are composed of groups, which in turn are composed of individual jobs. Organizations also display five key systems properties: inputs, transformations, and outputs; boundaries; feedback; equifinality; and alignment.

An organization-level diagnostic model was described and applied. It consists of environmental inputs; a set of design components called a strategic orientation; and a variety of outputs, such as performance, productivity, and stakeholder satisfaction. Diagnosis involves understanding each of the parts in the model and then assessing how the elements of the strategic orientation align with each other and with the inputs. Organization effectiveness is likely to be high when there is good alignment.

■ NOTES

1. D. Nadler, "Role of Models in Organizational Assessment," in *Organizational Assessment*, eds. E. Lawler III, D. Nadler, and C. Cammann (New York: John Wiley & Sons, 1980): 119–31; R. Keidel, *Seeing Organizational Patterns* (San Francisco: Berrett-Koehler, 1995); M. Harrison, *Diagnosing Organizations*, 2d ed. (Thousand Oaks, Calif.: Sage Publications, 1994).

2. D. Coghlan, "Organization Development through Interlevel Dynamics, *International Journal of Organizational Analysis* 2 (1994): 264–79.

3. M. Weisbord, "Organizational Diagnosis: Six Places to Look for Trouble with or without a Theory," *Group and Organizational Studies* 1 (1976): 430–37.

4. D. Nadler and M. Tushman, "A Diagnostic Model for Organization Behavior," in *Perspectives on Behavior in Organizations*, eds. J. Hackman, E. Lawler III, and L. Porter (New York: McGraw-Hill, 1977): 85–100.

5. J. Galbraith, *Competing with Flexible Lateral Organizations*, 2d ed. (Reading, Mass.: Addison-Wesley, 1994).

6. J. Kotter, *Organizational Dynamics: Diagnosis and Intervention* (Reading, Mass.: Addison-Wesley, 1978).

7. M. Tushman and E. Romanelli, "Organization Evolution: A Metamorphosis Model of Convergence and Reorientation," in *Research in Organizational Behavior*, vol. 7, eds. L. Cummings and B. Staw (Greenwich, Conn.: JAI Press, 1985); C. Worley, D. Hitchin, and W. Ross, *Integrated Strategic Change: How OD Builds Competitive Advantage* (Reading, Mass.: Addison-Wesley, 1996).

8. F. Emery and E. Trist, "The Causal Texture of Organizational Environments," *Human Relations* 18 (1965): 21–32; H. Aldrich, *Organizations and Environments* (Englewood Cliffs, N.J.: Prentice Hall, 1979).

9. M. Porter, *Competitive Strategy* (New York: Free Press, 1980).

10. Emery and Trist, "Causal Texture"; Aldrich, *Organizations and Environments*.

11. M. Porter, *Competitive Advantage* (New York: Free Press, 1985); C. Hill and G. Jones, *Strategic Management*, 3d ed. (Boston: Houghton Mifflin, 1995).

12. C. Hofer and D. Schendel, *Strategy Formulation: Analytical Concepts* (St. Paul, Minn.: West Publishing, 1978).

13. R. Hoff, "Inside Intel," *Business Week* (1 June 1992): 86–94.

14. J. Thompson, *Organizations in Action* (New York: McGraw-Hill, 1967); D. Gerwin, "Relationships between Structure and Technology," in Handbook of Organizational Design, vol. 2, eds. P. Nystrom and W. Starbuck (Oxford: Oxford University Press, 1981): 3–38.

15. J. Galbraith, *Organization Design* (Reading, Mass.: Addison-Wesley, 1977); D. Robey and C. Sales, *Designing Organizations*, 4th ed. (Homewood, Ill.: Irwin, 1994).

16. P. Lawrence and J. Lorsch, *Organization and Environment* (Cambridge: Harvard University Press, 1967).

17. V. Sathe, "Implications of Corporate Culture: A Manager's Guide to Acting," *Organizational Dynamics* (Autumn 1983): 5–23; E. Schein, *Organizational Culture and Leadership*, 2d ed. (San Francisco: Jossey-Bass, 1990).

18. E. Abrahamson and C. Fombrun, "Macrocultures: Determinants and Consequences," *Academy of Management Review* 19 (1994): 728–56.

19. Adapted from material in G. Willigan, "High-Performance Marketing: An Interview with Nike's Phil Knight," *Harvard Business Review* (July-August, 1992); D. Yang and M. Oneal, "Can Nike Just Do It?" *Business Week* (18 April 1994): 86–90; D. Rikert and C. Christensen, *Nike (A)* 9-395-025 (Boston: Harvard Business School, 1984); D. Rikert and C. Christensen, *Nike (B)* 9-385-027 (Boston: Harvard Business School, 1984).

6

Diagnosing Groups and Jobs

Chapter 5 introduced diagnosis as the second major phase in the model of planned change. Based on open-systems theory, a comprehensive diagnostic framework for organization-, group-, and job-level systems was described. The organization-level diagnostic model was elaborated and applied. After the organization level, the next two levels of diagnosis are the group and job. Many large organizations have groups or departments that are themselves relatively large, like the operating divisions at Viacom, Thomson Learning, or General Electric. Diagnosis of large groups can follow the dimensions and relational fits applicable to organization-level diagnosis. In essence, large groups or departments operate much like organizations, and their functioning can be assessed by diagnosing them as organizations.

Small departments and groups, however, can behave differently from large organizations and so they need their own diagnostic models to reflect those differences. In the first section of this chapter, we discuss the diagnosis of work groups. Such groups generally consist of a relatively small number of people working face-to-face on a shared task. Work groups are prevalent in all sizes of organizations. They can be relatively permanent and perform an ongoing function, or they can be temporary and exist only to perform a certain task or to make a specific decision.

Finally, we describe and apply a diagnostic model of individual jobs—the smallest unit of analysis in organizations. An individual job is constructed to perform a specific task or set of tasks. How jobs are designed can affect individual and organizational effectiveness.

GROUP-LEVEL DIAGNOSIS

Figure 6.1 replicates the comprehensive model introduced in Chapter 5 but highlights the group- and individual-level models. It shows the inputs, design components, outputs, and relational fits for group-level diagnosis.[1] The model is similar to other popular group-level diagnostic models, such as Hackman and Morris's task group design model,[2] McCaskey's framework for analyzing groups,[3] and Ledford, Lawler, and Mohrman's participation group design model.[4]

Inputs

Organization design is clearly the major input to group design. It consists of the design components characterizing the larger organization within which the group is embedded: technology, structure, measurement systems, and human resources systems, as well as organization culture. Technology can determine the characteristics of the group's task; structural systems can specify the level of coordination required among groups. The human resources and measurement systems, such as performance appraisal and reward systems, play an important role in determining team functioning.[5] For example, individually based performance appraisal and reward systems tend to interfere with team functioning because members may be

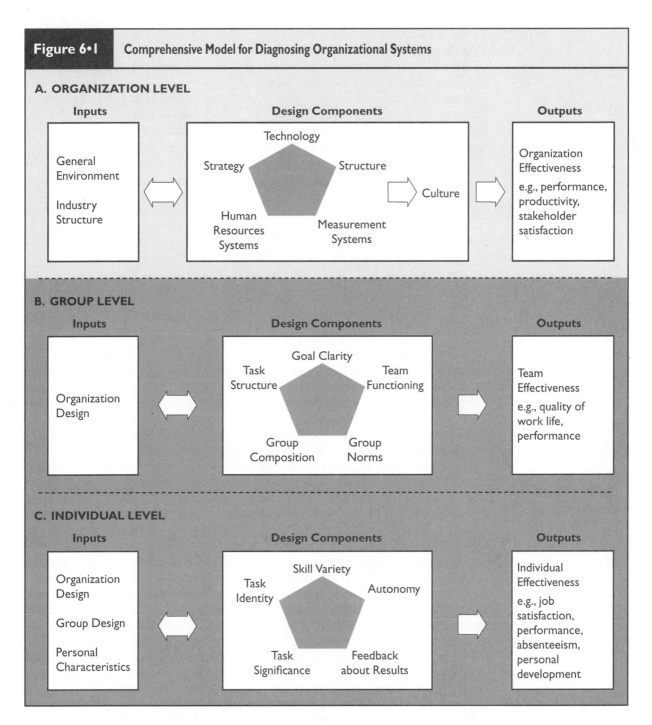

Figure 6•1   Comprehensive Model for Diagnosing Organizational Systems

more concerned with maximizing their individual performance to the detriment of team performance. Collecting information about the group's organization design context can greatly improve the accuracy of diagnosis.

Design Components

Figure 6.1(B) shows that groups have five major components: goal clarity, task structure, group composition, group functioning, and performance norms.

Goal clarity involves how well the group understands its objectives. In general, goals should be moderately challenging; there should be a method for measuring, monitoring, and feeding back information about goal achievement; and the goals should be clearly understood by all members.

Task structure is concerned with how the group's work is designed. Task structures can vary along two key dimensions: coordination of members' efforts and regulation of their task behaviors.[6] The coordination dimension involves the degree to which group tasks are structured to promote effective interaction among group members. Coordination is important in groups performing interdependent tasks, such as surgical teams and problem-solving groups. It is relatively unimportant, however, in groups composed of members who perform independent tasks, such as a group of telephone operators or salespeople. The regulation dimension involves the degree to which members can control their own task behaviors and be relatively free from external controls such as supervision, plans, and programs. Self-regulation generally occurs when members can decide on such issues as task assignments, work methods, production goals, and membership. (Interventions for designing group task structure are discussed in Chapter 16.)

Composition concerns the membership of groups. Members can differ on a number of dimensions having relevance to group behavior. Demographic variables, such as age, education, experience, and skills and abilities, can affect how people behave and relate to each other in groups. Demographics can determine whether the group is composed of people having task-relevant skills and knowledge, including interpersonal skills. People's internal needs also can influence group behaviors. Individual differences in social needs can determine whether group membership is likely to be satisfying or stressful.[7]

Group functioning is the underlying basis of group life. How members relate to each other is important in work groups because the quality of relationships can affect task performance. In some groups, for example, interpersonal competition and conflict among members result in their providing little support and help for each other. Conversely, groups may become too concerned about sharing good feelings and support and spend too little time on task performance. In organization development, considerable effort has been invested to help work group members develop healthy interpersonal relations, including an ability and a willingness to share feelings and perceptions about members' behaviors so that interpersonal problems and task difficulties can be worked through and resolved.[8] Group functioning therefore involves task-related activities, such as giving and seeking information and elaborating, coordinating, and evaluating activities; and the group-maintenance function, which is directed toward holding the group together as a cohesive team and includes encouraging, harmonizing, compromising, setting standards, and observing.[9] (Interpersonal interventions are discussed in Chapter 12.)

Performance norms are member beliefs about how the group should perform its task and include acceptable levels of performance.[10] Norms derive from interactions among members and serve as guides to group behavior. Once members agree on performance norms, either implicitly or explicitly, then members routinely perform tasks according to those norms. For example, members of problem-solving groups often decide early in the life of the group that decisions will be made through voting; voting then becomes a routine part of group task behavior. (Interventions aimed at helping groups to develop appropriate performance norms are discussed in Chapter 12.)

Outputs

Group effectiveness has two dimensions: performance and quality of work life. Performance is measured in terms of the group's ability to control or reduce costs, increase productivity, or improve quality. This is a "hard" measure of effectiveness. In addition, effectiveness is indicated by the group member's quality of work life. It concerns work satisfaction, team cohesion, and organizational commitment.

Fits

The diagnostic model in Figure 6.1(B) shows that group design components must fit inputs if groups are to be effective in terms of performance and the quality of work life. Research suggests the following fits between the inputs and design dimensions:

1. Group design should be congruent with the larger organization design. Organization structures with low differentiation and high integration should have work groups that are composed of highly skilled and experienced members performing highly interdependent tasks. Organizations with differentiated structures and formalized human resources and information systems should spawn groups that have clear, quantitative goals and support standardized behaviors. Although there is little direct research on these fits, the underlying rationale is that congruence between organization and group designs supports overall integration within the company. When group designs are not compatible with organization designs, groups often conflict with the organization.[11] They may develop norms that run counter to organizational effectiveness, such as occurs in groups supportive of horseplay, goldbricking, and other counterproductive behaviors.

2. When the organization's technology results in interdependent tasks, coordination among members should be promoted by task structures, composition, performance norms, and group functioning. Conversely, when technology permits independent tasks, the design components should promote individual task performance.[12] For example, when coordination is needed, task structure might physically locate related tasks together; composition might include members with similar interpersonal skills and social needs; performance norms would support task-relevant interactions; and healthy interpersonal relationships would be developed.

3. When the technology is relatively uncertain and requires high amounts of information processing and decision making, group task structure, composition, performance norms, and group functioning should promote self-regulation. Members should have the necessary freedom, information, and skills to assign members to tasks, to decide on production methods, and to set performance goals.[13] When technology is relatively certain, group designs should promote standardization of behavior, and groups should be externally controlled by supervisors, schedules, and plans.[14] For example, when self-regulation is needed, task structure might be relatively flexible and allow the interchange of members across group tasks; composition might include members with multiple skills, interpersonal competencies, and social needs; performance norms would support complex problem solving; and efforts would be made to develop healthy interpersonal relations.

Analysis

Application 6.1 presents an example of applying group-level diagnosis to a top-management team engaged in problem solving.

APPLICATION 6•1   Top-Management Team at Ortiv Glass Corporation

The Ortiv Glass Corporation produces and markets plate glass for use primarily in the construction and automotive industries. The multiplant company has been involved in OD for several years and actively supports participative management practices and employee-involvement programs. Ortiv's organization design is relatively organic, and the manufacturing plants are given freedom and encouragement to develop their own organization designs and approaches to participative management. It recently put together a problem-solving group made up of the top-management team at its newest plant.

The team consisted of the plant manager and the managers of the five functional departments reporting to him: engineering (maintenance), administration, human resources, production, and quality control. In recruiting managers for the new plant, the company selected people with good technical skills and experience in their respective functions. It also chose people with some managerial experience and a desire to solve problems collaboratively, a hallmark of participative management. The team was relatively new, and members had been working together for only about five months.

The team met formally for two hours each week to share pertinent information and to deal with plantwide issues affecting all of the departments, such as safety procedures, interdepartmental relations, and personnel practices. Members described these meetings as informative but often chaotic in terms of decision making. The meetings typically started late as members straggled in at different times. The latecomers generally offered excuses about more pressing problems occurring elsewhere in the plant. Once started, the meetings

were often interrupted by "urgent" phone messages for various members, including the plant manager, and in most cases the recipient would leave the meeting hurriedly to respond to the call.

The group had problems arriving at clear decisions on particular issues. Discussions often rambled from topic to topic, and members tended to postpone the resolution of problems to future meetings. This led to a backlog of unresolved issues, and meetings often lasted far beyond the two-hour limit. When group decisions were made, members often reported problems in their implementation. Members typically failed to follow through on agreements, and there was often confusion about what had actually been agreed upon. Everyone expressed dissatisfaction with the team meetings and their results.

Relationships among team members were cordial yet somewhat strained, especially when the team was dealing with complex issues in which members had varying opinions and interests. Although the plant manager publicly stated that he wanted to hear all sides of the issues, he often interrupted the discussion or attempted to change the topic when members openly disagreed in their views of the problem. This interruption was typically followed by an awkward silence in the group. In many instances when a solution to a pressing problem did not appear forthcoming, members either moved on to another issue or they informally voted on proposed options, letting majority rule decide the outcome. Members rarely discussed the need to move on or vote; rather, these behaviors emerged informally over time and became acceptable ways of dealing with difficult issues. ■

The group is having a series of ineffective problem-solving meetings. Members report a backlog of unresolved issues, poor use of meeting time, lack of follow-through and decision implementation, and a general dissatisfaction with the team meetings. Examining group inputs and design components and how the two fit can help explain the causes of those group problems.

The key issue in diagnosing group inputs is the design of the larger organization within which the group is embedded. The Ortiv Glass Corporation's design is relatively differentiated. Each plant is allowed to set up its own organization design. Similarly, although no specific data are given, the company's technology, structure, measurement systems, human resources systems, and culture appear to promote flexible and innovative behaviors at the plant level. Indeed, freedom to innovate in the manufacturing plants is probably an outgrowth of the firm's OD activities and participative culture.

In the case of decision-making groups such as this one, organization design also affects the nature of the issues that are worked on. The team meetings appear to be devoted to problems affecting all of the functional departments. This suggests that the problems entail high interdependence among the functions; consequently, high coordination among members is needed to resolve them. The team meetings also seem to include many issues that are complex and not easily solved, so there is probably a relatively high amount of uncertainty in the technology or work process. The causes of the problems or acceptable solutions are not readily available. Members must process considerable information during problem solving, especially when there are different perceptions and opinions about the issues.

Diagnosis of the team's design components answers the following questions:

1. *How clear are the group's goals?* The team's goals seem relatively clear: they are to solve problems. There appears to be no clear agreement, however, on the specific problems to be addressed. As a result, members come late because they have "more pressing" problems needing attention.

2. *What is the group's task structure?* The team's task structure includes face-to-face interaction during the weekly meetings. That structure allows members from different functional departments to come together physically to share information and to solve problems mutually affecting them. It facilitates coordination of problem solving among the departments in the plant. The structure also seems to provide team members with the freedom necessary to regulate their task behaviors in the meetings. They can adjust their behaviors and interactions to suit the flow of the discussion and problem-solving process.

3. *What is the composition of the group?* The team is composed of the plant manager and managers of five functional departments. All members appear to have task-relevant skills and experience, both in their respective functions and in their managerial roles. They also seem to be interested in solving problems collaboratively. That shared interest suggests that members have job-related social needs and should feel relatively comfortable in group problem-solving situations.

4. *What are the group's performance norms?* Group norms cannot be observed directly but must be inferred from group behaviors. The norms involve member beliefs about how the group should perform its task, including acceptable levels of performance. A useful way to describe norms is to list specific behaviors that complete the sentences "A good group member should...." and "It's okay to...." Examination of the team's problem-solving behaviors suggests the following performance norms are operating in the example:

   - "It's okay to come late to team meetings."
   - "It's okay to interrupt meetings with phone messages."
   - "It's okay to leave meetings to respond to phone messages."
   - "It's okay to hold meetings longer than two hours."
   - "A good group member should not openly disagree with others' views."
   - "It's okay to vote on decisions."
   - "A good group member should be cordial to other members."
   - "It's okay to postpone solutions to immediate problems."
   - "It's okay not to follow through on previous agreements."

5. *What is the nature of team functioning in the group?* The case strongly suggests that interpersonal relations are not healthy on the management team. Members do not seem to confront differences openly. Indeed, the plant manager purposely intervenes when conflicts emerge. Members feel dissatisfied with the meetings, but they spend little time talking about those feelings. Relationships are strained, but members fail to examine the underlying causes.

The problems facing the team can now be explained by assessing how well the group design fits the inputs. The larger organization design of Ortiv is relatively differentiated and promotes flexibility and innovation in its manufacturing plants. The firm supports participative management, and the team meetings can be seen as an attempt to implement that approach at the new plant. Although it is too early to tell whether the team will succeed, there does not appear to be significant incongruity between the larger organization design and what the team is trying to do. Of course, team problem solving may continue to be ineffective, and the team might revert to a more autocratic approach to decision making. In such a case, a serious mismatch between the plant management team and the larger company would exist, and conflict between the two would likely result.

The team's issues are highly interdependent and often uncertain, and meetings are intended to resolve plantwide problems affecting the various functional departments. Those problems are generally complex and require the members to process a great deal of information and create innovative solutions. The team's task structure and composition appear to fit the nature of team issues. The face-to-face meetings help to coordinate problem solving among the department managers, and except for the interpersonal skills, members seem to have the necessary task-relevant skills and experience to drive the problem-solving process. There appears, however, to be a conflict in the priority between the problems to be solved by the team and the problems faced by individual managers.

More important, the key difficulty seems to be a mismatch between the team's performance norms and interpersonal relations and the demands of the problem-solving task. Complex, interdependent problems require performance norms that support sharing of diverse and often conflicting kinds of information. The norms must encourage members to generate novel solutions and to assess the relevance of problem-solving strategies in light of new issues. Members need to address explicitly how they are using their knowledge and skills and how they are weighing and combining members' individual contributions.

In our example, the team's performance norms fail to support complex problem solving; rather, they promote a problem-solving method that is often superficial, haphazard, and subject to external disruptions. Members' interpersonal relationships reinforce adherence to the ineffective norms. Members do not confront personal differences or dissatisfactions with the group process. They fail to examine the very norms contributing to their problems. In this case, diagnosis suggests the need for group interventions aimed at improving performance norms and developing healthy interpersonal relations.

INDIVIDUAL-LEVEL DIAGNOSIS

The lowest level of organizational diagnosis is the individual job or position. An organization consists of numerous groups; a group, in turn, is composed of several individual jobs. This section discusses the inputs, design components, and relational fits for diagnosing jobs. The model shown in Figure 6.1(C) is similar to other popular job diagnostic frameworks, such as Hackman and Oldham's job diagnostic survey and Herzberg's job enrichment model.[15]

Inputs

Three major inputs affect job design: organization design, group design, and the personal characteristics of jobholders.

Organization design is concerned with the larger organization within which the individual job is the smallest unit. Organization design is a key part of the larger context surrounding jobs. Technology, structure, measurement systems, human resources systems, and culture can have a powerful impact on the way jobs are designed and on people's experiences in jobs. For example, company reward systems can orient employees to particular job behaviors and influence whether people see job performance as fairly rewarded. In general, technology characterized by relatively uncertain tasks and low interdependency is likely to support job designs allowing employees flexibility and discretion in performing tasks. Conversely, low-uncertainty work systems are likely to promote standardized job designs requiring routinized task behaviors.[16]

Group design concerns the larger group or department containing the individual job. Like organization design, group design is an essential part of the job context. Group task structure, goal clarity, composition, performance norms, and group functioning serve as inputs to job design. They typically have a more immediate impact on jobs than do the larger, organization-design components. For example, group task structure can determine how individual jobs are grouped together—as in groups requiring coordination among jobs or in ones comprising collections of independent jobs. Group composition can influence the kinds of people who are available to fill jobs. Group performance norms can affect the kinds of job designs that are considered acceptable, including the level of jobholders' performances. Goal clarity helps members to prioritize work, and group functioning can affect how powerfully the group influences job behaviors. When members maintain close relationships and the group is cohesive, group norms are more likely to be enforced and followed.[17]

Personal characteristics of individuals occupying jobs include their age, education, experience, and skills and abilities. All of these can affect job performance as well as how people react to job designs. Individual needs and expectations can also affect employee job responses. For example, individual differences in growth need—the need for self-direction, learning, and personal accomplishment—can determine how much people are motivated and satisfied by jobs with high levels of skill variety, autonomy, and feedback about results.[18] Similarly, work motivation can be influenced by people's expectations that they can perform a job well and that good job performance will result in valued outcomes.[19]

Design Components

Figure 6.1(C) shows that individual jobs have five key dimensions: skill variety, task identity, task significance, autonomy, and feedback about results.[20]

Skill variety identifies the degree to which a job requires a range of activities and abilities to perform the work. Assembly-line jobs, for example, generally have limited skill variety because employees perform a small number of repetitive activities. Most professional jobs, on the other hand, include a great deal of skill variety because people engage in diverse activities and employ several different skills in performing their work.

Task identity measures the degree to which a job requires the completion of a relatively whole, identifiable piece of work. Skilled craftspeople, such as tool-and-die makers and carpenters, generally have jobs with high levels of task identity. They are able to see a job through from beginning to end. Assembly-line jobs involve only a limited piece of work and score low on task identity.

Task significance identifies the degree to which a job has a significant impact on other people's lives. Custodial jobs in a hospital are likely to have more task significance than similar jobs in a toy factory because hospital custodians are likely to see their jobs as affecting someone else's health and welfare.

Autonomy indicates the degree to which a job provides freedom and discretion in scheduling the work and determining work methods. Assembly-line jobs generally have little autonomy: the work pace is scheduled, and people perform preprogrammed tasks. College teaching positions have more autonomy: professors usually can determine how a course is taught, even though they may have limited say over class scheduling.

Feedback about results involves the degree to which a job provides employees with direct and clear information about the effectiveness of task performance. Assembly-line jobs often provide high levels of feedback about results, whereas college professors must often contend with indirect and ambiguous feedback about how they are performing in the classroom.

Those five job dimensions can be combined into an overall measure of job enrichment. Enriched jobs have high levels of skill variety, task identity, task significance, autonomy, and feedback about results. They provide opportunities for self-direction, learning, and personal accomplishment at work. Many people find enriched jobs internally motivating and satisfying. (Job enrichment is discussed more fully in Chapter 16.)

Fits

The diagnostic model in Figure 6.1(C) suggests that job design must fit job inputs to produce effective job outputs, such as high quality and quantity of individual performance, low absenteeism, and high job satisfaction. Research reveals the following fits between job inputs and job design:

1. Job design should be congruent with the larger organization and group designs within which the job is embedded.[21] Both the organization and the group serve as a powerful context for individual jobs or positions. They tend to support and reinforce particular job designs. Highly differentiated and integrated organizations and groups that permit members to self-regulate their behavior fit enriched jobs. These larger organizations and groups promote autonomy, flexibility, and innovation at the individual job level. Conversely, bureaucratic organizations and groups relying on external controls are congruent with job designs scoring low on the five key dimensions. Both organizations and groups reinforce standardized, routine jobs. As suggested earlier, congruence across different levels of organization design promotes integration of the organization, group, and job levels. Whenever the levels do not fit each other, conflict is likely to emerge.

2. Job design should fit the personal characteristics of the jobholders if they are to perform effectively and derive satisfaction from work. Generally, enriched jobs fit people with strong growth needs.[22] These people derive satisfaction and accomplishment from performing jobs involving skill variety, autonomy, and feedback about results. Enriched jobs also fit people possessing moderate to high levels of task-relevant skills, abilities, and knowledge. Enriched jobs generally require complex information processing and decision making; people must have comparable skills and abilities to perform effectively. Jobs scoring low on the five job dimensions generally fit people with rudimentary skills and abilities and with low growth needs. Simpler, more routinized jobs requiring limited skills and experience fit better with people who place a low value on opportunities for self-direction and learning. In addition, because people can grow through

education, training, and experience, job design must be monitored and adjusted from time to time.

Analysis

Application 6.2 presents an example of applying individual-level diagnosis to job design. The plant discussed there seemed to have problems implementing new, more enriched job designs. Production was below expectations, and employee absenteeism and turnover were higher than average. Employees were complaining that the jobs were less challenging than expected and that management failed to follow through on promised opportunities for decision making. Examination of inputs and job design features and how the two fit can help explain the causes of these problems.

Diagnosis of individual-level inputs answers the following questions:

1. *What is the design of the larger organization within which the individual jobs are embedded?* Although the example says little about the new plant design, a number of inferences are possible. Management at the new plant was trying to design more enriched jobs than were provided at Mot's older plants. This suggests that the culture of the plant was supportive of employee involvement, at least during the initial design and start-up stages. At the organization level, there seemed little need for flexible and innovative responses; consequently, the plant design is likely to have been more formal and bureaucratic than innovative and integrated. The market for surgical sutures was stable and production methods routinized, with changes in technology or scheduling rare.

2. *What is the design of the group containing the individual jobs?* Individual jobs were grouped together according to the type of suture produced. Although people spent most of their time working on individual jobs—either swaging, inspecting, or handwinding—they did meet weekly to share information and to solve common problems. Interaction during task performance seemed limited because of highly scheduled work flow. However, some interaction between the swaging and inspection jobs did occur because inspectors handed unacceptable sutures back to swagers to be redone.

3. *What are the personal characteristics of jobholders?* People were recruited for the new plant because of their desire for enriched jobs and participation in decision making. This suggests that employees likely had strong growth needs. Moreover, the recruiting process explicitly promoted enriched jobs and employee decision making, and thus employees were also likely to have strong expectations about such job characteristics.

Diagnosis of individual jobs involves the following job dimensions:

1. *How much skill variety is included in the jobs?* The individual jobs in the new plant seemed to have low to moderate amounts of skill variety. Although some additional set-up, inspection, and scheduling activities were added to the swaging and handwinding jobs, these jobs primarily involved a limited set of repetitive activities. The inspection job included a bit more skill variety—gathering samples of product, examining them for defects, recording results, and either passing the product to handwinders or back to swagers for redoing. The job rotation scheme was an attempt to enhance skill variety by giving employees a greater number of tasks across the different jobs. Unfortunately, because people

APPLICATION 6•2 Job Design at Mot Surgical Corporation

Mot Surgical Corporation is a subsidiary of a large pharmaceutical company that produces drugs and related medical products. Mot specializes in surgical sutures and has three manufacturing plants. At the time of the case in 1980, Mot's parent corporation had supported employee involvement for several years. It had encouraged its subsidiaries to increase employee participation and to design meaningful jobs. The newest plant in the southwestern United States was seen as a potential site to enrich jobs that at Mot's older plants had been routinized for years.

Traditionally, the jobs involved in producing surgical sutures were divided according to the three main stages of production. First, the job of swager involved attaching a surgical needle to a filament made of a catgut or synthetic fiber. The needle and filament were placed in a press, and the press joined the two together. The swaging activities were of a short time cycle, highly standardized, and repetitive; workers sat at individual presses turning out dozens of finished sutures per hour. Second, the job of inspector involved examining the finished swaging product for defects. Product quality was especially important because the condition of sutures can affect the outcome of surgery. Inspectors took samples of swaging product and visibly examined them. The job took extreme concentration because defects were difficult to detect. Inspectors passed poor-quality work back to relevant swagers and passed good product on to the next production stage. Third, the job of handwinder involved taking acceptable swaging product and winding it by hand into a figure eight for packaging. Like swaging, handwinding activities were highly routinized and repetitive; handwinders sat at individual workstations and wound literally thousands of figure eights per hour.

The activities surrounding the suture jobs were also highly programmed and scheduled. The market for surgical sutures was relatively stable. Production runs were long and scheduled well in advance, and changes in schedule were rare. Similarly, the production methods associated with swaging, inspection, and handwinding were highly programmed, and technical changes in production were infrequent. The primary goal of management was the production of large quantities of acceptable product.

Before hiring in the new plant began, the three suture jobs were placed into discrete groups according to the specific type of suture produced. People in each product group were to be trained in all three jobs. Members would stay on a job for a specified period of time and then rotate to another job. Performance of the swaging and handwinding jobs also included some minor setup, inspection, and scheduling activities.

Weekly meetings also were planned so that employees could share information, solve common problems, and make work-related decisions. The new, more enriched jobs were expected to result in high productivity and quality of work life.

Mot made great efforts to recruit people who were likely to respond favorably to enriched jobs. Newspaper advertisements and job interviews explicitly mentioned the enriched nature of the new jobs and the promise that employees would be involved in decision making. Potential recruits were shown the new plant setup and asked about their desire to learn new things and to be involved in decision making. Initially, about thirty people were hired and trained in the new job; additional employees were assimilated into the plant over the next few months. The training program was oriented to learning the swaging, inspection, and handwinding jobs and to gaining problem-solving skills.

As training progressed and the plant gradually started production, several unexpected problems emerged. First, employees found it difficult to rotate among the different jobs without a considerable loss of production. The swaging, inspection, and handwinding tasks involved entirely different kinds of manual dexterity and mental concentration. Each time people switched from one job to another, much relearning and practice were necessary to achieve a normal level of production. The net result of this rotation was lower-than-expected productivity. When this problem persisted, workers were urged to stay on one particular job.

A second problem concerned employee participation in decision making. During the early stages of the plant startup, workers had ample opportunities for decision making. They were involved in solving certain break-in problems and deciding on housekeeping, personnel, and operating issues. They were undergoing training and had time to devote to problem solving without heavy pressures for production. Over time, however, plant operations became more routine and predictable, and there was less need for employee decision making. Moreover, increased pressures for production cut into the limited time devoted to decision making.

A third problem involved employee behaviors and attitudes. After six months of operation, employee absenteeism and turnover were higher than the local industry average. People complained that the job was more routine and boring than they had expected. They felt that management had sold them a bill of goods about opportunities for decision making. These behaviors and attitudes were especially prevalent among those who were hired first and had participated in the initial recruiting and startup. ∎

had problems maintaining high levels of production when they rotated jobs, they were urged to stay on one job.

2. *How much task identity do the jobs contain?* The jobs seemed to include moderate amounts of task identity. Each job produced a small yet identifiable piece of work. The swagers, in attaching a needle to a filament, produced a completed suture. Inspectors performed most of the activities needed to ensure product quality. The handwinders, in preparing sutures for packaging, probably had the lowest task identity. The grouping of the three jobs into discrete product groups was an attempt to increase task identity because employees could see how the three jobs fit together to produce a suture ready for packaging.

3. *How much task significance is involved in the jobs?* All three jobs seemed to score high on this feature. Surgical sutures are an integral part of surgery, and the jobs contributed to helping physicians heal people and save lives.

4. *How much autonomy is included in the jobs?* The jobs appeared to contain almost no freedom in either work schedules or work methods. Each job was highly routinized. The little autonomy there was in making decisions at the weekly meetings had decreased over time. Increased pressures for production also reduced the opportunities for decision making.

5. *How much feedback about results do the jobs contain?* Employees were provided with direct and clear information about their performances. The swagers and handwinders did minor inspection tasks, and the former received continual feedback from inspectors about the quality of their swaging.

When the job characteristics are examined together, the jobs appear to contain moderate levels of enrichment. Feedback about results and task significance are fairly high; task identity is moderate; skill variety and autonomy are low to moderate. Over time, however, the level of enrichment dropped because skill variety and autonomy were decreased. Indeed, the jobs in the new plant came to resemble those in Mot's older plants.

Mot's problems with reduced performance and employee withdrawal and dissatisfaction can be explained by assessing how well the job designs fit the inputs. The new plant design seems only partially to fit the job designs. The plant seems more formal and certain than flexible and innovative, and this fits well with jobs consisting of limited amounts of autonomy and skill variety. The plant programmed production rigidly, and the job designs reflect this standardization. The organization culture of promoting quality of work life seems to conflict with the way the jobs were designed, however. Initial attempts to rotate jobs and to involve employees in decision making gave way to more traditional job designs. Over time, pressures for production and fewer opportunities for decision making displaced the initial focus on quality of work life. The plant's espoused culture was incongruent with the way jobs finally developed. This incongruity was especially troublesome for the initial recruits who were led to expect a more enriched work life.

The various product groups seem to fit well with the job designs. The groups' task structures promoted only limited interaction among jobholders, and this was consistent with the individualized nature of each job. Moreover, the reduced emphasis on group decision making was congruent with jobs that have become more routine and scheduled over time.

The technology of producing sutures is highly certain and includes limited interdependence among the different tasks. Tasks that are certain require little information processing and decision making. Routinized jobs fit such tasks, and the jobs in the plant gradually became routinized to fit the high level of technical certainty. The plant's initial attempts to enrich jobs in a situation of high technical certainty seem misguided. Indeed, job rotation disrupted the routine, repetitive nature of the tasks and resulted in poor performance. The limited technical interdependence seems to fit the individualized focus of the job designs. Again, attempts at group problem solving and decision making probably provided more member interaction than was technically needed. The meetings might have contributed to lowered productivity by reducing time for individual performance.

Employee withdrawal and dissatisfaction seem directly related to a mismatch between the job designs and people's growth needs. People with strong growth needs like enriched jobs allowing self-direction, challenge, and learning. Although the initial job designs were intended to provide such opportunities, the resulting designs were routine and boring. Employees could not satisfy their needs by performing such jobs, and worse yet, they felt betrayed by a company that had promised enriched jobs.

Examination of the fits between the job designs and the inputs suggests an intervention dilemma in this case. Should the plant continue to maintain the fit between technology and job design and risk alienating or losing many of its initial recruits? If so, interventions probably should be aimed at changing the plant's espoused culture and recruiting and training practices. Alternatively, should the plant attempt to bring about a better fit between its current employees and job design and risk lowered or more costly production? If so, interventions should probably be aimed at job enrichment and at reducing pressures for production from the parent corporation. (Interventions for matching people, technology, and job design are discussed in Chapter 16.)

■ SUMMARY

In this chapter, diagnostic models associated with groups and individuals were described and applied. Each of the models derive from the open-systems view of organizations developed in Chapter 5. Diagnostic models include the input, design component (transformation processes), and output dimensions needed to understand groups and individual jobs.

Group diagnostic models take the organization's design as the primary input; examine goal clarity, task structure, group composition, performance norms, and group functioning as the key design components; and list group performance and member quality of work life as the outputs. As with any open-systems model, the alignment of these parts is the key to understanding effectiveness.

At the individual job level, organization design, group design, and characteristics of each job are the salient inputs. Task variety, task significance, task identity, autonomy, and feedback work together to produce outputs of work satisfaction and work quality.

■ NOTES

1. S. Cohen, "Designing Effective Self-Managing Work Teams," in *Advances in Interdisciplinary Studies of Work Teams,* vol. 1, ed. M. Beyerlein (Greenwich, Conn.: JAI Press, 1995).

2. J. Hackman and C. Morris, "Group Tasks, Group Interaction Process, and Group Performance Effectiveness: A Review and Proposed Integration," in *Advances in Experimental Social Psychology,* vol. 9, ed. L. Berkowitz (New York:

Academic Press, 1975): 45–99; J. Hackman, ed., *Groups That Work (and Those That Don't): Creating Conditions for Effective Teamwork* (San Francisco: Jossey-Bass, 1989).

3. M. McCaskey, "Framework for Analyzing Work Groups," *Harvard Business School Case 9-480-009* (Boston: Harvard Business School, 1997).

4. G. Ledford, E. Lawler, and S. Mohrman, "The Quality Circle and Its Variations," in *Productivity in Organizations: New Perspectives from Industrial and Organizational Psychology*, eds. J. Campbell, R. Campbell, and Associates (San Francisco: Jossey-Bass, 1988): 255–94.

5. D. Ancona and D. Caldwell, "Bridging the Boundary: External Activity and Performance in Organizational Teams," *Administrative Science Quarterly* 37 (1992): 634–65; Cohen, "Self-Managing Work Teams"; S. Mohrman, S. Cohen, and A. Mohrman, *Designing Team-Based Organizations* (San Francisco: Jossey-Bass, 1995).

6. G. Susman, *Autonomy at Work* (New York: Praeger, 1976); T. Cummings, "Self-Regulating Work Groups: A Socio-Technical Synthesis," *Academy of Management Review* 3 (1978): 625–34; J. Slocum and H. Sims, "A Typology for Integrating Technology, Organization, and Job Design," *Human Relations* 33 (1980): 193–212.

7. J. R. Hackman and G. Oldham, *Work Redesign* (Reading, Mass.: Addison-Wesley, 1980).

8. E. Schein, *Process Consultation*, vols. I–II (Reading, Mass.: Addison-Wesley, 1987).

9. W. Dyer, *Team Building*, 3d ed. (Reading, Mass.: Addison-Wesley, 1994).

10. Hackman and Morris, "Group Tasks"; T. Cummings,

"Designing Effective Work Groups," in *Handbook of Organizational Design*, vol. 2, eds. P. Nystrom and W. Starbuck (Oxford, U.K.: Oxford University Press, 1981): 250–71.

11. Cummings, "Effective Work Groups."

12. Susman, *Autonomy at Work*; Cummings, "Self-Regulating Work Groups"; Slocum and Sims, "Typology."

13. Cummings, "Self-Regulating Work Groups"; Slocum and Sims, "Typology."

14. Ibid.

15. Hackman and Oldham, *Work Redesign*; F. Herzberg, "One More Time: How Do You Motivate Employees?" *Harvard Business Review* 46 (1968): 53–62.

16. J. Pierce, R. Dunham, and R. Blackburn, "Social Systems Structure, Job Design, and Growth Need Strength: A Test of a Congruence Model," *Academy of Management Journal* 22 (1979): 223–40.

17. Susman, *Autonomy at Work*; Cummings, "Self-Regulating Work Groups"; Slocum and Sims, "Typology."

18. Hackman and Oldham, *Work Redesign*; Pierce, Dunham, and Blackburn, "Social Systems Structure."

19. E. Lawler III, *Motivation in Work Organizations* (Monterey, Calif.: Brooks/Cole, 1973).

20. Hackman and Oldham, *Work Redesign*.

21. Pierce, Dunham, and Blackburn, "Social Systems Structure"; Susman, *Autonomy at Work*; Cummings, "Self-Regulating Work Groups"; Slocum and Sims, "Typology."

22. Hackman and Oldham, *Work Redesign*; Pierce, Dunham, and Blackburn, "Social Systems Structure."

7. Collecting and Analyzing Diagnostic Information

Organization development is vitally dependent on organization diagnosis: the process of collecting information that will be shared with the client in jointly assessing how the organization is functioning and determining the best change intervention. The quality of the information gathered, therefore, is a critical part of the OD process. In this chapter, we discuss several key issues associated with collecting and analyzing diagnostic data on how an organization or department functions.

Data collection involves gathering information on specific organizational features, such as the inputs, design components, and outputs presented in Chapters 5 and 6. The process begins by establishing an effective relationship between the OD practitioner and those from whom data will be collected and then choosing data-collection techniques. Four methods can be used to collect data: questionnaires, interviews, observations, and unobtrusive measures. Data analysis organizes and examines the information to make clear the underlying causes of an organizational problem or to identify areas for future development. The next step in the cyclical OD process is the feedback of data to the client system, an important process described in Chapter 8. The overall process of data collection, analysis, and feedback is shown in Figure 7.1.

THE DIAGNOSTIC RELATIONSHIP

In most cases of planned change, OD practitioners play an active role in gathering data from organization members for diagnostic purposes. For example, they might interview members of a work team about causes of conflict among members; they might survey employees at a large industrial plant about factors contributing to poor product quality. Before collecting diagnostic information, practitioners need

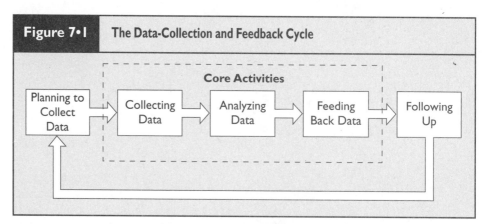

| Figure 7•1 | The Data-Collection and Feedback Cycle |

Core Activities

Planning to Collect Data → Collecting Data → Analyzing Data → Feeding Back Data → Following Up

SOURCE: D. Nadler, *Feedback and Organization Development: Using Data-Based Methods*, page 43. © 1977 by Addison-Wesley Publishing Co., Inc. Reprinted by permission of Addison Wesley Longman.

to establish a relationship with those who will provide and subsequently use it. Because the nature of that relationship affects the quality and usefulness of the data collected, it is vital that OD practitioners clarify for organization members who they are, why the data are being collected, what the data gathering will involve, and how the data will be used.[1] That information can help allay people's natural fears that the data might be used against them and gain members' participation and support, which are essential to developing successful interventions.

Establishing the diagnostic relationship between the consultant and relevant organization members is similar to forming a contract. It is meant to clarify expectations and to specify the conditions of the relationship. In those cases where members have been directly involved in the entering and contracting process described in Chapter 4, the diagnostic contract will typically be part of the initial contracting step. In situations where data will be collected from members who have not been directly involved in entering and contracting, however, OD practitioners will need to establish a diagnostic contract as a prelude to diagnosis. The answers to the following questions provide the substance of the diagnostic contract:[2]

1. *Who am I?* The answer to this question introduces the OD practitioner to the organization, particularly to those members who do not know the consultant and yet will be asked to provide diagnostic data.

2. *Why am I here, and what am I doing?* These answers are aimed at defining the goals of the diagnosis and data-gathering activities. The consultant needs to present the objectives of the action research process and to describe how the diagnostic activities fit into the overall developmental strategy.

3. *Who do I work for?* This answer clarifies who has hired the consultant, whether it be a manager, a group of managers, or a group of employees and managers. One way to build trust and support for the diagnosis is to have those people directly involved in establishing the diagnostic contract. Thus, for example, if the consultant works for a joint labor–management committee, representatives from both sides of that group could help the consultant build the proper relationship with those from whom data will be gathered.

4. *What do I want from you, and why?* Here, the consultant needs to specify how much time and effort people will need to give to provide valid data and subsequently to work with these data in solving problems. Because some people may not want to participate in the diagnosis, it is important to specify that such involvement is voluntary.

5. *How will I protect your confidentiality?* This answer addresses member concerns about who will see their responses and in what form. This is especially critical when employees are asked to provide information about their attitudes or perceptions. OD practitioners can either ensure confidentiality or state that full participation in the change process requires open information sharing. In the first case, employees are frequently concerned about privacy and the possibility of being punished for their responses. To alleviate concern and to increase the likelihood of obtaining honest responses, the consultant may need to assure employees of the confidentiality of their information, perhaps through explicit guarantees of response anonymity. In the second case, full involvement of the participants in their own diagnosis may be a vital ingredient of the change process. If sensitive issues arise, assurances of confidentiality can co-opt the OD practitioner and thwart meaningful diagnosis. The consultant is bound to keep confidential the issues that are most critical for the group or organization to

understand.[3] OD practitioners must think carefully about how they want to handle confidentiality issues.

6. ***Who will have access to the data?*** Respondents typically want to know whether they will have access to their data and who else in the organization will have similar access. The OD practitioner needs to clarify access issues and, in most cases, should agree to provide respondents with their own results. Indeed, the collaborative nature of diagnosis means that organization members will work with their own data to discover causes of problems and to devise relevant interventions.

7. ***What's in it for you?*** This answer is aimed at providing organization members with a clear delineation of the benefits they can expect from the diagnosis. This usually entails describing the feedback process and how they can use the data to improve the organization.

8. ***Can I be trusted?*** The diagnostic relationship ultimately rests on the trust established between the consultant and those providing the data. An open and honest exchange of information depends on such trust, and the practitioner should provide ample time and face-to-face contact during the contracting process to build this trust. This requires the consultant to listen actively and discuss openly all questions raised by participants.

Careful attention to establishing the diagnostic relationship helps to promote the three goals of data collection.[4] The first and most immediate objective is to obtain valid information about organizational functioning. Building a data-collection contract can ensure that organization members provide honest, reliable, and complete information.

Data collection also can rally energy for constructive organizational change. A good diagnostic relationship helps organization members start thinking about issues that concern them, and it creates expectations that change is possible. When members trust the consultant, they are likely to participate in the diagnostic process and to generate energy and commitment for organizational change.

Finally, data collection helps to develop the collaborative relationship necessary for effecting organizational change. The diagnostic stage of action research is probably the first time that most organization members meet the OD practitioner, and it can be the basis for building a longer-term relationship. The data-collection contract and subsequent data-gathering and feedback activities provide members with opportunities for seeing the consultant in action and for knowing her or him personally. If the consultant can show employees that she or he is trustworthy, is willing to work with them, and is able to help improve the organization, then the data-collection process will contribute to the longer-term collaborative relationship so necessary for carrying out organizational changes.

METHODS FOR COLLECTING DATA

The four major techniques for gathering diagnostic data are questionnaires, interviews, observations, and unobtrusive measures. Table 7.1 briefly compares the methods and lists their major advantages and problems. No single method can fully measure the kinds of variables important to OD because each has certain strengths and weaknesses.[5] For example, perceptual measures, such as questionnaires and surveys, are open to self-report biases, such as respondents' tendency to give socially desirable answers rather than honest opinions. Observations, on the other hand,

Table 7•1	A Comparison of Different Methods of Data Collection	
METHOD	**MAJOR ADVANTAGES**	**MAJOR POTENTIAL PROBLEMS**
Questionnaires	1. Responses can be quantified and easily summarized 2. Easy to use with large samples 3. Relatively inexpensive 4. Can obtain large volume of data	1. Nonempathy 2. Predetermined questions/missing issues 3. Overinterpretation of data 4. Response bias
Interviews	1. Adaptive—allows data collection on a range of possible subjects 2. Source of "rich" data 3. Empathic 4. Process of interviewing can build rapport	1. Expense 2. Bias in interviewer responses 3. Coding and interpretation difficulties 4. Self-report bias
Observations	1. Collects data on behavior, rather than reports of behavior 2. Real time, not retrospective 3. Adaptive	1. Coding and interpretation difficulties 2. Sampling inconsistencies 3. Observer bias and questionable reliability 4. Expense
Unobtrusive measures	1. Nonreactive—no response bias 2. High face validity 3. Easily quantified	1. Access and retrieval difficulties 2. Validity concerns 3. Coding and interpretation difficulties

SOURCE: D. Nadler, *Feedback and Organization Development: Using Data-Based Methods*, page 119. © 1977 by Addison-Wesley Publishing Co., Inc. Reprinted by permission of Addison Wesley Longman.

are susceptible to observer biases, such as seeing what one wants to see rather than what is really there. Because of the biases inherent in any data-collection method, we recommend that more than one method be used when collecting diagnostic data. If data from the different methods are compared and found to be consistent, it is likely that the variables are being measured validly. For example, questionnaire measures of job discretion could be supplemented with observations of the number and kinds of decisions employees are making. If the two kinds of data support one another, job discretion is probably being accurately assessed. If the two kinds of data conflict, then the validity of the measures should be examined further—perhaps by using a third method, such as interviews.

Questionnaires

One of the most efficient ways to collect data is through *questionnaires*. Because they typically contain fixed-response queries about various features of an organization, these paper-and-pencil measures can be administered to large numbers of people simultaneously. Also, they can be analyzed quickly, especially with the use of computers, thus permitting quantitative comparison and evaluation. As a result, data can easily be fed back to employees. Numerous basic resource books on survey methodology and questionnaire development are available.[6]

Questionnaires can vary in scope, some measuring selected aspects of organizations and others assessing more comprehensive organizational characteristics. They also can vary in the extent to which they are either standardized or tailored to a specific organization. Standardized instruments generally are based on an explicit model of organization, group, or individual effectiveness and contain a predetermined set of questions that have been developed and refined over time. For example, Table 7.2 presents a standardized questionnaire for measuring the job-design dimensions identified in Chapter 6: skill variety, task identity, task significance, autonomy, and feedback about results. The questionnaire includes three items or questions for each dimension, and a total score for each job dimension is computed simply by adding the responses for the three relevant items and arriving at a total score from three (low) to twenty-one (high). The questionnaire has wide applicability. It has been used in a variety of organizations with employees in both blue-collar and white-collar jobs.

Several research organizations have been highly instrumental in developing and refining surveys. The Institute for Social Research at the University of Michigan (http://www.isr.umich.edu) and the Center for Effective Organizations at the University of Southern California (http://www.marshall.usc.edu/ceo) are two prominent examples. Two of the institute's most popular measures of organizational dimensions are the *Survey of Organizations* and the *Michigan Organizational Assessment Questionnaire*. Few other instruments are supported by such substantial reliability and validity data.[7] Other examples of packaged instruments include Weisbord's *Organizational Diagnostic Questionnaire*, Dyer's *Team Development Survey*, and Hackman and Oldham's *Job Diagnostic Survey*.[8] In fact, so many questionnaires are available that rarely would an organization have to create a totally new one. However, because every organization has unique problems and special jargon for referring to them, almost any standardized instrument will need to have organization-specific additions, modifications, or omissions.

Customized questionnaires, on the other hand, are tailored to the needs of a particular client. Typically, they include questions composed by consultants or organization members, receive limited use, and do not undergo longer-term development. They can be combined with standardized instruments to provide valid and reliable data focused toward the particular issues facing an organization.

Questionnaires, however, have a number of drawbacks that need to be taken into account in choosing whether to employ them for data collection. First, responses are limited to the questions asked in the instrument. They provide little opportunity to probe for additional data or to ask for points of clarification. Second, questionnaires tend to be impersonal, and employees may not be willing to provide honest answers. Third, questionnaires often elicit response biases, such as the tendency to answer questions in a socially acceptable manner. This makes it difficult to draw valid conclusions from employees' self-reports.

Interviews

A second important measurement technique is the *individual* or *group interview*. Interviews are probably the most widely used technique for collecting data in OD. They permit the interviewer to ask the respondent direct questions. Further probing and clarification is, therefore, possible as the interview proceeds. This flexibility is invaluable for gaining private views and feelings about the organization and for exploring new issues that emerge during the interview.

Interviews may be highly structured, resembling questionnaires, or highly unstructured, starting with general questions that allow the respondent to lead the way. Structured interviews typically derive from a conceptual model of organization functioning; the model guides the types of questions that are asked. For example, a structured interview based on the organization-level design components identified in Chapter 5 would ask managers specific questions about organization structure, measurement systems, human resources systems, and organization culture.

Table 7•2	Job Design Questionnaire

Here are some statements about your job. How much do you agree or disagree with each?

MY JOB:	STRONGLY DISAGREE	DISAGREE	SLIGHTLY DISAGREE	UNDECIDED	SLIGHTLY AGREE	AGREE	STRONGLY AGREE
1. provides much variety	[1]	[2]	[3]	[4]	[5]	[6]	[7]
2. permits me to be left on my own to do my own work	[1]	[2]	[3]	[4]	[5]	[6]	[7]
3. is arranged so that I often have the opportunity to see jobs or projects through to completion. .	[1]	[2]	[3]	[4]	[5]	[6]	[7]
4. provides feedback on how well I am doing as I am working	[1]	[2]	[3]	[4]	[5]	[6]	[7]
5. is relatively significant in our organization	[1]	[2]	[3]	[4]	[5]	[6]	[7]
6. gives me considerable opportunity for independence and freedom in how I do my work . . .	[1]	[2]	[3]	[4]	[5]	[6]	[7]
7. gives me the opportunity to do a number of different things	[1]	[2]	[3]	[4]	[5]	[6]	[7]
8. provides me an opportunity to find out how well I am doing	[1]	[2]	[3]	[4]	[5]	[6]	[7]
9. is very significant or important in the broader scheme of things. .	[1]	[2]	[3]	[4]	[5]	[6]	[7]
10. provides an opportunity for independent thought and action. .	[1]	[2]	[3]	[4]	[5]	[6]	[7]
11. provides me with a great deal of variety at work	[1]	[2]	[3]	[4]	[5]	[6]	[7]
12. is arranged so that I have the opportunity to complete the work I start.	[1]	[2]	[3]	[4]	[5]	[6]	[7]
13. provides me with the feeling that I know whether I am performing well or poorly	[1]	[2]	[3]	[4]	[5]	[6]	[7]
14. is arranged so that I have the chance to do a job from the beginning to the end (i.e., a chance to do the whole job).	[1]	[2]	[3]	[4]	[5]	[6]	[7]
15. is one where a lot of other people can be affected by how well the work gets done	[1]	[2]	[3]	[4]	[5]	[6]	[7]

Scoring:

Skill variety. . . . . questions 1, 7, 11
Task identity . . . . questions 3, 12, 14
Task significance . . . . questions 5, 9, 15
Autonomy . . . . questions 2, 6, 10
Feedback about results. . . . . questions 4, 8, 13

SOURCE: Reproduced by permission of E. Lawler, S. Mohrman, and T. Cummings, Center for Effective Organizations, University of Southern California.

Unstructured interviews are more general and include broad questions about organizational functioning, such as:

- What are the major goals or objectives of the organization or department?
- How does the organization currently perform with respect to these purposes?
- What are the strengths and weaknesses of the organization or department?
- What barriers stand in the way of good performance?

Although interviewing typically involves one-to-one interaction between an OD practitioner and an employee, it can be carried out in a group context. Group interviews save time and allow people to build on others' responses. A major drawback, however, is that group settings may inhibit some people from responding freely.

A popular type of group interview is the *focus group* or *sensing meeting*.[9] These are unstructured meetings conducted by a manager or a consultant. A small group of ten to fifteen employees is selected representing a cross section of functional areas and hierarchical levels or a homogenous grouping, such as minorities or engineers. Group discussion is frequently started by asking general questions about organizational features and functioning, an intervention's progress, or current performance. Group members are then encouraged to discuss their answers more fully. Consequently, focus groups and sensing meetings are an economical way to obtain interview data and are especially effective in understanding particular issues in greater depth. The richness and validity of the information gathered will depend on the extent to which the manager or consultant develops a trust relationship with the group and listens to member opinions.

Another popular unstructured group interview involves assessing the current state of an intact work group. The manager or consultant generally directs a question to the group, calling its attention to some part of group functioning. For example, group members may be asked how they feel the group is progressing on its stated task. The group might respond and then come up with its own series of questions about barriers to task performance. This unstructured interview is a fast, simple way to collect data about group behavior. It allows members to discuss issues of immediate concern and to engage actively in the questioning and answering process. This technique is limited, however, to relatively small groups and to settings where there is trust among employees and managers and a commitment to assessing group processes.

Interviews are an effective method for collecting data in OD. They are adaptive, allowing the interviewer to modify questions and to probe emergent issues during the interview process. They also permit the interviewer to develop an empathetic relationship with employees, frequently resulting in frank disclosure of pertinent information.

A major drawback of interviews is the amount of time required to conduct and analyze them. Interviews can consume a great deal of time, especially if interviewers take full advantage of the opportunity to hear respondents out and change their questions accordingly. Personal biases also can distort the data. Like questionnaires, interviews are subject to the self-report biases of respondents and, perhaps more important, to the biases of the interviewer. For example, the nature of the questions and the interactions between the interviewer and the respondent may discourage or encourage certain kinds of responses. These problems suggest that interviewing takes considerable skill to gather valid data. Interviewers must be able to understand their own biases, to listen and establish empathy with respondents, and to change questions to pursue issues that develop during the course of the interview.

Observations

One of the more direct ways of collecting data is simply to *observe* organizational behaviors in their functional settings. The OD practitioner may do this by walking casually through a work area and looking around or by simply counting the occurrences of specific kinds of behaviors (for example, the number of times a phone call is answered after three rings in a service department). Observation can range from complete participant observation, in which the OD practitioner becomes a member of the group under study, to more detached observation, in which the observer is clearly not part of the group or situation itself and may use film, videotape, and other methods to record behaviors.

Observations have a number of advantages. They are free of the biases inherent in self-report data. They put the practitioner directly in touch with the behaviors in question, without having to rely on others' perceptions. Observations also involve real-time data, describing behavior occurring in the present rather than the past. This avoids the distortions that invariably arise when people are asked to recollect their behaviors. Finally, observations are adaptive in that the consultant can modify what he or she chooses to observe, depending on the circumstances.

Among the problems with observations are difficulties interpreting the meaning underlying the observations. Practitioners may need to devise a coding scheme to make sense out of observations, and this can be expensive, take time, and introduce biases into the data. Because the observer is the data-collection instrument, personal bias and subjectivity can distort the data unless the observer is trained and skilled in knowing what to look for; how, where, and when to observe; and how to record data systematically. Another problem concerns sampling: observers not only must decide which people to observe; they also must choose the time periods, territory, and events in which to make those observations. Failure to attend to these sampling issues can result in highly biased samples of observational data.

When used correctly, observations provide insightful data about organization and group functioning, intervention success, and performance. For example, observations are particularly helpful in diagnosing the interpersonal relations of members of work groups. As discussed in Chapter 6, interpersonal relationships are a key component of work groups; observing member interactions in a group setting can provide direct information about the nature of those relationships.

Unobtrusive Measures

Unobtrusive data are not collected directly from respondents but from secondary sources, such as company records and archives. These data are generally available in organizations and include records of absenteeism or tardiness; grievances; quantity and quality of production or service; financial performance; meeting minutes; and correspondence with key customers, suppliers, or governmental agencies.

Unobtrusive measures are especially helpful in diagnosing the organization, group, and individual outputs presented in Chapters 5 and 6. At the organization level, for example, market share and return on investment usually can be obtained from company reports. Similarly, organizations typically measure the quantity and quality of the outputs of work groups and individual employees. Unobtrusive measures also can help to diagnose organization-level design components—structure, work systems, control systems, and human resources systems. A company's organization chart, for example, can provide useful information about organization structure. Information about control systems usually can be obtained by examining the firm's management information system, operating procedures, and accounting practices. Data about human resources systems often are included in a company's personnel manual.

Unobtrusive measures provide a relatively objective view of organizational functioning. They are free from respondent and consultant biases and are perceived as being "real" by many organization members. Moreover, unobtrusive measures tend to be quantified and reported at periodic intervals, permitting statistical analysis of behaviors occurring over time. Examining monthly absenteeism rates, for example, might reveal trends in employee withdrawal behavior.

The major problems with unobtrusive measures occur in collecting such information and drawing valid conclusions from it. Company records may not include data in a form that is usable by the consultant. If, for example, individual performance data are needed, the consultant may find that many firms only record production information at the group or departmental level. Unobtrusive data also may have their own built-in biases. Changes in accounting procedures and in methods of recording data are common in organizations, and such changes can affect company records independently of what is actually happening in the organization. For example, observed changes in productivity over time might be caused by modifications in methods of recording production rather than by actual changes in organizational functioning.

Despite these drawbacks, unobtrusive data serve as a valuable adjunct to other diagnostic measures, such as interviews and questionnaires. Archival data can be used in preliminary diagnosis, identifying those organizational units with absenteeism, grievance, or production problems. Then, interviews might be conducted or observations made in those units to discover the underlying causes of the problems. Conversely, unobtrusive data can be used to crosscheck other forms of information. For example, if questionnaires reveal that employees in a department are dissatisfied with their jobs, company records might show whether that discontent is manifested in heightened withdrawal behaviors, in lowered quality work, or in similar counterproductive behaviors.

Application 7.1 describes the use of multiple methods to collect diagnostic data in an information systems division of a multihospital system. The consultants used all four techniques described previously: interviews, questionnaires, observations, and unobtrusive measures. The multiple methods provided a comprehensive diagnosis of the issues facing the division.

SAMPLING

Before discussing how to analyze data, the issue of *sampling* needs to be emphasized. Application of the different data-collection techniques invariably raises the following questions: "How many people should be interviewed and who should they be?" "What events should be observed and how many?" "How many records should be inspected and which ones?"[10]

Sampling is not an issue in many OD cases. Because practitioners collect interview or questionnaire data from all members of the organization or department in question, they do not have to worry about whether the information is representative of the organization or unit.

Sampling becomes an issue in OD, however, when data are collected from selected members, behaviors, or records. This is often the case when diagnosing organization-level issues or large systems. In these cases, it may be important to ensure that the sample of people, behaviors, or records adequately represents the characteristics of the total population. For example, a sample of fifty employees might be

APPLICATION 7·1   Collecting Diagnostic Data in the Information Systems Division

The Information Systems (IS) Division of the St. Joseph Healthcare System is a moderate-size organization providing a variety of information services to a corporate office and seven hospitals in California and Texas. It is located in southern California and employs about two hundred people, some of whom are located in the hospitals. The division vice president and Sharon Carlson, the head of OD for the division, were concerned about a number of persistent problems facing the organization: an unclear mission, high levels of customer dissatisfaction, and an organization structure that provided neither sound performance nor employee satisfaction. After preliminary discussions with an OD consultant team familiar with the health-care system, Carlson decided to hire the team to conduct an intensive diagnosis of the division as a prelude to developing solutions to the problems.

The consultants met first with the division's top-management team to discuss the purpose and strategy for the diagnosis, as well as plans for feeding the data back to organization members. The strategy for collecting data included in-depth interviews with managers; focus group meetings with a sample of division employees; in-depth interviews with corporate managers responsible for the division and for the hospitals that were division customers; a short questionnaire for all members; collection of archival data from previous studies concerning project performance and customer satisfaction; and documentation from the recently completed strategic planning process. The consultants also were allowed to observe members on the job and at meetings.

Data collection started with the interviews and focus groups, which took about an hour each. Interviews with corporate and division management focused on the purpose of the division, perceptions of its organization, and opinions about its effectiveness. In focus groups of random samples of employees, members discussed the things they liked about the division, things they did not like, and barriers to change. During the focus groups, the consultants contracted with different members to observe their work during the day.

Data from the interviews and focus groups, as well as information from previous studies, were used to construct a five-page questionnaire. It was composed of items from stan-

dardized surveys, items from prior surveys administered in the division, and items constructed especially for the division. The survey asked about the clarity of the division's goals, characteristics of its structure, levels of satisfaction, and other issues brought up in the interviews. A pretest of the survey permitted an assessment of the questionnaire's measurement properties, and several items were modified. The survey was then sent to all members of the division and returned to the consultant team's office for analysis.

The consultants also examined division records and analyzed prior customer satisfaction studies. They met with Carlson on a regular basis to report progress and to schedule additional data-collection activities.

The different data-collection methods enabled the consultants to piece together a comprehensive account of the IS division's current situation. One set of problems, for example, involved the relationships among the division, the corporate office, and the hospitals. The corporate office wanted centralized computing and standardized programs, but the hospitals wanted local computing control and customized software solutions. The IS division was caught in the middle; its mission and goals were unclear for reasons largely not under its control. Another set of problems concerned the division's structure. The annual budgeting process separated capital investment decisions from ongoing product development decisions. As a result, hospital requests for support that were not budgeted for a year in advance could not be honored and led to beliefs that the IS division was unresponsive. This structural problem was verified in the survey and observation data. Employees felt frustrated; believed projects rarely were completed within time, cost, and quality standards; and operated within conflicting standards of achievement.

The consultant team put these findings together in a feedback report, outlining how the data were collected, describing the major problems observed, and making recommendations for change. The report included tables and charts illustrating the diagnostic findings. An important outcome for the division was recognizing that many of the persistent problems could not be solved by an internal OD project but required work at the division's boundaries. ■

used to assess the perceptions of all three hundred members of a department. A sample of production data might be used to evaluate the total production of a work group. OD practitioners often find that it is more economical and quicker to gather a sampling of diagnostic data than to collect all possible information. If done correctly, the sample can provide useful and valid information about the entire organization or unit.

Sampling design involves considerable technical detail, and consultants may need to become familiar with basic references in this area or to obtain professional help.[11] The first issue to address is *sample size,* or how many people, events, or records are needed to carry out the diagnosis or evaluation. This question has no simple answer: the necessary sample size is a function of population size, the confidence desired in the quality of the data, and the resources (money and time) available for data collection.

First, the larger the population (for example, number of organization members or total number of work outcomes) or the more complex the client system (for example, the number of salary levels that must be sampled or the number of different functions), the more difficult it is to establish a "right" sample size. As the population increases in size and complexity, the less meaning one can attach to simple measures, such as an overall average score on a questionnaire item. Because the population comprises such different types of people or events, more data are needed to ensure an accurate representation of the potentially different subgroups. Second, the larger the proportion of the population that is selected, the more confidence one can have about the quality of the sample. If the diagnosis concerns an issue of great importance to the organization, then extreme confidence may be needed, indicative of a very large sample size. Third, limited resources constrain sample size. If resources are limited but the required confidence is high, then questionnaires will be preferred over interviews because more information can be collected per member per dollar.

The second issue to address is *sample selection.* Probably the most common approach to sampling diagnostic data in OD is a simple *random sample,* in which each member, behavior, or record has an equal chance of being selected. For example, assume that an OD practitioner would like to select fifty people randomly out of the three hundred employees at a manufacturing plant. Using a complete list of all three hundred employees, the consultant can generate a random sample in one of two ways. The first method is to use a random number table printed in the back of almost any statistics text; the consultant would pick out the employees corresponding to the first fifty numbers under three hundred beginning anywhere in the table. The second method is to pick every sixth name (300/50 = 6) starting anywhere in the list.

If the population is complex or many subgroups need to be represented in the sample, a *stratified sample* may be more appropriate than a random one. In a stratified sample, the population of members, events, or records is segregated into a number of mutually exclusive subpopulations and a random sample is taken from each subpopulation. For example, members of an organization might be divided into three groups (managers, white-collar workers, and blue-collar workers), and a random sample of members, behaviors, or records could be selected from each grouping to reach diagnostic conclusions about each of the groups.

Adequate sampling is critical to gathering valid diagnostic data, and the OD literature has paid little attention to this issue. OD practitioners should gain rudimentary knowledge in this area and use professional help if necessary.

TECHNIQUES FOR ANALYZING DATA

Data analysis techniques fall into two broad classes: qualitative and quantitative. Qualitative techniques generally are easier to use because they do not rely on numerical data. That fact also makes them easier to understand and interpret. Quantitative techniques, on the other hand, can provide more accurate readings of the organizational problem.

Qualitative Tools

Of the several methods for summarizing diagnostic data in qualitative terms, two of the most important are content analysis and force-field analysis.

Content Analysis

A popular technique for assessing qualitative data, especially interview data, is *content analysis*, which attempts to summarize comments into meaningful categories. When done well, a content analysis can reduce hundreds of interview comments into a few themes that effectively summarize the issues or attitudes of a group of respondents. The process of content analysis can be quite formal, and specialized references describe this technique in detail.[12] In general, however, the process can be broken down into three major steps. First, responses to a particular question are read to gain familiarity with the range of comments made and to determine whether some answers are occurring over and over again. Second, based on this sampling of comments, themes are generated that capture recurring comments. Themes consolidate different responses that say essentially the same thing. For example, in answering the question "What do you like most about your job?" different respondents might list their co-workers, their supervisors, the new machinery, and a good supply of tools. The first two answers concern the social aspects of work, and the second two address the resources available for doing the work. Third, the respondents' answers to a question are then placed into one of the categories. The categories with the most responses represent those themes that are most often mentioned.

Force-Field Analysis

A second method for analyzing qualitative data in OD derives from Kurt Lewin's three-step model of change. Called *force-field analysis*, this method organizes information pertaining to organizational change into two major categories: forces for change and forces for maintaining the status quo or resisting change.[13] Using data collected through interviews, observation, or unobtrusive measures, the first step in conducting a force-field analysis is to develop a list of all the forces promoting change and all those resisting it. Then, based either on the OD practitioner's personal belief or perhaps on input from several members of the client organization, a determination is made of which of the positive and which of the negative forces are most powerful. One can either rank the order or rate the strength of the different forces.

Figure 7.2 illustrates a force-field analysis of the performance of a work group. The arrows represent the forces, and the length of the arrows corresponds to the strength of the forces. The information could have been collected in a group interview in which members were asked to list those factors maintaining the current level of group performance and those factors pushing for a higher level. Members also could have been asked to judge the strength of each force, with the average judgment shown by the length of the arrows.

This analysis reveals two strong forces pushing for higher performance: pressures from the supervisor of the group and competition from other work groups performing similar work. These forces for change are offset by two strong forces for maintaining the status quo: group norms supporting present levels of performance and well-learned skills that are resistant to change. According to Lewin, efforts to change to a higher level of group performance, shown by the darker band in Figure 7.2, should focus on reducing the forces maintaining the status quo. This might entail changing the group's performance norms and helping members to learn new skills. The reduction of forces maintaining the status quo is likely to result in

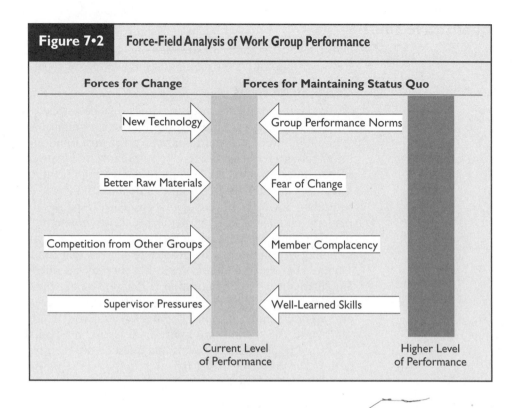

Figure 7·2   Force-Field Analysis of Work Group Performance

Forces for Change   Forces for Maintaining Status Quo

New Technology   Group Performance Norms

Better Raw Materials   Fear of Change

Competition from Other Groups   Member Complacency

Supervisor Pressures   Well-Learned Skills

Current Level
of Performance

Higher Level
of Performance

organizational change with little of the tension or conflict typically accompanying change caused by increasing the forces for change.

Quantitative Tools

Methods for analyzing quantitative data range from simple descriptive statistics of items or scales from standard instruments to more sophisticated, multivariate analysis of the underlying instrument properties and relationships among measured variables.[14] The most common quantitative tools are means, standard deviations, frequency distributions, scattergrams, correlation coefficients, and difference tests. These measures are routinely produced by most statistical computer software packages. Therefore, mathematical calculations are not discussed here.

Means, Standard Deviations, and Frequency Distributions

One of the most economical and straightforward ways to summarize quantitative data is to compute a *mean* and *standard deviation* for each item or variable measured. These represent the respondents' average score and the spread or variability of the responses, respectively. These two numbers easily can be compared across different measures or subgroups. For example, Table 7.3 shows the means and standard deviations for six questions asked of one hundred employees concerning the value of different kinds of organizational rewards. Based on the five-point scale ranging from one (very low value) to five (very high value), the data suggest that challenging work and respect from peers are the two most highly valued rewards. Monetary rewards, such as pay and fringe benefits, are not as highly valued.

But the mean can be a misleading statistic. It only describes the average value and thus provides no information on the distribution of the responses. Different patterns of responses can produce the same mean score. Therefore, it is important to use the standard deviation along with the frequency distribution to gain a clearer

Table 7•3	Descriptive Statistics of Value of Organizational Rewards	
ORGANIZATIONAL REWARDS	**MEAN**	**STANDARD DEVIATION**
Challenging work	4.6	0.76
Respect from peers	4.4	0.81
Pay	4.0	0.71
Praise from supervisor	4.0	1.55
Promotion	3.3	0.95
Fringe benefits	2.7	1.14

Number of respondents = 100.
1 = very low value; 5 = very high value.

understanding of the data. The *frequency distribution* is a graphical method for displaying data that shows the number of times a particular response was given. For example, the data in Table 7.3 suggest that both pay and praise from the supervisor are equally valued with a mean of 4.0. However, the standard deviations for these two measures are very different at 0.71 and 1.55, respectively. Table 7.4 shows the frequency distributions of the responses to the questions about pay and praise from the supervisor. Employees' responses to the value of pay are distributed toward the higher end of the scale, with no one rating it of low or very low value. In contrast, responses about the value of praise from the supervisor fall into two distinct groupings: twenty-five employees felt that supervisor praise has a low or very low value, whereas seventy-five people rated it high or very high. Although both rewards have

Table 7•4	Frequency Distributions of Responses to "Pay" and "Praise from Supervisor" Items	
Pay (Mean = 4.0)		
RESPONSE	**NUMBER CHECKING EACH RESPONSE**	**GRAPH***
(1) Very low value	0	
(2) Low value	0	
(3) Moderate value	25	XXXXX
(4) High value	50	XXXXXXXXXX
(5) Very high value	25	XXXXX
Praise from Supervisor (Mean = 4.0)		
RESPONSE	**NUMBER CHECKING EACH RESPONSE**	**GRAPH***
(1) Very low value	15	XXX
(2) Low value	10	XX
(3) Moderate value	0	
(4) High value	10	XX
(5) Very high value	65	XXXXXXXXXXXXX

*Each X = five people checking the response.

the same mean value, their standard deviations and frequency distributions suggest different interpretations of the data.

In general, when the standard deviation for a set of data is high, there is considerable disagreement over the issue posed by the question. If the standard deviation is small, the data are similar on a particular measure. In the example described above, there is disagreement over the value of supervisory praise (some people think it is important but others do not), but there is fairly good agreement that pay is a reward with high value.

Scattergrams and Correlation Coefficients

In addition to describing data, quantitative techniques also permit OD consultants to make inferences about the relationships between variables. Scattergrams and correlation coefficients are measures of the strength of a relationship between two variables. For example, suppose the problem being faced by an organization is increased conflict between the manufacturing department and the engineering design department. During the data-collection phase, information about the number of conflicts and change orders per month over the past year is collected. The data are shown in Table 7.5 and plotted in a scattergram in Figure 7.3.

A *scattergram* is a diagram that visually displays the relationship between two variables. It is constructed by locating each case (person or event) at the intersection of its value for each of the two variables being compared. For example, in the month of August, there were eight change orders and three conflicts, whose intersection is shown on Figure 7.3 as an X.

Three basic patterns can emerge from a scattergram, as shown in Figure 7.4. The first pattern is called a positive relationship because as the values of x increase, so do the values of y. The second pattern is called a negative relationship because as the values of x increase, the values of y decrease. Finally, there is the "shotgun" pattern wherein no relationship between the two variables is apparent. In the example shown in Figure 7.3, an apparently strong positive relationship exists between the number of change orders and the number of conflicts between the engineering design department and the manufacturing department. This suggests that change orders may contribute to the observed conflict between the two departments.

Table 7·5	Relationship Between Change Orders and Conflicts	
MONTH	**NUMBER OF CHANGE ORDERS**	**NUMBER OF CONFLICTS**
April	5	2
May	12	4
June	14	3
July	6	2
August	8	3
September	20	5
October	10	2
November	2	1
December	15	4
January	8	3
February	18	4
March	10	5

The *correlation coefficient* is simply a number that summarizes data in a scattergram. Its value ranges between +1.0 and –1.0. A correlation coefficient of +1.0 means that there is a perfect, positive relationship between two variables, whereas a correlation of –1.0 signifies a perfectly negative relationship. A correlation of 0 implies a "shotgun" scattergram where there is no relationship between two variables.

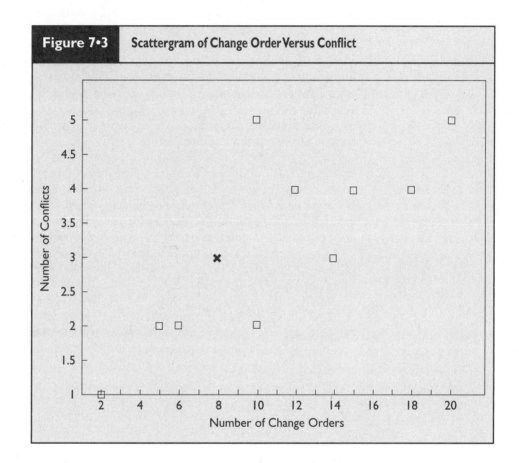

Figure 7•3   Scattergram of Change Order Versus Conflict

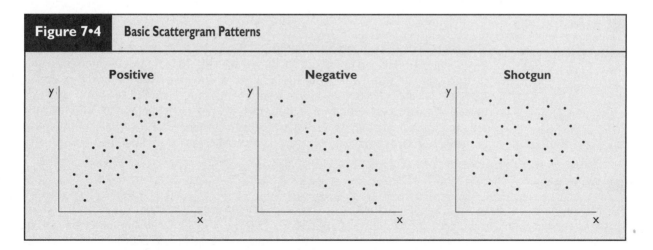

Figure 7•4   Basic Scattergram Patterns

Difference Tests

The final technique for analyzing quantitative data is the *difference test*. It can be used to compare a sample group against some standard or norm to determine whether the group is above or below that standard. It also can be used to determine whether two samples are significantly different from each other. In the first case, such comparisons provide a broader context for understanding the meaning of diagnostic data. They serve as a "basis for determining 'how good is good or how bad is bad.'"[15] Many standardized questionnaires have standardized scores based on the responses of large groups of people. It is critical, however, to choose a comparison group that is similar to the organization being diagnosed. For example, if one hundred engineers take a standardized attitude survey, it makes little sense to compare their scores against standard scores representing married males from across the country. On the other hand, if industry-specific data are available, a comparison of sales per employee (as a measure of productivity) against the industry average would be valid and useful.

The second use of difference tests involves assessing whether two (or more) groups differ from one another on a particular variable, such as job satisfaction or absenteeism. For example, job satisfaction differences between an accounting department and a sales department can be determined with this tool. Given that each group took the same questionnaire, their means and standard deviations can be used to compute a difference score (t-score or z-score) indicating whether the two groups are statistically different. The larger the difference score relative to the sample size and standard deviation for each group, the more likely that one group is more satisfied than the other.

Difference tests also can be used to determine whether a group has changed its score on job satisfaction or some other variable over time. The same questionnaire can be given to the same group at two points in time. Based on the group's means and standard deviations at each point in time, a difference score can be calculated. The larger the score, the more likely that the group actually changed its job satisfaction level.

The calculation of difference scores can be very helpful for diagnosis but requires the OD practitioner to make certain assumptions about how the data were collected. These assumptions are discussed in most standard statistical texts, and OD practitioners should consult them before calculating difference scores for purposes of diagnosis or evaluation.[16]

■ SUMMARY

This chapter described several different methods for collecting and analyzing diagnostic data. Because diagnosis is an important step that occurs frequently in the planned change process, a working familiarity with these techniques is essential. Methods of data collection include questionnaires, interviews, observation, and unobtrusive measures. Methods of analysis include qualitative techniques, such as content and force-field analysis, and quantitative techniques, such as the determination of mean, standard deviation, correlation coefficient, as well as difference tests.

■ NOTES

1. S. Mohrman, T. Cummings, and E. Lawler III, "Creating Useful Knowledge with Organizations: Relationship and Process Issues," in *Producing Useful Knowledge for Organiza-tions*, eds. R. Kilmann and K. Thomas (New York: Praeger, 1983): 613–24; C. Argyris, R. Putnam, and D. Smith, eds., *Action Science* (San Francisco: Jossey-Bass, 1985); E. Lawler

III, A. Mohrman, S. Mohrman, G. Ledford Jr., and T. Cummings, *Doing Research That Is Useful for Theory and Practice* (San Francisco: Jossey-Bass, 1985).

2. D. Nadler, *Feedback and Organization Development: Using Data-Based Methods* (Reading, Mass.: Addison-Wesley, 1977): 110–14.

3. W. Nielsen, N. Nykodym and D. Brown, "Ethics and Organizational Change," *Asia Pacific Journal of Human Resources* 29 (1991).

4. Nadler, *Feedback,* pp. 105–7.

5. W. Wymer and J. Carsten, "Alternative Ways to Gather Opinion," *HR Magazine* (April 1992): 71–78.

6. Examples of basic resource books on survey methodology include: L. Rea, R. Parker, and A. Shrader, *Designing and Conducting Survey Research: A Comprehensive Guide* (San Francisco: Jossey Bass, 1997); S. Seashore, E. Lawler III, P. Mirvis, and C. Cammann, *Assessing Organizational Change* (New York: Wiley Interscience, 1983); J. Van Mannen and J. Dabbs, *Varieties of Qualitative Research* (Beverly Hills, Calif.: Sage Publications, 1983); E. Lawler III, D. Nadler, and C. Cammann, *Organizational Assessment: Perspectives on the Measurement of Organizational Behavior and the Quality of Worklife* (New York: Wiley-Interscience, 1980); Nadler, *Feedback;* S. Sudman and N. Bradburn, *Asking Questions* (San Francisco: Jossey-Bass, 1983).

7. J. Taylor and D. Bowers, *Survey of Organizations: A Machine Scored Standardized Questionnaire Instrument* (Ann Arbor: Institute for Social Research, University of Michigan, 1972); C. Cammann, M. Fichman, G. Jenkins, and J. Klesh, "Assessing the Attitudes and Perceptions of Organizational Members," in *Assessing Organizational Change: A Guide to Methods, Measures, and Practices,* eds. S. Seashore, E. Lawler III, P. Mirvis, and C. Cammann (New York: Wiley Interscience, 1983): 71–138.

8. M. Weisbord, "Organizational Diagnosis: Six Places to Look for Trouble with or without a Theory," *Group and Organization Studies* 1 (1976): 430–37; R. Preziosi, "Organizational Diagnosis Questionnaire," in *The 1980 Handbook for Group Facilitators,* ed. J. Pfeiffer (San Diego: University Associates, 1980); W. Dyer, *Team Building: Issues and Alternatives* (Reading, Mass.: Addison-Wesley, 1977); J. Hackman and G. Oldham, *Work Redesign* (Reading, Mass.: Addison-Wesley, 1980).

9. J. Fordyce and R. Weil, *Managing WITH People,* 2d ed. (Reading, Mass.: Addison-Wesley, 1979); W. Wells, "Group Interviewing," in *Handbook of Marketing Research,* ed. R. Ferder, (New York: McGraw-Hill, 1977); R. Krueger, *Focus Groups: A Practical Guide for Applied Research,* 2d ed. (Thousand Oaks, Calif.: Sage Publications, 1994).

10. C. Emory, *Business Research Methods* (Homewood, Ill.: Richard D. Irwin, 1980): 146.

11. W. Deming, *Sampling Design* (New York: John Wiley, 1960); L. Kish, *Survey Sampling* (New York: John Wiley, 1995).

12. B. Berelson, "Content Analysis," *Handbook of Social Psychology,* ed. G. Lindzey (Reading, Mass.: Addison-Wesley, 1954); K. Krippendorf, *Content Analysis: An Introduction to Its Methodology* (Thousand Oaks, Calif.: Sage Publications, 1980); W. Weber, *Basic Content Analysis* (Thousand Oaks, Calif.: Sage Publications, 1990).

13. K. Lewin, *Field Theory in Social Science* (New York: Harper and Row, 1951).

14. More sophisticated methods of quantitative analysis are found in the following sources: W. Hays, *Statistics* (New York: Holt, Rinehart, & Winston, 1963); J. Nunnally and I. Bernstein, *Psychometric Theory,* 3d ed. (New York: McGraw-Hill, 1994); F. Kerlinger, *Foundations of Behavioral Research,* 2d ed. (New York: Holt, Rinehart, & Winston, 1973); J. Cohen and P. Cohen, *Applied Multiple Regression/Correlation Analysis for the Behavioral Sciences,* 2d ed. (Hillsdale, N.J.: Lawrence Erlbaum Associates, 1983); E. Pedhazur, *Multiple Regression in Behavioral Research* (New York: Harcourt Brace, 1997).

15. A. Armenakis and H. Field, "The Development of Organizational Diagnostic Norms: An Application of Client Involvement," *Consultation* 6 (Spring 1987): 20–31.

16. Cohen and Cohen, *Applied Multiple Regression.*

8

Feeding Back Diagnostic Information

Perhaps the most important step in the diagnostic process is feeding back diagnostic information to the client organization. Although the data may have been collected with the client's help, the OD practitioner usually is responsible for organizing and presenting them to the client. Properly analyzed and meaningful data can have an impact on organizational change only if organization members can use the information to devise appropriate action plans. A key objective of the feedback process is to be sure that the client has ownership of the data.

As shown in Figure 8.1, the success of data feedback depends largely on its ability to arouse organizational action and to direct energy toward organizational problem solving. Whether feedback helps to energize the organization depends on the *content* of the feedback data and on the *process* by which they are fed back to organization members.

In this chapter, we discuss criteria for developing both the content of feedback information and the processes for feeding it back. If these criteria are overlooked, the client is not apt to feel ownership of the problems facing the organization. A flexible and potentially powerful technique for data feedback that has arisen out of the wide use of questionnaires in OD work is known as *survey feedback*. Its central role in many large-scale OD efforts warrants a special look.

DETERMINING THE CONTENT OF THE FEEDBACK

In the course of diagnosing the organization, a large amount of data is collected. In fact, there is often more information than the client needs or could interpret in a realistic period of time. If too many data are fed back, the client may decide that changing is impossible. Therefore, OD practitioners need to summarize the data in ways that enable clients to understand the information and draw action implications from it. The techniques for data analysis described in Chapter 7 can inform this task. Additional criteria for determining the content of diagnostic feedback are described below.

Several characteristics of effective feedback data have been described in the literature.[1] They include the following nine properties:

1. *Relevant.* Organization members are likely to use feedback data for problem solving when they find the information meaningful. Including managers and employees in the initial data-collection activities can increase the relevance of the data.

2. *Understandable.* Data must be presented to organization members in a form that is readily interpreted. Statistical data, for example, can be made understandable through the use of graphs and charts.

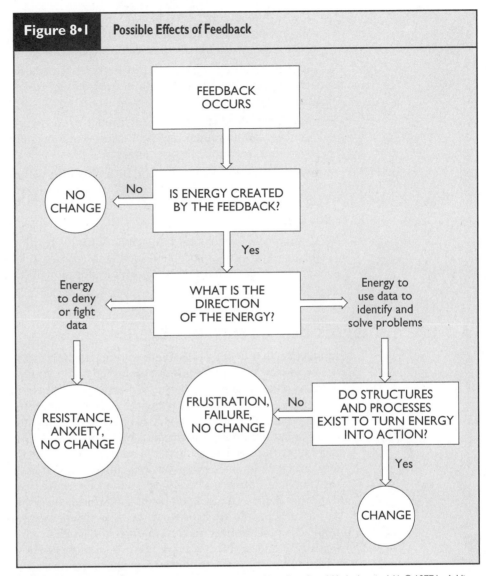

Figure 8•1   Possible Effects of Feedback

SOURCE: D. Nadler, *Feedback and Organization Development: Using Data-Based Methods*, page 146. © 1977 by Addison-Wesley Publishing Co., Inc. Reprinted by permission of Addison Wesley Longman.

3. *Descriptive.* Feedback data need to be linked to real organizational behaviors if they are to arouse and direct energy. The use of examples and detailed illustrations can help employees gain a better feel for the data.

4. *Verifiable.* Feedback data should be valid and accurate if they are to guide action. Thus, the information should allow organization members to verify whether the findings really describe the organization. For example, questionnaire data might include information about the sample of respondents as well as frequency distributions for each item or measure. Such information can help members verify whether the feedback data accurately represent organizational events or attitudes.

5. *Timely.* Data should be fed back to members as quickly as possible after being collected and analyzed. This will help ensure that the information is still valid and is linked to members' motivations to examine it.

6. *Limited.* Because people can easily become overloaded with too much information, feedback data should be limited to what employees can realistically process at one time.

7. *Significant.* Feedback should be limited to those problems that organization members can do something about because it will energize them and help direct their efforts toward realistic changes.

8. *Comparative.* Feedback data can be ambiguous without some benchmark as a reference. Whenever possible, data from comparative groups should be provided to give organization members a better idea of how their group fits into a broader context.

9. *Unfinalized.* Feedback is primarily a stimulus for action and thus should spur further diagnosis and problem solving. Members should be encouraged, for example, to use the data as a starting point for more in-depth discussion of organizational issues.

CHARACTERISTICS OF THE FEEDBACK PROCESS

In addition to providing effective feedback data, it is equally important to attend to the process by which that information is fed back to people. Typically, data are provided to organization members in a meeting or series of meetings. Feedback meetings provide a forum for discussing the data, drawing relevant conclusions, and devising preliminary action plans. Because the data might include sensitive material and evaluations about organization members' behaviors, people may come to the meeting with considerable anxiety and fear about receiving the feedback. This anxiety can result in defensive behaviors aimed at denying the information or providing rationales. More positively, people can be stimulated by the feedback and the hope that desired changes will result from the feedback meeting.

Because people are likely to come to feedback meetings with anxiety, fear, and hope, OD practitioners need to manage the feedback process so that constructive discussion and problem solving occur. The most important objective of the feedback process is to ensure that organization members *own* the data. Ownership is the opposite of resistance to change and refers to people's willingness to take responsibility for the data, their meaning, and the consequences of using them to devise a change strategy.[2] If the feedback session results in organization members rejecting the data as invalid or useless, then the motivation to change is lost and members will have difficulty engaging in a meaningful process of change.

Ownership of the feedback data is facilitated by the following five features of successful feedback processes:[3]

1. *Motivation to work with the data.* People need to feel that working with the feedback data will have beneficial outcomes. This may require explicit sanction and support from powerful groups so that people feel free to raise issues and to identify concerns during the feedback sessions. If people have little motivation to work with the data or feel that there is little chance to use the data for change, then the information will not be owned by the client system.

2. *Structure for the meeting.* Feedback meetings need some structure or they may degenerate into chaos or aimless discussion. An agenda or outline and a

discussion leader can usually provide the necessary direction. If the meeting is not kept on track, especially when the data are negative, ownership can be lost in conversations that become too general. When this happens, the energy gained from dealing directly with the problem is lost.

3. *Appropriate attendance.* Generally, people who have common problems and can benefit from working together should be included in the feedback meeting. This may involve a fully intact work team or groups comprising members from different functional areas or hierarchical levels. Without proper representation in the meeting, ownership of the data is lost because participants cannot address the problem(s) suggested by the feedback.

4. *Appropriate power.* It is important to clarify the power possessed by the group. Members need to know on which issues they can make necessary changes, on which they can only recommend changes, and over which they have no control. Unless there are clear boundaries, members are likely to have some hesitation about using the feedback data for generating action plans. Moreover, if the group has no power to make changes, the feedback meeting will become an empty exercise rather than a real problem-solving session. Without the power to address change, there will be little ownership of the data.

5. *Process help.* People in feedback meetings require assistance in working together as a group. When the data are negative, there is a natural tendency to resist the implications, deflect the conversation onto safer subjects, and the like. An OD practitioner with group process skills can help members stay focused on the subject and improve feedback discussion, problem solving, and ownership.

When combined with effective feedback data, these features of successful feedback meetings enhance member ownership of the data. They help to ensure that organization members fully discuss the implications of the diagnostic information and that their conclusions are directed toward relevant and feasible organizational changes.

Application 8.1 presents excerpts from some training materials that were delivered to a group of internal facilitators at a *Fortune* 100 telecommunications company.[4] It describes how the facilitators were trained to deliver the results of a survey concerning problem solving, team functioning, and perceived effectiveness.

SURVEY FEEDBACK

Survey feedback is a process of collecting and feeding back data from an organization or department through the use of a questionnaire or survey. The data are analyzed, fed back to organization members, and used by them to diagnose the organization and to develop interventions to improve it. Because questionnaires often are used in organization diagnosis, particularly in OD efforts involving large numbers of participants, and because it is a powerful intervention in its own right, survey feedback is discussed here as a special case of data feedback.

As discussed in Chapter 1, survey feedback is a major technique in the history and development of OD. Originally, this intervention included only data from questionnaires about members' attitudes. However, attitudinal data can be supplemented with interview data and more objective measures, such as productivity, turnover, and absenteeism.[5] Another trend has been to combine survey feedback with other OD interventions, including work design, structural change, large-group interventions, and intergroup relations. These change methods are the

APPLICATION 8•1   Training OD Practitioners in Data Feedback

Following deregulation of the telecommunications industry, GTE of California initiated a large-scale organization change to adapt to a rapidly changing environment. A key feature of the change was the implementation of an employee involvement (EI) process by management and the Communications Workers of America union. EI had as its stated goals the improvement of productivity and quality of work life. As part of that effort, the Center for Effective Organizations at the University of Southern California assisted the organization in collecting and feeding back implementation data on the EI intervention.

The data collected included observation of various work processes and problem-solving meetings; unobtrusive measures such as minutes from all meetings, quarterly income statements, operational reports, and communications; and questionnaire and interview data. A three-page questionnaire was administered every three months and asked participants on EI problem-solving teams for their perceptions of team functioning and performance. Internal EI facilitators were appointed from both management and union employees, and part of their work required them to feed back the results of the quarterly surveys.

To provide timely feedback to the problem-solving teams, the EI facilitators were trained to deliver survey feedback. Some of the material developed for that training is summarized below.

I. Planning for a Survey-Feedback Session

The success of a survey-feedback meeting often has more to do with the level of preparation for the meeting than with anything else. There are several things to do in preparing for a survey-feedback meeting.

A. *Distribute copies of the feedback report in advance.* This enables people to devote more time at the meeting to problem solving and less to just digesting the data. This is especially important when a large quantity of data is being presented.

B. *Think about substantive issues in advance.* Formulate your own view of what the data suggest about the strengths and weaknesses of the group. Does the general picture appear to be positive or problematic? Do the data fit the experience of the group as you know it? What issues do the data suggest need group attention? Is the group likely to avoid any of these issues? If so, how will you help the group confront the difficult issues?

C. *Make sure you can answer likely technical questions about the data.* Survey data have particular strengths and weaknesses. Be able to acknowledge that the data are not perfect, but that a lot of effort has gone into ensuring that they are reliable and valid.

D. *Plan your introduction to the survey-feedback portion of the meeting.* Make the introduction brief and to the point. Remind the group of why it is considering the data, set the stage for problem solving by pointing out that many groups find such data helpful in tracking their progress, and be prepared to run through an example that shows how to understand the feedback data.

II. Problem Solving with Survey-Feedback Data

A. *Chunk the feedback.* If a lot of data are being fed back, use your knowledge of the group and the data to present small portions of data. Stop periodically to see if there are questions or comments about each section or "chunk" of data.

B. *Stimulate discussion on the data.* What follows are various ways to help get the discussion going.

1. Help clarify the meaning of the data by asking
   • What questions do you have about what the data mean?
   • What does [a specific number] mean?
   • Does anything in the data surprise you?
   • What do the data tell you about how we're doing as a group?

2. Help develop a shared diagnosis about the meaning of the data by commenting
   • What I hear people saying is. . . . Does everyone agree with that?
   • Several people are saying that . . . is a problem. Do we agree that this is something the group needs to address?
   • Some people seem to be saying . . . while other comments suggest. . . . Can you help me understand how the group sees this?
   • The group has really been struggling with [specific issue that the facilitator is familiar with], but the data say that we are strong on this. Can someone explain this?

3. Help generate action alternatives by asking
   • What are some of the things we can do to resolve . . . ?
   • Do we want to brainstorm some action steps to deal with . . . ?

C. *Focus the group on its own data.* The major benefit of survey feedback for EI teams will be in learning about the group's own behavior and outcomes. Often, however, groups will avoid dealing with issues concerning their own group in favor of broader and less helpful discussions about what other groups are doing right and wrong.

Comments you might use to help get the group on track include

- What do the data say about how we are doing as a group?
- There isn't a lot we can do about what other groups are doing. What can we do about the things that are under *our* control?
- The problem you are mentioning sounds like one this group also is facing [explain]. Is that so?

D. *Be prepared for problem-solving discussions that are only loosely connected to the data.* It is more important for the group to use the data to understand itself better and to solve problems than it is to follow any particular steps in analyzing the data. Groups often are not very systematic in how they analyze survey-feedback data. They may ignore issues that seem obvious to them and instead focus on one or two issues that have meaning for them.

E. *Hot issues and how to deal with them.* Survey data can be particularly helpful in addressing some hot issues within the group that might otherwise be overlooked. For example, a group often will prefer to portray itself as very effective when group members privately acknowledge that such is not the case. If the data show problems that are not being addressed, you can raise this issue as a point for discussion. If someone denies that group members feel there is a problem, you can point out that the data come from the group and that group members reported such-and-such on the survey. Be careful not to use a parental tone; if you sound like you're wagging your finger at or lecturing the group, you're likely to get a negative reaction. Use the data to raise issues for discussion in a less emotional way.

Ultimately, the group must take responsibility for its own use of the data. There will be times when you see the issues differently from the way group members see them or times when it appears certain to you that the group has a serious problem that it refuses to acknowledge. A facilitator cannot push a group to do something it's not ready to do, but he or she can poke the group at times to find out if it is ready to deal with tough issues. "A little irritation is what makes a pearl in the oyster." ■

outcome of the planning and implementation phase following from survey feedback and are described fully in Chapters 12 through 20.

What Are the Steps?

Survey feedback generally involves the following five steps:[6]

1. *Members of the organization, including those at the top, are involved in preliminary planning of the survey.* In this step, all parties must be clear about the level of analysis (organization, department, or small group) and the objectives of the survey. Because most surveys derive from a model about organizational or group functioning, organization members must, in effect, approve that diagnostic framework. This is an important initial step in gaining ownership of the data and in ensuring that the right problems and issues are addressed by the survey.

    Once the objectives are determined, the organization can use one of the standardized questionnaires described in Chapter 7, or it can develop its own survey instrument. If the survey is developed internally, pretesting the questionnaire is essential to ensure that it has been constructed properly. In either case, the survey items need to reflect the objectives established for the survey and the diagnostic issues being addressed.

2. *The survey instrument is administered to all members of the organization or department.* That breadth of data collection is ideal, but it may be necessary to administer the instrument to a sample of members because of cost or time constraints. If so, the size of the sample should be as large as possible to improve the motivational basis for participation in the feedback sessions.

3. *The OD consultant usually analyzes the survey data, tabulates the results, suggests approaches to diagnosis, and trains client members to lead the feedback process.*

4. *Data feedback usually begins at the top of the organization and cascades downward to groups reporting to managers at successively lower levels.* This waterfall approach ensures that all groups at all organizational levels involved in the survey receive appropriate feedback. Most often, members of each organization group at each level discuss and deal with *only* that portion of the data involving their particular group. They, in turn, prepare to introduce data to groups at the next lower organizational level if appropriate.

   Data feedback also can occur in a "bottom-up" approach. Initially, the data for specific work groups or departments are fed back and action items proposed. At this point, the group addresses problems and issues within its control. The group notes any issues that are beyond its authority and suggests actions. That information is combined with information from groups reporting to the same manager, and the combined data are fed back to the managers who review the data and the recommended actions. Problems that can be solved at this level are addressed. In turn, their analyses and suggestions regarding problems of a broader nature are combined, and feedback and action sessions proceed up the hierarchy. In such a way, the people who most likely will carry out recommended action get the first chance to propose suggestions.

5. *Feedback meetings provide an opportunity to work with the data.* At each meeting, members discuss and interpret their data, diagnose problem areas, and develop action plans. OD practitioners can play an important role during these meetings,[7] facilitating group discussion to produce accurate understanding, focusing the group on its strengths and weaknesses, and helping to develop effective action plans.

Although the preceding steps can have a number of variations, they generally reflect the most common survey-feedback design.[8] Application 8.2 presents a contemporary example of how the survey-feedback methodology can be adapted to serve strategic purposes. The application describes how Prudential Real Estate Affiliates combines attitudinal surveys with hard measures to increase change ownership in real estate sales offices.[9]

Survey Feedback and Organizational Dependencies

Traditionally, the steps of survey feedback have been applied to work groups and organizational units with little attention to dependencies among them. Research suggests, however, that the design of survey feedback should vary depending on how closely the participating units are linked with one another.[10] When the units are relatively independent and have little need to interact, survey feedback can focus on the dynamics occurring within each group and can be applied to the groups separately. When there is greater dependency among units and they need to coordinate their efforts, survey feedback must take into account relationships among the units, paying particular attention to the possibility of intergroup

APPLICATION 8•2   Operations Review and Survey Feedback at Prudential Real Estate Affiliates

Prudential Real Estate Affiliates, Inc. (PREA) is a subsidiary of the Prudential Insurance Company of America. Throughout the United States, it franchises the Prudential name to independently owned and operated real estate offices that help people buy and sell homes and commercial real estate. PREA works with approximately twelve hundred of these offices. Although some real estate firms are large, multioffice organizations, many are small independent offices with an owner/manager and several sales associates. PREA's primary work is to help the offices do their job better by offering a range of support services, including technical support, sales training, advertising, and business assistance.

PREA has adapted successfully the survey-feedback technology to assist their customers in improving profitability, productivity, and sales associate work satisfaction. The survey-feedback methodology is called an "operations review." It is a voluntary service annually provided free of charge to any office. PREA describes the operations review as an "interactive process." Each office manager is required to gather internal information about its operations and to send the data to PREA. In addition, each sales associate completes a confidential 43-item opinion survey that is returned directly to PREA for analysis.

These data are entered into a database, and a four-color report is produced. The report is then fed back to the owner/manager of a single office or to the management team in the larger offices. In the best cases, all or part of the data is then shared with the sales associates at a sales meeting. The data are discussed, areas of improvement are identified, and action plans are developed. "When there are discrepancies, especially on the sales force attitudes, it is a great opportunity for discussion," says Skip Newberg, one of the process designers.

The data are presented in three major areas: financial performance, including income, expense, and profit ratios; productivity, including units sold or revenues per full-time sales associate; and management practices, including office climate, service orientation, and sales associates' attitudes. The data for each question are presented in colorful graphs that compare the office's productivity with that of similar offices (in terms of size or structure) and with the productivity of the top-performing sales office in the country. "Presenting the data in this simple way has an impact. Reams of computer printouts with numbers are not interesting. . . . Graphs and colors grab a manager's attention," says Newberg.

Although the financial and productivity data are important, it is the management practices data that get the most attention in the feedback process. Newberg believes that "the power is not in the printed book; the power is in the skill of

the people who sit down with the sales office people and help them interpret it. A skilled person can show an office their strengths and weaknesses in such a way that they can use the data to make improvements." The "management practices" section examines three areas that are related to sales office performance: climate, service orientation, and fundamental attitudes. *Climate* refers to the associates' perceptions of the extent and degree to which their work and well being are promoted by management and other associates. It also indicates the degrees to which associates have a sense of pride in their office. Items in the survey, such as "This real estate office is considered to be a leader by others in the market" and "We get a lot of customers in this office based on customer referrals" are two statements that tap that dimension. *Service orientation* refers to an office's emphasis on service quality and customer satisfaction. To assess this dimension, the survey asks sales associates to agree or disagree with statements such as "Our office places so much emphasis on selling to customers that it is difficult to serve customers properly" and "Our advertising is consistent with the service we deliver." Finally, *fundamental attitudes* of sales associates and their perceptions of management's attitudes can range from optimistic to pessimistic. The survey taps these attitudes with statements such as "Clients have no loyalty regardless of how you treat them" and "Giving customers truly excellent custom service takes too much; it's just not worth it."

Including sales office performance next to sales associates' opinions and attitudes provides an important motivational aspect to the feedback process. Newberg believes that "there isn't a manager alive who doesn't want to know how they compare to their peers. The profit and productivity information gets the office's attention and makes it easier to get the message across." The message he refers to is the results of research conducted by PREA. It has produced some remarkable evidence of relationships between sales office performance and the attitudes and opinions of the sales associates. For example, PREA's research has provided strong evidence of a positive relationship between the fundamental attitudes of sales associates and sales office profitability.

Invariably during the feedback session, owner/managers or senior managers say, "OK, that's great, sales associate attitudes and office performance are related. But how can I improve sales associate attitudes?" Glenn Sigmund, a PREA manager who has worked extensively with the operations review, says, "If we can get managers to this point, we have their interest, motivation, and most importantly, commitment to address change." Additional research by PREA found certain key behaviors, practices, and policies that were directly related to positive scores on fundamental attitudes, service orientation, and office climate. These practices and policies give the sales office something tangible to work with and implement.

Response to the system has been favorable. More than twenty thousand sales associates have taken the survey, and many offices are back for the third year of feedback. One CEO from a large multioffice firm said, "This is one of the most valuable services PREA offers. Our managers see it as a great tool and one of the best mechanisms for feedback from our sales associates to check how we're really doing." Another manager in a smaller office reported that "the operations review has had a definite impact. It helps us focus on carrying out our business plan and increase profits. We also use it to help our sales associates plan how to improve their own effectiveness." ■

conflict. In these situations, the survey-feedback process needs to be coordinated across the interdependent groups. The process will typically be managed by special committees and task forces representing the groups. They will facilitate the intergroup confrontation and conflict resolution generally needed when relations across groups are diagnosed.

Limitations of Survey Feedback

Although the use of survey feedback is widespread in contemporary organizations, the following limits and risks have been identified:[11]

1. *Ambiguity of purpose.* Managers and staff groups responsible for the survey-feedback process may have difficulty reaching sufficient consensus about the purposes of the survey, its content, and how it will be fed back to participants. Such confusion can lead to considerable disagreement over the data collected and paralysis about doing anything with them.

2. *Distrust.* High levels of distrust in the organization can render the survey feedback ineffective. Employees need to trust that their responses will remain anonymous and that management is serious about sharing the data and solving problems jointly.

3. *Unacceptable topics.* Most organizations have certain topics that they do not want examined. This can severely constrain the scope of the survey process, particularly if the neglected topics are important to employees.

4. *Organizational disturbance.* The survey-feedback process can unduly disturb organizational functioning. Data collection and feedback typically infringe on employee work time. Moreover, administration of a survey can call attention to issues with which management is unwilling to deal, and can create unrealistic expectations about organizational improvement.

Results of Survey Feedback

Survey feedback has been used widely in business organizations, schools, hospitals, federal and state governments, and the military, including the army, navy, air force, and marines. The navy has used survey feedback in more than five hundred navy commands. More than 150,000 individual surveys were given, and a large bank of computerized research data was generated. Promising results were noted between survey indices and nonjudicial punishment rates, incidence of drug abuse reports, and performance of ships undergoing refresher training (a postoverhaul training and evaluation period).[12] Positive results have been reported in such diverse areas as an industrial organization in Sweden and the Israeli Army.[13]

One of the most important studies of survey feedback was done by Bowers, who conducted a five-year longitudinal study (the Intercompany Longitudinal Study) of twenty-three organizations in fifteen companies involving more than fourteen thousand people in both white-collar and blue-collar positions.[14] In each of the twenty-three organizations studied, repeat measurements were taken. The study compared survey feedback with three other OD interventions: interpersonal process consultation, task process consultation, and laboratory training. The study reported that survey feedback was the most effective of the four treatments and the only one "associated with large across-the-board positive changes in organization climate."[15]

In the first edition of this book, we questioned these findings on a number of methodological grounds, concluding it was not surprising that "survey feedback comes out best in research done by the Institute for Social Research, the largest survey feedback organization in the world." Since then, a more critical and comprehensive study provided alternative explanations for the findings of the original study.[16] Although pointing to the original study as a seminal piece, the critique discovered methodological problems in the research itself. It did not question the original conclusion that survey feedback is effective in achieving organizational change, but it did question the fairness of the procedure employed for evaluating the other intervention techniques. It suggested that any conclusions to be drawn from action research studies should be based, at least in part, on objective operating data.

Comprehensive reviews of the literature reveal differing perspectives on the effects of survey feedback. In one review, survey feedback's biggest impact was on attitudes and perceptions of the work situation. The study suggested that survey feedback might best be viewed as a bridge between the diagnosis of organizational problems and the implementation of problem-solving methods because little evidence suggests that survey feedback alone will result in changes in individual behavior or organizational output.[17] This view is supported by recent research suggesting that the more the data were used to solve problems between initial surveys and later surveys, the more the data improved.[18] Another study suggested that survey feedback has positive effects on both outcome variables (for example, productivity, costs, and absenteeism) and process variables (for example, employee openness, decision making, and motivation) in 53 percent and 48 percent, respectively, of the studies measuring those variables. When compared with other OD approaches, survey feedback was only bettered by interventions using several approaches together—for example, change programs involving a combination of survey feedback, process consultation, and team building.[19] On the other hand, another review found that, in contrast to laboratory training and team building, survey feedback was least effective, with only 33 percent of the studies that measured hard outcomes reporting success. The success rate increased to 45 percent, however, when survey feedback was combined with team building.[20] Finally, a meta-analysis of OD process interventions and individual attitudes suggested that survey feedback was not significantly associated with overall satisfaction or attitudes about co-workers, the job, or the organization. Survey feedback was able to account for only about 11 percent of the variance in satisfaction and other attitudes.[21]

Studies of specific survey-feedback interventions identify conditions that improve the success of this technique. One study in an urban school district reported difficulties with survey feedback and suggested that its effectiveness depends partly on the quality of those leading the change effort, members' understanding of the process, the extent to which the survey focuses on issues important to participants, and the degree to which the values expressed by the survey are congruent with those of the respondents.[22] Another study in the military concluded that survey feedback works best when supervisors play an active role in feeding back data to employees and helping them to work with the data.[23] Similarly, a field study of funeral cooperative societies concluded that the use and dissemination of survey results increased when organization members were closely involved in developing and carrying out the project and when the consultant provided technical assistance in the form of data analysis and interpretation.[24] Finally, a long-term study of survey feedback in an underground mining operation suggested that continued, periodic use of survey feedback can produce significant changes in organizations.[25]

■ SUMMARY

This chapter described the process of feeding back data to a client system. It concerned identifying the content of the data to be fed back and designing a feedback process that ensures ownership of the data. Feeding back data is a central activity in almost any OD program. If members own the data, they will be motivated to solve organizational problems. A special application of the data-collection and feedback process is called survey feedback. It is one of the most accepted processes in organization development, enabling practitioners to collect diagnostic data from a large number of organization members and to feed back that information for purposes of problem solving. Survey feedback highlights the importance of contracting appropriately with the client system, establishing relevant categories for data collection, and feeding back the data as necessary steps for diagnosing organizational problems and developing interventions for resolving them.

■ NOTES

1. S. Mohrman, T. Cummings, and E. Lawler III, "Creating Useful Knowledge with Organizations: Relationship and Process Issues," in *Producing Useful Knowledge for Organizations,* eds. R. Kilmann and K. Thomas (New York: Praeger, 1983): 613–24.

2. C. Argyris, *Intervention Theory and Method: A Behavioral Science View* (Reading, Mass.: Addison-Wesley, 1970); P. Block, *Flawless Consulting: A Guide to Getting Your Expertise Used,* 2d ed. (San Francisco: Jossey-Bass, 1999).

3. D. Nadler, *Feedback and Organization Development: Using Data-Based Methods* (Reading, Mass.: Addison-Wesley, 1977): 156–58.

4. G. Ledford and C. Worley, "Some Guidelines for Effective Survey Feedback" (working paper, Center for Effective Organizations, University of Southern California, Los Angeles, 1987).

5. D. Nadler, P. Mirvis, and C. Cammann, "The Ongoing Feedback System: Experimenting with a New Managerial Tool," *Organizational Dynamics* 4 (Spring 1976): 63–80.

6. F. Mann, "Studying and Creating Change," in *The Planning of Change,* eds. W. Bennis, K. Benne, and R. Chin (New York: Holt, Rinehart, & Winston, 1964): 605–15;

Nadler, *Feedback;* J. Wiley, "Making the Most of Survey Feedback as a Strategy for Organization Development," *OD Practitioner* 23 (1991): 1–5; A. Church, A. Margiloff, and C. Coruzzi, "Using Surveys for Change: An Applied Example in a Pharmaceuticals Organization," *Leadership and Organization Development Journal* 16 (1995): 3–12; J. Folkman and J. Zenger, *Employee Surveys That Make a Difference: Using Customized Feedback Tools to Transform Your Organization* (New York: Executive Excellence, 1999).

7. Ledford and Worley, "Effective Survey Feedback."

8. N. Margulies and J. Wallace, *Organizational Change* (Glenville, Ill.: Scott, Foresman, 1973).

9. This application was contributed by S. Newberg and G. Sigmund of Prudential Real Estate Affiliates, Inc.

10. M. Sashkin and R. Cooke, "Organizational Structure as a Moderator of the Effects of Data-Based Change Programs" (paper delivered at the thirty-sixth annual meeting of the Academy of Management, Kansas City, 1976); D. Nadler, "Alternative Data-Feedback Designs for Organizational Intervention," *The 1979 Annual Handbook for Group Facilitators,* eds. J. Jones and J. Pfeiffer (LaJolla, Calif.: University Associates, 1979): 78–92.

11. S. Seashore, "Surveys in Organizations," in *Handbook of Organizational Behavior,* ed. J. Lorsch (Englewood Cliff, N.J.: Prentice Hall, 1987): 142.

12. R. Forbes, "Quo Vadis: The Navy and Organization Development" (paper delivered at the Fifth Psychology in the Air Force Symposium, United States Air Force Academy, Colorado Springs, Colo., April 8, 1976).

13. S. Rubenowitz, Goteborg, Sweden: Goteborg Universitet, personal communication, 1988; D. Eden and S. Shlomo, "Survey-Based OD in the Israel Defense Forces: A Field Experiment" (undated manuscript, Tel Aviv University).

14. D. Bowers, "OD Techniques and Their Result in 23 Organizations: The Michigan ICL Study," *Journal of Applied Behavioral Science* 9 (January-March 1973): 21–43.

15. Ibid., p. 42.

16. W. Pasmore, "Backfeed, The Michigan ICL Study Revisited: An Alternative Explanation of the Results," *Journal of Applied Behavioral Science* 12 (April-June 1976): 245–51; W. Pasmore and D. King, "The Michigan ICL Study Revisited: A Critical Review" (working paper 548, Krannert Graduate School of Industrial Administration, West Lafayette, Ind., 1976).

17. F. Friedlander and L. Brown, "Organization Development," in *Annual Review of Psychology,* eds. M. Rosenzweig and L. Porter (Palo Alto, Calif.: Annual Reviews, 1974).

18. D. Born and J. Mathieu, "Differential Effects of Survey-Guided Feedback: The Rich Get Richer and the Poor Get Poorer," *Group and Organization Management* 21 (1996): 388–404.

19. J. Porras and P. O. Berg, "The Impact of Organization Development," *Academy of Management Review* 3 (April 1978): 249–66.

20. J. Nicholas, "The Comparative Impact of Organization Development Interventions on Hard Criteria Measures," *Academy of Management Review* 7 (October 1982): 531–42.

21. G. Neuman, J. Edwards, and N. Raju, "Organizational Development Interventions: A Meta-Analysis of Their Effects on Satisfaction and Other Attitudes," *Personnel Psychology* 42 (1989): 461–83.

22. S. Mohrman, A. Mohrman, R. Cooke, and R. Duncan, "Survey Feedback and Problem-Solving Intervention in a School District: 'We'll Take the Survey But You Can Keep the Feedback,'" in *Failures in Organization Development and Change,* eds. P. Mirvis and D. Berg (New York: John Wiley & Sons, 1977): 149–90.

23. F. Conlon and L. Short, "An Empirical Examination of Survey Feedback as an Organizational Change Device," *Academy of Management Proceedings* (1983): 225–29.

24. R. Sommer, "An Experimental Investigation of the Action Research Approach," *Journal of Applied Behavioral Science* 23 (1987): 185–99.

25. J. Gavin, "Observation from a Long-Term Survey-Guided Consultation with a Mining Company," *Journal of Applied Behavioral Science* 21 (1985): 201–20.

9

Designing Interventions

An organization development intervention is a sequence of activities, actions, and events intended to help an organization improve its performance and effectiveness. Intervention design, or action planning, derives from careful diagnosis and is meant to resolve specific problems and to improve particular areas of organizational functioning identified in the diagnosis. OD interventions vary from standardized programs that have been developed and used in many organizations to relatively unique programs tailored to a specific organization or department.

This chapter describes criteria that define effective OD interventions and then identifies contingencies that guide successful intervention design. Finally, the various types of OD interventions presented in this book are reviewed. Parts 3 through 6 of this book describe fully the major interventions used in OD today.

WHAT ARE EFFECTIVE INTERVENTIONS?

The term *intervention* refers to a set of sequenced planned actions or events intended to help an organization increase its effectiveness. Interventions purposely disrupt the status quo; they are deliberate attempts to change an organization or subunit toward a different and more effective state. In OD, three major criteria define an effective intervention: (1) the extent to which it fits the needs of the organization; (2) the degree to which it is based on causal knowledge of intended outcomes; and (3) the extent to which it transfers change-management competence to organization members.

The first criterion concerns the extent to which the intervention is relevant to the organization and its members. Effective interventions are based on valid information about the organization's functioning; they provide organization members with opportunities to make free and informed choices; and they gain members' internal commitment to those choices.[1]

Valid information is the result of an accurate diagnosis of the organization's functioning. It must reflect fairly what organization members perceive and feel about their primary concerns and issues. Free and informed choice suggests that members are actively involved in making decisions about the changes that will affect them. It means that they can choose not to participate and that interventions will not be imposed on them. Internal commitment means that organization members accept ownership of the intervention and take responsibility for implementing it. If interventions are to result in meaningful changes, management, staff, and other relevant members must be committed to carrying them out.

The second criterion of an effective intervention involves knowledge of outcomes. Because interventions are intended to produce specific results, they must be based on valid knowledge that those outcomes actually can be produced. Otherwise there is no scientific basis for designing an effective OD intervention. Unfortunately, and in contrast to other applied disciplines such as medicine and engineering, knowledge of intervention effects is in a rudimentary stage of development in OD. Much of the evaluation research lacks sufficient rigor to make strong causal inferences about the success or failure of change programs. (Chapter 11 discusses how to evaluate OD programs rigorously.) Moreover, few attempts have been made to examine the comparative effects of different OD techniques. All of these factors make it difficult to know whether one method is more effective than another.

Despite these problems, more attempts are being made to assess systematically the strengths and weaknesses of OD interventions and to compare the impact of different techniques on organization effectiveness.[2] Many of the OD interventions that will be discussed here in Parts 3 through 6 have been subjected to evaluative research, which is explored in the appropriate chapters along with respective change programs.

The third criterion of an effective intervention involves the extent to which it enhances the organization's capacity to manage change. The values underlying OD suggest that organization members should be better able to carry out planned change activities on their own following an intervention. They should gain knowledge and skill in managing change from active participation in designing and implementing the intervention. Competence in change management is essential in today's environment, where technological, social, economic, and political changes are rapid and persistent.

HOW TO DESIGN EFFECTIVE INTERVENTIONS

Designing OD interventions requires paying careful attention to the needs and dynamics of the change situation and crafting a change program that will be consistent with the previously described criteria of effective interventions. Current knowledge of OD interventions provides only general prescriptions for change. There is scant precise information or research about how to design interventions or how they can be expected to interact with organizational conditions to achieve specific results.[3] Moreover, because the ability to implement most OD interventions is highly dependent on the skills and knowledge of the change agent, the design of an intervention will depend to some extent on the expertise of the practitioner.

Two major sets of contingencies that can affect intervention success have been discussed in the OD literature: those having to do with the change situation (including the practitioner) and those related to the target of change. Both kinds of contingencies need to be considered in designing interventions.

Contingencies Related to the Change Situation

Researchers have identified a number of contingencies present in the change situation that can affect intervention success. These include individual differences among organization members (for example, needs for autonomy), organizational factors (for example, management style and technical uncertainty), and dimensions of the change process itself (for example, degree of top-management support). Unless these factors are taken into account in designing an intervention, it will have little impact on organizational functioning or, worse, it may produce negative results. For example, to resolve motivational problems among blue-collar workers in an oil refinery, it is important to know whether interventions intended to improve motivation (for example, job enrichment) will succeed with the kinds of people who work there. In many cases, knowledge of these contingencies results in modifying or adjusting the change program to fit the setting. In applying a reward-system intervention to an organization, the changes might have to be modified depending on whether the firm wants to reinforce individual or team performance.

Although knowledge of contingencies is still at a rudimentary stage of development in OD, researchers have discovered several situational factors that can affect intervention success.[4] These factors include contingencies for many of the interventions reviewed in this book, and they will be discussed in respective chapters describing the change programs. More generic contingencies that apply to all OD interventions are presented below. They include the following situational factors that must be considered in designing any intervention: the organization's readiness for change, its change capability, its cultural context, and the change agent's skills and abilities.

Readiness for Change

Intervention success depends heavily on the organization being ready for planned change. Indicators of readiness for change include sensitivity to pressures for change, dissatisfaction with the status quo, availability of resources to support change, and commitment of significant management time. When such conditions are present, interventions can be designed to address the organizational issues uncovered during diagnosis. When readiness for change is low, however, interventions need to focus first on increasing the organization's willingness to change.[5]

Capability to Change

Managing planned change requires particular knowledge and skills (as outlined in Chapter 10), including the ability to motivate change, to lead change, to develop political support, to manage the transition, and to sustain momentum. If organization members do not have these capabilities, then a preliminary training intervention may be needed before members can engage meaningfully in intervention design.

Cultural Context

The national culture within which the organization is embedded can exert a powerful influence on members' reactions to change, so intervention design must account for the cultural values and assumptions held by organization members. Interventions may have to be modified to fit the local culture, particularly when OD practices developed in one culture are applied to organizations in another culture.[6] For example, a team-building intervention designed for top managers at an American firm may need to be modified when applied to the company's foreign subsidiaries. (Chapter 21 will describe the cultural values of different countries and show how interventions can be modified to fit different cultural contexts.)

Capabilities of the Change Agent

Many failures in OD result when change agents apply interventions beyond their competence. In designing interventions, OD practitioners should assess their experience and expertise against the requirements needed to implement the intervention effectively. When a mismatch is discovered, practitioners can explore whether the intervention can be modified to fit their talents better, whether another intervention more suited to their skills can satisfy the organization's needs, or whether they should enlist the assistance of another change agent who can guide the process more effectively. The ethical guidelines under which OD practitioners operate require full disclosure of the applicability of their knowledge and expertise to the client situation. Practitioners are expected to intervene within their capabilities or to recommend someone more suited to the client's needs.

Contingencies Related to the Target of Change

OD interventions seek to change specific features or parts of organizations. These targets of change are the main focus of interventions, and researchers have identified two key contingencies related to change targets that can affect intervention success: the organizational issues that the intervention is intended to resolve and the level of organizational system at which the intervention is expected to have a primary impact.

Organizational Issues

Organizations need to address certain issues to operate effectively. Figure 9.1 lists these issues along with the OD interventions that are intended to resolve them. (The parts and chapters of this book that describe the specific interventions are also identified in the figure.) It shows the following four interrelated issues that are key targets of OD interventions:

1. *Strategic issues.* Organizations need to decide what products or services they will provide and the markets in which they will compete, as well as how to relate to their environments and how to transform themselves to keep pace with changing conditions. These strategic issues are among the most critical facing organizations in today's changing and highly competitive environments. OD methods aimed at these issues are called strategic interventions. The methods are among the most recent additions to OD and include integrated strategic change, mergers and acquisitions, transorganizational development, and organization learning.

2. *Technology and structure issues.* Organizations must decide how to divide work into departments and then how to coordinate among those departments to support strategic directions. They also must make decisions about how to deliver products or services and how to link people to tasks. OD methods for dealing with these structural and technological issues are called technostructural interventions and include OD activities relating to organization design, employee involvement, and work design.

3. *Human resources issues.* These issues are concerned with attracting competent people to the organization, setting goals for them, appraising and rewarding their performance, and ensuring that they develop their careers and manage stress. OD techniques aimed at these issues are called human resources management interventions.

4. *Human process issues.* These issues have to do with social processes occurring among organization members, such as communication, decision making, leadership, and group dynamics. OD methods focusing on these kinds of issues are called human process interventions; included among them are some of the most common OD techniques, such as conflict resolution and team building.

Consistent with system theory as described in Chapter 5, these organizational issues are interrelated and need to be integrated with each other. The double-headed arrows connecting the different issues in Figure 9.1 represent the fits or linkages among them. Organizations need to match answers to one set of questions with answers to other sets of questions to achieve high levels of effectiveness. For example, decisions about gaining competitive advantage need to fit with choices about organization structure, setting goals for and rewarding people, communication, and problem solving.

Figure 9•1   Types of OD Interventions and Organizational Issues

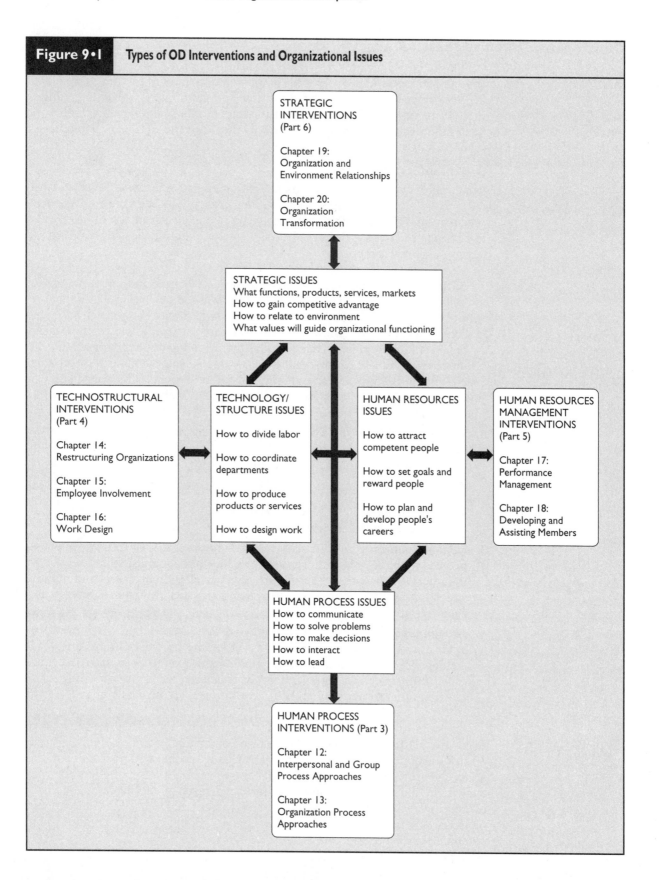

The interventions presented in this book are intended to resolve these different concerns. As shown in Figure 9.1, particular OD interventions apply to specific issues. Thus, intervention design must create change methods appropriate to the organizational issues identified in diagnosis. Moreover, because the organizational issues are themselves linked together, OD interventions similarly need to be integrated with one another. For example, a goal-setting intervention that tries to establish motivating goals may need to be integrated with supporting interventions, such as a reward system that links pay to goal achievement. The key point is to think systemically. Interventions aimed at one kind of organizational issue will invariably have repercussions on other kinds of issues. Careful thinking about how OD interventions affect the different kinds of issues and how different change programs might be integrated to bring about a broader and more coherent impact on organizational functioning are critical to effective intervention.

Organizational Levels

In addition to facing interrelated issues, organizations function at different levels—individual, group, organization, and transorganization. Thus, organizational levels are targets of change in OD. Table 9.1 lists OD interventions in terms of the level of organization that they primarily affect. For example, some technostructural interventions affect mainly individuals and groups (for example, work design), whereas others impact primarily the total organization (for example, structural design).

It is important to emphasize that only the primary level affected by the intervention is identified in Table 9.1. Many OD interventions also have a secondary impact on the other levels. For example, structural design affects mainly the organization level but can have an indirect effect on groups and individuals because it sets the broad parameters for designing work groups and individual jobs. Again, practitioners need to think systemically. They must design interventions to apply to specific organizational levels, address the possibility of cross-level effects, and perhaps integrate interventions affecting different levels to achieve overall success.[7] For example, an intervention to create self-managed work teams may need to be linked to organization-level changes in measurement and reward systems to promote team-based work.

OVERVIEW OF INTERVENTIONS

The OD interventions discussed in Parts 3 through 6 of this book are briefly described below. They represent the major organizational change methods used in OD today.

Human Process Interventions

Part 3 of the book presents interventions focusing on people within organizations and the processes through which they accomplish organizational goals. These processes include communication, problem solving, group decision making, and leadership. This type of intervention is deeply rooted in the history of OD. It represents the earliest change programs characterizing OD, including the T-group and the organizational confrontation meeting. Human process interventions derive mainly from the disciplines of psychology and social psychology and the applied fields of group dynamics and human relations. Practitioners applying these interventions generally value human fulfillment and expect that organizational effectiveness follows from improved functioning of people and organizational processes.[8]

Table 9•1	Types of Interventions and Organizational Levels		
INTERVENTIONS	**Primary Organizational Level Affected**		
	INDIVIDUAL	**GROUP**	**ORGANIZATION**
Human process (Part 3)			
T-groups	X	X	
Process consultation		X	
Third-party intervention	X	X	
Team building		X	
Organization confrontation meeting		X	X
Intergroup relations		X	X
Large-group interventions			X
Grid organization development		X	X
Technostructural (Part 4)			
Structural design			X
Downsizing			X
Reengineering		X	X
Parallel structures		X	X
High-involvement organizations	X	X	X
Total quality management		X	X
Work design	X	X	
Human resources management (Part 5)			
Goal setting	X	X	
Performance appraisal	X	X	
Reward systems	X	X	X
Career planning and development	X		
Managing workforce diversity	X	X	
Employee wellness	X		
Strategic (Part 6)			
Integrated strategic change			X
Transorganization development			X
Mergers and acquisitions integration			X
Culture change			X
Self-designing organizations		X	X
Organization learning and knowledge management		X	X

Chapter 12 discusses human process interventions related to interpersonal relationships and group dynamics. These include the following four interventions:

1. **T-group.** This traditional change method provides members with experiential learning about group dynamics, leadership, and interpersonal relations. The basic T-group brings ten to fifteen strangers together with a professional trainer to examine the social dynamics that emerge from their interactions. Members gain feedback about the impact of their own behaviors on each other and learn about group dynamics.

2. **Process consultation.** This intervention focuses on interpersonal relations and social dynamics occurring in work groups. Typically, a process consultant helps

group members diagnose group functioning and devise appropriate solutions to process problems, such as dysfunctional conflict, poor communication, and ineffective norms. The aim is to help members gain the skills and understanding necessary to identify and solve problems themselves.

3. *Third-party intervention.* This change method is a form of process consultation aimed at dysfunctional interpersonal relations in organizations. Interpersonal conflict may derive from substantive issues, such as disputes over work methods, or from interpersonal issues, such as miscommunication. The third-party intervener helps people resolve conflicts through such methods as problem solving, bargaining, and conciliation.

4. *Team building.* This intervention helps work groups become more effective in accomplishing tasks. Like process consultation, team building helps members diagnose group processes and devise solutions to problems. It goes beyond group processes, however, to include examination of the group's task, member roles, and strategies for performing tasks. The consultant also may function as a resource person offering expertise related to the group's task.

Chapter 13 presents human process interventions that are more systemwide than those described in Chapter 12. They typically focus on the total organization or an entire department, as well as on relations between groups. These include the following four change programs:

1. *Organization confrontation meeting.* This change method mobilizes organization members to identify problems, set action targets, and begin working on problems. It is usually applied when organizations are experiencing stress and when management needs to organize resources for immediate problem solving. The intervention generally includes various groupings of employees in identifying and solving problems.

2. *Intergroup relations.* These interventions are designed to improve interactions among different groups or departments in organizations. The microcosm group intervention involves a small group of people whose backgrounds closely match the organizational problems being addressed. This group addresses the problem and develops means to solve it. The intergroup conflict model typically involves a consultant helping two groups understand the causes of their conflict and choose appropriate solutions.

3. *Large-group interventions.* These interventions involve getting a broad variety of stakeholders into a large meeting to clarify important values, to develop new ways of working, to articulate a new vision for the organization, or to solve pressing organizational problems. Such meetings are powerful tools for creating awareness of organizational problems and opportunities and for specifying valued directions for future action.

4. *Grid organization development.* This normative intervention specifies a particular way to manage an organization. It is a packaged OD program that includes standardized instruments for measuring organizational practices and specific procedures for helping organizations to achieve the prescribed approach.

Technostructural Interventions

Part 4 of the book presents interventions focusing on an organization's technology (for example, task methods and job design) and structure (for example, division of labor and hierarchy). These change methods are receiving increasing attention in OD, especially in light of current concerns about productivity and organizational effectiveness. They include approaches to employee involvement, as well as methods for designing organizations, groups, and jobs. Technostructural interventions are rooted in the disciplines of engineering, sociology, and psychology and in the applied fields of sociotechnical systems and organization design. Practitioners generally stress both productivity and human fulfillment and expect that organization effectiveness will result from appropriate work designs and organization structures.[9]

In Chapter 14, we discuss the following three technostructural interventions concerned with restructuring organizations:

1. *Structural design.* This change process concerns the organization's division of labor—how to specialize task performances. Interventions aimed at structural design include moving from more traditional ways of dividing the organization's overall work (such as functional, self-contained–unit, and matrix structures) to more integrative and flexible forms (such as process-based and network-based structures). Diagnostic guidelines exist to determine which structure is appropriate for particular organizational environments, technologies, and conditions.

2. *Downsizing.* This intervention reduces costs and bureaucracy by decreasing the size of the organization through personnel layoffs, organization redesign, and outsourcing. Each of these downsizing methods must be planned with a clear understanding of the organization's strategy.

3. *Reengineering.* This recent intervention radically redesigns the organization's core work processes to create tighter linkage and coordination among the different tasks. This work-flow integration results in faster, more responsive task performance. Reengineering is often accomplished with new information technology that permits employees to control and coordinate work processes more effectively. Reengineering often fails if it ignores basic principles and processes of OD.

Chapter 15 is concerned with *employee involvement* (EI). This broad category of interventions is aimed at improving employee well-being and organizational effectiveness. It generally attempts to move knowledge, power, information, and rewards downward in the organization. EI includes parallel structures (such as cooperative union–management projects and quality circles), high-involvement plants, and total quality management.

Chapter 16 discusses *work design.* These change programs are concerned with designing work for work groups and individual jobs. The intervention includes engineering, motivational, and sociotechnical systems approaches that produce traditionally designed jobs and work groups; enriched jobs that provide employees with greater task variety, autonomy, and feedback about results; and self-managing teams that can govern their own task behaviors with limited external control.

Human Resources Management Interventions

Part 5 of the book focuses on personnel practices used to integrate people into organizations. These practices include career planning, reward systems, goal setting, and performance appraisal—change methods that traditionally have been associated with the personnel function in organizations. In recent years, interest has grown in integrating human resources management with OD. Human resources management interventions are rooted in the disciplines of economics and labor relations and in the applied personnel practices of wages and compensation, employee selection and placement, performance appraisal, and career development. Practitioners in this area typically focus on the people in organizations, believing that organizational effectiveness results from improved practices for integrating employees into organizations.

Chapter 17 deals with interventions concerning performance management, including the following change programs:

1. *Goal setting.* This change program involves setting clear and challenging goals. It attempts to improve organization effectiveness by establishing a better fit between personal and organizational objectives. Managers and subordinates periodically meet to plan work, review accomplishments, and solve problems in achieving goals.

2. *Performance appraisal.* This intervention is a systematic process of jointly assessing work-related achievements, strengths, and weaknesses. It is the primary human resources management intervention for providing performance feedback to individuals and work groups. Performance appraisal represents an important link between goal setting and reward systems.

3. *Reward systems.* This intervention involves the design of organizational rewards to improve employee satisfaction and performance. It includes innovative approaches to pay, promotions, and fringe benefits.

Chapter 18 focuses on these three change methods associated with developing and assisting organization members:

1. *Career planning and development.* This intervention helps people choose organizations and career paths and attain career objectives. It generally focuses on managers and professional staff and is seen as a way of improving the quality of their work life.

2. *Managing workforce diversity.* This change program makes human resources practices more responsive to a variety of individual needs. Important trends, such as the increasing number of women, ethnic minorities, and physically and mentally challenged people in the workforce, require a more flexible set of policies and practices.

3. *Employee wellness.* These interventions include employee assistance programs (EAPs) and stress management. EAPs are counseling programs that help employees deal with substance abuse and mental health, marital, and financial problems that often are associated with poor work performance. Stress management programs help workers cope with the negative consequences of stress at work. They help managers reduce specific sources of stress, such as role conflict and ambiguity, and provide methods for reducing such stress symptoms as hypertension and anxiety.

Strategic Interventions

Part 6 of the book considers interventions that link the internal functioning of the organization to the larger environment and transform the organization to keep pace with changing conditions. These change programs are among the newest additions to OD. They are implemented organizationwide and bring about a fit between business strategy, structure, culture, and the larger environment. The interventions derive from the disciplines of strategic management, organization theory, open-systems theory, and cultural anthropology.

In Chapter 19, we discuss the following major interventions for managing organization and environment relationships:

1. *Integrated strategic change.* This comprehensive OD intervention describes how planned change can make a value-added contribution to strategic management. It argues that business strategies and organizational systems must be changed together in response to external and internal disruptions. A strategic change plan helps members manage the transition between a current strategy and organization design and the desired future strategic orientation.

2. *Transorganization development.* This intervention helps organizations enter into alliances, partnerships, and joint ventures to perform tasks or solve problems that are too complex for single organizations to resolve. It helps organizations recognize the need for partnerships and develop appropriate structures for implementing them.

3. *Merger and acquisition integration.* This intervention describes how OD practitioners can assist two or more organizations to form a new entity. Addressing key strategic, leadership, and cultural issues prior to the legal and financial transaction helps to smooth operational integration.

Chapter 20 addresses three major interventions for transforming organizations:

1. *Culture change.* This intervention helps organizations develop cultures (behaviors, values, beliefs, and norms) appropriate to their strategies and environments. It focuses on developing a strong organization culture to keep organization members pulling in the same direction.

2. *Self-designing organizations.* This change program helps organizations gain the capacity to alter themselves fundamentally. It is a highly participative process involving multiple stakeholders in setting strategic directions and designing and implementing appropriate structures and processes. Organizations learn how to design and implement their own strategic changes.

3. *Organization learning and knowledge management.* This intervention describes two interrelated change processes: organization learning (OL), which seeks to enhance an organization's capability to acquire and develop new knowledge, and knowledge management (KM), which focuses on how that knowledge can be organized and used to improve organization performance. These interventions move the organization beyond solving existing problems so as to become capable of continuous improvment.

■ SUMMARY

This chapter presented an overview of interventions currently used in OD. An intervention is a set of planned activities intended to help an organization improve its performance and effectiveness. Effective interventions are designed to fit the needs of the organization, are based on causal knowledge of intended outcomes, and transfer competence to manage change to organization members.

Intervention design involves understanding situational contingencies such as individual differences among organization members and dimensions of the change process itself. Four key organizational factors—readiness for change, capability to change, cultural context, and the capabilities of the change agent—affect the design and implementation of almost any intervention.

Furthermore, OD interventions seek to change specific features or parts of organizations. These targets of change can be classified based on the organizational issues that the intervention is intended to resolve and the level of organizational system at which the intervention is expected to have a primary impact. Four types of OD interventions are addressed in this book: (1) human process programs aimed at people within organizations and their interaction processes; (2) technostructural methods directed at organization technology and structures for linking people and technology; (3) human resources management interventions focused at integrating people into the organization successfully; and (4) strategic programs targeted at how the organization uses its resources to gain a competitive advantage in the larger environment. For each type of intervention, specific change programs at different organization levels are discussed in Parts 3 through 6 of this book.

■ NOTES

1. C. Argyris, *Intervention Theory and Method: A Behavioral Science View* (Reading, Mass.: Addison-Wesley, 1970).

2. T. Cummings, E. Molloy, and R. Glen, "A Methodological Critique of 58 Selected Work Experiments," *Human Relations* 30 (1977): 675–708; T. Cummings, E. Molloy, and R. Glen, "Intervention Strategies for Improving Productivity and the Quality of Work Life," *Organizational Dynamics* 4 (Summer 1975): 59–60; J. Porras and P. O. Berg, "The Impact of Organization Development," *Academy of Management Review* 3 (1978): 249–66; J. Nicholas, "The Comparative Impact of Organization Development Interventions on Hard Criteria Measures," *Academy of Management Review* 7 (1982): 531–42; R. Golembiewski, C. Proehl, and D. Sink, "Estimating the Success of OD Applications," *Training and Development Journal* 72 (April 1982): 86–95.

3. D. Warrick, "Action Planning," in *Practicing Organization Development*, eds. W. Rothwell, R. Sullivan, and G. McClean (San Diego: Pfeiffer, 1995).

4. Nicholas, "Comparative Impact"; J. Porras and P. Robertson, "Organization Development Theory: A Typology and Evaluation," in *Research in Organizational Change and Development*, vol. 1, eds. R. Woodman and W. Pasmore (Greenwich, Conn.: JAI Press, 1987): 1–57.

5. T. Stewart, "Rate Your Readiness for Change," *Fortune* (7 February 1994): 106–10.

6. G. Hofstede, *Culture's Consequences* (Beverly Hills, Calif.: Sage, 1980); K. Johnson, "Estimating National Culture and O.D. Values," in *Global and International Organization Development*, eds. P. Sorensen Jr., T. Head, K. Johnson, et al. (Champaign, Ill.: Stipes, 1995): 266–81.

7. D. Coghlan, "Rediscovering Organizational Levels for OD Interventions," *Organization Development Journal* 13 (1995): 19–27.

8. F. Friedlander and L. D. Brown, "Organization Development," *Annual Review of Psychology* 25 (1974): 313–41.

9. E. Lawler III, *The Ultimate Advantage* (San Francisco: Jossey-Bass, 1992).

10

Leading and Managing Change

After diagnosis reveals the causes of problems or opportunities for development, organization members begin planning and subsequently leading and implementing the changes necessary to improve organization effectiveness and performance. A large part of OD is concerned with interventions for improving organizations. The previous chapter discussed the design of interventions and introduced the major ones currently used in OD. Chapters 12 through 20 describe those interventions in detail. This chapter addresses the key activities associated with successfully leading and managing organizational changes.

Change can vary in complexity from the introduction of relatively simple processes into a small work group to transforming the strategies and design features of the whole organization. Although change management differs across situations, in this chapter we discuss tasks that must be performed in managing any kind of organizational change. (Tasks applicable to specific kinds of changes are examined in the intervention chapters in Parts 3 through 6.)

OVERVIEW OF CHANGE ACTIVITIES

The OD literature has directed considerable attention to leading and managing change. Much of the material is highly prescriptive, advising managers about how to plan and implement organizational changes. Traditionally, change management has focused on identifying sources of resistance to change and offering ways to overcome them.[1] More recent contributions have challenged the focus on resistance and have been aimed at creating visions and desired futures, gaining political support for them, and managing the transition of the organization toward them.[2]

The diversity of practical advice for managing change can be organized into five major activities, as shown in Figure 10.1. The activities contribute to effective change management and are listed roughly in the order in which they typically are performed. Each activity represents a key element in change leadership.[3] The first activity involves *motivating change* and includes creating a readiness for change among organization members and helping them address resistance to change. Leadership must create an environment in which people accept the need for change and commit physical and psychological energy to it. Motivation is a critical issue in starting change because ample evidence indicates that people and organizations seek to preserve the status quo and are willing to change only when there are compelling reasons to do so. The second activity is concerned with *creating a vision* and is closely aligned with leadership activities. The vision provides a purpose and reason for change and describes the desired future state. Together, they provide the "why" and "what" of planned change. The third activity involves *developing political support* for change. Organizations are composed of powerful individuals and groups that can either block or promote change, and leaders and change agents need to gain their support to implement changes. The fourth activity is concerned with *managing the transition* from the current state to the desired future

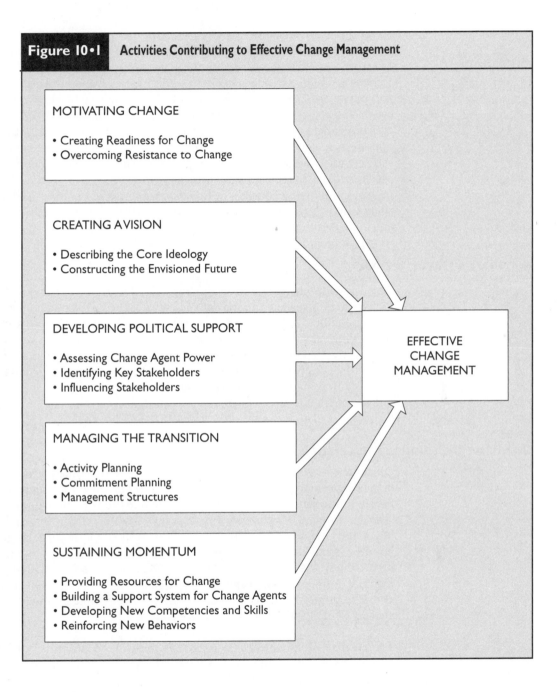

Figure 10•1   Activities Contributing to Effective Change Management

MOTIVATING CHANGE

• Creating Readiness for Change
• Overcoming Resistance to Change

CREATING A VISION

• Describing the Core Ideology
• Constructing the Envisioned Future

DEVELOPING POLITICAL SUPPORT

• Assessing Change Agent Power
• Identifying Key Stakeholders
• Influencing Stakeholders

MANAGING THE TRANSITION

• Activity Planning
• Commitment Planning
• Management Structures

SUSTAINING MOMENTUM

• Providing Resources for Change
• Building a Support System for Change Agents
• Developing New Competencies and Skills
• Reinforcing New Behaviors

EFFECTIVE CHANGE MANAGEMENT

state. It involves creating a plan for managing the change activities as well as planning special management structures for operating the organization during the transition. The fifth activity involves *sustaining momentum* for change so that it will be carried to completion. This includes providing resources for implementing the changes, building a support system for change agents, developing new competencies and skills, and reinforcing the new behaviors needed to implement the changes.

Each of the activities shown in Figure 10.1 is important for managing change. Although little research has been conducted on their relative contributions, organizational leaders must give careful attention to each activity when planning and implementing organizational change. Unless individuals are motivated and committed to change, unfreezing the status quo will be extremely difficult. In the absence of vision, change is likely to be disorganized and diffuse. Without the support of powerful individuals and groups, change may be blocked and possibly sabotaged. Unless the transition process is managed carefully, the organization will have difficulty functioning while it moves from the current state to the future state. Without efforts to sustain momentum for change, the organization will have problems carrying the changes through to completion. Thus, all five activities must be managed effectively to realize success.

In the following sections of this chapter, we discuss more fully each of these change activities, directing attention to how the activities contribute to planning and implementing organizational change.

MOTIVATING CHANGE

Organizational change involves moving from the known to the unknown. Because the future is uncertain and may adversely affect people's competencies, worth, and coping abilities, organization members generally do not support change unless compelling reasons convince them to do so. Similarly, organizations tend to be heavily invested in the status quo, and they resist changing it in the face of uncertain future benefits. Consequently, a key issue in planning for action is how to motivate commitment to organizational change. As shown in Figure 10.1, this requires attention to two related tasks: creating readiness for change and overcoming resistance to change.

Creating Readiness for Change

One of the more fundamental axioms of OD is that people's readiness for change depends on creating a felt need for change. This involves making people so dissatisfied with the status quo that they are motivated to try new work processes, technologies, or ways of behaving. Creating such dissatisfaction can be difficult, as anyone knows who has tried to lose weight, stop smoking, or change some other habitual behavior. Generally, people and organizations need to experience deep levels of hurt before they will seriously undertake meaningful change. For example, IBM, GM, and Sears experienced threats to their very survival before they undertook significant change programs. The following three methods can help generate sufficient dissatisfaction to produce change:

1. *Sensitize organizations to pressures for change.* Innumerable pressures for change operate both externally and internally to organizations. As described in Chapter 1, modern organizations face unprecedented environmental pressures to change themselves, including heavy foreign competition, rapidly changing technology, and the draw of global markets. Internal pressures to change include new leadership, poor product quality, high production costs, and excessive employee absenteeism and turnover. Before these pressures can serve as triggers for change, however, organizations must be sensitive to them. The pressures must pass beyond an organization's threshold of awareness if managers are to respond to them. Many organizations, such as Kodak, Apple, Polaroid, and Jenny Craig, set their thresholds of awareness too high and neglected pressures for change until those pressures reached disastrous levels.[4] Organizations can make themselves more sensitive to pressures for change by encouraging

leaders to surround themselves with devil's advocates;[5] by cultivating external networks that comprise people or organizations with different perspectives and views; by visiting other organizations to gain exposure to new ideas and methods; and by using external standards of performance, such as competitors' progress or benchmarks,[6] rather than the organization's own past standards of performance. At Wesley Long Community Hospital, in Greensboro, North Carolina, for example, managers visited the Ritz-Carlton Hotel, Marconi Commerce Systems' high-involvement plant, and other hospitals known for high quality to gain insights about revitalizing their own organization.

2. *Reveal discrepancies between current and desired states.* In this approach to generating a felt need for change, information about the organization's current functioning is gathered and compared with desired states of operation. (See "Creating a Vision" later in this chapter for more information about desired future states.) These desired states may include organizational goals and standards, as well as a general vision of a more desirable future state.[7] Significant discrepancies between actual and ideal states can motivate organization members to initiate corrective changes, particularly when members are committed to achieving those ideals. A major goal of diagnosis, as described in Chapters 5 and 6, is to provide members with feedback about current organizational functioning so that the information can be compared with goals or with desired future states. Such feedback can energize action to improve the organization. At Waste Management, Sunbeam, and Banker's Trust, for example, financial statements had reached the point at which it was painfully obvious that drastic renewal was needed.[8]

3. *Convey credible positive expectations for the change.* Organization members invariably have expectations about the results of organizational changes. The contemporary approaches to planned change described in Chapter 2 suggest that these expectations can play an important role in generating motivation for change.[9] The expectations can serve as a self-fulfilling prophecy, leading members to invest energy in change programs that they expect will succeed. When members expect success, they are likely to develop greater commitment to the change process and to direct more energy into the constructive behaviors needed to implement it.[10] The key to achieving these positive effects is to communicate realistic, positive expectations about the organizational changes. Organization members also can be taught about the benefits of positive expectations and be encouraged to set credible positive expectations for the change program.

Overcoming Resistance to Change

Change can generate deep resistance in people and in organizations, thus making it difficult, if not impossible, to implement organizational improvements.[11] At a personal level, change can arouse considerable anxiety about letting go of the known and moving to an uncertain future. People may be unsure whether their existing skills and contributions will be valued in the future, or have significant questions about whether they can learn to function effectively and to achieve benefits in the new situation. At the organization level, resistance to change can come from three sources.[12] *Technical resistance* comes from the habit of following common procedures and the consideration of sunk costs invested in the status quo. *Political resistance* can arise when organizational changes threaten powerful stakeholders, such as top executive or staff personnel, or call into question the past decisions of leaders. Organization change often implies a different allocation of already scarce resources, such as capital, training budgets, and good people. Finally, *cultural resistance* takes the form of systems and procedures that reinforce the status quo, promoting conformity to existing values, norms, and assumptions about how things should operate.

There are at least three major strategies for dealing with resistance to change:[13]

1. ***Empathy and support.*** A first step in overcoming resistance is to learn how people are experiencing change. This strategy can identify people who are having trouble accepting the changes, the nature of their resistance, and possible ways to overcome it, but it requires a great deal of empathy and support. It demands a willingness to suspend judgment and to see the situation from another's perspective, a process called *active listening.* When people feel that those people who are responsible for managing change are genuinely interested in their feelings and perceptions, they are likely to be less defensive and more willing to share their concerns and fears. This more open relationship not only provides useful information about resistance but also helps establish the basis for the kind of joint problem solving needed to overcome barriers to change.

2. ***Communication.*** People resist change when they are uncertain about its consequences. Lack of adequate information fuels rumors and gossip and adds to the anxiety generally associated with change. Effective communication about changes and their likely results can reduce this speculation and allay unfounded fears. It can help members realistically prepare for change.

   However, communication is also one of the most frustrating aspects of managing change. Organization members constantly receive data about current operations and future plans as well as informal rumors about people, changes, and politics. Managers and OD practitioners must think seriously about how to break through this stream of information. One strategy is to make change information more salient by communicating through a new or different channel. If most information is delivered through memos and emails, then change information can be sent through meetings and presentations. Another method that can be effective during large-scale change is to substitute change information for normal operating information deliberately. This sends a message that changing one's activities is a critical part of a member's job.

3. ***Participation and involvement.*** One of the oldest and most effective strategies for overcoming resistance is to involve organization members directly in planning and implementing change. Participation can lead both to designing high-quality changes and to overcoming resistance to implementing them.[14] Members can provide a diversity of information and ideas, which can contribute to making the innovations effective and appropriate to the situation. They also can identify pitfalls and barriers to implementation. Involvement in planning the changes increases the likelihood that members' interests and needs will be accounted for during the intervention. Consequently, participants will be committed to implementing the changes because doing so will suit their interests and meet their needs. Moreover, for people having strong needs for involvement, the act of participation itself can be motivating, leading to greater effort to make the changes work.[15]

Application 10.1 describes how Ralph Stayer struggled to motivate change in Johnsonville Sausage.[16] The CEO clearly understood the need for change, and he had to find ways to get his employees involved. After several ill-fated attempts, he achieved the motivation he was looking for by finding the areas where his interests intersected with the interests of his workforce.

APPLICATION 10•1   Motivating Change at Johnsonville Sausage

In the early 1980s, Johnsonville Sausage was a successful Wisconsin manufacturer. It was growing at an annual rate of 20 percent and steadily increasing market shares in neighboring states. The quality of its products was high, and the organization was a respected member of the community. But CEO Ralph Stayer was worried. As a medium-sized organization, Johnsonville Sausage was neither large enough to promote and advertise its products on the same scale as large producers nor small enough to provide superior customer service as a local producer.

Of more concern was that the organization's members did not seem to be aware of the problem and did not care. Every day, Stayer observed people bored by their jobs and making thoughtless mistakes. They mislabeled products, used the wrong ingredients in a batch of sausage and, in an extreme case, drove the prongs of a forklift through a new wall. Although no one was deliberately wasting money, it was obvious to Stayer that people were not taking responsibility for their work. How could the organization survive a competitive challenge when no one cared about the organization and its success?

Over time, Stayer tried many tactics to get his workforce to change. Strategic planning exercises resulted in carefully drawn organization charts and reports that described who was responsible for what and who would report to whom. The discussions were thoughtful and detailed, but nothing happened. In the mid-1980s, after much soul searching and an employee survey that confirmed his fears about the state of the workforce, Stayer decided that the best way to improve the company was to increase the workers' involvement. He announced, "From now on, you are all responsible for making your own decisions." The problem was that no one had asked for more responsibility. Despite the workers' best efforts, the organization floundered. People had become accustomed to Stayer making all of the decisions, and he became frustrated when they didn't make the decisions he wanted. Not only was the organization resisting change, but Stayer himself was contributing to the problem. "I didn't really want them to make independent decisions. I wanted them to make the de-

cisions I would have made. Deep down, I was still in love with my own control; I was just making people guess what I wanted instead of telling them."

Ordering change and watching it go nowhere helped Stayer learn that he didn't control people directly but that he could control and manage the context within which people worked. He began by helping people to see the issues that needed changing and by overcoming resistance through participation and involvement. For example, he began sending customer letters directly to the line workers who, coming face-to-face with customer complaints, began to understand how their work affected others. Similarly, when complaints about working on weekends surfaced, managers encouraged the workers to look at the problem. Through the workers' initiatives, it became clear that overtime and customer complaints were the result of worker tardiness and absenteeism, sloppy maintenance, slow shift startups, and other behaviors entirely under their control. Once the employees began to see themselves as part of the problem, change came fairly quickly.

How the quality-control process was changed provides another example of motivating change through participation. In the company's sausage-making process, the package-ready sausage was inspected for taste, flavor, color, and texture by the quality department. Stayer reasoned that by checking the product after it was made, management had assumed responsibility for quality. Instead, the people who made the sausage were given the responsibility for tasting the product. Teams of workers began tasting the sausage every morning and discussing how to improve it. They asked for information about costs and customer reactions and used that to improve processes. Eventually, work design, compensation systems, and performance-appraisal systems also were changed. Johnsonville Sausage became a benchmark of self-management, highlighted by author Tom Peters and declared one of *Business Week*'s Management Meccas. All of this because Ralph Stayer figured out how to motivate his workforce to change. ■

CREATING A VISION

The second activity in leading and managing change involves creating a vision of what members want the organization to look like or become. It is one of the most popular yet least understood practices in management.[17] Generally, a vision describes the core values and purpose that guide the organization as well as an envisioned future toward which change is directed. It provides a valued direction for designing, implementing, and assessing organizational changes. The vision also can energize commitment to change by providing members with a common goal and a compelling rationale for why change is necessary and worth the effort. However, if the vision is seen as impossible or promotes changes that the organization cannot implement, it actually can depress member motivation. For example, George Bush's unfulfilled "thousand points of light" vision was emotionally appealing, but it was too vague and contained little inherent benefit. In contrast, John Kennedy's vision of "putting a man on the moon and returning him safely to the earth" was just beyond engineering and technical feasibility. In the context of the 1960s, it was bold, alluring, and vivid; it provided not only a purpose but a valued direction as well.[18] Recent research suggests that corporations with carefully crafted visions can significantly outperform the stock market over long periods of time.[19]

Creating a vision is considered a key element in most leadership frameworks.[20] Organization or subunit leaders are responsible for effectiveness, and they must take an active role in describing a desired future and energizing commitment to it. In many cases, leaders encourage participation in developing the vision to gain wider input and support. For example, they involve subordinates and others who have a stake in the changes. The popular media frequently offer accounts of executives who have helped to mobilize and direct organizational change, including Nobuhiko Kawamoto of Honda and Jack Welch at General Electric. Describing a desired future is no less important for people leading change in small departments and work groups than for senior executives. At lower organizational levels, there are ample opportunities to involve employees directly in the visioning process.

Developing a vision is heavily driven by people's values and preferences for what the organization should look like and how it should function. The envisioned future represents people's ideals, fantasies, or dreams of what they would like the organization to look like or become. Unfortunately, dreaming about the future is discouraged in most organizations[21] because it requires creative and intuitive thought processes that tend to conflict with the rational, analytical methods prevalent there. Consequently, leaders may need to create special conditions in which to describe a desired future such as off-site workshops or exercises that stimulate creative thinking.

Research by Collins and Porras suggests that compelling visions are composed of two parts: (1) a relatively stable core ideology that describes the organization's core values and purpose, and (2) an envisioned future with bold goals and a vivid description of the desired future state that reflects the specific change under consideration.[22]

Describing the Core Ideology

The fundamental basis of a vision for change is the organization's core ideology. It describes the organization's core values and purpose and is relatively stable over time. *Core values* typically include three to five basic principles or beliefs that have stood the test of time and best represent what the organization stands for. Although the vision ultimately describes a desired future, it must acknowledge the organization's historical roots, the intrinsically meaningful core values and principles that have guided and will guide the organization over time. Core values are not "espoused values"; they are the "values in use" that actually inform members what is important in the organization. The retailer Nordstrom, for example, has clear values around the importance of customer service; toymaker Lego has distinct values around the importance of families; and the Disney companies have explicit values around wholesomeness and imagination. These values define the true nature of these firms and cannot be separated from them. Thus, core values are not determined or designed; they are discovered and described through a process of inquiry.

Members can spend considerable time and energy discovering their organization's core values through long discussions about organizational history, key events, founder's beliefs, the work people actually do, and the "glue" that holds the organization together.[23] In many cases, organizations want the core values to be something they are not. For example, many U.S. firms want "teamwork" to be a core value despite strong cultural norms and organizational practices that reward individuality.

The organization's *core purpose* is its reason for being, the idealistic motivation that brings people to work each day. A core purpose is not a strategy. Purpose describes why the organization exists; strategy describes how an objective will be achieved. Organizations often create a slogan or metaphor that captures the real reason they are in business. For example, part of Disneyland's return to prominence in the late 1980s and 1990s was guided by the essential purpose of "creating a place where people can feel like kids again." Similarly, Apple's original vision of "changing the way people do their work" described well the benefits the organization was providing to its customers and society at large. Many Apple employees previously had experienced the drudgery of a boring job, an uninspired boss, or an alienating workplace, and it was alluring to be part of a company that was changing work into something more challenging, creative, or satisfying.

The real power of an organization's core ideology is its stability over time and the way it can help the organization change itself. Core values and purpose provide guidelines for the strategic choices that will work and can be implemented versus those that will not work because they contradict the real nature of the organization's identity. An envisioned future can be compelling and emotionally powerful to members only if it aligns with and supports the organization's core values and purpose.

Constructing the Envisioned Future

The core ideology provides the context for the envisioned future. Unlike core values and purpose, which are stable aspects of the organization and must be discovered, the envisioned future is specific to the change project at hand and must be created. The envisioned future varies in complexity and scope depending on the changes being considered. A relatively simple upgrading of a work group's word-processing software requires a less complex envisioned future than the transformation of a government bureaucracy.

The envisioned future typically includes the following elements that can be communicated to organization members:[24]

1. ***Bold and valued outcomes.*** Descriptions of envisioned futures often include specific performance and human outcomes that the organization or unit would like to achieve. These valued outcomes can serve as goals for the change process and standards for assessing progress. For example, BHAGs (Big, Hairy, Audacious Goals) are clear, tangible, energizing targets that serve as rallying points for organization action. They can challenge members to meet clear target levels of sales growth or customer satisfaction, to overcome key competitors, to achieve role-model status in the industry, or to transform the organization in some meaningful way. For example, in 1990 Wal-Mart Stores made a statement of intent "to become a $125 billion company by the year 2000." (Net sales in 1999 exceeded $137.6 billion.) Following the downsizing of the U.S. military

budget, Rockwell proposed the following bold outcome for its change efforts: "Transform this company from a defense contractor into the best diversified high-technology company in the world."

2. **Desired future state.** This element of the envisioned future specifies, in vivid detail, what the organization should look like to achieve bold and valued outcomes. It is a passionate and engaging statement intended to draw organization members into the future. The organizational features described in the statement help define a desired future state toward which change activities should move. This aspect of the visioning process is exciting and compelling. It seeks to create a word picture that is emotionally powerful to members and motivates them to change.

Application 10.2 describes the elements of the vision at MicroStrategy.[25] The company's vision is powerful and compelling, and its CEO works hard to communicate the message.

DEVELOPING POLITICAL SUPPORT

From a political perspective, organizations can be seen as loosely structured coalitions of individuals and groups having different preferences and interests.[26] For example, shop-floor workers may want secure, high-paying jobs, and top executives may be interested in diversifying the organization into new businesses. The marketing department might be interested in developing new products and markets, and the production department may want to manufacture standard products in the most efficient way. These different groups or coalitions compete with one another for scarce resources and influence. They act to preserve or enhance their self-interests while managing to arrive at a sufficient balance of power to sustain commitment to the organization and achieve overall effectiveness.

Given this political view, attempts to change the organization may threaten the balance of power among groups, thus resulting in political conflicts and struggles.[27] Individuals and groups will be concerned with how the changes affect their own power and influence, and they will act accordingly. Some groups will become less powerful; others will gain influence. Those whose power is threatened by the change will act defensively and seek to preserve the status quo. For example, they may try to present compelling evidence that change is unnecessary or that only minor modifications are needed. On the other hand, those participants who will gain power from the changes will push heavily for them, perhaps bringing in seemingly impartial consultants to legitimize the need for change. Consequently, significant organizational changes are frequently accompanied by conflicting interests, distorted information, and political turmoil.

Methods for managing the political dynamics of organizational change are relatively recent additions to OD. Traditionally, OD has neglected political issues mainly because its humanistic roots promoted collaboration and power sharing among individuals and groups.[28] Today, change agents are paying increased attention to power and political activity, particularly as they engage in strategic change involving most parts and features of organizations. Some practitioners are concerned, however, about whether power and OD are compatible. A growing number of advocates suggest that OD practitioners can use power in positive ways.[29] They can build their own power base to gain access to other power holders within the organization. Without such access, those who influence or make decisions may not have the advantage of an OD perspective. OD practitioners can use power strategies that are

APPLICATION 10·2   Michael Saylor and MicroStrategy's Envisioned Future

MicroStrategy develops and produces data-mining and decision-support software. Its products allow organizations to understand their interactions with customers and suppliers and their internal business processes. This information enables the organization to improve operations, analyze marketing effectiveness, and create and deliver targeted, one-to-one marketing campaigns to customers. For example, MicroStrategy software helps McDonald's determine which promotions bring in the largest number of middle-class men during lunch hour. It also makes information available to employees. Using their software, British retailer Marks and Spencer put a 600-gigabyte data warehouse into the hands of eight hundred employees.

Michael Saylor, MicroStrategy's co-founder and CEO, built a vision based on a set of clear values and beliefs about the future. For example, the company's values, including long-term commitment and changing the world, differ markedly from what he sees as the values of the typical Silicon Valley high-technology startups. In those companies, everyone is busy looking out for themselves. "There's no honor among thieves," Saylor says. "It consists of a bunch of venture capitalists who don't have a long-term commitment to their investments, employees who don't have a long-term commitment to their company, and companies that don't have a long-term commitment to their customers."

Saylor's values led to the following statement of the organization's mission and purpose:

Intelligence Everywhere.

The purpose is supported by a BHAG and an envisioned future. In addition, with the help of co-founder Sanju Bansal, MicroStrategy has begun to implement the organization necessary to bring the vision into reality. The BHAG has been articulated as follows:

> We think we have found the next great market—the ability to provide information to everybody, everywhere, anytime, and to automate sales and marketing of services. . . . We have multidecades of growth ahead of us. . . . We will have finished when we employ 20,000 or 30,000 or 40,000 people and we're a $10 billion company, and everybody on the planet lives every hour of every day dependent upon our technology.

The envisioned future is a story about the firm and its destiny. Everyone makes decisions. The CEO wants to know how to make the company more profitable. An e-tailer needs to know what her customers really want to buy. An investor wonders how his portfolio can yield higher returns. A mother wants to select the best doctor for her child's surgery. Saylor's organization sees a future world where information flows freely in a frictionless market; a win–win situation where decision makers can obtain all the information they need and corporations can profit from the data warehouses; a society where a person can ask any question, anytime, anywhere, and receive the answer when and where it's needed via an everyday electronic device, such as the phone, an e-mail access, or a pager.

Saylor molds his company around the vision of what a company should be.

- New hires—even seasoned executives—must complete six-week "boot camp" and pass tests on the company's software and marketing message.

- At an annual one-week "university," all employees must attend classes from 8 a.m. to 6 p.m., with a mandatory study hall from 8 to 10 p.m. Once a year, Saylor takes all employees on an ocean cruise—no spouses invited. "Our culture is part intellectual, part military, part fraternity, part religion."

- When MicroStrategy went public in 1998, Saylor and other founders did not sell their stock. Rather, they took a one-time dividend before the offering and created an ownership structure in which insiders get ten votes for each share of stock and outside shareholders get one vote per share. All of this is to ensure a long-term commitment to and ownership of the organization.

- Each product, although grounded in the realities of business today, is a part of the vision. For example, the Telepath product provides subscribers with information about their investment portfolios, including when a stock hits a certain price level or when the portfolio dips below a certain rate of return. But Saylor looks beyond the simple product to what it represents and how it contributes to the vision: "What made Edison great? He gave us light. GE. We bring good things to life. They built generators, and they build dynamos to pump electricity. I want to see a world where we have universal intelligence, and that will mean 10,000 intelligence dynamos. There ought to be dynamos everywhere, spinning data, always delivering the right information to the right person. I want to know when my wife's in the hospital or my boat is smacked or my equities are in trouble or the government's unstable and something has happened to my hometown. I think that people will surrender their personal information to a centralized intelligence dynamo . . . because the cost of not doing so is an early death, an accidental death, a lack of an opportunity, a lack of income, a lack of happiness." One analyst went so far as to say, "He can make his products sound like they're the solution to world hunger."

So far, the vision has worked. Employee retention and devotion are extraordinarily high for the industry, with a turnover rate less than 10 percent. The company's performance has improved from losses on $5 million in sales in 1994 to a net income of $6 million on sales of $106 million in 1998. It moved from the ninth-largest vendor of decision-support software in 1995 to number four in 1998. ■

open and aboveboard to get those in power to consider OD applications. They can facilitate processes for examining the uses of power in organizations and help power holders devise more creative and positive strategies than political bargaining, deceit, and the like. They can help power holders confront the need for change and can help ensure that the interests and concerns of those with less power are considered. Although OD professionals can use power constructively in organizations, they probably will continue to be ambivalent and tense about whether such uses promote OD values and ethics or whether they represent the destructive, negative side of power. That tension seems healthy, and we hope that it will guide the wise use of power in OD.

As shown in Figure 10.2, managing the political dynamics of change includes the following activities: assessing the change agent's power, identifying key stakeholders, and influencing stakeholders.

Assessing Change Agent Power

The first task is to evaluate the change agent's own sources of power. This agent may be the leader of the organization or department undergoing change, or he or she may be the OD consultant if professional help is being used. By assessing their own power base, change agents can determine how to use it to influence others to

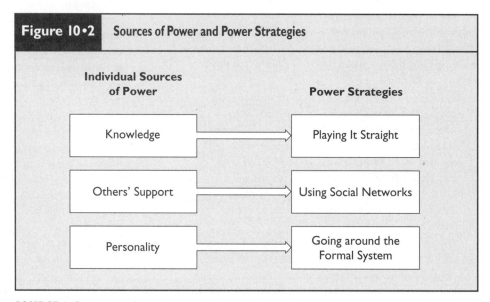

Figure 10•2   **Sources of Power and Power Strategies**

SOURCE: L. Greiner and V. Schein, *Power and Organization Development: Mobilizing Power to Implement Change*, page 52. © 1988 by Addison-Wesley Publishing Co., Inc. Reprinted by permission of Addison Wesley Longman.

support changes. They also can identify areas in which they need to enhance their sources of power.

Greiner and Schein, in the first OD book written entirely from a power perspective, identified three key sources of personal power in organizations (in addition to one's formal position): knowledge, personality, and others' support.[30] Knowledge bases of power include having expertise that is valued by others and controlling important information. OD professionals typically gain power through their expertise in organizational change. Personality sources of power can derive from change agents' charisma, reputation, and professional credibility. Charismatic leaders can inspire devotion and enthusiasm for change from subordinates. OD consultants with strong reputations and professional credibility can wield considerable power during organizational change. Others' support can contribute to individual power by providing access to information and resource networks. Others also may use their power on behalf of the change agent. For example, leaders in organizational units undergoing change can call on their informal networks for resources and support, and encourage subordinates to exercise power in support of the change.

Identifying Key Stakeholders

Having assessed their own power bases, change agents can identify powerful individuals and groups with an interest in the changes, such as staff groups, unions, departmental managers, and top-level executives. These key stakeholders can thwart or support change, and it is important to gain broad-based support to minimize the risk that a single interest group will block the changes. Identifying key stakeholders can start with the simple question "Who stands to gain or to lose from the changes?" Once stakeholders are identified, creating a map of their influence may be useful.[31] The map could show relationships among the stakeholders in terms of who influences whom and what the stakes are for each party. This would provide change agents with information about which people and groups need to be influenced to accept and support the changes.

Influencing Stakeholders

This activity involves gaining the support of key stakeholders to motivate a critical mass for change. There are at least three major strategies for using power to influence others in OD: playing it straight, using social networks, and going around the formal system.[32] Figure 10.2 links these strategies to the individual sources of power discussed above.

The strategy of playing it straight is very consistent with an OD perspective, and thus it is the most widely used power strategy in OD. It involves determining the needs of particular stakeholders and presenting information about how the changes can benefit them. This relatively straightforward approach is based on the premise that information and knowledge can persuade people about the need and direction for change. The success of this strategy relies heavily on the change agent's knowledge base. He or she must have the expertise and information to persuade stakeholders that the changes are a logical way to meet their needs. For example, a change agent might present diagnostic data, such as company reports on productivity and absenteeism or surveys of members' perceptions of problems, to generate a felt need for change among specific stakeholders. Other persuasive evidence might include educational material and expert testimony, such as case studies and research reports, demonstrating how organizational changes can address pertinent issues.

The second power strategy, using social networks, is more foreign to OD and includes forming alliances and coalitions with other powerful individuals and groups, dealing directly with key decision makers, and using formal and informal contacts to gain information. In this strategy, change agents attempt to use their social relationships to gain support for changes. As shown in Figure 10.2, they use the individual power base of others' support to gain the resources, commitment, and political momentum needed to implement change. This social networking might include, for example, meeting with other powerful groups and forming alliances to support specific changes. This would likely involve ensuring that the interests of the different parties—labor and management, for example—are considered in the change process. Many union and management quality-of-work-life efforts involve forming such alliances. This strategy also might include using informal contacts to discover key roadblocks to change and to gain access to major decision makers who need to sanction the changes.

The power strategy of going around the formal system is probably least used in OD and involves purposely circumventing organizational structures and procedures to get the changes made. Existing organizational arrangements can be roadblocks to change, and working around the barriers may be more expedient and effective than taking the time and energy to remove them. As shown in Figure 10.2, this strategy relies on a strong personality base of power. The change agent's charisma, reputation, or professional credibility lend legitimacy to going around the system and can reduce the likelihood of negative reprisals. For example, managers with reputations as winners often can bend the rules to implement organizational changes. Their judgment is trusted by those whose support they need to enact the changes. This power strategy is relatively easy to abuse, however, and OD practitioners should consider carefully the ethical issues and possible unintended consequences of circumventing formal policies and practices.

Application 10.3 shows how one manager used the personal power bases of expertise and reputation to form social networks with key stakeholders and gained support for a statewide change in the public schools.[33]

MANAGING THE TRANSITION

Implementing organizational change involves moving from the existing organization state to the desired future state. Such movement does not occur immediately but, as shown in Figure 10.3, instead requires a transition state during which the organization learns how to implement the conditions needed to reach the desired future. Beckhard and Harris pointed out that the transition state may be quite different from the present state of the organization and consequently may require special management structures and activities.[34] They identified three major activities and

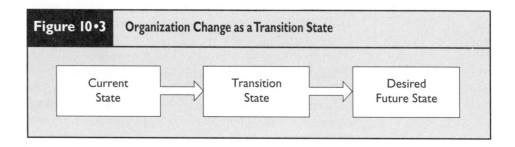

| Figure 10•3 | Organization Change as a Transition State |

Current State → Transition State → Desired Future State

APPLICATION 10·3

Using Social Networks to Implement Change in a Public Education Institution

Tom, the chief administrative officer for a California county office of education, had learned through his seven-year tenure that implementing a technology infrastructure in the public school system was not an easy or smooth process. Many districts and school offices, each with its own county offices of education, had to be coordinated. It was nearly impossible to control at a statewide level and no efforts were being made to streamline an already overly bureaucratic oversight process. To make matters worse, money was being expended on a variety of projects that rarely related to other projects and seldom required an evaluation process upon exhaustion of funding.

In 1998, however, Tom was asked to oversee a statewide initiative to provide technical connectivity to disadvantaged school systems. Children in schools where the parents' average income was lower did not have as many opportunities to work with computers and the Internet. As part of the initiative, he identified a process for implementing the change. Over the years, Tom had developed relationships with high-technology companies from Silicon Valley to deliver technology-based solutions for his local county jurisdiction. He thought about how he might use those relationships to bring Internet connections, hardware, and software to the schools that needed it most.

With the help of schools that chose to apply for aid, Tom and his staff developed partnerships with network engineering and design firms, hardware manufacturers, software developers, Internet service providers (ISPs), application service providers (ASPs), and learning service providers (LSPs). Working together, the parties designed hardware and software packages that bundled quality products and services specifically created for school systems. Through Tom's leadership, a coordination team that specialized in technology tools for schools was launched to offer consulting services to those who wanted to learn how best to move technology into the curriculum.

The technology companies provided products and services to school systems within forty-four of the fifty-eight counties in the state. They learned about educational processes and procedures that were later used to improve the design of their own hardware and software systems. In addition, those companies learned how to serve the specific needs of the public education system market. At the same time, schools began benefiting in financial and practical ways from services designed to meet their needs. In 1999, Tom resigned from his position within the county office of education and became president of a nonprofit organization working to enact the change on a statewide basis. ■

structures to facilitate organizational transition: activity planning, commitment planning, and change-management structures.

Activity Planning

This involves making a road map for change, citing specific activities and events that must occur if the transition is to be successful. Activity planning should clearly identify, temporally orient, and integrate discrete change tasks and should link these tasks to the organization's change goals and priorities. Activity planning also should gain top-management approval, be cost effective, and remain adaptable as feedback is received during the change process.

An important feature of activity planning is that visions and desired future states can be quite general when compared with the realities of implementing change. As a result, it may be necessary to supplement them with midpoint goals as part of the activity plan.[35] Such goals represent desirable organizational conditions between the current state and the desired future state. For example, if the organization is implementing continuous improvement processes, an important midpoint goal can be the establishment of a certain number of improvement teams focused on understanding and controlling key work processes. Midpoint goals are clearer and more detailed than desired future states, and thus they provide more concrete and manageable steps and benchmarks for change. Activity plans can use midpoint goals to provide members with the direction and security they need to work toward the desired future.

Commitment Planning

This activity involves identifying key people and groups whose commitment is needed for change to occur and formulating a strategy for gaining their support. Although commitment planning is generally a part of developing political support, discussed above, specific plans for identifying key stakeholders and obtaining their commitment to change need to be made early in the change process.

Change-Management Structures

Because organizational transitions tend to be ambiguous and to need direction, special structures for managing the change process need to be created. These management structures should include people who have the power to mobilize resources to promote change, the respect of the existing leadership and change advocates, and the interpersonal and political skills to guide the change process. Alternative management structures include the following:[36]

- The chief executive or head person manages the change effort.
- A project manager temporarily is assigned to coordinate the transition.
- The formal organization manages the change effort in addition to supervising normal operations.
- Representatives of the major constituencies involved in the change jointly manage the project.
- Natural leaders who have the confidence and trust of large numbers of affected employees are selected to manage the transition.
- A cross section of people representing different organizational functions and levels manages the change.
- A "kitchen cabinet" representing people whom the chief executive consults with and confides in manages the change effort.

Application 10.4 shows how the St. Anthony Hospital System used a set of committees to manage the implementation of total quality management, charging them to promote and oversee the changes.

SUSTAINING MOMENTUM

Once organizational changes are under way, explicit attention must be directed to sustaining energy and commitment for implementing them. The initial excitement and activity of changing often dissipate in the face of practical problems of trying to learn new ways of operating. A strong tendency exists among organization members to return to what is learned and well known unless they receive sustained support and reinforcement for carrying the changes through to completion. In this section, we present approaches for sustaining momentum for change. The subsequent tasks of assessing and stabilizing changes are discussed in Chapter 11. The following five activities can help to sustain momentum for carrying change through to completion: providing resources for change, building a support system for change agents, developing new competencies and skills, reinforcing new behaviors, and staying the course.

APPLICATION 10·4   Transition Management at St. Anthony Hospital System

The management team at St. Anthony's, a two-hospital system in the midwestern United States, decided to implement a total quality management system. The decision was in response to difficulties in retaining physicians and insurance contracts because of deteriorating clinical quality and patient care. The hospitals also were preparing for reaccreditation by the Joint Commission on Accreditation of Healthcare Organizations and were aware of the commission's increased emphasis on quality measurement. In collaboration with an external OD practitioner, the hospitals recognized that the change could not be implemented overnight and that TQM effort represented a major transition in the hospital's culture and operating procedures.

To facilitate the process, a long-term change plan was developed to gain the appropriate level of knowledge and commitment to implement the desired changes. It called for the establishment of a steering committee that would oversee the efforts of two "executive quality councils" (EQCs). The steering committee would be responsible primarily for reviewing organizational policies that might impact program implementation and for interfacing with the corporate office regarding TQM implementation. The EQCs would be responsible mainly for the day-to-day decisions governing TQM implementation at their respective hospitals. These

councils either would disappear after implementation or would become the formal operating structure governing the organization.

The change plan also called for members of the steering committee and the EQCs to be educated over a six- to nine-month period regarding the definition and implementation of TQM. The steering committee and the EQCs would be responsible for diagnosing each hospital's strengths and weaknesses, developing a communication plan to inform the staff about the changes, and creating new information and control systems to monitor the results of quality-improvement projects. The councils also would be responsible for establishing quality-improvement teams, monitoring their efforts, and rewarding and recognizing quality improvements.

The selection of steering committee and EQC members was given special attention. The steering committee comprised the top medical staff, key members of the corporate organization, and the senior administrators from both hospitals. The EQCs were made up of the senior hospital managers, local physicians, appropriate representatives from the corporate office, and midlevel hospital managers. These memberships ensured that all important stakeholders were represented and given a voice in the design and implementation of the TQM effort. ■

Providing Resources for Change

Implementing organization change generally requires additional financial and human resources, particularly if the organization continues day-to-day operations while trying to change itself. These extra resources are needed for such change activities as training, consultation, data collection and feedback, and special meetings. Extra resources also are helpful to provide a buffer as performance drops during the transition period. Organizations can underestimate seriously the need for special resources devoted to the change process. Significant organizational change invariably requires considerable management time and energy, as well as the help of consultants. A separate "change budget" that exists along with capital and operating budgets can earmark the resources needed for training members in how to behave differently and for assessing progress and making necessary modifications in the change program.[37] Unless these extra resources are planned for and provided, meaningful change is less likely to occur.

Building a Support System for Change Agents

Organization change can be difficult and filled with tension, not only for participants but for change agents as well.[38] They often must give members emotional support, but they may receive little support themselves. They often must maintain "psychological distance" from others to gain the perspective needed to lead the change process. This separation can produce considerable tension and isolation, and change agents may need to create their own support system to help them cope with such problems. A support system typically consists of a network of people with whom the change agent has close personal relationships—people who can give emotional support, serve as a sounding board for ideas and problems, and challenge untested assumptions. For example, OD professionals often use trusted colleagues as "shadow consultants" to help them think through difficult issues with clients and to offer conceptual and emotional support. Similarly, a growing number of companies, such as Intel, Procter & Gamble, BHP-Copper, TRW, and Texas Instruments, are forming internal networks of change agents to provide mutual learning and support.

Developing New Competencies and Skills

Organizational changes frequently demand new knowledge, skills, and behaviors from organization members. In many cases, the changes cannot be implemented unless members gain new competencies. For example, employee-involvement programs often require managers to learn new leadership styles and new approaches to problem solving. Change agents must ensure that such learning occurs. They need to provide multiple learning opportunities, such as traditional training programs, on-the-job counseling and coaching, and experiential simulations, covering both technical and social skills. Because it is easy to overlook the social component, change agents may need to devote special time and resources to helping members gain the social skills needed to implement changes. Ford's new CEO, Jacques Nasser, is supporting the organization's efforts to increase the speed of decision making through a concerted emphasis on "teaching." Through small-group discussions of strategy, providing all employees with a computer, assignments to develop new ideas, and 360-degree feedback, Ford managers are learning new skills and a new mindset to support the organization's need for faster decision making.[39]

Reinforcing New Behaviors

In organizations, people generally do those things that bring them rewards. Consequently, one of the most effective ways to sustain momentum for change is to reinforce the kinds of behaviors needed to implement the changes. This can be accomplished by linking formal rewards directly to the desired behaviors. For example, Integra Financial encouraged more teamwork by designing a rewards and recognition program in which the best team players got both financial rewards and management attention, and a variety of behaviors aimed at promoting self-interest were directly discouraged.[40] (Chapter 17 discusses several reward-system interventions.) In addition, desired behaviors can be reinforced more frequently through informal recognition, encouragement, and praise. Perhaps equally important are the intrinsic rewards that people can experience through early success in the change effort. Achieving identifiable early successes can make participants feel good about themselves and their behaviors, and thus reinforce the drive to change.

Staying the Course

Change requires time, and many of the expected financial and organizational benefits from change lag behind its implementation. If the organization changes again too quickly or abandons the change before it is fully implemented, the desired results may never materialize. There are two primary reasons that managers do not

APPLICATION 10•5   Sustaining Momentum for Change at Eastern Occupational Center

Eastern Occupational Center provides occupational training for students and adults located within two unified school districts. Eastern employs a large number of full- and part-time faculty members who teach courses in such areas as welding, typing, food service, child care, and automotive repair. Several administrative departments provide management and support services to the faculty, and the heads of those departments report to the director of the center.

In 1987, the director contacted an external OD consultant for help in solving a recurrent problem between members of the faculty and members of the administrative departments. The symptoms included a great deal of conflict and disagreement. The faculty complained that the administrators changed rules and procedures too quickly and often failed to follow through on promises for more support. The members of the administrative departments, on the other hand, complained that the teachers were late in filling out important reports and often were unrealistic in asking for resources. Both sides showed a strong willingness to resolve the issues.

After initial contracting with the director and the department heads, the consultant gathered diagnostic data mainly through interviewing members from the administrative and teacher groups. The data were fed back to the director and

department heads, who spent time analyzing them and developing a number of solutions to the intergroup conflict. Some of the solutions were relatively simple, such as improving the layout of reports, but others required major changes in how members related to one another and how managers led their departments. The director and department heads realized that implementing these behavioral changes would require considerable training and skill development, and they consequently budgeted extra funds for such activities.

Over the next six months, the consultant led a number of training sessions for the administrators and faculty, emphasizing skill development in active listening, communication, conflict resolution, and problem solving. The center's director and department heads supplemented the training with goal-setting and performance-appraisal activities aimed at identifying and assessing the new behaviors being learned. These activities helped reinforce the new skills and behaviors. By making the behaviors part of the goals and performance appraisal, change agents motivated members to learn how to perform them. The new behaviors contributed much to improving relationships between the administrators and the teachers. ■

keep a steady focus on change implementation. First, many managers fail to anticipate the decline in performance, productivity, or satisfaction as change is implemented. Organization members need time to practice, develop, and learn new behaviors; they do not abandon old ways of doing things and adopt a new set of behaviors overnight. Moreover, change activities, such as training, extra meetings, and consulting assistance, are extra expenses added onto current operating expenditures. There should be little surprise, therefore, that effectiveness declines before it gets better. However, perfectly good change projects often are abandoned when questions are raised about short-term performance declines. Patience and trust in the diagnosis and intervention design work are necessary.

Second, many managers do not keep focused on a change because they want to implement the next big idea that comes along. When organizations change before they have to in response to the latest management fad, a "flavor-of-the-month" cynicism can develop. As a result, organization members provide only token support to a change under the (accurate) notion that the current change won't last. Successful organizational change requires persistent leadership that does not waiver unnecessarily.

Application 10.5 describes how one organization, the Eastern Occupational Center, sustained momentum for change by providing members with the new skills needed to enact the changes and by reinforcing the new behaviors through goal setting and performance appraisal.

SUMMARY

In this chapter, we described five kinds of activities that change agents must carry out when planning and implementing changes. The first activity is motivating change, which involves creating a readiness for change among organization members and overcoming their resistance. The second activity concerns creating a vision that builds on an organization's core ideology. It describes an envisioned future that includes a bold and valued outcome and a vividly described desired future state. The core ideology and envisioned future articulate a compelling reason for implementing change. The third task for change agents is developing political support for the changes. Change agents first must assess their own sources of power, then identify key stakeholders whose support is needed for change and devise strategies for gaining their support. The fourth activity concerns managing the transition of the organization from its current state to the desired future state. This requires planning a road map for the change activities, as well as planning how to gain commitment for the changes. It also may involve creating special change-management structures. The fifth change task is sustaining momentum for the changes so that they are carried to completion. This includes providing resources for the change program, creating a support system for change agents, developing new competencies and skills, reinforcing the new behaviors required to implement the changes, and staying the course.

NOTES

1. J. Kotter and L. Schlesinger, "Choosing Strategies for Change," *Harvard Business Review* 57 (1979): 106–14; R. Ricardo, "Overcoming Resistance to Change," *National Productivity Review* 14 (1995): 28–39; A. Armenakis, S. Harris, and K. Mossholder, "Creating Readiness for Organizational Change," *Human Relations* 46 (1993): 681–704.

2. E. Dent and S. Goldberg, "Challenging 'Resistance to Change,'" *Journal of Applied Behavioral Science* 35 (March 1999): 25; M. Weisbord, *Productive Workplaces* (San Francisco: Jossey-Bass, 1987); R. Beckhard and R. Harris, *Organizational Transitions: Managing Complex Change*, 2d ed. (Reading, Mass.: Addison-Wesley, 1987); R. Beckhard and W. Pritchard, *Changing the Essence* (San Francisco: Jossey-Bass, 1991); J. Collins and J. Porras, *Built to Last* (New York: Harper Business, 1994); J. Conger, G. Spreitzer, and E. Lawler, *The Leader's Change Handbook* (San Francisco: Jossey-Bass, 1999).

3. Conger, Spreitzer, and Lawler, *Change Handbook*.

4. N. Tichy and M. Devanna, *The Transformational Leader* (New York: John Wiley & Sons, 1986); Armenakis, Harris, and Mossholder, "Creating Readiness."

5. R. Cosier and C. Schwenk, "Agreement and Thinking Alike: Ingredients for Poor Decisions," *Academy of Management Executive* 4 (1990): 69–74.

6. S. Walleck, D. O'Halloran, and C. Leader, "Benchmarking World-Class Performance," *McKinsey Quarterly* 1 (1991).

7. W. Burke, *Organization Development: A Normative View* (Reading, Mass.: Addison-Wesley, 1987); Collins and Porras, *Built to Last*.

8. R. Charan and G. Colvin, "Why CEOs Fail," *Fortune* (21 June 1999): 69–78.

9. D. Eden, "OD and Self-Fulfilling Prophesy: Boosting Productivity by Raising Expectations," *Journal of Applied Behavioral Science* 22 (1986): 1–13; D. Cooperrider, "Positive Image, Positive Action: The Affirmative Basis of Organizing," in *Appreciative Management and Leadership: The Power of Positive Thought and Actions in Organizations*, eds., S. Srivastva, D. Cooperrider, and associates (San Francisco: Jossey-Bass, 1990).

10. Eden, "OD and Self-Fulfilling Prophesy," p. 8.

11. Kotter and Schlesinger, "Choosing Strategies"; P. Block, *Flawless Consulting: A Guide to Getting Your Expertise Used* (Austin, Tex.: Learning Concepts, 1981); P. Strebel, "Why Do Employees Resist Change?" *Harvard Business Review* (May-June 1996): 86–93.

12. N. Tichy, "Revolutionize Your Company," *Fortune* (13 December 1993): 114–18.

13. D. Kirkpatrick, ed., *How to Manage Change Effectively* (San Francisco: Jossey-Bass, 1985).

14. V. Vroom and P. Yetton, *Leadership and Decision Making* (Pittsburgh: University of Pittsburgh Press, 1973).

15. T. Cummings and E. Molloy, *Improving Productivity and the Quality of Work Life* (New York: Praeger, 1977).

16. R. Stayer, "How I Learned to Let My Workers Lead," *Harvard Business Review* (November-December 1990): 66–83; J. Byrne, "Management Meccas," *Business Week* (18 September 1995).

17. Collins and Porras, *Built to Last;* T. Stewart, "A Refreshing Change: Vision Statements That Make Sense," *Fortune* (30 September 1996): 195–96; T. Stewart, "Why Value Statements Don't Work," *Fortune* (10 June 1996): 137–38.

18. P. Senge, *The Fifth Discipline* (New York: Doubleday, 1990).

19. Collins and Porras, *Built to Last.*

20. J. Kotter, *Leading Change* (Boston: Harvard Business School Press, 1994); W. Bennis and B. Nanus, *Leadership* (New York: Harper & Row, 1985); J. O'Toole, *Leading Change: Overcoming the Ideology of Comfort and the Tyranny of Custom* (San Francisco: Jossey-Bass, 1995); F. Hesselbein, M. Goldsmith, R. Beckhard, eds., *The Leader of the Future* (San Francisco: Jossey-Bass, 1995).

21. Tichy and Devanna, *Transformational Leader.*

22. Collins and Porras, *Built to Last.*

23. T. Stewart, "Company Values That Add Value," *Fortune* (8 July 1996): 145–47; J. Pearce II and F. David, "Corporate Mission Statements: The Bottom Line," *Academy of Management Executive* 1 (1987): 109–15.

24. Collins and Porras, *Built to Last.*

25. D. Roth, "The Value of Vision," *Fortune* (24 May 1999): 285–88; J. Novack, "Database Evangelist," *Forbes* (7 September 1998): 66; a variety of information, including data from the annual report, was utilized from the company's website: http://www.microstrategy.com.

26. J. Pfeffer, *Power in Organizations* (New York: Pitman, 1982).

27. D. Nadler, "The Effective Management of Change," in *Handbook of Organizational Behavior,* ed. J. Lorsch (Englewood Cliffs, N.J.: Prentice Hall, 1987): 358–69.

28. C. Alderfer, "Organization Development," *Annual Review of Psychology* 28 (1977): 197–223.

29. T. Bateman, "Organizational Change and the Politics of Success," *Group and Organization Studies* 5 (June 1980): 198–209; A. Cobb and N. Margulies, "Organization Development: A Political Perspective," *Academy of Management Review* 6 (1981): 49–59; A. Cobb, "Political Diagnosis: Applications in Organization Development," *Academy of Management Review* 11 (1986): 482–96; L. Greiner and V. Schein, *Power and Organization Development: Mobilizing Power to Implement Change* (Reading, Mass.: Addison-Wesley, 1988); D. Buchanan and R. Badham, "Politics and Organizational Change: The Lived Experience," *Human Relations* 52 (1999): 609–11.

30. Greiner and Schein, *Power and Organization Development.*

31. Nadler, "Effective Management"; Beckhard and Pritchard, *Changing the Essence.*

32. Greiner and Schein, *Power and Organization Development.*

33. Christine Mattos wrote and contributed this application.

34. Beckhard and Harris, *Organizational Transitions.*

35. Ibid.

36. Ibid.

37. C. Worley, D. Hitchin, and W. Ross, *Integrated Strategic Change: How OD Helps to Build Competitive Advantage* (Reading, Mass.: Addison-Wesley, 1996).

38. M. Beer, *Organization Change and Development: A Systems View* (Santa Monica, Calif.: Goodyear, 1980).

39. S. Wetlaufer, "Driving Change: An Interview with Ford Motor Company's Jacques Nasser," *Harvard Business Review* (March-April 1999): 76–88.

40. A. Fisher, "Making Change Stick," *Fortune* (17 April 1995): 121–31.

11

Evaluating and Institutionalizing Organization Development Interventions

This chapter focuses on the final stage of the organization development cycle—evaluation and institutionalization. *Evaluation* is concerned with providing feedback to practitioners and organization members about the progress and impact of interventions. Such information may suggest the need for further diagnosis and modification of the change program, or it may show that the intervention is successful. *Institutionalization* involves making a particular change a permanent part of the organization's normal functioning. It ensures that the results of successful change programs persist over time.

Evaluation processes consider both the implementation success of the intended intervention and the long-term results it produces. Two key aspects of effective evaluation are measurement and research design. The institutionalization or long-term persistence of intervention effects is examined in a framework showing the organization characteristics, intervention dimensions, and processes contributing to institutionalization of OD interventions in organizations.

EVALUATING ORGANIZATION DEVELOPMENT INTERVENTIONS

Assessing organization development interventions involves judgments about whether an intervention has been implemented as intended and, if so, whether it is having desired results. Managers investing resources in OD efforts increasingly are being held accountable for results—being asked to justify the expenditures in terms of hard, bottom-line outcomes. More and more, managers are asking for rigorous assessment of OD interventions and are using the results to make important resource allocation decisions about OD, such as whether to continue to support the change program, to modify or alter it, or to terminate it and try something else.

Traditionally, OD evaluation has been discussed as something that occurs *after* the intervention. Chapters 12 through 20, for example, present evaluative research about the interventions after discussions of the respective change programs. That view can be misleading, however. Decisions about the measurement of relevant variables and the design of the evaluation process should be made early in the OD cycle so that evaluation choices can be integrated with intervention decisions.

There are two distinct types of OD evaluation—one intended to guide the implementation of interventions and another to assess their overall impact. The key issues in evaluation are measurement and research design.

Implementation and Evaluation Feedback

Most discussions and applications of OD evaluation imply that evaluation is something done after intervention. It is typically argued that once the intervention is implemented, it should be evaluated to discover whether it is producing intended effects. For example, it might be expected that a job enrichment program would lead to higher employee satisfaction and performance. After implementing job enrichment, evaluation would involve assessing whether these positive results indeed did occur.

This after-implementation view of evaluation is only partially correct. It assumes that interventions have been implemented as intended and that the key purpose of evaluation is to assess their effects. In many, if not most, organization development programs, however, implementing interventions cannot be taken for granted.[1] Most OD interventions require significant changes in people's behaviors and ways of thinking about organizations, but they typically offer only broad prescriptions for how such changes are to occur. For example, job enrichment (see Chapter 16) calls for adding discretion, variety, and meaningful feedback to people's jobs. Implementing such changes requires considerable learning and experimentation as employees and managers discover how to translate these general prescriptions into specific behaviors and procedures. This learning process involves much trial and error and needs to be guided by information about whether behaviors and procedures are being changed as intended.[2] Consequently, we should expand our view of evaluation to include both *during-implementation* assessment of whether interventions are actually being implemented and *after-implementation* evaluation of whether they are producing expected results.

Both kinds of evaluation provide organization members with feedback about interventions. Evaluation aimed at guiding implementation may be called *implementation feedback,* and assessment intended to discover intervention outcomes may be called *evaluation feedback.*[3] Figure 11.1 shows how the two kinds of feedback fit with the diagnostic and intervention stages of OD. The application of OD to a particular organization starts with a thorough diagnosis of the situation (Chapters 5 through 8), which helps identify particular organizational problems or areas for improvement, as well as likely causes underlying them. Next, from an array of possible interventions (Chapters 12 through 20), one or some set is chosen as a means

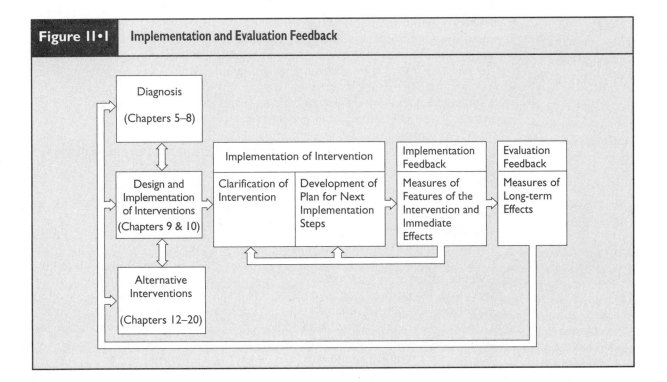

Figure 11•1   Implementation and Evaluation Feedback

of improving the organization. The choice is based on knowledge linking interventions to diagnosis (Chapter 9) and change management (Chapter 10).

In most cases, the chosen intervention provides only general guidelines for organizational change, leaving managers and employees with the task of translating those guidelines into specific behaviors and procedures. Implementation feedback informs this process by supplying data about the different features of the intervention itself and data about the immediate effects of the intervention. These data, collected repeatedly and at short intervals, provide a series of snapshots about how the intervention is progressing. Organization members can use this information, first, to gain a clearer understanding of the intervention (the kinds of behaviors and procedures required to implement it) and, second, to plan for the next implementation steps. This feedback cycle might proceed for several rounds, with each round providing members with knowledge about the intervention and ideas for the next stage of implementation.

Once implementation feedback informs organization members that the intervention is sufficiently in place, evaluation feedback begins. In contrast to implementation feedback, it is concerned with the overall impact of the intervention and with whether resources should continue to be allocated to it or to other possible interventions. Evaluation feedback takes longer to gather and interpret than does implementation feedback. It typically includes a broad array of outcome measures, such as performance, job satisfaction, absenteeism, and turnover. Negative results on these measures tell members either that the initial diagnosis was seriously flawed or that the wrong intervention was chosen. Such feedback might prompt additional diagnosis and a search for a more effective intervention. Positive results, on the other hand, tell members that the intervention produced expected outcomes and might prompt a search for ways to institutionalize the changes, making them a permanent part of the organization's normal functioning.

An example of a job enrichment intervention helps to clarify the OD stages and feedback linkages shown in Figure 11.1. Suppose the initial diagnosis reveals that employee performance and satisfaction are low and that jobs being overly structured and routinized is an underlying cause of this problem. An inspection of alternative interventions to improve productivity and satisfaction suggests that job enrichment might be applicable for this situation. Existing job enrichment theory proposes that increasing employee discretion, task variety, and feedback can lead to improvements in work quality and attitudes and that this job design and outcome linkage is especially strong for employees who have growth needs—needs for challenge, autonomy, and development. Initial diagnosis suggests that most of the employees have high growth needs and that the existing job designs prevent the fulfillment of these needs. Therefore, job enrichment seems particularly suited to this situation.

Managers and employees now start to translate the general prescriptions offered by job enrichment theory into specific behaviors and procedures. At this stage, the intervention is relatively broad and must be tailored to fit the specific situation. To implement the intervention, employees might decide on the following organizational changes: job discretion can be increased through more participatory styles of supervision; task variety can be enhanced by allowing employees to inspect their job outputs; and feedback can be made more meaningful by providing employees with quicker and more specific information about their performances.

After three months of trying to implement these changes, the members use implementation feedback to see how the intervention is progressing. Questionnaires and interviews (similar to those used in diagnosis) are administered to measure the different features of job enrichment (discretion, variety, and feedback) and to assess employees' reactions to the changes. Company records are analyzed to show the short-term effects on productivity of the intervention. The data reveal that productivity and satisfaction have changed very little since the initial diagnosis. Employee perceptions of job discretion and feedback also have shown negligible change, but perceptions of task variety have shown significant improvement. In-depth discussion and analysis of this first round of implementation feedback help supervisors gain a better feel for the kinds of behaviors needed to move toward a participatory leadership style. This greater clarification of one feature of the intervention leads to a decision to involve the supervisors in leadership training to develop the skills and knowledge needed to lead participatively. A decision also is made to make job feedback more meaningful by translating such data into simple bar graphs, rather than continuing to provide voluminous statistical reports.

After these modifications have been in effect for about three months, members institute a second round of implementation feedback to see how the intervention is progressing. The data now show that productivity and satisfaction have moved moderately higher than in the first round of feedback and that employee perceptions of task variety and feedback are both high. Employee perceptions of discretion, however, remain relatively low. Members conclude that the variety and feedback dimensions of job enrichment are sufficiently implemented but that the discretion component needs improvement. They decide to put more effort into supervisory training and to ask OD practitioners to provide online counseling and coaching to supervisors about their leadership styles.

After four more months, a third round of implementation feedback occurs. The data now show that satisfaction and performance are significantly higher than in the first round of feedback and moderately higher than in the second round. The data also show that discretion, variety, and feedback are all high, suggesting that the job enrichment intervention has been successfully implemented. Now evaluation feedback is used to assess the overall effectiveness of the program.

The evaluation feedback includes all the data from the satisfaction and performance measures used in the implementation feedback. Because both the immediate and broader effects of the intervention are being evaluated, additional outcomes are examined, such as employee absenteeism, maintenance costs, and reactions of other organizational units not included in job enrichment. The full array of evaluation data might suggest that after one year from the start of implementation, the job enrichment program is having expected effects and thus should be continued and made more permanent.

Measurement

Providing useful implementation and evaluation feedback involves two activities: selecting the appropriate variables and designing good measures.

Selecting Variables

Ideally, the variables measured in OD evaluation should derive from the theory or conceptual model underlying the intervention. The model should incorporate the key features of the intervention as well as its expected results. The general diagnostic models described in Chapters 5 and 6 meet this criteria, as do the more specific models introduced in Chapters 12 through 20. For example, the job-level diagnostic model described in Chapter 6 proposes several major features of work: task variety, feedback, and autonomy. The theory argues that high levels of these elements can be expected to result in high levels of work quality and satisfaction. In addition, as we shall see in Chapter 16, the strength of this relationship varies with the degree of employee growth need: the higher the need, the more that job enrichment produces positive results.

The job-level diagnostic model suggests a number of measurement variables for implementation and evaluation feedback. Whether the intervention is being implemented could be assessed by determining how many job descriptions have been rewritten to include more responsibility or how many organization members have received cross-training in other job skills. Evaluation of the immediate and long-term impact of job enrichment would include measures of employee performance and satisfaction over time. Again, these measures would likely be included in the initial diagnosis, when the company's problems or areas for improvement are discovered.

Measuring both intervention and outcome variables is necessary for implementation and evaluation feedback. Unfortunately, there has been a tendency in OD to measure only outcome variables while neglecting intervention variables altogether.[4] It generally is assumed that the intervention has been implemented, and attention, therefore, is directed to its impact on such organizational outcomes as performance, absenteeism, and satisfaction. As argued earlier, implementing OD interventions generally takes considerable time and learning. It must be empirically determined that the intervention has been implemented; it cannot simply be assumed. Implementation feedback serves this purpose, guiding the implementation process and helping to interpret outcome data. Outcome measures are ambiguous without knowledge of how well the intervention has been implemented. For example, a negligible change in measures of performance and satisfaction could mean that the wrong intervention has been chosen, that the correct intervention has not been implemented effectively, or that the wrong variables have been measured. Measurement of the intervention variables helps determine the correct interpretation of outcome measures.

As suggested above, the choice of intervention variables to measure should derive from the conceptual framework underlying the OD intervention. OD research and theory increasingly have come to identify specific organizational changes needed to implement particular interventions (much of that information is discussed in Chapters 12 through 20). These variables should guide not only implementation of the intervention but also choices about what change variables to measure for evaluative purposes. Additional sources of knowledge about intervention variables can be found in the numerous references at the end of each of the intervention chapters in this book and in several of the books in the Wiley Series on Organizational Assessment and Change.[5]

The choice of what outcome variables to measure also should be dictated by intervention theory, which specifies the kinds of results that can be expected from particular change programs. Again, the material in this book and elsewhere identifies numerous outcome measures, such as job satisfaction, intrinsic motivation, organizational commitment, absenteeism, turnover, and productivity.

Historically, OD assessment has focused on attitudinal outcomes, such as job satisfaction, while neglecting hard measures, such as performance. Increasingly, however, managers and researchers are calling for development of behavioral measures of OD outcomes. Managers are interested primarily in applying OD to change work-related behaviors that involve joining, remaining, and producing at work, and are assessing OD more frequently in terms of such bottom-line results. Macy and Mirvis have done extensive research to develop a standardized set of behavioral outcomes for assessing and comparing intervention results.[6] Table 11.1 lists

Table 11•1	Behavioral Outcomes for Measuring OD Interventions: Definitions and Recording Categories

BEHAVIORAL DEFINITIONS	RECORDING CATEGORIES
Absenteeism: each absence or illness over four hours	*Voluntary:* short-term illness (less than three consecutive days), personal business, family illness *Involuntary:* long-term illness (more than three consecutive days), funerals, out-of-plant accidents, lack of work temporary layoff), presanctioned days off *Leaves:* medical, personal, maternity, military, and other (e.g., jury duty)
Tardiness: each absence or illness under four hours	*Voluntary:* same as absenteeism *Involuntary:* same as absenteeism
Turnover: each movement beyond the organizational boundary	*Voluntary:* resignation *Involuntary:* termination, disqualification, requested resignation, permanent layoff, retirement, disability, death
Internal employment stability: each movement within the organizational boundary	*Internal movement:* transfer, promotion, promotion with transfer *Internal stability:* new hires, layoffs, rehires
Strikes and work stoppages: each day lost as a result of strike or work stoppage	*Sanctioned:* union-authorized strike, company-authorized lockout *Unsanctioned:* work slowdown, walkout, sitdown
Accidents and work-related illness: each recordable injury illness, or death from a work-related accident or from exposure to the work environment	*Major:* OSHA accident, illness, or death which results in medical treatment by a physician or registered professional person under standing orders from a physician *Minor:* non-OSHA accident or illness which results in one-time treatment and subsequent observation not requir-professional care *Revisits:* OSHA and non-OSHA accident or illness which requires subsequent treatment and observation
Grievances: written grievance in accordance with labor–management contract	*Stage:* recorded by step (first through arbitration)
Productivity:* resources used in production of acceptable outputs (comparison of inputs with outputs)	*Output:* product or service quantity (units or $) *Input:* direct and/or indirect (labor in hours or $)
Production quality: resources used in production of unacceptable outputs	*Resource utilized:* scrap (unacceptable in-plant products in units or $); customer returns (unacceptable out-of-plant products in units or $); recoveries (salvageable products in units or $); rework (additional direct and/or indirect labor in hours or $)
Downtime: unscheduled breakdown of machinery	*Downtime:* duration of breakdown (hours or $) *Machine repair:* nonpreventive maintenance ($)
Inventory, material, and supply variance: unscheduled resource utilization	*Variance:* over- or underutilization of supplies, materials, inventory (resulting from theft, inefficiency, and so on)

*Reports only labor inputs.

SOURCE: B. Macy and P. Mirvis, "Organizational Change Efforts: Methodologies for Assessing Organizational Effectiveness and Program Costs Versus Benefits," *Evaluation Review* 6, pp. 306–10. Copyright © 1982 by Sage Publications, Inc. Reprinted by permission of Sage Publications, Inc.

eleven outcomes, including their behavioral definitions and recording categories. The outcomes are in two broad categories: *participation-membership,* including absenteeism, tardiness, turnover, internal employment stability, and strikes and work stoppages; and *performance on the job,* including productivity, quality, grievances, accidents, unscheduled machine downtime and repair, material and supply overuse, and inventory shrinkage. All of the outcomes should be important to most managers, and they represent generic descriptions that can be adapted to both industrial and service organizations.

Designing Good Measures

Each of the measurement methods described in Chapter 7 has advantages and disadvantages. Many of these characteristics are linked to the extent to which a measurement is operationally defined, reliable, and valid. These assessment characteristics are discussed below.

1. *Operational definition.* A good measure is operationally defined; that is, it specifies the empirical data needed, how they will be collected and, most important, how they will be converted from data to information. For example, Macy and Mirvis developed operational definitions for the behavioral outcomes listed in Table 11.1 (see Table 11.2).[7] They consist of specific computational rules that can be used to construct measures for each of the behaviors. Most of the behaviors are reported as rates adjusted for the number of employees in the organization and for the possible incidents of behavior. These adjustments make it possible to compare the measures across different situations and time periods. These operational definitions should have wide applicability across both industrial and service organizations, although some modifications, deletions, and additions may be necessary for a particular application.

   Operational definitions are extremely important in measurement because they provide precise guidelines about what characteristics of the situation are to be observed and how they are to be used. They tell OD practitioners and the client system exactly how diagnostic, intervention, and outcome variables will be measured.

2. *Reliability.* Reliability concerns the extent to which a measure represents the "true" value of a variable; that is, how accurately the operational definition translates data into information. For example, there is little doubt about the accuracy of the number of cars leaving an assembly line as a measure of plant productivity; although it is possible to miscount, there can be a high degree of confidence in the measurement. On the other hand, when people are asked to rate their level of job satisfaction on a scale of 1 to 5, there is considerable room for variation in their response. They may just have had an argument with their supervisor, suffered an accident on the job, been rewarded for high levels of productivity, or been given new responsibilities. Each of these events can sway the response to the question on any given day. The individuals' "true" satisfaction score is difficult to discern from this one question, and the measure lacks reliability.[8]

   OD practitioners can improve the reliability of their measures in four ways. First, rigorously and operationally define the chosen variables. Clearly specified operational definitions contribute to reliability by explicitly describing how collected data will be converted into information about a variable. An explicit description helps to allay the client's concerns about how the information was collected and coded.

Table 11•2	Behavioral Outcomes for Measuring OD Interventions: Measures and Computational Formulae

BEHAVIORAL MEASURE*	COMPUTATIONAL FORMULA
Absenteeism rate** (monthly)	$$\frac{\Sigma \text{ Absence days}}{\text{Average workforce size} \times \text{Working days}}$$
Tardiness rate** (monthly)	$$\frac{\Sigma \text{ Tardiness incidents}}{\text{Average workforce size} \times \text{Working days}}$$
Turnover rate (monthly)	$$\frac{\Sigma \text{ Turnover incidents}}{\text{Average workforce size}}$$
Internal stability rate (monthly)	$$\frac{\Sigma \text{ Internal movement incidents}}{\text{Average workforce size}}$$
Strike rate (yearly)	$$\frac{\Sigma \text{ Striking Workers} \times \text{Strike days}}{\text{Average workforce size} \times \text{Working days}}$$
Accident rate (yearly)	$$\frac{\Sigma \text{ of Accidents, illnesses}}{\text{Total yearly hours worked}} \times 200{,}000***$$
Grievance rate (yearly)	Plant: $$\frac{\Sigma \text{ Grievance incidents}}{\text{Average workforce size}}$$ Individual: $$\frac{\Sigma \text{ Aggrieved individuals}}{\text{Average workforce size}}$$
Productivity:****	$$\frac{\text{Output of goods or services (units or \$)}}{\text{Direct and/or indirect labor (hours or \$)}}$$
Total	
Below standard	Actual versus engineered standard
Below budget	Actual versus budgeted standard
Variance	Actual versus budgeted variance
Per employee	Output/average workforce size
Quality:****	
Total	Scrap + Customer returns + Rework − Recoveries ($, units, or hours)
Below standard	Actual versus engineered standard
Below budget	Actual versus budgeted standard
Variance	Actual versus budgeted variance
Per employee	Total/average workforce size
Downtime	Labor ($) + Repair costs or dollar value of replaced equipment ($)
Inventory, supply, and material usage	Variance (actual versus standard utilization) ($)

*All measures reflect the number of incidents divided by an exposure factor that represents the number of employees in the organization and the possible incidents of behavior (e.g., for absenteeism, the average workforce size × the number of working days). Mean monthly rates (i.e., absences per workday) are computed and averaged for absenteeism, leaves, and tardiness for a yearly figure and summed for turnover, grievances, and internal employment stability for a yearly figure. The term *rate* refers to the number of incidents per unit of employee exposure to the risk of such incidences during the analysis interval.

**Sometimes combined as number of hours missing/average workforce size × working days.

***Base for 100 full-time equivalent workers (40 hours × 50 weeks).

****Monetary valuations can be expressed in labor dollars, actual dollar costs, sales dollars; overtime dollar valuations can be adjusted to base year dollars to control for salary, raw material, and price increases.

SOURCE: B. Macy and P. Mirvis, "Organizational Change Efforts: Methodologies for Assessing Organizational Effectiveness and Program Costs Versus Benefits," *Evaluation Review* 6, pp. 306–10. Copyright © 1982 by Sage Publications, Inc. Reprinted by permission of Sage Publications, Inc.

Second, use multiple methods to measure a particular variable. As discussed in Chapter 7, the use of questionnaires, interviews, observations, and unobtrusive measures can improve reliability and result in more comprehensive understanding of the organization. Because each method contains inherent biases, several different methods can be used to triangulate on dimensions of organizational problems. If the independent measures converge or show consistent results, the dimensions or problems likely have been diagnosed accurately.[9]

Third, use multiple items to measure the same variable on a questionnaire. For example, in Hackman and Oldham's Job Diagnostic Survey for measuring job characteristics (Chapter 16), the intervention variable "autonomy" has the following operational definition: the average of respondents' answers to the following three questions (measured on a seven-point scale):[10]

1. The job permits me to decide *on my own* how to go about doing the work.

2. The job denies me any chance to use my personal initiative or judgment in carrying out the work. (reverse scored)

3. The job gives me considerable opportunity for independence and freedom in how I do the work.

By asking more than one question about "autonomy," the survey increases the accuracy of its measurement of this variable. Statistical analyses (called *psychometric tests*) are readily available for assessing the reliability of perceptual measures, and OD practitioners should apply these methods or seek assistance from those who can apply them.[11] Similarly, there are methods for analyzing the content of interview and observational data, and OD evaluators can use these methods to categorize such information so that it can be understood and replicated.[12]

Fourth, use standardized instruments. A growing number of standardized questionnaires are available for measuring OD intervention and outcome variables. For example, the Center for Effective Organizations at the University of Southern California (http://www.marshall.usc.edu/ceo) and the Institute for Social Research at the University of Michigan (http://www.isr.umich.edu) have developed comprehensive survey instruments to measure the features of many of the OD interventions described in this book, as well as their attitudinal outcomes.[13] Considerable research and testing have gone into establishing measures that are reliable and valid. These survey instruments can be used for initial diagnosis, for guiding implementation of interventions, and for evaluating immediate and long-term outcomes.

3. *Validity.* Validity concerns the extent to which a measure actually reflects the variable it is intended to reflect. For example, the number of cars leaving an assembly line might be a reliable measure of plant productivity, but it may not be a valid measure. The number of cars is only one aspect of productivity; they may have been produced at an unacceptably high cost. Because the number of cars does not account for cost, it is not a completely valid measure of plant productivity.

OD practitioners can increase the validity of their measures in several ways. First, ask colleagues and clients if a proposed measure actually represents a particular variable. This is called *face validity* or *content validity.* If experts and clients agree that the measure reflects the variable of interest, then there is increased confidence in the measure's validity. Second, use multiple measures of the same variable, as described in the section about reliability, to make preliminary assessments of the measure's *criterion* or *convergent validity*. That is, if several different measures of the same variable correlate highly with each other, especially if one or more of the other measures has been validated in prior research, then there is increased confidence in the measure's validity. A special case of criterion validity, called *discriminant validity*, exists when the proposed measure does not correlate with measures that it is not supposed to correlate with. For example, there is no good reason for daily measures of assembly-line productivity to correlate with daily air temperature. The lack of a correlation would be one indicator that the number of cars is measuring productivity and not some other variable. Finally, *predictive validity* is demonstrated when the variable of interest accurately forecasts another variable over time. For example, a measure of team cohesion can be said to be valid if it accurately predicts improvements in team performance in the future.

It is difficult, however, to establish the validity of a measure until it has been used. To address this concern, OD practitioners should make heavy use of content validity processes and use measures that already have been validated. For example, presenting proposed measures to colleagues and clients for evaluation prior to measurement has several positive effects: it builds ownership and commitment to the data-collection process and improves the likelihood that the client system will find the data meaningful. Using measures that have been validated through prior research improves confidence in the results and provides a standard that can be used to validate any new measures used in collecting the data.

Research Design

In addition to measurement, OD practitioners must make choices about how to design the evaluation to achieve valid results. The key issue is how to design the assessment to show whether the intervention did in fact produce the observed results. This is called *internal validity*. The secondary question of whether the intervention would work similarly in other situations is referred to as *external validity*. External validity is irrelevant without first establishing an intervention's primary effectiveness, so internal validity is the essential minimum requirement for assessing OD interventions. Unless managers can have confidence that the outcomes are the result of the intervention, they have no rational basis for making decisions about accountability and resource allocation.

Assessing the internal validity of an intervention is, in effect, testing a hypothesis—namely, that specific organizational changes lead to certain outcomes. Moreover, testing the validity of an intervention hypothesis means that alternative hypotheses or explanations of the results must be rejected. That is, to claim that an intervention is successful, it is necessary to demonstrate that other explanations—in the form of rival hypotheses—do not account for the observed results. For example, if a job enrichment program appears to increase employee performance, such other possible explanations as new technology, improved raw materials, or new employees must be eliminated.

Accounting for rival explanations is not a precise, controlled, experimental process such as might be found in a research laboratory.[14] OD interventions often have a number of features that make determining whether they produced observed results difficult. They are complex and often involve several interrelated changes that obscure whether individual features or combinations of features are accounting for the results. Many OD interventions are long-term projects and take considerable time to produce desired outcomes. The longer the time period of the change program, the greater are the chances that other factors, such as technology improvements, will emerge to affect the results. Finally, OD interventions almost always are applied to existing work units rather than to randomized groups of organization members. Ruling out alternative explanations associated with randomly selected intervention and comparison groups is, therefore, difficult.

Given the problems inherent in assessing OD interventions, practitioners have turned to *quasi-experimental research designs*.[15] These designs are not as rigorous and controlled as are randomized experimental designs, but they allow evaluators to rule out many rival explanations for OD results other than the intervention itself. Although several quasi-experimental designs are available, those with the following three features[16] are particularly powerful for assessing changes:

1. *Longitudinal measurement.* This involves measuring results repeatedly over relatively long time periods. Ideally, the data collection should start before the change program is implemented and continue for a period considered reasonable for producing expected results.

2. *Comparison unit.* It is always desirable to compare results in the intervention situation with those in another situation where no such change has taken place. Although it is never possible to get a matching group identical to the intervention group, most organizations include a number of similar work units that can be used for comparison purposes.

3. *Statistical analysis.* Whenever possible, statistical methods should be used to rule out the possibility that the results are caused by random error or chance. Various statistical techniques are applicable to quasi-experimental designs, and OD practitioners should apply these methods or seek help from those who can apply them.[17]

Table 11.3 provides an example of a quasi-experimental design having these three features. The intervention is intended to reduce employee absenteeism. Measures of absenteeism are taken from company monthly records for both the intervention and comparison groups. The two groups are similar yet geographically separate subsidiaries of a multiplant company. Table 11.3 shows each plant's monthly absenteeism rate for four consecutive months both before and after the start of the intervention. The plant receiving the intervention shows a marked decrease in absenteeism in the months following the intervention, whereas the control plant shows comparable levels of absenteeism in both time periods. Statistical analyses of these data suggest that the abrupt downward shift in absenteeism following the intervention was not attributable to chance variation. This research design and the data provide relatively strong evidence that the intervention was successful.

Table 11•3	Quasi-Experimental Research Design								
	Monthly Absenteeism (%)								
	SEPT.	OCT.	NOV.	DEC.		JAN.	FEB.	MAR.	APR.
Intervention group	5.1	5.3	5.0	5.1	Start of intervention	4.6	4.0	3.9	3.5
Comparison group	2.5	2.6	2.4	2.5		2.6	2.4	2.5	2.5

Quasi-experimental research designs using longitudinal data, comparison groups, and statistical analysis permit reasonable assessments of intervention effectiveness. Repeated measures often can be collected from company records without directly involving members of the experimental and comparison groups. These unobtrusive measures are especially useful in OD assessment because they do not interact with the intervention and affect the results. More obtrusive measures, such as questionnaires and interviews, are reactive and can sensitize people to the intervention. When this happens, it is difficult to know whether the observed findings are the result of the intervention, the measuring methods, or some combination of both.

Multiple measures of intervention and outcome variables should be applied to minimize measurement and intervention interactions. For example, obtrusive measures such as questionnaires could be used sparingly, perhaps once before and once after the intervention. Unobtrusive measures, such as the behavioral outcomes shown in Tables 11.1 and 11.2, could be used repeatedly, thus providing a more extensive time series than the questionnaires. When used together, the two kinds of measures should produce accurate and nonreactive evaluations of the intervention.

The use of multiple measures also is important in assessing perceptual changes resulting from interventions. Considerable research has identified three types of change—alpha, beta, and gamma—that occur when using self-report, perceptual measures.[18]

Alpha change refers to movement along a measure that reflects stable dimensions of reality. For example, comparative measures of perceived employee discretion might show an increase after a job enrichment program. If this increase represents alpha change, it can be assumed that the job enrichment program actually increased employee perceptions of discretion.

Beta change involves the recalibration of the intervals along some constant measure of reality. For example, before-and-after measures of perceived employee discretion can decrease after a job enrichment program. If beta change is involved, it can explain this apparent failure of the intervention to increase discretion. The first measure of discretion may accurately reflect the individual's belief about the ability to move around and talk to fellow workers in the immediate work area. During implementation of the job enrichment intervention, however, the employee may learn that the ability to move around is not limited to the immediate work area. At a second measurement of discretion, the employee, using this new and recalibrated understanding, may rate the current level of discretion as lower than before.

Gamma change involves fundamentally redefining the measure as a result of an OD intervention. In essence, the framework within which a phenomenon is viewed changes. For example, the presence of gamma change would make it difficult to compare measures of employee discretion taken before and after a job enrichment program. The measure taken after the intervention might use the same words, but they represent an entirely different concept. As described above, the term "discretion" may originally refer to the ability to move about the department and interact with other workers. After the intervention, discretion might be defined in terms of the ability to make decisions about work rules, work schedules, and productivity levels. In sum, the job enrichment intervention changed the way discretion is perceived and how it is evaluated.

These three types of change apply to perceptual measures. When other than alpha changes occur, interpreting measurement changes becomes far more difficult. Potent OD interventions may produce both beta and gamma changes, which severely complicates interpretations of findings reporting change or no change.

Further, the distinctions among the three different types of change suggest that the heavy reliance on questionnaires, so often cited in the literature, should be balanced by using other measures, such as interviews and unobtrusive records. Analytical methods have been developed to assess the three kinds of change, and OD practitioners should gain familiarity with these recent techniques.[19]

Application 11.1 describes the evaluation of a culture change process that involved outdoor experiential training as a key component. It is an example of how one organization used data collected from employees and managers as both implementation and evaluation feedback. The material presented so far in this chapter can be used to assess the evaluation's effectiveness. What are the strengths and weaknesses of the assessment? How could it have been improved? Do you see any evidence of alpha, beta, or gamma change? How much confidence do you have in the recommendations?

INSTITUTIONALIZING INTERVENTIONS

Once it is determined that a change has been implemented and is effective, attention is directed at institutionalizing the changes—making them a permanent part of the organization's normal functioning. Lewin described change as occurring in three stages: unfreezing, moving, and refreezing. Institutionalizing an OD intervention concerns refreezing. It involves the long-term persistence of organizational changes: to the extent that changes persist, they can be said to be institutionalized. Such changes are not dependent on any one person but exist as a part of the culture of an organization. This means that numerous others share norms about the appropriateness of the changes.

How planned changes become institutionalized has not received much attention in the OD literature. Rapidly changing environments have led to admonitions from consultants and practitioners to "change constantly," to "change before you have to," and "if it's not broke, fix it anyway." Such a context has challenged the utility of the institutionalization concept. Why endeavor to make any change permanent given that it may require changing again soon? However, the admonitions also have resulted in institutionalization concepts being applied in new ways. Change itself has become the focus of institutionalization. Total quality management, organization learning, integrated strategic change, and self-design interventions all are aimed at enhancing the organization's capability for change.[20] In this vein, processes of institutionalization take on increased utility. This section presents a framework identifying factors and processes that contribute to the institutionalization of OD interventions, including the process of change itself.

Institutionalization Framework

Figure 11.2 presents a framework that identifies organization and intervention characteristics and institutionalization processes affecting the degree to which change programs are institutionalized.[21] The model shows that two key antecedents—organization and intervention characteristics—affect different institutionalization processes operating in organizations. These processes, in turn, affect various indicators of institutionalization. The model also shows that organization characteristics can influence intervention characteristics. For example, organizations having powerful unions may have trouble gaining internal support for OD interventions.

APPLICATION 11•1   Evaluating the Effect of Outdoor-Based Experience Training on an Organization's Culture

Southern California Edison is a large investor-owned electric utility serving the southern California area. The customer service division (CSD) is responsible for repair and installation of the electric distribution systems, customer billing and collections, and responses to requests for information. CSD employs more than five thousand employees.

In 1991, a strategic change program redefined the mission and purpose of the CSD. The process identified the utility's bureaucratic culture as a key barrier to achieving the organization's goals, and a task force was created to initiate a culture change process. Several consulting firms were asked to make presentations. Among them was a supplier of outdoor experiential training. Rather than using traditional classroom techniques, these methods transfer concepts like problem solving, accountability, group interaction skills, and teamwork through physically challenging exercises. The task force believed that such a nontraditional approach might help organization members think in new ways and thereby support culture change.

In cooperation with this training organization, a change program was designed that put the organization's top six hundred managers through a three-day outdoor experience to introduce and practice key concepts and ideas. Shortly thereafter, a pilot group of frontline employees and supervisors participated in a similar program, and then undertook team projects to address key operational problems. The idea was to get people who had just been in the training to apply their new skills to real organizational issues. Finally, the task force contracted with another outside consultant to evaluate the training's impact on work and performance.

The evaluation consultant interviewed members of the task force and consultants from the training organization to understand the cultural values desired by the strategic change initiative, the intent of the program, and the concepts that would be used by the training organization. Based on these interviews, the consultant worked with the task force members to brainstorm items and questions that might be used in a survey to understand the extent to which these concepts, values, and skills were present or desired. These items were pretested with a small group of managers and employees to assess their reliability. The proposed evaluation design included preexperience interviews and surveys, postexperience interviews and surveys, observation and tracking of the postexperience teams' performance, and collection of work and performance data at the individual level. In addition, a group of managers and employees who did not go through the training was identified as a control group.

As the training program unfolded, interview and survey data were collected and fed back to the task force. The initial data from the early training sessions were used to make adjustments in the content and flow of the three-day experience. In addition, the data pointed out that managers and employees feared that more than training would be necessary to change their behaviors. Between the outdoor experience and a short follow-up workshop, participants reported a significant decline in their belief that project teams would get the support of management. The item about whether they would get the necessary resources remained the lowest-rated item across the two surveys. As a result, the task force was alerted early to the need for supporting changes in the work design, structure, reward system, and senior management's symbolic leadership. Task force members began to share this information with other task forces working in these areas.

After the last group of employees had been through the training, the consultant identified and quantified the benefits of the organizational change project. The following items summarize the consultant's findings:

1. *Intervention design.* The structuring of the culture change process was cause for concern. The training was rated highly (95 percent rated it positive or very positive), but participants noted that although top management went through a similar outdoor experience and could speak the "language" introduced during the sessions, middle managers had been left out. It was difficult to get middle management to approve resources for the problem-solving teams. Nonparticipants reported feeling "left out."

2. *Group functioning.* All participants reported improvements in their work group's functioning and believed that the project teams were functioning well. The survey data supported this observation: 83 percent of respondents believed relationships within groups had improved and 79 percent of the respondents believed relationships among groups had improved. The most highly rated changes in the surveys were the ability to value others, understanding how personal behavior impacts others, and learning to trust others.

3. *Project team performance.* The data from the project teams suggested that all project teams were able to achieve, or were able to demonstrate sufficiently the likelihood of achieving, improved operating performance at their work locations. This was noteworthy given that all of the teams were cross-functional; solving these more complex problems is inherently more difficult and time consuming. Yet within six months of training, the five pilot teams were able to generate more than $60,000 in cost savings at their locations.

Assuming that local best practices could be shared and implemented in other locations allowed a direct corporatewide contribution of more than $1.5 million. These cost-savings estimates were made using generally conservative figures and did not include the savings or advantages associated with improved customer satisfaction or service quality levels. However, other costs were not included, such as the opportunity costs of teams meeting on company time.

In addition, all project teams reported substantial difficulty in meeting their objectives. Barriers included differing time schedules, lack of management support, and finding out that other groups (as part of other corporate change initiatives) were working on the same problem. In the three teams where the cost savings were the highest, the involvement, support, and participation of a manager or supervisor was reported as an important ingredient.

The researcher concluded that the outdoor-based training experience had produced some important results. In particular, expected savings generated by the team would clearly cover the cost of the training, and many participants reported that they were applying what they had learned from the training in their work and in their personal lives. The regional manager was strongly supportive of the effort. He had initiated efforts to address concerns about management support in the middle and lower levels. Finally, the design clearly communicated expectations that the program and the projects should contribute to bottom-line results.

However, the consultant also concluded that significant problems remained. A recent reorganization was limiting the regional manager's ability to drive the local organizations toward an aligned set of policies and structures. In addition, other corporate programs with similar objectives were competing for attention, resources, and time. The consultant recommended that management examine the fit between the organization's design, other organizational changes taking place, and the desired behaviors and attitudes of its employees. In general the workforce was receiving mixed messages about what was important at CSD; such misalignment would likely suppress the long-term impact from any strategic change initiative. The consultant therefore recommended that further funding for the program be suspended unless and until management developed a consistent strategy for supporting not only cultural change but the organizational changes necessary to support it. ■

Organization Characteristics

Figure 11.2 shows that the following three key dimensions of an organization can affect intervention characteristics and institutionalization processes.

1. *Congruence.* This is the degree to which an intervention is perceived as being in harmony with the organization's managerial philosophy, strategy, and structure; its current environment; and other changes taking place.[22] When an intervention is congruent with these dimensions, the probability is improved that it will be institutionalized. Congruence can facilitate persistence by making it easier to gain member commitment to the intervention and to diffuse it to wider segments of the organization. The converse also is true: many OD interventions promote employee participation and growth. When applied in highly bureaucratic organizations with formalized structures and autocratic managerial styles, participative interventions are not perceived as congruent with the organization's managerial philosophy.

2. *Stability of environment and technology.* This involves the degree to which the organization's environment and technology are changing. Unless the change target is buffered from these changes or unless the changes are dealt with directly by the change program, it may be difficult to achieve long-term intervention stability.[23] For example, decreased demand for the firm's products or services can lead to reductions in personnel that may change the composition of the groups involved in the intervention. Conversely, increased product demand can curtail institutionalization by bringing new members on board at a rate faster than they can be socialized effectively.

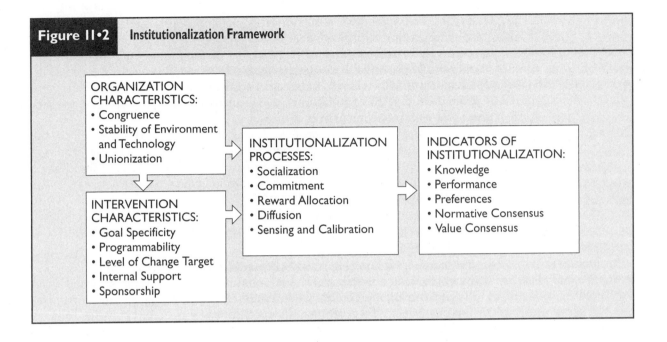

Figure 11·2   Institutionalization Framework

ORGANIZATION CHARACTERISTICS:
- Congruence
- Stability of Environment and Technology
- Unionization

INTERVENTION CHARACTERISTICS:
- Goal Specificity
- Programmability
- Level of Change Target
- Internal Support
- Sponsorship

INSTITUTIONALIZATION PROCESSES:
- Socialization
- Commitment
- Reward Allocation
- Diffusion
- Sensing and Calibration

INDICATORS OF INSTITUTIONALIZATION:
- Knowledge
- Performance
- Preferences
- Normative Consensus
- Value Consensus

3. *Unionization.* Diffusion of interventions may be more difficult in unionized settings, especially if the changes affect union contract issues, such as salary and fringe benefits, job design, and employee flexibility. For example, a rigid union contract can make it difficult to merge several job classifications into one, as might be required to increase task variety in a job enrichment program. It is important to emphasize, however, that unions can be a powerful force for promoting change, particularly when a good relationship exists between union and management.

Intervention Characteristics

Figure 11.2 shows that the following five major features of OD interventions can affect institutionalization processes:

1. *Goal specificity.* This involves the extent to which intervention goals are specific rather than broad. Specificity of goals helps direct socializing activities (for example, training and orienting new members) to particular behaviors required to implement the intervention. It also helps operationalize the new behaviors so that rewards can be linked clearly to them. For example, an intervention aimed only at increasing product quality is likely to be more focused and readily put into operation than a change program intended to improve quality, quantity, safety, absenteeism, and employee development.

2. *Programmability.* This involves the degree to which the changes can be programmed or the extent to which the different intervention characteristics can be specified clearly in advance to enable socialization, commitment, and reward allocation.[24] For example, job enrichment specifies three targets of change: employee discretion, task variety, and feedback. The change program can be planned and designed to promote those specific features.

3. *Level of change target.* This concerns the extent to which the change target is the total organization, rather than a department or small work group. Each

level of organization has facilitators and inhibitors of persistence. Departmental and group change are susceptible to countervailing forces from others in the organization. These can reduce the diffusion of the intervention and lower its ability to impact organization effectiveness. However, this does not preclude institutionalizing the change within a department that successfully insulates itself from the rest of the organization. Such insulation often manifests itself as a subculture within the organization.[25]

Targeting the intervention to wider segments of the organization, on the other hand, also can help or hinder change persistence. A shared belief about the intervention's value can be a powerful incentive to maintain the change, and promoting a consensus across organizational departments exposed to the change can facilitate institutionalization. But targeting the larger system also can inhibit institutionalization. The intervention can become mired in political resistance because of the "not invented here" syndrome or because powerful constituencies oppose it.

4. *Internal support.* This refers to the degree to which there is an internal support system to guide the change process. Internal support, typically provided by an internal consultant, can gain commitment for the changes and help organization members implement them. External consultants also can provide support, especially on a temporary basis during the early stages of implementation. For example, in many interventions aimed at implementing high-involvement organizations (see Chapter 15), both external and internal consultants provide change support. The external consultant typically brings expertise on organizational design and trains members to implement the design. The internal consultant generally helps members relate to other organizational units, resolve conflicts, and legitimize the change activities within the organization.

5. *Sponsorship.* This concerns the presence of a powerful sponsor who can initiate, allocate, and legitimize resources for the intervention. Sponsors must come from levels in the organization high enough to control appropriate resources, and they must have the visibility and power to nurture the intervention and see that it remains viable. There are many examples of OD interventions that persisted for several years and then collapsed abruptly when the sponsor, usually a top administrator, left the organization. There also are numerous examples of middle managers withdrawing support for interventions because top management did not include them in the change program.

Institutionalization Processes

The framework depicted in Figure 11.2 shows the following five institutionalization processes that can directly affect the degree to which OD interventions are institutionalized.

1. *Socialization.* This concerns the transmission of information about beliefs, preferences, norms, and values with respect to the intervention. Because implementation of OD interventions generally involves considerable learning and experimentation, a continual process of socialization is necessary to promote persistence of the change program. Organization members must focus attention on the evolving nature of the intervention and its ongoing meaning. They must communicate this information to other employees, especially new members. Transmission of information about the intervention helps bring new members onboard and allows participants to reaffirm the beliefs, norms, and values underlying the intervention.[26] For example, employee involvement programs

often include initial transmission of information about the intervention, as well as retraining of existing participants and training of new members. Such processes are intended to promote persistence of the program as both new behaviors are learned and new members are introduced.

2. *Commitment.* This binds people to behaviors associated with the intervention. It includes initial commitment to the program, as well as recommitment over time. Opportunities for commitment should allow people to select the necessary behaviors freely, explicitly, and publicly. These conditions favor high commitment and can promote stability of the new behaviors. Commitment should derive from several organizational levels, including the employees directly involved and the middle and upper managers who can support or thwart the intervention. In many early employee involvement programs, for example, attention was directed at gaining workers' commitment to such programs. Unfortunately, middle managers were often ignored and considerable management resistance to the interventions resulted.

3. *Reward allocation.* This involves linking rewards to the new behaviors required by an intervention. Organizational rewards can enhance the persistence of interventions in at least two ways. First, a combination of intrinsic and extrinsic rewards can reinforce new behaviors. Intrinsic rewards are internal and derive from the opportunities for challenge, development, and accomplishment found in the work. When interventions provide these opportunities, motivation to perform should persist. This behavior can be further reinforced by providing extrinsic rewards, such as money, for increased contributions. Because the value of extrinsic rewards tends to diminish over time, it may be necessary to revise the reward system to maintain high levels of desired behaviors.

    Second, new behaviors will persist to the extent that rewards are perceived as equitable by employees. When new behaviors are fairly compensated, people are likely to develop preferences for those behaviors. Over time, those preferences should lead to normative and value consensus about the appropriateness of the intervention. For example, many employee involvement programs fail to persist because employees feel that their increased contributions to organizational improvements are unfairly rewarded. This is especially true for interventions relying exclusively on intrinsic rewards. People argue that an intervention that provides opportunities for intrinsic rewards also should provide greater pay or extrinsic rewards for higher levels of contribution to the organization.

4. *Diffusion.* This refers to the process of transferring interventions from one system to another. Diffusion facilitates institutionalization by providing a wider organizational base to support the new behaviors. Many interventions fail to persist because they run counter to the values and norms of the larger organization. Rather than support the intervention, the larger organization rejects the changes and often puts pressure on the change target to revert to old behaviors. Diffusion of the intervention to other organizational units reduces this counterimplementation force. It tends to lock in behaviors by providing normative consensus from other parts of the organization. Moreover, the *act* of transmitting institutionalized behaviors to other systems reinforces commitment to the changes.

5. *Sensing and calibration.* This involves detecting deviations from desired intervention behaviors and taking corrective action. Institutionalized behaviors invariably encounter destabilizing forces, such as changes in the environment, new technologies, and pressures from other departments to nullify changes. These factors cause some variation in performances, preferences, norms, and

values. To detect this variation and take corrective actions, organizations must have some sensing mechanism. Sensing mechanisms, such as implementation feedback, provide information about the occurrence of deviations. This knowledge can then initiate corrective actions to ensure that behaviors are more in line with the intervention. For example, if a high level of job discretion associated with a job enrichment intervention does not persist, information about this problem might initiate corrective actions, such as renewed attempts to socialize people or to gain commitment to the intervention.

Indicators of Institutionalization

Institutionalization is not an all-or-nothing concept but reflects degrees of persistence of an intervention. Figure 11.2 shows five indicators of the extent of an intervention's persistence. The extent to which the following factors are present or absent indicates the degree of institutionalization.

1. *Knowledge.* This involves the extent to which organization members have knowledge of the behaviors associated with an intervention. It is concerned with whether members know enough to perform the behaviors and to recognize the consequences of that performance. For example, job enrichment includes a number of new behaviors, such as performing a greater variety of tasks, analyzing information about task performance, and making decisions about work methods and plans.

2. *Performance.* This is concerned with the degree to which intervention behaviors are actually performed. It may be measured by counting the proportion of relevant people performing the behaviors. For example, 60 percent of the employees in a particular work unit might be performing the job enrichment behaviors described above. Another measure of performance is the frequency with which the new behaviors are performed. In assessing frequency, it is important to account for different variations of the same essential behavior, as well as highly institutionalized behaviors that need to be performed only infrequently.

3. *Preferences.* This involves the degree to which organization members privately accept the organizational changes. This contrasts with acceptance based primarily on organizational sanctions or group pressures. Private acceptance usually is reflected in people's positive attitudes toward the changes and can be measured by the direction and intensity of those attitudes across the members of the work unit receiving the intervention. For example, a questionnaire assessing members' perceptions of a job enrichment program might show that most employees have a strong positive attitude toward making decisions, analyzing feedback, and performing a variety of tasks.

4. *Normative consensus.* This focuses on the extent to which people agree about the appropriateness of the organizational changes. This indicator of institutionalization reflects how fully changes have become part of the normative structure of the organization. Changes persist to the degree members feel that they should support them. For example, a job enrichment program would become institutionalized to the extent that employees support it and see it as appropriate to organizational functioning.

5. *Value consensus.* This is concerned with social consensus on values relevant to the organizational changes. Values are beliefs about how people ought or ought not to behave. They are abstractions from more specific norms. Job enrichment,

for example, is based on values promoting employee self-control and responsibility. Different behaviors associated with job enrichment, such as making decisions and performing a variety of tasks, would persist to the extent that employees widely share values of self-control and responsibility.

These five indicators can be used to assess the level of institutionalization of an OD intervention. The more the indicators are present in a situation, the higher will be the degree of institutionalization. Further, these factors seem to follow a specific development order: knowledge, performance, preferences, norms, and values. People must first understand new behaviors or changes before they can perform them effectively. Such performance generates rewards and punishments, which in time affect people's preferences. As many individuals come to prefer the changes, normative consensus about their appropriateness develops. Finally, if there is normative agreement about the changes reflecting a particular set of values, over time there should be some consensus on those values among organization members.

Given this developmental view of institutionalization, it is implicit that whenever one of the last indicators is present, all the previous ones are automatically included as well. For example, if employees normatively agree with the behaviors associated with job enrichment, then they also have knowledge about the behaviors, can perform them effectively, and prefer them. An OD intervention is fully institutionalized only when all five factors are present.

Application 11.2 describes Hewlett-Packard's successful history of institutionalizing a new set of behaviors through structural change. It describes how culture and reward systems can play a strong role in both supporting and constraining change.[27]

■ SUMMARY

We discussed in this chapter the final two stages of planned change—evaluating interventions and institutionalizing them. Evaluation was discussed in terms of two kinds of necessary feedback: implementation feedback, concerned with whether the intervention is being implemented as intended, and evaluation feedback, indicating whether the intervention is producing expected results. The former comprises collected data about features of the intervention and its immediate effects, which are fed back repeatedly and at short intervals. The latter comprises data about the long-term effects of the intervention, which are fed back at long intervals.

Evaluation of interventions also involves decisions about measurement and research design. Measurement issues focus on selecting variables and designing good measures. Ideally, measurement decisions should derive from the theory underlying the intervention and should include measures of the features of the intervention and its immediate and long-term consequences. Further, these measures should be operationally defined, reliable, and valid and should involve multiple methods, such as a combination of questionnaires, interviews, and company records.

Research design focuses on setting up the conditions for making valid assessments of an intervention's effects. This involves ruling out explanations for the observed results other than the intervention. Although randomized experimental designs are rarely feasible in OD, quasi-experimental designs exist for eliminating alternative explanations.

OD interventions are institutionalized when the change program persists and becomes part of the organization's normal functioning. A framework for understanding and improving the institutionalization of interventions identified organization characteristics (congruence, stability of environment and technology, and

APPLICATION 11·2   Institutionalizing Structural Change at Hewlett-Packard

In March 1999, Hewlett-Packard (HP) CEO Lewis Platt announced a major strategic change. HP's $7.6 billion instruments division, the business on which the company had been founded, was to be spun off as a stand-alone organization. In addition, he would step down as CEO after eight years in the position and over thirty years in the company. This structural change was the latest in a long line of successful structural changes that have consistently sparked revenue and profit growth as well as stock price appreciation. Few organizations have implemented as many major changes and still maintained both strong financial performance and corporate reputation. HP's history of seeing the need for, implementing, and reaping the benefits of structural change is a testament to its ability to institutionalize change, as these examples demonstrate.

HP is perennially one of the most admired companies in the United States according to *Fortune*'s ratings. Since its founding in 1939, HP has implemented successfully no fewer than a dozen major organizational changes, including the transition from a high-tech entrepreneurial startup to a professionally managed company; from a small instruments business to a leading computer company; from a company oriented around complex-instruction-set computing technology to reduced-instruction-set computing technology; from a technology/engineering-based company to a market/brand-driven company; and most recently, from a "pure products" company to an e-services company. This latest transformation will be implemented by Carly Fiorina, the company's first CEO to come from outside the HP culture.

HP's electronics and computer business is characterized by highly volatile technological and market change. It must quickly adopt, innovate, and implement a variety of technological and organizational changes just to survive. HP's traditional and current strategies are built on innovation, differentiation, and high quality. Another important feature of HP, and one of its more enduring characteristics, is the "HP way"—a cultural artifact that supports a participative management style and emphasizes commonness of purpose and teamwork on one hand and individual freedom and initiative on the other. The HP way is not a formal policy and is therefore difficult to define. As one manager stated in the late 1970s, "There's something useful in not being too precise—a value to fuzziness. No one can really define the HP way. If it weren't fuzzy, it would be a rule! This way leaves room for the constant microreconciliations needed in a changing world. [HP] is designed as an adaptive company." Over time, however, the HP way has been both a constraint to and a facilitator of change.

For example, the HP way has been at the root of the company's difficulties in institutionalizing structural and behavioral changes to bring about more cooperation among the computer divisions. The initial structural change occurred in 1982 when HP transformed itself from a producer of high-quality electronic measuring instruments into a computer company. At the time, computers and computer-related equipment only accounted for about one-third of revenues and HP was structured into more than fifty highly autonomous and decentralized product divisions focused on specialized niche markets. Individual engineers came up with innovative ideas and "bootstrapped" new products any way they could. Organization members were encouraged to work with other engineers in other departments within the same division, but there was little incentive to coordinate the development of technologies across divisions. This focus on the individual was supported by a performance management system that measured and rewarded "sustained contributions"; the key to success for an individual was working with many people in the division. HP prospered by maximizing each of its parts.

Former CEO John Young's decision to focus on computers fundamentally shifted the keys to success. Computer production required a coordinated effort among the different component divisions and market shares large enough to encourage software vendors to write programs for their machines. In a culture that supported individual contributions over divisional cooperation, Young placed all the instruments divisions into one group and all the computer divisions into another group, a basic design that persisted until the recent spin-off of the instruments business. In addition, he centralized research, marketing, and manufacturing, which had previously been assigned to the divisions. Problems quickly arose. In one case, the company's new and highly touted graphics printer would not work with its HP3000 minicomputer. The operating software, made by a third HP division, would not allow the two pieces of hardware to interface.

In response, the computer group formed committees to figure out what new technologies to pursue, which to ignore, which of HP's products should be saved, and which would be shelved. As the committees came up with recommendations, the committees themselves kept multiplying. The company's entrenched culture, built around the HP way's philosophy of egalitarianism and mutual respect, promoted consensus: Everyone had to have a hand in making a decision.

By 1988, the organization chart still showed a predominantly decentralized divisional structure. What it didn't show was the overwhelming number of committees that slowed decision making and product development. In one case, it took seven months and nearly one hundred people on nine committees to name the company's new software product. This web of committees, originally designed to foster communication among HP's operating divisions, had pushed up costs and slowed development. In the rapidly changing world of software, personal computers, minicomputers, and printers, the culture was hamstringing the organization's success. The ethic of individual freedom balanced by teamwork had produced an unwieldy bureaucracy.

After a series of delays of important new products, John Young reorganized the computer group. In late 1990, he eliminated most of the committees and removed layers of management by dividing the computer business into two groups: one to handle personal computers and peripherals sold through dealers, and the other to handle sales of workstations and minicomputers to big customers. To match the organization structure, the previously centralized corporate salesforce was split and assigned to particular divisions. This change focused HP's computer systems on the market and restored much of the autonomy to the divisions. The balance between individuality and common purpose that characterized the original HP way was unleashed, leading to several years of strong revenue and profit growth.

In 1993, and before he was officially installed as the new CEO, Platt announced that HP would pursue the convergence of several base technologies, such as wireless communication, printing, and measurement, to create whole new products for the converging computer, communication, and consumer electronics markets. Implementing such a strategy again depended on strong coordination among HP's product divisions. To insure that the gains in cooperation were not lost as HP embarked on its new strategy, CEO Platt tied division managers' incentive compensation to working cooperatively with other divisions to create new products that used multiple-division technologies.

The new structure was also a big success. Growth in the printer and PC markets drove revenues from $13.2 billion in 1990 to $38.4 billion in 1996, with profits growing in the same proportions. HP had once again revived itself. In 1996, they were the fifth most admired company in the United States. In the Internet world, however, their success was short-lived, and critics argued that Platt's subsequent attention to "soft" issues such as work/life balance and promoting diversity, rather than launching an Internet strategy, resulted in stalled growth. For 1997 and 1998, and aided by the Asian financial crisis, growth rates slipped to single digits.

In the summer of 1998, Platt believed that HP had simply become too big and complex, and he began to consider major changes. Clues for the restructuring came on the heels of a change initiated by two key managers: Ann Livermore, head of software and support, and William Russell, head of the Unix computer business. These two long-standing but independent computer groups began working to commercialize a set of Web technologies. They pulled more than twenty stand-alone products from the two divisions into simple, problem-solving packages. Their efforts resulted in a proposal to merge the two divisions which Platt approved in October 1999.

When Platt announced his decision to spin off the instruments business and step down as CEO, he also decentralized the structure, already considered highly decentralized by most standards, by giving the four key division heads CEO-like authority. Although the announcements delighted Wall Street analysts, it was only the beginning.

Shortly after being named HP's fourth CEO, Carly Fiorina laid out her agenda: create a compelling vision for HP, implement a structure to support the vision, and launch a marketing campaign to build the HP brand. The vision called for a shift from a stand-alone products company to an e-services company. The structural change involved merging the four major product divisions into a group focused on computing and a group focused on printing. This structure for the first time united HP's laser and inkjet printing divisions and furthered the opportunities for computer products to coordinate their activities. The two remaining executives were assigned marketing responsibilities to focus on key customers. In November, Fiorina announced a major marketing campaign focused on the HP way's value of innovation.

The lessons of history have not been lost on the new CEO. The structural changes have been backed up with changes in the compensation system. HP executive and managerial rewards, traditionally in the form of raises, bonuses, and profit sharing, but not stock options, are being revamped to include stock tied to overall company performance. By paying close attention to the implementation of structural change, HP has made great strides in institutionalizing individual cooperation and interdivisional coordination. ■

unionization) and intervention characteristics (goal specificity, programmability, level of change target, internal support, and sponsorship) that affect institutionalization processes. The framework also described specific institutionalization processes (socialization, commitment, reward allocation, diffusion, and sensing and calibration) that directly affect indicators of intervention persistence (knowledge, performance, preferences, normative consensus, and value consensus).

■ NOTES

1. T. Cummings and E. Molloy, *Strategies for Improving Productivity and the Quality of Work Life* (New York: Praeger, 1977); J. Whitfield, W. Anthony, and K. Kacmar, "Evaluation of Team-Based Management: A Case Study," *Journal of Organizational Change Management* 8, 2 (1995): 17–28.

2. S. Mohrman and T. Cummings, "Implementing Quality-of-Work-Life Programs by Managers," in *The NTL Manager's Handbook*, eds. R. Ritvo and A. Sargent (Arlington, Va.: NTL Institute, 1983): 320–28; T. Cummings and S. Mohrman, "Self-Designing Organizations: Towards Implementing Quality-of-Work-Life Innovations," in *Research in Organizational Change and Development*, vol. 1, eds. R. Woodman and W. Pasmore (Greenwich, Conn.: JAI Press, 1987): 275–310.

3. T. Cummings, "Institutionalizing Quality-of-Work-Life Programs: The Case for Self-Design" (paper delivered at the annual meeting of the Academy of Management, Dallas, Tex., August 1983).

4. Cummings and Molloy, *Strategies.*

5. P. Goodman, *Assessing Organizational Change: The Rushton Quality of Work Experiment* (New York: John Wiley & Sons, 1979); A. Van de Ven and D. Ferry, eds., *Measuring and Assessing Organizations* (New York: John Wiley & Sons, 1985); E. Lawler III, D. Nadler, and C. Cammann, eds., *Organizational Assessment: Perspectives on the Measurement of Organizational Behavior and Quality of Work Life* (New York: John Wiley & Sons, 1980); A. Van de Ven and W. Joyce, eds., *Perspectives on Organizational Design and Behavior* (New York: John Wiley & Sons, 1981); S. Seashore, E. Lawler III, P. Mirvis, and C. Cammann, eds., *Assessing Organizational Change: A Guide to Methods, Measures, and Practices* (New York: Wiley-Interscience, 1983).

6. B. Macy and P. Mirvis, "Organizational Change Efforts: Methodologies for Assessing Organizational Effectiveness and Program Costs Versus Benefits," *Evaluation Review* 6 (1982): 301–72.

7. Macy and Mirvis, "Organizational Change Efforts."

8. J. Nunnally, *Psychometric Theory*, 2d ed. (New York: McGraw-Hill, 1978); J. Kirk and M. Miller, *Reliability and Validity in Qualitative Research* (Beverly Hills, Calif.: Sage Publications, 1985).

9. D. Miller, *Handbook of Research Design and Social Measurement* (Thousand Oaks, Calif.: Sage Publications, 1991); N. Denzin and Y. Lincoln, eds., *Handbook of Qualitative Research* (Thousand Oaks, Calif.: Sage Publications, 1994).

10. R. Hackman and G. Oldham, *Work Redesign* (Reading, Mass.: Addison-Wesley, 1980): 275–306.

11. Nunnally, *Psychometric Theory.*

12. C. Selltiz, M. Jahoda, M. Deutsch, and S. Cook, *Research Methods in Social Relations*, rev. ed. (New York: Holt, Rinehart, & Winston, 1966): 385–440.

13. J. Taylor and D. Bowers, *Survey of Organizations: A Machine-Scored Standardized Questionnaire Instrument* (Ann Arbor: Institute for Social Research, University of Michigan, 1972); *Comprehensive Quality-of-Work-Life Survey* (Los Angeles: Center for Effective Organizations, University of Southern California, 1981); C. Cammann, M. Fichman, G. D. Jenkins, and J. Klesh, "Assessing the Attitudes and Perceptions of Organizational Members," in *Assessing Organizational Change: A Guide to Methods, Measures, and Practices*, eds. S. Seashore, E. Lawler III, P. Mirvis, and C. Cammann (New York: Wiley-Interscience, 1983): 71–119.

14. R. Bullock and D. Svyantek, "The Impossibility of Using Random Strategies to Study the Organization Development Process," *Journal of Applied Behavioral Science* 23 (1987): 255–62.

15. D. Campbell and J. Stanley, *Experimental and Quasi-Experimental Design for Research* (Chicago: Rand McNally, 1966); T. Cook and D. Campbell, *Quasi-Experimentation: Design and Analysis Issues for Field Settings* (Chicago: Rand McNally, 1979).

16. E. Lawler III, D. Nadler, and P. Mirvis, "Organizational Change and the Conduct of Assessment Research," in *Assessing Organizational Change: A Guide to Methods, Measures and Practices*, eds. S. Seashore, E. Lawler III, P. Mirvis, and C. Cammann (New York: Wiley-Interscience, 1983): 19–47.

17. Cook and Campbell, *Quasi-Experimentation.*

18. R. Golembiewski and R. Munzenrider, "Measuring Change by OD Designs," *Journal of Applied Behavioral Science* 12 (April-June 1976): 133–57.

19. A. Bedeian, A. Armenakis, and R. Gilson, "On the Measurement and Control of Beta Change," *Academy of Management Review* 5 (1980): 561–66; W. Randolph and R. Edwards, "Assessment of Alpha, Beta and Gamma Changes in a University-Setting OD Intervention," *Academy of Management Proceedings* (1978): 313–17; J. Terborg, G. Howard, and S. Maxwell, "Evaluating Planned Organizational Change: A Method for Assessing Alpha, Beta, and Gamma Change," *Academy of Management Review* 7 (1982): 292–95; M. Buckley and A. Armenakis, "Detecting Scale

Recalibration in Survey Research," *Group and Organization Studies* 12 (1987): 464–81; R. Millsap and S. Hartog, "Alpha, Beta, and Gamma Change in Evaluation Research: A Structural Equation Approach," *Journal of Applied Psychology* 73 (1988): 574–84.

20. D. Ciampa, *Total Quality: A User's Guide for Implementation* (Reading, Mass.: Addison-Wesley, 1992); P. Senge, *The Fifth Discipline* (New York: Doubleday, 1990); Cummings and Mohrman, "Self-Designing Organizations"; C. Worley, D. Hitchin, and W. Ross, *Integrated Strategic Change* (Reading, Mass.: Addison-Wesley, 1996).

21. This section is based on the work of P. Goodman and J. Dean, "Creating Long-Term Organizational Change," in *Change in Organizations,* ed. P. Goodman (San Francisco: Jossey-Bass, 1982): 226–79. To date, the framework is largely untested and unchallenged. Ledford's process model of persistence (see note 22) is the only other model proposed to explain institutionalization. The empirical support for either model, however, is nil.

22. G. Ledford, "The Persistence of Planned Organizational Change: A Process Theory Perspective" (Ph.D. diss., University of Michigan, 1984).

23. L. Zucker, "Normal Change or Risky Business: Institutional Effects on the 'Hazard' of Change in Hospital Organizations, 1959–1979," *Journal of Management Studies* 24 (1987): 671–700.

24. S. Mohrman and T. Cummings, *Self-Designing Organizations: Learning How to Create High Performance* (Reading, Mass.: Addison-Wesley, 1989).

25. J. Martin and C. Siehl, "Organizational Cultures and Counterculture: An Uneasy Symbiosis," *Organizational Dynamics* (1983): 52–64; D. Meyerson and J. Martin, "Cultural Change: An Integration of Three Different Views," *Journal of Management Studies* 24 (1987): 623–47.

26. L. Zucker, "The Role of Institutionalization in Cultural Persistence," *American Sociological Review* 42 (1977): 726–43.

27. R. Von Werssowetz and M. Beer, "Human Resources at Hewlett-Packard," *Harvard Business School Case 9-482-125* (Boston: Harvard Business School, 1982); B. Buell and R. Hof, "Hewlett-Packard Rethinks Itself," *Business Week* (1 April 1991): 76–79; R. Hof, "Suddenly, Hewlett-Packard Is Doing Everything Right," *Business Week* (23 March 1992): 88–89; "Can John Young Redesign Hewlett-Packard," *Business Week* (6 December 1982): 72–78; J. Levine, "Mild-Mannered Hewlett-Packard Is Making Like Superman," *Business Week* (7 March 1988): 110–14; R. Hof, "Hewlett-Packard Digs Deep for a Digital Future," *Business Week* (18 October 1993): 72–75; A. Fisher, "America's Most Admired Corporations," *Fortune* (4 March 1996): 90–98; P. Burrows with P. Elstrom, "The Boss," *Business Week* (2 August 1999): 76–83; D. Hamilton, "H-P to Relaunch Its Brand, Adopt New Logo," *Wall Street Journal* (16 November 1999): B6; D. Hamilton and S. Thurm, "H-P to Spin Off Its Measurement Operations," *Wall Street Journal* (3 March 1999): A3; E. Nee, "Lew Platt: Why I Dismembered HP," *Fortune* (29 March 1999): 167–69.

■ It's Your Turn

Dear Steve,

I enjoyed seeing you at the OD Network conference. I've been trying to reach you by phone, but no luck, so I thought I would drop you an email. Your secretary said you were on a job out of state. I've been working with several clients and my teaching load is getting pretty hectic. Are you interested in working together again? I've been contacted by Newfangled Software to discuss some management training, possibly OD. It seems like you worked for them several years ago. Is this correct or have I got my organizations mixed up?

Hope to hear from you soon and maybe we can work something out at Newfangled.

Tom

Dear Tom,

Sorry to have missed your calls, but I was in Oklahoma City doing some work with the State Department. Thanks for the email, although it triggered some old memories. Excuse my rambling in what I will share with you about Newfangled Software. Please keep this confidential. Yes, you were right about me working with them. I looked in my records and it was nine years ago. I've been keeping in touch indirectly with how things are going there through some of my old contacts.

Their president, David Dyer, has been under severe pressure from three of their five board members. I can't say he doesn't deserve at least some of the blame for their current problems, although I suspect the board members have their own political agendas. I was contacted by a guy named Irwin from their training department to go on their annual retreat with the middle and top managers. Irwin is okay, and if he has a fault, it's his taking his work too seriously, given the current culture at Newfangled. Initially I was to do some manage-

ment development training on a very superficial level. David Dyer had only been there for several months. Irwin and I decided it would be prudent to go easy at first until David got the lay of the land. Irwin, not David, was my contact person because Irwin was responsible for all of the management and technical training.

Anyway, the three-day retreat was "weird" but, reflecting on things, not at all unusual. The retreat started when we were all loaded up in a bus. None of the participants was told where they were going, so it was to be a big surprise. We traveled about three hours to a dude ranch in the local mountains. I was supposed to provide the training for one afternoon and the following morning. Irwin helped out. We did a few icebreaker exercises, followed by some kind of nonthreatening team exercise. This was followed by reports from the teams on what they thought were effective supervision skills. It was really low-key stuff. I arranged the teams to be composed of managers from both middle and top levels.

You know, I can remember what happened as if it were yesterday. David remained real aloof. I had previously arranged for him, like everyone else, to be in a team. He joked around with several other men for about thirty minutes before joining his team. Meanwhile, his team went to work without him. He finally joined them but did not say much. After a few minutes he got up and went over to another team and talked with them about the tennis game they'd had the previous day. I did not confront him at the time, which, reflecting on things, may have been a mistake on my part. But I rationalized that he was new and wanted to get to know his people on a social basis. Besides, don't we OD types say we should take our clients "where they're at?"

Well, that was the afternoon session. Not exactly a roaring success, but a number of the participants were really getting into the exercises. The next morning went about the same. David played the part of the social butterfly. His behavior was a bit obvious to others. Reflecting back on things, I think he was intimidated. This was his first president position. We had a team-building exercise followed by a discussion on how departments, in general, could work better together—nothing specific. I remember one fellow got real annoyed at some of the other teams for joking around. He said something to the effect that this was why it took so long for new products to get out the door. Several others agreed, but then David said what we were doing in the teams was just a fun game and did not mean anything. The morning session ended okay, for the most part, although David and several others left early.

Nothing more happened with me and the company. Irwin called me to say his budget had been cut, and they were not able to do any more training for a while. I read between the lines and politely wished him well. Several years ago, I heard from a friend, Patricia Kingsley, who I have worked with on other jobs. She said she had been recruited to conduct training at Newfangled's annual retreat. They flew over a thousand miles to a retreat at Cape Cod. Big bucks on this trip. It was for five days, and she was to provide training for four half-day sessions. Halfway through the first session, David recruited three of his top administrators and they went for a canoe ride. Patricia said you could hear them out on the lake laughing and carrying on while the rest of the team was working. At each of the other three sessions, participation dropped off dramatically until she ended up with less than a quarter of the people in the last session. She said she had never seen anything like it.

Their training sessions occur every May, so it looks like it's your turn. No consultant seems to get past the annual retreat. I'd like to work with you again, but I think it would be in everyone's best interest that I pass on this one. The pay is good and you may get a good vacation out of it. On the other hand, don't take your lack of success personally. You may have a different experience because the board may have made some changes. Stay in touch and give me a call.

Sincerely,

Steve

Questions

1. Assume that you are going to meet with Irwin to discuss the training session for the next management retreat. What contracting issues are most important for you?

2. How will you address the issue of David's past behavior?

Source: Reprinted and adapted with permission from a case titled "The OD Letters" that appeared in D. Harvey and D. Brown, *An Experiential Approach to Organization Development* (Upper Saddle River, N.J.: Prentice Hall, 1996).

■ Sunflower Incorporated

Sunflower Incorporated is a large distribution company with more than five thousand employees and gross sales of more than $700 million (1991). The company purchases and distributes salty snack foods and liquor to independent retail stores throughout the United States and Canada. The snack foods include corn chips, potato chips, cheese curls, tortilla chips, and peanuts. The United States and Canada are divided into twenty-two regions, each with its own central warehouse, salespeople, finance department, and purchasing department. The company distributes national as well as local brands and packages some items under private labels. The head office encourages each region to be autonomous because of local tastes and practices. The northeast United States, for example, consumes a greater percentage of Canadian whisky and American bourbon, and the West consumes more light liquors, such as vodka, gin, and rum. Snack foods in the Southwest often are seasoned to reflect Mexican tastes.

Early in 1989, Sunflower began using a financial reporting system that compared sales, costs, and profits across regions. Management was surprised to learn that profits varied widely. By 1990, the differences were so great that management decided some standardization was necessary. They believed that highly profitable regions were sometimes using lower-quality items, even seconds, to boost profit margins. This practice could hurt Sunflower's image. Other regions were facing intense price competition in order to hold market share. National distributors were pushing hard to increase their market share. Frito-Lay, Borden Foods, Nabisco, Procter & Gamble (Pringles), and Standard Brands (Planter's peanuts) were pushing hard to increase market share by cutting prices and launching new products.

As these problems accumulated, Leon Steelman, president of Sunflower, decided to create a new position to monitor pricing and purchasing practices. Agnes Albanese was hired from the finance department of a competing organization. Her new title was director of pricing and purchasing, and she reported to the vice president of finance, Al Mobley. Steelman and Mobley gave Albanese great latitude in organizing her job and encouraged her to establish whatever rules and procedures were necessary. She could gather information from each region, and each region was notified of her appointment by an official memo sent to regional managers. A copy of that memo was posted on each warehouse bulletin board, and the announcement was made in the company newspaper.

After three weeks on the job, Albanese decided that pricing and purchasing decisions should be standardized across regions. As a first step, she wanted the financial executive in each region to notify her of any local price change greater than 3 percent. She also decided that all new contracts for local purchases of more than five thousand dollars should be cleared through her office. (Approximately 60 percent of items distributed in the regions was purchased in large quantities and supplied from the home office. The other 40 percent was purchased and distributed within the region.) Albanese believed that the only way to standardize operations was for each region to notify the home office in advance of any change in prices or purchases. She discussed the proposed policy with Mobley. He agreed and they submitted a formal proposal to the president and board of directors, who approved the plan. Sunflower was moving into the peak holiday season, so Albanese wanted to implement the new procedures right away. She decided to send an email to the financial and purchasing executives in each region notifying them of the new procedures. The change would be inserted in all policy and procedure manuals throughout Sunflower within four months.

Albanese showed a draft of the email to Mobley and invited his comments. Mobley said the Internet was an excellent idea but wondered if it was sufficient. The regions handle hundreds of items and were used to decentralized decision making. Mobley suggested that Albanese visit the regions and discuss purchasing and pricing policies with the executives. Albanese refused, saying that the trips would be expensive and time-consuming. She had so many things to do at headquarters that a trip was impossible. Mobley also suggested waiting to implement the procedures until after the annual company meeting in three months. Albanese said this would take too long because the procedures would not take effect until after the peak sales season. She believed the procedures were needed now, and she sent out the email the next day.

During the next few days, replies came in from most of the regions. The executives were in agreement with the content of the email and said they would be happy to cooperate.

Eight weeks later, Albanese had not received notices from any regions about local price or purchase changes. Other executives who had visited regional warehouses indicated to her that the regions were busy as usual. Regional executives seemed to be following usual procedures for that time of year.

Questions

1. How well did Albanese manage the pricing and purchasing changes at Sunflower? Were the changes implemented successfully? How would you find this out?

2. What might Albanese have done differently? What should she do now?

Source: Adapted by permission of the publisher from R. Daft, *Organization Theory and Design* (St. Paul: West, 1983), pp. 334–36.

■ The Torenton Mine (A)

The Client

The body of ore now being mined at Torenton was first discovered in 1967 far beneath the snow-covered peak of Antler Mountain. More than nine years later, after an investment of more than a half-billion dollars, Torenton's first ore car emerged from the tunnel precisely on schedule—a modern-day marvel of engineering and technical acumen. From the outset, Torenton was one of the safest and most efficient hard rock mines in the industry.

By 1981, nearly eighteen hundred employees worked at Torenton, producing more than thirty thousand tons of rock each day. They came from all areas of the nation and, for most of them, Torenton was the first mine they had ever seen. Torenton had no labor unions, and the majority of employees apparently had little desire for one. The wage and benefits policies were highly competitive for the industry and certainly better than those of other regional employers. Experienced miners regarded Torenton as something resembling a country club, an odd association for those uninitiated to the rigors of mining. As with most mines, Torenton's workforce structure became dense with engineering and technical personnel as one ascended the hierarchy.

Torenton was an operating company that belonged to a large mining corporation. As such, the corporate office dictated many of the mining policies. Staff departments often had dual reporting relationships with local and corporate management. Emerging from the tradition of mining, expertise in technical matters far exceeded the company's sophistication in managing human resources.

The Consulting System

My association with Torenton began in early 1974. At the time, I had been involved in OD for eight years but had never worked with a mining company. As a graduate faculty member in an industrial/organizational psychology program, I had colleagues and students as resources. Sometimes during the course of my work I managed a temporary team of as many as twenty-five people; at other times I worked only with one or two colleagues.

For the most part, the senior-level staff members of the consulting team were other faculty, and the support staff tended to consist of advanced graduate students.

The First Attitude Survey

The OD process at Torenton began in 1973. Concerned about a turnover rate for hourly employees of more than 14 percent per month, the company hired a consultant to conduct an attitude survey of these employees. A sample of 20 percent of the workforce participated in face-to-face interviews and completed written questionnaires. The consultant made a report to the management committee, which comprised all department heads and the general manager. Although the data pointed out interdepartmental conflicts and problems with vertical communication occurring above the first line of supervision, the managers concluded that the supervisors needed human relations training.

The Training Program

Following that decision, the HR manager invited me to conduct a supervisory training program at Torenton. The original request was in the form of a work order to "fix the supervisors," but the managers proved flexible enough to consider an alternate proposal that called for everyone in a supervisory position to complete a two-day training program in basic human relations skills. The training relied heavily on a behavior modeling approach, but also included more philosophical discussions of such concepts as Theories X and Y.

For most first-line supervisors, this training represented their initial exposure to management education. The written and verbal feedback was mostly positive, although as many as one-fourth of the participants commented on the implied shift in management style communicated by the program's emphases. This was one of the early signs of potential differences in client–consultant theories of action. But the most pernicious snag in the program occurred when we decided to *practice*, not just talk about, certain management principles during the management committee's training workshop. In the process of working on a group problem-solving exercise, the second most influential member walked out, seeming to end any further OD processes and perhaps any additional behavioral science programs.

The Second Attitude Survey and the First Feedback

Although the training session with the top team ended in disarray, the HR manager—with the consent of the general manager—invited me to prepare a proposal for a follow-up attitude survey of hourly employees. The motivation for doing this stemmed partly from the HR manager's desire to estimate the impact of the supervisory training. Moreover, the turnover rates for hourly employees remained at about 10 percent per month. I developed a written questionnaire from sixty-one face-to-face interviews, a literature review, and items from the 1973 survey. The questionnaire was administered during working hours in the summer of 1975. Before doing this, I was allowed to work underground as a miner for about one month so that I could better understand the miner's world.

In negotiating this contract, I argued for the inclusion of a feedback component to the program that would call for employees to meet in "family groups" to review the data. Although implementation was problematic, feedback sessions were held with all hourly crews. The format provided employees with comprehensive survey reports for their crews and for the company as a whole, and it enabled them not only to comment on companywide issues but also to engage in action planning for change. Sessions were held during working hours in meeting rooms at the mine.

The managers actually had little conception of what might result when they granted permission to hold the feedback sessions. Discussions of the management philosophy possibly associated with a survey feedback program (SFP) had been held with the management committee, but their comprehension was superficial at best. This confusion became dramatically evident during a last-minute confrontation that occurred the day before the first scheduled feedback session. At that time, the general manager had to be reconvinced that employees needed to have access to the data during a feedback meeting. Also, it was not management's style (theory of action) to become involved in programs the way we expected. Typically, they hired a contractor to take on a task and report to the client following completion of the work. Because we were dealing with processes and relationships, however, our work required violations of the norms of appropriate contractor behavior.

The 1975 SFP supported a number of changes, and within a year the managers had revised some major policies and instituted new programs: a highly criticized attendance policy was revised, the employee orientation program was redesigned, a credit union was established, and a preventive maintenance program was implemented. The HR manager acted as the internal change agent, providing continuity and direction both during and after the major programmatic activities.

Countering Apathy with Evidence

Although the SFP appeared to be a major success, the top managers remained cool toward behavioral science interventions. They viewed these programs as a nuisance, part of the modern management style but unrelated to such important matters as productivity—and certainly inconsistent with the style of a "real" mine boss.

With the support of the HR manager, I launched a study to evaluate the degree of relationship between employee attitudes and job behaviors. Evidence suggested that, on the average, mining crews supervised by bosses with high ratings in consideration and participatory practices outproduced crews whose supervisors had low ratings by more than a half-million dollars in ore per year. Data on the relationship of job morale to criteria of safety and turnover also had impressive cost implications. These results were summarized in a report titled *Attitudes Count!*

We did not imply that attitudes and supervisory style were the sole factors affecting these criteria; given our correlational research design, we had to be extremely cautious in interpreting these findings. The managers seemed aware of the limits of these data but were intrigued nonetheless. Although we suggested conducting a controlled experiment, the

HR manager and others felt that the essential point had been made—that is, that a *probable* relationship existed between attitudes/style and outcomes—and that further study would have only questionable value.

Reactions to the report held one major surprise. To this point the managers had said that attitudes were mostly irrelevant; now they switched to saying, "Of course! We all know the happy worker is a productive worker. So what's so new about this?" Although the response was unenthusiastic, criticism of the survey program diminished markedly following publication of the report.

Consultation Skills

Because much of the follow-up work of the 1975 survey fell onto the HR staff, I suggested arranging a consultation skills workshop for this group. Through that training I hoped to enhance the effectiveness and scope of organization interventions by the HR function. A program based on Argyris's model for intervention was implemented during a six-month period (1976–1977). In the program, the Model I and Model II theories of action were described, and the staff, using role plays and actual consultations in the mine, diagnosed their models in use, discussing the appropriateness and feasibility of consultations with either model. The results were quite mixed. Some HR staff members felt disappointed, for they had wanted to improve their skills in a win–lose model of intervention. Others felt discouraged because of the apparent discrepancy between the organization's current state and the state it needed to achieve to implement Model II strategies.

Throughout the project, the few skeptics remained unconvinced but other HR staff members found that Torenton's climate was more receptive to Model II approaches than they had anticipated. The management actions of the 1980s particularly reflected this. I must attribute the survival of these ideas in the midst of disbelief and disillusionment to the HR manager, who continued to foster and reward Model II approaches made by his staff.

More Human Relations Training

The 1975 SFP extended well into 1976, followed by the consultation skills training and a series of re-ports based on the survey and productivity data. In preparation for their survey feedback sessions, supervisors had participated in training in 1974 and in 1975–1976. By the end of 1977, the HR manager reported that human relations skills needed reinforcement. I was asked to conduct another on-site training program, this time without the participation of the top managers. I was pleased with continuing the training, but also felt that the limited time allocated for it would make the effort more symbolic than functional. Our research had identified supervisory consideration, participatory practices, and the giving of feedback as critical factors with high criterion relationships. The training design was largely based on the outcomes of our action research.

The training experience was unremarkable, but the idea that we were continuing to emphasize supervisory behaviors of consideration, participation, and feedback seemed to convey a political message of sorts to the trainees. They interpreted the consistency of our training messages over the years to mean that this "new style" had the backing of the top managers. The irony of this interpretation was that the top managers, by authorizing the human relations program but failing to participate in it, were labeled hypocrites by the trainees, who asked such questions as, "How can they tell us that we should let our 'hands' participate when they won't even participate in the training they're sending us to, or when they don't give us a 'say' around here?"

Some Unsolicited Feedback

Prior to the training program, the consultants asked the management committee if it would be interested in a further appraisal of the organization based on the perceptions of the supervisors in the training session (both the 1973 and 1975 surveys had focused primarily on the hourly employees). The managers said they were interested, but their decision was unenthusiastic.

This latest survey reflected the verbal input of the training participants who—characteristic of the mine employees—knew how to criticize but not how to praise. We entitled the report *Problems of Supervision* because of the overriding tone of the supervisors' comments. The report criticized highly the upper managers' style of operation and their attention to supervisors' concerns.

The management committee reacted vehemently to the report. The general manager accused the consultants of fabricating the results because none of his managers had ever indicated the existence of problems so pervasive and deeply felt as the report suggested. Although we convinced him that the data came from the supervisory staff, we could not dispel the impression that we had somehow evoked only the most critical statements.

One must consider the validity of the general manager's impression. During the latest round of training our access to the top group had been restricted. We unequivocally believed that the top team members needed training. We also believed that for OD to succeed in this organization continuous efforts were needed to keep the management committee involved so that all of our consultations did not become the functional responsibility of one department—human resources. The survey of supervisors was directed toward increasing the managers' awareness and commitment. Were we making our own feelings about the top managers apparent by the way we collected data—that is, did we bias the responses?

I find it hard to answer this with absolute certainty. We believe we did not bias the responses and, while gathering the data, we actually were surprised by the paucity of positive comments. We did, however, readily accept this negativism as another confirmation of the mine staff's prevailing norm of informing people only about their mistakes. Moreover, most of the information we ordinarily received in off-the-record communications criticized some dimension of organizational life and thus corroborated the criticisms we heard while conducting the training survey. This seemed to highlight the nature of communications of employees to consultants, and it possibly reflected a slowly evolving definition of our roles vis-à-vis the employees.

An Organizationwide Survey Feedback Program

Remarkably, this management group persevered: although we consultants were more and more frequently perceived as bearers of bad tidings, when the management committee approved plans for a third attitude survey, it asked me to submit a proposal. My plan called for all employees in all departments to become involved in both the survey and feedback activities. After considering the rationale for an organizationwide program, the committee gave its approval.

Although I have no proof of this, I conjecture that their surprise at the results of the unsolicited survey may have heightened the managers' curiosity about "concealed" attitudes held by those in staff groups and the ranks of management. This hypothesized interest could have provoked greater support for surveying heretofore neglected segments of the organization.

By the time of the third attitude survey, Torenton had almost seventeen hundred employees. With all departments and all levels involved in the SFP, we had to establish mechanisms for following up the feedback sessions. The management committee designated a systemwide survey committee to track major departmental and organizational problems, but once again the HR staff bore primary responsibility for ensuring long-term follow-up. Consultations and work with the survey and feedback data continued well into early 1980.

The HR staff members each facilitated an average of twenty-five feedback sessions. The frequent repetitions of complaints and pointed attacks on company practices took their toll on the staff. This, combined with the staff's attempts to follow up on issues and convince various managers to implement myriad changes, led some HR personnel to experience emotional burnout. The managers, feeling pressure from all sides to make changes stimulated by survey and feedback data, eventually called for an end to "all this survey talk" so that employees could "get back to work."

Changes were evident at all levels of the organization, both during and following the program. In most feedback sessions, participants agreed on local actions and provided input for wider decision making. The follow-up by the survey committee virtually ensured that the commitments would be implemented, because mine managers resented being reminded by committee members to do something. Months later, departments continued to analyze survey data to obtain potential support for systemwide decisions. We action researchers made sure we knew how the survey and feedback input was used. Clearly, few people in the organization had any idea of the far-ranging impact of the program. Company communications regarding the follow-up of the SFP were typically neglected.

A Period of Integration

A hiatus in the consultations took place in 1980. During that time, information from the survey continued to serve as justification for policy changes or program design, but external consultations consisted primarily of advisory sessions with the HR manager and the implementation of some personnel research projects, such as selection research and performance appraisal development. The follow-up work from the survey did, however, include the attendance of a large number of middle and senior managers at external management programs. The orientation of those programs was quite compatible with the directions of the project's work. Also significant was the company's decision in 1980 to enact a policy providing for the annual human relations training of all supervisory personnel.

Since the completion of the survey, I had requested another tour of work underground on a mining crew. Although I undertook that action to increase my personal understanding of the mining profession, it also affected the managers' perceptions of my involvement with them and their organization. Throughout this tour of work, I could contrast my underground experiences in 1975 with the organizational realities of 1979. The improvements were dramatic, particularly in the domain of supervisor–employee relationships. A new order of management prevailed at Torenton.

Replication of the Organizationwide Survey Feedback Program

The survey concept gradually had become an institutionalized communications tool because the company adopted a policy of conducting periodic employee attitude surveys and made explicit reference to them in the employees' handbook. The managers asked me to submit a proposal for an attitude survey in late 1980. Other consultants entered bids, but our expertise with Torenton weighed heavily in favor of our project staff. To a large extent, the survey made in early 1981 replicated—with some improvements—the one made in 1978.

Institutionalization had some apparent consequences. Employees were better informed not only about the process, but—more important—about the potential of this program. They knew its limits, and thus were less optimistic that substantial changes would result. We consultants felt concerned about our changing role in an institutionalized program, and wondered if the same impetus for change would exist in a program that was becoming increasingly routine and for which the sluggish change processes of previous SFPs seemed to produce a general lowering of expectations.

To our surprise, the increased sophistication of the employees regarding the style and philosophy of survey feedback efforts caused managers and department heads to become significantly more involved in this program. One manifestation of this increased involvement was the managers' tendency to schedule ongoing feedback meetings with their staffs following the initial survey feedback sessions. Another indication was the conceptual exploration of quality circle programs by the most influential members of the top staff.

While we were concluding our work with Torenton on the fourth survey, the downturn in the national economy began to affect the mining industry. Because of this, the managers scuttled many of the intended follow-up programs and redirected their attention to the more pressing issue of survival. Despite this, our observation of the mine during the hard times indicated that the organization had become a far more collaborative system than it was before.

■ The Torenton Mine (B)

Behavioral Indices

Although assessing the project's contributions to organizational effectiveness and health is difficult, I can speculate as to how the intervention possibly influenced such indicators as the turnover, productivity, and safety records of the mine from 1974 to 1981.

Turnover

Because a major rationale for conducting the first and second survey programs was Torenton's high rate of turnover, the decline in turnover from an annual rate of 117.6 percent (9.8 percent per month) in 1974 to one of 18 percent (1.5 percent per month) in 1981 suggests that the organization successfully solved the problem of employee attrition (see Exhibit 1). Although one might argue that economic fluctuations could provide a more parsimonious explanation for this trend, I would counter this partially by noting that even in the prosperous period of the late 1970s, attrition rates fell substantially. Other counterarguments point to organizational changes resulting directly or indirectly from the SFPs, including a major revision in the attendance policy, an expanded screening and orientation program, vastly improved transfer and promotion systems, a definable shift in supervisory style to a more participative approach, and a variety of new communications channels.

One might reasonably argue that turnover reductions could have been solely a reflection of structural change—in this case, an improved attendance policy. To address this objection, one must examine the data on absenteeism. The policy prior to the intervention gave supervisors total discretion in declaring absences excused or unexcused, and it set an upper limit of six excused absences per year. The new policies allowed supervisors little input into deciding the nature of the absence, and it permitted an employee to take off as many as twelve days per year. One might predict that this policy change would lead to an increase in absenteeism and a decline in turnover, if other factors such as supervisor relationships, work group climate, and communications remained the same. Before the

change, the absenteeism rates for hourly employees were 11.1 percent (1974) and 9.5 percent (1975). The new policy took effect in January 1976 and, following this, absenteeism rates were 7.5 percent (1976), 7.3 percent (1977), 8.0 percent (1978), 8.2 percent (1979), 8.5 percent (1980), and 8.2 percent (1981). This seems to suggest that other factors such as those mentioned above had indeed improved.

These arguments increase the plausibility of attributing improvements to the interventions, but action research as a design strategy leaves much to be desired when one attempts to corroborate a view scientifically. To increase credibility in the data, one might use a control group against which to contrast trends. Fortunately, we could obtain turnover data from another mine that produced the same ore, was located in the same region, and was owned and operated by the same corporation. This second mine differed from Torenton in that it employed about twenty-five hundred workers (Torenton employed eighteen hundred) and had been in operation for more than twenty-five years. More critically, this other mine did not have an ongoing program of behavioral science intervention. It did, of course, make "normal" efforts to improve—that is, without the assistance of external consultants. From 1974 to 1981, this comparison mine reduced its turnover rate from 3.7 percent per month to 1.6 percent, representing an improvement of 58 percent. The turnover rate at Torenton declined from 9.8 percent to 1.5 percent, an improvement of 85 percent. Because Torenton had a higher turnover rate in 1974, this comparison could be misleading and should be considered only as suggestive of the pace of improvement at Torenton.

Productivity

A second criterion—mining productivity—traditionally has been measured according to a complex formula of "feet per manshift." One can account partially for the erratic performance graph shown in Exhibit 1 by noting that a hiring boom took place in 1978 and 1979. The dip in feet per manshift in 1976 was thought to reflect the mine's changing from developmental to production mining as Torenton began producing ore for the market. In general, the

Exhibit 1

Monthly Averages for Turnover, Productivity, and Safety for the Period 1974–1981

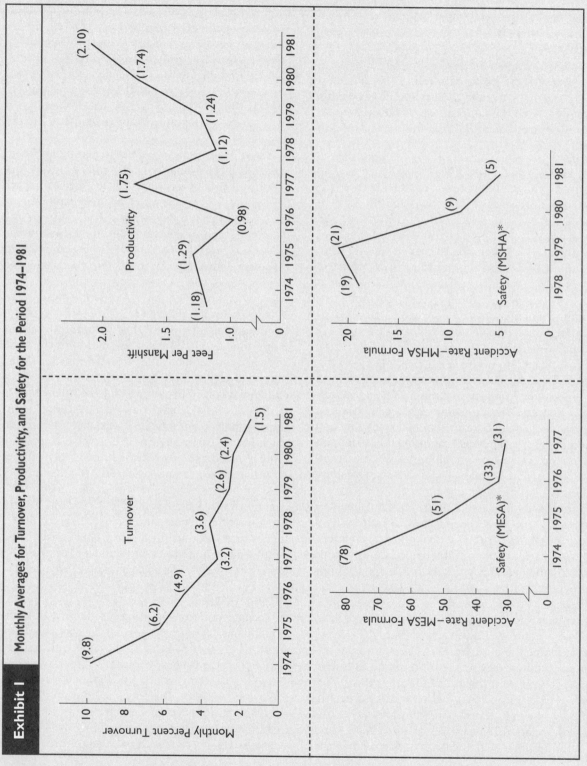

* MESA: Mine Enforcement Safety Administration; MSHA: Mine Safety and Health Administration.

trend suggests an improvement in mining effectiveness and, as most mine operators would realize, this occurred despite major additions to safety procedures that greatly slowed ore production.

A look at the comparison mine gives one a better perspective on Torenton's progress. The technology of the two mines differed only slightly, and any technological changes—such as advances in methods or tools—were relatively minor in both settings during the period. The other mine used a productivity index known as "tons per manshift." In 1974, the comparison mine had a productivity rate of 34.9. Productivity there declined steadily until 1979, after which it showed some recovery, but as of 1981 productivity remained at 32.3 tons per manshift and failed to regain the 1974 level. During the same period, Torenton moved from a productivity level of 1.18 feet per manshift (1974) to one of 2.10 (1981). Because of the different scales of measurement, perhaps one can only state that the data imply that Torenton gradually improved its performance during the period by more than 75 percent, although the comparison mine showed a slight decline.

Safety

The third criterion is safety, and the method for assessing it changed in 1977 from the MESA (Mine Enforcement Safety Administration) formula to the MSHA (Mine Safety and Health Administration) formula. Exhibit 1 describes a relatively continuous improvement in each graph, but inconsistencies in computational procedures do not allow a simple assertion of safety progression during the 1974–1981 period. Informal judgments by Torenton's safety personnel, however, suggest this was the case.

Using the same MESA and MSHA formulas for the comparison mine, one finds that the MESA rates moved from thirty-eight in 1974 to a high of forty-seven in 1976 before dropping to twenty-nine in 1977. The MSHA rates moved from eight in 1978 to a high of ten in 1979 and then declined in 1981. The degree of change, using either formula, seems more marked at Torenton. According to mine officials at Torenton, however, this may have been partly an artifact of the interpretations given the MESA and MSHA formulas by the two mines when they were first presented by the government agencies.

As an alternative means of gauging the Torenton safety record, we considered industry records for this period from the appropriate mining sector—that is, metal and nonmetal mining (cf. *Statistical Abstract of the United States: 1982–1983*, 1983, p. 718). Data from 1974 to 1980 show a slight increase in the rate of nonfatal injuries per million work hours (twenty-four to twenty-eight) as well as in the rate of nonfatal injuries per one thousand workers (forty-four to fifty-one). This seems to suggest that Torenton's trend toward fewer on-the-job injuries ran counter to the industry pattern.

Questions

1. How would you evaluate the organizational development process that was carried out at the Torenton Mine?

2. Do you believe the hard measures of turnover, productivity, and safety are related to the survey feedback effort? What other plausible explanations exist? How would you determine the true impact of the survey feedback process?

Source: Adapted with permission from NTL Institute, "Observations from a Long-Term, Survey-Guided Consultation with a Mining Company," by James F. Gavin, *Journal of Applied Behavioral Science,* 21, 2 (copyright 1985): 201–20.

Initiating Change in the Manufacturing and Distribution Division of PolyProd

Information management has become a critical competency in modern high-technology firms. These companies simply cannot afford to waste time reinventing or rejustifying existing methodologies, and costly errors—even injuries—can result from not having and following appropriate operating procedures. However, the burgeoning quantity of data, information, and knowledge that must be retrieved and used has begun to tax some companies' abilities to keep up. In addition, many of the people within these organizations are not trained properly or are unwilling to deal with formal information systems.

Identifying the Need for Improved Information Management

You are Roberta Jackson, a concerned, experienced first-level project manager working at the headquarters site of the manufacturing and distribution division (M&DDiv) of PolyProd, a corporation that develops, markets, and manufactures a variety of high-technology products for industry and home use. Based on your experience and some informal information that you have collected, you are convinced that failing to improve current information management practices will cost PolyProd millions of dollars in direct expenses and could contribute to long-term market share declines in PolyProd products. As a result, you believe it is necessary to change M&DDiv's documentation processes and procedures that govern the creation and use of the specifications and formal procedures required by the manufacturing organization.

You anticipate that such an undertaking will involve change and project management techniques traditional in large engineering firms, and that it should proceed along well-trodden paths: You will plan the project, sell it to management and obtain the authority to begin, and then allocate resources and monitor progress until you can declare victory. The following sections describe the M&DDiv's organization, the documentation system, and other factors contributing to the current situation.

The M&DDiv Organization and Culture

M&DDiv manufactures and distributes a small but lucrative subset of PolyProd's products and has five locations around the world. The headquarters organization, located in the United States, centrally manages the other four sites in Canada, Asia, Africa, and Europe but also allows them a lot of autonomy in decision making. Each location houses both manufacturing and distribution processes.

The variety and complexity of M&DDiv's products have increased markedly, as have the speed, intricacy, and expense of the unique high-volume automated manufacturing processes that produce the products. As a result, M&DDiv has been growing rapidly during its entire eleven-year history, experiencing exponential increases in locations, sales, capital equipment, product lines, and personnel. Such support systems as the information and knowledge management system have struggled to keep up with the growth. Moreover, the required hiring of many inexperienced or temporary personnel has stretched the ability of M&DDiv to maintain the culture of PolyProd. These trends are expected to continue unabated in the foreseeable future.

The company's business strategy charters the headquarters site with designing products and their manufacturing methodologies, and then with transferring the maturing manufacturing processes offshore to take advantage of the lower tax rates and cheaper labor at the four production locations. The key success factors for the headquarters site are rapid design innovation and minimum elapsed time between design acceptance and volume manufacturability. The priorities of the production sites are shippable-product volume, quality, and cost-effectiveness.

Over the last several years, friction has been increasing between headquarters and the other locations. The managers and employees at the sites generally are dissatisfied with what they regard as a patronizing and demanding attitude, and they resent policies and assignments unilaterally sent out by headquarters. Headquarters staff, in turn, resent the fierce and sometimes unnecessary individualism of the other locations. Throughout M&DDiv, there is a subtle but strong resistance to large-scale or externally initiated change. This is especially true when the change involves converging all sites in a single process or technology. Much of this results from the pressures of maintaining high production levels; unproven change simply is too risky. Historically, any attempt to institute a change by dictate has been doomed to failure. For example, announced changes typically take three to five years to institutionalize, and even after that time, there is considerable residual resistance or grudging compliance. It is common for otherwise successful projects to wither and die from lack of implementation support.

Headquarters has its own internal issues. First, it has a long-standing tradition of conservatism and hardened reluctance to change. Second, it is still reeling from the rapid growth that has transformed it from a small, independent factory into the hub of a global business. Finally, it is suffering from a discontinuity in its own cultural history: rapid hiring and promotion, insufficient mentoring, heavy outsourcing and downsizing of certain competencies, and extensive use of a temporary workforce in non-engineering areas have put extreme pressures on the once homogenous and intensely loyal culture.

In a static, stable environment, the existing relationship between headquarters and the other locations might be considered an acceptable cost of doing business. In M&DDiv, however, the stakes are far too high to maintain the status quo. Anticipated continued growth will magnify all problems exponentially, and the seriousness of the problems very well might inhibit or halt that growth. Because M&DDiv's revenue represents a significant portion of PolyProd's bottom line, much of PolyProd's total growth is contingent on M&DDiv's continued expansion. If M&DDiv falters, PolyProd well might follow.

The Documentation Problem

At PolyProd, quality is everything. The company simply cannot allow bad products to reach the customer, but neither can it afford to scrap good products that may have failed too-stringent tests. The precision high-volume manufacturing processes used by all M&DDiv sites use rigorous quality control procedures to ensure the highest yield of good products and the lowest scrap. This is achieved by statistical analyses of interim results and by standardizing tasks and tooling as much as possible. This, in turn, hinges on a huge quantity of documentation, including material and process specifications, operating instructions, maintenance information, replication data (for example, bills of materials, assembly and checkout instructions), and the like. In summary, good products require either good documentation or expensive workarounds and corrections.

The Documentation System

The documentation system consists of a number of components: an electronic "vault" where a variety of documents are kept; the computer systems and networks that allow access to the vault; the documents (electronic files) themselves; the protocols for routing and approving revisions; and, perhaps most critical and most dangerous, all of the people who interact with these components. To be effective, a documentation system has to be developed carefully, maintained actively, and protected closely from inappropriate alteration. Because products and their production equipment migrate between sites, the documentation also must be portable and usable without extensive revision.

When a new product design is initiated, a suite of drawings and other specifications is created immediately and remains with the project for its whole life. The design engineer's early sketches and notes are entered into the electronic vault, where they are protected against loss and inadvertent change. As experiments are done and prototypes are created, test results and design refinements are added to the vault. As the design moves into the premanufacturing stage, parts lists, materials specifications, assembly instructions, test procedures, and quality criteria are added to the file. When the automated equipment to produce the product in volume is designed, its information joins the product's information in the vault.

The vault provides functions other than safekeeping. Accessed through workstations throughout the site, the vault allows engineers to sign out documents for revision, printing, or online viewing. Every time a change is made, the vault's software tracks the differences between the old and new versions, records who made the changes, and routes the revised documentation by email through an approval team. Once approved, the revised document replaces the original version, which then is archived automatically to provide an audit trail. Throughout its life, a document may be entirely electronic and viewed only online, printed and bound, printed when needed and then discarded, or some combination of these media.

Virtually every department in the factory uses these documents. The research and design (R&D) department designs the product; manufacturing engineering uses the product specifications to design production equipment; materials engineering uses the same specifications to select the plastics and metals used to make the product; materials procurement uses the materials engineering documents to order the supplies for the production line; capital purchasing uses the manufacturing engineering documents to let contracts for the production lines; technical writing groups use all of these documents to create user manuals and other printed materials to ship with the final product; and traffic combs through the data to estimate the number and types of shipping containers and vehicles that will be needed. When the product is actually manufactured, the production departments continually refer to the documentation for instructions on how to operate, test, and repair their equipment; how to order and load raw materials into the machinery; how to test the products; and how to judge the product's quality.

When headquarters prepares to send a product and its production equipment to one of the other locations, the documentation is supposed to be sent first. The documentation is used at the new location to train employees, to guide the preparation of the new facility, and to ensure that all of the supply chain components are in place to provide raw materials and outbound shipping. Much of the documentation is translated into the local language for use by semiskilled production workers once the production line is running at the new location.

Every department at every location is both a consumer and a producer of documentation, and all are completely interdependent. A single error in a specification can cascade into a multimillion-dollar disaster in the form of incorrect raw materials, a product that passes tests but doesn't work for the customer, a production line that won't fit inside the factory building, or a huge fine from U.S. Customs for mistakenly exporting restricted technology.

The Current Situation

Various departments within M&DDiv have invested heavily in the human resources, tools, and time needed to create and maintain the documentation process. Despite this investment, M&DDiv's documentation is still regarded as unsatisfactory by most employees and management. For example, there is widespread dissatisfaction with the documentation system in the design departments at headquarters. Because of past bad experiences with outdated or incorrect documentation, users distrust all documentation's accuracy and find the vault hard to access. The quality department is distressed by the delays in the correction and update cycle. Technical writers are unhappy with the general usability of the required word processors, graphics programs, and the vault; they also feel artistically constrained when asked to use standard templates or designs for their documents. The writers get little cooperation from the subject matter experts and reviewers they rely on for information and feel that creating a finished document can take four to five times as much time and effort as it should take.

The headquarters document control supervisors and technical-writing supervisors also are frustrated. Their personal workloads have ballooned to unmanageable levels as they added staff to keep up with the increasing documentation requirements of M&DDiv's growing number of products. At the same time, they are permitted to hire only temporary resources; qualified candidates have become increasingly hard to find, and they take everything they have learned with them when their finite-length contracts end.

The production sites share all of these concerns and have unique issues of their own. They are frustrated by their inability to get correct and complete documentation when a manufacturing process transfers from headquarters, although the documentation is supposed to arrive long before the manufacturing process arrives. They often must convert unusual file formats or struggle to rewrite U.S.-idiomatic information to meet the needs of their local users. They also often feel that they need to invent their own document designs because global designs are still pending or are too specific to another location's needs.

Contributing Factors

As your early interest in overcoming these problems increased, you conducted an informal analysis based on interviews and observations at all five locations. You have concluded that there are a number of interrelated causes producing M&DDiv's documentation problems.

The primary issue is the lack of an overriding vision or strategy to guide the creation of a full and robust documentation system. To be fair, several years ago, M&DDiv's senior management chartered a documentation quality effort. That effort, however, was implemented only partially, and the project lost momentum after some early successes. This sent a signal—to both the headquarters site and the production locations—that documentation was not really so important after all, much to the relief of those who considered documentation-related tasks a distraction from their "real work." As the rigor of document-creation and -maintenance rules began to wane, the quality of the documents and the processes they supported began to deteriorate again. This continuing gradual slide at each of the locations is exacerbated by the lack of coordination among the sites. Decisions are made independently, based on local or perceived larger-scope needs, or occasionally on policies that were developed during the short-lived documentation-quality project. Few people consider a time horizon farther out than one year, and even fewer look forward with a global perspective.

There are severe integration problems among locations. The production entities are concerned with document control and simplicity. Headquarters has difficulty in simply collecting the information in the first place, and with keeping it up-to-date and complete as the subject matter rapidly evolves during the design and tuning phases. Headquarters often uses the documentation as repositories of historical or justification information, and this use confuses and annoys the production sites, which require only the minimum information necessary to manufacture products.

There also are internal integration problems within each location. Responsibility for different aspects of the documentation falls within several organizations: creation and storage technology in one organization; the formal processes for acquisition and control in another; best-practice consulting in a third; and technical writers scattered throughout several other departments with their customers (for example, some writers sit within R&D, some work with manufacturing engineering, and still others are in the quality department). There are no rewards for communicating or collaborating, and the groups frequently develop similar or conflicting solutions to what turn out to be common problems.

Day-to-day operation also is less than optimal. The majority of involved personnel have little or no training or experience in the field of documentation. This has led to quality problems, arbitrary decision making, inappropriate prioritizing of tasks and objectives, and several blind-alley projects (that is, projects that start successfully but run into insurmountable barriers and are abandoned). Many writers and document controllers are former production line operators who show little interest or aptitude during times of high need. Few of the external temporary personnel have formal technical writing experience; most are recently graduated English or journalism majors. The technical writing supervisors all moved laterally from production and received no special training or mentoring; this results in inefficiency and quality problems within their departments.

Generally, each of the problems and frustrations outlined above is restricted to the departments immediately affected. The various symptoms are highly distributed, frequently are noticeable only at the lowest levels of the organization, and often are concealed beneath their effects. For example, raw material rejection in the receiving department might increase without anyone questioning whether the inspection checklist itself was incorrect, or a growing headcount in the support department might not be linked with a particular manufacturing location's use of an obsolete adjustment procedure. These problems usually would be examined by the immediate department supervisor without regard to a larger context, and would seldom be visible to upper management or someone with a less parochial viewpoint.

Until you began talking with people at all sites, most people were aware only of their own difficulties with the documentation, and were surprised by your interest. You found that the overall sense of "shared pain" in the organization was very low, and that upper management was completely unaware of the magnitude, frequency, and very real cost of the problems.

Aside from a few informal company networks and councils, there are no worldwide efforts to resolve these problems from a system perspective. Most of the separate organizations recognize the local aspects of the problems, and in isolation, some have projects in place to improve their own processes. There is, however, no movement toward a larger-scale solution.

It is clear that M&DDiv is in a state of uneasy stasis and that external stimulus—you—will be needed to begin a resolution.

Your Plan to Initiate Change

You have decided to conduct an informal discussion with Stewart Jones (the M&DDiv executive you deem to be the most likely potential sponsor for the project) to get a preliminary opinion on whether your project would be worth proposing formally. You have planned your approach carefully.

Because of the engineering-intense environment in M&DDiv, you know that you must follow a defined, rational project management methodology—overt touchy-feely techniques would be rejected out of hand. You understand, too, that changing the documentation process will require equal parts of cultural change and process improvement.

You understand the dynamics of M&DDiv management: they seem powerless to force change on the different geographic locations, and they are unable and unwilling to spend much time trying to reach consensus on the need for standardizing anything. Going to the top won't help. Because you are dealing with many branches of a very large organization, you face a Catch-22 situation: when you appeal up the organization chart to a level that has the power to command all relevant organizations, that person is so removed from the problem that he or she is unwilling to consider it unless it has huge demonstrable impact.

Questions

1. What is your assessment of your (Roberta's) efforts to date?

2. How will you convince Stewart Jones to allow you to proceed with the project? What arguments might you use?

3. Describe how you will develop a change process and the critical issues you will face in managing the change.

Source: Copyright 2000 by Clarity and Brian B. Egan. Adapted with permission.

Human Process Interventions

3

12

Interpersonal and Group Process Approaches

This chapter discusses change programs relating to interpersonal relations and group dynamics. These change programs are among the earliest ones devised in OD and represent attempts to improve people's working relationships with one another. The interventions are aimed at helping group members assess their interactions and devise more effective ways of working together. These interventions represent a basic skill requirement for an OD practitioner.

T-groups, derived from the early laboratory training stem of OD, are used today mainly to help managers learn about the effects of their behavior on others. Process consultation is another OD technique for helping group members understand, diagnose, and improve their behaviors. Through process consultation, the group should become better able to use its own resources to identify and solve interpersonal problems that often block the solving of work-related problems. Third-party interventions focus directly on dysfunctional interpersonal conflict. This approach is used only in special circumstances and only when both parties are willing to engage in the process of direct confrontation.

Team building is aimed both at helping a team perform its tasks better and at satisfying individual needs. Through team-building activities, group goals and norms become clearer. In addition, team members become better able to confront difficulties and problems and to understand the roles of individuals within the team. Among the specialized team-building approaches presented are interventions associated with ongoing teams and with such temporary teams as project teams and task forces.

T-GROUPS

As discussed in Chapter 1, sensitivity training, or the T-group, is an early forerunner of modern OD interventions. Its direct use in OD has lessened considerably. The National Training Laboratories (NTL) and UCLA are among the few remaining organizations that offer T-groups on a regular basis. OD practitioners often attend T-groups to improve their own functioning. For example, T-groups can help OD practitioners become more aware of how others perceive them and thus increase their effectiveness with client systems. In addition, OD practitioners often recommend that organization members attend a T-group to learn how their behaviors affect others and to develop more effective ways of relating to people.

What Are the Goals?

T-groups traditionally are designed to provide members with experiential learning about group dynamics, leadership, and interpersonal relations. The basic T-group consists of ten to fifteen strangers who meet with a professional trainer to explore the social dynamics that emerge from their interactions. Modifications of this basic design have generally moved in two directions. The first path has used T-group methods to help individuals gain deeper personal understanding and development. This intrapersonal focus typically is called an encounter group or a personal-growth group. It generally is considered outside the boundaries of OD and should be conducted only by professionally trained clinicians. The second direction uses T-group techniques to explore group dynamics and member relationships within an intact work group. Considerable training in T-group methods and group dynamics should be acquired before trying these interventions. This group focus has led to the OD intervention called team building, which is discussed later in this chapter.

After an extensive review of the literature, Campbell and Dunnette listed six overall objectives common to most T-groups, although not every practitioner need accomplish every objective in every T-group.[1] These objectives are

1. Increased understanding, insight, and self-awareness about one's own behavior and its impact on others, including the ways in which others interpret one's behavior.

2. Increased understanding and sensitivity about the behavior of others, including better interpretation of both verbal and nonverbal clues, which increases awareness and understanding of what other people are thinking and feeling.

3. Better understanding and awareness of group and intergroup processes, both those that facilitate and those that inhibit group functioning.

4. Increased diagnostic skills in interpersonal and intergroup situations. In Campbell and Dunnette's view, accomplishing the first three objectives provides the basic tools for accomplishing the fourth objective.

5. Increased ability to transform learning into action so that real-life interventions will be successful in increasing member satisfaction, output, or effectiveness.

6. Improvement in individuals' ability to analyze their own interpersonal behavior as well as to learn how to help themselves and others with whom they come in contact achieve more satisfying, rewarding, and effective interpersonal relationships.

These goals seem to meet many T-group applications, although any one training program may emphasize one goal more than the others. One trainer may emphasize understanding group process as applied to organizations; another may focus on group process as a way of developing individuals' understanding of themselves and others; and a third trainer may concentrate primarily on interpersonal and intrapersonal learning.

Application Stages

Application 12.1 illustrates the activities occurring in a typical unstructured strangers T-group, one of the most popular approaches.

The Results of T-Groups

T-groups have been among the most controversial topics in organization development, and probably more has been written about them than about any other single topic in OD. A major issue of concern relates to the effectiveness of T-groups—their impact on both the individual and the organization.

Campbell and Dunnette reviewed a large number of published articles on T-groups and criticized them for their lack of scientific rigor.[2] Argyris, on the other hand, criticized Campbell and Dunnette, arguing that a different kind of scientific

APPLICATION 12·1   Unstructured Strangers T-Group

A typical T-group session for strangers might consist of five or six T-groups of ten to fifteen members who have signed up for a session conducted by the National Training Laboratories, UCLA's Ojai program, a university, or a similar organization. The T-group sessions may be combined with cognitive learning, such as brief lectures on general theory, designed exercises, or management games.

Each T-group comprises people who have not previously known one another. If several people from the same organization attend, they are put into different T-groups. At the beginning of the training session, the trainer makes a brief and ambiguous statement about either his or her role or some ground rules and lapses into silence. Because the trainer has not taken a leadership role or provided goals for the group, a dilemma of leadership and agenda is created. The group must work out its own methods to proceed further; it must fill the void left by the lack of a leader or of group objectives.

As the group fills the void, the individuals' behaviors become the "here-and-now" basic data for the learning experiences. As the group struggles with procedure, individual members try out different behaviors and roles, many of which are unsuccessful. One T-group member might make a number of direct, forceful, and unsuccessful attempts to take over the leadership role, trying first one style, then another. Finally, he or she conspicuously withdraws from the group, falls silent, and appears to be thinking about other things. Group members might observe that this person has two basic styles of working with others; when one style is unsuccessful, he or she adopts the other—withdrawal.

As appropriate, the trainer will make an "intervention," an observation or comment about the group, its behavior, or the activities that are taking place. The type and nature of the intervention will vary, depending on the purpose of the laboratory and the trainer's own style. Usually, the trainer encourages individuals to understand what is going on in the group, their own feelings and behaviors, and the impact their behavior has on themselves and others. The primary emphasis is on the here-and-now experience, rather than on anecdotes or "back at the ranch" experiences.

The emphasis on openness and leveling in a supportive and caring environment enables the participants to gain insight into their own and others' feelings and behaviors. A better understanding of group dynamics also can make them more productive individuals. ∎

rigor is necessary for evaluating T-groups.[3] Although there are obvious methodological problems, the studies generally support the notion that T-group training does bring about change in the individual back in his or her work situation.[4] Among the most frequently found changes are increased flexibility in role behavior; more openness, receptivity, and awareness; and more open communication, with better listening skills and less dependence on others. However, because the goals of many T-group designs are not carefully spelled out, because there are so many variations in design, and particularly because many of the research designs do not carefully measure an individual's real work climate and culture, the findings are not highly predictable. Further, some individuals do not attend T-group sessions voluntarily, and little knowledge is available about the differences between those who want to attend and those who are forced to attend.

In considering the value of T-groups for organizations, the evidence is even more mixed. One comparative study of different human process interventions showed that T-groups had the least impact on measures of process (for example, openness and decision making) and outcome (for example, productivity and costs).[5] Another comparative study showed, however, that structured T-groups had the most impact on hard measures, such as productivity and absenteeism.[6] The T-groups in this study were structured so that learning could be explicitly transferred back to the work setting. A third comparative study showed that although T-groups improved group process, they failed to improve the organizational culture surrounding the groups and to gain peer and managerial support in the organization.[7] Finally, in a meta-analysis of sixteen studies, researchers concluded that laboratory training interventions had significant, positive effects on overall employee satisfaction and other attitudes.[8]

In his review of the T-group literature, Kaplan concluded that despite their tarnished reputation, such interventions "can continue to serve a purpose they are uniquely suited for, to provide an emotional education and to promote awareness of relationships and group process."[9] To accomplish these purposes, T-groups must be competently run so that there is a minimal risk of hurting participants; they selectively must include only those people who want to attend; and they need to be relevant to the wider organizational context so that participants can apply their learning at work.

PROCESS CONSULTATION

Process consultation (PC) is a general framework for carrying out helping relationships.[10] It is oriented to helping managers, employees, and groups assess and improve *processes,* such as communication, interpersonal relations, decision making, and task performance. Schein argues that effective consultants and managers should be good helpers, aiding others in getting things done and in achieving the goals they have set.[11] Thus, PC is more a philosophy than a set of techniques aimed at performing this helping relationship. The philosophy ensures that those who are receiving the help own their problems, gain the skills and expertise to diagnose them, and solve them themselves. Thus, it is an approach to helping people and groups help themselves.

Schein defines process consultation as "the creation of a relationship that permits the client to perceive, understand, and act on the process events that occur in [her/his] internal and external environment in order to improve the situation as defined by the client."[12] The process consultant does not offer expert help in the form of solutions to problems, as in the doctor–patient model. Rather, the process consultant works to develop relationships, observes groups and people in action, helps them diagnose the way they are carrying out tasks, and helps them learn how to be more effective.

Principles of Process Consultation

PC follows closely the phases of planned change described in Chapter 2: entering, defining the relationship, selecting an approach, gathering data and making a diagnosis, intervening, reducing the involvement, and terminating the relationship. When used in process consultation, however, these stages are not so clear-cut. As a philosophy of helping in relationships, Schein proposes ten principles to guide the process consultant's actions.[13]

1. *Always try to be helpful.* Process consultants must be mindful of their intentions, and each interaction must be oriented toward being helpful.

2. *Always stay in touch with the current reality.* Each interaction should produce diagnostic information about the current situation. It includes data about the client's opinions, beliefs, and emotions; the system's current functioning; and the practitioner's reactions, thoughts, and feelings.

3. *Access your ignorance.* An important source of information about current reality is the practitioner's understanding of what is known, what is assumed, and what is not known. Process consultants must use themselves as instruments of change.

4. *Everything you do is an intervention.* Any interaction in a consultative relationship generates information as well as consequences. Simply conducting preliminary interviews with group members, for example, can raise members' awareness of a situation and help them see it in a new light.

5. *The client owns the problem and the solution.* This is a key principle in all OD practice. Practitioners help clients solve their own problems and learn to manage future change.

6. *Go with the flow.* When process consultants access their own ignorance, they often realize that there is much about the client system and its culture that they do not know. Thus, practitioners must work to understand the client's motivations and perceptions.

7. *Timing is crucial.* Observations, comments, questions, and other interventions intended to be helpful may work in some circumstances and fail in others. Process consultants must be vigilant to occasions when the client is open (or not open) to suggestions.

8. *Be constructively opportunistic with confrontive interventions.* Although process consultants must be willing to go with the flow, they also must be willing to take appropriate risks. From time to time and in their best judgment, practitioners must learn to take advantage of "teachable moments." A well-crafted process observation or piece of feedback can provide a group or individual with great insight into their behavior.

9. *Everything is information; errors will always occur and are the prime source for learning.* Process consultants never can know fully the client's reality and invariably will make mistakes. The consequences of these mistakes, the unexpected and surprising reactions, are important data that must be used in the ongoing development of the relationship.

10. *When in doubt, share the problem.* The default intervention in a helping relationship is to model openness by sharing the dilemma of what to do next.

Group Process

Process consultation deals primarily with five important interpersonal and group processes: communications, the functional roles of group members, the ways in which the group solves problems and makes decisions, group norms development, and the use of leadership and authority.

Communications

One of the process consultant's areas of interest is the nature and style of communication at both the overt and covert levels. At the overt level, communication issues involve who talks to whom, for how long, and how often. One method for describing group communication is to keep a time log of how often and to whom people talk. For example, at an hour-long meeting conducted by a manager, the longest anyone other than the manager got to speak was one minute, and that minute was allotted to the assistant manager. Rather than telling the manager that he is cutting people off, the consultant can give descriptive feedback by citing the number of times others tried to talk and the amount of time they were given. The consultant must make certain that the feedback is descriptive and not evaluative (good or bad), unless the individual or group is ready for evaluative feedback.

By keeping a time log, the consultant also can note who talks and who interrupts. Frequently, certain people are perceived as being quiet, when in fact they have tried to say something and have been interrupted. Such interruptions are one of the most effective ways of reducing communications and decreasing participation in a meeting.

Body language and other nonverbal behavior also can be a highly informative method for understanding communication processes.[14] For example, at another meeting conducted by a manager, the animated discussion at the start of the meeting was interrupted by the second-in-command, who said, "This is a problem-solving meeting, not a gripe session." As the manager continued to talk, the fourteen other members present assumed expressions of concentration. Within twenty-five minutes, all of them had folded their arms and were leaning backward, a sure sign that they were blocking out or shutting off the message. Within ten seconds of the manager's subsequent statement, "We are interested in getting your ideas," those present unfolded their arms and began to lean forward, a clear nonverbal sign that they were involved once again.

At the covert or hidden level of communication, sometimes one thing is said but another meant, thus giving a double message. Luft has described this phenomenon in what is called the *Johari Window*.[15] Figure 12.1, a diagram of the Johari Window, shows that some personal issues are perceived by both the individual and others (cell 1). Other people are aware of their own issues, but they conceal them from others (cell 2). People with certain feelings about themselves or others in the work group may not share with others unless they feel safe and protected; by not revealing reactions they feel might be hurtful or impolite, they lessen the degree of communication.

Cell 3 comprises personal issues that are unknown to the individual but that are communicated clearly to others. For example, an individual may shout, "I'm not

Figure 12•1	Johari Window	
Unknown to Others	**Known to Others**	
Known to Self, Unknown to Others	Known to Self and Others	**Known to Self**
Unknown to Self or Others	Unknown to Self, Known to Others	**Unknown to Self**

SOURCE: Adapted by permission of the publisher from J. Luft, "The Johari Window," *Human Relations Training News* 5 (1961): 6–7.

angry," as he or she slams a fist on the table, or say, "I'm not embarrassed at all," as he or she blushes scarlet. Typically, cell-3 communication conveys double messages. For example, one manager who made frequent business trips invariably told his staff to function as a team and to make decisions in his absence. The staff, however, consistently refused to do this because it was clear to them, and to the process consultant, that the manager was really saying, "Go ahead as a team and make decisions in my absence, but be absolutely certain they are the exact decisions I would make if I were here." Only after the manager participated in several meetings in which he received feedback was he able to understand that he was sending a double message. Thereafter, he tried both to accept decisions made by others and to use management by objectives with his staff and with individual managers.

Cell 4 of the Johari Window represents those personal aspects that are unknown to either the individual or others. Because such areas are outside the realm of the process consultant and the group, focus is typically on the other three cells.

The consultant can encourage individuals to be more open with others about their views, opinions, concerns, and emotions, thus reducing cell 2. Further, the consultant can help individuals give feedback to others, thus reducing cell 3. Reducing the size of these two cells helps improve the communication process by enlarging cell 1, the "self" that is open to both the individual and others.

Functional Roles of Group Members

The process consultant must be keenly aware of the different roles individual members take on in a group. Both upon entering and while remaining in a group, the individual must determine a self-identity, influence, and power that will satisfy personal needs while working to accomplish group goals. Preoccupation with individual needs or power struggles can reduce the effectiveness of a group severely, and unless the individual can expose and share those personal needs to some degree, the group is unlikely to be productive. Therefore, the process consultant must help the group confront and work through these needs. Emotions are facts, but frequently they are regarded as side issues to be avoided. Whenever an individual, usually the leader, says to the group, "Let's stick with the facts," it can be a sign that the emotional needs of group members are not being satisfied and, indeed, are being disregarded as irrelevant.

Two other functions need to be performed if a group is to be effective: (1) task-related activities, such as giving and seeking information and elaborating, coordinating, and evaluating activities; and (2) group-maintenance actions, directed toward holding the group together as a cohesive team, including encouraging, harmonizing, compromising, setting standards, and observing. Most ineffective groups perform little group maintenance, and this is a primary reason for bringing in a process consultant.

The process consultant can help by suggesting that some part of each meeting be reserved for examining these functions and periodically assessing the feelings of the group's members. As Schein points out, however, the basic purpose of the process consultant is not to take on the role of expert but to help the group share in its own diagnosis and do a better job in learning to diagnose its own processes: "It is important that the process consultant encourage the group not only to allocate time for diagnosis but to take the lead itself in trying to articulate and understand its own processes."[16] Otherwise, the group may default and become dependent on the supposed expert. In short, the consultant's role is to make comments and to assist with diagnosis, but the emphasis should be on facilitating the group's understanding and articulation of its own processes.

Group Problem Solving and Decision Making

To be effective, a group must be able to identify problems, examine alternatives, and make decisions. The first part of this process is the most important. Groups often fail to distinguish between problems (either task-related or interpersonal) and symptoms. Once the group identifies the problem, a process consultant can help the group analyze its approach, restrain the group from reacting too quickly and making a premature diagnosis, or suggest additional options.

For example, a consultant was asked to process a group's actions during a three-hour meeting that had been taped. The tapes revealed that premature rejection of a suggestion had severely retarded the group's process. After one member's suggestion at the beginning of the meeting was quickly rejected by the manager, he repeated his suggestion several times in the next hour. Each time his suggestion was rejected quickly. During the second hour, this member became quite negative, opposing most of the other ideas offered. Finally, toward the end of the second hour, he brought up his proposal again. At that time, it was thoroughly discussed and then rejected for reasons that the member accepted.

During the third hour, this person was one of the most productive members of the group, offering constructive and worthwhile ideas, suggestions, and recommendations. In addition, he was able to integrate the comments of others, to modify them, and to come up with useful, integrated new suggestions. However, it was not until his first suggestion had been thoroughly discussed (even though it was finally rejected) that he was able to become a truly constructive member of the group.

Once the problem has been identified, a decision must be made. One way of making decisions is to ignore a suggestion. For example, when one person makes a suggestion, someone else offers another before the first has been discussed. A second method is to give decision-making power to the person in authority. Sometimes decisions are made by minority rule, the leader arriving at a decision and turning for agreement to several people who will comply. Frequently, silence is regarded as consent. Decisions also can be made by majority rule, consensus, or unanimous consent.

The process consultant can help the group understand how it makes its decisions and the consequences of each decision process, as well as help diagnose which type of decision process may be the most effective in a given situation. Decision by unanimous consent or consensus, for example, may be ideal in some circumstances but too time-consuming or costly in other situations.

Group Norms and Growth

Especially if a group of people works together over a period of time, it develops group norms or standards of behavior about what is good or bad, allowed or forbidden, right or wrong. There may be an explicit norm that group members are free to express their ideas and feelings, whereas the implicit norm is that one does not contradict the ideas or suggestions of certain group members (usually the more powerful ones). The process consultant can be very helpful in assisting the group to understand and articulate its own norms and to determine whether those norms are helpful or dysfunctional. By understanding its norms and recognizing which ones are helpful, the group can grow and deal realistically with its environment, make optimum use of its own resources, and learn from its own experiences.[17]

Leadership and Authority

A process consultant needs to understand processes of leadership and how different leadership styles can help or hinder a group's functioning. In addition, the consultant can help the leader adjust her or his style to fit the situation. An important step in that process is for the leader to gain a better understanding of her or his own behavior and the group's reaction to that behavior. It also is important that the leader become aware of alternative behaviors. For example, after gaining a better understanding of her or his assumptions about human behavior, the leader may do a better job of testing and perhaps changing those assumptions.

Basic Process Interventions

For each of the five interpersonal and group processes described above, a variety of interventions may be used. In broad terms, these are aimed at making individuals and groups more effective.[18]

Individual Interventions

These interventions are designed to help people be more effective or to increase the information they have about their "blind spot" in the Johari Window. Before process consultants can give individual feedback, they first must observe relevant events, ask questions to understand the issues fully, and make certain that the feedback is given to the client in a usable manner. The following are guidelines[19] for effective feedback.

- The giver and receiver must have consensus on the receiver's goals.
- The giver should emphasize description and appreciation.
- The giver should be concrete and specific.
- Both giver and receiver must have constructive motives.
- The giver should not withhold negative feedback if it is relevant.
- The giver should own his or her observations, feelings, and judgments.
- Feedback should be timed to when the giver and receiver are ready.

Group Interventions

These interventions are aimed at the process, content, or structure of the group. Process interventions sensitize the group to its own internal processes and generate interest in analyzing those processes. Interventions include comments, questions, or observations about

- relationships between and among group members
- problem solving and decision making
- the identity and purpose of the group.

Content interventions help the group determine what it works on. They include comments, questions, or observations about

- group membership
- agenda setting, review, and testing procedures
- interpersonal issues
- conceptual inputs on task-related topics.

Structural interventions help the group examine the stable and recurring methods it uses to accomplish tasks. They include comments, questions, or observations about the following:

- methods for dealing with external issues, such as inputs, resources, and customers
- methods for determining goals, developing strategies, accomplishing work, assigning responsibility, monitoring progress, and addressing problems
- relationships to authority, formal rules, and levels of intimacy.

Application 12.2 presents an example of process consultation with the top-management team of a manufacturing firm.[20]

When Is Process Consultation Appropriate?

Process consultation, a general model for helping relationships, has wide applicability in organizations. Because PC helps people and groups own their problems and diagnose and resolve them, it is most applicable in the following circumstances:[21]

1. The client has a problem but does not know its source or how to resolve it.
2. The client is unsure of what kind of help or consultation is available.
3. The nature of the problem is such that the client would benefit from involvement in its diagnosis.
4. The client is motivated by goals that the consultant can accept, and the consultant has some capacity to enter into a helping relationship directed at reaching those goals.
5. The client ultimately knows what interventions are most applicable.
6. The client is capable of learning how to assess and resolve her or his own problem.

Results of Process Consultation

Although process consultation is an important part of organization development and has been widely practiced over the past thirty-five years, only a modest amount of research addresses its effect on improving the ability of groups to accomplish work. The few studies that have been conducted have produced little hard evidence of effectiveness. Research findings on process consultation are unclear, especially because the findings relate to task performance.

A number of difficulties arise in trying to measure performance improvements as a result of process consultation. One problem is that most process consultation is conducted with groups performing mental tasks (for example, decision making); the outcomes of such tasks are difficult to evaluate. A second difficulty with measuring PC's effects occurs because in many cases process consultation is combined with other interventions in an ongoing OD program. Isolating the impact of process consultation from other interventions is difficult.

Kaplan's review of process consultation studies underscored the problems of measuring performance effects.[22] It examined published studies in three categories: (1) reports in which process intervention is the causal variable but performance is measured inadequately or not at all, (2) reports in which performance is measured but process consultation is not isolated as the independent variable (the case in many instances), and (3) research in which process consultation is isolated as the causal variable and performance is adequately measured. The review suggests that process consultation has positive effects on participants, according to self-reports of greater personal involvement, higher mutual influence, group effectiveness, and similar variables. However, very little, if any, research clearly demonstrates that

APPLICATION 12•2   Process Consultation at Action Company

This application, a story often told by Ed Schein and documented in several of his books about process consultation and culture, involves the senior management team of an organization that he worked with over several years. It illustrates well several of the principles of process consultation, such as accessing your ignorance, always trying to be helpful, and understanding that errors are the prime source of learning.

The Action Company was a large and innovative high-technology organization. One salient feature of their executive committee meetings was long and loud discussions. Members interrupted each other constantly, often got into shouting matches, drifted off the subject, and moved from one agenda point to another without any clear sense of what had been decided. Based on his beliefs about the nature of effective groups and his experiences with group dynamics training, the process consultant made several initial interventions as an "expert" consultant. For example, whenever he saw an opportunity, he would ask the group to consider the consequences of interrupting each other repeatedly. This had the effect of communicating his belief that their process was "bad" and interfered with the group's task and effectiveness. He pointed out how important ideas were being lost and potentially important ideas were not getting a full discussion. The group invariably responded with agreement and a resolution to do better, but within ten minutes were back to the same pattern.

As the process consultant reflected on these early interventions, he noticed that he was imposing on the group his own beliefs about what an ideal team should look like and how it should behave. This group, on the other hand, was clearly on a different path. Over time, he discovered that this group had a different set of shared assumptions that were driving their behaviors. In short, the group was trying to arrive at the "truth." Their assumption was that truth was revealed in ideas and actions that could withstand argument and debate. If an idea could survive intense scrutiny, it must be true and was worth pursuing.

Once he understood this basic premise, the process consultant asked himself what he could do that would be more helpful to the group. His answer was to work within the group's assumptions that were driving their behavior rather than imposing his beliefs on them. He had to learn that the primary task of the group, as *they* saw it, was to develop ideas that were so sound they could afford to bet the company on them. Generating ideas and evaluating them were therefore the two most crucial functions that they worked on in meetings.

Two kinds of interventions grew out of this insight. First, he noticed that ideas were in fact being lost because so much information was being processed so rapidly. Partly for his own sake and partly because he thought it might help, he went to the flipchart and wrote down the main ideas as they came out.

These ideas, incomplete or undeveloped because the presenter had been interrupted, led to the second kind of intervention. Instead of punishing the group for its "bad" behavior, as he had done in the early stages of the consultation, he looked for opportunities to turn the conversation back over to the person with the idea. For example, he would say, "John, you were trying to make a point. Did we get all of that?" This created the opportunity to get the idea out without drawing unnecessary attention to the reason why it had not gotten out in the first place. The combination of these two kinds of interventions focused the group on the ideas that were not on the flipchart and helped them navigate through their complex agenda. Ideas that were about to be lost were written down, resurrected, and given a fair chance.

The lesson was clear. Until the process consultant understood what the group really was trying to do, he could not focus on the right processes nor did he know how to intervene helpfully. He had to sense what the primary task was and where the group was getting stuck (incomplete idea formulation and too-quick evaluation) before he could determine what kind of intervention would be "facilitative." ∎

objective task effectiveness was increased. In most cases, either the field studies did not directly measure performance or the effect of process intervention was confounded with other variables.

A third problem with assessing the performance effects of process consultation is that much of the relevant research has used people's perceptions rather than hard performance measures as the index of success.[23] Although much of this research shows positive results, these findings should be interpreted carefully until further research is done using more concrete measures of performance.

THIRD-PARTY INTERVENTIONS

Third-party intervention focuses on conflicts arising between two or more people within the same organization. Conflict is inherent in groups and organizations and can arise from a variety of sources, including differences in personality, task orientation, and perceptions among group members, as well as competition for scarce resources. To emphasize that conflict is neither good nor bad per se is important. Conflict can enhance motivation and innovation and lead to greater understanding of ideas and views. On the other hand, it can prevent people from working together constructively, destroying necessary task interactions among group members. Consequently, third-party intervention is used primarily in situations in which conflict significantly disrupts necessary task interactions and work relationships among members.

Third-party intervention varies considerably depending on the kind of issues underlying the conflict. Conflict can arise over substantive issues, such as work methods, pay rates, and conditions of employment; or it can emerge from interpersonal issues, such as personalities and misperceptions. When applied to substantive issues, conflict resolution interventions often involve resolving labor–management disputes through arbitration and mediation. The methods used in such substantive interventions require considerable training and expertise in law and labor relations and generally are not considered part of OD practice. For example, when union and management representatives cannot resolve a joint problem, they can call upon the Federal Mediation and Conciliation Service to help them resolve the conflict. In addition, "alternative dispute resolution" (ADR) practices increasingly are offered in lieu of more expensive and time-consuming court trials.[24] Conflicts also may arise at the boundaries of the organization, such as between suppliers and the company or between a company and a public policy agency.[25]

When conflict involves interpersonal issues, however, OD has developed approaches that help control and resolve it. These third-party interventions help the parties interact with each other directly, facilitating their diagnosis of the conflict and how to resolve it. That ability to facilitate conflict resolution is a basic skill in OD and applies to all of the process interventions discussed in this chapter. Consultants, for example, frequently help organization members resolve interpersonal conflicts that invariably arise during process consultation and team building.

Third-party consultation interventions cannot resolve all interpersonal conflicts in organizations, nor should they. Many times, interpersonal conflicts are not severe or disruptive enough to warrant attention. At other times, they simply may burn themselves out. Evidence also suggests that other methods may be more appropriate under certain conditions. For example, managers tend to control the process and outcomes of conflict resolution actively when they are under heavy time pressures, when the disputants are not expected to work together in the future, and when the resolution of the dispute has a broad impact on the organization.[26] Under those conditions, the third party may resolve the conflict unilaterally with little input from the conflicting parties.

An Episodic Model of Conflict

Interpersonal conflict often occurs in iterative, cyclical stages known as "episodes." An episodic model is shown in Figure 12.2. At times, issues underlying a conflict are latent and do not present any manifest problems for the parties. Then something triggers the conflict and brings it into the open. For example, a violent disagreement or frank confrontation can unleash conflictual behavior. Because of the

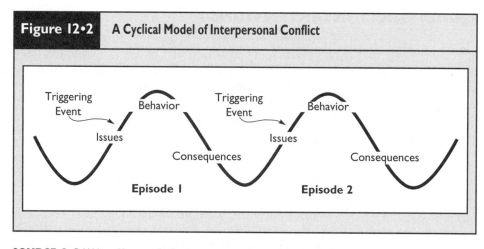

Figure 12·2   A Cyclical Model of Interpersonal Conflict

Triggering Event → Behavior

Issues

Consequences

Episode 1

Triggering Event → Behavior

Issues

Consequences

Episode 2

SOURCE: R. G. Walton, *Managing Conflict: Interpersonal Dialogue and Third Party Roles*, page 67. © 1987 by Addison-Wesley Publishing Co., Inc. Reprinted by permission of Addison Wesley Longman.

negative consequences of that behavior, the unresolved disagreement usually becomes latent again. And again, something triggers the conflict, making it overt, and so the cycle continues with the next conflict episode.

Conflict has both costs and benefits to the antagonists and to those in contact with them. Unresolved conflict can proliferate and expand. An interpersonal conflict may be concealed under a cause or issue that serves to make the conflict appear more legitimate. Frequently, the overt conflict is only a symptom of a deeper problem.

The episode model identifies four strategies for conflict resolution. The first three attempt to control the conflict, and only the last approach tries to change the basic issues underlying it.[27] The first strategy is to prevent the ignition of conflict by arriving at a clear understanding of the triggering factors and thereafter avoiding or blunting them when the symptoms occur. For example, if conflict between the research and production managers is always triggered by new product introductions, then senior management can warn them that conflict will not be tolerated during the introduction of the latest new product. However, this approach may not always be functional and merely may drive the conflict underground until it explodes. As a control strategy, however, this method may help to achieve a temporary cooling-off period.

The second control strategy is to set limits on the form of the conflict. Conflict can be constrained by informal gatherings before a formal meeting or by exploration of other options. It also can be limited by setting rules and procedures specifying the conditions under which the parties can interact. For example, a rule can be instituted that union officials can attempt to resolve grievances with management only at weekly grievance meetings.

The third control strategy is to help the parties cope differently with the consequences of the conflict. The third-party consultant may work with the people involved to devise coping techniques, such as reducing their dependence on the relationship, ventilating their feelings to friends, and developing additional sources of emotional support. These methods can reduce the costs of the conflict without resolving the underlying issues.

The fourth method is an attempt to eliminate or to resolve the basic issues causing the conflict. As Walton points out, "There is little to be said about this objective because it is the most obvious and straightforward, although it is often the most difficult to achieve."[28]

Facilitating the Conflict Resolution Process

Walton has identified a number of factors and tactical choices that can facilitate the use of the episode model in resolving the underlying causes of conflict.[29] The following ingredients can help third-party consultants achieve productive dialogue between the disputants so that they examine their differences and change their perceptions and behaviors: mutual motivation to resolve the conflict; equality of power between the parties; coordinated attempts to confront the conflict; relevant phasing of the stages of identifying differences and of searching for integrative solutions; open and clear forms of communication; and productive levels of tension and stress.

Among the tactical choices identified by Walton are those having to do with diagnosis, the context of the third-party intervention, and the role of the consultant. One of the tactics in third-party intervention is the gathering of data, usually through preliminary interviewing. Group-process observations can also be used. Data gathering provides some understanding of the nature and the type of conflict, the personality and conflict styles of the individuals involved, the issues and attendant pressures, and the participants' readiness to work together to resolve the conflict.

The context in which the intervention occurs is also important. Consideration of the neutrality of the meeting area, the formality of the setting, the appropriateness of the time for the meeting (that is, a meeting should not be started until a time has been agreed on to conclude or adjourn), and the careful selection of those who should attend the meeting are all elements of this context.

In addition, the third-party consultant must decide on an appropriate role to assume in resolving conflict. The specific tactic chosen will depend on the diagnosis of the situation. For example, facilitating dialogue of interpersonal issues might include initiating the agenda for the meeting, acting as a referee during the meeting, reflecting and restating the issues and the differing perceptions of the individuals involved, giving feedback and receiving comments on the feedback, helping the individuals diagnose the issues in the conflict, providing suggestions or recommendations, and helping the parties do a better job of diagnosing the underlying problem.

The third-party consultant must develop considerable skill at diagnosis, intervention, and follow-up. The third-party intervener must be highly sensitive to his or her own feelings and to those of others. He or she also must recognize that some tension and conflict are inevitable and that although there can be an optimum amount and degree of conflict, too much conflict can be dysfunctional for both the people involved and the larger organization. The third-party consultant must be sensitive to the situation and able to use a number of different intervention strategies and tactics when intervention appears to be useful. Finally, she or he must have professional expertise in third-party intervention and must be seen by the parties as neutral or unbiased regarding the issues and outcomes of the conflict resolution.

Application 12.3 describes an attempt to address conflict in an information technology unit.[30] How does this description fit with the process described above? What would you have done differently?

TEAM BUILDING

Team building refers to a broad range of planned activities that help groups improve the way they accomplish tasks and help group members enhance their interpersonal

APPLICATION 12•3   Conflict Management at Balt Healthcare Corporation

Pete and Dan were managers in an IT department that was part of the information services group at Balt Healthcare Corporation, a large organization that provided health-care products to a global market. Pete was the general manager of the IT department and had been working in the unit for most of his 16 years with Balt. The IT department had global responsibility for developing and maintaining the organization's intranets, Websites, and internal networks. Pete ran his department with a traditional and formal management style where communication traveled vertically through the hierarchy.

Dan recently had been assigned to Pete's department to operate a small experimental group charged with developing e-commerce solutions for the organization and the industry. This was state-of-the-art development work with enormous future implications for the organization as it explored the possibility of sales, business-to-business, and other supply chain opportunities on the Internet. Dan, in contrast to Pete, had a management style that stressed the value of open communication channels to promote teamwork and collaboration.

The biggest challenge in Dan's work was managing the transition from design into production. Senior management at Balt believed that by assigning Dan's team to Pete's organization, the resources required to manage this transition would be more readily available to Dan's group. In fact, it was generally agreed that Pete's strengths complimented Dan's weaknesses. Whereas Dan was a better designer, Pete had operational expertise that would help in bringing Dan's ideas online.

Unfortunately, the trouble started almost as soon as the assignment was announced. Although in front of their bosses Pete had agreed to work with Dan to make the project a success, his support was lukewarm at best. Dan and Pete had a history of conflict in the organization. Neither one respected the other's style, and prior conflicts had been swept under the carpet, creating a considerable amount of pent-up animosity. Operationally, when Dan's group needed resources to bring an idea online, Pete announced that all of his people were busy and that he couldn't assign anyone to help. Similarly, anytime Dan needed access to a piece of hardware within the IT unit, Pete made it complicated to get that access. Dan became increasingly frustrated by Pete's lack of cooperation and he was quite open about his feelings of being sabotaged. His complaints reached the highest levels of management as well as other members of the information services staff.

After several frustrating attempts to speak with Pete about the situation, Dan consulted Marilyn, the vice president for information services. Marilyn, like others in the organization, was aware of the conflict. She requested assistance from the human resources manager and an organization development specialist. The OD specialist met with Pete and Dan separately to understand the history of the conflict and each individual's contribution to it. Although different styles were partly to blame, the differences in the two work processes were also contributing to the problem. Pete's organization was primarily routine development and maintenance tasks that allowed for considerable preplanning and scheduling of resources. Dan's project, however, was highly creative and unpredictable. There was little opportunity to give Pete advance notice regarding the experimental team's needs for equipment and other resources.

The OD specialist recommended several strategies to Marilyn, including a direct confrontation, the purchase of additional hardware and software, and mandating the antagonists' cooperation. Marilyn responded that there was no available budget for purchasing new equipment and admitted that she did not have any confidence in her ability to facilitate the needed communication and leadership for her staff. She asked the OD specialist to facilitate a more direct process. Agreements were made in writing about how the process would work, including Marilyn meeting with Dan and Pete to discuss the problem between them and how it was affecting the organization. But Marilyn did not follow through on the agreement. She never met with Pete and Dan at the same time and, as a result, the messages she sent to each were inconsistent. In fact, during their separate conversations, it appeared that Marilyn began supporting Pete and began criticizing Dan. Dan began to withdraw, productivity in both groups suffered, and he became more hostile, stubborn, and bitter.

In the end, Dan felt sabotaged not only by Pete but by Marilyn as well. He took a leave of absence based on Marilyn's advice. His project was left without a leader and he ended up leaving the organization. Pete stayed on, but staff at all levels of the organization were upset that his behavior had not been questioned. Similarly, the organization lost a lot of respect for Marilyn's ability to address conflict. Losses in productivity and morale among staff in many areas in the organization resulted from the conflict between two employees. ■

and problem-solving skills. Organizations comprise many permanent and temporary groups, and team building is an effective approach to improving teamwork and task accomplishment in such environments. It can help problem-solving groups make maximum use of members' resources and contributions. It can help members develop a high level of motivation to implement group decisions. Team building also can help groups overcome specific problems, such as apathy and general lack of member interest; loss of productivity; increasing complaints within the group; confusion about assignments; low participation in meetings; lack of innovation and initiation; increasing complaints from those outside the group about the quality, timeliness, and effectiveness of services and products; and hostility or conflicts among members.

It is equally important that team building can facilitate other OD interventions, such as employee involvement, work design, restructuring, and strategic change. Those change programs typically are designed by management teams and implemented through various committees and work groups. Team building can help the groups design high-quality change programs and ensure that the programs are accepted and implemented by organization members. Indeed, most technostructural, human resources management, and strategic interventions depend on some form of team building for effective implementation.

The importance of team building is well established, and its use is expected to grow even faster in the coming years. Management teams are encountering issues of greater complexity and uncertainty, especially in such fast-growing industries as electronics, entertainment, information technology and processing, and health and financial services. Team building can provide the kind of teamwork and problem-solving skills needed to tackle such issues. As manufacturing and service technologies continue to develop—for example, just-in-time inventory systems, manufacturing cells, robotics, and service quality concepts—there is increasing pressure on organizations to implement team-based work designs. Team building can assist in the development of group goals and norms that support high productivity and quality of work life. The globalization of work and organizations implies that people from different cultures and geographic locations will increasingly interact over complex management and operational tasks. Team building is an excellent vehicle for examining cross-cultural issues and their impact on decision making and problem solving. When such groups represent the senior management of an organization, team building can help establish a coherent corporate strategy and can promote the kind of close cooperation needed to make this new form of governance effective.[31] Finally, in today's business situation, mergers and acquisitions are increasing rapidly. The success of these endeavors depends partly on getting members from different organizations to work together effectively. Team building can facilitate the formation of a unified team with common goals and procedures.

In the OD literature, team building is not clearly differentiated from process consultation. This confusion exists because most team building includes process consultation—helping the group diagnose and understand its own internal processes. However, process consultation is a more general approach to helping relationships than is team building. Team building focuses explicitly on helping groups perform tasks and solve problems more effectively. Process consultation, on the other hand, is concerned with establishing effective helping relationships in organizations. It is seen as key to effective management and consultation and can be applied to any helping relationship, from subordinate development to interpersonal relationships to group development. Thus, team building consists of process consultation plus other, more task-oriented interventions.

Dyer has developed a checklist for identifying whether a team-building program is needed and whether the organization is ready to start such a program (Table 12.1).[32] If the problem is a structural or technical one, an intergroup issue, an administrative mistake, or a conflict between only two people, team building would not be an appropriate change strategy.

Team-Building Activities

A team is a group of interdependent people who share a common purpose, have common work methods, and hold each other accountable.[33] The nature of that interdependence varies, creating the following types of teams: groups reporting to

---

Table 12•1	Team-Building Checklist

I. Problem identification: To what extent is there evidence of the following problems in your work unit?

	LOW EVIDENCE		SOME EVIDENCE		HIGH EVIDENCE
1. Loss of production or work-unit output	1	2	3	4	5
2. Grievances or complaints within the work unit	1	2	3	4	5
3. Conflicts or hostility between unit members	1	2	3	4	5
4. Confusion about assignments or unclear relationships between people	1	2	3	4	5
5. Lack of clear goals or low commitment to goals	1	2	3	4	5
6. Apathy or general lack of interest or involvement of unit members	1	2	3	4	5
7. Lack of innovation, risk taking, imagination, or taking initiative	1	2	3	4	5
8. Ineffective staff meetings	1	2	3	4	5
9. Problems in working with the boss	1	2	3	4	5
10. Poor communications: people afraid to speak up, not listening to each other, or not talking together	1	2	3	4	5
11. Lack of trust between boss and members or between members	1	2	3	4	5
12. Decisions are made that people do not understand or agree with	1	2	3	4	5
13. Good work is not recognized or rewarded	1	2	3	4	5
14. Lack of encouragement for working together in a better team effort	1	2	3	4	5

Scoring: Add the scores for the fourteen items. If your score is between 14 and 28, there is little evidence your unit needs team building. If your score is between 29 and 42, there is some evidence but no immediate pressure, unless two or three items are very high. If your score is between 43 and 56, you should think seriously about planning the team-building program. If your score is over 56, team building should be top priority for your work unit.

II. Are you (or your manager) prepared to start a team-building program? Consider the following statements. To what extent do they apply to you or your department?

	LOW		MEDIUM		HIGH
1. You are comfortable in sharing organizational leadership and decision making with subordinates and prefer to work in a participative atmosphere.	1	2	3	4	5
2. You see a high degree of interdependence as necessary among functions and workers in order to achieve your goals.	1	2	3	4	5

Continued on page 233

the same supervisor, manager, or executive; groups involving people with common organizational goals; temporary groups formed to do a specific, one-time task; groups consisting of people whose work roles are interdependent; and groups whose members have no formal links in the organization but whose collective purpose is to achieve tasks they cannot accomplish alone. In addition, there are a number of

Table 12•1	Team-Building Checklist, *continued*				
		LOW		MEDIUM		HIGH

		LOW		MEDIUM		HIGH
3.	The external environment is highly variable or changing rapidly, and you need the best thinking of all your staff to plan for these conditions.	1	2	3	4	5
4.	You feel you need the input of your staff to plan major changes or develop new operating policies and procedures.	1	2	3	4	5
5.	You feel that broad consultation among your people as a group in goals, decisions, and problems is necessary on a continuing basis.	1	2	3	4	5
6.	Members of your management team are (or can become) compatible with each other and are able to create a collaborative rather than a competitive environment.	1	2	3	4	5
7.	Members of your team are located close enough to meet together as needed.	1	2	3	4	5
8.	You feel you need to rely on the ability and willingness of subordinates to resolve critical operating problems directly and in the best interest of the company or organization.	1	2	3	4	5
9.	Formal communication channels are not sufficient for the timely exchange of essential information, views, and decisions among your team members.	1	2	3	4	5
10.	Organization adaptation requires the use of such devices as project management, task forces, or ad hoc problem-solving groups to augment conventional organization structure.	1	2	3	4	5
11.	You feel it is important to bring out and deal with critical, albeit sensitive, issues that exist in your team.	1	2	3	4	5
12.	You are prepared to look at your own role and performance with your team.	1	2	3	4	5
13.	You feel there are operating or interpersonal problems that have remained unsolved too long and need the input from all group members.	1	2	3	4	5
14.	You need an opportunity to meet with your people to set goals and develop commitment to these goals.	1	2	3	4	5

Scoring: If your total score is between 50 and 70, you probably are ready to go ahead with the team-building program. If your score is between 35 and 49, you probably should talk the situation over with your team and others to see what would need to be done to get ready for team building. If your score is between 14 and 34, you probably are not prepared to start team building.

SOURCE: W. Dyer, *Team Building: Issues and Alternatives*, pages 42–46. © 1987 by Addison-Wesley Publishing Co., Inc. Reprinted by permission of Addison Wesley Longman.

factors that affect the outcomes of any specific team-building activity: the length of time allocated to the activity, the team's willingness to look at the way in which it operates, the length of time the team has been working together, and the team's permanence. Consequently, the results of team-building activities can range from comparatively modest changes in the team's operating mechanisms (for example, meeting more frequently or gathering agenda items from more sources) to much deeper changes (for example, modifying team members' behavior patterns or the nature and style of the group's management, or developing greater openness and trust).

In general, team-building activities can be classified as follows: (1) activities relevant to one or more individuals; (2) activities specific to the group's operation and behavior; and (3) activities affecting the group's relationship with the rest of the organization. Usually, a specific team-building activity will overlap these three categories. On occasion, a change in one area will have negative results in other areas. A very cohesive team may increase its isolation from other groups, leading to intergroup conflict or other dysfunctional results, which in turn can have a negative impact on the total organization unless the team develops sufficient diagnostic skills to recognize and deal with such results.

Activities Relevant to One or More Individuals

People come into groups and organizations with varying needs and wants for achievement, inclusion, influence, and belonging. These needs and wants can be supported and nurtured by the team's structure and process or they can be discouraged. Almost all team-building efforts result in one or more of the members gaining a better understanding of the way authority, inclusion, emotions, control, and power affect problem solving and other group processes. Such activities provide information so that people have a clearer sense of how their needs and wants can or will be supported. This information then gives group members a choice about their level of involvement, commitment, and investment in the team's functioning.

For example, in one team, the typical decision-making process included the leader having several agenda items for discussion. Each of the items, however, had a predetermined set of actions that she wanted the group to take. Most members were frustrated by their inability to influence decision making. During the team-building process, group members asked whether the boss really wanted ideas and contributions from group members. They gave specific examples of the leader's not-so-subtle manipulation to arrive at preconceived decisions and described how they felt about it. At the end of the discussion, the boss indicated her willingness to be challenged about such preconceived decisions, and the other team members expressed their increased willingness to engage in problem-solving discussions, their trust in the leader, and their ability to make the challenge without fear of reprisal.

Sometimes, the team-building process generates pressures on individual members, such as requests for higher levels of task performance. Such requests could have negative results unless accompanied by agreement for further one-to-one negotiations among team members. If these demands are made of the boss, for example, he or she may feel a loss of power and authority unless the team can agree on ways in which the boss can be kept informed about what is happening. Methods to meet these needs for control and influence without causing feelings of isolation can be explored.

Activities Oriented to the Group's Operation and Behavior

The most common focus of team building activities is behavior related to task performance and group process. In an effective team, task behavior and group process must be integrated with each other as well as with the needs and wants of the people making up the group. Team-building activities often begin by clarifying the team's purpose, priorities, goals, and objectives. This establishes a framework within which further work can be done. In most team-building activities, groups spend some time finding ways to improve the mechanisms that structure their approach to work. A group may discuss how a meeting agenda is created, the efficiency of key work processes, or strategies for lowering costs. In addition, groups often examine their communications patterns and determine ways in which they can be improved. Frequently, this leads to dropping some communications patterns and establishing new ones that are more open and conducive to problem solving in nature.

Another group operation issue is the effective use of time. To improve in this area, the group may examine its present planning mechanisms, introduce better ones, and identify ways for using its skills and knowledge more effectively. The group also may make decisions about reorganizing and redistributing the workload. As the group develops over time, it tends to become more aware of the need for action plans about problems or tasks as well as for better self-diagnosis about the effectiveness of its task-accomplishment processes.

Frequently, groups examine and diagnose the nature of their problem-solving techniques. Specific items usually are diagnosed in the earlier stage of team building, and as teams mature they broaden the scope of these diagnostic efforts to include areas that are more directly related to interpersonal styles and their impact on other group members. Throughout this process, group norms become clearer, and the group can provide more opportunity for members to satisfy individual needs within the group. As a result, the team is much more willing to take risks within both the team and the organization. Team members become more capable of facing difficulties and problems, not only within their own group but also within the larger organization. A spirit of openness, trust, and risk taking develops.

Activities Affecting the Group's Relationship with the Rest of the Organization

As the team gains a better understanding of itself and becomes better able to diagnose and solve its own problems, it focuses on its role within the organization. A group's relationship to the larger organizational context is an important aspect of group effectiveness.[34] As a result, the team may perceive a need to clarify its organizational role and to consider how this role can be improved or modified. Sometimes, the team may recognize a need for more collaboration with other parts of the organization and so try to establish working parties or project teams that cross the boundaries of existing teams.

As the team becomes more cohesive, it usually exerts a stronger influence on the other subsystems of the organization. Because that is one area in which team building can have negative effects, the process consultant must help the group understand its role within the organization, develop its own diagnostic skills, and examine alternative action plans so that intergroup tensions and conflicts do not expand.

Types of Team Building

Family Group Diagnostic Meeting

The family group diagnostic meeting involves the individual "family" group—where all team members report to the same supervisor, manager, or executive. This process, which has been described by a number of authors, is aimed at getting a general reading on the overall performance of the group, including current problems that should be worked on in the future.[35] This technique allows the work group to get away from the work itself to gather data about its current performance and to formulate plans for future action. Normally, the immediate supervisor of a work group discusses the concept with the process consultant, and if both agree that there is a need for such an approach, the idea is discussed with the group to obtain members' reactions.

If the reactions are favorable, the leader or process consultant may ask the group, before the meeting, to consider areas in which performance is good and areas that need improvement. Group members also may be asked to consider their work relationships with one another and with other groups in the organization. In advance of a general meeting, the consultant may interview some or all members of the work group to gather preliminary data or merely ask all of the members to think about these and similar problems. Then the group assembles for a meeting that may last one or two days.

The diagnostic data can be made public in a number of ways. One method brings the total group together for a discussion, with everyone presenting ideas to the entire group. Another approach breaks the group into smaller groups in which more intensive discussions can take place and has the subgroups report back to the larger group. A third technique has individuals pair up, discuss their ideas, and then report to the entire group. Finally, the consultant can feed back to the group his or her diagnostic findings collected before the meeting so that the total group can process the data and determine whether they are correct and relevant.

After the data have been made public, the issues identified are discussed and categorized (categories might include, for example, planning, interdepartmental scheduling, and tight resources). Next, the group begins to develop action plans. The primary objective of the family group diagnostic meeting, however, is to bring to the surface problems and issues that need to be addressed. Taking specific action usually is reserved for a later time.

The advantage of the family group diagnostic meeting is that it allows a group to participate in generating the data necessary to identify its own strengths, weaknesses, and problem areas. The use of a process consultant is helpful but not essential. A key issue, however, is making certain that the participants recognize that their primary objective is to identify problems rather than to solve them. As Beer has noted, "All the advantages of direct involvement are inherent in this model, although there may be limited openness if the group has had no previous development and a supportive climate does not exist."[36]

Family Group Team-Building Meeting

The family group team-building meeting occurs with a permanent work group, a management team, or a temporary, project-type team. It is one of the most widely used OD interventions.

The team development process involves helping the group learn to identify, diagnose, and solve problems with the help of an OD practitioner. The problems may involve the tasks or activities the group must perform, the process by which it goes about accomplishing the tasks, or interpersonal conflict between two or more team members. French and Bell have defined team development as "an inward look by the team at its own performance, behavior, and culture for the purposes of dropping out dysfunctional behaviors and strengthening functional ones."[37]

The first intervention is to gather data through the use of questionnaires or, more commonly, through interviews. The nature of the data gathered will vary, depending on the purpose of the team-building program, the consultant's knowledge about the organization and its culture, and the people involved. The consultant already may have obtained a great deal of data by sitting in as a process observer at staff and other meetings. The data gathered also will depend on what other OD efforts have taken place in the organization. By whatever method obtained, however, the data usually include information on leadership styles and behavior; goals, objectives, and decision-making processes; such variables of organizational culture as trust, communication patterns, and interpersonal relationships and processes; barriers to effective group functioning; and task and related technical problems.

Frequently, but not always, the data-gathering stage is initiated only after the manager and her or his group have agreed that team development is a process in which they wish to engage and have set a date for an off-site meeting. This sequence ensures that organization members have freedom of choice and that the data-gathering stage is conducted as close to the actual meeting as possible. The off-site meeting may last from a day and a half to a week, with the average being about three days. The meeting is held away from the organization to reduce the number of interruptions and other pressures that might inhibit the process.

At the beginning of the meeting, the consultant feeds back the information that has been collected. This information usually is categorized by major themes, and the group must establish the agenda by placing priorities on these themes. Based on his or her knowledge of the data and the group, the consultant may help in setting the agenda or may act solely as a process observer, feeding back to the group his or her observations of what the group is doing.

As Beer points out, the consultant can play several different roles during the team-development meeting.[38] One role is that of process consultant, helping the group to understand and diagnose its own group process. The consultant also may function as a resource person, offering expertise as a behavioral scientist, or as a teacher, giving information about such areas as group dynamics, conflict resolution, and leadership. However, the primary role of the consultant is to assist the group in learning to identify, diagnose, and solve its own problems.

During the meeting, the group should develop action plans for becoming more effective. Frequently, merely discussing the barriers leads to improving the effectiveness of the group. One meeting, however, is rarely enough to effect major change. Instead, a series of meetings usually is needed to ensure permanent change.

Application 12.4 presents an example of a family group team-building meeting involving a top-management team.

The Manager's Role in Team Building

Ultimately, the manager is responsible for group functioning, although this responsibility obviously must be shared by the group itself. Therefore, it is management's task to develop a work group that can stop regularly to analyze and diagnose its own effectiveness and work process. With the group's involvement, the manager must diagnose the group's effectiveness and take appropriate actions if the work unit shows signs of operating difficulty or stress.

Many managers, however, have not been trained to perform the data gathering, diagnosis, planning, and action necessary to maintain and improve their teams continually. Thus, the issue of who should lead a team-building session is a function of managerial capability. The initial use of a consultant usually is advisable if a manager is aware of problems, feels that she or he may be part of the problem, and believes that some positive action is needed to improve the operation of the unit, but is not sure how to go about it. Dyer has provided a checklist for assessing the need for a consultant (Table 12.2). Some of the questions ask the manager to examine problems and establish the degree to which she or he feels comfortable in trying out new and different things, the degree of knowledge about team building,

APPLICATION 12·4   Building the Executive Team at Caesars Tahoe

Caesars Tahoe is a casino, hotel, and entertainment complex on the south shore of Lake Tahoe, Nevada. As part of the Caesars World chain, including Caesars Palace in Las Vegas, Caesars in Atlantic City, and the riverboat Caesars Indiana, Caesars Tahoe enjoys a reputation as a "high-end" experience. Its history is laced with stories of celebrities, athletes, and some of the wealthiest people in the world winning and losing millions of dollars gambling in its casinos. Originally established as an alternative to the Las Vegas desert, Caesars Tahoe is the third-largest facility in town in terms of casino floor space and number of rooms, but it has the largest showroom for headline talent, the highest gambling limits, and the highest proportion of table games such as craps, blackjack, and roulette.

In 1995, the Caesars World organization was purchased by the ITT conglomerate, was spun off into the Starwood Resorts organization when ITT reorganized in 1997, and then was sold to Park Place Entertainment when Starwood decided to focus on nongaming properties. As of late 1999, the Caesars World corporate office was waiting for the transaction with Park Place to be closed formally.

The executive team at Caesars Tahoe consisted of an executive vice president and general manager (GM) for the property and seven direct reports. The marketing function was divided into three segments, each headed by a vice president. Far East marketing was responsible for recruiting "million-dollar players" from the South Pacific region; national marketing was responsible for working with other Caesars properties to ensure that "high rollers" from the United States were well attended to; and casino marketing handled the more traditional promotion activities of advertising, special events coordination, entertainment bookings, and convention marketing. The hotel vice president was responsible for the front desk, housekeeping, maintenance, food and beverage service, and so on. The casino operations vice president managed all gambling operations. In addition, there was a vice president for human resources and a chief financial officer. The vice presidents for casino marketing and casino operations had been with the property for ten and twenty years, respectively. No other member of the team had been with the property more than two years. In fact, the current GM was the thirteenth in twenty years.

The GM contacted an external OD consultant to help the executive team improve teamwork and clarify the core values of the organization. General changes in the gaming industry, higher than normal turnover levels in the hotel and casino, concerns over whether the Caesars "brand" had suffered in all the corporate portfolio adjustments, and conflicts among his senior managers prompted his call. His own vision for the property included growing the property, reestablishing the Caesars brand, and investing in human resources. Interviews with the members of the executive committee confirmed his initial descriptions about the team and the organization's situation.

In consultation with the GM, the corporate OD consultant, and the human resources vice president, an agenda was developed that addressed the goals and vision for the property, team processes and roles, and action plans for the future. A two-day off-site meeting was arranged at a local resort.

The workshop kicked off on the evening before the meeting with a welcome and overview of the agenda by the GM and a stakeholder mapping exercise that clarified the current mission of the property. Team members were excused for the evening with the thoughts of the exercise fresh in their minds. On the morning of the first day, executive committee members were encouraged to share their expectations for the meeting and to develop specific norms that would guide their behaviors during the two-day meeting. This process was aided by an exercise in which the group members shared their experiences about the best team they had ever worked on and in that way identified characteristics of effective teams. The norms and characteristics were placed on flipcharts and hung on the wall of the meeting room. All members agreed to behave according to the norms and to assess periodically how well the norms were being followed. The consultant agreed to provide feedback on norm compliance during the session.

The group then participated in a problem-solving exercise that prompted members to collaborate on a task. The task generated important data about the group's functioning. Those observations were discussed, as were insights about the team gleaned from the results of an interpersonal style instrument completed by members prior to the meeting. The nature of the conflicts among members also was discussed. From this new basis of group understanding, the executive committee began to discuss their hopes and visions for the property. The first day ended with several unfinished lists of value statements, core purposes, and thoughts about the strategies and markets served by the organization. An evaluation of the day asked for an overall rating and comments about what the group should stop, start, and continue to do.

The next day began by feeding back the data from the evaluation, which suggested that most people were satisfied with the accomplishments of the first day but that important issues still needed to be addressed. Although the agenda called for a flow similar to that of the day before, moving back and forth between teamwork-related activities and discussions about the property's future, the consultant wrote several important topics on a flipchart and asked the group to identify the most important agenda items. Quickly they decided that they wanted to finish the core-values work and then discuss their core purpose.

The consultant facilitated the conversation that was now clearly under the control of the group members. Within a couple of hours, they group had produced a list of core values, developed a process for involving the rest of the organization in creating a final list of values, and crafted a core purpose that described the essence of the organization. Based on this work, the group moved to some initial discussions about its vision for the future. In addition, the group generated a list of key action items necessary to realize that vision. This was especially tricky given the uncertain demands of the new

owner, but the group decided that it was important to have a clear strategy for themselves so that any demands from the new parent could be evaluated. Members also reasoned that the parent might ask them what they thought was possible and they wanted to be ready.

The meeting ended with the completion of a responsibility chart to clarify task completion expectations and accountabilities among the team members. A final evaluation of the meeting included process observations by the team members about how they had worked together and statements about their satisfaction with the results of the meeting. They all agreed that they had made important decisions and were leaving with substantial results. ∎

whether the boss might be a major source of difficulty, and the openness of group members.

Basically, the role of the consultant is to work closely with the manager (and members of the unit) to a point at which the manager is capable of engaging in

Table 12•2	Assessing the Need for a Consultant

SHOULD YOU USE AN OUTSIDE CONSULTANT TO HELP IN TEAM BUILDING? (Circle the appropriate response.)

1.	Does the manager feel comfortable in trying out something new and different with the staff?	Yes	No	?
2.	Is the staff used to spending time in an outside location working on issues of concern to the work unit?	Yes	No	?
3.	Will group members speak up and give honest data?	Yes	No	?
4.	Does your group generally work together without a lot of conflict or apathy?	Yes	No	?
5.	Are you reasonably sure that the boss is not a major source of difficulty?	Yes	No	?
6.	Is there a high commitment by the boss and unit members to achieving more effective team functioning?	Yes	No	?
7.	Is the personal style of the boss and his or her management philosophy consistent with a team approach?	Yes	No	?
8.	do you feel you know enough about team building to begin a program without help?	Yes	No	?
9.	Would your staff feel confident enough to begin a team-building progam without outside help?	Yes	No	?

Scoring: If you have circled six or more "yes" responses, you probably do not need an outside consultant. If you have circled four or more "no" responses, you probably do need a consultant. If you have a mixture of "yes," "no," and ? responses, invite a consultant to talk over the situation and make a joint decision.

SOURCE: W. Dyer, *Team Building: Issues and Alternatives*, pages 42–46. © 1987 by Addison-Wesley Publishing Co., Inc. Reprinted by permission of Addison Wesley Longman.

team-development activities as a regular and ongoing part of overall managerial responsibilities. Assuming that the manager wants and needs a consultant, the two should work together as a team in developing the initial program, keeping in mind that (1) the manager ultimately is responsible for all team-building activities, even though the consultant's resources are available, and (2) the goal of the consultant's presence is to help the manager learn to continue team-development processes with minimum consultant help or without the ongoing help of the consultant.

Thus, in the first stages the consultant might be much more active in data gathering, diagnosis, and action planning, particularly if a one- to three-day off-site workshop is considered. In later stages, the consultant takes a much less active role, with the manager becoming more active and serving as both manager and team developer.

When Is Team Building Applicable?

Team building is applicable in a large number of situations, from starting a new team, to resolving conflicts among members, to revitalizing a complacent team. Lewis[39] has identified the following conditions as best suited to team building:

1. Patterns of communication and interaction are inadequate for good group functioning.
2. Group leaders desire an integrated team.
3. The group's task requires interaction among members.
4. The team leader will behave differently as the result of team building, and members will respond to the new behavior.
5. The benefits outweigh the costs of team building.
6. Team building must be congruent with the leader's personal style and philosophy.

The Results of Team Building

The research on team building has a number of problems. First, it focuses mainly on the feelings and attitudes of group members. Little evidence supports that group performance improves as a result of team-building experiences. One study, for example, found that team building was a smashing success in the eyes of the participants.[40] However, a rigorous field test of the results over time showed no appreciable effects on either the team's functioning and efficiency or the larger organization's functioning and efficiency. Second, the positive effects of team building typically are measured over relatively short time periods. Evidence suggests that the positive effects of off-site team building are short-lived, often fading after the group returns to the organization. Third, team building rarely occurs in isolation. Usually it is carried out in conjunction with other interventions leading to or resulting from team building itself. For this reason it is difficult to separate the effects of team building from those of the other interventions.[41]

Studies of the empirical literature present a mixed picture of the impact of team building on group performance. One review showed that team building improves process measures, such as employee openness and decision making, about 45 percent of the time and improves outcome measures, such as productivity and costs, about 53 percent of the time.[42] Another review revealed that team building positively affects hard measures of productivity, employee withdrawal, and costs about 50 percent of the time.[43] Still another review concluded that team building cannot be linked convincingly to improved performance. Of the thirty studies reviewed, only ten tried to measure changes in performance. Although these changes were generally positive, the studies' research designs were relatively weak, reducing confidence in the findings.[44] One review concluded that process interventions, such as team building and process consultation, are most likely to improve process variables, such as decision making, communication, and problem solving.[45]

Boss conducted extensive research on arresting the potential fade-out effects of off-site team building.[46] He proposed that the tendency for the positive behaviors developed at off-site team building to regress once the group is back in the organization can be checked by conducting a follow-up intervention called personal management interview (PMI). PMI is done soon after the off-site team building and involves the team leader, who first negotiates roles with each member and then holds weekly or biweekly meetings with each member to improve communication, resolve problems, and increase personal accountability. Boss feels that effective leader and member relationships provide the constant contact and reinforcement necessary for the longer-term success of team building. PMI is a structured approach to maintaining effective superior–subordinate relations.

Boss has presented evidence to support the effectiveness of PMI in sustaining the long-term effects of off-site team building.[47] He compared the long-term effects of team building in ten teams that had engaged in off-site team building, and a control group with no intervention. The data showed that all teams having off-site team building improved their effectiveness as measured soon after the intervention. However, only those teams subsequently engaged in PMIs were able to maintain those effectiveness levels; the other teams showed a substantial regression of effects over time. The data further showed that PMI can help to maintain the level of group effectiveness over a three-year period.

Buller and Bell have attempted to differentiate the effects of team building from the effects of other interventions that occur along with team building.[48] Specifically, they tried to separate the effects of team building from the effects of goal setting, an intervention aimed at setting realistic performance goals and developing action plans for achieving them. In a rigorous field experiment, Buller and Bell examined the differential effects of team building and goal setting on productivity measures of underground miners. The results showed that team building affects the *quality* of performance and goal setting affects the *quantity* of performance. This differential impact was explained in terms of the nature of the mining task. The task of improving the quality of performance was more complex, unstructured, and interdependent than was the task of achieving quantity. This suggests that team building can improve group performance, particularly on tasks that are complex, unstructured, and interdependent. That the advantages of combining both interventions were inconclusively identified in the Buller and Bell study suggests the need for additional studies of the differential impact of team building and other interventions such as goal setting.

■ SUMMARY

In this chapter, we presented human process interventions aimed at interpersonal relations and group dynamics. Among the earliest interventions in OD, these change programs help people gain interpersonal skills, work through interpersonal conflicts, and develop effective groups. The first intervention discussed was the T-group, the forerunner of modern OD change programs. T-groups typically consist of a small number of strangers who meet with a professional trainer to explore the social dynamics that emerge from their interactions. OD practitioners often attend

T-groups themselves to improve their interpersonal skills or they recommend that managers attend a T-group to learn more about how their behaviors affect others.

Process consultation is used not only as a way of helping groups become effective but also as a means whereby groups learn to diagnose and solve their own problems and continue to develop their competence and maturity. Important areas of activity include communications, roles of group members, difficulties with problem-solving and decision-making norms, and leadership and authority. The basic difference between process consultation and third-party intervention is that the latter focuses on interpersonal dysfunctions in social relationships between two or more individuals within the same organization and is targeted toward resolving direct conflict between those individuals.

Team building is directed toward improving group effectiveness and the ways in which members of teams work together. These teams may be permanent or temporary, but their members have either common organizational aims or work activities. The general process of team building, like process consultation, tries to equip a group to handle its own ongoing problem solving. Selected aspects of team building include the family group diagnostic meeting and the family group team-building meeting.

■ NOTES

1. J. Campbell and M. Dunnette, "Effectiveness of T-Group Experiences in Managerial Training and Development," *Psychological Bulletin* 70 (August 1968): 73–103.

2. Ibid.

3. M. Dunnette, J. Campbell, and C. Argyris, "A Symposium: Laboratory Training," *Industrial Relations* 8 (October 1968): 1–45.

4. Campbell and Dunnette, "Effectiveness of T-Group Experiences"; R. House, "T-Group Education and Leadership Effectiveness: A Review of the Empirical Literature and a Critical Evaluation," *Personnel Psychology* 20 (Spring 1967): 1–32; J. Campbell, M. Dunnette, E. Lawler III, and K. Weick, *Managerial Behavior, Performance, and Effectiveness* (New York: McGraw-Hill, 1970): 292–98.

5. J. Porras and P. O. Berg, "The Impact of Organization Development," *Academy of Management Review* 3 (April 1978): 249–66.

6. J. Nicholas, "The Comparative Impact of Organization Development Interventions on Hard Criteria Measures," *Academy of Management Review* 7 (October 1982): 531–42.

7. D. Bowers, "OD Techniques and Their Results in 23 Organizations: The Michigan IGL Study," *Journal of Applied Behavioral Science* 9 (January-February 1973): 21–43.

8. G. Neuman, J. Edwards, and N. Raju, "Organizational Development Interventions: A Meta-Analysis of Their Effects on Satisfaction and Other Attitudes," *Personnel Psychology* 42 (1989): 461–83.

9. R. Kaplan, "Is Openness Passé?" *Human Relations* 39 (November 1986): 242.

10. E. Schein, *Process Consultation Volume II: Lessons for Managers and Consultants* (Reading, Mass.: Addison-Wesley, 1987).

11. Ibid., pp. 5–17.

12. E. Schein, *Process Consultation Revisited* (Reading, Mass.: Addison-Wesley, 1998): 20.

13. Ibid.

14. J. Fast, *Body Language* (Philadelphia: Lippincott, M. Evans, 1970).

15. J. Luft, "The Johari Window," *Human Relations Training News* 5 (1961): 6–7.

16. E. Schein, *Process Consultation: Its Role in Organization Development* (Reading, Mass.: Addison-Wesley, 1969): 44.

17. N. Clapp, "Work Group Norms: Leverage for Organizational Change, Theory and Application" (undated working paper, Block Petrella Weisbord, Plainfield, N.J); R. Allen and S. Pilnick, "Confronting the Shadow Organization: How to Detect and Defeat Negative Norms," *Organizational Dynamics* (Spring 1973): 3–18.

18. Schein, *Process Consultation Revisited,* p. 147.

19. J. Gibb, "Defensive Communication," *Journal of Communication* 11 (1961): 141–48; Schein, *Process Consultation Revisited.*

20. Schein, *Process Consultation Revisited*, pp. 167–68; E. Schein, *Organization Culture and Leadership*, 2d ed. (San Francisco: Jossey-Bass, 1992).

21. Schein, *Process Consultation Volume II*, pp. 32–34.

22. R. Kaplan, "The Conspicuous Absence of Evidence That Process Consultation Enhances Task Performance," *Journal of Applied Behavioral Science* 15 (1979): 346–60.

23. G. Lippitt, *Organizational Renewal* (New York: Appleton-Century-Crofts, 1969); C. Argyris, *Organization and Innovation* (Homewood, Ill.: Richard D. Irwin, 1965).

24. People interested in finding assistance might want to contact The Society of Professionals in Dispute Resolution (SPIDR) at http://www.spidr.org.

25. D. Kolb and associates, *When Talk Works: Profiles of Mediators* (San Francisco: Jossey-Bass, 1994).

26 R. Lewicki and B. Sheppard, "Choosing How to Intervene: Factors Affecting the Use of Process and Outcome Control in Third-Party Dispute Resolution," *Journal of Occupational Behavior* 6 (January 1985): 49–64; H. Prein, "Strategies for Third-Party Intervention," *Human Relations* 40 (1987): 699–720.

27. R. Walton, *Managing Conflict: Interpersonal Dialogue and Third-Party Roles*, 2d ed. (Reading, Mass.: Addison-Wesley, 1987).

28. Ibid., pp. 81–82.

29. Ibid., pp. 83–110.

30. This application was developed by Christine Mattos.

31. T. Patten, *Organizational Development Through Team Building* (New York: John Wiley & Sons, 1981): 2; D. Stepchuck, "Strategies for Improving the Effectiveness of Geographically Distributed Work Teams" (unpublished Master's thesis, Pepperdine University, 1994).

32. W. Dyer, *Team Building: Issues and Alternatives*, 2d ed. (Reading, Mass.: Addison-Wesley, 1987).

33. J. Katzenbach and D. Smith, *The Wisdom of Teams* (Boston: Harvard Business School Press, 1993).

34. D. Ancona and D. Caldwell, "Bridging the Boundary: External Activity and Performance in Organizational Teams," *Administrative Science Quarterly* 37 (4, 1992): 634–65; S. Cohen, "Designing Effective Self-Managing Work Teams" (paper presented at the Theory Symposium on Self-Managed Work Teams, Denton, Tex., June 4–5, 1993).

35. M. Beer, "The Technology of Organization Development," in *Handbook of Industrial and Organizational Psychology*, ed. M. Dunnette (Chicago: Rand McNally, 1976): 937–93; W. French and C. Bell, *Organization Development: Behavioral Science Interventions for Organization Improvement* (Englewood Cliffs, N.J.: Prentice Hall, 1978).

36. Beer, "Technology of Organization Development," p. 37.

37. French and Bell, *Organization Development*, p. 115.

38. Beer, "Technology of Organization Development."

39. J. Lewis III, "Management Team Development: Will It Work for You?" *Personnel* (July-August 1975): 14–25.

40. D. Eden, "Team Development: A True Field Experiment at Three Levels of Rigor," *Journal of Applied Psychology* 70 (1985): 94–100.

41. R. Woodman and J. Sherwood, "The Role of Team Development in Organizational Effectiveness: A Critical Review," *Psychological Bulletin* 88 (July-November 1980): 166–86.

42. Porras and Berg, "Impact of Organization Development."

43. Nicholas, "Comparative Impact."

44. Woodman and Sherwood, "Role of Team Development."

45. R. Woodman and S. Wayne, "An Investigation of Positive-Finding Bias in Evaluation of Organization Development Interventions," *Academy of Management Journal* 28 (December 1985): 889–913.

46. R. W. Boss, "Team Building and the Problem of Regression: The Personal Management Interview as an Intervention," *Journal of Applied Behavioral Science* 19 (1983): 67–83.

47. Ibid.

48. R. Buller and C. Bell Jr., "Effects of Team Building and Goal Setting: A Field Experiment," *Academy of Management Journal* 29 (1986): 305–28.

Organization Process Approaches

In Chapter 12, we presented interventions aimed at improving interpersonal and group processes. This chapter describes systemwide process interventions—change programs directed at improving such processes as organizational problem solving, leadership, visioning, and task accomplishment between groups—for a major subsystem or for an entire organization.

The first type of intervention, the organization confrontation meeting, is among the earliest organizationwide process approaches. It helps mobilize the problem-solving resources of a major subsystem or whole organization by encouraging members to identify and confront pressing issues.

The second organization process approach is called intergroup relations. It consists of two interventions: the intergroup conflict resolution meeting and microcosm groups. Both interventions are aimed at diagnosing and addressing important organizational-level processes, such as conflict, the coordination of organizational units, and diversity. The intergroup conflict intervention is specifically oriented toward conflict processes, whereas the microcosm group is a more generic systemwide change strategy.

A third systemwide process approach, the large-group intervention, has received considerable attention recently and is one of the fastest-growing areas in OD. Large-group interventions get a "whole system into the room"[1] and create processes that allow a variety of stakeholders to interact simultaneously. A large-group intervention can be used to clarify important organizational values, develop new ways of looking at problems, articulate a new vision for the organization, solve cross-functional problems, restructure operations, or devise an organizational strategy. It is a powerful tool for addressing organizational problems and opportunities and for accelerating the pace of organizational change.

The final section of this chapter describes a normative approach to OD: Blake and Mouton's Grid® Organization Development. It is a popular intervention, particularly in large organizations. Grid OD is a packaged program that organizations can purchase and train members to use. In contrast to modern contingency approaches, the Grid proposes one best way to manage organizations. Consequently, OD practitioners increasingly have questioned its applicability and effectiveness in contemporary organizations.

ORGANIZATION CONFRONTATION MEETING

The *confrontation meeting* is an intervention designed to mobilize the resources of the entire organization to identify problems, set priorities and action targets, and begin working on identified problems. Originally developed by Beckhard,[2] the intervention can be used at any time but is particularly useful when the organization is in stress and when there is a gap between the top and the rest of the organization (such as when a new top manager joins the organization). General Electric's "Work-Out" program is a recent example of how the confrontation meeting has been adapted to fit today's organizations.[3] Although the original model involved only managerial and professional people, it has since been used successfully with technicians, clerical personnel, and assembly workers.

Application Stages

The organization confrontation meeting typically involves the following steps:

1. A group meeting of all those involved is scheduled and held in an appropriate place. Usually the task is to identify problems about the work environment and the effectiveness of the organization.

2. Groups are appointed representing all departments of the organization. Thus, each group might have one or more members from sales, purchasing, finance, operations, and quality assurance. For obvious reasons, a subordinate should not be in the same group as his or her boss, and top management should form its own group. Group size can vary from five to fifteen members, depending on such factors as the size of the organization and available meeting places.

3. The point is stressed that the groups are to be open and honest and to work hard at identifying problems they see in the organization. No one will be criticized for bringing up problems and, in fact, the groups will be judged on their ability to do so.

4. The groups are given an hour or two to identify organization problems. Generally, an OD practitioner goes from group to group, encouraging openness and assisting the groups with their tasks.

5. The groups then reconvene in a central meeting place. Each group reports the problems it has identified and sometimes offers solutions. Because each group hears the reports of all the others, a maximum amount of information is shared.

6. Either then or later, the master list of problems is broken down into categories. This can be done by the participants, by the person leading the session, or by the manager and his or her staff. This process eliminates duplication and overlap and allows the problems to be separated according to functional or other appropriate areas.

7. Following problem categorization, participants are divided into problem-solving groups whose composition may, and usually does, differ from that of the original problem-identification groups. For example, all operations problems may be handled by people in that subunit. Or task forces representing appropriate cross sections of the organization may be formed.

8. Each group ranks the problems, develops a tactical action plan, and determines an appropriate timetable for completing this phase of the process.

9. Each group then periodically reports its list of priorities and tactical plans of action to management or to the larger group.

10. Schedules for periodic (frequently monthly) follow-up meetings are established. At these sessions, the team leaders report either to top management, to the other team leaders, or to the group as a whole regarding their team's progress and plans for future action. The formal establishment of such follow-up meetings ensures both continuing action and the modification of priorities and timetables as needed.

Application 13.1 presents the Work-Out process at General Electric Medical Systems business. It shows how the basic framework of a confrontation meeting can be adapted to address organizational problems such as productivity and employee involvement.[4]

Results of Confrontation Meetings

Because organization confrontation meetings often are combined with other approaches, such as survey feedback, determining specific results is difficult. In many cases, the results appear dramatic in mobilizing the total resources of the organization for problem identification and solution. Beckhard cites a number of specific examples in such different organizations as a food products manufacturer, a military products manufacturer, and a hotel.[5] Positive results also were found in a confrontation meeting with forty professionals in a research and development firm.[6]

The organization confrontation meeting is a promising approach for mobilizing organizational problem solving, especially in times of low performance. Although the results of its use appear impressive, little systematic study of this intervention has been done. There is a clear need for evaluative research.

INTERGROUP RELATIONS INTERVENTIONS

The ability to diagnose and understand intergroup relations is important for OD practitioners because (1) groups often must work with and through other groups to accomplish their goals; (2) groups within the organization often create problems and place demands on each other; and (3) the quality of the relationships between groups can affect the degree of organizational effectiveness. Two OD interventions—microcosm groups and intergroup conflict resolution—are described here. A microcosm group uses members from several groups to help solve organization-wide problems. Intergroup issues are explored in this context, and then solutions are implemented in the larger organization. Intergroup conflict resolution helps two groups work out dysfunctional relationships. Together, these approaches help improve intergroup processes and lead to organizational effectiveness.

Microcosm Groups

A *microcosm group* consists of a small number of individuals who reflect the issue being addressed.[7] For example, a microcosm group composed of members representing a spectrum of ethnic backgrounds, cultures, and races can be created to address diversity issues in the organization. This group, assisted by OD practitioners, can create programs and processes targeted at specific problems. In addition to addressing diversity problems, microcosm groups have been used to carry out organization diagnoses, solve communications problems, integrate two cultures, smooth the transition to a new structure, and address dysfunctional political processes.

Microcosm groups work through "parallel processes," which are the unconscious changes that take place in individuals when two or more groups interact.[8] After groups interact, members often find that their characteristic patterns of roles and interactions change to reflect the roles and dynamics of the group with whom they were relating. Put simply, groups seem to "infect" and become "infected" by the other groups. The following example given by Alderfer[9] helps to clarify how parallel processes work.

An organizational diagnosis team had assigned its members to each of five departments in a small manufacturing company. Members of the team had interviewed

APPLICATION 13•1   A Work-Out Meeting at General Electric Medical Systems Business

As part of the large-scale change effort, Jack Welch and several managers at General Electric devised a method for involving many organization members in the change process. Work-Out is a process for gathering the relevant people to discuss important issues and develop a clear action plan. The program has four goals: to use employees' knowledge and energy to improve work, to eliminate unnecessary work, to build trust through a process that allows and encourages employees to speak out without being fearful, and to engage in the construction of an organization that is ready to deal with the future.

At GE Medical Systems (GEMS), internal consultants conducted extensive interviews with managers throughout the organization. The interviews revealed considerable dissatisfaction with existing systems, including performance management (too many measurement processes, not enough focus on customers, unfair reward systems, and unrealistic goals), career development, and organizational climate. Managers were quoted as saying:

> I'm frustrated. I simply can't do the quality of work that I want to do and know how to do. I feel my hands are tied. I have no time. I need help on how to delegate and operate in this new culture.

> The goal of downsizing and delaying is correct. The execution stinks. The concept is to drop a lot of "less important" work. This just didn't happen. We still have to know all the details, still have to follow all the old policies and systems.

In addition to the interviews, Jack Welch spent some time at GEMS headquarters listening and trying to understand the issues facing the organization.

Based on the information compiled, about fifty GEMS employees and managers gathered for a five-day Work-Out session. The participants included the group executive who oversaw the GEMS business, his staff, employee relations managers, and informal leaders from the key functional areas who were thought to be risk takers and who would challenge the status quo. Most of the work during the week was spent unraveling, evaluating, and reconsidering the structures and processes that governed work at GEMS. Teams of managers

and employees addressed business problems. Functional groups developed visions of where their operations were headed. An important part of the teams' work was to engage in "bureaucracy busting" by identifying CRAP (Critical Review APpraisals) in the organization. Groups were asked to list needless approvals, policies, meetings, and reports that stifled productivity. In an effort to increase the intensity of the work and to encourage free thinking, senior managers were not a part of these discussions.

At the end of the week, the senior management team listened to the concerns, proposals, and action plans from the different teams. During the presentations, senior GEMS managers worked hard to understand the issues, communicate with the organization members, and build trust by sharing information, constraints, and opportunities. Most of the proposals focused on ways to reorganize work and improve returns to the organization. According to traditional Work-Out methods, managers must make instant, on-the-spot decisions about each idea in front of the whole group. The three decision choices are approval; rejection with clear reasons; and need more data, with a decision to be made within a month.

The five-day GEMS session ended with individuals and functional teams signing close to one hundred written contracts to implement the new processes and procedures or drop unnecessary work. The contracts were between people, between functional groups, and between levels of management, and organizational contracts affecting all members. One important outcome of the Work-Out effort at GEMS was a decision to involve suppliers in its internal email network. Through that interaction, GEMS and a key supplier eventually agreed to build new-product prototypes together, and their joint efforts have led to further identification of ways to reduce costs, improve design quality, or decrease cycle times.

Work-Out at GE has been very successful but hard to measure in dollar terms. Since 1988, hundreds of Work-Outs have been held, and the concept has continued to evolve into best-practice investigations, process mapping, and change-acceleration programs. The Work-Out process, however, clearly is based on the confrontation meeting model, where a large group of people gathers to identify issues and plan actions to address problems. ■

each department head and several department members, and had observed department meetings. The team was preparing to observe their first meeting of department heads and were trying to anticipate the group's behavior. At first they seemed to have no "rational" basis for predicting the top group's behavior because they "had no data" from direct observation. They decided to role-play the group meeting they had never seen. Diagnostic team members behaved as they thought the department heads would, and the result was uncanny. Team members found that they easily became engaged with one another in the simulated department-head meeting; emotional involvement occurred quickly for all participants. When the team actually was able to observe a department-head meeting, they were amazed at how closely the simulated meeting had approximated the actual session.

Thus, if a small and representative group can intimately understand and solve a complex organizational problem for themselves, they are in a good position to recommend action to address the problem in the larger system.

Application Stages

The process of using a microcosm group to address organizationwide issues involves the following five steps:

1. *Identify an issue.* This step involves finding a systemwide problem to be addressed. This may result from an organizational diagnosis or may be an idea generated by an organization member or task force. For example, one microcosm group charged with improving organizational communications was started by a division manager. He was concerned that the information provided by those reporting directly to him differed from the data he received from informal conversations with people throughout the division.

2. *Convene the group.* Once an issue is identified, the microcosm group can be formed. The most important convening principle is that group membership needs to reflect the appropriate mix of stakeholders related to the issue. If the issue is organizational communication, then the group should contain people from all hierarchical levels and functions, including staff groups and unions, if applicable. If the issue is integrating two corporate cultures following a merger, the microcosm group should contain people from both organizations who understand their respective cultures. Following the initial setup, the group itself becomes responsible for determining its membership. It will decide whether to add new members and how to fill vacant positions.

   Convening the group also draws attention to the issue and gives the group status. Members also need to be perceived as credible representatives of the problem. This will increase the likelihood that organization members will listen to and follow the suggestions they make.

3. *Provide group training.* Once the microcosm group is established, training is provided in group problem solving and decision making. Team-building interventions also may be appropriate. Group training focuses on establishing a group mission or charter, working relationships among members, group decision-making norms, and definitions of the problem to be addressed.

   From a group-process perspective, OD practitioners may need to observe and comment on how the group develops. Because the group is a microcosm of the organization, it will tend, through its behavior and attitudes, to reflect the problem in the larger organization. For example, if the group is addressing communication problems in the organization, it is likely to have its own difficulties with communication. Recognizing within the group the problem or issue it was formed to address is the first step toward solving the problem in the larger system.

4. *Address the issue.* This step involves solving the problem and implementing solutions. OD practitioners may help the group diagnose, design, implement, and evaluate changes. A key issue is gaining commitment in the wider organization

to implementing the group's solutions. The following factors can facilitate such ownership. First, a communication plan should link group activities to the organization. This may include publishing minutes from team meetings; inviting organization members, such as middle managers, union representatives, or hourly workers, into the meetings; and making presentations to different organizational groups. Second, group members need to be visible and accessible to management and labor. This can ensure that the appropriate support and resources are developed for the recommendations. Third, problem-solving processes should include an appropriate level of participation by organization members. Different data collection methods can be used to gain member input and to produce ownership of the problem and solutions.

5. *Dissolve the group.* The microcosm group can be disbanded following successful implementation of changes. This typically involves writing a final report or holding a final meeting.

Results of Microcosm Groups

The microcosm group intervention derives from an intergroup relations theory developed by Alderfer and has been applied by him to communications and race-relations problems. A microcosm group that addressed communications issues improved the way meetings were conducted; developed a job posting, career development, and promotion program; and conducted new-employee orientations.[10] In addition, the group assisted in the development, administration, and feedback of an organizationwide employee opinion survey. Alderfer also reported seven years of longitudinal data on a race-relations advisory group in a large organization.[11] Over time, white members showed significant improvements in their race-relations perceptions; African Americans consistently perceived more evidence of racism in the organization; and attendance at the meetings varied both over time and by race. In addition to the intragroup data, the case documented several changes in the organization, including the development of a race-relations competency document, the implementation of a race-relations workshop, and the creation of an upward-mobility policy.

A dearth of research exists on microcosm groups, partly because it is difficult to measure parallel processes and associate them with measures of organizational processes. More research on this intervention is needed.

Resolving Intergroup Conflict

The *intergroup conflict* intervention is designed specifically to help two groups or departments within an organization resolve dysfunctional conflicts. Intergroup conflict is neither good nor bad in itself, and in some cases, conflict among departments is necessary and productive for organizations.[12] This applies where there is little interdependence among departments and conflict or competition among them can spur higher levels of productivity. For example, organizations structured around different product lines might want to promote competition among the product groups. This might increase each group's productivity and add to the overall effectiveness of the firm.

In other organizations, especially those with very interdependent departments, conflict may become dysfunctional.[13] Two or more groups may grow polarized, and their continued conflict may result in the development of defensiveness and negative stereotypes of the other group. Polarization can be revealed in such statements as: "Any solution they come up with is wrong," "We find that nobody in that group will cooperate with us," or "What do you expect of those idiots?"

Particularly when intergroup communication is necessary, the amount and quality of communication usually drops off. Groups begin seeing the others as "the enemy" rather than in positive or even neutral terms. As the amount of communication decreases, the amount of mutual problem solving falls off as well. The tendency increases for one group to sabotage the efforts of the other group, either consciously or unconsciously.

Application Stages

A basic strategy for improving interdepartmental or intergroup relationships is to change the perceptions (perhaps, more accurately, misperceptions) that the two groups have of each other. One formal approach for accomplishing this, originally described by Blake and his associates, consists of a ten-step procedure.[14]

1. A consultant external to the two groups obtains their agreement to work directly on improving intergroup relationships. (The use of an outside consultant is highly recommended because without the moderating influence of such a neutral third party, it is almost impossible for the two groups to interact without becoming deadlocked and polarized in defensive positions.)

2. A time is set for the two groups to meet—preferably away from their normal work situations.

3. The consultant, together with the managers of the two groups, describes the purpose and objectives of the meeting—to develop better mutual relationships, explore the perceptions the groups have of each other, and formulate plans for improving the relationship. The two groups are presented the following or similar questions: "What qualities or attributes best describe our group?" "What qualities or attributes best describe the other group?" and "How do we think the other group will describe us?" Then, the two groups are encouraged to establish norms of openness for feedback and discussion.

4. The two groups are assigned to separate rooms and asked to write their answers to the three questions. Usually, an outside consultant works with each group to help the members become more open and to encourage them to develop lists that accurately reflect their perceptions, both of their own image and of the other group.

5. After completing their lists, the two groups reconvene. A representative from each group presents the written statements. Only the two representatives are allowed to speak. The primary objective at this stage is to make certain that the images, perceptions, and attitudes are presented as accurately as possible and to avoid the arguments that might arise if the two groups openly confronted each other. Questions, however, are allowed to ensure that both groups clearly understand the written lists. Justifications, accusations, or other statements are not permitted.

6. When it is clear that the two groups thoroughly understand the content of the lists, they separate again. By this point, a great number of misperceptions and discrepancies have been brought to light.

7. The task of the two groups (almost always with a consultant as a process observer) is to analyze and review the reasons for the discrepancies. The emphasis is on solving the problems and reducing the misperceptions. The actual or implicit question is not whether the perception of the other group is right or wrong but rather "How did these perceptions occur? What actions on the part of our group may have contributed to this set of perceptions?"

8. When the two groups have worked through the discrepancies, as well as the areas of common agreement, they meet to share both the identified discrepancies and their problem-solving approaches to those discrepancies. Because the primary focus is on the behavior underlying the perceptions, free, open discussion is encouraged between the two groups, and their joint aim is to develop an overall list of remaining and possible sources of friction and isolation.

9. The two groups are asked to develop specific plans of action for solving specific problems and for improving their relationships.

10. When the two groups have gone as far as possible in formulating action plans, at least one follow-up meeting is scheduled so that the groups can report on actions that have been implemented, identify any further problems that have emerged, and, where necessary, formulate additional action plans.

In addition to this formal approach to improving interdepartmental or intergroup relationships are a number of more informal procedures. Beckhard asks each of the two groups to develop a list of what irritates or exasperates them about the other group and to predict what they think the other group will say about them.[15] A more simplified approach, although perhaps not as effective, is to bring the two groups together, dispense with the written lists developed in isolation, and discuss only common problems and irritations.

Different approaches to resolving intergroup conflict form a continuum from behavioral solutions to attitudinal change solutions.[16] Behavioral methods are oriented to keeping the relevant parties physically separate and specifying the limited conditions under which interaction will occur. Little attempt is made to understand or change how members of each group see the other. Conversely, attitudinal methods, such as exchanging group members or requiring intense interaction with important rewards or opportunities clearly tied to coordination, are directed at changing how each group perceives the other. Here, it is assumed that perceptual distortions and stereotyping underlie the conflict and need to be changed to resolve it.

Most of the OD solutions to intergroup conflict reviewed in this section favor attitudinal change strategies. However, such interventions typically require considerably more skill and time than do the behavioral solutions. Changing attitudes is difficult in conflict situations, especially if the attitudes are deep-seated and form an integral part of people's personalities. Attitudinal change interventions should be reserved for those situations in which behavioral solutions might not work.

Behavioral interventions seem most applicable in situations in which task interdependence between the conflicting groups is relatively low and predictable. For example, the task interaction between the production and maintenance departments might be limited to scheduled periodic maintenance on machines. Here, higher management can physically separate the departments and specify the limited conditions under which they should interact. Where the shared task requires only limited interaction, that interaction can be programmed and standardized.

Attitudinal change interventions seem necessary when task interdependence between the conflicting groups is high and unpredictable, such as might be found between the research and production departments during a new product introduction. Here, the two departments need to work together closely, often at unpredictable times and with novel, complex issues. When conflicts arise because of misperceptions, they must be worked through in terms of people's perceptions and attitudes. The shared task does not permit physical separation or limited, specific interaction. It is in these highly interdependent and unpredictable task situations that the conflict resolution interventions discussed in this section are most appropriate.

Application 13.2 presents an example of intergroup conflict resolved by an attitudinal change intervention.[17] The method temporarily exchanged personnel between the conflicting departments and was carried out by management without the help of an OD consultant. The change method takes considerable time and seems most applicable to conflicts that do not have to be resolved immediately.

Results of Intergroup Conflict Interventions

A number of studies have been done on the effects of intergroup conflict resolution. In his original study, Blake reported vastly improved relationships between the union and management.[18] In a later study, Bennis used Blake's basic design to improve relationships between two groups of U.S. State Department officials—high-level administrative officers and officers in the foreign service.[19] Initially, there was much mutual distrust, negative stereotyping, blocked communication, and hostility between the two groups. "Each 'side' perceived the other as more threatening than any realistic overseas enemy."[20] Although no hard data were obtained, the intervention seemed to improve relationships so that the two groups "at least understood the other side's point of view."

Golembiewski and Blumberg used a modification of the Blake design that involved an exchange of "images" not only among organizational units but also among individuals in the marketing division of a large firm.[21] An attitude questionnaire was used to make before-and-after comparisons. The results were measured and found to be different for more or less "deeply involved" individuals or units. In general, the more deeply involved people or units (promotion, regions and divisions, and sales) reflected more positive attitudes toward collaboration and had greater feelings of commitment to the success of the entire organization. Less deeply involved positions or units (such areas as sales training, hospital sales, and trade relations) did not show any particular trends in attitudinal changes, either positive or negative.

French and Bell, who used a somewhat similar design, reported that they were able to work successfully with three groups simultaneously.[22] They obtained positive results in their work with key groups in an Indian tribal organization—the tribal council, the tribal staff, and the Community Action Program (CAP). The researchers asked each group to develop perceptions of the other two, as well as of itself, and to share those perceptions in the larger group. The tribal council developed four lists—both favorable and unfavorable items about the tribal staff, a similar list about the CAP, and predictions as to what the staff and CAP would say about the council.

Once each group had developed its lists, the results were shared in a three-group meeting, and participants worked through the similarities and dissimilarities in the various lists. According to the researchers, the use of this method reduces intergroup problems and frictions and increases communications and interactions.

Huse and Beer have described positive results arising from periodic cross-departmental meetings in which personnel in one department would meet, in sequence, with those from other departments to discuss perceptions, expectations, and strong and weak points about one another.[23] Interviews indicated that the participants found the meetings extremely helpful. As one engineer said, "Before we had these meetings, I really wasn't concerned about the people in the other departments except to feel that they weren't doing their job. After we held the interdepartmental meetings, I began to understand some of their problems. I began to listen to them and to work with them."[24]

In another study, Huse found that bringing representatives of different groups together to work on common work-related problems had a marked effect, not only

APPLICATION 13•2   Intergroup Relations at Canadian-Atlantic

Canadian-Atlantic, a transportation conglomerate headquartered in Vancouver, British Columbia, experienced intense conflict between research managers and operating managers at the home office. Research managers were responsible for developing operational innovations for everything from loading railroad cars to increasing operational efficiency. Operations managers were responsible for scheduling and running trains.

Operations managers had absolutely no use for research personnel, claiming that research personnel took far too long to do projects. One manager said, "A 50-percent solution when we need it is much better than a 100-percent solution ten years from now when the crisis is over." Operations managers also were offended by the complicated terminology and jargon used by research personnel. The latter had developed several useful innovations, such as automated loading platforms and training simulators, but resistance to the innovations was great. Research personnel wanted to cooperate with operations managers, but they could not go along with certain requests, such as releasing half-completed innovations or watering down their ideas for less-educated personnel in

operations. One manager commented that the extent of communication between research and operations "was just about zero, and both groups are beginning to like it that way."

The vice president of research and development (R&D) was worried. He believed that intergroup hostility was reducing dramatically his department's effectiveness. Morale was low, and operations managers had little interest in new developments. The R&D vice president persuaded the company president to rotate managers between operations and research. Initially, one manager from each department was exchanged. Later, two and three were exchanged simultaneously. Each rotation lasted about six months. After two-and-one-half years, the relationship between the departments was vastly improved, with key individuals understanding both points of view and working to integrate the existing differences. One operations manager enjoyed the work in research so much that he asked to stay on there, and the operations vice president tried to hire two of the R&D managers to work permanently in his division. ■

on relationships among a number of different manufacturing groups but also on the quality of the product, which increased 62 percent.[25] The basic tactic in this study was to ensure that when a work-related problem arose, representatives of two or more groups worked jointly on the problem.

Based on their experience at TRW Systems, Fordyce and Weil developed a modified approach whereby each group builds three lists—one containing "positive feedback" items (those things the group values and likes about the other group), a "bug" list (those things the group dislikes about the other group), and an "empathy" list (predictions about what the other group's list contains).[26] When the groups come together, they build a master list of major concerns and unresolved problems, which are assigned priorities and developed into an agenda. When they have completed the task, the subgroups report the results of their discussions to the total group, which then develops a series of action steps for improving the relations between the groups and commits itself to following through. For each action step, specific responsibilities are assigned, and an overall schedule is developed for prompt completion of the action steps.

In conclusion, the technology for improving intergroup relations is promising. A greater distinction between attitudinal and behavioral changes needs to be made in planning effective intergroup interventions. A greater variety of interventions that addresses the practical difficulties of bringing two groups together also is necessary. Finally, more knowledge is needed about how culture affects intergroup conflict and how interventions need to be adjusted in cross-cultural situations.[27] Growing knowledge and theory suggest that conflict can be either functional or dysfunctional, depending on the circumstances. Further research is needed to identify when conflict should be intensified and when it should be reduced. In short, conflict should be managed.[28]

LARGE-GROUP INTERVENTIONS

The third systemwide process intervention is called *large-group intervention.* Such change programs have been referred to variously as "search conferences," "open-space meetings," "open-systems planning," and "future searches."[29] They focus on issues that affect the whole organization or large segments of it, such as developing new products or services, responding to environmental change, or introducing new technology. The defining feature of large-group intervention is the bringing together large numbers of organization members and other stakeholders, often more than one hundred, for a two- to four-day meeting or conference. Here, conference attendees work together to identify and resolve organizationwide problems, to design new approaches to structuring and managing the firm, or to propose future directions for the organization. Large-group interventions are among the fastest-growing OD applications. Only a handful of these change efforts had been conducted when this text was revised in 1993, but the number and type of large-group interventions have increased rapidly since then.

Large-group interventions can vary on several dimensions, including purpose, size, length, structure, and number. The purpose of these change methods can range from solving particular organizational problems to envisioning future strategic directions. Large-group interventions have been run with groups of less than fifty to more than two thousand participants and have lasted between one and five days. Some large-group processes are relatively planned and structured; others are more informal.[30] Some interventions involve a single large-group meeting; others include a succession of meetings to accomplish systemwide change in a short period of time.[31]

Despite these differences, most large-group interventions have similar conceptual foundations and methods. These interventions have evolved over the past thirty years and represent a combination of open-systems applications and "futuring" and "visioning" exercises. Open-systems approaches direct attention to how organizations interact with and are shaped by their environments. They suggest that an organization's current state is the result of the intentional and unintentional interaction among many groups and individuals both inside and outside the organization. Changing the organization's vision, structure, strategy, or work therefore requires the deliberate, face-to-face coordination of these groups. Four key assumptions[32] underlie this approach.

1. *Organization members' perceptions play a major role in environmental relations.* They determine which parts of the environment are attended to or ignored as well as what value is placed on those parts. Such perceptions provide the basis for planning and implementing specific actions in relation to the environment.

2. *Organization members must share a common view of the environment to permit coordinated action toward it.* Without a shared view of the environment, conflicts can arise about what parts of the environment are important and about what value should be placed on different parts. Such perceptual disagreements make planning and implementing a coherent strategy difficult.[33]

3. *Organization members' perceptions must accurately reflect the condition of the environment if organizational responses are to be effective.* Members can misinterpret environmental information, ignore important forces, or attend to

negligible events. Such misperceptions can render organizational responses to the environment inappropriate or ineffective. For example, managers at Coca-Cola misperceived the market for soft drinks and introduced New Coke. Sales failed to meet expectations, and New Coke had to be withdrawn from the market.

4. *Organizations cannot only adapt to their environment; they must create it proactively.* Organizations often are discussed in terms of their dependency on environments and on how they should adapt to environmental forces. But it also is possible for organizations to plan proactively for a desired environment and then take action against the existing environment to move it in the desired direction. For example, when Alcoa first started to manufacture aluminum building materials, there was little demand for them. Rather than wait to see whether the market developed, Alcoa entered the construction business and pioneered the use of aluminum building materials.

Futuring and visioning exercises help guide members in creating "images of potential" toward which the organization can grow and develop.[34] Focusing on the organization's potential rather than its problems is aligned with contemporary approaches to planned change described in Chapter 2. It can increase members' energy for change and build a broad consensus toward a new future.

Application Stages

Conducting a large-group intervention generally involves preparing for the meeting, conducting it, and following up on outcomes. These activities are described below.

Preparing for the Large-Group Meeting

A design team comprising OD practitioners and several organization members is formed to organize the event. The team generally addresses three key ingredients for successful large-group meetings: a compelling meeting theme, appropriate participants, and relevant tasks to address the theme.

1. *Compelling meeting theme.* Large-group interventions require a compelling reason or focal point for change. Although "people problems" can be an important focus, more powerful reasons for large-group efforts include managing impending mergers or reorganizations, responding to environmental threats and opportunities, or proposing radical organizational changes.[35] Whatever the focal point for change, senior leaders need to make clear to others the purpose of the large-group meeting. Ambiguity about the reason for the intervention can dissipate participants' energy and commitment to change. For example, a large-group meeting that successfully envisioned a hospital's future organization design was viewed as a failure by a few key managers who thought that the purpose was to cut costs from the hospital's budget. Their subsequent lack of support stalled the change effort.

2. *Appropriate participants.* A fundamental goal of large-group interventions is to "get the whole system in the room." This involves inviting as many people as possible who have a stake in the conference theme and who are energized and committed to conceiving and initiating change. Senior managers, suppliers, union leaders, internal and external customers, trade group representatives, government and regulatory officials, and organization members from a variety of jobs, genders, races, and ages are potential participants.

3. *Relevant tasks to address the conference theme.* As described below, these tasks typically are assigned to several subgroups responsible for examining the theme and drawing conclusions for action. Generally, participants rely on their own experience and expertise to address systemwide issues, rather than drawing on resources from outside of the large-group meeting. This ensures that the meeting can be completed within the allotted time and that members can participate fully as important sources of information.

Conducting the Meeting

The flow of events in a large-group meeting can vary greatly, depending on its purpose and the framework adopted. Most large-group processes, however, fit within two primary frameworks: open-systems methods and open-space methods.

Open-Systems Methods. A variety of large-group approaches, such as search conferences, open-systems planning, and real-time strategic change, have their basis in open-systems methods. These approaches help organizations assess their environments systematically and develop strategic responses to them. They help organization members develop a strategic mission for relating to the environment and influencing it in favorable directions. Open-systems methods begin with a diagnosis of the existing environment and how the organization relates to it. They proceed to develop possible future environments and action plans to bring them about.[36] These steps are described below.

1. *Map the current environment surrounding the organization.* In this step, the different domains or parts of the environment are identified and prioritized. This involves listing all external groups directly interacting with the organization, such as customers, suppliers, or government agencies, and ranking them in importance. Participants then are asked to describe each domain's expectations for the organization's behavior.

2. *Assess the organization's responses to environmental expectations.* This step asks participants to describe how the organization currently addresses the environmental expectations identified in step 1.

3. *Identify the core mission of the organization.* This step helps to identify the underlying purpose or core mission of the organization, as derived from how it responds to external demands. Attention is directed at discovering the mission as it is revealed in the organization's behavior, not as it is pronounced in the organization's official statement of purpose. This is accomplished by examining the organization and environment transactions identified in steps 1 and 2 and then assessing the values that seem to underlie those interactions. These values provide clues about the actual identity or mission of the organization.

4. *Create a realistic future scenario of environmental expectations and organization responses.* This step asks members to project the organization and its environment into the near future, assuming no real changes in the organization. It asks participants to address the question, "What will happen if the organization continues to operate as it does at present?" Participant responses are combined to develop a likely organization future under the assumption of no change.

5. *Create an ideal future scenario of environmental expectations and organization responses.* Members are asked to create alternative, desirable futures. This involves going back over steps 1, 2, and 3 and asking what members ideally would like to see happen in the near future in both the environment and the

organization. People are encouraged to fantasize about desired futures without worrying about possible constraints.

6. *Compare the present with the ideal future and prepare an action plan for reducing the discrepancy.* This last step identifies specific actions that will move both the environment and the organization toward the desired future. Planning for appropriate interventions typically occurs in three timeframes: tomorrow, six months from now, and two years from now. Participants also decide on a follow-up schedule for sharing the flow of actions and updating the planning process.

There are a number of variations on this basic model, each of which follows a similar pattern of creating common ground, discussing the issues, and devising an agenda for change. For example, search conferences begin with an exercise called "appreciating the past," which asks participants to examine the significant events, milestones, and highlights of the organization's previous thirty years (or less, in the case of newer organizations).[37] It demonstrates that participants share a common history, although they may come from different organizations, departments, age groups, or hierarchical levels.

Once common ground is established, members can discuss the systemwide issue or theme. To promote widespread participation, members typically organize into subgroups of eight to ten people representing as many stakeholder viewpoints as possible. The subgroups may address a general question (for example, "What are the opportunities for new business in our global market?") or focus on a specific issue (for example, "How can we improve quality and cut costs on a particular product line?"). Subgroup members brainstorm answers to these questions, record them on flipchart paper, and share them with the larger group. The whole group compares responses from the subgroups and identifies common themes. Other methods, such as presentations to the large group, small-group meetings on particular aspects of the conference theme, or spontaneous meetings of interest to the participants, are used to discuss the conference theme and distribute information to members.

The final task of large-group meetings based on open-systems methods is creating an agenda for change. Participants are asked to reflect on what they have learned at the meeting and to suggest changes for themselves, their department, and the whole organization. Members from the same department often are grouped together to discuss their proposals and decide on action plans, timetables, and accountabilities. Action items for the total organization are referred to a steering committee that addresses organizationwide policy issues and action plans. At the conclusion of the large-group meeting, the departmental subgroups and the steering committee report their conclusions to all participants and seek initial commitment to change.

Application 13.3 describes a large-group intervention to address the complex issue of how to manage forests in North America.[38] The Seventh American Forest Congress followed an open-systems model to design and implement its large-group meeting.

Open-Space Methods. The second approach to large-group interventions is distinguished by its lack of formal structure. Open-space methods temporarily restructure or "self-organize" participants around interests and topics associated with the conference theme. They generally follow these steps:[39]

1. *Set the conditions for self-organizing.* In the first step, the OD practitioner or manager responsible for the large-group intervention sets the stage by

APPLICATION 13•3   The Seventh American Forest Congress

The use and management of America's forests traditionally have been governed by regular Forest Congresses that were convened by a friendly but somewhat exclusive group of landowners, government agencies, timber companies, and recreational users. Legislation and government regulation followed from the advice of the congresses. The congresses of 1882 and 1905 established, respectively, the National Forest System and the U.S. Forest Service. A third congress, in 1946, considered reforestation issues after significant stands of timber were used for the war effort. The Fourth, Fifth, and Sixth Congresses met at intervals of about a decade (1953, 1963, and 1975), mostly to refine the multiple-use policy that governed forest use. Changes in the timber industry and government policy, increasing product demand, a confusing maze of court rulings, and the proliferation of groups with an interest in forest policy polarized a once-workable system for mediating differences. As a result, no congress was called in the 1980s, and not until 1994 were steps made to find a new way to bring stakeholders together to hammer out the increasingly problematic issues of forest use.

In 1994, a small group of diverse stakeholders met to commit together to a new path. That group's recommendation was to move away from the failed approaches of the past that stressed listening to or pleading with experts seated together on a stage and left groups talking past one another. The complex issues, elusive answers, and sharpening conflict demanded a wholly different paradigm. The steering group's executive committee, what became known as the Seventh American Forest Congress's board of directors, devised a core vision that called for high participation of very diverse groups talking with each other in a process that encouraged brand-new forms of much more open communication and ways of working together. The board also acknowledged that deeply rooted problems required a process rather than a solution and a new means for empowering the system of conflicting interests to resolve its own problems.

Out of this initial effort came detailed plans that would make the Seventh American Forest Congress in February 1996 a midpoint in a broad process of large-scale change among forestry's diverse interests. From July 1995 until late January 1996, about ninety local meetings were arranged to feed the eventual work of the congress. Roundtable sessions were organized in local areas to collect opinions and mirrored the expected mix of demographics, professions, and interests. Fifty-one of these roundtable sessions were conducted with the assistance of experienced facilitators, and each lasted at least a day. Thirty-nine collaborative meetings were conducted by individual interested parties (for example, professional groups, timber producers, and communities). Both types of pre-congress groups were required to develop common ground, not necessarily consensus, in three areas: a new vision for forest use, principles for achieving that vision, and essential next steps for moving toward the vision. The results of these local sessions provided the working raw materials for the large, diverse, and inclusive Seventh Congress.

From the outset, organizers stressed just how different the Seventh Congress would be. The program brochure promised that "this will not be like any convention you have attended previously." It was to be clearly purposeful and would use the latest methods in large-group facilitation: "Together, you will agree on a shared vision for the future of America's forests, a set of guiding principles, and the next steps necessary to realize the vision based on principles. This will be accomplished through interaction sessions using state-of-the-art methods in large-group facilitation." Rather than throttle voices, the congress specifically embraced and celebrated the diversity of interests around forest-use policy. It was to be a citizen's congress with no delegates, no invitations, and no maximum level of attendance. Anyone who wished to attend the congress could register. Of course, congress organizers had prepared to conduct a large-scale interactive process event. A design team selected by the board of directors attended six two-day sessions to put together a process and assemble the logistics for carrying out the congress.

The fifteen hundred participants were placed at tables of no more than ten people each. Table members were selected to maximize the diversity of interests represented at the congress. The design team created a "script" that would lead table members through a process of refining a vision for America's forests and the principles for the use and care of those forests. Members then would consider the next steps to be taken by the system of interests to achieve the common vision both at the national level and in local environments. The congress would finish by obtaining the individual commitments of every participant to put congress outcomes into practice. The keys to success included the creation of effective teams out of highly diverse table members; the use of processes that explicitly took into account the explosive potential for conflict and hence kept interest focused on talking with tablemates and not talking at the congress as a whole; and finally congress leaders' and facilitators' taking no substantive stance on the issues but letting the congress find and empower itself through the process.

In the first day's activities, the process and goals were outlined, table teams were built, members worked toward refining a common vision, and table members participated in different "concurrent dialogue sessions" that brought back emerging views and principles to their tables. The real key to the first session was the building of the table teams. Ten diverse people with passionately held points of view were put together and given tasks that forced them to seek and cultivate common bonds. Before moving on to working with more substantive issues, table members shared information about themselves and established commitments to each other that would carry their work through the congress. In the first round of activity, each table had a trained facilitator. After the first round, tablemates chose facilitators and recorders from their own ranks. Once table members established commitments to each other, they began the process of creating a common database for the congress. The first task was to brainstorm the items that made each member feel good and not so good about what is happening to America's forests. From the very start, table members had to deal face-to-face with the hottest issues of the congress.

With dissatisfaction out in the open and systematically identified, table members turned their attention to developing the vision. Vision elements were taken from the prior work of the roundtables and collaborative meetings. Every table was asked to react to each of those elements. Each member could express her or his reaction by giving the statement a green light for solid agreement, a yellow light indicating less than full support but willingness to go along, or a red light for complete disagreement. Table members were asked to tally their responses to more than a dozen of these vision statement elements and to focus their discussion on finding common ground.

In the afternoon of the first day, table members could choose to attend breakout groups called concurrent dialogue sessions. The topics of those sessions had been predefined based on inputs from the roundtables. Table teams sent members to the sessions to bring back ideas and points of view emerging elsewhere. In each dialogue session a trained facilitator helped the group broaden various perspectives on forest issues. At the end of the day, team members reported the results of the dialogue sessions to their tables.

The second day's work began with a second round of concurrent dialogue sessions and feedback about the results of the first day's activities, especially congresswide tallies of vision statements and views about what was and was not working in America's forests. With this context established, table members refined the principles by which the common vision could be achieved. Table members attended concurrent dialogue sessions on particular principles, much like the

sessions of the previous day. The purpose of these sessions was to revise the principles and supporting statements and to generate principles that were missing after the roundtable process. The work of the dialogue sessions was reported to the whole congress on the following day.

In the last phases of the congress, participants began to feel empowered by the process. Instead of holding to a rigid schedule, the design team restructured the last day-and-a-half of the congress based on real-time feedback from the participants. Congress members worked first at their tables to develop advice to the board of directors for steps to be taken at the national level. Afterward, the now highly practiced participants decided to go to their "back-home" teams—formed by zip-code membership—to work out ways to translate the vision and principles into realities at the local level, the resources needed to do so, and the kinds of processes needed to link the work of the congress to the local areas. In addition, the early commitment to the process even thwarted an attempt to organize a walkout: two of the more vocal members, advocating personal agendas, failed to divide and disrupt the congress. Another indicator of the acceptance of the process was that literally thousands of actions were developed to support the principles.

Early reactions to the vision elements resulted in a large percentage of "red" or complete-disagreement votes. But the final tally of the congress recorded that of the thirteen considered pieces to the vision statement, more than a third of them received green lights from more than 80 percent of the participants. For example, 90 percent of the participants agreed that in the future the forests would be held in a variety of public, private, tribal, land-grant, and trust ownerships by owners whose rights, objectives, and expectations would be respected and who would understand and accept their responsibilities as stewards. Key statements of principle also received strong support. Back-home steps included reconvening local meetings within sixty days to review the results of the congress and to share the process of how those results were obtained. Advice to the congress board of directors reflected a deep interest in the new process that had been used. In fact, most of the comments dealt not with the contentious substantive issues, but with how to make the process run even more smoothly in the future. This, of course, was a key lesson: members were taking back process, not the better-honed conflict that had characterized traditional methods of dealing with forest policy. ■

announcing the theme of the session and the norms that will govern it. In addition, participants are informed that the meeting will consist of small-group discussions convened by the participants and addressing any topic they believe critical to the theme of the conference. Two sets of norms govern how open-space methods are applied, and although the norms may sound ambiguous, they are critical to establishing the conditions for a successful meeting.

The first set of norms concerns the "Law of Two Feet." It encourages people to take responsibility for their own behavior; to go to meetings and discussions where they are learning, contributing, or in some way remaining interested. Moving from group to group is legitimized by the roles of "butterflies" and "bumblebees." Butterflies attract others into spontaneous conversations and, in fact, may never attend a formal meeting. Bumblebees go from group to group and sprinkle knowledge, information, or new ideas into different meetings.

The second set of norms is labeled the "Four Principles." The first principle is "whoever comes is the right people." It is intended to free people to begin conversations with anyone at any time. It also signals that the quality of a conversation is what's most important, not who's involved. The second principle, "Whatever happens is the only thing that could have," infuses the group with responsibility, encourages participants to be flexible, and prepares them to be surprised. "Whenever it starts is the right time" is the third principle and is aimed at encouraging creativity and following the natural energy in the group. The final principle, "When it is over, it is over," allows people to move on and not feel like they have to meet for a certain time period or satisfy someone else's requirements.

2. **Create the agenda.** The second step in open-space interventions is to develop a road map for the remainder of the conference. This is accomplished by asking participants to describe a topic related to the conference theme that they have passion for and interest in discussing. This topic is written on a large piece of paper, announced to the group, and then posted on the community bulletin board where meeting topics and locations are displayed.[40] The person announcing the topic agrees to convene the meeting at the posted time and place. This process continues until everyone who wants to define a topic has been given the chance to speak. The final activity in this step asks participants to sign up for as many of the sessions as they have interest in. The open-space meeting begins with the first scheduled sessions.

3. **Coordinate activity through information.** During an open-space session, there are two ways to coordinate activities. First, each morning and evening a community meeting is held to announce new topics that have emerged for which meeting dates and times have been assigned, or to share observations and learnings. Second, as the different meetings occur, the conveners produce one-page summaries of what happened, who attended, what subjects were discussed, and what recommendations or actions were proposed. Typically, this is done on computer in a room dedicated for this purpose. These summaries are posted near the community bulletin board in an area often labeled "newsroom." Participants are encouraged to visit the newsroom and become familiar with what other groups have been discussing. The summaries also can be printed and copied for conference participants.

Application 13.4 provides a more detailed description of how an open-space meeting is conducted.[41] The consultant organization believed the open-space design allowed them to discuss a variety of issues in a flexible format and gave them the opportunity to network with colleagues in ways that a normal annual meeting would not have supported.

APPLICATION 13·4   Open-Space Meeting at a Consulting Firm

A worldwide consulting organization used an open-space design to address the future of the organization as part of its annual meeting. The meeting began with a day of traditional reports on past performance, market trends, and awards for outstanding consultants. The next morning, the 320 principals assembled in the conference center ballroom.

Day One

When people walked into the room, 320 chairs were arranged in three concentric circles. Many paused at the door as they arrived, looked around with raised eyebrows, and tried to decide where to sit. The open-space event was opened by the general manager who spoke about the organization's future and how it might be positioned for success. During his talk, he made several comments about how unusual it was for the organization to try this kind of meeting.

He then introduced a consultant who described what they would be doing and how they would do it. He told them that they would create their own agenda and run their own meetings for the next two days around issues that they really cared about. He described the importance of a few simple principles and laws (the Law of Two Feet and the Four Principles). Side murmurs and appreciative laughter were heard as he spoke.

The consultant then invited participants to think about issues related to the future of the organization about which they were passionate and willing to initiate a conversation. Participants were asked to come to the center of the circle, write their issue on a piece of paper and sign it, and announce their topic and their name to the group. Then they were instructed to go to the wall labeled "Community Bulletin Board," select a time and location for their meeting from the available openings, and hang their topic on the wall in that space. The community bulletin board had been arranged so that each meeting would last about an hour at a particular meeting place in the conference center. Eight time slots and 15 meeting spaces were available in the two days after the first morning, creating 120 meeting spaces.

There was a long pause, but after some time, someone rose, picked up a piece of paper, and began to write on it. Others followed and soon a dozen people were writing and announcing their topic and their name. When the initial flow waned, people who had been hesitating were urged to take the plunge and a number did. In about fifteen minutes, more than fifty topics were announced and posted. After being given a final opportunity to propose a topic, the participants were asked to go to the community bulletin board and sign

their names to any and all topics that they wanted to attend. People sat around and chatted until there was space at the wall and then went over to sign their names. In another fifteen minutes most of the topics had some names on them; a number were of high interest and attracted many signatures.

Once a person declared a topic and picked a time and place, her or his responsibility was to show up and convene the meeting. After the meeting was over, this person was to type up a summary of who was there and what happened on one of the fifteen computers arranged around the other walls of the ballroom. Following this initial set of instructions and agenda-setting activities, the participants were dismissed to start their meetings. The consultant was available to help with any problems, but the program was simple and self-instructing.

Some groups were clearly led by the convener; others had free-flow give-and-take. One group of six or seven took to working out a complex technical problem. Another group of twenty debated the necessity for certain corporate policies and appropriate actions to take. A third group was inventing new processes for integrating and educating midcareer hires. The groups were relatively stable, with people occasionally joining or leaving. One group that didn't have time to decide on the action steps it wanted after a lively discussion noted that a similar topic was being discussed on the next day and agreed to show up in that time space. Other small groups of people, in central gathering places, were meeting and working intently, apparently on business issues. The annual meeting convened attendees from many countries, and this was the one time during the year when they were all together. The open-space design provided a lot of agenda flexibility and time and space for easy networking.

During the afternoon, reports were filed, printed, and posted on a wall near the ballroom entrance. As people discovered them, the readers began to collect and converse. The page-length reports were numbered in order of their printing and posting, so that on subsequent visits to this "newsroom," it was easy to remember what had been read. The "Evening News," or final session of the first day, held in the ballroom at 5:45 p.m., was brief. A few announcements were made, along with a reminder about the next day's Morning News session. No activities were planned for the evening, and people went off to do whatever they wished.

Day Two

The second day began as the first had ended, in the large circles in the ballroom. The consultant asked if people wished to raise any new topics. After a long pause, one man came out to write on the newsprint. Several people followed him and another eight to ten topics were posted. The consultant then explained that a book summarizing all the discussions would be published and in their hands the next morning. The only requirement was that meeting conveners had to submit their summary reports before 6:30 that evening.

The second day was similar to the first, but with a more relaxed flow. Groups were meeting all over the place and this way of working was becoming familiar. People regularly checked in at the wall to see where they wanted to go or to read the long list of reports. At the Evening News, some announcements were made and the consultant explained that the next day would be spent prioritizing the sixty-seven issues that had been reported out. At 6:30 p.m., when the computers shut down, 102 pages were printed with a table of contents, a one-page description of the event that produced the book, and a simple ballot for voting on the top ten priorities. This went off to the copy center, where it was reproduced and bound with a cover page overnight.

Day Three

The next morning, the 320 attendees assembled to start the day's schedule. First, they picked up a copy of the book of reports, read and selected their ten most important issues, and then keyed in their votes on the computers. Second, after a short break, they returned to the ballroom to hear the results. The overall frequency distribution was displayed for the group. The titles of the fifteen top priorities were written on flipcharts and posted around the ballroom and adjoining anteroom space. People were given an opportunity to visit any or all of the stations and record two types of information on them: (1) any other related issues and (2) action steps that they wanted to see occur. The person who convened each of the top-priority sessions was asked to record the comments of those who came by. The final event of this open-space assembly was a commentary by the firm's manager about each issue, what had been written about it, and how the action items would be carried out. ■

Following up on Meeting Outcomes

Follow-up efforts are vital to implementing the action plans from large-scale interventions. These efforts involve communicating the results of the meeting to the rest of the organization, gaining wider commitment to the changes, and structuring the change process. In those cases where all the members of the organization were involved in the large-group meeting, implementation can proceed immediately according to the timetable included in the action plans.

Results of Large-Group Interventions

In the past decade, the number of case studies describing the methods and results of large-group interventions has increased dramatically. Such interventions have been conducted widely, at Hewlett-Packard, AT&T, AMI Presbyterian St. Luke's Hospital, Boeing, Kodak, and Rockport, among other companies; around a variety of themes or issues, including natural resources conservation, community development, and strategic change; and in a variety of countries, including Pakistan, Australia, England, and India.[42] Despite the proliferation of practice, however, little systematic research has been done on the interventions' effects. Because these change efforts often set the stage for subsequent OD interventions, it is difficult to isolate their specific results from those of the other changes. Anecdotal evidence from practitioners suggests the following benefits from large-group interventions: increased energy toward organizational change, improved feelings of community, ability to see outside the box, increased speed of change, and improved relationships with stakeholders.[43] Clearly, systematic research is needed on this important systemwide process intervention.

GRID ORGANIZATION DEVELOPMENT: A NORMATIVE APPROACH

Normative approaches to systemwide process intervention suggest that there is one best way to manage all organizations. This contrasts sharply with modern contingency theory and open-systems approaches, which propose that managerial practices should vary depending on the organization's environment, technology, and member needs and values. Two interventions represent the primary normative approaches. Likert's System 4 model was described in Chapter 1 as an important element in the history of OD, but its application in current organizations has declined substantially. Blake and Mouton's Grid® Organization Development, however, has been applied extensively and continues in use today.

Like Likert's System 4 process, Grid OD originated from research about managerial and organizational effectiveness.[44] Data gathered on organizational excellence from 198 organizations located in the United States, Japan, and Great Britain found that the two foremost barriers to excellence were planning and communications.[45] Each of these barriers was researched further to understand its roots, and the research resulted in a normative model of leadership—the Managerial Grid.

According to the Managerial Grid, an individual's style can be described according to his or her concern for production and concern for people.[46] A *concern for production* covers a range of behaviors, such as accomplishing productive tasks, developing creative ideas, making quality policy decisions, establishing thorough and high-quality staff services, or creating efficient workload measurements. Concern for production is not limited to things but also may involve human accomplishment within the organization, regardless of the assigned tasks or activities. A *concern for people* encompasses a variety of issues, including concern for the individual's personal worth, good working conditions, a degree of involvement or commitment to completing the job, security, a fair salary structure and fringe benefits, and good social and other relationships. Each dimension is measured on a nine-point scale and results in 81 possible leadership styles.

For example, 1,9 managers have a low concern for production and a high concern for people: they view people's feelings, attitudes, and needs as valuable in their own right. This type of manager strives to provide subordinates with work conditions that provide ease, security, and comfort. On the other hand, 9,1 managers have a high concern for production but a low concern for people: they minimize the attitudes and feelings of subordinates and give little attention to individual creativity, conflict, and commitment. As a result, the focus is on the work organization.

Blake and Mouton proposed that the 9,9 managerial style is the most effective in overcoming the communications barrier to corporate excellence. The basic assumptions behind this managerial style differ qualitatively and quantitatively from those underlying the other managerial styles, which assume there is an inherent conflict between the needs of the organization and the needs of people. By showing a high concern for both people and production, managers allow employees to think and to influence the organization, thus promoting active support for organizational plans. Employee participation means that better communication is critical; therefore, necessary information is shared by all relevant parties. Moreover, better communication means self-direction and self-control, rather than unquestioning, blind obedience. Organizational commitment arises out of discussion, deliberation, and debate over major organizational issues.

Application Stages

One of the most structured interventions in OD, Blake and Mouton's Grid® Organization Development has two key objectives: to improve planning by developing a strategy for organizational excellence based on clear logic, and to help managers gain the necessary knowledge and skills to supervise effectively. It consists of six phases designed to analyze an entire business and to overcome the planning and communications barriers to corporate excellence.

Phase 1—The Grid Seminar

In this one-week program, participants analyze their personal styles on the Managerial Grid and learn team methods of problem solving. Top management attends the seminar and then leads the next level of management through a similar experience. In addition to assessing themselves using questionnaires and case studies, participants receive feedback on their styles from other group members.

Phase 2—Teamwork Development

In this phase of the Grid program, managers are expected to do team development in at least two different groups—with their own bosses and with their immediate subordinates. As with the Grid seminar itself, the team-building phase usually is conducted in an off-the-job setting so that team members can work without interruption. As in the seminar, team building generally starts with top management—the manager and the corporate staff, or the manager and the department, division, or plant staff. Typically, a steering committee or OD coordinator ensures that the team-building efforts are coordinated throughout the organization, provides materials, and establishes overall priorities.

Phase 3—Intergroup Development

Although an organization may have various sections or units, each with specialized tasks and different goals, it still must work as a whole if it is to achieve organizational excellence. A fair amount of intergroup or interdepartmental conflict is present in most organizations. Each group builds negative stereotypes of other groups, and this conflict can escalate easily into subtle or overt power struggles that result in win–lose situations. Improving intergroup relations involves the following steps: (1) before the sessions, each person prepares a written description of the actual working relationship, as contrasted with the ideal relationship; (2) each group isolates itself for several days to summarize its perceptions of the actual and ideal relationships; (3) the two groups meet and limit their interaction to comparing their perceptions via a spokesperson; and (4) the two groups then work on making the relationship more productive. The action step is completed when both groups have a clear understanding of the specific actions each group will take and how those actions will be followed up.

Phase 4—Developing an Ideal Strategic Organization Model

The top managers in the organization now work toward achieving a model of organizational excellence, incorporating six basic factors: (1) clear definitions of minimum and optimum organizational financial objectives; (2) clear, explicit definitions of the character and nature of organizational activities; (3) clear operational definitions of the character and scope of markets, customers, or clients; (4) an organizational structure that integrates operations for synergistic results; (5) basic policies for organizational decision making; and (6) approaches to implement growth capacity and avoid stagnation or obsolescence.

Phase 5—Implementing the Ideal Strategic Model

Blake and Mouton point out that if the first four phases have been completed successfully, many of the barriers to implementation will have been remodeled or reduced already, managers will have a good understanding of Grid theories, and communication blocks will have been identified and resolved. Implementing the ideal strategic model thus becomes a matter of keeping in mind certain considerations. First, the nature of the organization and its market or environment defines business segments contained within the ideal strategic model. Second, specific organizational units, such as cost centers or profit centers, are identified. Third, planning teams are appointed for each autonomous unit. The planning team is responsible for preparing and testing the unit's operation in accordance with the specifics of the ideal strategic model for the larger organization. Fourth, because the units cannot be completely autonomous, an overall headquarters entity must be established. At a minimum, this organization must have the ability to develop executive talent, gather investment capital, and provide service to the entire organization more cheaply or efficiently than can be done by the local decision centers or autonomous units. Finally, the planning coordinator and the corporate strategy-implementation committee need to ensure that the implementation plan is understood clearly while it is proceeding so that enthusiasm for the change can be maintained and resistance to the development and to implementation of the ideal strategic model can be minimized.

Phase 6—Systematic Critique

The final phase in achieving ideal organizational excellence is the systematic effort to examine the organization's progress toward that goal, including formal and informal measurement and evaluation of direction, rate, quality, and quantity of progress. Phase 6 also allows for the systematic planning of future development activities. Because communication and planning are the greatest barriers to organizational excellence, this critique becomes more important as an organization goes through the Grid process.

Application 13.5 presents an example of Grid® Organization Development in a large manufacturing plant.[47]

Results of Grid Organization Development

Grid® Organization Development has been adopted in whole or in part by many organizations; phases 1, 2, and 3, which apply mainly to communication barriers, are especially popular.[48] Research about the effectiveness of the Grid is mixed, however. On the positive side, Blake and Mouton collected data on two similar organizations and found the one that went through the six Grid phases improved profitability significantly, whereas the control organization did not.[49] One example of a Grid failure, on the other hand, is a study that examined the impact of Grid® Organizational Development in six geographic districts of a large federal agency. The researchers assessed the organizational climate of each district to determine the extent to which the organization was moving toward 9,9 management. The results showed no significant climate changes in any of the six districts. That failure of the Grid program was attributed mainly to the lack of top-management support for the program.[50]

In conclusion, like Likert's System 4 Management, Grid® Organization Development is a normative intervention that proposes one most-effective way to manage organizations—9,9 management. In recent years, the program authors have extended the approach to fit different professions, expanded applications into international arenas, and added a third motivational dimension to the grid.[51] Contingency theory and the mixed research results suggest that the Grid can be successful, but not in all situations.

APPLICATION 13·5   Grid Organization Development at the Sigma Plant

One of the earliest and most extensive applications of the Grid occurred at the Sigma plant of a large, multiplant company. Sigma employed about four thousand employees, including eight hundred managers and technical staff. A major impetus underlying the program was the merger of the parent company with another firm. This disrupted a long-standing relationship between Sigma and the parent company, and required Sigma to operate more autonomously than it had in the past. This new method of operating was especially difficult because of strained relationships among Sigma's departments and between levels of management. A new plant manager experienced difficulty obtaining acceptance for and cooperation with suggested improvements.

The Grid was considered a possible method for resolving these problems. Sigma's top managers met with a Grid consultant who had been working in other parts of the parent company; they also attended a Grid seminar held outside the company. The managers gathered enough positive information about the Grid to decide to develop their own program with the consultant's help. The first phase of the Grid began with forty senior managers attending a one-week managerial Grid seminar. This phase continued for about eight months until all eight hundred managers and technical staff had completed the seminar. By that time, the earlier participants had begun later phases of the Grid.

Those later phases included a number of activities intended to solve specific problems:

1. A management team used problem-solving approaches learned in the Grid seminar to keep all levels of management informed during union contract negotiations.

2. Management teams were established to work out programs for reducing the costs of utilities and maintenance materials and supplies.

3. A new series of Grid programs was extended to lower-level supervisors, including the labor force; union officers were invited to attend the sessions.

4. A safety program based on Grid methods was implemented.

5. The plant manager initiated a program in which supervisors and subordinates jointly set performance goals.

An evaluation of the Grid program by an external team showed a sharp increase in productivity and a comparably sharp decrease in controllable costs. About 44 percent of the increase in profitability resulted from a reduction in controllable costs, which was primarily traceable to the reduction of labor costs. About 13 percent of the decrease in controllable costs could be attributed to better operating procedures and higher hourly productivity, which resulted in an increase of several million dollars in profit. Comments by plant personnel showed a favorable response to the program's impact on efficiency.

Other measures also showed the positive impact of the program. The number of meetings (for a sample of managers) increased by 41 percent, and more emphasis was placed on teamwork and problem solving. Post hoc analyses of value and attitude changes showed changes consistent with the norms and values taught in the Grid program. One of the most important aspects of this program was that the top managers were instructors for the phase 1 training sessions. These same managers were among those showing the most improvement, as reported by their subordinates. ■

■ SUMMARY

This chapter described four types of systemwide process interventions: confrontation meetings, intergroup interventions, large-group interventions, and Grid® Organization Development. The organization confrontation meeting is a way of mobilizing resources for organizational problem solving and seems especially relevant for organizations undergoing stress. The intergroup relations approaches are designed to help solve a variety of organizational problems. Microcosm groups can be formed to address particular issues and use parallel processes to diffuse group solutions to the organization. The intergroup conflict resolution approach involves a method for mitigating dysfunctional conflicts between groups or departments. Conflict can be dysfunctional in situations in which groups must work together. It may, however, promote organizational effectiveness when departments are relatively independent of each other. Large-group interventions are designed to focus the energy and attention of a "whole system" around organizational processes such as a vision, strategy, or culture. It is best used when the organization is about to begin a large-scale change effort or is facing a new situation. These three process interventions do not claim universal success; each works best only in certain situations.

Grid® Organization Development is a normative program that proposes one best way to manage organizations. Although its authors claim that it can be successful in all situations, research assessing normative models is mixed, suggesting that the Grid can be successful under certain conditions and that more research is needed to pinpoint what those conditions are.

■ NOTES

1. M. Weisbord, *Productive Workplaces* (San Francisco: Jossey-Bass, 1987).

2. R. Beckhard, "The Confrontation Meeting," *Harvard Business Review* 4 (1967): 149–55.

3. B. B. Bunker and B. Alban, *Large Group Interventions* (San Francisco: Jossey-Bass, 1997); N. Tichy and S. Sherman, *Control Your Destiny or Someone Else Will* (New York: HarperCollins, 1993).

4. This application was adapted from material in Bunker and Alban, *Large Group Interventions,* and in Tichy and Sherman, *Control Your Destiny.*

5. R. Beckhard, *Organization Development: Strategies and Models* (Reading, Mass.: Addison-Wesley, 1969).

6. W. Bennis, *Organization Development: Its Nature, Origins, and Prospects* (Reading, Mass.: Addison-Wesley, 1969): 7.

7. C. Alderfer, "An Intergroup Perspective on Group Dynamics," in *Handbook of Organizational Behavior,* ed. J. Lorsch (Englewood Cliffs, N.J.: Prentice Hall, 1987): 190–222; C. Alderfer, "Improving Organizational Communication Through Long-Term Intergroup Intervention," *Journal of Applied Behavioral Science* 13 (1977): 193–210; C. Alderfer, R. Tucker, C. Alderfer, and L. Tucker, "The Race Relations Advisory Group: An Intergroup Intervention," in *Organizational Change and Development,* vol. 2, eds. W. Pasmore and R. Woodman (Greenwich, Conn.: JAI Press, 1988): 269–321.

8. Alderfer, "Intergroup Perspective."

9. Ibid., p. 210.

10. Alderfer, "Improving Organizational Communication."

11. Alderfer et al., "Race Relations Advisory Group."

12. K. Jehn, "A Multimethod Examination of the Benefits and Detriments of Intragroup Conflict," *Administrative Science Quarterly* 40 (1995): 256–83.

13. D. Tjosvold, "Cooperation Theory and Organizations," *Human Relations* 37 (1984): 743–67.

14. R. Blake, H. Shepard, and J. Mouton, *Managing Intergroup Conflict in Industry* (Houston, Tex.: Gulf, 1954).

15. Beckhard, *Organization Development.*

16. E. Neilson, "Understanding and Managing Intergroup Conflict," in *Organizational Behavior and Administration,* eds. P. Lawrence, L. Barnes, and J. Lorsch (Homewood, Ill.: Richard D. Irwin, 1976): 291–305.

17. R. Daft, *Organization Theory and Design,* 6th ed. (Cincinnati, Ohio: South-Western College Publishing, 1998): 503.

18. Blake, Shepard, and Mouton, *Managing Intergroup Conflict.*

19. Bennis, *Organization Development.*

20. Ibid., p. 4.

21. R. Golembiewski and A. Blumberg, "Confrontation as a Training Design in Complex Organizations: Attitudinal Changes in a Diversified Population of Managers," *Journal of Applied Behavioral Science* 3 (1967): 525–47.

22. W. French and C. Bell, *Organization Development: Behavioral Science Interventions for Organization Improvement* (Englewood Cliffs, N.J.: Prentice Hall, 1978).

23. E. Huse and M. Beer, "Eclectic Approach to Organizational Development," *Harvard Business Review* 49 (1971): 103–13.

24. Ibid., p. 112.

25. E. Huse, "The Behavioral Scientist in the Shop," *Personnel* 44 (May-June 1965): 8–16.

26. J. Fordyce and R. Weil, *Managing WITH People* (Reading, Mass.: Addison-Wesley, 1971).

27. A. Hubbard, "Cultural and Status Differences in Intergroup Conflict Resolution: A Longitudinal Study of a

Middle East Dialogue Group in the United States," *Human Relations* 52 (1999): 303–23.

28. K. Thomas, "Conflict and Conflict Management," in *Handbook of Industrial and Organizational Psychology,* ed. M. Dunnette (Chicago: Rand McNally, 1976): 889–936.

29. Weisbord, *Productive Workplaces;* M. Weisbord, *Discovering Common Ground* (San Francisco: Berrett-Koehler, 1993); Bunker and Alban, *Large Group Interventions;* H. Owen, *Open Space Technology: A User's Guide* (Potomac, Md.: Abbott, 1992).

30. Owen, *Open Space Technology.*

31. D. Axelrod, "Getting Everyone Involved," *Journal of Applied Behavioral Science* 28 (1992): 499–509.

32. T. Cummings and S. Srivastva, *Management of Work: A Socio-Technical Systems Approach* (San Diego, Calif.: University Associates, 1977): 112–16.

33. L. Bourgeois, "Strategic Goals, Perceived Uncertainty, and Economic Performance in Volatile Environments," *Academy of Management Journal* 28 (1985): 548–73; C. West Jr., and C. Schwenk, "Top Management Team Strategic Consensus, Demographic Homogeneity, and Firm Performance: A Report of Resounding Nonfindings," *Academy of Management Journal* 17 (1996): 571–76.

34. F. Emery and E. Trist, *Towards a Social Ecology* (New York: Plenum Publishing, 1973); R. Beckhard and R. Harris, *Organizational Transitions: Managing Complex Change,* 2d ed. (Reading, Mass.: Addison-Wesley, 1987); R. Lippitt, "Future Before You Plan," in *The NTL Manager's Handbook* (Arlington, Va.: NTL Institute, 1983): 38–41.

35. Weisbord, *Productive Workplaces.*

36. C. Krone, "Open Systems Redesign," in *Theory and Method in Organization Development: An Evolutionary Process,* ed. J. Adams (Arlington, Va.: NTL Institute for Applied Behavioral Science, 1974): 364–91; G. Jayaram, "Open Systems Planning," in *The Planning of Change,* 3d ed., eds. W. Bennis, K. Benne, R. Chin, and K. Corey (New York: Holt, Rinehart, & Winston, 1976): 275–83; R. Beckhard and R. Harris, *Organizational Transitions: Managing Complex Change,* 2d ed. (Reading, Mass.: Addison-Wesley, 1987); Cummings and Srivastva, *Management of Work.*

37. Weisbord, *Productive Workplaces.*

38. This application was submitted by Roland Sullivan, designer and co-lead facilitator of the Seventh American Forest Congress.

39. Bunker and Alban, *Large Group Interventions;* Owen, *Open Space Technology.*

40. Owen, *Open Space Technology.*

41. Adapted from an example provided in Bunker and Alban, *Large Group Interventions.*

42. Weisbord, *Common Ground;* Owen, *Open Space Technology.*

43. R. Purser, S. Cabana, M. Emery, and F. Emery, "Search Conferencing: Accelerating Large-Scale Strategic Planning," in *Fast Cycle Organization Development,* ed. M. Anderson (Cincinnati, Ohio: South-Western College Publishing, 2000); D. Coghlan, "The Process of Change through Inter-level Dynamics in a Large-Group Intervention for a Religious Organization," *Journal of Applied Behavioral Science* 34 (1998): 105–20.

44. R. Blake and J. Mouton, *The Managerial Grid* (Houston, Tex.: Gulf, 1964); R. Blake, J. Mouton, L. Barnes, and L. Greiner, "Breakthrough in Organization Development," *Harvard Business Review* 42 (1964): 133–55; R. Blake and J. Mouton, *Corporate Excellence Through Grid Organization Development: A Systems Approach* (Houston, Tex.: Gulf, 1968); R. Blake and J. Mouton, *Building a Dynamic Corporation Through Grid Organization Development* (Reading, Mass.: Addison-Wesley, 1969); R. Blake and A. McCanse, *Leadership Dilemmas—Grid Solutions* (Houston, Tex.: Gulf, 1991).

45. Blake and Mouton, *Corporate Excellence.*

46. Blake and Mouton, *Managerial Grid.*

47. Blake et al., "Breakthrough."

48. "Using the Managerial Grid to Ensure MBO," *Organizational Dynamics* 2 (Spring 1974): 55; J. Flower, "Human Change by Design: Excerpts from a Conversation with Robert R. Blake," *Healthcare Forum Journal* 35 (1992): http://www.well.com/user/bbear/blake.html.

49. Blake and Mouton, *Managerial Grid,* pp. 178–79. A more complete description is given in R. Blake and J. Mouton, *Organizational Change by Design* (Austin, Tex.: Scientific Methods, 1976): 1–16.

50. L. Greiner, D. Leitch, and L. Barnes, "The Simple Complexity of Organization Climate in a Government Agency" (undated manuscript).

51. Flower, "Human Change."

■ The Metric Division Case

You are a member of the corporate OD staff of a large conglomerate of companies manufacturing household hardware goods. As is typical of your work, you were asked to make a presentation to a management team in one of the companies concerning the different kinds of management development programs and activities that the corporation offers. The contact in this case comes from the personnel manager of the Metric Division. This division recently has been reorganized so that now it is totally responsible for an entire product line. (An organization chart for the division is shown in Exhibit 1.) The top-management staff has been in place for five months, and the division president is interested in the available options for management development of his subordinates. Joan, the personnel manager, has shared with you her perception that Joe, the division head, wants to get off to a good start in the

new structure and is looking for perks for his people—programs they can attend to increase their knowledge and skills.

At a staff meeting of Metric Division management, you presented the various kinds of training programs and consultation services that your corporate group offers. The presentation covered individual skill-oriented programs as well as on-site action research or OD interventions, including team development. During a brief discussion of the kinds of things that enhance team effectiveness, the national sales manager, Don, commented that some of the ideas you were covering might be helpful to the staff. You discussed the need to do some diagnosis before launching into a developmental program. Don further stated that he thought it would be very helpful to have someone interview all the members of the staff to determine what could be done to help them work together more effectively. A more general discussion ensued; everyone, including Joe,

| Exhibit 1 | Metric Division Organization Chart |

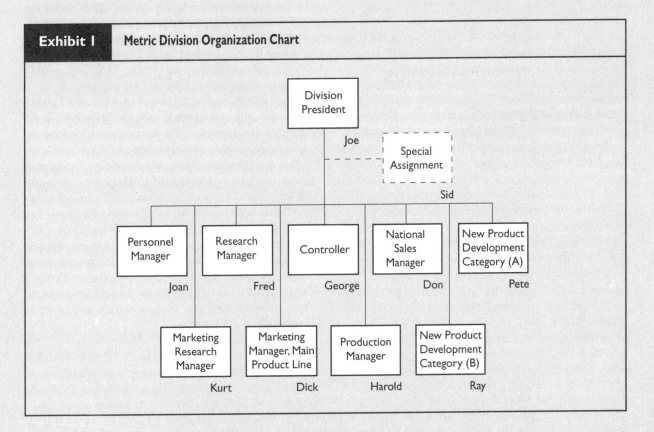

agreed verbally to have you conduct a diagnosis to help them decide whether some special developmental effort was warranted.

You interviewed each member of the staff for sixty to ninety minutes each over the next ten days. Your contract around the interviews included the following aspects:

1. *Anonymity:* Interviewees should use names only if it was alright for others to see that name in some paraphrase of their comments.

2. *Feedback:* You would provide a summary of the interview data for the team to look at together in order to decide collectively whether there was sufficient need to spend time on particular issues to improve their functioning.

3. *Action planning:* The staff has agreed to one three-hour session to look at your feedback summary and to decide whether to go ahead with any developmental efforts.

It is now three days before the scheduled feedback meeting. The following information is the summary of the interviews with each staff member, including Joe.

Summary of Verbatim Responses to Questions

What does this staff do well as a team?

Not a team yet but does have common thread of loyalty to Joe—doesn't function as a team on group decisions, however. We don't listen, though we talk a hell of a lot and say little. In crisis we band together. One-on-ones don't contribute to team concept.

Share information well. Have mutual and high regard for one another.

Not too much as a team yet—mainly a source of information from each other. Effective in information sharing.

Cope fairly well with business situations, such as profit position—good willingness to recognize others' problems.

Bring keen interest and desire to do well, but not that many things done well as a team. There's a question of functional as opposed to division responsibility.

What does this staff not do well as a team?

Nothing really as a team—"Don't really know what we do well."

Identify and solve or decide on issues of divisional nature (things like examining ourselves as a division—how we operate, how we function as management group within a division). Not agreed as a staff that we should even do that.

Might be unreal, but I don't feel the staff does very well at solving problems. We don't address issues, clarify data, or go for resolution very well. All problems are treated alike, and we need ground rules for the kinds of problems to be solved by the group at the right time and by the right people. We're less effective as a team than we are in pairs or in one-to-one situations.

Where we have tried to problem solve, I think we've been less effective than we could have been —not too much practice at it.

Deal in abstract matters—tendency not to resolve such issues but rather to let them disappear. We're a business-oriented group that deals best with dollars and things.

We don't question one another—don't feel we're open to looking at each other's worlds—don't have overriding sense of owning divisionwide problems—still some functionalism present. Look to Joe for decisions.

As a team, we haven't come to grips with anything of great relevance to the business decision-making process—probably have avoided it.

Haven't learned to resolve issues quickly and provide input to areas outside our area.

We don't routinely as a group discuss division problems, only in a crisis when we're trying to put out a fire. Do a lot of one-on-one in staff meeting, especially sales and marketing, while rest of us sit there not knowing what's going on or how to contribute. Subjects get so specific you're out in center field. We don't discuss business needs like development—we as staff don't know what's going on in any depth.

We debate and discuss a subject forever—for example, name tags discussion. Joe lets discussion ramble. Someone ought to be process observer and pull us up short if wasting time.

How effective do you feel staff meetings are?

Semieffective—information mode—do well. However, when a specific problem arises, we don't do as well. Don't attack a problem in an orderly way. We would like a more systematic approach. Must utilize staff time more effectively.

Don't feel everyone's on board. Issues of new versus old still present and get in the way. We are more just a group of functional heads around the table. Staff meeting not effective at all. Question about how to conduct a staff meeting—never complete an agenda. What should these meetings be—information sharing, decision making, or what? What does Joe really want?

Meetings seem to be a waste of time in terms of moving the business ahead, but helpful as a learning device. There's not a lot of building, and we talk to Joe, rather than each other. Heavy loading of marketing people probably skews perspective of staff. Must decide on how we want to use the staff. Are we really going to be a problem-solving group, or just an information-sharing team? We should agree to define our role if we are serious about it.

Not very effective if you expect problem solving or decision making, but effective as information sharing—depends on question of role. I'd like it to be a problem-solving group for division—size might make it difficult.

Compared with my previous experiences, I think they're more effective; however, we seem unable to generate agenda items and deal with them.

Staff meetings are pretty ineffective. No one questions why we're there.

Relatively ineffective. Misapplication of time for majority of people there. We wait for our issue to come up. We should deal with issues that transcend total division—convene relevant staff on business issues.

We confirm previously made decisions and disguise this as decision making.

We don't discriminate between major and minor issues; we handle them the same way—from a million-dollar problem to name tags for a sales meeting.

Staff expertise could be productive if applied to bigger, longer-range problems instead of this being done by individuals.

Staff meetings ramble. Joe likes everyone to have an opportunity to talk. I like meetings crisp and to the point; we are better organized with agendas and minutes and follow-up. Size of staff affects this also—in long run we should reduce size.

How effective do you feel the organization structure of the division is in facilitating getting the work done?

Has some problems—the nontraditional marketing organization gives me some concerns. I don't see any real negatives though.

Very effective. We've gotten along very well as a division in an operating business fashion. Feel more strongly about our unit as opposed to former structure.

My only other comment would be about the number of marketing people on the staff, which may risk tilting the direction toward marketing too much.

Reasonably effective.

I'm pleased with it. We do fundamental things well, but administratively we're not that effective (except controller's function).

Not bad. Some communication problem between operations and marketing. Size of staff might make forming a team more difficult.

We're set up the way we should be, but having nine people report to Joe may preclude us from dealing with things as a staff. We might have to trim the number to operate truly as a staff team.

We should improve interaction of staff—not confine it to staff meetings—and improve productive exchange among members.

We should (1) identify people relevant to decision; (2) clearly identify others as resource; (3) get primary options out quickly; (4) avoid continual competitiveness and dwelling on minor aspects, such as name tags.

If I had responsibility for all aspects of business and could get all people working together as a team, I'd do even a better job.

We should be organized to maximize development, and I don't think we are. Development is not fully coordinated but is going on in several separate areas.

In the long run, the division should be organized around our businesses. Our division should be organized so that a person responsible for a given product line should have all aspects: research, operations, marketing, and so forth.

With three marketing jobs, I have concern we have too many people on staff—eleven people cut air time for each. I have to deal with three guys instead of one to get job done, which takes time.

Present structure requires several people in each function to zero in on work direction, and this is time consuming.

What are the goals or priorities of this staff, and how do you feel about them?

None that explicit. Implicit goals to learn how to function under this kind of structure. What is our role? We could use explicit goals and priorities.

What goals? We still don't have the clear-cut goals I'd like to see.

We have some clear-cut goals and priorities as a division, and each function is contributing separately. Staff should help achieve them in a synergistic fashion.

We don't have goals as a group, but individually we probably do. One commonly shared goal might be to move staff meetings along more expeditiously.

No specific set of goals for staff, aside from business objectives.

Not come to grips yet—no list, but a goal could be the establishment of process (climate) and relationship that would lead to accomplishment of our business objectives.

Absence of goals and priorities linked to plan and to how we solve issues. As raw materials costs rise, goals should be defined. Everybody keeps asking what the goals and objectives are. They want the boss to restate them: (1) to achieve the profit objectives—most important; (2) make products *x* and *y* successful new businesses; (3) increase the profitability of business; (4) weave us into an effective operating division.

Goals have not been communicated to staff accurately and emphatically enough. We develop strategies for top management, but we don't discuss them. They are developed between marketing and Joe. We don't develop them jointly and therefore have to run to find out what they are.

We don't talk in staff about priorities—we decide in our own minds. Joe never says exactly what we are going to do. Joe should go off and lay out plan and come back and we will critique; instead, it's taken for granted. Joe's a great guy, however; don't get me wrong.

Goals and priorities not fully coordinated—for example, where we stand on the new generation of products. Is anyone working on them, and if not, shouldn't we be?

What helps you get your job done?

The learning part of my job has clearly been helped by the staff, and exposure to individuals has helped me work more effectively with them.

They're still bringing me onboard. Very helpful efforts to bring me up to date. Willingness to help has been gratifying.

Fair exchange of information among ourselves, facilitated by personal respect. Posting from staff is important—extent to which they get involved in my work is important.

Timely provision of information in an easily digested form capable of being passed on—"completed staff work"—we're getting better, but I'm still rewriting a lot. Lack of organizational status; for example, when marketing doesn't dominate the business to an unhealthy degree.

When staff involves and uses me as a resource and they do it early enough.

Complete confidence of boss, accessibility of other levels within organization and other functions (point of relevant information), plus effective support of other functions. Resource application from other functional heads is very important, and that deployment is critical.

Staff's commitment to giving me resources to do my job. They have restraints.

Pete, Dick—less exchange or help from them. They are too into their own bag. We could counsel each other better, but we don't.

If division does well and I don't, I suffer. If division does not do well and I do, I suffer.

Support of staff to make new products division successful is very helpful.

Joe is a leader and very supportive, is trusting and stays cool in face of problems. Without that kind of boss my job would be twice as difficult.

Helps—knowing what total decision is and knowing Joe's onboard so I can go ahead with money, time, and so on, knowing I have authority once decision is made.

Joe's saying that you have authority and responsibilities—he does not nitpick things. He leaves you on your own to run your job.

Question is how to make my organization fit into overall operation of division.

What gets in the way of getting your job done?

Not having it clear in our minds what our individual roles and responsibilities are—"Where should we be getting into the act?"

One-to-one decisions as opposed to those that have impacts on other areas—time restraints, schedules, time demands. Inability to sit down and make decisions together quickly.

Tendency of senior marketing personnel to delegate market research could create problems for me. Question of trust and respect of market research professionalism raises a concern.

Not enough interaction between functions; for example, development guys across units don't interchange their knowledge and take advantage of individual capabilities.

Not getting into a situation until it's cast in concrete—it becomes more difficult to be of constructive help then.

What would you like your boss to do more or less of?

Continue leaning on me for input—more leadership in staff meetings and more decisiveness when there are disagreements among us. Less detail orientation on some items, as it could be a waste of his time.

Be more available to each of the functions. Work at continuing interface relationships. Fewer one-on-one decisions where decision makes impact on my area.

Get himself away from details of day-to-day business. Ask more often, "What do you need or want from me?" Keep himself oriented to how business is operating and just trust staff more for their functional expertise. He gets problems transferred to him.

Apply decisive leadership abilities more—he's hedging to be nice right now. More appreciation/involvement in developing aspects of business and in long-term issues transcending all groups. Less orientation to brand detail.

Boss—as a resource; give more of his time. Less of sending signals to rest of organization (my area of organization) without touching base with me first; for example, discussing with agency what he feels is working with our advertising program. Express where he thinks business is capable of going—his assessment. What he thinks we can and should be doing.

Joe must recognize that president's job is different; principal function is to mold different functions together toward common objective. Need to find his philosophy and express to group what the role of president is.

Could reach out more to staff to do and define his job. Perhaps staff should tell him how we see his role.

What would you like your peers to do more or less of?

I wish the staff as a totality would become less sensitive to people running across functional lines to get information from individuals directly involved. We're too compartmentalized.

Would like group to be more sensitive to the sales organization situation and help us to become more effective as a line function. In other words, use us more. I would hope individuals would resolve possible disagreements before meetings to avoid taking up others' time.

Make me more aware of their planning needs earlier. Be less independent of each other.

Set climate in their organization that would allow all expertise, regardless of level, to surface. Give their people more lead time.

Help discipline staff to allocate appropriate amount of time to big versus little issues.

Give me more time to discuss my business with them.

Like more opportunity to participate in their business and broader aspects of business; for example, I'd like to feel people are tapping me for my expertise in technical research and development.

Express goals and strategies for business and functional areas more. Not in detail, but overview.

More working as team and less perpetuating one-on-one interaction, especially when subject cuts across many functions.

Which, if any, of your relationships with members of this staff do you feel could be improved? How would you start to do this?

Relations with production could be worked on. Communications among functions at plant levels could be improved. Division professional services, too—have started discussions on this with Don. We're defining the problem now.

We've done some fence mending with Harold and are off to a good start with technical research, financial, and sales. Have innate rivalries with new-products development group, and Pete and I would have to work on and set the right climate. Could be sharing of ideas and data that we are both developing.

Harold and I have good workaday relationship. George and I still sorting out our different styles—I'm too loose and we're in process of bending. Don's fine, still finding his way—Dick and I have good relationship, he keeps me aware and involved but doesn't always respond to things I'd like to see done; he must keep me aware of things I need to know—Pete and I still working on relationships, I think he believes I intrude into nuts and bolts too much. Ray believes I don't spend enough time with him and his function. Fred and I have clear understanding. I have little contact with Kurt and would like more participation and counseling in staff meetings. Pleased with relationship with Joan—would like a stronger functional voice at times.

Relationship between Dick and me one of standard politeness; don't get along, contribute little to each other.

My best relationship is with Fred.

I could improve my relationship with George. I have to get his confidence that I'm not managing the numbers to make them look better than they are.

Harold and I have a good relationship. He makes it clear that I should handle relationships with his subs through him. We could keep each other posted more.

Dick—slightly strained relationship. We are hesitant to give each other advice. I get the feeling of a competitive relationship.

Joan and I are fine, and George and Don also.

Initially, there was an old-guard and new-guard feeling with Dick and Sid, who have been with the company for years—I believe that's going away.

Dick is obviously smart and ambitious; he's willing to speak long and specifically on any and all subjects. I feel he overwhelms our organization and shuts off many because it turns into a philosophical discussion between Joe and Dick. Pete is not about to let Dick be crown prince and throws in his points also; this cuts off air time for others. They love to debate. Don also takes his share of air time.

Pete's feeling of competition and of being alone in getting new product off the ground getting in way.

Sid undecided about whether he is coming back and so on is getting in the way. Dick has fine connections and pushes through decisions. Sid always plays it cagey.

Questions

1. What are the major issues you think the team is facing?

2. What would you do next with the data? Who would see them? In what form?

3. Assuming the team agreed, what course of action would you recommend after the feedback meeting?

Source: Adapted by permission of the publisher from M. Plovnick, R. Fry, and W. Burke, *Organization Development: Exercises, Cases, and Readings* (Boston: Little, Brown, 1982), pp. 109–17. This case is an adaptation of a teaching case developed by James Shonk, president, J. H. Shonk & Associates, Ridgefield, Conn.

■ Exley Chemical Company

The Exley Chemical Company is a major chemical manufacturer making primarily industrial chemicals, plastics, and consumer products. Company sales and profits have grown, and its ratio of net profits to sales is about average for the industry, but in the last year or so both sales and profits have been disappointing (see Exhibit 1).

Because new products constantly are being introduced into the line and methods are changing constantly, the relative importance of different product groups always is shifting. For example, changes in percentage of total sales were experienced by the major product groups over a five-year period (see Exhibit 2).

The Organization

The general organization structure is shown in Exhibit 3. Production is carried on in four plants located across the United States, each of which has a plant manager. The marketing manager handles sales and marketing services, including the field salesforce, with twenty district managers, and twenty-five industrial sales representatives.

All research is administered and performed at the corporate research laboratory, including the research for the development section, which is responsible for the development and improvement of production processes. The engineering department handles all planning and construction and the development of new processes and pilot-plant operations.

Furthermore, to manage the increasing number of new products being developed, a product development division was established about three years ago. Prior to that, new products developed by the research division were passed on to the engineering division from the pilot-plant operation. Unfortunately, this method was inadequate for the complex coordination of these projects, so the new division was established. The product development division was charged with coordinating efforts in developing new products, including recommending manufacturing capacity, sales programs, and so on. The division was to conduct surveys to analyze market potential for new products and recommend development or production based on the results of those surveys. During the period following the creation of the product development division, problems emerged.

The Situation

Conflicts were created with several other departments. For example, the product development division started using a small force of specialty salespeople to conduct pilot marketing programs—an initiative that was not well received by the marketing department. Also, the product division was given responsibility for market research, but the tasks of sales analysis and forecasting remained in the marketing division. Finally, a product manager was appointed for each separate group of products and was made responsible for the coordination of all company activities for that product group. This resulted in more problems, including the following:

1. The product manager often needs to visit customers to get more realistic input on market conditions, but that is resented by marketing executives. They feel that all customer

Exhibit 1	Annual Sales

YEAR	SALES
Five years ago	$ 81,000,000
Three years ago	93,000,000
Two years ago	108,000,000
Last year	111,000,000

Exhibit 2	Changes in Percentages of Sales by Product Group

	Percentage of Sales	
PRODUCT GROUP	FIVE YEARS AGO	LAST YEAR
Chemicals	61	55
Plastics	31	33
Consumer	8	12
Total	100	100

relations should be handled through marketing because the visits confuse the customer. "Judging from what I've seen, product development couldn't care less about what we are doing in terms of integrating our markets," said the marketing vice president.

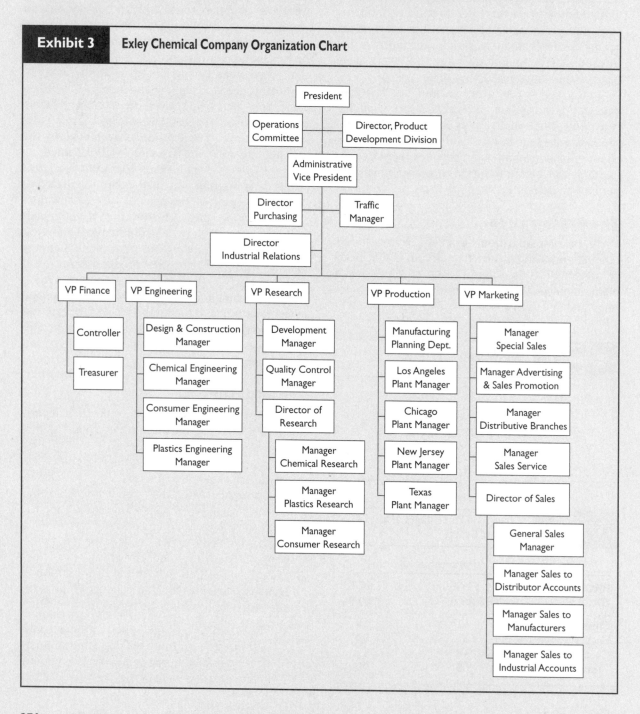

Exhibit 3 **Exley Chemical Company Organization Chart**

President
- Operations Committee
- Director, Product Development Division

Administrative Vice President
- Director Purchasing
- Traffic Manager
- Director Industrial Relations

VP Finance
- Controller
- Treasurer

VP Engineering
- Design & Construction Manager
- Chemical Engineering Manager
- Consumer Engineering Manager
- Plastics Engineering Manager

VP Research
- Development Manager
- Quality Control Manager
- Director of Research
  - Manager Chemical Research
  - Manager Plastics Research
  - Manager Consumer Research

VP Production
- Manufacturing Planning Dept.
- Los Angeles Plant Manager
- Chicago Plant Manager
- New Jersey Plant Manager
- Texas Plant Manager

VP Marketing
- Manager Special Sales
- Manager Advertising & Sales Promotion
- Manager Distributive Branches
- Manager Sales Service
- Director of Sales
  - General Sales Manager
  - Manager Sales to Distributor Accounts
  - Manager Sales to Manufacturers
  - Manager Sales to Industrial Accounts

2. Sales executives question the sales estimates issued by the product managers. The estimates usually are based on the total product market rather than on Exley's share, a basis that often inflates sales estimates. "The product development group is aggressive and they want to grow, but you have to grow within guidelines. The product guys are going to have to learn to work with the other divisions," said a sales manager.

3. At a recent meeting of the Chemical Manufacturers' Association, a product manager learned that a competitor was about to patent a new polymer production process that presumably will reduce costs by about one-third. Exley's research person in charge of polymers said that Exley has several interesting possibilities which might break in a few months. "I think corporate headquarters needs to integrate operations better. We can't be a bunch of entrepreneurs around here. We've got to have more teamwork on these projects," said a project manager.

4. The manager of sales proposed to the consumer products group that Exley's antifreeze be promoted to retail outlets. He has forwarded the proposal to the project manager with a note: "Our customers feel this is a hot idea; can production supply the needed quantities at a competitive price?" The product manager has found that the two people in research and engineering who are most knowledgeable regarding this product now are deeply involved in a new project, so little has been done to date. "The big frustration is that you can't get help from other departments, if it doesn't have a large return for them. Each division head works on the project that makes the most for their division, but these are not necessarily the best from a corporate standpoint," said the product manager.

Questions

1. What are the sources of conflict at Exley Chemical Company?

2. In this situation, do you recommend a large-group intervention or an intergroup relations intervention? Why?

3. Design an intervention to address the problem.

Source: Adapted with permission from D. Harvey and D. Brown, *An Experiential Approach to Organization Development* (Upper Saddle River, N.J.: Prentice Hall, 1996).

Technostructural Interventions

4

14

Restructuring Organizations

In this chapter, we begin to examine technostructural interventions—change programs focusing on the technology and structure of organizations. Increasing global competition and rapid technological and environmental changes are forcing organizations to restructure themselves from rigid bureaucracies to leaner, more flexible structures. These new forms of organizing are highly adaptive and cost efficient. They often result in fewer managers and employees and in streamlined work flows that break down functional barriers.

Interventions aimed at structural design include moving from more traditional ways of dividing the organization's overall work, such as functional, self-contained-unit, and matrix structures, to more integrative and flexible forms, such as process-based and network-based structures. Diagnostic guidelines help determine which structure is appropriate for particular organizational environments, technologies, and conditions.

Downsizing seeks to reduce costs and bureaucracy by decreasing the size of the organization. This reduction in personnel can be accomplished through layoffs, organization redesign, and outsourcing, which involves moving functions that are not part of the organization's core competence to outside contractors. Successful downsizing is closely aligned with the organization's strategy.

Reengineering radically redesigns the organization's core work processes to give tighter linkage and coordination among the different tasks. This work-flow integration results in faster, more responsive task performance. Reengineering often is accomplished with new information technology that permits employees to control and coordinate work processes more effectively.

STRUCTURAL DESIGN

Organization structure describes how the overall work of the organization is divided into subunits and how these subunits are coordinated for task completion. It is a key feature of an organization's strategic orientation.[1] Based on a contingency perspective shown in Figure 14.1, organization structures should be designed to fit with at least five factors: the environment, organization size, technology, organization strategy, and worldwide operations. Organization effectiveness depends on the extent to which its structures are responsive to these contingencies.[2]

Organizations traditionally have structured themselves into one of three forms: functional departments that are task specialized; self-contained units that are oriented to specific products, customers, or regions; or matrix structures that combine both functional specialization and self-containment. Faced with accelerating changes in competitive environments and technologies, however, organizations increasingly have redesigned their structures into more integrative and flexible forms. These more recent innovations include process-based structures that design subunits around the organization's core work processes, and network-based structures

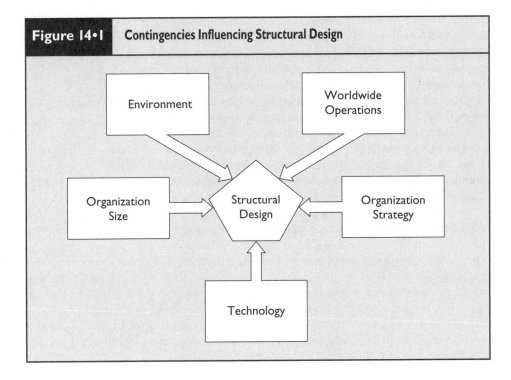

Figure 14•1 | **Contingencies Influencing Structural Design**

that link the organization to other, interdependent organizations. The advantages, disadvantages, and contingencies of the different structures are described below.

The Functional Organization

Perhaps the most widely used organizational structure in the world today is the basic *functional structure,* depicted in Figure 14.2. The organization usually is subdivided into functional units, such as engineering, research, operations, human resources, finance, and marketing. This structure is based on early management

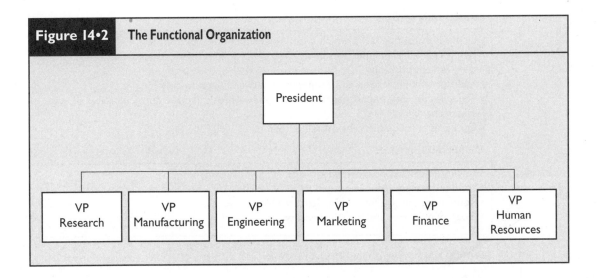

Figure 14•2 | **The Functional Organization**

theories regarding specialization, line and staff relations, span of control, authority, and responsibility.[3] The major functional subunits are staffed by specialists in such disciplines as engineering and accounting. It is considered easier to manage specialists if they are grouped together under the same head and if the head of the department has training and experience in that particular discipline.

Table 14.1 lists the advantages and disadvantages of functional structures. On the positive side, functional structures promote specialization of skills and resources by grouping people who perform similar work and face similar problems. This grouping facilitates communication within departments and allows specialists to share their expertise. It also enhances career development within the specialty, whether it be accounting, finance, engineering, or sales. The functional structure reduces duplication of services because it makes the best use of people and resources.

On the negative side, functional structures tend to promote routine tasks with a limited orientation. Department members focus on their own tasks, rather than on the organization's total task. This can lead to conflict across functional departments when each group tries to maximize its own performance without considering the performances of other units. Coordination and scheduling among departments can be difficult when each emphasizes its own perspective. As shown in Table 14.1, the functional structure tends to work best in small- to medium-sized firms in environments that are relatively stable and certain. These organizations typically have a small number of products or services, and coordination across specialized units is

Table 14•1	Advantages, Disadvantages, and Contingencies of the Functional Form

ADVANTAGES

- Promotes skill specialization
- Reduces duplication of scarce resources and uses resources full time
- Enhances career development for specialists within large departments
- Facilitates communication and performance because superiors share expertise with their subordinates
- Exposes specialists to others within the same specialty

DISADVANTAGES

- Emphasizes routine tasks, which encourages short time horizons
- Fosters parochial perspectives by managers, which limit their capabilities for top-management positions
- Reduces communication and cooperation between departments
- Multiplies the interdepartmental dependencies, which can make coordination and scheduling difficult
- Obscures accountability for overall outcomes

CONTINGENCIES

- Stable and certain environment
- Small to medium size
- Routine technology, interdependence within functions
- Goals of efficiency and technical quality

SOURCE: Adapted by permission of the publisher from J. McCann and J. R. Galbraith, "Interdepartmental Relations," in *Handbook of Organizational Design: Remodeling Organizations and Their Environment,* eds. P. C. Nystrom and W. H. Starbuck, vol. 2 (New York: Oxford University Press, 1981): 61.

relatively easy. This structure also is best suited to routine technologies in which there is interdependence within functions, and to organizational goals emphasizing efficiency and technical quality.

The Self-Contained-Unit Organization

The *self-contained-unit structure* represents a fundamentally different way of organizing. Also known as a product or divisional structure, it was developed at about the same time by General Motors, Sears, Standard Oil of New Jersey (Exxon), and DuPont.[4] It groups organizational activities on the basis of products, services, customers, or geography. All or most of the resources necessary to accomplish a specific objective are set up as a self-contained unit headed by a product or division manager. For example, General Electric has plants that specialize in making jet engines and others that produce household appliances. Each plant manager reports to a particular division or product vice president, rather than to a manufacturing vice president. In effect, a large organization may set up smaller (sometimes temporary) special-purpose organizations, each geared to a specific product, service, customer, or region. A typical product structure is shown in Figure 14.3. It is interesting to note that the formal structure within a self-contained unit often is functional in nature.

Table 14.2 lists the advantages and disadvantages of self-contained-unit structures. These organizations recognize key interdependencies and coordinate resources toward an overall outcome. This strong outcome orientation ensures departmental accountability and promotes cohesion among those contributing to the product. These structures provide employees with opportunities for learning new skills and expanding knowledge because workers can move more easily among the different specialties contributing to the product. As a result, self-contained-unit structures are well suited for developing general managers.

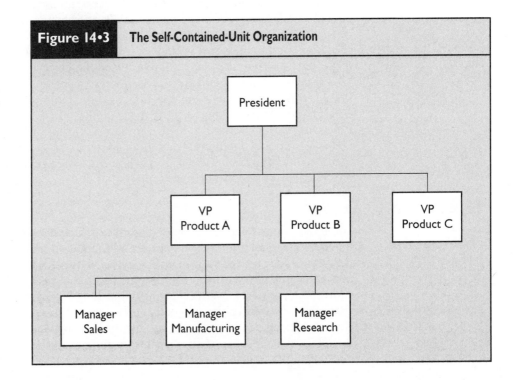

Figure 14·3   The Self-Contained-Unit Organization

Table 14•2	Advantages, Disadvantages, and Contingencies of the Self-Contained-Unit Form

ADVANTAGES

- Recognizes sources of interdepartmental dependencies
- Fosters an orientation toward overall outcomes and clients
- Allows diversification and expansion of skills and training
- Ensures accountability by departmental managers and so promotes delegation of authority and responsibility
- Heightens departmental cohesion and involvement in work

DISADVANTAGES

- May use skills and resources inefficiently
- Limits career advancement by specialists to movements out of their departments
- Impedes specialists' exposure to others within the same specialties
- Puts multiple-role demands on people and so creates stress
- May promote departmental objectives, as opposed to overall organizational objectives

CONTINGENCIES

- Unstable and uncertain environments
- Large size
- Technological interdependence across functions
- Goals of product specialization and innovation

SOURCE: Adapted by permission of the publisher from J. McCann and J. R. Galbraith, "Interdepartmental Relations," in *Handbook of Organizational Design: Remodeling Organizations and Their Environment,* eds. P. C. Nystrom and W. H. Starbuck, vol. 2 (New York: Oxford University Press, 1981): 61.

Self-contained-unit organizations do have certain problems. They may not have enough specialized work to use people's skills and abilities fully. Specialists may feel isolated from their professional colleagues and may fail to advance in their career specialty. The structures may promote allegiance to department rather than organization objectives. They also place multiple demands on people, thereby creating stress.

The self-contained-unit structure works best in conditions almost the opposite of those favoring a functional organization, as shown in Table 14.2. The organization needs to be relatively large to support the duplication of resources assigned to the units. Because each unit is designed to fit a particular niche, the structure adapts well to uncertain conditions. Self-contained units also help to coordinate technical interdependencies falling across functions and are suited to goals promoting product or service specialization and innovation.

The Matrix Organization

Some OD practitioners have focused on maximizing the strengths and minimizing the weaknesses of both the functional and the self-contained-unit structures, and this effort has resulted in the *matrix organization.*[5] It superimposes the lateral structure of a product or project coordinator on the vertical functional structure, as shown in Figure 14.4. Matrix organizational designs originally evolved in the aerospace industry where changing customer demands and technological conditions caused managers to focus on lateral relationships between functions to develop a flexible and adaptable system of resources and procedures, and to achieve a series of project objectives. Matrix organizations now are used widely in manufacturing, service, nonprofit, governmental, and professional organizations.[6]

Every matrix organization contains three unique and critical roles: the top manager, who heads and balances the dual chains of command; the matrix bosses (functional, product, or area), who share subordinates; and the two-boss managers, who report to two different matrix bosses. Each of these roles has its own unique requirements. For example, functional matrix bosses are expected to maximize their respective technical expertise within constraints posed by market realities. Two-boss managers, however, must accomplish work within the demands of supervisors who want to achieve technical sophistication on the one hand, and to meet customer expectations on the other. Thus, a matrix organization has more than its matrix structure. It also must be reinforced by matrix processes, such as performance management systems that get input from both functional and project bosses, by matrix leadership behavior that operates comfortably with lateral decision making, and by a matrix culture that fosters open conflict management and a balance of power.[7]

Matrix organizations, like all organization structures, have both advantages and disadvantages, as shown in Table 14.3. On the positive side, this structure allows multiple orientations. Specialized, functional knowledge can be applied to all projects. New products or projects can be implemented quickly by using people flexibly

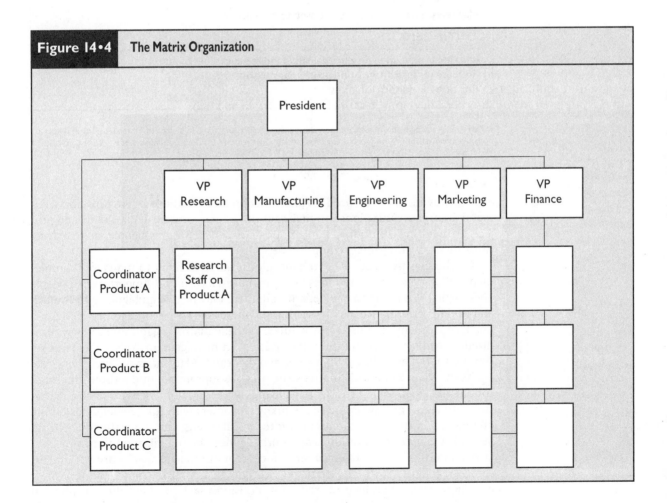

Figure 14•4   **The Matrix Organization**

Table 14•3	Advantages, Disadvantages, and Contingencies of the Matrix Form

ADVANTAGES

- Makes specialized, functional knowledge available to all projects
- Uses people flexibly, because departments maintain reservoirs of specialists
- Maintains consistency between different departments and projects by forcing communication between managers
- Recognizes and provides mechanisms for dealing with legitimate, multiple sources of power in the organization
- Can adapt to environmental changes by shifting emphasis between project and functional aspects

DISADVANTAGES

- Can be very difficult to introduce without a preexisting supportive management climate
- Increases role ambiguity, stress, and anxiety by assigning people to more than one department
- Without power balancing between product and functional forms, lowers overall performance
- Makes inconsistent demands, which may result in unproductive conflicts and short-term crisis management
- May reward political skills as opposed to technical skills

CONTINGENCIES

- Dual focus on unique product demands and technical specialization
- Pressure for high information processing capacity
- Pressure for shared resources

SOURCE: Adapted by permission of the publisher from J. McCann and J. R. Galbraith, "Interdepartmental Relations," in *Handbook of Organizational Design: Remodeling Organizations and Their Environment,* eds. P. C. Nystrom and W. H. Starbuck, vol. 2 (New York: Oxford University Press, 1981): 61.

and by moving between product and functional orientations as circumstances demand. Matrix organizations can maintain consistency among departments and projects by requiring communication among managers. For many people, matrix structures are motivating and exciting.

On the negative side, these organizations can be difficult to manage. To implement and maintain them requires heavy managerial costs and support. When people are assigned to more than one department, there may be role ambiguity and conflict, and overall performance may be sacrificed if there are power conflicts between functional departments and project structures. To make matrix organizations work, organization members need interpersonal and conflict management skills. People can get confused about how the matrix works, and that can lead to chaos and inefficiencies.

As shown in Table 14.3, matrix structures are appropriate under three important conditions.[8] First, there must be outside pressures for a dual focus. That is, a matrix structure works best when there are many customers with unique demands on the one hand and strong requirements for technical sophistication on the other hand. Second, a matrix organization is appropriate when the organization must process a large amount of information. Circumstances requiring such capacity are few and include the following: when external environmental demands change unpredictably and there is considerable uncertainty in decision making; when the organization produces a broad range of products or services, or offers those outputs to a large number of different markets, and there is considerable complexity in decision making; and when there is reciprocal interdependence among the tasks in the organization's technical core and there is considerable pressure on communication and coordination systems. Third, and finally, there must be pressures for shared resources. When customer demands vary greatly and technological requirements are strict, valuable human and physical resources are likely to be scarce. The matrix works well under those conditions because it facilitates the sharing of scarce resources. If any of the foregoing conditions is not met, a matrix organization is likely to fail.

Process-Based Structures

A radically new logic for structuring organizations is to form multidisciplinary teams around core processes, such as product development, order fulfillment, sales generation, and customer support.[9] As shown in Figure 14.5, *process-based structures* emphasize lateral rather than vertical relationships.[10] All functions necessary to produce a product or service are placed in a common unit usually managed by someone called a "process owner." There are few hierarchical levels, and the senior executive team is relatively small, typically consisting of the chair, the chief operating officer, and the heads of a few key support services such as strategic planning, human resources, and finance.

Process-based structures eliminate many of the hierarchical and departmental boundaries that can impede task coordination and slow decision making and task

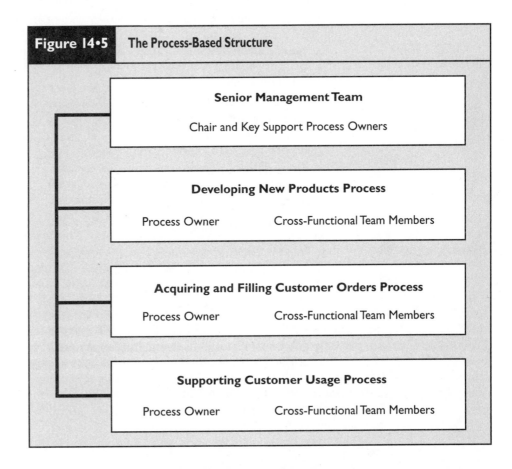

Figure 14•5   **The Process-Based Structure**

Senior Management Team

Chair and Key Support Process Owners

Developing New Products Process

Process Owner   Cross-Functional Team Members

Acquiring and Filling Customer Orders Process

Process Owner   Cross-Functional Team Members

Supporting Customer Usage Process

Process Owner   Cross-Functional Team Members

performance. They reduce the enormous costs of managing across departments and up and down the hierarchy. Process-based structures enable organizations to focus most of their resources on serving customers, both inside and outside the firm.

The use of process-based structures is growing rapidly in a variety of manufacturing and service companies. Typically referred to as "horizontal," "boundaryless," or "team-based" organizations, they are used to enhance customer service at such firms as American Express Financial Advisors, The Associates, Duke Power, 3M, Xerox, General Electric Capital Services, and the National & Provincial Building Society in the United Kingdom. Although there is no one right way to design process-based structures, the following features characterize this new form of organizing.[11]

- *Processes drive structure.* Process-based structures are organized around the three to five key processes that define the work of the organization. Rather than products or functions, processes define the structure and are governed by a "process owner." Each process has clear performance goals that drive task execution.
- *Work adds value.* To increase efficiency, process-based structures simplify and enrich work processes. Work is simplified by eliminating nonessential tasks and reducing layers of management, and it is enriched by combining tasks so that teams perform whole processes.
- *Teams are fundamental.* Teams are the key organizing feature in a process-based structure. They manage everything from task execution to strategic planning, are typically self-managing, and are responsible for goal achievement.
- *Customers define performance.* The primary goal of any team in a process-based structure is customer satisfaction. Defining customer expectations and designing team functions to meet those expectations command much of the team's attention. The organization must value this orientation as the primary path to financial performance.
- *Teams are rewarded for performance.* Appraisal systems focus on measuring team performance against customer satisfaction and other goals, and then provide real recognition for achievement. Team-based rewards are given as much, if not more, weight than is individual recognition.
- *Teams are tightly linked to suppliers and customers.* Through designated members, teams have timely and direct relationships with vendors and customers to understand and respond to emerging concerns.
- *Team members are well informed and trained.* Successful implementation of a process-based structure requires team members who can work with a broad range of information, including customer and market data, financial information, and personnel and policy matters. Team members also need problem-solving and decision-making skills and abilities to address and implement solutions.

Table 14.4 lists the advantages and disadvantages of process-based structures. The most frequently mentioned advantage is intense focus on meeting customer needs, which can result in dramatic improvements in speed, efficiency, and customer satisfaction. Process-based structures remove layers of management, and consequently information flows more quickly and accurately throughout the organization. Because process teams comprise different functional specialties, boundaries between departments are removed, thus affording organization members a

Table 14•4	Advantages, Disadvantages, and Contingencies of the Process-Based Form

ADVANTAGES

- Focuses resources on customer satisfaction
- Improves speed and efficiency, often dramatically
- Adapts to environmental change rapidly
- Reduces boundaries between departments
- Increases ability to see total work flow
- Enhances employee involvement
- Lowers costs because of less overhead structure

DISADVANTAGES

- Can threaten middle managers and staff specialists
- Requires changes in command-and-control mindsets
- Duplicates scarce resources
- Requires new skills and knowledge to manage lateral relationships and teams
- May take longer to make decisions in teams
- Can be ineffective if wrong processes are identified

CONTINGENCIES

- Uncertain and changing environments
- Moderate to large size
- Nonroutine and highly interdependent technologies
- Customer-oriented goals

broad view of the work flow and a clear line of sight between team performance and organization effectiveness. Process-based structures also are more flexible and adaptable to change than are traditional structures.

A major disadvantage of process-based structures is the difficulty of changing to this new organizational form. These structures typically require radical shifts in mindsets, skills, and managerial roles—changes that involve considerable time and resources and can be resisted by functional managers and staff specialists. Moreover, process-based structures may result in expensive duplication of scarce resources and, if teams are not skilled adequately, in slower decision making as they struggle to define and reach consensus. Finally, implementing process-based structures relies on properly identifying key processes needed to satisfy customer needs. If critical processes are misidentified or ignored altogether, performance and customer satisfaction are likely to suffer.

Table 14.4 shows that process-based structures are particularly appropriate for highly uncertain environments where customer demands and market conditions are changing rapidly. They enable organizations to manage nonroutine technologies and coordinate work flows that are highly interdependent. Process-based structures generally appear in medium- to large-sized organizations having several products or projects. They focus heavily on customer-oriented goals and are found in both domestic and global organizations.

Application 14.1 describes the process-based structure implemented by the Military Aircraft and Missiles Group of Boeing.[12]

APPLICATION 14•1   Boeing's Military Aircraft and Missile Group's Process Structure

The Military Aircraft and Missile Group, a major division within Boeing, is home to the Airlift and Tanker (A&T) Program. This program designs, manufactures, and supports the C–17 aircraft, which transports people and oversized cargo around the world. The C–17, for example, was used to evacuate citizens to safety from a civil war in Liberia, deliver half the cargo in the United Nations' Bosnia peacekeeping effort, and fly hurricane relief supplies to the Caribbean. The C–17 development program began in 1982. An enormous technical challenge, the program fell behind on cost and schedule requirements and was threatened with cancellation. The recent success of the program, including a 1998 Malcolm Baldrige National Quality Award, is partly the result of its implementing a process-based structure that allows the A&T program to focus on customer requirements, manage the technical challenges, and develop partnerships with its unions and suppliers. The Aircraft and Missile Group's process structure is shown in Figure 14.6.

The key, valued-added processes in the structure—acquiring business, planning and controlling programs, defining products, managing suppliers, producing the aircraft, and supporting the delivered product, are governed by two important support activities, managing the enterprise and supporting and servicing the business. Elements of each process are described below:

- The *acquire business* process consists of developing winning strategies, developing proposals, and negotiating contracts.
- The *plan and control program* process involves adminis-

tering contracts, managing changes, managing material requirements, and managing risks.
- The *define the product* process includes managing the product from design to manufacture, providing integrated logistical support planning, and performing systems engineering services.
- The *manage suppliers* process involves selecting, negotiating, and managing vendors.
- The *production* process contains all of the activities required to fabricate parts and tools, assemble the aircraft, and certify factory processes.
- The *support the delivered product* process consists of all the aftermarket services, such as providing technical assistance, spare parts, repairs, and other product support activities.

The *manage the enterprise* support process is staffed by the leadership team, who oversees strategic planning and goal setting, operational planning, managing technology development, and developing the workforce activities. The *support and services* process handles human resources activities, safety, facilities management, financial, and information systems services to support the core processes. These two support processes are an important feature of the basic structure. They contain activities and routines, including process-based management tools, an integrated people system, and an integrated planning process, that enable A&T's members to achieve outstanding productivity, work satisfaction, and other outcomes. ∎

Figure 14•6   AT&T's Process-Based Structure

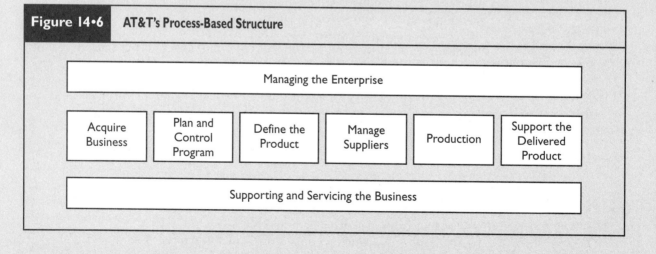

Managing the Enterprise

| Acquire Business | Plan and Control Program | Define the Product | Manage Suppliers | Production | Support the Delivered Product |

Supporting and Servicing the Business

Network-Based Structures

A *network-based structure* manages the diverse, complex, and dynamic relationships among multiple organizations or units, each specializing in a particular business function or task.[13] Some confusion over the definition of a network has been clarified recently by a typology describing four basic types of networks.[14]

- An *internal market network* exists when a single organization establishes each subunit as an independent profit center that is allowed to buy and sell services and resources from each other as well as from the external market. Asea Brown Boveri's (ABB) fifty worldwide businesses consist of twelve hundred companies organized into forty-five hundred profit centers that conduct business with each other.

- A *vertical market network* is composed of multiple organizations linked to a focal organization that coordinates the movement of resources from raw materials to end consumer. Nike, for example, has its shoes manufactured in different plants and then organizes their distribution through retail outlets.

- An *intermarket network* represents alliances among a variety of organizations in different markets and is exemplified by the Japanese *keiretsu* and the Korean *chaebol.*

- An *opportunity network* is the most advanced form of network structure. It is a temporary constellation of organizations brought together to pursue a single purpose. Once accomplished, the network disbands.

These types of networks can be distinguished from one another in terms of whether they are single or multiple organizations, single or multiple industry, and stable or temporary.[15] For example, an internal market network is a stable, single-organization, single-industry structure; an opportunity network is a temporary, multiple-organization structure that can span several different industries.

As shown in Figure 14.7, the network structure redraws organizational boundaries and links separate business units to facilitate task interaction. The essence of networks is the relationships among organizations that perform different aspects of work. In this way, organizations do the things that they do well; for example, manufacturing expertise is applied to production, and logistical expertise is applied to distribution. Network organizations use strategic alliances, joint ventures, research and development consortia, licensing agreements, and wholly owned subsidiaries to design, manufacture, and market advanced products, enter new international markets, and develop new technologies.

Network-based structures are known by a variety of names, including shamrock organizations and virtual, modular, or cellular corporations.[16] Less formally, they have been described as "pizza" structures, spiderwebs, starbursts, and cluster organizations. Companies such as Apple Computer, Benetton, Sun Microsystems, Liz Claiborne, MCI WorldCom, and Merck have implemented fairly sophisticated vertical market and intermarket network structures. Opportunity networks also are commonplace in the construction, fashion, and entertainment industries, as well as in the public sector.[17]

Network structures typically have the following characteristics.

- ***Vertical disaggregation.*** This refers to the breaking up of the organization's business functions, such as production, marketing, and distribution, into separate organizations performing specialized work. In the film industry, for example,

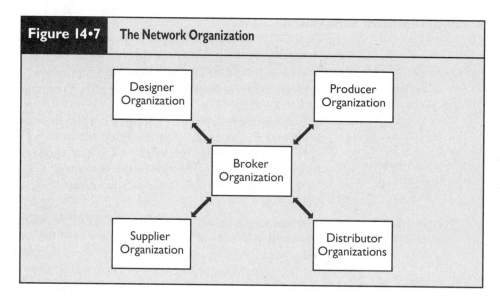

Figure 14•7   The Network Organization

separate organizations providing transportation, cinematography, special effects, set design, music, actors, and catering all work together under a broker organization, the studio. The particular organizations making up the opportunity network represent an important factor in determining its success.[18] More recently, disintermediation, or the replacement of whole steps in the value chain by information technology, specifically the Internet, has fueled the development and numbers of network structures.

- *Brokers.* Networks often are managed by broker organizations that locate and assemble member organizations. The broker may play a central role and subcontract for needed products or services, or it may specialize in linking equal partners into a network. In the construction industry, the general contractor typically assembles and manages drywall, mechanical, electrical, plumbing, and other specialties to erect a building.

- *Coordinating mechanisms.* Network organizations generally are not controlled by hierarchical arrangements or plans. Rather, coordination of the work in a network falls into three categories: informal relationships, contracts, and market mechanisms. First, coordination patterns can depend heavily on interpersonal relationships among individuals who have a well-developed partnership. Conflicts are resolved through reciprocity; network members recognize that each likely will have to compromise at some point. Trust is built and nurtured over time by these reciprocal arrangements. Second, coordination can be achieved through formal contracts, such as ownership control, licensing arrangements, or purchase agreements. Finally, market mechanisms, such as spot payments, performance accountability, and information systems, ensure that all parties are aware of each others' activities.

Network structures have a number of advantages and disadvantages, as shown in Table 14.5.[19] They are highly flexible and adaptable to changing conditions. The ability to form partnerships with different organizations permits the creation of a "best-of-the-best" company to exploit opportunities, often global in nature. They enable each member to exploit its distinctive competence. They can accumulate and apply sufficient resources and expertise to large, complex tasks that single organizations cannot perform. Perhaps most important, network organizations can have synergistic effects whereby members build on each other's strengths and competencies, creating a whole that exceeds the sum of its parts.

The major problems with network organizations are in managing such complex structures. Galbraith and Kazanjian describe network structures as matrix organizations extending beyond the boundaries of single firms but lacking the ability to appeal to a higher authority to resolve conflicts.[20] Thus, matrix skills of managing lateral relations across organizational boundaries are critical to administering network structures. Most organizations, because they are managed hierarchically, can be expected to have difficulties managing lateral relations. Other disadvantages of network organizations include the difficulties of motivating organizations to join such structures and of sustaining commitment over time. Potential members may not want to give up their autonomy to link with other organizations and, once linked, they may have problems sustaining the benefits of joining together. This is especially true if the network consists of organizations that are not the "best of breed." Finally, joining a network may expose the organization's proprietary knowledge and skills to others.

As shown in Table 14.5, network organizations are best suited to highly complex and uncertain environments where multiple competencies and flexible responses are needed. They seem to apply to organizations of all sizes, and they deal

Table 14•5	Advantages, Disadvantages, and Contingencies of the Network-Based Form

ADVANTAGES
- Enables highly flexible and adaptive response to dynamic environments
- Creates a "best-of-the-best" organization to focus resources on customer and market needs
- Enables each organization to leverage a distinctive competency
- Permits rapid global expansion
- Can produce synergistic results

DISADVANTAGES
- Managing lateral relations across autonomous organizations is difficult
- Motivating members to relinquish autonomy to join the network is troublesome
- Sustaining membership and benefits can be problematic
- May give partners access to proprietary knowledge/technology

CONTINGENCIES
- Highly complex and uncertain environments
- Organizations of all sizes
- Goals of organizational specialization and innovation
- Highly uncertain technologies
- Worldwide operations

with complex tasks or problems involving high interdependencies across organizations. Network structures fit with goals that emphasize organization specialization and innovation. They also fit well in organizations with worldwide operations.

Application 14.2 describes how MCI's network structure was configured to align with its strategy and how relationships are managed.[21]

DOWNSIZING

Downsizing refers to interventions aimed at reducing the size of the organization.[22] This typically is accomplished by decreasing the number of employees through layoffs, attrition, redeployment, or early retirement or by reducing the number of organizational units or managerial levels through divestiture, outsourcing, reorganization, or delayering. In practice, downsizing generally involves layoffs where a certain number or class of organization members is no longer employed by the organization. Although traditionally associated with lower-level workers, downsizing increasingly has claimed the jobs of staff specialists, middle managers, and senior executives.

An important consequence of downsizing has been the rise of the contingent workforce. These less expensive temporary or permanent part-time workers often are hired by the organizations that just laid off thousands of employees. A study by the American Management Association found that nearly a third of the 720 firms in the sample had rehired recently terminated employees as independent contractors or consultants because the downsizings had not been matched by an appropriate reduction in or redesign of the workload.[23] Overall cost reduction was achieved by replacing expensive permanent workers with a contingent workforce.

Over the past decade, most major U.S. corporations and government agencies have engaged in downsizing activities. For example, a study of more than thirty-five hundred companies found that 59 percent had fired at least 5 percent of their workers at least once between 1980 and 1994, and one-third of those companies downsized more than 15 percent of their workforce at least once.[24] In addition, 650,000 people were laid off in 1998, and more than 207,000 layoffs were announced in the first four months of 1999.[25] Other organizations have downsized through redeploying workers from one function or job to another. For example, AT&T, IBM, Boeing, Sears, and Xerox cut nearly a quarter-million jobs in 1993 and hired more than 63,000 in 1996.[26] Similarly, in 1996 IBM laid off more than 69,000 people but increased its workforce by 16,000 that same year as its demand was shifting from hardware to software and services.[27]

Downsizing is generally a response to at least four major conditions. First, it is associated increasingly with mergers and acquisitions. One in nine job cuts during 1998 were the result of the integration of two organizations.[28] Second, it can result from organization decline caused by loss of revenues and market share and by technological and industrial change. In southern California, an economy traditionally dependent on the defense industry, more than one hundred thousand jobs have been lost to relocation or elimination as that industry has contracted and consolidated. Third, downsizing can occur when organizations implement one of the new organizational structures described above. For example, creation of network-based structures often involves outsourcing work to other firms that is not essential to the organization's core competence. Fourth, downsizing can result from beliefs and social pressures that smaller is better.[29] In the United States, there is strong conviction that organizations should be leaner and more flexible. Hamel and Prahalad warned, however, that organizations must be careful that downsizing is not a

APPLICATION 14·2   Working the Network Structure at MCI

From its founding in 1968, MCI has made a business out of attacking telecommunications industry leader AT&T, and its growth was partly attributable to the networklike organization structure it adopted, mostly because it had to. Because it was a start-up organization, no one in the United States would sell it operating equipment, so MCI sought out international suppliers and telecommunications services using hardware and software developed in whole or in part by others. In an industry where new products routinely become obsolete in a year, MCI claimed that it is more efficient to spend time looking for innovative subcontractors than to develop its own technology. "I have access to the intellectual assets of nine thousand [other firms'] engineers," Rick Liebhaber, a former MCI executive once said. "If I did my own development, what would I have, five hundred engineers?"

An important ingredient to MCI's success was a clear understanding of its distinctive competence. Founder Bob McGowan never lost sight of what business his company was in, so he never succumbed to the temptations of pursuing new technologies or fads that were "outside the company's purview." MCI's key strengths were in marketing and managing relationships with subcontractors. With respect to marketing, its "Friends and Family" marketing scheme, introduced in the early 1990s, was recognized as one of the best marketing programs in any industry. It increased long-distance revenues by $1.2 billion annually. In addition, the company's 1-800-COLLECT campaign significantly increased its share of the $3 billion collect-call market. MCI also had special competencies in pulling together new telecommunications packages that could serve a customer better; rapidly and effectively integrating the work of outsiders was a special competence MCI sought to maintain.

MCI's ability to leverage its marketing expertise in relationships with other organizations through a network structure allowed the company to become the second-largest enterprise in the long-distance market. An examination of its current and past strategies and structures provides insight to the strengths of a network organization. For example, chairman Bert Roberts, Jr., suggested that MCI's strategic plan called for a reposturing of the company into a "leadership role, not a following role." The manifestation of that plan was a program called "networkMCI." Introduced in January 1995, it was a $20-billion, six-year strategy to integrate MCI's current voice and data services with a new local phone network and the latest in digital wireless services. Naturally, implementing the strategy relied largely on marketing savvy and partnerships with other organizations.

For instance, the company spent more than $2 billion of networkMCI's $20-billion budget to build local phone net-

works in twenty cities and it plans to provide local service in two hundred cities early in the next decade. If the past holds true, it will do so through a network of suppliers offering MCI the best technology available. A small advanced-technology staff searches globally for leading-edge technologies to adopt. The company was the first to recognize Corning Glass's fiber-optic cable as an outstanding medium for communications and implemented the technology before the competition did so.

Another plank in its networkMCI implementation is its relationship with Nextel Communications, a builder and provider of wireless digital networks that MCI will market. In February 1995, MCI acquired a 17-percent stake in Nextel, and spent $150 million for a stake in In-Flight Phone, which has contracts to operate air-to-ground phones on Continental Airlines and USAir.

Internationally, MCI accepted $4.3 billion from British Telecommunications PLC (BT) in exchange for a 20-percent stake in the company. MCI will market services in North and South America, and BT will market to the rest of the world. In addition, MCI and BT together worked with Japan's Nippon Telegraph and Telephone Corporation to market to the Far East. In Mexico, MCI formed a joint venture with Grupo Financiero Banamex-Accival, a financial syndicate that wants to challenge the established Mexican phone company. North of the border, MCI joined forces with Stentor, a Canadian phone company group, to create a digital network that will link the United States and Canada.

The network structure is an obvious part of MCI's international strategy in the North American Free Trade Agreement (NAFTA) market. Many of the company's existing U.S. business customers also have set up business in Mexico and Canada to take advantage of NAFTA, and MCI followed them there. Once the communication networks were in place in Mexico and Canada, MCI created a three-country market for long-distance telecommunications that offered services such as Friends & Family throughout North America. Hence, it has a deal with Banamex, which has a private network that links its 650 branch offices throughout Mexico. MCI invested $150 million in 1994 and $300 million more over the next several years for a 45-percent stake in a joint venture with Banamex to build a public network to 250 cities.

A closer look at how MCI relates to its technology suppliers provides some insights on the workings of a network structure. By partnering with other companies in technology development, MCI's network structure provides a great deal of flexibility. For example, MCI reaps the benefits of more than nine thousand research and development engineers not on its payroll. The research and development facility in Richardson, Texas, is known as an "engineering developmental lab" because technologies developed by dozens of indepen-dent contractors from all over the world are tested, perfect-ed, and then integrated into the MCI network.

To induce subcontractors to push their technologies to the limit, the company uses two suppliers for every network function—fiber-optics, switching, and the like—then uses au-tomated measurement systems embedded in the network to track the reliability of the vendors' equipment. It renews con-tracts on an annual basis, and suppliers know that if their equipment does not work or is not technologically advanced, they are not going to be an MCI supplier for very long.

For example, two large companies, one in the United States and the other in Japan, supplied MCI with laser tech-nology that powered fiber-optic cable at a capacity of 405 megabytes per second (which translates to simultaneous transmission of six thousand phone calls per second). When the second vendor jumped to 565 megabytes, it won the con-tract to provide laser technology for all of MCI's new routes. When the first vendor later jumped to 810 megabytes, it won the next contract.

Vendors that lose out on new contracts aren't discarded; the "losing" laser-technology supplier still has equipment on MCI's network and is eligible for new contracts if it improves its technology. "MCI sticks with every potential supplier," Rick Liebhaber said. "Suppliers basically want to be the best and we help them reach their objectives by providing high standards. Sticking with creative vendors also means that MCI

will help out if and when the vendor's quality falls short—working together with them on quality control projects aimed at bringing performance up to snuff."

Using networks of subcontractors can lead to some in-teresting relationships. There are times when MCI is simulta-neously providing service to a customer, subcontracting a service from that customer, and competing with the same firm. More than once, MCI management has found itself in the position of bidding against one of its own customers for a contract. Ironically, what the competitor/customer was offer-ing as part of its service was service it was purchasing from MCI. Although some managers wanted to stop selling to cus-tomers that were bidding against them, the more sales the customer/competitors made using MCI service as a part of their offerings, the more revenue MCI made from dealing with them. The key is, "We need to remember which rela-tionship we're working on when we're talking," Liebhaber said. "When competing, I deal with a firm just the way I deal with any other competitor." If the organizations can manage those relationships in a rational way, each organization can gather strengths from the other.

"It's how you put it all together that makes the difference. That's where we add the value," said Liebhaber. "You see, we understand our business. Our business is not engineering or manufacturing. Our business is service. So it's how you put the pieces of technology together—that's MCI's creativity. We know those are our strengths." ■

symptom of "corporate anorexia."[30] Organizations may downsize for their own sake and not think about future growth. They may lose key employees who are necessary for future success, cutting into the organization's core competencies and leaving a legacy of mistrust among members. In such situations, it is questionable whether downsizing is developmental as defined in OD.

Application Stages

Successful downsizing interventions tend to proceed by the following steps:[31]

1. *Clarify the organization's strategy.* As a first step, organization leaders specify corporate strategy and communicate clearly how downsizing relates to it. They seek to inform members that downsizing is not a goal in itself, but a restructur-ing process for achieving strategic objectives. Leaders need to provide visible and consistent support throughout the process. They can provide opportunities for members to voice their concerns, ask questions, and obtain counseling if necessary.

2. *Assess downsizing options and make relevant choices.* Once corporate strategy is clear, the full range of downsizing options can be identified and assessed. Table 14.6 describes three primary downsizing methods: workforce reduction, organi-zation redesign, and systemic change. A specific downsizing strategy may use

elements of all three approaches. *Workforce reduction* is aimed at reducing the number of employees, usually in a relatively short timeframe. It can include attrition, retirement incentives, outplacement services, and layoffs. *Organization redesign* attempts to restructure the firm to prepare it for the next stage of growth. This is a medium-term approach that can be accomplished by merging organizational units, eliminating management layers, and redesigning tasks. *Systemic change* is a longer-term option aimed at changing the culture and strategic orientation of the organization. It can involve interventions that alter the responsibilities and work behaviors of everyone in the organization and that promote continual improvement as a way of life in the firm.

Case, a manufacturer of heavy construction equipment, used a variety of methods to downsize, including eliminating money-losing product lines; narrowing the breadth of remaining product lines; bringing customers to the company headquarters to get their opinions of new product design (which surprisingly resulted in maintaining, rather than changing, certain preferred features, thus holding down redesign costs); shifting production to outside vendors; restructuring debt; and spinning off most of its 250 stores. Eventually, these changes led to closing five plants and to payroll reductions of almost 35 percent.[32] The number of jobs lost would have been much greater, however, if Case had not implemented a variety of downsizing methods.

Unfortunately, organizations often choose obvious solutions for downsizing, such as layoffs, because they can be implemented quickly. This action produces a climate of fear and defensiveness as members focus on identifying who will be separated from the organization. Examining a broad range of options and considering the entire organization rather than only certain areas can help allay

Table 14•6	Three Downsizing Tactics		
DOWNSIZING TACTIC	**CHARACTERISTICS**	**EXAMPLES**	
Workforce reduction	Aimed at headcount reduction Short-term implementation Fosters a transition	Attrition Transfer and outplacement Retirement incentives Buyout packages Layoffs	
Organization redesign	Aimed at organization change Moderate-term implementation Fosters transition and, potentially, transformation	Eliminate functions Merge units Eliminate layers Eliminate products Redesign tasks	
Systemic redesign	Aimed at culture change Long-term implementation Fosters transformation	Change responsibility Involve all constituents Foster continuous improvement and innovation Simplification Downsizing: a way of life	

SOURCE: K. Cameron, S. Freeman, and A. Mishra, "Best Practices in White-Collar Downsizing: Managing Contradictions," *Academy of Management Executive* 5 (1991): 62.

fears that favoritism and politics are the bases for downsizing decisions. Moreover, participation of organization members in such decisions can have positive benefits. It can create a sense of urgency for identifying and implementing options to downsizing other than layoffs. Participation can provide members with a clearer understanding of how downsizing will proceed and can increase the likelihood that whatever choices are made are perceived as reasonable and fair.

3. *Implement the changes.* This stage involves implementing methods for reducing the size of the organization. Several practices characterize successful implementation. First, downsizing is best controlled from the top down. Many difficult decisions are required, and a broad perspective helps to overcome people's natural instincts to protect their enterprise or function. Second, identify and target specific areas of inefficiency and high cost. The morale of the organization can be hurt if areas commonly known to be redundant are left untouched. Third, link specific actions to the organization's strategy. Organization members need to be reminded consistently that restructuring activities are part of a plan to improve the organization's performance. Finally, communicate frequently using a variety of media. This keeps people informed, lowers their anxiety over the process, and makes it easier for them to focus on their work.

4. *Address the needs of survivors and those who leave.* Most downsizing eventually involves reduction in the size of the workforce, and it is important to support not only employees who remain with the organization but also those who leave. When layoffs occur, employees are generally asked to take on additional responsibilities and to learn new jobs, often with little or no increase in compensation. This added workload can be stressful, and when combined with anxiety over past layoffs and possible future ones, it can lead to what researchers have labeled the "survivor syndrome."[33] This syndrome involves a narrow set of self-absorbed and risk-averse behaviors that can threaten the organization's survival. Rather than working to ensure the organization's success, survivors often are preoccupied with whether additional layoffs will occur, with guilt over receiving pay and benefits while co-workers are struggling with termination, and with the uncertainty of career advancement.

   Organizations can address these survivor concerns with communication processes that increase the amount and frequency of information provided. Communication should shift from explanations about who left or why to clarification of where the company is going, including its visions, strategies, and goals. The linkage between employees' performance and strategic success is emphasized so that remaining members feel they are valued. Organizations also can support survivors through training and development activities that prepare them for the new work they are being asked to perform. Senior management can promote greater involvement in decision making, thus reinforcing the message that people are important to the future success and growth of the organization.

   Given the negative consequences typically associated with job loss, organizations have developed an array of methods to help employees who have been laid off. These include outplacement counseling, personal and family counseling, severance packages, office support for job searches, relocation services, and job retraining. Each service is intended to assist employees in their transition to another work situation.

5. *Follow through with growth plans.* This final stage of downsizing involves implementing an organization renewal and growth process. Failure to move quickly to implement growth plans is a key determinate of ineffective downsizing.[34]

For example, a study of 1,020 human resource directors reported that only 44 percent of the companies that had downsized in the previous five years shared details of their growth plans with employees; only 34 percent told employees how they would fit into the company's new strategy.[35] Organizations must ensure that employees understand the renewal strategy and their new roles in it. Employees need credible expectations that, although the organization has been through a tough period, their renewed efforts can move it forward.

Application 14.3 describes the process of a strategically focused downsizing effort at Arizona Public Service Company.[36]

Results of Downsizing

The empirical research on downsizing is mostly negative. A review conducted by the National Research Council concluded, "From the research produced thus far, downsizing as a strategy for improvement has proven to be, by and large, a failure."[37] A number of studies have documented the negative productivity and employee consequences. One survey of 1,005 companies that used downsizing to reduce costs reported that fewer than half of the firms actually met cost targets. Moreover, only 22 percent of the companies achieved expected productivity gains, and consequently about 80 percent of the firms needed to rehire some of the same people that they had previously terminated. Fewer than 33 percent of the companies surveyed reported that profits increased as much as expected, and only 21 percent achieved satisfactory improvements in shareholder return on investment.[38] Another survey of 1,142 downsized firms found that only about a third achieved productivity goals.[39] In addition, the research points to a number of problems at the individual level, including increased stress and illness, loss of self-esteem, reduced trust and loyalty, and marriage and family disruptions.[40]

Research on the effects of downsizing on financial performance also shows negative results. One study examined an array of financial performance measures, such as return on sales, assets, and equity, in 210 companies that announced layoffs.[41] It found that increases in financial performance in the first year following the layoff announcements were not followed by performance improvements in the next year. In no case did a firm's financial performance after a layoff announcement match its maximum levels of performance in the year before the announcement. These results suggest that layoffs may result in initial improvements in financial performance, but such gains are temporary and not sustained at even pre-layoff levels. In a similar study of sixteen firms that wrote off more than 10 percent of their net worth in a five-year period, stock prices, which averaged 16 percent below the market average before the layoff announcements, increased on the day that the restructuring was announced but then began a steady decline. Two years after the layoff announcements, ten of the sixteen stocks were trading below the market by 17 percent to 48 percent, and twelve of the sixteen were below comparable firms in their industries by 5 to 45 percent.[42]

These research findings paint a rather bleak picture of the success of downsizing. The results must be interpreted cautiously, however, for three reasons. First, many of the survey-oriented studies received responses from human resources specialists who might have been naturally inclined to view downsizing in a negative light. Second, the studies of financial performance may have included a biased sample of firms. If the companies selected for analysis had been poorly managed, then downsizing alone would have been unlikely to improve financial performance. There is

APPLICATION 14•3 The Strategic Downsizing Process at Arizona Public Service Company

The Arizona Public Service Company (APS) engaged in a strategic approach to downsizing in 1990. At the time, it was struggling with high costs, low customer-service ratings, and an inwardly focused bureaucracy insensitive to changes in the electric power industry. Three years later, APS was cited as one of the best power companies in the United States. The company's power plants have had the best power availability factor, a measure of its capacity to meet customer demand, in thirty-five years, and customer-service ratings are at record high levels. At the time of its strategic restructuring, APS made a commitment to the regulatory body that it would not file for a rate increase before 1993. As 1993 drew to a close, the company had exceeded its goal to lower costs and had canceled the proposed rate increase. CEO Mark De Michele credits the success of the turnaround with the process used to conduct the downsizing. It had four phases: strategic analysis, structural redesign, redeployment, and renewal.

Strategic analysis consisted of understanding the competitive context and the goals APS should strive to achieve. Competition from power companies inside and outside its operating area, technological and regulatory reform, and its poor operating results required that APS formulate goals around reduced costs and improved customer service. These two goals became the foundation for the vision statement "Top Five by '95" which drove the subsequent revitalization effort. A third goal was to change APS's culture to emphasize customer service rather than engineering.

Structural redesign involved determining the kind of organization that would best enable employees to accomplish strategic goals. De Michele and his senior management team recognized that reaching these goals required a new organization. The new APS needed to have fewer levels and more decision-making power in the hands of lower-level employees, fewer people (although they weren't sure exactly how many fewer), and, perhaps most important, the right mix of people with skills and motivation to achieve the goals after restructuring.

The company formed three teams and hired consultants to redesign the company's three major areas: generation and transmission, customer service, and staff services. The teams reviewed the work in each area, the best practices for performing the work (compared with other top utilities), and the number of people required. A companywide employee suggestion program generated more than two thousand ideas for getting more work done with fewer people. Although not all of the suggestions could be addressed, this initial step sent an important signal that employee input would to be an important part of the new organization.

The details of structure and size emerged from this analysis. Workforce reductions, to the extent they were required, were the outcome, not the objective. And although the process did lead to substantial reductions in number of employees, everyone knew that the reductions had not been arbitrary but were the result of a reasoned analysis and would lead to a more competitive company.

Redeployment, or staffing the new organization, was the third phase. By the time the redeployment effort was completed, the new organization chart had one thousand fewer positions, a decrease of approximately 15 percent. The redeployment phase had four key activities: position descriptions, communication, application and review, and employee assistance. Developing position descriptions required APS managers and supervisors to articulate the required competencies for each position in the new structure.

Communications represented a crucial step in the redeployment phase. De Michele made numerous presentations to managers, supervisors, and employees and spent 30 to 40 percent of his time meeting with large groups of employees on a regular basis, invariably answering tough questions about what workers could expect. Employees often asked, "How do we know the selection process will be fair?" "Isn't it true that you have a specific number of cuts in mind?" and "How do we know that this is not going to happen again?" In response, De Michele explained the review and appeal process described below, challenged employees to observe the selections that were made before questioning the fairness of the process, emphasized that positioning the right people in the right jobs was critical to the future of the company, and stated that he could not promise that there would be no changes in the future. In addition, senior management was to be affected by the restructuring as well. Early in the process, De Michele announced that there would be three fewer senior officers. Because those officers had been with the company a long time and were well respected by their peers, it was evident that management was making tough decisions about its own.

The application and review process sought to place the right employee in the right position to accomplish the goals of lower costs and high customer satisfaction. Employees were encouraged to apply for any and all positions for which they believed they were qualified. Then each applicant for each position was rated according to the minimum requirements and competencies for the job. Issues such as affirmative action and absenteeism also were considered. To ensure fairness, all assessment forms required the signatures of a manager and his or her manager before they were passed to the review board.

The review board consisted of a retiring officer and two senior managers and ensured that the "best" employee was selected for each available position. It was assisted by the company's affirmative action group and outside legal counsel. APS also set up an appeals board to examine any complaints or grievances raised by employees who did not agree with the review board's decision. The appeals board had wide latitude to investigate allegations and render decisions. When the review board's decisions were reversed, the manager who had filled out the assessment form developed a solution for the aggrieved employee, such as finding another place in the department or elsewhere.

The final activity in deployment was an internal placement and employee assistance program to handle those negatively affected by the process. APS defined "negatively affected" as employees who were not offered a position, employees offered jobs for which the midpoint of their new pay scale was 10 percent less than their former pay scale, or employees whose new assignment was seventy-five miles or more from their former work site. These people were offered career counseling workshops, outplacement assistance, enhanced severance packages, and other support services.

Renewal was the final phase of restructuring. APS took specific steps to aid in recovery and contribute to an ongoing process of recovery. Shortly after redeployment, at a meeting of all managers, the officer team discussed the company's mission, values, and strategic goals. The vision "Top Five by '95" became the companywide theme. Following De Michele's presentation, the officers commented on how they envisioned their future roles in the organization. In addition, managers participated in a case study scenario that highlighted the need for managers to work with their employees in facilitating the transition. The meeting was partly a celebration of the newly selected organization and partly a preparation for the work ahead. In the months that followed, managers and supervisors were given leadership training relevant to the new organization.

The renewal phase at APS was integrated with ongoing strategic planning. The vision "Top Five by '95" was translated into specific operational goals, and each area and department was expected to contribute to the strategic goals of lower costs and better customer service. Other changes included a revised appraisal system and a planning process that specifically linked corporate goals to the frontline activities in the company. The company continues to use the selection criteria developed during the redeployment process for staffing decisions. ■

some empirical support for this view because low-performing firms are more likely to engage in downsizing than are high-performing firms.[43]

Third, disappointing results may be a function of the way downsizing was implemented. A number of organizations have posted solid financial returns following downsizing, such as Florida Power and Light, General Electric, Motorola, Texas Instruments, Boeing, Chrysler, and Hewlett-Packard.[44] A study of thirty downsized firms in the automobile industry showed that those companies that implemented effectively the process described above scored significantly higher on several performance measures than did firms that had no downsizing strategy or that implemented the steps poorly.[45] Several studies have suggested that where downsizing programs adopt appropriate OD interventions or apply strategies similar to the process outlined above, they generate more positive individual and organizational results.[46] Thus, the success of downsizing efforts may depend as much on how effectively the intervention is applied as on the size of the layoffs or the amount of delayering.

REENGINEERING

The final restructuring intervention is reengineering—the fundamental rethinking and radical redesign of business processes to achieve dramatic improvements in performance.[47] Reengineering transforms how organizations traditionally produce and deliver goods and services. Beginning with the Industrial Revolution, organizations have increasingly fragmented work into specialized units, each focusing on a limited part of the overall production process. Although this division of labor has enabled organizations to mass-produce standardized products and services efficiently, it can be overly complicated, difficult to manage, and slow to respond to the rapid and unpredictable changes experienced by many organizations today. Reengineering addresses these problems by breaking down specialized work units into more integrated, cross-functional work processes. This streamlines work processes and makes them faster and more flexible; consequently, they are more responsive to changes in competitive conditions, customer demands, product life cycles, and technologies.[48]

As might be expected, reengineering requires an almost revolutionary change in how organizations design their structures and their work. It addresses fundamental issues about why organizations do what they do, and why do they do it in a particular way. Reengineering identifies and questions the often unexamined assumptions underlying how organizations perform work. This effort typically results in radical changes in thinking and work methods—a shift from specialized jobs, tasks, and structures to integrated processes that deliver value to customers. Such revolutionary change differs considerably from incremental approaches to performance improvement, such as continuous improvement and total quality management (Chapter 15), which emphasize incremental changes in existing work processes. Because reengineering radically alters the status quo, it seeks to produce dramatic increases in organization performance.

In radically changing business processes, reengineering frequently takes advantage of new information technology. Modern information technologies, such as teleconferencing, expert systems, shared databases, and wireless communication, can enable organizations to reengineer. They can help organizations to break out of traditional ways of thinking about work and embrace entirely new ways of producing and delivering products. At IBM Credit, for example, an integrated information system with expert systems technology enables one employee to handle all stages of the credit-delivery process. This eliminates the handoffs, delays, and errors that derived from the traditional work design, in which different employees performed sequential tasks.

Whereas new information technology can enable organizations to reengineer themselves, existing technology can thwart such efforts.[49] Many reengineering projects fail because existing information systems do not provide the data needed to operate integrated business processes. The systems do not allow interdependent departments to interface with each other; they often require new information to be entered by hand into separate computer systems before people in different work areas can access it. Given the inherent difficulty in trying to support process-based work with specialized information systems, organizations have sought to develop information technologies that are more suited to reengineered work. The most popular software system, SAP, was developed by a German company of the same name. With SAP, firms can standardize their information systems because the software processes data on a range of tasks and links it all together, thus integrating the information flow among different parts of the business. Because they believe that SAP may be the missing technological link to reengineering, many of the largest consulting firms that provide reengineering services, such as Anderson Consulting, Deloitte Touche, and PriceWaterhouseCoopers, have developed their own SAP consultants.

Reengineering also is associated with interventions having to do with downsizing, the shift from functional to process-based structures, and work design (Chapter 16). Although these interventions have different conceptual and applied backgrounds, they overlap considerably in practice. Reengineering can result in production and delivery processes that require fewer people and fewer layers of management. Conversely, downsizing may require subsequent reengineering interventions. When downsizing occurs without fundamental changes in how work is performed, the same tasks simply are being performed with a smaller number of people. Thus, expected cost savings may not be realized because lower productivity offsets lower salaries and fewer benefits.

Reengineering also can be linked to transformation of organization structures and work design. Its focus on work processes helps to break down the vertical orientation of functional and self-contained-unit organizations. The endeavor identifies and assesses core business processes and redesigns work to account for key task interdependencies running through them. That typically results in new jobs or teams that emphasize multifunctional tasks, results-oriented feedback, and employee empowerment—characteristics associated with motivational and sociotechnical approaches to work design. Regrettably, reengineering has failed to apply these approaches' attention to individual differences in people's reactions to work to its own work-design prescriptions. It advocates enriched work and teams, without consideration for the wealth of research that shows that not all people are motivated to perform such work.[50]

Application Stages

Reengineering is a relatively new intervention and is still developing applied methods. Early applications emphasized identifying which business processes to reengineer and technically assessing the work flow. More recent efforts have extended reengineering practice to address issues of managing change, such as how to deal with resistance to change and how to manage the transition to new work processes.[51] The following application steps are included in most reengineering efforts, although the order may change slightly from one situation to another.[52]

1. *Prepare the organization.* Reengineering begins with clarification and assessment of the organization's context, including its competitive environment, strategy, and objectives. This effort establishes the need for reengineering and the strategic direction that the process should follow. Changes in an organization's competitive environment can signal a need for radical change in how it does business. As preparation for reengineering at GTE Telephone Operations, for example, executives determined that although deregulation had begun with coin-operated telephones and long-distance service, it soon would spread to the local network. They concluded that this would present an enormous competitive challenge and that the old way of doing business, reinforced by years of regulatory protection, would seriously saddle the organization with high costs.[53]

2. *Specify organization strategy and objectives.* The business strategy determines the focus of reengineering and guides decisions about the business processes that are essential for strategic success. In the absence of such information, the organization may reengineer extraneous processes or ones that could be outsourced. GTE executives recognized that the keys to the firm's success in a more competitive environment were low costs and customer satisfaction. Consequently, they set dramatic goals of doubling revenues while halving costs and reducing product development time by 75 percent. Defining these objectives gave the reengineering effort a clear focus.

A final task in this preparation step is to communicate clearly throughout the organization why reengineering is necessary and the direction it will take. GTE's communications program lasted a year and a half, and helped ensure that members understood the reasons underlying the program and the magnitude of the changes to be made. Senior executives were careful to communicate, both verbally and behaviorally, that they were fully committed to the change effort. Demonstration of such unwavering support seems necessary if organization members are to challenge their traditional thinking about how business should be conducted.

3. *Fundamentally rethink the way work gets done.* This step lies at the heart of reengineering and involves these activities: identifying and analyzing core business processes, defining their key performance objectives, and designing new processes. These tasks are the real work of reengineering and typically are performed by a cross-functional team who is given considerable time and resources to accomplish them.[54]

   a. *Identify and analyze core business processes.* Core processes are considered essential for strategic success. They include activities that transform inputs into valued outputs. Core processes typically are assessed through development of a process map that lists the different activities required to deliver an organization's products or services. GTE determined that its core processes could be characterized as "choose, use, and pay." Customers first choose a telephone carrier, then use its services, and pay for them. GTE developed a process map for these core processes that included the work flow for getting customers to choose, use, and pay for the firm's service.

   Analysis of core business processes can include assigning costs to each of the major phases of the work flow to help identify costs that may be hidden in the activities of the production process. Traditional cost-accounting systems do not store data in process terms; they identify costs according to categories of expense, such as salaries, fixed costs, and supplies.[55] This method of cost accounting can be misleading and can result in erroneous conclusions about how best to reduce costs. For example, the material control department at a Dana Corporation plant in Plymouth, Minnesota, changed from a traditional to a process-based accounting system.[56] The traditional accounting system showed that salaries and fringe benefits accounted for 82 percent of total costs—an assessment that suggested workforce downsizing was the most effective way to lower costs. The process-based accounting system revealed a different picture, however: it showed that 44 percent of the department's costs involved expediting, resolving, and reissuing orders from suppliers and customers. In other words, almost half of their costs were associated with reworking deficient orders.

   Business processes also can be assessed in terms of value-added activities—the amount of value contributed to a product or service by a particular step in the process. For example, as part of its invoice collection process, Corky's Pest Control, a small service business dependent on a steady stream of cash payments, provides its customers with a self-addressed, stamped envelope. Although this adds an additional cost to each account, it more than pays for itself in customer loyalty and retention, and reduced accounts receivables and late payments handling. Conversely, organizations often engage in process activities that have little or no added value. For instance, in a Denver hospital an employee on each workshift checked a pump that circulated oxygen. Eight years earlier, the pump had failed and caused a death.

Since that time, a new pump had been installed with fault-protection equipment and control sensors that no longer required the physical inspection. Yet because of habit, the checking process remained in place and drained resources that could be used more productively in other areas.

b. *Define performance objectives.* Challenging performance goals are set in this step. The highest possible level of performance for any particular process is identified, and dramatic goals are set for speed, quality, cost, or other measures of performance. These standards can derive from customer requirements or from benchmarks of the best practices of industry leaders. For example, at Andersen Windows, the demand for unique window shapes pushed the number of different products from 28,000 to more than 86,000 in 1991.[57] The pressure on the shop floor for a "batch of one" resulted in 20 percent of all shipments containing at least one order discrepancy. As part of its reengineering effort, Andersen set targets for ease of ordering, manufacturing, and delivery. Each retailer and distributor was sold an interactive, computerized version of its catalogue that allowed customers to design their own windows. The resulting design is then given a unique "license plate number" and the specifications are sent directly to the factory. By 1995, new sales had tripled at some retail locations, the number of products had increased to 188,000, and fewer than one in two hundred shipments had a discrepancy.

c. *Design new processes.* The last task in this third step of reengineering is to redesign current business processes to achieve breakthrough goals. It often starts with a clean sheet of paper and addresses the question "If we were starting this company today, what processes would we need to create a sustainable competitive advantage?" These essential processes are then designed according to the following guidelines:[58]

- Begin and end the process with the needs and wants of the customer.
- Simplify the current process by combining and eliminating steps.
- Use the "best of what is" in the current process.
- Attend to both technical and social aspects of the process.
- Do not be constrained by past practice.
- Identify the critical information required at each step in the process.
- Perform activities in their most natural order.
- Assume the work gets done right the first time.
- Listen to people who do the work.

An important activity that appears in many successful reengineering efforts is implementing "early wins" or "quick hits." Analysis of existing processes often reveals obvious redundancies and inefficiencies for which appropriate changes may be authorized immediately. These early successes can help generate and sustain momentum in the reengineering effort.

4. *Restructure the organization around the new business processes.* This last step in reengineering involves changing the organization's structure to support the new business processes. This endeavor typically results in the kinds of process-based structures that were described earlier in this chapter. An important element of this restructuring is implementing new information and measurement systems that reinforce a shift from measuring behaviors, such as absenteeism and grievances, to assessing outcomes, such as productivity, customer satisfaction, and

cost savings. Moreover, information technology is one of the key drivers of reengineering because it can drastically reduce the cost and time associated with integrating and coordinating business processes.

Reengineered organizations typically have the following characteristics:[59]

- *Work units change from functional departments to process teams.* The Principal Financial Group's Individual Insurance Department was structured according to product lines, such as life, health, and auto insurance.[60] Following reengineering, the department organized around cross-functional presale teams aimed at developing and building customer relationships and postsale teams that maintained them.

- *Jobs change from simple tasks to multidimensional work.* The postsale team was responsible for a field-support process called licensing and contracting. Under the old structure, this was a sixteen-step effort that involved nine people in different departments and on different floors in Principal's home office. Following reengineering, the process consists of only six steps and involves only three people who are cross-trained to perform the various tasks.

- *People's roles change from controlled to empowered.* At Hallmark Circuits, the reengineering effort resulted not only in changed jobs and processes, but in increased employee involvement as well. Production teams meet twice daily to discuss problems; hiring decisions are made by a four-person team of employees; major equipment purchases are jointly determined by management and employees; and the manufacturing group plays a big role in deciding whether to bid on or take new jobs.[61]

- *The focus of performance measures and compensation shifts from activities to results.* Reengineered organizations routinely collect and report measures of customer satisfaction, operating costs, and productivity to all teams and then tie these measures to pay. In this way, teams and their members are rewarded for working smarter, not harder.

- *Organization structures change from hierarchical to flat.* As described earlier, the favored structure of the reengineered organization is process-based. Rather than having layers of management, the organization has empowered, cross-functional, and well-educated process teams that collect information, make decisions about task execution, and monitor their performance.

- *Managers change from supervisors to coaches; executives change from scorekeepers to leaders.* In process-based structures, the role of management and leadership changes drastically. A new set of skills is required, including facilitation, resource acquisition, information sharing, supporting, and problem solving.

Application 14.4 describes the reengineering efforts at Schlage. It highlights the importance of focusing on large, strategically important, cross-functional processes and on the enabling role of information technology.[62]

Results from Reengineering

The results from reengineering vary widely. Industry journals and the business press regularly contain accounts of dramatic business outcomes attributable to reengineering. On the other hand, the bestselling book on reengineering reported that as many as 70 percent of the efforts failed to meet their cost, cycle time, or productivity objectives.[63] One study polled 497 companies in the United States and

APPLICATION 14•4   Reengineering Schlage Lock Company

The Schlage Lock Company, a part of Ingersoll-Rand Company, makes conventional key and combination locks. Although it offers service directly to companies and builders that need locks for specific sites or projects, Schlage's primary customer base comprises retailers, home improvement stores, and some general merchandisers. The company has approximately twenty-five hundred employees and maintains facilities in five locations: San Francisco; San Jose; Tecate, Mexico; Security, Colorado; and Lenexa, Kansas.

In 1991, as part of an ongoing performance-improvement effort, Schlage Lock Company initiated a business reengineering program. At the time when the decision to undertake reengineering was made, Schlage was not in crisis. The company recognized, however, that its position in the industry likely would slip over the coming decade if it did not take steps to alter its methods of operation. Part of the concern stemmed from major changes in the way retailers were operating. The high-volume, "value" retailers such as Wal-Mart, Home Depot, and Price/Costco brought new purchasing and distribution methods to the industry. Quick deliveries were required to maintain volumes on the one hand and keep inventories low on the other. Manufacturers were required to bear the risk of carrying inventory.

Under this pressure, flexible production scheduling becomes a crucial capability for manufacturers, especially when customer demands do not follow expectations. Thanks to high volumes and computer tracking, retailers try to respond to consumer trends with as little delay as possible. Unfortunately for manufacturers, this kind of micromarketing means they are expected to respond with equal rapidity. Projections based on last year's sales are no longer adequate; production must be based on last month's or even last week's sales, and the time to get an item into and through production must be very short.

Schlage recognized that the changes in the way its customers did business would require fundamental changes in its manufacturing operations, information systems, marketing, sales, and administrative practices. It also recognized that making these changes required substantial employee development, as well as reasons and opportunities for employees to become involved in meeting company goals.

In preparing for its reengineering effort, Schlage adopted a strategic plan with a mission statement that staked the organization to world-class order management and manufacturing systems. In addition, it defined its primary reengineering goals as increasing throughput and productivity, reducing operations costs, and improving customer relations. The centerpiece of the strategic plan was the recognition that a new information system would be critical in the restructuring. A

Strategic Information Systems Plan (SISP) task force was established to oversee the effort, and the team spent five months interviewing sixty Schlage employees from its various facilities. Interviewees were asked about their job responsibilities, how the information systems were used, and how they completed their work. The initial SISP interviews were intended to understand how the current information system operated. "We had a lot of custom [software] programs, in house," explained Brent Elliott, the Schlage manager charged with implementing the SISP. "And what we came up with is [that] we could actually go in and implement new systems to basically automate our existing practices. But as we looked at where we were going strategically, we felt that just automating our current practices wasn't going to be enough for the future. We had to do something a lot more dramatic than just automating our current processes." The interview data and task force discussions had pointed up another, more important problem.

What the team discovered was that Schlage's manufacturing processes also had to be reengineered. Its traditional manufacturing pattern was based on a traditional job-design model. A single task was assigned to each employee, who would perform only that task. The approach was not well managed and created several inefficiencies. In particular, differing work habits and experience often left some employees idle while others were backlogged. Significant bottlenecks throughout the system caused increased costs and inflexibility.

A long string of solid profits meant that these kinds of inefficiencies generally were ignored. However, in the context of the flexibility required by customers' new demands, such a system could not continue. Moreover, the pressure of increased competition forced the company to recognize the importance of improving manufacturing flexibility and efficiency. Management looked at the inefficiencies as an opportunity to push production beyond the targeted goals.

After a thorough review of the existing methods, the manufacturing process was reengineered into a series of worker cells, with each cell having responsibility for a particular group of product lines. Members of each cell would be cross-trained so that as labor needs changed with each step along the production process, the work group could adapt by shifting resources to their most valued use. An important side benefit to the change was that Schlage employees would gain a better understanding of the entire business process from product development to production through marketing and sales, and a better understanding of how their work fit into the company's overall success.

Consequently, manufacturing process reengineering became an important part of the SISP process. As manufacturing issues were being addressed, the original SISP team addressed the core information processing systems of order entry, product costing, design for producibility, bill of materials, master scheduling, order management, and business systems support.

The interview data provided the important baseline information needed to form a reengineered information systems plan. The plan included communication goals, measurements, and performance guidelines as well as a commitment to training employees and managers on the new systems. It proposed streamlining current information processes in each of the critical information systems areas, then evaluating computer applications to determine the software that best supported those processes.

The SISP team's findings suggested that by using more packaged applications and fewer vendors, the systems could become more integrated, more flexible, and more user-friendly. In working toward that vision, the team evaluated several mainframe computer platforms as well as local- and wide-area network technologies to link engineering and sales offices with manufacturing and warehousing facilities. Several consultants were used to help in the selection process.

The reengineering process was implemented by creating a team for each of the company's five facilities. Claudia Melteff, the company's director of human resources, refers to these groups as "Tiger Teams." "It's an Army term," she explained. "The idea is it's a group that goes in and blitzes an area. We pulled together the brightest and the best and let them have a go at reorganizing." Each facility also has a "champion" who has responsibility for making sure that resources are obtained and time schedules are adhered to. The champions, under Elliott's supervision, are accountable for implementing the new effort and for making sure company objectives are met.

The reengineering effort at Schlage, still in progress, did have a few bumps in the road. "If there was a serious shortcoming to Schlage's approach," said Melteff, "it occurred at the mid-management level." The traditional company culture focused on a management development process that promoted people according to on-the-job experience and outside education financed by a tuition reimbursement program. There were very few internal management training classes. The shift to a cellular structure, however, implied that many mid-management positions would be deleted or changed substantially. The mistake occurred in skipping over midlevel managers in the training programs that were a part of the reengineering effort. Failure to include them in the reorganization discounted their contribution to the organization, created distrust, and, in some cases, produced hostility to change. "We thought we could prevail by addressing everything with logic, but if you can't manage the feelings, that's where problems occur," Melteff noted. "People aren't dumb. When a shake-up of any kind occurs, they know it's going to affect them, and their first reaction is going to be emotional." The irony is that companies want people who are emotionally connected to their work but then cannot understand resistance to proposed changes. ■

1,245 companies in Europe, and found that 60 percent of U.S. firms and 75 percent of European firms had engaged in at least one reengineering project. Eighty-five percent of the firms reported little or no gain from the efforts.[64] Despite its popularity, reengineering is only beginning to be evaluated systematically, and there is little research to help unravel the disparate results.[65]

One evaluation of business process reengineering examined more than one hundred companies' efforts.[66] In-depth analyses of twenty reengineering projects found that eleven cases had total business unit cost reductions of less than 5 percent, whereas six cases had total cost reductions averaging 18 percent. The primary difference was the scope of the business process selected. Reengineering key value-added processes significantly affected total business unit costs; reengineering narrow business processes did not.

Similarly, performance improvements in particular processes were associated strongly with changes in six key levers of behavior, including structure, skills, information systems, roles, incentives, and shared values. Efforts that addressed all six levers produced average cost reductions in specific processes by 35 percent; efforts that affected only one or two change levers reduced costs by 19 percent. Finally, the percentage reduction in total unit costs was associated with committed leadership. Similarly, a survey of twenty-three "successful" reengineering cases found that they were characterized by a clear vision of the future, specific goals for change, use of information technology, top management's involvement and commitment, clear milestones and measurements, and the training of participants in process analysis and teamwork.[67]

SUMMARY

This chapter presented interventions aimed at restructuring organizations. Several basic structures, such as the functional structure, the self-contained unit, and the matrix configuration, dominate most organizations. Two newer forms, process-based and network-based structures, were also described. Each of these structures has corresponding strengths and weaknesses, and supportive conditions must be assessed when determining which structure is an appropriate fit with the organization's environment.

Two restructuring interventions were described: downsizing and reengineering. Downsizing decreases the size of the organization through workforce reduction or organizational redesign. It generally is associated with layoffs where a certain number or class of organization members is no longer employed by the organization. Downsizing can contribute to organization development by focusing on the organization's strategy, using a variety of downsizing tactics, addressing the needs of all organization members, and following through with growth plans. Reengineering is the fundamental rethinking and radical redesign of business processes to achieve dramatic improvements in performance. It seeks to transform how organizations traditionally produce and deliver goods and services. A typical reengineering project prepares the organization, rethinks the way work gets done, and restructures the organization around the newly designed core processes.

NOTES

1. M. Tushman and E. Romanelli, "Organizational Evolution: A Metamorphosis Model of Convergence and Reorientation," in *Research in Organizational Behavior*, vol. 7, eds. L. Cummings and B. Staw (Greenwich, Conn.: JAI Press, 1985); C. Worley, D. Hitchin, and W. Ross, *Integrated Strategic Change* (Reading, Mass.: Addison-Wesley, 1996).

2. P. Lawrence and J. Lorsch, *Organization and Environment: Managing Differentiation and Integration* (Cambridge: Harvard Graduate School of Business, Administration Division of Research, 1967); J. R. Galbraith, *Organization Design* (Reading, Mass.: Addison-Wesley, 1977): 5.

3. L. Gulick and L. Urwick, eds., *Papers on the Science of Administration* (New York: Institute of Public Administration, Columbia University, 1937); M. Weber, *The Theory of Social and Economic Organization*, eds. A. Henderson and T. Parsons (Glencoe, Ill.: Free Press, 1947).

4. A. Chandler, *Strategy and Structure: Chapters in the History of the Industrial Enterprise* (Cambridge, Mass.: MIT Press, 1962).

5. S. Davis and P. Lawrence, *Matrix* (Reading, Mass.: Addison-Wesley, 1977); H. Kolodny, "Managing in a Matrix," *Business Horizons* 24 (March-April 1981): 17–35.

6. Davis and Lawrence, *Matrix*.

7. W. Joyce, "Matrix Organization: A Social Experiment," *Academy of Management Journal* 29 (1986): 536–61; C. Worley and C. Teplitz, "The Use of 'Expert Power' as an Emerging Influence Style within Successful U.S. Matrix Organizations," *Project Management Journal* (1993): 31–36.

8. Davis and Lawrence, *Matrix*.

9. J. Byrne, "The Horizontal Corporation," *Business Week* (20 December 1993): 76–81; S. Mohrman, S. Cohen, and A. Mohrman, *Designing Team-Based Organizations* (San Francisco: Jossey-Bass, 1995); R. Ashkenas, D. Ulrich, T. Jick, and S. Kerr, *The Boundaryless Organization* (San Francisco: Jossey-Bass, 1995).

10. J. Galbraith, E. Lawler, and associates, *Organizing for the Future: The New Logic for Managing Complex Organizations* (San Francisco: Jossey-Bass, 1993).

11. Byrne, "Horizontal Corporation."

12. This application was based on materials and interview data provided by Debbie Collard, director, Continuous Quality Improvement, Airlift and Tanker Programs, Boeing, December 1999.

13. W. Halal, "From Hierarchy to Enterprise: Internal Markets Are the New Foundation of Management," *Academy of Management Executive* 8, 4 (1994): 69–83; C. Snow, R. Miles, and H. Coleman Jr., "Managing 21st Century Network Organizations," *Organizational Dynamics* 20 (1992): 5–19; S. Tully, "The Modular Corporation," *Fortune* (8 February 1993): 106–14; R. Rycroft, "Managing Complex Networks: Key to 21st Century Innovation Success," *Research-Technology Management* (May-June 1999): 13–18.

14. R. Chisolm, *Developing Network Organizations: Learning from Theory and Practice* (Reading, Mass.: Addison-Wesley, 1998); R. Achrol, "Changes in the Theory of Interorganizational Relations in Marketing: Toward a Network Paradigm," *Journal of the Academy of Marketing Science* 25 (1997): 56–71.

15. C. Snow, "Twenty-First Century Organizations: Implications for a New Marketing Paradigm," *Journal of the Academy of Marketing Science* 25 (1997): 72–74.

16. W. Davidow and M. Malone, *The Virtual Corporation: Structuring and Revitalizing the Corporation of the 21st Century* (New York: Harper Business, 1992); J. Bryne, R. Brandt, and O. Port, "The Virtual Corporation," *Business Week* (8 February 1993): 98–102; Tully, "The Modular Corporation"; R. Keidel, "Rethinking Organizational Design," *Academy of Management Executive* 8 (1994): 12–30; C. Handy, *The Age of Unreason* (Cambridge, Mass.: Harvard Business School Press, 1989); R. Miles, C. Snow, J. Mathews, G. Miles, and H. Coleman, "Organizing in the Knowledge Age: Anticipating the Cellular Form," *Academy of Management Executive* 11 (1997): 7–20.

17. W. Powell, "Neither Market Nor Hierarchy: Network Forms of Organization," in *Research in Organizational Behavior,* vol. 12, eds. B. Staw and L. Cummings (Greenwich, Conn.: JAI Press, 1990): 295–336; M. Lawless and R. Moore, "Interorganizational Systems in Public Service Delivery: A New Application of the Dynamic Network Framework," *Human Relations* 42 (1989): 1167–84; M. Gerstein, "From Machine Bureaucracies to Networked Organizations: An Architectural Journey," in *Organizational Architecture,* eds. D. Nadler, M. Gerstein, R. Shaw, and associates (San Francisco: Jossey-Bass, 1992): 11–38.

18. D. Tapscott, *The Digital Economy* (New York: McGraw-Hill, 1996); Bryne, Brandt, and Port, "Virtual Corporation."

19. Bryne, Brandt, and Port, "Virtual Corporation"; G. Dess, A. Rasheed, K. McLaughlin, and R. Priem, "The New Corporate Architecture," *Academy of Management Executive* 9 (1995): 7–20.

20. J. Galbraith and R. Kazanjian, *Strategy Implementation: Structure, Systems and Process,* 2d ed. (St. Paul: West, 1986): 159–60.

21. This application is adapted from material in M. Lewyn, "MCI: Attacking on All Fronts," *Business Week* (13 June 1994); from T. Peters, *Liberation Management* (New York: Knopf, 1992); and from information provided by Michael Bendon.

22. W. Cascio, "Downsizing: What Do We Know? What Have We Learned?" *Academy of Management Executive* 7 (1993): 95–104.

23. J. Laabs, "Has Downsizing Missed its Mark?" *Workforce* (April 1999): 30–37.

24. J. Morris, W. Cascio, and C. Young, "Downsizing after All These Years: Questions and Answers about Who Did It, How Many Did It, and Who Benefited from It," *Organizational Dynamics* (Winter 1999): 78–87.

25. "Layoffs Continue, Despite the Strong Economy," *HR Focus* (1 September 1999): 5.

26. Laabs, "Has Downsizing Missed Its Mark?"

27. Ibid.

28. Ibid.

29. W. McKinley, C. Sanchez, and A. Schick, "Organizational Downsizing: Constraining, Cloning, Learning," *Academy of Management Executive* 9 (1995): 32–44.

30. G. Hamel and C. Prahalad, *Competing for the Future* (Cambridge, Mass: Harvard Business School Press, 1994).

31. K. Cameron, S. Freeman, and A. Mishra, "Best Practices in White-Collar Downsizing: Managing Contradictions," *Academy of Management Executive* 5 (1991): 57–73; K. Cameron, "Strategies for Successful Organizational Downsizing," *Human Resource Management* 33 (1994): 189–212; R. Marshall and L. Lyles, "Planning for a Restructured, Revitalized Organization," *Sloan Management Review* 35 (1994): 81–91; N. Polend, "Downsizing and Organization Development: An Opportunity Missed, but Not Lost" (unpublished senior project, The Union Institute, 1999).

32. K. Kelly, "Case Digs out from Way Under," *Business Week* (14 August 1995).

33. J. Brockner, "The Effects of Work Layoffs on Survivors: Research, Theory and Practice," in *Research in*

Organizational Behavior, vol. 10, eds. B. M. Staw and L. L. Cummings (Greenwich, Conn.: JAI Press, 1989): 213–55; J. Byrne, "The Pain of Downsizing," *Business Week* (9 May 1994).

34. Marshall and Lyles, "Planning for a Restructured, Revitalized Organization."

35. J. E. Rogdon, "Lack of Communication Burdens Restructurings," *Wall Street Journal* (2 November 1992): B1.

36. Adapted from Marshall and Lyles, "Planning for a Restructured, Revitalized Organization."

37. D. Druckman, J. Singer, and H. Van Cott, eds., *Enhancing Organizational Performance* (Washington, D.C.: National Academy Press, 1997).

38. A. Bennett, "Downsizing Doesn't Necessarily Bring an Upswing in Corporate Profitability," *Wall Street Journal* (6 June 1991): B1; Cascio, "Downsizing."

39. R. Henkoff, "Getting beyond Downsizing," *Fortune* (1 October 1994): 58.

40. R. Cole, "Learning from Learning Theory: Implications for Quality Improvements of Turnover, Use of Contingent Workers, and Job Rotation Policies," *Quality Management Journal* 1 (1993): 1–25; K. Kozlowski, G. Chao, E. Smith, and J. Hedlund, "Organizational Downsizing: Strategies, Interventions, and Research Implications" in *International Review of Industrial and Organizational Psychology* (New York: Wiley, 1993); Druckman, Singer, and Van Cott, eds., *Enhancing Organizational Performance;* B. Luthans and S. Sommer, "The Impact of Downsizing on Workplace Attitudes," *Group and Organization Management* (March 1999): 46–55.

41. W. McKinley, A. G. Schick, J. L. Sun, and A. P. Tang, "The Financial Environment of Layoffs: An Exploratory Study" (working paper, Southern Illinois University at Carbondale, 1994).

42. Cascio, "Downsizing."

43. Morris, Cascio, and Young, "Downsizing."

44. J. Byrne, "There Is an Upside to Downsizing," *Business Week* (9 May 1994).

45. Cameron, Freeman, and Mishra, "Best Practices."

46. Cameron, Freeman, and Mishra, "Best Practices"; Kozlowski et al., "Organizational Downsizing"; J. Davy, A. Kinicki, and C. Schreck, "Developing and Testing a Model of Survivor Responses to Layoffs," *Journal of Vocational Behavior* 38 (1991): 302–17; K. Labich, "How to Fire People and Still Sleep at Night," *Fortune* (10 June 1996): 65–72; D. Feldman and C. Leana, "Better Practices in Managing Layoffs," *Human Resource Management Journal* 33 (1995): 239–60; J. Byrne, "Why Downsizing Looks Different These Days," *Business Week* (10 October 1994).

47. M. Hammer and J. Champy, *Reengineering the Corporation* (New York: HarperCollins, 1993); T. Stewart, "Reengineering: The Hot New Managing Tool," *Fortune* (23 August 1993): 41–48; J. Champy, *Reengineering Management* (New York: HarperCollins, 1994).

48. R. Kaplan and L. Murdock, "Core Process Redesign," *McKinsey Quarterly* 2 (1991): 27–43.

49. Tapscott, *Digital Economy.*

50. J. Moosbruker and R. Loftin, "Business Process Redesign and Organizational Development: Enhancing Success by Removing the Barriers," *Journal of Applied Behavioral Science* (September 1998): 286–97.

51. M. Miller, "Customer Service Drives Reengineering Effort," *Personnel Journal* 73 (1994): 87–93.

52. Kaplan and Murdock, "Core Process Redesign"; R. Manganelli and M. Klein, *The Reengineering Handbook* (New York: AMACOM, 1994).

53. D. P. Allen and R. Nafius, "Dreaming and Doing: Reengineering GTE Telephone Operations," *Planning Review* (June-July 1993): 28–31.

54. J. Katzenbach and D. Smith, "The Rules for Managing Cross-Functional Reengineering Teams," *Planning Review* (March-April 1993): 12–13; A. Nahavandi and E. Aranda, "Restructuring Teams for the Re-Engineered Organization," *Academy of Management Executive* 8 (1994): 58–68.

55. M. O'Guin, *The Complete Guide to Activity Based Costing* (Englewood Cliffs, N.J.: Prentice Hall, 1991); H. Johnson and R. Kaplan, *Relevance Lost: The Rise and Fall of Management Accounting* (Cambridge, Mass.: Harvard Business School Press, 1987).

56. T. P. Pare, "A New Tool for Managing Costs," *Fortune* (14 June 1993): 124–29.

57. J. Martin, "Are You as Good as You Think You Are?" *Fortune* (30 September 1996): 142–52.

58. Hammer and Champy, *Reengineering the Corporation.*

59. Ibid.

60. C. Rohm, "The Principal Insures a Better Future by Reengineering Its Individual Insurance Deparment," *National Productivity Review* 12 (1992): 55–65.

61. R. Riggs, "Employees Re-Engineer Firm," *San Diego Union Tribune* (23 October 1993): C1–C2.

62. J. McCloud, "Changing Customer Demands Serve as Impetus for BPR at Schlage Lock Co.," *Industrial Engineering* 25 (1994): 30–37.

63. Hammer and Champy, *Reengineering the Corporation.*

64. CSC Index, "State of Reengineering Report, 1994," *Economist* (2 July 1994): 6.

65. Champy, *Reengineering Management;* K. Jensen, "The Effects of Reengineering on Injury Frequency" (unpublished Master's thesis, Pepperdine University, 1993);

Druckman, Singer, and Van Cott, eds., *Enhancing Organizational Performance.*

66. G. Hall, J. Rosenthal, and J. Wade, "How to Make Reengineering Really Work," *Harvard Business Review* (November-December 1993): 119–31.

67. J. Dixon, "Business Process Reengineering: Improving in New Strategic Directions," *California Management Review* 36 (1994): 93–108.

15

Employee Involvement

Faced with competitive demands for lower costs, higher performance, and greater flexibility, organizations are increasingly turning to employee involvement (EI) to enhance the participation, commitment, and productivity of their members. This chapter presents OD interventions aimed at moving decision making downward in the organization, closer to where the actual work takes place. This increased employee involvement can lead to quicker, more responsive decisions, continuous performance improvements, and greater employee flexibility, commitment, and satisfaction.

Employee involvement is a broad term that has been variously referred to as "empowerment," "participative management," "work design," "industrial democracy," and "quality of work life." It covers diverse approaches to gaining greater participation in relevant workplace decisions. Organizations, such as General Mills, AT&T, and Intel, have enhanced worker involvement through enriched forms of work; others, such as GTE and Ford, have increased participation by forming employee involvement teams that develop suggestions for improving productivity and quality; Southwest Airlines, Shell Oil, and Nucor Steel have sought greater participation through union–management cooperation on performance and quality-of-work-life issues; and still others, such as Texas Instruments, Solar Turbines, 3M, the IRS, and Motorola, have improved employee involvement by emphasizing participation in quality improvement approaches.

As described in Chapter 1, current EI approaches evolved from earlier quality-of-work-life efforts in Europe, Scandinavia, and the United States. The terms *employee involvement* and *empowerment* gradually have replaced the designation *quality of work life*, particularly in the United States. A current definition of EI includes four elements that can promote meaningful involvement in workplace decisions: power, information, knowledge and skills, and rewards. These components of EI combine to exert powerful effects on productivity and employee well-being.

The following major EI applications are discussed in this chapter: parallel structures, including cooperative union–management projects and quality circles; high-involvement organizations; and total quality management. Two additional EI approaches, work design and reward system interventions, are discussed in Chapters 16 and 17, respectively.

EMPLOYEE INVOLVEMENT: WHAT IS IT?

Employee involvement is the current label used to describe a set of practices and philosophies that started with the quality-of-work-life movement in the late 1950s. The phrase *quality of work life* was used to stress the prevailing poor quality of life at the workplace.[1] As described in Chapter 1, both the term QWL and the meaning attributed to it have undergone considerable change and development. In this section, we provide a working definition of EI, document the growth of EI practices in the United States and abroad, and clarify the important and often misunderstood relationship between EI and productivity.

A Working Definition of Employee Involvement

Employee involvement seeks to increase members' input into decisions that affect organization performance and employee well-being.[2] It can be described in terms of four key elements that promote worker involvement:[3]

1. *Power.* This element of EI includes providing people with enough authority to make work-related decisions covering various issues such as work methods, task assignments, performance outcomes, customer service, and employee selection. The amount of power afforded employees can vary enormously, from simply asking them for input into decisions that managers subsequently make, to managers and workers jointly making decisions, to employees making decisions themselves.

2. *Information.* Timely access to relevant information is vital to making effective decisions. Organizations can promote EI by ensuring that the necessary information flows freely to those with decision authority. This can include data about operating results, business plans, competitive conditions, new technologies and work methods, and ideas for organizational improvement.

3. *Knowledge and skills.* Employee involvement contributes to organizational effectiveness only to the extent that employees have the requisite skills and knowledge to make good decisions. Organizations can facilitate EI by providing training and development programs for improving members' knowledge and skills. Such learning can cover an array of expertise having to do with performing tasks, making decisions, solving problems, and understanding how the business operates.

4. *Rewards.* Because people generally do those things for which they are recognized, rewards can have a powerful effect on getting people involved in the organization. Meaningful opportunities for involvement can provide employees with internal rewards, such as feelings of self-worth and accomplishment. External rewards, such as pay and promotions, can reinforce EI when they are linked directly to performance outcomes that result from participation in decision making. (Reward systems are discussed more fully in Chapter 17.)

Those four elements—power, information, knowledge and skills, and rewards—contribute to EI success by determining how much employee participation in decision making is possible in organizations. The farther that all four elements are moved downward throughout the organization, the greater the employee involvement. Furthermore, because the four elements of EI are interdependent, they must be changed together to obtain positive results. For example, if organization members are given more power and authority to make decisions but do not have the information or knowledge and skill to make good decisions, then the value of involvement is likely to be negligible. Similarly, increasing employees' power, information, and knowledge and skills but not linking rewards to the performance consequences of changes gives members little incentive to improve organizational performance. The EI methods that will be described in this chapter vary in how much involvement is afforded employees. Parallel structures, such as union–management cooperative efforts and quality circles, are limited in the degree that the four elements of EI are moved downward in the organization; high-involvement organizations and total quality management provide far greater opportunities for involvement.

The Diffusion of Employee Involvement Practices

The number of organizations using employee involvement practices is growing in both the United States and Europe. In the most comprehensive, long-term study of EI applications so far, Lawler, Mohrman, and Ledford surveyed the *Fortune* 1000 at four time periods: 1987, 1990, 1993, and 1996.[4] Their data show positive trends in EI use among these firms over that time period, including both a growing number of firms applying EI and a greater percentage of the workforce included in such programs. Despite these positive trends, however, their research reveals that the scope and depth of EI interventions are relatively modest. Data from 1996 show that about one-third of the companies surveyed reported no significant involvement efforts and approximately the same percentage revealed limited attempts at getting employees involved in decision making. Thus, although many large organizations are using EI practices, there is considerable room for their diffusion across organizations and throughout the workforce.

Similarly, EI has prospered outside of the United States. Countries using EI in western Europe include France, Germany, Denmark, Sweden, Norway, Holland, Italy, and, to a lesser extent, Great Britain.[5] Although the tremendous changes currently taking place in countries such as Russia, Czechoslovakia, Hungary, Bulgaria, and the former Republic of Yugoslavia may have dampened EI efforts, several programs are actively underway.[6] Canada, Mexico, India, and Japan also are using EI. Internationally, EI may be considered a set of processes directed at changing the structure of the work situation within a particular cultural environment and under the influence of particular values and philosophies. As a result, in some instances EI has been promoted by unions; in others, by management. In some cases, it has been part of a pragmatic approach to increasing productivity; in other cases, it has been driven by socialist values.[7]

How Employee Involvement Affects Productivity

An assumption underlying much of the EI literature is that such interventions will lead to higher productivity. Although this premise has been based mainly on anecdotal evidence and a good deal of speculation, there is now a growing body of research findings to support that linkage.[8] Studies have found a consistent relationship between EI practices and such productivity measures as financial performance, customer satisfaction, labor hours, and waste rates.

Attempts to explain this positive linkage traditionally have followed the idea that giving people more involvement in work decisions raises their job satisfaction and, in turn, their productivity. There is growing evidence that this satisfaction-causes-productivity premise is too simplistic and sometimes wrong.

A more realistic explanation for how EI interventions can affect productivity is shown in Figure 15.1. EI practices, such as participation in workplace decisions, can improve productivity in at least three ways.[9] First, such interventions can improve communication and coordination among employees and organizational departments, and help integrate the different jobs or departments that contribute to an overall task.

Second, EI interventions can improve employee motivation, particularly when they satisfy important individual needs. Motivation is translated into improved performance when people have the necessary skills and knowledge to perform well and when the technology and work situation allow people to affect productivity.

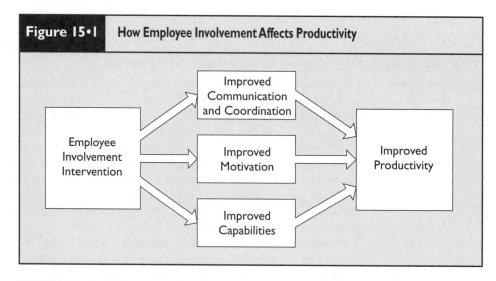

Figure 15·1   How Employee Involvement Affects Productivity

For example, some jobs are so rigidly controlled and specified that individual motivation can have little impact on productivity.

Third, EI practices can improve the capabilities of employees, thus enabling them to perform better. For example, attempts to increase employee participation in decision making generally include skill training in group problem solving and communication.

Figure 15.2 shows the secondary effects of EI. These practices increase employee well-being and satisfaction by providing a better work environment and a more fulfilling job. Improved productivity also can increase satisfaction, particularly when it leads to greater rewards. Increased employee satisfaction, deriving from EI interventions

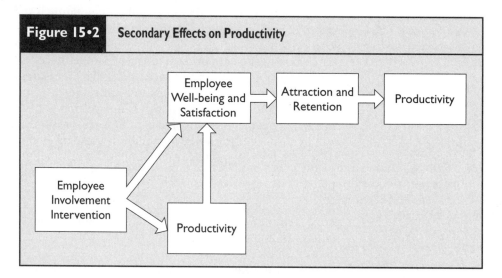

Figure 15·2   Secondary Effects on Productivity

and increased productivity, ultimately can have a still greater impact on productivity by attracting good employees to join and remain with the organization.

In sum, EI interventions are expected to increase productivity by improving communication and coordination, employee motivation, and individual capabilities. They also can influence productivity by means of the secondary effects of increased employee well-being and satisfaction. Although a growing body of research supports these relationships,[10] there is considerable debate over the strength of the association between EI and productivity.[11] Recent data support the conclusion that relatively modest levels of EI produce moderate improvements in performance and satisfaction and that higher levels of EI produce correspondingly higher levels of performance.[12]

EMPLOYEE INVOLVEMENT APPLICATIONS

This section describes three major EI applications that vary in the amount of power, information, knowledge and skills, and rewards that are moved downward through the organization (from least to most involvement): parallel structures, including cooperative union–management projects and quality circles; high-involvement organizations; and total quality management.

Parallel Structures

Parallel structures involve members in resolving ill-defined, complex problems and build adaptability into bureaucratic organizations.[13] Also known as "collateral structures," "dualistic structures," or "shadow structures,"[14] parallel structures operate in conjunction with the formal organization. They provide members with an alternative setting in which to address problems and to propose innovative solutions free from the formal organization structure and culture. For example, members may attend periodic off-site meetings to explore ways to improve quality in their work area or they may be temporarily assigned to a special project or facility to devise new products or solutions to organizational problems. Parallel structures facilitate problem solving and change by providing time and resources for members to think, talk, and act in completely new ways. Consequently, norms and procedures for working in parallel structures are entirely different from those of the formal organization. This section describes the application steps associated with most parallel structures; discusses two specific applications, cooperative union–management projects and quality circles; and reviews the research on their effectiveness.

Application Stages

Parallel structures fall at the lower end of the EI scale. Member participation typically is restricted to making proposals and to offering suggestions for change because subsequent decisions about implementing the proposals are reserved for management. Membership in parallel structures also tends to be limited, primarily to volunteers and to numbers of employees for which there are adequate resources. Management heavily influences the conditions under which parallel structures operate. It controls the amount of authority that members have in making recommendations, the amount of information that is shared with them, the amount of training they receive to increase their knowledge and skills, and the amount of monetary rewards for participation. Because parallel structures offer limited amounts of EI, they are most appropriate for organizations with little or no history of employee participation, top-down management styles, and bureaucratic cultures.

Parallel structures typically are implemented in the following steps:[15]

1. *Define the purpose and scope.* This first step involves defining the purpose for the parallel structure and initial expectations about how it will function. Organizational diagnosis can help clarify which specific problems and issues to address, such as productivity, absenteeism, or service quality. In addition, management training in the use of parallel structures can include discussions about the commitment and resources necessary to implement them; the openness needed to examine organizational practices, operations, and policies; and the willingness to experiment and learn.

2. *Form a steering committee.* Parallel structures typically use a steering committee composed of acknowledged leaders of the various functions and constituencies within the formal organization. This committee performs the following tasks:

   • refining the scope and purpose of the parallel structure
   • developing a vision for the effort
   • guiding the creation and implementation of the structure
   • establishing the linkage mechanisms between the parallel structure and the formal organization
   • creating problem-solving groups and activities
   • ensuring the support of senior management.

   OD practitioners can play an important role in forming the steering committee. First, they can help develop and maintain group norms of learning and innovation. These norms set the tone for problem solving throughout the parallel structure. Second, they can help the committee create a vision statement that refines the structure's purpose and promotes ownership of it. Third, they can help committee members develop and specify objectives and strategies, organizational expectations and required resources, and potential rewards for participation in the parallel structure.

3. *Communicate with organization members.* The effectiveness of a parallel structure depends on a high level of involvement from organization members, and . communicating the purpose, procedures, and rewards of participation can promote that involvement. Moreover, employee participation in developing a structure's vision and purpose can increase ownership and visibly demonstrate the "new way" of working. Continued communication concerning parallel structure activities can ensure member awareness.

4. *Form employee problem-solving groups.* These groups are the primary means of accomplishing the purpose of the parallel learning structure. Their formation involves selecting and training group members, identifying problems for the groups to work on, and providing appropriate facilitation. Selecting group members is important because success often is a function of group membership.[16] Members need to represent the appropriate hierarchical levels, expertise, functions, and constituencies that are relevant to the problems at hand. This allows the parallel structure to identify and communicate with the formal structure. It also provides the necessary resources to solve the problems.

   Once formed, the groups need appropriate training. This may include discussions about the vision of the parallel structure, the specific problems to be addressed, and the way those problems will be solved. As in the steering committee, group norms promoting openness, creativity, and integration need to be established.

Another key resource for parallel structures is facilitation for the problem-solving groups. Although this can be expensive, it can yield important benefits in problem-solving efficiency and quality. Group members are being asked to solve problems by cutting through traditional hierarchical and functional boundaries. Facilitators can pay special attention to processes that require disparate groups to cooperate. They can help members identify and resolve problem-solving issues within and between groups.

5. *Address the problems and issues.* Generally, groups in parallel structures solve problems by using an action research process. They diagnose specific problems, plan appropriate solutions, and implement and evaluate them. Problem solving can be facilitated when the groups and the steering committee relate effectively to each other. This permits the steering committee to direct problem-solving efforts in an appropriate manner, to acquire the necessary resources and support, and to approve action plans. It also helps ensure that the groups' solutions are linked appropriately to the formal organization. In this manner, early attempts at change will have a better chance of succeeding.

6. *Implement and evaluate the changes.* This step involves implementing appropriate organizational changes and assessing the results. Change proposals need the support of the steering committee and the formal authority structure. As changes are implemented, the organization needs information about their effects. This lets members know how successful the changes have been and if they need to be modified. In addition, feedback on changes helps the organization learn to adapt and innovate.

Cooperative Union–Management Projects

Cooperative union–management projects are one of the oldest EI applications of parallel structures. They are associated with the original QWL movement and its focus on workplace change, although more recent approaches have broadened that focus to include productivity improvement. Cooperative union–management projects are relatively new to OD in the United States, but such dual involvement has a long history in other countries, particularly the Scandinavian countries. These interventions tend to have the following structural characteristics:[17]

- *Steering committee.* This top-level labor–management committee serves as the basic center for planning. It is created during the project start-up phase and comprises key representatives from management, such as a president or chief operating officer, and each of the unions and employee groups involved in the project, such as local union presidents. The steering committee's mandate is to begin activities directed at improving both the quality of working life and the effectiveness of the organization. Members are encouraged to be open about the need for improvements in productivity. Unionists are told that because projects are jointly controlled efforts, they need not fear an organization's productivity motives. Indeed, many unions distrust a management philosophy that does not express concern for higher productivity or the quality of its product or service.

- *Multiple-level committees.* Because the steering committee may not be able to oversee all aspects of a project, it often is necessary to establish more than one labor–management committee at a number of selected levels in the organization to reflect the differing interests and knowledge. For example, the steering committee can be amplified and assisted by working committees at the plant, department, and shop-floor levels. These lower-level committees deal with day-to-day project activities.

- *Ad hoc committees.* In many instances, labor–management committees initiate particular projects that involve the workers and managers in a specific part of the organization. At the same time, employees themselves frequently initiate action toward a particular goal. In such cases, an ad hoc committee is established to bring about change. Such committees are charged with a specific task and have a limited lifetime.

- *External consultants.* External change agents act as third-party facilitators, offering guidance and assistance to the labor–management committees and problem-solving and teamwork training for all participants. In most projects, the steering committee selects the consultants.[18]

- *External researchers.* In some projects, researchers are brought in to assess the overall results of the intervention. In those cases, separate roles for the change agents and the evaluation researchers are created. It is assumed that keeping these functions separate enables consultants to be concerned with client needs and researchers to do a more objective assessment of the intervention.[19]

Excellent descriptions of cooperative union–management projects are available in the literature, featuring longitudinal discussions of problems, successes, and partial failures. The projects include a large metropolitan hospital,[20] a large international company called the "National Processing Case,"[21] and the Bolivar plant of Harman International Industries.[22] Union–management cooperative projects have been carried out in most industrial and public sectors in the United States. Both managers and unionists realize that their fates are positively correlated and that both parties must be jointly involved in enhancing the quality of work life and productivity.[23] Almost every major union and corporation has become involved in these efforts, including UAW, Communications Workers of America, Ford, General Motors, and AT&T.[24]

Application 15.1 presents an example of a cooperative union–management program at GTE of California.[25]

Quality Circles

Quality circles, or "employee involvement teams" as they are often called in the United States, were at one time the most popular parallel structure approach to EI. Originally developed in Japan in the mid-1950s, quality circles consist of small groups of employees who meet voluntarily to identify and solve productivity problems. The group method of problem solving and the participative management philosophy associated with it are natural outgrowths of Japanese managerial practices. The Japanese emphasize decentralized decision making and use the small group as the organization unit to promote collective decision making and responsibility.[26] Various estimates once put the total circle membership at as many as ten million Japanese workers.[27]

Quality circles were introduced in the United States in the mid-1970s. Their growth through the early 1980s was nothing short of astounding, with some four thousand companies adopting some version of the circles approach. The popularity of quality circles can be attributed in part to the widespread drive to emulate Japanese management practices and to achieve the quality improvements and cost savings associated with those methods. What may be overlooked, however, is the Japanese philosophy of decentralized, collective decision making, which supports and nurtures the circles approach. Thus, quality circles may be more difficult to

APPLICATION 15•1   Union–Management Cooperation at GTE of California

GTE of California (GTEC) and the Communications Workers of America embarked on a cooperative union–management project during the fall of 1984. This OD effort was in response to the court-ordered breakup of AT&T, which forced firms in the telecommunications industry to rethink the way that they conducted business. Over time, the deregulation of the industry would remove the protective shield of guaranteed returns on investment, monopoly territories, and "cradle-to-grave" employment that had characterized operations.

Under the new conditions, GTEC management and union leadership believed strongly that the company's usual way of operating in the regulatory environment would need to change. The traditional approach to managing the business was characterized by centralized decision making and work planning, lackadaisical service orientation, and little cross-functional teamwork. The advent of deregulation was coupled with tremendous technological changes in information processing and service delivery and a broadening of the belief that workers should have more say in decisions that affect them. The old way of managing produced low morale and mediocre service in this changing environment. Consequently, management and union officials felt the need for improved adaptability and productivity and a more customer-oriented workforce.

For some time, union leadership had been researching worker participation and union–management cooperation at its national office in Washington, D.C. This research was limited, however, because no one had implemented such interventions during a period of rapid deregulation. At the same time, GTEC senior management had been meeting with other telephone companies to discuss how to meet the challenges posed by deregulation, technological change, and increased worker sophistication. These discussions consistently pointed out that effective organizations in deregulated environments were more decentralized in their decision making. But, given decades of regulatory tradition, the means to accomplish such an organizational change were not clear.

Working with OD consultants from the University of Southern California's Center for Effective Organizations, senior managers and union leaders began discussing how to increase worker participation and decentralize decision making without treading on traditional collective bargaining issues. These discussions resulted in a cooperative union–management partnership called Employee Involvement. The purpose of the EI process was to improve employees' quality of working life and productivity. The group of senior managers and union officials became the steering committee for the project and developed a vision of the EI process and its objectives.

The steering committee established a parallel structure to guide implementation of the EI process with the twenty-six thousand employees at GTEC. It comprised three area coordinating committees responsible for implementing the EI process in their respective geographic regions. Each coordinating committee created support committees for the functional areas in its region. The support committees, in turn, established EI teams that would identify and solve work-related problems in the different units of the company. Each committee and team was staffed with both union and management personnel as appropriate.

As part of the early implementation activities, all organization members attended a two-hour orientation meeting that described the goals, structure, and implementation of the EI process. This orientation was conducted by both GTEC management and local union presidents. In addition, a three-day union–management training program was conducted for all supervisors and union officials (local presidents and stewards). During the first two days of training, union leaders and GTEC managers were trained separately in their respective roles and responsibilities in the EI process. On the third day, the managers and union officials were brought together to discuss how the implementation of EI would proceed in their particular departments. Members of the support committees and employee involvement teams attended a five-day training program focusing on meeting-management skills, problem-solving techniques, and group dynamics. They were also provided with internal facilitators if needed.

Over the next several months, the EI teams focused on quality-of-work-life issues, such as the provision of bottled drinking water, rather than on productivity-related changes. Responsible committees were concerned about this limited focus and modified the process to align it more closely with EI's productivity objectives. For example, the problem-solving training was changed to emphasize performance issues. In addition, the composition and responsibilities of the different committees were revised to increase senior management and union leadership involvement and accountability. At the organizational level, a new incentive compensation system was initiated. This system rewarded cross-functional teamwork and generated many ideas for employee involvement. Finally, facilitators were assigned permanently to functional areas to focus on operating problems.

The EI process produced many successes. One team, established in early 1985, worked for more than two years to simplify the way field employees reported their time at work. These efforts produced savings of more than $3 million by increasing the amount of productive time that employees spent in the field and by consolidating several offices that had been used to collect, collate, and report work-time information. Between 1987 and 1988, an evaluation of the EI process concluded that the program had produced a net savings (after the costs of training and dedicated personnel) of more than $1 million. In 1991, GTEC surpassed its competition in measures of customer satisfaction for large- and medium-sized busi-

nesses to become the benchmark for others. In addition, several cost measures also decreased significantly. The EI program survived through two union contract negotiations and massive corporate changes that reduced the size of the workforce by consolidating work functions and business units and standardizing systems and equipment. ■

implement in the more autocratic, individualistic situations that characterize many American companies.[28]

Although quality circles are implemented in different ways, a typical program is illustrated in Figure 15.3. Circle programs generally are implemented with a parallel structure consisting of several circles, each having three to fifteen members. Membership is voluntary, and members of a circle share a common job or work area. Circles meet once each week for about one hour on company time. Several consulting companies have developed training packages as part of standardized programs for implementing quality circles. Members are trained in different problem identification and analysis techniques and they apply their training to identify,

| Figure 15•3 | Quality Circles Program Structure |

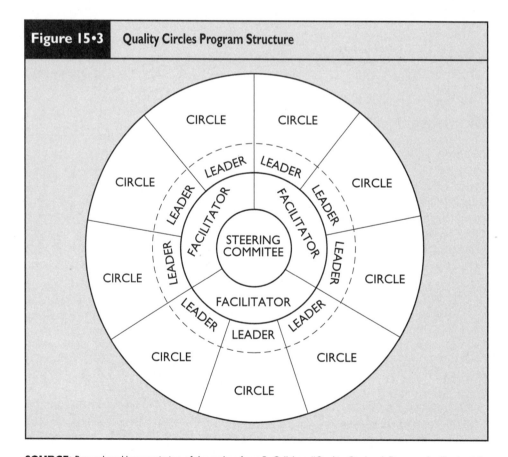

SOURCE: Reproduced by permission of the author from R. Callahan, "Quality Circles: A Program for Productivity Improvement Through Human Resource Development" (unpublished paper, Albers School of Business, Seattle University, 1982): p. 16.

analyze, and recommend solutions to work-related problems. When possible, they implement solutions that affect only their work area and do not require higher management approval.

Each circle has a leader, who is typically the supervisor of the work area represented by circle membership. The leader trains circle members and guides the weekly meetings, setting the agenda and facilitating the problem-solving process.

Facilitators can be a key part of a quality circles program. They coordinate the activities of several circles and may attend the meetings, especially during the early development stages. Facilitators train circle leaders and help them start the circles. They also help circles obtain needed inputs from support groups and keep upper management apprised of progress. Because facilitators are the most active promoters of the program, their role may be full time.

A steering committee is the central coordinator of the quality circles program. Generally, it is composed of the facilitators and representatives of the major functional departments in the organization. The steering committee determines the policies and procedures of the program and the issues that fall outside of circle attention, such as wages, fringe benefits, and other topics normally covered in union contracts. The committee also coordinates training programs and guides program expansion. Large quality circles programs might have several steering committees operating at different levels.

Application 15.2 presents a classic example of a quality circles program in the warehouse department of the H•E•B Grocery Company.[29] The study reports mixed results but identifies the organizational conditions needed to implement effective quality circles.

Results of Parallel Structure Approaches

A large body of literature exists on the implementation and impact of parallel structure approaches to EI. The business and popular press are full of glowing reports about the benefit of union–management cooperative projects, quality circles, and other parallel structure interventions. Parallel structures create a source of involvement beyond that found in most bureaucratic organizations. For many people, especially lower-level employees, this opportunity to influence the formal organization leads to increased work satisfaction and task effectiveness.[30] Among the reported results are reductions in costs, improvements in the quality and quantity of production, and increased member skill development, motivation, organizational commitment, and satisfaction.[31] These results suggest that employee involvement can affect both the organization, through group ideas that are implemented, and the individual, through membership in a problem-solving group.

There are also many case studies of parallel structures. For example, a study at General Motors' central foundry division showed that the parallel organization saved sixty thousand labor-hours per year in one plant, with similar savings across the entire division.[32] Other publicized successes using cooperative union–management projects are the Harman plant in Bolivar and the Rockwell International plant in Battle Creek, Michigan (a joint UAW–GM effort); the Rushton Mines in Pennsylvania; and more recently, the Magma Copper Company (now BHP Copper) in Arizona. These types of studies, however, often raise more questions than they answer about the ability of EI interventions to affect organizational outcomes, and they often challenge the validity of the reported successes.[33]

Large-sample studies of parallel structures typically report mixed results. For example, in a study of five plant-level union–management projects, only two of the five plants reported improvements in productivity and union–management

APPLICATION 15•2   Quality Circles at H•E•B Grocery Company

A quality circles program was implemented as a pilot project at a large warehouse of the H•E•B Grocery Company in Texas. Department management of this eighty-person, two-shift warehousing operation volunteered to adopt the program, which was part of a larger corporate strategy to increase employee involvement. This choice emerged from a survey in which employees indicated a desire to be better informed about department events and to have greater involvement in problem solving. All but four workers volunteered to be part of the pilot circles.

The program consisted of four circles, each composed of ten people representing a cross section of workers familiar with the warehousing operation. The circles met for two hours at two-week intervals. Because of the large number of workers who wished to participate in the program, management held periodic rotations, replacing some circle members with new volunteers. One rotation occurred after five months: twelve workers dropped out, several more left the department, and twenty-nine employees joined the circles.

Each circle had a worker-leader trained in communication techniques, group process, and problem-solving skills. The leaders also formed a leader circle that met regularly to exchange ideas, concerns, and information and to coordinate the four circles. Supervisors were trained and served as resources to the circles. Similarly, members of the corporate human resources department served as facilitators. They helped the leaders train circle members, attended the meetings, and provided process facilitation. The department head and several top managers formed the steering committee to guide the project. Circle suggestions were reported to department management, which worked closely with employees to implement the suggestions.

Researchers conducted a thorough evaluation of the quality circles program. They compared the warehouse department with a similar control group that had not participated in the program. Comparison measures included survey data at three points in time: five months before the program, three months after its beginning, and ten months after the program started. Also included were unobtrusive measures of productivity, absenteeism, and accidents collected at four-week intervals beginning one year before the program. The researchers also conducted formal, open-ended interviews with selected warehouse managers and circle members and observed the circles in action once a month. All documentation that emerged from the circles was examined.

In contrast to the control group, the warehouse department showed slightly more positive trends in productivity during the course of the circles program. Specifically, the quantity of production increased slightly, and small decreases

were shown in costs, absenteeism, labor expense, overtime, and accidents. The survey data showed that the attitudes of warehouse employees changed little during the program but, unexpectedly, the attitudes of members of the control group suffered in regard to feeling informed, being involved in decision making, and receiving feedback from supervisors. The researchers attributed this deterioration in morale to the disruption caused by a rapid expansion in the workload of the comparison unit. Because the expansion affected both the warehouse and the control group, the researchers concluded that the circles program might have buffered warehouse employees during this disruption, accounting for the stability of attitudes during the program.

Examination of the interview and observational data revealed a more negative assessment of the circles program. Its initial months were marked by a flurry of activity and improvement suggestions. Among the outcomes were efforts to improve equipment maintenance procedures, reduce warehouse congestion, and prevent damage. After several months, attendance at the meetings began to wane, and the circle members found it increasingly difficult to identify significant issues within their sphere of expertise and influence. Supervisors also started to admit that the circles were draining time and energy from the department.

A second flurry of activity and enthusiasm for the program took place soon after the voluntary rotation of members into and out of the program. With time, this energy also subsided as members became frustrated with the difficulty of systematic problem solving, the slowness of any implementation of ideas, and the failure of the program to affect their jobs. As the workload of the warehouse increased, management allowed the circles to become inactive by neglecting the project.

Interview data showed that participants in the program felt they had accomplished something worthwhile, had learned a lot, and had enjoyed the circles. Nonparticipants or those who dropped out of the circles felt that the program never really dealt with significant issues. It is interesting that those who didn't participate or dropped out showed a marked worsening of attitudes during the program, compared with active participants. This unexpected downturn was attributed to disillusionment with the program and to feelings that some participants were wasting time. Supervisors felt that the payback was not worth the time spent in the meetings. The human resources personnel judged the program a successful step toward employee involvement in H•E•B.

Observations and interviews suggested several reasons why the program gradually died. The level of group functioning did not noticeably improve during the program, and there was no indication that systematic problem-solving techniques were followed. Implementation of several ideas was unduly delayed in bureaucratic channels, resulting in member perceptions of low management commitment to the program. Although many circle members reported satisfaction with the program, little indication was evident that their enthusiasm translated into greater motivation on the job. Indeed, many of the most active participants became disenchanted with their jobs and sought ways to enter the supervisory ranks. Some members also felt that they were being inadequately compensated for generating money-saving ideas for the company.

The researchers concluded that, as a pilot project, the quality circles program was successful. The company learned about the level of commitment and energy required to sustain such programs and continued to experiment with other approaches to employee involvement, holding more realistic expectations. The rigorous and contradictory nature of the assessment measures strongly suggests that research on quality circles must go beyond glowing testimonials and superficial reports of worker enthusiasm to include whether such programs effect valued individual and organizational outcomes. ■

relationships. In three of the five plants, relations among managers improved and grievance levels decreased.[34] Another study covering twenty-five manufacturing plants showed that involvement in joint union–management programs had no impact on economic performance.[35] Similarly, in a review of more than one hundred citations, Ledford, Lawler, and Mohrman concluded that the existing research showed no clear positive or negative trend in the productivity effects of quality circles.[36] Although the evidence of attitudinal effects was more extensive than that of productivity effects, the studies reviewed still showed mixed results for attitudinal changes. For example, in one study using a rigorous research design, participation in a quality circle was positively related to measures of personal competence and interpersonal trust but was not related to an increased sense of participation.[37] On the other hand, more recent data suggest stronger relationships between employee participation and direct performance outcomes, such as productivity, customer satisfaction, quality, and speed; profitability; and employee satisfaction.[38]

Probably the most extensive assessment of union–management cooperative projects was conducted by researchers from the University of Michigan's Institute for Social Research (ISR).[39] Over a period of at least three years, the ISR studied eight major projects implemented during the 1970s. Although the projects showed some improvements in employee attitudes, the productivity outcomes were unimpressive. Only two projects showed improvements in productivity—an auto parts factory where employee performance increased sharply after instituting a productivity-related reward system, and a coal mine where productivity improved slightly after implementing job training and autonomous work groups. The other projects either showed no productivity increases or failed to provide productivity data that could be analyzed. Interesting to note, all four projects from the public sector had no measures of productivity—the engineering department of a federal utility company, a hospital, a municipal transit system, and a municipal government.

The ISR researchers explained the meager productivity results in terms of the projects' mistakes. All of the projects were pioneering efforts and hardly could be expected to avoid the mistakes. More recent union–management cooperative projects seem to be doing better: "The newer projects tend to be much better linked to the management and union hierarchies, receive better assistance from a widening circle of experienced consultants, have more realistic goals, and use more sharply focused organizational change strategies."[40] A 1994 study by the Commission on the Future of Worker–Management Relations supported that conclusion. It found that systematically implemented programs often improve productivity and almost always increase investment in employee skills and knowledge.[41]

In an attempt to discover which parallel structure intervention features contribute most to program success, two researchers conducted a large-scale study of quality circles in nine organizational units of a large, multidivisional firm.[42] Their findings suggest that parallel structures are more successful to the extent that they include or have access to the necessary skills and knowledge to address problems systematically; formalize meetings, record keeping, and communication channels; integrate themselves both horizontally and vertically with the rest of the company; and become a regular part of the formal organization, rather than a special or extraparallel set of activities. A recent study of parallel structures composed of employee- involvement teams suggests that unless these structures are carefully integrated with the formal organization, they are unlikely to have much impact and will be abandoned.[43]

These findings are consistent with a number of other factors contributing to program success.[44] First, parallel structures are highly dependent on group members having sufficient group process, problem-solving, and presentation skills and adequate task-relevant information.[45] Second, lower-level managers need to support the program and have participatory leadership styles if workers are to gain the necessary freedom to engage in problem solving. Third, not all people can be expected to react favorably to participation: some workers have low social needs and prefer to work alone, rather than in groups; some do not want greater participation at work. Fourth, top-management support is necessary both to start the program and to implement many of the subsequent solutions. Unless management is willing to authorize necessary resources to make suggested improvements, circle members are likely to become disenchanted, seeing the program more as window dressing than as meaningful participation.

Finally, court rulings in the early 1990s challenged the legality of some EI approaches under provisions of the National Labor Relations Act (NLRA). This law, passed by Congress in 1935, gives employees the right to form labor unions and decrees that employers must bargain in good faith with representatives of those organizations. In protecting employees' rights to collective bargaining, the NLRA precludes certain employer unfair labor practices, one of which is aimed at employer domination of a labor organization. Under the law, a committee or team of workers that meets to address issues related to wages, hours, or conditions of work can be considered a "labor organization." If management creates the team, provides it with resources, or influences it in any way, then management may be found to dominate this so-called labor organization. In two legal cases involving Electromation, Inc., and DuPont, the court ruled that, in setting up employee teams or committees to address such issues as communication, cost cutting, and safety, the companies had created labor organizations and had dominated them unfairly. Although the NLRA does not outlaw EI teams per se, such interventions may be legally questionable in situations where teams address issues traditionally reserved for bargaining and where management influences or controls the teams. In response to these rulings, Congress passed legislation in 1996 to amend the National Labor Relations Act. The Teamwork for Employees and Management Act of 1995 preserves legitimate employee involvement programs without infringing on the rights of employees to bargain collectively.

High-Involvement Organizations

Over the past several years, an increasing number of employee involvement projects have been aimed at creating high-involvement organizations (HIOs). These interventions create organizational conditions that support high levels of employee participation. What makes HIOs unique is the comprehensive nature of their design process. Unlike parallel structures that do not alter the formal organization, in HIOs almost all organization features are designed jointly by management and workers to promote high levels of involvement and performance, including structure, work design, information and control systems, physical layout, personnel policies, and reward systems.

Features of High-Involvement Organizations

High-involvement organizations are designed with features congruent with one another. For example, in HIOs employees have considerable influence over decisions. To support such a decentralized philosophy, members receive extensive training in problem-solving techniques, plant operation, and organizational policies. In addition, both operational and issue-oriented information is shared widely and is obtained easily by employees. Finally, rewards are tied closely to unit performance, as well as to knowledge and skill levels. These disparate aspects of the organization are mutually reinforcing and form a coherent pattern that contributes to employee involvement. Table 15.1 presents a list of compatible design

Table 15•1	Design Features for a Participative System

☐ ORGANIZATIONAL STRUCTURE

1. Flat
2. Lean
3. Minienterprise-oriented
4. Team-based
5. Participative council or structure

☐ JOB DESIGN

1. Individually enriched
2. Self-managing teams

☐ INFORMATION SYSTEM

1. Open
2. Inclusive
3. Tied to jobs
4. Decentralized; team-based
5. Participatively set goals and standards

☐ CAREER SYSTEM

1. Tracks and counseling available
2. Open job posting

☐ SELECTION

1. Realistic job preview
2. Team-based
3. Potential and process-skill oriented

☐ TRAINING

1. Heavy commitment
2. Peer training
3. Economic education
4. Interpersonal skills

☐ REWARD SYSTEM

1. Open
2. Skill-based
3. Gain sharing or ownership
4. Flexible benefits
5. All salaried workforce
6. Egalitarian perquisites

☐ PERSONNEL POLICIES

1. Stability of employment
2. Participatively established through representative group

☐ PHYSICAL LAYOUT

1. Around organizational structure
2. Egalitarian
3. Safe and pleasant

SOURCE: Reproduced by permission of the publisher from Edward E. Lawler III, "Increasing Worker Involvement to Enhance Organizational Effectiveness: Design Features for a Participation System," in *Change in Organizations*, eds. P. S. Goodman and associates (San Francisco: Jossey-Bass, 1982): 298–99.

elements characterizing HIOs,[46] and most such organizations include several if not all of the following features:

- *Flat, lean organization structures* contribute to involvement by pushing the scheduling, planning, and controlling functions typically performed by management and staff groups toward the shop floor. Similarly, minienterprise, team-based structures that are oriented to a common purpose or outcome help focus employee participation on a shared objective. Participative structures, such as work councils and union–management committees, create conditions in which workers can influence the direction and policies of the organization.

- *Job designs* that provide employees with high levels of discretion, task variety, and meaningful feedback can enhance involvement. They enable workers to influence day-to-day workplace decisions and to receive intrinsic satisfaction by performing work under enriched conditions. Self-managed teams encourage employee responsibility by providing cross-training and job rotation, which give people a chance to learn about the different functions contributing to organizational performance.

- *Open information systems* that are tied to jobs or work teams provide the necessary information for employees to participate meaningfully in decision making. Goals and standards of performance that are set participatively can provide employees with a sense of commitment and motivation for achieving those objectives.

- *Career systems* that provide different tracks for advancement and counseling to help people choose appropriate paths can help employees plan and prepare for long-term development in the organization. Open job posting, for example, makes employees aware of jobs that can further their development.

- *Selection* of employees for high-involvement organizations can be improved through a realistic job preview providing information about what it will be like to work in such situations. Team member involvement in a selection process oriented to potential and process skills of recruits can facilitate a participative climate.

- *Training* employees for the necessary knowledge and skills to participate effectively in decision making is a heavy commitment in HIOs. This effort includes education on the economic side of the enterprise, as well as interpersonal skill development. Peer training is emphasized as a valuable adjunct to formal, expert training.

- *Reward systems* can contribute to employee involvement when information about them is open and the rewards are based on acquiring new skills, as well as sharing gains from improved performance. Similarly, participation is enhanced when people can choose among different fringe benefits and when reward distinctions among people from different hierarchical levels are minimized.

- *Personnel policies* that are participatively set and encourage stability of employment provide employees with a strong sense of commitment to the organization. People feel that the policies are reasonable and that the firm is committed to their long-term development.

- *Physical layouts* of organizations also can enhance employee involvement. Physical designs that support team structures and reduce status differences among employees can reinforce the egalitarian climate needed for employee participation. Safe and pleasant working conditions provide a physical environment conducive to participation.

These HIO design features are mutually reinforcing. "They all send a message to people in the organization that says they are important, respected, valued, capable of growing, and trusted and that their understanding of and involvement in the total organization is desirable and expected."[47] Moreover, these design components tend to motivate and focus organizational behavior in a strategic direction, and thus can lead to superior effectiveness and competitive advantage, particularly in contrast to more traditionally designed organizations.[48]

Application Factors

At present, there is no universally accepted approach to implementing the high-involvement features described here. The actual implementation process often is specific to the situation, and little systematic research has been devoted to understanding the change process itself.[49] Nevertheless, at least two distinct factors seem to characterize how HIOs are implemented. First, implementation generally is guided by an explicit statement of values that members want the new organization to support. Typically, such values as teamwork, equity, quality, and empowerment guide the choice of specific design features. Values that are strongly held and widely shared by organization members can provide the energy, commitment, and direction needed to create high-involvement organizations. A second feature of the implementation process is its participative nature. Managers and employees take active roles in choosing and implementing the design features. They may be helped by OD practitioners, but the locus of control for the change process resides clearly within the organization. This participative change process is congruent with the high-involvement design being created. In essence, high-involvement design processes promote high-involvement organizations.

Results of High-Involvement Organizations

A survey of ninety-eight HIOs showed that about 75 percent of them perceived their performance, relative to competitors, as better than average on quality of work life, customer service, productivity, quality, and grievance rates.[50] Voluntary turnover was two percent, substantially below the national average of 13.2 percent; return on investment was almost four times greater than industry averages; and return on sales was more than five times greater. Another study of the financial performance of U.S. companies from 1972 to 1992 revealed that the five top-performing firms—Plenum Publishing, Circuit City, Tyson Foods, Wal-Mart, and Southwest Airlines—all relied heavily on EI practices for competitive advantage rather than on those factors typically associated with financial success, such as market leadership, profitable industries, unique technology, and strong barriers to entry.[51]

Such results cannot be expected in all situations. The following situational contingencies seem to favor high-involvement organizations: interdependent technologies, small organization size, new plant startups, and conditions under which quality is an important determinant of operating effectiveness.

Application 15.3 presents an example of how Chrysler applied high-involvement principles to its Neon automobile.[52] The Neon drew critical acclaim for its short design time and was introduced in Japan to compete with Toyota's and Honda's popular subcompacts.

APPLICATION 15•3 Chrysler Corporation Moves Toward High Involvement

In 1989, Chrysler Corporation decided to build the new Neon subcompact at its Belvidere, Illinois, plant and discontinue the Horizon Omni and Sundance Shadow. Although important differences exist, Neon was to be to Chrysler what the Saturn was to General Motors, a totally new American car with the quality and price that would rival similar Japanese models. It also represented Chrysler's first strong implementation of high-involvement principles; the cornerstone concept to the design, engineering, and production of the Neon was worker participation. The major impetus behind the project was top management's belief that high-involvement concepts would provide the kind of well-trained, flexible workforce needed to produce high-quality cars efficiently at low cost. In addition, Chrysler's 1.35-defects-per-car quality rating was well above industry leader Toyota, which reported only .74 defects per car. The high-involvement transformation was expected to make significant improvements in Chrysler quality.

By 1992, seven permanent "process teams," each with approximately thirty-five hourly workers and managers, were established from the Belvidere plant. The teams went to Chrysler's Technology Center in Auburn Hills, Michigan, to assist in the design of the car, its parts, the production process, and the production tools. This involved working with design and process engineers on prototypes, engines, and assembly. Almost half of the plant's workers went to the Technology Center during the design phase.

This design process was a significant deviation from the traditional method. Under the old way, engineering design was completely separated from manufacturing and production. Each new car was elegantly conceived and then handed over to manufacturing to produce. More often than not, the design was not producible. If manufacturing had a problem, the engineering group might consider alterations in the design if there was sufficient time before production was scheduled. Otherwise, it was manufacturing's problem.

But under Chrysler's "platform" approach, designers, assembly-line workers, fabricators, suppliers, and managers all came together in the same room. Not surprisingly, there was a considerable amount of resistance. The engineers' status was threatened by hourly workers telling a professional what couldn't be done. Similarly, the hourly worker felt uncomfortable because the engineers rarely listened to, let alone implemented, any suggestions from the plant. Several meetings were required to build the trust necessary for complete collaboration.

As a result of the early cooperation between production and engineering, the production ramp-up process went more smoothly. In one case, workers showed the engineers how a particular part could not be attached because the bumper assembly blocked the air gun; the engineers redesigned the bumper. Together, the engineers and the assembly workers designed the Neon in just thirty-one months, five months ahead of schedule, and tying Honda for the fastest vehicle development time.

The design and development process was supported by a high-involvement communications and suggestion program, more egalitarian structures and processes, and extensive training for the Belvidere workers. For example, worker suggestions pass through an Individual Quality Participation process. Under a prior, neglected system, suggestions struggled through a slow and bureaucratic structure, and employees rarely were given credit when their ideas were implemented. Under the new system, each suggestion goes to a manager who has one day to get it to someone who can act on it. The second person has two days to respond. By day four, the worker who made the suggestion is given feedback on the status of the idea. Millions of dollars have been saved by these suggested changes that ranged from small process improvements, like how to reduce the number of times a worker needs to replenish the bolts from inventory, to larger ones, like changing from cardboard shipping containers to reusable plastic ones.

Egalitarian structure and process changes were evident as well, although they were not radical departures from the old governance principles. Within Chrysler, the Neon organization followed a traditional, but considerably flatter, functional structure. Belvidere's organization structure was relatively flat, with only three levels separating the plant manager from the workers. Supervisors coordinated interactions with other workers and across different shifts. They treated workers more as colleagues than as subordinates; they involved them in decision making and helped them develop appropriate skills. Workers were empowered and customer-focused, and they used principles of total quality management. Under the United Auto Workers' contract, the Belvidere plant workers kept their narrowly defined jobs, although production workers in the stamping plant had only one classification and performed fifteen different jobs. However, in the rest of the plant, workers were given much more ability to rotate to different positions, and there was a strong attempt to fit the employee to the work that best suited his or her talents and personality.

Other processes also supported worker involvement in ongoing plant operations. For example, everyone at the Belvidere plant punches a time clock, even the plant manager, and all of Neon's thirty-two hundred workers share in the company's profits. In an important symbolic change, the plant manager spends a large amount of time on the factory floor interacting with workers. Under the old plant regime, workers were told what to do and to keep their mouths shut. Now, says one twenty-eight-year veteran, there's a "little bit of listen. I ain't saying it's 100 percent yet. I'd be lying if I said it was. But it's a lot better than it used to be." What makes the symbolism work is a direct and open climate. People talk openly to the plant manager and to each other about the current defects that have been found. More important, the conversation often centers on how the customer will never see the defect because it was found and fixed, and how processes were implemented to ensure that it will not occur again.

One of the biggest enablers of worker involvement in the design and production effort was worker education. Every worker, hourly and salaried, attended a variety of training sessions. Early orientation sessions, for example, featured descriptions of the new car and introduced the new emphasis on quality. Videos of the plant manager and local union president talking about the Neon project were followed by pre-

sentations on quality and exercises to practice with the new tools. More specialized training was also offered. Eight coordinators from the plant worked with the production personnel and engineers to design and deliver the focused training modules. All in all, more than 948,000 labor-hours of training were designed and delivered by factory workers.

The results from the new design and production process were impressive. Annual grievances declined from about three thousand before worker involvement to just fifty-one in 1993. The car was a critical success before it was commercially available; it was named 1994 Car of the Year by *Automobile* magazine. The first Neon rolled off the assembly line on November 10, 1993, but was known as the 1995 Neon because it met 1995 federal safety and emission standards. Finally, consultants and industry analysts familiar with the Belvidere plant were impressed by the differences in employee attitudes and the participative climate. ∎

Total Quality Management

Total quality management (TQM) is the most recent and, along with high-involvement organizations, the most comprehensive approach to employee involvement. Also known as "continuous process improvement" and "continuous quality," TQM grew out of a manufacturing emphasis on quality control and represents a long-term effort to orient all of an organization's activities around the concept of quality.[53] Quality is achieved when organizational processes reliably produce products and services that meet or exceed customer expectations. Although it is possible to implement TQM without employee involvement, member participation in the change process increases the likelihood that it will become part of the organization's culture. Quality improvement processes were popular in the 1990s, and many organizations, including Morton Salt, Weyerhaeuser, Xerox, Boeing's Airlift and Tanker Program, Motorola, and Analog Devices, incorporated TQM interventions. Today, continuous quality improvement is essential for global competitiveness.

Like high-involvement designs, TQM increases workers' knowledge and skills through extensive training, provides relevant information to employees, pushes decision-making power downward in the organization, and ties rewards to performance. When implemented successfully, TQM also is aligned closely with a firm's overall business strategy and attempts to change the entire organization toward continuous quality improvement.[54]

The principles underlying TQM can be understood by examining the careers of W. Edwards Deming and Joseph M. Juran, the fathers of the modern quality movement. They initially introduced TQM to U.S. companies during World War II, but in an odd twist of fate following the war, they found their ideas taking hold more in Japan than in the United States.[55] Based on the pioneering work of Walter A. Shewhart of Bell Laboratories, Deming applied statistical techniques to improve product quality at defense plants. When the war ended, U.S. businesses turned to mass-production techniques and emphasized quantity over quality to satisfy postwar demand. Deming was known for his statistical and sampling expertise, and General

Douglas MacArthur asked him to conduct a census of the Japanese population. During his work in Japan, Deming began discussions with Japanese managers about rebuilding their manufacturing base. He advocated a disciplined approach of "plan–do–check–adjust" to identify and improve manufacturing processes that affected product quality. For example, he suggested that ensuring the quality of inputs was a better way of minimizing deviations in an operating process than inspecting finished goods. With such an approach, the Japanese could produce world-class–quality products and restore their country economically. Deming's ideas eventually were codified into the "Fourteen Points" and the "Seven Deadly Sins" of quality summarized in Table 15.2. In honor of the ideas that helped rejuvenate the Japanese economy, the Union of Japanese Scientists and Engineers (JUSE) created the Deming Award to distinguish annually the best in quality manufacturing.

At about the same time, Juran's publication of the *Quality Control Handbook* in 1951 identified two sources of quality problems: avoidable and unavoidable costs. Avoidable costs included hours spent reworking defective products, processing complaints, and scrapping otherwise useful material. Unavoidable costs included work associated with inspection and other preventive measures. He suggested that when organizations focused on unavoidable costs to maintain quality, an important opportunity was being missed, and he advocated that an organization focus on avoidable costs that could be found in any process or activity, not just in manufacturing.

The popularity of TQM in the United States can be traced to a 1980 NBC television documentary titled, "If Japan Can . . . Why Can't We?" The documentary chronicled Deming's work with the Japanese and his concern that U.S. companies would not listen to him after the war. The documentary had a powerful impact on firms facing severe competition, particularly from the Japanese, and many companies, including Ford Motor Company, General Motors, Dow Chemical, and Hughes Aircraft, quickly sought Deming's advice. Another important influence on the TQM movement in the United States was Philip Crosby's book *Quality Is Free*.[56] He showed that improved quality can lower overall costs, dispelling the popular belief that high quality means higher total costs for the organization. With fewer parts

Table 15•2	Deming's Quality Guidelines

THE FOURTEEN POINTS

1. Create a constancy of purpose
2. Adopt a new philosophy
3. End the practice of purchasing at lowest prices
4. Institute leadership
5. Eliminate empty slogans
6. Eliminate numerical quotas
7. Institute on-the-job training
8. Drive out fear
9. Break down barriers between departments
10. Take action to accomplish the transformation
11. Improve constantly and forever the process of production and service
12. Cease dependence on mass inspection
13. Remove barriers to pride in workmanship
14. Retrain vigorously

THE SEVEN DEADLY SINS

1. Lack of constancy of purpose
2. Emphasizing short-term profits and immediate dividends
3. Evaluation of performance, merit rating, or annual review
4. Mobility of top management
5. Running a company only on visible figures
6. Excessive medical costs
7. Excessive costs of warranty

reworked, less material wasted, and less time spent inspecting finished goods, the organization's total costs actually can decline. Deming also believed that if the principles of quality were put in place, reduced costs would be a natural by-product of increased quality.

In 1987, Congress established the Malcolm Baldrige National Quality Award. It recognizes large and small organizations in services and manufacturing for quality achievement along seven dimensions: leadership, strategic planning, customer and market focus, information and analysis, human resources focus, process management, and business results. Health care and educational categories were added in 1999. Competition for the award has grown enormously. Some large organizations have spent millions of dollars to prepare for the contest; others have applied just to receive the extensive feedback from the board of examiners on how to improve quality; and still others feel compelled to apply because customers insist that they show progress in process improvement.

In 1992, the Rochester Institute of Technology and *USA Today* started the annual Quality Cup to honor quality improvement teams of five to twenty people.[57] One of the 1998 winners was the University of California at Irvine, which developed the BY-PASS system that allows people to purchase parking permits online, thus saving the university $1.4 million dollars over the past five years and saving faculty, staff, and students countless hours of standing in line. Another quality award is the Shingo Prize for companies that achieve highly efficient production methods. The 1999 Shingo prize winners were from Mexico and the United States.[58] Numerous states have initiated their own quality awards. At the national level, the Carey Award and the President's Quality Award are given to federal agencies in a Malcolm Baldrige Award–like contest and the Hammer Awards are given as part of the National Performance Review for innovation and quality improvement in the federal government.

TQM is a growing industry itself, with consulting firms, university courses, training programs, and professional associations related to quality improvement diffusing rapidly across industrial nations. The quality approach is supported by at least four major associations: the American Society for Quality (ASQ), the Association for Quality and Participation (AQP) (formerly the International Quality Circle Association), the Quality and Productivity Management Association (QPMA), and the American Productivity and Quality Center (APQC). The ASQ has more than one hundred thousand members, and the AQP has more than ten thousand members. These associations actively support TQM by sponsoring quality training workshops and conferences and serving as clearinghouses for important information on TQM programs. The APQC, for example, has assembled a database of best-practices information so that organizations can compare their processes against the best in the world. AQP is an excellent source of information and training in employee involvement, union partnerships, and quality tools. ASQ has gained prominence as the administrator of the Malcolm Baldrige Award and is known for its course offerings in TQM. The International Organization for Standardization (ISO) also supports TQM. Its ISO 9000 standard applies to quality systems, and certification requires firms to document key goals and processes, to demonstrate compliance, and to create processes for improvement.

Application Stages

TQM typically is implemented in five major steps:

1. *Gain long-term senior management commitment.* This stage involves helping senior executives understand the importance of long-term commitment to

TQM. Without a solid understanding of TQM and the key success factors for implementation, managers often believe that workers are solely responsible for quality. Yet only senior executives have the authority and larger perspective to address the organizationwide, cross-functional issues that hold the greatest promise for TQM's success.

Senior managers' role in TQM implementation includes giving direction and support throughout the change process. For example, establishing organizationwide TQM generally takes three or more years, although technical improvements to the workflow can be as quick as six to eight months. The longer-term and more difficult parts of implementation, however, involve changes in the organization's support systems, such as customer service, finance, sales, and human resources. Often these systems are frozen in place by old policies and norms that can interfere with the new approach. Senior managers have to confront those practices and create new ones that support TQM and the organization's strategic orientation.

Top executives also must be willing to allocate significant resources to TQM implementation, particularly to make large investments in training. For example, as part of its Baldrige Award preparation, Motorola developed Motorola University, a training organization that teaches in twenty-seven languages. Departments at Motorola allocate at least 1.5 percent of their budgets to education, and every employee must take a minimum of forty hours of training a year. This effort supports Motorola's goals of "six sigma" quality (a statistical measure of product quality that implies 99.9997 percent perfection) and of having a workforce that is able to read, write, solve problems, and do math at the seventh-grade level or above. When several business units within Motorola achieved the six-sigma target, the company demonstrated its commitment to continuously improving quality with a new target of tenfold improvement in key goals.

Finally, senior managers need to clarify and communicate throughout the organization a totally new orientation to producing and delivering products and services. At Volvo, for example, CEO Soren Gyll says that the company's three core values—quality, environmental concern and, especially, safety—must never be compromised. Managers are challenged to create a climate "where people can use their analytical skills and their creativity to continuously improve the organization's overall effectiveness and efficiency."

2. *Train members in quality methods.* TQM implementation requires extensive training in the principles and tools of quality improvement. Depending on the organization's size and complexity, such training can be conducted in a few weeks to more than two years. Members typically learn problem-solving skills and simple *statistical process control* (SPC) techniques, usually referred to as the seven tools of quality. At Cedar-Sinai Hospital in Los Angeles, all employees take a three-day course on the applicability of brainstorming, histograms, flowcharts, scatter diagrams, Pareto charts, cause-and-effect diagrams, control charts, and other problem-solving procedures. This training is the beginning of a long-term process in continuous improvement. The knowledge gained is used to understand variations in organizational processes, to identify sources of avoidable costs, to select and prioritize quality improvement projects, and to monitor the effects of changes on product and service quality. By learning to analyze the sources of variation systematically, members can improve the reliability of product manufacturing or service delivery. For example, HCA's West Paces Ferry Hospital used TQM methods to reduce direct costs attributable to antibiotic waste.[59] It used flowcharts, fishbone diagrams, and Pareto charts to

determine the major causes of unused intravenous preparations. Changes in the antibiotic delivery process resulted in reduced costs of antibiotics to the hospital of 44.5 percent and to patients of 45 percent.

3. *Start quality improvement projects.* In this phase of TQM implementation, individuals and work groups apply the quality methods to identify the few projects that hold promise for the largest improvements in organizational processes. They identify output variations, intervene to minimize deviations from quality standards, monitor improvements, and repeat this quality improvement cycle indefinitely. Identifying output variations is a key aspect of TQM. Such deviations from quality standards typically are measured by the percentage of defective products or, in the case of customer satisfaction, by on-time delivery percentages or customer survey ratings. For example, VF Corporation, a leading retail apparel firm, found that retailers were out of stock on 30 percent of their items 100 percent of the time. In response, VF revamped its systems to fill orders within twenty-four hours 95 percent of the time.

    TQM is concerned not only with variations in the quality of finished products and services but also with variations in the steps of a process that produce a product or service and the levels of internal customer satisfaction. For example, Eastman Chemical Company established a patent process improvement team to enhance the relationship between scientists and lawyers in applying for patent approvals. The team, made up of inventors, lab managers, and attorneys, doubled the number of patent attorneys and relocated their offices near the labs. Attorneys now meet with scientists during the experimental phase of research to discuss ways to increase the chances of yielding a patentable product or process. Patent submissions have increased by 60 percent, and the number of patents issued to the company has doubled.[60]

    Based on the measurement of output variations, each individual or work group systematically analyzes the cause of variations using SPC techniques. For example, product yields in a semiconductor manufacturing plant can go down for many reasons, including a high concentration of dust particles, small vibrations in the equipment, poor machine adjustments, and human error. Quality improvement projects often must determine which of the possible causes is most responsible, and, using that information, run experiments and pilot programs to determine which adjustments will cause output variations to drop and quality to improve. Those adjustments that do reduce variations are implemented across the board. Members continue to monitor the quality process to verify improvement and then begin the problem-solving process again for continuous improvement.

4. *Measure progress.* This stage of TQM implementation involves measuring organizational processes against quality standards. Knowing and analyzing the competition's performance are essential for any TQM effort because it sets minimum standards of cost, quality, and service and ensures the organization's position in the industry over the short run. For the longer term, such analytical efforts concentrate on identifying world-class performance, regardless of industry, and creating stretch targets, also known as *benchmarks*. Benchmarks represent the best in organizational achievements and practices for different processes and generally are accepted as "world class." For example, Alaska Airlines is considered the benchmark of customer service in the airline industry, while Disney's customer-service orientation is considered a world-class benchmark.

    The implied goal in most TQM efforts is to meet or exceed a competitor's benchmark. Alcoa's chairman, Paul H. O'Neill, charged all of the company's business units with closing the gap between Alcoa and its competitor's benchmarks by 80 percent within two years.[61] In aluminum sheet for beverage cans, for example, Japan's Kobe Steel, Ltd., was the benchmark, and Wall Street estimated that achieving O'Neill's goal would increase Alcoa's earnings by one dollar per share. The greatest leverage for change often is found in companies from unrelated industries, however. For example, Alcoa might look to Alaska Airlines or Disney to get innovative ideas about customer service. Understanding benchmarks from other industries challenges an organization's thinking about what is possible and promotes what is referred to as "out-of-the-box thinking."

5. *Rewarding accomplishment.* In this final stage of TQM implementation, the organization links rewards to improvements in quality. TQM does not monitor and reward outcomes normally tracked by traditional reward systems, such as the number of units produced. Such measures do not necessarily reflect product quality and can be difficult to replace because they are ingrained in the organization's traditional way of doing business. Rather, TQM rewards members for "process-oriented" improvements, such as increased on-time delivery, gains in customers' perceived satisfaction with product performance, and reductions in *cycle time,* the time it takes a product or service to be conceived, developed, produced, and sold. Rewards usually are designed initially to promote finding solutions to the organization's key problems. The linkage between rewards and process-oriented improvements reinforces the belief that continuous improvements, even small ones, are an important part of the new organizational culture associated with TQM. According to a survey of five hundred firms in four countries, conducted by Ernst and Young and the American Quality Foundation, more than half of the U.S. companies studied linked executive pay to improving quality and achieving benchmarks.[62]

TQM has continued to evolve in most industrialized countries. Early adopters of this intervention focused on trying to identify and solve the key problems facing the organization to improve performance and customer satisfaction. Organizations with mature TQM programs have shifted their attention from retrospective problem solving to proactive problem anticipation and prevention. For example, one of the Conference Board's longest-running quality councils held a two-day workshop using TQM principles to forecast the needs of human resources management. The council, which is made up of organizations with mature TQM systems, examined how human resources planning could integrate career planning, training, and management succession. It also discussed how the human resources function could evolve to a more strategic role in organization change. This shift from reaction to anticipation seems to be a hallmark of mature, successful TQM programs.

Application 15.4 describes a TQM intervention at L.L.Bean. It shows how competing for the Malcolm Baldrige National Quality Award can lead to significant change, even for an organization with an already high level of customer service.[63]

Results of Total Quality Management

TQM's emergence in the United States and the variation in how it is applied across organizations have made rigorous evaluation of results difficult. Much of the evidence is anecdotal. Winners of the Malcolm Baldrige National Quality Award, including Federal Express, Xerox, the Cadillac Division of General Motors, and Motorola, have received considerable attention. For example, Motorola's manufacturing organization reduced the number of parts in its cellular phones by 70 percent and cut the time required to build a cellular phone from forty hours to four; it reduced defects by

APPLICATION 15•4   Total Quality Management at L.L.Bean

Customers of L.L.Bean know that they are the boss. They can order hunting equipment twenty-four hours a day. They can request fishing poles to arrive, via Federal Express, within two days—at no extra charge. And they can return broken car racks after years of use. To say that the Maine-based mail-order company has a reputation for superior customer service is an understatement. The company's history is replete with stories of employees who went out of their way for a customer. L.L.Bean has a reputation that dates back to 1912, when founder Leon Leonwood Bean made good on nearly an entire shipment of hunting shoes that came back to him with defective stitching.

That reputation prompted Leon Gorman, the grandson of Bean and current chairman of L.L.Bean, to apply for the Malcolm Baldrige National Quality Award in the service category in 1988, the first year the award came out. Despite its reputation, L.L.Bean won no award that year, although it was one of two companies that qualified for a site visit. No award was given that year in the service category.

At the time, Gorman noted that L.L.Bean "will be under a great deal of pressure to renew and enhance our quality improvement efforts to make sure we live up to our reputation." Consequently, the company used feedback from the Baldrige committee as diagnostic information to carry out Gorman's desire to renew and enhance the company's quality improvement efforts. This resulted in a change program that focused first on employee involvement and then on process improvement.

The Baldrige feedback prompted Bean to take a hard look at its quality culture. Although members of the award committee had been impressed with Bean's customer service and cited it as "world class," they thought that the firm was not achieving customer satisfaction in a productive way. Bean had been satisfying customers through a guarantee-based approach to quality; in fact, they pioneered the "no-questions-asked" guarantee. The Baldrige committee members thought that Bean should not rely on a guarantee but should ensure that things happen right the first time. A favorite company story illustrates the situation: A customer service representative in Freeport, Maine, once strapped a canoe on his car and drove it to a customer in New York, who was leaving the next morning for a hunting trip. Although this certainly demonstrated exemplary customer service, the award committee noted that it also served as a sign that something was wrong. The canoe had been ordered in plenty of time to be shipped; had the order been processed properly in the first place, there would have been no need for heroics.

The diagnostic information also revealed that Bean needed to have more employee involvement. This came as a sur-

prise to management because the firm prided itself on a participative culture. L.L.Bean had been one of the first organizations in the United States to implement quality circles ten years earlier. Certainly, managers argued, the employee who delivered the canoe was involved. What members of L.L.Bean had trouble understanding was the practice of letting people take responsibility for their work and the work quality. In fact, decision making at L.L.Bean had usually taken place at a high level.

Based on the diagnostic feedback, the organization first developed a definition for what was referred to as "total quality" (TQ). It proposed that "total quality involves managing an enterprise to maximize customer satisfaction in the most efficient and effective way possible by totally involving people in improving the way work is done." In short, the company defined TQ as the way to involve its people and to improve customer-service processes.

Next, L.L.Bean focused on training. It spent approximately ten months familiarizing its three thousand employees with TQ methods and what quality means to the firm. First, all salaried employees in the organization received three days of TQ training, and then all hourly workers received one day. Senior executives were trained first so that each level within the company was capable of supporting total quality as the next level down learned about it.

During this training period, Bean's human resources department explored ways to change the infrastructure of the company to support greater employee involvement in decisions that affect quality. It concluded that because L.L.Bean is a service organization, decisions that influence quality occur every time a customer calls one of its phone centers and talks to a customer service representative. Thus, frontline, customer-contact employees needed to be knowledgeable and empowered. This would require a new managerial role aimed at involving employees and helping them develop the necessary expertise.

Soon after the training, Bean enlisted seventy members to devise ways to put the knowledge into action and to challenge the status quo. They formed seven cross-functional teams composed of both managers and workers. One team defined the manager's role in a quality-oriented organization as that of coach and developer, and created a program to help managers acquire the knowledge and skills to fill this new role. Another team constructed a feedback instrument as part of a management development process. The tool eventually became part of a performance management process that linked managers' compensation to improvements in such behaviors as being "aspiring and focused, ethical and compassionate, customer focused and aligned, effective and efficient, challenging and empowering, open and innovating, and re-warding and developing."

Employee involvement also paid big dividends in L.L.Bean's process improvement efforts. At the manufacturing division, a manager of footwear production shut down an entire work line, despite tremendous productivity pressures, and spent the morning teaching workers how a shoe is costed out. He explained each of the operations involved in making a shoe and described the cost of each task and of the materials involved. He then took employees back to the production line and asked them to discover ways that they could save money based on what they had learned in the morning. Employees found enough savings that day to pay for all the training conducted in the department for the entire year. In another case, stockers who replenish shelves in Bean's retail store swapped jobs temporarily with pickers who gather store orders from inventory in the distribution center. They applied TQ methods, such as work-flow mapping, to understand the work relationship between the store and the distribution center. In the old process, retail workers placed orders with the distribution center for items running low in the store. Pickers at the distribution center gathered those items on rolling carts, packed them in boxes, and loaded them onto trucks. When the items arrived at the store, stockers unloaded and unwrapped them and put them on rolling carts for transportation to the shelves. When the employees saw both sides of the work process, they realized that there was no reason for packaging the items. Now, the pickers simply roll the carts holding items directly on to trucks so that stockers can roll them right off.

To support these process improvements, L.L.Bean's staff groups also changed. The human resources department, for example, expanded its role to help employees understand and manage the TQ process. The department reengineered itself from a functional structure to a customer-oriented organization. Now, service teams made up of human resources specialists support each of L.L.Bean's major divisions with process improvement techniques, health and safety advice, employee relations help, and training.

Most gratifying to L.L.Bean is that through all the changes, customer satisfaction remained high and job satisfaction among the workforce increased more than 12 percent. Although L.L.Bean is only halfway through its TQ intervention, it has experienced increased profitability, return on sales, and return on equity. ■

80 percent and saved $962 million in inspection and reworking costs; it set a goal of tenfold improvement in quality within five years and exceeded that goal within three years.[64] The U.S. Commerce Department's National Institute of Standards and Technology routinely tracks the stock performance of Baldrige Award winners compared to a Standard & Poor's 500 index fund. The Baldrige winners outperformed the index fund by a ratio of 2.6 to 1 and outperformed the S&P 500 significantly between 1994 and 1999.[65]

A 1998 survey of the *Fortune* 1000 companies showed that about 66 percent have implemented some form of TQM, although that percentage is down from a high of 76 percent in 1993.[66] Furthermore, 76 percent of the companies rated their TQM experience as either positive or very positive. The research also found that TQM is often associated with the implementation of other EI interventions. As organizations enact process improvements, they may need to make supporting changes in reward systems and work design. Finally, the study revealed that TQM was positively associated with performance outcomes, such as productivity, customer service, product/service quality, and profitability, as well as with human outcomes, such as employee satisfaction and quality of work life.

Other studies also suggest positive TQM results. In a Conference Board study of 149 large organizations, more than 30 percent reported improved financial performance. Another study of the twenty highest-point-scorers in the Baldrige competition reported improved employee relations, product quality, and customer satisfaction and lowered costs compared with other Baldrige applicants.[67] These results should be interpreted cautiously, however, because most of the studies lack sufficient scientific rigor.

A more balanced picture of TQM effects is provided by a study of fifty-four firms of different sizes, both adopters and nonadopters of TQM. It found that TQM firms significantly outperformed non-TQM firms. The source of the performance advantage was not the tools and techniques of TQM, however, but the culture, empowerment, and commitment that came from successful implementation. The study concluded that "these tacit resources, and not TQM tools and techniques, drive TQM success," and that "organizations that acquire them can outperform competitors with or without the accompanying TQM ideology."[68]

Although reports of TQM success are plentiful in the popular literature, there are also reports of problems.[69] At Florida Power and Light, executives were divided over whether TQM actually had helped the organization, and a new CEO's interviews with employees found widespread resentment toward the process. It is clear that more systematic research is needed to assess whether these positive outcomes are valid and, if so, whether similar results can be expected across a wide range of organizational applications.

■ SUMMARY

This chapter described employee involvement interventions. These technostructural change programs are aimed at moving organization decision making downward to improve responsiveness and performance and to increase member flexibility, commitment, and satisfaction. Different approaches to EI can be described by the extent to which power, information, knowledge and skills, and rewards are shared with employees.

The relationship between EI and productivity can be oversimplified. Productivity can be increased through improved employee communication, motivation, and skills and abilities. It also can be affected through increased worker satisfaction, which in turn results in productive employees joining and remaining with the organization.

Major EI interventions are parallel structures, including cooperative union–management projects and quality circles; high-involvement designs; and TQM. The results of these approaches tend to be positive, and the quality of research supporting these interventions is increasing.

■ NOTES

1. L. Davis, "Enhancing the Quality of Work Life: Developments in the United States," *International Labour Review* 116 (July-August 1977): 53–65.

2. D. Glew, A. O'Leary-Kelly, R. Griffin, and D. Van Fleet, "Participation in Organizations: A Preview of the Issues and Proposed Framework for Future Analysis," *Journal of Management* 21, 3 (1995): 395–421.

3. E. Lawler III, *High-Involvement Management* (San Francisco: Jossey-Bass, 1986).

4. E. Lawler III, S. Mohrman, and G. Ledford, *Strategies for High-Performance Organizations* (San Francisco: Jossey-Bass, 1998).

5. M. Marchington, A. Wilkinson, and P. Ackers, "Understanding the Meaning of Participation: Views from the Workplace," *Human Relations* 47, 8 (1994): 867–94; C. Goulden, "Supervisory Management and Quality Circle Performance: An Empirical Study," *Journal of Management Development* 14, 7 (1995): 15–27.

6. D. Welsh, F. Luthans, and S. Sommer, "Managing Russian Factory Workers: The Impact of U.S.-Based Behavioral and Participative Techniques," *Academy of Management Journal* 36, 1 (1993): 58–79; D. Jones, "Employee Participation During the Early Stages of Transition: Evidence from Bulgaria," *Economic and Industrial Democracy* 16, 1 (1995): 111–35.

7. C. Cooper and E. Mumford, *The Quality of Working Life in Western and Eastern Europe* (Westport, Conn.: Greenwood Press, 1979); P. Sorenson, T. Head, N. Mathys, J. Preston, and D. Cooperrider, *Global and Organizational Development* (Champaign, Ill.: Stipes, 1995).

8. M. Kizilos, "The Relationship Between Employee Involvement and Organization Performance" (unpublished Ph.D. diss., University of Southern California, 1995); M. Huselid, "The Impact of Human Resource Management Practices on Turnover, Productivity, and Corporate Financial Performance," *Academy of Management Journal* 38 (1995): 635–72; M. Kizilos, T. Cummings, and A. Strickstein, "Achieving Superior Customer Service Through Employee Involvement," *Academy of Management Best Paper Proceedings* (1994): 197–201; J. Arthur, "Effects of Human Resources Systems on Manufacturing Performance and Turnover," *Academy of Management Journal* 37 (1994): 670–87; A. Kalleberg and J. Moody, "Human Resource Management and Organizational Performance," *American Behavioral Scientist* 37 (1994): 948–62; D. Denison, *Corporate Culture and Organizational Effectiveness* (New York: John Wiley & Sons, 1990); G. Hansen and B. Wernerfelt, "Determinates of Firm Performance: The Relative Importance of Economic and Organizational Factors," *Strategic Management Journal* 10 (1989): 399–411.

9. E. Lawler III and G. Ledford, "Productivity and the Quality of Work Life," *National Productivity Review* 2 (Winter 1981–82): 23–36.

10. Glew et al., "Participation in Organizations"; J. Wagner, "Participation's Effects on Performance and Satisfaction: A Reconsideration of Research Evidence," *Academy of Management Review* 19 (1994): 312–30.

11. G. Ledford and E. Lawler, "Research on Employee Participation: Beating a Dead Horse?" *Academy of Management Review* 19 (1994): 633–36.

12. Lawler, Mohrman, and Ledford, *Strategies*, p. 150.

13. G. Bushe and A. Shani, "Parallel Learning Structure Interventions in Bureaucratic Organizations," in *Research in Organizational Change and Development*, vol. 4, eds. W. Pasmore and R. Woodman (Greenwich, Conn.: JAI Press, 1990): 167–94.

14. D. Zand, "Collateral Organization: A New Change Strategy," *Journal of Applied Behavioral Science* 10 (1974): 63–89; S. Goldstein, "Organizational Dualism and Quality Circles," *Academy of Management Review* 10 (1985): 504–17; V. Schein and L. Greiner, "Can Organization Development Be Fine Tuned to Bureaucracies?" *Organizational Dynamics* (Winter 1977): 48–61.

15. D. Zand, *Information, Organization, and Power: Effective Management in the Knowledge Society* (New York: McGraw-Hill, 1981): 57–88; G. Bushe and A. Shani, *Parallel Learning Structures: Increasing Innovation in Bureaucracies* (Reading, Mass.: Addison-Wesley, 1991).

16. C. Worley and G. Ledford, "The Relative Impact of Group Process and Group Structure on Group Effectiveness" (paper presented at the Western Academy of Management, Spokane, Wash., April 1992).

17. L. Davis and C. Sullivan, "A Labor–Management Contract and Quality of Working Life," *Journal of Occupational Behavior* 1 (1979): 29–41; E. Lawler III and J. Drexler Jr., "Dynamics of Establishing Cooperative Quality-of-Worklife Projects," *Monthly Labor Review* 101 (March 1978): 23–28; D. Nadler, M. Hanlon, and E. Lawler III, "Factors Influencing the Success of Labor–Management Quality of Work Life Projects" (research paper, Columbia University Graduate School of Business, April 1978).

18. M. Duckles, R. Duckles, and M. Maccoby, "The Process of Change at Bolivar," *Journal of Applied Behavioral Science* 13 (1977): 387–499.

19. D. Nadler, G. Jenkins, P. Mirvis, and B. Macy, "A Research Design and Measurement Package for the Assessment of Quality of Work Interventions," *Proceedings of the Academy of Management* (1975): 87–102.

20. D. Nadler, "Hospitals, Organized Labor, and Quality of Work: An Intervention Case Study," *Journal of Applied Behavioral Science* 14 (1978): 366–81.

21. J. Drexler Jr., "A Union Management Cooperative Project to Improve the Quality of Work Life," *Journal of Applied Behavioral Science* 13 (1977): 373–86.

22. Duckles, Duckles, and Maccoby, "Change at Bolivar," pp. 387–499.

23. D. Dinnocenzo, "Labor–Management Cooperation," *Training and Development Journal* 43 (May 1989): 35–40; K. Ropp, "State of the Unions," *Personnel Administrator* 32 (July 1987): 36–40; M. Hilton, "Union and Management: A Strong Case for Cooperation," *Training and Development Journal* 41 (January 1987): 54–55.

24. Lawler, *High-Involvement Management*.

25. C. Worley, "Implementing Strategic Change at GTE of California" (working paper, Pepperdine University, 1993).

26. G. Munchus III, "Employer–Employee Based Quality Circles in Japan: Human Resource Policy Implications for American Firms," *Academy of Management Review* 8 (1983): 255–61.

27. R. Callahan, "Quality Circles: A Program for Productivity Improvement Through Human Resource Development" (unpublished paper, Albers School of Business, Seattle University, 1982).

28. Munchus, "Quality Circles in Japan," pp. 255–61.

29. S. Mohrman and L. Novelli, "Learning from a Quality Circles Program" (working paper, Center for Effective Organizations, University of Southern California, 1982).

30. Zand, *Collateral Organization.*

31. A. Honeycutt, "The Key to Effective Quality Circles," *Training and Development Journal* 43 (May 1989): 81–84; E. Yager, "The Quality Circle Explosion," *Training and Development Journal* 35 (April 1981): 93–105; "A Quality Circle Nets a Nice Round Figure," *Supervisory Management* 40 (1995): 7.

32. E. Miller, "The Parallel Organization Structure at General Motors—An Interview with Howard C. Carlson," *Personnel* (September-October 1978): 64–69.

33. M. Barrick and R. Alexander, "A Review of Quality Circle Efficacy and the Existence of Positive-Findings Bias," *Personnel Psychology* 40 (1987): 579–92; J. Vogt and B. Hunt, "What Really Goes Wrong with Participative Groups," *Training and Development Journal* 42 (May 1988): 96–100; R. Steel and G. Shane, "Evaluation Research on Quality Circles: Technical and Analytical Implications," *Human Relations* 39 (1986): 449–68.

34. G. Bushe, "Developing Cooperative Labor–Management Relations in Unionized Factories: A Multiple Case Study of Quality Circles and Parallel Organizations Within Joint Quality of Work Life Projects," *Journal of Applied Behavioral Science* 24 (1988): 129–50.

35. H. Katz, T. Kochan, and M. Weber, "Assessing the Effects of Industrial Relations Systems and Efforts to Improve the Quality of Working Life on Organizational Effectiveness," *Academy of Management Journal* 28 (1985): 509–26.

36. G. Ledford Jr., E. Lawler III, and S. Mohrman, "The Quality Circle and Its Variations," in *Enhancing Productivity: New Perspectives from Industrial and Organizational Psychology,* eds. J. P. Campbell and J. R. Campbell (San Francisco: Jossey-Bass, 1988): 225–94.

37. R. Steel and R. Lloyd, "Cognitive, Affective, and Behavioral Outcomes of Participation in Quality Circles: Conceptual and Empirical Findings," *Journal of Applied Behavioral Science* 24 (1988): 1–17.

38. Lawler, Mohrman, and Ledford, *Strategies,* pp. 112–13; D. Tjosvold, "Making Employee Involvement Work: Co-operative Goals and Controversy to Reduce Costs," *Human Relations* 51 (1998): 210–14.

39. Lawler and Ledford, "Productivity."

40. Ibid., p. 35.

41. "Employee Participation and Labor–Management Cooperation in American Workplaces," *Challenge* 38 (1995): 38–46.

42. S. Mohrman and G. Ledford Jr., "The Design and Use of Effective Employee Participation Groups," *Human Resource Management* 24 (1985): 413–28.

43. E. Lawler III and S. Mohrman, "Quality Circles after the Fad," *Harvard Business Review* 85 (1985): 64–71; Mohrman and Ledford Jr., "Design and Use."

44. Callahan, "Quality Circles."

45. C. Worley, "Implementing Participation Strategies in Hospitals: Correlates of Effective Problem-Solving Teams," *Public Administration and Management: An Interactive Journal* 5 (2000): http://www.pamij.com; D. Collins, "Self-Interests and Group Interests in Employee Involvement Programs: A Case Study," *Journal of Labor Research* 16 (1995): 57–79.

46. Lawler, *High-Involvement Management.*

47. E. Lawler III, "Increasing Worker Involvement to Enhance Organizational Effectiveness," in *Change in Organizations,* ed. P. Goodman (San Francisco: Jossey-Bass, 1982): 299; R. Walton, "From Control to Commitment in the Workplace," *Harvard Business Review* 63 (1985): 76–84.

48. Lawler, *High-Involvement Management;* E. Lawler, *The Ultimate Advantage* (San Francisco: Jossey-Bass, 1992).

49. Glew et al., "Participation in Organizations."

50. G. Ledford, "High-Involvement Organizations" (working paper, Center for Effective Organizations, University of Southern California, 1992).

51. J. Pfeffer, "Producing Sustainable Competitive Advantage Through the Effective Management of People," *Academy of Management Executive* 9, 1 (1995): 55–69.

52. This application was adapted from information provided in M. Hequet, "Working Involvement Lights up Neon," *Training* 31 (1994): 23–29.

53. The authors wish to thank Miriam Y. Lacey, associate professor of Organization Behavior, Pepperdine University, and Debbie Collard, director, Continuous Quality Improvement, Airlift and Tanker Programs, Boeing, for their helpful comments on this section.

54. Y. Shetty, "Product Quality and Competitive Strategy," *Business Horizons* (May-June 1987): 46–52; D. Garvin, "Competing on the Eight Dimensions of Quality," *Harvard Business Review* (November-December 1987): 101–09; D. Garvin, *Managing Quality: The Strategic and Competitive Edge* (New York: Free Press, 1988); "The Quality Imperative," *Business Week,* Special Issue (25 October 1991): 34.

55. W. Deming, *Quality, Productivity, and Competitive Advantage* (Cambridge: MIT Center for Advanced Engineering Study, 1982); W. Deming, *Out of the Crisis* (Cambridge: MIT Press, 1986); J. Juran, *Quality Control Handbook,* 3d ed. (New York: McGraw-Hill, 1974); J. Juran, *Juran on the Leadership for Quality: An Executive Handbook* (New York: Free Press, 1989).

56. P. Crosby, *Quality Is Free* (New York: McGraw-Hill, 1979); P. Crosby, *Quality Without Tears* (New York: McGraw-Hill, 1984).

57. J. Hillkirk, "New Award Cites Teams with Dreams," *USA Today* (10 April 1992): 1, 4, 5b; http://www.quality-cup.org.

58. Information on the Shingo Prize and the recipients can be found at http://www.shingoprize.com.

59. C. Caldwell, J. McEachern, and V. Davis, "Measurement Tools Eliminate Guesswork," *Healthcare Forum Journal* (July-August 1990): 23–27.

60. "Quality Imperative," *Business Week,* p. 152.

61. Ibid., p. 14.

62. Ibid., p. 14.

63. Adapted from D. Anfuso, "L.L.Bean's Quality Management Efforts Put People Before Processes," *Personnel Journal* 73 (1994): 72–83.

64. R. Shaffer, "Why Motorola Is Expensive—And Still a Bargain," *Forbes* 146 (1990): 102; E. Segalla, "All for Quality, and Quality for All," *Training and Development Journal* 43 (1989): 36–45; B. Avishai and W. Taylor, "Customers Drive a Technology-Driven Company: An Interview with George Fisher," *Harvard Business Review* 67 (1989): 106–14; K. Bhote, "Motorola's Long March to the Malcolm Baldrige National Quality Award," *National Productivity Review* 8 (1989): 365–75; "Quality at Motorola," various internal company documents from January 1988 to June 1990.

65. "Betting to Win on the Baldie Winners," *Business Week* (18 October 1993): 8; additional information about this study can be found at http://www.nist.gov/public_affairs/stockstudy.htm.

66. Lawler, Mohrman, and Ledford, *Strategies.*

67. U.S. General Accounting Office, *Management Practices: U.S. Companies Improve Performance Through Quality Efforts* (Gaithersburg, Md.: Author, 1991).

68. T. Powell, "Total Quality Management as a Competitive Advantage: A Review and Empirical Study," *Strategic Management Journal* 16 (1995): 15–37.

69. "Is the Baldrige Overblown?" *Fortune* (1 July 1991): 62–65.

16

Work Design

This chapter is concerned with work design—creating jobs and work groups that generate high levels of employee fulfillment and productivity. This technostructural intervention can be part of a larger employee involvement application, or it can be an independent change program. Work design has been researched and applied extensively in organizations. Recently, organizations have tended to combine work design with formal structure and supporting changes in goal setting, reward systems, work environment, and other performance management practices. These organizational factors can help structure and reinforce the kinds of work behaviors associated with specific work designs. (How performance management interventions can support work design is discussed in Chapter 17.)

This chapter examines three approaches to work design. The engineering approach focuses on efficiency and simplification, and results in traditional job and work group designs. Traditional jobs involve relatively routine and repetitive forms of work, where little interaction among people is needed to produce a service or product. Telephone operators and data-entry positions are examples of this job design. Traditional work groups are composed of members performing routine yet interrelated tasks. Member interactions are typically controlled by rigid work flows, supervisors, and schedules, such as might be found on assembly lines.

A second approach to work design rests on motivational theories and attempts to enrich the work experience. Job enrichment involves designing jobs with high levels of meaning, discretion, and knowledge of results. A well-researched model focusing on job attributes has helped clear up methodological problems with this important intervention.

The third and most recent approach to work design derives from sociotechnical systems methods, and seeks to optimize both the social and the technical aspects of work systems. This method has led to a popular form of work design called "self-managed teams" which are composed of multiskilled members performing interrelated tasks. Members are given the knowledge, information, and power necessary to control their own task behaviors with relatively little external control. New support systems and supervisory styles are needed to manage them.

The chapter describes each of these perspectives on work design, and then presents a contingency framework for integrating the approaches based on personal and technical factors in the workplace. When work is designed to fit these factors, it is both satisfying and productive.

THE ENGINEERING APPROACH

The oldest and most prevalent approach to designing work is based on engineering concepts and methods. It proposes that the most efficient work designs can be determined by clearly specifying the tasks to be performed, the work methods to be used, and the work flow among individuals. The engineering approach is based on the pioneering work of Frederick Taylor, the father of scientific management. He developed methods for analyzing and designing work and laid the foundation for the professional field of industrial engineering.[1]

The *engineering approach* scientifically analyzes workers' tasks to discover those procedures that produce the maximum output with the minimum input of energies and resources.[2] This generally results in work designs with high levels of specialization and specification. Such designs have several benefits: they allow workers to learn tasks rapidly; they permit short work cycles so performance can take place with little or no mental effort; and they reduce costs because lower-skilled people can be hired and trained easily and paid relatively low wages.

The engineering approach produces two kinds of work design: traditional jobs and traditional work groups. When the work can be completed by one person, such as with bank tellers and telephone operators, traditional jobs are created. These jobs tend to be simplified, with routine and repetitive tasks having clear specifications concerning time and motion. When the work requires coordination among people, such as on automobile assembly lines, traditional work groups are developed. They are composed of members performing relatively routine yet related tasks. The overall group task is typically broken into simpler, discrete parts (often called jobs). The tasks and work methods are specified for each part, and the parts are assigned to group members. Each member performs a routine and repetitive part of the group task. Members' separate task contributions are coordinated for overall task achievement through such external controls as schedules, rigid work flows, and supervisors.[3] In the 1950s and 1960s, this method of work design was popularized by the assembly lines of American automobile manufacturers and was an important reason for the growth of American industry following World War II.

The engineering approach to job design is less an OD intervention than a benchmark in history. Critics of the approach argue that the method ignores workers' social and psychological needs. They suggest that the rising educational level of the workforce and the substitution of automation for menial labor point to the need for more enriched forms of work in which people have greater discretion and are more challenged. Moreover, the current competitive climate requires a more committed and involved workforce able to make online decisions and to develop performance innovations. Work designed with the employee in mind is more humanly fulfilling and productive than that designed in traditional ways. However, it is important to recognize the strengths of the engineering approach. It remains an important work design intervention because its immediate cost savings and efficiency can be measured readily, and because it is well understood and easily implemented and managed.

THE MOTIVATIONAL APPROACH

The *motivational approach* to work design views the effectiveness of organizational activities primarily as a function of member needs and satisfaction, and seeks to improve employee performance and satisfaction by enriching jobs. The motivational method provides people with opportunities for autonomy, responsibility, closure (that is, doing a complete job), and performance feedback. Enriched jobs are popular in the United States at such companies as AT&T Universal Card, TRW, Dayton Hudson, and GTE.

The motivational approach usually is associated with the research of Herzberg and of Hackman and Oldham. Herzberg's two-factor theory of motivation proposed that certain attributes of work, such as opportunities for advancement and recognition, which he called *motivators,* help increase job satisfaction.[4] Other attributes that Herzberg called *hygiene factors,* such as company policies, working conditions, pay, and supervision, do not produce satisfaction but rather prevent dissatisfaction—important contributors because only satisfied workers are motivated to produce. Successful job enrichment experiments at AT&T, Texas Instruments, and Imperial Chemical Industries helped to popularize job enrichment in the 1960s.[5]

Although Herzberg's motivational factors sound appealing, increasing doubt has been cast on the underlying theory. Motivation and hygiene factors are difficult to put into operation and measure, and that makes implementation and evaluation of the theory difficult. Furthermore, important worker characteristics that can affect whether people will respond favorably to job enrichment were not included in his theory. Finally, Herzberg's failure to involve employees in the job enrichment process itself does not suit most OD practitioners today. Consequently, a second, well-researched approach to job enrichment has been favored. It focuses on the attributes of the work itself and has resulted in a more scientifically acceptable theory of job enrichment than Herzberg's model. The research of Hackman and Oldham represents this more recent trend in job enrichment.[6]

The Core Dimensions of Jobs

Considerable research has been devoted to defining and understanding core job dimensions.[7] Figure 16.1 summarizes the Hackman and Oldham model of job design. Five core dimensions of work affect three critical psychological states, which in turn produce personal and job outcomes. These outcomes include high internal work motivation, high-quality work performance, satisfaction with the work, and low absenteeism and turnover. The five core job dimensions—skill variety, task identity, task significance, autonomy, and feedback from the work itself—are described below and associated with the critical psychological states that they create.

Skill Variety, Task Identity, and Task Significance

These three core job characteristics influence the extent to which work is perceived as meaningful. *Skill variety* refers to the number and types of skills used to perform a particular task. Employees at Lechmere's, a retail chain in Florida, can work as warehouse stock clerks, cashiers, and salespeople. The more tasks an individual performs, the more meaningful the job becomes. When skill variety is increased by moving a person from one job to another, a form of job enrichment called *job rotation* is accomplished. However, simply rotating a person from one boring job to another is not likely to produce the outcomes associated with a fully enriched job.

Task identity describes the extent to which an individual performs a whole piece of work. For example, an employee who completes an entire wheel assembly for an airplane, including the tire, chassis, brakes, and electrical and hydraulic systems, has more task identity and will perceive the work as more meaningful than someone who only assembles the braking subsystem. *Job enlargement,* another form of job enrichment that combines increases in skill variety with task identity, blends several narrow jobs into one larger, expanded job. For example, separate machine set-up, machining, and inspection jobs might be combined into one. This method can increase meaningfulness, job satisfaction, and motivation when employees comprehend and like the greater task complexity.

Task significance represents the impact that the work has on others. In jobs with high task significance, such as nursing, consulting, or manufacturing something like sensitive parts for the space shuttle, the importance of successful task completion creates meaningfulness for the worker.

Experienced meaningfulness is expressed as an average of these three dimensions. Thus, although it is advantageous to have high amounts of skill variety, task

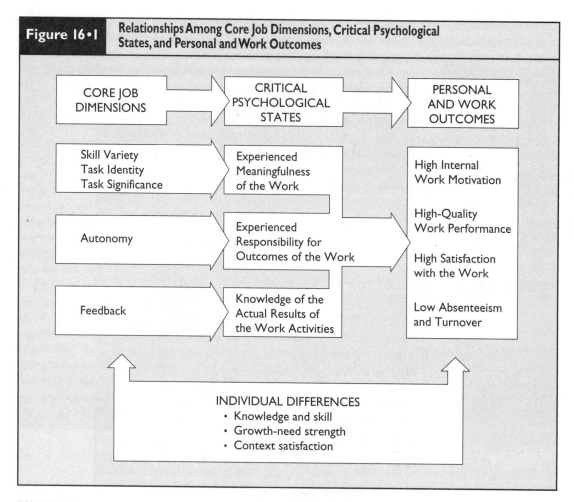

Figure 16•1   Relationships Among Core Job Dimensions, Critical Psychological States, and Personal and Work Outcomes

SOURCE: J. Hackman and G. Oldham, *Work Redesign*, page 90. © 1980 by Addison-Wesley Publishing Co., Inc. Reprinted by permission of Addison Wesley Longman.

identity, and task significance, a strong emphasis on any one of the three dimensions can, at least partially, make up for deficiencies in the other two.

Autonomy

This refers to the amount of independence, freedom, and discretion that the employee has to schedule and perform tasks. Salespeople, for example, often have considerable autonomy in how they contact, develop, and close new accounts, whereas assembly-line workers often have to adhere to work specifications clearly detailed in a policy-and-procedure manual. Employees are more likely to experience responsibility for their work outcomes when high amounts of autonomy exist.

Feedback from the Work Itself

This core dimension represents the information that workers receive about the effectiveness of their work. It can derive from the work itself, as when determining whether an assembled part functions properly, or it can come from such external sources as reports on defects, budget variances, customer satisfaction, and the like.

Because feedback from the work itself is direct and generates intrinsic satisfaction, it is considered preferable to feedback from external sources.

Individual Differences

Not all people react in similar ways to job enrichment interventions. Individual differences—among them, a worker's knowledge and skill levels, growth-need strength, and satisfaction with contextual factors—moderate the relationships among core dimensions, psychological states, and outcomes. "Worker knowledge and skill" refers to the education and experience levels characterizing the workforce. If employees lack the appropriate skills, for example, increasing skill variety may not improve a job's meaningfulness. Similarly, if workers lack the intrinsic motivation to grow and develop personally, attempts to provide them with increased autonomy may be resisted. (We will discuss growth needs more fully in the last section of this chapter.) Finally, contextual factors include reward systems, supervisory style, and co-worker satisfaction. When the employee is unhappy with the work context, attempts to enrich the work itself may be unsuccessful.

Application Stages

The basic steps for job enrichment as described by Hackman and Oldham include making a thorough diagnosis of the situation, forming natural work units, combining tasks, establishing client relationships, vertical loading, and opening feedback channels.[8]

Making a Thorough Diagnosis

The most popular method of diagnosing a job is through the use of the Job Diagnostic Survey (JDS) or one of its variations.[9] An important output of the JDS is the motivating potential score, which is a function of the three psychological states—experienced meaningfulness, autonomy, and feedback. The survey can be used to profile one or more jobs, to determine whether motivation and satisfaction are really problems or whether the job is low in motivating potential, and to isolate specific job aspects that are causing difficulties. Figure 16.2 shows two jobs. Job A in engineering maintenance is high on all of the core dimensions. Its motivating potential score is 260 (motivating potential scores average about 125). Job B, the routine and repetitive task of processing checks in a bank, has a motivating potential score of 30. The score is well below average and would be even lower except for the job's relatively high task significance. This job could be redesigned and improved.

The JDS also indicates how ready employees are to accept change. Employees who have high growth needs will respond more readily to job enrichment than will those with low or weak growth needs. A thorough diagnosis of the existing work system should be completed before implementing actual changes. The JDS measures satisfaction with pay, co-workers, and supervision. If there is high dissatisfaction with one or more of these areas, other interventions might be more helpful prior to work redesign.

Forming Natural Work Units

As much as possible, natural work units should be formed. Although there may be a number of technological constraints, interrelated task activities should be grouped together. The basic question in forming natural work units is "How can one increase 'ownership' of the task?" Forming such natural units increases two of the core dimensions—task identity and task significance—that contribute to the meaningfulness of work.

| Figure 16•2 | The JDS Diagnostic Profile for a "Good" and a "Bad" Job |

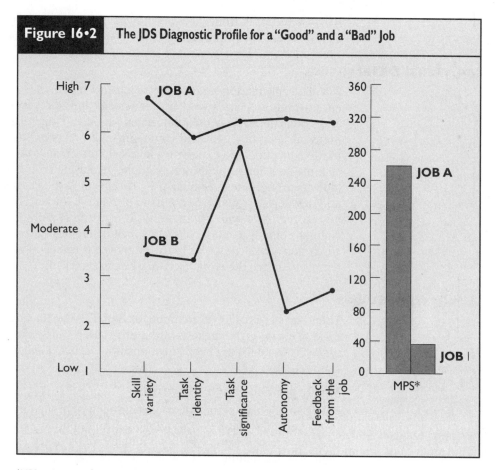

*MPS, motivating potential score.

Combining Tasks

Frequently, divided jobs can be put back together to form a new and larger one. In the Medfield, Massachusetts, plant of Corning Glass Works, the task of assembling laboratory hotplates was redesigned by combining a number of previously separate tasks. After the change, each hotplate was completely assembled, inspected, and shipped by one operator, resulting in increased productivity of 84 percent. Controllable rejects dropped from 23 percent to less than 1 percent, and absenteeism dropped from 8 percent to less than 1 percent.[10] A later analysis indicated that the change in productivity was the result of the intervention.[11] Combining tasks increases task identity and allows a worker to use a greater variety of skills. The hotplate assembler can identify with a product finished for shipment, and self-inspection of his or her work adds greater task significance, autonomy, and feedback from the job itself.

Establishing Client Relationships

When jobs are split up, the typical worker has little or no contact with, or knowledge of, the ultimate user of the product or service. Improvements often can be realized simultaneously on three of the core dimensions by encouraging and helping workers to establish direct relationships with the clients of their work. For example, when a typist in a typing pool is assigned to a particular department, feedback increases because of the additional opportunities for praise or criticism of his or her work. Because of the need to develop interpersonal skills in maintaining the client relationship, skill variety may increase. If the worker is given personal responsibility for deciding how to manage relationships with clients, autonomy is increased.

Three steps are needed to create client relationships: (1) the client must be identified; (2) the contact between the client and the worker needs to be established as directly as possible; and (3) criteria and procedures are needed by which the client can judge the quality of the product or service received and relay those judgments back to the worker. For example, even customer-service representatives and data-entry operations can be set up so that people serve particular clients. In the hotplate department, personal nametags can be attached to each instrument. The Indiana Bell Telephone Company found substantial improvements in satisfaction and performance when telephone directory compilers were given accountability for a specific geographic area.[12]

Vertical Loading

The intent of vertical loading is to decrease the gap between *doing* the job and *controlling* the job. A vertically loaded job has responsibilities and controls that formerly were reserved for management. Vertical loading may well be the most crucial of the job-design principles. Autonomy is invariably increased. This approach should lead to greater feelings of personal accountability and responsibility for the work outcomes. For example, at an IBM plant that manufactures circuit boards for personal computers, assembly workers were trained to measure the accuracy and speed of production processes and to test the quality of finished products. Their work is more "whole," they are more autonomous, and the engineers who used to measure and test are free to design better products and more efficient ways to manufacture them.[13]

Loss of vertical loading usually occurs when someone has made a mistake. Once a supervisor steps in, the responsibility may be removed indefinitely. For example, many skilled machinists have to complete forms to have maintenance people work on a machine. The supervisor automatically signs the slip rather than allowing the machinist either to repair the machine or ask directly for maintenance support.

Opening Feedback Channels

In almost all jobs, approaches exist to open feedback channels and help people learn whether their performance is remaining at a constant level, improving, or deteriorating. The most advantageous and least threatening feedback occurs when a worker learns about performance as the job is performed. In the hotplate department at Corning Glass Works, assembling the entire instrument and inspecting it dramatically increased the quantity and quality of performance information available to the operators. Data given to a manager or supervisor often can be given directly to the employee. Computers and other automated operations can be used to provide people with data not currently accessible to them. Many organizations simply have not realized the motivating impact of direct, immediate feedback.

Application 16.1 presents an example of job enrichment in a large data-entry operation where workers were not directly involved in the redesign process and where supervisors developed and implemented the changes.[14] Although the results were extremely positive, research suggests that employee participation in the change program might have produced even more beneficial outcomes.[15]

APPLICATION 16•1   Job Enrichment at the Travelers Insurance Companies

A job enrichment program took place in a data-entry operation of the Travelers Insurance Companies. Before the intervention, the department was ineffective: due dates and schedules frequently were missed and absenteeism was higher than average. The department consisted of ninety-eight data-entry clerks and verifiers, plus seven assignment clerks and a supervisor. The jobs were split up and highly standardized, providing workers with little opportunity for discretion, skill variety, and feedback. Typically, assignment clerks received jobs from user departments, reviewed the work for obvious errors, and put acceptable work into batches that could be completed in about one hour. If the clerks found errors, they gave the work to the supervisor who usually handled the problem by dealing with the user department. The data-entry clerks who were given the batches were told to enter only what they saw and not to correct any errors, no matter how obvious. All data entry was 100 percent verified, a task that resembled data entry and took almost as long. Errors detected in verification were given randomly to data-entry operators to be corrected.

Management and consultants felt that the problems experienced by the data-entry department were motivational. The supervisor spent most of his time responding to crises. He dealt almost daily with employee complaints, especially their apathy or outright hostility toward their jobs. Further diagnosis using the JDS showed that the data-entry and verifying jobs had extremely low motivating potential. Skill variety was low because operators used only a single skill—the ability to input or verify the data adequately. Task identity and task significance were not apparent. People did not perform a whole identifiable job, nor did they have any knowledge about the job's meaning to the user department or the ultimate customer. Autonomy was nonexistent because workers had no freedom to schedule work, to resolve problems, or even to correct obvious errors. Feedback about results was low because an operator who finished a batch of work rarely saw evidence of its quality.

Realizing the low motivating potential of the jobs, management decided to undertake a job enrichment program.

First, the consultants conducted an educational session with the supervisor, who was introduced to Hackman and Oldham's approach to job enrichment. Relevant job changes were designed using the following five implementation concepts:

1. *Natural work units.* Each operator was assigned continuing responsibility for certain accounts, rather than receiving batches at random.
2. *Task combination.* Some planning and controlling functions were combined with the task of data entry or verifying.
3. *Client relationships.* Each operator was given several channels of direct contact with clients. The operators inspected their incoming documents for correctness; when mistakes were found, they resolved them directly with the user departments.
4. *Feedback.* Operators received direct feedback about their work from clients and the computer department, including a weekly record of productivity and errors.
5. *Vertical loading.* Operators were permitted to correct obvious data errors and set their own schedules as long as they met department schedules. Some competent operators were given the option of not verifying their work and of making certain program changes.

The results of the job enrichment program were outstanding. The number of operators declined from ninety-eight to sixty, primarily through attrition, transfers to other departments, and promotions to higher-paying jobs. The quantity of work increased 39.6 percent, while the percentage of operators performing poorly declined from 11.1 percent to 5.5 percent. Absenteeism declined 24.1 percent, and employee satisfaction increased significantly. Because of these improvements, management permitted operators to work with fewer external controls. Perhaps more important, the supervisor no longer had to spend his time supervising behavior and dealing with crises, but could devote time to developing feedback systems, setting up work modules, and leading the job enrichment effort. ■

Barriers to Job Enrichment

As the application of job enrichment has spread, a number of obstacles to significant job restructuring have been identified. Most of these barriers exist in the organizational context within which the job design is executed. Other organizational systems and practices, whether technical, managerial, or personnel, can affect both the implementation of job enrichment and the lifespan of whatever changes are made.

At least four organizational systems can constrain the implementation of job enrichment:[16]

1. *The technical system.* The technology of an organization can limit job enrichment by constraining the number of ways jobs can be changed. For example, long-linked technology like that found on an assembly line can be highly programmed and standardized, thus limiting the amount of employee discretion that is possible. Technology also may set an "enrichment ceiling." Some types of work, such as continuous-process production systems, may be naturally enriched so there is little more that can be gained from a job enrichment intervention.

2. *The personnel system.* Personnel systems can constrain job enrichment by creating formalized job descriptions that are rigidly defined and limit flexibility in changing people's job duties. For example, many union agreements include such narrowly defined job descriptions that major renegotiation between management and the union must occur before jobs can be significantly enriched.

3. *The control system.* Control systems, such as budgets, production reports, and accounting practices, can limit the complexity and challenge of jobs within the system. For example, a company working on a government contract may have such strict quality control procedures that employee discretion is effectively curtailed.

4. *The supervisory system.* Supervisors determine to a large extent the amount of autonomy and feedback that subordinates can experience. To the extent that supervisors use autocratic methods and control work-related feedback, jobs will be difficult, if not impossible, to enrich.

Once these implementation constraints have been overcome, other factors determine whether the effects of job enrichment are strong and lasting.[17] Consistent with the contingency approach to OD, the staying power of job enrichment depends largely on how well it fits and is supported by other organizational practices, such as those associated with training, compensation, and supervision. These practices need to be congruent with and to reinforce jobs having high amounts of discretion, skill variety, and meaningful feedback.

Results of Job Enrichment

Hackman and Oldham reported data from the JDS on more than one thousand people in about one hundred different jobs in more than a dozen organizations.[18] In general, they found that employees whose jobs were high on the core dimensions were more satisfied and motivated than were those whose jobs were low on the dimensions. The core dimensions also were related to such behaviors as absenteeism and performance, although the relationship was not strong for performance. In addition, they found that responses were more positive for people with high growth needs than for those with weaker ones. Similarly, recent research has shown that enriched jobs are strongly correlated with mental ability.[19] Enriching the jobs of workers with low growth needs or with low knowledge and skills is more likely to produce frustration than satisfaction.

An impressive amount of research has been done on Hackman and Oldham's approach to job enrichment. In addition, a number of studies have extended and refined their approach, including a modification of the original JDS instrument to produce more reliable data[20] and the incorporation of such other moderators as the need for achievement and job longevity.[21] In general, research has supported the proposed relationships between job characteristics and outcomes, including the moderating effects of growth needs, knowledge and skills, and context satisfaction.[22] In regard to context satisfaction, for example, research indicates that employee turnover, dissatisfaction, and withdrawal are associated with dark offices, a lack of privacy, and high worker densities.[23]

Reviews of the job enrichment research also report positive effects. An analysis of twenty-eight studies concluded that the job characteristics are positively related to job satisfaction, particularly for people with high growth needs.[24] Another review concluded that job enrichment is effective at reducing employee turnover.[25] A different examination of twenty-eight job enrichment studies reported overwhelmingly positive results.[26] Improvements in quality and cost measures were reported slightly more frequently than improvements in employee attitudes and quantity of production. However, the studies suffered from methodological weaknesses which suggest that the positive findings should be viewed with some caution. Another review of sixteen job enrichment studies showed mixed results.[27] Thirteen of the programs were developed and implemented solely by management. These studies showed significant reduction in absenteeism, turnover, and grievances, and improvements in production quality in only about half of the cases where these variables were measured. The three studies with high levels of employee participation in the change program showed improvements in these variables in all cases where they were measured. Although it is difficult to generalize from such a small number of studies, employee participation in the job enrichment program appears to enhance the success of such interventions.

Finally, a comprehensive meta-analysis of more than seventy-five empirical studies of the Hackman and Oldham model found modest support for the overall model.[28] Although some modifications to the model appear warranted, the studies suggested that many of the more substantive criticisms were unfounded. For example, research supported the conclusion that the relationships between core job characteristics and psychological outcomes were stronger and more consistent than the relationships between core job dimensions and work performance, although these latter relationships did exist and were meaningful. The researchers also found support for the proposed linkages among core job dimensions, critical psychological states, and psychological outcomes. It is interesting that the job feedback dimension emerged as the strongest and most consistent predictor of both psychological and behavioral work outcomes. The researchers suggested that of all job characteristics, increasing feedback had the most potential for improving work productivity and satisfaction. The role of growth-need strength as a moderator was also supported, especially between core dimensions and work performance. Clearly, research supporting the job enrichment model is plentiful. Although the evidence suggests that the model is not perfect, it does appear to be a reasonable guide to improving the motivational outcomes of work.

THE SOCIOTECHNICAL SYSTEMS APPROACH

The *sociotechnical systems (STS) approach* currently is the most extensive body of scientific and applied work underlying employee involvement and innovative work designs. Its techniques and design principles derive from extensive action research in both public and private organizations across diverse national cultures. This section reviews the conceptual foundations of the STS approach and then describes its most popular application—self-managed work teams.

Conceptual Background

Sociotechnical systems theory was developed originally at the Tavistock Institute of Human Relations in London and has spread to most industrialized nations in a little more than fifty years. In Europe and particularly Scandinavia, STS interventions are almost synonymous with work design and employee involvement. In Canada and the United States, STS concepts and methods underlie many of the innovative work designs and team-based structures that are so prevalent in contemporary organizations. Intel Corporation, United Technologies, General Mills, and Procter & Gamble are among the many organizations applying the STS approach to transforming how work is designed and performed.

STS theory is based on two fundamental premises: that an organization or work unit is a combined, social-plus-technical system (sociotechnical), and that this system is open in relation to its environment.[29]

Sociotechnical System

The first assumption suggests that whenever human beings are organized to perform tasks, a joint system is operating—a sociotechnical system. This system consists of two independent but related parts: a social part including the people performing the tasks and the relationships among them, and a technical part comprising the tools, techniques, and methods for task performance. These two parts are independent of each other because each follows a different set of behavioral laws. The social part operates according to biological and psychosocial laws, whereas the technical part functions according to mechanical and physical laws. Nevertheless, the two parts are related because they must act together to accomplish tasks. Hence, the term *sociotechnical* signifies the joint relationship that must occur between the social and technical parts, and the word *system* communicates that this connection results in a unified whole.

Because a sociotechnical system is composed of social and technical parts, it follows that it will produce two kinds of outcomes: products, such as goods and services; and social and psychological consequences, such as job satisfaction and commitment. The key issue is how to design the relationship between the two parts so that both outcomes are positive (referred to as *joint optimization*). Sociotechnical practitioners design work and organizations so that the social and technical parts work well together, producing high levels of product and human satisfaction. This effort contrasts with the engineering approach to designing work, which focuses on the technical component, worries about fitting people in later, and often leads to mediocre performance at high social costs. The STS approach also contrasts with the motivational approach that views work design in terms of human fulfillment and can lead to satisfied employees but inefficient work processes.

Environmental Relationship

The second major premise underlying STS theory is that such systems are open to their environments. As discussed in Chapter 5, open systems must interact with their environments to survive and develop. The environment provides the STS with necessary inputs of energy, raw materials, and information, and the STS provides the environment with products and services. The key issue here is how to design the interface between the STS and its environment so that the system has sufficient freedom to function while exchanging effectively with the environment. In what is typically called *boundary management*, STS practitioners structure environmental relationships both to protect the system from external disruptions and to facilitate the exchange of necessary resources and information. This enables the STS to adapt to changing conditions and to influence the environment in favorable directions.

In summary, STS theory suggests that effective work systems jointly optimize the relationship between their social and technical parts. Moreover, such systems effectively manage the boundary separating and relating them to the environment. This allows them to exchange with the environment while protecting themselves from external disruptions.

Self-Managed Work Teams

The most prevalent application of the STS approach is self-managed work teams.[30] Alternatively referred to as self-directed, self-regulating, or high-performance work teams, these work designs consist of members performing interrelated tasks.[31] Self-managed teams typically are responsible for a complete product or service, or a major part of a larger production process. They control members' task behaviors and make decisions about task assignments and work methods. In many cases, the team sets its own production goals within broader organizational limits and may be responsible for support services, such as maintenance, purchasing, and quality control. Team members generally are expected to learn many if not all of the jobs within the team's control and frequently are paid on the basis of knowledge and skills rather than seniority. When pay is based on performance, team rather than individual performance is the standard.

Self-managed work teams are being implemented at a rapid rate across a range of industries and organizations, such as Intel, Sherwin-Williams, General Mills, Quantum, General Electric, and Motorola. A 1996 survey of *Fortune* 1000 companies found that 78 percent of these firms were using self-managed work teams, a 50 percent increase from 1987.[32] Although this work design typically does not cover a majority of the workforce, this represents an impressive increase in the use of self-managed teams.

Figure 16.3 is a model explaining how self-managed work teams perform. It summarizes current STS research and shows how teams can be designed for high performance. Although the model is based mainly on experience with teams that perform the daily work of the organization (work teams), it also has relevance to

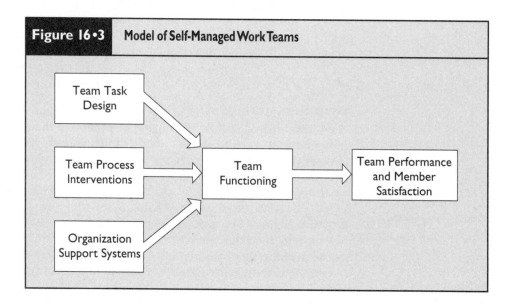

Figure 16•3   Model of Self-Managed Work Teams

Team Task Design → Team Functioning

Team Process Interventions → Team Functioning

Organization Support Systems → Team Functioning

Team Functioning → Team Performance and Member Satisfaction

other team designs, such as problem-solving teams, management teams, cross-functional integrating teams, and employee involvement teams.[33] The model shows that team performance and member satisfaction follow directly from how well the team functions: how well members communicate and coordinate with each other, resolve conflicts and problems, and make and implement task-relevant decisions. Team functioning, in turn, is influenced by three major inputs: team task design, team process interventions, and organization support systems. Because these inputs affect how well teams function and subsequently perform, they are key intervention targets for designing and implementing self-managed work teams.

Team Task Design

Self-managed work teams are responsible for performing particular tasks; consequently, how the team is designed for task performance can have a powerful influence on how well it functions. Task design generally follows from the team's mission and goals that define the major purpose of the team and provide direction for task achievement. When a team's mission and goals are closely aligned with corporate strategy and business objectives, members can see how team performance contributes to organization success. This can increase member commitment to team goals.

Team task design links members' behaviors to task requirements and to each other. It structures member interactions and performances. Three task design elements are necessary for creating self-managed work teams: task differentiation, boundary control, and task control.[34] *Task differentiation* involves the extent to which the team's task is autonomous and forms a relatively self-completing whole. High levels of task differentiation provide an identifiable team boundary and a clearly defined area of team responsibility. At Johnsonville Sausage, for example, self-managed teams comprise seven to fourteen members. Each team is large enough to accomplish a set of interrelated tasks but small enough to allow face-to-face meetings for coordination and decision making. In many hospitals, self-managed nursing teams are formed around interrelated tasks that together produce a relatively whole piece of work. Thus, nursing teams may be responsible for particular groups of patients, such as those in intensive care or undergoing cancer treatments, or they may be accountable for specific work processes, such as those in the laboratory, pharmacy, or admissions office.

Boundary control involves the extent to which team members can influence transactions with their task environment—the types and rates of inputs and outputs. Adequate boundary control includes a well-defined work area; group responsibility for boundary-control decisions, such as quality assurance (which reduces dependence on external boundary regulators, such as inspectors); and members sufficiently trained to perform tasks without relying heavily on external resources. Boundary control often requires deliberate cross-training of team members to take on a variety of tasks. This makes members highly flexible and adaptable to changing conditions. It also reduces the need for costly overhead because members can perform many of the tasks typically assigned to staff experts, such as those in quality control, planning, and maintenance.

Task control involves the degree to which team members can regulate their own behavior to provide services or to produce finished products. It includes the freedom to choose work methods, to schedule activities, and to influence production goals to match both environmental and task demands. Task control relies heavily on team members having the power and authority to manage equipment, materials, and other resources needed for task performance. This "work authority" is essential if members are to take responsibility for getting the work accomplished. Task control also requires that team members have accurate and timely information about team performance to allow them to detect performance problems and make necessary adjustments.

Task control enables self-managed work teams to observe and control technical variances as quickly and as close to their source as possible. Technical variances arise from the production process and represent significant deviations from specific goals or standards. In manufacturing, for example, abnormalities in raw material, machine operation, and work flow are sources of variance that can adversely affect the quality and quantity of the finished product. In service work, out-of-the-ordinary requests, special favors or treatment, or unique demands create variances that can place stress on the process. Technical variances traditionally are controlled by support staff and managers, but this can take time and add greatly to costs. Self-managed work teams, on the other hand, have the freedom, skills, and information needed to control technical variances online when they occur. This affords timely responses to production problems and reduces the amount of staff overhead needed.

Team Process Interventions

A second key input to team functioning involves team process interventions. As described in Chapter 12, teams may develop ineffective social processes that impede functioning and performance, such as poor communication among members, dysfunctional roles and norms, and faulty problem solving and decision making. Team process interventions, such as process consultation and team building, can resolve such problems by helping members address process problems and moving the team to a more mature stage of development. Because self-managed work teams need to be self-reliant, members generally acquire their own team process skills. They may attend appropriate training programs and workshops or they may learn on the job by working with OD practitioners to conduct process interventions on their own teams. Although members' process skills generally are sufficient to resolve most of the team's process problems, OD experts occasionally may need to supplement the team's skills and help members address problems that they are unable to resolve.

Organization Support Systems

The final input to team functioning is the extent to which the larger organization is designed to support self-managed work teams. The success of such teams clearly depends on support systems that are quite different from traditional methods of managing.[35] For example, a bureaucratic, mechanistic organization is not highly conducive to self-managed teams. An organic structure, with flexibility among units, relatively few formal rules and procedures, and decentralized authority, is much more likely to support and enhance the development of self-managed work teams. This explains why such teams are so prevalent in high-involvement organizations (described in Chapter 15). Their different features, such as flat, lean structures, open information systems, and team-based selection and reward practices, all reinforce teamwork and responsible self-management.

A particularly important support system for self-managed work teams is the external leadership. Self-managed teams exist along a spectrum from having only mild influence over their work to near-autonomy. In many circumstances, such teams take on a variety of functions traditionally handled by management. These can include assigning members to individual tasks, determining the methods of work, scheduling, setting production goals, and selecting and rewarding members. These activities do not make external supervision obsolete, however. That leadership role usually is changed to two major functions: working with and developing team members, and assisting the team in managing its boundaries.[36]

Working with and developing team members is a difficult process and requires a different style of managing than do traditional systems. The team leader (often called a team facilitator) helps team members organize themselves in a way that allows them to become more independent and responsible. She or he must be familiar with team-building approaches and must assist members in learning the skills to perform their jobs. Recent research suggests that the leader needs to provide expertise in self-management.[37] This may include encouraging team members to be self-reinforcing about high performance, to be self-critical of low performance, to set explicit performance goals, to evaluate goal achievement, and to rehearse different performance strategies before trying them.

If team members are to maintain sufficient autonomy to control variance from goal attainment, the leader may need to help them manage team boundaries. Where teams have limited control over their task environment, the leader may act as a buffer to reduce environmental uncertainty. This can include mediating and negotiating with other organizational units, such as higher management, staff experts, and related work teams. Research suggests that better managers spend more time in lateral interfaces.[38]

These new leadership roles require new and different skills, including knowledge of sociotechnical principles and group dynamics, understanding of both the task environment and the team's technology, and ability to intervene in the team to help members increase their knowledge and skills. Leaders of self-managed teams also should have the ability to counsel members and to facilitate communication among them.

Many managers have experienced problems trying to fulfill the complex demands of leading self-managed work teams. The most typical complaints mention ambiguity about responsibilities and authority, lack of personal and technical skills and organizational support, insufficient attention from higher management, and feelings of frustration in the supervisory job.[39] Attempts to overcome these problems have been made in the following areas.[40]

1. *Recruitment and selection.* Recruitment has been directed at selecting team leaders with a balanced mixture of technical and social skills. Those with extensive technical experience have been paired with more socially adept leaders so that both can share skills and support each other.

2. *Training.* Extensive formal and on-the-job training in human relations, group dynamics, and leadership styles have been instituted for leaders of self-managed work teams. Such training is aimed at giving leaders concepts for understanding their roles, as well as hands-on experience in team building, process consultation, and third-party intervention (see Chapter 12).

3. *Evaluation and reward systems.* Attempts have been made to tie team leader rewards to achievements in team development. Leaders prepare developmental plans for individual workers and the team as a whole, and set measurable benchmarks for progress. Performance appraisals of leaders are conducted within a group format, with feedback supplied by team members, peers, and higher-level management.

4. *Leadership support systems.* Leaders of self-managed work teams have been encouraged to develop peer support groups. Team leaders can meet off site to share experiences and to address issues of personal and general concern.

5. *Use of freed-up time.* Team leaders have been provided with a mixture of strategies to apply their talents beyond the immediate work team. A team leader has more time when the team has matured and taken on many managerial functions. In those cases, team leaders have been encouraged to become involved in such areas as higher-level planning and budgeting, companywide training and development, and individual career development.

Application Stages

STS work designs have been implemented in a variety of settings, including manufacturing firms, hospitals, schools, and government agencies. Although the specific implementation strategy is tailored to the situation, a common method of change underlies many of these applications. It generally involves high worker participation in work design and implementation. Such participative work design allows employees to translate their special knowledge of the work situation into relevant designs, and employees with ownership over the design process are likely to be highly committed to implementing the outcomes.[41]

STS applications generally proceed in six steps:[42]

1. *Sanctioning the design effort.* At this step, workers receive the necessary protection and support to diagnose their work system and to create an appropriate work design. In many unionized situations, top management and union officials jointly agree to suspend temporarily the existing work rules and job classifications so that employees have the freedom to explore new ways of working. Management also may provide workers with sufficient time and external help to diagnose their work system and devise alternative work structures. In cases of redesigning existing work systems, normal production demands may be reduced during the redesign process. Also, workers may be given some job and wage security so that they feel free to try new designs without fear of losing their jobs or money.

2. *Diagnosing the work system.* This step includes analyzing the work system to discover how it is operating. Knowledge of existing operations (or of intended operations, in the case of a new work system) is the basis for creating an appropriate work design. STS practitioners have devised diagnostic models applicable to work systems that make products or deliver services. The models analyze a system's technical and social parts and assess how well the two fit each other. The task environment facing the system also is analyzed to see how well it is meeting external demands, such as customer quality requirements.

3. *Generating appropriate designs.* Based on the diagnosis, the work system is redesigned to fit the situation. Although this typically results in self-managed work teams, it is important to emphasize that the diagnosis may reveal that tasks are not very interdependent and that an individual-job work design, such as an enriched job, might be more appropriate. Two important STS principles guide the design process.

The first principle, *compatibility,* suggests that the process of designing work should fit the values and objectives underlying the approach. For example, the major goals of STS design are joint optimization and boundary management. A work-design process compatible with those objectives would be highly participative, involving those having a stake in the work design, such as employees, managers, engineers, and staff experts. They would jointly decide how to create the social and technical components of work, as well as the environmental exchanges. This participative process increases the likelihood that design choices will be based simultaneously on technical, social, and environmental criteria. How well the compatibility guideline is adhered to can determine how well the work design subsequently is implemented.[43]

The second design principle is called *minimal critical specification*. It suggests that STS designers should specify only those critical features needed to implement the work design. All other features of the design should be left free to vary with the circumstances. In most cases, minimal critical specification identifies what is to be done, not how it will be accomplished. This allows employees considerable freedom to choose work methods, task allocations, and job assignments to match changing conditions.

The output of this design step specifies the new work design. In the case of self-managed teams, this includes the team's mission and goals, an ideal work flow, the skills and knowledge required of team members, a plan for training members to meet those requirements, and a list of the decisions the team will make now as well as the ones it should make over time as members develop greater skills and knowledge.

4. *Specifying support systems.* As suggested above, organizational support systems may have to be changed to support new work designs. When self-managed teams are designed, for example, the basis for pay and measurement systems may need to change from individual to team performance to facilitate necessary task interaction among workers.

5. *Implementing and evaluating the work designs.* This stage involves making necessary changes to implement the work design and evaluating the results. For self-managing teams, implementation generally requires a great amount of training so that workers gain the necessary technical and social skills to perform multiple tasks and to control task behaviors. It also may entail developing the team through various team-building and process-consultation activities. OD consultants often help team members carry out these tasks with a major emphasis on helping them gain competence in this area. Evaluation of the work design is necessary both to guide the implementation process and to assess the overall effectiveness of the design. In some cases, the evaluation information suggests the need for further diagnosis and redesign efforts.

6. *Continual change and improvement.* This last step points out that STS designing never is complete but rather continues as new things are learned and new conditions are encountered. Thus, the ability to design and redesign work continually needs to be built into existing work designs. Members must have the skills and knowledge to assess their work unit continually and to make necessary changes and improvements. From this view, STS designing rarely results in a stable work design but instead provides a process for modifying work continually to fit changing conditions and to make performance improvements.

Application 16.2 describes how one of ASEA Brown Boveri's plants implemented self-managed teams.[44] It clearly demonstrates the importance of aligning the systems to support self-management as well as the process of gradually increasing the team's autonomy and responsibility.

Results of Self-Managed Teams

Research on STS design efforts is extensive. For example, a 1994 bibliography by researchers at Eindhoven University of Technology in The Netherlands found

APPLICATION 16•2   Moving to Self-Managed Teams at ABB

The ASEA Brown Boveri (ABB) Industrial Systems plant in Columbus, Ohio, was part of ABB's Industrial and Building Systems division. It produced low-volume, made-to-order industrial process and quality control systems. A single system included mechanical and hydraulic machinery, high-speed computer processors, and high-speed/high-accuracy measurement sensors that incorporated infrared, microwave, and other optical technologies packaged for severe environments. Customers for these control systems included the pulp and paper, chemical, petrochemical, pharmaceutical, metals, textiles, and food industries.

Overall demand for industrial control systems expanded steadily during the 1980s. But in 1990, demand dropped sharply and competition from international manufacturers increased. Ken Morris became vice president of manufacturing at the Columbus plant in 1991. Unfortunately, Morris arrived at a time when the manufacturing performance at the Columbus plant had not kept pace with the global market. Overhead costs above industry averages and low quality of suppliers' products combined to produce a net loss for four straight years. Morris recognized another sign of trouble when he repeatedly observed employees from different departments meeting separately with the same customers and not communicating with the other departments about the discussions they had with their mutual customers. "We had a silo-based organization. No one knew what the other was doing," Morris explained.

Based on this and other information, Morris's original idea was to create more flexibility for employees to work with customers and suppliers. "I had done a lot of reading about teams," he said, "and I knew that a lot of folks in the industry were talking about moving to total quality management or teams over the next few years. But I wasn't interested in teaming for teaming's sake. Whatever we did had to keep us alive, and I didn't have years to do it. I had to do something now." Morris laid out a change plan that would radically reshape the structure and systems that governed the Columbus plant. At the center of the reorganization was the concept of the high-performance work system. Eventually, nineteen teams—twelve production process teams and seven continuous improvement teams—would be the fundamental work units of the 186-employee plant.

ABB's move to a high-performance, team-based work system proceeded in a stepwise fashion, each step building on the previous one. Morris began the effort by preparing both his leadership team and the plant's employees for the coming changes. An off-site meeting was used to educate members of his leadership staff on the basics of team-based organizations and to gain their ownership in the plant's new direction. One

output of the retreat was the formation of a "high-performance work system" design team that worked for six months to create a change plan. Another important output was the new mission for the ABB Columbus plant: "To become recognized as the best time-based competitor in the world" by developing a customer-focused environment with a passion for process management and waste reduction, and a desire to unleash the power of people. Morris also began to hold quarterly meetings with all plant employees and to share information with them about competitors, the industry, planning, and financial conditions. For most employees, the inaugural quarterly meeting was the first time they had heard that the plant was operating at a loss.

Implementing the high-performance work system at ABB Columbus was formally initiated by adopting a set of industry benchmarks for products and processes in 1991. These quality measurements became the first goals for the plant's production system. In this way, Morris and his team hoped to get the manufacturing and supply processes under control. Implementation continued with technical changes in the work flow, including adoption of a just-in-time production process and installation of a new, fully integrated management information system. These changes dramatically increased the interdependency between steps in the work flow. The organization structure was changed from functional silos to a process-based structure in November 1993.

As the structure evolved, ABB emphasized training as a key to its success. "Education and training shifted us to the paradigm we wanted. Without that investment, we would have only seen incremental improvements," said Morris. "The quantum improvements we achieved were possible because we created a new vision of what was possible and then taught ourselves how to achieve it." Every ABB employee participated in a rigorous program of high-performance work systems, just-in-time manufacturing systems, conflict resolution, and ISO 9000 standards and processes. As noted by human resources internal consultant Mari Jo Cary, "The high-performance work system created a business environment to produce a quality product and on-time delivery at the right price for our customers." Plant employees continued to spend 4.5 percent of their time on training and education. These preparatory changes allowed for establishing the first process teams and process improvement teams following the restructuring.

The movement toward a team-based organization was slow and frustrating. The changes came at a time of falling production that increased unit costs and rising turnover at all levels of the organization. Furthermore, negative attitudes toward teams surfaced in the 1992 employee survey. Employee complaints continued to rise about the frequency of meetings, team goals that seemed unreachable, and the time it took to operate as a team.

The twelve process teams were formed around three key product lines and five support processes, such as supply management, engineering, metal fabrication, traffic management, and financial and human resources support. Each team consisted of six to fifteen members who, in addition to their manufacturing responsibilities, could serve as a coordinator for one of the seven team functions: time management, quality, safety, just-in-time processes, supply management, communications, and continuous improvement. Each team was chartered by its process owner—a senior-level manager for that product line who was responsible for two or three teams. Each charter described the team's purpose and vision, the roles and responsibilities of team members, processes for selection and dismissal, and norms of team member behavior.

While the production and support process teams were charged with meeting the benchmark standards for cycle time, quality, and cost, the seven process improvement teams worked to enhance efficiency and effectiveness within and across the production process teams. For example, a supply management process improvement team initiated a supplier excellence certification process. Each supplier was rated on a "report card." Those who didn't rate well were eliminated from the list of eligible suppliers; those who rated well received contracts. Eventually, continuous improvement in the supply management process led to elimination of all inspections of incoming material, the direct delivery of supplies to the point of use rather than into inventory, the elimination of a 115,000-square-foot storage facility, and the creation of a planner/supply management expert role for each production process team.

A key feature of ABB's transition to a fully self-managed team environment was the teams' gradual adoption of more and more responsibility and decision-making authority. ABB developed twenty-four "points of implementation," outlining responsibilities common to all teams. These twenty-four key team functions ranged from simple tasks (for example, housekeeping, equipment maintenance, and control of scrap material), to more difficult functions (for example, vacation scheduling, control of materials and inventory, and job design), to advanced team functions (for example, conflict resolution, selection of new members, and, ultimately, compensation decisions). Initially, all teams were assigned a low level of accountability and empowerment (level 1) for each of the twenty-four points. At that stage, the team had little ownership for the function. Although the process owner worked

with the team, accountability for team behaviors rested with that owner. Higher levels of empowerment increased the amounts of responsibility, authority, and accountability over key functions. At level 4, the team developed and implemented plans without review, and team accountability rested with team members. Boundary management and compensation decisions were shared with the process owner.

To reach the highest level of autonomy and accountability (level 4), a team first had to be introduced to the meaning and concept of the particular function. The team's next step was to take the function and create a plan to implement and perform ongoing management of that function. The third step was to demonstrate that it had the ability to implement the plan and manage the function without assistance. As the final step in becoming accountable for a function, the process owner signified that the team was fully empowered for future actions within this function. These points of implementation laid out a clear road map for each team and provided it with clear boundaries regarding its level of autonomy, responsibility, and accountability.

By 1995, each team was completely self-managed. All functions traditionally conducted by a manager or team leader were handled by the team. Teams answered directly to their process owner and customers, and in 1996 began conducting their own performance evaluations using a 360-degree process. When the teams required knowledge or skills outside of their existing capabilities, they called upon subject-matter experts within the plant who provided support in such areas as order management, price/cost quoting, material sourcing and control, production, inventory control, product quality, packing, and invoicing.

The results of ABB's effort were impressive. By 1994, the Columbus plant had achieved the following performance improvements:

- Warranty costs had been reduced by 74 percent.
- Revenue generated per person was up 212 percent.
- Work-in-progress turnover was up 222 percent.
- Total cycle time had been reduced from 16.2 weeks to 4.3 weeks, a 73-percent reduction.
- Seven managers and twenty-five supervisors had been replaced with five process owners.

By 1995, the Columbus plant had posted a profit for the first time since 1990, and all key financial and performance objectives were met or exceeded. In addition, its 95.3 percent on-time-to-customer rating was recognized as a best-in-class benchmark, and the plant was named among *Industry Week's* top ten plants. ■

3,082 English-language studies.[45] As with reports on job enrichment, most of the published reports on self-managed teams show favorable results.[46]

A series of famous case studies at General Foods' Gaines Pet Food/Topeka plant, the Saab-Scania engine assembly plant, and Volvo's Kalmar and Udevalla plants provide one set of positive findings. The Gaines Pet Food plant operated at an overhead rate that was 33 percent below that of traditional plants.[47] It reported annual variable cost savings of six hundred thousand dollars, one of the best safety records in the company, turnover rates far below average, and high levels of job satisfaction. A long-term, external evaluation of the groups at Gaines plant attributed savings related to work innovation at about $1 million a year, and despite a variety of problems, productivity increased in every year but one over a decade of operation.[48] The plant has maintained one of the highest product quality ratings at General Foods since its opening.

Extensive research on self-managing groups has been done by Saab-Scania.[49] The first group was established in 1969, and four years later there were 130 production groups. These groups have generally shown improvements in production and employee attitudes and decreases in unplanned work stoppages and turnover rates. It is interesting that workers from the United States who have visited Saab's engine assembly plant reported that work was too fast and that lunch breaks were too short.[50] A Saab executive commented that the visitors had not stayed long enough to understand the design fully, causing their complaint that the pace was too fast.

The widely publicized use of self-managing groups at Volvo's automotive plant in Kalmar, Sweden, also has shown positive results.[51] The Kalmar factory opened in July 1974 and by the following year it was operating at 100 percent efficiency. As a reference point, highly productive automobile plants normally operate at about 80 percent of engineering standards. Interviews with workers and union officials indicated that the quality of work life was considerably better than in assembly jobs that they had held in the past. Volvo's Udevalla plant also reported significant quality improvements and higher productivity than comparable plants.[52]

A second set of studies supporting the positive impact of sociotechnical design teams comes from research comparing self-managed teams with other interventions. For example, probably one of the most thorough assessments of self-managing groups is a longitudinal study conducted in a midwestern U.S. food-processing plant.[53] Self-managed groups were created as part of an overall revamping of a major part of the plant's production facilities. The effects of the intervention were extremely positive. One year after startup, production was 133 percent higher than originally planned, while start-up costs were 7.7 percent lower than expected. Fewer workers were needed to operate the plant than engineers had projected, with an annual savings in fixed-labor expense of $264,000. Employee attitudes were extremely positive toward the group design. These positive effects did not result solely from the self-managing design, however. The intervention also included survey feedback for diagnostic purposes and changes in technology, the physical work setting, and management. These kinds of changes, common in self-managing group projects, facilitate the development of self-managed teams.

This study also permitted a comparison of self-managing groups with job enrichment, which occurred in another department of the company. Both interventions included survey feedback. The self-managing project involved technological changes, whereas the job enrichment program did not. The results showed that the interventions had similar positive effects in terms of employee attitudes, but only the self-managing project had significant improvements in productivity and costs.

Again, the productivity improvements cannot be attributed solely to the self-managed teams but also were the result of the technological changes.

More recently, a rigorous field experiment in a telecommunications company compared self-managed teams with traditionally designed work groups performing the same types of tasks. The study found significant differences between the two groups in job satisfaction, growth-needs satisfaction, social-needs satisfaction, and group satisfaction. Self-managing group members and higher-level managers perceived group performance as superior to traditionally managed groups. In contrast to these overall findings, however, objective measures of service quality and customer satisfaction did not differ between the two types of groups.[54]

A third set of positive results comes from reviews, or meta-analyses, of other studies. One review examined sixteen studies and showed that when productivity, costs, and quality were measured, improvements occurred in more than 85 percent of the cases.[55] Significant reductions in employee turnover and absenteeism rates and improvements in employee attitudes were reported in about 70 percent of the cases where these variables were measured. Certain methodological weaknesses in the studies suggest, however, that the positive results should be viewed carefully. Another review of twelve studies of self-managed groups showed improvements in hard performance measures in about 67 percent of the cases where such measures were taken.[56] Both of these reviews also included job enrichment studies, as reported earlier in this chapter. The relative impact of self-managing groups seems about equal to that of job enrichment, especially when the latter includes worker participation in the design process.

Three more recent meta-analyses also provide general support for self-managed teams. In a review of all STS work design studies conducted in the 1970s, researchers found a strong positive relationship between the installation of self-managed teams and attitudinal and economic gains.[57] These designs were found to increase employee satisfaction; to reduce production costs through group member innovations; and to decrease absenteeism, turnover, and accident rates. The researchers reported little evidence for claims of increased productivity primarily because of the lack of sufficient reported data. In a technical and comprehensive meta-analysis, researchers concluded that self-managed teams do produce increases in productivity and reductions in escape behavior, such as absenteeism, but that these effects varied widely. Higher results were associated with high levels of work-group autonomy, supporting changes in the reward system, interventions that did not include technological changes, and applications outside of the United States.[58] Finally, a detailed and comprehensive meta-analysis of 131 North American field experiments reported that work innovations, such as autonomous and semiautonomous work groups, were more likely to have a positive impact on financial performance measures, including costs, productivity, and quality, than were behavioral or attitudinal variables.[59] Considerable variation in the size of the positive effect, however, led the researchers to suggest that organization change was risky. Only when such other organizational features as reward systems, information systems, and performance appraisal systems changed simultaneously was the probability of positive results increased.

Although the majority of studies report positive effects of self-managing groups, some research suggests a more mixed assessment. A field experiment studying the long-term effects of self-managed groups showed improvements in job satisfaction but no effects on job motivation, work performance, organizational commitment, mental health, or voluntary turnover.[60] The company did lower indirect overhead costs, however, by reducing the number of supervisors. This study, which received an award from the Academy of Management for quality research, concluded that the major benefits of self-managed teams are economic, deriving from the need for less supervision. Another study found that the introduction of self-managed teams into an independent insurance agency threatened the personal control and autonomy of individual employees.[61] The groups that were implemented without employee participation exerted strong pressures to follow rigid procedures. Group leaders focused on the concerns of younger, inexperienced employees and ignored older workers' requests for less red tape and more freedom. The older employees felt that the groups undermined their individual discretion, autonomy, and initiative. The study concluded that unless self-managed teams are implemented and managed properly, individual members' autonomy and motivation can be constrained inadvertently.

DESIGNING WORK FOR TECHNICAL AND PERSONAL NEEDS

This chapter has described three approaches to work design: engineering, motivational, and sociotechnical. Tradeoffs and conflicts among the approaches must be recognized. The engineering approach produces traditional jobs and work groups and focuses on efficient performance. It downplays employee needs and emphasizes economic outcomes. The motivational approach designs jobs that are stimulating and demanding and highlights the importance of employee need satisfaction. Research suggests, however, that increased satisfaction may not generate improvements in productivity. Finally, the sociotechnical systems approach integrates social and technical aspects, but has not produced consistent research results on its success. In this final section, we attempt to integrate the three perspectives by providing a contingency framework that suggests that any of the three approaches can be effective when applied in the appropriate circumstances. Work design involves creating jobs and work groups for high levels of employee satisfaction and productivity. A large body of research shows that achieving such results depends on designing work to match specific factors operating in the work setting, factors that involve the technology for producing goods and services and the personal needs of employees. When work is designed to fit or match these factors, it is most likely to be both productive and humanly satisfying.

The technical and personal factors affecting work design success provide a contingency framework for choosing among the four different kinds of work designs discussed in the chapter: traditional jobs, traditional work groups, enriched jobs, and self-managed teams.

Technical Factors

Two key dimensions can affect change on the shop floor: technical interdependence, or the extent to which cooperation among workers is required to produce a product or service; and technical uncertainty, or the amount of information processing and decision making employees must do to complete a task.[62] In general, the degree of technical interdependence determines whether work should be designed for individual jobs or for work groups. When interdependence is low and there is little need for worker cooperation—as, for example, in field sales and data entry—work can be designed for individual jobs. Conversely, when interdependence is high and employees must cooperate—as in production processes like coal mining, assembly lines, and writing software—work should be designed for groups composed of people performing interacting tasks.

The second dimension, technical uncertainty, determines whether work should be designed for external forms of control, such as supervision, scheduling, or standardization, or for worker self-control. When technical uncertainty is low and little information has to be processed by employees, work can be designed for external control, such as might be found on assembly lines and in other forms of repetitive work. On the other hand, when technical uncertainty is high and people must process information and make decisions, work should be designed for high levels of employee self-control, such as might be found in professional work and troubleshooting tasks.

Figure 16.4 shows the different types of work designs that are most effective, from a purely technical perspective, for different combinations of interdependence and uncertainty. In quadrant 1, where technical interdependence and uncertainty are both low, such as might be found in data entry, jobs should be designed traditionally with limited amounts of employee interaction and self-control. When task interdependence is high but uncertainty is low (quadrant 2), such as work occurring on assembly lines, work should be designed for traditional work groups in which employee interaction is scheduled and self-control is limited. In quadrant 3, where technical interdependence is low but uncertainty is high, such as in field sales, work should be structured for individual jobs with internal forms of control, such as in enriched jobs. Finally, when both technical interdependence and uncertainty are high (quadrant 4), such as might be found in a continuous-process chemical plant, work should be designed for self-managed teams in which members have the multiple skills, discretion, and information necessary to control their interactions around the shared tasks.

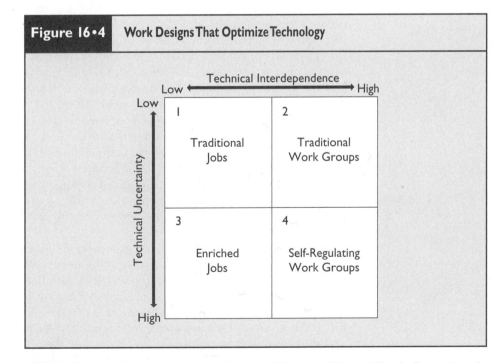

Figure 16•4   Work Designs That Optimize Technology

Technical Interdependence
Low ←———————————→ High

Technical Uncertainty
Low

1	2
Traditional Jobs	Traditional Work Groups
3	4
Enriched Jobs	Self-Regulating Work Groups

High

SOURCE: Reproduced by permission of the publisher from T. Cummings, "Designing Work for Productivity and Quality of Work Life," *Outlook* 6 (1982): 39.

Personal-Need Factors

Most of the research identifying individual differences in work design has focused on selected personal traits. Two types of personal needs can influence the kinds of work designs that are most effective: social needs, or the desire for significant social relationships; and growth needs, or the desire for personal accomplishment, learning, and development.[63] In general, the degree of *social needs* determines whether work should be designed for individual jobs or work groups. People with low needs for social relationships are more likely to be satisfied working on individualized jobs than in interacting groups. Conversely, people with high social needs are more likely to be attracted to group forms of work than to individualized forms.

The second individual difference, *growth needs*, determines whether work designs should be routine and repetitive or complex and challenging. People with low growth needs generally are not attracted to jobs offering complexity and challenge (that is, enriched jobs) but are more satisfied performing routine forms of work that do not require high levels of decision making. On the other hand, people with high growth needs are satisfied with work offering high levels of discretion, skill variety, and meaningful feedback. Performing enriched jobs allows them to experience personal accomplishment and development.

That some people have low social and growth needs often is difficult for OD practitioners to accept, particularly in light of the social and growth values underlying much OD practice. It is important to recognize, however, that individual differences do exist. Assuming that all people have high growth needs or want high levels of social interaction can lead to inappropriate work designs. For example, a new manager of a clerical support unit was astonished to find the six members using typewriters, even though a significant portion of the work consisted of retyping memos and reports that were produced frequently but changed very little from month to month. In addition, the unit had a terrible record of quality and on-time production. The manager quickly ordered new word processors and redesigned the work flow to increase interaction among members. Worker satisfaction declined, interpersonal conflicts increased, and work quality and on-time performance remained poor. An assessment of the effort revealed that all six of the staff members had low growth needs and low needs for inclusion in group efforts. In the words of one worker, "All I want is to come into work, do my job, and get my paycheck."

It is important to emphasize that people who have low growth or social needs are not inferior to those placing a higher value on those factors; they simply are different. It is necessary also to recognize that people can change their needs through personal growth and experience. OD practitioners must be sensitive to individual differences in work design and careful not to force their own values on others. Many consultants, eager to be seen on the cutting edge of practice, recommend self-managed teams in all situations, without careful attention to technological and personal considerations.

Figure 16.5 shows the different types of work designs that are most effective for the various combinations of social and growth needs. When employees have relatively low social and growth needs (quadrant 1), traditional jobs are most effective. In quadrant 2, where employees have high social needs but low growth needs, traditional work groups, such as might be found on an assembly line, are most appropriate. These allow for some social interaction but limited amounts of challenge and discretion. When employees have low social needs but high growth needs (quadrant 3), enriched jobs are most satisfying. Here, work is designed for individual jobs that have high levels of task variety, discretion, and feedback about results. A research scientist's job is likely to be enriched, as is that of a skilled craftsperson.

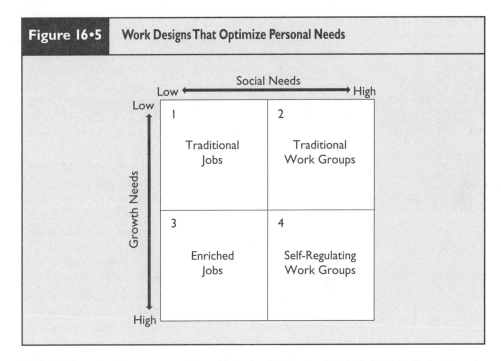

Figure 16·5   Work Designs That Optimize Personal Needs

SOURCE: Reproduced by permission of the publisher from T. Cummings, "Designing Work for Productivity and Quality of Work Life," *Outlook* 6 (1982): 40.

Finally, in quadrant 4, where employees have high social and growth needs, work should be designed for self-managed teams that offer significant social interaction around complex and challenging tasks. A team of astronauts in a space shuttle resembles a self-managed work group, as does a group managing the control room of an oil refinery or a group of nurses in a hospital unit.

Meeting Both Technical and Personal Needs

Jointly satisfying technical and human needs to achieve work-design success is likely to occur only in limited circumstances. When the technical conditions of a company's production processes (as shown in Figure 16.4) are compatible with the personal needs of its employees (as shown in Figure 16.5), the respective work designs combine readily and can satisfy both. On General Motors' assembly lines, for example, the technology is highly interdependent but low in uncertainty (quadrant 2 in Figure 16.4). Much of the production is designed around traditional work groups in which task behaviors are standardized and interactions among workers are scheduled. Such work is likely to be productive and fulfilling to the extent that General Motors' production workers have high social needs and low growth needs (quadrant 2 in Figure 16.5).

When technology and people are incompatible—for example, when an organization has quadrant 1 technology and quadrant 4 worker needs—at least two kinds of changes can be made to design work that satisfies both requirements.[64] One strategy is to change technology or people to bring them more into line with each other. This is a key point underlying sociotechnical systems approaches. For example, technical interdependence can be reduced by breaking long assembly lines into more discrete groups. In Sweden, Volvo redesigned the physical layout and technology for assembling automobiles and trucks to promote self-managed teams.

Modifying people's needs is more complex and begins by matching new or existing workers to available work designs. For example, companies can assess workers' needs through standardized paper-and-pencil tests and use the information gleaned from them to counsel employees and help them locate jobs compatible with their needs. Similarly, employees can be allowed to volunteer for specific work designs—a common practice in STS projects. This matching process is likely to require high levels of trust and cooperation between management and workers, as well as a shared commitment to designing work for high performance and employee satisfaction.

A second strategy for accommodating both technical and human requirements is to leave the two components unchanged and create compromise work designs that only partially fulfill the demands of either component. The key issue is to decide to what extent one contingency will be satisfied at the expense of the other. For example, when capital costs are high relative to labor costs, such as in highly automated plants, work design is likely to favor the technology. Conversely, in many service jobs where labor is expensive relative to capital, organizations may design work for employee motivation and satisfaction at the risk of shortchanging their technology. These examples suggest a range of possible compromises based on different weightings of technical and human demands. Careful assessment of both types of contingencies and of the cost–benefit tradeoffs is necessary to design an appropriate compromise work design.

Clearly, the strategy of designing work to bring technology and people more into line with each other is preferable to the compromise work design strategy. Although the latter approach seems necessary when there are heavy constraints on changing the contingencies, in many cases those constraints are more imagined than real. The important thing is to understand the technical and personal factors existing in a particular situation and to design work accordingly. Traditional jobs and traditional work groups will be successful in certain situations (as shown in Figures 16.4 and 16.5); in other settings, enriched jobs and self-managed teams will be more effective.

■ SUMMARY

In this chapter, we discussed three different approaches to work design and described a contingency framework to determine the approach most likely to result in high productivity and worker satisfaction. The contingency framework reconciles the strengths and weaknesses of each approach. The engineering approach produces traditional jobs and traditional work groups. Traditional jobs are highly simplified and involve routine and repetitive forms of work, rather than coordination among people to produce a product or service. Traditional jobs achieve high productivity and worker satisfaction in situations characterized by low technical uncertainty and interdependence and low growth and social needs.

Traditional work groups are composed of members who perform routine yet interrelated tasks. Member interactions are controlled externally, usually by rigid work flows, schedules, and supervisors. Traditional work groups are best suited to conditions of low technical uncertainty but high technical interdependence. They fit people with low growth needs but high social needs.

The motivational approach produces enriched jobs involving high levels of skill variety, task identity, task significance, autonomy, and feedback from the work itself. Enriched jobs achieve good results when the technology is uncertain but does not require high levels of coordination and when employees have high growth needs and low social needs.

Finally, the sociotechnical systems approach is associated with self-managed teams. These groups are composed of members performing interrelated tasks. Members are given the multiple skills, autonomy, and information necessary to control their own task behaviors with relatively little external control. Many OD practitioners argue that self-managed teams represent the work design of the 1990s because high levels of technical uncertainty and interdependence are prevalent in today's workplaces and because today's workers often have high growth and social needs.

■ NOTES

1. F. Taylor, *The Principles of Scientific Management* (New York: Harper & Row, 1911).

2. Ibid.

3. T. Cummings, "Self-Regulating Work Groups: A Socio-Technical Synthesis," *Academy of Management Review* 3 (1978): 625–34; G. Susman, *Autonomy at Work* (New York: Praeger, 1976); J. Slocum and H. Sims, "A Typology of Technology and Job Redesign," *Human Relations* 33 (1983): 193–212.

4. F. Herzberg, B. Mausner, and B. Snyderman, *The Motivation to Work* (New York: John Wiley & Sons, 1959); F. Herzberg, "The Wise Old Turk," *Harvard Business Review* 52 (September-October 1974): 70–80; F. Herzberg and Z. Zautra, "Orthodox Job Enrichment: Measuring True Quality in Job Satisfaction," *Personnel* 53 (September-October 1976): 54–68.

5. M. Myers, *Every Employee a Manager* (New York: McGraw-Hill, 1970); R. Ford, *Motivation Through the Work Itself* (New York: American Management Association, 1969); W. Paul, K. Robertson, and F. Herzberg, "Job Enrichment Pays Off," *Harvard Business Review* 45 (March-April 1969): 61–78.

6. J. Hackman and G. Oldham, *Work Redesign* (Reading, Mass.: Addison-Wesley, 1980).

7. A. Turner and P. Lawrence, *Industrial Jobs and the Worker* (Cambridge, Mass.: Harvard Graduate School of Business Administration, Division of Research, 1965); J. Hackman and G. Oldham, "Development of the Job Diagnostic Survey," *Journal of Applied Psychology* 60 (April 1975): 159–70; H. Sims, A. Szilagyi, and R. Keller, "The Measurement of Job Characteristics," *Academy of Management Journal* 19 (1976): 195–212.

8. Hackman and Oldham, *Work Redesign*; J. Hackman, G. Oldham, R. Janson, and K. Purdy, "A New Strategy for Job Enrichment," *California Management Review* 17 (Sum-

mer 1975): 57–71; R. Walters, *Job Enrichment for Results: Strategies for Successful Implementation* (Reading, Mass.: Addison-Wesley, 1975); J. Hackman, "Work Design," in *Improving Life at Work: Behavioral Science Approaches to Organizational Change*, eds. J. Hackman and L. L. Suttle (Santa Monica, Calif.: Goodyear, 1977): 96–163.

9. J. Hackman and G. Oldham, *The Diagnostic Survey: An Instrument for the Diagnosis of Jobs and the Evaluation of Job Redesign Projects*, Technical Report No. 4 (New Haven, Conn.: Yale University, Department of Administrative Sciences, 1974); Sims, Szilagyi, and Keller, "Measurement"; M. Campion, "The Multimethod Job Design Questionnaire," *Psychological Documents* 15 (1985): 1; J. Idaszak and F. Drasgow, "A Revision of the Job Diagnostic Survey: Elimination of a Measurement Artifact," *Journal of Applied Psychology* 72 (1987): 69–74.

10. E. Huse and M. Beer, "Eclectic Approach to Organizational Development," *Harvard Business Review* 49 (September-October 1971): 103–12.

11. A. Armenakis and H. Field, "Evaluation of Organizational Change Using Nonindependent Criterion Measures," *Personnel Psychology* 28 (Spring 1975): 39–44.

12. R. Ford, "Job Enrichment Lessons from AT&T," *Harvard Business Review* 51 (January-February 1973): 96–106.

13. R. Henkoff, "Make Your Office More Productive," *Fortune* (25 February 1991): 84.

14. Hackman et al., "New Strategy."

15. I. Seeborg, "The Influence of Employee Participation in Job Redesign," *Journal of Applied Behavioral Science* 14 (1978): 87–98.

16. G. Oldham and J. Hackman, "Work Design in the Organizational Context," in *Research in Organizational Behavior*, vol. 2, eds. B. Staw and L. Cummings (Greenwich, Conn.: JAI Press, 1980): 247–78; J. Cordery and T. Wall,

"Work Design and Supervisory Practice: A Model," *Human Relations* 38 (1985): 425–41.

17. Hackman and Oldham, *Work Redesign.*

18. Ibid.

19. M. Campion, "Interdisciplinary Approaches to Job Design: A Constructive Replication with Extensions," *Journal of Applied Psychology* 73 (1988): 467–81.

20. C. Kulik, G. Oldham, and P. Langner, "Measurement of Job Characteristics: Comparison of the Original and the Revised Job Diagnostic Survey," *Journal of Applied Psychology* 73 (1988): 426–66; Idaszak and Drasgow, "Revision of the Job Diagnostic Survey."

21. R. Steers and D. Spencer, "The Role of Achievement Motivation in Job Design," *Journal of Applied Psychology* 62 (1977): 472–79; J. Champoux, "A Three-Sample Test of Some Extensions to the Job Characteristics Model," *Academy of Management Journal* 23 (1980): 466–78; R. Katz, "The Influence of Job Longevity on Employee Reactions to Task Characteristics," *Human Relation* 31 (1978): 703–25.

22. R. Zeffane, "Correlates of Job Satisfaction and Their Implications for Work Redesign," *Public Personnel Management* 23 (1994): 61–76.

23. G. Oldham and Y. Fried, "Employee Reactions to Workspace Characteristics," *Journal of Applied Psychology* 72 (1987): 75–80.

24. B. Loher, R. Noe, N. Moeller, and M. Fitzgerald, "A Meta-Analysis of the Relation of Job Characteristics to Job Satisfaction," *Journal of Applied Psychology* 70 (1985): 280–89.

25. B. McEvoy and W. Cascio, "Strategies for Reducing Employee Turnover: A Meta-Analysis," *Journal of Applied Psychology* 70 (1985): 342–53.

26. T. Cummings and E. Molloy, *Improving Productivity and the Quality of Work Life* (New York: Praeger, 1977).

27. J. Nicholas, "The Comparative Impact of Organization Development Interventions on Hard Criteria Measures," *Academy of Management Review* 7 (1982): 531–42.

28. Y. Fried and G. Ferris, "The Validity of the Job Characteristics Model: A Review and Meta-Analysis," *Personnel Psychology* 40 (1987): 287–322.

29. E. Trist, B. Higgin, H. Murray, and A. Pollock, *Organizational Choice* (London: Tavistock, 1963); T. Cummings and S. Srivastva, *Management of Work: A Socio-Technical Systems Approach* (San Diego: University Associates, 1977); A. Cherns, "Principles of Sociotechnical Design Revisited," *Human Relations* 40 (1987): 153–62.

30. Cummings, "Self-Regulating Work Groups"; J. Hackman, *The Design of Self-Managing Work Groups,* Technical Report No. 11 (New Haven, Conn.: Yale University, School of Organization and Management, 1976); Cummings and Srivastva, *Management of Work;* Susman, *Autonomy at Work;* H. Sims and C. Manz, "Conversations Within Self-Managed Work Groups," *National Productivity Review* 1 (Summer 1982): 261–69; T. Cummings, "Designing Effective Work Groups," in *Handbook of Organizational Design: Remodeling Organizations and Their Environments,* vol. 2, eds. P. C. Nystrom and W. H. Starbuck (New York: Oxford University Press, 1981): 250–71.

31. C. Manz, "Beyond Self-Managing Teams: Toward Self-Leading Teams in the Workplace," in *Research in Organizational Change and Development,* vol. 4, eds. W. Pasmore and R. Woodman (Greenwich, Conn.: JAI Press, 1990): 273–99; C. Manz and H. Sims Jr., "Leading Workers to Lead Themselves: The External Leadership of Self-Managed Work Teams," *Administrative Science Quarterly* 32 (1987): 106–28.

32. E. Lawler, S. Mohrman, and G. Ledford, *Strategies for High-Performance Organizations* (San Francisco: Jossey-Bass, 1998).

33. B. Dumaine, "The Trouble with Teams," *Fortune* (5 September 1994): 86–92.

34. Cummings, "Self-Regulating Work Groups."

35. Cummings, "Self-Regulating Work Groups"; J. Pearce II and E. Ravlin, "The Design and Activation of Self-Regulating Work Groups," *Human Relations* 40 (1987): 751–82; J. R. Hackman, "The Design of Work Teams," in *Handbook of Organizational Behavior,* ed. J. Lorsch (Englewood Cliffs, N.J.: Prentice Hall, 1987): 315–42.

36. Ibid.

37. C. Manz and H. Sims, "The Leadership of Self-Managed Work Groups: A Social Learning Theory Perspective" (paper delivered at meeting of National Academy of Management, New York, August 1982); C. Manz and H. Sims Jr., "Searching for the 'Unleader': Organizational Member Views on Leading Self-Managed Groups," *Human Relations* 37 (1984): 409–24.

38. H. Mintzberg, *The Nature of Managerial Work* (New York: Harper & Row, 1973); L. Sayles, *Managerial Behavior: Administration in Complex Organizations* (New York: McGraw-Hill, 1964).

39. R. Walton and L. Schlesinger, "Do Supervisors Thrive in Participative Work Systems?" *Organizational Dynamics* 8 (Winter 1979): 25–38.

40. Ibid.

41. M. Weisbord, "Participative Work Design: A Personal Odyssey," *Organizational Dynamics* (1984): 5–20.

42. T. Cummings, "Socio-Technical Systems: An Intervention Strategy," in *New Techniques in Organization Development*, ed. W. Burke (New York: Basic Books, 1975): 228–49; Cummings and Srivastva, *Management of Work;* Cummings and Molloy, *Improving Productivity.*

43. Cherns, "Sociotechnical Design Revisited."

44. This application was submitted by Joseph Whittinghill of Rayner and Associates, Freeland, Wash.

45. F. van Eijnatten, S. Eggermont, G. de Goffau, and I. Mankoe, *The Socio-Technical Systems Design Paradigm* (Eindhoven, The Netherlands: Eindhoven University of Technology, 1994).

46. P. Goodman, R. Devadas, and T. Hughson, "Groups and Productivity: Analyzing the Effectiveness of Self-Managing Teams," in *Productivity in Organizations*, eds. J. Campbell, R. Campbell, and associates (San Francisco: Jossey-Bass, 1988): 295–325.

47. R. Walton, "How to Counter Alienation in the Plant," *Harvard Business Review* 12 (November-December 1972): 70–81.

48. R. Schrank, "On Ending Worker Alienation: The Gaines Pet Food Plant," in *Humanizing the Workplace,* ed. R. Fairfield (Buffalo: Prometheus Books, 1974): 119–20, 126; R. Walton, "Teaching an Old Dog Food New Tricks," *Wharton Magazine* 4 (Winter 1978): 42; L. Ketchum, "Innovating Plant Managers Are Talking About . . . " (presentation at the International Conference on the Quality of Working Life, Toronto, August 30–September 3, 1981): 2–3; H. Simon et al., "General Foods Topeka: Ten Years Young" (presentation at the International Conference on the Quality of Working Life, Toronto, August 30–September 3, 1981): 5–7.

49. J. Norsted and S. Aguren, *The Saab-Scania Report* (Stockholm: Swedish Employer's Confederation, 1975).

50. "Doubting Sweden's Way," *Time* (10 March 1975): 40.

51. P. Gyllenhammèr, *People at Work* (Reading, Mass.: Addison-Wesley, 1977): 15–17, 43, 52–53; B. Jünsson, "Corporate Strategy for People at Work—The Volvo Experience" (presentation at the International Conference on the Quality of Working Life, Toronto, August 30–September 3, 1981); N. Tichy and J. Nisberg, "When Does Work Restructuring Work? Organizational Innovations at Volvo and GM," *Organizational Dynamics* 5 (Summer 1976): 73.

52. J. Kapstein and J. Hoerr, "Volvo's Radical New Plant: The Death of the Assembly Line?" *Business Week* (28 August 1989): 92–93.

53. W. Pasmore, "The Comparative Impacts of Sociotechnical System, Job-Redesign, and Survey-Feedback Interventions," in *Sociotechnical Systems: A Source Book,* eds. W. Pasmore and J. Sherwood (San Diego: University Associates, 1978): 291–300.

54. S. Cohen and G. Ledford Jr., "The Effectiveness of Self-Managing Teams: A Quasi-Experiment," *Human Relations* 47 (1994): 13–43.

55. Cummings and Molloy, *Improving Productivity.*

56. Nicholas, "Comparative Impact."

57. Pearce and Ravlin, "Design and Activation."

58. R. Beekun, "Assessing the Effectiveness of Sociotechnical Interventions: Antidote or Fad?" *Human Relations* 42 (1989): 877–97.

59. B. Macy, P. Bliese, and J. Norton, "Organizational Change and Work Innovation: A Meta-Analysis of 131 North American Field Experiments—1961–1990," in *Research in Organizational Change and Development,* vol. 7, eds. R. Woodman and W. Pasmore (Greenwich, Conn.: JAI Press, 1994).

60. T. Wall, N. Kemp, P. Jackson, and C. Clegg, "Outcomes of Autonomous Workgroups: A Long-Term Field Experiment," *Academy of Management Journal* 29 (June 1986): 280–304.

61. C. Manz and H. Angle, "Can Group Self-Management Mean a Loss of Personal Control: Triangulating a Paradox," *Group and Organization Studies* 11 (December 1986): 309–34.

62. T. Cummings, "Self-Regulating Work Groups"; Susman, *Autonomy at Work;* Slocum and Sims, "Typology of Technology"; M. Kiggundu, "Task Interdependence and Job Design: Test of a Theory," *Organizational Behavior and Human Performance* 31 (1983): 145–72.

63. Hackman and Oldham, *Work Redesign;* K. Brousseau, "Toward a Dynamic Model of Job–Person Relationships: Findings, Research Questions, and Implications for Work System Design," *Academy of Management Review* 8 (1983): 33–45; G. Graen, T. Scandura, and M. Graen, "A Field Experimental Test of the Moderating Effects of Growth Needs Strength on Productivity," *Journal of Applied Psychology* 71 (1986): 484–91.

64. T. Cummings, "Designing Work for Productivity and Quality of Work Life," *Outlook* 6 (1982): 35–39.

The Lizard Lick Fine Paper Mill

The Lizard Lick Fine Paper Mill is located in Lizard Lick, South Carolina. It is one of more than a dozen plants operated by the paper division of a large natural resources company. The mill is the primary employer in a radius of seventy-five miles and has been supporting the community of Lizard Lick since 1944. In fact, its opening was contemporaneous with D–Day and the Allied invasion of Europe. The small community has never been the same since the mill was constructed.

The primary output of the mill is a roll of "fine paper" that weighs about one thousand pounds. It is distinguished from kraft paper or newsprint by its white color, smoothness, and fiber content for use as stationery or in photocopiers and printers. Fine paper is produced in a four-step process. The first step, pulping, involves turning "chips" or finely chopped wood into a soup by adding water and chemicals. The second step is called "liquoring." Here, the pulp is heated in large cauldrons that allow the chemicals to break down the cellulose in the wood to form a thick paste. A large, thin screen is dipped into the paste, and the screen and paste are rolled, heated, and compressed until the paste is of a consistency that can be separated from the screen and further rolled and dried. That third step is carried out by a continuous-process machine roughly the size of a football field. Finally, the long sheet of fine paper is rolled onto a giant spool and placed in finished inventory. Each step in the process is linked tightly to the next process and a breakdown anywhere in the process can cause expensive shutdowns of the whole plant. Like all paper plants, the mill is located next to a railroad where the large rolls of paper are loaded into boxcars for shipment to customers such as Hallmark, Xerox, and other large paper users. The plant operates around the clock, and four shift crews of about 80 people each are required to operate the plant's core processes. Overall, the plant employs about 550 people. In addition, the plant includes support operations in bleaching, power generation, and the wood yard. An organization chart is shown in Exhibit 1.

Riding the wave of reconstruction in the years following World War II, the Lizard Lick Mill built a reputation of high productivity, reaching a record of

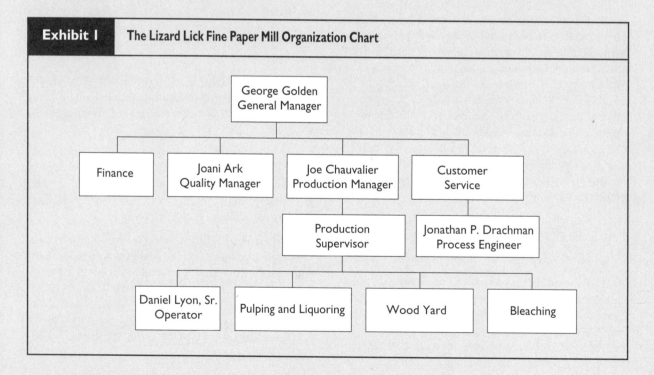

Exhibit 1 — The Lizard Lick Fine Paper Mill Organization Chart

seven hundred tons per day in 1982. It was not unusual for Lizard Lick to obtain a return on assets (ROA) of 32 percent. The plant's productivity and operating results were reflected in a reward system that paid out handsome bonuses to salaried workers for exceeding the budgeted targets. The mill always has been viewed as the flagship of the parent company, and employees have sought management opportunities at Lizard Lick to ensure career success.

Over the last several years, however, Lizard Lick has been a disappointment to the company. ROA has dropped to 7 percent, productivity has plummeted to 550 tons per day, and quality has declined significantly. For example, customer complaints are up 50 percent, and the costs associated with a customer returning rolls of damaged paper or rolls that did not meet the customer's requirements have increased to $500,000 per year. Operating costs are the highest in the division. People say morale is low and as evidence point to 11 percent absenteeism along with increases in days off because of injury .

The plant manager, George Golden, has called you in as an internal OD consultant to help him manage the change process at Lizard Lick. In your preparing for the work, you discovered that George was sent to Lizard Lick three years ago, as the final stepping-stone on his ascendance to corporate management. His charge was to return Lizard Lick to its position of prominence within the organization. George is known throughout the division as a hard driving, no nonsense, hands-on manager. He is very comfortable setting high standards and holding people accountable for results.

On your first trip to the mill, you stop by George's office and ask him for some background information. He tells you, "What we have here in Lizard Lick is a mill that is completely out of control. For example, my chips cost me 20 percent more today than they did three years ago, and the supply of chips is unpredictable. This is complicated by escalating chemical costs, which fortunately I've been able to curtail by buying for two years in advance, which represents a 12 percent savings. Our real problem however is unfair pricing by our competition, whose prices are irresponsibly low and who are not factoring in these new costs of doing business.

"Furthermore, the Japanese are killing us. They claim to be selling product at an acceptable margin to them, when in fact we know that they've got to be selling it below cost. What they're after is market share. It is impossible to produce paper at the costs they are claiming. My only recourse has been to dedicate valuable time away from my mill lobbying against these unfair practices in Washington, D.C.

"While waiting for long-term relief from the U.S. government, I have got to reduce my costs. This morning I was forced to take a hard line, and I said the following to my staff: 'You people are not doing your job in terms of managing costs for my mill. As of the end of this quarter, I expect a 10 percent reduction in all your areas or there will be a few changes made around here. Please let me know if I can help you in any way.'"

Following some contracting with George about your role, the two of you agree that you should interview several of the key people in the mill. Your interviews and observations are summarized below.

Joe Chauvalier, the production manager at the Lizard Lick Mill, came up through the ranks. While working as a machine tender, he developed a tremendous ability for papermaking. His co-workers say that Joe can "smell good paper from bad." He and his workers view fine papermaking as an art requiring years of on-the-job experience to develop the right feel for a good batch. Last March he celebrated his twenty-second anniversary with the company, the last ten years of which he has been production manager. "I am really frustrated in my job. I'm expected to make significant reductions in mill costs while being forced to allocate my resources toward all these corporate improvement programs. At one point they had me shutting down production to share performance data with hourly employees. We finally gave that up and got back to work. But my people and I are still spending 80 percent of our time in meetings—there's just no time to run the operation. Life was simpler when we could just focus on producing tons off the machine, but now that we are more quality conscious, we don't send just anything to our customers: we pull off the bad paper and absorb the cost ourselves. I'm worried about this quarter's financial results."

Joani Ark was appointed by George to be quality manager for the Lizard Lick Mill. She has been with the company four years and in the quality manager job for fourteen months. Energetic, bright, and hard working, Joani has had some difficulty defining her role in the improvement process, particularly vis-à-vis Joe Chauvalier, who feels free to off-load various tasks to her (for example, set up tracking systems, charter task forces, hire hourly workers, organize mill picnics). Because they both report to George it is important that they comfortably coordinate their activities, but there seems to be confusion about who leads what and who supports what. Joani says, "George has regularly scheduled one-on-one meetings with each of his direct reports as well as others in the mill. He's very proud of his open-door policy. The problem for me is that it seems everyone receives a piece of his time except me. When I arrive for my appointment, Big George usually has someone in with him and is running late. His secretary asks me to come back later. Upon my return, Joe is usually in with George talking about production scheduling or some mill problem, so I wait. When Joe comes out, he has a list of things for me to do, and George is otherwise occupied again. In truth, I don't feel focused in my job. I am convinced that the best impact I can have on the mill is to search out ways to define more clearly our customers' needs for paper and help people develop processes that will improve our ability to meet those needs, but somehow I seem to have trouble finding the time to focus on this. Sometimes I think the only one who understands what I'm saying is Jackie Drachman."

Jonathan (Jackie) P. Drachman is an intense, quiet worker with a penchant for data analysis. When he was growing up, his schoolmates were convinced he was a genius. As process engineer, Jackie tracks performance data that shows how well the fine paper machine is working: tons per hour, cost, machine uptime, recovery (broke analysis), paper quality parameters (moisture, basis weight, caliper, percent ash), and energy usage. In the past, he liked to play around with ratios, trends, and new data classifications. When he discovered something of interest, he would route it to George and the management team.

As of late, Jackie has seemed detached and listless. He tells you, "I don't know what all the fuss is about—people asking if I'm okay and all. Of course I'm okay. My job isn't as much fun since I figured out that no one was reading, let alone acting, on my reports. Everyone is so busy, with the waste task force, the chip ordering task force, the cost reduction task force, the new recruit task force, the preventive maintenance task force, the chemical futures task force, and the on-time delivery task force, that there's no time or inclination to look at my analyses. I decided to test this conclusion by not sending out my weekly update on upstream causes of downstream problems. It's been seven weeks now, and not one person has asked about my reports, so I guess it's true—no one was using them. It's just a little depressing to think I was putting all my passions to work in an area that wasn't valued."

The heart of the paper mill is the fine paper machine, which is run by operator Daniel Lyon, Sr. A union employee for fourteen years, Danny has seen managers and programs come and go. The one constant has been the fine paper machine. Danny watches over it and tends it like a favorite car, tweaking it to keep it perfect. "Tons produced and reduced costs are the big goals around here," he says. "When the machine breaks down, production stops and we waste large batches of paper. Breakdowns are my biggest problem. I served on a preventive maintenance task force where we worked with the machine vendor to predict the life cycle of various parts. The idea was to empty and shut down the machine on a routine basis so parts could be replaced before they broke. But we were losing too much production time and missing deliveries, you know. Usually maintenance didn't have the right parts on hand, so we'd shut down for nothing. Deliveries are too important to our customers to shut down deliberately. We've asked corporate for a new machine."

Questions

1. What is your diagnosis of the Lizard Lick plant's problems?

2. What kind of contract do you want to have with George? Who is your client?

3. What employee involvement interventions might be appropriate in this situation?

4. Develop an implementation plan assuming you had everyone's agreement to proceed.

Source: Adapted with permission from Miriam Y. Lacey, Pepperdine University, The George L. Graziadio School of Business Management, Culver City, California. All rights reserved.

■ City of Carlsbad, California: Restructuring the Public Works Department (A)

In 1995, the City of Carlsbad, California, an ocean-front community of about seventy-five thousand people, was emerging from the worst recession in its history. In response to a call from the city council and nationwide efforts to operate governments in a more businesslike manner, the city manager led the organization through a comprehensive strategic planning process. Through highly participative methods, including focus groups and a large-group community visioning process, a new city mission and vision (Exhibit 1) and a set of values to guide decision making (Exhibit 2) were developed. In addition, several important strategic initiatives were started, including a new information system and a revised performance appraisal and incentive compensation process.

The strategic initiatives and the city manager's assessment of the organization's design pointed to misalignments in the city's structure. The city manager convened a small representative task force of managers to design a new structure. The result was a reorganization of the city into five major service areas (MSAs), including community development, safety services (for example, fire, police), and public works.

An evaluation of the entire strategic change effort suggested that a large majority of the internal and external stakeholders viewed the changes positively and believed that they had improved customer focus and employee commitment. The results also promised to reduce operating costs and to create an organization that could absorb the expected growth in demand for new and better services.

The Public Works Department

The largest of the new MSAs, public works, comprised six previously independent departments responsible for engineering services; parks, streets, facilities, and fleet maintenance; and a legally separate water district owned by the city (Exhibit 3). The new organization was expected to design, construct, and maintain the infrastructure for the growing city.

Exhibit 1	City of Carlsbad Mission and Vision Statement

Our mission is to provide top-quality services to our citizens and customers in a manner that enhances the quality of life for all who live, work, and play in Carlsbad.

Exhibit 2	City of Carlsbad Values

We believe *these values are important to achieve our desired future as employees for the City of Carlsbad. They are chosen freely, prized publicly, and acted upon again and again.*

- **Integrity**–An organization and workforce distinguished by sound moral and ethical character
- **Trust**–A workplace characterized by widespread belief in the integrity, reliability, and ability of employees
- **Competence**–A workplace characterized by employees who have the skills and training to do their jobs
- **Accountability**–An environment characterized by employees who are willing to be responsible
- **Teamwork**–A workplace that encourages the use of teams to accomplish organizational goals and objectives
- **Quality**–An environment characterized by employees with passion for excellence
- **Empowerment**–Employees who have the authority, responsibility, and accountability to decide and act

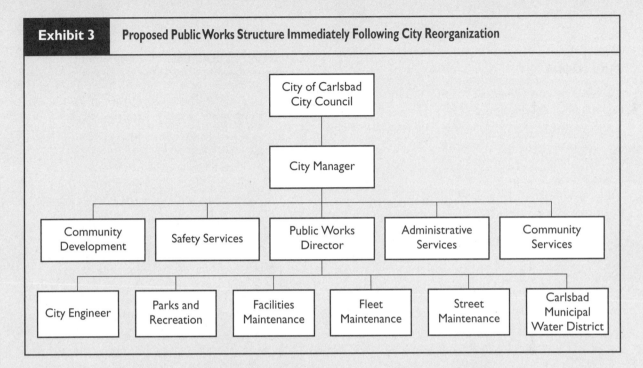

The new public works director was excited about the prospect of designing his new MSA according to the vision and values created by the city during its strategic change efforts. In line with those values, he saw the opportunity to implement the new design in participative and empowering ways, and he wanted to take advantage of the city's general plan that called for new buildings to house the engineering staff and the public works yard.

After consultation with an OD practitioner, the city manager commissioned diagnostic interviews and focus groups with a variety of employees and other stakeholders. The data can be summarized as follows:

- Each of the previously independent departments had its own way of doing things. Each was suspicious of the reasons for the structural change. The water district employees were particularly cohesive.

- Many of the work processes in each department were similar. For example, the buildings, parks, and streets departments each had equipment and work assignments involving the maintenance of restrooms, painting, landscaping, and light construction. The engineering department for the water district was largely redundant with the city engineering department, and both the city and the water district owned several identical pieces of large and expensive equipment.

- Each department had members with long and short tenures.

- Most of the departments lacked formal goals and planning processes.

- The current public works director also was acting as the city engineer.

- The engineering department was anticipating an increased workload over the next ten years as the city continued growing; workloads in the maintenance groups were expected to grow over time but lag the growth rates in engineering.

- Almost all of the employees enjoyed working for the City of Carlsbad and intended to stay.

The public works director and the OD consultants worked together to understand implications of those data and to design an action plan to describe and refine the new structure.

Questions

1. What is your diagnosis of the situation in the public works department?

2. How would you proceed from this point?

3. What interventions would you recommend and why?

4. Develop an action plan for implementation for your preferred intervention.

Source: Adapted with permission of Christopher G. Worley, Pepperdine University, Culver City, Calif., © 2000.

Human Resources Management Interventions

5

17 Performance Management

In this chapter, we discuss human resources management interventions concerned with managing individual and group performance. Performance management involves goal setting, performance appraisal, and reward systems that align member work behavior with business strategy, employee involvement, and workplace technology. Goal setting describes the interaction between managers and employees in jointly defining member work behaviors and outcomes. Orienting employees to the appropriate kinds of work outcomes can reinforce the work designs described in Chapter 16 and support the organization's strategic objectives. Goal setting can clarify the duties and responsibilities associated with a particular job or work group. When applied to jobs, goal setting can focus on individual goals and can reinforce individual contributions and work outcomes. When applied to work groups, it can be directed at group objectives and can reinforce members' joint actions and overall group outcomes. One popular and classic approach to goal setting is called management by objectives.

Performance appraisal involves collecting and disseminating performance data to improve work outcomes. It is the primary human resources management intervention for providing performance feedback to individuals and work groups. Performance appraisal is a systematic process of jointly assessing work-related achievements, strengths, and weaknesses. It also can facilitate career counseling, provide information about the strength and diversity of human resources in the company, and link employee performance with rewards.

Reward systems are concerned with eliciting and reinforcing desired behaviors and work outcomes. They can support goal setting and feedback systems by rewarding the kinds of behaviors required to implement a particular work design or support a business strategy. Like goal setting, rewards systems can be oriented to individual jobs and goals or to group functions and objectives. Moreover, they can be geared to traditional work designs that require external forms of control or to enriched, self-regulating designs that require employee self-control. Several innovative and effective reward systems are used in organizations today.

Performance management interventions traditionally are implemented by the human resources department within organizations, whose managers have special training in these areas. Because of the breadth and depth of knowledge required to carry out these kinds of change programs successfully, practitioners tend to specialize in one part of the human resources function, such as performance appraisal or compensation.

Recently, interest in integrating human resources management with organization development has been growing. In many companies, such as AG Communication Systems, Caesars World, GTE, Colgate-Palmolive, Johnson & Johnson, and Sun Microsystems, organization development is a separate function of the human resources department. As OD practitioners increasingly have become involved in organization design and employee involvement, they have realized the need to change personnel practices to bring them more in line with the new designs and processes. Consequently, personnel specialists now frequently help initiate OD projects. For example, a large electronics firm expanded the role of compensation specialists to include initiation of work-design projects. The compensation people at this firm, who traditionally were consulted by OD practitioners after the work design had taken place, were dissatisfied with this secondary role and wanted to be more proactive. In most cases, personnel practitioners continue to specialize in their respective area, but they become more sensitive to and competent in organization development. Similarly, OD practitioners continue to focus on planned change while becoming more knowledgeable about human resources management.

We begin by describing a performance management model. It shows how goal setting, performance appraisal, and rewards are closely linked and difficult to separate in practice, but how each element is distinct and has its own dynamics. Following the model, each aspect of performance management is discussed and its impact on performance is evaluated.

A MODEL OF PERFORMANCE MANAGEMENT

Performance management is an integrated process of defining, assessing, and reinforcing employee work behaviors and outcomes.[1] Organizations with a well-developed performance management process often outperform those without this element of organization design.[2] As shown in Figure 17.1, performance management includes practices and methods for goal setting, performance appraisal, and reward systems. These practices jointly influence the performance of individuals and work groups. Goal setting specifies the kinds of performances that are desired; performance appraisal assesses those outcomes; reward systems provide the reinforcers to ensure that desired outcomes are repeated. Because performance management occurs in a larger organizational context, at least three contextual factors determine how these practices affect work performance: business strategy, workplace technology, and employee involvement.[3] High levels of work performance tend to occur when goal setting, performance appraisal, and reward systems are aligned jointly with these contextual factors.

Business strategy defines the goals and objectives that are needed for an organization to compete successfully, and performance management focuses, assesses, and reinforces member work behaviors toward those objectives. This ensures that work behaviors are strategically driven.

Workplace technology affects whether performance management practices should be based on the individual or the group. When technology is low in interdependence and work is designed for individual jobs, goal setting, performance appraisal, and reward systems should be aimed at individual work behaviors. Conversely, when technology is highly interdependent and work is designed for groups, performance management should be aimed at group behaviors.[4]

Finally, the level of employee involvement in an organization should determine the nature of performance management practices. When organizations are highly bureaucratic with low levels of participation, goal setting, performance appraisal, and reward systems should be formalized and administered by management and staff personnel. In high-involvement situations, on the other hand, performance management should be heavily participative, with both management and employees setting goals and appraising and rewarding performance. In high-involvement organizations, for example, employees participate in all stages of performance

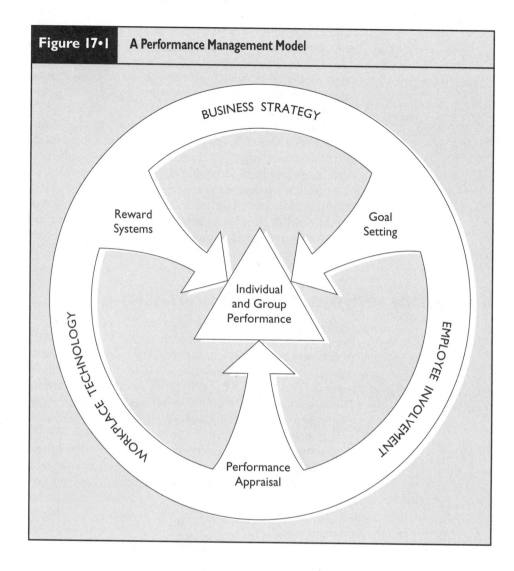

Figure 17•1   A Performance Management Model

management, and are heavily involved in both designing and administering its practices.

GOAL SETTING

Goal setting involves managers and subordinates in jointly establishing and clarifying employee goals. In some cases, such as management by objectives, it also can facilitate employee counseling and support. The process of establishing challenging goals involves managing the level of participation and goal difficulty. Once goals have been established, the way they are measured is an important determinant of member performance.[5]

Goal setting can affect performance in several ways. It influences what people think and do by focusing their behavior in the direction of the goals, rather than elsewhere. Goals energize behavior, motivating people to put forth the effort to reach difficult goals that are accepted, and when goals are difficult but achievable, goal setting prompts persistence over time. Goal-setting interventions have been implemented in such organizations as GE, 3M, AT&T Universal Card, and Occidental Petroleum's subsidiary Oxy-USA.

Characteristics of Goal Setting

An impressive amount of research underlies goal-setting interventions and practices,[6] and has revealed that goal setting works equally well in both individual and group settings.[7] This research has identified two major processes that affect positive outcomes: establishment of challenging goals and clarification of goal measurement.

Establishing Challenging Goals

The first element of goal setting concerns establishing goals that are perceived as challenging but realistic and to which there is a high level of commitment. This can be accomplished by varying the goal difficulty and the level of employee participation in the goal-setting process. Increasing the difficulty of employee goals, also known as "stretch goals," can increase their perceived challenge and enhance the amount of effort expended to achieve them.[8] Thus, more difficult goals tend to lead to increased effort and performance, as long as they are seen as feasible. If goals are set too high, however, they may lose their motivating potential and employees will give up when they fail to achieve them. An important method for increasing the acceptance of a challenging goal is to collect benchmarks or best-practice referents. When employees see that other people, groups, or organizations have achieved a specified level of performance, they are more motivated to achieve that level themselves.

Another aspect of establishing challenging goals is to vary the amount of participation in the goal-setting process. Having employees participate can increase motivation and performance, but only to the extent that members set higher goals than those typically assigned to them. Participation also can convince employees that the goals are achievable and can increase their commitment to achieving them.

All three contextual factors play an important role in establishing challenging goals. First, there must be a clear "line of sight" between the business strategy goals and the goals established for individuals or groups. When the group is trying to achieve goals that are not aligned with the business strategy, performance can suffer and organization members can become frustrated. Second, employee participation in goal setting is more likely to be effective if employee involvement policies in the organization support it. Under such conditions, participation in goal setting is likely to be seen as legitimate, resulting in the desired commitment to challenging goals. Third, when tasks are highly interdependent and work is designed for groups, group-oriented participative goal setting tends to increase commitment.[9]

Clarifying Goal Measurement

The second element in the goal-setting process involves specifying and clarifying the goals. When given specific goals, workers perform higher than when they are simply told to "do their best" or when they receive no guidance at all. Specific goals reduce ambiguity about expectations and focus the search for appropriate behaviors.

To clarify goal measurement, objectives should be operationally defined. For example, a group of employees may agree to increase productivity by 5 percent, a challenging and specific goal. But there are a variety of ways to measure productivity, and it is important to define the goal operationally to be sure that the measure can be influenced by employee or group behaviors. For example, a productivity goal defined by sales per employee may be inappropriate for a manufacturing group.

Clarifying goal measurement also requires that employees and supervisors negotiate the resources necessary to achieve the goals—for example, time, equipment, raw materials, and access to information. If employees cannot have appropriate resources, the targeted goal may have to be revised.

Contextual factors also play an important role in the clarifying process. Goal specification and clarity can be difficult in high-technology settings where the work often is uncertain and highly interdependent. Increasing employee participation in clarifying goal measurement can give employees ownership of a nonspecific but challenging goal. Employee involvement policies also can impact the way goals are clarified. The entire goal-setting process can be managed by employees and work teams when employee involvement policies and work designs favor it. Finally, the process of specifying and clarifying goals is extremely difficult if the business strategy is unclear. Under such conditions, attempting to gain consensus on the measurement and importance of goals can lead to frustration and resistance to change.

Application Stages

Based on these features of the goal-setting process, OD practitioners have developed specific approaches to goal setting. The following steps characterize those applications:

1. *Diagnosis.* The first step is a thorough diagnosis of the job or work group; employee needs; and the three context factors, business strategy, workplace technology, and level of employee involvement. This provides information about the nature and difficulty of specific goals, the appropriate types and levels of participation, and the necessary support systems.

2. *Preparation for goal setting.* This step prepares managers and employees to engage in goal setting, typically by increasing interaction and communication between managers and employees, and offering formal training in goal-setting methods. Specific action plans for implementing the program also are made at this time.

3. *Setting of goals.* In this step challenging goals are established and methods for goal measurement are clarified. Employees participate in the process to the extent that contextual factors support such involvement and to the extent that they are likely to set higher goals than those assigned by management.

4. *Review.* At this final step the goal-setting process is assessed so that modifications can be made, if necessary. The goal attributes are evaluated to see whether the goals are energizing and challenging and whether they support the business strategy and can be influenced by the employees.

Management by Objectives

A common form of goal setting used in organizations is *management by objectives* (MBO). This method is chiefly an attempt to align personal goals with business strategy by increasing communications and shared perceptions between the manager and subordinates, either individually or as a group, and by reconciling conflict where it exists.

All organizations have goals and objectives; all managers have goals and objectives. In many instances, however, those goals are not stated clearly, and managers and subordinates have misunderstandings about what those objectives are. MBO is an approach to resolving these differences in perceptions and goals. MBO can be defined as systematic and periodic manager–subordinate meetings designed to accomplish organizational goals by joint planning of the work, periodic reviewing of accomplishments, and mutual solving of problems that arise in the course of getting the job done.

MBO has its origin in two different backgrounds—organizational and developmental. The organizational root of MBO was developed by Peter Drucker, who emphasized that organizations need to establish objectives in eight key areas: "market standing; innovation; productivity; physical and financial resources; profitability; manager performance and development; worker performance and attitude; and public responsibility."[10] Drucker's work was expanded by Odiorne, whose first book on MBO stressed the need for quantitative measurement.[11]

According to Levinson,[12] MBO's second root is found in the work of McGregor, who stressed the qualitative nature of MBO and its use for development and growth on the job.[13] McGregor attempted to shift emphasis from identifying weaknesses to analyzing performance in order to define strengths and potentials. He believed that this shift could be accomplished by having subordinates reach agreement with their boss on major job responsibilities; then, individuals could develop short-term performance goals and action plans for achieving those goals, thus allowing them to appraise their own performance. Subordinates then would discuss the results of this self-appraisal with their supervisors and develop a new set of performance goals and plans. This emphasis on mutual understanding and performance rather than personality would shift the supervisor's role from judge to helper, thereby reducing both role conflict and ambiguity. The second root of MBO reduces role ambiguity by making goal setting more participative and transactional, by increasing communication between role incumbents, and by ensuring that both individual and organizational goals are identified and achieved.

An MBO program often goes beyond the one-on-one, manager–subordinate relationship to focus on problem-solving discussions involving work teams as well. Setting goals and reviewing individual performance are considered within the larger context of the job. In addition to organizational goals, the MBO process gives attention to individuals' personal and career goals and tries to make those and the organizational goals more complementary. The target-setting procedure allows real (rather than simulated) subordinate participation in goal setting, with open, problem-centered discussions among team members, supervisors, and subordinates.

There are six basic steps in implementing an MBO process.[14]

1. *Work group involvement.* In the first step of MBO, the members of the primary work group define overall group and individual goals and establish action plans for achieving them. If this step is omitted or if organizational goals and strategies are unclear, the effectiveness of an MBO approach may be greatly reduced over time.

2. *Joint manager–subordinate goal setting.* Once the work group's overall goals and responsibilities have been determined, attention is given to the job duties and responsibilities of the individual role incumbents. Roles are carefully examined in light of their interdependence with the roles of others outside the work group.

3. *Establishment of action plans for goals.* The subordinate develops action plans for goal accomplishment, either in a group meeting or in a meeting with the immediate manager. The action plans reflect the individual style of the subordinate, not that of the supervisor.

4. *Establishment of criteria, or yardsticks, of success.* At this point, the manager and subordinate agree on the success criteria for the goals that have been established—criteria that are not limited to easily measurable or quantifiable data. A more important reason for jointly developing the success criteria is to ensure that the manager and subordinate have a common understanding of the task and what is expected of the subordinate. Frequently, the parties involved discover that they have not reached a mutual understanding. The subordinate and the manager may have agreed on a certain task, but in discussing how to measure its success, they find that they have not been communicating clearly. Arriving at joint understanding and agreement on success criteria is the most important step in the entire MBO process.

5. *Review and recycle.* Periodically, the manager reviews work progress, either in the larger group or with the subordinate. There are three stages in this review process. First, the subordinate takes the lead, reviewing progress and discussing achievements and the obstacles faced. Next, the manager discusses work plans and objectives for the future. Last, after the action plans have been made, a more general discussion covers the subordinate's future ambitions and other factors of concern. In this final phase, a great deal of coaching and counseling usually takes place.

6. *Maintenance of records.* In many MBO programs, the working documents of the goals, criteria, yardsticks, priorities, and due dates are forwarded to a third party. Although the evidence is indirect, it is likely that the MBO program, as an OD effort, suffers when the working papers are reviewed regularly by a third party, such as higher management or the personnel department. Experience shows that when the working papers routinely are passed on, they are less likely to reflect open, honest communication within the supervisor-subordinate pair or the work group. Often they represent instead an effort to impress the third party or to comply with institutionalized rules and procedures.

Application 17.1 describes how a performance management process was designed at Monsanto Company. It shows how goal-setting processes can be linked with business strategies and performance appraisal processes.[15]

Effects of Goal Setting and MBO

Goal setting has been researched extensively and shown to be a particularly effective OD intervention. The research results on MBO generally are positive but less consistent than the findings on goal setting.

Goal setting appears to produce positive results over a wide range of jobs and organizations. It has been tested on data-entry operators, logging crews, clerical workers, engineers, and truck drivers, and it has produced performance improvements of between 11 and 27 percent.[16] Moreover, four meta-analyses of the extensive empirical evidence supporting goal setting concluded that the proposed effects of goal difficulty, goal specificity, and participation in goal setting generally are substantiated across studies and with both groups and individuals.[17] Longitudinal analyses support the conclusion that the gains in performance are not short-lived.[18] A recent field study of the goal-setting process, however, failed to replicate the typical positive linear relationship between goal difficulty and performance, raising some concern about the generalizability of the method from the laboratory to practice.[19] Additional research has attempted to identify potential factors moderating the results

APPLICATION 17•1   The Performance Enhancement Process at Monsanto

The Chemical Group of the Monsanto Company is a global provider of chemicals, plastics, and fibers. Previously the centerpiece in Monsanto's corporate strategy, the Chemical Group's role was changing as Monsanto restructured its business from commodity and specialty chemicals to biotechnology-based products and health care. As part of that role change, the business was asked to become a cash generator with a workforce that had been through divestitures, downsizings, and other dramatic changes.

In 1991, the human resources department was reorganized into a development group and an administration group. The development group's first assignment was to redesign the performance management system in light of the Chemical Group's new role and the existing workforce. A task force was formed to design a long-range human resources strategy where the new performance management system would be the key implementation vehicle.

Interviews with more than fifteen hundred organization members, a literature review on performance management, and a review of best practices at other firms resulted in several key conclusions. First, human resources management practices can have a major impact on organization performance. Second, performance management systems typically constrain rather than promote employee contributions to performance. Third, traditional MBO processes were ineffective, contrary to empowerment values, and focused more on past accomplishments than on future development. Based on this diagnosis, the task force recommended adopting a Performance Enhancement Process (PEP) based on the following design principles:

- Focus on development rather than judgment.
- Focus employee effort on continuous improvement of work processes.
- Simplify goal setting.
- Shift the focus from individuals to teams; from supervisory judgment to supervisory coaching.
- Clarify roles and increase the amount of feedback.

The designed PEP process included direction setting and performance planning, individual development, and continual coaching. Direction setting and performance planning initiate the PEP process and occur at the beginning of a yearly performance management cycle. The supervisor and employee meet to establish job accountabilities and goals, and they agree on a competency profile that the employee is expected to demonstrate in his or her current job. Job accountabilities are the actual behaviors that directly contribute to achieving the organization's objectives. They define the reason why the job exists. Work goals are the specific accomplishments to be

achieved during the year. The PEP process suggests that there should be no more than five goals and that one of them should be related to the development of the employee.

Direction setting and performance planning ensure that employees have a clear line of sight between their work and the achievement of the organization's objectives. In addition, this part of the PEP process is designed to be developmental and future oriented. It tries to avoid the negative dynamics of setting low goals that are not challenging, using fuzzy language that allows differing interpretations of accomplishments, or specifying a long list of assumptions about what might go wrong that would prevent a fair appraisal. Rather, through discussion, the employee and supervisor understand and agree on the direction the employee's work should take.

Finally, a competency expectation profile is developed. The task force defined competency as a combination of knowledge, skills, and behaviors that drive performance, and identified twelve core competencies that all employees should develop, such as commitment to task, appreciating differences, and customer focus. Each competency was defined differently depending on a particular stage in a person's career. Together, the supervisor and employee decide on the competencies the employee needs to demonstrate during the performance appraisal cycle.

Individual development and continual coaching are the next components of the PEP process. The key to the success of these components is the transformed role of the supervisor from judge to coach. First, the employee evaluates his or her performance according to the stated accountabilities, goals, and competencies. The supervisor cannot edit this form, the employee is asked to sign the self-assessment, and it becomes a part of the employee's permanent record. The supervisor's input to the self-assessment is a "coaching dialogue" that occurs over time and clarifies the supervisor's view of the employee's performance. Second, the supervisor and employee agree on a list of peers, colleagues, internal customers, and others who provide feedback from multiple viewpoints to the employee on the demonstration of his or her competencies. The feedback is summarized and given to the employee, who compares the feedback with the self-assessment and the competency profile developed at the beginning of the cycle. The employee notes discrepancies and uses them in developing the next competency profile.

The supervisor facilitates the feedback process. He or she helps identify raters, collects the data, and is available to the employee for help in interpretation. The data do not go into the employee's permanent file. The supervisor is removed from being the omniscient observer, and a more structured and developmental approach to feedback is achieved. ∎

of goal setting, including task uncertainty, amount and quality of planning, personal need for achievement, education, past goal successes, and supervisory style.[20] Some support for the moderators has been found. For example, when the technical context is uncertain, goals tend to be less specific and people need to engage in more search behavior to establish meaningful goals.

The body of research concerning MBO also is large but provides mixed support. Huse and Kay were among the first to report statistically documented results of an MBO program at General Electric.[21] They found consistently positive results in terms of managerial help in performing work, agreement on goals, attitudes toward performance discussions, and current and future performance improvements. But they also reported problems when organizational goals were emphasized over developmental goals. Other research also has reported mixed results. Raia, for example, conducted longitudinal studies at Purex and found positive improvements in productivity, communications, performance evaluation, and goal awareness.[22] However, many of the managers felt that the MBO program was not linked to the organization's systems and that it placed too much emphasis on paperwork and production. Carroll and Tosi conducted a long-term study of an MBO program at Black & Decker,[23] first evaluating the program and then using those data to help the company revise and improve it. This resulted in greater use of and satisfaction with the program. The researchers concluded that top-management support of MBO is the most important factor in implementing such programs. A study of an MBO program at the College of Business and Economics at Idaho State University showed mixed results.[24] Faculty reported decreases in teaching and research performance and in satisfaction as a result of MBO. However, an examination of records showed a slight increase in research output and a large improvement in service activities. The researchers explained the discrepancy between faculty assessments and college records as resulting from faculty discontent with the program. The educators perceived that the MBO program infringed on their academic freedom and autonomy.

The existing research suggests that a properly designed MBO program can have positive organizational results. Many programs are short-lived, however, and wither on the vine because they have been installed without adequate diagnosis of the context factors. In particular, MBO can focus too much on vertical alignment of individual and organizational goals and not enough on the horizontal issues that exist when tasks or groups are interdependent. The following conditions have been found to promote MBO success:[25]

- Installation of the program must be preceded by adequate diagnosis.
- The program must take the entire organization into account, including the support and reward systems.
- Managers must be willing to participate.
- The program must be tailored to the specific organization.
- Other interventions, such as team building or changes in organizational structure, may need to take place before the installation of an MBO program.

MBO programs that overemphasize measurement, do not emphasize the discretionary opportunities open to the individual, lack participation by subordinates (with the manager imposing goals), use a win–lose or reward–punishment psychology, and overemphasize paperwork and red tape are doomed to fail.

PERFORMANCE APPRAISAL

Performance appraisal is a feedback system that involves the direct evaluation of individual or work group performance by a supervisor, manager, or peers. Most organizations have some kind of evaluation system that is used for performance feedback, pay administration, and, in some cases, counseling and developing employees.[26] Thus, performance appraisal represents an important link between goal-setting processes and reward systems. One survey of more than five hundred firms found that 90 percent used performance appraisal to determine merit pay increases, 87 percent used it to review performance, and 79 percent used it as the opportunity to set goals for the next period.[27]

Abundant evidence, however, indicates that organizations do a poor job appraising employees.[28] One study found that 32 percent of managers surveyed rated their performance appraisal process as very ineffective.[29] Consequently, a growing number of firms have sought ways to improve performance appraisal. Some innovations have been made in enhancing employee involvement, balancing organizational and employee needs, and increasing the number of raters.[30] These newer forms of appraisal are being used in such organizations as AT&T, Raychem, Levi Strauss, Intel, and Monsanto.

The Performance Appraisal Process

Table 17.1 summarizes several common elements of performance appraisal systems.[31] For each element, two contrasting features are presented, representing traditional bureaucratic approaches and newer, high-involvement approaches. Performance appraisals are conducted for a variety of purposes, including affirmative action, pay and promotion decisions, and human resources planning and development.[32] Because each purpose defines what performances are relevant and how they should be measured, separate appraisal systems are often used. For example, appraisal methods for pay purposes are often different from systems that assess employee development or promotability. Employees also have a variety of reasons for wanting appraisal, such as receiving feedback for career decisions, getting a raise, and being promoted. Rather than trying to meet these multiple purposes with a few standard appraisal systems, the new appraisal approaches are more tailored to

Table 17•1	Performance Appraisal Elements	
ELEMENTS	**TRADITIONAL APPROACHES**	**HIGH-INVOLVEMENT APPROACHES**
Purpose	Organizational, legal Fragmented	Developmental Integrative
Appraiser	Supervisor, managers	Appraisee, co-workers, and others
Role of appraisee	Passive, recipient	Active participant
Measurement	Subjective Concerned with validity	Objective and subjective
Timing	Periodic, fixed, administratively driven	Dynamic, timely, employee- or work-driven

balance the multiple organizational and employee needs. This is accomplished by actively involving the appraisee, co-workers, and managers in assessing the purposes of the appraisal at the time it takes place and adjusting the process to fit that purpose. Thus, at one time the appraisal process might focus on pay decisions, another time on employee development, and still another time on employee promotability. Actively involving all relevant participants can increase the chances that the purpose of the appraisal will be correctly identified and understood and that the appropriate appraisal methods will be applied.

The new methods tend to expand the appraiser role beyond managers to include multiple raters, such as the appraisee, co-workers, and others having direct exposure to the employee's performance. Also known as *360-degree feedback,* this broader approach is used more for member development than for compensation purposes.[33] This wider involvement provides a number of different views of the appraisee's performance. It can lead to a more comprehensive assessment of the employee's performance and can increase the likelihood that both organizational and personal needs will be taken into account. The key task is to form an overarching view of the employee's performance that incorporates all of the different appraisals. Thus, the process of working out differences and arriving at an overall assessment is an important aspect of the appraisal process. This improves the appraisal's acceptance, the accuracy of the information, and its focus on activities that are critical to the business strategy.

The newer methods also expand the role of the appraisee. Traditionally, the employee is simply a receiver of feedback. The supervisor unilaterally completes a form concerning performance on predetermined dimensions, usually personality traits, such as initiative or concern for quality, and presents its contents to the appraisee. The newer approaches actively involve appraisees in all phases of the appraisal process. The appraisee joins with superiors and staff personnel in gathering data on performance and identifying training needs. This active involvement increases the likelihood that the content of the performance appraisal will include the employee's views, needs, and criteria, along with those of the organization. This newer role for employees increases their acceptance and understanding of the feedback process.

Performance measurement is typically the source of many problems in appraisal because it is seen as subjective. Traditionally, performance evaluation focused on the consistent use of prespecified traits or behaviors. To improve consistency and validity of measurement, considerable training is used to help raters (supervisors) make valid assessments. This concern for validity stems largely from legal tests of performance appraisal systems and leads organizations to develop measurement approaches, such as the behaviorally anchored rating scale (BARS) and its variants. In newer approaches validity is not only a legal or methodological issue but a social issue as well; all appropriate participants are involved in negotiating acceptable ways of measuring and assessing performance. Increased participation in goal setting is a part of this new approach. All participants are trained in methods of measuring and assessing performance. Because it focuses on both objective and subjective measures of performance, the appraisal process is more understood, accepted, and accurate.

The timing of performance appraisals traditionally is fixed by managers or staff personnel and is based on administrative criteria, such as yearly pay decisions. Newer approaches increase the frequency of feedback. Although it may not be practical to increase the number of formal appraisals, the frequency of informal feedback can increase, especially when strategic objectives change or when the technology is highly uncertain. In those situations, frequent performance feedback is necessary for appropriate adaptations in work behavior. The newer approaches to appraisal increase the timeliness of feedback and give employees more control over their work.

Application Stages

The process of implementing a performance appraisal system has received increasing attention. OD practitioners have recommended the following six steps:[34]

1. *Select the right people.* For political and legal reasons, the design process needs to include human resources staff, legal representatives, senior management, and system users. Failure to recognize performance appraisal as part of a complex performance management system is the single most important reason for design problems. Members representing a variety of functions need to be involved in the design process so that the essential strategic and organizational issues are addressed.

2. *Diagnose the current situation.* A clear picture of the current appraisal process is essential to designing a new one. Diagnosis involves assessing the contextual factors (business strategy, workplace technology, and employee involvement), current appraisal practices and satisfaction with them, work design, and the current goal-setting and reward system practices. This information is used to define the current system's strengths and weaknesses.

3. *Establish the system's purposes and objectives.* The ultimate purpose of an appraisal system is to help the organization achieve better performance. Managers, staff, and employees can have more specific views about how the appraisal process can be used. Potential purposes can include serving as a basis for rewards, career planning, human resources planning, and performance improvement or simply giving performance feedback.

4. *Design the performance appraisal system.* Given the agreed-upon purposes of the system and the contextual factors, the appropriate elements of an appraisal system can be established. These should include choices about who performs the appraisal, who is involved in determining performance, how performance is measured, and how often feedback is given. Criteria for designing an effective performance appraisal system include timeliness, accuracy, acceptance, understanding, focus on critical control points, and economic feasibility.

   First, the timeliness criterion recognizes the time value of information. Individuals and work groups need to get performance information before evaluation or review. When the information precedes performance evaluation, it can be used to engage in problem-solving behavior that improves performance and satisfaction. Second, the information contained in performance feedback needs to be accurate. Inaccurate data prevent employees from determining whether their performance is above or below the goal targets and discourage problem-solving behavior. Third, the performance feedback must be accepted and owned by the people who use it. Participation in the goal-setting process can help to ensure this commitment to the performance appraisal system. Fourth, information contained in the appraisal system needs to be understood if it is to have problem-solving value. Many organizations use training to help employees understand the operating, financial, and human resources data that will be fed back to them. Fifth, appraisal information should focus on critical control points. The information received by employees must be aligned with important elements of the business strategy, employee performance, and reward system.

For example, if the business strategy requires cost reduction but workers are measured and rewarded on the basis of quality, the performance management system may produce the wrong kinds of behavior. Finally, the economic feasibility criterion suggests that an appraisal system should meet a simple cost–benefit test. If the costs associated with collecting and feeding back performance information exceed the benefits derived from using the information, then a simpler system should be installed.

5. *Experiment with implementation.* The complexity and potential problems associated with performance appraisal processes strongly suggest using a pilot test of the new process to spot, gauge, and correct any flaws in the design before it is implemented systemwide.

6. *Evaluate and monitor the system.* Although the experimentation step may have uncovered many initial design flaws, ongoing evaluation of the system once it is implemented is important. User satisfaction, from human resources staff, manager, and employee viewpoints, is an essential input. In addition, the legal defensibility of the system should be tracked by noting the distribution of appraisal scores against age, sex, and ethnic categories.

Application 17.2 describes the design and redesign of a performance appraisal process for the managers of New York City. It demonstrates how using (and not using) several of the design steps discussed above can affect the appraisal implementation.

Effects of Performance Appraisal

Research strongly supports the role of feedback on performance. One study concluded that objective feedback as a means for improving individual and group performance has been "impressively effective"[35] and has been supported by a large number of literature reviews over the years.[36] Another researcher concluded that "objective feedback does not usually work, it virtually always works."[37] In field studies where performance feedback contained behavior-specific information, median performance improvements were over 47 percent; when the feedback concerned less-specific information, median performance improvements were over 33 percent. In a meta-analysis of performance appraisal interventions, feedback was found to have a consistently positive effect across studies.[38] In addition, although most appraisal research has focused on the relationship between performance and individuals, several studies have demonstrated a positive relationship between group performance and feedback.[39] Because these results often vary across settings and even within studies,[40] more research is clearly needed in this area.

REWARD SYSTEMS

Organizational rewards are powerful incentives for improving employee and work group performance. As pointed out in Chapter 16, rewards also can produce high levels of employee satisfaction. OD traditionally has relied on intrinsic rewards, such as enriched jobs and opportunities for decision making, to motivate employee performance. Early quality-of-work-life interventions were based mainly on the intrinsic satisfaction derived from performing challenging, meaningful types of work. More recently, OD practitioners have expanded their focus to include extrinsic rewards: pay; various incentives, such as stock options, bonuses, and gain sharing; promotions; and benefits. They have discovered that both intrinsic and extrinsic rewards can enhance performance and satisfaction.[41]

APPLICATION 17·2   Performance Appraisal in New York City

In the government of one of the largest cities in the world, appraising the performance of thousands of supervisors and managers is a herculean task. In the late 1980s, a task force reviewing the city's charter argued that a new performance evaluation system was needed to overcome several perceived managerial problems, such as deteriorating service levels and low productivity. The existing system had been all but discredited: it was suffering from typical rating errors, and managers generally found it difficult to use. The task force recommended a new system that focused on managerial accountability and was linked to rewards. The city's personnel department began the task of developing a new system ". . . to identify strengths, deficiencies, and development needs; to assess potential for reassignment and advancement; to award pay increases; and to make decisions as to retention or removal during the probationary periods."

The Managerial Performance Appraisal System (MPAS) was a comprehensive, results-oriented approach with a strong management-by-objectives flavor. Goals set by the city would govern the establishment of goals at successively lower levels. Discussions between each manager and his or her supervisor would focus on the manager's key responsibilities, expected results, performance standards or the basis for evaluation of actual results, and action plans. The outcome of the discussion was to be recorded on a specially designed form. Managers and their supervisors would review results and revise standards, if appropriate, in formal and informal progress meetings.

Performance was to be assessed in terms of five levels, ranging from outstanding to unsatisfactory. Each level was defined by "the extent to which expected results were exceeded, attained, or not attained," including other such considerations as goal difficulty, importance, and extenuating circumstances. In addition, performance assessment was expected to cover such things as strengths and deficiencies in performance, personal development plans, and salary and career development recommendations.

Implementation of the MPAS included training and briefings for top-level executives and training for all other managers. The initial plans for top-executive training were found to be unrealistic—the executives would not devote the time needed to attend a seven-session course—and a two-session program had to be devised. Moreover, the city's political leadership lacked commitment, and this contributed to lower-level managers attaching little credence to the system. Managers saw no tangible benefits, and many refused to adopt the participatory style required by the new system; they resisted the planning and quantification of standards, and they disliked the extra paperwork.

It rapidly became apparent that the new system was not being taken seriously. It was too complex and too demanding of managers' time, and it interfered with operations. The system was reviewed by a private citizens' group at the request of the mayor's office. The group recommended that the system be streamlined to focus only on essential elements and to interfere as little as possible with ongoing operations.

Taking into account comments received from all quarters, the reconvened design team from the personnel department began to rethink the appraisal system. It came up with a much simpler scheme, having fewer purposes, called the Managerial Performance Evaluation (MPE) system. The emphasis in this system was on salary review, but it was designed to allow other purposes to be included later. At the heart of the system's documentation was a one-page form. The philosophy remained results oriented, but the system operated in a somewhat simpler fashion: The discussion between manager and supervisor of key responsibilities and performance expectations remained, but with less emphasis on quantification. Expectations could be set out in other terms—timeliness, quality, or behavior—if appropriate.

The assessment process was also simplified: There was to be a narrative assessment of actual performance and a rating for each key responsibility. An overall rating was required to take into account the key responsibility ratings and any other significant performance events. There were three rating levels: outstanding, satisfactory, and unsatisfactory.

Mayoral support for the new system was sought and received. The new system was implemented and monitored using limited training but was supported by a guidance booklet. The strong mayoral support helped to generate acceptance of the revised system, and managers found MPE easier to operate than MPAS.

There were still a few problems, however. Because salary increases were tied closely to the performance evaluation, the definition of the rating level "satisfactory" caused some concern. It was intended to reflect fully acceptable or good performance but was seen by some as implying only marginal performance. There was a fear that too many "outstanding" ratings would be given because of the possible stigma attaching to "satisfactory." Doubts were expressed as to whether pay increases actually would be linked to performance. The consequences of the performance ratings had been explained (for example, larger-than-average increases would be paid to outstanding managers), but there was uncertainty about the actual size of the increase that would be associated with "outstanding" or "satisfactory" performance. A related difficulty was that of managers not being given "unsatisfactory" ratings where performance merited it because this would result in the denial of an increase. Despite these difficulties, an audit of the early stages of the revised system showed that MPE was off to a promising start: the large majority of managers had been able to define measurable performance expectations; progress in meeting them was being measured; and the appropriateness of performance expectations was being assessed in light of the initial experience with the system. ■

OD practitioners increasingly are attending to the design and implementation of reward systems. This recent attention to rewards has derived partly from research in organization design and employee involvement. These perspectives treat rewards as an integral part of organizations.[42] They hold that rewards should be congruent with other organizational systems and practices, such as the organization's structure, top management's human relations philosophy, and work designs. Many features of reward systems contribute to both employee fulfillment and organizational effectiveness. In this section, we describe how rewards affect individual and group performance and then discuss three specific rewards: pay, promotions, and benefits.

How Rewards Affect Performance

Considerable research has been done on how rewards affect individual and group performance. The most popular model describing this relationship is value expectancy theory. In addition to explaining how performance and rewards are related, it suggests requirements for designing and evaluating reward systems.

The *value expectancy model*[43] posits that employees will expend effort to achieve performance goals that they believe will lead to outcomes that they value. This effort will result in the desired performance goals if the goals are realistic, if employees fully understand what is expected of them, and if they have the necessary skills and resources. Ongoing motivation depends on the extent to which attaining the desired performance goals actually results in valued outcomes. Consequently, key objectives of reward systems interventions are to identify the intrinsic and extrinsic outcomes (rewards) that are highly valued and to link them to the achievement of desired performance goals.

Based on value expectancy theory, the ability of rewards to motivate desired behavior depends on these six factors:[44]

1. *Availability.* For rewards to reinforce desired performance, they must be not only desired but also available. Too little of a desired reward is no reward at all. For example, pay increases are often highly desired but unavailable. Moreover, pay increases that are below minimally accepted standards may actually produce negative consequences.[45]

2. *Timeliness.* Like effective performance feedback, rewards should be given in a timely manner. A reward's motivating potential is reduced to the extent that it is separated in time from the performance it is intended to reinforce.

3. *Performance contingency.* Rewards should be closely linked with particular performances. If the goal is met, the reward is given; if the target is missed, the reward is reduced or not given. The clearer the linkage between performance and rewards, the better able rewards are to motivate desired behavior. Unfortunately, this criterion often is neglected in practice. Forty percent of employees nationwide believe that there is no linkage between pay and performance.[46] From

another perspective, merit increases in 1988 were concentrated between 4 and 5 percent nationwide. That is, almost everyone, regardless of performance level, got about the same raise.

4. *Durability.* Some rewards last longer than others. Intrinsic rewards, such as increased autonomy and pride in workmanship, tend to last longer than extrinsic rewards. Most people who have received a salary increase realize that it gets spent rather quickly.

5. *Equity.* Satisfaction and motivation can be improved when employees believe that the pay policies of the organization are equitable or fair. Internal equity concerns comparison of personal rewards to those holding similar jobs or performing similarly in the organization. Internal inequities typically occur when employees are paid a similar salary or hourly wage regardless of their level of performance. External equity concerns comparison of rewards with those of other organizations in the same labor market. When an organization's reward level does not compare favorably with the level of other organizations, employees are likely to feel inequitably rewarded.

6. *Visibility.* To leverage a reward system, it must be visible. Organization members must be able to see who is getting the rewards. Visible rewards, such as placement on a high-status project, promotion to a new job, and increased authority, send signals to employees that rewards are available, timely, and performance contingent.

Reward systems interventions are used to elicit and maintain desired levels of performance. To the extent that rewards are available, durable, equitable, timely, visible, and performance contingent, they can support and reinforce organizational goals, work designs, and employee involvement. The next sections describe three types of rewards—pay, fringe benefits, and promotions—that are particularly effective in improving employee performance and satisfaction.

Pay

In recent years, interest has grown in using various forms of pay to improve employee satisfaction and increase both individual and organizational performance. This has resulted in a number of innovative pay schemes, including skill-based pay, all-salaried workforce, lump-sum salary increases, performance-based pay, and gain sharing.[47] Each of these systems is described and discussed below.

Skill-Based Pay Plans

Traditionally, organizations design pay systems by evaluating jobs. The characteristics of a particular job are determined, and pay is made comparable to what other organizations pay for jobs with similar characteristics. This job evaluation method tends to result in pay systems with high external and internal equity. However, it fails to reward employees for all of the skills that they have, discourages people from learning new skills, and results in a view of pay as an entitlement.[48]

Some organizations, such as General Mills, Northern Telecom, United Technologies, and General Foods, have worked to resolve these problems by designing pay systems according to people's skills and abilities. By focusing on the individual, rather than the job, skill-based pay systems reward learning and growth. Typically, employees are paid according to the number of different jobs that they can perform. For example, in General Mill's Squeeze-It plant, new employees are paid a starting wage at the low end of the skilled worker wage rate for premium employers in the community. They are then assigned to any one of four skill blocks corresponding to a particular set of activities in the production process. For each skill block there are three levels of skill. Pay is based on the level of skill in each of the skill blocks; the more proficient the skill in each block and the more blocks one is proficient at, the higher the pay. After all skill blocks are learned at the highest level, the top rate is given.[49] This progression in skills typically takes two years to complete, and employees are given support and training to learn the new jobs.

Skill-based pay systems have a number of benefits. They contribute to organizational effectiveness by providing a more flexible workforce and by giving employees a broad perspective on how the entire plant operates. This flexibility can result in leaner staffing and fewer problems with absenteeism, turnover, and work disruptions. Skill-based pay can lead to durable employee satisfaction by reinforcing individual development and by producing an equitable wage rate.[50]

The two major drawbacks of skill-based pay schemes are the tendency to "top out" and the lack of performance contingency. Top-out occurs when employees learn all the skills there are to learn and then run up against the top end of the pay scale, with no higher levels to attain. Some organizations have resolved this topping-out effect by installing a gain-sharing plan after most employees have learned all relevant jobs. Gain sharing, discussed later in this section, ties pay to organizational effectiveness, allowing employees to push beyond previous pay ceilings. Other organizations have resolved this effect by making base skills obsolete and adding new ones, thus raising the standards of employee competence. Skill-based pay systems also require a heavy investment in training, as well as a measurement system capable of telling when employees have learned the new jobs. They typically increase direct labor costs, as employees are paid highly for learning multiple tasks. In addition, because pay is based on skill and not performance, the workforce could be highly paid and flexible but not productive.

Like most new personnel practices, limited evaluative research exists on the effectiveness of these interventions. Long-term assessment of the Gaines Pet Food plant reveals that the skill-based pay plan has contributed to both organizational effectiveness and employee satisfaction. Several years after the plant opened, workers' attitudes toward pay were significantly more positive than those of people working in other similar plants that did not have skill-based pay. Gaines workers reported much higher levels of pay satisfaction, as well as feelings that their pay system was fairly administered.[51]

A national survey of skill-based pay plans sponsored by the U.S. Department of Labor concluded that such systems increase workforce flexibility, employee growth and development, and product quality and quantity while reducing staffing needs, absenteeism, and turnover.[52] These results appear contingent on management commitment to the plan and having the right kind of people, particularly those with interpersonal skills, motivation, and a desire for growth and development. This study also showed that skill-based pay is applicable across a variety of situations, including both manufacturing and service industries, production and staff employees, new and old sites, and unionized and nonunionized settings. Finally, in a 1996 survey of 212 *Fortune* 1000 companies, 42 percent indicated that skill-based pay systems were successful or very successful, down from 52 percent in 1993.[53]

Application 17.3 describes the development of a skill-based pay system at Sola Ophthalmics.[54] It demonstrates the importance of employee involvement in the design process and how skill-based pay systems can support work design interventions.

APPLICATION 17·3   Skill-Based Pay at Sola Ophthalmics

Sola Ophthalmics, a division of Pilkington Visioncare, manufactures premium-quality contact lenses. Poor performance in the face of increasing market demand led the firm to examine its manufacturing process and compensation system. The manufacturing process consisted of three major stages, with each stage handled by a different section of the company. In the first stage, employees from the "base curve" section lathed the curve of the lens that fits against the eye. During the second stage, employees in the "front curve" section lathed the customer's prescribed amount of optical correction on the front of the lens. Employees in the "finishing" section polished and buffed the edge and surfaces of the lens to make it microscopically smooth. In all, twenty-six different jobs had to be completed to manufacture a lens ready for packaging.

Diagnosis of the manufacturing process found that each section saw its goal as getting the product quickly out of its area and into the next. Within sections, employees tended to view their jobs in the same way: they performed their assigned task as quickly as possible and passed the product on to the next employee. This resulted in uneven quality, a large amount of wasted material, and frustrated employees.

To remedy these problems, the manufacturing process was reorganized into modules giving teams of twenty-five workers responsibility for all three manufacturing processes. This solved some problems but created new ones as well. The new work design put much more emphasis on managing the work flow within each module. This required having workers who were not only well trained but also capable of handling a variety of jobs so that they could assist with the work flow as needed.

Unfortunately, Sola's existing compensation system gave employees little incentive to learn new jobs or to perform a variety of tasks. It assigned manufacturing employees to one of three job grades on the basis of the sophistication or difficulty of the particular job that they performed. An employee who knew a variety of lower-rated jobs and who therefore was extremely valuable to a work module might have a job grade of only 2, whereas an employee who knew only one, but more difficult, job might have a job grade of 3. Employees perceived this system of compensation as unfair, and management readily acknowledged its inequity.

"We recognized that we needed a different compensation system, one that would rate employees not only by the difficulty of the job they perform but also by the number of jobs they are capable of performing," said Richard Bunning, director of human resources at Sola. With the strong support of the manufacturing director, he convened a task force of manufacturing supervisors to develop a proposal for implementing a skill-based pay system at Sola. The proposal supported the need to reward employees for the number of different jobs that they could perform.

Top management accepted the proposal, and Bunning and his task force were made responsible for working out the details of the new reward system. Bunning's first move was to present the task force's proposal to all manufacturing employees through small-group discussions. This elicited their input, addressed their concerns, and gained their support.

The task force then developed a rating system for the jobs within each manufacturing module. Using input from managers and employees, the rating system examined each job in terms of the difficulty of learning it, the importance of the job, and its affect on manufacturing cost. Based on a point system developed through extensive discussion and employee input, the twenty-six existing jobs were placed into clusters of similar ratings. This resulted in an eight-level hierarchy of jobs, with the lowest-level cluster of easy jobs (entry level) receiving a point value of 1 and the highest-level cluster receiving a point value of 8. In line with the clusters, new pay grades were established.

In the next step, each employee's current skill level was assessed and assigned to one of the new clusters. Most employees were assigned to a cluster rating of 2 or 3, although some experienced employees ended up in clusters 4 and 5. The task force had ensured that no employee would drop to a lower pay scale even if assigned to a lower skill cluster. Instead, the employee would be given time to cross-train into extra jobs to maintain his or her pay level.

Once the skill clusters, pay grades, and employee assignments were established, Sola still had to deal with a variety of implementation and management details. The following are some of the more important policies it developed:

- Before the implementation of the pay program, employees who initially qualified for an increase in pay grade would receive a bonus instead of a promotional increase to avoid immediately raising the labor-cost base. A one-grade increase would merit forty hours' pay; a two-grade increase, sixty hours' pay; and so on.
- Following implementation, employees would receive a 5-percent increase per grade whenever they were promoted to a higher level.
- Cross-training would be guided by "skill depth" charts. Each job would have only two or three employees trained in a backup capacity to limit the amount of cross-training. Thus, cross-training just for the sake of promotions would be avoided.

The new plan was implemented in January 1987 and was supported almost universally by employees and managers.

Managers felt that the new pay system met expectations in supporting the manufacturing modules. It provided an incentive to employees to cross-train and to cooperate in moving among various jobs to enhance the work flow within their modules. The module manufacturing system itself has led to dramatic gains in productivity. Although a direct causal relationship between the skill-based pay system and its effect on productivity cannot be determined, a positive correlation between each module's productivity and the average skill depth of its employees was shown. In addition, average pay levels actually have decreased because many new employees were hired at the lowest pay rate. Further, by initially paying bonuses instead of giving promotional increases to employees who had been upgraded, average pay increases for existing employees were minimized.

After two years, the skill-based pay system continued to flourish. Bunning cited four reasons for its success. First, the organization was ready for change. Second, skill-based pay was not viewed as a cure-all but rather as a supportive system designed to meet the need for achieving profitability and developing a flexible, well-trained workforce. Third, broad employee involvement was encouraged through the task force. Fourth, there was close cooperation and commitment by manufacturing management and the human resources department. ■

All-Salaried Workforce

An increasing number of companies, such as IBM, Gillette, and Dow Chemical, are adopting all-salaried pay systems that treat managers and workers the same in terms of pay administration and some fringe benefits.[55] Typically, such systems pay all employees on a salary basis. People do not punch time clocks or lose pay when they are late, and they have generous sick leave and absenteeism privileges. Employees generally prefer all-salaried plans because they allow more freedom about when to start and stop work and because they treat workers more maturely than do hourly wage systems. All-salaried plans also can improve organizational effectiveness by making the organization a more attractive place to work, thus reducing turnover.

A major problem with all-salaried workforces is that some employees abuse the plan by chronically staying home or coming late to work. Although there is conflicting evidence about whether all-salaried plans increase or reduce absenteeism and tardiness, negative effects generally can be avoided by combining the plan with a more participative approach to management. Eaton Corporation, for example, employs all-salaried workforce as a prelude to job enrichment and participative management. Egalitarian personnel practices are seen as a necessary precondition to meaningful work redesign.

Lump-Sum Salary Increases

Traditionally, organizations have distributed annual pay increases by adjusting the regular paychecks of employees. For example, weekly paychecks are increased to reflect the annual raise. This tradition has two major drawbacks. It makes employees wait a full year before they receive the full amount of their annual increase. Second, it makes the raise hardly visible to employees because once added to regular pay checks, it may mean little change in take-home pay.

Aetna, BFGoodrich, Timex, and Westinghouse, among others, have tried to make annual salary increases more flexible and visible[56] by instituting a lump-sum increase program that gives employees the freedom to decide when they receive their annual raise. For example, an employee can choose to receive it all at once at the start of the year. The money advanced to the employee is treated as a loan, usually at a modest interest rate. If the person quits before the end of the year, the proportion of the raise that has not been earned has to be paid back.

Lump-sum increase programs can contribute to employee satisfaction by tailoring the annual raise to individual needs. Such programs can improve organizational effectiveness by making the organization more attractive and reducing turnover. They can increase employee motivation in situations where pay is linked to performance. By making the amount of the salary increase highly visible, employees can see a clear relationship between their performance and their annual raise. The major disadvantages of lump-sum programs are the extra costs of administering the plan and the likelihood that some employees will quit and not pay back the company.

Performance-Based Pay Systems

Organizations have devised many ways of linking pay to performance,[57] making it the fastest-growing segment of pay-based reward systems development. One study estimated that almost two-thirds of medium- and large-sized businesses have some form of performance-based pay system for nonexecutives. They are used in such organizations as Monsanto, Behlen Mfg., DuPont, American Express, and Herman Miller.[58] Such plans tend to vary along three dimensions: (1) the organizational unit by which performance is measured for reward purposes—an individual, group, or organization basis; (2) the way performance is measured—the subjective measures used in supervisors' ratings or objective measures of productivity, costs, or profits; and (3) what rewards are given for good performance—salary increases, stock, or cash bonuses. Table 17.2 lists different types of performance-based pay systems varying along these dimensions and rates them in terms of other relevant criteria.

In terms of linking pay to performance, individual pay plans are rated highest, followed by group plans and then organization plans. The last two plans score lower on this factor because pay is not a direct function of individual behavior. At the group and organization levels, an individual's pay is influenced by the behavior of others and by external market conditions. Generally, stock and bonus plans tie pay to performance better than do salary plans. The amount of awarded stock may vary sharply from year to year, whereas salary increases tend to be more stable because organizations seldom cut employees' salaries. Finally, objective measures of performance score higher than subjective measures. Objective measures are more credible, and people are more likely to see the link between pay and objective measures.

Most of the pay plans in Table 17.2 do not produce negative side effects, such as workers falsifying data and restricting performance. The major exceptions are individual bonus plans. These plans, such as piece-rate systems, tend to result in negative effects, particularly when trust in the plan is low. For example, if people feel that piece-rate quotas are unfair, they may hide work improvements for fear that quotas may be adjusted higher.

As might be expected, group- and organization-based pay plans encourage cooperation among workers more than do individual plans. Under the former, it is generally to everyone's advantage to work well together because all share in the financial rewards of higher performance. The organization plans also tend to promote cooperation among functional departments. Because members from different departments feel that they can benefit from each others' performance, they encourage and help each other make positive contributions.

From an employee's perspective, Table 17.2 suggests that the least acceptable pay plans are individual bonus programs. Employees tend to dislike such plans because they encourage competition among individuals and because they are difficult to administer fairly. Such plans may be inappropriate in some technical contexts.

Table 17•2	Ratings of Various Pay-for-Performance Plans*				
		TIE PAY TO PERFORMANCE	**PRODUCE NEGATIVE SIDE EFFECTS**	**ENCOURAGE COOPERATION**	**EMPLOYEE ACCEPTANCE**
SALARY REWARD					
Individual plan	Productivity	4	1	1	4
	Cost-effectiveness	3	1	1	4
	Superiors' rating	3	1	1	3
Group	Productivity	3	1	2	4
	Cost-effectiveness	3	1	2	4
	Superiors' rating	2	1	2	3
Organizationwide	Productivity	2	1	3	4
	Cost-effectiveness	2	1	2	4
STOCK/BONUS REWARD					
Individual plan	Productivity	5	3	1	2
	Cost-effectiveness	4	2	1	2
	Superiors' rating	4	2	1	2
Group	Productivity	4	1	3	3
	Cost-effectiveness	3	1	3	3
	Superiors' rating	3	1	3	3
Organizationwide	Productivity	3	1	3	4
	Cost-effectiveness	3	1	3	4
	Profit	2	1	3	3

*Ratings: 1 = lowest rating, 5 = highest rating.

SOURCE: Reproduced by permission of the publisher from E. Lawler III, "Reward Systems," in *Improving Life at Work*, eds. J. Hackman and J. Suttle (Santa Monica, Calif.: Goodyear, 1977): 195.

For example, technical innovations typically lead engineers to adjust piece-rate quotas upward because employees should be able to produce more with the same effort. Workers, on the other hand, often feel that the performance worth of such innovations does not equal the incremental change in quotas, thus resulting in feelings of pay inequity. Table 17.2 suggests that employees tend to favor salary increases to bonuses. This follows from the simple fact that a salary increase becomes a permanent part of a person's pay, but a bonus does not.

The overall ratings in Table 17.2 suggest that no one pay-for-performance plan scores highest on all criteria. Rather, each plan has certain strengths and weaknesses that depend on a variety of contingencies. As business strategies, organization performance, and other contingencies change, the pay-for-performance system also must change. At Lincoln Electric, a long-time proponent and model for incentive pay, growth into international markets, poor managerial decisions, and other factors have put pressure on the bonus plan. In one instance, a poor acquisition decision hurt earnings and left the organization short of cash for the bonus payout. The organization borrowed money rather than risk losing employees' trust. Financially weakened by the acquisition, and in combination with the other changes,

Lincoln Electric has initiated a planned change effort to examine its pay-for-performance process and recommend a new approach.[59]

When all criteria are taken into account, however, the best performance-based pay systems seem to be group and organization bonus plans that are based on objective measures of performance and individual salary-increase plans. These plans are relatively good at linking pay to performance. They have few negative side effects and at least modest employee acceptance. The group and organization plans promote cooperation and should be used where there is high task interdependence among workers, such as might be found on assembly lines. The individual plan promotes competition and should be used where there is little required cooperation among employees, such as in field sales jobs.

Gain Sharing

As the name implies, gain sharing involves paying employees a bonus based on improvements in the operating results of an organization. Although not traditionally associated with employee involvement, gain sharing increasingly has been included in comprehensive employee involvement projects. Many organizations, such as Georgia-Pacific, Huffy Bicycle Company, Inland Container Corp., TRW, and General Electric, are discovering that when designed correctly, gain-sharing plans can contribute to employee motivation, involvement, and performance.

Developing a gain-sharing plan requires making choices about the following design elements:[60]

- *Process of design.* This factor concerns whether the plan will be designed participatively or in a top-down manner. Because the success of gain sharing depends on employee acceptance and cooperation, it is recommended that a task force composed of a cross section of employees design the plan and be trained in gain-sharing concepts and practice. The task force should include people who are credible and represent both management and nonmanagement interests.

- *Organizational unit covered.* The size of the unit included in the plan can vary widely, from departments or plants with less than fifty employees to companies with several thousand people. A plan covering the entire plant would be ideal in situations where there is a freestanding plant with good performance measures and an employee size of less than five hundred. When the number of employees exceeds five hundred, multiple plans may be installed, each covering a relatively discrete part of the company.

- *Bonus formula.* Gain-sharing plans are based on a formula that generates a bonus pool, which is divided among those covered by the plan. Although most plans are custom-designed, there are two general considerations about the nature of the bonus formula. First, a standard of performance must be developed that can be used as a baseline for calculating improvements or losses. Some plans use past performance to form a historical standard, whereas others use engineered or estimated standards. When available, historical data provide a relatively fair standard of performance; engineer-determined data can work, however, if there is a high level of trust in the standard and how it is set. Second, the costs included in arriving at the bonus must be chosen. The key is to focus on those costs that are most controllable by employees. Some plans use labor costs as a proportion of total sales; others include a wider range of controllable costs, such as those for materials and utilities.

- *Sharing process.* Once the bonus formula is determined, it is necessary to decide how to share gains when they are obtained. This decision includes choices about what percentage of the bonus pool should go to the company and what percentage to employees. In general, the company should take a low-enough percentage to ensure that the plan generates a realistic bonus for employees. Other decisions about dividing the bonus pool include who will share in the bonus and how the money will be divided among employees. Typically, all employees included in the organizational unit covered by the plan share in the bonus. Most plans divide the money on the basis of a straight percentage of total salary payments.

- *Frequency of bonus.* Most plans calculate a bonus monthly. This typically fits with organizational recording needs and is frequent enough to spur employee motivation. Longer payout periods generally are used in seasonal businesses or where there is a long production or billing cycle for a product or service.

- *Change management.* Organizational changes, such as new technology and product mixes, can disrupt the bonus formula. Many plans include a steering committee to review the plan and to make necessary adjustments, especially in light of significant organizational changes.

- *The participative system.* Many gain-sharing plans include a participative system that helps to gather, assess, and implement employee suggestions and improvements. These systems generally include a procedure for formalizing suggestions and different levels of committees for assessing and implementing them.

Although gain-sharing plans are tailored to each situation, three major plans are used most often: the Scanlon plan, the Rucker plan, and Improshare. The most popular program is the Scanlon plan, used in such firms as Donnelly Corporation, De Soto, Midland-Ross, and Dana Corporation. The Rucker plan and Improshare use different bonus formulas and place less emphasis on worker participation than does the Scanlon plan.[61]

Named after Joe Scanlon, a union leader in the mid-1930s, the Scanlon plan is both an incentive plan and a management philosophy. Scanlon believed in a participative philosophy in which managers and workers share information, problems, goals, and ideas. Moreover, he felt that a company's pay system should be tied to that philosophy by rewarding cooperation and problem solving. Based on these beliefs, the Scanlon plan uses a participative suggestion system involving different levels of worker–management committees. The committees solicit employee suggestions, assess them, and see that promising improvements are implemented.

The incentive part of the Scanlon plan generally includes a bonus formula based on a ratio measure comparing total sales volume to total payroll expenses. This measure of labor cost efficiency is relatively responsive to employee behaviors and is used to construct a historical base rate at the beginning of the plan. Savings resulting from improvements over this base make up the bonus pool. The bonus is often split equally between the company and employees, with all members of the organization receiving bonuses of a percentage of their salaries.

Gain-sharing plans tie the goals of workers to the organization's goals. It is to the financial advantage of employees to work harder, to cooperate with each other, to make suggestions, and to implement improvements. Reviews of the empirical literature and individual studies suggest that when such plans are implemented properly, organizations can expect specific improvements.[62] A study sponsored by the General Accounting Office found that plans in place more than five years averaged annual savings of 29 percent in labor costs;[63] there also is evidence to suggest that they work in 50 to 80 percent of the reported cases.[64] A report on four case studies in manufacturing and service settings noted significant increases in productivity (32 percent in manufacturing and 11 percent in services), as well as in several other measures.[65] A longitudinal field study employing experimental and control groups supports gain sharing's positive effect over time and even after the group's bonus was discontinued.[66] Other reported results include enhanced coordination and teamwork; cost savings; acceptance of technical, market, and methods changes; demands for better planning and more efficient management; new ideas as well as effort; reductions in overtime; more flexible union–management relations; and greater employee satisfaction.[67]

Gain-sharing plans are better suited to certain situations than to others, and Table 17.3 lists conditions favoring such plans. In general, gain sharing seems suited

Table 17·3	Conditions Favoring Gain-Sharing Plans

ORGANIZATIONAL CHARACTERISTIC	FAVORABLE CONDITION
Size	Small unit, usually less than five hundred employees
Age	Old enough that the learning curve has flattened and standards can be set based on performance history
Financial measures	Simple, with a good history
Market for output	Good, can absorb additional production
Product costs	Controllable by employees
Organizational climate	Open, high level of trust
Style of management	Participative
Union status	No union, or one that is favorable to a cooperative effort
Overtime history	Limited to no use of overtime in past
Seasonal nature of business	Relatively stable across time
Work floor interdependence	High to moderate interdependence
Capital investment plans	Little investment planned
Product stability	Few design changes
Comptroller/chief financial officer	Trusted, able to explain financial measures
Communication policy	Open, willing to share financial results
Plant manager	Trusted, committed to plan, able to articulate goals and ideals of plan
Management	Technically competent, supportive of participative management style, good communication skills, able to deal with suggestions and new ideas
Corporate position (if part of larger organization)	Favorable to plan
Workforce	Technically knowledgeable, interested in participation and higher pay, financially knowledgeable and interested
Plant support services	Maintenance and engineering groups competent, willing, and able to respond to increased demands

SOURCE: E. Lawler III, *Pay and Organization Development*, page 144. © 1981 by Addison-Wesley Publishing Co., Inc. Reprinted by permission of Addison Wesley Longman.

to small organizations with a good market, simple measures of historical performance, and production costs controllable by employees. Product and market demand should be relatively stable, and employee–management relations should be open and based on trust. Top management should support the plan, and support services should be willing and able to respond to increased demands. The workforce should be interested in and knowledgeable about gain sharing and should be technically proficient in its tasks.

Promotions

Like decisions about pay increases, many decisions about promotions and job movements in organizations are made in a top-down, closed manner: higher-level managers decide whether lower-level employees will be promoted. This process can be secretive, with people often not knowing that a position is open, that they are being considered for promotion, or the reasons why some people are promoted but others are not. Without such information, capable people who might be interested in a new job may be overlooked. Furthermore, because employees may fail to see the connection between good performance and promotions, the motivational potential of promotions is reduced.

Fortunately, this is changing. Most organizations today have tried to reduce the secrecy surrounding promotions and job changes by openly posting the availability of new jobs and inviting people to nominate themselves.[68] Although open job posting entails extra administrative costs, it can lead to better promotion decisions. Open posting increases the pool of available personnel by ensuring that interested people will be considered for new jobs and that capable people will be identified. Open posting also can increase employee motivation by showing that a valued reward is available and contingent on performance.

Some organizations have increased the accuracy and equity of job-change decisions by including peers and subordinates in the decision-making process. Peer and subordinate judgments about a person's performance and promotability help bring all relevant data to bear on promotion decisions. Such participation can increase the accuracy of these decisions and can make people feel that the basis for promotions is equitable. In many self-regulating work teams, for example, the group interviews and helps select new members and supervisors. This helps ensure that new people will fit in and that the group is committed to making that happen. Evidence from high-involvement plants suggests that participation in selecting new members can lead to greater group cohesiveness and task effectiveness.[69]

Benefits

In addition to pay and promotions, organizations provide a variety of other extrinsic rewards in the form of benefits. Some of these are mandated by law, such as unemployment insurance and workers' compensation; others are a matter of long tradition, such as paid vacations and health insurance; and still others have emerged to keep pace with the needs of the changing labor force, such as maternity leave, educational benefits, retirement plans, and child care. Organizations, such as Genentech, Johnson & Johnson, Xerox, Allstate, and Bank of America, increasingly are using benefits to attract and retain good employees, to help them better integrate work with home life, and to improve the quality of work life. These benefits can translate into economic gains through reduced absenteeism and turnover, and greater organizational commitment and performance.

Examples of some of the more recent trends in benefits include various forms of early and flexible retirement and preretirement counseling to meet the demands of the greying labor force. Maternity and paternity leaves and child care are designed to satisfy the needs of dual-career couples and single parents. For example, Genentech underwrites half the operating expenses of its child care facility, and Johnson & Johnson, along with ten other corporations, formed an alliance among 145 providers to offer child and dependent care services. There also has been increased attention to providing educational programs, financial services, and pension and investing plans to help employees develop themselves and prepare for secure futures.

Organizations generally provide equal benefit packages to all employees at similar organizational levels. Employees are treated essentially the same, with major differences occurring between hierarchical levels, which therefore tests the equity criterion. This approach also does not account for the kinds of benefits that different people value and therefore may not pass the availability test. For example, younger workers may want more vacation time, whereas older employees may desire more retirement benefits. By treating employees the same, a company spends money for benefits that some people do not value. This also can lead to employee dissatisfaction and reduced motivation. Finally, benefits cannot be manipulated during the year and fail to be timely or performance contingent.

Most large companies are tailoring benefit plans to employee needs through the use of cafeteria-style programs.[70] These plans give employees some choice over how they receive their total fringe-benefit payment. The company tells workers how much it will spend on the total benefit package, and employees use that amount to buy only the fringe benefits they want. In some plans, the employee can spend less than the allocated amount and receive the balance as an increase in pay. For example, one employee might decide to sign up for a less expensive health maintenance organization benefit plan and allocate the remaining amount toward a cash payment; another might allocate the benefit amount equally between paid vacations, life insurance, and health insurance. These plans also allow the employee to purchase additional benefits, such as life, dental, optical, and family health insurance, often at preferred rates.

A flexible benefit program can contribute to employee satisfaction by providing only those benefits that people value. It can increase organizational effectiveness by making the company an attractive place to work, thus reducing absenteeism and turnover. The plan also can improve employee understanding of the firm's benefits. At American Can, for example, the employee's family often becomes involved in discussing and choosing benefits.

The major drawbacks of the plan include the extra costs to administer it and the fact that the costs and availability of many fringe benefits are based on the number of people covered by them. For small organizations, this latter difficulty may require special agreements with insurance companies or entail added risks in implementing the plan.

Some organizations also are concerned that cafeteria-style benefit plans might be misused: employees might not take enough insurance in favor of a cash payment and leave themselves vulnerable to financial problems if illness or other problems occur. Although some evidence suggests that employees will act responsibly when given the choice, organizations may want to ensure that everyone has a minimum level of coverage. TRW, a pioneer in flexible benefits programs, provides all employees with minimum levels of important benefits and allows people to supplement them as desired. This plan has been operating since 1974 and permits new choices each year. More than 80 percent of employees changed their benefits program when the new plan was introduced, suggesting that the traditional fringe-benefit program had failed to match most workers' needs.[71]

Many companies did not adopt cafeteria-style plans in the 1980s because they were uncertain about tax laws and legal implications. However, the Deficit Reduction Act of 1984 both clarified and set rules for such plans.[72] First, the act identified which benefits were nontaxable and could be included in cafeteria-style programs—for example, health, accident, medical, and life insurance; dependent-care assistance; and group legal services. Second, the act prohibited preferential or discriminatory treatment of employees and set out certain reporting requirements. One expert predicted that the 1984 law would encourage the growth of cafeteria-style plans.[73]

Reward-System Process Issues

Thus far, we have discussed different reward systems and assessed their strengths and weaknesses. Considerable research has been conducted on the process aspect of reward systems. *Process* refers to how pay and other rewards typically are administered in the organization. At least two process issues affect employees' perceptions of the reward system: who should be involved in designing and administering the reward system, and what kind of communication should exist with respect to rewards.[74]

Traditionally, reward systems are designed by top managers and compensation specialists and are simply imposed on employees. Although this top-down process may result in a good system, it cannot ensure that employees will understand and trust it. In the absence of trust, workers are likely to have negative perceptions of the reward system. There is growing evidence that employee participation in the design and administration of a reward system can increase employee understanding and can contribute to feelings of control over and commitment to the plan.

Lawler and Jenkins described a small manufacturing plant where a committee of workers and managers designed a pay system, after studying alternative plans and collecting salary survey data.[75] This resulted in a plan that gave control over salaries to members of work groups. Team members behaved responsibly in setting wage rates. They gave themselves 8 percent raises, which fell at the fiftieth percentile in the local labor market. Moreover, the results of a survey administered six months after the start of the new pay plan showed significant improvements in turnover, job satisfaction, and satisfaction with pay and its administration. Lawler attributed these improvements to employees having greater information about the pay system. Participation led to employee ownership of the plan and feelings that it was fair and trustworthy.

Communication about reward systems also can have a powerful impact on employee perceptions of pay equity and on motivation. Most organizations maintain secrecy about pay rates, especially in the managerial ranks. Managers typically argue that secrecy is preferred by employees. It also gives managers freedom in administering pay because they do not have to defend their judgments. There is evidence to suggest, however, that pay secrecy can lead to dissatisfaction with pay and to reduced motivation. Dissatisfaction derives mainly from people's misperceptions about their pay relative to the pay of others. Research shows that managers tend to overestimate the pay of peers and of people below them in the organization and that they tend to underestimate the pay of superiors. These misperceptions contribute to dissatisfaction with pay because regardless of a manager's pay level, it will seem small in comparison to the perceived pay level of subordinates and peers. Perhaps worse, potential promotions will appear less valuable than they actually are.

Secrecy can reduce motivation by obscuring the relationship between pay and performance. For organizations having a performance-based pay plan, secrecy prevents employees from testing whether the organization is actually paying for performance; employees come to mistrust the pay system, fearing that the company has something to hide. Secrecy can also reduce the beneficial impact of accurate performance feedback. Pay provides people with feedback about how they are performing in relation to some standard. Because managers overestimate the pay of peers and subordinates, they will consider their own pay low and thus perceive performance feedback more negatively than it really is. Such misperceptions about performance discourage those managers who are actually performing effectively.

For organizations having a history of secrecy, initial steps toward an open reward system should be modest. For example, an organization could release information on pay ranges and median salaries for different jobs. Organizations with unions generally publish such data for lower-level jobs, and extending that information to all jobs would not be difficult. Once organizations have established higher levels of trust about pay, they might publicize information about the size of raises and who receives them. Finally, as organizations become more democratic, with high levels of trust among managers and workers, they can push toward complete openness about all forms of rewards.

It is important to emphasize that both the amount of participation in designing reward systems and the amount of frankness in communicating about rewards should fit the rest of the organization design and managerial philosophy. Clearly, high levels of participation and openness are congruent with democratic organizations. It is questionable whether authoritarian organizations would tolerate either one.

■ SUMMARY

This chapter presented three types of human resources management interventions—goal setting, performance appraisal, and rewards systems. Although all three change programs are relatively new to organization development, they offer powerful methods for managing employee and work group performance. They also help enhance worker satisfaction and support work design, business strategy, and employee involvement practices.

Principles contributing to the success of goal setting include establishing challenging goals and clarifying measurement. These are accomplished by setting difficult but feasible goals, managing participation in the goal-setting process, and being sure that the goals can be measured and influenced by the employee or work group. The most common form of goal setting—management by objectives—depends on top-management support and participative planning to be effective.

Performance appraisals represent an important link between goal setting and reward systems. As part of an organization's feedback and control system, they provide employees and work groups with information they can use to improve work outcomes. Appraisals are becoming more participative and developmental. An increasing number of people are involved in collecting performance data, evaluating an employee's performance, and determining how the appraisee can improve.

Reward systems interventions elicit and maintain desired performance. They can be oriented to both individual jobs or work groups and affect both performance and employee well-being. Three major kinds of reward systems interventions are the design of pay, promotions, and benefits.

The more innovative pay plans include skill-based pay, all-salaried workforce, lump-sum salary increases, performance-based pay, and gain sharing. Each of the plans has strengths and weaknesses when measured against criteria of performance contingency, equity, availability, timeliness, durability, and visibility. Interventions regarding promotions include open posting of jobs and inviting people to nominate themselves for job openings. Involving peers and subordinates in promotion decisions can increase the accuracy and equity of such changes. Flexible benefit programs give employees some discretion in allocating their total benefit payment. The critical process of implementing a reward system involves decisions about who should be involved in designing and administering it and how much information about pay should be communicated.

■ NOTES

1. A. Mohrman, S. Mohrman, and C. Worley, "High-Technology Performance Management," in *Managing Complexity in High-Technology Organizations,* eds. M. Von Glinow and S. Mohrman (New York: Oxford University Press, 1990): 216–36.

2. D. McDonald and A. Smith, "A Proven Connection: Performance Management and Business Results," *Compensation and Benefits Review* 27 (1995): 59–64.

3. J. Riedel, D. Nebeker, and B. Cooper, "The Influence of Monetary Incentives on Goal Choice, Goal Commitment, and Task Performance," *Organizational Behavior and Human Decision Processes* 42 (1988): 155–80; P. Earley, T. Connolly, and G. Ekegren, "Goals, Strategy Development, and Task Performance: Some Limits on the Efficacy of Goal Setting," *Journal of Applied Psychology* 74 (1989): 24–33; N. Perry, "Here Come Richer, Riskier Pay Plans," *Fortune* (19 December 1988): 50–58; E. Lawler III, *High-Involvement Management* (San Francisco: Jossey-Bass, 1986); A. Mohrman, S. Resnick-West, and E. Lawler III, *Designing Performance Appraisal Systems* (San Francisco: Jossey-Bass, 1990).

4. Mohrman, Mohrman, and Worley, "High-Technology Performance Management."

5. E. Locke and G. Latham, *A Theory of Goal Setting and Task Performance* (Englewood Cliffs, N.J.: Prentice Hall, 1990).

6. Locke and Latham, *Theory of Goal Setting;* E. Locke, R. Shaw, L. Saari, and G. Latham, "Goal Setting and Task Performance: 1969–1980," *Psychological Bulletin* 97 (1981): 125–52; M. Tubbs, "Goal Setting: A Meta-Analytic Examination of the Empirical Evidence," *Journal of Applied Psychology* 71 (1986): 474–83.

7. A. O'Leary-Kelly, J. Martocchio, and D. Frink, "A Review of the Influence of Group Goals on Group Performance," *Academy of Management Journal* 37 (1994): 1285–1301.

8. S. Sherman, "Stretch Goals: The Dark Side of Asking for Miracles," *Fortune* (13 November 1995): 231–32; S.

Tully, "Why to Go for Stretch Targets," *Fortune* (14 November 1994): 145–58.

9. D. Crown and J. Rosse, "Yours, Mine, and Ours: Facilitating Group Productivity Through the Integration of Individual and Group Goals," *Organizational Behavior and Human Decision Processes* 64, 2 (1995): 138–50.

10. P. Drucker, *The Practice of Management* (New York: Harper & Row, 1954): 63.

11. G. Odiorne, *Management by Objectives* (New York: Pittman, 1965).

12. H. Levinson, "Management by Objectives: A Critique," *Training and Development Journal* 26 (1972): 410–25.

13. D. McGregor, "An Uneasy Look at Performance Appraisal," *Harvard Business Review* 35 (May-June 1957): 89–94.

14. E. Huse and E. Kay, "Improving Employee Productivity Through Work Planning," in *The Personnel Job in a Changing World,* ed. J. Blood (New York: American Management Association, 1964): 301–15.

15. This application was adapted from T. Jones, "Performance Management in a Changing Context: Monsanto Pioneers a Competency-Based, Developmental Approach," *Human Resource Management* 34 (1995): 425–42.

16. Locke and Latham, *Theory of Goal Setting.*

17. Tubbs, "Goal Setting"; R. Guzzo, R. Jette, and R. Katzell, "The Effects of Psychologically Based Intervention Programs on Worker Productivity: A Meta-Analysis," *Personnel Psychology* 38 (1985): 275–91; A. Mento, R. Steel, and R. Karren, "A Meta-Analytic Study of the Effects of Goal Setting on Task Performance: 1966–1984," *Organizational Behavior and Human Decision Processes* 39 (1987): 52–83; O'Leary-Kelly, Martocchio, and Frink, "Influence of Group Goals."

18. C. Pearson, "Participative Goal Setting as a Strategy for Improving Performance and Job Satisfaction: A Longitudinal Evaluation with Railway Track Maintenance

Gangs," *Human Relations* 40 (1987): 473–88; R. Pritchard, S. Jones, P. Roth, K. Stuebing, and S. Ekeberg, "Effects of Group Feedback, Goal Setting, and Incentives on Organizational Productivity," *Journal of Applied Psychology* 73 (1988): 337–58.

19. S. Yearta, S. Maitlis, and R. Briner, "An Exploratory Study of Goal Setting in Theory and Practice: A Motivational Technique That Works?" *Journal of Occupational and Organizational Psychology* 68 (1995): 237–52.

20. R. Steers, "Task-Goal Attributes: Achievement and Supervisory Performance," *Organizational Behavior and Human Performance* 13 (1975): 392–403; G. Latham and G. Yukl, "A Review of Research on the Application of Goal Setting in Organizations," *Academy of Management Journal* 18 (1975): 824–45; R. Steers and L. Porter, "The Role of Task-Goal Attributes in Employee Performance," *Psychological Bulletin* 81 (1974): 434–51; Earley, Connolly, and Ekegren, "Goals"; J. Hollenbeck and A. Brief, "The Effects of Individual Differences and Goal Origin on Goal Setting and Performance," *Organizational Behavior and Human Decision Processes* 40 (1987): 392–414.

21. Huse and Kay, "Improving Employee Productivity," pp. 301–15.

22. A. Raia, "Goal Setting and Self-Control: An Empirical Study," *Journal of Management Studies* 2 (1965): 34–53; A. Raia, "A Second Look at Management Goals and Controls," *California Management Review* 8 (1965): 49–58.

23. S. Carroll and W. Tosi Jr., *Management by Objectives* (New York: Macmillan, 1973): 23.

24. D. Terpstra, P. Olson, and B. Lockeman, "The Effects of MBO on Levels of Performance and Satisfaction Among University Faculty," *Group and Organization Studies* 7 (1982): 353–66.

25. R. Byrd and J. Cowan, "MBO: A Behavioral Science Approach," *Personnel* 51 (March-April 1974): 42–50.

26. G. Latham and R. Wexley, *Increasing Productivity Through Performance Appraisal* (Reading, Mass.: Addison-Wesley, 1981).

27. C. Peck, "Pay and Performance: The Interaction of Compensation and Performance Appraisal," *Research Bulletin* 155 (New York: Conference Board, 1984).

28. E. Lawler III, *Pay and Organization Development* (Reading, Mass.: Addison-Wesley, 1981): 113; Mohrman, Resnick-West, and Lawler, *Designing Performance Appraisal Systems.*

29. D. Antonioni, "Improve the Performance Management Process Before Discounting Performance Ap-

praisals," *Compensation and Benefits Review* 26 (3, 1994): 29–37.

30. S. Mohrman, G. Ledford Jr., E. Lawler III, and A. Mohrman, "Quality of Work Life and Employee Involvement," in *International Review of Industrial and Organizational Psychology 1986,* eds. C. Cooper and I. Robertson (New York: John Wiley, 1986); G. Yukl and R. Lepsinger, "How to Get the Most out of 360-Degree Feedback," *Training* 32, 21 (1995): 45–50.

31. Mohrman et al., "Quality of Work Life."

32. E. Huse, "Performance Appraisal—A New Look," *Personnel Administration* 30 (March-April 1967): 3–18.

33. S. Gebelein, "Employee Development: Multi-Rater Feedback Goes Strategic," *HR Focus* 73, 1 (1996): 1, 4; B. O'Reilly, "360 Feedback Can Change Your Life," *Fortune* (17 October 1994): 93–100.

34. Mohrman, Resnick-West, and Lawler, *Designing Performance Appraisal Systems;* E. Lawler, "Performance Management: The Next Generation," *Compensation and Benefits Review* 26, 3 (1994): 16–19.

35. J. Fairbank and D. Prue, "Developing Performance Feedback Systems," in *Handbook of Organizational Behavior Management,* ed. L. Frederiksen (New York: John Wiley & Sons, 1982).

36. R. Ammons, *Knowledge of Performance: Survey of Literature, Some Possible Applications and Suggested Experimentation,* USAF WADC Technical Report 5414 (Wright-Patterson Air Force Base, Ohio: Wright Air Development Center, Aero Medical Laboratory, 1954); J. Adams, "Response Feedback and Learning," *Psychology Bulletin* 70 (1968): 486–504; J. Annett, *Feedback and Human Behavior* (Baltimore, Md.: Penguin, 1969); J. Sassenrath, "Theory and Results on Feedback and Retention," *Journal of Educational Psychology* 67 (1975): 894–99; F. Luthans and T. Davis, "Behavioral Management in Service Organizations," in *Service Management Effectiveness,* eds. D. Bowen, R. Chase, and T. Cummings (San Francisco: Jossey-Bass, 1989): 177–210.

37. R. Kopelman, *Managing Productivity in Organizations* (New York: McGraw-Hill, 1986).

38. Guzzo, Jette, and Katzell, "Psychologically Based Intervention Programs."

39. D. Nadler, "The Effects of Feedback on Task Group Behavior: A Review of the Experimental Research," *Organizational Behavior and Human Performance* 23 (1979): 309–38; D. Nadler, C. Cammann, and P. Mirvis, "Developing a Feedback System for Work Units: A Field Experiment

in Structural Change," *Journal of Applied Behavioral Science* 16 (1980): 41–62; J. Chobbar and J. Wallin, "A Field Study on the Effect of Feedback Frequency on Performance," *Journal of Applied Psychology* 69 (1984): 524–30.

40. F. Luthans, "The Exploding Service Sector: Meeting the Challenge Through Behavioral Management," *Journal of Organizational Change Management* 1 (1988): 18–28; F. Balcazar, B. Hopkins, and Y. Suarez, "A Critical Objective Review of Performance Feedback," *Journal of Organizational Behavior Management* 7 (1986): 65–89; R. Waldersee and F. Luthans, "A Theoretically Based Contingency Model of Feedback: Implications for Managing Service Employees," *Journal of Organizational Change Management* 3 (1990): 46–56.

41. W. Scott, J. Farh, and P. Podsakoff, "The Effects of 'Intrinsic' and 'Extrinsic' Reinforcement Contingencies on Task Behavior," *Organizational Behavior and Human Decision Processes* 41 (1988): 405–25; E. Lawler III, *Strategic Pay* (San Francisco: Jossey-Bass, 1990).

42. E. Lawler, *Rewarding Excellence: Pay Strategies for the New Economy* (San Francisco: Jossey-Bass, 2000).

43. J. Campbell, M. Dunnette, E. Lawler III, and K. Weick, *Managerial Behavior, Performance, and Effectiveness* (New York: McGraw-Hill, 1970).

44. S. Kerr, "Risky Business: The New Pay Game," *Fortune* (22 July 1996): 94–96.

45. C. Worley, D. Bowen, and E. Lawler III, "On the Relationship Between Objective Increases in Pay and Employees' Subjective Reactions," *Journal of Organization Behavior* 13 (1992): 559–71.

46. Perry, "Richer, Riskier Pay Plans."

47. S. Tully, "Your Paycheck Gets Exciting," *Fortune* (1 November 1993): 83–98.

48. V. Gibson, "The New Employee Reward System," *Management Review* (February 1995): 13–18.

49. G. Ledford and G. Bergel, "Skill-Based Pay Case Number 1: General Mills," (skill-based pay seminar materials, American Compensation Association, Scottsdale, Ariz., 1990).

50. Lawler, *Pay and Organization Development*, p. 66; E. Lawler and G. Ledford Jr., "Skill-Based Pay," *Personnel* 62 (1985): 30–37.

51. Lawler, *Pay and Organization Development*, p. 66.

52. N. Gupta, G. D. Jenkins Jr., and W. Curington, "Paying for Knowledge: Myths and Realities," *National Productivity Review* (Spring 1986): 107–23.

53. E. Lawler III, S. Mohrman, and G. Ledford, *Strategies for High-Performance Organizations* (San Francisco: Jossey-Bass, 1998).

54. W. Wagel, "At Sola Ophthalmics, Paying for Skills Pays Off!" *Personnel* 66 (March 1989): 20–25.

55. Lawler, *Pay and Organization Development*, pp. 62–65.

56. Ibid., pp. 69–72.

57. Ibid., p. 113.

58. H. Gleckman, S. Atchison, T. Smart, and J. Bryne, "Bonus Pay: Buzzword or Bonanza?" *Business Week* (14 November 1994): 62–67.

59. Z. Schiller, "A Model Incentive Plan Gets Caught in a Vise," *Business Week* (22 January 1996): 89–90.

60. Lawler, *Pay and Organization Development*, pp. 134–43; M. Schuster, J. Schuster, and M. Montague, "Excellence in Gainsharing: From the Start to Renewal," *Journal for Quality and Participation* 17, 3 (1994): 18–25; D. Band, G. Scanlon, and C. Tustin, "Beyond the Bottom Line: Gainsharing and Organization Development," *Personnel Review* 23, 8 (1994): 17–32; J. Belcher, "Gainsharing and Variable Pay: The State of the Art," *Compensation and Benefits Review* 26, 3 (1994): 50–60.

61. Lawler, *Pay and Organization Development*, pp. 146–54.

62. J. Ramquist, "Labor–Management Cooperation: The Scanlon Plan at Work," *Sloan Management Review* (Spring 1982): 49–55; T. Cummings and E. Molloy, *Improving Productivity and the Quality of Work Life* (New York: Praeger, 1977): 249–60; R. J. Bullock and E. Lawler III, "Gainsharing: A Few Questions, and Fewer Answers," *Human Resource Management* 23 (1984): 23–40; C. Miller and M. Schuster, "A Decade's Experience with the Scanlon Plan: A Case Study," *Journal of Occupational Behavior* 8 (April 1987): 167–74; T. Welbourne and L. Gomez-Meija, "Gainsharing: A Critical Review and a Future Research Agenda," *Journal of Management* 21, 3 (1995): 559–609; W. Imberman, "Is Gainsharing the Wave of the Future," *Management Accounting* 77 (1977): 35–40; D. Collins, *Gainsharing and Power: Lessons from Six Scanlon Plans* (Ithaca, N.Y.: ILR Press of Cornell University Press, 1998).

63. General Accounting Office, *Productivity Sharing Programs: Can They Contribute to Productivity Improvement?* (Washington, D.C.: Author, 1981).

64. Bullock and Lawler, "Gainsharing"; C. O'Dell, *People, Performance, and Pay* (Houston, Tex.: American Productivity Center, 1987).

65. E. Doherty, W. Nord, and J. McAdams, "Gainsharing and Organization Development: A Productive Synergy," *Journal of Applied Behavioral Science* 25 (1989): 209–29.

66. S. Hanlon, D. Meyer, and R. Taylor, "Consequences of Gainsharing: A Field Experiment Revisited," *Group and Organization Management* 19, 1 (1994): 87–111.

67. E. Lawler III, "Gainsharing Theory and Research: Findings and Future Directions," in *Organizational Change and Development,* vol. 2, eds. W. Pasmore and R. Woodman (Greenwich, Conn.: JAI Press, 1988): 323–44.

68. E. Lawler III, "Reward Systems," in *Improving Life at Work,* eds. J. Hackman and J. Suttle (Santa Monica, Calif.: Goodyear, 1977): 176.

69. R. Walton, "How to Counter Alienation in the Plant," *Harvard Business Review* 50 (November-December 1972): 70–81.

70. Lawler, "Reward Systems," pp. 180–82; J. Haslinger, "Flexible Compensation: Getting a Return on Benefit Dollars," *Personnel Administrator* 30 (1985): 39–46.

71. Lawler, "Reward Systems," p. 182.

72. G. Dessler, *Human Resource Management* (New York: Prentice Hall, 1996).

73. Ibid.

74. Lawler, *Pay and Organization Development,* pp. 101–11.

75. E. Lawler III and G. Jenkins, *Employee Participation in Pay Plan Development* (unpublished technical report to U.S. Department of Labor, Ann Arbor, Mich.; Institute for Social Research, University of Michigan, 1976).

18

Developing and Assisting Members

This chapter presents three human resources management interventions concerned with developing and assisting the well-being of organization members. First, organizations have had to adapt their career planning and development processes to a variety of trends. For example, people have different needs and concerns as they progress through their career stages; technological changes have altered organizational structures and systems dramatically; and global competition has forced organizations to redefine how work gets done. These processes and concerns have forced individuals and organizations to redefine the social contract that binds them together. Career planning and development interventions can help deal effectively with these issues. Second, increasing workforce diversity provides an especially challenging environment for human resources management. The mix of genders, ages, value orientations, thinking styles, and ethnic backgrounds represented in the modern workforce is increasingly varied. Management's perspectives, strategic responses, and implementation approaches can help address pressures posed by this diversity. Finally, wellness interventions, such as employee assistance and stress management programs, are addressing several important social trends, such as fitness and health consciousness, drug and alcohol abuse, and work–life balance.

CAREER PLANNING AND DEVELOPMENT INTERVENTIONS

Career planning and development have been receiving increased attention in organizations. Growing numbers of managers and professional staff are seeking more control over their work lives. As organizations downsize and restructure, there is less trust in the organization to provide job security. Employees are not willing to have their careers "just happen" and are taking an active role in planning and managing them. This is particularly true for women, midcareer employees, and college recruits, who are increasingly asking for career planning assistance.[1] For example, a recent study by the Hay Group found that technology professionals were willing to leave their jobs for better career development opportunities.[2] On the other hand, organizations are becoming more and more reliant on their "intellectual capital." Providing career planning and development opportunities for organization members helps to recruit and retain skilled and knowledgeable workers. Many talented job candidates, especially minorities and women, are showing a preference for employers who offer career advancement opportunities.

Many organizations—General Electric, Xerox, Intel, Ciba-Geigy, Cisco Systems, Quaker Oats, and Novotel UK, among others—have adopted career planning and development programs. These programs have attempted to improve the quality of work life for managers and professionals, to improve their performance, to increase employee retention, and to respond to equal employment and affirmative action legislation. Companies have discovered that organizational growth and effectiveness require career development programs to ensure that needed talent will be available. Competent managers are often the scarcest resource. Many companies also have experienced the high costs of turnover among recent college graduates, including MBAs, which can reach 50 percent after five years. Career planning and development help attract and hold such highly talented employees and can increase the chances that their skills and knowledge will be used.

Recent legislation and court actions have motivated many firms to set up career planning and development programs for minority and female employees, who are in short supply at the middle- and upper-management levels. Organizations are discovering that the career development needs of women and minorities often require special programs and the use of nontraditional methods, such as integrated systems for recruitment, placement, and development. Similarly, age-discrimination laws have led many organizations to set up career programs aimed at older managers and professionals. Thus, career planning and development are increasingly being applied to people at different ages and stages of development—from new recruits to those nearing retirement age.

Finally, career planning and development interventions increasingly have been used in cases of "career halt" where layoffs and job losses have resulted from organization decline, downsizing, reengineering, and restructuring. These abrupt halts to career progress can have severe human consequences, and human resources practices have been developed for helping members cope with these problems.

Career planning is concerned with individuals choosing occupations, organizations, and positions at each stage of their careers. Career development involves helping employees attain career objectives.[3] Although both of these interventions generally are aimed at managerial and professional employees, a growing number of programs are including lower-level employees, particularly those in white-collar jobs.

Career Stages

A career consists of a sequence of work-related positions occupied by a person during the course of a lifetime.[4] Traditionally, careers were judged in terms of advancement and promotion upward in the organizational hierarchy. Today, they are defined in more holistic ways to include a person's attitudes and experiences. For example, a person can remain in the same job, acquiring and developing new skills, and have a successful career without ever getting promoted. Similarly, people may move horizontally through a series of jobs in different functional areas of the firm. Although they may not be promoted upward in the hierarchy, their broadened job experiences constitute a successful career.

Considerable research has been devoted to understanding how aging and experience affect people's careers. This research has drawn on the extensive work done on adult growth and development[5] and has adapted that developmental perspective to work experience.[6] Results suggest that employees progress through at least four distinct career stages as they mature and gain experience. Each stage has unique concerns, needs, and challenges.

1. *The establishment stage (ages 21–26 years).* This phase is the outset of a career when people are generally uncertain about their competence and potential. They are dependent on others, especially bosses and more experienced employees, for guidance, support, and feedback. At this stage, people are making initial choices about committing themselves to a specific career, organization, and job. They are exploring possibilities while learning about their own capabilities.

2. *The advancement stage (ages 26–40 years).* During this phase, employees become independent contributors who are concerned with achieving and advancing in

their chosen careers. They have typically learned to perform autonomously and need less guidance from bosses and closer ties with colleagues. This settling-down period also is characterized by attempts to clarify the range of long-term career options.

3. *The maintenance stage (ages 40–60 years).* This phase involves leveling off and holding on to career successes. Many people at this stage have achieved their greatest advancements and are now concerned with helping less-experienced subordinates. For those who are dissatisfied with their career progress, this period can be conflictual and depressing, as characterized by the term "midlife crisis." People often reappraise their circumstances, search for alternatives, and redirect their career efforts. Success in these endeavors can lead to continuing growth, whereas failure can lead to early decline.

4. *The withdrawal stage (ages 60 years and above).* This final stage is concerned with leaving a career. It involves letting go of organizational attachments and getting ready for greater leisure time and retirement. The employee's major contributions are imparting knowledge and experience to others. For those people who are generally satisfied with their careers, this period can result in feelings of fulfillment and a willingness to leave the career behind.

The different career stages represent a broad developmental perspective on people's jobs. They provide insight about the personal and career issues that people are likely to face at different career phases. These issues can be potential sources of stress. Employees are likely to go through the phases at different rates, and to experience personal and career issues differently at each stage. For example, one person may experience the maintenance stage as a positive opportunity to develop less-experienced employees; another person may experience the maintenance stage as a stressful leveling off of career success.

Career Planning

Career planning involves setting individual career objectives. It is highly personalized and generally includes assessing one's interests, capabilities, values, and goals; examining alternative careers; making decisions that may affect the current job; and planning how to progress in the desired direction. This process results in people choosing occupations, organizations, and jobs. It determines, for example, whether individuals will accept or decline promotions and transfers and whether they will stay or leave the company for another job or for retirement.

The four career stages can be used to make career planning more effective. Table 18.1 shows the different career stages and the career planning issues relevant at each phase. Applying the table to a particular employee involves first diagnosing the person's existing career stage—establishment, advancement, maintenance, or withdrawal. Next, available career planning resources are used to help the employee address pertinent issues. Career planning programs include some or all of the following resources:

- communication about career opportunities and resources available to employees within the organization
- workshops to encourage employees to assess their interests, abilities, and job situations and to formulate career development plans
- career counseling by managers or human resources personnel

Table 18•1	Career Stages and Career Planning Issues
CAREER STAGE	**CAREER-PLANNING ISSUES**
Establishment	What are alternative occupations, organizations, and jobs? What are my interests and capabilities? How do I get the work accomplished? Am I performing as expected? Am I developing the necessary skills for advancement?
Advancement	Am I advancing as expected? How can I advance more effectively? What long-term options are available? How do I get more exposure and visibility? How do I develop more effective peer relationships? How do I better integrate career choices with my personal life?
Maintenance	How do I help others become established and advance? Should I reassess myself and my career? Should I redirect my actions?
Withdrawal	What are my interests outside of work? What postretirement work options are available to me? How can I be financially secure? How can I continue to help others?

- self-development materials, such as books, videotapes, and other media, directed toward identifying life and career issues
- assessment programs that provide various tests of vocational interests, aptitudes, and abilities relevant to setting career goals.

Application 18.1 describes the career planning resources available at Pacific Bell.[7] It provides an example of the range of resources that can be provided and how these programs can be implemented flexibly.

According to Table 18.1, employees who are just becoming established in careers can be stressed by concerns for identifying alternatives, assessing their interests and capabilities, learning how to perform effectively, and finding out how they are doing. At this stage, the company should provide considerable communication and counseling about available career paths and the skills and abilities needed to progress in them. Workshops, self-development materials, and assessment techniques should be aimed at helping employees assess their interests, aptitudes, and capabilities and at linking that information to possible careers and jobs. Considerable attention should be directed to giving employees continual feedback about job performance and to counseling them about how to improve it. The supervisor–subordinate relationship is especially important for these feedback and development activities.

People at the advancement stage are mainly concerned with getting ahead, discovering long-term career options, and integrating career choices, such as transfers or promotions, with their personal lives. Here, the company should provide employees with communication and counseling about challenging assignments and

APPLICATION 18•1   Career Planning Centers at Pacific Bell

Pacific Bell, a Pacific Telesis company, provides local telephone products and services to residential and business customers throughout California. The company operates ten career centers, each managed by an on-site career development specialist with at least ten months of intensive on-the-job training. In addition, the company operates two mobile vans that serve the career needs of employees in outlying areas.

Employees come to the center on their own or may be referred by their managers or a medical health services counselor. Their visits are completely confidential.

Each center has a reference library of print, audio, and video resources on career planning, retirement planning, job titles, and corporate culture. Employees have access to the company's job posting systems and computerized, self-guided career–life planning programs. All of the center's resources are linked to the corporate business plan. The center's staff also provides workshops on résumé writing, interviewing, group interpretation of career assessments, and career planning.

An employee can make an appointment with the career development specialist who will help him or her examine personal skills, interests, abilities, and values and identify appropriate career choices. The counseling process helps the worker answer the questions, "Who am I? How am I seen? Where do I want to go? How do I get there?"

The specialist will help employees research career options within the company or outside, if necessary, and to ap-praise their skills and abilities realistically against the job requirements. Personal issues affecting career options are considered and incorporated into each employee's individualized plan. Specialists also provide ongoing support while employees are making job changes and transitions.

Brian Cowgill, the career counselor who provides clinical supervision to the northern California centers, says that the centers were created in response to Pacific Bell's strategic changes as well as to changes in the work environment and employees' values and needs. "Pacific Bell has changed its corporate mission to be more focused on the customer," says Cowgill. "As a result, job descriptions and job duties have changed for many employees. They are challenged to examine their interests and abilities in order to keep up with the changing work environment."

In addition, employee values have shifted. For example, younger employees are challenging old assumptions about work and are feeling the need to explore all the options open to them. Employee loyalty and commitment are low, especially among the newly hired who have highly sought skills and knowledge. A flattening of organizational structures leaves these employees with fewer opportunities for upward advancement, and they are actively making themselves available to the highest bidder. The career centers enable these employees to discover how best to use their skills and abilities. ■

possibilities for more exposure and demonstration of skills. It should help clarify the range of possible long-term career options and provide members with some idea about where they stand in achieving them. Workshops, developmental materials, and assessment methods should be aimed at helping employees develop wider collegial relationships, join with effective mentors and sponsors, and develop more creativity and innovation. These activities also should help people assess both career and personal life spheres and integrate them more successfully.

At the maintenance stage, individuals are concerned with helping newer employees become established and grow in their careers. This phase also may involve a reassessment of self and career and a possible redirection to something more rewarding. The firm should provide individuals with communications about the broader organization and how their roles fit into it. Workshops, developmental materials, counseling, and assessment techniques should be aimed at helping employees to assess and develop skills in order to train and coach others. For those experiencing a midlife crisis, career planning activities should be directed at helping them to reassess their circumstances and to develop in new directions. Midlife crises generally are caused by perceived threats to people's career or family identities.[8] Career planning should help people deal effectively with identity issues, especially in the context of an ongoing career. This may include workshops and close interpersonal counseling to help people confront identity issues and reorient their thinking about themselves in relation to work and family. These activities also might help employees deal with the emotions evoked by a midlife crisis and develop the skills and confidence to try something new.

Employees who are at the withdrawal stage can experience stress about disengaging from work and establishing a secure leisure life. Here, the company should provide communications and counseling about options for postretirement work and financial security, and it should convey the message that the employee's experience in the organization is still valued. Retirement planning workshops and materials can help employees gain the skills and information necessary to make a successful transition from work to nonwork life. They can prepare people to shift their attention away from the organization to other interests and activities.

Effective career planning and development requires a comprehensive program integrating both corporate business objectives and employee career needs. As shown in Figure 18.1, this is accomplished through human resources planning aimed at developing and maintaining a workforce to meet business objectives. It

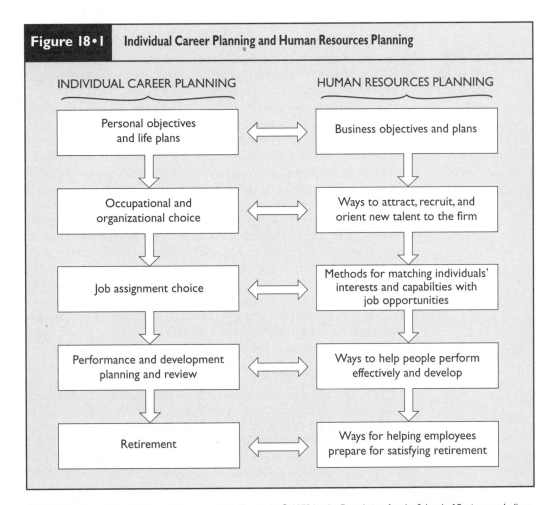

Figure 18•1   Individual Career Planning and Human Resources Planning

INDIVIDUAL CAREER PLANNING

- Personal objectives and life plans
- Occupational and organizational choice
- Job assignment choice
- Performance and development planning and review
- Retirement

HUMAN RESOURCES PLANNING

- Business objectives and plans
- Ways to attract, recruit, and orient new talent to the firm
- Methods for matching individuals' interests and capabilties with job opportunities
- Ways to help people perform effectively and develop
- Ways for helping employees prepare for satisfying retirement

SOURCE: Adapted from *Business Horizons*, vol. 16. Copyright © 1973 by the Foundation for the School of Business at Indiana University. Used with permission.

includes recruiting new talent, matching people to jobs, helping them develop careers and perform effectively, and preparing them for satisfactory retirement. Career planning activities feed into and support career development and human resources planning activities.

Application 18.2 describes how Colgate-Palmolive, an international consumer-products company, revised career planning to integrate better with business strategy and human resources planning.[9]

Career Development

Career development helps individuals achieve their career objectives. It follows closely from career planning and includes organizational practices that help employees implement those plans. These may include skill training, performance feedback and coaching, planned job rotation, mentoring, and continuing education.

Career development can be integrated with people's career needs by linking it to different career stages. As described earlier, employees progress through distinct career stages, each with unique issues relevant to career planning: establishment, advancement, maintenance, and withdrawal. Career development interventions help members implement these plans. Table 18.2 identifies career development interventions, lists the career stages to which they are most relevant, and defines their key purposes and intended outcomes. It shows that career development practices may apply to one or more career stages. Performance feedback and coaching, for example, are relevant to both the establishment and advancement stages. Career development interventions also can serve a variety of purposes, such as helping members identify a career path or providing feedback on career progress and work effectiveness. They can contribute to different organizational outcomes such as lowering turnover and costs and enhancing member satisfaction.

Career development interventions traditionally have been applied to younger employees who have a longer time period to contribute to the firm than do older members. Managers often stereotype older employees as being less creative, alert, and productive than younger workers and consequently provide them with less career development support.[10] Similarly, Table 18.2 suggests that the OD field has been relatively lax in developing methods for helping older members cope with the withdrawal stage because only two of the eleven interventions presented there apply to the withdrawal stage—consultative roles and phased retirement. This relative neglect can be expected to change in the near future, however, as the U.S. workforce continues to grey. To sustain a highly committed and motivated workforce, organizations increasingly will have to address the career needs of older employees. They will have to recognize and reward the contributions that older workers make to the company. Workforce diversity interventions, discussed later in this chapter, are a positive step in that direction.

Realistic Job Preview

This intervention provides organization members with realistic expectations about the job during the recruitment process. It provides recruits with information about whether the job is likely to be consistent with their needs and career plans. Such knowledge is especially useful during the establishment stage, when people are most in need of realistic information about organizations and jobs. It also can help employees during the advancement stage, when job changes are likely to occur because of promotion.

Research suggests that people may develop unrealistic expectations about the organization and job.[11] They can suffer from "reality shock" when those expectations

APPLICATION 18•2   Linking Career Planning, Human Resources Planning, and Strategy at Colgate-Palmolive

Colgate-Palmolive Co. is a global manufacturer and marketer of consumer products, with about 70 percent of its annual $8 billion in sales of personal and household-care products deriving from international markets. To support its global business strategy, the company organized into five worldwide business units in 1989—oral care, personal care, hard-surface care, fabric care, and pet nutrition—but soon discovered a significant gap between its business strategy and the human resources necessary to implement it. Consequently, a Global Human Resources Strategy (GHRS) team was formed to devise ways to integrate business strategy with human resources planning and career planning.

The GHRS team's first task was to articulate a human resources vision based on three key values needed to compete globally: care, teamwork, and continuous improvement. This effort resulted in the following vision statement:

> We care about people. Colgate people, consumers, shareholders, and our business partners. We are committed to act with compassion, integrity, and honesty in all situations, to listen with respect to others and to value cultural differences. We are also committed to protect our global environment and enhance the local communities where we work.

> We are all part of a global team, committed to working together across functions, across countries, and throughout the world. Only by sharing ideas, technologies, and talents can we sustain profitable growth.

> We are committed to getting better every day in all we do, as individuals and as teams. By better understanding consumers' and customers' expectations, and by continuously working to innovate and improve our products, services, and processes, we will "become the best."

The GHRS team circulated the vision statement among the firm's senior executives. After extensive discussion, they revised and approved it. Based on principles espoused in the vision, the team then worked on crafting a human resources strategy that would align with business objectives. First, they interviewed managers from Colgate businesses around the world. "The line managers provided invaluable perspective and insight as to the needs of the organization and the role of HR in achieving business goals," said Brian Smith, director of global human resource strategy.

The interviews revealed the need for human resources support in several areas, including career planning, education and training, and strategy implementation. Colgate needed a comprehensive career planning system so that sufficient numbers of managers with the right skills would be available to fill forecasted job openings. Employees, on the other hand, needed a meaningful career planning system to help them determine what experiences and skills they would need to achieve their own career objectives. Colgate also needed education and training programs that could be applied across business units around the world to reduce the waste and redundancy of the current approach to training where each business unit developed unique programs. Finally, to implement product strategies, the business units needed certain reservoirs of talent, skills, and knowledge. This would require career planning and development on a global scale.

Based on the interview data, the GHRS team coordinated the design of human resources practices for each of the major business functions in the firm. To that end the team created functional design teams, each chaired by the senior manager of the respective business function and including line managers from the business functions as well as appropriate human resources specialists. The design teams first identified global competencies needed to perform the different business functions at Colgate and then designed appropriate career paths and training programs that would allow employees to acquire those competencies.

The manufacturing design team, for example, headed by the manufacturing vice president, identified three sets of global manufacturing competencies: functional/technical, managerial, and leadership. The functional/technical cluster comprised skills and knowledge associated with financial analysis, safety, and production management. The managerial competencies included expertise in negotiation, relationship building, and innovation. The leadership skills involved mobilizing and inspiring people toward a common vision and strategy. To gain the job experiences necessary to learn these competencies, the manufacturing team identified the following career paths: functional/technical competencies could be learned in entry-level positions; managerial competencies could be acquired through job rotation, promotion, and special job assignments both domestically and globally; leadership competencies could be gained with experience in higher-level director and vice president positions. To support these career paths, the manufacturing team designed appropriate training programs as well as performance management processes to monitor and reward learning and performance for each level in the career tracks.

At the conclusion of the functional design teams' efforts in 1992, the GHRS team sponsored a Global Human Resources Conference to launch implementation of the human resources strategy and practices throughout Colgate. More than two hundred human resources leaders from business units around the world attended the weeklong conference. Also present were Colgate's chairman, president, chief operating officer, division presidents, and global business leaders. The conference described the new human resources strategy and practices and linked them directly to business strategy and objectives. It reaffirmed senior management's commitment to the human resources vision, and resulted in specific plans to implement the functional career paths, training programs, and performance management systems across business units worldwide. Colgate's human resources leaders left the conference with renewed energy for the human resources strategy and with clear directions for implementing it across the global businesses. ∎

Table 18•2	Career Development Interventions		
INTERVENTION	**CAREER STAGE**	**PURPOSE**	**INTENDED OUTCOMES**
Realistic job preview	Establishment Advancement	To provide members with an accurate expectation of work requirements	Reduce turnover Reduce training costs Increase commitment Increase job satisfaction
Job pathing	Establishment Advancement	To provide members with a sequence of work assignments leading to a career objective	Reduce turnover Build organizational knowledge
Performance feedback and coaching	Establishment Advancement	To provide members with knowledge about their career progress and work effectiveness	Increase productivity Increase job satisfaction Monitor human resources development
Assessment centers	Establishment Advancement	To select and develop members for managerial and technical jobs	Increase person–job fit Identify high-potential candidates
Mentoring	Establishment Advancement Maintenance	To link a less-experienced member with a more-experienced member for member development	Increase job satisfaction Increase member motivation
Developmental training	Establishment Advancement Maintenance	To provide education and training opportunities that help members achieve career goals	Increase organizational capability
Work–life balance planning	Establishment Advancement Maintenance	To help members balance work and personal goals	Improve quality of life Increase productivity
Job rotation and challenging assignments	Advancement Maintenance	To provide members with interesting work	Increase job satisfaction Maintain member motivation
Dual-career accommodations	Advancement Maintenance	To assist members with significant others to find satisfying work assignments	Attract and retain high-quality members Increase job satisfaction
Consultative roles	Maintenance Withdrawal	To help members fill productive roles later in their careers	Increase problem-solving capacity Increase job satisfaction
Phased retirement	Withdrawal	To assist members in moving into retirement	Increase job satisfaction Lower stress during transition

are not fulfilled and may leave the organization or stay and become disgruntled and unmotivated. To overcome these problems, organizations such as Texas Instruments, Prudential Insurance, and Johnson & Johnson provide new recruits with information about both the positive and negative aspects of the company and the job. They furnish recruits with booklets, talks, and site visits showing what organizational life is really like. Such information reduces the chances that employees will develop unrealistic job expectations and become disgruntled and leave the company.[12] This can lead to reduced turnover and training costs, and increased organizational commitment and job satisfaction.[13]

Application 18.3 describes a highly innovative but demanding realistic job preview program at an auto assembly plant.[14]

Job Pathing

This intervention provides members with a carefully developed sequence of work assignments leading to a career objective, although the notion of a job path in the new economy is being challenged.[15] It helps members in the establishment and advancement stages of their careers. Job pathing helps employees develop skills, knowledge, and competencies by performing jobs that require new skills and abilities. Research suggests that employees who receive challenging job assignments early in their careers do better in later jobs.[16] Career pathing allows for a gradual stretching of people's talents by moving them through selected jobs of increasing challenge and responsibility. As a person gains experience and demonstrates competence in the job, she or he moves to another job with more advanced skills and knowledge. Performing well on one job increases the chance of being assigned to a more demanding job.

The keys to effective job pathing are to identify the skills an employee needs for a certain target job and then to lay out a sequence of interim jobs that will provide those experiences. The interim jobs should provide enough challenge to stretch a person's learning capacity without overwhelming the employee or withholding the target job too long. Some banks, for example, have used job pathing to provide employees with a specific series of jobs for learning how to become a branch manager. In one Los Angeles bank, the jobs in the path include teller, loan officer, credit manager, and commercial loan manager. A job pathing process was also evident at Colgate-Palmolive (Application 18.2). By identifying the necessary competencies in technical and managerial career tracks, the company provided employees with clear paths to higher-level jobs. Job pathing reduces turnover by offering opportunities for advancement. It also can build organizational knowledge. As employees advance along career paths, they gain skills and experience to resolve organizational problems, to assist in large-scale organization change, and to transfer their accumulated knowledge to new members.

Performance Feedback and Coaching

One of the most effective interventions during the establishment and advancement phases includes feedback about job performance and coaching to improve performance. As suggested in the discussions of goal setting and performance appraisal interventions (Chapter 17), employees need continual feedback about goal achievement as well as necessary support and coaching to improve their performances. Feedback and coaching are particularly relevant when employees are establishing careers. They have concerns about how to perform the work, whether they are performing up to expectations, and whether they are gaining the necessary skills for advancement. A manager can facilitate career establishment by providing feedback on performance, coaching, and on-the-job training. These activities can help

APPLICATION 18•3   Realistic Job Preview at Nissan

James Mandelker had two minutes to grab fifty-five nuts, bolts, and washers; assemble them in groups of five; and attach them in order of size to a metal rack. But he fumbled nervously with several pieces and finished the task seconds after his allotted time. "I've got to get a little better at this, don't I?" he frowned, as he pulled the last of the fasteners out of a grimy plastic tray. His tester, Gloria Macaluso, encouraged him: "You're close. For the first night, you're probably doing a little better than normal."

James is trying to get a job at the Nissan Motor Manufacturing Corporation plant in Smyrna, Tennessee. The thirty-one-year-old department-store employee will be devoting seventy hours worth of his nights and weekends during the next few months doing similar exercises. James and about 270 other job seekers are participating in Nissan's preemployment program. In exchange for a shot at highly paid assembly-line jobs and Nissan's promise not to inform their employers, these moonlighters will work as many as 360 hours

without being paid. They will be tested and instructed in employment fundamentals by the Japanese automaker. "We hope the process makes it plain to people what the job is," says Thomas P. Groom, Nissan's manager of employment. "It's an indoctrination process as well as a screening tool."

Not all participants are fully satisfied with the program. One candidate who works as a machine adjuster at an envelope factory says the long preemployment period "worries you, because you get your hopes up." And some candidates bemoan the lack of pay for their time. But many participants feel that the training and experience outweigh the unpaid work required to get hired. For one thing, they get a shot at some of the best-paying jobs in the state. If they are not hired, they can take elsewhere the skills they have learned there. Loraine Olsen, a press operator who went through the program, said, "It gave me a chance to see what Nissan expected of me without their having to make a commitment to me or me to them." ■

employees get the job done while meeting their career development needs. Companies such as Intel and Monsanto, for example, use performance feedback and coaching for employee career development. They separate the career development aspect of performance appraisal from the salary review component, thus ensuring that employees' career needs receive as much attention as salary issues. Feedback and coaching interventions can increase employee performance and satisfaction,[17] and provide a systematic way to monitor the development of human resources in the firm.

Assessment Centers

This intervention was traditionally designed to help organizations select and develop employees with high potential for managerial jobs. More recently, assessment centers have been extended to career development and to selection of people to fit new work designs, such as self-managing teams.[18] Assessment centers are popular both in Europe and the United States; more than 70 percent of large organizations in the United Kingdom and more than two thousand U.S. companies have some form of assessment center.[19] When used to evaluate managerial capability, assessment centers typically process twelve to fifteen people at a time and require them to spend two to three days on site. Participants are given a comprehensive interview, take several tests of mental ability and knowledge, and participate in individual and group exercises intended to simulate managerial work. An assessment team consisting of experienced managers and human resources specialists observes the behaviors and performance of each candidate. This team arrives at an overall assessment of each participant's managerial potential, including a rating on several items believed to be relevant to managerial success in the organization, and pass the results to management for use in making promotion decisions.

Assessment centers have been applied to career development as well, where the emphasis is on feedback of results to participants. Trained staff help participants hear and understand feedback about their strong and weak points. They help participants become clearer about career advancement and identify training experiences and job assignments to promote that progress. When used for developmental purposes, assessment centers can provide employees with the support and direction needed for career development. They can demonstrate that the company is a partner rather than an adversary in that process. Although assessment centers can help people's careers at all stages of development, they seem particularly useful at the advancement stage, when employees need to assess their talents and capabilities in light of long-term career commitments. Research suggests that assessment centers can promote career advancement to the extent that participants are willing to work on the center's recommendations for development.[20] When participants develop themselves in such areas as clarity about career motivation and ability to work with others, their probability of promotion increases.

Assessment centers are being used increasingly to select members for new work designs. They provide comprehensive information about how recruits are likely to perform in such settings, which can increase the fit between the employee and the job and consequently lead to higher levels of employee performance and satisfaction. Application 18.4 shows how such centers can be used for selection purposes in a team-based organization.[21] It illustrates how this intervention can help organizations select the right people, shorten training cycles, and improve productivity.

Mentoring

One of the most useful ways to help employees advance in their careers is sponsorship.[22] This involves establishing a close link between a manager or someone more experienced and another organization member who is less experienced. Mentoring is a powerful intervention that assists members in the establishment, advancement, and maintenance stages of their careers. For those in the establishment stage, a sponsor or mentor takes a personal interest in the employee's career and guides and sponsors it. This ensures that a person's hard work and skill translate into actual opportunities for promotion and advancement.[23] For older employees in the maintenance stage, mentoring provides opportunities to share knowledge and experience with others who are less experienced. Older managers may mentor younger employees who are in the establishment and advancement career stages. Mentors do not have to be the direct supervisors of the younger employees but can be hierarchically or functionally distant from them. Other mentoring opportunities include temporarily assigning veteran managers to newer managers to help them gain managerial skills and knowledge. For example, during the startup of a new manufacturing plant, the plant manager, who was in the advancement career stage, was assisted by a veteran with years of experience in manufacturing management. The veteran was temporarily located at the new plant to help the plant manager develop the skills and knowledge to get the plant operating and to manage it. Once a month, a consultant helped the two managers examine their relationship and set action plans for improving the mentoring process.

Several of Boeing's divisions have well-developed mentoring processes. High-potential members are identified and paired with a corporate manager who volunteers to be a mentor. The mentor helps the employee gain the skills, experience, and visibility necessary for advancement in the company. Senior executives strongly support the mentoring program and believe that it is necessary for managerial success. They believe that "mentoring improves the pool of talent for management and technical jobs and helps to shape future leaders. It is also an effective vehicle for moving knowledge through the organization from the people who have the most experience."[24]

APPLICATION 18·4   Assessment Center for Employee Selection at Hamilton-Standard

The Hamilton-Standard Commercial Aircraft Electronics Division of United Technologies manufactures environmental and jet engine control systems for commercial aerospace applications. In 1991, the division moved to Colorado Springs when it was awarded a contract on the Boeing 777. To achieve demanding standards of quality, cost, and time, Hamilton-Standard used a high-involvement work design. This design included a relatively flat hierarchy and self-managed work teams composed of members who were certified in a variety of technical, business, and interpersonal skills. The teams were highly flexible and able to follow the product through all areas of production. Although a number of workers, staff members, and managers moved with the division to Colorado Springs, the increased scale of operations needed for the Boeing contract required hiring and training a large number of new team members over the next eighteen to twenty-four months—a daunting task in a new geographic location.

To find the right people for the team-based structure, Hamilton-Standard created an assessment center. It was run by division personnel, including existing team members, staff, and managers, who underwent extensive training to learn how to review résumés, conduct interviews, and assess experiential exercises. The assessment center included a number of activities aimed at evaluating the ability of job applicants to work in teams, make decisions, and learn new skills.

Preliminary assessment began with an information session for candidates who submitted résumés to the division. Groups of about 150 applicants engaged in an interactive, two-hour meeting that addressed the firm's products and expectations for new employees. Candidates also discovered what they could expect from Hamilton-Standard in terms of compensation, benefits, work environment, and developmental opportunities. At the end of the session, participants were invited to complete formal job applications, which subsequently were reviewed to identify high-potential candidates who would be asked to participate in the center's evaluation process.

The assessment center was designed to evaluate sixty-five to seventy candidates in a single day—typically a Saturday, to accommodate recruits who were employed elsewhere. In the

week before they attended the center, candidates completed a battery of tests that measured generic work skills, social competence, and mathematical knowledge. These assessments helped Hamilton-Standard identify applicants' strengths and weaknesses and became part of the data subsequently used to accept or reject candidates.

At the assessment center, candidates underwent two interviews—one oriented to technical competence and the other to business knowledge. They also participated in a team-consensus exercise aimed at assessing team skills and decision-making capability. The technical interview presented candidates with a flowchart of the manufacturing process and asked them to identify areas in which they could add value. Their responses enabled interviewers to assess technical depth and breadth, ability to learn, and desire to be cross-functional. The business interview evaluated candidates' understanding of material flow processes, configuration management, computers, finance, and human resources practices. In the consensus exercise, participants worked in small teams to build a model airplane. Their behaviors were observed and assessed on such team-performance criteria as participation, support of the process, interpersonal skills, quality of thought, and flexibility.

At the conclusion of the assessment center activities, results of the tests, interviews, and exercise were entered into a spreadsheet to facilitate comparison among candidates and to help focus selection decisions. Evaluators then met as a team to examine the records, to discuss each candidate, and to make final selections. Consistent with Hamilton-Standard's team-based culture, all hiring decisions were made by group consensus.

The assessment center enabled Hamilton-Standard to recruit extremely capable people who fit well with a team-based work structure. In less than two years, the division was able to hire, train, and retain a talented, cross-functional workforce with certified skills covering more than fifty-two areas. To date, the teams have been effective at improving customer-acceptance rates while lowering costs, thus making Hamilton-Standard a highly competitive supplier of aerospace electronics. ■

Research suggests that mentoring is relatively prevalent in organizations. A survey of 1,250 top executives showed that about two-thirds had a mentor or sponsor during their early career stages, when learning, growth, and advancement were most prominent. The executives reported that effective mentors were willing to share knowledge and experience, were knowledgeable about the company and the use of power, and were good counselors. In contrast to executives who did not have mentors, those having them received slightly more compensation, had more advanced college degrees, had engaged in career planning prior to mentoring, and were more satisfied with their careers and their work.[25]

Although research shows that mentoring can have positive outcomes, artificially creating such relationships when they do not occur naturally is difficult.[26] Some organizations have developed workshops in which managers are trained to become effective mentors. Others, such as IBM and AT&T, include mentoring as a key criterion for paying and promoting managers. In a growing number of cases, companies are creating special mentoring programs for women and minorities who have traditionally had difficulties cultivating developmental relationships.

Developmental Training

This intervention helps employees gain the skills and knowledge for training and coaching others. It may include workshops and training materials oriented to human relations, communications, active listening, and mentoring. It can also involve substantial investments in education, such as tuition reimbursement programs that assist members in achieving advanced degrees. Developmental training interventions generally are aimed at increasing the organization's reservoir of skills and knowledge. This enhances its capability to implement personal and organizational strategies.

A large number of organizations offer developmental training programs, including Procter & Gamble, Cisco Systems, IBM, and Hewlett-Packard. Many of these efforts are directed at midcareer managers who generally have good technical skills but only rudimentary experience in coaching others. In-house developmental training typically involves preparatory reading, short lectures, experiential exercises, and case studies on such topics as active listening, defensive communication, personal problem solving, and supportive relationships. Participants may be videotaped training and coaching others, and the tapes may be reviewed and critiqued by participants and staff. Classroom learning is often rotated with on-the-job experiences, and there is considerable follow-up and recycling of learning. Numerous consulting firms also offer workshops and structured learning materials on developmental training, and an extensive practical literature exists in this area.[27]

Work–Life Balance Planning

This relatively new OD intervention helps employees better integrate and balance work and home life. Restructuring, downsizing, and increased global competition have contributed to longer work hours and more stress. Baby-boomers approaching fifty years of age and others are rethinking their priorities and seeking to restore some balance in a work-dominated life. Organizations, such as Corning Glass Works, Hewlett-Packard, Infonet, and the City of Phoenix, are responding to these concerns so they can attract, retain, and motivate the best workforce. More balanced work and family lives can benefit both employees and the company through increased creativity, morale, and effectiveness, and reduced turnover.

Work–life balance planning involves a variety of programs to help members better manage the interface between work and family. These include such organizational practices as flexible hours, job sharing, and daycare, as well as interventions to help employees identify and achieve both career and family goals. A popular program is called *middlaning*, a metaphor for a legitimate, alternative career track that acknowledges choices about living life in the "fast lane."[28] Middlaning helps people redesign their work and income-generating activities so that more time and energy are available for family and personal needs. It involves education in work addiction, guilt, anxiety, and perfectionism; skill development in work contract negotiation; examination of alternatives such as changing careers, free-lancing, and entrepreneuring; and exploration of options for controlling financial pressures by improving income/expense ratios, limiting "black hole" worries such as college tuition for children and retirement expenses, and replacing financial worrying with financial planning. Because concerns about work–life balance are unlikely to abate and may even increase in the near future, we can expect requisite OD interventions, such as middlaning, to proliferate throughout the public and private sectors.

Job Rotation and Challenging Assignments

The purpose of these interventions is to provide employees with the experience and visibility needed for career advancement or with the challenge needed to revitalize a stagnant career at the maintenance stage. Unlike job pathing, which specifies a sequence of jobs to reach a career objective, job rotation and challenging assignments are less planned and may not be as oriented to promotion opportunities.

Members in the advancement stage may be moved into new job areas after they have demonstrated competence in a particular work specialty. Companies such as Corning Glass Works, Hewlett-Packard, American Crystal Sugar Company, and Fidelity Investments identify "comers" (managers under forty years old with potential for assuming top management positions) and "hipos" (high-potential candidates) and provide them with cross-divisional job experiences during the advancement stage. These job transfers provide managers with a broader range of skills and knowledge as well as opportunities to display their managerial talent to a wider audience of corporate executives. Such exposure helps the organization identify members who are capable of handling senior executive responsibilities; it helps the members decide whether to seek promotion to higher positions or to particular departments. To reduce the risk of transferring employees across divisions or functions, some firms, such as Procter & Gamble, Heublein, and Continental Can, have created "fallback positions." These jobs are identified before the transfer, and employees are guaranteed that they can return to them without negative consequences if the transfers or promotions do not work out. Fallback positions reduce the risk that employees in the advancement stage will become trapped in a new job assignment that is neither challenging nor highly visible in the company.

In the maintenance stage, challenging assignments can help revitalize veteran employees by providing them with new challenges and opportunities for learning and contribution. Research on enriched jobs suggests that people are most responsive to them during the first one to three years on a job, when enriched jobs are likely to be seen as challenging and motivating.[29] People who have leveled off and remain on enriched jobs for three years or more tend to become unresponsive to them. They are no longer motivated and satisfied by jobs that may no longer seem enriched. One way to prevent this loss of job motivation, especially among midcareer employees who are likely to remain on jobs for longer periods of time than people in the establishment and advancement phases, is to rotate workers to new, more challenging jobs at about three-year intervals, or to redesign their jobs at those times. Such job changes would keep employees responsive to challenging jobs and sustain motivation and satisfaction during the maintenance phase.[30]

A growing body of research suggests that "plateaued employees" (those with little chance of further advancement) can have satisfying and productive careers if they accept their new role in the company and are given challenging assignments with high performance standards.[31] Planned rotation to jobs requiring new skills can provide that challenge. However, a firm's business strategy and human resources philosophy must reinforce lateral (as opposed to strictly vertical) job changes if plateaued employees are to adapt effectively to their new jobs.[32] Firms with business strategies emphasizing stability and efficiency of operations, such as the U.S. Post Office and McDonald's, are likely to have more plateaued employees at the maintenance stage than are companies with strategies promoting development and growth, such as Microsoft and Intel. The human resources systems of firms with stable growth strategies should be especially aimed at helping plateaued employees lower their aspirations for promotion and withdraw from the tournament mobility track. Moreover, such firms should enforce high performance standards so that high-performing plateaued employees (solid citizens) are rewarded, and low performers (deadwood) are encouraged to seek help or to leave the firm.

Dual-Career Accommodations

These are practices for helping employees cope with the problems inherent in "dual careers"—that is, both the employee and a spouse or significant other pursuing full-time careers. Dual careers are becoming more prevalent as women increasingly enter the workforce. The U.S. Department of Labor reports that more than 80 percent of all marriages involve dual careers.[33] Although these interventions can apply to all career stages, they are especially relevant during advancement. One of the biggest problems created by dual careers is job transfers, which are likely to occur during the advancement stage. Transfer to another location usually means that the working partner must also relocate. In many cases, the company employing the partner must either lose the employee or arrange a transfer to the same location. Similar problems can occur in recruiting employees. A recruit may not join an organization if its location does not provide career opportunities for the partner.

Because partners' careers can affect the recruitment and advancement of employees, organizations are devising policies to accommodate dual-career employees. A survey of companies reported the following dual-career accommodations: recognition of problems in dual careers, help with relocation, flexible working hours, counseling for dual-career employees, family daycare centers, improved career planning, and policies making it easier for two members of the same family to work in the same organization or department.[34] Some companies have also established cooperative arrangements with other firms to provide sources of employment for the other partner.[35] General Electric, for example, has created a network with other firms to share information about job opportunities for dual-career couples. (Chapter 19 describes interventions aimed at interorganizational networking.)

Consultative Roles

These provide late-career employees with opportunities to apply their wisdom and knowledge to helping others develop in their careers and solve organizational problems. Such roles, which can be structured around specific projects or problems, involve offering advice and expertise to those responsible for resolving the issues. For example, a large aluminum forging manufacturer was having problems developing accurate estimates of the cost of producing new products. The sales and estimating departments lacked the production experience to make accurate bids for potential new business, thus either losing customers or losing money on products. The company temporarily assigned an old-line production manager who was nearing retirement to consult with the salespeople and estimators about bidding on new business. The consultant applied his years of forging experience to help the sales and estimating people make more accurate estimates. In about a year, the sales staff and estimators gained the skills and invaluable knowledge necessary to make more accurate bids. Perhaps equally important, the preretirement production manager felt that he had made a significant contribution to the company—something he had not experienced for years.

In contrast to mentoring roles, consultative roles are not focused directly on guiding or sponsoring younger employees' careers. They are directed at helping others deal with complex problems or projects. Similarly, in contrast to managerial positions, consultative roles do not include the performance evaluation and control inherent in being a manager. They are based more on wisdom and experience than on authority. Consequently, consultative roles provide an effective transition for moving preretirement managers into more support-staff positions. They free up managerial positions for younger employees while allowing older managers to apply their experience and skills in a more supportive and less threatening way than might be possible from a strictly managerial role.

When implemented well, consultative roles can increase the organization's problem-solving capacity. They enable experienced employees to apply their skills and knowledge to resolving important problems, and can increase members' work satisfaction in the maintenance or withdrawal career stages. They provide senior employees with meaningful work as they begin to move from the workforce to retirement.

Phased Retirement

This provides older employees with an effective way of withdrawing from the organization and establishing a productive leisure life. It includes various forms of part-time work. Employees gradually devote less of their time to the organization and more time to leisure pursuits (which to some might include developing a new career). Phased retirement allows older employees to make a gradual transition from organizational to leisure life. It enables them to continue contributing to the firm while it gives them time to establish themselves outside of work. For example, people may use the extra time off work to take courses, to gain new skills and knowledge, and to create opportunities for productive leisure. IBM, for example, offers tuition rebates for courses on any topic taken within three years of retirement.[36] Many IBM preretirees have used this program to prepare for second careers.

Equally important, phased retirement lessens the reality shock often experienced by those who retire all at once. It helps employees grow accustomed to leisure life and withdraw emotionally from the organization. A growing number of companies have some form of phased retirement. Pepperdine University and the University of Southern California, for example, implemented a phased retirement program for professors, which allows them some choice about part-time employment starting at age fifty-five. The program is intended to provide more promotional positions for younger academics and to give older professors greater opportunities to establish a leisure life and still enjoy many benefits of the university.

Organization Decline and Career Halt

In recent years, the United States has experienced an enormous amount of organization decline, downsizing, and restructuring across a variety of smokestack, service, government, and high-technology industries. Decreasing and uneven demand for products and services; growing numbers of mergers, acquisitions, divestitures, and failures; and increasing restructurings to operate leaner and more efficiently have resulted in layoffs, reduced job opportunities, and severe career disruptions for a large number of managers and employees.[37] Between January 1995 and December 1997 (the most recent data available), more than 3.6 million workers over 20 years old were laid off.[38] The human costs of these changes and restructurings are enormous.

People inevitably experience a halt in their career development and progression, resulting in dangerous increases in personal stress, financial and family disruption, and loss of self-esteem. Fortunately, a growing number of organizations are managing decline in ways that are effective for both the organization and the employee. One set of human resources practices involves alternatives to the layoffs that typically occur when firms have to downsize or cut back operations.[39] For example, Polaroid has used job sharing, in which two people share one full-time job; Pacific Northwest Bell has encouraged workers to take unpaid leaves with jobs guaranteed on their return; Hewlett-Packard has experimented with work sharing, in which members take cuts in pay and agree to work fewer hours; Natomas has used across-the-board pay cuts to keep people employed; 3M has offered early retirement with full pension credit to twenty-year employees who are at least fifty-five years old; Union Bank and Xerox have offered part-time consulting jobs to employees who agree to resign or retire early; and many firms have moved employees from unhealthy to healthy units and businesses within the organization.

Organizations have also developed human resources practices for managing decline in those situations where layoffs are unavoidable, such as plant closings, divestitures, and business failures. The following methods can help people deal more effectively with layoffs and premature career halts:[40]

- equitable layoff policies spread throughout organizational ranks, rather than focused on specific levels of employees, such as shop-floor workers or middle managers

- keeping people informed about organizational problems and possibilities of layoffs so that they can reduce ambiguity and prepare themselves for job changes

- setting realistic expectations, rather than offering excessive hope and promises, so that employees can plan for the organization's future and for their own

- generous relocation and transfer policies that help people make the transition to a new work situation

- helping people find new jobs, including outplacement services and retraining

- treating people with dignity and respect, rather than belittling or humiliating them because they are unfortunate enough to be in a declining business that can no longer afford to employ them.

In today's environment, organization decline, downsizing, and restructuring will continue. As a result, the Workforce Investment Act of 1998 helps people affected by career halt and downsizing.[41] OD practitioners are likely to become increasingly involved in helping people manage career dislocation and halt. The methods described above can help organizations manage the human resources consequences of decline, but a great deal more research is needed to assess the effects of these strategies and to identify factors contributing to their success. Because career disruption and halt can be extremely stressful, the interventions described in the section on employee wellness play an important role in managing the human consequences of organization decline.

WORKFORCE DIVERSITY INTERVENTIONS

Several profound trends are shaping the labor markets of modern organizations. Researchers suggest that contemporary workforce characteristics are radically different from what they were just twenty years ago. Employees represent every ethnic background and color; range from highly educated to illiterate; vary in age from eighteen to eighty; may appear perfectly healthy or may have a terminal illness; may be single parents or part of dual-income, divorced, same-sex, or traditional families; and may be physically or mentally challenged.

Workforce diversity is more than a euphemism for cultural or ethnic differences. Such a definition is too narrow and focuses attention away from the broad range of issues that a diverse workforce poses. Diversity results from people who bring different resources and perspectives to the workplace and who have distinctive needs, preferences, expectations, and lifestyles.[42] Organizations must design human resources systems that account for these differences if they are to attract and retain a productive workforce and if they want to turn diversity into a competitive advantage.[43]

Figure 18.2 presents a general framework for managing diversity in organizations.[44] First, the model suggests that an organization's diversity approach is a function of *internal and external pressures* for and against diversity. Pro-diversity forces argue that organization performance is enhanced when the workforce's diversity is embraced as an opportunity. But diversity is often discouraged by those who fear that too many perspectives, beliefs, values, and attitudes dilute concerted action. Second, *management's perspective and priorities* with respect to diversity can range from resistance to active learning and from marginal to strategic. For example, organizations can resist diversity by implementing only legally mandated policies such as affirmative action, equal employment opportunity, or Americans with Disabilities Act requirements. On the other hand, a learning and strategic perspective can lead management to view diversity as a source of competitive advantage. For example, a health-care organization with a diverse customer base can improve perceptions of service quality with physician diversity. Third, within management's

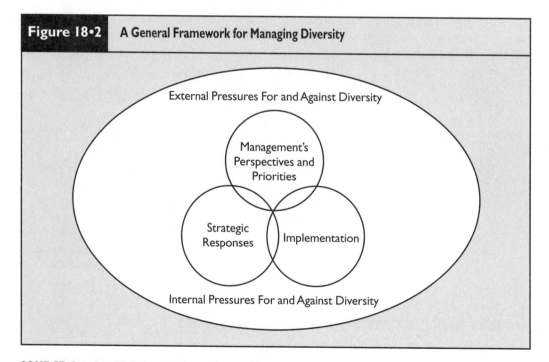

| **Figure 18•2** | **A General Framework for Managing Diversity** |

External Pressures For and Against Diversity

Management's Perspectives and Priorities

Strategic Responses   Implementation

Internal Pressures For and Against Diversity

SOURCE: Dass, P., and B. Parker. (1999) "Strategies for Managing Human Resource Diversity: From Resistance to Learning," *Academy of Management Executive,* 13, p. 69.

priorities, the organization's *strategic responses* can range from reactive to proactive. Diversity efforts at Texaco and Denny's had little momentum until a series of embarrassing race-based events forced a response. Fourth, the organization's *implementation style* can range from episodic to systemic. A diversity approach will be most effective when the strategic responses and implementation style fit with management's intent and internal and external pressures.

Unfortunately, organizations have tended to address workforce diversity pressures in a piecemeal fashion; only 5 percent of more than fourteen hundred companies surveyed thought they were doing a "very good job" of managing diversity.[45] As each trend makes itself felt, the organization influences appropriate practices and activities. For example, as the percentage of women in the workforce increased, many organizations simply added maternity leaves to their benefits packages; as the number of physically challenged workers increased and when Congress passed the Americans with Disabilities Act in 1990, organizations changed their physical settings to accommodate wheelchairs. Demographers warn, however, that these trends are not only powerful by themselves but will likely interact with each other to force organizational change. Thus, a growing number of organizations, such as MBNA Corporation, Lockheed Martin, the St. Paul Companies, Levi Strauss, Procter & Gamble, Monsanto, and Wisconsin Electric, are taking bolder steps. They are not only adopting learning perspectives with respect to diversity, but systemically weaving diversity-friendly values and practices into the cultural fabric of the organization.

Many of the OD interventions described in this book can be applied to the strategic responses and implementation of workforce diversity, as shown in Table 18.3. It summarizes several of the internal and external pressures facing organizations, including age, gender, disability, culture and values, and sexual orientation.[46] The table also reports the major trends characterizing those dimensions, organizational implications and workforce needs, and specific OD interventions that can address those implications.

Age

The average age of the U.S. workforce is rising and changing the distribution of age groups. Between 1998 and 2008, the category of workers aged twenty-five to fifty-four years will grow 5.5 percent, and the fifty-five and over age category is expected to increase almost 48 percent. This skewed distribution is mostly the result of the baby boom between 1946 and 1964. As a result, organizations will face a predominantly middle-aged and older workforce. Even now, many organizations are reporting that the average age of their workforce is over forty. Such a distribution will place special demands on the organization.

For example, the personal needs and work motivation of the different cohorts will require differentiated human resources practices. Older workers place heavy demands on health-care services, are less mobile, and will have fewer career advancement opportunities. This situation will require specialized work designs that account for physical capabilities of older workers, career development activities that address and use their experience, and benefit plans that accommodate their medical and psychological needs. Demand for younger workers, on the other hand, will be intense. To attract and retain this more mobile group, jobs will have to be more challenging, advancement opportunities more prevalent, and an enriched quality of work life more common.

Organization development interventions, such as work design, wellness programs (discussed below), career planning and development, and reward systems

Table 18•3	Workforce Diversity Dimensions and Interventions		
WORKFORCE DIFFERENCES	**TRENDS**	**IMPLICATIONS AND NEEDS**	**INTERVENTIONS**
Age	Median age up Distribution of ages changing	Health care Mobility Security	Wellness program Job design Career planning and development Reward systems
Gender	Percentage of women increasing Dual-income families	Child care Maternity/paternity leave Single parents	Job design Fringe benefit rewards
Disability	The number of people with disabilities entering the work-force is increasing	Job challenge Job skills Physical space Respect and dignity	Performance management Job design Career planning and development
Culture and values	Rising proportion of immigrant and minority-group workers Shift in rewards	Flexible organizational policies Autonomy Affirmation Respect	Career planning and development Employee involvement Reward systems
Sexual orientation	Number of single-sex households up More liberal attitudes toward sexual orientation	Discrimination	Equal employment opportunities Fringe benefits Education and training

must be adapted to these different age groups. For the older employee, work designs can reduce the physical components or increase the knowledge and experience components of a job. At Builder's Emporium, a chain of home improvement centers, the store clerk job was redesigned to eliminate heavy lifting by assigning night crews to replenish shelves and emphasizing sales ability instead of strength. Younger workers will likely require more challenge and autonomy. Wellness programs can be used to address the physical and mental health of both generations. Career planning and development programs will have to recognize the different career stages of each cohort and offer resources tailored to that stage. Finally, reward system interventions may offer increased health benefits, time off, and other perks for the older worker while using promotion, ownership, and pay to attract and motivate the scarcer, younger workforce.

Gender

Another important trend is the increasing percentage of female workers in the labor force. By the year 2008, almost 48 percent of the U.S. workforce will be women, and they will represent more than half of the new entrants between 1998 and 2008. The organizational implications of these trends are sobering. Three-quarters of all working women are in their childbearing years, and more than half of all mothers work. Health-care costs will likely increase at even faster rates, and costs associated with absenteeism and turnover will rise. In addition, demands for child care, maternity and paternity leaves, and flexible working arrangements will place pressure on work systems to maintain productivity and teamwork. From a management perspective, there will be more men and women working together as peers, more women entering the executive ranks, greater diversity of management styles, and changing definitions of managerial success.

Work design, reward systems, and career development are among the more important interventions for addressing issues arising out of the gender trend. For example, jobs can be modified to accommodate the special demands of working mothers. A number of organizations, such as Digital Equipment, Steelcase, and Hewlett-Packard, have instituted job sharing, by which two people perform the tasks associated with one job. The firms have done this to allow their female employees to pursue both family and work careers. Reward system interventions, especially fringe benefits, can be tailored to offer special leaves to both mothers and fathers, child-care options, flexible working hours, and health and wellness benefits. Career development interventions help maintain, develop, and retain a competent and diverse workforce. Organizations such as Polaroid, Hoechst Celanese, and Ameritech have instituted job pathing, challenging assignments, and mentoring programs to retain key female members.

Disability

A third trend is the increasing number of men and women with disabilities entering the workforce. The workforce of the twenty-first century will comprise people with a variety of physical and mental disabilities. For example, the high school dropout rate has remained above 4 percent throughout the 1990s, and approximately 21 percent of the population over age 16 have only rudimentary reading and writing skills. In a world of knowledge work, the lack of education or an inability to learn is a profoundly debilitating condition. More and more organizations will employ physically handicapped people, especially as the number of younger workers declines, creating a great demand for labor. In 1990, the federal Americans with Disabilities Act banned all forms of discrimination on the basis of physical or mental disability in the hiring and promotion process. It also required many organizations to modify physical plants and office buildings to accommodate people with disabilities.

The organizational implications of the disability trend represent both opportunity and adjustment. The productivity of physically and mentally disabled workers often surprises managers, and training is required to increase managers' awareness of this opportunity. Employing disabled workers, however, also means a need for more comprehensive health care, new physical workplace layouts, new attitudes toward working with the disabled, and challenging jobs that use a variety of skills.

OD interventions, including work design, career planning and development, and performance management, can be used to integrate the disabled into the workforce. For example, traditional approaches to job design can simplify work to permit physically handicapped workers to complete an assembly task. Career planning and development programs need to focus on making disabled workers aware of career opportunities. Too often, these employees do not know that advancement is possible, and they are left feeling frustrated. Career tracks need to be developed for these workers.

Performance management interventions, including goal setting, monitoring, and coaching performance, aligned with the workforce's characteristics are important. At Blue Cross and Blue Shield of Florida, for example, a supervisor learned sign language to communicate with a deaf employee whose productivity was low but whose quality of work was high. Two other deaf employees were transferred to that supervisor's department, and over a two-year period, the performance of the deaf workers improved 1,000 percent with no loss in quality.

Culture and Values

Immigration into the United States from the Pacific Rim, South America, Europe, the Middle East, and the former Soviet states will drastically alter the cultural diversity of the workplace. Between 1998 and 2008, the U.S. civilian labor force will increase by 12 percent, while the Asian and Hispanic population in the United States will increase by 40 and 37 percent, respectively. Approximately six hundred thousand people will immigrate (legally and illegally) into the United States, mostly from Latin America and Asia, and about two-thirds of those immigrants will enter the workforce. In California, 50 percent of the population will be people of color by the year 2005, and they will speak more than eighty languages.

Cultural diversity has broad organizational implications. Different cultures represent a variety of values, work ethics, and norms of correct behavior. Not all cultures want the same things from work, and simple, piecemeal changes in specific organizational practices will be inadequate if the workforce is culturally diverse. Management practices will have to be aligned with cultural values and support both career and family orientations. English is a second language for many people, and jobs of all types (processing, customer contact, production, and so on) will have to be adjusted accordingly. Finally, the organization will be expected to satisfy both extrinsic and monetary needs, as well as intrinsic and personal growth needs.

Several planned change interventions, including employee involvement, reward systems, and career planning and development, can be used to adapt to cultural diversity. Employee involvement practices can be adapted to the needs for participation in decision making. People from certain cultures, such as Scandinavia, are more likely to expect and respond to high-involvement policies; other cultures, such as Latin America, view participation with reservation. (See the discussion of cultural values in Chapter 21.) Participation in an organization can take many forms, from suggestion systems and attitude surveys to high-involvement work designs and performance management systems. Organizations can maximize worker productivity by basing the amount of power and information workers have on cultural and value orientations.

Reward systems can focus on increasing flexibility. For example, flexible working hours that permit employees to arrive at and leave work within specified periods enable them to meet personal obligations without sacrificing organizational objectives. Many organizations have implemented this innovation, and most report that the positive benefits outweigh the costs. Work locations also can be varied. Many organizations (e.g., Pacific Telesis, Eddie Bauer, and Marriott) allow workers to spend part of their time telecommuting from home. Other flexible benefits, such as floating holidays, allow people from different cultures to match important religious and family occasions with work schedules.

Child-care and dependent-care assistance also support different lifestyles. For example, at Stride Rite Corporation, the Stride Rite Intergenerational Day Care Center houses fifty-five children between the ages of fifteen months and six years as well as twenty-four elders over sixty years old. The center was established after an organizational survey determined that 25 percent of employees provided some sort of elder care and that an additional 13 percent anticipated doing so within five years.

Finally, career planning and development programs can help workers identify advancement opportunities that are in line with their cultural values. Some cultures value technical skills over hierarchical advancement; others see promotion as a prime indicator of self-worth and accomplishment. By matching programs with people, job satisfaction, productivity, and employee retention can be improved.

Sexual Orientation

Finally, diversity in sexual and affectional orientation, including gay, lesbian, and bisexual individuals and couples, increasingly is affecting the way that organizations think about human resources. Accurate data on the number of gays and lesbians in the workforce are difficult to obtain because laws and social norms do not support self-disclosure of a person's sexual orientation. However, related data suggest that this dimension of workforce diversity is gaining in significance. A 1998 U.S. Census report showed the number of same-sex-partner households as 1.67 million, and a number of studies have estimated the number of gays and lesbians at between 6 and 10 percent of the population.

The primary organizational implication of sexual orientation diversity is discrimination. People can have strong emotional reactions to sexual orientation. When these feelings interact with the gender, culture, and values trends described above, the likelihood of both overt and unconscious discrimination is high. An important aspect to this discrimination is the misperceived relationship between sexual orientation and AIDS/HIV. Overall, although 47,000 new cases of HIV and AIDS were reported in the twelve months ending July 1999, the data suggest that the growth of AIDS/HIV is lowest within the gay and lesbian community and highest among drug users and teenagers. The common perception, however, does not fit the facts. Gay men and lesbians often are reticent to discuss how organizational policies can be less discriminatory because they fear their openness will lead to unfair treatment.

Interventions aimed at this dimension of workforce diversity are relatively new in OD and are being developed as organizations encounter sexual orientation issues in the workplace. The most frequent response is education and training. This intervention increases members' awareness of the facts and decreases the likelihood of overt discrimination. Human resources practices having to do with equal employment opportunity (EEO) and fringe benefits also can help to address sexual orientation parity issues. Some organizations have modified their EEO statements to address sexual orientation. Firms such as Advanced Micro Devices, Fujitsu, Ben & Jerry's, and Dow Chemical have communicated strongly to members and outsiders that decisions with respect to hiring, promotion, transfer, and so on cannot (and will not) be made with respect to a person's sexual orientation. Similarly, organizations are increasingly offering domestic-partner benefit plans. Companies such as Microsoft, Apple, Lotus Development Corporation, and Inprise/Borland have extended health-care and other benefits to the same-sex partners of their members. A 1992 *Newsweek* poll found that 78 percent of the respondents favored extending employee benefits to the domestic partners of lesbians and gay men.

Workforce diversity interventions are growing rapidly in OD. A national survey revealed that 75 percent of firms either have, or plan to begin, diversity efforts.[47] Research suggests that diversity interventions are especially prevalent in large organizations with diversity-friendly senior management and human resources policies.[48] Although existing evidence shows that diversity interventions are growing in popularity, there is still ambiguity about the depth of organizational commitment to such practices and their personal and organizational consequences. A great deal more research is needed to understand these newer interventions and their outcomes.

Application 18.5 describes a workforce diversity intervention at Baxter Exports, showing how diversity can exist in many areas and how organizations can employ a range of interventions to make the workplace more flexible.[49]

EMPLOYEE WELLNESS INTERVENTIONS

In the past decade, organizations have become increasingly aware of the relationship between employee wellness and productivity.[50] The estimated cost to industry from stress-related ailments is more than $200 billion per year[51] and is an increasingly global phenomenon. In the United Kingdom, stress and stress-related illness cost industry and taxpayers £12 *billion* each year.[52] Employee assistance programs (EAPs) and stress management interventions have grown because organizations are taking more responsibility for the welfare of their employees. Companies such as Johnson & Johnson, Weyerhaeuser, Federal Express, Quaker Oats, GTE, and Abbott Laboratories are sponsoring a wide range of fitness and wellness programs.

In this section, we discuss two important wellness interventions—EAPs and stress management. EAPs are primarily reactive efforts that identify, refer, and treat employee problems (e.g., drug abuse, marital difficulties, or depression) that affect worker performance. Stress management, both proactive and reactive, is concerned with helping employees alleviate or cope with the negative consequences of stress at work.

Employee Assistance Programs

Forces affecting psychological and physical problems at the workplace are increasing. The 1992 National Household Survey on Drug Abuse reported that 66.5 percent of current illicit drug users then 18 years or older were working full- or part-time. Similarly, alcohol and other drug use costs U.S. business an estimated $102 billion per year in lost productivity, accidents, and turnover.[53] Britain's Royal College of Psychiatrists suggested that up to 30 percent of employees in British companies would experience mental health problems and that 115 million workdays were lost each year as a result of depression.[54] Other factors, too, have contributed to increased problems: altered family structures, the growth of single-parent households, the increase in divorce, greater mobility, and changing modes of child rearing are all fairly recent phenomena that have added to the stress experienced by employees. These trends indicate that an increasing number of employees need assistance with personal problems, and the research suggests that EAP use increases during downsizing and restructuring.[55]

EAPs help identify, refer, and treat workers whose personal problems affect their performance.[56] Initially started in the 1940s to combat alcoholism, these programs have expanded to deal with emotional, family, marital, and financial problems, and, more recently, drug abuse. EAPs can be either broad programs that address a full range of issues or more focused programs dealing with specific problems, such as drug or alcohol abuse.

Central to the philosophy underlying EAPs is the belief that although the organization has no right to interfere in the private lives of its employees, it does have a right to impose certain standards of work performance and to establish sanctions when these are not met. Anyone whose work performance is impaired because of a personal problem is eligible for admission into an EAP program. Successful EAPs have been implemented at General Motors, Johnson & Johnson, Motorola, Burlington Northern Railroad, and Dominion Foundries and Steel Company. Although limited, some research has demonstrated that EAPs can positively affect

APPLICATION 18•5   Embracing Employee Diversity at Baxter Export

Baxter Export Corporation is an 85-person unit responsible for international logistics at Baxter Healthcare, a $5.4 billion maker of health-care products. Their diversity practices are the first steps in response to an eighteen-month study by Baxter International. A survey of one thousand employees found that among salaried employees, most work–life tensions were driven by the need for greater balance and the desire for flexibility.

Work–life tensions are prevalent at Baxter Export. The pressures of a globally competitive business require analysts, who make around $40,000 annually, to manage the flow of catheters, dialysis solutions, intravenous tubes, and other products to subsidiaries and customers around the world. As a result, many two-income families have been forced into intensive arrangements.

One analyst's day ends with emails and voicemails from Saudi Arabia, Oman, and Panama; a conference call that runs over the allotted time; and the anxiety from expectations that dinner should be ready by 5:30. An on-time dinner is important because her husband, who has picked up their three-year-old from day care and their seven-year-old from grade school, has to leave for one of his two night jobs. The week will also include a Cub Scout meeting, grocery shopping, other kids' activities, and errands. "We're kind of used to it . . . it's our life," the analyst says.

Another employee's day begins at 6:30 a.m. because it's easier to communicate with customers in South Africa and New Zealand, and she can pick up her daughter from daycare by 4 p.m. Getting home sooner is also important because of the full-time care required by her mother-in-law, who recently was diagnosed with cancer. "I was working overtime, often until 7 p.m.," she explains. "I'd get home in time to give my daughter her bottle, then put her to sleep. I said: 'this is ridiculous.'" The flexible work hours and at least one day a week spent telecommuting ease the burden.

At Baxter Export, 30 percent of its employees use telecommuting, job-sharing, or working part-time to build flexibility into their schedules. John Linder, the manager who oversees the analysts, is convinced that acknowledging and easing tensions in the workplace is good business. Although he doesn't work at home himself, he believes that his people are 10 percent more productive on the days they telecommute. Baxter's willingness to accommodate problems, he adds, also pays off in higher commitment. Still, telecommuters are held to rules that limit disruption. They can't work more than two days a week out of the office. Any more than that and it begins to affect the cohesiveness of the group. In addition, everyone has to be in on Wednesdays for meetings, and they must pay for call-waiting on their home phones (Latin American customers, especially, don't like voicemail).

With all their flexibility, however, Baxter Export employees still struggle to find balance. Most spend forty-five to fifty hours a week on the job. There is a solution, but it is no easy fix: the division is entering a thorough restructuring that is altering not just its own jobs and processes but also those throughout the corporation.

Griff Lewis, the executive vice president who oversees Baxter Export, notes that the unit's volume is growing at 12 percent to 15 percent per year, and he does not have the budget to add corresponding staff. Just to keep people's hours reasonable, never mind reducing them, he has to find ways to lift productivity—rethinking processes, redesigning jobs, and eliminating unnecessary tasks.

Over the next five years, therefore, Baxter will have to move to an automated allocation system that requires overseas customers, rather than Baxter Export analysts, to prepare demand forecasts and enter orders. That system would route orders directly to U.S. warehouses and, as a result, decrease each analyst's workload by three days per month within two years. Also, Lewis expects to standardize processes across the 120 countries his department services, eliminating extraneous tasks and allowing employees to address mostly exceptional orders and higher-level issues.

Already, such schemes have relieved the sixty-hour weeks that were commonplace a few years ago. Lewis's restructuring is complicated by his division's web of relationships with the many units of its global parent. Baxter's U.S. manufacturing division, for instance, maintains as little inventory as possible. When demand overseas exceeds expectations, Lewis' analysts cannot always find product easily. If managers in Brazil cram in last-minute orders to meet quarterly quotas, someone at Baxter Exports has to work late to meet requirements on time.

The attempts to build flexibility into the work schedules and think systemically about reducing the hours worked at Baxter Export is one of the reason Baxter Healthcare ranked 19th on *Business Week*'s 1997 annual survey of work and family strategies in corporate America. ∎

absenteeism, turnover, and job performance.[57] At AT&T, for example, fifty-nine employees who were close to losing their jobs were enrolled in an EAP and successfully returned to work. Hiring and training replacements would have been much more costly than the expense of the EAP.[58]

The Employee Assistance Program Model

Figure 18.3 displays the components of a typical EAP. They include the identification and referral of employees into the program, management of the EAP process, and problem diagnosis and treatment.

1. *Identification and referral.* The first step in an EAP is entry into the program, through formal or informal referral. In the case of formal referrals, the process involves identifying employees who are having work performance problems and getting them to consider entering the EAP. Identifying these employees is

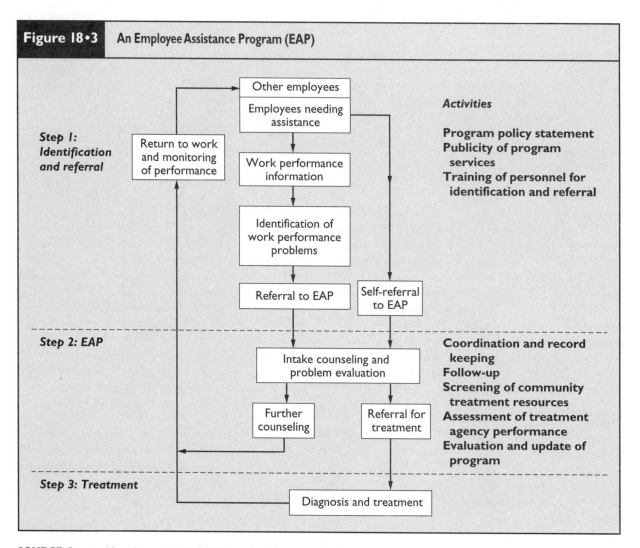

Figure 18•3   **An Employee Assistance Program (EAP)**

closely related to the performance management process discussed in Chapter 17. Performance records need to be maintained and corrective action taken whenever performance falls below an acceptable standard. During action planning to improve performance, managers can point out to appraisees the existence of support services, such as the EAP. A formal referral takes place if the performance of an employee continues to deteriorate and the manager decides that EAP services are required. An informal referral occurs when an employee initiates admission to an EAP even though performance problems may not exist or may not have been detected.

As shown in Figure 18.3, several organizational activities support this initial step in the EAP process. First, a written policy with clear procedures regarding the EAP is necessary. Second, top management and the human resources department must publicly support the EAP, and publicity about the program should be well distributed. Third, training and development programs should equip supervisors to identify and document performance problems effectively, to carry out performance improvement action planning, and to develop appropriate methods for referring employees to the EAP. Finally, the confidentiality of employees using the program must be safeguarded to gain the support of the workforce.

2. *EAP office.* The second component of an EAP is the work performed in the program office, where people with problems are linked with treatment resources. The EAP office accepts an employee into the program, provides problem evaluation and initial counseling, refers the employee to treatment resources and agencies, monitors the employee's progress during treatment, and reintegrates the employee into the workforce. In some EAPs, especially in large organizations, the actual counseling and treatment resources are located in-house. In most EAPs, however, the employee is referred to outside agencies that contract with the organization to perform treatment services. In all cases, a clear procedure for helping the employee return to the workforce is crucial and must be managed to maintain confidentiality.

   Good management is required for an effective EAP. For example, the program's relationship to disciplinary procedures must be clear. In some organizations, corrective actions are suspended if the employee seeks EAP help; in others, the two processes are not connected. Maintaining confidential records about treatment also is essential. In-house resources have the disadvantage of appearing to compromise this important program element, but they may offer some cost savings. If external treatment resources are used, care must be taken to screen and qualify those resources.

3. *Treatment.* The third EAP component is the treatment of the employee's problem. Potential resources include inpatient and outpatient care, social services, and self-help groups. The resources tapped by EAPs will vary from program to program.

Implementing an Employee Assistance Program

EAPs can be flexible and customized to fit various organizational philosophies and employee problems. Practitioners have suggested the following seven steps in establishing an EAP:[59]

1. *Develop an EAP policy and procedure.* Establish specific guidelines concerning the EAP and its availability to employees and their families. Policies concerning

confidentiality, disciplinary procedures, communication, training, and overall program philosophy should be included. Use senior management and union involvement (where appropriate) in developing the guidelines to elicit worker commitment.

2. *Select and train a program coordinator.* A person should be designated by the organization as the EAP coordinator. This person is responsible for overall coordination of program activities, such as training, handling program publicity, evaluating program activities, troubleshooting to ensure the quick resolution of problems, and providing ongoing program support.

3. *Obtain employee/union support for the EAP.* Program effectiveness demands employee or union support for EAP implementation. Obtaining that support may require meeting with key employee or union representatives to get their input in defining significant features of the EAP, including office location, staffing, participation on an EAP advisory committee, and employee/union attendance at EAP training; to review significant policy and/or procedural components to ensure support; and to share endorsements from other organizations where EAPs have been implemented.

4. *Publicize the program.* Communicating about the EAP's availability and increasing employee awareness of its procedures, resources, and benefits should be a high priority. Both formal and informal referrals to the program assume that managers and employees are aware of its existence. If it is not well publicized or if people do not know how to contact the program office, then participation may be below expected levels.

5. *Establish relationships with health-care providers and insurers.* All applicable health insurance policies should be reviewed to determine coverage for mental health and chemical dependency treatment. Although most policies include this coverage, reimbursement procedures often vary. This information needs to be summarized for EAP users so that all parties are aware of potential costs and responsibilities. EAP staff should be prepared to advise employees seeking treatment about expected insurance coverage and any personal expenses related to treatment. Potential providers of EAP treatment services should be interviewed, screened, and selected, and appropriate procedures should be developed for making referrals and maintaining confidentiality.

6. *Schedule EAP training.* The legal climate surrounding EAPs, referrals, and employee discipline requires that EAP training methods and materials be up-to-date and accurate. Training should include role plays about handling difficult employees as well as methods for referring workers to the program.

7. *Continually administer and manage the plan.* A plan should be developed for reviewing program effectiveness. This typically involves auditing procedures, measuring system-user satisfaction, and determining whether treatment options should be added or deleted. Ongoing training of EAP staff also should occur, emphasizing the changing legal requirements of EAPs, new counseling or treatment options, organizational changes that may affect program use, and behaviors that focus on service quality.

Application 18.6 describes the evolution of an EAP and wellness program at Johnson & Johnson.[60] and demonstrates how such programs can be implemented in large, decentralized organizations.

APPLICATION 18•6 **Johnson & Johnson's Employee Assistance and Live for Life Programs**

Johnson & Johnson (J&J) is the most diversified health-care corporation in the world. It grosses more than $6.5 billion a year and employs approximately seventy-five thousand people at 165 companies in fifty-six countries. Its philosophy is embodied in a document called "Our Credo." A section of this document makes a commitment to the welfare of its employees.

The J&J companies are decentralized and directly responsible for their own operations. Corporate management is committed to this structure because of the many proven advantages to the businesses and people involved, such as the development of general managers, faster product development, and a closer connection with the customer.

Based on a successful pilot project in the Ethicon division of J&J, top management decided to implement EAPs throughout the rest of the company. The J&J EAPs are in-house treatment programs that offer employees and family members confidential, professional assistance for problems related to alcohol and drug abuse, as well as marital, family, emotional, and mental health difficulties. Treatment of the whole person underlies the counseling effort. The major goal is to help clients assume responsibility for their own behavior and, if it is destructive to themselves or others, to modify it. This process is supported with a variety of therapies that clearly recognize that any one method is not a panacea for resolving the client's problems. Employees can enter an EAP by self-referral or by counseling from their supervisor. The program emphasizes the necessity of maintaining complete confidentiality when counseling the employee or family member to protect both the client's dignity and job.

J&J's employee assistance program is committed publicly to resolving the major health problem in the country—substance abuse and addiction. The program is specifically designed to identify, intervene, and treat substance abuse and addiction, as well as the family problems associated with this disease.

The implementation of EAPs throughout the firm was accomplished in three phases. The first phase consisted of contacting the managers and directors of personnel for each of the decentralized divisions and assessing their divisions' EAP needs. An educational process was initiated to inform managers and directors about the employee assistance program. This EAP training then was conducted in each of the personnel departments of the divisions. The second phase included a formal presentation to the management board of each division. It included information about the EAP and about an alcohol and drug component for executives. In the third phase, cost estimates were developed for EAP use and for employment of an EAP administrator to implement the program in each division. In addition, the corporate director of assistance programs established a quality assurance program to review all EAP activities biennially.

The EAPs were implemented between 1980 and 1985. More than 90 percent of all domestic employees have direct access to an EAP, and the remaining employees have telephone access. There are employee assistance programs at all major J&J locations throughout the United States, Puerto Rico, and Canada. Programs also are operating in Brazil and England. A study of J&J's EAP in the New Jersey area showed that clients with drug abuse, emotional, or mental health problems who availed themselves of EAP services were treated at substantial savings to the company.

More recently, EAPs have been integrated with J&J's wellness program known as Live for Life. This program was initiated by the chairman of the board in 1977, when he committed to provide all employees and their families with the opportunity to become the healthiest employees of any corporation in the world. The Live for Life program offered classes in nutrition, weight reduction, and smoking cessation. In addition, small gymnasiums with workout equipment, aerobics rooms, and swimming pools were made available. Now known as Live for Life Assistance programs, health, safety, benefits, wellness, and employee assistance programs work together to promote employee well-being in the workplace. ■

Stress Management Programs

Concern has been growing in organizations about managing the dysfunction caused by stress. Stress is linked to the following illnesses: hypertension, heart attacks, diabetes, asthma, chronic pain, allergies, headache, backache, various skin disorders, cancer, immune system weakness, and decreases in the number of white blood cells and changes in their function. It can also lead to alcoholism and drug abuse, two problems that are reaching epidemic proportions in organizations and society. For organizations, these personal effects can result in costly health benefits, absenteeism, turnover, and low performance. One study reported that one in three workers said they have thought about quitting because of stress; one in two workers said job stress reduced their productivity; and one in five workers said they took sick leave in the month preceding the survey because of stress.[61] Another study estimates that each employee who suffers from a stress-related illness loses an average of sixteen days of work per year.[62] Finally, the Research Triangle Institute estimated the annual cost to the U.S. economy from stress-related disorders at $187 billion. Other estimates are more conservative, but they invariably run into the billions of dollars.[63]

Like other human resources management interventions, stress management is often facilitated by practitioners with special skills and knowledge—typically psychologists, physicians, and other health professionals specializing in work stress. Recently, some OD practitioners have gained competence in this area, and there has been a growing tendency to include stress management as part of larger OD efforts. The concept of stress is best understood in terms of a model that describes the organizational and personal conditions contributing to the dysfunctional consequences of stress. Two key types of stress management interventions may be used: those aimed at the diagnosis or awareness of stress and its causes, and those directed at changing the causes and helping people cope with stress.

Definition and Model

Stress refers to the reaction of people to their environments. It involves both physiological and psychological responses to environmental conditions, causing people to change or adjust their behaviors. Stress is generally viewed in terms of the fit of people's needs, abilities, and expectations with environmental demands, changes, and opportunities.[64] A good person–environment fit results in positive reactions to stress; a poor fit leads to the negative consequences already described. Stress is generally positive when it occurs at moderate levels and contributes to effective motivation, innovation, and learning. For example, a promotion is a stressful event that is experienced positively by most employees. On the other hand, stress can be dysfunctional when it is excessively high (or low) or persists over a long period of time. It can overpower a person's coping abilities and cause physical and emotional exhaustion. For example, a boss who is excessively demanding and unsupportive can cause subordinates undue tension, anxiety, and dissatisfaction. Those factors, in turn, can lead to withdrawal behaviors, such as absenteeism and turnover; to ailments, such as headaches and high blood pressure; and to lowered performance. Situations in which there is a poor fit between employees and the organization produce negative stress consequences.

A tremendous amount of research has been conducted on the causes and consequences of work stress. Figure 18.4, a model summarizing stress relationships, identifies specific occupational stressors that may result in dysfunctional consequences. People's individual differences determine the extent to which the stressors are perceived negatively. For example, people with strong social support experience the stressors as less stressful than those who do not have such support. This greater perceived stress can lead to such negative consequences as anxiety, poor decision making, increased blood pressure, and low productivity.

The stress model shows that almost any dimension of the organization (e.g., working conditions, structure, role, or relationships) can cause negative stress. This suggests that much of the material covered so far in this book provides knowledge about work-related stressors, and implies that virtually all of the OD interventions

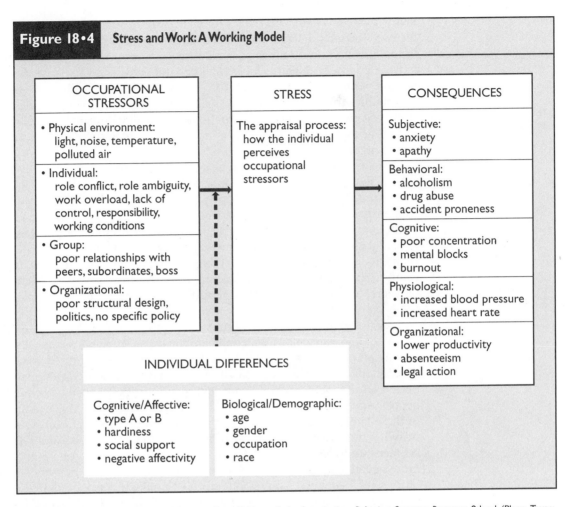

Figure 18•4   Stress and Work: A Working Model

OCCUPATIONAL STRESSORS

- Physical environment:
  light, noise, temperature,
  polluted air
- Individual:
  role conflict, role ambiguity,
  work overload, lack of
  control, responsibility,
  working conditions
- Group:
  poor relationships with
  peers, subordinates, boss
- Organizational:
  poor structural design,
  politics, no specific policy

STRESS

The appraisal process:
how the individual
perceives
occupational
stressors

CONSEQUENCES

Subjective:
- anxiety
- apathy

Behavioral:
- alcoholism
- drug abuse
- accident proneness

Cognitive:
- poor concentration
- mental blocks
- burnout

Physiological:
- increased blood pressure
- increased heart rate

Organizational:
- lower productivity
- absenteeism
- legal action

INDIVIDUAL DIFFERENCES

Cognitive/Affective:
- type A or B
- hardiness
- social support
- negative affectivity

Biological/Demographic:
- age
- gender
- occupation
- race

SOURCE: Reprinted from J. Gibson, J. Ivancevich, and J. Donnelly Jr., *Organizations: Behaviors, Structure, Processes,* 8th ed. (Plano, Texas: Business Publications, 1994): 266. Reprinted with permission of The McGraw-Hill Companies.

included in the book can play a role in stress management. Process consultation, third-party intervention, survey feedback, intergroup relations, structural design, employee involvement, work design, goal setting, reward systems, and career planning and development all can help alleviate stressful working conditions. Thus, to some degree stress management has been under discussion throughout this book. Here, the focus is on those occupational stressors and stress-management techniques that are unique to the stress field and that have received the most systematic attention from stress researchers.

Occupational Stressors. Figure 18.4 identifies several organizational sources of stress, including structure, role on the job, physical environment, and relationships. Extensive research has been done on three key organizational sources of stress: the individual items related to work overload, role conflict, and role ambiguity.

Work overload can be a persistent source of stress, especially among managers and white-collar employees having to process complex information and make difficult decisions. Quantitative overload consists of having too much to do in a given time period. Qualitative overload refers to having work that is too difficult for one's abilities and knowledge. A review of the research suggests that work overload is highly related to managers' needs for achievement and so it may be partly self-inflicted.[65] Research relating workload to stress outcomes reveals that both too much or too little work can have negative consequences. Apparently, when the amount of work is in balance with people's abilities and knowledge, stress has a positive impact on performance and satisfaction, but when workload either exceeds employees' abilities (overload) or fails to challenge them (underload), people experience stress negatively. This negative experience can lead to lowered self-esteem and job dissatisfaction, nervous symptoms, increased absenteeism, and reduced participation in organizational activities.[66]

People's roles at work also can be a source of stress. A *role* can be defined as the sum total of expectations that the individual and significant others have about how the person should perform a specific job. The employee's relationships with peers, supervisors, vendors, customers, and others can result in diverse expectations about how a particular role should be performed. The employee must be able to integrate these expectations into a meaningful whole to perform the role effectively. Problems arise when there is role ambiguity and the person does not clearly understand what others expect of her or him, or when there is role conflict and the employee receives contradictory expectations that cannot be satisfied at the same time.[67]

Extensive studies of role ambiguity and conflict suggest that both conditions are prevalent in organizations, especially among managerial jobs where clarity often is lacking and job demands often are contradictory.[68] For example, managerial job descriptions typically are so general that it is difficult to know precisely what is expected on the job. Similarly, managers spend most of their time interacting with people from other departments, and opportunities for conflicting demands abound in these lateral relationships. Role ambiguity and conflict can cause severe stress, resulting in increased tension, dissatisfaction, and withdrawal, and reduced commitment and trust in others. Some evidence suggests that role ambiguity has a more negative impact on managers than does role conflict. In terms of individual differences, people with a low tolerance for ambiguity respond more negatively to role ambiguity than others do; introverts and people who are more flexible react more negatively to role conflict than others do.[69]

Individual Differences. Figure 18.4 identifies several individual differences affecting how people respond to occupational stressors: hardiness, social support, age, education, occupation, race, negative affectivity, and Type A behavior pattern. Much research has been devoted to the Type A behavior pattern, which is characterized by impatience, competitiveness, and hostility. Type A personalities (in contrast to Type Bs) invest long hours working under tight deadlines. They put themselves under extreme time pressure by trying to do more and more work in less and less time. Type B personalities, on the other hand, are less hurried, aggressive, and hostile than Type As. Extensive research shows that Type A people are especially prone to stress. For example, a longitudinal study of thirty-five hundred men found that Type As had twice as much heart disease, five times as many second heart attacks, and twice as many fatal heart attacks as did Type Bs.[70] Researchers explain Type A susceptibility to stress in terms of an inability to deal with uncertainty, such as might occur with qualitative overload and role ambiguity. To work rapidly and meet pressing deadlines, Type As need to be in control of the situation. They do not allocate enough time for unforeseen disturbances and consequently experience extreme tension and anxiety when faced with unexpected events.[71]

Unfortunately, the proportion of Type A managers in organizations may be quite large. One study showed that 60 percent of the managers were clearly Type A and only 12 percent were distinctly Type B.[72] In addition, a short questionnaire measuring Type A behaviors and given to members of several MBA classes and executive programs has found that Type As outnumber Type Bs by about five to one. These results are not totally surprising because many organizations (and business schools) reward aggressive, competitive, workaholic behaviors. Indeed, Type A behaviors can help managers achieve rapid promotion in many companies. Ironically, however, those same behaviors may be detrimental to effective performance at top organizational levels where tasks and decision making require the kind of patience, tolerance for ambiguity, and attention to broad issues often neglected by Type As.

Diagnosis and Awareness of Stress and Its Causes

Stress management is directed at preventing negative stress outcomes either by changing the organizational conditions causing the stress or by enhancing employees' abilities to cope with them. This preventive approach starts from a diagnosis of the current situation, including employees' self-awareness of their own stress and its sources. This diagnosis provides the information needed to develop an appropriate stress management program.[73] Two methods for diagnosing stress are the following:

Charting Stressors. Such charting involves identifying organizational and personal stressors operating in a particular situation. It is guided by a conceptual model like that shown in Figure 18.4, and it measures potential stressors affecting employees negatively. Data can be collected through questionnaires and interviews about environmental and personal stressors. Researchers at the University of Michigan's Institute for Social Research have developed standardized instruments for measuring most of the stressors shown in Figure 18.4. It is important to obtain perceptual measures because people's cognitive appraisal of the situation makes a stressor stressful. Most organizational surveys measure dimensions potentially stressful to employees, such as work overload, role conflict and ambiguity, promotional issues, opportunities for participation, managerial support, and communication. Similarly, there are specific instruments for measuring the individual differences, such as hardiness, social support, and Type A or B behavior pattern. In addition to perceptions of stressors, it is necessary to measure stress consequences, such as subjective moods, performance, job satisfaction, absenteeism, blood pressure, and cholesterol level. Various instruments and checklists have been developed for obtaining people's perceptions of negative consequences, and these can be supplemented with hard measures taken from company records, medical reports, and physical examinations. Once measures of the stressors and consequences are obtained, the two sets of data must be related to reveal which stressors contribute most to negative stress in the situation under study. For example, a relational analysis might show that qualitative overload and role ambiguity are highly related to employee fatigue, absenteeism, and poor performance, especially for Type A employees. This kind of information points to specific organizational conditions that must be improved to reduce stress. Moreover, it identifies the kinds of employees who may need special counseling and training in stress management. Organizations such as AT&T, the U.S. Department of Defense, and the Los Angeles Police Department periodically chart stressors to assess the health of their employees and to make necessary improvements.

Health Profiling. This method is aimed at identifying stress symptoms so that corrective action can be taken. It starts with a questionnaire asking people for their medical history; personal habits; current health; and vital signs, such as blood pressure, cholesterol level, and triglyceride levels. It also may include a physical examination if some of the information is not readily available. Information from the questionnaire and physical examination is then analyzed, usually by a computer that calculates the individual's health profile. This profile compares the individual's characteristics with those of an average person of the same gender, age, and race. The profile identifies the person's future health prospect, typically by placing her or him in a health-risk category with a known probability of fatal disease, such as cardiovascular risk. The health profile also indicates how the health risks can be reduced by making personal and environmental changes such as dieting, exercising, or traveling.

Many firms cannot afford to do their own health profiling and contract with health firms to do it on a fee basis per employee (usually ranging from $125 to $400 for a one- to five-hour examination). Other firms have extensive in-house health and stress-management programs. At one program, health profiling was an initial diagnostic step. Each participant first went through a rigorous physical and medical history examination to determine personal health risks and to establish a basis for prescribing an individualized health program. Company officials reported that the program had positive results: "It has generated good public interest, helped recruiting efforts, and provided better all-around fitness for participants in the program. Individual health screening has uncovered six cases of early-stage cancer and a number of cases of high blood pressure and heart disease."[74]

Alleviating Stressors and Coping with Stress

After diagnosing the presence and causes of stress, the next step in stress management is to do something about it. Interventions for reducing negative stress tend to fall into two groups: those aimed at changing the organizational conditions causing stress and those directed at helping people to cope better with stress. Because stress results from the interaction between people and the environment, both strategies are needed for effective stress management.

This section first presents two methods for alleviating stressful organizational conditions: role clarification and supportive relationships. These efforts are aimed at decreasing role ambiguity and conflict and improving poor relationships, key sources of managerial stress. Then, two interventions aimed at helping people to cope more positively with stress are discussed: stress inoculation training and health and fitness facilities. These can help employees alleviate stress symptoms and prepare themselves for handling stressful situations.

Role Clarification. This involves helping employees better understand the demands of their work roles. A manager's role is embedded in a network of relationships with other managers, each of whom has specific expectations about how the manager should perform the role. Role clarification is a systematic process for revealing others' expectations and arriving at a consensus about the activities constituting a particular role. There are several role clarification methods, among them job expectation technique (JET) and role analysis technique (RAT)[75] and they follow a similar strategy. First, the people relevant to defining a particular role are identified (e.g., members of a managerial team, a boss and subordinate, and members of other departments relating to the role holder) and brought together at a meeting, usually in a location away from the organization.

Second, the role holder discusses her or his perceived job duties and responsibilities and the other participants are encouraged to comment and to agree or disagree with the role holder's perceptions. An OD practitioner may act as a process consultant to facilitate interaction and reduce defensiveness. Third, when everyone has reached consensus on defining the role, the role holder is responsible for writing a description of the activities that are seen now as constituting the role. A copy of the role description is distributed to all participants to ensure that they fully understand and agree with the role definition. Fourth, the participants periodically check to see whether the role is being performed as intended and make modifications if necessary.

Role clarification can be used to define a single role or the roles of members of a group. It has been used in such companies as Alcoa, Sherwin-Williams, Johnson & Johnson, and Honeywell to help management teams arrive at agreed-upon roles for members. The process is generally included as part of initial team-building meetings for new management teams starting high-involvement plants. Managers share perceptions and negotiate about one another's roles as a means of determining areas of discretion and responsibility. Role clarity is particularly important in new plant situations where managers are trying to implement participative methods. The ambiguity of such settings can be extremely stressful, and role clarification can reduce stress by helping managers translate such ambiguous concepts as "involvement" and "participation" into concrete role behaviors.

Research on role clarification supports these benefits. One study found that it reduced stress and role ambiguity and increased job satisfaction.[76] Another study reported that it improved interpersonal relationships among group members and contributed to improved production and quality.[77] These findings should be interpreted carefully, however, because both studies had weak research designs and used only perceptual measures.

Supportive Relationships. This involves establishing trusting and genuinely positive relationships among employees, including bosses, subordinates, and peers. Supportive relations have been a hallmark of organization development and are a major part of such interventions as team building, intergroup relations, employee involvement, work design, goal setting, and career planning and development. Considerable research shows that supportive relationships can buffer people from stress.[78] When people feel that relevant others really care about what happens to them and are willing to help, they can cope with stressful conditions. The pioneering coal mining studies which gave rise to sociotechnical systems theory found that miners needed the support from a cohesive work group to deal effectively with the stresses of underground mining.

Recent research on the boss–subordinate relationship suggests that a supportive boss can provide subordinates with a crucial defense against stress. A study of managers at an AT&T subsidiary undergoing turmoil because of the company's corporate breakup showed that employees who were under considerable stress but felt that their boss was supportive suffered half as much illness, depression, impaired sexual performance, and obesity as employees reporting to an unsupportive boss. A study of U.S. Defense Department employees at air force bases in the Midwest showed that the single organizational dimension accounting for higher levels of cholesterol was having a boss who was too bossy.[79]

This research suggests that organizations must become more aware of the positive value of supportive relationships in helping employees cope with stress. They may need to build supportive, cohesive work groups in situations that are particularly stressful, such as introducing new products, solving emergency problems, and handling customer complaints. For example, firms such as Procter & Gamble and Alcoa have recognized that internal OD consultation can be extremely stressful, and so have encouraged internal OD practitioners to form support teams to help each other cope with the demands of the role. Equally important, organizations need to direct more attention to ensuring that managers provide the support and encouragement necessary to help subordinates cope with stress. For example, the

University of Southern California's executive programs often include a module on helping subordinates cope with stress, and firms are training managers to be more sensitive to stress and more supportive and helpful to subordinates.

Stress Inoculation Training. Companies have developed programs to help employees acquire the skills and knowledge to cope more positively with stressors. Participants are first taught to understand stress warning signals, such as difficulty in making decisions, disruption in sleeping and eating habits, and greater frequencies of headaches and backaches. Then they are encouraged to admit that they are overstressed (or understressed) and to develop a concrete plan for coping with the situation. One strategy is to develop and use a coping self-statement procedure. Participants verbalize a series of questions or statements each time they experience negative stress. The following sample questions or statements[80] are addressed to the four stages of the stress-coping cycle:

- preparation (What am I going to do about these stressors?)
- confrontation (I must relax and stay in control.)
- coping (I must focus on the present set of stressors.)
- self-reinforcement (I handled it well.)

Stress inoculation training is aimed at helping employees cope with stress rather than at changing the stressors themselves. Its major value is sensitizing people to the presence of stress and preparing them to take personal action. Self-appraisal and self-regulation of stress can free people from total reliance on others for stress management. Given the multitude of organizational conditions that can cause stress, such self-control is a valuable adjunct to interventions aimed at changing the conditions themselves.

Health Facilities. A growing number of organizations are providing facilities for helping employees cope with stress. Elaborate exercise facilities are maintained by such firms as Xerox, Weyerhaeuser, and PepsiCo. Similarly, more than five hundred companies (e.g., Exxon, Mobil, and Chase Manhattan Bank) operate corporate cardiovascular fitness programs. Before starting such programs, employees must take an exercise tolerance test and have the approval of either a private or a company doctor. Each participant is then assigned a safe level of heart response to the various parts of the fitness program. Preliminary evidence suggests that fitness programs can reduce absenteeism and coronary risk factors, such as high blood pressure, body weight, percentage of body fat, and triglyceride levels.[81] A review of the research, however, suggests that fitness programs primarily result in better mental health and resistance to stress and that such organizational improvements as reduced absenteeism and turnover and improved performance are more uncertain.[82]

In addition to exercise facilities, some companies, such as McDonald's and Equitable Life Assurance Society, provide biofeedback facilities in which managers take relaxation breaks using biofeedback devices to monitor respiration and heart rate. Feedback of such data helps managers lower their respiration and heart rates. Some companies provide time for employees to meditate, and other firms have stay-well programs that encourage healthy diets and lifestyles.

Application 18.7 presents an example of a stress-management intervention at Metropolitan Hospital,[83] and emphasizes the need for diagnosing stressors as a prelude to developing specific stress-management interventions.

APPLICATION 18•7   Stress Management at Metropolitan Hospital

This stress management program was carried out over a two-year period at Metropolitan Hospital. Initial impetus for the project was widespread complaints from middle managers about feeling stressed, overworked, and subject to unexpected changes in policies and procedures. Top administrators sought help in dealing with these problems from external OD consultants who had skills and experience in stress management.

The initial step of the project consisted of diagnosing the causes and consequences of experienced stress at the hospital. Understanding the sources of stress was seen as a necessary prelude to developing an appropriate plan for managing stress. The consultants developed a questionnaire to collect data from the forty-five middle managers responsible for almost every phase of hospital operation. Design of the questionnaire was guided by a conceptual model of stress similar to that shown in Figure 18.3. The questionnaire included items about various organizational stressors, including both ongoing, recurrent stressors and those associated with recent changes. It also included questions about each manager's use of stress management techniques, such as exercise, nutritional awareness, and the creation of support systems. The questionnaire ended with items about experienced strain (e.g., irritability, sleep difficulty, and changes in eating and drinking patterns) and longer-term stress effects (e.g., health conditions, satisfaction, and work effectiveness).

Analysis of the diagnostic data showed that many of the organizational change events and ongoing working conditions were significantly related to managers' levels of strain and longer-term stress effects. Among the most stressful organizational change events were major and frequent changes in instructions, policies, and procedures; numerous unexpected crises and deadlines; and sudden increases in the activity level or pace of work. The ongoing working conditions that contributed most to negative stress included quantitative work overload, feedback only when performance is unsatisfactory, lack of confidence in management, and role conflict and ambiguity. The managers reported little if any use of stress management techniques to help them to cope with these stressors. Only 20 percent engaged in regular physical exercise and, surprisingly, 60 percent had marginally or poorly balanced diets. Among the most commonly reported health problems were tension headaches, diarrhea or constipation, common colds, and backaches.

Working from the diagnostic data, and with the help of the consultants, senior management implemented several organizational improvements. To reduce work overload and role ambiguity, each managerial position was analyzed in terms of work distribution, job requirements, and performance standards. This analysis resulted in more balanced workloads across the jobs and in clearer job descriptions. Hospital administrators also began working with department managers to define job expectations and to provide ongoing performance feedback. The managers were given training in how to organize their workload and time more productively and how to delegate work to subordinates more effectively.

The "firefighting" climate at the hospital had caused many managers to focus on their own departments while neglecting important lateral relationships with other units. Monthly cross-departmental meetings were implemented to improve lateral relations among department heads and supervisors. Efforts also were made to provide an organizational climate supporting the building of peer support groups.

To reduce uncertainty about organizational changes, senior managers spent more time informing and educating managers about forthcoming changes. Top management also held quarterly information meetings with first-line supervisors to clear up misunderstandings, misinterpretations, and rumors.

The above changes were aimed at reducing organizational stressors and other measures were taken to help managers identify and cope more effectively with stress. The hospital instituted yearly physical examinations to detect stress-related problems. It also trained managers to identify stress symptoms and problems both in themselves and in subordinates. The hospital developed an exercise club and various sports activities and offered weekly yoga classes. It also created a training program combining nutritional awareness with techniques for coping with tension headaches and backaches. Fresh fruit was made available as an alternative to doughnuts in all meetings and training sessions.

Initial reactions to the stress management program were positive, and the hospital is assessing the longer-term effects of the intervention. Measures of stressors and experienced stress will be taken every twelve to eighteen months to monitor the program so that changes can be made as necessary. ■

■ SUMMARY

This chapter presented three major human resources interventions: career planning and development, workforce diversity interventions, and employee wellness programs. Although these kinds of change programs generally are carried out by human resources specialists, a growing number of OD practitioners are gaining competence in these areas and the interventions are increasingly being included in OD programs.

Career planning involves helping people choose occupations, organizations, and jobs at different stages of their careers. Employees typically pass through four different career stages—establishment, advancement, maintenance, and withdrawal—with different career planning issues relevant to each stage. Major career planning practices include communication, counseling, workshops, self-development materials, and assessment programs. Career planning is a highly personalized process that includes assessing one's interests, values, and capabilities; examining alternative careers; and making relevant decisions.

Career development helps employees achieve career objectives. Effective efforts in that direction include linking corporate business objectives, human resources needs, and the personal needs of employees. Different career development needs and practices exist and are relevant to each of the four stages of people's careers.

Workforce diversity interventions are designed to adapt human resources practices to an increasingly diverse workforce. Demographic, gender, disability, and culture and values trends point to a more complex set of human resources demands. Within such a context, OD interventions (e.g., job design, performance management, and employee involvement practices) have to be adapted to a diverse set of personal preferences, needs, and lifestyles.

Employee wellness interventions, such as employee assistance programs and stress management, recognize the important link between worker health and organizational productivity. EAPs identify, refer, and treat employees and their families for such problems as marital problems, drug and alcohol abuse, emotional disturbances, and financial difficulties. EAPs preserve the dignity of the individual but also recognize the organization's right to expect certain work behaviors. EAPs typically include identifying and referring an employee to the program; managing the program effectively to offer adequate resources and ensure confidentiality; and diagnosing and treating the employee's problem.

Stress management is concerned with helping employees to cope with the negative consequences of stress at work. The concept of stress involves the fit of people's needs, abilities, and expectations with environmental demands, changes, and opportunities. A good person–environment fit results in positive reactions to stress, such as motivation and innovation, and a poor fit results in negative effects, such as headaches, backaches, and cardiovascular disease. A model for understanding work-related stress includes occupational stressors; individual differences, which affect how people respond to the stressors; and negative stress outcomes. Occupational stressors include work overload and role ambiguity and conflict. People with a Type A behavior pattern, characterized by impatience, competitiveness, and hostility, are especially prone to stress. The two main steps in stress-management are diagnosing stress and its causes, and alleviating stressors and helping people to cope with stress. Two methods for diagnosing stress are charting stressors and health profiling. Techniques for alleviating stressful conditions include role clarification and supportive relationships. Means for helping workers cope with stress are stress inoculation training and participation in activities at health and fitness facilities.

■ NOTES

1. J. Fierman, "Beating the Midlife Career Crisis," *Fortune* (6 September 1993): 52–62; L. Richman, "How to Get Ahead in America," *Fortune* (16 May 1994): 46–54.

2. "IT Workers Expect Career Development and Job Satisfaction," *HR Focus* (1 August 1999): 4.

3. D. Hall and J. Goodale, *Human Resource Management: Strategy, Design, and Implementation* (Glenview, Ill.: Scott, Foresman, 1986): 392.

4. D. Feldman, *Managing Careers in Organizations* (Glenview, Ill.: Scott, Foresman, 1988).

5. E. Erikson, *Childhood and Society* (New York: Norton, 1963); G. Sheehy, *Passages: Predictable Crises of Adult Life* (New York: E. P. Dutton, 1974); D. Levinson, *Seasons of a Man's Life* (New York: Alfred A. Knopf, 1978); R. Gould, *Transformations: Growth and Change in Adult Life* (New York: Simon & Schuster, 1978).

6. D. Super, *The Psychology of Careers* (New York: Harper & Row, 1957); D. T. Hall, *Careers in Organizations* (Santa Monica, Calif.: Goodyear, 1976); E. Schein, *Career Dynamics: Matching Individual and Organizational Needs* (Reading, Mass.: Addison-Wesley, 1978); L. Baird and K. Kram, "Career Dynamics: The Superior/Subordinate Relationship," *Organizational Dynamics* 11 (Spring 1983): 46–64; J. Slocum and W. Cron, "Job Attitudes and Performance During Three Career Stages" (working paper, Edwin L. Cox School of Business, Southern Methodist University, Dallas, Tex., 1984).

7. Adapted from D. Jamieson and J. O'Mara, *Managing Workforce 2000: Gaining the Diversity Advantage* (San Francisco: Jossey-Bass, 1991): 57.

8. M. McGill, "Facing the Mid-Life Crisis," *Business Horizons* 16 (November 1977): 5–13.

9. D. Anfuso, "Colgate's Global HR Unites Under One Strategy," *Personnel Journal* 74, 10 (1995): 44–48; D. McNamara, "Developing Global Human Resource Competencies" (presentation to the Conference Board Quality Council II, Chicago, April 11, 1996).

10. B. Rosen and T. Jerdee, "Too Old or Not Too Old," *Harvard Business Review* 55 (November-December 1977): 97–106; N. Munk, "Finished at Forty," *Fortune* (1 February 1999): 50–66.

11. J. Wanous, "Realistic Job Previews for Organizational Recruitment," *Personnel* 52 (1975): 58–68.

12. J. Wanous, "Effects of a Realistic Job Preview on Job Acceptance, Job Attitudes, and Job Survival," *Journal of Applied Psychology* 58 (1973): 327–32; J. Wanous, "Realistic Job Previews: Can a Procedure to Reduce Turnover Also Influence the Relationship Between Abilities and Performance?" *Personnel Psychology* 31 (Summer 1978): 249–58; S. Premack and J. Wanous, "A Meta-Analysis of Realistic Job Preview Experiments," *Journal of Applied Psychology* 70 (1985): 706–19.

13. B. M. Meglino, A. DeNisi, S. Youngblood, and K. Williams, "Effects of Realistic Job Previews: A Comparison Using an Enhancement and a Reduction Preview," *Journal of Applied Psychology* 73 (1988): 259–66; J. Vandenberg and V. Scarpello, "The Matching Method: An Examination of the Processes Underlying Realistic Job Previews," *Journal of Applied Psychology* 75 (1990): 60–67.

14. Adapted from D. Buss, "Job Tryouts Without Pay Get More Testing in U.S. Auto Plants," *Wall Street Journal* (10 January 1985): section 2, 29.

15. L. Thurow, "Building Wealth," *Atlantic Monthly* (June 1999): 57–69.

16. D. Bray, R. J. Campbell, and D. Grant, *Formative Years in Business: A Long Term AT&T Study of Managerial Lives* (New York: John Wiley & Sons, 1974).

17. F. Balcazar, B. Hopkins, and Y. Suarez, "A Critical Objective Review of Performance Feedback," *Journal of Organizational Behavior Management* 7 (1986): 65–89; J. Chobbar and J. Wallin, "A Field Study on the Effect of Feedback Frequency on Performance," *Journal of Applied Psychology* 69 (1984): 524–30; R. Waldersee and F. Luthans, "A Theoretically Based Contingency Model of Feedback: Implications for Managing Service Employees," *Journal of Organizational Change Management* 3 (1990): 46–56.

18. G. Thornton, *Assessment Centers* (Reading, Mass.: Addison-Wesley, 1992); A. Engelbrecht and H. Fischer, "The Managerial Performance Implications of a Developmental Assessment Center Process," *Human Relations* 48 (1995): 387–404.

19. Thornton, Assessment Centers; P. Griffiths and P. Goodge, "Development Centres: The Third Generation," *Personnel Management* 26, 6 (1994): 40–43; P. Geradus, W. Jansen, and F. DeJongh, *Assessment Centres: A Practical Handbook* (New York: John Wiley & Sons, 1998).

20. R. Jones and M. Whitmore, "Evaluating Developmental Assessment Centers as Interventions," *Personnel Psychology* 48 (1995): 377–88.

21. J. Kirksey and R. Zawacki, "Assessment Center Helps Find Team-Oriented Candidates," *Personnel Journal* 73 (1994): 92.

22. J. Clawson, "Mentoring in Managerial Careers," in *Family and Career*, ed. C. B. Derr (New York: Praeger, 1980); K. Kram, *Mentoring at Work* (Glenview, Ill.: Scott, Foresman, 1984); A. Geiger-DuMond and S. Boyle, "Mentoring: A Practitioner's Guide," *Training and Development* (March 1995): 51–54; G. Shea, *Mentoring: How to Develop Successful Mentor Behaviors* (Menlo Park, Calif.: Crisp Publications, 1998).

23. E. Collins and P. Scott, "Everyone Who Makes It Has a Mentor," *Harvard Business Review* 56 (July-August 1978): 100; M. Murray, *Beyond the Myths and Magic of Mentoring* (San Francisco: Jossey-Bass, 1991).

24. Geiger-DuMond and Boyle, "Mentoring," p. 51.

25. G. Roche, "Much Ado about Mentors," *Harvard Business Review* 57 (January-February 1979): 14–28.

26. Hall and Goodale, *Human Resource Management*, pp. 373–74.

27. See, for example, D. Kolb, D. Rubin, and J. McIntyre, *Organizational Psychology: Readings on Human Behavior in Organizations*, 4th ed. (New York: Prentice Hall, 1984).

28. D. Hitchin and J. Hitchin, "Middlaning: Living a Reasonable and Appropriately Balanced Life," *Graziadio Business Report* (Summer 1998): http://bschool.pepperdine.edu/gbr/982/middlani.html.

29. R. Katz, "Time and Work: Towards an Integrative Perspective," in *Research in Organizational Behavior*, vol. 2, eds. B. Staw and L. Cummings (New York: JAI Press, 1979): 81–127.

30. K. Brousseau, "Toward a Dynamic Model of Job-Person Relationships: Findings, Research Questions, and Implications for Work System Design," *Academy of Management Review* 8 (January 1983): 33–45.

31. J. Carnazza, A. Korman, T. Ference, and J. Stoner, "Plateaued and Non-Plateaued Managers: Factors in Job Performance," *Journal of Management* 7 (1981): 7–27.

32. J. Slocum, W. Cron, R. Hansen, and S. Rawlings, "Business Strategy and the Management of the Plateaued Performer," *Academy of Management Journal* 28 (1985): 133–54.

33. R. Karanbayya and A. Reilly, "Dual Earner Couples: Attitudes and Actions in Restructuring Work for Family," *Journal of Organizational Behavior* 13 (1992): 585–603; J. Schneer and F. Reitman, "Effects of Alternate Family Structures on Managerial Careers," *Academy of Management Journal* 36 (1993): 830–43.

34. D. T. Hall and M. Morgan, "Career Development and Planning," in *Contemporary Problems in Personnel*, 3d ed., eds. K. Pearlman, F. Schmidt, and W. C. Hamnek (New York: John Wiley & Sons, 1983): 232–33.

35. M. Bekas, "Dual-Career Couples—A Corporate Challenge," *Personnel Administrator* (April 1984): 37–44.

36. J. Ivancevich and W. Glueck, *Foundations of Personnel/Human Resource Management*, 3d ed. (Plano, Tex.: Business Publications, 1986): 541.

37. J. Nocera, "Living with Layoffs," *Fortune* (1 April 1996): 69–71.

38. These data are collected biannually by the U.S. Bureau of Labor Statistics and can be accessed at http://stats.bls.gov/newsrels.htm.

39. L. Perry, "Least-Cost Alternatives to Layoffs in Declining Industries," *Organizational Dynamics* 14 (1986): 48–61; J. Treece, "Doing It Right, till the Last Whistle," *Business Week* (6 April 1992): 58–59.

40. D. Cook and G. Ferris, "Strategic Human Resource Management and Firm Effectiveness in Industries Experiencing Decline," *Human Resource Management* 25 (Fall 1986): 441–58; R. Sutton, K. Eisenhardt, and J. Jucker, "Managing Organizational Decline: Lessons from Atari," *Organizational Dynamics* 14 (Spring 1986): 17–29; K. Cameron, S. Freeman, and A. Mishra, "Best Practices in White-Collar Downsizing: Managing Contradictions," *Academy of Management Executive* 5 (1991): 57–73; K. Cameron, "Strategies for Successful Organizational Downsizing," *Human Resource Management* 33 (1994): 189–212.

41. For information on the Workforce Investment Act, go to http://usworkforce.org.

42. Jamieson and O'Mara, *Managing Workforce 2000*.

43. F. Rice, "How to Make Diversity Pay," *Fortune* (8 August 1994): 78–86; R. Thomas Jr., "From Affirmative Action to Affirming Diversity," *Harvard Business Review* (March-April 1990): 107–17; K. Labich, "Making Diversity Pay," *Fortune* (9 September 1996): 177–80.

44. P. Dass and B. Parker, "Strategies for Managing Human Resource Diversity: From Resistance to Learning," *Academy of Management Executive* 13 (1999): 68–80.

45. Rice, "How to Make Diversity Pay," p. 79.

46. This section benefited greatly from the advice and assistance of Pat Pope, president of Pope and Associates, Cincinnati, Ohio. Much of the data and many examples

cited in support of each trend can be found in the following references and Websites: Munk, "Finished at Forty"; M. Galen, "Equal Opportunity Diversity: Beyond the Numbers Game," *Business Week* (14 August 1995): 60–61; K. Hammon and A. Palmer, "The Daddy Trap," *Business Week* (21 September 1998): 56–64; H. Kahan and D. Mulryan, "Out of the Closet," *American Demographics* (May 1995): 40–47; http://stats.bls.gov; http://nces.ed.gov; http://census.gov; http://cdc.gov.

47. Towers Perrin, *Workforce 2000 Today: A Bottom-Line Concern—Revisiting Corporate Views on Workforce Change* (New York: Author, 1992).

48. S. Rynes and B. Rosen, "A Field Survey of Factors Affecting the Adoption and Perceived Success of Diversity Training," *Personnel Psychology* 48 (1995): 247–70; K. Labich, "Making Diversity Pay."

49. This application was adopted from material in K. Hammonds, "Case Study: One Company's Delicate Balancing Act," *Business Week* (15 September 1997): 102–04.

50. J. Blair and M. Fotter, *Challenges in Health Care Management* (San Francisco: Jossey-Bass, 1990).

51. K. Warner, T. Wickizer, R. Wolfe, J. Schildroth, and M. Samuelson, "Economic Implications of the Workplace Health Promotion Programs: Review of the Literature," *Journal of Occupational Medicine* 30 (1988): 106–12; G. Pfeiffer, *WorkCare Group,* information found at http://www.jps.net/dkgamow/clarsrch.htm, accessed on January 15, 2000; additional data can be found at the National Institute of Drug Abuse, http://www.nida.hih.gov/.

52. These data were found at http://www.successunlimited.co.uk/costs.htm, accessed January 14, 2000.

53. S. Savitz, "Mental Health Plans Help Employees, Reduce Costs," *Best's Review* 96, 3 (1995): 60–62.

54. C. Hodges, "Growing Problem of Stress at Work Alarms Business," *People Management* 1, 9 (1995): 14–15.

55. W. Lissy and M. Morgenstern, "Employees Turn to EAPs During Downsizing," *Compensation and Benefits Review* 27, 3 (1995): 16.

56. Hall and Goodale, *Human Resource Management,* p. 554.

57. M. Shain and J. Groenveld, *Employee Assistance Programs: Philosophy, Theory, and Practice* (Lexington, Mass.: D. C. Heath, 1980).

58. Ivancevich and Glueck, *Foundations of Personnel,* p. 706.

59. J. Spicer, ed., *The EAP Solution* (Center City, Minn.: Hazelden, 1987).

60. Adapted from T. Desmond, "An Internal Broadbrush Program: J & J's Live for Life Assistance Program," in *The EAP Solution,* ed. J. Spicer (Center City, Minn.: Hazelden, 1987): 148–56.

61. T. O'Boyle, "Fear and Stress in the Office Take Toll," *Wall Street Journal* (6 November 1990): B1, B3; A. Riecher, "Job Stress: What It Can Do to You," *Bryan-College Station Eagle* (15 August 1993): D1.

62. D. Allen, "Less Stress, Less Litigation," *Personnel* (January 1990): 32–35; D. Hollis and J. Goodson, "Stress: The Legal and Organizational Implications," *Employee Responsibilities and Rights Journal* 2 (1989): 255–62.

63. D. Ganster and J. Schaubroeck, "Work Stress and Employee Health," *Journal of Management* 17 (1991): 235–71; T. Stewart, "Do You Push Your Employees Too Hard?" *Fortune* (22 October 1990): 121–28.

64. T. Cummings and C. Cooper, "A Cybernetic Framework for Studying Occupational Stress," *Human Relations* 32 (1979): 395–418.

65. J. French and R. Caplan, "Organization Stress and Individual Strain," in *The Failure of Success,* ed. A. Morrow (New York: AMACOM, 1972).

66. Ibid.

67. R. Kahn, D. Wolfe, R. Quinn, J. Snoek, and R. Rosenthal, *Organizational Stress* (New York: John Wiley & Sons, 1964).

68. C. Cooper and J. Marshall, "Occupational Sources of Stress: A Review of the Literature Relating to Coronary Heart Disease and Mental Ill Health," *Journal of Occupational Psychology* 49 (1976): 11–28; C. Cooper and R. Payne, *Stress at Work* (New York: John Wiley & Sons, 1978).

69. Cooper and Marshall, "Occupational Sources."

70. R. Rosenman and M. Friedman, "The Central Nervous System and Coronary Heart Disease," *Hospital Practice* 6 (1971): 87–97.

71. D. Glass, *Behavior Patterns, Stress and Coronary Disease* (Hillsdale, N.J.: Lawrence Erlbaum, 1977); V. Price, *Type A Behavior Pattern* (New York: Academic Press, 1982).

72. J. Howard, D. Cunningham, and P. Rechnitzer, "Health Patterns Associated with Type A Behavior: A Managerial Population," *Journal of Human Stress* 2 (1976): 24–31.

73. See, for example, the Addison-Wesley series on occupational stress: L. Warshaw, *Managing Stress* (Reading, Mass.: Addison-Wesley, 1982); A. McClean, *Work Stress*

(Reading, Mass.: Addison-Wesley, 1982); A. Shostak, *Blue-Collar Stress* (Reading, Mass.: Addison-Wesley, 1982); L. Moss, *Management Stress* (Reading, Mass.: Addison-Wesley, 1982); L. Levi, *Preventing Work Stress* (Reading, Mass.: Addison-Wesley, 1982); J. House, *Work Stress and Social Support* (Reading, Mass.: Addison-Wesley, 1982).

74. J. Ivancevich and M. Matteson, "Optimizing Human Resources: A Case for Preventive Health and Stress Management," *Organizational Dynamics* 9 (Autumn 1980): 7–21.

75. E. Huse and C. Barebo, "Beyond the T-Group: Increasing Organizational Effectiveness," *California Management Review* 23 (1980): 104–17; I. Dayal and J. Thomas, "Operation KPE: Developing a New Organization," *Journal of Applied Behavioral Science* 4 (1968): 473–506.

76. Huse and Barebo, "Beyond the T-Group."

77. Dayal and Thomas, "Operation KPE."

78. House, *Work Stress and Social Support*.

79. D. Goleman, "Stress: It Depends on the Boss," *International Herald Tribune* 10 (February 1984).

80. Ivancevich and Matteson, "Optimizing Human Resources," p. 19.

81. J. Zuckerman, "Keeping Managers in Good Health," *International Management* 34 (January 1979): 40.

82. L. Falkenberg, "Employee Fitness Programs: Their Impact on the Employee and the Organization," *Academy of Management Review* 12 (1987): 511–22.

83. J. Adams, "Improving Stress Management: An Action Research-Based OD Intervention," in *The Cutting Edge: Current Theory and Practice in Organization Development*, ed. W. Burke (San Diego: University Associates, 1978): 245–61.

■ Ring and Royce Electronics

Ring and Royce (R&R) was a medium-sized electronic component designer and manufacturer in southern California, with annual sales of about $100 million. Fully 80 percent of R&R revenues came from government and military contracts for small, specially designed electronic devices. The company was functionally organized with a president who reported to a group vice president of the parent corporation. Reporting to the president were vice presidents of human resources, engineering design, production and assembly, marketing and contract administration, and finance and accounting. The company was over thirty years old and had an excellent reputation in the small electronic components market.

Most of the work performed by the company fell under the rubric of design and development engineering. R&R usually bid on and won military contracts that called for specially designed components for state-of-the-art navigational systems, test systems, and aircraft. The company also maintained a small production and final assembly plant. The design and development group, however, was regarded as the high-status group.

A strong engineering orientation dominated the company culture. The president was an engineer and had close ties with the engineering design department. Traditionally, the route to high levels of management was through the engineering department. Most of the employees and managers there were professionals, many of them with advanced degrees. Production and assembly, on the other hand, were low-status areas, and few people from those departments ever were promoted into senior management positions. Any engineer with managerial aspirations learned quickly to move out of assembly into engineering design. Although this was a topic of concern and conversation among the employees, most workers attributed this orientation to the company's success clearly being linked with engineering innovations. Paralleling the career progression norms and engineering orientation, the engineering design department was staffed predominantly by males and the production and assembly departments were staffed primarily by females.

In 1986, the U.S. government, as part of a routine audit of military contractors, cited serious shortcomings in R&R's affirmative action compliance. It noted, for example, that there were no women or minorities in senior management; that there were only a few people of color in middle management ranks; and that the only positions of responsibility held by women and minorities were lead positions in the production and final assembly departments. Otherwise, women held only low-level staff or clerical positions in administration and human resources. People of color were found mostly in the production and final assembly plant as hourly workers. The audit noted that unless this situation changed within twelve months, the government would have no choice but to cancel the pending and existing contracts that had been awarded to Ring and Royce.

Organization development activities were not new to Ring and Royce. Two internal OD practitioners, one male and one female, reported to the vice president of human resources. In a conversation with the vice president, the two internal consultants noted that they recently had attended a workshop on workforce diversity and that some of the methods described there might be appropriate to use at R&R. The vice president asked the internal consultants to contact the workshop presenter and develop a response to the government audit. As the presenter, you meet with the internal OD practitioners and the vice president of human resources and suggest that a logical first step is to study the organization to understand how employees and managers see the promotion and career opportunities. This would also allow the organization to develop a diversity profile that could serve as a baseline against which to judge progress in meeting the government's requirements.

Together, you and the internal consultants conduct a study on the career planning and development practices of R&R, the distribution of women and people of color in the organization, and the attitudes of the current workforce toward promotion opportunities and diversity. The findings of your study are summarized below.

1. The study confirmed the government's audit in terms of the low percentage of women and minorities in supervisory and lead positions (except in production and final assembly) and their absence from middle and senior management levels.

2. The availability of women and minority engineers is very low. They usually are very young, recent college graduates, and are in great demand. It is costly to identify and recruit these engineers, and once hired, these employees are not likely to be serious management candidates for several years.

3. Women and minority engineers who are hired and trained by the organization gain considerable experience and expertise, and as a result, become hot commodities. They are the objects of considerable effort by headhunters who recruit them away from R&R to larger organizations capable of paying significantly higher salaries and offering a number of perquisites that R&R cannot match, including more-rapid promotion.

4. Of the women currently in the R&R workforce, just under half of them are single mothers and only 20 percent have any technical training. Turnover is low, but absenteeism is relatively high.

5. Of the minorities currently in the R&R workforce, only 25 percent have a technical or bachelor's degree; 77 percent have been with R&R less than three years; and the turnover within this group is significantly higher than the overall company average.

6. The female employees had relatively uniform attitudes. First, there was little interest in advancement or promotion. They equated promotion with longer hours, travel, and higher stress. Because many of the women had school-age children, these job characteristics conflicted with their needs to be at home at a specific time each day. Second, there was great interest in acquiring additional technical training. However, this too was seen as requiring extra time that would detract from the time they wanted to spend with their children.

7. Important differences were identified between the male and female employees. For example, male and female supervisors had different ways of describing an effective manager. Males viewed promotability in terms of the things that were noticed by managers one and two levels above them in the hierarchy. That is, they were very clear about what their bosses wanted and were very visible in going about meeting these needs. They spent most of their time doing these results-oriented activities, often to the exclusion of other, equally important but less visible, tasks. Women, on the other hand, viewed promotable managers as people who did all things as well as possible. They defined success in terms of balancing and maximizing, within given contraints, a whole set of objectives.

8. These differences partially explained, but did not justify, senior management's perceptions of their workers. Male supervisors were viewed in a more positive light. They were seen as being better at identifying priorities and achieving results, while women supervisors were viewed as more reliable but not very astute politically. In addition, management did not see the female managers as aggressive, wondered about their ability to make difficult personnel and human resources decisions, and believed them to be less interested in technical matters. Female supervisors were "too concerned with maintaining good relationships at work, rather than posting good performance results."

9. The study also found that most men identified a higher-level manager whom they considered to be a mentor. Most women did not identify a mentor. They suggested that the rumor and gossip mill were all too quick to question a female supervisor working closely with a male manager. Taking on a mentor was seen as a large risk to a woman's integrity and reputation.

After reviewing the results of the study, the vice president of human resources has asked you and the internal practitioners to recommend a course of action.

Questions

1. What summary conclusions do you have about Ring and Royce, and how will you organize the study findings to support those conclusions?

2. How might R&R go about increasing its compliance with affirmative action regulations?

3. What sources of resistance exist within the organization?

Source: Reproduced with permission from Walter L. Ross, Covey Leadership Center, Provo, Utah, and Christopher G. Worley, Pepperdine University, The George L. Graziadio School of Business and Management, Culver City, California.

■ Precision Instruments (A)*

In the spring of 1988, the new building that everyone at Precision Instruments had been hearing about for over a year was nearly completed. Most people at Precision were eager to make the five-mile move from their cramped quarters in a crowded industrial park to the secluded location on the edge of the forest. Although Precision's cofounders Jim Hart, Don McBride, and Harold Phelps were anxious to move and felt that the new building would reinforce company confidence in their relatively young company, they wondered how the move would change the company that they had worked so hard to build.

Company History and Background

Initial Meeting of Precision's Cofounders

Precision Instruments designed, marketed, and manufactured gauges and other instruments that measured the pressure, temperature, density, and related properties of flowing materials. These instruments were used mainly in process industries such as petroleum, chemicals, paper, food processing, and mining. Precision was founded in 1975, but the association of Jim Hart and Don McBride, the two cofounders with experience in the instruments business, began long before the formation of Precision. Jim and Don met when they were studying mechanical engineering at the University of Illinois. After graduation, they both went to work for Blacker and Cromwell, a Houston-based instruments firm, founded in the late 1800s, that had been the world's second-largest producer of instruments for the process industries.

Several years later Jim and Don had become, respectively, the sales manager and marketing manager at Blacker. They had a lot of influence on the way things were run in the company because the president had no previous experience in the instruments business. Running a business like Blacker required some knowledge of fluid design, mechanical design, and electronics, as well as information about the habits and needs of the few key industries that used Blacker's products. In spite of their influence, however, when Don and Jim told the president that they wanted to redesign the product line and make several major innovations, he vetoed the idea. He said that Blacker's long-time customers wouldn't tolerate a major change in the entire product line.

However, Jim and Don felt that the innovations would be very profitable, and they began to think about making the new products themselves.

Their chance to go into business together came when Harold Phelps, a wealthy Louisiana plumbing contractor and an old friend of Jim's showed up on Jim's doorstep saying that he wanted to get out of the plumbing business and that he would like to go into business with Jim. Jim asked Don if he would like to join them, and the three of them decided that because instruments was the only business they knew, they'd better go into instruments.

Precision's Earliest Days

Jim and Don both felt that the major weakness of their biggest competitors (Tanner Controls and Blacker and Cromwell) was that they had grown up rapidly and haphazardly when the instruments business was still very young. Because they couldn't really anticipate the needs of their customers, both Tanner and Blacker developed a broad line of products, many of which had overlapping functions. Because the products were developed at various times, even products that performed very similar functions contained few common parts. Jim and Don believed that producing very different products with overlapping functions forced their competitors to make small, unprofitable production runs and to maintain large, costly inventories. They proposed that their new organization and its customers would be better served by a product line that was designed in a modular fashion (where all products were made of a few basic interchangeable parts).

Drawing on their long experience in the instruments business, Jim and Don designed a product line that could be built in a modular fashion and that also contained many small improvements that Jim and Don knew customers wanted.

---

*This is a disguised case.

Although Harold contributed most of Precision's initial capital, the cofounders decided that each man would own a third of the business. The three also decided that either Jim or Don should act as president of the company. Jim had a couple of years' more experience than Don, so they decided that Jim should be the president. When the decision was made, Don told Jim, "Now that you're president, I know we're still going to try and agree on everything cooperatively, but if a decision needs to be made, I want you to know that you have the final say. I don't believe in running a company by a committee, and I'll bow to your final decision in any matter."

Precision's Move to Oregon

The three founders decided to establish their headquarters in a semirural part of Oregon. Their plan was to contract out the production of parts to machine shops, as they had done at Blacker. While they were investigating machine shops, one of their friends stopped by to ask how the business was developing. When they told him about their plan to subcontract their production work, he told them that they could make a lot more money by having their own machines. To convince them of the soundness of his idea, the next day he brought in plans for a minimum-size machine shop as well as estimates showing that all of the necessary machinery could be obtained and used for about $100,000 annually. Convinced that their friend's idea was sound, Jim and Don worked through him to purchase the machinery in Houston and arranged to have it shipped to Oregon. They also obtained a line of credit with a sympathetic local banker that helped them move into a more permanent building.

As Precision prepared to produce its first products, Don began to set up a sales organization. At Precision, Don planned to market the products through a network of sales representatives. He had perfected this idea at Blacker, and now he knew whom to contact and how to interest people in Precision's new products.

When production began, the three cofounders assumed a kind of informal division of labor. Jim took care of decision and engineering while Don tried to interest customers in the product. Mean-while, Harold, with substantial help from Jim and Don, took charge of the manufacturing area. Although Harold didn't know a lot about the technical details of making the product, he developed excellent relationships with the workers and was a source of encouragement to them, especially when the company was just beginning to get on its feet. Harold spent most of his time on the shop floor talking to the workers and monitoring the progress of various production runs.

Although each man had one focus area, all of them were very concerned about the success of the business and spent long hours keeping informed about all of the developments in their new company.

Because most prospective customers preferred to buy their instruments from established suppliers whose products had been tested both in the laboratory and in the field, Precision's sales initially were not too large. The company's first projections had predicted a "cash-out position for the first three and one half years," and Precision didn't actually break even until thirty-eight months after it was started. During the first year of business, none of the cofounders drew any salaries. They also stretched out their payables and avoided all nonessential expenses; however, they always paid their employees on time.

In 1990, about fifteen years after Precision was founded, Don was reminiscing about starting the company, and he said that he looked on the company's early days as "one of the best times in my life. Even though our families were eating fried bread, we believed that we were building something that would be good for the community and good for a lot of people, and we were prepared to give it everything we had."

Precision's Increasing Success

Once Precision's customers had a chance to test the soundness of the products and the staying power of Precision, sales began to skyrocket. The modular design, which enabled Precision to guarantee shorter delivery times and which required customers to stock fewer spare parts, became very popular. By 1980, the company was so successful that the founders decided to go public in order to raise the capital that they would need for further expansion.

By the spring of 1988, Precision had expanded its total plant size from 2,500 to 55,000 square feet and had acquired an additional building. The workforce had grown from 10 or 15 people who had been personal friends of the cofounders to 150 machinists, engineers, and office personnel. Although the local machinists union once had tried to organize Precision's workers, they were unable to raise the support required to call for a National Labor Relations Board (NLRB) election. Five years after the unionization attempt, Don recalled that "When the Machinists' workers tried to unionize us, it just made Jim and me seethe inside. We've tried to bend over backward to do right by our employees. Sometimes we've even taken money out of our own pockets to make this a better place to work. The people in the shop wouldn't understand this, but it's the truth. We provide a lot of jobs and pay a lot of taxes, but you just can't make those people understand basic economic principles."

Precision's monetary growth had been as spectacular as its physical growth. Its sales had increased at a compound rate of more than 40 percent a year, and earnings and stock prices had followed suit (Exhibit 1). Productivity, especially in the manufacturing area, was very high. When customers or friends came to see Jim, Don, or Harold, the cofounders often bragged about how hard their people worked and said that the work ethic was stronger in the Northwest than in any other part of the country. The cofounders based pay increases strictly on merit, and it was not uncommon for a machinist to get a 25 or 30 percent raise in a single year. Also, Jim, Don, and Harold were preparing to implement a profit-sharing plan that would give the company employees 50 percent of all operating income after operating income reached 18 percent of net sales. The first profit-sharing checks were to be distributed in June 1988, and the accounting department had estimated that most employees would receive checks for about 10 percent of their gross salary. (In the production area, most workers would receive between $1,500 and $2,500.) In December 1987, *Business Week* named Precision, along with Mattel, Kodak, and two other large companies, "one of the five best growth companies of the year."

To accommodate their rapid growth, Jim, Don, and Harold made plans to build a large new plant in a picturesque wooded area. The plant would be designed to accommodate a larger inventory, several

Exhibit 1	Five-Year Financial Summary* (in millions, except where noted)				
	1988	1987	1986	1985	1984
Net sales	$13.68	$9.45	$7.16	$4.66	$2.61
Cost of goods sold	7.57	4.71	3.84	2.71	1.50
Gross profit	6.11	4.74	3.32	1.95	1.11
Operating income	2.71	1.94	1.27	.59	.32
Net earnings	1.52	1.03	.64	.28	.15
Earnings per share (in dollars)	.70	.52	.36	.16	.09
Year-end backlog	8.02	6.64	7.07	4.13	2.68
Total assets	15.67	8.92	5.34	3.92	2.60
Stockholders' equity	6.01	4.41	1.95	1.23	.91
Stock price (high and low bid, in dollars)	$12^3/4$ to $7^5/8$	$6^3/4$ to $5^1/2$	$4^5/8$ to $2^5/8$	$2^5/8$ to $1^1/8$	$1^1/2$ to 1

*Year ended March 31.

new machines, more office space, and a fully computerized design and manufacturing system.

The cofounders wanted a building that would impress customers and suppliers and that would communicate the idea that Precision was a very successful and rapidly growing company. Therefore, they hired some of Portland's best architects, interior designers, and landscapers to help them design their showplace. When the plans were finally completed, they called for an artificial lake (complete with ducks), a nine-hole golf course, facilities for badminton and volleyball, and a storage facility for the recently acquired company plane.

The cofounder's offices were to be furnished with solid mahogany desks, leather chairs and couches, Persian rugs, rare plants, and fine paintings. Vice presidents' offices and reception areas were to be smaller-scale, less expensively furnished replicas of the executive offices.

The production area was designed as a large, well-lighted, adequately heated and ventilated room that would be easy to clean and maintain, and that would accommodate the rapid growth in orders that the founders anticipated.

Finally, in the spring of 1988, the 135,000-square-foot building was ready for occupancy. Jim and Don had decided on a moving date, and many of the employees had made arrangements to use their own cars and trucks to help the company move. Many of the employees were anxious to move into the new building and were proud of the company's physical and financial growth. However, the move was not the only change that would soon occur in the company. One month before the moving date, Harold announced that he would retire as soon as the company was settled into its new location. Although Jim and Don wondered how things would change when they moved out of the place where they had "made the company work," they felt that the move marked an important step forward in the life of their company.

■ Precision Instruments (B)

In April of 1991, just three years after Precision's move to the new building, Jim Hart was looking at the preliminary financial results for the year and wondering what had gone wrong. During the company's first two years in the new building, Precision's financial performance (Exhibit 1) had been much lower than the cofounders had expected, and this year's figures were not looking much better. Also, the machinists were again trying to unionize Precision, and they seemed to be having some success. The head foreman had mentioned that some of the production workers seemed frustrated and dissatisfied and felt that a union would improve the situation, but Jim wasn't sure why the workers were upset. As Jim wondered what he could do to turn the company around, he thought about some of the problems he and Don had faced during the last three years.

Precision's "Growing Pains"

When Precision's cofounders planned for the new building, they expected that Precision's rapid growth would continue for several years. However, an economic downturn occurred soon after the company moved and the projected sales growth did not materialize. Precision, therefore, had to absorb the costs associated with a building that was bigger than necessary. Initially Jim and Don were not very concerned about this situation because they expected that when the economy recovered, orders would increase. However, although orders eventually picked up, earnings remained low.

Just after the company moved, a major patent infringement suit diverted some of Jim's attention from the problem of easing the transition to the new building. In mid-1986, one of Precision's competitors filed a suit claiming that Precision's newest and most profitable product infringed on the competitor's patents. Initially, while evidence was being gathered, Precision was allowed to make the product. However, in early 1990, both the district and the appeals courts handed down judgments against Precision. Although Precision was filing an appeal with the Supreme Court, the district and appeals courts had prohibited the company from manufac-

Exhibit 1	Two-Year Financial Summary* (in millions, except where noted)	
	1990	**1989**
Net sales	$19.20	$16.02
Cost of goods sold	11.85	9.71
Gross profit	7.35	6.31
Operating income	1.96	1.22
Net earnings	.63	.61
Earnings per share (in dollars)	.28	.28
Year-end backlog	11.96	9.90
Total assets	22.98	18.52
Stockholders' equity	7.43	6.70
Stock price (high and low bid, in dollars)	$9^{1}/_{2}$ to $6^{1}/_{4}$	$9^{1}/_{2}$ to $7^{1}/_{2}$

*Year ended March 31.

turing the product. By early 1991, Precision had incurred well over a million dollars in legal fees, and Jim, Don, and other top managers had spent many hours in meetings with Precision's attorneys. Also, during a recent meeting about the audit of Precision's 1991 financial results, Precision's auditors informed Jim that in the light of the court verdicts, the auditors would probably have to issue a qualified opinion about Precision's 1991 financial statements.

In addition to outside economic and legal pressures, Jim and Don had to cope with many problems associated with increasing the size of their company. For example, when the company moved, about fifty people joined the company. Several of the new hires were engineers who were brought into the design department to help increase the rate of new product development. Jim, Don, and the vice president of engineering worked hard to shape the design department into a creative and productive unit that would be able to meet Precision's future product development needs. Although Precision's products were selling well, Jim and Don felt that if Precision was going to be able to meet the customers' changing product requirements, the company needed a team of design engineers who were aware of the latest technologies in the process industries and were designing products compatible with those technologies. Also, Jim and Don wanted to expand Precision's product line to include several highly specialized instruments that Precision could not have afforded to make when it was smaller. To develop these new products effectively, Precision increased its engineering design staff from twenty to twenty-eight and installed a CAD–CAM (computer-aided design–computer-aided manufacturing) system.

The CAD-CAM system was installed not only to help the engineering department but also to help the production staff. The system was supposed to make instrument design and production easier by allowing engineers to design products at computer screens and by maintaining, among other things, complete and accurate records of sales, inventories, and the status of finished and semifinished goods. Although the system's manufacturers had assured Precision that the system would increase productivity, so far, the system had not achieved the desired results. The system had been very expensive to install and difficult to operate. Also, many of the people who were supposed to use the myriad reports generated by the computer found the system confusing and preferred to do things the old way. One production control manager expressed the feelings of many of Precision's middle managers when he said, "I get a big pile of computer reports every week, and I don't even know what most of them are about. I just pile them in a corner and get on with my work."

Problems Among the Precision Workers

As Jim thought about the various problems he'd faced during the last three years, he decided that none of them was as difficult or as baffling as a major production problem that had increased in severity recently. Production had been somewhat sluggish ever since the move. At first, Jim attributed the problem to the difficulties associated with working in a new environment and with trying to integrate newly hired workers into the production team. However, productivity never really picked up and, in fact, it remained lower than it had been at the old plant. During the last six months, the productivity problem seemed to have worsened: scrap rates and absenteeism had increased, and the value of finished products produced per labor hour had decreased. Total production was substantially below the goal, and foremen and production control managers reported that workers seemed restless and spent a lot of time discussing their complaints with each other. Jim also had heard rumors that the recent unionization drive actually was being conducted at the request of Precision workers. In fact, the union had received support from 37 percent of Precision's workers (which was enough to call for an NLRB election sometime in June).

Jim was very concerned about the problems in the production area. He knew that to regain financial strength, the company needed to increase productivity. He also was opposed to working with a union, and he even felt a bit angry that some of the workers apparently wanted a union. He believed he'd always treated the production workers "right." (Pay and benefits at Precision were somewhat higher than at other manufacturing operations in the area. Precision's shop was the cleanest and most comfortable in the area. The company had no salary grades and gave raises only on the basis of performance. High producers regularly received raises of up to 25 percent, and no one was stuck in a situation where he or she couldn't make more money by improving performance.) Jim couldn't understand why the workers wanted a union, and he felt that having to go through an NLRB election was an unjustified "slap in the face." Nevertheless, he realized that he couldn't do anything about the problems until he knew what was causing them, so he decided to invite several production workers from various functions (receiving/shipping, machines, assembly, testing, among other) into his office for a frank discussion of the problems in the shop.

Jim's Discussion with Production Workers

A week after he decided to talk to some of the production workers, Jim met in his office with fifteen people who worked on the shop floor. When everyone arrived, Jim told the workers, "I know that things aren't going very well in the shop, and I'd like to find out why. I've heard that some of the workers are unhappy, and I want to solve the problems you're having back there so that you can start really producing again. During this meeting, I want you to tell me what you think needs to be changed, and I'll just listen to you."

Ted Lockhart (age fifty-five, a machinist who had worked for Precision about ten years) started the discussion: "I think that the first thing we've got to do is get decent materials. I get a lot of bad materials at my workstation, and when I point it out to the head man, he just tells me to go ahead and 'machine it any way you can.' I know that materials like that never make it past the test, so they just have to be scrapped or reworked. It seems to me that the company can't possibly be making money when we machine the same material three or four times and then just end up scrapping it."

Helen Stone (age thirty-five, assembly worker, four years with the company): "Yeah, I've seen a lot of bad material down in assembly. Sometimes the parts are so bent out of shape that we can't even fit the pieces together. I put a lot of stuff in the scrap bin, and that's probably not helping the company any."

Lyle Duncan (age twenty-six, machinist, three years with the company): "When I get bad materials, the lead man just tells me to 'go ahead and machine it or we'll never get this order out on time.' I don't see why we are promising these deadlines that we can't possibly meet. I mean, I've heard that we're promising to deliver things in four weeks. Everyone knows that's completely ridiculous because it takes us four weeks just to get the raw stock. I don't think it's very good for business to be promising stuff you can't deliver. Won't that make our customers unhappy with us?"

Stan Healy (age forty, test technician, six years with the company): "You know it's real hard for a guy to work on an order when he knows that it's going to end up in the scrap bin. It's hard to feel like you're getting anywhere."

Paul Linton (age thirty-two, shipping/receiving worker, five years with the company): "Another thing that makes it real hard for a guy to keep going is the fact that we don't get profit sharing anymore. The first year it was really great. Guys were walking around with checks for $2,000, and they really felt good about it. Now, they keep telling us that we're almost near the goal and then, at the end of the year, we find that we've worked our hearts out for nothing. Now it's gotten to the point where it seems like we won't get the money no matter how hard we work."

Lyle: "Yeah, when I came here, they told me that about 10 percent of my salary would come from profit sharing. So far, I haven't seen even a penny of profit sharing, and I kind of feel like they almost lied to me when I got my job here."

Ted: "Profit sharing is not the only thing I'm worried about. It seems like, ever since we moved over here, the office people have gotten a lot of nice things and that we haven't gotten anything."

Stan: "Every time people talk to us they say that the office is doing well, but the shop needs a lot of improvement. It seems to me like we've been out back working really hard while the office people have just been up here enjoying all the fancy furniture and plush carpeting that we bought when we moved over here."

Scott Price (age thirty-eight, tool shop employee, two years with the company): "My wife's a secretary up here in the office, and when I come up to see her, people are always telling me that I shouldn't be up here because I might get the new carpets dirty. When people say that, I feel like telling them that the shop made the money that bought these carpets, so we have a right to walk on them."

Helen: "There's been some talk in the shop that we're going to have separate Christmas parties and picnics from the office. That doesn't seem very good to me because I think we've all worked hard to make this company successful and we shouldn't go around thinking that some of us are better than others."

Ted: "Yeah, in the old days, everybody knew each other, and we all worked together to get the job done. If we needed to get a rush order done, everyone stayed late and helped get it out. Now, it's like everyone cares more about their own department than about the company, and we have to go through miles of red tape to get anything done. At the old place, 'us' was the company. Now it seems like 'us' means that department. I don't even know everyone in the shop anymore, and when an engineer sends down more specifications that have mistakes in them, it takes me two or three days to get a hold of him, and then he wants to meet me in his office and not down at my workstation where he can really see the problem."

Paul: "Before we got so big, we were really a company. Now, it seems like the shop's been pushed way out in the back and like people don't know that the shop's part of Precision."

Helen: "When we moved over here, I was really proud of the way the company had grown, and it was a big motivation for me. But it seems like ever since we've been over here, management hasn't told us what's been going on. With Harold gone, we don't see anyone from the office anymore, and we're in the dark about management's real attitudes toward us."

After listening to the employees for a few more minutes, Jim thanked them for the information and told them to go back to work. Jim was somewhat surprised by what he'd heard in the meeting. He'd been aware of most of the problems that the workers had mentioned, but he felt that they were overstating the seriousness of the situation. He wondered if the people in the meeting really understood the problems he had to deal with. He wasn't sure that the workers would understand that he sometimes had to accept unsatisfactory materials in order to maintain his relationship with an important supplier or that short delivery time was one of Precision's most important selling points. He could understand the workers' distress about profit sharing, but he wished that they would realize that everyone in the company had been hurt by the earnings drop and that he and Don were trying very hard to get earnings back up. He also wondered if talking to the president of the company had made the workers air their grievances more loudly than usual. Jim decided that, before he tried to do anything, he needed to get more objective data about the situation in the shop.

The next day, as Jim was thinking about how he could get more information about the problems in the production area, he got a call from Mark Garrett, a professor of business administration at a nearby university. Mark was an old friend of Jim's and a Precision stockholder. He told Jim that he was very interested in finding out more about small, highly successful companies like Precision and that he wanted to send a casewriter out to Precision to learn about what had made Precision successful.

Jim responded by saying, "I'd be glad to let you learn more about us if you could also help us learn a little about ourselves. Production has been pretty slow around here for a while, and in fact, I told everyone that I'm going to insist on seeing some improvement this month and I'm not going to accept any excuses. I go back to the shop every week and try to get a feel for what's going on. We've got it organized so that the materials move around the shop in kind of a "U"—they come in on one side, go down through the machining and chemical treatment, and then back up through assembly, test, and shipping. That makes it very easy for me to get around and see how everyone's doing. Lately, it seems like things have been a little slow, but I'm not sure exactly why. I talked to some of the workers yesterday, but I'm not sure how much of what they said was just 'letting off steam.' It would really help me if you could come in and ask people 'what things keep you from being as productive as you'd like to be?' and then get back to me about it. I think that part of the problem is that they just don't understand the things we have to do, but I want to make sure that there is not something that needs to be fixed so that we can get them producing for us again."

Jim and Mark agreed that the casewriter would interview twenty-five people and ask them about productivity and other issues that could be included in a case. The casewriter would then prepare a summary of interviewee comments and send it to Jim. In order to get the best possible data, Mark and Jim agreed that the interviewees would not be identified in the final report.

The Casewriter's Report

Six weeks after the first interviews, a summary of the interviewees' comments arrived in the mail. Jim was interested in knowing what the casewriter had found; so he began skimming the report which grouped excerpts from the interviews into several categories. As Jim looked at the report, several comments caught his attention:

In the smaller plant, we had a better atmosphere. People cared about making the goal. Now people say "so what?" [over eight years with the company]

People know that certain things have to be done, but they don't really care. [two years with company]

It's not pay and benefits. If a person feels good he'll break his back to do a good job. Management needs to motivate properly—there's a lack of positive input to the employees. [five years]

The production problem doesn't have a lot to do with pay. There's just no motivation to do your best work. Everyone likes to be noticed, and people need recognition. [one year]

Sometimes I wonder if Jim cares about the company anymore. Besides owning Precision, he owns a small paper plant near here, a company that leases private planes, and a Burger King franchise. Last year, he was the campaign manager for a man who ran for political office. I wonder if he has the time to invest here that he used to. I know we see him a lot less in the shop, and I wonder if the whole company feels the loss. I think this lawsuit really frustrates him and makes him want to spend more time on other things. [over eight years]

In the old plant, Jim came out and talked to people every day. Now, we'll go four or five months without seeing him. [over eight years]

Right now, there's no two-way communication with management. They don't come back here, and it seemed like it got a lot worse when we moved. [over eight years]

The main reason we want the union is we feel that management hasn't listened to what we have to offer in the way of suggestions to improve the company. [over six years]

I think that the machinists are out for their own personal gain and don't care whether the company goes under or not. But I still think that organizing as a bargaining unit is a good idea so that we can get a better line of communication with management. There's a lot more to the communication problem than meets the eye. There are certain things that management is keeping under wraps. We don't understand why management is doing these things. [two years]

I think that one of the biggest reasons that people want a union is that they want to be able to bargain with Jim on salary. Some of the ways they have put together here to give raises are quite strange. Jim still approves everyone's salary personally, and a lot of complaints and evaluations wind up in a guy's file without him being told anything about it. Then they use your file to hold you back; there are a lot of petty reasons why they hold people back here. [over eight years]

The only way to get ahead is by apple polishing. The only other way is by blood relation. I want the union here so I can have job security and so the foreman couldn't fire anybody on a whim anymore. [five years]

The atmosphere at Precision is uncertain. You're never really sure how you're doing or when your supervisor is going to come down on you. [seven years]

We had a fire in the receiving area the other day, and all of the guys pitched in and put it out. The next day we got a memo that said only people who are authorized to put out fires should do so. But nobody knows who these people are. [four years]

The first year we were in the building, we worked a lot of crazy hours and then we didn't get profit sharing. When the profit was shown, it turned out they'd bought machinery and office furniture, and it seemed to the men that they'd just hidden the money. [over eight years]

Profit sharing's a joke. The first year, we got $1,900, but since then we haven't gotten anything because we're paying for their precious building. [over eight years]

People just don't believe they can get a profit sharing anymore. [four years]

If I could change anything at Precision, I'd like to see the departments working together again. For instance, purchasing should work more with us so that we would get the right materials and so that we wouldn't have to do things over again. [seven years]

I wonder about the future of the company because sometimes I see things that just aren't like they should be. We have merchandise that's not finished that was counted as finished goods in last year's inventory. [three years]

I wonder if we need all of these luxuries that we've got here. Maybe we'd do better if we spent less on the building. [four years]

After reading the report, Jim wasn't sure what to do. He wanted to bring up productivity, but he didn't know what he should do first.

Questions

1. What are the different sources of Precision Instruments' problems?

2. Identify and describe the different performance management systems.

3. How and where would you intervene?

Strategic Interventions

6

19

Organization and Environment Relationships

This chapter concerns interventions that address the relationship between an organization and its environment. These change programs are relatively recent additions to the OD field. They focus on helping organizations position themselves strategically in their competitive environments and achieve a better fit with the external forces affecting their goal achievement and performance. Practitioners are discovering that additional knowledge and skills in such areas as competitive strategy, finance, marketing, and political science are necessary to implement these strategic interventions.

Organizations are open systems and must relate to their environments. They must acquire the resources and information needed to function; they must deliver products or services that are valued by customers. An organization's strategy—how it acquires resources and delivers outputs—is shaped by particular aspects and features of the environment. Cigarette manufacturers, faced with increasing regulation and declining demand in the United States, increased distribution to non-U.S. countries and diversified into other industries, such as foods, beverages, and consumer products. Thus, organizations can devise a number of responses for managing environmental interfaces, from internal administrative responses, such as creating special units to scan the environment, to external collective responses, such as forming strategic alliances with other organizations.

The interventions described in this chapter help organizations gain a comprehensive understanding of their environments and devise appropriate responses to external demands. Integrated strategic change is a comprehensive OD intervention aimed primarily at a single organization or business unit. It suggests that business strategy and organization design must be changed together to respond to external and internal disruptions. A strategic change plan can help members manage the transition between the current strategic orientation and the desired future strategic orientation.

Transorganizational development is concerned with helping organizations join into partnerships with other organizations to perform tasks or to solve problems that are too complex and multifaceted for single organizations to resolve. These multiorganization systems abound in today's environment and include joint ventures, strategic alliances, research and development consortia, and public–private partnerships. They tend to be loosely coupled and nonhierarchical, and consequently, they require methods different from most traditional OD interventions which are geared to single organizations. These methods involve helping organizations recognize the need for partnerships and developing coordinating structures for carrying out multiorganization activities.

Mergers and acquisitions represent the combination of two or more organizations into one entity. These complex strategic changes involve integrating many of the interventions previously discussed in this text, including human process, technostructural, and human resources management interventions. Research and practice in mergers and acquisitions strongly suggest that OD practices can contribute to implementation success.

ORGANIZATION AND ENVIRONMENT FRAMEWORK

This section provides a framework for understanding how environments affect organizations and, in turn, how organizations can affect environments. The framework is based on the concept, described in Chapter 5, that organizations and their subunits are open systems existing in environmental contexts. Environments can be described in two ways. First, there are different *types* of environments that consist of specific components or forces. To survive and grow, organizations must understand these different environments, select appropriate parts to respond to, and develop effective relationships with them. A manufacturing firm, for example, must understand raw materials markets, labor markets, customer segments, and production technology alternatives. It then must select from a range of raw material suppliers, applicants for employment, customer demographics, and production technologies to achieve desired outcomes effectively. Organizations are thus dependent on their environments. They need to manage external constraints and contingencies and take advantage of external opportunities. They also need to influence the environment in favorable directions through such methods as political lobbying, advertising, and public relations.

Second, several useful *dimensions* capture the nature of organizational environments. Some environments are rapidly changing and complex, and so require different organizational responses than do environments that are stable and simple. For example, chewing gum manufacturers face a stable market and use well-understood production technologies. Their strategy and organization design issues are radically different from those of software developers who face product life cycles measured in months instead of years, where labor skills are rare and hard to find, and where demand can change drastically overnight.

In this section, first we describe different types of environments that can affect organizations. Then we identify environmental dimensions that influence organizational responses to external forces. Finally, we review the different ways that organizations can respond to their environments. This material provides an introductory context for describing interventions that concern organization and environment relationships: integrated strategic change, transorganizational development, and mergers and acquisitions.

Environmental Types

Organizational environments are everything beyond the boundaries of organizations that can directly or indirectly affect performance and outcomes. That includes external agents that directly affect the organization, such as suppliers, customers, regulators, and competitors, as well as indirect influences in the wider cultural, political, and economic context. These two classes of environments are called the task environment and the general environment, respectively.[1] We will also describe the enacted environment, which reflects members' perceptions of the general and task environments.

As described in Chapter 5, the *general environment* consists of all external forces that can influence an organization. It can be categorized into technological, legal and regulatory, political, economic, social, and ecological components. Each of these forces can affect the organization in both direct and indirect ways. For example, economic recessions can directly impact demand for a company's product. The general environment also can affect organizations indirectly by virtue of the linkages between external agents. For example, an organization may have trouble obtaining raw materials from a supplier because the supplier is embroiled in a labor dispute with a national union, a lawsuit with a government regulator, or a boycott by a consumer group. Thus, components of the general environment can affect the organization without having any direct connection to it.

The *task environment* consists of the specific individuals and organizations that interact directly with the organization and can affect goal achievement: customers, suppliers, competitors, producers of substitute products or services, labor unions, financial institutions, and so on. These direct relationships are the medium through which organizations and environments mutually influence one another. Customers, for example, can demand changes in the organization's products, and the organization can try to influence customers' tastes and desires through advertising.

The *enacted environment* consists of the organization's perception and representation of its general and task environments. Weick suggested that environments must be perceived before they can influence decisions about how to respond to them.[2] Organization members must actively observe, register, and make sense of the environment before it can affect their decisions about what actions to take. Thus, only the enacted environment can affect which organizational responses are chosen. The general and task environments, however, can influence whether those responses are successful or ineffective. For example, members may perceive customers as relatively satisfied with their products and may decide to make only token efforts at developing new products. If those perceptions are wrong and customers are dissatisfied with the products, the meager product development efforts can have disastrous organizational consequences. As a result, an organization's enacted environment should accurately reflect its general and task environments if members' decisions and actions are to be effective.

Environmental Dimensions

Environments can also be characterized along dimensions that describe the organization's context and influence its responses. One perspective views environments as information flows and suggests that organizations need to process information to discover how to relate to their environments.[3] The key dimension of the environment affecting information processing is *information uncertainty,* or the degree to which environmental information is ambiguous. Organizations seek to remove uncertainty from the environment so that they know best how to transact with it. For example, organizations may try to discern customer needs through focus groups and surveys and attempt to understand competitor strategies through press releases, salesforce behaviors, and knowledge of key personnel. The greater the uncertainty, the more information processing is required to learn about the environment. This is particularly evident when environments are complex and rapidly changing. These kinds of environments pose difficult information processing problems for organizations. For example, global competition, technological change, and financial markets have created highly uncertain and complex environments for many multinational firms and have severely strained their information processing capacity.

Another perspective views environments as consisting of resources for which organizations compete.[4] The key environmental dimension is *resource dependence,* or the degree to which an organization relies on other organizations for resources. Organizations seek to manage critical sources of resource dependence while remaining as autonomous as possible. For example, firms may contract with several suppliers of the same raw material so that they are not overly dependent on one vendor. Resource dependence is extremely high for an organization when other organizations control critical resources that cannot be obtained easily elsewhere. Resource criticality and availability determine the extent to which an organization is dependent on the environment and must respond to its demands. An example is the tight labor market for information systems experts experienced by many firms in the late 1990s.

These two environmental dimensions—information uncertainty and resource dependence—can be combined to show the degree to which organizations are constrained by their environments and consequently must be responsive to their demands.[5] As shown in Figure 19.1, organizations have the most freedom from external forces when information uncertainty and resource dependence are both low. In such situations, organizations do not need to respond to their environments and can behave relatively independently of them. U.S. automotive manufacturers faced these conditions in the 1950s and operated with relatively little external constraint or threat. Organizations are more constrained and must be more responsive to external demands as information uncertainty and resource dependence increase. They must perceive the environment accurately and respond to it appropriately. As described in Chapter 1, organizations such as financial institutions, high-technology firms, and health-care facilities are facing unprecedented amounts of environmental uncertainty and resource dependence. Their existence depends on recognizing external challenges and responding quickly and appropriately to them.

Figure 19•1	Environmental Dimensions and Organizational Transactions

		RESOURCE DEPENDENCE	
		Low	High
INFORMATION UNCERTAINTY	Low	Minimal environmental constraint and need to be responsive to environment	Moderate constraint and responsiveness to environment
	High	Moderate constraint and responsiveness to environment	Maximal environmental constraint and need to be responsive to environment

SOURCE: Adapted from H. Aldrich, *Organizations and Environments* (New York: Prentice Hall, 1979): 133.

Organizational Responses

Organizations must have the capacity to monitor and make sense of their environments if they are to respond appropriately. They must identify and attend to those environmental factors and features that are highly related to goal achievement and performance. Moreover, they must have the internal capacity to develop effective responses. Organizations employ a number of methods to influence and respond to their environments, to buffer their technology from external disruptions, and to link themselves to sources of information and resources. These responses are generally designed by senior executives responsible for setting corporate strategy and managing external relationships. Three classes of responses are described below: administrative, competitive, and collective.

Administrative Responses

The most common organizational responses to the environment are administrative, including the formation or clarification of the organization's mission; the development of objectives, policies, and budgets; or the creation of scanning units. These responses can be either proactive or reactive and are aimed at defining the organization's purpose and key tasks in relationship to particular environments. As discussed in Chapter 10, an organization's *mission* describes its long-term purpose, including the products or services to be offered and the markets to be served. An effective mission clearly differentiates the organization from others in its competitive environment.[6] For example, 3M's core purpose is to solve unsolved problems innovatively. 3M is distinguished from its competitors by its attention to unsolved problems and its core competence of innovation. Similarly, an organization's *objectives, policies, and budgets* signal which parts of the environment are important. They allocate and direct resources to particular environmental relationships.[7] Intel's new product development objectives and allocation of more than 20 percent of revenues to research and development signal the importance of its linkage to the technological environment. Finally, organizations may create *scanning units*, such as market research and regulatory relations departments, to respond administratively to the environment. These units scan particular parts or aspects of the environment, interpret relevant information, and communicate it to decision makers who develop appropriate responses.[8] Scanning units generally include specialists with expertise in a particular segment of the environment. For example, market researchers provide information to marketing executives about customer tastes and preferences. Such information guides choices about product development, pricing, and advertising.

Competitive Responses

Competitive responses to the environment typically are associated with for-profit firms but can also apply to nonprofit and governmental organizations. Such actions seek to enhance the organization's performance by establishing a competitive advantage over its rivals. To sustain competitive advantage, organizations must achieve an external position vis-à-vis their competitors or perform internally in ways that are unique, valuable, and difficult to imitate.[9]

Uniqueness. An organization first must identify the bundle of resources and processes that make it distinct from other firms. These can include financial resources, such as access to low-cost capital; reputational resources, such as brand image or a history of product quality; technological resources, such as patents or a strong research and development department; and human resources, such as excellent labor–management relationships or scarce and valuable skill sets. Based on this list, the organization then determines how the resources apply to key organizational processes—regular patterns of organizational activity that involve a sequence of tasks performed by individuals.[10] For example, a software development process combines computer resources, software programs, typing skills, knowledge of computer languages, and customer requirements. Other organizational processes include new product development, strategic planning, appraising member performance, making sales calls, fulfilling customer orders, and the like. Processes and capabilities that are unique to the organization are called *distinctive competencies* and represent the cornerstone of competitive advantage.[11]

Value. Organizations achieve competitive advantage when their resources and processes deliver outputs that either warrant a higher-than-average price or are exceptionally low in cost. Both advantages are valuable according to a performance/price criterion. Products and services with highly desirable features or capabilities, although expensive, are valuable because of their ability to satisfy customer demands for high quality or some other performance dimension. Mercedes automobiles are valuable because the perceived benefits of ownership, including engineering performance, reliability, and prestige, exceed the price paid. On the other hand, outputs that cost little to produce are valuable because of their ability to satisfy customer demands at a low price. Chevrolet automobiles are valuable because they provide basic transportation at a low price. Mercedes and Chevrolet are both profitable, but achieve that outcome through different value propositions.

Imitability. Finally, sustainable competitive advantage is achieved when unique and valuable resources and processes are difficult to mimic or duplicate by other organizations.[12] For example, organizations can protect their competitive advantage by making it difficult for other firms to identify their distinctive competence. Disclosing unimportant information at trade shows or forgoing superior profits can make it difficult for competitors to identify an organization's strengths. Organizations can aggressively pursue a range of opportunities, thus raising the cost for competitors who try to replicate their success. Organizations can seek to retain key human resources through attractive compensation and reward practices like those described in Chapter 17, thereby making it more difficult and costly for competitors to attract such talent.

Collective Responses

Organizations can cope with problems of environmental dependence and uncertainty through increased coordination with other organizations. Collective responses help control interdependencies among organizations and include such methods as bargaining; contracting; coopting; and creating joint ventures, federations, strategic alliances, and consortia.[13] Contemporary organizations increasingly are turning to joint ventures and partnerships with other organizations to manage environmental uncertainty and perform tasks that are too costly and complicated for single organizations to perform. These multiorganization arrangements are being used as a means of sharing resources for large-scale research and development, for spreading the risks of innovation, for applying diverse expertise to complex problems and tasks, and for overcoming barriers to entry into foreign markets. For example, pharmaceutical firms are forming strategic alliances to distribute noncompeting medications and avoid the high costs of establishing sales organizations; firms from different countries are forming joint ventures to overcome restrictive trade barriers; and high-technology firms are forming research consortia to undertake significant and costly research and development for their industries.

Major barriers to collective responses in the United States are organizations' drive to act autonomously and government policies discouraging coordination among organizations, especially in the same industry. On the other hand, Japanese industrial and economic policies promote cooperation among organizations, thus giving them a competitive advantage in responding to complex and dynamic global environments.[14] For example, the Japanese government traditionally has provided financial assistance and support to cooperative research efforts among Japanese consumer product manufacturers. The resulting technological developments enabled such firms as Matsushita, Canon, and Sony to reduce American competitors' market shares dramatically.

The three interventions discussed in this chapter derive from this organization and environment framework. They help organizations assess their environments and make appropriate responses to them. The first intervention, integrated strategic change, focuses on how to coordinate administrative and competitive responses for a single organization or strategic business unit. The next two interventions, transorganization development and mergers and acquisitions, broaden the scope from single to multiple organizations. These interventions endeavor to coordinate administrative, competitive, and collective responses.

INTEGRATED STRATEGIC CHANGE

Integrated strategic change (ISC) is a recent intervention that brings an OD perspective to traditional strategic planning. It was developed in response to managers' complaints that good business strategies often are not implemented. The research suggested that too little attention was being given to the change process and human resources issues necessary to execute the strategy.[15] For example, the predominant paradigm in strategic planning and implementation artificially separates strategic thinking from operational and tactical actions; it ignores the contributions that planned change processes can make to implementation.[16] In the traditional process, senior managers and strategic planning staff prepare economic forecasts, competitor analyses, and market studies. They discuss these studies and rationally align the firm's strengths and weaknesses with the environmental opportunities and threats to form the organization's strategy.[17] Implementation occurs as middle managers, supervisors, and employees hear about the new strategy through memos, restructuring announcements, changes in job responsibilities, or new departmental objectives. Consequently, because participation has been limited to top management, there is little understanding of the need for change and little ownership of the new behaviors, initiatives, and tactics required to achieve the announced objectives.

Key Features

ISC, in contrast, was designed to be a highly participative process. It has three key features:[18]

1. The relevant unit of analysis is the organization's *strategic orientation* comprising its strategy and organization design. Strategy and the design that supports it must be considered as an integrated whole.

2. Creating the strategic plan, gaining commitment and support for it, planning its implementation, and executing it are treated as one integrated process. The ability to repeat such a process quickly and effectively when conditions warrant represents a sustainable competitive advantage.[19]

3. Individuals and groups throughout the organization are integrated into the analysis, planning, and implementation process to create a more achievable plan, to maintain the firm's strategic focus, to direct attention and resources on the organization's key competencies, to improve coordination and integration within the organization, and to create higher levels of shared ownership and commitment.

Application Stages

The ISC process is applied in four phases: performing a strategic analysis, exercising strategic choice, designing a strategic change plan, and implementing the plan. The four steps are discussed sequentially here but actually unfold in overlapping and integrated ways. Figure 19.2 displays the steps in the ISC process and its change components. An organization's existing strategic orientation, identified as its current strategy (S1) and organization design (O1), are linked to its future strategic orientation (S2/O2) by the strategic change plan.

1. *Performing the strategic analysis.* The ISC process begins with a diagnosis of the organization's readiness for change and its current strategy and organization (S1/O1). The most important indicator of readiness is senior management's willingness and ability to carry out strategic change. Greiner and Schein suggest that the two key dimensions in this analysis are the leader's willingness and commitment to change and the senior team's willingness and ability to follow the leader's initiative.[20] Organizations whose leaders are not willing to lead and whose senior managers are not willing and able to support the new strategic direction when necessary should consider team-building processes to ensure their commitment.

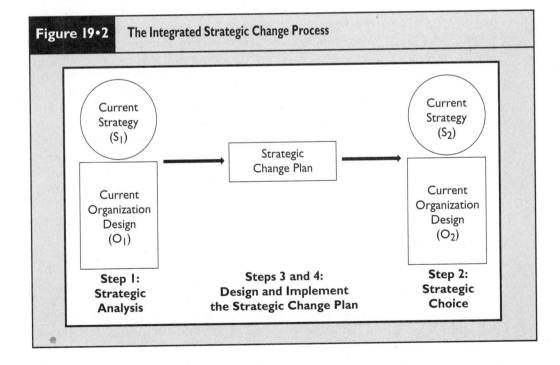

Figure 19·2	The Integrated Strategic Change Process

Current Strategy (S1)

Current Organization Design (O1)

Strategic Change Plan

Current Strategy (S2)

Current Organization Design (O2)

Step 1: Strategic Analysis

Steps 3 and 4: Design and Implement the Strategic Change Plan

Step 2: Strategic Choice

The second stage in strategic analysis is understanding the current strategy and organization design. The process begins with an examination of the organization's industry as well as its current financial performance and effectiveness. This information provides the necessary context to assess the current strategic orientation's viability. Porter's model of industry attractiveness[21] as well as the environmental framework introduced at the beginning of this chapter are the two most relevant models for analyzing the environment. Next, the current strategic orientation is described to explain current levels of performance and human outcomes. Several models for guiding this diagnosis exist.[22] For example, the current strategic orientation can be assessed according to the model and methods introduced in Chapter 5. The strategy is represented by the organization's mission, goals and objectives, intent, and business policies. The organization design is described by the structure, work, information, and human resource systems. Other models for understanding the organization's strategic orientation include the competitive positioning model[23] and other typologies.[24] These frameworks assist in assessing customer satisfaction; product and service offerings; financial health; technological capabilities; and organizational culture, structure, and systems.

Strategic analysis actively involves organization members in the process. Search conferences; employee focus groups; interviews with salespeople, customers, purchasing agents; and other methods allow a variety of employees and managers to participate in the diagnosis and increase the amount and relevance of the data collected. This builds commitment to and ownership of the analysis; should a strategic change effort result, members are more likely to understand why and be supportive of it.

2. *Exercising strategic choice.* Once the existing strategic orientation is understood, a new one must be designed. For example, the strategic analysis may reveal misfits among the organization's environment, strategic orientation, and performance. These misfits can be used as inputs to workshops where the future strategy and organization design are crafted. Based on this analysis, senior management formulates visions for the future and broadly defines two or three alternative sets of objectives and strategies for achieving those visions. Market forecasts, employees' readiness and willingness to change, competitor analyses, and other projections can be used to develop the alternative future scenarios.[25] The different sets of objectives and strategies also include projections about the organizational design changes that will be necessary to support each alternative. Although participation from other organizational stakeholders is important in the alternative generation phase, choosing the appropriate strategic orientation ultimately rests with top management and cannot easily be delegated. Senior executives are in the unique position of viewing strategy from a general management position. When major strategic decisions are given to lower-level managers, the risk of focusing too narrowly on a product, market, or technology increases.

This step determines the content or "what" of strategic change. The desired strategy (S2) defines the products or services to offer, the markets to be served, and the way these outputs will be produced and positioned. The desired organization design (O2) specifies the organizational structures and processes necessary to support the new strategy. Aligning an organization's design with a particular strategy can be a major source of superior performance and competitive advantage.[26]

3. *Designing the strategic change plan.* The strategic change plan is a comprehensive agenda for moving the organization from its current strategy and organization design to the desired future strategic orientation. It represents the process or "how" of strategic change. The change plan describes the types, magnitude, and schedule of change activities, as well as the costs associated with them. It also specifies how the changes will be implemented, given power and political issues, the nature of the organizational culture, and the current ability of the organization to implement change.[27]

4. *Implementing the strategic change plan.* The final step in the ISC process is the actual implementation of the strategic change plan. This draws heavily on knowledge of motivation, group dynamics, and change processes. It deals continuously with such issues as alignment, adaptability, teamwork, and organizational and personal learning. Implementation requires senior managers to champion the different elements of the change plan. They can, for example, initiate action and allocate resources to particular activities, set high but achievable goals, and provide feedback on accomplishments. In addition, leaders must hold people accountable to the change objectives, institutionalize each change that occurs, and be prepared to solve problems as they arise. This final point recognizes that no strategic change plan can account for all of the contingencies that emerge. There must be a willingness to adjust the plan as implementation unfolds to address unforseen and unpredictable events and to take advantage of new opportunities.

Application 19.1 describes an integrated strategic change intervention at Magma Copper Company and demonstrates how powerful the process can be, even in the face of influential suppliers and significant changes in ownership.

TRANSORGANIZATIONAL DEVELOPMENT

Transorganizational development (TD) is a form of planned change aimed at helping organizations develop collective and collaborative strategies with other organizations. Many of the tasks, problems, and issues facing organizations today are too complex and multifaceted to be addressed by a single organization. Multiorganization strategies and arrangements are increasing rapidly in today's highly competitive, global environment. In the private sector, research and development consortia allow companies to share resources and risks associated with large-scale research efforts. For example, Sematech involved many large organizations, such as Intel, AT&T, IBM, Xerox, and Motorola, that joined together to improve the competitiveness of the U.S. semiconductor industry. Joint ventures, such as Fuji-Xerox, between domestic and foreign firms can help overcome trade barriers and facilitate technology transfer across nations. The New United Motor Manufacturing, Inc., in Fremont, California, for example, is a joint venture between General Motors and Toyota to produce automobiles using Japanese teamwork methods. In the public sector, partnerships between government and business provide the resources and initiative to undertake complex urban renewal projects, such as Baltimore's Inner Harbor Project and Pittsburgh's Neighborhood Housing Services. Alliances among public service agencies in a region, such as the Human Services Council of Grand River, Michigan, and OuR TOWN, a cooperative project between local governments to promote rural tourism, can help coordinate services, promote economies, and avoid costly overlap and redundancy.

APPLICATION 19•1　Managing Strategic Change at Magma Copper Company

In 1995, Magma Copper Company was the tenth-largest copper mining and refining organization in the world. It operated mines in Arizona, Nevada, and South America. Smelting and refining operations were located outside of Tucson, Arizona, in one of the industry's largest complexes. Magma operated in a commodity industry where firms were "price takers." The price of copper was dictated by the market, and firms had little opportunity to influence buyers or differentiate the product. In addition, the market for copper was global with significant demand existing outside the United States. Industry analysts were predicting both increasing demand and steady prices over the next ten years. Competitors were located around the world, many of them subsidized by their governments. As a result of these conditions, cost and productivity were important strategic objectives.

Magma initiated a strategic change effort labeled "Division 2000." Corporate management and several internal OD consultants believed that the traditional ways of managing copper companies could be improved to impact performance dramatically. Although Magma's stock price and future earnings projections were rated highly by financial analysts, a well-publicized turnaround effort within the smelting and refining division produced industry-leading productivity outcomes and pointed out that capital-intensive processes could be improved with significant attention to social and human concerns. The Division 2000 project sought to extend those learnings and to understand how the organization might be organized and managed in the future.

The strategic analysis process took place over several months. The corporation's readiness for change was indicated by senior management's commitment to the Division 2000 project. The CEO, the president of the smelting and refining division, and the general managers of the mining divisions each provided budget support, people, and time. In addition, the unions believed that Division 2000 was an important opportunity to build on the partnership that had been created during successful negotiations two years earlier.

The business units engaged in a diagnostic process that examined their key operating goals and policies as well as their structures, information systems, reward systems, human resources systems, and cultures. Using mostly internal resources and guided by an external consultant, each division was encouraged to use a process that best fit its situation. One mining division convened a large-group meeting, another mine held small-group interviews, and the smelting and refining division used a task force. The results of the strategic analysis were compiled by the division and submitted to a group of managers and internal consultants acting as a steering committee.

Understanding the culture was an important characteristic of the diagnosis. In 1992, Magma Copper had adopted a unique vision and philosophy called the "Voice of Magma" that outlined the values that should guide individual behaviors. To reinforce those values, a significant investment in interpersonal relations training provided a social technology for organization members to interact with each other. A distinctive vocabulary accompanied the technology; people worked to achieve "breakthrough results" in their jobs and sought to build "extraordinary relationships" with other members. Each of the divisions undertook a qualitative assessment to determine the extent to which the social technology was operating in the division and could represent an important change lever.

Following the analysis, each division as well as the corporate office engaged in a process of visioning their desired strategic orientation. The corporate office provided financial, productivity, and people-oriented goals as inputs to the process. The divisions were asked to determine the extent to which they believed they could contribute to each of the goals and to commit to those goals over the next five years. In addition, the divisions were asked to "stand in the future" and describe the organization that would be necessary to achieve the goals and that they would want to work in. Again, the business units were asked to think about organization features such as information systems, relationships and culture, structure, work design, and human resources systems. In essence, they were being asked to design an organization that not only operated at low cost and high productivity but also produced desirable human outcomes.

The strategic choice phase generated considerable energy and enthusiasm in the organization. For example, requests from several divisions for information about cutting-edge examples in other organizations led to a two-day conference on best practices. Consultants were brought in to describe world-class benchmarks of different organization design systems as well as the change processes that were used to produce them. It was attended by more than one hundred employees, union leaders, managers, and corporate staff. It not only helped educate the organization on what was possible; it also helped members see what would be involved in making the changes they were considering.

The steering committee compiled the divisions' descriptions of their desired strategic orientations. The committee's first task was to ensure that the goals committed to by the divisions sufficiently covered the goals set out by the corporate staff. In a couple of cases, some renegotiation was necessary to satisfy the corporation's objectives completely. Their second task was to look at the organizational features. Recommendations were made to the organization's senior management regarding policies and design elements that might be centralized and standardized and those that should be left to the division for implementation. Finally, the steering committee examined the data to understand the areas that needed the most attention and that might help to develop a strategic change plan.

The last step in the process was to gain approval of the recommendations and to commission the divisions to develop strategic change plans. The output of this process would be a "transformation agenda" that would include the activities needed to achieve their desired strategic orientations as well as budget estimates that would feed into the corporation's budgeting process. However, approval by the corporation's senior leadership was delayed. First, Magma Copper announced on December 1, 1995, its intention to merge with the Australian firm, Broken Hills Proprietary Company, Ltd., a diversified natural resources organization. As the merger activities accelerated, management's attention was shifted away from the Division 2000 project. Second, labor negotiations had begun with serious discussions about governance and partnership. Both management and labor were interested in extending the groundbreaking agreement that won them national attention, and the Division 2000 process had raised important questions about how that partnership would evolve. The negotiating group requested that the Division 2000

process be put on hold as these discussions took place. As a result, formal approval of the steering committee recommendations did not come.

But that did not stop the process. Based on several change principles raised during the best-practices conference, three divisions proceeded with the design and development of change plans for moving their organizations forward. In one mining division, a sociotechnical analysis of the work flow and a mandate from the division manager to leverage the interpersonal skills of the workforce produced proposals for a new division structure focused on teams and important innovations in the information system. The smelting and refining division conducted a five-day workshop to identify the key systems requiring urgent attention and formed task forces to use a "self-design" process that would move the division toward its desired strategic orientation.

All of these change initiatives occurred even as the price of copper fell from about $1.25 per pound to less than a dollar. The commitment to change raised by the process and the involvement of people in creating their futures generated substantive change ideas to help the organization lower costs and improve productivity. In addition, the new BHP Copper group is serving as an important source of change ideas and processes for the rest of the BHP organization. ■

Transorganizational Systems and Their Problems

Cummings has referred to these multiorganization structures as *transorganizational systems* (TSs)—groups of organizations that have joined together for a common purpose.[28] TSs include a range of collective responses, including licensing agreements, strategic alliances, joint ventures, and public–private partnerships. They are functional social systems existing intermediately between single organizations and societal systems. TSs make decisions and perform tasks on behalf of their member organizations, although members maintain their separate organizational identities and goals. This separation distinguishes them from mergers and acquisitions. In contrast to most organizations, TSs tend to be underorganized: relationships among member organizations are loosely coupled; leadership and power are dispersed among autonomous organizations, rather than hierarchically centralized; and commitment and membership are tenuous as member organizations act to maintain their autonomy while jointly performing.

These characteristics make creating and managing TSs difficult.[29] Potential member organizations may not perceive the need to join with other organizations. They may be concerned with maintaining their autonomy or have trouble identifying potential partners. U.S. firms, for example, are traditionally "rugged individualists" preferring to work alone rather than to join with other organizations. Even if organizations decide to join together, they may have problems managing their relationships and controlling joint performances. Because members typically are accustomed to hierarchical forms of control, they may have difficulty managing lateral relations among independent organizations. They also may have difficulty managing different levels of commitment and motivation among members and sustaining membership over time.

Application Stages

Given these problems, transorganizational development has evolved as a unique form of planned change aimed at creating TSs and improving their effectiveness. In laying out the conceptual boundaries of TD, Cummings described the practice of TD as following the phases of planned change appropriate for underorganized systems (see Chapter 2).[30] These stages parallel other process models that have been proposed for creating and managing joint ventures, strategic alliances, and interorganizational collaboration.[31] The four stages are shown in Figure 19.3, along with key issues that need to be addressed at each stage. The stages and issues are described below.

1. *Identification stage.* This initial stage of TD involves identifying potential member organizations of the TS. For example, in the case of a strategic alliance or joint venture, this stage involves identifying the potential partners best suited to achieving the organization's objectives. Identifying potential members can be difficult because organizations may not perceive the need to join together or may not know enough about each other to make membership choices. These problems are typical when trying to create a new TS. Relationships among potential members may be loosely coupled or nonexistent; thus, even if organizations see the need to form a TS, they may be unsure about who should be included.

    The identification stage is generally carried out by one or a few organizations interested in exploring the possibility of creating a TS. Change agents work with these initiating organizations to clarify their own goals, such as product or technology exchange, learning, or market access; to explore alternatives to collaboration, including internal development, purchasing skills or resources, or making an acquisition; and understanding the tradeoff between the loss of autonomy and the value of collaboration. OD practitioners also help specify criteria for

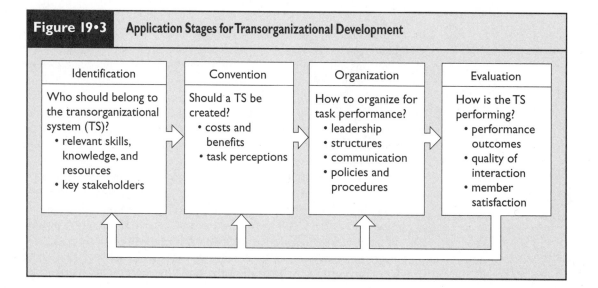

Figure 19•3	Application Stages for Transorganizational Development

Identification	Convention	Organization	Evaluation
Who should belong to the transorganizational system (TS)? • relevant skills, knowledge, and resources • key stakeholders	Should a TS be created? • costs and benefits • task perceptions	How to organize for task performance? • leadership • structures • communication • policies and procedures	How is the TS performing? • performance outcomes • quality of interaction • member satisfaction

membership in the TS and identify organizations meeting those standards. Because TSs are intended to perform specific tasks, a practical criterion for membership is how much organizations can contribute to task performance. Potential members can be identified and judged in terms of the skills, knowledge, and resources that they bring to bear on the TS task. TD practitioners warn, however, that identifying potential members also should take into account the political realities of the situation.[32] Consequently, key stakeholders who can affect the creation and subsequent performance of the TS are identified as possible members.

During the early stages of creating a TS, there may be insufficient leadership and cohesion among participants to choose potential members. In these situations, participants may contract with an outside change agent who can help them achieve sufficient agreement on TS membership. In several cases of TD, change agents helped members to create a special leadership group that could make decisions on behalf of the participants.[33] This leadership group comprised a small cadre of committed members and was able to develop enough cohesion among members to carry out the identification stage.

2. *Convention stage.* Once potential members of the TS are identified, the convention stage is concerned with bringing them together to assess whether creating a TS is desirable and feasible. This face-to-face meeting enables potential members to explore mutually their motivations for joining and their perceptions of the joint task. They work to establish sufficient levels of motivation and of task consensus to form the TS.

Like the identification stage, this phase of TD generally requires considerable direction and facilitation by change agents. Existing stakeholders may not have the legitimacy or skills to perform the convening function, and change agents can serve as conveners if they are perceived as legitimate and credible by the attending organizations. In many TD cases, conveners came from research centers or universities with reputations for neutrality and expertise in TD.[34] Because participating organizations tend to have diverse motives and views and limited means for resolving differences, change agents may need to structure and manage interactions to facilitate airing of differences and arriving at consensus about forming the TS. They may need to help organizations work through differences and reconcile self-interests with those of the larger TS.

3. *Organization stage.* When the convention stage results in a decision to create a TS, members then begin to organize themselves for task performance. This involves establishing structures and mechanisms that promote communication and interaction among members and that direct joint efforts to the task at hand.[35] For example, members may create a coordinating council to manage the TS, and they might assign a powerful leader to head that group. They might choose to formalize exchanges among members by developing rules, policies, and formal operating procedures. When members are required to invest large amounts of resources in the TS, such as might occur in an industry-based research consortium, the organizing stage typically includes voluminous contracting and negotiating about members' contributions and returns. Here, corporate lawyers and financial analysts play key roles in structuring the TS. They determine how costs and benefits will be allocated among member organizations as well as the legal obligations, decision-making responsibilities, and contractual rights of members.

In the case of strategic alliances and joint ventures, explicit strategies must be created for how the TS will perform its work. Change agents can help members define competitive advantage for the TS as well as the structural requirements necessary to support achievement of its goals.

4. *Evaluation stage.* This final stage of TD involves assessing how the TS is performing. Members need feedback so that they can identify problems and begin to resolve them. Feedback data generally include performance outcomes and member satisfactions, as well as indicators of how well members are interacting jointly. Change agents, for example, can periodically interview or survey member organizations about various outcomes and features of the TS and feed that data back to TS leaders. Such information will enable leaders to make necessary operational modifications and adjustments. It may signal the need to return to previous stages of TD to make necessary corrections, as shown by the feedback arrows in Figure 19.2.

Application 19.2 describes how a TD process was applied to develop a national coal policy that integrated both business and environmental points of view.[36] The change agents included members from both industry and environmental groups, as well as academic practitioners from Georgetown University.

Roles and Skills of the Change Agent

Transorganizational development is a relatively new application of planned change, and practitioners are still exploring appropriate roles and skills. They are discovering the complexities of working with underorganized systems comprising multiple organizations. This contrasts sharply with OD, which has traditionally been applied in single organizations that are heavily organized. Consequently, the roles and skills relevant to OD need to be modified and supplemented when applied to TD.

The major role demands of TD derive from the two prominent features of TSs: their underorganization and their multiorganization composition. Because TSs are underorganized, change agents need to play activist roles in creating and developing them.[37] They need to bring structure to a group of autonomous organizations that may not see the need to join together or may not know how to form an alliance. The activist role requires a good deal of leadership and direction, particularly during the initial stages of TD. For example, change agents may need to educate potential TS members about the benefits of joining together. They may need to structure face-to-face encounters aimed at sharing information and exploring interaction possibilities.

Because TSs are composed of multiple organizations, change agents need to maintain a neutral role, treating all members alike.[38] They need to be seen by members as working on behalf of the total system, rather than as being aligned with particular members or views. When change agents are perceived as neutral, TS members are more likely to share information with them and to listen to their inputs. Such neutrality can enhance change agents' ability to mediate conflicts among members. It can help them uncover diverse views and interests and forge agreements among stakeholders. Change agents, for example, can act as mediators, ensuring that members' views receive a fair hearing and that disputes are equitably resolved. They can help to bridge the different views and interests and achieve integrative solutions.

Given these role demands, the skills needed to practice TD include political and networking abilities.[39] Political competence is needed to understand and resolve the conflicts of interest and value dilemmas inherent in systems made up of multiple organizations, each seeking to maintain autonomy while jointly interacting.

APPLICATION 19·2   The National Coal Policy Project

The OPEC (Organization of Petroleum-Exporting Countries) oil embargo of 1973 made many Americans aware that the United States was too dependent on foreign oil as a source of energy. Coal was a promising alternative to oil—especially because the United States had substantial reserves of coal available. However, the development of coal reserves was not being pursued actively, largely because of the ecological problems associated with both its mining and its use. Environmentalists and coal industry representatives had often clashed in the courts, in Congress, and in the regulatory agencies over issues related to coal development. Many environmentalists had come to view their industrial counterparts as motivated only by profit and insensitive to ecological concerns; many industry members, in turn, saw environmentalists as radicals who wanted only to stop business growth.

Jerry Decker, a corporate energy manager from Dow Chemical Company, was dissatisfied enough with the situation to set about determining if environmental and business advocates could have a meaningful discussion on the issues. Decker and an environmentalist counterpart, Larry Moss, former president of the Sierra Club, persuaded representatives from industry and environmental groups to participate in a test meeting. The success of this meeting led them to examine future relationships and to establish the National Coal Policy Project (NCPP). The purpose of the project was to see if a consensus on national coal policy could be developed using nontraditional methods of collaboration.

Identifying the relevant members for the NCPP was a fairly straightforward process for Decker and Moss. The question, however, was whether to invite more than just environmental or industry stakeholders. For example, should outside parties likely to be affected by the process be asked to join the project? These included the transportation industry (trucking and railroads), labor unions, farmers and ranchers, consumers, and government officials who might have to help in implementing NCPP recommendations. Ultimately, Decker and Moss decided to focus only on environmental and industry representatives to enhance the likelihood of agreement among such "strange bedfellows."

Bringing together NCPP members proved to be more difficult. Decker was a respected leader in industry and trusted by even the most impassioned environmentalists. Moss, however, evoked mixed opinions. Several stakeholders claimed that he had "pronuclear" views, that he had little experience in coal issues, and that he was using the project to develop contacts for his newly established consulting firm. Another observer, however, described him as "one of the nation's most effective and best-known environmentalists."

Most of the coal-producing and coal-consuming industries contacted by Decker and Moss were willing to participate in the project. The exceptions included the aluminum and paper industries that expressed a preference for continuing the traditional methods of resolving their disputes with environmentalists. In addition, the president of one powerful coal industry lobby privately expressed his support for the NCPP but believed that his participation might be seen as a conciliatory move that would diminish his stature as a strong lobbyist. He nominated a less well-known member from his board of directors.

The response from the environmental groups was mixed. Of the groups that declined to participate, some questioned whether such a project could possibly succeed in resolving the issues. Others, operating on a limited budget, were reluctant to spare personnel and financial resources for such an experimental effort. Still others questioned the appropriateness of resolving issues outside of the established forums developed by Congress, the courts, and the regulatory agencies.

Despite the concerns of many potential stakeholders, the NCPP formally began its work in January 1977. With the help of the Center for Strategic and International Studies (CSIS) at Georgetown University, the project was organized into five task forces devoted to air pollution, mining, transportation, energy pricing, and fuel utilization and conservation. Each task force had an equal number of representatives from industry and environmental groups and was co-chaired by a member of each group. Each task force met several times during the year that the project took place, frequently making field trips to mining sites or other areas that would provide useful information for task force discussions. The task forces were assisted by a plenary group composed of task force co-chairs Decker and Moss, a project director from CSIS, and plenary chairman Frank Quinn, a labor mediator from Temple University.

Following a year of discussions, participants of the NCPP held a news conference in Washington, D.C., to announce a set of two hundred recommendations covering various aspects of coal policy in the United States. Two of the NCPP's recommendations were drafted into bills introduced to the U.S. House of Representatives in 1980. HR 1430, an amendment to the Clean Air Act, proposed a streamlined procedure for licensing new coal-fired power plants while providing funds to interest groups seeking to participate in the licensing process. HR 1431 sought to authorize the Environmental Protection Agency to institute an emission tax and rebate plan giving coal-using firms an incentive to reduce their emissions. Although both measures were considered twice by the

House, neither bill was enacted. Other NCPP recommendations were adopted by the Office of Surface Mining.

Finally, many NCPP participants cited a change in their attitudes as an outcome of the project. John Corcoran, industry chair of the mining task force, recalled that before the NCPP, "I knew a few environmentalists and I came to the judgment they were all misguided." Following participation, he observed, "If I were opening a new surface mine or constructing a coal-burning facility involving unique or sensitive environmental issues, I am convinced that reviewing my plans and my projects with concerned environmental groups like those involved in the NCPP project could save months and perhaps years of litigation." Additional evidence of changed attitudes was provided by a survey that found participants reporting a higher level of understanding of the concerns and interests of both sides. ■

Political savvy can help change agents manage their own roles and values in respect to those power dynamics. It can help them to avoid being coopted by certain TS members and thus losing their neutrality.

Networking skills are also indispensable to TD practitioners. These include the ability to manage lateral relations among autonomous organizations in the relative absence of hierarchical control. Change agents must be able to span the boundaries of diverse organizations, link them together, and facilitate exchanges among them. They must be able to form linkages where none existed and to transform networks into operational systems capable of joint task performance.

Defining the roles and skills of TD practitioners is still in a formative stage. Our knowledge in this area will continue to develop as more experience is gained with TSs. Change agents are discovering, for example, that the complexity of TSs requires a team consulting approach, involving practitioners with different skills and approaches working together to promote TS effectiveness. Initial reports of TD practice suggest that such change projects are large scale and long term,[40] typically involving multiple, simultaneous interventions aimed at both the total TS and its constituent members. The stages of TD application are protracted, requiring considerable time and effort to identify relevant organizations, to convene them, and to organize them for task performance.

MERGERS AND ACQUISITIONS

Mergers and acquisitions (M&As) involve the combination of two organizations. The term *merger* refers to the integration of two previously independent organizations into a completely new organization; *acquisition* involves the purchase of one organization by another for integration into the acquiring organization. M&As are distinct from TSs, such as alliances and joint ventures, because at least one of the organizations ceases to exist. The stressful dynamics associated with M&As led one researcher to call them the "ultimate change management challenge."[41]

M&A Rationale

Organizations have a number of reasons for wanting to acquire or merge with other firms, including diversification or vertical integration; gaining access to global markets, technology, or other resources; and achieving operational efficiencies, improved innovation, or resource sharing.[42] As a result, M&As have become a preferred method for rapid growth and strategic change. For example, the value of U.S. domestic M&A transactions was more than $488 billion in 1997 and more than $800 billion in 1998.[43] The total value of M&A activity on a worldwide basis was expected to exceed $2 trillion in 1999. Recent large transactions include Chrysler and Daimler-Benz, CBS and Viacom, Ford and Volvo, Boeing and McDonnell Douglas, and WorldCom and MCI. Despite M&A popularity, they have a questionable record of success.[44] Among the reasons commonly cited for merger failure are inadequate due diligence processes, lack of a compelling strategic rationale, unrealistic expectations of synergy, paying too much for the transaction, conflicting corporate cultures, and failure to move quickly.[45]

M&A interventions typically are preceded by an examination of corporate and business strategy. Corporate strategy describes the range of businesses within which the firm will participate, and business strategy specifies how the organization will compete in any particular business. Organizations must decide whether their corporate and strategic goals should be achieved through administrative or competitive responses, such as ISC, or through collective responses, such as TD or M&As. Mergers and acquisitions are preferred when internal development is too slow, or when alliances or joint ventures do not offer sufficient control over key resources to meet the firm's objectives.

M&As are complex strategic changes that involve various legal and financial requirements beyond the scope of this text. OD practitioners are encouraged to seek out and work with specialists in these other relevant disciplines. The focus here is on how OD can contribute to M&A success.

Application Stages

Mergers and acquisitions involve three major phases as shown in Table 19.1: precombination, legal combination, and operational combination.[46] OD practitioners

Table 19•1	Major Phases and Activities in Merger and Acquisitions	
MAJOR M&A PHASES	**KEY STEPS**	**OD AND CHANGE MANAGEMENT ISSUES**
Precombination	• Search for and select candidate • Create M&A team • Establish business case • Perform due diligence assessment • Develop merger integration plans	• Ensure that candidates are screened for cultural as well as financial, technical, and physical asset criteria • Define a clear leadership structure • Establish a clear strategic vision, competitive strategy, and systems integration potential • Specify the desirable organization design features • Specify an integration action plan
Legal combination	• Complete financial negotiations • Close the deal • Announce the combination	
Operational combination	• Day 1 activities • Organizational and technical integration activities • Cultural integration activities	• Implement changes quickly • Communicate • Solve problems together and focus on the customer • Conduct an evaluation to learn and identify further areas of integration planning

can make substantive contributions to the precombination and operational combination phases as described below.

Precombination Phase

This first phase consists of planning activities designed to ensure the success of the combined organizations. The organization that initiates the strategic change must identify a candidate organization, work with it to gather information about each other, and plan the implementation and integration activities. The evidence is growing that precombination phase activities are critical to M&A success.[47]

1. *Search for and select candidate.* This involves developing screening criteria to assess and narrow the field of candidate organizations, agreeing on a first-choice candidate, assessing regulatory compliance, establishing initial contacts, and formulating a letter of intent. Criteria for choosing an M&A partner can include leadership and management characteristics, market access resources, technical or financial capabilities, physical facilities, and so on. OD practitioners can add value at this stage of the process by encouraging screening criteria that include managerial, organizational, and cultural components as well as technical and financial aspects. In practice, financial issues tend to receive greater attention at this stage, with the goal of maximizing shareholder value. Failure to attend to cultural and organizational issues, however, can result in diminished shareholder value during the operational combination phase.[48]

    Identifying potential candidates, narrowing the field, agreeing on a first choice, and checking regulatory compliance are relatively straightforward activities. They generally involve investment brokers and other outside parties who have access to databases of organizational, financial, and technical information. The final two activities, making initial contacts and creating a letter of intent, are aimed at determining the candidate's interest in the proposed merger or acquisition.

2. *Create an M&A team.* Once there is initial agreement between the two organizations to pursue a merger or acquisition, senior leaders from the respective organizations appoint an M&A team to establish the business case, to oversee the due diligence process, and to develop a merger integration plan.[49] This team typically comprises senior executives and experts in such areas as business valuation, technology, organization, and marketing. OD practitioners can facilitate formation of this team through human process interventions, such as team building and process consultation, and help the team establish clear goals and action strategies. They also can help members define a clear leadership structure, apply relevant skills and knowledge, and ensure that both organizations are represented appropriately. The group's leadership structure, or who will be accountable for the team's accomplishments, is especially critical. In an acquisition, an executive from the acquiring firm is typically the team's leader. In a merger of equals, the choice of a single individual to lead the team is more difficult, but must be made. The outcome of this decision and the process used to make it form the first outward symbol of how this strategic change will be conducted.

3. *Establish the business case.* The purpose of this activity is to develop a prima facie case that combining the two organizations will result in a competitive advantage that exceeds their separate advantages.[50] It includes specifying the strategic vision, competitive strategy, and systems integration potential for the M&A. OD practitioners can facilitate this discussion to ensure that each issue is fully explored. If the business case cannot be justified on strategic, financial,

and operational grounds, the M&A should be revisited, terminated, or another candidate should be sought.

Strategic vision represents the organizations' combined capabilities. It synthesizes the strengths of the two organizations into a viable new organization. For example, AT&T had a clear picture of its intentions in acquiring NCR: to "link people, organizations, and their information in a seamless global computer network."

Competitive strategy describes the business model for how the combined organization will add value in a particular product market or segment of the value chain, how that value proposition is best performed by the combined organization (compared with competitors), and how that proposition will be difficult to imitate. The purpose of this activity is to force the two organizations to go beyond the rhetoric of "these two organizations should merge because it's a good fit." The AT&T and NCR acquisition struggled, in part, because NCR management was told simply to "look for synergies."[51]

Systems integration specifies how the two organizations will be combined. It addresses how and if they can work together. It includes such key questions as Will one firm be acquired and operated as a wholly owned subsidiary? Does the transaction imply a merger of equals? Are layoffs implied, and if so, where? On what basis can promised synergies or cost savings be achieved?

4. *Perform a due diligence assessment.* This involves evaluating whether the two organizations actually have the managerial, technical, and financial resources that each assumes the other possesses. It includes a comprehensive review of each organization's articles of incorporation, stock option plans, organization charts, and so on. Financial, human resources, operational, technical, and logistical inventories are evaluated along with other legally binding issues. The discovery of previously unknown or unfavorable information can stop the M&A process from going forward.

Although due diligence assessment traditionally emphasizes the financial aspects of M&As, this focus is increasingly being challenged by evidence that culture clashes between two organizatons can ruin expected financial gains.[52] Thus, attention to the cultural features of M&As is becoming more prevalent in due diligence assessment. For example, Abitibi-Price applied a cultural screen as part of its due diligence activities along with financial and operational criteria. The process sought to identify the fit between Abitibi's values and those of possible merger candidates. Stone Consolidated emerged as both a good strategic and cultural fit with Abitibi. This cultural assessment contributed heavily to the success of the subsequent merger.

The scope and detail of due diligence assessment depend on knowledge of the candidate's business, the complexity of its industry, the relative size and risk of the transaction, and the available resources. Due diligence activities must reflect symbolically the vision and values of the combined organizations. An overly zealous assessment, for example, can contradict promises of openness and trust made earlier in the transaction. Missteps at this stage can lower or destroy opportunities for synergy, cost savings, and improved shareholder value.[53]

5. *Develop merger integration plans.* This stage specifies how the two organizations will be combined.[54] It defines integration objectives; the scope and timing of integration activities; organization design criteria; Day 1 requirements; and who does what, where, and when. The scope of these plans depends on how integrated the organizations will be. If the candidate organization will operate as an independent subsidiary with an "arm's-length" relationship to the parent,

merger integration planning need only specify those systems that will be common to both organizations. A full integration of the two organizations requires a more extensive plan.

Merger integration planning starts with the business case conducted earlier and involves more detailed analyses of the strategic vision, competitive strategy, and systems integration for the M&A. For example, assessment of the organizations' markets and suppliers can reveal opportunities to serve customers better and to capture purchasing economies of scale. Examination of business processes can identify best operating practices; which physical facilities should be combined, left alone, or shutdown; and which systems and procedures are redundant. Capital budget analysis can show which investments should be continued or dropped. Typically, the M&A team appoints subgroups composed of members from both organizations to perform these analyses. OD practitioners can conduct team building and process consultation interventions to improve how those groups function.

Next, plans for designing the combined organization are developed. They include the organization's structure, reporting relationships, human resources policies, information and control systems, operating logistics, work designs, and customer-focused activities.

The final task of integration planning involves developing an action plan for implementing the M&A. This specifies tasks to be performed, decision-making authority and responsibility, and timelines for achievement. It also includes a process for addressing conflicts and problems that will invariably arise during the implementation process.

Legal Combination Phase

This phase of the M&A process involves the legal and financial aspects of the transaction. The two organizations settle on the terms of the deal, register the transaction with and gain approval from appropriate regulatory agencies, communicate with and gain approval from shareholders, and file appropriate legal documents. In some cases, an OD practitioner can provide advice on negotiating a fair agreement, but this phase generally requires knowledge and expertise beyond that typically found in OD practice.

Operational Combination Phase

This final phase involves implementing the merger integration plan. In practice, it begins during due diligence assessment and may continue for months or years following the legal combination phase.[55] M&A implementation includes the three kinds of activities described below.

1. *Day 1 activities.* These include communications and actions that offically start the implementation process. For example, announcements may be made about key executives of the combined organization, the location of corporate headquarters, the structure of tasks, and areas and functions where layoffs will occur. M&A practitioners pay special attention to sending important symbolic messages to organization members, investors, and regulators about the soundness of the merger plans and those changes that are critical to accomplishing strategic and operational objectives.[56]

2. *Operational and technical integration activities.* These involve the physical moves, structural changes, work designs, and procedures that will be implemented to accomplish the strategic objectives and expected cost savings of the

M&A. The merger integration plan lists these activities, which can be large in number and range in scope from seemingly trivial to quite critical. For example, American Airlines' acquisition of Reno Air involved changing Reno's employee uniforms, the signage at all airports, marketing and public relations campaigns, repainting airplanes, and integrating the route structures, among others. When these integration activities are not executed properly, the M&A process can be set back. American's poor job of clarifying the wage and benefit programs caused an unauthorized pilot "sickout" that cancelled many flights and left thousands of travelers stranded. Finally, integrating the reservation, scheduling, and pricing systems was a critical activity. Failure to execute this task quickly could have caused tremendous logistical problems, increased safety risks, and further alienated customers.

3. *Cultural integration activities.* These tasks are aimed at building new values and norms in the organization. Successful implementation melds both the technical and cultural aspects of the combined organization. For example, members from both organizations can be encouraged to solve business problems together, thus addressing operational and cultural integration issues simultaneously.[57]

The M&A literature contains several practical suggestions for managing the operational combination phase. First, the merger integration plan should be implemented sooner rather than later, and quickly rather than slowly. Integration of two organizations generally involves aggressive financial targets, short timelines, and intense public scrutiny.[58] Moreover, the change process is often plagued by culture clashes and political fighting. Consequently, organizations need to make as many changes as possible in the first one hundred days following the legal combination phase.[59] Quick movement in key areas has several advantages: it preempts unanticipated organization changes that might thwart momentum in the desired direction, it reduces organization members' uncertainty about when things will happen, and it reduces the anxiety of the activity's impact on the individual's situation. All three of these conditions can prevent desired collaboration and other benefits from occurring.

Second, integration activities must be communicated clearly and in a timely fashion to a variety of stakeholders, including shareholders, regulators, customers, and organization members. M&As can increase uncertainty and anxiety about the future, especially for members of the involved organizations who often inquire, "Will I have a job? Will my job change? Will I have a new boss?" These kind of questions can dominate conversations, reduce productive work, and spoil opportunities for collaboration. To reduce ambiguity, organizations can provide concrete answers through a variety of channels including company newsletters, email and intranet postings, press releases, video and in-person presentations, one-on-one interaction with managers, and so on.

Third, members from both organizations need to work together to solve implementation problems and to address customer needs. Such coordinated tasks can clarify work roles and relationships; they can contribute to member commitment and motivation. Moreover, when coordinated activity is directed at customer service, it can assure customers that their interests will be considered and satisfied during the merger.

Fourth, organizations need to assess the implementation process continually to identify integration problems and needs. The following questions can guide the assessment process:[60]

- Have savings estimated during precombination planning been confirmed or exceeded?
- Has the new entity identified and implemented shared strategies or opportunities?
- Has the new organization been implemented without loss of key personnel?
- Was the merger and integration process seen as fair and objective?
- Is the combined company operating efficiently?
- Have major problems with stakeholders been avoided?
- Did the process proceed according to schedule?
- Were substantive integration issues resolved?
- Are people highly motivated (more so than before)?

Mergers and acquisitions are among the most complex and challenging interventions facing organizations and OD practitioners. Application 19.3 describes the M&A process at Daimler-Benz and Chrysler. It clearly demonstrates the importance of cultural issues in mergers and the role that organization development can play in the process.[61]

■ SUMMARY

In this chapter, we presented interventions aimed at improving organization and environment relationships. Organizations are open systems that exist in environmental contexts and they must establish and maintain effective linkages with the environment to survive and prosper. Three types of environments affect organizational functioning: the general environment, the task environment, and the enacted environment. Only the last environment can affect organizational choices about behavior, but the first two impact the consequences of those actions. Two environmental dimensions, information uncertainty and resource dependence, affect the degree to which organizations are constrained by their environments and need to be responsive to them. For example, when information uncertainty and resource dependence are high, organizations are maximally constrained and need to be responsive to their environments.

Integrated strategic change is a comprehensive intervention for addressing organization and environment issues. It gives equal weight to the strategic and organizational factors affecting organization performance and effectiveness. In addition, these factors are highly integrated during the process of assessing the current strategy and organization design, selecting the desired strategic orientation, developing a strategic change plan, and implementing it.

Transorganizational development is a form of planned change aimed at helping organizations create partnerships with other organizations to perform tasks or to solve problems that are too complex and multifaceted for single organizations to carry out. Because these multiorganization systems tend to be underorganized, TD follows the stages of planned change relevant to underorganized systems: identification, convention, organization, and evaluation. TD is a relatively new application of planned change, and appropriate change-agent roles and skills are being formulated.

Mergers and acquisitions involve combining two or more organizations to achieve strategic and financial objectives. It generally involves three phases:

APPLICATION 19·3   Merging Mercedes and Chrysler

On November 17, 1998, Daimler-Benz, Germany's most revered brand name, and Chrysler, America's number-three car company, merged to become the world's fifth-largest car maker. The $40.5 billion merger was the largest merger in the history of the automobile manufacturing business.

The process began in the early 1990s when Daimler executives began asking the question, What is happening in the international motor industry? Their discussions led to the conclusion that Mercedes automobiles were reaching the limits of their market. Although they sold a little more than 508,000 vehicles in 1993, the likelihood of ever selling more than a million in the "already mature" markets was slight. Daimler's marquis name brand made it difficult to enter emerging and other high-volume markets. Moreover, if Mercedes remained in a specialized niche, they might not be able to benefit quickly from new technologies. Innovators would have little incentive to license their advanced technology to a small market player. As a result, Daimler began looking for a partner who could increase its scope of operations.

The process heated up during the mid-1990s because of overcapacity in the global automotive industry. Daimler examined every automotive manufacturer in the world and concluded that Chrysler was the top candidate because of its complementary product line and geographical distribution. The two companies began the first of three rounds of talks in 1995. Their first attempt at working together was an ill-fated Latin American joint venture. In 1997, they began a second round of merger discussions, but shortly after the talks began, Ford was expressed interest in a joint venture and approached Daimler. That deal fell through when the Ford family wanted too much ownership control. The third round of talks between Daimler and Chrysler culminated in the May 7, 1998, merger announcement. In the announcement, Jurgen Schrempp and Robert Eaton were named co-chairs of DaimlerChrysler, a merger of equals.

Wall Street gave the merger an instant blessing. The business case looked very good along product, geography, and financial lines, but there were concerns about the differences in culture. First, there was very little product overlap. Mercedes luxury cars competed in a segment beyond Chrysler's target markets, which included minivans, pickup trucks, and sport-utility vehicles. The only models competing against each other were the Jeep Grand Cherokee and Mercedes M-class. Second, each company had a strong geographic presence where the other was weak: Chrysler was focused on North America (93 percent of revenues) whereas Mercedes received 63 percent of its sales from Europe. The combination allowed both firms to make a strong entry into the Latin American market. Third, both organizations had healthy balance sheets.

However, strong reservations emerged concerning the cultural fit. Organizationally, Chrysler was a lean, centralized, low-cost producer; Mercedes was a high-quality, bureaucratic, and staid organization. Cultural artifacts were easy to identify. For example, meetings at Chrysler were typically under an hour and involved little documentation; Daimler meetings were long periods of time spent poring over reams of reports. Moreover, German and American social cultures are quite different in terms of risk, individualism, and punctuality.

Still, the two organizations saw great opportunities in cost savings, especially in logistics, purchasing, and finance. Subsequent announcements promised savings of $1.4 billion in the first year of operations. According to Gary Verlade, DaimlerChrysler AG executive vice president of global procurement and supply, the new organization would be able to optimize worldwide capacity, enjoy increased purchasing power with suppliers, and capitalize on cost savings derived from shared technology. He suggested that it would take between three and five years to consolidate purchasing for the two companies—an aggressive target. Combining manufacturing would take much longer.

Prior to the formal close of the transaction, the integration team announced the structure and principles for the postmerger consolidation process. First, Thomas Stallkamp, Chrysler's president, was announced as head of the integration effort. Second, issue resolution teams were established to help address key concerns. The first five teams were banded under the category of global automotive integration, which included product development, volume production, global sales and marketing, raw materials and parts sourcing, and global automotive strategizing. Others were grouped under companywide functions such as finance, human resources, information technology, and research and development. Issue resolution teams would report to an integration team, which would report to the DaimlerChrysler board every four weeks. Third, the integration process was to be shaped by eight basic principles, including:

1. Maintain the base: The store has to remain open during remodeling.
2. Focus on "value-drivers," those activities that create the greatest near-term customer value.
3. Maintain and build on the strengths of both companies to create a whole greater than the sum of its parts.
4. Decide and implement swiftly.
5. Affected parties are participating parties.

6. Pragmatism must come before perfectionism.

7. Accommodate change.

8. Despite the effort and urgency, remember that post-merger integration is temporary.

Shortly after the merger was finalized in November, Schrempp and Eaton named the senior executives for the new organization as well as the key structural features. The organization was to have dual headquarters, Auburn Hills, Michigan, in North America, and Stuttgart, in Germany. The purpose of having two headquarters was to avoid confusion as to whether the new organization was Chrysler or Daimler dominated. In addition, initial consolidation and integration would occur in the finance, purchasing, and other staff organizations.

More than a year after the merger was announced, DaimlerChrysler has withstood a number of challenges, almost all of which can be seen as originating in the different cultures. This includes a large exodus of Chrysler employees, problems achieving promised synergies, and difficulties merging human resources practices.

Perhaps the most symbolic of the problems Daimler-Chrysler faced in its execution of the postmerger integration was the September 1999 announcement that Stallkamp, the head of the integration team, was leaving the organization. He joined several other key Chrysler executives who had left the organization because of their perception that the new organization was going to be more German than American. Some executives reported that they feared being hobbled by the more deliberate, stodgy German process of management. Schrempp's style was more hierarchical and control oriented, and contrasted sharply with Chrysler's matrix management style that encourages teamwork and produces surprisingly harmonious results. Then in October 1999, Shrempp an-

nounced a restructuring of the organization into three groups: Chrysler, Mercedes, and commercial products. This structure gave considerable autonomy to the North American organization, in effect putting further integration efforts on hold and raising concerns over whether the new organization would be able to deliver on its promised $1.4 billion in cost savings.

In fact, the integration effort had run into several snags. Stallkamp's integration team had identified about five hundred potential changes with the top ninety-eight changes expected to produce the promised savings. Finance and purchasing were considered top candidates for savings, but the purchasing integration went more slowly than expected because of differences in their purchasing specifications for steel and other materials and their different ways of approaching supplier relationships. In addition, squabbles among the integration team slowed decision making. Whenever a conflict arose concerning where to cut costs, powerful members pushed the decision up to the board.

A related problem the organization had to face was the different human resources practices, most importantly compensation. Executive pay at Chrysler was much higher than at Daimler-Benz. In addition, there were big differences between European and American union contracts, including benefits and vacation time, that were driven by different cultural assumptions. For example, Daimler employees flew first class whereas only senior executives were allowed to fly first class at Chrysler. Like many other seemingly mundane issues, the travel policy became a sore point and took more than six months to resolve. With respect to the compensation problem, the new board had to approve drastic changes in pay packages to put German executives on an equal footing with their American counterparts. This made realizing the promised cost savings more difficult. ■

precombination, legal combination, and operational combination. The M&A process has been dominated by financial and technical concerns, but experience and research strongly support the contribution that OD practitioners can make to M&A success.

■ NOTES

1. R. Miles, *Macro Organization Behavior* (Santa Monica, Calif.: Goodyear, 1980); R. Daft, *Organization Theory and Design* (Cincinnati, Ohio: South-Western College Publishing, 1998).

2. K. Weick, *The Social Psychology of Organizing*, 2d ed. (Reading, Mass.: Addison-Wesley, 1979).

3. J. Galbraith, *Competing with Flexible Lateral Organizations*, 2d ed. (Reading, Mass.: Addison-Wesley, 1994); P. Evans

and T. Wurster, "Strategy and the New Economics of Information," *Harvard Business Review* 75 (1997): 70–83.

4. J. Pfeffer and G. Salancik, *The External Control of Organizations: A Resource Dependence Perspective* (New York: Harper & Row, 1978).

5. H. Aldrich, *Organizations and Environments* (New York: Prentice Hall, 1979); L. Hrebiniak and W. Joyce, "Organizational Adaptation: Strategic Choice and Environmental Determinism," *Administrative Science Quarterly* 30 (1985): 336–49.

6. J. Collins and J. Porras, "Building Your Company's Vision," *Harvard Business Review* (September-October 1996): 65–77; D. Calfee, "Get Your Mission Statement Working," *Management Review* (January 1993): 54–57; J. Pearce II and F. David, "Corporate Mission Statements: The Bottom Line," *Academy of Management Executive* 1 (1987): 109–16; F. David, "How Companies Define Their Mission," *Long-Range Planning* 22 (1989): 90–97; Peter F. Drucker Foundation, *The Drucker Foundation Self-Assessment Tool: Process Guide* (San Francisco: Peter F. Drucker Foundation and Jossey-Bass, 1999), http://www.pfdf.org/leaderbooks/sat/mission.html.

7. C. Hofer and D. Schendel, *Strategy Formulation: Analytic Concepts* (St. Paul, Minn.: West Publishing, 1978).

8. Pfeffer and Salancik, *External Control of Organizations*.

9. J. Barney, *Gaining and Sustaining Competitive Advantage* (Reading, Mass.: Addison-Wesley, 1996).

10. R. Nelson and S. Winter, *An Evolutionary Theory of Economic Change* (Cambridge, Mass.: Belknap Press, 1982).

11. P. Selznick, *Leadership in Administration* (New York: Harper & Row, 1957); M. Peteraf, "The Cornerstones of Competitive Advantage: A Resource-Based View," *Strategic Management Journal* 14 (1993): 179–92.

12. R. Grant, *Contemporary Strategy Analysis,* 3d ed. (Malden, Mass.: Blackwell, 1998); Barney, *Competitive Advantage*.

13. Aldrich, *Organizations and Environments*.

14. W. Ouchi, *The M-Form Society: How American Teamwork Can Recapture the Competitive Edge* (Reading, Mass.: Addison-Wesley, 1984); L. Thurow, *Head to Head: The Coming Economic Battle Among Japan, Europe, and America* (New York: William Morrow, 1992).

15 M. Jelinek and J. Litterer, "Why OD Must Become Strategic," in *Organizational Change and Development*, vol. 2, eds. W. Pasmore and R. Woodman (Greenwich, Conn.: JAI Press, 1988): 135–62; A. Bhambri and L. Pate, "Introduction—The Strategic Change Agenda: Stimuli, Processes, and Outcomes," *Journal of Organization Change Management* 4 (1991): 4–6; D. Nadler, M. Gerstein, R. Shaw, and associates, eds., *Organizational Architecture* (San Francisco: Jossey-Bass, 1992); C. Worley, D. Hitchin, and W. Ross, *Integrated Strategic Change: How Organization Development Builds Competitive Advantage* (Reading, Mass.: Addison-Wesley, 1996).

16. C. Worley, D. Hitchin, R. Patchett, R. Barnett, and J. Moss, "Unburn the Bridge, Get to Bedrock, and Put Legs on the Dream: Looking at Strategy Implementation with Fresh Eyes" (paper presented to the Western Academy of Management, Redondo Beach, Calif., March 1999).

17. H. Mintzberg, *The Rise and Fall of Strategic Planning* (New York: Free Press, 1994).

18. Worley, Hitchin, and Ross, *Integrated Strategic Change*.

19. P. Senge, *The Fifth Discipline* (New York: Doubleday, 1990); E. Lawler, *The Ultimate Advantage* (San Francisco: Jossey-Bass, 1992); Worley, Hitchin, and Ross, *Integrated Strategic Change*.

20. L. Greiner and V. Schein, *Power and Organization Development* (Reading, Mass.: Addison-Wesley, 1988).

21. M. Porter, *Competitive Strategy* (New York: Free Press, 1980).

22. Grant, *Contemporary Strategy Analysis*.

23. M. Porter, *Competitive Advantage* (New York: Free Press, 1985).

24. R. Miles and C. Snow, *Organization Strategy, Structure, and Process* (New York: McGraw-Hill, 1978); M. Tushman and E. Romanelli, "Organizational Evolution: A Metamorphosis Model of Convergence and Reorientation," in *Research in Organizational Behavior*, vol. 7, eds. L. Cummings and B. Staw (Greenwich, Conn.: JAI Press, 1985).

25. J. Naisbitt and P. Aburdene, *Reinventing the Corporation* (New York: Warner Books, 1985); A. Toffler, *The Third Wave* (New York: McGraw-Hill, 1980); A. Toffler, *The Adaptive Corporation* (New York: McGraw-Hill, 1984); M. Weisbord, *Productive Workplaces* (San Francisco: Jossey-Bass, 1987).

26. E. Lawler III, *The Ultimate Advantage* (San Francisco: Jossey-Bass, 1992); M. Tushman, W. Newman, and E. Romanelli, "Convergence and Upheaval: Managing the Unsteady Pace of Organizational Evolution," *California Management Review* 29 (1987): 1–16; Nadler et al., *Organizational Architecture*; R. Buzzell and B. Gale, *The PIMS Principles* (New York: Free Press, 1987).

27. L. Hrebiniak and W. Joyce, *Implementing Strategy* (New York: Macmillan, 1984); J. Galbraith and R. Kazanjian, *Strategy Implementation: Structure, Systems, and Process,* 2d ed. (St. Paul, Minn.: West Publishing, 1986).

28. T. Cummings, "Transorganizational Development," in *Research in Organizational Behavior,* vol. 6, eds. B. Staw and L. Cummings (Greenwich, Conn.: JAI Press, 1984): 367–422.

29. B. Gray, "Conditions Facilitating Interorganizational Collaboration," *Human Relations* 38 (1985): 911–36; K. Harrigan and W. Newman, "Bases of Interorganization Co-Operation: Propensity, Power, Persistence," *Journal of Management Studies* 27 (1990): 417–34; Cummings, "Transorganizational Development."

30. Cummings, "Transorganizational Development."

31. C. Raben, "Building Strategic Partnerships: Creating and Managing Effective Joint Ventures," in *Organizational Architecture,* eds. Nadler et al. (San Francisco: Jossey-Bass, 1992): 81–109; B. Gray, *Collaborating: Finding Common Ground for Multiparty Problems* (San Francisco: Jossey-Bass, 1989); Harrigan and Newman, "Bases of Interorganization Co-operation"; P. Lorange and J. Roos, "Analytical Steps in the Formation of Strategic Alliances," *Journal of Organizational Change Management* 4 (1991): 60–72; B. Gomes-Casseres, "Managing International Alliances: Conceptual Framework," *Harvard Business School Note 9-793-133* (Boston: Harvard Business School Publishing, 1993).

32. D. Boje, "Towards a Theory and Praxis of Transorganizational Development: Stakeholder Networks and Their Habitats" (working paper 79-6, Behavioral and Organizational Science Study Center, Graduate School of Management, University of California, Los Angeles, February 1982); B. Gricar, "The Legitimacy of Consultants and Stakeholders in Interorganizational Problems" (paper presented at annual meeting of the Academy of Management, San Diego, Calif., August 1981); T. Williams, "The Search Conference in Active Adaptive Planning," *Journal of Applied Behavioral Science* 16 (1980): 470–83; B. Gray and T. Hay, "Political Limits to Interorganizational Consensus and Change," *Journal of Applied Behavioral Science* 22 (1986): 95–112.

33. E. Trist, "Referent Organizations and the Development of Interorganizational Domains" (paper presented at annual meeting of the Academy of Management, Atlanta, August 1979).

34. Cummings, "Transorganizational Development."

35. Raben, "Building Strategic Partnerships."

36. Adapted from Gray and Hay, "Political Limits."

37. Cummings, "Transorganizational Development."

38. Ibid.

39. B. Gricar and D. Brown, "Conflict, Power, and Organization in a Changing Community," *Human Relations* 34 (1981): 877–93.

40. Cummings, "Transorganizational Development."

41. T. Galpin and D. Robinson, "Merger Integration: The Ultimate Change Management Challenge," *Mergers and Acquisitions* 31(1997): 24–29.

42. M. Marks and P. Mirvis, *Joining Forces: Making One Plus One Equal Three in Mergers, Acquisitions, and Alliances* (San Francisco: Jossey-Bass, 1998).

43. R. Smith and I. Walter, "1998 Global Capital Market Activity and Market Shares of Leading Competitors." http:\\www.stern.edu/~rsmith/Gorilla_Tables.htm, accessed December 2, 1999.

44. A variety of studies have questioned whether merger and acquisition activity actually generates benefits to the organization or its shareholders, including M. Porter, "From Competitive Advantage to Corporate Strategy," *Harvard Business Review* (May-June 1978): 43–59; "Merger Integration Problems," *Leadership and Organization Development Journal* 19 (1998): 59–60; "Why Good Deals Miss the Bull's-Eye: Slow Integration, Poor Communication Torpedo Prospects for Creating Value," *Mergers and Acquisitions* 33 (1999): 5; T. Brush, "Predicted Change in Operational Synergy and Post-Acquisition Performance of Acquired Businesses," *Strategic Management Journal* 17 (1996): 1–24; and P. Zweig with J. Perlman, S. Anderson, and K. Gudridge, "The Case Against Mergers," *Business Week* (30 October 1995): 122–30. The research includes an A. T. Kearney study of 115 multibillion-dollar, global mergers between 1993 and 1996 where 58 percent failed to create "substantial returns for shareholders," measured by tangible returns in the form of dividends and stock price appreciation; a Mercer Management Consulting study of all mergers from 1990 to 1996 where nearly half "destroyed" shareholder value; a PriceWaterhouseCoopers study of 97 acquirers that completed deals worth $500 million or more from 1994 to 1997 and where two-thirds of the buyer's stocks dropped on announcement of the transaction and "a year later" a third of the losers still were lagging the levels of peer-company shares or the stock market in general; and a European study of 300 companies that found that planning for restructuring was poorly thought out and underfunded. Similarly, despite the large

amount of writing on the subject, a large proportion of firms involved in mergers have not gotten the message that postmerger integration is the key to success. For example, in the A. T. Kearny study, only 39 percent of the cases had set up a management team in the first one hundred days and only 28 percent had a clear vision of corporate goals when the acquisition began.

45. Zweig et al., "Case Against Mergers."

46. Marks and Mirvis, *Joining Forces;* R. Ashkenas, L. DeMonaco, and S. Francis, "Making the Deal Real: How GE Capital Integrates Acquisitions," *Harvard Business Review* (January-February 1998); B. Brunsman, S. Sanderson, and M. Van de Voorde. "How to Achieve Value Behind the Deal During Merger Integration," *Oil and Gas Journal* 96 (1998): 21–30; A. Fisher, "How to Make a Merger Work," *Fortune* (24 January 1994): 66–70; K. Kostuch, R. Malchione, and I. Marten, "Post-Merger Integration: Creating or Destroying Value?" *Corporate Board* 19 (1998): 7–11; A. Kruse, "Merging Cultures: How OD Adds Value in Mergers and Acquisitions" (presentation to the ODNetwork meeting, San Diego, Calif., October 1999); M. Sirower, "Constructing a Synergistic Base for Premier Deals," *Mergers and Acquisitions* 32 (1998): 42–50; D. Jemison and S. Sitkin, "Corporate Acquisitions: A Process Perspective," *Academy of Management Review* 11 (1986): 145–63.

47. Ashkenas, DeMonaco, and Francis, "Making the Deal Real"; G. Ledford, C. Siehl, M. McGrath, and J. Miller, "Managing Mergers and Acquisitions" (working paper, Center for Effective Organizations, University of Southern California, Los Angeles, 1985).

48. Ledford et al., "Managing Mergers and Acquisitions"; B. Blumenthal, "The Right Talent Mix to Make Mergers Work," *Mergers and Acquisitions* (September-October 1995): 26–31; A. Buono, J. Bowditch, and J. Lewis, "When Cultures Collide: The Anatomy of a Merger," *Human Relations* 38 (1985): 477–500; D. Tipton, "Understanding Employee Views Regarding Impending Mergers to Minimize Integration Turmoil" (unpublished Master's thesis, Pepperdine University, 1998).

49. Marks and Mirvis, *Joining Forces;* Ashkenas, DeMonaco, and Francis, "Making the Deal Real."

50. Sirower, "Constructing a Synergistic Base"; Brunsman, Sanderson, and Van de Voorde, "How to Achieve Value."

51. Sirower, "Constructing a Synergistic Base."

52. Ledford et al., "Managing Mergers and Acquisitions."

53. S. Elias, "Due Diligence," http://www.eliasondeals.com/duedilig.html, 1998.

54. Brunsman, Sanderson, and Van de Voorde. "How to Achieve Value."

55. Ashkenas, DeMonaco, and Francis, "Making the Deal Real."

56. Ashkenas, DeMonaco, and Francis, "Making the Deal Real"; Brunsman, Sanderson, and Van de Voorde. "How to Achieve Value."

57. Galpin and Robinson, "Merger Integration."

58. Ibid.

59. Ashkenas, DeMonaco, and Francis, "Making the Deal Real."

60. Kostuch, Malchione, and Marten, "Post-Merger Integration."

61. A. Taylor, "The Germans Take Charge Creating DaimlerChrysler," *Fortune* (11 January 1999): 92–98; J. Muller, "Lessons from a Casualty of the Culture Wars," *Business Week* (29 November 1999): 198; J. Muller with K. Kerwin and J. Ewing, "Man with a Plan," *Business Week* (4 October 1999): 34; J. Muller, "The One-Year Itch at Daimler-Chrysler," *Business Week* (15 November 1999): 42–43; T. Schellhardt, "A Marriage of Unequals," *Wall Street Journal* (8 April 1999): R8; S. Lipin and B. Mitchener, "Daimler–Chrysler Merger to Produce $3 Billion in Savings, Revenue Gains in 3–5 Years," *Wall Street Journal* (8 May 1998): A10; B. Vlasic with K. Kerwin, D. Woodruff, T. Peterson, and L. N. Spiro, "The First Global Car Colossus," *Business Week* (18 May 1998): 40–47.

20

Organization Transformation

This chapter presents interventions aimed at transforming organizations. It describes activities directed at changing the basic character or culture of the organization. These interventions bring about important alignments among the organization's strategies, design elements, and culture, and between the organization and its competitive environment.[1] They are directed mostly at the culture or dominant paradigm within the organization. These frame-breaking and sometimes revolutionary interventions typically go beyond improving the organization incrementally and focus on changing the way it views itself and its environment.

Organization transformations can occur in response to or in anticipation of major changes in the organization's environment or technology. In addition, these changes often are associated with significant alterations in the firm's business strategy, which, in turn, may require modifying corporate culture as well as internal structures and processes to support the new direction. Such fundamental change entails a new paradigm for organizing and managing organizations. It involves qualitatively different ways of perceiving, thinking, and behaving in organizations. Movement toward this new way of operating requires top managers to take an active leadership role. The change process is characterized by considerable innovation and learning and continues almost indefinitely as organization members discover new ways of improving the organization and adapting it to changing conditions.

Organization transformation is a recent advance in organization development, and there is some confusion about its meaning and definition. This chapter starts with a description of several major features of transformational change. Against this background, three kinds of interventions are discussed: culture change, self-design, and organization learning and knowledge management.

An organization's culture is the pattern of assumptions, values, and norms that are shared by organization members. A growing body of research has shown that culture can affect strategy formulation and implementation as well as the firm's ability to achieve high levels of performance. Culture change involves helping senior executives and administrators diagnose existing culture and make necessary alterations in the basic assumptions and values underlying organizational behaviors.

Self-designing organizations are those that have gained the capacity to alter themselves fundamentally. Creating them is a highly participative process in which multiple stakeholders set strategic directions, design appropriate structures and processes, and implement them. This intervention includes considerable innovation and learning as organizations design and implement significant changes.

Organization learning and knowledge management refer to the capacity of an organization to change and improve.[2] Distinct from individual learning, this intervention helps the organization move beyond solving existing problems and gain the capability to improve continuously. It results in the development of a learning organization where empowered members take responsibility for strategic direction.

CHARACTERISTICS OF TRANSFORMATIONAL CHANGE

In the past decade, a large number of organizations radically altered how they operate and relate to their environments. Increased foreign competition forced many industries to downsize and become leaner, more efficient, and flexible. Deregulation pushed organizations in the financial services, telecommunications, and airline industries to rethink business strategies and reshape how they operate. Public demand for less government and lowered deficits forced public sector agencies to streamline operations and to deliver more for less. Rapid changes in technologies rendered many organizational practices obsolete, pushing firms to be continually innovative and nimble.

Organization transformation implies radical changes in how members perceive, think, and behave at work. These changes go far beyond making the existing organization better or fine-tuning the status quo. They are concerned with fundamentally altering the organizational assumptions about its functioning and how it relates to the environment. Changing these assumptions entails significant shifts in corporate philosophy and values and in the numerous structures and organizational arrangements that shape members' behaviors. Not only is the magnitude of change greater, but the change fundamentally alters the qualitative nature of the organization.

Organization transformation interventions are recent additions to OD and still are in a formative stage of development. For example, organization learning was originally discussed in the late 1950s but did not reach prominence until the early 1990s. Examination of the rapidly growing literature on the topic suggests, however, the following distinguishing features of these revolutionary change efforts.

Change Is Triggered by Environmental and Internal Disruptions

Organizations are unlikely to undertake transformational change unless significant reasons to do so emerge. Power, sentience, and expertise are vested in the existing organizational arrangements, and when faced with problems, members are more likely to fine-tune those structures than to alter them drastically. Thus, in most cases, organizations must experience or anticipate a severe threat to survival before they will be motivated to undertake transformational change. Such threats arise when environmental and internal changes render existing organizational strategies and designs obsolete. The changes threaten the very existence of the organization as it presently is constituted.

In studying a large number of organization transformations, Tushman, Newman, and Romanelli showed that transformational change occurs in response to at least three kinds of disruption:[3]

1. *Industry discontinuities*—sharp changes in legal, political, economic, and technological conditions that shift the basis for competition within industries

2. *Product life cycle shifts*—changes in product life cycle that require different business strategies

3. *Internal company dynamics*—changes in size, corporate portfolio strategy, executive turnover, and the like.

These disruptions severely jolt organizations and push them to alter business strategy and, in turn, their mission, values, structure, systems, and procedures.

Change Is Systemic and Revolutionary

Transformational change involves reshaping the organization's culture and design elements. These changes can be characterized as systemic and revolutionary because the entire nature of the organization is altered fundamentally. Typically driven by senior executives, change may occur rapidly so that it does not get mired in politics, individual resistance, and other forms of organizational inertia.[4] This is particularly pertinent to changing the different features of the organization, such as structure, information systems, human resources practices, and work design. These features tend to reinforce one another, thus making it difficult to change them in a piecemeal manner.[5] They need to be changed together and in a coordinated fashion so that they can mutually support each other and the new cultural values and assumptions.[6] Transformational change, however, is distinguished from other types of strategic change by its attention to the people side of the organization. For a change to be labeled transformational, a majority of individuals in an organization must change their behavior.[7]

Long-term studies of organizational evolution underscore the revolutionary nature of transformational change.[8] They suggest that organizations typically move through relatively long periods of smooth growth and operation. These periods of convergence or evolution are characterized by incremental changes. At times, however, most organizations experience severe external or internal disruptions that render existing organizational arrangements ineffective. Successful firms respond to these threats to survival by transforming themselves to fit the new conditions. These periods of total system and quantum changes represent abrupt shifts in the organization's structure, culture, and processes. If successful, the shifts enable the organization to experience another long period of smooth functioning until the next disruption signals the need for drastic change.[9]

These studies of organization evolution and revolution point to the benefits of implementing transformational change as rapidly as possible. The faster the organization can respond to disruptions, the quicker it can attain the benefits of operating in a new way. Rapid change enables the organization to reach a period of smooth growth and functioning sooner, thus providing it with a competitive advantage over those firms that change more slowly.

Change Demands a New Organizing Paradigm

Organizations undertaking transformational change are, by definition, involved in second-order or gamma types of change.[10] Gamma change involves discontinuous shifts in mental or organizational frameworks.[11] Creative metaphors, such as "organization learning" or "continuous improvement," often are used to help members visualize the new paradigm.[12] During the 1980s, increases in technological change, concern for quality, and worker participation led to at least one shift in organizing paradigm. Characterized as the transition from a "control-based" to a "commitment-based" organization, the features of the new paradigm included leaner, more flexible structures; information and decision making pushed down to the lowest levels; decentralized teams and business units accountable for specific products, services, or customers; and participative management and teamwork. This new organizing paradigm is well suited to changing conditions.

Change Is Driven by Senior Executives and Line Management

A key feature of organization transformation is the active role of senior executives and line managers in all phases of the change process.[13] They are responsible for the strategic direction and operation of the organization and actively lead the transformation. They decide when to initiate transformational change, what the change should be, how it should be implemented, and who should be responsible for directing it. Because existing executives may lack the talent, energy, and commitment to undertake these tasks, they may be replaced by outsiders who are recruited to lead the change. Research on transformational change suggests that externally recruited executives are three times more likely to initiate such change than are existing executive teams.[14]

The critical role of executive leadership in transformational change is clearly emerging. Lucid accounts of transformational leaders describe how executives, such as Jack Welch at General Electric, Max DuPree at Herman Miller, and Sir Colin Marshall at British Airways, actively manage both the organizational and personal dynamics of transformational change.[15] The work of Nadler, Tushman, and others points to three key roles for executive leadership of such change:[16]

1. *Envisioning.* Executives must articulate a clear and credible vision of the new strategic orientation. They also must set new and difficult standards for performance, and generate pride in past accomplishments and enthusiasm for the new strategy.

2. *Energizing.* Executives must demonstrate personal excitement for the changes and model the behaviors that are expected of others. They must communicate examples of early success to mobilize energy for change.

3. *Enabling.* Executives must provide the resources necessary for undertaking significant change and use rewards to reinforce new behaviors. Leaders also must build an effective top-management team to manage the new organization and develop management practices to support the change process.

Continuous Learning and Change

Transformational change requires considerable innovation and learning.[17] Organizational members must learn how to enact the new behaviors required to implement new strategic directions. This typically is a continuous learning process of trying new behaviors, assessing their consequences, and modifying them if necessary. Because members usually must learn qualitatively different ways of perceiving, thinking, and behaving, the learning process is likely to be substantial and to involve much unlearning. It is directed by a vision of the future organization and by the values and norms needed to support it. Learning occurs at all levels of the organization, from senior executives to lower-level employees.

Because the environment itself is likely to be changing during the change process, transformational change rarely has a delimited timeframe but is likely to persist as long as the firm needs to adapt to change. Learning how to manage change in a continuous manner can help the organization keep pace with a dynamic environment. It can provide the built-in capacity to fit the organization continually to its environment.

CULTURE CHANGE

The topic of organization culture has become extremely important to American companies in the past ten years, and culture change is the most common form of organization transformation. The number of culture change interventions has grown accordingly. Organization culture is also the focus of growing research and

OD application and has spawned a number of bestselling management books start-ing with *Theory Z, The Art of Japanese Management,* and *In Search of Excellence* and, more recently, *Built to Last* and *Corporate Culture and Performance.*[18] Organization cul-ture is seen as a major strength of such companies as Herman Miller, Intel, PepisCo, Motorola, Hewlett-Packard, Xerox, McDonald's, and Levi Strauss. A growing num-ber of managers appreciate the power of corporate culture in shaping employee be-liefs and actions. A well-conceived and well-managed organization culture, closely linked to an effective business strategy, can mean the difference between success and failure in today's demanding environments.

Concept of Organization Culture

Despite the increased attention and research devoted to corporate culture, there is still some confusion about what the term *culture* really means when applied to or-ganizations.[19] Examination of the different definitions suggests that organization culture is the pattern of basic assumptions, values, norms, and artifacts shared by organization members. These shared meanings help members make sense out of everyday life in the organization. The meanings signal how work is to be done and evaluated, and how employees are to relate to each other and to significant others, such as customers, suppliers, and government agencies.

As shown in Figure 20.1, organization culture includes four major elements ex-isting at different levels of awareness:[20]

1. *Artifacts.* Artifacts are the highest level of cultural manifestation. These are the visible symbols of the deeper levels of culture, such as norms, values, and basic

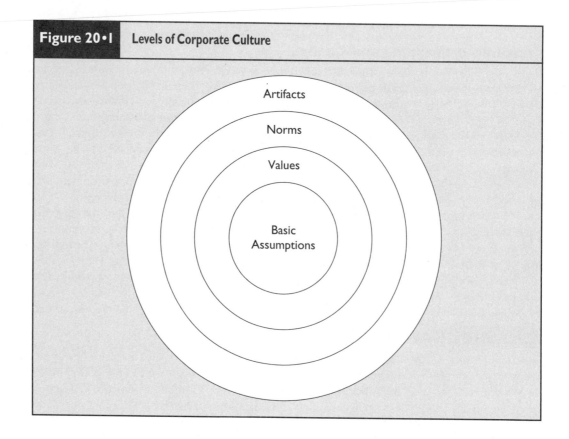

Figure 20•1   Levels of Corporate Culture

assumptions. They include observable behaviors of members, as well as the structures, systems, procedures, rules, and physical aspects of the organization. At Nordstrom, a high-end retail department store, the policy and procedure manual is rumored to be one sentence, "Do whatever you think is right." In addition, stores promote from within; pay commissions on sales to link effort and compensation; provide stationery for salespeople to write personal notes to customers, and expect buyers to work as salespeople to better understand the customer's expectations. By itself, artifacts provide little information about the real culture of the organization; but they are clearly a function of the deeper assumptions.

2. *Norms.* Just below the surface of cultural awareness are norms guiding how members should behave in particular situations. These represent unwritten rules of behavior. At Nordstom, norms dictate that it's okay for members to go the extra mile to satisfy customer requests, and it's not okay for salespeople to process customers who were working with another salesperson.

3. *Values.* The next-deeper level of awareness includes values about what ought to be in organizations. Values tell members what is important in the organization and what deserves their attention. Because Nordstrom values customer service, the sales representatives pay strong attention to how well the customer is treated. Obviously, this value is supported by the norms and artifacts.

4. *Basic assumptions.* At the deepest level of cultural awareness are the taken-for-granted assumptions about how organizational problems should be solved. These basic assumptions tell members how to perceive, think, and feel about things. They are nonconfrontable and nondebatable assumptions about relating to the environment and about human nature, human activity, and human relationships. For example, a basic assumption at Nordstrom is that it is morally right to treat people with dignity and that customers treated with extraordinary service will become loyal and frequent shoppers.

Corporate culture is the product of long-term social learning and reflects what has worked in the past.[21] It represents those basic assumptions, values, norms, and artifacts that have worked well enough to be passed on to succeeding generations of employees. For example, the cultures of many companies (e.g., IBM, J.C.Penney, Sony, and Hewlett-Packard) are deeply rooted in the firm's history. They were laid down by a strong founder and have been reinforced by top executives and corporate success into customary ways of perceiving and acting. These customs provide organization members with clear and widely shared answers to such practical issues as "what really matters around here," "how do we do things around here," and "what we do when a problem arises."[22]

Organization Culture and Organization Effectiveness

The interest in organization culture derives largely from its presumed impact on organization effectiveness. There is considerable speculation and increasing research suggesting that organization culture can improve its ability to implement new business strategies as well as to achieve high levels of performance.

Organizations in many industries, such as energy, banking, and electronics, have faced increasingly complex and changing environments brought on by deregulation, technological revolutions, foreign competition, and unpredictable markets. Many firms (e.g., PepsiCo, American Express, and Prudential Insurance) attempted to adapt to those conditions by changing business strategy and moving into new, unfamiliar areas. Unfortunately, efforts to implement a new strategy can fail because a company's culture is unsuited to the new business.[23] An organization culture that once was a source of strength for a company can become a major liability in successfully implementing a new strategy. For example, Walt Disney's death was a major blow to the organization. His image and reputation were almost palpable at the company's studios in Burbank, California. Managers and executives became overly cautious, continuously asking themselves, "What would Walt have done?" Disney's performance began to slide as these "hero worshipers" continued to produce an outdated line of family films. When CEO Michael Eisner came aboard, he reassigned and replaced many managers. As a result, the new managers, most of whom had never met Disney, began to create a culture that was more sophisticated than stodgy, more adventurous than cautious, more ambitious than content.[24]

The growing appreciation that culture can play a significant role in implementing new strategy has fueled interest in the topic, especially in those firms needing to adapt to turbulent environments. A number of independent consultants and consulting firms have increasingly focused on helping firms implement new strategies by bringing culture more in line with the new direction.[25] Indeed, much of the emphasis in the 1970s on formulating business strategy shifted to organization culture in the 1980s as firms discovered cultural roadblocks to implementing a strategy. Along with this emerging focus on organization culture, however, came the sobering reality that cultural change is an extremely difficult and long-term process. Some experts doubt whether large firms actually can bring about fundamental changes in their cultures; those who have accomplished such feats estimate that the process takes from six to fifteen years.[26] For example, AT&T has struggled for years to change from a service-oriented telephone company to a market-oriented communications business. Its reconfiguration into three separate companies is thought to be partly the result of AT&T's inability to merge its culture with NCR, which it acquired in 1991.[27] Efforts to serve different markets in different ways have been hindered by strong values and norms instilled at the turn of the twentieth century—values that required company workers to treat all customers equally.

Evidence suggests that, in addition to affecting the implementation of business strategy, corporate culture can affect organization performance. Comparative studies of Japanese and American management methods suggest that the relative success of Japanese companies in the 1980s could be partly explained by their strong corporate cultures emphasizing employee participation, open communication, security, and equality.[28] One study of American firms showed a similar pattern of results.[29] Using survey measures of culture and Standard & Poor's financial ratios as indicators of organizational effectiveness, the research examined the relationship between culture and effectiveness for thirty-four large U.S. companies over a five-year period. The firms represented twenty-five different industries, and more than forty-three thousand people responded to the survey instrument. The results show that firms whose cultures support employee participation in decision making, adaptable work methods, sensible work designs, and reasonable and clear goals perform significantly higher (financial ratios about twice as high) than do companies scoring low on those factors. Moreover, the employee participation element of corporate culture only showed differences in effectiveness among the firms after three years; the other measures of culture showed differences in all five years. This suggests that changing some parts of corporate culture, such as participation, should be considered as a long-term investment.

More recently, a study of 207 firms in twenty-two different industries between 1987 and 1991 examined the relationship between culture and performance.[30] The researchers examined relationships between financial performance and the strength of a culture, the strategic appropriateness of a culture, and the adaptiveness of a culture. First, there were no significant performance differences between organizations with widely shared values and those with little agreement around cultural assumptions. Second, there was a significant relationship between culture and performance when the organization emphasized the "right" values—values that were critical to success in a particular industry. Finally, performance results over time supported cultures that emphasized anticipating and adapting to environmental change.

These findings suggest that the strength of an organization's culture can be both an advantage and a disadvantage. Under stable conditions, widely shared and strategically appropriate values can contribute significantly to organization performance. However, if the environment is changing, strong cultures can be a liability. Unless they also emphasize adaptiveness, the organization may experience wide swings in performance during transformational change.

Diagnosing Organization Culture

Culture change interventions generally start by diagnosing the organization's existing culture to assess its fit with current or proposed business strategies. This requires uncovering and understanding the shared assumptions, values, norms, and artifacts that characterize an organization's culture. OD practitioners have developed a number of useful approaches for diagnosing organization culture. These fall into three different yet complementary perspectives: the behavioral approach, the competing values approach, and the deep assumption approach. Each diagnostic perspective focuses on particular aspects of organization culture, and together the approaches can provide a comprehensive assessment of these complex phenomena.

The Behavioral Approach

This method of diagnosis emphasizes the surface level of organization culture—the pattern of behaviors that produce business results.[31] It is among the more practical approaches to culture diagnosis because it assesses key work behaviors that can be observed.[32] The behavioral approach provides specific descriptions about how tasks are performed and how relationships are managed in an organization. For example, Table 20.1 summarizes the organization culture of an international banking division as perceived by its managers. The data were obtained from a series of individual and group interviews asking managers to describe "the way the game is played," as if they were coaching a new organization member. Managers were asked to give their impressions in regard to four key relationships—companywide, boss–subordinate, peer, and interdepartment—and in terms of six managerial tasks—innovating, decision making, communicating, organizing, monitoring, and appraising/rewarding. These perceptions revealed a number of implicit norms for how tasks are performed and relationships managed at the division.

Cultural diagnosis derived from a behavioral approach can also be used to assess the cultural risk of trying to implement organizational changes needed to support a new strategy. Significant cultural risks result when changes that are highly important to implementing a new strategy are incompatible with the existing patterns of behavior. Knowledge of such risks can help managers determine whether implementation plans should be changed to manage around the existing culture, whether the culture should be changed, or whether the strategy itself should be modified or abandoned.

Table 20·1	Summary of Corporate Culture at an International Banking Division

RELATIONSHIPS	CULTURE SUMMARY
Companywide	Preserve your autonomy. Allow area managers to run the business as long as they keep the profit budget.
Boss–subordinate	Avoid confrontations. Smooth over disagreements. Support the boss.
Peer	Guard information; it is power. Be a gentleman or lady.
Interdepartment	Protec your department's bottom line. Form alliances around specific issues. Guard your turf.

TASKS	CULTURE SUMMARY
Innovating	Consider it risky. Be a quick second.
Decision making	Handle each deal on its own merits. Gain consensus. Require many sign-offs. Involve the right people. Seize the opportunity.
Communicating	Withhold information to control adversaries. Avoid confrontation. Be a gentleman or lady.
Organizing	Centralize power. Be autocratic.
Monitoring	Meet short-term profit goals.
Appraising and rewarding	Reward the faithful. Choose the best bankers as managers. Seek safe jobs.

The Competing Values Approach

This perspective assesses an organization's culture in terms of how it resolves a set of value dilemmas.[33] The approach suggests that an organization's culture can be understood in terms of two important "value pairs"; each pair consists of contradictory values placed at opposite ends of a continuum, as shown in Figure 20.2. The two value pairs are (1) internal focus and integration versus external focus and differentiation and (2) flexibility and discretion versus stability and control. Organizations continually struggle to satisfy the conflicting demands placed on them by these competing values. For example, when faced with the competing values of internal versus external focus, organizations must choose between attending to the integration problems of internal operations or the competitive issues in the external environment. Too much emphasis on the environment can result in neglect of internal efficiencies. Conversely, too much attention to the internal aspects of organizations can result in missing important changes in the competitive environment.

The competing values approach commonly collects diagnostic data about the competing values with a survey designed specifically for that purpose.[34] It provides measures of where an organization's existing values fall along each of the dimensions. When taken together, these data identify an organization's culture as falling into one of the four quadrants shown in Figure 20.2: clan culture, adhocracy culture, hierarchical culture, and market culture. For example, if an organization's values are focused on internal integration issues and emphasize innovation and flexibility, it manifests a clan culture. On the other hand, a market culture characterizes values that are externally focused and emphasize stability and control.

The Deep Assumptions Approach

This final diagnostic approach emphasizes the deepest levels of organization culture—the generally unexamined, but tacit and shared assumptions that guide member behavior and that often have a powerful impact on organization effectiveness. Diagnosing culture from this perspective typically begins with the most tangible level of awareness and then works down to the deep assumptions.

Diagnosing organization culture at the deep assumptions level poses at least three difficult problems for collecting pertinent information.[35] First, culture reflects shared assumptions about what is important, how things are done, and how people should behave in organizations. People generally take cultural assumptions for granted and rarely speak of them directly. Rather, the company's culture is implied in concrete behavioral examples, such as daily routines, stories, rituals, and language. This means that considerable time and effort must be spent observing, sifting

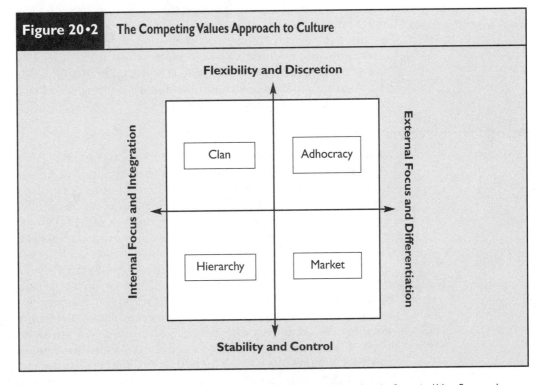

Figure 20·2   **The Competing Values Approach to Culture**

Flexibility and Discretion

Internal Focus and Integration

External Focus and Differentiation

Clan

Adhocracy

Hierarchy

Market

Stability and Control

SOURCE: Cameron and Quinn, *Diagnosing and Changing Organizational Culture Based on the Competing Values Framework*, page 32. © 1999 Addison-Wesley Publishing Co., Inc. Reprinted by permission of Addison Wesley Longman.

through, and asking people about these cultural outcroppings to understand their deeper significance for organization members. Second, some values and beliefs that people espouse have little to do with the ones they really hold and follow. People are reluctant to admit this discrepancy, yet somehow the real assumptions underlying idealized portrayals of culture must be discovered. Third, large, diverse organizations are likely to have several subcultures, including countercultures going against the grain of the wider organization culture. Assumptions may not be shared widely and may differ across groups in the organization. This means that focusing on limited parts of the organization or on a few select individuals may provide a distorted view of the organization's culture and subcultures. All relevant groups in the organization must be discovered and their cultural assumptions sampled. Only then can practitioners judge the extent to which assumptions are shared widely.

OD practitioners emphasizing the deep assumptions approach have developed a number of useful techniques for assessing organization culture.[36] One method involves an iterative interviewing process involving both outsiders and insiders.[37] Outsiders help members uncover cultural elements through joint exploration. The outsider enters the organization and experiences surprises and puzzles that are different from what was expected. The outsider shares these observations with insiders, and the two parties jointly explore their meaning. This process involves several iterations of experiencing surprises, checking for meaning, and formulating hypotheses about the culture. It results in a formal written description of the assumptions underlying an organizational culture.

A second method for identifying the organization's basic assumptions brings together a group of people for a culture workshop—for example, a senior management team or a cross section of managers, old and new members, labor leaders, and staff.[38] The group first brainstorms a large number of artifacts, such as behaviors, symbols, language, and physical space arrangements. From this list, the values and norms that would produce such artifacts are deduced. In addition, the values espoused in formal planning documents are listed. Finally, the group attempts to identify the assumptions that would explain the constellation of values, norms, and artifacts. Because they generally are taken for granted, they are difficult to articulate. A great deal of process consultation skill is required to help organization members see the underlying assumptions.

Application Stages

There is considerable debate over whether changing something as deep-seated as organization culture is possible.[39] Those advocating culture change generally focus on the more superficial elements of culture, such as norms and artifacts. These elements are more changeable than the deeper elements of values and basic assumptions. They offer OD practitioners a more manageable set of action levers for changing organizational behaviors. Some would argue, however, that unless the deeper values and assumptions are changed, organizations have not really changed the culture.

Those arguing that implementing culture change is extremely difficult, if not impossible, typically focus on the deeper elements of culture (values and basic assumptions). Because these deeper elements represent assumptions about organizational life, members do not question them and have a difficult time envisioning anything else. Moreover, members may not want to change their cultural assumptions. The culture provides a strong defense against external uncertainties and threats.[40] It represents past solutions to difficult problems. Members also may have vested interests in maintaining the culture. They may have developed personal stakes, pride, and power in the culture and may strongly resist attempts to change it. Finally, cultures that provide firms with a competitive advantage may be difficult to imitate, thus making it hard for less successful firms to change their cultures to approximate the more successful ones.[41]

Given the problems with cultural change, most practitioners in this area suggest that changes in corporate culture should be considered only after other, less difficult and less costly solutions have been applied or ruled out.[42] Attempts to overcome cultural risks when strategic changes are incompatible with culture might include ways to manage around the existing culture. Consider, for example, a single-product organization with a functional focus and a history of centralized control that is considering an ambitious product-diversification strategy. The firm might manage around its existing culture by using business teams to coordinate functional specialists around each new product. Another alternative to changing culture is to modify strategy to bring it more in line with culture. The single-product organization just mentioned might decide to undertake a less ambitious strategy of product diversification.

Despite problems in changing corporate culture, large-scale cultural change may be necessary in certain situations: if the firm's culture does not fit a changing environment; if the industry is extremely competitive and changes rapidly; if the company is mediocre or worse; if the firm is about to become a very large company; or if the company is smaller and growing rapidly.[43] Organizations facing these conditions need to change their cultures to adapt to the situation or to operate at higher levels of effectiveness. They may have to supplement attempts at cultural change with other approaches, such as managing around the existing culture and modifying strategy.

Although knowledge about changing corporate culture is in a formative stage, the following practical advice can serve as guidelines for cultural change:[44]

1. *Formulate a clear strategic vision.* Effective cultural change should start from a clear vision of the firm's new strategy and of the shared values and behaviors needed to make it work.[45] This vision provides the purpose and direction for cultural change. It serves as a yardstick for defining the firm's existing culture and for deciding whether proposed changes are consistent with core values of the organization. A useful approach to providing clear strategic vision is development of a statement of corporate purpose, listing in straightforward terms the firm's core values. For example, Johnson & Johnson calls its guiding principles "Our Credo." It describes several basic values that guide the firm, including, "We believe our first reponsibility is to the doctors, nurses and patients, to mothers and all others who use our products and services"; "Our suppliers and distributors must have an opportunity to make a fair profit"; "We must respect [employees'] dignity and recognize their merit"; and "We must maintain in good order the property we are privileged to use, protecting the environment and natural resources."[46]

2. *Display top-management commitment.* Cultural change must be managed from the top of the organization. Senior managers and administrators have to be strongly committed to the new values and need to create constant pressures for change. They must have the staying power to see the changes through.[47] For example, Jack Welch, CEO at General Electric, has enthusiastically pushed a policy of cost cutting, improved productivity, customer focus, and bureaucracy busting for more than ten years to every plant, division, group, and sector in his organization. His efforts were rewarded with a *Fortune* cover story lauding his organization for creating more than $52 billion in shareholder value during his tenure.[48]

3. *Model culture change at the highest levels.* Senior executives must communicate the new culture through their own actions. Their behaviors need to symbolize the kinds of values and behaviors being sought. In the few publicized cases of successful culture change, corporate leaders have shown an almost missionary zeal for the new values; their actions have symbolized the values forcefully.[49] For example, Jim Treybig, CEO of Tandem, the computer manufacturer, decided not to fire an employee whose performance had slipped until he could investigate the reason for the employee's poor performance. It turned out that the employee was having family problems, and therefore Treybig gave him another chance. To the people at Tandem, the story symbolized the importance of consideration in leading people.[50] Donald Kendall, the chief executive of PepsiCo, demonstrated the kind of ingenuity and dedication he expects from his staff by using a snowmobile to get to work in a blizzard.

4. *Modify the organization to support organizational change.* Cultural change generally requires supporting modifications in organizational structure, human resources systems, information and control systems, and management styles. These organizational features can help to orient people's behaviors to the new culture.[51] They can make people aware of the behaviors required to get things done in the new culture and can encourage performance of those behaviors. For example, Phil Condit and Harry Stonecipher of Boeing realized that more than culture change in the commercial aircraft division was necessary to turn around the organization's poor performance in 1997 and 1998. To alter the "warm and fuzzy" culture of the division radically, they initiated workforce reductions, fired key executives, made changes in the production standards, and initiated continuous improvement processes in production. These changes reinforced and symbolized the importance of financial performance, accountability, and global leadership in the industry.[52]

5. *Select and socialize newcomers and terminate deviants.* One of the most effective methods for changing corporate culture is to change organizational membership. People can be selected and terminated in terms of their fit with the new culture. This is especially important in key leadership positions, where people's actions can significantly promote or hinder new values and behaviors. For example, Gould, in trying to change from an auto parts and battery company to a leader in electronics, replaced about two-thirds of its senior executives with people more in tune with the new strategy and culture. Jan Carlzon of Scandinavian Airlines (SAS) replaced thirteen out of fifteen top executives in his turnaround of the airline. Another approach is to socialize newly hired people into the new culture. People are most open to organizational influences during the entry stage, when they can be effectively indoctrinated into the culture. For example, companies with strong cultures like Samsung, Procter & Gamble, and 3M attach great importance to socializing new members into the company's values.

6. *Develop ethical and legal sensitivity.* Cultural change can raise significant tensions between organization and individual interests, resulting in ethical and legal problems for practitioners. This is particularly pertinent when organizations are trying to implement cultural values promoting employee integrity, control, equitable treatment, and job security—values often included in cultural change efforts. Statements about such values provide employees with certain expectations about their rights and about how they will be treated in the organization. If the organization does not follow through with behaviors and procedures supporting

and protecting these implied rights, it may breach ethical principles and, in some cases, legal employment contracts. Recommendations for reducing the chances of such ethical and legal problems include setting realistic values for culture change and not promising what the organization cannot deliver; encouraging input from throughout the organization in setting cultural values; providing mechanisms for member dissent and diversity, such as internal review procedures; and educating managers about the legal and ethical pitfalls inherent in cultural change and helping them develop guidelines for resolving such issues.

Application 20.1 presents an example of culture change at Levi Strauss. The example illustrates the importance of a vision statement and the executive commitment required to bring about transformational change in an organization.[53] The Levi Strauss organization came under considerable scrutiny during 1999 because of its poor financial performance. The organization's values and cultural approach have been listed as potential contributors to the problem. However, the organization has continued to strive for the values they espouse.

SELF-DESIGNING ORGANIZATIONS

A growing number of researchers and practitioners have called for self-designing organizations that have the built-in capacity to transform themselves to achieve high performance in today's competitive and changing environment.[54] Mohrman and Cummings have developed a self-design change strategy that involves an ongoing series of designing and implementing activities carried out by managers and employees at all levels of the firm.[55] The approach helps members translate corporate values and general prescriptions for change into specific structures, processes, and behaviors suited to their situations. It enables them to tailor changes to fit the organization and helps them continually to adjust the organization to changing conditions.

The Demands of Transformational Change

Mohrman and Cummings developed the self-design strategy in response to a number of demands facing organizations engaged in transformational change. These demands strongly suggest the need for self-design, in contrast to more traditional approaches to organization change that emphasize ready-made programs and quick fixes. Although organizations prefer the control and certainty inherent in programmed change, the five requirements for organizational transformation reviewed below argue against this strategy:

1. Transformational change generally involves altering most features of the organization and achieving a fit among them and with the firm's strategy. This suggests the need for a *systemic* change process that accounts for these multiple features and relationships.

2. Transformational change generally occurs in situations experiencing heavy change and uncertainty. This means that changing is never totally finished, as new structures and processes will continually have to be modified to fit changing conditions. Thus, the change process needs to be *dynamic and iterative,* with organizations continually changing themselves.[56]

3. Current knowledge about transforming organizations provides only general prescriptions for change. Organizations need to learn how to translate that

APPLICATION 20•1   Values Drive Culture and Operations at Levi Strauss

Levi Strauss and Company, one of the world's largest makers of blue jeans and other apparel, has been engaged in a culture change effort that began in 1985. Following a meeting with a small number of minority and women managers who believed there were invisible barriers to advancement, CEO Robert D. Haas, the great-great-grandnephew of founder Levi Strauss, organized an off-site retreat that paired white senior managers with minority and women managers. The two-and-one-half days of discussions produced painful realizations about how the firm treated its people. What the small group had identified was not so much a diversity problem as a leadership and culture problem.

Today, Levi Strauss is focused on managing in a way that balances business concerns with a set of values that honor diversity, empowerment, and openness. The company has "struggled mightily" to live up to a vision of how to run a modern corporation—a vision set forth by Haas who has demonstrated unswerving commitment to it for more than ten years. As part of a mission of "responsible commercial success," the following Aspiration Statement hangs on office and factory walls throughout the organization and guides all major decisions.

Aspirations Statement

We all want a company that our people are proud of and committed to where all employees have an opportunity to contribute, learn, grow, and advance based on merit, not politics, or background. We want our people to feel respected, treated fairly, listened to, and involved. Above all, we want satisfaction from accomplishments and friendships, balanced personal and professional lives, and to have fun in our endeavors.

When we describe the kind of Levi Strauss and Company we want in the future what we are talking about is building on the foundation we have inherited: affirming the best of our Company's traditions, closing gaps that may exist between principles and practices, and updating some of our values to reflect contemporary circumstances.

What Type of Leadership Is Necessary to Make Our Aspirations a Reality?

NEW BEHAVIORS: Leadership that exemplifies directness, openness to influence, commitment to the success of others, and willingness to acknowledge our own contributions to problems, personal ac-

countability, teamwork, and trust. Not only must we model these behaviors, but we must coach others to adopt them.

DIVERSITY: Leadership that values a diverse workforce (age, sex, ethnic group, etc.) at all levels of the organization, diversity in experience, and a diversity in perspectives. We have committed to taking full advantage of the rich backgrounds and abilities of all our people and to promote a greater diversity in positions of influence. Differing points of view will be sought; diversity will be valued and honestly rewarded, not suppressed.

RECOGNITION: Leadership that provides greater recognition—both financial and psychic—for individuals and teams that contribute to our success. Recognition must be given to all who contribute: those who create and innovate and those who continually support day-to-day business requirements.

ETHICAL MANAGEMENT PRACTICES: Leadership that epitomizes the stated standards of ethical behavior. We must provide clarity about our expectations and must enforce these standards throughout the corporation.

COMMUNICATIONS: Leadership that is clear about company, unit, and individual goals and performance. People must know what is expected of them and receive timely, honest feedback on their performance and career aspirations.

EMPOWERMENT: Leadership that increases the authority and responsibility of those closest to our products and customers. By actively pushing the responsibility, trust, and recognition into the organization, we can harness and release the capabilities of all our people.

Haas believes that successful corporations are more than just strategies and structures. "This is where values come in. In a more volatile and dynamic business environment, the controls have to be conceptual. . . . Values provide a common language for aligning a company's leadership and its people" to the strategy. He set out to make each of his workers, from the factory floor on up, feel as if they are an integral part of the making and selling of blue jeans. All views on all issues—no matter how controversial—are encouraged, heard, and respected. The chairman does not tolerate harassment of any kind. Nor will he do business with suppliers or customers who violate Levi's strict standards regarding work environment and ethics. For example, Levi's board voted unanimously to pull its business out of China in protest of human rights violations even though it cost about $40 million of revenues.

"We are not doing this because it makes us feel good—although it does. We are not doing this because it is politically correct. We are doing this because we believe in the interconnection between liberating the talents of our people and business success." However, the simple truth is, living up to a value system as comprehensive as Levi's is difficult. It takes hours and hours of work by both managers and organization members.

To implement his vision, Haas began at the top. "The first responsibility for me and for my team [was] to examine critically our own behaviors and management styles in relation to the behaviors and values that we profess and to work to become more consistent with the values that we are articulating. . . . You can't be one thing and say another. People have unerring detection systems for fakes, and they won't put up with them. They won't put values into practice if you're not." The most difficult changes were in behaviors that had made managers successful in the past. Activities that were productive under the old culture were counterproductive in the flatter, more responsive, and empowered organization that top management was trying to implement.

To push his vision into the organization, Haas commissioned a set of training courses, such as leadership week, making ethical decisions, and managing diversity. Specifically designed not to be "skill-building" courses, the sessions were more like highly experiential seminars. During the sessions, managers and employees grappled with their own prejudices, attempted to make difficult decisions using the aspirations statement as a guide, and built a support network that helped in applying the ideas in the workplace. To reinforce the importance of the training, senior management attended the courses, came back to teach in them, and, in some cases, went through the courses again as participants to gain additional insights and ideas.

In addition, aspirations management was given some teeth by making it an important part of the performance management system. It includes a 360-degree-like feedback process; each manager develops an "aspirational objective"; and one-third of an employee's evaluation is based on "aspirational" behavior. The aspirations statement has also affected the way work is designed. A new team-based organization and incentive pay system means that a worker's appraisals and compensation depend on other workers. Although more aligned with the values of the organization, the work design produces difficult tests for management. For example, when workers think that someone is faking sick days or lollygagging on a sewing machine, tempers flare. Employee Salvador Salas notes that if someone calls attention to a worker's laziness, the worker will just "flip him off." Supervisor Gracie Cortez says that "it gets tough out there." She finds herself intervening to prevent "big fights." Says plant manager Edward Alvarez, "Peer pressure can be vicious and brutal." Empowerment and teamwork can be alien, uncomfortable concepts for those in the manufacturing plant who have spent their working lives taking orders.

After ten years of work, Haas is a long way from realizing his vision. "We are only a few steps along in our journey," he agrees. "We are far from perfect. We are far from where we want to be. But the goal is out there, and it's worth striving for." ▪

information into specific structures, processes, and behaviors appropriate to their situations. This generally requires considerable on-site innovation and learning as members learn by doing—trying out new structures and behaviors, assessing their effectiveness, and modifying them if necessary. Transformational change needs to facilitate this *organizational learning.*[57]

4. Transformational change invariably affects many organization stakeholders, including owners, managers, employees, and customers. These different stakeholders are likely to have different goals and interests related to the change process. Unless the differences are revealed and reconciled, enthusiastic support for change may be difficult to achieve. Consequently, the change process must attend to the interests of *multiple stakeholders.*[58]

5. Transformational change needs to occur at *multiple levels of the organization* if new strategies are to result in changed behaviors throughout the firm. Top executives must formulate a corporate strategy and clarify a vision of what the organization needs to look like to support it. Middle and lower levels of the organization need

to put those broad parameters into operation by creating structures, procedures, and behaviors to implement the strategy.[59]

Application Stages

The self-design strategy accounts for these demands of organization transformation. It focuses on all features of the organization (for example, structure, human resources practices, and technology) and designs them to support the business strategy mutually. It is a dynamic and an iterative process aimed at providing organizations with the built-in capacity to change and redesign themselves continually as the circumstances demand. The approach promotes organizational learning among multiple stakeholders at all levels of the firm, providing them with the knowledge and skills needed to transform the organization and continually to improve it.

Figure 20.3 outlines the self-design approach. Although the process is described in three stages, in practice the stages merge and interact iteratively over time. Each stage is described below:

1. *Laying the foundation.* This initial stage provides organization members with the basic knowledge and information needed to get started with organization transformation. It involves three kinds of activities. The first is acquiring knowledge about how organizations function, about organizing principles for achieving high performance, and about the self-design process. This information is generally gained through reading relevant material, attending in-house workshops, and visiting other organizations that successfully have transformed themselves. This learning typically starts with senior executives or with those managing the transformation process and cascades to lower organizational levels if a decision is made to proceed with self-design. The second activity in laying the foundation involves valuing—determining the corporate values that will guide the transformation process. These values represent those performance outcomes and organizational conditions that will be needed to implement the corporate strategy. They are typically written in a values statement that is discussed and negotiated among multiple stakeholders at all levels of the organization. The third activity is diagnosing the current organization to determine what needs to

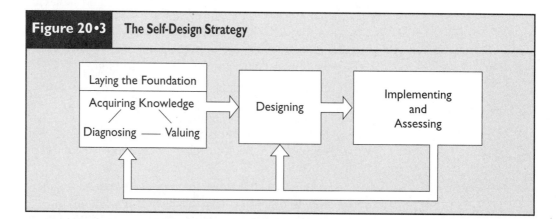

Figure 20•3	The Self-Design Strategy

Laying the Foundation

Acquiring Knowledge

Diagnosing — Valuing

Designing

Implementing and Assessing

SOURCE: S. Mohrman and T. Cummings, *Self-Designing Organizations: Learning How to Create High Performance*, page 37. © 1989 by Addison-Wesley Publishing Co., Inc. Reprinted by permission of Addison Wesley Longman.

be changed to enact the corporate strategy and values. Organization members generally assess the different features of the organization, including its performance. They look for incongruities between its functioning and its valued performances and conditions. In the case of an entirely new organization, members diagnose constraints and contingencies in the situation that need to be taken into account in designing the organization.

2. *Designing.* In this second stage of self-design, organization designs and innovations are generated to support corporate strategy and values. Only the broad parameters of a new organization are specified; the details are left to be tailored to the levels and groupings within the organization. Referred to as minimum specification design, this process recognizes that designs need to be refined and modified as they are implemented throughout the firm.

3. *Implementing and assessing.* This last stage involves implementing the designed organization changes. It includes an ongoing cycle of action research: changing structures and behaviors, assessing progress, and making necessary modifications. Information about how well implementation is progressing and how well the new organizational design is working is collected and used to clarify design and implementation issues and to make necessary adjustments. This learning process continues not only during implementation but indefinitely as members periodically assess and improve the design and alter it to fit changing conditions. The feedback loops shown in Figure 20.3 suggest that the implementing and assessing activities may lead back to affect subsequent designing, diagnosing, valuing, and acquiring knowledge activities. This iterative sequence of activities provides organizations with the capacity to transform and improve themselves continually.

The self-design strategy is applicable to existing organizations needing to transform themselves, as well as to new organizations just starting out. It is also applicable to changing the total organization or subunits. The way self-design is managed and unfolds can also differ. In some cases, it follows the existing organization structure, starting with the senior executive team and cascading downward across organizational levels. In other cases, the process is managed by special design teams that are sanctioned to set broad parameters for valuing and designing for the rest of the organization. The outputs of these teams then are implemented across departments and work units, with considerable local refinement and modification. Application 20.2 presents an example of self-design at a highly innovative and rapidly growing glassmaking company.

ORGANIZATION LEARNING AND KNOWLEDGE MANAGEMENT

The third organizational transformation intervention is aimed at helping organizations develop and use knowledge to change and improve themselves continually. It includes two interrelated change processes: organization learning (OL) which enhances an organization's capability to acquire and develop new knowledge, and knowledge management (KM) which focuses on how that knowledge can be organized and used to improve performance. Both OL and KM are crucial in today's complex, rapidly changing environments, and their importance is likely to increase in the future. They can be a source of strategic renewal, and they can enable organizations to acquire and apply knowledge more quickly and effectively than competitors thus establishing a sustained competitive advantage.[60] Moreover, when

APPLICATION 20•2   Self-Design at Mega Glass Company

In the mid-1980s, Mega Glass Company was one of the fastest-growing and most successful firms in the United States. Started only a few years earlier by a group of entrepreneurs and experienced glassmakers, Mega had grown rapidly into the nation's fourth-largest glass company through selected acquisitions, innovative products and production methods, and skillful financial management. In the face of this success, two key problems were emerging. First, senior executives were uncertain about how to maintain this entrepreneurial spirit as Mega grew older and larger. They feared that the company would become bureaucratized. Second, managers believed that they had already reaped most of the benefits that could be obtained from cost cutting and reducing slack resources, and they sought other means of achieving performance gains.

A company task force was formed to recommend solutions to these emerging problems. After reading relevant material, visiting other firms, and consulting with experts, the task force recommended to senior management the need to move toward a corporate culture promoting involvement and innovation at all levels of the firm. It argued that Mega's rapid growth had been managed primarily from the top of the company and that middle managers and employees had been left out of the decision-making and growth process. They would need to be more involved in the future if Mega hoped to continue to improve and innovate in the competitive glassmaking industry. After extensive discussion and debate, senior management decided to initiate a companywide change process aimed at enhancing involvement, innovation, and performance and at keeping the entrepreneurial spirit alive as the company continued to expand and grow.

As a first step toward change, senior executives met for several days to discuss Mega's strategic direction and to clarify the kinds of values and norms that would be needed to implement it. The outcome of this meeting was the first draft of a vision statement for Mega. It laid out the firm's dynamic, flexible approach to business and identified a number of corporate values, including participative decision making, management by continuous dialogue, employee growth and learning, attractive rewards, customer service, and ethical and legal behaviors. The key issue now was to translate these abstractions into concrete structures, processes, and behaviors throughout the firm.

Senior executives decided to get professional help to manage the change process and contacted university-based action researchers with experience in transformational change. After initial discussion and contracting, the researchers suggested that the top three levels of management at Mega should meet for a series of intense workshops to gain knowledge about organization change, to review the values statement, and to assess preliminarily how well those values were being enacted at Mega. The initial workshop took place at corporate headquarters and included about forty-five senior executives, from the president and his staff down to managers of production plants and distribution centers. Participants gained knowledge of how organizations function, innovations to achieve high performance, and a self-design strategy to manage transformational change.

Against this conceptual background, the second workshop addressed the values statement and assessed how well the values were being enacted at Mega. Participants had a spirited debate about the values and whether they were realistic for a company that had grown rapidly with a firm management hand and a history of cost cutting and pruning of slack resources. Members were asked to assess how consistently Mega operated on each of the separate value statements. They identified five major areas of inconsistency, including rewards based on skills and achievement, the continual upgrading of employee skills, open feedback and information exchange, flexible approaches to problem solving, and identification with the customer. Members formed corporatewide task forces around each of these inconsistencies to assess further why these values were not being implemented and to suggest ways to reduce the inconsistencies. A similar process of clarifying and assessing company values was initiated at lower levels of Mega, down through the production plants.

Over the next two years, the task forces designed organizational changes aimed at promoting the corporate values. Included among these were greater information sharing between headquarters and plant personnel, a more development-oriented performance appraisal system, open job posting, performance-based reward structures, and employee involvement methods, such as self-managing teams and employee-management committees. At the plant levels, similar suggestions for improvement were initiated. For example, one plant that had been experiencing labor problems started an employee-involvement program jointly managed by union officials and managers. This effort did much to turn around the poor labor climate and productivity of the plant. Also, a new plant was designed and implemented using high-involvement concepts, such as self-managing teams, a flat hierarchy, skill-based pay, gain-sharing, and realistic job previews. All of these changes took place with the guidance of the company's values and strategic direction.

When implementing these changes throughout Mega, periodic measures were taken of how well the changes were progressing and whether they were achieving expected results. This information was collected by the various task forces and plant-level design teams through surveys, company records, and selected interviews. The data pointed out areas where the implementation process was bogging down and enabled members to make necessary modifications. For example, methods for communicating between headquarters staff and the plant personnel were revised based on members' reactions to initial communication efforts. Similarly, the team structures in the new plant were modified based on early experience with the initial designs. This feedback and adjustment process did not go smoothly all the time because members sometimes denied the feedback data and failed to make necessary alterations in the organizational improve-

ment. That was part of the learning process, however, and members of Mega gradually came to realize the benefits of assessing and altering the improvements.

At this time, Mega has implemented its strategic direction and enacted its corporate values to support that direction. There have been some dramatic successes, such as the turnaround of the unionized plant, and some initial disappointments, such as in the technical startup of a new plant. The company is continuing to grow rapidly through additional acquisitions, productivity improvements, and innovative products. Perhaps equally important, Mega is building in the capacity to change and improve itself continually at all levels of the firm. ∎

knowledge is translated into new products and services, it can become a key source of wealth creation for organizations.[61] OL and KM are among the most widespread and fastest-growing interventions in OD. They are the focus of an expanding body of research and practice, and have been applied in such diverse firms as Anderson Consulting, Boeing, General Motors, Microsoft, Mobil Oil, and the U.S. Army.

Conceptual Framework

Like many new interventions in OD, there is some ambiguity about the concepts underlying OL and KM. Sometimes the terms "organization learning" and "knowledge management" are used interchangeably to apply to the broad set of activities through which organizations learn and organize knowledge; other times, they are used separately to emphasize different aspects of learning and managing knowledge. This confusion derives in part from the different disciplines and applications traditionally associated with OL and KM.

OL interventions emphasize the organizational structures and social processes that enable employees and teams to learn and to share knowledge. They draw heavily on the social sciences for conceptual grounding and on OD interventions, such as team building, structural design, and employee involvement, for practical guidance. In organizations, OL change processes typically are associated with the human resources function and may be assigned to a special leadership role, such as chief learning officer.

KM interventions, on the other hand, focus on the tools and techniques that enable organizations to collect, organize, and translate information into useful knowledge. They are rooted conceptually in the information and computer sciences and, in practice, emphasize electronic forms of knowledge storage and transmission such as intranets, data warehousing, and knowledge repositories. Organizationally, KM applications often are located in the information systems function and may be under the direction of a chief technology officer.

There is also confusion about the concept of organization learning itself, about whether it is an individual- or organization-level process. Some researchers and practitioners describe OL as individual learning that occurs within an organization context; thus, i is the aggregate of individual learning processes occurring within an organization.[62] Others characterize it in terms of organization processes and structures; they emphasize how learning is embedded in routines, policies, and organization cultures.[63] Snyder has proposed an integration of the two perspectives that treats organization learning as a relative concept.[64] Individuals do learn in organizations but that learning may or may not contribute to organization learning. Learning is organizational to the extent that

- It is done to achieve organization purposes.
- It is shared or distributed among members of the organization.
- Learning outcomes are embedded in the organization's systems, structures, and culture.

To the extent that these criteria are met, organization learning is distinct from individual learning. Thus, it is possible for individual members to learn while the organization does not. For example, a member may learn to serve the customer better without ever sharing such learning with other members. Conversely, it is possible for the organization to learn without individual members learning. Improvements in equipment design or work procedures, for example, reflect OL, even if these changes are not understood by individual members. Moreover, because organization learning serves the organization's purposes and is embedded in its structures, it stays with the organization, even if members change.

A key premise underlying much of the literature on OL and KM is that such interventions will lead to higher organization performance. Although their positive linkage to performance is assumed, the mechanisms through which OL and KM translate into performance improvements are rarely identified or explained. Understanding those mechanisms, however, is essential for applying these change processes in organizations.

Based on existing research and practice, Figure 20.4 provides an integrative framework for understanding OL and KM interventions,[65] summarizing the elements of these change processes and showing how they combine to affect

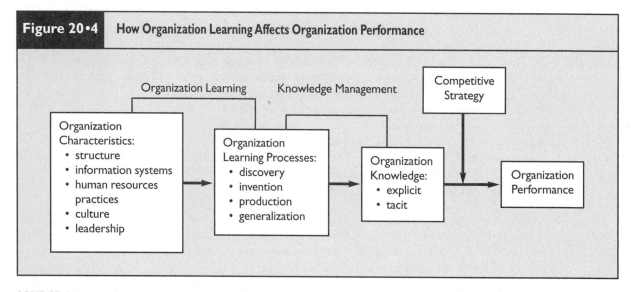

Figure 20•4   How Organization Learning Affects Organization Performance

SOURCE: Reproduced by permission from W. Snyder and T. Cummings, "Organization Learning Disorders: Conceptual Model and Intervention Hypotheses," *Human Relations* 51 (1998): 873–895.

organization performance. This framework suggests that specific characteristics, such as structure and human resources systems, influence how well organization learning processes are carried out. These learning processes affect the amount and kind of knowledge that an organization possesses; that knowledge, in turn, directly influences performance outcomes, such as product quality and customer service. As depicted in Figure 20.4, the linkage between organization knowledge and performance depends on the organization's competitive strategy. Organization knowledge will lead to high performance to the extent that it is both relevant and applied effectively to the strategy. For example, customer-driven organizations require timely and relevant information about customer needs. Their success relies heavily on members having that knowledge and applying it effectively in their work with customers.

Figure 20.4 also shows how OL and KM are interrelated. OL interventions address how organizations can be designed to promote effective learning processes, and how those learning processes themselves can be improved. KM interventions focus on the outcomes of learning processes, on how strategically relevant knowledge can be effectively organized and used throughout the organization. Each of the key elements of OL and KM—organization characteristics, organization learning processes, and organization knowledge—are described below along with the interventions typically associated with them.

Characteristics of a Learning Organization

As shown in Figure 20.4, there are several organization features that can promote effective learning processes including structure, information systems, human resources practices, culture, and leadership. Consequently, many of the interventions described in this book can help organizations develop more effective learning capabilities. Human resources management interventions—performance appraisal, reward systems, and career planning and development—can reinforce members' motivation to gain new skills and knowledge. Technostructural interventions, such as process-based and network structures, self-managing work teams, and reengineering, can provide the kinds of lateral linkages and teamwork needed to process, develop, and share diverse information and knowledge. Human process changes, including team building, search conferences, and intergroup relations interventions, can help members develop the kinds of healthy interpersonal relationships that underlie effective OL. Strategic interventions, such as integrated strategic change and transorganizational development, can help organizations gain knowledge about their environments and develop values and norms that promote OL.

OL practitioners have combined many of these interventions into the design and implementation of what is commonly referred to as the *learning organization,* a term used to describe organizations that are capable of effective learning.[66] Much of the literature on the learning organization is prescriptive and proposes how organizations should be designed and managed to promote effective learning. Although there is relatively little systematic research to support these premises, there is growing consensus among researchers and practitioners about specific organizational features that characterize the learning organization.[67] These qualities are mutually reinforcing and fall into five interrelated categories.

Structure

Learning organizations are structured to facilitate OL. Their structures emphasize teamwork, strong lateral relations, and networking across organizational boundaries both internal and external to the firm. These features promote the information sharing, systems thinking, and openness to information that are necessary for OL. They help members scan wider parts of the organization and its environment and reduce barriers to shared learning. Learning organizations also have relatively flat managerial hierarchies that enhance opportunities for employee involvement in the organization. Members are empowered to make relevant decisions and to influence the organization significantly, thus nurturing the personal mastery and efficacy that are essential to OL.

Information Systems

Organization learning involves gathering and processing information, and consequently, the information systems of learning organizations provide an infrastructure for OL. Organizations traditionally rely on information systems for control purposes: they use information to detect and correct errors in organizational functioning. In today's environments where learning is directed increasingly at transformational change, organizations require more sophisticated information systems to support these higher levels of OL. They need systems that facilitate rapid acquisition, processing, and sharing of rich, complex information and that enable people to manage knowledge for competitive advantage. For example, Monsanto has developed a "knowledge management architecture" that uses Lotus Notes to link salespeople, account managers, and competitor analysts to shared customer and competitor databases that are updated continually.[68] Change processes aimed at information systems will be discussed more thoroughly below when KM interventions are described.

Human Resources Practices

Because organization members are the ultimate creators and users of OL, the human resources practices of learning organizations are designed to promote member learning. These include appraisal and reward systems that account for long-term performance and knowledge development; they reinforce the acquisition and sharing of new skills and knowledge. For example, General Mills uses skill-based pay to motivate employees to learn multiple skills and jobs. Similarly, the training and development programs of learning organizations emphasize continuous learning and improvement. They are directed at enhancing human capital and opportunities for OL. Taco, a New England pump and valve manufacturer, has developed a "learning center" that includes classrooms, a computer lab, and a library.[69] Employees take advantage of more than six dozen courses offered at the center to improve their work skills and, in some cases, to earn college credit or a high school equivalency diploma.

Organization Culture

The shared assumptions, values, and norms that form an organization's culture can influence strongly how members gather, process, and share information. Learning organizations have strong cultures that promote openness, creativity, and experimentation among members. These values and norms provide the underlying social support needed for successful learning. They encourage members to acquire, process, and share information; they nurture innovation and provide the freedom to try new things, to risk failure, and to learn from mistakes. Hewlett-Packard, for example, has strong values and norms fostering innovation and experimentation.[70] Members are encouraged to think and behave differently. Mistakes and errors are treated as a normal part of the innovation process, and members actively learn from their failures how to change and improve both themselves and the organization.

Leadership

Like most interventions aimed at organization transformation, OL and KM depend heavily on effective leadership throughout the organization. The leaders of learning organizations are actively involved in OL.[71] They model the openness, risk taking, and reflection necessary for learning. They also communicate a compelling vision of the learning organization and provide the empathy, support, and personal advocacy needed to lead others in that direction. During Motorola's early efforts at total quality management, for example, CEO Bob Galvin championed the quality vision, attended the first classes on quality, and placed it first on the agenda at his monthly executive meetings.[72]

Organization Learning Processes

The organization characteristics described above affect how well members carry out organization learning processes. As shown in Figure 20.4, these processes consist of four interrelated activities: discovery, invention, production, and generalization.[73] Learning starts with discovery when errors or gaps between desired and actual conditions are detected. For example, sales managers may discover that sales are falling below projected levels and set out to solve the problem. Invention is aimed at devising solutions to close the gap between desired and current conditions, and includes diagnosing the causes of the gap and creating appropriate solutions to reduce it. The sales managers may learn that poor advertising is contributing to the sales problem and may devise a new sales campaign to improve sales. Production processes involve implementing solutions, and generalization includes drawing conclusions about the effects of the solutions and extending that knowledge to other relevant situations. For instance, the new advertising program would be implemented, and if successful, the managers might use variations of it with other product lines. Thus, these four learning processes enable members to generate the knowledge necessary to change and improve the organization.

Organizations can apply the learning processes described above to three levels of learning.[74] The lowest level is called *single-loop learning* or *adaptive learning* and is focused on learning how to improve the status quo. This is the most prevalent form of learning in organizations and enables members to reduce errors or gaps between desired and existing conditions. It can produce incremental change in how organizations function. The sales managers described above engaged in single-loop learning when they looked for ways to reduce the difference between current and desired levels of sales.

Double-loop learning or *generative learning* is aimed at changing the status quo. It operates at a more abstract level than does single-loop learning because members learn how to change the existing assumptions and conditions within which single-loop learning operates. This level of learning can lead to transformational change, where the status quo itself is radically altered. For example, the sales managers may learn that sales projections are based on faulty assumptions and models about future market conditions. This knowledge may result in an entirely new conception of future markets with corresponding changes in sales projections and product development plans. It may lead the managers to drop some products that had previously appeared promising, develop new ones that were not considered before, and alter advertising and promotional campaigns to fit the new conditions.

The highest level of OL is called *deuterolearning,* which involves learning how to learn. Here learning is directed at the learning process itself and seeks to improve how organizations perform single- and double-loop learning. For example, the sales managers might periodically examine how well they perform the processes of discovery, invention, production, and generalization. This could lead to improvements and efficiencies in how learning is conducted throughout the organization.

Practitioners have developed change strategies designed specifically for organization learning processes. Although these interventions are relatively new in OD and do not follow a common change process, they tend to focus on cognitive aspects of learning and how members can become more effective learners. In describing these change strategies, we draw heavily on the work of Argyris and Schon and of Senge and his colleagues because it is the most developed and articulated work in OL practice.[75]

From this perspective, organization learning is not concerned with the organization as a static entity but as an active process of sense making and organizing. Members socially construct the organization as they continually act and interact with each other and learn from those actions how to organize themselves for productive achievement. This active learning process enables members to develop, test, and modify mental models or maps of organizational reality. Called *theories in use*, these cognitive maps inform member behavior and organizing.[76] They guide how members make decisions, perform work, and organize themselves. Unfortunately, members' theories in use can be faulty, resulting in ineffective behaviors and organizing efforts. They can be too narrow and fail to account for important aspects of the environment; they can include erroneous assumptions that lead to unexpected negative consequences. Effective OL can resolve these problems by enabling members to learn from their actions how to detect and correct errors in their mental maps, and thus it can promote more effective organizing efforts.

The predominant mode of learning in most organizations is ineffective, however, and may even intensify errors. Referred to as *Model I* learning, it includes values and norms that emphasize unilateral control of environments and tasks, and protection of oneself and others from information that may be hurtful.[77] These norms result in a variety of defensive routines that inhibit learning, such as withholding information and feelings, competition and rivalry, and little public testing of theories in use and the assumptions underlying them. Model I is limited to single-loop learning, where existing theories in use are reinforced.

A more effective approach to learning, called *Model II,* is based on values promoting valid information, free and informed choice, internal commitment to the choice, and continuous assessment of its implementation.[78] This results in minimal defensiveness with greater openness to information and feedback, personal mastery and collaboration with others, and public testing of theories in use. Model II applies to double-loop learning, where theories in use are changed, and to deutero-learning, where the learning process itself is examined and improved.

OL interventions are aimed at helping organization members learn how to change from Model I to Model II learning. Like all learning, this change strategy includes the learning processes of discovery, invention, production, and generalization. Although the phases are described linearly below, in practice they form a recurrent cycle of overlapping learning activities.

1. *Discover theories in use and their consequences.* This first step involves uncovering members' mental models or theories in use and the consequences that follow from behaving and organizing according to them. Depending on the size of the client system, this may directly involve all members, such as a senior executive team, or it may include representatives of the system, such as a cross section of members from different levels and areas.

OL practitioners have developed a variety of techniques to help members identify their theories in use. Because these theories generally are taken for granted and rarely examined, members need to generate and analyze data to infer the theories' underlying assumptions. One approach is called *dialogue*, a variant of the human process interventions described in Chapter 12.[79] It involves members in genuine exchange about how they currently address problems, make decisions, and interact with each other and relevant others, such as suppliers, customers, and competitors. Participants are encouraged to be open and frank with each other, to behave as colleagues, and to suspend individual assumptions as much as possible. OL practitioners facilitate dialogue sessions using many of the human process tools described in Chapter 12, such as process consultation and third-party intervention. Dialogue can result in clearer understanding of existing theories in use and their behavioral consequences and enable members to uncover faulty assumptions that lead to ineffective behaviors and organizing efforts.

A second method of identifying theories in use involves constructing an *action map* of members' theories and their behavioral consequences.[80] OL practitioners typically interview members about recurrent problems in the organization, explanations of why they are occurring, actions that are taken to resolve them, and outcomes of those behaviors. Based on this information, an action map is constructed showing interrelationships among the values underlying theories in use, the action strategies that follow from them, and the results of those actions. Such information is fed back to members so that they can test the validity of the map, assess the effectiveness of their theories in use, and identify factors that contribute to functional and dysfunctional learning in the organization.

A third technique for identifying theories in use and revealing assumptions is called the *left-hand, right-hand column.*[81] It starts with each member selecting a specific example of a situation where she or he was interacting with others in a way that produced ineffective results. The example is described in the form of a script and is written on the right side of a page. For instance, it might include statements such as, "I told Larry that I thought his idea was good." "Joyce said to me that she did not want to take the assignment because her workload was too heavy." On the left-hand side of the page, the member writes what she or he was thinking but not saying at each phase of the exchange. For example, "When I told Larry that I thought his idea was good, what I was really thinking is that I have serious reservations about the idea, but Larry has a fragile ego and would be hurt by negative feedback." "Joyce said she didn't want to take the assignment because her workload is too heavy, but I know it's because she doesn't want to work with Larry." This simple yet powerful exercise reveals hidden assumptions that guide behavior and can make members aware of how erroneous or untested assumptions can undermine work relationships.

A fourth method that helps members identify how mental models are created and perpetuated is called the *ladder of inference,* as shown in Figure 20.5.[82] It demonstrates how far removed from concrete experience and selected data are the assumptions and beliefs that guide our behavior. The ladder shows vividly how members' theories in use can be faulty and lead to ineffective actions. People may draw invalid conclusions from limited experience; their cultural and personal biases may distort meaning attributed to selected data. The ladder of inference can help members understand why their theories in use may be invalid and why their behaviors and organizing efforts are ineffective. Members can start with descriptions of actions that are not producing intended results

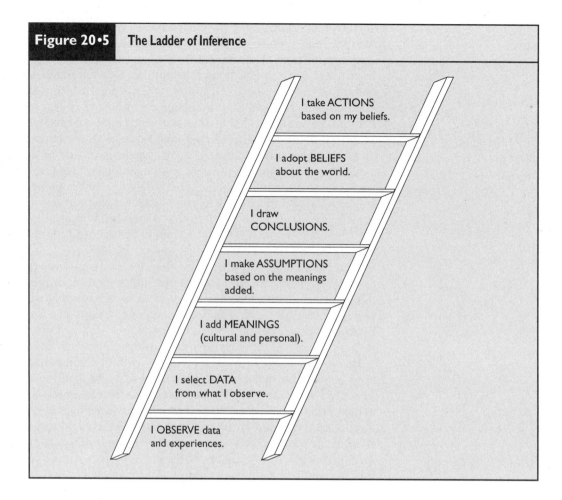

Figure 20•5   The Ladder of Inference

I take ACTIONS based on my beliefs.

I adopt BELIEFS about the world.

I draw CONCLUSIONS.

I make ASSUMPTIONS based on the meanings added.

I add MEANINGS (cultural and personal).

I select DATA from what I observe.

I OBSERVE data and experiences.

and then back down the ladder to discover the reasons underlying those ineffective behaviors. For example, a service technician might withhold from management valuable yet negative customer feedback about product quality, resulting in eventual loss of business. Backing down the ladder, the technician could discover an untested belief that upper management does not react favorably to negative information and may even "shoot the messenger." This belief may have resulted from assumptions and conclusions that the technician drew from observing periodic layoffs and from hearing widespread rumors that the company is out to get troublemakers and people who speak up too much. The ladder of inference can help members understand the underlying reasons for their behaviors and help them confront the possibility that erroneous assumptions are contributing to ineffective actions.

2. *Invent and produce more effective theories in use.* Based on what is discovered in the first phase of this change process, members invent and produce theories in use that lead to more effective actions and that are more closely aligned with Model II learning. This involves double-loop learning as members try to create and enact new theories. In essence, members learn by doing; they learn from their invention and production actions how to invent and produce more effective theories in use.

As might be expected, learning how to change theories in use can be extremely difficult. There is a strong tendency for members to revert to habitual behaviors and modes of learning. They may have trouble breaking out of existing mindsets and seeing new realities and possibilities. OL practitioners have developed both behavioral and conceptual interventions to help members overcome these problems.

Behaviorally, practitioners help members apply the values underlying Model II learning—valid information, free choice, and internal commitment—to question their experience of trying to behave more consistently with Model II.[83] They encourage members to confront and talk openly about how habitual actions and learning methods prevent them from creating and enacting more effective theories. Once these barriers to change are discussed openly, members typically discover that they are changeable. This shared insight often leads to the invention of more effective theories for behaving, organizing, and learning. Subsequent experimentation with trying to enact those theories in the workplace is likely to produce more effective change because the errors that invariably occur when trying new things now can be discussed and hence corrected.

Conceptually, OL practitioners teach members *system thinking* to help them invent more effective theories in use.[84] It provides concepts and tools for detecting subtle but powerful structures that underlie complex situations. Learning to see such structures can help members understand previously unknown forces operating in the organization. This information is essential for developing effective theories for organizing, particularly in today's complex, changing world.

Systems thinking generally requires a radical shift in how members view the world: from seeing parts to seeing wholes; from seeing linear cause–effect chains to seeing interrelationships, from seeing static entities to seeing processes of change. Practitioners have developed a variety of exercises and tools to help members make this conceptual shift. These include systems diagrams for displaying circles of influence among system elements; system archetypes describing recurrent structures that affect organizations; computerized microworlds where new strategies can be tried out under conditions that permit experimentation and learning; and games and experiential exercises demonstrating systems principles.[85]

3. ***Continuously monitor and improve the learning process.*** This final stage involves deuterolearning—learning how to learn. Here, learning is directed at the learning process itself and at how well Model II learning characteristics are reflected in it. This includes assessing OL strategies and the organizational structures and processes that contribute to them. Members assess periodically how well these elements facilitate single- and double-loop learning. They generalize positive findings to new or changing situations and make appropriate modifications to improve OL. Because these activities reflect the highest and most difficult level of OL, they depend heavily on members' capability to do Model II learning. Members must be willing to question openly their theories in use about OL; they must be willing to test publicly the effectiveness both of their learning strategies and of the wider organization.

Organization Knowledge

The key outcome of organization learning processes is organization knowledge. It includes what members know about organizational processes, products, customers, and competitive environments. Such knowledge may be *explicit* and exist in codified forms such as documents, manuals, and databases; or it may be *tacit* and reside mainly in members' skills, memories, and intuitions.[86] Fueled by innovations in information technology, KM interventions have focused heavily on codifying organization knowledge so it can be readily accessed and applied to organizational tasks. Because tacit knowledge is difficult if not impossible to codify, attention also has been directed at how such knowledge can be shared informally across members and organizational units.

Organization knowledge contributes to organization performance to the extent that it is relevant and applied effectively to the organization's competitive strategy, as shown in Figure 20.4. Moreover, organization knowledge is particularly valuable when it is unique and cannot easily be obtained by competitors.[87] Thus, organizations seek to develop or acquire knowledge that distinctly adds value for customers and that can be leveraged across products, functions, business units, or geographical regions. For example, Wal-Mart excels at managing its unique distribution system across a wide variety of regional stores. Honda is particularly successful at leveraging its competence in producing motors across a number of product lines, including automobiles, motorcycles, and lawn mowers.[88]

Because organization knowledge plays a crucial role in linking organization learning processes to organization performance, increasing attention is being directed at how firms can acquire and use it effectively. Two of the more popular books on innovation and global competition include the term "knowledge" in their titles: Leonard-Barton's *Wellsprings of Knowledge: Building and Sustaining the Sources of Innovation*[89] and Nonaka and Takeuchi's *The Knowledge-Creating Company: How Japanese Companies Foster Creativity and Innovation for Competitive Advantage*.[90] They show how many Japanese companies and such American firms as Hewlett-Packard and Motorola achieve competitive advantage through building and managing knowledge effectively. These knowledge capabilities have been described as "core competencies,"[91] "invisible assets,"[92] and "intellectual capital,"[93] thus suggesting their contribution to organization performance.

There is growing emphasis both in the accounting profession and in many industries on developing measures that capture knowledge capital.[94] For many organizations, the value of intellectual assets far exceeds the value of physical and financial assets;[95] intellectual assets are usually worth three to four times tangible book value.[96] Moreover, the key components of cost in many of today's organizations are research and development, intellectual assets, and services rather than materials and labor, which are the focus of traditional cost accounting. Dow Chemical, for example, has developed a process for measuring and managing intellectual capital.[97] The method first defines the role of knowledge in the firm's business strategy, then assesses current knowledge assets and deficiencies, and finally assembles a knowledge portfolio. This process enables Dow to manage knowledge almost as rigorously as it manages its tangible assets.

KM interventions are growing rapidly in OD and include a range of change strategies and methods. Although there is no universal approach to KM, these change processes address the essential steps for generating, organizing, and distributing knowledge within organizations.

1. *Generating knowledge.* This stage involves identifying the kinds of knowledge that will create the most value for the organization and then creating mechanisms for increasing that stock of knowledge. It starts with examination of the organization's competitive strategy; how it seeks to create customer value to achieve profitable results. Strategy provides the focus for KM; it identifies those

areas where knowledge is likely to have the biggest payoff. For example, competitive strategies that emphasize customer service, such as those found at McKinsey and Nordstrom, place a premium on knowledge about customer needs, preferences, and behavior. Strategies favoring product development, like those at Microsoft and Hoffman-LaRoche, benefit from knowledge about research and development. Strategies focusing on operational excellence, such as those at Motorola and Chevron, value knowledge about manufacturing and quality improvement processes.

Once the knowledge required for competitive strategy is identified, organizations need to devise mechanisms for acquiring or creating that knowledge. Externally, organizations can acquire other companies that possess the needed knowledge, or they can rent it from knowledge sources such as consultants and university researchers.[98] Internally, organizations can facilitate *communities of practice:* informal networks among employees performing similar work who share expertise and solve problems together.[99] They can also create more formal groups for knowledge generation, such as R&D departments, corporate universities, and centers of excellence. Organizations can bring together people with different skills, ideas, and values to generate new products or services. Called *creative abrasion,* this process breaks traditional frames of thinking by having diverse perspectives rub creatively against each other to develop innovative solutions.[100]

2. ***Organizing knowledge.*** This phase includes putting valued knowledge into a form that organizational members can use readily. It also may involve refining knowledge to increase its value to users. KM practitioners have developed tools and methods for organizing knowledge that form two broad strategies: codification and personalization.[101]

   Codification approaches rely heavily on information technology. They categorize and store knowledge in databases where it can be assessed and used by appropriate members. This strategy works best for explicit forms of knowledge that can be extracted from people, reports, and other data sources, and then organized into meaningful categories called "knowledge objects" that can be reused for various purposes. The economic rationale underlying this strategy is to invest once in a knowledge asset and then to reuse it many times. At Ernst & Young's Center for Business Knowledge, for example, key knowledge objects are extracted from consulting reports, benchmark data, and market segmentation analyses, and then placed in an electronic repository for people to use.[102] This enables Ernst & Young to apply its knowledge assets across various projects and clients, thus achieving scale in knowledge reuse to grow its business.

   Personalization strategies for organizing knowledge focus on the people who develop knowledge and on how they can share it person-to-person. This approach emphasizes tacit knowledge, which cannot be codified and stored effectively in computerized information systems. Such knowledge is typically accessed through personal conversations, direct contact, and on-going dialogue with the people who possess it. Thus, KM practitioners have developed a variety of methods for facilitating personal exchanges between those with tacit knowledge and those seeking it. For example, McKinsey fosters networking among its employees through transferring people across offices, encouraging the prompt return of phone calls from colleagues, brainstorming sessions, and cross-functional project teams.[103] Hughes, Microsoft, and Time-Life have created "knowledge maps" that identify valued competencies, skills, and knowledge and show people where to go and whom to contact to access them.[104]

3. *Distributing knowledge.* This final stage of KM creates mechanisms for members to gain access to needed knowledge. It overlaps with the previous phase of KM and involves making knowledge easy for people to find and encouraging its use and reuse. KM practitioners have developed a variety of methods for distributing knowledge, generally grouped as three approaches: self-directed distribution, knowledge services and networks, and facilitated transfer.[105]

Self-directed methods rely heavily on member control and initiative for knowledge distribution. They typically include databases for storing knowledge and locator systems for helping members find what they want. Databases can include diverse information such as articles, analytical reports, customer data, and best practices. Locator systems can range from simple phone directories to elaborate search engines. Self-directed knowledge transfer can involve either "pull" or "push" systems.[106] The former lets members pull down information they need, when they need it; the latter makes knowledge available to members by sending it out to them. Arthur Anderson, for example, has developed a "target push" system directed at users' interests and work context; it proactively delivers material that is likely to be helpful and relevant.[107]

Knowledge services and networks promote knowledge transfer by providing specific assistance and organized channels for leveraging knowledge throughout the organization. KM services include a variety of support for knowledge distribution, such as help desks, information systems, and knowledge packages. They also may involve special units and roles that scan the flow of knowledge and organize it into more useful forms, such as "knowledge departments," "knowledge managers," or "knowledge integrators."[108] Knowledge networks create linkages among organizational members for sharing knowledge and learning from one another. These connections can be electronic, such as those occurring in chat rooms, intranets, and discussion databases, or they may be personal like those taking place in talk rooms, knowledge fairs, and communities of practice.

Facilitated transfer of organization knowledge involves specific people who assist and encourage knowledge distribution. These people are trained to help members find and transmit knowledge as well as gain access to databases and other knowledge services. They also may act as change agents helping members implement knowledge to improve organization processes and structures. For example, Amoco's "Shared Learning Program" includes dedicated practitioners, called "quality/progress professionals," who coach employees in best practices and how to use them.[109]

Application 20.3 describes how KM interventions helped BP Amoco revitalize itself. It shows how KM can facilitate organization transformation and contribute to performance improvements.[110]

Outcomes of OL and KM

Given the current popularity of OL and KM interventions, research about their effects in organizations is growing. The Center for Organizational Learning at MIT is engaged in research efforts that include the Dialogue Project[111] and the New Management Style Project.[112] These research activities focus on particular aspects of OL processes. For example, dialogue was viewed as the primary method for improving customer service at Federal Express.[113] Other organizations claim considerable success with the ladder of inference, the left-hand/right-hand column tool, and systems

APPLICATION 20•3   Knowledge Management at BP Amoco

BP Amoco is one of the most profitable oil companies in the world today. In the past decade, it has changed from a large, stodgy bureaucracy with mediocre performance and enormous debt to a much smaller, flexible organization with drastically reduced costs and debt and surging oil reserves, production output, and profits. To accomplish this radical transformation, BP downsized and restructured itself into a learning organization where people, teams, and informal networks generate and share knowledge to add value to what they do.

BP's change process began in 1992 under CEO David Simon and was subsequently led by John Browne, who became CEO in 1995. Browne was a strong advocate of OL and KM and sought ways to foster their application throughout the firm. To spearhead this effort, Browne asked Kent Greenes to head a team charged with improving performance by sharing best practices, reusing knowledge, and accelerating learning. The team first assembled a portfolio of 15 projects where KM was likely to have the greatest payoffs. These included helping BP enter the Japanese retail market, reducing downtime at a polyethylene plant, and cutting the costs of a refinery turnaround—a scheduled shutdown and refurbishment—in Holland. To ensure success, projects were sponsored by specific business units that agreed to pay for them. Moreover, project outcomes were tied to the business units' "performance contracts" for financial, environmental, and other results. In BP's culture, these agreements are considered unbreakable, and executives will do almost anything to fulfill them.

Greenes' team used a number of KM tools to facilitate the projects. The Dutch refinery, for example, received a "peer assist" from other refineries having experience in turnarounds. This consisted of a two-day meeting where people with refinery turnaround experience shared their knowledge with the Dutch employees before the project began. It resulted in a $9 million savings. Another technique was adapted from the U.S. Army. Called "after-action reviews," it consists of answering the following questions after taking action: What was supposed to happen? What actually happened? Why is there a difference? What can we learn and do from this? A more elaborate version of this process, "the retrospect," was also applied at BP. The outcomes of these learning tools were used to develop a Web-based folder of information and knowledge including email hyperlinks to people with expertise to share.

Greenes' team also used information technology to enable employees to connect, communicate, and share knowledge. One method, called "connect," is a voluntary intranet directory listing people's expertise; about twelve thousand BP employees initially put themselves into this database. Another tool, "virtual team network," enables people from BP's different geographic locations to work together. It includes desktop videoconferencing, multimedia email, and a real-time shared whiteboard.

In 1999, two years after the start of BP's KM projects, documented savings were $260 million with another $400 million anticipated. Perhaps more important, about one-third of the firm's 90 business units had applied KM tools and ideas, and more were becoming involved rapidly. More than three hundred employees had become part-time knowledge managers, expanding greatly the work of Greenes' team. ∎

thinking. The CEO for Analog Devices described how systems thinking and total quality management principles were able to drive down failure rates, defects per unit, and manufacturing cycle times. Despite these success stories, there appears to be considerable room for improving OL interventions. Argyris and Schon state that they are unaware of any organization that has fully implemented a double-loop learning (Model II) system.[114]

A recent study of KM in 431 U.S. and European firms also suggests that organizations may have more problems implementing KM practices than is commonly reported in the popular media.[115] Only 46 percent of the companies reported above-average performance in "generating new knowledge." Ratings were even lower for "embedding knowledge in processes, products, and/or services" (29 percent) and "transferring existing knowledge into other parts of the organization" (13 percent). Another study of 31 KM projects across 20 organizations revealed that KM contributed to the fundamental transformation of only three of the firms studied.[116] Many of the companies, however, reported operational improvements in product development, customer support, software development, patent management, and education and training. Studies of transfer of best practices and KM by the American Productivity & Quality Center reveal a number of performance improvements in such companies as Buckman Laboratories, Texas Instruments, CIGNA Property & Casualty, and Chevron.[117] Among the reported outcomes were increases in new product sales, manufacturing capacity, and corporate profits, as well as reductions in costs, service delivery time, and start-up time for new ventures. Because most of the existing reports of OL and KM outcomes are case studies or anecdotal reports, more systematic research is need to assess the effects of these popular interventions.

■ SUMMARY

In this chapter, we presented interventions for helping organizations transform themselves. These changes can occur at any level in the organization, but their ultimate intent is to change the total system. They typically happen in response to or in anticipation of significant environmental, technological, or internal changes. These changes may require alterations in the firm's strategy, as described in Chapter 19, but are mostly aimed at altering corporate culture, vision, and mental models within the organization.

Corporate culture includes the pattern of basic assumptions, values, norms, and artifacts shared by organization members. It influences how members perceive, think, and behave at work. Corporate culture affects whether firms can implement new strategies and whether they can operate at high levels of excellence. Culture change interventions start with diagnosing the organization's existing culture. This can include assessing the cultural risks of making organizational changes needed to implement strategy. Changing corporate culture can be extremely difficult and requires clear strategic vision, top-management commitment, symbolic leadership, supporting organizational changes, selection and socialization of newcomers and termination of deviants, and sensitivity to legal and ethical issues.

A self-design change strategy helps a firm gain the built-in capacity to design and implement its own organizational transformation. Self-design involves multiple levels of the firm and multiple stakeholders and includes an iterative series of activities: acquiring knowledge, valuing, diagnosing, designing, implementing, and assessing.

Organization learning and knowledge management interventions help organizations develop and use knowledge to change and improve themselves continually. Organization learning interventions address how organizations can be designed to promote effective learning processes and how those learning processes themselves can be improved. An organization designed to promote learning over a sustained period of time is called a learning organization. Knowledge management focuses on how that knowledge can be organized and used to improve organization performance.

■ NOTES

1. C. Lundberg, "On Organizational Learning: Implications and Opportunities for Expanding Organizational Development," in *Research in Organizational Change and Development*, vol. 3, eds. W. Pasmore and R. Woodman (Greenwich, Conn.: JAI Press, 1989): 61–82.

2. M. Fiol and M. Lyles, "Organizational Learning," *Academy of Management Review* 10 (1985): 803–13; J. March and H. Simon, *Organizations* (New York: John Wiley, 1958).

3. M. Tushman, W. Newman, and E. Romanelli, "Managing the Unsteady Pace of Organizational Evolution," *California Management Review* (Fall 1986): 29–44.

4. Ibid.

5. A. Meyer, A. Tsui, and C. Hinings, "Guest Co-Editors Introduction: Configurational Approaches to Organizational Analysis," *Academy of Management Journal* 36 (1993): 1175–95.

6. D. Miller and P. Friesen, *Organizations: A Quantum View* (Englewood Cliffs, N.J.: Prentice Hall, 1984).

7. B. Blumenthal and P. Haspeslagh, "Toward a Definition of Corporate Transformation," *Sloan Management Review* 35 (1994): 101–07.

8. Tushman, Newman, and Romanelli, "Managing the Unsteady Pace"; L. Greiner, "Evolution and Revolution as Organizations Grow," *Harvard Business Review* (July-August 1972): 37–46.

9. M. Tushman and E. Romanelli, "Organizational Evolution: A Metamorphosis Model of Convergence and Reorientation," in *Research in Organizational Behavior*, vol. 7, eds. L. Cummings and B. Staw (Greenwich, Conn.: JAI Press, 1985): 171–222.

10. J. Bartunek and M. Louis, "Organization Development and Organizational Transformation," in *Research in Organizational Change and Development*, vol. 2, eds. W. Pasmore and R. Woodman (Greenwich, Conn.: JAI Press, 1988): 97–134.

11. R. Golembiewski, K. Billingsley, and S. Yeager, "Measuring Change and Persistence in Human Affairs: Types of Changes Generated by OD Designs," *Journal of Applied Behavioral Science* 12 (1975): 133–57.

12. J. Sackmann, "The Role of Metaphors in Organization Transformation," *Human Relations* 42 (1989): 463–85.

13. R. Waldersee, "Becoming a Learning Organization: The Transformation of the Workplace," *Journal of Management Development* 16 (1997): 262–74; A. Pettigrew, *The Awakening Giant: Continuity and Change in Imperial Chemical Industries* (Oxford: Blackwell, 1985); A. Pettigrew, "Context and Action in the Transformation of the Firm," *Journal of Management Studies* 24 (1987): 649–70; Tushman and Romanelli, "Organizational Evolution."

14. M. Tushman and B. Virany, "Changing Characteristics of Executive Teams in an Emerging Industry," *Journal of Business Venturing* (1986): 37–49; L. Greiner and A. Bhambri, "New CEO Intervention and Dynamics of Deliberate Strategic Change," *Strategic Management Journal* 10 (Summer 1989): 67–86.

15. N. Tichy and M. Devanna, *The Transformational Leader* (New York: John Wiley, 1986); M. DuPree, *Leadership Jazz* (New York: Doubleday, 1992); Blumenthal and Haspeslagh, "Corporate Transformation"; N. Tichy and S. Sherman, *Control Your Destiny or Someone Else Will* (New York: Doubleday, 1993).

16. P. Nutt and R. Backoff, "Facilitating Transformational Change," *Journal of Applied Behavioral Science* 33 (1997): 490–508; M. Tushman, W. Newman, and D. Nadler, "Executive Leadership and Organizational Evolution: Managing Incremental and Discontinuous Change," in *Corporate Transformation: Revitalizing Organizations for a Competitive World*, eds. R. Kilmann and T. Covin (San Francisco: Jossey-Bass, 1988): 102–30; W. Bennis and B. Nanus, *Leaders: The Strategies for Taking Charge* (New York: Harper & Row, 1985); Pettigrew, "Context and Action."

17. T. Cummings and S. Mohrman, "Self-Designing Organizations: Towards Implementing Quality-of-Work-Life Innovations," in *Research in Organizational Change and Development*, vol. 1, eds. R. Woodman and W. Pasmore (Greenwich, Conn.: JAI Press, 1987): 275–310.

18. W. Ouchi, *Theory Z: How American Business Can Meet the Japanese Challenge* (Reading, Mass.: Addison-Wesley, 1979); R. Pascale and A. Athos, *The Art of Japanese Management* (New York: Simon & Schuster, 1981); T. Deal and A. Kennedy, *Corporate Cultures* (Reading, Mass.: Addison-Wesley, 1982); T. Peters and R. Waterman, *In Search of Excellence* (New York: Harper & Row, 1982); T. Peters and N. Austin, *A Passion for Excellence* (New York: Random House, 1985); J. Pfeffer, *Competitive Advantage Through People* (Cambridge: Harvard Business School, 1994); J. Collins and J. Porras, *Built to Last* (New York: Harper Business, 1994); J. Kotter and J. Heskett, *Corporate Culture and Performance* (New York: Free Press, 1992).

19. D. Meyerson and J. Martin, "Cultural Change: An Integration of Three Different Views," *Journal of Management*

Studies 24 (1987): 623–47; D. Denison and G. Spreitzer, "Organizational Culture and Organizational Development: A Competing Values Approach," in *Research in Organizational Change and Development,* vol. 5, eds. R. Woodman and W. Pasmore (Greenwich, Conn.: JAI Press, 1991): 1–22; E. Schein, *Organizational Culture and Leadership,* 2d ed. (San Francisco: Jossey-Bass, 1992).

20. Schein, Organizational Culture; R. Kilmann, M. Saxton, and R. Serpa, eds., *Gaining Control of the Corporate Culture* (San Francisco: Jossey-Bass, 1985).

21. Schein, *Organizational Culture.*

22. M. Louis, "Toward a System of Inquiry on Organizational Culture" (paper delivered at the Western Academy of Management meetings, Colorado Springs, Colo., April 1982).

23. E. Abrahamson, and C. J. Fombrun, "Macrocultures: Determinants and Consequences," *Academy of Management Journal* 19 (1994): 728–55.

24. B. Dumaine, "Creating a New Company Culture," *Fortune* (15 January 1990): 127–31.

25. B. Uttal, "The Corporate Culture Vultures," *Fortune* (17 October 1983): 66–72.

26. Ibid., p. 70.

27. D. Kirkpatrick, "AT&T Has the Plan," *Fortune* (16 October 1995); A. Kupfer, "AT&T Ready to Run, Nowhere to Hide," *Fortune* (29 April 1996): 116–26.

28. Ouchi, *Theory Z;* Pascale and Athos, *Japanese Management.*

29. D. Denison, "The Climate, Culture, and Effectiveness of Work Organizations: A Study of Organizational Behavior and Financial Performance" (Ph.D. diss., University of Michigan, 1982).

30. Kotter and Heskett, *Corporate Culture.*

31. D. Hanna, *Designing Organizations for High Performance* (Reading, Mass.: Addison-Wesley, 1988).

32. H. Schwartz and S. Davis, "Matching Corporate Culture and Business Strategy," *Organizational Dynamics* (Summer 1981): 30–48; S. Davis, *Managing Corporate Culture* (Cambridge, Mass.: Ballinger, 1984).

33. K. Cameron and R. Quinn, *Diagnosing and Changing Organizational Culture* (Reading, Mass.: Addison-Wesley, 1999); Denison and Spreitzer, "Organizational Culture"; R. E. Quinn, *Beyond Rational Management: Mastering the Paradoxes and Competing Demands of High Performance* (San Francisco: Jossey-Bass, 1988).

34. R. Quinn and G. Spreitzer, "The Psychometrics of the Competing Values Culture Instrument and an Analysis of the Impact of Organizational Culture on Quality of Life," in *Research in Organizational Change and Development,* vol. 5, eds. R. Woodman and W. Pasmore (Greenwich, Conn.: JAI Press, 1991): 115–42.

35. Schein, *Organizational Culture.*

36. R. Zammuto and J. Krakower, "Quantitative and Qualitative Studies of Organizational Culture," in *Research in Organizational Change and Development,* vol. 5, eds. R. Woodman and W. Pasmore (Greenwich, Conn.: JAI Press, 1991): 83–114; Quinn and Spreitzer, "Psychometrics."

37. Schein, *Organizational Culture.*

38. E. Schein, *The Corporate Culture Survival Guide* (San Francisco: Jossey-Bass, 1999).

39. P. Frost, L. Moore, M. Louis, C. Lundberg, and J. Martin, eds., *Organizational Culture* (Beverly Hills, Calif.: Sage, 1985): 95–196.

40. Meyerson and Martin, "Cultural Change."

41. J. Barney, "Organizational Culture: Can It Be a Source of Sustained Competitive Advantage?" *Academy of Management Review* 11 (1986): 656–65.

42. Uttal, "Corporate Culture Vultures."

43. Ibid., p. 70.

44. Schein, *Corporate Culture Survival Guide;* Schwartz and Davis, "Matching Corporate Culture"; Uttal, "Corporate Culture Vultures"; Davis, *Managing Corporate Culture;* Kilmann, Saxton, and Serpa, *Gaining Control;* Frost et al., *Organizational Culture;* V. Sathe, "Implications of Corporate Culture: A Manager's Guide to Action," *Organizational Dynamics* (Autumn 1983): 5–23; B. Drake and E. Drake, "Ethical and Legal Aspects of Managing Corporate Cultures," *California Management Review* (Winter 1988): 107–23.

45. C. Worley, D. Hitchin, and W. Ross, *Integrated Strategic Change* (Reading, Mass.: Addison-Wesley, 1996); R. Beckhard and W. Pritchard, *Changing the Essence* (San Francisco: Jossey-Bass, 1992).

46. F. Aguilar and A. Bhambri, *Johnson and Johnson (A)* (Boston: HBS Case Services, 1983).

47. Dumaine, "Creating a New Company Culture"; C. O'Reilly, "Corporations, Culture, and Commitment: Motivation and Social Control in Organizations," *California Management Review* 31 (Summer 1989): 9–25; Pettigrew, "Context and Action."

48. Tichy and Sherman, *Control Your Destiny;* B. Morris, "The Wealth Builders," *Fortune* (11 December 1995): 80–96.

49. Dumaine, "Creating a New Company Culture."

50. Ibid.

51. Tichy and Sherman, *Control Your Destiny.*

52. K. Labich, "Boeing Finally Hatches a Plan," *Fortune* (1 March 1999): 101–06.

53. T. Plouffe, manager, Organization Effectiveness, Levi's Canada, personal communication, January 4, 1996; R. Mitchell, "Managing by Values: Is Levi Strauss' Approach Visionary—or Flaky?" *Business Week* (1 August 1994): 46–56; R. Howard, "Values Make the Company: An Interview with Robert Haas," *Harvard Business Review* (September-October 1990): 133–44.

54. B. Hedberg, P. Nystrom, and W. Starbuck, "Camping on Seesaws: Prescriptions for a Self-Designing Organization," *Administrative Science Quarterly* 21 (1976): 41–65; K. Weick, "Organization Design: Organizations as Self-Designing Systems," *Organizational Dynamics* 6 (1977): 30–46.

55. S. Mohrman and T. Cummings, *Self-Designing Organizations: Learning How to Create High Performance* (Reading, Mass.: Addison-Wesley, 1989); Cummings and Mohrman, "Self-Designing Organizations."

56. P. Lawrence and D. Dyer, *Renewing American Industry* (New York: Free Press, 1983).

57. C. Argyris, R. Putnam, and D. Smith, *Action Science* (San Francisco: Jossey-Bass, 1985); C. Lundberg, "On Organizational Learning: Implications and Opportunities for Expanding Organizational Development," in *Research on Organizational Change and Development*, vol. 3, eds. R. Woodman and W. Pasmore (Greenwich, Conn.: JAI Press, 1989): 61–82; P. Senge, *The Fifth Discipline* (New York: Doubleday, 1990).

58. M. Weisbord, *Productive Workplaces* (San Francisco: Jossey-Bass, 1987); R. Freeman, *Strategic Management* (Boston: Ballinger, 1984).

59. Miller and Friesen, *Organizations.*

60. M. Crossan, H. Lane, and R. White, "An Organizational Learning Framework: From Intuition to Institution," *Academy of Management Review* 24 (1999): 522–37; S. Prokesch, "Unleashing the Power of Learning: An Interview with British Petroleum's John Browne," *Harvard Business Review* (September-October 1997): 147–68; J.-C. Spender, "Making Knowledge the Basis of a Dynamic Theory of the Firm," *Strategic Management Journal* 17

(1996): 45–62; R. Strata, "Organizational Learning: The Key to Management Innovation," *Sloan Management Review* 30 (1989): 63–74.

61. D. Teece, "Capturing Value from Knowledge Assets: The New Economy, Market for Know-How, and Intangible Assets," *California Management Review* 40 (Spring 1998): 55–79.

62. C. Argyris and D. Schon, *Organizational Learning: A Theory of Action Perspective* (Reading, Mass.: Addison-Wesley, 1978); C. Argyris and D. Schon, *Organizational Learning II: Theory, Method, and Practice* (Reading, Mass.: Addison-Wesley, 1996); Senge, *Fifth Discipline.*

63. P. Adler and R. Cole, "Designed for Learning: A Tale of Two Auto Plants," *Sloan Management Review* 34 (1993): 85–94; S. Cook and D. Yanow, "Culture and Organizational Learning," *Journal of Management Inquiry* 2 (1993): 373–90; G. Huber, "The Nontraditional Quality of Organizational Learning," *Organization Science* 2 (1991): 88–115.

64. W. Snyder, "Organization Learning and Performance: An Exploration of the Linkages Between Organizational Learning, Knowledge, and Performance" (unpublished Ph.D. diss., University of Southern California, Los Angeles, 1996).

65. This framework draws heavily on the work of W. Snyder and T. Cummings, "Organization Learning Disorders: Conceptual Model and Intervention Hypotheses," *Human Relations* 51 (1998): 873–95.

66. Senge, *Fifth Discipline;* S. Chawla and J. Renesch, eds., *Learning Organizations: Developing Cultures for Tomorrow's Workplace* (Portland, OR: Productivity Press, 1995).

67. M. McGill, J. Slocum, and D. Lei, "Management Practices in Learning Organizations," *Organizational Dynamics* (Autumn 1993): 5–17; E. Nevis, A. DiBella, and J. Gould, "Understanding Organizations as Learning Systems," *Sloan Management Review* (Winter 1995): 73–85.

68. T. Stewart, "Getting Real About Brain Power," *Fortune* (27 November 1995): 201–03.

69. T. Stewart, "How a Little Company Won Big by Betting on Brainpower," *Fortune* (4 September 1995): 121–22.

70. Nevis, DiBella, and Gould, "Understanding Organizations."

71. M. Beer, "Leading Learning and Learning to Lead: An Action Learning Approach to Developing Organizational Fitness," in *The Leader's Change Handbook: An Essential*

Guide to Setting Direction and Action Taking, eds. J. Conger, G. Spreitzer, and E. Lawler III (San Francisco: Jossey-Bass, 1999): 127–61.

72. Ibid.

73. J. Dewey, *How We Think* (Boston: D.C. Heath, 1933).

74. Argyris and Schon, *Organizational Learning;* Argyris and Schon, *Organizational Learning II;* Senge, *Fifth Discipline.*

75. Argyris and Schon, *Organizational Learning II;* Senge, *Fifth Discipline;* P. Senge, C. Roberts, R. Ross, B. Smith, and A. Kleiner, *The Fifth Discipline Fieldbook: Strategies for Building a Learning Organization* (New York: Doubleday, 1995).

76. Argyris and Schon, *Organizational Learning II.*

77. Ibid.

78. Argyris and Schon, *Organizational Learning II ;* C. Argyris, *Intervention Theory and Method* (Reading, Mass.: Addison-Wesley, 1970).

79. Senge, *Fifth Discipline.*

80. Argyris and Schon, *Organizational Learning II.*

81. Argyris and Schon, *Organizational Learning II;* Senge et al., *Fifth Discipline Fieldbook;* B. Dumaine, "Mr. Learning Organization," *Fortune* (17 October 1994): 147–57.

82. Senge et al., *Fifth Discipline Fieldbook.*

83. Argyris and Schon, *Organizational Learning II ;* Argyris, *Intervention Theory and Method.*

84. Senge, *Fifth Discipline.*

85. Ibid.

86. M. Polanyi, *The Tacit Dimension* (New York: Doubleday, 1966); I. Nonaka and H. Takeuchi, *The Knowledge-Creating Company: How Japanese Companies Foster Creativity and Innovation for Competitive Advantage* (New York: Oxford University Press, 1995).

87. J. Barney, "Looking Inside for Competitive Advantage," *Academy of Management Executive* 9 (4, 1995): 49–61; M. Peteraf, "The Cornerstones of Competitive Advantage," *Strategic Management Journal* 14, 3 (1993): 179–92; Worley, Hitchin, and Ross, *Integrated Strategic Change.*

88. Snyder, *Organization Learning.*

89. D. Leonard-Barton, *Wellsprings of Knowledge: Building and Sustaining the Sources of Innovation* (Boston: Harvard Business School Press, 1995).

90. Nonaka and Takeuchi, *Knowledge Creating.*

91. C. Prahalad and G. Hamel, "The Core Competencies of the Corporation," *Harvard Business Review* 68 (1990): 79–91.

92. H. Itami, *Mobilizing for Invisible Assets* (Cambridge: Harvard University Press, 1987).

93. L. Edvinsson and M. Malone, *Intellectual Capital: Realizing Your Company's True Value by Finding Its Hidden Brainpower* (New York: Harper Business, 1997); T. Stewart, *Intellectual Capital: The New Wealth of Organizations* (New York: Doubleday, 1997); J. Nahapiet and S. Ghoshal, "Social Capital, Intellectual Capital, and the Organizational Advantage," *Academy of Management Review* 23 (1998): 242–66.

94. Edvinsson and Malone, *Intellectual Capital;* Stewart, *Intellectual Capital;* R. Kaplan and D. Norton, *The Balanced Scorecard* (Boston: Harvard Business School Press, 1996); K. Svieby, *The New Organizational Wealth: Managing and Measuring Knowledge-Based Assets* (San Francisco: Berrett-Koehler, 1977).

95. Edvinsson and Malone, *Intellectual Capital.*

96. C. Handy, *The Age of Unreason* (Boston: Harvard Business School Press, 1991).

97. T. Stewart, "Intellectual Capital," *Fortune* (3 October 1994): 68–74.

98. V. Anand, C. Manz, and W. Glick, "An Organizational Memory Approach to Information Management," *Academy of Management Review* 23 (1998): 796–809.

99. J. Lave and E. Wenger, *Situated Learning: Legitimate Peripheral Participation* (New York: Cambridge University Press, 1993); J. Brown and P. Duguid, "Organizational Learning and Communities of Practice: Towards a Unified View of Working, Learning, and Innovation," *Organization Science* 2 (1991): 40–57.

100. Leonard-Barton, *Wellsprings of Knowledge;* D. Leonard-Barton and S. Sensiper, "The Role of Tacit Knowledge in Group Innovation," *California Management Review* 40 (Spring 1998): 112–32.

101. M. Hansen, N. Nohria, and T. Tierney, "What's Your Strategy for Managing Knowledge?" *Harvard Business Review* (March-April 1999): 106–16.

102. Ibid.

103. Ibid.

104. T. Davenport and L. Prusak, *Working Knowledge: How Organizations Manage What They Know* (Boston: Harvard Business School Press, 1998).

105. C. O'Dell and C. Grayson, *If Only We Knew What We Know* (New York: Free Press, 1998).

106. D. Garvin and A. March, *A Note on Knowledge Management* (Boston: Harvard Business School Publishing, 1997).

107. Ibid.

108. O'Dell and Grayson, *If Only We Knew.*

109. Ibid.

110. Prokesch, "Unleashing the Power"; T. Stewart, "Telling Tales at BP Amoco," *Fortune* (7 June 1999): 220–24.

111. E. Schein, "On Dialogue, Culture, and Organizational Learning," *Organizational Dynamics* (Fall 1993): 40–51; W. Isaacs, "Dialogue, Collective Thinking, and Organizational Learning," *Organizational Dynamics* (Fall 1993): 24–39.

112. R. Strata, "Organizational Learning: The Key to Management Innovation," *Sloan Management Review* (Spring 1989): 63–74.

113. Dumaine, "Mr. Learning Organization."

114. Argyris and Schon, *Organizational Learning II*, p. 112.

115. R. Ruggles, "The State of the Notion: Knowledge Management in Practice," *California Management Review* 40 (Spring 1998): 80–89.

116. Davenport and Prusak, *Working Knowledge.*

117. O'Dell and Grayson, *If Only We Knew.*

Rondell Data Corporation

"God damn it, he's done it again!" Frank Forbus threw the stack of prints and specifications on his desk in disgust. The model 802 wide-band modulator, released for production the previous Thursday, had just come back to Frank's engineering services department with a caustic note that began, "This one can't be produced, either. . . ." It was the fourth time production had returned the design.

Forbus, director of engineering for the Rondell Data Corporation, was normally a quiet person. But the model 802 was stretching his patience; it was beginning to look like other new products that had hit delays and problems in the transition from design to production during the eight months Frank had worked for Rondell. These problems were nothing new at the sprawling, old Rondell factory. Frank's predecessor in the engineering job had run afoul of them, too, and finally had been fired for protesting too vehemently about the other departments. But the model 802 should have been different. Frank had met two months earlier (on July 3, 1978) with the firm's president, Bill Hunt, and with factory superintendent Dave Schwab to smooth the way for the new modulator design. He thought back to the meeting . . .

"Now, we all know there's a tight deadline on the 802," Bill Hunt said, "and Frank's done well to ask us to talk about its introduction. I'm counting on both of you to find any snags in the system, and to work together to get that first production run out by October 2. Can you do it?"

"We can do it in production if we get a clean design two weeks from now, as scheduled," answered Dave Schwab, the factory superintendent. "Frank and I have already talked about that, of course. I'm setting aside time in the card room and the machine shop, and we'll be ready. If the design goes over schedule, though, I'll have to fill in with other runs, and it will cost us a bundle to break in for the 802. How does it look in engineering, Frank?"

"I've just reviewed the design for the second time," Frank replied. "If Ron Porter can keep the salespeople out of our hair, and avoid any more last-minute changes, we've got a shot. I've pulled the draftspeople off of three other overdue jobs to get this one out. But, Dave, that means we can't spring engineers loose to confer with your production people on manufacturing problems."

"Well, Frank, most of those problems are caused by the engineers, and we need them to resolve the difficulties. We've all agreed that production bugs come from both of us bowing to sales pressure, and putting equipment into production before the designs are really ready. That's just what we're trying to avoid on the 802. But I can't have five hundred people sitting on their hands waiting for an answer from your people. We'll have to have *some* engineering support."

Bill Hunt broke in, "So long as you two can talk calmly about the problem I'm confident you can resolve it. What a relief it is, Frank, to hear the way you're approaching this. With Kilmann (the previous director of engineering), this conversation would have been a shouting match. Right, Dave?" Dave nodded and smiled.

"Now there's one other thing you both should be aware of," Hunt continued. "Doc Reeves and I talked last night about a new filtering technique, one that might improve the signal-to-noise ratio of the 802 by a factor of two. There's a chance Doc can come up with it before the 802 reaches production, and if it's possible, I'd like to use the new filters. That would give us a real jump on the competition."

Four days after that meeting, Frank found that two of his key people on the 802 design had been called to the production department for an emergency consultation about a problem in final assembly: two halves of a new data transmission interface wouldn't fit together because recent changes in the front end required a different chassis design for the rear end.

One week later, Doc Reeves proudly walked into Frank's office with the new filter design. "This won't affect the other modules of the 802 much," Doc had said. "Look, it takes three new cards, a few connectors, some changes in the wiring harness, and some new shielding, and that's all."

Frank tried to resist the last-minute design changes, but Bill Hunt had stood firm. With considerable overtime by the engineers and draftspeople, engineering services still should be able to finish the blueprints in time.

Two engineers and three draftspeople went onto twelve-hour days to get the 802 ready, but the prints were still five days late reaching Dave Schwab. Two days later, the prints came back to Frank, heavily annotated in red. Schwab had worked all day Saturday to review the job and had found more than a dozen discrepancies in the prints—most of them caused by the new filter design and insufficient checking time before release. Correction of these design faults gave rise to a new generation of discrepancies; Schwab's cover note on the second return of the prints indicated that he had had to release the machine capacity reserved for the 802. On the third iteration, Schwab committed his photo and plating capacity to another rush job. The 802 would be at least one month late getting into production. Ron Porter, the vice president for sales, was furious. His customer needed 100 units *now*. Rondell was the customer's only late supplier.

"Here we go again," thought Forbus.

COMPANY HISTORY

Rondell Data Corporation traced its lineage through several generations of electronics technology. Its original founder, Bob Rondell, launched the firm in 1920 as Rondell Equipment Co. to manufacture several electrical testing devices he had invented as an engineering faculty member at a large university. The firm began manufacturing radio broadcasting equipment in 1947 and data transmission equipment in the early 1960s. A well-established corps of direct sales representatives, mostly engineers, called on industrial, scientific, and government accounts but concentrated heavily on original equipment manufacturers. In this market, Rondell had a long-standing reputation as a source of high-quality, innovative designs. The firm's salespeople fed a continual stream of challenging problems into the engineering department, where the creative genius of Doc Reeves and several dozen other engineers "converted problems to solutions" (as the sales brochure bragged). Product design formed the spearhead of Rondell's growth.

By 1978, Rondell offered a wide range of products in its two major lines. Broadcast equipment sales had benefited from the growth of UHF television and FM radio and accounted for 35 percent of company sales. Data transmission had blossomed and an increasing number of orders called for unique specifications, ranging from specialized display panels to entirely untried designs.

The company had grown from one hundred employees in 1947 to more than eight hundred in 1978. (Exhibits 1 and 2 show the current organization chart and the backgrounds of key employees.) Bill Hunt, who had been a student of the company's founder, had presided over most of that growth and took great pride in preserving the family spirit of the old organization. Informal relationships among Rondell's veteran employees formed the backbone of the firm's day-to-day operations; all managers relied on personal contact, and Hunt often insisted that the absence of bureaucratic red tape was a key factor in recruiting outstanding engineering talent. The personal management approach extended throughout the factory. All exempt employees were paid a straight salary and a share of the profits. Rondell boasted an extremely loyal group of senior employees, and very low turnover in nearly all areas of the company.

The highest turnover job in the firm was director of engineering services. Forbus had joined Rondell in January 1978, replacing Jim Kilmann, who had lasted only ten months. Kilmann, in turn, had replaced Tom MacLeod, a talented engineer who had made a promising start but had taken to drinking after a year in the job. MacLeod's predecessor had been a genial oldtimer, who retired at seventy, after thirty years in charge of engineering. (Doc Reeves had refused the directorship in each of the recent changes, saying, "Hell, that's no promotion for a bench man like me. I'm no administrator.")

For several years, the firm had experienced a steadily increasing number of disputes between research, engineering, sales, and production people; disputes generally centered on the problem of new-product introduction. Quarrels between departments became more numerous under MacLeod, Kilmann, and Forbus. Some managers associated these disputes with the company's recent decline in profitability—a decline that, despite higher sales and gross revenues, was beginning to bother people in 1977. Hunt commented:

Better cooperation, I'm sure, could increase our output by 5 to 10 percent. I'd hoped Kilmann could solve the problems, but pretty obviously he was too young—too arrogant. People like him—that conflict type of personality—bother me. I don't like strife, and with him it seemed I spent all my time smoothing out arguments. Kilmann tried to tell everyone else how to run their departments, without having his own house in order. That approach just wouldn't work here at Rondell. Frank Forbus, now, seems much more in tune with our style of organization. I'm really hopeful now.

Still, we have just as many problems now as we did last year. Maybe even more. I hope Frank can get a handle on engineering services soon.

Engineering Department Research

According to the organization chart, Forbus was in charge of both research (the product development function) and engineering services (engineering support). To Forbus, however, the relationship with research was not so clear-cut:

Doc Reeves is one of the world's unique people, and none of us would have it any other way. He's a creative genius. Sure, the chart says he works for me, but we all know Doc does his own thing. He's not the least bit interested in management routines, and I can't count on him to take any responsibility in scheduling projects, or checking budgets, or what have you. But as long as Doc is

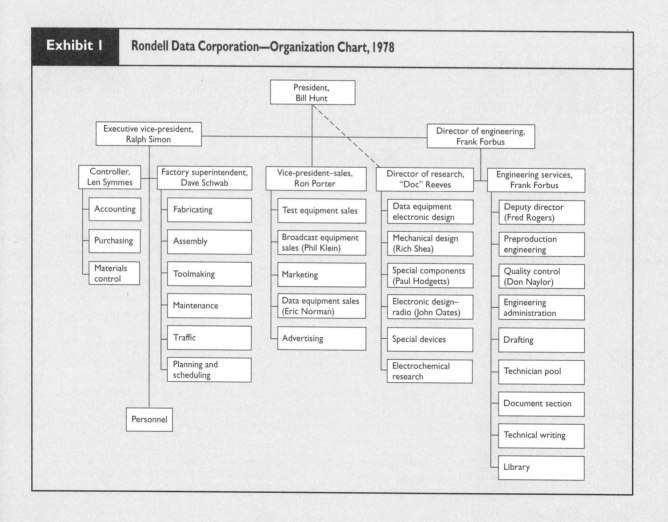

Exhibit 1   Rondell Data Corporation—Organization Chart, 1978

President, Bill Hunt

Executive vice-president, Ralph Simon

Director of engineering, Frank Forbus

- Controller, Len Symmes
  - Accounting
  - Purchasing
  - Materials control
- Factory superintendent, Dave Schwab
  - Fabricating
  - Assembly
  - Toolmaking
  - Maintenance
  - Traffic
  - Planning and scheduling
- Vice-president–sales, Ron Porter
  - Test equipment sales
  - Broadcast equipment sales (Phil Klein)
  - Marketing
  - Data equipment sales (Eric Norman)
  - Advertising
- Director of research, "Doc" Reeves
  - Data equipment electronic design
  - Mechanical design (Rich Shea)
  - Special components (Paul Hodgetts)
  - Electronic design–radio (John Oates)
  - Special devices
  - Electrochemical research
- Engineering services, Frank Forbus
  - Deputy director (Fred Rogers)
  - Preproduction engineering
  - Quality control (Don Naylor)
  - Engineering administration
  - Drafting
  - Technician pool
  - Document section
  - Technical writing
  - Library

Personnel

director of research, you can bet this company will keep on leading the field. He has more ideas per hour than most people have per year, and he keeps the whole engineering staff fired up. Everybody loves Doc—and you can count me in on that, too. In a way, he works for me, sure. But that's not what's important.

Doc Reeves—unhurried, contemplative, casual, and candid—tipped his stool back against the wall

Exhibit 2	Background of Selected Executives		

EXECUTIVE	POSITION	AGE	BACKGROUND
Bill Hunt	President	63	Engineering graduate of an Ivy League college. Joined the company in 1946 as an engineer. Worked exclusively on development for over a year and then split his time between development and field sales work until he became assistant to the president in 1956. Became president in 1960. Together, Hunt and Simon hold enough stock to command effective control of the company.
Ralph Simon	Executive vice president	65	Joined company in 1945 as a traveling representative. In 1947 became Rondell's leading salesperson for broadcast equipment. In 1954 was made treasurer but continued to spend time selling. In 1960 was appointed executive vice president with direct responsibility for financial matters and production.
Ron Porter	Vice president of sales	50	BS in engineering. Joined the company in 1957 as a salesperson. Was influential in establishing the data transmission product line and did early selling himself. In 1967 was made sales manager. Extensive contacts in trade associations and industrial shows. Appointed vice president of sales in 1974.
Dave Schwab	Production manager	62	Trade school graduate; veteran of both World War II and Korean War. Joined Rondell in 1955. Promoted to production manager seven months later after exposure of widespread irregularities in production and control departments. Reorganized production department and brought a new group of production specialists to the company.
Frank Forbus	Director of engineering	40	Master's degree in engineering. Previously division director of engineering in large industrial firm. Joined the company in 1977 as director of engineering, replacing an employee who had been dismissed because of an inability to work with sales and production personnel. As director of engineering, had administrative responsibility for research personnel and complete responsibility for engineering services.
Ed Reeves	Director of research	47	Joined Rondell in 1960. Worked directly with Hunt to develop major innovations in data transmission equipment. Appointed director of research in 1967.
Les Symmes	Controller	43	Joined company in 1955 while attending business college. Held several jobs, including production scheduling, accounting, and cost control. Named controller in 1972.

of his research cubicle and talked about what *was* important:

> Development engineering. That's where the company's future rests. Either we have it there, or we don't have it.
>
> There's no kidding ourselves that we're anything but a bunch of Rube Goldbergs here. But that's where the biggest kicks come from—from solving development problems and dreaming up new ways of doing things. That's why I so look forward to the special contracts we get involved in. We accept them not for the revenue they represent but because they subsidize the basic development work that goes into all our basic products.
>
> This is a fantastic place to work. I have a great crew and they can really deliver when the chips are down. Why, Bill Hunt and I (he gestured toward the neighboring cubicle, where the president's name hung over the door) are likely to find as many people here at work at 10 p.m. as at 3 p.m. The important thing here is the relationships between people; they're based on mutual respect, not on policies and procedures. Administrative red tape is a pain. It takes away from development time.
>
> Problems? Sure, there are problems now and then. There are power interests in production, where they sometimes resist change. But I'm not a fighting man, you know. I suppose if I were, I might go in there and push my weight around a little. But I'm an engineer, and can do more for Rondell sitting right here, or working with my own people. That's what brings results.

Other members of the research department echoed these views and added additional sources of satisfaction from their work. They were proud of the personal contacts built with customers' technical staffs—contacts that increasingly involved travel to the customer's factories to serve as expert advisers in preparation of overall system design specifications. The engineers also were delighted with the department's encouragement of their personal development, continuing education, and independence on the job.

But there were problems, too. Rich Shea, of the mechanical design section, noted:

> In the old days I really enjoyed the work—and the people I worked with. But now there's a lot of irritation. I don't like someone breathing down my neck. You can be hurried into jeopardizing the design.

John Oates, head of the radio electronic design section, was another designer with definite views:

> Production engineering is almost nonexistent in this company. Very little is done by the preproduction section in engineering services. Frank Forbus has been trying to get preproduction into the picture, but he won't succeed because you can't start from such an ambiguous position. There have been three directors of engineering in three years. Frank can't hold his own against the others in the company. Kilmann was too aggressive. Perhaps no amount of tact would have succeeded.

Paul Hodgetts was head of special components of the R&D department. Like the rest of the department, he valued bench work. But he complained of engineering services:

> The services don't do things we want them to do. Instead, they tell *us* what they're going to do. I should probably go to Frank, but I don't get any decisions there. I know I should go through Frank, but this holds things up, so I often go direct.

Engineering Services Department

The engineering services department (ESD) provided ancillary services to R&D and served as liaison between engineering and the other Rondell departments. Among its main functions were drafting, managing the central technicians' pool, scheduling and expediting engineering products, documentation and publication of parts lists and engineering orders, preproduction engineering (consisting of the final integration of individual design components into mechanically compatible packages), and quality control (including initial inspection of incoming parts and materials, and final inspection of subassemblies and finished equipment). Top management's description of the department included the line, "ESD is responsible for maintaining cooperation with other departments, providing services to the development engineers, and freeing more valuable people in R&D from essential activities that are diversions from and beneath their main competence."

Many of the seventy-five ESD employees were located in other departments. Quality control people were scattered through the manufacturing and receiving areas, and technicians worked primarily in the research area or the prototype fabrication room. The remaining ESD personnel were assigned to leftover nooks and crannies near production or engineering sections. Forbus described his position:

My biggest problem is getting acceptance from the people I work with. I've moved slowly rather than risk antagonism. I saw what happened to Kilmann, and I want to avoid that. But although his precipitate action had won over a few of the younger R&D people, he certainly didn't have the department's backing. Of course, it was the resentment of other departments that eventually caused his discharge. People have been slow accepting me here. There's nothing really overt, but I get a negative reaction to my ideas.

My role in the company has never been well-defined, really. It's complicated by Doc's unique position, of course, and also by the fact that ESD sort of grew by itself over the years, as the design engineers concentrated more and more on the creative parts of product development. I wish I could be more involved in the technical side. That's been my training, and it's a lot of fun. But in our setup, the technical side is the least necessary for me to be involved in.

Schwab is hard to get along with. Before I came and after Kilmann left, there were six months when no one was really doing any scheduling. No work loads were figured, and unrealistic promises were made about releases. This puts us in an awkward position. We've been scheduling way beyond our capacity to manufacture or engineer.

Certain people within R&D, for instance John Oates, understand scheduling well and meet project deadlines, but this is not generally true of the rest of the R&D department, especially the mechanical engineers, who won't commit themselves. Most of the complaints come from sales and production department heads because items, such as the 802, are going to production before they are fully developed, under pressure from sales to get the unit out, and this snags the whole process. Somehow, engineering services should

be able to intervene and resolve these complaints, but I haven't made much headway so far.

I should be able to go to Hunt for help, but he's too busy most of the time, and his major interest is the design side of engineering, where he got his own start. Sometimes he talks as though he's the engineering director as well as president. I have to put my foot down; there are problems here that the front office just doesn't understand.

Salespeople often were observed taking their problems directly to designers, although production frequently threw designs back at R&D, claiming they could not be produced and demanding the prompt attention of particular design engineers. The latter were frequently observed in conference with production supervisors on the assembly floor. Frank continued:

The designers seem to feel they're losing something when one of us tries to help. They feel it's a reflection on them to have someone take over what they've been doing. They seem to want to carry a project right through to the final stages, particularly the mechanical people. Consequently, engineering services people are used below their capacity to contribute, and our department is denied functions it should be performing. There's not as much use made of engineering services as there should be.

An ESD technician supervisor added his comments:

Production picks out the engineer who'll be the "bum of the month." They pick on every little detail instead of using their heads and making the minor changes that have to be made. The people with fifteen to twenty years of experience shouldn't have to prove their ability any more, but they spend four hours defending themselves and four hours getting the job done. I have no one to go to when I need help. Frank Forbus is afraid. I'm trying to help him but he can't help me at this time. I'm responsible for fifty people and I've got to support them.

Fred Rodgers, whom Forbus had brought with him to the company as an assistant, gave another view of the situation:

I try to get our people in preproduction to take responsibility but they're not used to it, and people in other departments don't usually see them as best qualified to solve the problem. There's a real barrier for a newcomer here. Gaining people's confidence is hard. More and more, I'm wondering whether there really is a job for me here. [Rodgers left Rondell a month later.]

Another subordinate of Forbus gave his view:

If Doc gets a new product idea, you can't argue. But he's too optimistic. He judges that others can do what he does—but there's only one Doc Reeves. We've had nine hundred production change orders this year—they changed two thousand five hundred drawings. If I were in Frank's shoes, I'd put my foot down on all this new development. I'd look at the reworking we're doing and get production set up the way I wanted it. Kilmann was fired when he was doing a good job. He was getting some system in the company's operations. Of course, it hurt some people. There is no denying that Doc is the most important person in the company. What gets overlooked is that Hunt is a close second, not just politically but in terms of what he contributes technically and in customer relations.

This subordinate explained that he sometimes went out into the production department but that Schwab, the production head, resented this. Production personnel said that Kilmann had failed to show respect for oldtimers and was always meddling in other departments' business. This was the reason for his being fired, they contended. Don Taylor, in charge of quality control, commented:

I am now much more concerned with administration and less with work. It is one of the evils you get into. There is tremendous detail in this job. I listen to everyone's opinion. Everybody is important. There shouldn't be distinctions—distinctions between people. I'm not sure whether Frank has to be a fireball like Kilmann. I think the real question is whether Frank is getting the job done. I know my job is essential; I want to supply service to the more talented people and give them information so they can do their jobs better.

Sales Department

Ron Porter was angry. His job was supposed to be selling, but instead it had turned into settling disputes inside the plant and making excuses to waiting customers. He jabbed a finger toward his desk:

You see that telephone? I'm actually afraid nowadays to hear it ring. Three times out of five, it will be a customer who's hurting because we've failed to deliver on schedule. The other two calls will be from production or ESD, telling me some schedule has slipped again.

The model 802 is typical. Absolutely typical. We padded the delivery date by six weeks to allow for contingencies. Within two months, the slack had evaporated. Now it looks like we'll be lucky to ship it before Christmas. (It was now November 28.) We're *ruining* our reputation in the market. Why, just last week one of our best customers—people we've worked with for fifteen years—tried to hang a penalty clause on their latest order.

We shouldn't have to be after the engineers all the time. They should be able to see what problems they create without our telling them.

Phil Klein, head of broadcast sales under Porter, noted that many sales decisions were made by top management. He thought that sales was understaffed and had never really been able to get on top of the job.

We have grown further and further away from engineering. The director of engineering does not pass on the information that we give him. We need better relationships there. It is very difficult for us to talk to customers about development problems without technical help. We need each other. The whole of engineering is now too isolated from the outside world. The morale of ESD is very low. They're in a bad spot—they're not well organized.

People don't take much to outsiders here. Much of this is because the expectation is built by top management that jobs will be filled from the bottom. So it's really tough when an outsider like Frank comes in.

Eric Norman, order and pricing coordinator for data equipment, talked about his relationships with the production department:

Actually, I get along with them fairly well. Oh, things could be better, of course, if they were more cooperative generally. They always seem to say, "It's my bat and my ball, and we're playing by my rules." People are afraid to make production mad; there's a lot of power in there.

But you've got to understand that production has its own set of problems. And nobody in Rondell is working any harder than Dave Schwab to try to straighten things out.

Production Department

Schwab had joined Rondell just after the Korean War, in which he had seen combat duty at the Yalu River and intelligence duty at Pyong Yang. Both experiences had been useful in his first year of civilian employment at Rondell. The wartime factory superintendent and several middle managers had apparently been engaging in highly questionable side deals with Rondell's suppliers. Schwab gathered the evidence, revealed the situation to Hunt, and had stood by the president in the ensuing unsavory situation. Seven months after joining the company, Schwab was named factory superintendent.

Schwab's first move had been to replace the fallen managers with a new team from outside the corporation. This group did not share the traditional Rondell emphasis on informality and friendly personal relationships, and had worked long and hard to install systematic manufacturing methods and procedures. Before the reorganization, production had controlled purchasing, stock control, and final quality control (where final assembly of products in cabinets was accomplished). Because of the wartime events, management decided on a checks-and-balances system of organization and removed these three departments from production jurisdiction. The new production managers felt they had been unjustly penalized by the reorganization, particularly because they had uncovered the behavior that was detrimental to the company in the first place.

By 1978, the production department had grown to five hundred employees, of whom 60 percent worked in the assembly area—an unusually pleasant environment that had been commended by *Factory* magazine for its colorful decoration, cleanli-

ness, and low noise level. Another 30 percent of the workforce, mostly skilled machinists, staffed the finishing and fabrication department. The remaining employees performed scheduling, supervisory, and maintenance duties. Production workers were not union members, were paid by the hour, and participated in both the liberal profit-sharing program and the stock purchase plan. Morale in production was traditionally high, and turnover was extremely low.

Schwab commented:

To be efficient, production has to be a self-contained department. We have to control what comes into the department and what goes out. That's why purchasing, inventory control, and quality ought to run out of this office. We'd eliminate a lot of problems with better control there. Why, even Don Naylor of QC would rather work for me than for ESD; he's said so himself. We understand his problems better.

The other departments should be self-contained, too. That's why I always avoid the underlings, and go straight to the department heads with any questions. I always go down the line.

I have to protect my people from outside disturbances. Look what would happen if I let unfinished, half-baked designs in here—there'd be chaos. The bugs have to be found before the drawings go into the shop, and it seems I'm the one who has to find them. Look at the 802, for example. [Dave had spent most of Thanksgiving Day (it was now November 28) red-penciling the latest set of prints.] ESD should have found every one of those discrepancies. They just don't check drawings properly. They change most of the things I flag, but then they fail to trace through the impact of those changes on the rest of the design. I shouldn't have to do that.

And those engineers are tolerance crazy. They want everything to a millionth of an inch. I'm the only one in the company who's had any experience with actually machining things to a millionth of an inch. We make sure that the things that engineers say on their drawings actually have to be that way and whether they're obtainable from the kind of raw material we buy.

That shouldn't be production's responsibility, but I have to do it. Accepting bad prints wouldn't let us ship the order any quicker. We'd only make a lot of junk that had to be reworked. And that would take even longer.

This way, I get to be known as the bad guy, but I guess that's just part of the job. [Schwab paused and smiled wryly.] Of course, what really gets them is that I don't even have a degree.

Schwab had fewer bones to pick with the sales department, because he said that they trusted him.

When *we* give Ron Porter a shipping date, he knows the equipment will be shipped *then*.

You've got to recognize, though, that all of our new product problems stem from sales making absurd commitments on equipment that hasn't been developed fully. That *always* means trouble. Unfortunately, Hunt always backs sales up, even when they're wrong. He always favors them over us.

Ralph Simon, executive vice president of the company, had direct responsibility for Rondell's production department. He said:

There really shouldn't be a dividing of departments among top management in the company. The president should be czar over all. The production people ask me to do something for them, and I really can't do it. It creates bad feelings between engineering and production, this special attention that they [R&D] get from Bill. But then Hunt likes to dabble in design. Schwab feels that production is treated like a poor relation.

Executive Committee

At the executive committee meeting on December 6, it was duly recorded that Schwab had accepted the prints and specifications for the model 802 modulator and had set December 29 as the shipping date for the first ten pieces. Hunt, as chairperson, shook his head and changed the subject quickly when Forbus tried to initiate discussion of interdepartmental coordination.

The executive committee itself was a brainchild of Rondell's controller, Len Symmes, who was well aware of the disputes that plagued the company. Symmes had convinced Hunt and Simon to meet every two weeks with their department heads; the meetings were formalized with Hunt, Simon, Porter, Schwab, Forbus, Reeves, Symmes, and the personnel director attending. Symmes explained his intent and the results:

Doing things collectively and informally just doesn't work as well as it used to. Things have been gradually getting worse for at least two years now. We had to start thinking in terms of formal organization relationships. I did the first organization chart, and the executive committee was my idea, too—but neither idea is contributing much help, I'm afraid. It takes top management to make an organization click. The rest of us can't act much differently until the top people see the need for us to change.

I had hoped the committee especially would help get the department managers into a constructive planning process. It hasn't worked out that way, because Mr. Hunt really doesn't see the need for it. He uses the meetings as a place to pass on routine information.

Merry Christmas

It was December 22, and Forbus was standing awkwardly in front of Hunt's desk. "Frank, I didn't know whether to tell you now, or after the holiday," Hunt said, "but I figured you'd work right through Christmas Day if we didn't have this talk, and that just wouldn't have been fair to you. I can't understand why we have such poor luck in the engineering director's job lately. And I don't think it's entirely your fault. But. . .

Frank only heard half of Hunt's words, and said nothing in response. He'd be paid through February 28. . . . He should use the time for searching. . . . Hunt would help all he could. . . . Jim Kilmann was supposed to be doing well at his own new job, and might need more help.

Frank cleaned out his desk and numbly started home. The electronic carillon near his house was playing a Christmas carol. Frank thought again of Hunt's rationale: conflict still plagued Rondell—and Frank had not made it go away. Maybe somebody else could do it.

"And what did Santa Claus bring you, Frankie?" he asked himself. "The sack. Only the empty sack."

Questions

1. What is your diagnosis of the strategy and organization design at Rondell? How well does Rondell's strategic orientation fit with its external environment?

2. How would you work with Bill Hunt and the executive committee to bring about strategic change at Rondell?

Source: Reprinted with permission of the author, John A. Seeger, Bently College, Waltham, Mass.

■ Managing Strategy at Caesars Tahoe

Caesars Tahoe General Manager David Attaway prepared to face his executive committee. While the sun was shining on the perfect Lake Tahoe morning, the information he was about to present was anything but a fair-weather forecast. He had just received the property's 1997 financial goal from the parent company, Caesars World, and he knew it would be a tough goal to meet given the challenges that 1996 had presented. Caesars World consisted of four properties—Caesars Palace in Las Vegas, Caesars in Atlantic City, another property in Canada, and Caesars Tahoe. Additionally, the parent of Caesars World, ITT Corporation, was placing increasing emphasis on cash flow and sustained earnings improvement. Attaway knew that some carefully formulated strategic plans were needed for Caesars Tahoe to meet its aggressive financial goal for 1997. Moreover, sustaining earnings improvement there in subsequent years would continue to be a challenge.

For the past eight years, the Lake Tahoe tourism market had been flat, with no change in sight. Increased competition from Las Vegas and nearby Reno, Nevada, only added to the ongoing challenge. The situation would be an easier one to remedy if the tough regulatory environment would allow the company to expand its facilities. How easy it would be if Tahoe were like Las Vegas, where hotel room additions could be had for the capital expense and potentially could add tenfold to revenues. But Tahoe was not Las Vegas, so there would be no new hotel rooms at Caesars Tahoe to help meet the financial goals.

Since entering the gaming industry, Attaway had watched it grow from a business with a colorful history of underworld involvement, owned primarily by private concerns and centered in Las Vegas, to a widely respected and accepted industry, operated by public corporations in twenty-five states, and with annual gross revenues of $39.4 billion. Indeed, with the acquisition by ITT Corporation, Caesars World had a parent among the blue-chip corporations in the United States.

With the industry's rapid expansion, customers had many choices. The various gaming venues, particularly in Las Vegas, offered an "experience" to the increasingly sophisticated customer. Erupting volcanoes, giant pyramids, live street shows, and other "WOW" attractions drew visitors from around the world. Additionally, hotel expansions provided opportunities for great room and package values.

Among the new entrants in the market each year were major hotel companies, riverboat operations, cruise ships, and Native American reservations. In addition, the traditional sources of revenue were shifting. Slot machine revenue was increasing at a stronger pace than table games, such as blackjack and craps, proving that customer mix and preference had shifted. In addition, at some of the new Las Vegas properties, gaming was no longer the major revenue source. As much as 60 percent of revenues were coming from retail operations, food, beverage, and hotel room sales. This represented a major shift in thinking and operating.

Attaway decided that the first things the executive committee would need to tackle were the strategic challenges, including an understanding of the market drivers and the specific elements facing Caesars Tahoe.

Caesars Tahoe— An Historic Perspective

Caesars Tahoe has been in business for seventeen years. The property was built in 1978 and leased by Caesars World in 1979. It was the last of the four major Lake Tahoe properties to be built. Different from most lease situations, Caesars World was responsible for financing the completion of construction on the building. The lease is for a period of twenty-five years, expiring in 2004, with two twenty-five-year renewal options.

Since opening, there have been ten chief operating officers and numerous changes in strategic focus. To illustrate, the first five years of operation were marked by major financial losses, and the property's business focus was exclusively on the volatile high-end customer. Any long-term focus was sacrificed for short-term gains. Local business was not cultivated and, as a result, the property had to work hard at attracting local clientele. What resulted was a general lack of direction and confusion among the staff.

Lake Tahoe—A National Treasure

Lake Tahoe lies between two cities: Reno, Nevada, with an area population of 250,000, is ninety minutes away by car; and Sacramento, California, with a population of 1.7 million, is a two-hour drive to the west. The lake is twenty-two miles long and twelve miles wide. The surface of the lake is 6,229 feet above sea level. Surrounding mountains form what is considered the Lake Tahoe basin, with the highest peak at about eleven thousand feet. Temperatures range from a low of 16 degrees F in the winter to a high of about 80 degrees F in the summer.

Caesars location on the south shore of Lake Tahoe is at once an asset and a liability. As a popular tourist area, with a year-round population of thirty-five thousand and annual visitors numbering over two million, the natural beauty of the area is the major attraction. But that same scenic beauty is also highly regulated by environmental restrictions that had virtually stopped growth at the lake. Attractions could not be built because of these restrictions, leaving the lake's natural attraction the most significant source of tourism.

Summer and winter are the lake's biggest seasons in terms of visitor volumes, with summer busier on a week-to-week basis. However, the period from June through September typically accounts for 40 percent of the annual gaming revenue. During both seasons, weekends and holidays attract the lion's share of visitors to the area. In the "shoulder" months—those between the summer and winter seasons—visitor counts decrease significantly. These months continue to be a time of great challenge for local business.

The Competitive Environment

Overview

Caesars Tahoe's competition on the south shore is, for the most part, limited to the three other major casino properties: Harrah's, Harvey's, and the Horizon. These properties, along with Caesars, are located within a several-block area of one another, an area commonly referred to as the "casino core." There is also a stand-alone Harrah's satellite casino, called Bill's, located between Harrah's and Caesars, as well as a small hotel/casino located just outside the casino core, called the Lakeside Inn. The total rooms available within the casino core is 2,350.

The Embassy Suites, along with several other mid-size properties, are the only other notable hotel properties on the south shore, and there are few national motel chains. Most of the motels are small, individually owned operations. Rooms available on the California side total seven thousand, many of which are old and in disrepair.

The competition outside the basin is fierce. With more rooms than customers and hotel occupancy rates declining, Reno attracts business with value packages and low room rates. On average, Reno room rates are in the $50 to $60 range, less than half of Caesars Tahoe's average room rate.

Las Vegas, just an hour by air from Reno, San Francisco, and Los Angeles, offers value and an "experience." Unsurpassed growth and the ability to offer thrills and attractions have made Las Vegas one of the top travel destinations in the United States. Las Vegas rooms number approximately one hundred thousand, with ten thousand more rooms planned in the next several years. In 1995, thirty million people visited Las Vegas. Although questions have arisen about the sustainability of such incredible growth, visitors keep coming and the city keeps booming.

In California, gaming concerns are represented by Native Americans, most notably Cache Creek, just outside Sacramento. There also are plans for a casino outside Placerville, which is located approximately ninety miles from Lake Tahoe.

The Competitors

Harrah's Tahoe is Caesars Tahoe's toughest competitor. Harrah's has been in business on the south shore for forty years. Its location as the most accessible casino property for California visitors has only added to its sustained success, and walk-in business makes up a large portion of its clientele. Reported operating income for 1995 was $37.5 million on revenues of $160 million (compared with an operating income of $11.4 million on $107.2 million in revenue for Caesars). Its continued growth in a flat market appears to be supported by an aggressive approach to controlling expenses.

The company is known for its consistency and often is considered the "McDonald's" of the industry. Harrah's customers have come to expect reasonably priced products and services in a clean and friendly environment. With multiple properties throughout the United States, Harrah's vast marketing network allows it to serve the midmarket customer extremely well. Customers are loyal, and Harrah's markets its properties in a way that encourages repeat visits.

In Lake Tahoe, Harrah's has the only buffet with a view of the lake. There are 535 guest rooms and approximately ninety thousand square feet of casino space. For the past decade, the Harrah's Tahoe target market has been the dollar-plus slot player. Their ratio of table-game revenues to slot revenues is 0.60:1, compared with 1.4:1 for Caesars. Although Harrah's Tahoe is no longer an official five-star property, according to the Mobile travel guide, the customer perception of five-star quality endures.

Harvey's, located directly across the street from Harrah's, is the largest of the casino core properties, with 744 guest rooms and one hundred thousand feet of casino space. Their ratio of table-game revenues to slot revenues is 0.40:1. It is connected via underground tunnel to Harrah's. Family-owned for fifty years, Harvey's went public in 1994, and had 1995 operating income of $22.6 million on revenues of $130.6 million. They have several other properties outside of Lake Tahoe, most notably a joint venture with the Hard Rock Cafe in Las Vegas.

Despite Harvey's mass marketing approach, the company is not considered a strong marketer and is associated with a lack of identity. Recently, several members of top management at Harrah's moved over to Harvey's, which may strengthen its position in the future. To date, the company appears to have failed to take advantage of its size relative to its position in the market.

The *Horizon,* located across the street from Caesars Tahoe, is owned and operated by a hotel holding company and is associated with no other identifiable casino company. The property, with 537 rooms and a forty-thousand-square-foot casino, is barely surviving financially. There was an operating loss of $2.5 million in 1995 on revenues of $36.5 million. The Horizon competes through somewhat desperate measures, such as unusual betting options and low price, and the company depends heavily on the walk-in business such options generate. At one time or another, all three major properties—Harrah's, Harvey's, and Caesars—have considered purchasing the Horizon, either individually or as a group. That remains a viable option but no one has moved forward to date because of perceived cost and the current lease agreement with the same property owner that leases Caesars Tahoe.

Political and Regulatory Environment

The south shore of Lake Tahoe is located in both Nevada and California, and presents a unique governmental structure, unlike any other in the nation. One city and two county governments oversee the area, governed by the Tahoe Regional Planning Agency (TRPA), a bi-state agency created by the U.S. Congress. The TRPA oversees all building, signage, land usage, transportation, and general development issues to ensure that environmental standards are maintained.

Casinos in the region may do nothing that expands current cubic volume, and noncasino hotel growth must be mitigated by the retirement of 1.3 existing rooms for every new room constructed. The focus of the TRPA does appear to be changing. The addition of Steve Wynn, chairman of the Mirage and part-time Lake Tahoe resident, to the TRPA board may signal the beginning of an agency more focused on environmental priorities as opposed to micromanaging local business growth. But until the law that governs the TRPA changes, the high level of regulation will continue to prevail.

Two chambers of commerce support the south shore: the Tahoe–Douglas Chamber and the South Lake Tahoe Chamber. Few of the small businesses associated with the chambers have the dollars available for additional marketing. Local business also is supported by the Lake Tahoe Visitors Authority, a community marketing organization, and the South Tahoe Gaming Alliance (STGA), a committee composed of all the local gaming concerns. The STGA's function is to consolidate gaming issues and maintain a unified front with various agencies.

The Infrastructure

Transportation to and from the Tahoe basin is extremely difficult. For example, the most common route into the south shore from northern California, U.S. Highway 50, often is reduced to a two-lane highway in the winter. During major snow storms, which are not unusual, the road is closed completely. Highway 50 continues north toward Reno and is the main route for visitors from the Reno area. In the early 1980s, three-quarters of a million travelers passed through the South Lake Tahoe Airport annually. Today, that number is virtually zero because the airport no longer serves commercial carriers as a result of legal battles over environmental restrictions, inability to compete on a low-cost basis, and general uncertainty in the market. The Reno Tahoe International Airport, located in Reno, is a ninety-minute drive.

The budget squeeze that has hit many local governments has affected Lake Tahoe as well. The poor condition of sidewalks, roads, and other city and county areas is testimony to the lack of funds available. There is a redevelopment plan in place for rejuvenating selected areas of the city. Financed primarily through private funding, the plan has three phases, and two are TRPA approved—the Ski Run and Park Avenue projects. None of the three projects provide for additional hotel rooms, but significant remodeling of existing rooms will be allowed.

- The Ski Run project, located approximately one and a half miles from Caesars and about a quarter-mile from the base of Heavenly Valley Ski Resort, is under way and scheduled for completion in 1997. It includes construction of a new hotel and general rejuvenation of the intersection.

- The Park Avenue project, scheduled to begin in 1997 and to be completed in 1999, covers a fourteen-acre area just three blocks from Caesars Tahoe. It includes a central transportation area, with a gondola to and from Heavenly Valley, an ice rink, a multiplex movie theater, shops, and

seven hundred upscale hotel rooms. For the purposes of the Ski Run and Park Avenue projects, the TRPA has permitted one-for-one room replacement instead of the current 1.3 rooms retired for every new room constructed. As yet, funding has not been secured for this project.

- A third project is still awaiting approval. It is to be located directly across the street from the Park Avenue project. The proposal for Project Three includes a convention center, additional retail space, an information building, a park with a "miniature" Lake Tahoe, and replacement of existing rooms with upscale rooms. There are mixed opinions on the probable success of Project Three. To date, no approvals have been awarded.

The Caesars Tahoe Customer

For the past decade, an increasing trend away from visits driven solely by gaming activities has developed. As gaming proliferates across the country, visitors to northern Nevada seek a more diversified experience. Similar to guests aboard a cruise ship, more and more visitors approach gaming as another amenity, along with food, entertainment, and retail opportunities. The Caesars Tahoe experience appears to be similar, with customer revenues generated by food and beverage, hotel, and entertainment sales, as well as the casino.

Customers at Caesars Tahoe, as in most casino operations, are ranked by earning potential or EP, the mathematical probability expressed as the amount of money the casino will win based on the type of game, length of time, and amount of average bet played by a particular individual. For example, if John Doe plays blackjack and bets an average amount of $100 for one hour, the calculation of his EP would be as follows:

$$\$100 \times 90 \text{ bets (the average number of blackjack hands per hour)} = \$9,000$$

$$\$9,000 \times 1.5\% \text{ (the theoretical win percentage ascribed to blackjack)} = \$135 \text{ per hour played}$$

This means that the amount the casino should theoretically win per hour from John Doe would be $135. Each customer's EP is calculated on the basis of their individual play and is an estimate derived from observed behavior. In most cases, the estimated total time played—in John Doe's case, total hours of play at all games—is used to determine trip earning potential.

EP calculation is important because it serves as a guideline in determining what level of free services or "complimentaries" a customer receives from the property. Complimentaries or "comps" are used as a marketing tool to support a guest's visit with free hotel rooms, food, beverages, transportation to and from the property, and, in some cases, discounts on losses. The complimentary amount provided is determined as a percentage of the customer's EP. As a general rule, comps represent 30 to 40 percent of earning potential at Caesars Tahoe.

Although the margins on the high-roller business can be great, comps still represent a significant portion of the expense associated with obtaining and maintaining business from a particular customer. Because of the significant opportunities to realize a greater margin on certain customers, there is tremendous pressure within the industry to attract qualified players. The trends are toward continually raising the bar with extra benefits to the customer in an attempt to attract him or her to the property. Without the volumes to support the escalating expense, Caesars Tahoe will have a more difficult time competing in the high-roller marketplace in the future.

The comped customer is a significant revenue source for Caesars Tahoe, but the importance of walk-in business cannot be overlooked. Each year, over a million people walk through the doors of Caesars Tahoe. The trends show that they are younger, looking for entertainment, and tend to spend less time on gaming. When they are involved in gaming, they tend to prefer slot machines to table games. They are more price and value conscious, loyal only to the extent that a good deal is available.

Unlike Las Vegas, where visitors come from diverse markets, visitors from northern California represent 68 percent of the south shore's total numbers. Additionally, convention and wholesale business continues to provide revenue opportunities. Convention business, like the rest of the Tahoe market, has been flat for years. Convention room nights in 1995 totaled 15,000, and wholesale room nights numbered 17,649. Caesars Tahoe recently completed a $500,000 renovation of the convention area, including audiovisual and decorative upgrades. The largest convention business segment comes from the west coast, followed by the east coast and midwest, in descending order. The sales staff is looking forward to developing a strong relationship with ITT Sheraton for the opportunities it may provide for Caesars Tahoe to tap into its national market resources.

Hotel business has been flat to declining overall, with total room nights in the hotel off by 7,000 between 1995 and 1996. Regular cash sale room nights totaled 61,397 in 1995, with comp sales at 37,354 room nights. The average day room rate (ADR) for Caesars Tahoe in 1995 was $113.08, compared with $104.07 for the South shore. There has been an effort to increase the ADR at Caesars Tahoe.

The Resource Base

The Physical Plant

Caesars Tahoe has 440 rooms, forty thousand square feet of casino space, a fifteen-thousand-square-foot convention center, three gourmet restaurants, a twenty-four-hour coffee shop and room service, a health spa/pool area, and a shopping galleria with approximately ten leased retail outlets. In addition, there is a wedding chapel located on property and operated by a leasee. Planet Hollywood, the restaurant chain, opened at Caesars Tahoe in 1994, turning a previously under-performing area (a cabaret bar) into a performing asset. Nero's 2000, Caesars Tahoe's own nightclub, provided additional operating income of $1 million in 1995. Plans for 1996 include the renovation of the twenty-four-hour coffee shop into a 250-seat buffet.

Caesars Tahoe itself operates the building as a leasee to the property owner. There is a fixed payment of approximately $4 million per year plus 20 percent of any pretax net profit (earnings before interest and taxes). The lease is up for renewal in the year 2004.

Human Resources

There are approximately eighteen hundred employees who work full-time for Caesars Tahoe. Turnover is high (around 60 percent annually) and is consistent with the other Lake Tahoe resort properties. High turnover is partly the result of seasonality and partly resort living, which couples low-wage, entry-level positions with a relatively high cost of living. The average starting wage at Caesars Tahoe is about $6.00 per hour. Although turnover is high, there still is a core group of long-term employees. Close to 50 percent of the Caesars Tahoe employee base has been with the company for more than five years. This stable employee base is beneficial in some ways, but it tends to create pockets of low morale and motivation. In some departments, there is little management depth. Lake Tahoe, like many resort areas, has an extremely limited labor pool. The majority of Caesars employees live in California. The average residency is three years. Much of the hiring for the summer months is accomplished through college student recruiting outside of Lake Tahoe. Attracting and retaining good employees always has been and continues to be a challenge for all of the Lake Tahoe casino properties.

Reputation

Like the lake, Caesars brand image—the Roman theme—is both an asset and a liability. The Caesars brand is recognized worldwide. Although mostly associated with Caesars Palace in Las Vegas, its reputation for high-rollers, sports figures, and entertainers extends to all of its properties. The theme and reputation allow the company to differentiate itself in the Tahoe marketplace because no other area casino has the same distinctive brand image. However, the theme's image of grandeur, luxury, and wealth also has proven intimidating for guests. For this reason, Caesars Tahoe has been inconsistent in its use of the brand during its seventeen years in Lake Tahoe.

The Caesars Tahoe Executive Committee Challenge

Refocusing his executive team on the key strategic issues was Attaway's foremost objective. Many questions needed answers. What services should Caesars Tahoe offer? Should the company change its scope and customer focus? Which market segments were working well and which still needed targeting: high rollers or customers with smaller gaming budgets, or both? What about the company's current basis for competing? How should Caesars Tahoe differentiate itself, both locally and within other markets such as Reno and Las Vegas? What are additional revenue sources? How can the company gain from its relationship with its parent Caesars World? With ITT Sheraton and ITT Corporation? How best to deliver the earnings goals to the parents? And perhaps most troubling to Attaway, what were the strategic issues that he and his team had failed to identify? With information and questions in hand, Attaway prepared to face his executive committee.

Questions

1. Perform a strategic analysis of the Caesars Tahoe organization. What are the key issues (opportunities and constraints) facing this property?

2. Design a strategic change process that you would propose to Attaway.

Source: "The Executive Committee Challenge," by Barbara Falvey and David Attaway, 1997. The case was adapted and reproduced with permission of Barbara Falvey.

Special Applications of Organization Development

7

21

Organization Development in Global Settings

This chapter describes the practice of organization development in international settings. It presents the contingencies and practice issues associated with OD in organizations outside the United States, in worldwide organizations, and in global social change organizations. The increasing applicability and effectiveness of OD in countries and cultures outside of the United States is debatable, however. Because OD was developed predominantly by American and Western European practitioners, its practices and methods are heavily influenced by the values and assumptions of industrialized cultures. Thus, the traditional approaches to planned change may promote management practices that conflict with the values and assumptions of other societies. Some practitioners believe, on the other hand, that OD can result in organizational improvements in any culture. Despite different points of view on this topic, the practice of OD in international settings can be expected to expand dramatically. The rapid development of foreign economies and firms, along with the evolution of the global marketplace, is creating organizational needs and opportunities for change.

In designing and implementing planned change for organizations operating outside the United States, OD practice must account for two important contingencies: alignment between the cultural values of the host country and traditional OD values, and the host country's level of economic development. Preliminary research suggests that failure to adapt OD interventions to these cultural and economic contingencies can produce disastrous results.[1]

In worldwide organizations, OD is used to help firms operate in multiple countries. Referred to as global, multinational, or transnational corporations, these firms must fit their organizational methods and procedures to different cultures. OD can help members gain the organizational skills and knowledge needed to operate across cultural boundaries, enhancing organizational effectiveness through better alignment of people and systems with international strategy.

Finally, OD is playing an increasingly important role in global social change. Practitioners using highly participative approaches are influencing the development of evolving countries, providing a voice to underrepresented social classes, and bridging the gap between cultures facing similar social issues. The application of planned change processes in these settings represents one of the newest and most exciting areas of OD.

ORGANIZATION DEVELOPMENT OUTSIDE THE UNITED STATES

Organization development is being practiced increasingly in organizations outside of the United States.[2] Survey feedback interventions have been used at Air New Zealand and at the Air Emirates (United Arab Republic); work design interventions have been implemented in Gamesa (Mexico); merger and acquisition integration interventions have been used in Korea, The Netherlands, and Europe; and reward system changes have been implemented at the Weili Washing Machine Factory in

Zhongshan, China.[3] This international diffusion of OD derives from three important trends: the rapid development of foreign economies, the increasing worldwide availability of technical and financial resources, and the emergence of a global economy.[4]

The dramatic restructuring of socialist economies and the rapid economic growth of developing countries are numbing in scope and impact. The World Bank projects that world gross domestic product growth will average about 3.5 percent between 1996 and 2005, whereas projected growth in Latin America and the Caribbean is 3.8 percent, in East Asia 7.9 percent, and in South Asia 5.4 percent. The European Union continues its push for integration with the printing of the Euro currency, the admission of new countries, and the rationalizing of economic standards. The political transformation of Russia and of Eastern European countries such as Poland and East Germany is producing new growth-oriented economies. The abolishment of apartheid has placed South Africa on a progressive development path, and China continues its economic experiments in geographic areas such as Hong Kong and Shanghai and in privatization of government-controlled organizations.

Organizations operating in these rejuvenated or newly emerging economies are increasingly turning to OD practices to solve problems and improve effectiveness. In Germany, for example, industrial expansion following reunification was fueled partly by immigrants filling factory jobs. The *Learnstatt* concept, a form of quality circles, developed from courses in which immigrants were being taught to speak German. In such organizations as Kraftwerk Union AG and BMW, new ideas about work processes were introduced during the language training to make the classes more interesting and applicable. Eventually, those groups began to discuss ways to improve manufacturing efficiency.[5] Other interventions, including codetermination, work councils, and extensive apprenticeship programs, represent efforts to increase employee empowerment in German organizations.

The second trend contributing to OD applications in global settings is the unprecedented availability of technological and financial resources on a worldwide scale. The development of the Internet, the World Wide Web, and e-commerce has increased foreign governments' and organizations' access to enormous information resources and fueled growth and development. The increased availability of capital and technology, for example, was cited as a primary reason for the rise of Chilean firms in the 1980s.[6] Information technology, in particular, is making the world "smaller" and more interdependent. As organizations outside the United States adopt new technology, the opportunity increases to apply techniques that facilitate planned change. OD interventions can smooth the transition to a new reporting structure, clarify roles and relationships, and reduce the uncertainty associated with implementing new techniques and practices.

The final trend fueling international OD applications is the emergence of a global economy. The Asian financial crisis in 1999 aptly demonstrated how interdependent the world's markets have become. Many foreign organizations are maturing and growing by entering the global business community. This international expansion is aided by lowered trade barriers, deregulation, and privatization. The established relationships and local knowledge that once favored only a small number of worldwide organizations no longer are barriers to entry into many countries.[7] As organizations expand globally, they are faced with adapting structures, information systems, coordinating processes, and human resources practices to worldwide operations in a variety of countries. This has led to OD interventions geared to planned change across different cultures and economies.

The success of OD in settings outside the United States depends on two key contingencies: cultural context and economic development. First, OD interventions need to be responsive to the cultural values and organizational customs of the host country if the changes are to produce the kinds of positive results shown in the United States.[8] For example, team-building interventions in Latin American countries can fail if there is too much emphasis on personal disclosure and interpersonal relationships. Latin Americans typically value masculinity and a devotion to family, avoid conflict, and are status conscious. They may be suspicious of human process interventions that seek to establish trust, openness, and equality and consequently may resist them actively. The more that a country's cultural values match the traditional values of OD, the less likely it is that an intervention will have to be modified. Second, a country's economic development can affect the success of OD interventions.[9] For example, organizations operating in countries with moderate levels of economic development may need business-oriented interventions more than OD kinds of changes. Indeed, there is little to be gained from addressing interpersonal conflict in a top-management team if the organization has difficulty getting products shipped or delivering service.

Cultural Context

Researchers have proposed that applying OD in different countries requires a "context-based" approach to planned change.[10] This involves fitting the change process to the organization's cultural context, including the values held by members in the particular country or region. These beliefs inform people about which behaviors are important and acceptable in their culture. Cultural values play a major role in shaping the customs and practices that occur within organizations as well, influencing how members react to phenomena having to do with power, conflict, ambiguity, time, and change.

There is a growing body of knowledge about cultural diversity and its effect on organizational and management practices.[11] Researchers have identified five key values that describe national cultures and influence organizational customs: context orientation, power distance, uncertainty avoidance, achievement orientation, and individualism (Table 21.1).[12]

Context Orientation

This value describes how information is conveyed and time is valued in a culture. In low-context cultures, such as Scandinavia and the United States, information is communicated in words and phrases. By using more specific words, more meaning is expressed. In addition, time is viewed as discrete and linear—as something that can be spent, used, saved, or wasted. In high-context cultures, on the other hand, the communication medium reflects the message more than the words, and time is a fluid and flexible concept. For example, social cues in Japan and Venezuela provide as much, if not more, information about a particular situation than do words alone. Organizations in high-context cultures emphasize ceremony and ritual. How one behaves is an important signal of support and compliance with the way things are done. Structures are less formal in high-context cultures; there are few written policies and procedures to guide behavior. Because high-context cultures view time as fluid, punctuality for appointments is less a priority than is maintaining relationships.

Power Distance

This value concerns the way people view authority, status differences, and influence patterns. People in high power distance regions, such as Latin America and

Table 21·1	Cultural Values and Organization Customs		
VALUE	**DEFINITION**	**ORGANIZATION CUSTOMS WHEN THE VALUE IS AT ONE EXTREME**	**REPRESENTATIVE COUNTRIES**
Context	The extent to which words carry the meaning of a message; how time is viewed	Ceremony and routines are common. Structure is less formal; fewer written policies exist. People are often late for appointments.	*High:* Asian and Latin American countries *Low:* Scandinavian countries, United States
Power distance	The extent to which members of a society accept that power is distributed unequally in an organization	Decision making is autocratic. Superiors consider subordinates as part of a different class. Subordinates are closely supervised. Employees are not likely to disagree. Powerful people are entitled to privileges.	*High:* Latin American and Eastern European countries *Low:* Scandinavian countries
Uncertainty avoidance	The extent to which members of an organization tolerate the unfamiliar and unpredictable	Experts have status/authority. Clear roles are preferred. Conflict is undesirable. Change is resisted. Conservative practices are preferred.	*High:* Asian countries *Low:* European countries
Achievement orientation	The extent to which organization members value assertiveness and the acquisition of material goods	Achievement is reflected in wealth and recognition. Decisiveness is valued. Larger and faster are better. Gender roles are clearly differentiated.	*High:* Asian and Latin American countries, South Africa *Low:* Scandinavian countries
Individualism	The extent to which people believe they should be responsible for themselves and their immediate families	Personal initiative is encouraged. Time is valuable to individuals. Competitiveness is accepted. Autonomy is highly valued.	*High:* United States *Low:* Latin American and Eastern European countries

Eastern Europe, tend to favor unequal distributions of power and influence, and consequently autocratic and paternalistic decision-making practices are accepted. Organizations in high power distance cultures tend to be highly centralized with several hierarchical levels and a large proportion of supervisory personnel. Subordinates in these organizations represent a lower social class. They expect to be supervised closely and believe that power holders are entitled to special privileges. Such practices would be inappropriate in low power distance regions, such as Scandinavia, where participative decision making and egalitarian methods prevail.

Uncertainty Avoidance

This value reflects a preference for conservative practices and familiar and predictable situations. People in high uncertainty avoidance regions, such as Asia, prefer stable routines, resist change, and act to maintain the status quo. They do not like conflict and believe that company rules should not be broken. In regions where uncertainty avoidance is low, such as in many European countries, ambiguity is less threatening. Organizations in these cultures tend to favor fewer rules, higher levels of participation in decision making, more organic structures, and more risk taking.

Achievement Orientation

This value concerns the extent to which the culture favors the acquisition of power and resources. Employees from achievement-oriented cultures, such as Asia and Latin America, place a high value on career advancement, freedom, and salary growth. Organizations in these cultures pursue aggressive goals and have high levels of stress and conflict. Organizational success is measured in terms of size, growth, and speed. On the other hand, workers in cultures where achievement is less of a driving value, such as those in Scandinavia, prize the social aspects of work including working conditions and supervision, and typically favor opportunities to learn and grow at work.

Individualism

This value is concerned with looking out for oneself as opposed to one's group or organization. In high individualism cultures, such as the United States and Canada, personal initiative and competitiveness are valued strongly. Organizations in individualistic cultures often have high turnover rates and individual rather than group decision-making processes. Employee empowerment is supported when members believe that it improves the probability of personal gain. These cultures encourage personal initiative, competitiveness, and individual autonomy. Conversely, in low individualism countries, such as Taiwan, Japan, and Peru, allegiance to one's group is paramount. Organizations operating in these cultures tend to favor cooperation among employees and loyalty to the company.

Economic Development

In addition to cultural context, an important contingency affecting OD success internationally is a country's level of industrial and economic development. It can be judged from social, economic, and political perspectives.[13] For example, economic development can be reflected in a country's management capability as measured by information systems and skills; decision-making and action-taking capabilities; project planning and organizing abilities; evaluation and control technologies; leadership, motivational, and reward systems; and human selection, placement, and development levels. Similarly, the United Nations' Human Development Programme has created a Human Development Index that assesses a country's economic development in terms of life expectancy, educational attainment, and income.

Subsistence Economies

Countries such as Bangladesh, Nepal, Afghanistan, India, and Nigeria have relatively low degrees of development and their economies are agriculturally based. Their populations consume most of what they produce, and any surplus is used to barter for other needed goods and services. A large proportion of the population is unfamiliar with the concept of "employment." Working for someone else in exchange for wages is not common or understood, and consequently few large organizations exist outside of the government. In subsistence economies, OD interventions emphasize global social change and focus on creating conditions for sustainable social and economic progress. These change methods are described in the last section of this chapter.

Industrializing Economies

These countries, which include South Africa, the Philippines, Brazil, Iran, and the People's Republic of China, are moderately developed and tend to be rich in natural resources. An expanding manufacturing base that accounts for increasing amounts of the country's gross domestic product fuels economic growth. The rise of manufacturing also contributes to the formation of a class system including upper-, middle-, and low-income groups. Organizations operating in these nations generally focus on efficiency of operations and revenue growth. Consequently, OD interventions address strategic, structural, and work design issues.[14] They help organizations identify domestic and international markets, develop clear and appropriate goals, and structure themselves to achieve efficient performance and market growth.

Industrial Economies

Highly developed countries, such as Scandinavia, Japan, France, and the United States, emphasize nonagricultural industry. In these economies, manufactured goods are exported and traded with other industrialized countries; investment funds are available both internally and externally; the workforce is educated and skilled; and technology often is substituted for labor. Because the OD interventions described in this book were developed primarily in industrial economies, they can be expected to have their strongest effects in those contexts. Their continued success cannot be ensured, however, because these countries are advancing rapidly to postindustrial conditions. Here, OD interventions will need to fit into economies driven by information and knowledge, where service outpaces manufacturing, and where national and organizational boundaries are more open and flexible.

How Cultural Context and Economic Development Affect OD Practice

The contingencies of cultural context and economic development can have powerful effects on the way OD is carried out in different countries.[15] They can determine whether change processes proceed slowly or quickly; involve few or many members; are directed by hierarchical authority or by consensus; and focus on business, organizational, or human process issues. When the two contingencies are considered together, they reveal four different international settings for OD practice, as shown in Figure 21.1. These different situations reflect the extent to which a country's culture fits with traditional OD values of direct and honest communication, sharing power, and improving their effectiveness and the degree to which the

Figure 21•1	**The Cultural and Economic Contexts of International OD Practice**

country is economically developed.[16] In Figure 21.1, the degree of economic development is restricted to moderately and highly industrialized regions. Subsistence economies are not included because they afford little opportunity to practice traditional OD; in those contexts, a more appropriate strategy is global social change, discussed later in this chapter. In general, however, the more developed the economy, the more OD is applied to the organizational and human process issues described in this book. In less developed situations, OD focuses on business issues, such as procuring raw materials, producing efficiently, and marketing successfully.[17] On the other hand, when the country's culture supports traditional OD values, the planned change process can be applied with only small adjustments.[18] The more the cultural context differs from OD's traditional values profile, the more the planned change process will need to be modified to fit the situation.

Low Cultural Fit, Moderate Industrialization

This context is least suited to traditional OD practice. It includes industrializing economies with cultural values that align poorly with OD values, including many Middle East nations, such as Iraq, Iran, and the United Arab Republic; the South Pacific region, including Malaysia and the Philippines; and certain South American countries, such as Brazil, Ecuador, Guatemala, and Nicaragua. These regions are highly dependent on their natural resources and have a relatively small manufacturing base. They tend to be high-context cultures with values of high power distance and achievement orientation and of moderate uncertainty avoidance. They are not a bad fit with OD values because these cultures tend toward moderate or high levels of collectivism, especially in relation to family.

These settings require change processes that fit local customs and that address business issues. As might be expected, little is written on applying OD in these countries, and there are even fewer reports of OD practice. Cultural values of high power distance and achievement are inconsistent with OD activities emphasizing openness, collaboration, and empowerment. Moreover, executives in industrializing economies frequently equate OD with human process interventions, such as team building, conflict management, and process consultation. They perceive OD as too soft to meet their business needs. For example, Egyptian and Filipino managers tend to be autocratic, engage in protracted decision making, and focus on economic and business problems. Consequently, organizational change is slow paced, centrally controlled, and aimed at achieving technical rationality and efficiency.[19]

Not all organizations are influenced similarly by these contextual forces. In an apparent exception to the rule, the president of Semco S/A (Brazil), Ricardo Semler, has designed a highly participative organization.[20] Most Semco employees set their own working hours and approve hires and promotions. Information flows downward through a relatively flat hierarchy, and strategic decisions are made participatively by companywide vote. Brazil's cultural values are not as strong on power distance and masculinity as in other Latin American countries, and that may explain the apparent success of this high-involvement organization. It suggests that OD interventions can be implemented within this cultural context when strongly supported by senior management.

Application 21.1 describes a work design intervention in a plant in Egypt. It demonstrates some of the difficulties associated with planned change in industrializing countries whose cultural context does not fit with traditional OD values. It also demonstrates some of the ingredients for successful OD in these situations.[21]

APPLICATION 21•1   Job Enrichment in an Egyptian Organization

Plant A, in Cairo, Egypt, produces electrical and communications equipment for both the government and the public markets. It is the largest factory of its kind in Egypt and works closely with its government customers to produce what is needed and to coordinate its actions. This particular facility's development over the years had been based on a foreign model of how a factory of this type should be designed. As one of the many government-owned factories built in the last twenty years, its form has also been strongly affected by the Egyptian social and legal environment. For example, the factory was functionally organized, but it also has a few matrix project groups reporting to the chairman of the board. The board is composed of a politically appointed chairman, a vice chairman for finance and administration, and one for commerce. It also consists of a technical vice chairman, a representative of the user govenmental agency, and three members elected from among the workers and employees. Although the influence of these elected board members is nearly nil, legislation does exist in Egypt to call for workers' elections for board members. The chairman serves as the CEO, and the vice chairmen serve as operating executives. The factory falls under the authority of the technical vice chairman, as do all the other production units except the special matrix groups.

The primary consultant to the factory had been a member of its board of directors for five years, but at the time of the research his relationship was informal, existing primarily through his friends and associates still at the factory. As a result of discussions with the consultant, management agreed to focus on a particular unit in the factory to carry out action research on work design and job enrichment. Management believed that this unit had an atmosphere of low morale, high absenteeism, turnover percentages higher than desired, and an evident need for improving productivity and reducing reject rates. The focus unit contained 176 employees including a manager and his assistant, twenty engineers, and thirty-six supervisors (seventeen men and nineteen women). There were ninety-six assembly workers on a one-shift operation, and of these, only eighteen were men. The fourteen clerks and cleaning personnel were all male.

The plant's organization and job design were heavily influenced by the English manufacturing firms whose products it was producing and assembling. The work design had come directly from the production specifications and, without any significant alteration, it was set up to operate the same way in Egypt. The production process in the plant consisted of fifty-two separate, specialized, and inspected operations, each one done by one worker and taking six to nine minutes to complete. The work flowed through two U-shaped facilities with assembly and inspection completed in one section, then load-ing and packing completed nearby. People interacted only when they moved an assembled piece from one stage to the next. Technical advisors from the foreign firms were present in the factory but they took no active part in this project or the job redesign effort.

The overall design of the research followed an action research approach of involving the organization in identifying its own problems and opportunities, designing solutions to these, and then testing and modifying the solutions as appropriate. The board proposed and approved a step-by-step strategy. The first step was to train designated personnel about the concepts of OD and the action research process. These programs were conducted in Arabic and covered the basic theories of work motivation, job design, group leadership, problem analysis, and evaluation techniques.

The second step involved diagnostic activities. Complete data were collected about the organization's structure and its production rates over the past six months. In addition, pre-intervention data were collected from the unit chosen to receive special attention for comparison with data to be collected after the intervention. These data included reject rates, damaged parts costs, and turnover and absenteeism rates. Observations and interviews were used to generate information about the climate of the organization and also about how work was being performed and the related morale factors. An oral questionnaire, given to a sample group of members of the test unit, asked about work conditions and attitudes about work. Four special meetings of members from all levels of the organization and led by the consultant, the vice chairman, and the research and development manager were held to collect ideas and suggestions about the research. The results were tabulated and then discussed with the research team and the chairman of the board.

From all of this information, the following problem statement and research hypothesis were developed: "At present in the test unit, there is an atmosphere of low morale and job dissatisfaction. It is hypothesized that this is resulting from the boredom and fatigue associated with the nature of the work in the test unit." (This is a direct quotation from the consultant's report, translated into English.) Based on these conclusions, problem-solving meetings were set up in the test unit with the managers and the research team. A brainstorming design was used to generate ideas. The agreed-upon solution was that "restructuring the work functions and positions in the test unit in order to decrease work fatigue and monotony would lead to an increase in job satisfaction and raise morale, thus reducing absenteeism, turnover, and improving productivity" (another quotation from the consultant's report). This solution was reviewed and agreed on by higher-level management. Through this process, all levels of the organization became involved in the project, and although management had a chance to review the suggestions from the research team, the workers felt that the solutions were a result of their own participation. After a solution to the identified problems was reached, the next step was to design the implementation procedures.

A training program was used to explain the principles of a job enrichment process. A force-field analysis (see Chapter 7) guided the implementation process. The objective of the job enrichment program was to let each individual accomplish a complete operation to whatever extent was possible. Where this was not feasible, the objective was to design the job so that it could be completed in full by a small group of workers under the leadership of one supervisor. Of the test unit's fifty-two operations, the first twenty-six were combined and placed with a group of six employees working together with one foreman. Other assembly and test operations were combined to give a person a whole job, and job rotation and job sharing were introduced to reduce the boredom produced by certain tasks. In addition, an inspection operation was redesigned to eliminate continuous operation of a piece of equipment that exposed personnel to harmful radiation.

The implementation plan called for a two-week pilot test to address morale and productivity problems. After two days, the results were so negative that the experiment was stopped, and the sources of the poor results were investigat-ed. Three issues required attention. First, more training in the new work procedures was proposed for the experimental unit. Second, the active interest of everyone in the plant interfered with and in some cases actually interrupted the work. In response, a special location was provided where interested employees could observe the new project, but they could not interfere or offer "helpful" recommendations. Third, it was discovered that two supervisors' opposition to the project had never been dealt with effectively, and they actively were sabotaging the project. These two supervisors were disciplined and moved away from the test unit. The high level of worker commitment made it easy to address these issues, and another two-week pilot test was initiated.

After the operators were retrained and the test redesigned, the second trial run produced both hard and soft results. First, the production rate at the beginning of the test period was slightly lower than normal but soon climbed above the previous rate and in only two weeks showed an 11 percent improvement. In addition, the proportion of rejected to accepted parts decreased 6 percent, and the costs of damaged parts decreased 25 percent. Second, the duration of the test was not long enough to determine significance in the absenteeism or turnover statistics, but there was much evidence of increased job interest and involvement. Moreover, employee morale and work attitudes improved, and interviews with and observations of the workers revealed that they were reacting positively to being a part of an effort to improve their jobs. ■

High Cultural Fit, Moderate Industrialization

This international context includes subsistence and industrializing economies with cultures that align with traditional OD values. Such settings support the kinds of OD processes described in this book, especially technostructural and strategic interventions that focus on business development. According to data on economic development and cultural values, relatively few countries fit this context. India's industrial base is growing rapidly and may fit this contingency. Similarly, South Africa's recent political and cultural changes make it one of the most interesting settings in which to practice OD.[22]

South Africa is an industrializing economy. Its major cities are the manufacturing hubs of the economy, although agriculture and mining still dominate in rural areas. The country's values are in transition and may become more consistent with OD values. South Africans customarily have favored a low-context orientation; relatively high levels of power distance; and moderate levels of individualism, uncertainty avoidance, and achievement orientation. Organizations typically have been bureaucratic with authoritarian management, established career paths, and job security primarily for Caucasian employees. These values and organizational conditions are changing, however, as the nation's political and governance structures are transformed. Formerly, apartheid policies reduced uncertainty and defined power differences among citizens. Today, free elections and the abolishment of apartheid have increased uncertainty drastically and established legal equality among the races. These changes are likely to move South Africa's values closer to those underlying OD.[23] If so, OD interventions should become increasingly relevant to that nation's organizations.

A study of large South African corporations suggests the directions that OD is likely to take in that setting.[24] The study interviewed internal OD practitioners about key organizational responses to the political changes in the country, such as the free election of Nelson Mandela, abolishment of apartheid, and the Reconstruction and Development Program. Change initiatives at Spoornet, Eskom, and Telkom, for example, centered around two strategic and organizational issues. First, the political changes opened up new international markets, provided access to new technologies, and exposed these organizations to global competition. Consequently, these firms initiated planned change efforts to create corporate visions and identify strategies for entering new markets and acquiring new technologies. Second, the political changes forced corporations to modify specific human resources and organizational practices. The most compelling change was mandated affirmative action quotas. At Spoornet, Eskom, and Telkom, apartheid was thoroughly embedded in the organizations' structures, policies, and physical arrangements. Thus, planned change focused on revising human resources policies and practices. Similarly, organizational structures that had fit well within the stable environment of apartheid were outmoded and too rigid to meet the competitive challenges of international markets. Planned changes for restructuring these firms were implemented as part of longer-term strategies to change corporate culture toward more egalitarian and market-driven values.

Low Cultural Fit, High Industrialization

This international setting includes industrialized countries with cultures that fit poorly with traditional OD values. Many countries in Central America, Eastern Asia, and Eastern Europe fit this description. Reviews of OD practice in those regions suggest that planned change includes all four types of interventions described in this book, although the change process itself is adapted to local conditions.[25] For example, Mexico, Venezuela, China, Japan, and Korea are high-context cultures where knowledge of local mannerisms, customs, and rituals is required to understand the meaning of communicated information.[26] To function in such settings, OD practitioners not only must know the language but the social customs as well. Similarly, cultural values emphasizing high levels of power distance, uncertainty avoidance, and achievement orientation foster organizations where roles, status differences, and working conditions are clear; where autocratic and paternalistic decisions are expected; and where the acquisition of wealth and influence by the powerful is accepted. OD interventions that focus on social processes and employee empowerment are not favored naturally in this cultural context and consequently need to be modified to fit the situations.

Asian organizations, such as Matsushita, Nissan, Toyota, Fujitsu, NEC, and Hyundai, provide good examples of how OD interventions can be tailored to this global setting. These firms are famous for continuous improvement and TQM practices; they adapt these interventions to fit the Asian culture. Roles and behaviors required to apply TQM are highly specified, thereby holding uncertainty to a relatively low level. Teamwork and consensus decision-making practices associated with quality improvement projects also help to manage uncertainty. When large numbers of employees are involved, information is spread quickly and members are kept informed about the changes taking place. Management controls the change process by regulating the implementation of suggestions made by the problem-solving groups. Because these interventions focus on work processes, teamwork and employee involvement do not threaten the power structure. Moreover, TQM and continuous improvement do not alter the organization radically but produce small, incremental changes that can add up to impressive gains in long-term productivity and cost reduction.

In these cultures, OD practitioners also tailor the change process itself to fit local conditions. Mexican companies, for example, expect OD practitioners to act as experts and to offer concrete advice on how to improve the organization. To be successful, OD practitioners need sufficient status and legitimacy to work with senior management and to act in expert roles.[27] Status typically is associated with academic credentials, senior management experience, high-level titles, or recommendations by highly placed executives and administrators. As might be expected, the change process in Latin America is autocratic and driven downward from the top of the organization. Subordinates or lower-status people generally are not included in diagnostic or implementation activities because inclusion might equalize power differences and threaten the status quo. Moreover, cultural norms discourage employees from speaking out or openly criticizing management. There is relatively little resistance to change because employees readily accept changes dictated by management.

In Asia, OD is an orderly process, driven by consensus and challenging performance goals.[28] Organizational changes are implemented slowly and methodically, so trust builds and change-related uncertainty is reduced. Changing too quickly is seen as arrogant, divisive, and threatening. At the China Association for the International Exchange of Personnel, the move from a government bureau to a "market-facing" organization has been gradual but consistent. Managers have been encouraged to contact more and more foreign organizations, to develop relationships and contracts, and to learn marketing and organization development skills. Because Asian values promote a cautious and somewhat closed culture that prizes consensus, dignity, and respect, OD tends to be impersonal and to focus mainly on work-flow improvements. Human process issues are rarely addressed because people are expected to act in ways that do not cause others to "lose face" or to bring shame to the group.

High Cultural Fit, High Industrialization

This last setting includes industrialized countries with cultural contexts that fit well with traditional OD values. Much of the OD practice described in this book was developed in these situations, particularly in the United States.[29] To extend our learning, we will focus on how OD is practiced in other nations in this global setting, including the Scandinavian countries—Sweden, Norway, Finland, and Denmark— and countries with a strong British heritage, such as Great Britain, Northern Ireland, Australia, and New Zealand.

Scandinavians enjoy a high standard of living and strong economic development.[30] Because their cultural values most closely match those traditionally espoused in OD, organizational practices are highly participative and egalitarian. OD practice tends to mirror these values. Multiple stakeholders, such as managers, unionists, and staff personnel, actively are involved in all stages of the change process, from entry and diagnosis to intervention and evaluation. This level of involvement is much higher than typically occurs in the United States. It results in a change process that is heavily oriented to the needs of shop-floor participants.

Norwegian labor laws, for example, give unionists the right to participate in technological innovations that can affect their work lives. Such laws also mandate that all employees in the country have the right to enriched forms of work.

Given this cultural context, Scandinavian companies pioneered sociotechnical interventions to improve productivity and quality of work life.[31] Sweden's Saab-Scania and Volvo restructured automobile manufacturing around self-managed work groups. Denmark's Patent Office and Norway's Shell Oil demonstrated how union–management cooperative projects can enhance employee involvement throughout the organization. In many cases, national governments were involved heavily in these change projects by sponsoring industrywide improvement efforts. The Norwegian government, for example, was instrumental in introducing industrial democracy to that nation's companies. It helped union and management in selected industries implement pilot projects to enhance productivity and quality of work life. The results of these sociotechnical experiments were then diffused throughout the Norwegian economy. In many ways, the Scandinavian countries have gone further than other global regions in linking OD to national values and policies.

Countries associated with the United Kingdom tend to have values consistent with a low-context orientation, moderate to high individualism and achievement orientation, and moderate to low power distance and uncertainty avoidance. This cultural pattern results in personal relationships that often seem indirect to Americans. For example, a British subordinate who is told to think about a proposal is really being told that the suggestion has been rejected. These values also promote organizational policies that are steeped in formality, tradition, and politics. The United Kingdom's long history tends to reinforce the status quo, and consequently resistance to change is high.

OD practice in the United Kingdom parallels the cultural pattern described above. In Great Britain, for example, sociotechnical systems theory was developed by practitioners at the Tavistock Institute of Human Relations.[32] Applications, such as self-managed work groups, however, have not readily diffused within British organizations. The individualistic values and inherently political nature of this culture tend to conflict with interventions emphasizing employee empowerment and teamwork. In contrast, the Scandinavian cultures are far more supportive of sociotechnical practice and have been instrumental in diffusing it worldwide.

The emergence of the European Union has served as a catalyst for change in many British organizations. Companies such as Akzo Nobel, British Aerospace, International Computers Ltd. (ICL), and Reuters are actively engaged in strategic change interventions. At British Petroleum, chairman Robert B. Horton is implementing a flexible organization to compete better in the emerging economy. He is reducing the number of levels in the structure, discontinuing long-standing committees, eliminating staff, and empowering employees in teams.[33] More limited interventions, such as team building, conflict resolution, and work redesign, are being carried out in such organizations as Unilever and Smithkline Beecham.

WORLDWIDE ORGANIZATION DEVELOPMENT

An important trend facing many business firms is the emergence of a global marketplace. Driven by competitive pressures, lowered trade barriers, and advances in information technologies, the number of companies offering products and services in multiple countries is increasing rapidly. The organizational growth and complexity associated with worldwide operations pose challenging managerial problems.

Executives must choose appropriate strategic orientations for operating across cultures and geographical locations, and under diverse governmental and environmental requirements. They must be able to adapt corporate policies and procedures to a range of local conditions. Moreover, the tasks of controlling and coordinating operations in different nations place heavy demands on information and control systems and on managerial skills and knowledge.

Worldwide organization development applies to organizations that are operating across multiple geographic and cultural boundaries. This contrasts with OD in organizations that operate outside the United States but within a single cultural and economic context. This section describes the emerging practice of OD in worldwide organizations, a relatively new but important area of planned change.

What Is a Worldwide Organization?

Worldwide organizations can be defined in terms of three key facets.[34] First, they offer products or services in more than one country and actively manage substantial direct investments in those countries. Consequently, they must relate to a variety of demands, such as unique product requirements, tariffs, value-added taxes, transportation laws, and trade agreements. Second, worldwide firms must balance product and functional concerns with geographic issues of distance, time, and culture. American tobacco companies, for example, face technological, moral, and organizational issues in determining whether to market cigarettes in less-developed countries, and if they do, they must decide how to integrate manufacturing and distribution operations on a global scale. Third, worldwide companies must carry out coordinated activities across cultural boundaries using a wide variety of personnel. Workers with different cultural backgrounds must be managed in ways that support the overall goals and image of the organization.[35] The company must therefore adapt its human resources policies and procedures to fit the culture and accomplish operational objectives. From a managerial perspective, selecting executives to head foreign operations is an important decision in worldwide organizations.

Worldwide Strategic Orientations

A key contingency in designing OD interventions in worldwide organizations is how products, organizational units, and personnel are arranged to form strategic orientations that enable firms to compete in the global marketplace.[36] Worldwide organizations can offer certain products or services in some countries and not in others; they can centralize or decentralize operations; and they can determine how to work with people from different cultures. Despite the many possible combinations of characteristics, researchers have found that worldwide organizations generally implement one of three types of strategic orientations: global, multinational, or transnational. Table 21.2 presents these orientations in terms of the diagnostic framework described in Chapter 5. Each strategic orientation is geared to specific market, technological, and organizational requirements. OD interventions that can help organizations to meet these demands also are included in Table 21.2.

Global Orientation

This orientation is characterized by a strategy of marketing standardized products in different countries. It is an appropriate orientation when there is little economic reason to offer products or services with special features or locally available options. Manufacturers of office equipment, consumer goods, computers, tires, and containers, for example, can offer the same basic product in almost any country.

Table 21•2	Characteristics and Interventions for Worldwide Strategic Orientations				
WORLDWIDE STRATEGIC ORIENTATION	**STRATEGY**	**STRUCTURE**	**INFORMATION SYSTEM**	**HUMAN RESOURCES**	**OD INTERVENTIONS**
Global	Standardized products Goals of efficiency through volume	Centralized, balanced, and coordinated activities Global product division	Formal	Ethnocentric selection	Career planning Role clarification Employee involvement Senior management team building Conflict management
Multinational	Tailored products Goals of local responsiveness through specialization	Decentralized operations; centralized planning Global geographic divisions	Profit centers	Regiocentric or polycentric selection	Intergroup relations Local management team building Management development Reward systems Strategic alliances
Transnational	Tailored products Goals of learning and responsiveness through integration	Decentralized, worldwide coordination Global matrix or network	Subtle, clan-oriented controls	Geocentric selection	Extensive selection and rotation Cultural development Intergroup relations Building corporate vision

The goal of efficiency dominates this orientation. Production efficiency is gained through volume sales and a small number of large manufacturing plants, and managerial efficiency is achieved by centralizing product design, manufacturing, distribution, and marketing decisions. Tight coordination is achieved by the close physical proximity of major functional groups and formal control systems that balance inputs, production, and distribution with worldwide demand. Many Japanese firms, such as Honda, Sony, NEC, and Matsushita, used this strategy in the 1970s and early 1980s to grow in the international economy. In Europe, Nestlé exploits economies of scale in marketing by advertising well-known brand names around the world. The increased number of microwaves and two-income families allowed Nestlé to push its Nescafé coffee and Lean Cuisine low-calorie frozen dinners to dominant market-share positions in Europe, North America, Latin America, and Asia. Similarly, Korean noodle maker, Nong Shim Company, avoided the 1999 financial crisis by staying focused on efficiency. Yoo Jong Suk, Nong Shim's head of strategy, went against recommendations to diversify and stated, "All we want is to be globally recognized as a ramyon maker."[37]

In the global orientation, the organization tends to be centralized with a global product structure. Presidents of each major product group report to the CEO and form the line organization. Each of these product groups is responsible for worldwide operations. Information systems in global orientations tend to be quite formal with local units reporting sales, costs, and other data directly to the product president. The predominant human resources policy integrates people into the organization through ethnocentric selection and staffing practices. These methods seek to fill key foreign positions with personnel, or expatriates, from the home country where the corporation headquarters is located.[38] Managerial jobs at Volvo and Michelin, for example, are occupied by Swedish and French citizens, respectively.[39] Ethnocentric policies support the global orientation because expatriate managers are more likely than host-country nationals to recognize and comply with the need to centralize decision making and to standardize processes, decisions, and relationships with the parent company. Although many Japanese automobile manufacturers have decentralized production, Nissan's global strategy has been to retain tight, centralized control of design and manufacturing, ensure that almost all of its senior foreign managers are Japanese, and have even low-level decisions emerge from face-to-face meetings in Tokyo.[40]

Several OD interventions can be used to support the global strategic orientation, including career planning, role clarification, employee involvement, conflict management, and senior management team building. Each of these interventions can help the organization achieve improved operational efficiency. For example, role clarification interventions, such as job enrichment, goal setting, and conflict management, can formalize and standardize organizational activities. This ensures that each individual knows specific details about how, when, and why a job needs to be done. As a result, necessary activities are described and efficient transactions and relationships are created.

Senior management team building can improve the quality of strategic decisions. Centralized policies make the organization highly dependent on this group and can exaggerate decision-making errors. In addition, interpersonal conflict can increase the cost of coordination or cause significant coordination mistakes. Process interventions at this level can help improve the speed and quality of decision making and improve interpersonal relationships.

Career planning can help home-country personnel develop a path to senior management by including foreign subsidiary experiences and cross-functional assignments as necessary qualifications for advancement. At the country level, career planning can emphasize that advancement beyond regional operations is limited for host-country nationals. OD can help here by developing appropriate career paths within the local organization or in technical, nonmanagerial areas. Finally, employee empowerment can support efficiency goals by involving members in efforts at cost reduction, work standardization, and minimization of coordination costs.

Multinational Orientation

This strategic orientation, characterized by a product line that is tailored to local conditions, is best suited to markets that vary significantly from region to region or country to country. At American Express, for example, charge card marketing is fitted to local values and tastes. The "Don't leave home without it" and "Membership has its privileges" themes seen in the United States were translated to "Peace of mind only for members" in Japan.[41]

The multinational orientation emphasizes a decentralized, global division structure. Each region or country is served by a divisional organization that operates autonomously and reports to headquarters. This results in a highly differentiated and loosely coordinated corporate structure. Operational decisions, such as product design, manufacturing, and distribution, are decentralized and tightly integrated at the local level. For example, laundry soap manufacturers offer product formulas, packaging, and marketing strategies that conform to the different environmental regulations, types of washing machines, water hardness, and distribution channels in each country. On the other hand, planning activities often are centralized at corporate headquarters to achieve important efficiencies necessary for worldwide coordination of emerging technologies and of resource allocation. A profit-center control system allows local autonomy as long as profitability is maintained. Examples of multinational corporations include Hoechst and BASF of Germany, IBM and Merck of the United States, and Honda of Japan. Each of these organizations encourages local subsidiaries to maximize effectiveness within their geographic region.

People are integrated into multinational firms through polycentric or regiocentric personnel policies because these firms believe that host-country nationals can understand native cultures most clearly.[42] By filling positions with local citizens who appoint and develop their own staffs, the organization aligns the needs of the market with the ability of its subsidiaries to produce customized products and services. The distinction between a polycentric and a regiocentric selection process is one of focus. In a polycentric selection policy, a subsidiary represents only one country; in the regiocentric selection policy, a slightly broader perspective is taken and key positions are filled by regional citizens (that is, people who might be called Europeans, as opposed to Belgians or Italians).

The decentralized and locally coordinated multinational orientation suggests the need for a complex set of OD interventions. When applied to a subsidiary operating in a particular country or region, the OD process described above for organizations outside the United States is relevant. The key is to tailor OD to fit the specific cultural and economic context where the subsidiary is located.

When OD is applied across different regions and countries, interventions must account for differences in cultural and economic conditions that can affect its success. Appropriate interventions for multinational corporations include intergroup relations, local management team building, sophisticated management selection and development practices, and changes to reward systems. Team building remains an important intervention. Unlike team building in global orientations, the local management team requires attention in multinational firms. This presents a challenge for OD practitioners because polycentric selection policies can produce management teams with different cultures at each subsidiary. Thus, a program developed for one subsidiary may not work with a different team at another subsidiary, given the different cultures that might be represented.

Intergroup interventions to improve relations between local subsidiaries and the parent company are also important for multinational companies. Decentralized decision making and regiocentric selection can strain corporate–subsidiary relations. Local management teams, operating in ways appropriate to their cultural context, may not be understood by corporate managers from another culture. OD practitioners can help both groups understand these differences by offering training in cultural diversity and appreciation. They also can smooth parent–subsidiary relationships by focusing on the profit-center control system or other criteria as the means for monitoring and measuring subsidiary effectiveness.

Management selection, development, and reward systems also require special attention in multinational firms. Managerial selection for local or regional subsidiaries requires finding technically and managerially competent people who also possess the interpersonal competence needed to interface with corporate headquarters. Because these people may be difficult to find, management development programs can teach these cross-cultural skills and abilities. Such programs typically involve language, cultural awareness, and technical training; they also can include managers and staff from subsidiary and corporate offices to improve communications between the two areas. Finally, reward systems need to be aligned with the decentralized structure. Significant proportions of managers' total compensation could be tied to local profit performance, thereby aligning reward and control systems.

Transnational Orientation

The transnational strategy combines customized products with both efficient and responsive operations; the key goal is learning. This is the most complex worldwide strategic orientation because transnationals can manufacture products, conduct research, raise capital, buy supplies, and perform many other functions wherever in the world the job can be done optimally. They can move skills, resources, and knowledge to regions where they are needed.

The transnational orientation combines the best of global and multinational orientations and adds a third attribute—the ability to transfer resources both within the firm and across national and cultural boundaries. Otis Elevator, a division of United Technologies, developed a new programmable elevator using six research centers in five countries: a United States group handled the systems integration; Japan designed the special motor drives that make the elevators ride smoothly; France perfected the door systems; Germany created the electronics; and Spain produced the small-geared components.[43] Other examples of transnational firms include General Electric, Asea Brown Boveri, Motorola, Electrolux, and Hewlett-Packard.

Transnational firms organize themselves into global matrix and network structures especially suited for moving information and resources to their best use. In the matrix structure, local divisions similar to the multinational structure are crossed with product groups at the headquarters office. The network structure treats each local office, including headquarters, product groups, and production facilities, as self-sufficient nodes that coordinate with each other to move knowledge and resources to their most valued place. Because of the heavy information demands needed to operate these structures, transnationals have sophisticated information systems. State-of-the-art information technology is used to move strategic and operational information throughout the system rapidly and efficiently. Organizational learning and knowledge management practices (Chapter 20) gather, organize, and disseminate the knowledge and skills of members who are located around the world.

People are integrated into transnational firms through a geocentric selection policy that staffs key positions with the best people, regardless of nationality.[44] This staffing practice recognizes that the distinctive competence of a transnational firm is its capacity to optimize resource allocation on a worldwide basis. Unlike global and multinational firms that spend more time training and developing managers to fit the strategy, the transnational firm attempts to hire the right person from the beginning. Recruits at any of Hewlett-Packard's foreign locations, for example, are screened not only for technical qualifications but for personality traits that match HP's cultural values.[45]

Transnational companies require OD interventions that can improve their ability to achieve efficient worldwide integration under highly decentralized decision-making conditions. These interventions include extensive management selection and development practices in support of the geocentric policies described above, intergroup relations, and development and communication of a strong corporate vision and culture. Knowledge management interventions help develop a worldwide repository of information that enables members' learning.

Effective transnational firms have well-developed vision and mission statements that communicate the values and beliefs underlying the firm's culture and guide its operational decisions. ABB's mission statement, for example, went through a multicultural rewriting when they recognized that talking about profit was an uncomfortable activity in some cultures.[46] OD processes that increase member participation in the construction or modification of these statements can help members gain ownership of them. Research into the development of corporate credos at the British computer manufacturer ICL, SAS, and Apple Computer showed that success was more a function of the heavy involvement of many managers than the quality of the statements themselves.[47]

Once vision and mission statements are crafted, management training can focus on clarifying their meaning, the values they express, and the behaviors required to support those values. This process of gaining shared meaning and developing a strong culture provides a basis for social control. Because transnationals need flexibility and coordination, they cannot rely solely on formal reports of sales, costs, or demand to guide behavior. This information often takes too much time to compile and distribute. Rather, the corporate vision and culture provide transnational managers with the reasoning and guidelines for why and how they should make decisions.

This form of social control supports OD efforts to improve management selection and development, intergroup relationships, and strategic change. The geocentric selection process can be supplemented by a personnel policy that rotates managers through different geographical regions and functional areas to blend people, perspectives, and practices. At such organizations as GE, ABB, Coca-Cola, and Colgate, a cadre of managers with extensive foreign experience is being developed. Rotation throughout the organization also improves the chances that when two organizational units must cooperate, key personnel will know each other and make coordination more likely. The corporate vision and culture can also become important tools in building cross-functional or interdepartmental processes for transferring knowledge, resources, or products. Moreover, they can provide guidelines for formulating and implementing strategic change, and serve as a social context for designing appropriate structures and systems at local subsidiaries.

Changing Worldwide Strategic Orientations

In addition to implementing planned changes that support the development of the three basic worldwide strategic orientations, OD can help firms change from one orientation to another. At first, OD can help organizations make the transition from a domestic to a worldwide strategic orientation. Researchers have found that many organizations that sell products or services to other countries start with either global or multinational orientations. They have also suggested that global and multinational organizations tend to evolve into a transnational orientation because of changes in the organization's environment, markets, or technologies.[48] In the global orientation, for example, environmental changes can reduce the need for centralized and efficient operations. The success of Japanese automobile manufacturers employing a global strategy caused employment declines in the U.S. auto industry and overall trade imbalances. Consumer and government reactions forced Japanese firms to become more responsive to local conditions. Conversely, consumer preference changes can reduce the needs for tailored products and locally responsive management that are characteristic of the multinational strategy. The typical response is to centralize many decisions and activities.

Thus, the evolution to a transnational orientation is a complex strategic change effort requiring the acquisition of two additional capabilities. First, global orientations need to adapt multinational policies, and multinational orientations need to become more global. Second, the organization needs to acquire the ability to transfer resources efficiently around the world. Much of the difficulty in evolving to a transnational strategy lies in developing these additional capabilities.

Changing from Domestic to Global or Multinational

Change from a domestic to a worldwide organization represents a dramatic shift in scope for most firms. The direction this change takes depends largely on the degree to which the worldwide market is homogeneous. Success in such a market depends on a global orientation of delivering standardized products or services to different countries in the most efficient manner. In more heterogeneous markets, success relies on a multinational orientation that customizes products and services to fit local conditions. Domestic organizations typically gain knowledge of worldwide markets through initial efforts to export products abroad. This can be accomplished by giving worldwide markets increased importance in the operating structure of the firm. For example, the company may create a special international division to handle all foreign sales of its products. The international division is primarily responsible for marketing and distribution, although it may be able to set up joint ventures, licensing agreements, distribution territories/franchises, sales offices, and in some cases, manufacturing plants. This initial movement into the international arena enables domestic organizations to learn about the demands of the global marketplace, thus providing knowledge about whether a global or multinational orientation is needed to compete successfully.

In addition to information about the market, organizations take into account their distinctive competencies when choosing an international strategy. They assess whether their culture and core competencies are more suited for centralized or decentralized decision making. Centralization favors a global orientation, and decentralization favors a multinational strategy.

Once companies develop a strategic orientation for competing internationally, they create an organization design to support it. Information like that found in Table 21.2 is useful for designing structures, information systems, and personnel practices for specific strategic orientations.

OD can help domestic organizations become international. Team building and large-group interventions, such as search conferences, can aid the process through which senior executives gather appropriate information about international markets, distinctive competencies, and culture, and choose a strategic orientation. Based on that decision, OD interventions can help the organization to implement the change. For instance, members can use integrated strategic management to design and manage the transition from the old strategic orientation to the new one. They can apply technostructural interventions to design an appropriate structure, to define new tasks and work roles, and to clarify reporting relationships between corporate headquarters and foreign-based units. Managers and staff can apply human resources management interventions to train and prepare managers and their families for international assignments and to develop selection methods and reward systems relevant to operating internationally.[49]

Application 21.2 describes the challenges Campbell Soup Company faced in moving to a worldwide strategy.[50] The story provides an opportunity to apply your knowledge of OD. What strategic orientation do you think Campbell should pursue? What OD interventions can help the firm compete in new markets?

Changing from Global to Transnational

In the transition from a global to a transnational orientation, the firm must acquire the know-how to operate a decentralized organization and learn to transfer knowledge, skills, and resources among disparate organizational units operating in different countries. In this situation, the administrative challenge is to encourage creative over centralized thinking and to let each functional area operate in a way that

APPLICATION 21·2   Campbell Soup Company Moves to a Worldwide Strategic Orientation

Campbell's soup is an American tradition. Its red-and-white label represents one of the strongest brands in the United States, although Campbell markets many other consumer products, such as V-8 juice, Pepperidge Farm baked goods, and Swanson's frozen foods. The company was started in 1869 by Joseph Campbell and Abram Anderson, but its initial growth was spurred by John Dorrance's technological innovation of canning condensed soup. The Dorrance family still owns more than 50 percent of the company.

Many of Campbell's products have enjoyed a dominant market share and solid financial performance over time. That performance has been supported by a divisional structure focused on each basic product line, plus an international division whose sales accounted for 18 to 20 percent of total revenues in the mid-1980s and less than 25 percent in 1993. Marketing and new product development have always been strengths of the Campbell organization. For example, between 1984 and 1986 the company introduced more than 290 new products, and led the domestic prepared foods industry in establishing regionalized marketing in the late 1980s. Finally, under the Dorrance family, the company always has possessed a strong, conservative, and almost secretive culture.

Like many domestic industries, however, Campbell's main markets have both matured and experienced increased competition. Campbell's sales have flattened in the United States, increasing only about 3 percent per year between 1990 and 1993. Canned soup, the company's mainstay, has lost ground to fresh and frozen foods, which are more in tune with today's health-conscious marketplace, forcing Campbell to introduce new products in this category. At the same time, Campbell's other products face tough competition. H.J. Heinz and General Foods, for example, have imitated Campbell's regionalized marketing strategy and caused Campbell to undertake large increases in advertising and marketing expenses.

In response to these issues, Campbell began a strategic change effort to implement a worldwide strategy. Campbell's new CEO, David Johnson, began devising the foreign strategy almost as soon as he took over the top job at Campbell in 1990. Johnson is well qualified to lead the change; he has plenty of overseas experience to help him. His career has included assignments as a marketing executive in South Africa for Colgate-Palmolive Co., and he ran WarnerLambert Co.'s Parke-Davis Group in Hong Kong. His initial actions at Campbell focused on earnings problems by cutting operating costs and closing or selling twenty plants. But he clearly believed that global growth was Campbell's ticket out of stagnation and announced that international sales should supply more than half of Campbell's revenues by the year 2000.

Prepared foods, however, are difficult to market globally. First, prepared foods are not as universal or as easily marketed as soap, cigarettes, or soda, which have allowed such domestic players as Procter & Gamble, Philip Morris, and Coca-Cola to expand abroad. Prepared foods may be the toughest products to sell overseas because of the broad range of items, and many of Campbell's products will have difficulty in foreign markets. Italians, not surprisingly, look down on canned pasta, so Franco-American SpaghettiOs cannot be offered there. Similarly, the average Pole consumes five bowls of soup a week—three times the American average—but 98 percent of Polish soups are homemade, and "Mom is one tough competitor." Second, Campbell faces several large competitors that have been active in the global market for years. For example, CPC International Inc. and H.J. Heinz Co. already have built healthy market shares abroad. CPC has established brands, such as Knorr powdered soups, in most of the foreign markets that Campbell would like to enter, and it owns 80 percent of the market in Argentina. Last year, 60 percent of CPC's $6.6 billion in sales originated outside North America. Similarly, Heinz is the dominant canned-soup maker in Britain.

Still, with the flat sales in the United States, Johnson has little choice but to make the change, which includes acquisitions, new product development, and marketing. Despite its domestic strength in marketing and new product development, the organization faces uphill struggles. Its acquisition history has been spotted. One of the company's biggest overseas ventures, the $400-million acquisition of Britain's Freshbake Foods Group PLC in 1988, was disappointing. Freshbake products lacked brand appeal and did not excite British consumers. More recently, Johnson tried to acquire Australia's Arnotts Ltd. As he saw it, the two companies were a natural fit. The $485-million-a-year cookie maker was a household name throughout Australia; Johnson was born in Australia; Arnotts was run by a Campbell's veteran; and Johnson believed that the cookie maker could benefit from Campbell's marketing competencies. In addition, Campbell already owned one-third of Arnotts' stock—a purchase dating back to 1985. Unfortunately for Campbell, what followed was a painful, costly, four-month struggle. Along the way, the local press painted Johnson and the company as Ugly Americans. When Campbell finally was allowed to increase its holdings to 58 percent in February 1993, it was at a cost of more than $200 million.

Johnson indicated that Campbell may increase its pace of acquisitions to fill in its emerging global network. He also suggested that he would be willing to borrow funds to make the acquisitions happen. Increasing debt would be quite a break from Campbell's past conservative, debt-averse culture.

Marketing and product development initiatives, however, have gone better. In Western Europe, the company's Pepperidge Farm cookies, renamed Biscuits Maison to appeal to continental palates, are fast gaining a following. In addition, Campbell's soup is being shipped to Asia, and a Hong Kong taste kitchen and research and development operation is testing new recipes for that market. In some markets, Campbell's intent is to create new products that appeal to distinctly regional tastes. Early results include a fiery cream of chile poblano soup for Mexico and a watercress and duck-gizzard soup for Hong Kong.

Campbell also has managed to overcome competitive and cultural obstacles in some countries. It has attacked Knorr's powdered soups in Argentina with advertisements that tout its Sopa de Campbell as "the Real Soup" and stress its list of fresh ingredients. Less than a year after introducing nine varieties of red-and-white-labeled soup in Buenos Aires, the company now claims 10 percent of the country's $50-million soup market. In Poland, Campbell advertises to working Polish mothers looking for convenience. But it acknowledges that learning what works best will take time. In many regions, consumers know nothing about Campbell or its products—a legacy of the company's insular history.

Johnson's biggest problem, however, is Campbell's culture. Conservative and paternalistic, the organization had a long-standing policy during the 1970s that no new product could be introduced unless it could show a profit within a year. Under the previous CEO, Gordon McGovern, some of the more stifling artifacts of the culture were changed. He permitted members to eat and drink coffee at their desks; he began wandering through the hallways without his suit coat on; he appointed the first two women vice presidents; and he changed several of the benefits, including the establishment of a daycare center and the creation of an allowance for employees who adopted children. Still, the organization's culture remained stodgy.

One of the most important problems Johnson faces is that, because of acquisition and operating problems in the past, managers in the organization have avoided taking assignments in foreign countries, and few Campbell executives now have any substantive overseas experience. ■

best suits its context. For example, if international markets require increasingly specialized products, then manufacturing needs to operate local plants and flexible delivery systems that can move raw materials to where they are needed, when they are needed. OD interventions that can help this transition include training efforts that increase the tolerance for differences in management practices, control systems, performance appraisals, and policies and procedures; reward systems that encourage entrepreneurship and performance at each foreign subsidiary; and efficient organization designs at the local level.

The global orientation strives to achieve efficiency through centralization and standardization of products and practices. In the case of organizational systems, this works against the establishment of highly specialized and flexible policies and resists the movement of knowledge, skills, and resources. Training interventions that help managers develop an appreciation for the different ways that effectiveness can be achieved will aid the global organization's move toward transnationalism.

Changes in reward systems also can help the global firm evolve. By changing from a highly quantitative, centralized, pay-for-performance system characteristic of a global orientation, the organization can reward people who champion new ideas and provide incentives for decentralized business units. This more flexible reward system promotes coordination among subsidiaries, product lines, and staff groups. In addition, the transition to a transnational orientation can be aided by OD practitioners working with individual business units, rather than with senior management at headquarters. Working with each subsidiary on issues relating to its own structure and function sends an important message about the importance of decentralized operations.

Finally, changing the staffing policy is another important signal to organization members that a transition is occurring. Under the global orientation, an ethnocentric policy supported standardized activities. By staffing key positions with the best people, rather than limiting the choice to just parent-country individuals, the symbols of change are clear and the rewards for supporting the new orientation are visible.

Changing from Multinational to Transnational

In moving from a multinational to a transnational orientation, products, technologies, and regulatory constraints can become more homogeneous and require more efficient operations. The competencies required to compete on a transnational basis, however, may be located in many different geographic areas. The need to balance local responsiveness against the need for coordination among organizational units is new to multinational firms. They must create interdependencies among organizational units through the flow of parts, components, and finished goods; the flow of funds, skills, and other scarce resources; or the flow of intelligence, ideas, and knowledge. For example, as part of Ford's transition to a transnational company, the redesign of the Tempo automobile was given to one person, David Price, an Englishman. He coordinated all features of the new car for both sides of the Atlantic and used the same platform, engines, and other parts. Ford used teleconferencing and computer links, as well as extensive air travel, to manage the complex task of meshing car companies on two continents.[51]

In such situations, OD is an important activity because complex interdependencies require sophisticated and nontraditional coordinating mechanisms.[52] OD interventions, such as intergroup team building or cultural awareness and interpersonal skills training, can help develop the communication linkages necessary for successful coordination. In addition, the inherently "matrixed" structures of worldwide firms and the cross-cultural context of doing business in different countries tend to create conflict. OD interventions, such as role clarification, third-party consultation, and mediation techniques, can help to solve such problems.

The transition to a transnational firm is difficult and threatens the status quo. Under the multinational orientation, each subsidiary is encouraged and rewarded for its creativity and independence. Transnational firms, however, are effective when physically or geographically distinct organizational units coordinate their activities. The transition from independent to interdependent business units can produce conflict as the coordination requirements are worked through. OD practitioners can help mitigate the uncertainty associated with the change by modifying reward systems to encourage cooperation and spelling out clearly the behaviors required for success.

GLOBAL SOCIAL CHANGE

The newest and perhaps most exciting applications of organization development in international settings are occurring in global social change organizations (GSCOs).[53] These organizations generally are not for profit and nongovernmental. They typically are created at the grassroots level to help communities and societies address such important problems as unemployment, race relations, sustainable development, homelessness, hunger, disease, and political instability. In international settings, GSCOs are heavily involved in the developing nations. Examples include the World Conservation Union, the Hunger Project, the Nature Conservancy, the Mountain Forum, International Physicians for the Prevention of Nuclear War, International Union for the Conservation of Nature and Natural Resources, and the Asian Coalition for Agrarian Reform and Rural Development. Many practitioners who help create and develop these GSCOs come from an OD background and have adapted their expertise to fit highly complex, global situations. This section describes global social change organizations and how OD is practiced in them.

Global Social Change Organizations: What Are They?

Global social change organizations are part of a social innovation movement to foster the emergence of a global civilization.[54] They exist under a variety of names, including development organizations (DOs), international nongovernmental organizations (INGOs), social movement organizations (SMOs), international private voluntary organizations, and bridging organizations.[55] They exist to address complex social problems, including overpopulation, ecological degradation, the increasing concentration of wealth and power, the lack of management infrastructures to facilitate growth, and the lack of fundamental human rights. The efforts of many GSCOs to raise awareness and mobilize resources toward solving these problems culminated in the United Nations' Conference on Environment and Development in Rio de Janeiro in June 1992, where leaders from both industrialized and less-developed countries met to discuss sustainable development.[56]

GSCOs have the following characteristics:[57]

- They assert, as their primary task, a commitment to serve as an agent of change in creating environmentally and socially sustainable world futures; their transformational missions are articulated around the real needs of people and the earth.

- They have discovered and mobilized innovative social-organizational architectures that make possible human cooperation across previously polarizing or arbitrarily constraining boundaries.

- They hold values of empowerment, or people-centered forms of action, in the accomplishment of their global change mission, emphasizing the central role of people as both means and ends in any development process.

- They are globally and locally linked in structure, membership, or partnership and thereby exist, at least in identity and practice (maybe not yet legally), as entities beyond the nation-state.

- They are multiorganizational and often cross-sectoral. They can be business, governmental, or not for profit. Indeed, many of the most significant global change organizing innovations involve multiorganization partnerships bridging sectoral boundaries in new hybrid forms of business, intergovernmental, and private voluntary sectors.

GSCOs therefore differ from traditional for-profit firms on several dimensions.[58] First, they typically advocate a mission of social change—the formation and development of better societies and communities. "Better" typically means more just (Amnesty International, Hunger Project), peaceful (International Physicians for the Prevention of Nuclear War), or ecologically conscious (Nature Conservancy, the Global Village of Beijing, the Mountain Forum, International Union for the Conservation of Nature and Natural Resources). Second, the mission is supported by a network structure. Most GSCO activity occurs at the boundary or periphery between two or more organizations.[59] Unlike most industrial firms that focus on internal effectiveness, GSCOs are directed at changing their environmental context. For example, World Vision coordinated the efforts of more than one hundred organizations to address the human consequences of Ceausescu's Romanian government.[60] Third, GSCOs generally have strong values and ideologies that justify and motivate organization behavior. These "causes" provide intrinsic rewards to GSCO members and a blueprint for action.[61] The ideological position that basic human rights include shelter has directed Habitat for Humanity to erect low-cost homes in Tijuana, Mexico, and other underdeveloped communities. Fourth, GSCOs interact with a broad range of external and often conflicting constituencies. To help the poor, GSCOs often must work with the rich; to save the ecology, they must work with developers; to empower the masses, they must work with the powerful few. This places a great deal of pressure on GSCOs to reconcile pursuit of a noble cause with the political reality of power and wealth. Fifth, managing these diverse external constituencies often creates significant organizational conflict. On the one hand, GSCOs need to create specific departments to serve and represent particular stakeholders. On the other hand, they are strongly averse to bureaucracy and desire collegial and consensus-seeking cultures. The conflicting perspectives of the stakeholders, the differentiated departments, and the ideological basis of the organization's mission can produce a contentious internal environment. For example, the International Relief and Development Agency was created to promote self-help projects in Third World countries using resources donated from First World countries. As the agency grew, departments were created to represent different stakeholders: a fund-raising group handled donors, a projects department worked in the Third World, a public relations department directed media exposure, and a policy information department lobbied the government. Each department adapted to fit its role. Fund-raisers and lobbyists dressed more formally, took more moderate political positions, and managed less participatively than did the projects departments. These differences were often interpreted in political and ideological terms, creating considerable internal conflict.[62] Sixth, GSCO membership often is transitory. Many people are volunteers, and the extent and depth of their involvement varies over time and by issue. Turnover is quite high.

Application Stages

Global social change organizations are concerned with creating sustainable change in communities and societies. This requires a form of planned change in which the practitioner is heavily involved, many stakeholders are encouraged and expected to participate, and "technologies of empowerment" are used.[63] Often referred to as "participatory action research,"[64] planned change in GSCOs typically involves three types of activities: building local organization effectiveness, creating bridges and linkages with other relevant organizations, and developing vertical linkages with policymakers.

Building the Local Organization

Although GSCOs are concerned primarily with changing their environments, a critical issue in development projects is recognizing the potential problems inherent in the GSCO itself. Because the focus of change is their environment, members of GSCOs are often oblivious to the need for internal development. Moreover, the complex organizational arrangements of a network make planned change in GSCOs particularly challenging.

OD practitioners focus on three activities in helping GSCOs build themselves into viable organizations: using values to create the vision, recognizing that internal conflict is often a function of external conditions, and understanding the problems of success. For leadership to function effectively, the broad purposes of the GSCO must be clear and closely aligned with the ideologies of its members. Singleness of purpose can be gained from tapping into the compelling aspects of the values and principles that the GSCO represents. For example, the Latin American Division of the Nature Conservancy holds an annual two-day retreat. Each participant prepares a white paper concerning his or her area of responsibility: the issues, challenges, major dilemmas or problems, and ideas for directions the division could take. Over the course of the retreat, participants actively discuss each paper. They have broad freedom to challenge the status quo and to question previous decisions. By the end of the retreat, discussions have produced a clear statement about the course that the division will take for the following year. People leave with increased clarity about and commitment to the purpose and vision of the division.[65]

Developing a shared vision results in the alignment of individual and organizational values. Because most activities occur at the boundary of the organization, members often are spread out geographically and are not in communication with each other. A clearly crafted vision allows people in disparate regions and positions to coordinate their activities. At the Hunger Project, for example, OD practitioners asked organization members, "What is your job or task in this organization?" The GSCO president responded, "That is simple. My work is to make the end of hunger an idea whose time has come." A receptionist answered, "My task in this organization is to end hunger. I don't just answer phones or set up meetings. In everything I do, I am working to end hunger."[66] Because of the diverse perspectives of the different stakeholders, GSCOs often face multiple conflicts. In working through them, the organizational vision can be used as an important rallying point for discovering how each person's role contributes to the GSCO's purpose. The affective component of the vision is what allows GSCO members to give purpose to their lives and work.[67]

Another way to manage conflict is to prevent its occurrence. At the Hunger Project, the "committed listener" and "breakthrough" processes give GSCO members an opportunity to seek help before conflict becomes dysfunctional. Every member of the organization has a designated person who acts as a committed listener. When things are not going well, or someone is feeling frustrated in his or her ability to accomplish a goal, he or she can talk it out with this colleague. The role of the committed listener is to listen intently, to help the individual understand the issues, and to think about framing or approaching the problem in new ways. This new perspective is called a "breakthrough"—a creative solution to a potentially conflictual situation.

Finally, a GSCO's success can create a number of problems. The very accomplishment of its mission can take away its reason for existence, thus causing an identity crisis. For example, a GSCO that succeeds in creating jobs for underprivileged youth can be dissolved because its funding is redirected toward organizations that have not yet met their goals, because its goals change, or simply because it has accomplished its purpose. During these times, the vital social role that these organizations play needs to be emphasized. GSCOs often represent bridges between the powerful and powerless, between the rich and poor, and between the elite and oppressed, and as such may need to be maintained as legitimate parts of the community.

Another problem can occur when GSCO success produces additional demands for greater formalization. New people must be hired and acculturated; greater control over income and expenditures has to be developed; new skills and behaviors have to be learned. The need for more formal systems often runs counter to ideological principles of autonomy and freedom and can produce a profound resistance to change. Employees' participation during diagnosis and implementation can help them commit to the new systems. In addition, new employment opportunities, increased job responsibilities, and improved capabilities to carry out the GSCO's mission can be used to encourage commitment and reduce resistance to the changes.

Alternatively, the organization can maintain its autonomy through structural arrangements. The Savings Development Movement (SDM) of Zimbabwe was a grassroots effort to organize savings clubs, the proceeds of which helped farmers buy seed in volume. Its success in creating clubs and helping farmers lower their costs caused the organization to grow very rapidly. Leaders chose to expand SDM not by adding staff but by working with the Ministry of Agriculture to provide technical support to the clubs and with the Ministry of Community Development and Women's Affairs to provide training. The savings clubs remained autonomous and locally managed. This reduced the need for formal systems to coordinate the clubs with government agencies. The SDM office staff did not grow, but the organization remained a catalyst, committed to expanding participation rather than providing direct services.[68]

Creating Horizontal Linkages

Successful social change projects often require a network of local organizations with similar views and objectives. Such projects as improving the availability of health services to refugees in Khartoum, turning responsibility for maintenance and control over small irrigation systems to local water users in Indonesia, or teaching leadership skills in South Africa require that multiple organizations interact.[69] Consequently, an important planned change activity in GSCOs is creating strong horizontal linkages to organizations in the community or society where the development project is taking place. For example, GSCOs aimed at job development not only must recruit, train, and market potential job applicants but also must develop relationships with local job providers and government authorities. The GSCO must help these organizations commit to the GSCO's vision, mobilize resources, and create policies to support development efforts.

The ability of GSCOs to sustain themselves depends on establishing linkages with other organizations whose cooperation is essential to preserving and expanding their efforts. Unfortunately, members of GSCOs often view local government officials, community leaders, or for-profit organizations as part of the problem. Rather than interacting with these stakeholders, GSCOs often "protect" themselves and their ideologies from contamination by these outsiders. Planned change efforts to overcome this myopia are similar to the transorganizational development interventions discussed in Chapter 19. GSCO members are helped to identify, convene, and organize these key external organizations. For example, following the earthquakes in Mexico City in 1985, the Committee of Earthquake Victims was established to prevent the government and landlords from evicting low-income tenants from their destroyed housing. The committee formed relationships with other GSCOs concerned with organizing the poor or with responding to the disaster. The committee also linked up with local churches, universities, charitable organizations, and poor urban neighborhood organizations. It bargained with the government and appealed to the media to scuttle attempts at widespread eviction proceedings. This pressure culminated in agreement around a set of principles for reconstruction in Mexico City.[70]

Developing Vertical Linkages

GSCOs also must create channels of communication and influence upward to governmental and policy-level decision-making processes. These higher-level decisions often affect the creation and eventual success of GSCO activities. For example, the Global Village of Beijing (GVB) is a nongovernmental organization that raises the environmental consciousness of people in China. GVB leveraged its relationships with journalists and the government to produce a weekly television series on government channels to discuss and promote environmentally friendly practices, such as recycling, and to expose the Chinese people to environmental projects in different countries. When the Chinese government proposed new environmental regulations and policies as part of the World Trade Organization admission process, GVB helped assess the proposals.[71]

Vertical linkages also can be developed by building on a strong record of success. The Institute of Cultural Affairs (ICA) is concerned with the "application of methods of human development to communities and organizations all around the world." With more than one hundred offices in thirty-nine nations, ICA trains and consults with small groups, communities, organizations, and voluntary associations, in addition to providing leadership training for village leaders, conducting community education programs, and running ecological preservation projects. Its reputation has led to recognition and credibility: it was given consultative status by the United Nations in 1985, and it has category II status with the Food and Agriculture Organization, working relation status with the World Health Organization, and consultative status with UNICEF.[72]

Application 21.3 describes the work of Floresta and gives a brief account of how the organization operates, including the process of change and development.[73] The opening of Floresta's Mexico program provides important clues about the development of vertical and horizontal linkages and how GSCOs work within a clear vision.

Change Agent Roles and Skills

Planned change in development organizations is a relatively new application of organization development in international settings. The number of practitioners is small but growing, and the skills and knowledge necessary to carry out OD in these situations are being developed. The grassroots, political, and ideological natures of many international GSCOs require change agent roles and skills that are quite different from those in more formal, domestic settings.[74] GSCO change agents typically occupy stewardship and bridging roles. The steward role derives from the ideological and grassroots activities associated with GSCOs. It asks the change agent to be a co-learner or co-participant in achieving global social change. This type of change is "sustainable," or ecologically, politically, culturally, and economically balanced. Change agents must therefore work from an explicit value base that is aligned with GSCO activities. For example, change agents are not usually asked, "What are your credentials to carry out this project?" Instead, practitioners are asked, "Do you share our values?" or "What do you think of the plight of the people we are serving?" Stewardship implies an orientation toward the development of sustainable solutions to local and global problems.

The second role, bridging, derives from the grassroots and political activities of many GSCOs. Bridging is an appropriate title for this role because it metaphorically reflects the core activities of GSCOs and the change agents who work with them. Both mainly are concerned with connecting and integrating diverse elements of societies and communities toward sustainable change, and with transferring ideas among individuals, groups, organizations, and societies.

Carrying out the steward and bridging roles requires communication, negotiation, and networking skills. Communication and negotiation skills are essential for GSCO change agents because of the asymmetrical power bases extant in grassroots development efforts. GSCOs are relatively powerless compared with governments, wealthy upper classes, and formal organizations. Given the diverse social systems involved, there often is no consensus about a GSCO's objectives. Moreover, different constituencies may have different interests, and there may be histories of antagonism

APPLICATION 21•3   Social and Environmental Change at Floresta

Floresta is a nongovernmental organization founded on the premise that many environmental and social problems can be addressed effectively by harnessing basic economic forces. Its mission is to attack the economic problems in developing countries that cause and are caused by deforestation. Deforestation can be stemmed if it is economically advantageous for people to change their practices and take care of their environment. Similarly, poverty can be addressed optimally by providing long-term opportunities for people to change their own situations.

Floresta brings hope and long-term opportunity to the people affected by these problems through technically appropriate, business-based programs that lead to self-sufficiency. This fundamental vision has remained unchanged for fourteen years.

Originally developed to meet the environmental, economic, and spiritual needs of the rural people of the Dominican Republic, Floresta provides local farmers with a loan of several thousand dollars each over a seven-year period through the Agroforestry Revolving Loan Fund. These loans are used to establish agroforests consisting of fast-growing trees that are harvested for wood products, as well as fruit trees and more traditional short-term crops. The loans are not a handout. The farmers begin to pay back their loans with their first tree harvest. That money is used to enter more farmers in the program. This process offers significant economic gains to the farmers (often up to a 500- or 600-percent increase in income) while healing environmental scars.

Although the loan fund is the heart of Floresta's program, farmers also receive technical training and marketing assistance. For example, agroforestry is different from traditional farming, and involves much more than simply planting trees. Each farmer must learn to plant, care for, and eventually harvest his or her trees in a sustainable manner. In addition, farmers receive training in soil care, harvesting, and marketing as well as financial planning assistance for the first surplus money they earn. Finally, a common problem faced by subsistence farmers is market access. The individual beneficiary must have not only a market for his or her products but also an economical way to get those products to that market. Floresta provides services in both of those areas.

More than three hundred families have benefited or are benefiting from Floresta's program in the Dominican Republic. Of these, twenty have completed repayment of their loans and now have self-sufficient, six-acre agroforestry farms that are producing at several times the rate of their former subsistence farms. They no longer have any obligation to Floresta, and the money that was loaned to them is now available to other needy farmers. The farmers, however, frequently are eager to continue their relationship with Floresta because of Floresta's marketing services and the community spirit that Floresta engenders. The farmers' achievements validate the Floresta model, supporting it with real-life success. A worldwide goal of one thousand families has been set for the year 2001.

Scott Sabin, executive director of Floresta, described his approach to social and environmental change as he brought the program into Mexico:

I first met the people in the Mixtec village of El Oro in 1996, and for the past year our team had been working closely with them to diagnose some of the economic and environmental problems of the region, and to begin to develop solutions. We have become quite comfortable with many of the local people and several of them typically accompany us as we visit some of the other villages in the municipality of Santo Domingo Nuxaa. The make up of the team varies, but usually consists of representatives from AMEXTRA, government forestry offices, local municipalities, and several other consultants. I represent Floresta. Over the past two years and many visits, we had built up quite a feeling of camaraderie.

Floresta partnered with the Mexican agency, AMEXTRA, to bring this team together and to ensure that Floresta's agroforestry program in Oaxaca would be well thought out and appropriate. Floresta has considerable experience in the Dominican Republic, but the mountains of Mexico are completely different ecologically, economically, and culturally. It is a big mistake to assume that the identical solution can work everywhere.

Working with the people of El Oro, we studied the local problems from both the community and technical perspectives. We worked to incorporate the community itself into the data collection and the investigation. For example, the Mixtec people tend to be cautious around outsiders. They also tend to be very communal, and every step along the way they voted as to whether or not they wished to continue working with us. So far we have passed all the votes unanimously, but stories of other development workers who had not been so fortunate always made me uneasy. Now we are working on implementing solutions and with promoters from El Oro, sharing these ideas with other communities.

Firewood and charcoal are the biggest sources of income for most of the villages. For example, I once observed and interviewed five family members, ranging in age from the mid-sixties to six, making charcoal. It was the primary source of income for the family. They had crops, too, but in years when there was drought, they were forced to rely more on charcoal. They were able to sell 25 kilogram bags of charcoal for 14 pesos a bag, or less than 2 dollars each. They made thirty bags of charcoal at a time and they did it about three times a year. Roughly calculated, this family of five subsisted on about 160 dollars per year.

The problem faced by the family is one of poverty, and tragically, the solution that they have chosen, the only solution they can choose, is leading toward their own ultimate demise and the destruction of the mountains around them. That is, an important cause of deforestation in the tropics is the subsistence farmer who must continually move to find fertile soil and who sells wood for fuel. Deforestation is a product of desperation and hunger, rather than of greed. Farmers are faced daily with the need to cut trees

for their immediate survival. It quickly becomes a vicious cycle, as the treeless hillsides erode at an alarming rate and the topsoil pollutes rivers and streams. Without vegetation, the hills no longer hold water and quickly become unproductive. Rural families are often left with no alternative but migration to overcrowded cities. Any solution to deforestation must address their needs first.

In the Mixteca, Floresta has helped the community of El Oro to establish nine agroforestry demonstration farms, a community tree nursery, and an Agroforestry Development Committee. It also is establishing connections between the local church and churches in the United States. A sawmill and community-based reforestation and forest management plan is envisioned for the next year. This will replace the concessions that currently are being sold to large logging companies. Together with the Mixtec people, who already realize the precarious nature of the situation, Floresta is helping to diversify and improve the rural economy. ■

among groups that make promulgation of the development project difficult. The steward and bridging roles require persuasive articulation of the GSCO's ideology and purpose at all times, under many conditions, and to everyone involved.

The change agent also must be adept at political compromise and negotiation. Asymmetrical power contexts represent strong challenges for stewardship and bridging. To accomplish sustainable change, important tradeoffs often are necessary. The effective change agent needs to understand the elements of the ideology that can and cannot be sacrificed and when to fight or walk away from a situation.

Networking skills represent a significant part of the action research process as applied in GSCO settings. Networking takes place at two levels. First, in the steward role, practitioners bring to the GSCO specific knowledge of problem solving, technologies of empowerment using processes that socially construct and make sense of the surrounding conditions, and organization design.[75] The participants bring local knowledge of political players, history, culture, and ecology. A "cogenerative dialogue" or "collective reflection" process emerges when these two frames of reference interact to produce new ideas, possibilities, and insights.[76] When both the practitioner and the participants contribute to sustainable solutions, the stewardship role is satisfied.

Second, in the bridging role, networking skills create conditions that enable diverse stakeholders to interact and solve common problems or address common issues. Change agents must be able to find common ground so that different constituencies can work together. Networking requires the capability to tap multiple sources of information and perspective, often located in very different constituencies. Action becomes possible through these networks.

But bridging also implies making linkages among individual, group, GSCO, and social levels of thought. Ideas are powerful fuel in international grassroots development projects. Breakthrough thinking by individuals to see things in new ways can provide the impetus for change at the group, GSCO, social, and global levels. This was demonstrated in the Live Aid rock concerts in 1988, the culmination of one man's concern over famine relief in Africa.[77]

The change agent in international GSCO settings must play a variety of roles and use many skills. Clearly, stewardship and bridging roles are important in facilitating GSCO accomplishment. Other roles and skills will likely emerge over time. Change agents, for example, are finding it increasingly important to develop "imaginal literacy" skills—the ability to see the possibilities, rather than the constraints, and the ability to develop sustainable solutions by going outside the boxes to create new ideas.[78]

■ SUMMARY

This chapter has examined the practice of international organization development in three areas. In organizations outside the United States, the traditional approaches to OD need to be adapted to fit the cultural and economic development context in which they are applied. This adaptation approach recognizes that OD practices may be culture-bound: what works in one culture may be inappropriate in another. The cultural contexts of different geographical regions were examined in terms of five values: context orientation, power distance, uncertainty avoidance, achievement orientation, and individualism. This approach also recognizes that not all OD interventions may be appropriate. The prevailing economic situation may strongly favor business-oriented over process-oriented interventions. The process of OD under different cultural and economic conditions was also described, although the descriptions are tentative. As OD matures, its methods will become more differentiated and adaptable.

OD activities to improve global, multinational, and transnational strategic orientations increasingly are in demand. Each of these strategies responds to specific environmental, technological, and economic conditions. Interventions in worldwide organizations require a strategic and organizational perspective on change to align people, structures, and systems.

Finally, OD process in global social change organizations was discussed. This relatively new application of OD promotes the establishment of a global civilization. Strong ideological positions regarding the fair and just distribution of wealth, resources, and power fuel this movement. By strengthening local organizations, building horizontal linkages with other like-minded GSCOs, and developing vertical linkages with policy-making organizations, a change agent can help the GSCO become more effective and alter its external context. To support roles of stewardship and bridging, change agents need communication, negotiation, and networking skills.

■ NOTES

1. L. Bourgeois and M. Boltvinik, "OD in Cross-Cultural Settings: Latin America," *California Management Review* 23 (Spring 1981): 75–81; L. Brown, "Is Organization Development Culture Bound?" *Academy of Management Newsletter* (Winter 1982); P. Evans, "Organization Development in the Transnational Enterprise," in *Research in Organizational Change and Development,* vol. 3, eds. R Woodman and W. Pasmore (Greenwich, Conn.: JAI Press, 1989): 1–38; R. Marshak, "Lewin Meets Confucius: A Re-View of the OD Model of Change," *Journal of Applied Behavioral Science* 29 (1997): 400–02; A. Chin and C. Chin, *Internationalizing OD: Cross-Cultural Experiences of NTL Members* (Alexandria, Va.: NTL Institute, 1997).

2. P. Sorensen Jr., T. Head, K. Johnson, N. Mathys, J. Preston, and D. Cooperrider, eds., *Global and International Organization Development* (Champaign, Ill.: Stipes, 1995); D. Berlew and W. LeClere, "Social Intervention in Curaçao: A Case Study," *Journal of Applied Behavioral Science* 10 (1974): 29–52; B. Myers and J. Quill, "The Art of O.D. in Asia: Never Take Yes for an Answer," *Proceedings of the O.D. Network Conference, Seattle* (Fall 1981): 52–58; R. Boss and M. Mariono, "Organization Development in Italy," *Group and Organization Studies* 12 (1987): 245–56.

3. B. Moore, "The Service Profit Chain—A Tale of Two Airlines" (unpublished Master's thesis, Pepperdine University, 1999); P. Engardino and L. Curry, "The Fifth Tiger Is on China's Coast," *Business Week* (6 April 1992): 43.

4. T. Peters, "Prometheus Barely Unbound," *Academy of Management Executive* 4 (1990): 70–84; Evans, "Organization Development," pp. 3–23; L. Thurow, *The Future of Capitalism* (New York: Morrow, 1996).

5. R. Pieper, "Organization Development in West Germany" in *Global and International Organization Development,* Sorensen et al., pp. 104–21.

6. C. Fuchs, "Organizational Development Under Political, Economic and Natural Crisis," in *Global and International Organization Development,* Sorensen et al., pp. 248–58.

7. "A Survey of Multinationals: Big Is Back," *Economist* 24 (June 1995).

8. Evans, "Organization Development," pp. 8–11; Brown, "Is Organization Development Culture Bound?"; Bourgeois and Boltvinik, "OD in Cross-Cultural Settings"; W. Ouchi, *Theory Z* (Reading, Mass.: Addison-Wesley, 1981).

9. T. Head, "The Role of a Country's Economic Development in Organization Development Implementation," in *Global and International Organization Development,* Sorensen et al., pp. 18–25; W. Woodworth, "Privatization in Belarussia: Organizational Change in the Former USSR," *Organization Development Journal* 3 (1993): 53–59.

10. E. Schein, *Organization Culture and Leadership,* 2d ed. (San Francisco: Jossey-Bass, 1992); Evans, "Organization Development," p. 11.

11. G. Hofstede, *Culture's Consequences* (Beverly Hills, Calif.: Sage, 1980); A. Jaeger, "Organization Development and National Culture: Where's the Fit?" *Academy of Management Journal* 11 (1986): 178–90; N. Margulies and A. Raia, "The Significance of Core Values on the Theory and Practice of Organizational Development," *Journal of Organizational Change and Management* 1 (1988): 6–17; A. Francesco and

B. Gold, *International Organizational Behavior* (Upper Saddle River, N.J.: Prentice Hall, 1998).

12. Hofstede, *Culture's Consequences;* E. Hall and M. Hall, "Key Concepts: Understanding Structures of Culture" in *International Management Behavior,* eds. H. Lane, J. DiStefano, and M. Maznevski, 3d ed. (Cambridge, Mass.: Blackwell); F. Kluckhohn and F. Strodtbeck, *Variations in Value Orientations* (Evanston, Ill.: Peterson, 1961); F. Trompenaars, *Riding the Waves of Culture* (London: Economist Press, 1993).

13. K. Murrell, "Management Infrastructure in the Third World," in *Global Business Management in the 1990s,* ed. R. Moran (New York: Beacham, 1990); The United Nations Development Programme, *Human Development Report* (New York: Oxford University Press, 1994); P. Kotler, *Marketing Management,* 9th ed. (Englewood Cliffs, N.J.: Prentice Hall, 1997).

14. B. Webster, "Organization Development: An International Perspective" (unpublished Master's thesis, Pepperdine University, 1995).

15. Jaeger, "Organization Development and National Culture."

16. The dearth of published empirical descriptions of OD in particular countries and organizations necessitates a regional focus. The risk is that these descriptions may generalize too much. Practitioners should take great care in applying these observations to specific situations.

17. Woodworth, "Privatization in Belarussia."

18. K. Johnson, "Estimating National Culture and O. D. Values," in *Global and International Organization Development,* Sorensen et al., pp. 266–81; Jaeger, "Organization Development and National Culture."

19. A. Shevat, "The Practice of Organizational Development in Israel," in *Global and International Organization Development,* Sorensen et al., pp. 180–83; W. Fisher, "Organization Development in Egypt," in *Global and International Organization Development,* Sorensen et al., pp. 184–90.

20. R. Semler, "All for One, One for All," *Harvard Business Review* (September-October 1989): 76–84.

21. This application is adapted from K. Murrell and M. Wahba, "Organization Development and Action Research in Egypt," *Organization Development Journal* 5 (1987): 57–63. A large amount of material is pulled directly from the article in an attempt to retain the language and tone of the intervention, which provides important evidence about how the basic action research process and its underlying values were adapted to fit the Egyptian context.

22. J. Preston, L. DuToit, and I. Barber, "A Potential Model of Transformational Change Applied to South Africa," in *Research in Organizational Change and Development,* vol. 9, eds. R. Woodman and W. Pasmore (Greenwich, Conn.: JAI Press, 1998); G. Sigmund, "Current Issues in South African Corporations: An Internal OD Perspective" (unpublished Master's thesis, Pepperdine University, 1996).

23. Johnson, "Estimating National Culture."

24. Sigmund, "Current Issues."

25. Webster, "Organization Development"; I. Perlaki, "Organization Development in Eastern Europe," *Journal of Applied Behavioral Science* 30 (1994): 297–312; J. Putti, "Organization Development Scene in Asia: The Case of Singapore," in *Global and International Organization Development,* Sorensen et al., pp. 215–23; M. Rikuta, "Organizational Development within Japanese Industry: Facts and Prospects," in *Global and International Organization Development,* Sorensen et al., pp. 231–47; J. Reeder, "When West Meets East: Cultural Aspects of Doing Business in Asia," *Business Horizons* (January-February 1987): 69–74; Myers and Quill, "Art of O.D."; I. Nonaka, "Creating Organizational Order out of Chaos: Self-Renewal in Japanese Firms," *California Management Review* (Spring 1988): 57–73; S. Redding, "Results-Orientation and the Orient: Individualism as a Cultural Determinant of Western Managerial Techniques," *International HRD Annual,* vol. 1 (Alexandria, Va.: American Society for Training & Development, 1985); K. Johnson, "Organizational Development in Venezuela," in *Global and International Organization Development,* Sorensen et al., pp. 259–64; Fuchs, "Organizational Development," R. Babcock and T. Head, "Organization Development in the Republic of China (Taiwan)," in *Global and International Organization Development,* Sorensen et al., pp. 224–30; R. Marshak, "Training and Consulting in Korea," *OD Practitioner* 25 (Summer 1993): 16–21.

26. Babcock and Head, "Organization Development"; Johnson, "Organizational Development."

27. Johnson, "Organizational Development"; A. Mueller, "Successful and Unsuccessful OD Interventions in a Venezuelan Banking Organization: The Role of Culture" (unpublished Master's thesis, Pepperdine University, 1995).

28. Rikuta, "Organizational Development."

29. Webster, "Organization Development"; B. Gustavsen, "The LOM Program: A Network-Based Strategy for Organization Development in Sweden," in *Research in Organizational Change and Development,* vol. 5, eds. R. Woodman and W. Pasmore (Greenwich, Conn.: JAI Press, 1991):

285–316; P. Sorensen Jr., H. Larsen, T. Head, and H. Scoggins, "Organization Development in Denmark," in *Global and International Organization Development,* Sorensen et al., pp. 48–64; A. Derefeldt, "Organization Development in Sweden," in *Global and International Organization Development,* Sorensen et al., pp. 65–73; J. Norsted and S. Aguren, *The Saab-Scania Report* (Stockholm: Swedish Employer's Confederation, 1975); B. Jonsson, "Corporate Strategy for People at Work—The Volvo Experience," (paper presented at the International Conference on the Quality of Working Life, Toronto, Canada, August 30–September 3, 1981).

30. Johnson, "Estimating National Culture."

31. Norsted and Aguren, *Saab-Scania Report,* Jonsson, "Corporate Strategy."

32. E. Trist, "On Socio-Technical Systems," in *The Planning of Change,* 2d ed., eds. W. Bennis, K. Benne, and R. Chin (New York: Holt, Rinehart & Winston, 1969): 269–72; A. Cherns, "The Principles of Sociotechnical Design," *Human Relations* 19 (1976): 783–92; E. Jacques, *The Changing Culture of a Factory* (New York: Dryden, 1952).

33. P. Nulty, "Batman Shakes BP to Bedrock," *Fortune* (19 November 1990): 155–62.

34. C. Bartlett and S. Ghoshal, *Transnational Management,* 3d ed. (Boston: Irwin McGraw-Hill, 2000).

35. H. Lancaster, "Global Managers Need Boundless Sensitivity, Rugged Constitutions," *Wall Street Journal* (13 October 1998): B1.

36. Bartlett and Ghoshal, *Transnational Management;* D. Heenan and H. Perlmutter, *Multinational Organization Development* (Reading, Mass.: Addison-Wesley, 1979); Evans, "Organization Development," pp. 15–16; Y. Doz, *Strategic Management in Multinational Companies* (Oxford: Pergamon Press, 1986); C. Bartlett, Y. Doz, and G. Hedlund, *Managing the Global Firm* (London: Routledge, 1990).

37. M. Ihlwan, "Doing a Bang-up Business," *Business Week* (18 May 1999): 50.

38. Heenan and Perlmutter, *Multinational Organization Development,* p. 13.

39. A. Borrus, "The Stateless Corporation," *Business Week* (14 May 1990): 103.

40. Ibid., p. 105.

41. J. Main, "How to Go Global—And Why," *Fortune* (28 August 1989): 76.

42. Heenan and Perlmutter, *Multinational Organization Development,* p. 20.

43. Borrus, "Stateless Corporation," p. 101.

44. Heenan and Perlmutter, *Multinational Organization Development*, p. 20.

45. Evans, "Organization Development."

46. T. Stewart, "A Way to Measure Worldwide Success," *Fortune* (15 March 1999): 196–98.

47. Evans, "Organization Development."

48. C. Bartlett and S. Ghoshal, "Organizing for Worldwide Effectiveness: The Transnational Solution," *California Management Review* (Fall 1988): 54–74.

49. R. Tung, "Expatriate Assignments: Enhancing Success and Minimizing Failure," *Academy of Management Executive* (Summer 1987): 117–26; J. Roure, J. Alvarez, C. Garcia-Pont, and J. Nueno, "Managing Internationally: The International Dimensions of the Managerial Task," *European Management Journal* 11 (1993): 485–92; A. Mamman, "Expatriate Adjustment: Dealing with Hosts' Attitudes in a Foreign Assignment," *Journal of Transitional Management Development* 1 (1995).

50. This application was derived from J. Weber, "Campbell: Now It's M-M-Global," *Business Week* (15 March 1993): 52–54; C. Dugas, "Marketing's New Look," *Business Week* (26 June 1987): 64–69; J. Weber, "M'm M'm Bad: Trouble at Campbell Soup," *Business Week* (September 1989): 68–70.

51. Main, "How to Go Global," p. 73.

52. Evans, "Organization Development in the Transnational Enterprise."

53. L. Brown and J. Covey, "Development Organizations and Organization Development: Toward an Expanded Paradigm for Organization Development," in *Research in Organizational Change and Development*, vol. 1, eds. R. Woodman and W. Pasmore (Greenwich, Conn.: JAI Press, 1987): 59–88; P. Tuecke, "Rural International Development," in *Discovering Common Ground*, ed. M. Weisbord (San Francisco: Berrett-Koehler, 1993).

54. P. Freire, *Pedagogy of the Oppressed* (Harmondsworth, England: Penguin, 1972); H. Perlmutter and E. Trist, "Paradigms for Societal Transition," *Human Relations* 39 (1986): 1–27; F. Westley, "Bob Geldof and Live Aid: The Affective Side of Global Social Innovation," *Human Relations* 44 (1991): 1011–36; D. Cooperrider and W. Pasmore, "Global Social Change: A New Agenda for Social Science," *Human Relations* 44 (1991): 1037–55; H. Perlmutter, "On the Rocky Road to the First Global Civilization," *Human Relations* 44 (1991): 897–920; E. Boulding, "The Old and New

Transnationalism: An Evolutionary Perspective," *Human Relations* 44 (1991): 789–805; P. Johnson and D. Cooperrider, "Finding a Path with a Heart: Global Social Change Organizations and Their Challenge for the Field of Organizational Development," in *Research in Organizational Change and Development*, vol. 5, eds. R. Woodman and W. Pasmore (Greenwich, Conn.: JAI Press, 1991): 223–84.

55. D. Cooperrider and T. Thachankary, "Building the Global Civic Culture: Making Our Lives Count," in *Global and International Organization Development*, Sorensen et al., pp. 282–306; Brown and Covey, "Development Organizations."

56. E. Smith, "Growth vs. Environment," *Business Week* (11 May 1992): 66–75.

57. D. Cooperrider and J. Dutton, *Organizational Dimensions of Global Change* (Newbury Park, Calif.: Sage, 1999): p. 12.

58. L. Brown, "Bridging Organizations and Sustainable Development," *Human Relations* 44 (1991): 807–31; Johnson and Cooperrider, "Finding a Path"; Cooperrider and Thachankary, "Building the Global Civil Culture."

59. L. D. Brown and D. Ashman, "Social Capital, Mutual Influence, and Social Learning in Intersectoral Problem Solving in Africa and Asia," in *Organizational Dimensions of Global Change*, eds. Cooperrider and Dutton (Newbury Park, Calif.: Sage, 1999): 139–167.

60. W. Pasmore, "OD and the Management of Global Social Change: Implications and Opportunities," *ODC Newsletter* (Winter 1994): 8–11.

61. F. Westley, "Not on Our Watch," in *Organizational Dimensions of Global Change*, Cooperrider and Dutton, pp. 88–113.

62. Brown and Covey, "Development Organizations."

63. Johnson and Cooperrider, "Finding a Path"; Cooperrider and Thachankary, "Building the Global Civic Culture."

64. W. Whyte, *Participatory Action Research* (Newbury Park, Calif.: Sage, 1991).

65. Johnson and Cooperrider, "Finding a Path," pp. 240–41.

66. Ibid., p. 237.

67. P. Vaill, "The Purposing of High Performing Organizations," *Organization Dynamics* 11 (Autumn 1982): 23–39.

68. M. Bratton, "Non-Governmental Organizations in Africa: Can They Influence Public Policy?" *Development and Change* 21 (1989): 81–118.

69. Brown and Ashman, "Social Capital"; L. DuToit, "Leadership for the Future: A Large Systems OD Intervention in South Africa," in *Global and International Organization Development,* eds. Sorensen et al. (Champaign, Ill.: Stipes, 1995): 203–14; L. DuToit, "Large Systems Change: Corporate Reaction to Transnational Demands in South Africa" (presentation to the 1995 OD Network, Seattle, Wash., 1995).

70. S. Annis, "What Is Not the Same about the Urban Poor: The Case of Mexico City," in *Strengthening the Poor: What Have We Learned?* ed. J. Lewis (Washington, D.C.: Overseas Development Council, 1988): 138–43.

71. Personal communication with members of the Global Village of Beijing, March 28, 2000.

72. Johnson and Cooperrider, "Finding a Path."

73. Information for this application was drawn from their Website, http://www.floresta.org, and links to various articles.

74. L. Brown and J. Covey, "Action Research for Grassroots Development: Collective Reflection and Development NGOS in Asia" (presentation at the Academy of Management, Miami, 1990).

75. D. Cooperrider and S. Srivastva, "Appreciative Inquiry in Organizational Life," in *Research in Organizational Change and Development,* vol. 1, eds. R. Woodman and W. Pasmore (Greenwich, Conn.: JAI Press, 1987): 129–69; Cooperrider and Dutton, *Organizational Dimensions of Global Change.*

76. Brown and Covey, "Action Research"; M. Elden and M. Levin, "Cogenerative Learning: Bringing Participation into Action Research," in *Participatory Action Research,* ed. W. Whyte (Newbury Park, Calif.: Sage, 1991): 127–42.

77. Westley, "Bob Geldof."

78. E. Boulding, *Building a Global Civic Culture: Education for an Interdependent World* (Syracuse, N.Y.: Syracuse University Press, 1988).

22

Organization Development in Health Care, School Systems, and the Public Sector

Organization development is practiced in various types of organizations in both the private and public sectors. In recent years we also have seen growing applications of OD in service industries. Traditionally, however, the published material on OD has focused on applications in industrial organizations. This raises an issue of how relevant much of that knowledge is to other kinds of organizations, such as hospitals, schools, and government agencies. There is considerable speculation and some evidence that traditional applications of OD may need to be modified if they are to extend beyond the narrow industrial model.

This chapter presents broad applications of OD in nonindustrial settings. In previous editions of this book, a person with knowledge and experience in OD in a particular kind of organization was asked to contribute a section for this chapter. For this edition, we asked Foster Mobley, of the Legacy Alliance, to examine OD in health care; Paul Spittler of the Anaheim Union High School District to describe how OD is applied in school systems; and Ray Patchett, city manager for the City of Carlsbad, California, to discuss OD applications in the public sector. Each author stresses the similarities and differences between OD as it is traditionally practiced in industrial organizations and how it applies in these nonindustrial settings. Their conclusions suggest the need for a greater diversity of diagnostic methods, interventions, and values when using OD in nonindustrial environments.

ORGANIZATION DEVELOPMENT IN HEALTH CARE*

Health care is a dynamic and complex industry undergoing fundamental structural change.[1] There is a basic redefinition of what health care comprises and how it is delivered to those in need. Moreover, there is a revolution in the marketplace, in which those who control many of the financial aspects of care are exercising control over those who decide upon and provide the care.[2] The debates affecting the eventual shape of prevention care, care delivery, financing, and access to care are being held in the halls of Congress, the boardrooms of large and small employers, and intensively, in the countless daily interactions between care providers and those they serve. Health care represents a difficult context within which to practice OD.

Consider this increasingly common scenario: A cardiac patient at a rural clinic outside Santa Fe, New Mexico, is diagnosed via telemedicine by the Mayo Clinic in Rochester, Minnesota. The prescribed treatment involves a combination of self-administered drug therapy (after the patient watches a twenty-minute video that describes the treatment and answers the most-asked questions), physical therapy (conducted in partnership between a home health agency and the local senior center), telephone support for monitoring and motivation (located in Greensboro, North Carolina), and nutritional support (provided by a local community agency). The local hospital, once the center of diagnostic and treatment activity in this

---

* Written by Foster W. Mobley, The Legacy Alliance.

example, received its revenues by providing all of these products and services. For organization development, there was a clear target of change. But in the changing environment of health care depicted by this scenario, the question must be asked, "What is the organization to be developed?"

This section describes some of the environmental trends shaping the industry, the implications of these changes on OD in health care, and the current and future success factors for practicing OD in this challenging arena.

Environmental Trends in Health Care

Practitioners and industry leaders acknowledge that the health-care industry is being reshaped by at least five environmental trends:[3]

1. *Changes in the definition of the "product" of health care.* Under the traditional structure of health care, hospitals, surgery centers, and rural health clinics had a simple product: healing for sick people. Significant costs and resources were devoted to treating chronic disease and the complications associated with the last several years of life. Today, the focus of providers is shifting from the treatment to the prevention of illness. There is growing attention to creating healthier lifestyles that improve the quality of life and prevent chronic disease in later years. A 1994 study concluded, "Americans are moving away from a narrow concept of health as the absence of disease to a broader definition that encompasses quality of life indicators."[4] This shift in values is congruent with important indicators of our health and wellness, such as better air quality, reduced crime, population control, and less stress. As witness to the importance of this shift, many hospitals are forging alliances with community groups and engaging in dialogue about a new definition of "healthier communities" and the role played by health-care providers.[5]

   This shift has important implications for how hospitals are organized and operated. For example, healthy people require less surgery than sick people, but surgery is an important source of revenue and status in a hospital. The result is intense competition among hospitals for both local and regional "centers of excellence." Hospitals are vying for status as the cardiac surgery, trauma, emergency, or pediatric care provider in a geographic area. One consequence of this competition is that many facilities are reducing the number of services offered, selectively implementing new technologies, and joining with other hospitals in strategic partnerships to provide a virtual network of services.

2. *Changes in how and where care is delivered.* The hospital is no longer the center of health-care delivery. How prevention or treatment takes place is a more relevant question than where it takes place. As a result, there has been an increased focus on the continuum of care—all the different organizations and people who provide various aspects of prevention, diagnosis, treatment, and monitoring. For example, the fastest-growing segment of the industry is self-care, where consumers administer preventive or remedial treatments to themselves or family members, typically at home. In addition, reductions in the size and cost of diagnostic equipment, like simple blood testing, have shifted many testing and monitoring capabilities to physician offices and the home. Finally, hospitals are providing patients and their families with information about self-treatment in order to reduce costs. For example, people with diabetes attending a self-care course on their illness showed a 69-percent decrease in their hospital admission rate.[6]

3. *Changes in the industry's structure.* In the past, health care was provided through a series of independent people and organizations coordinating the treatment of a patient. Insurance companies that paid the bills were independent of the physicians that provided the services, who were independent of the hospitals where acute diagnosis and treatment were provided. Other parts of the system, including some diagnostic services, laboratory services, hospice care, long-term care, home health, and physical therapy, also were pieces of a loose system that had little or no coordination.

For the past decade, the focus on cost and medical outcomes has resulted in a massive effort to join these independent parts in an integrated health-delivery system. For example, many physician practices joined with hospitals in legal partnerships to align their reimbursement incentives and work processes, and many hospitals and health systems joined together to create regional alliances that could capture market advantages and economies of scale. Despite the effort and optimism, a significant number of these "marriages" of former independent parts (and in some cases, competitors) failed to realize any significant improvement in economic and/or efficient performance. Today, the "unbundling" of these former partners is occurring at a rapid pace, and the rules for how they will once again work together to coordinate aspects of care for patients are still being written.

4. *Changes in how the "product" is paid for.* Over the past ten to twenty years, the average annual rate of health-care cost increase easily outpaced the rate of inflation. At least three groups, or payors, contributed to these increases. Because federal and state governments guarantee health-care services for the elderly, the indigent, and past and present military and government workers, those governments currently are responsible for more than 50 percent of all health-care expenditures in the United States. Secondary payors include companies providing health plans for their workers and insurance companies. Insurance companies create and manage health plans, including "managed care" products, whose financial viability is dependent on their effective management of treatment types, levels, and costs. Tertiary payors include individuals, some without insurance, purchasing health services on their own. Both public policy and marketplace initiatives have begun to control the runaway costs of health care.[7] One such initiative involves shifting control of the health-care dollar from physicians, hospitals, and health plans to employers.[8] In other initiatives, some state governments are beginning to mandate certain basics for the care of patients to combat perceived economic decisions that compromise care quality, such as requiring hospitals to care for new mothers and their babies for three days before discharge. These changes contributed to health-care cost reductions in 1994, and in 1995 the medical component of the consumer price index rose only 4.1 percent, the smallest increase since the index was created in 1984.[9]

Perhaps the biggest single change has occurred in how millions of Americans pay for their care. In particular, people have enrolled in managed care insurance programs, such as HMOs, and away from traditional fee-for-service programs. Estimates suggest that as many as 60 percent of Americans were enrolled in some kind of managed care plan in 1996. The primary reason for this shift seems to have been cost and quality: HMO coverage is provided at a significantly lower cost to the consumer, and studies indicate that the consumer perceives the overall level of quality to be equal to that of traditional forms of coverage.

5. *Changes in the role of information technology.* The use and influence of information technology on health-care delivery has been pervasive. For example,

electronic bedside terminals eliminate the need for a paper chart and instantaneously provide the physician's office and areas throughout the hospital with access to vital medical and business data. Health outcomes databases compare treatment methods and their efficacy across a broad base of providers of that treatment. Decision-support tools yield accurate and detailed cost and performance data to manage and improve each part of the work process, and telemedicine or communications and diagnostic tools allow a patient in one part of the country to be medically diagnosed in another part.

Implications for the Practice of Organization Development

In a discussion of chaos and change, Fred Massarik, a professor of OD, wrote:

> In essence, we now face frequently, more so than even in the immediate past, that point of discontinuity where old rules—or even fairly well-learned approaches for dealing with conventional change—fail us.... Given these circumstances, the top-notch OD practitioner of the next decade will need to become rapidly and responsively adaptable to a world that will not hold still, not even long enough for traditional diagnostic process and normal intervention design. High-speed heuristics, sometimes virtually on the spot, but rooted in a thorough understanding of underlying concepts, will become the order of the day.[10]

In this context, the organization development practitioner must practice and seek to influence the process and outcomes of change in health care. The implications of this condition include the following:

- *Industry restructuring will continue, including the abandoning of many previous merger and affiliation efforts.* This creates an intense need for attention to culture, human systems, and work processes/technologies. Defining and enacting new or changed relationships among providers of care, such as hospitals, physicians, and ancillary service providers, payors for that care, and communities of consumers still is considered by some to be the key to health-care's success.[11] Given the direction of many of these efforts, it creates a problem in trans-organization development, and OD practitioners must be versed in the processes and difficulties inherent in this intervention.[12]

- *In response to industry restructuring, changes in where health care is delivered, and the increasing pervasiveness of technology, there will be significant, negative costs to the people side of the enterprise.* Although stress, burnout, and voluntary termination are frequent topics in industry journals today, the human and social issues of morale, job satisfaction, commitment, quality of work life, and worker productivity and performance are equally important.[13] For example, one study found that 68 percent of health-care executives see burnout as a serious problem, 64 percent are physically exhausted by the end of the day, and 58 percent say emotional exhaustion is common.[14] Another survey of 681 hospitals reported that "poor employee morale is by far the worst human resources problem in the hospital industry."[15] The quality of work life for people in health care is under intense attack, and work performance may be a casualty of industry change. OD interventions that increase employee involvement and assist members in coping with stress clearly will be needed.

- *The structure of health-care organizations is being redefined by individuals with historically different, and possibly incomplete, skill sets.* Today's health-care organizations are being designed by leaders and managers not trained in organizational principles or large-scale change. Schein enumerates the following as some of these principles or skills: intervention skills, commitment to managing unpredictable contingencies, and the acceptance that all human systems are unique and unpredictable.[16] In the past eight years, health-care executives have paid somewhat more attention to organizational philosophies and design principles in their plans to implement various change strategies. Continuous quality improvement, core process reengineering, and work redesign interventions are becoming more and more prevalent. However, the industry, as a whole, is untrained and underprepared to address the types and magnitude of human system changes it now faces.

- *The practice of organization development is likely to be performed in a reactive rather than prospective manner.* The consummation (and in some cases, rapid abandonment) of alliances, acquisitions, and partnerships is driven more by fear of extinction than by concern for whether it will work from a people, cultural, and systems perspective. There was little prospective change planning in advance of most deals, leaving any and all integration work to be dealt with after the fact. Such omissions discount the impact and implications of areas of concern to OD practitioners.

  This fear has generally proven to be founded. The industry's merged organizations, partnerships, health-care systems, and alliances have failed to achieve the envisioned efficiency gains. Key parties in these efforts have reported that the amount of time and effort required to fully integrate was underestimated, the benefits from the integration did not appear as quickly as expected, and the speed with which the mergers and alliances were put together overlooked key issues that altogether prevented the benefits from occurring.

- *Organization development practitioners must respond to their clients' pressures for timely, results-focused actions.* Organization development in health care is more likely to be a "technique-driven" professional practice, in part to respond to the pace of change and perceived need for immediate results, rather than "a philosophy or attitude toward how one can best work with organizations."[17] For example, the merger/alliance activities under way suggest a need for intensive diagnoses around culture, key work processes, leadership effectiveness, and organization structure. Similarly, team-development interventions likely will increase as care delivery shifts from singular, functional contacts to a multidisciplinary, team-based approach.

  This solution-based approach to planned change will be challenged by executives' questionable skills in leading change. Moreover, these leaders tend to devote little time to activities they perceive as a "moderate" priority. Recent research by Boss and Golembiewski[18] found that the role of the chief executive or other organizational leader in successful OD interventions was essential. The issues of insufficient skill, time, and priority place OD interventions at great risk of failure.

- *Organization development in health care will expand beyond the boundaries of traditional health-care organizations.* Consider, once again, the scenario at the beginning of this section. The question was raised, "What is the organization to be developed?" Perhaps better questions would be, "What are the human, cultural, systems, and performance implications of this virtual delivery system, regardless of 'organization,' and what can the OD practitioner do to facilitate both growth and performance optimally?"

  Health-care providers are joining together formally and informally in a mission to transform the health status of entire communities. OD practitioners must help facilitate a clear definition among all new partners on what defines health to the organization, and they must help define what collaboration among various health-care providers and partners truly means. The boundaries between organizations in the business of health-care delivery are fading rapidly because of the increasing number of mergers and alliances as well as this healthier communities mission.

Current and Future Success Principles for OD in Health Care

These conditions suggest a set of principles and beliefs that describe effective OD interventions and OD practitioners in health care. This list is posed as a series of future challenges to the practice and practitioner of OD in health care.

- *Demonstrate the relevance of the subject to strategic performance.* A central debate in OD is whether it should be focused only on quality-of-work-life issues or if performance and systems improvement issues should be of equal importance. The pervasiveness and impact of industry restructuring strongly suggest that any organizational intervention that is not linked to strategic performance risks being labeled irrelevant. In the health-care industry, OD interventions must be linked clearly to issues of the organization's strategic performance—those things that help the organization achieve and sustain competitive advantage, such as cost position, clinical excellence, and market share. OD interventions must not be seen as irrelevant or inconsequential to the life-and-death matters in operating a health-care organization.

  Linking OD efforts to issues of strategic importance will require two things: the practitioner's ability to understand the business of health care and how OD skills and knowledge can impact organizational performance, and the careful identification of the issues selected for action. The increasingly connected relationships among external strategy, structural integration, and human systems enhancement will have to be the expanded domain of the OD practitioner in health care.

- *Demonstrate competence.* The changes taking place within health care will require constant reevaluation and redefinition of competences in a particular field or discipline. This will be as true for medical professionals and health-care managers as for OD practitioners. For example, continuing education is a necessity if managers are to be successful in today's managed care-driven environment.[19] That may include enhanced knowledge and skill for leaders in intervention technologies, exposure to important trends and regulatory issues, and practice in the principles of large-scale change. Leading health systems and hospitals already are providing skills and awareness training to managers in areas of leadership, strategy, restructuring clinical care, human resources issues, and change management.[20]

  Competence for health-care OD practitioners will be demonstrated in a variety of ways, some traditional and some new. For example, practitioners demonstrate competence each day through their ethical demeanor. And, in this dynamic environment, the competence of OD practitioners will be demonstrated by their mastery of conflict resolution skills. Flattened organizational structures and industrywide downsizing, two important accompaniments of the merger and alliance trend, significantly increase the potential for organizational conflict around ambiguous roles, power, and accountability. Although role and authority clarification interventions have always been in the OD practitioner's kit bag, the dynamism of the industry will foster these debates at a continuing and possibly accelerated pace. As described above, new competences will be required in strategy, in business issues, and in the ability to interject process comments into a business discussion while speaking the language of the organization's senior managers.

- *Facilitate integration among and between the diverse parts of the system.* A universal theme of the practice of OD in health care today is integration among traditional and nontraditional stakeholder groups. For example, medical staffs, physician offices, community agencies, and insurance companies typically are untouched by OD processes. Now, in addition to new opportunities for improving the health and performance within each of those groups, significant efforts are necessary to facilitate integration of those groups to improve health-care delivery and reduce cost. A good example is in the practice of community building currently under way among stakeholder groups such as medical practices, citizens, employers, and hospitals. The purpose of this intervention is to craft a common vision for what constitutes health for the entire community, across all health-care providers. OD practitioners are uniquely qualified to assist in developing such a vision. Many have the skills and knowledge to work in transorganizational settings and possess the technologies of large-group intervention to create such a process.

Conclusions

The health-care industry is changing fundamentally and offers unprecedented challenges and opportunities. OD practitioners can influence positive growth and development by linking their efforts to the strategies of the organization, demonstrating competence and integrity, and being able to facilitate integration of people and processes across traditional departmental and organizational boundaries.

This opportunity comes with a challenge. At a time when each dollar and every resource in health care is being closely scrutinized, the inherent value of the OD approach is being tested for validity. Clients, under increasing pressure to demonstrate the added value of key activities will, in turn, subject OD practitioners and their change interventions to the same testing. The practitioner must seek a balance between responsiveness and relevance while maintaining a commitment to the core values that have defined OD, namely the equal importance of human needs and the creation of a work environment that allows growth, fulfillment, and performance.[21]

ORGANIZATION DEVELOPMENT IN SCHOOL SYSTEMS*

Mark Twain once said, "In the first place God made idiots. This was for practice. Then He made school boards." Fortunately, modern critics of public schools are more kind in their analysis. Driven by greater social complexity and increasingly competitive demands of a global economy, societal pressure to improve educational effectiveness has increased during the past twenty years. Shifting demographics, for example, have produced a culturally diverse and multilingual student population. Other societal trends, such as increased rates of divorce and dual-career families, manifest themselves in children who arrive at school poorly prepared and lacking the supportive and active involvement of their parents. Schools are being asked to do more under more difficult circumstances.

---

* Written by Paul Spittler, Anaheim Union High School District.

In response to the challenges facing public education today, reformers advocate changes in all aspects of the bureaucratic network that constitutes and surrounds public education. Educational reform focuses on the individual school site as well as on the complex policy-making machinery that directs and simultaneously constrains schools. Reformers seek higher standards for all children, more demanding curricular content and instructional methodology, smaller class sizes, authentic measurement systems and greater accountability, and more effective school organizations. In short, it asks school personnel to attain higher standards, carry out their tasks differently, and organize differently to do so.[22]

As organizations, schools are regarded by educators as completely unique, distinct from other organizational types. However, practitioners of organizational change view schools as typical bureaucratic systems, not unlike other kinds of organizations. Comparative studies indicate that there is some validity in both these views. Schools share certain characteristics with all open systems and can be diagnosed and changed along variables common to all organizations. At the same time, schools differ from other organizations with respect to such things as the tasks they perform and the technologies they use to accomplish those tasks. Considering both the similarities and differences between schools and business organizations, OD programs designed for business and industry are neither entirely suited to nor entirely inappropriate for educational systems. OD techniques developed for other organizations can be used constructively in schools but only if they are refocused and modified to be responsive to the special needs of these systems.[23]

After exploring the characteristics of school systems and the implications for planned change processes, several high-involvement interventions that are currently being implemented in school are described.

Some Unique Characteristics of Schools

Schools differ from private-sector firms in their tasks and technologies, environments, members, and structures. The primary task carried out by schools is the transformation of young people through learning. This task differs from that of most business organizations in that it focuses on people, rather than on nonliving systems. Educating children is a complex and uncertain task. There is, for example, considerable ambiguity and disagreement concerning educational content of the required curriculum and little public consensus as to valid measures authenticating mastery of that curriculum.[24] Further, the technologies or methods used to carry out this task are ambiguous, particularly in their effectiveness. The impact of a particular teaching strategy may be difficult to discern, and its applicability may vary for students with different characteristics. These uncertainties create problems for the individual teacher as well as for the school as a whole.[25]

Not unlike business organizations, public schools are highly dependent on and vulnerable to their environments. Their enrollments rise and fall with birth and immigration rates, and their funding base erodes as citizens demand lower taxes. In addition, their customers are characterized by different and often mutually exclusive sets of interests. They are subject to close public scrutiny and to occasional "crises" that may arise within their communities.[26] Unfortunately, school administrators react to these forces by retrenching and defending, and their schools evolve into reactive, rather than proactive, organizations.[27]

However, public schools enjoy near-monopoly status and generally lack an environmental force for change matching that of competitive pressure. Although private schools have increased in number, their total share of the market is slight, accessible only to a relatively small percentage of the population.

Schools also are somewhat unique with respect to the qualifications and characteristics of their members. Teachers generally are better educated than are the people dealing with clients or working on the line in business or industrial organizations.[28] Teachers probably take a greater interest in their jobs than do people in many other organizations and derive more satisfaction from the intrinsic rewards of their work.[29] Teachers believe that it is their responsibility to solve many task-related problems—in some cases, autonomously in their own classrooms and, in other cases, cooperatively in communities and faculty senates.[30]

Although some structural differences exist between schools and other organizations, these differences are not always very great.[31] The administrative structures of schools originally were modeled after those of business organizations,[32] and schools have been characterized by their centrality of decision making and their standardization of activities.[33] However, schools also have been called "loosely structured"[34] and "loosely coupled"[35] organizations. Those labels have been applied partly because teachers carry out their work in self-contained classrooms; are highly autonomous; and are weakly interconnected in influence, interpersonal support, and the flow of information. Thus, the administrative (or vertical) structures of schools are well developed, but collegial (or horizontal) structures tend to be weak. Although these structural characteristics are similar to those of many business organizations, they are not entirely appropriate for schools, given the uncertainties of their tasks and technologies. Better developed collegial structures would be particularly useful in schools for solving the problems experienced by those directly responsible for carrying out the primary tasks of the organization.[36]

Implications for OD in Schools

The organizational characteristics of schools have important implications for the design of OD programs. First, schools traditionally have highly developed administrative structures that enable them to interact with their environments, although not necessarily in a proactive manner. For example, all schools are subject to public oversight concerning the academic achievement of their students. As a result, these sophisticated structures are quite good at collecting and reporting on the students' academic progress. Yet, despite the repetitive nature of annual standardized testing, few states have sought to achieve public consensus regarding the test instrument in advance of public criticism.

Second, the tasks performed by schools are somewhat uncertain. This uncertainty can create difficulties in task performance and can complicate other problems, including those of coordinating activities and allocating resources, that routinely must be solved by all organizations. In states with high levels of immigration, for example, the number of non–English-speaking students may change dramatically from one year to the next. Although teachers and other members of the school community may be able to solve some of these problems by relying on traditional authority structures, other problems may be resolved only through the use of collaborative decision-making structures which often do not exist.

Third, teachers committed to their work are likely to receive greater intrinsic rewards if task-related issues are resolved properly. However, teachers typically do not have access to structures for collaborative problem solving or do not possess the skills needed to use such structures effectively should they exist.[37]

Finally, despite their obvious bureaucratic characteristics, schools paradoxically may be regarded as underorganized systems (see Chapter 2). Communication among teachers is typically fragmented, curricular responsibilities between and within grade levels are frequently unclear, and the output requirements of the system are somewhat ambiguous. Correspondingly, many school districts exhibit characteristics of transorganizational systems (see Chapter 19). Schools within a given district can be said to be loosely coupled because leadership and power are typically dispersed among principals at largely autonomous school sites.

Those four points explain why many OD programs for schools focus heavily on creating collaborative decision-making structures that include teachers and parents and on helping participants develop the skills necessary to use such structures. These interventions can provide the school community with a base for identifying and solving problems that involve task and technological issues and that require the collective expertise of the entire school staff as well as the active support and involvement of parents.[38] Furthermore, they can provide a base for change initiation within schools[39] and can make them more proactive vis-à-vis their environments. And although the appropriateness of collaborative structures depends on the precise nature of the organization's environment and tasks,[40] substantial evidence suggests that collaborative decision-making structures are needed in most schools.[41]

High-Involvement Management in Schools

School reform stressing greater collaboration in decision making as a means of improving organizational performance is based on the principles of high-involvement management—a systemic change model that creates an environment where employees are motivated and empowered to become active in improving organizational performance.[42] The basic goal of high-involvement management applied to schools is to create an alternative to the traditional control-oriented hierarchy in which school district superintendents and school principals at the top are responsible for strategy, direction, and organizational performance and in which teachers feel victimized and constrained by a bureaucracy they cannot influence.[43] High-involvement management diffuses control throughout the organization such that all organizational stakeholders—including parents—can influence decisions, contribute to strategy and direction, and participate in improving organizational performance.

The high-involvement framework entails increasing the presence of four key organizational resources at the technical core of the organization: power, information, knowledge and skills, and rewards. These resources are believed to be closely linked to employees' capability and motivation to contribute to enhanced organizational performance.[44] Ideally, a high-involvement approach in schools would enable parents and teachers to influence the content of the curriculum, the delivery of that content, and the evaluation of student performance; it would allow them to participate in the creation of school district strategy and mission and specific educational goals; it would enable them to develop the skills necessary to use cooperative decision-making structures and to collect and assess performance data; it would provide them with ongoing task feedback; and it would reward teachers based on the improved academic performance of their students as well as on the development of their individual capabilities.

High-involvement principles have been found to be particularly appropriate in settings where the work is nonroutine, where organizational inputs are of a wide variety, and where the results of the task technologies are uncertain. Educational organizations fit these characteristics: work cannot be entirely preprogrammed, and teachers are called on to employ their judgment to tailor approaches to individual students.[45] High involvement is also appropriate where interdependence among various task contributors is high and where their activities must be coordinated in a manner that cannot be fully anticipated.[46] For example, the work of one high school teacher has a reciprocal impact on the work of another and vice versa.

Most important for educators, the effectiveness of high-involvement management has already been demonstrated. In private-sector service and manufacturing organizations, implementing high-involvement practices has had a positive influence on many organizational conditions, including levels of work quality, innovation, introduction of new technology, customer satisfaction, and quality of decision making; employee outcomes such as quality of work life and satisfaction; and financial outcomes such as efficiency and competitiveness.[47]

Two broad-based trends in educational management incorporate the principles of high-involvement management: total quality management and school-based management (SBM). Successful examples of both frameworks focus not only on the creation of collaborative decision-making structures, which include teachers and parents in addition to administrators, but also on the development of the requisite skills necessary to use such structures.

Total Quality Management

This intervention is the most recent and perhaps the most comprehensive approach to employee involvement (see Chapter 15). It is a long-term effort that orients all of an organization's activities around the concept of quality. TQM pushes decision-making power downward in the organization, provides relevant information to all employees, increases workers' knowledge and skills through extensive training, and ties rewards to organizational performance.

For Deming, a central figure in TQM, the key problem in American education is the absence of quality—meeting and exceeding the customer's needs and expectations and then continuing to improve. For him, the responsibility for quality lies with school administration, not with the student. Through evaluation systems that off-load the responsibility for quality onto the student, administrators abdicate their primary role of defining quality and improving work processes, and instead induce conflict, reduce cooperation, destroy intrinsic motivation, and cause morale and quality to suffer.[48]

Total quality initiatives have been ongoing in a variety of educational settings for nearly a decade. Deming's own *Out of the Crisis*[49] specifically identified public education as a service provider for which his "14 Points" would be appropriate. That same year, California's Sacramento County Office of Education began the first K–12 public education, organizationwide application of quality concepts in the United States, based on Deming's approach. Simultaneously, education literature began to appear that noted the parallels between independent research on improving school effectiveness and the Deming approach.[50] Further, beginning about 1989, Deming commenced annual seminars aimed especially at teachers. In 1990 Myron Tribus reported on the applications of Deming's principles in a Native American "alternative" school in Sitka, Alaska, and the American Association of School Administrators began its official study of the applicability of TQM to schools.[51] By 1994 more than 135 school districts were engaged in formal TQM programs nationally.[52]

In practice, successful TQM programs tend to be leader-initiated, long-term, and iterative in nature. Implementation of TQM typically is dependent on a number of team-based structures that operate parallel to traditional administrative authority. The teams arrive at decisions through group consensus, ground recommendations for action on valid data, determine valid criteria and strategies for measuring progress, and enjoy some degree of co-governance or collaborative decision making with the formal administrative leadership. In addition, extensive training is provided in a variety of areas to match the needs of the implementation process. In the early phases of implementation, training focuses on building an awareness of the quality philosophy. Then, as the organization moves forward, participants receive group process training and team-building assistance. Later, training in specific statistical tools is introduced in preparation for ongoing data gathering and analysis.[53]

TQM calls for total transformation rather than incremental movement in the pursuit of its objectives.[54] Its assumptions regarding human nature and behavior fit naturally with the assumptions of many educators.[55] In addition, the changes envisioned by the principles of TQM align closely with counterpart proposals in educational research for increasing educational effectiveness.[56] But, despite its popularity and track record of success in industrial, service, and governmental settings, little compelling evidence exists linking TQM with increased student achievement.[57]

School-Based Management

This intervention, also known as site-based management, involves the formal alteration of school governance structures. It is a form of decentralization that identifies the individual school as the primary unit of improvement and relies on the redistribution of decision-making authority to achieve and sustain educational improvements. Some formal authority to make decisions regarding budget, personnel, and educational programs is commonly distributed among site-level participants so that they can become directly involved in schoolwide decision making.[58]

Site-based management has almost as many variations as locations claiming to be site based, and they differ along every important dimension—who initiates it, who is involved, what they control, and whether they are accountable to an outside authority. Site-based management may be instituted by state law or administrative action, by a district, or by a school. It may or may not be linked to an accountability system with consequences tied to student performance. But, in all its iterations, school-based management is an attempt to transform schools into individual communities in which appropriate people participate constructively in major decisions that affect them.[59]

Most variants of SBM involve some sort of representative decision-making body that shares authority with the principal or acts in an advisory capacity. The composition of these councils, committees, or boards may vary tremendously and can include principals, teachers, and parents, as well as students, community residents, and business representatives. States or districts may specify the constituencies that must be represented on the councils or simply leave it to individual schools.

The state of Kentucky and the city of Chicago, for example, require virtually every school to have a school-based council, specify their makeup, and endow councils with extensive fiscal and policy authority. Maryland and Texas require schools to have school-based decision-making teams but, in contrast, do not specify their composition or legally transfer authority from the district to the school. These are only a few examples. According to one study, one-third of all school districts had some version of SBM between 1986 and 1990, and since 1990 at least five additional states have required it in some form.[60] During that same period, more than twenty states have passed legislation to permit the creation of "charter" schools, individual schools that are de facto school-based although they carry another title.[61]

Power and its delegation are central to SBM. In typically centralized school districts, many administrative decisions are made at the central office.[62] By contrast, school-based programs delegate decision-making authority to the school level, namely to principals, teachers, and parents, under the assumption that school-level actors are better positioned than district or state officials to make decisions for their organizations.[63]

Despite the current popularity of SBM, however, evidence of its impact on student performance is not compelling. A comprehensive literature review[64] concludes that there is little evidence that SBM has significantly enhanced conditions in schools and districts or improved students' academic performance, and a more recent Rand Corporation study reached the same conclusion.[65]

Classroom Interventions

Although not OD interventions per se, two instructional trends—integrated curriculum and cooperative learning—incorporate many of the principles of high-involvement management, altering the nature of power, information, knowledge and skills, and rewards within the classroom. Typically a team-based approach, integrated curriculum breaks down the traditional barriers among academic departments. Rather than viewing mathematics, science, language arts, fine arts, and social sciences as isolated subjects, integrated curriculum produces lessons that cut horizontally across departments, reintegrating and enriching student work. Similarly, cooperative learning specifically adopts a team-based approach to classroom work design and student learning.[66] Students work in cooperative learning teams and, to varying degrees, are evaluated based on the team's performance. Both of these instructional trends are project oriented, and students produce whole, identifiable pieces of work. Ideally, both approaches redefine the roles of teacher and student. Rather than delivering educational content to passive observers, the teacher becomes a facilitator for student-designed projects, and students take a more responsible role in the design of their own learning.

Conclusions

Reformers have called for large-scale change in educational systems that may require schools to become high-involvement organizations, capable of tapping the vast underutilized potential of teachers, parents, and the community to find better ways to educate children. Principals, teachers, and parents are not being asked simply to do their jobs better; they are being asked to do different jobs.

Principals are being asked to lead organizational transformation at a time when the task of educating children is more difficult than ever. Teachers are being asked to participate in improving the quality and performance of the school; to collectively solve problems and generate new and more effective approaches to teaching and learning; and to demonstrate new ways of relating to each other, to students, and to the community. Parents are being asked to participate more fully in the decisions affecting the direction, content, and delivery of their children's education.

This transformation process requires establishing new and effective structures and processes to promote broader participation in school governance, organizational improvement, and enhanced delivery of service; creating systems to measure results and share information; developing broader and deeper skills and knowledge through extensive training; and establishing appropriate systems to reward improvement.

A number of factors in schools make change of this magnitude especially difficult and present special challenges. The loose coupling of various aspects of schools and the isolated functioning of teachers conspire against a systemic approach to change. Schools do not have a tradition of strategy formulation and goal setting, nor are accountability and performance management systems well developed or accepted there. School participants will have to get used to examining results, talking about goals and how to achieve them, watching trends collectively, solving problems, and being held accountable.

There is a pressing need for additional experimentation and evaluation of new forms of school organization. In response, a number of demonstration schools have exhibited high-involvement characteristics,[67] including the School Development Program schools,[68] Accelerated Schools,[69] Essential Schools,[70] and the Pinellas County Schools.[71] SBM schools having success in reforming their approaches to teaching and learning are characterized by decentralized influence in decision making, broad information sharing, and high levels of knowledge and skills development.[72]

Much more research is required to test fully the efficacy of high-involvement approaches to school reform, and much of this will have to be action research. In particular, future researchers must consider how specific programs incorporate each of the four elements of high-involvement management. Most important, the connection between high involvement and enhanced student performance must be established convincingly.

ORGANIZATION DEVELOPMENT IN THE PUBLIC SECTOR*

Public sector organizations, such as federal, state, and local governments, operate in an environment of competing political, social, and economic forces. Calls for the government to become more citizen focused and to operate in a more businesslike manner are common. Legislation and programs aimed at improving government accountability, quality, and effectiveness are being introduced and adopted at all levels of government.[73] For example, the 1993 National Performance Review (NPR) initiative created by President Bill Clinton and run by Vice President Al Gore called for national agencies to transform themselves into high-quality, low-cost service providers[74] and outlined 384 recommendations for improvement. At the state level, initiatives to curb government revenues or taxing authority, such as California's Proposition 13 (adopted by voters in 1978), continue to be introduced.

In addition, public sector organizations face increasingly complex and significant challenges in responding to citizens, crafting public policy, and providing public services. Their record of success has been spotty at best with trust in government falling dramatically. In 1964, 75 percent of Americans said that they trusted the federal government to do the right thing "just about always" or "most of the time." By 1994, three out of four Americans said they mistrusted government.[75] Similarly, public participation, once the hallmark of the American democratic process, is suffering. Voter turnout has dropped from more than 63 percent in 1960 to 49 percent in 1996.[76] As a result, public sector organizations are engaging in a tremendous effort to develop greater public trust and confidence in government as they move into the twenty-first century.

For example, many governments are attempting to be more productive, efficient, and effective by downsizing and privatizing public services[77] and introducing technology to increase effectiveness and productivity. The International City/County Management Association has initiated a nationwide performance measurement initiative aimed at improving public sector effectiveness. City governments, such as that of Phoenix, Arizona, are competing with the private sector through managed competition programs. Other cities, such as Carlsbad and Irvine, California, are implementing performance management compensation systems

---

*Written by Raymond R. Patchett, City Manager, City of Carlsbad, California.

that reward employees based on competencies and the achievement of goals. All are being introduced to translate legislative mandates into measurable results and outcomes, such as citizen satisfaction and service quality.

These types of changes suggest a vital and important OD role in the public sector. Planned organization change efforts in the public sector can be as successful as those in private organizations,[78] and OD interventions are becoming more common and accepted in government. For example, community visioning processes are being conducted to connect government with its citizens; technology is being introduced to help governments operate electronically and be more effective; team building is being conducted for elected officials and staff at all levels of the organization; and performance management and compensation programs are being implemented. These OD interventions, and others included in this book, are helping public sector organizations respond to the citizenry and transform themselves into citizen-focused, customer-driven, results-oriented public sector organizations.

Although public sector OD applications are becoming more common, they face a unique set of circumstances, including a complex political and administrative environment. Interventions often are conducted in the public arena among a number of stakeholders, each of whom has legitimate standing in the decision-making process. The climate and support for OD is complicated further by the structure of public sector organizations. Although the legislative and political arena is interdependent with the administrative domain, it is highly unlikely that both will be involved in the same OD intervention. If they are, each domain has a different role and operates based on different and sometimes competing values. To conduct planned change initiatives effectively, OD practitioners must recognize and appreciate these differences. This section highlights some key differences between the public and private sectors and discusses some of the implications for applying OD in public sector organizations.

Comparing Public and Private Sector Organizations

Public sector OD initiatives need to recognize the political nature of government and be aware of the differences between public and private sector organizations. This discussion draws on the writing and research of Bob Golembiewski, John Bryson, H. George Frederickson, and John Nalbandian. Public and private sector organizations differ along four key dimensions: values and structure, the multiplicity of decision makers, stakeholder diversity and access, and the extent of intergovernmental relationships. Each of these differences is discussed along with its implications for OD practice.

Values and Structure

Public and private sector organizations differ in important ways with respect to their values and structures. In private sector companies, the key values are profitability and the creation of competitive advantage. The board of directors, who represent the shareholders, and the management team, who are tasked with implementing a strategy, share these values. Although public sector organizations share a similar structural arrangement of representation and implementation, there are crucial differences in purpose and role that hold important implications for OD practice.

In contrast to the private sector, the overarching purpose of public sector organizations is to understand and promote the public good and demonstrate responsiveness to public wants and needs. The public good is addressed through policies and programs that support a broad array of citizen needs and must, by law, be discussed and adopted in an open forum. Responsiveness is reflected in demands for representation, efficiency, individual rights, and social equity.[79] In service of these values and purposes, public sector organizations also adopt a representation–implementation structural form. The representative function is known as the political or legislative domain, and the implementation function is known as the administrative domain.

The political–administrative structure reflects the values and roles inherent in government organizations. In the classic theory of public administration, the political domain is led by elected representatives who pass legislation and enabling statutes in service of the public good. In turn, they delegate implementation of programs and statutes to administrative agencies.[80] The political domain includes both elected and politically appointed officials, and the administrative group includes the merit-based civil service and certain executives, such as city managers, who are appointed on the basis of professional rather than political criteria.[81] This structure mirrors the private sector's distinction between a board of directors and management.

Unlike private sector organizations, however, the purposes and values within public sector organizations are not shared necessarily by the representative and implementation functions. For example, politicians serve at the pleasure of the public. Although private sector board members are elected representatives of the shareholders, their elections are not as open and public as are those of political officeholders. Politicians must compete to get elected and continue to posture and compete to get reelected. As a result, political values of social equity and representation are reflected in an open and public process where the particular interests and values of a diverse set of constituencies are brought together to produce a common view of the public good. Clearly, politics is the art and science of government.[82]

Moreover, the political function is responsible for the establishment and oversight of an organization that is designed to implement the outcomes of the legislative process. Generally, the mission of the administrative function is regulation of the laws and delivery of public services or goods. The legislative mandates, rules, and procedures established to run public sector organizations make them less flexible than most private sector organizations and constrain their ability to act outside of their legislative framework. Thus, the administrative function values partisan neutrality; selection and promotion on the basis of merit, specialization, and expertise; the use of information for analyzing public policy issues; recordkeeping for purposes of continuity; application of the work ethic; and the justification of decisions based on efficiency (achieving the most productivity for the money available) or economy (achieving a given level of productivity for as little money as possible) or both.[83] When elected officials are responding to the citizenry or setting policy, the political domain's values of representation and social equity may override the administrative values of efficiency. When such value conflicts occur, administrators are often caught in the tension between politics and their mandate to run an efficient organization.

These value differences have contributed to the perception of government as a bureaucracy, which simply refers to the administration of a government through bureaus staffed with nonelected officials. Perceptions of bureaucracy are often negative, however, and include indifferent people exercising power through strict adherence to inflexible policies, rules, and procedures. Although public and private sector organizations can take on the characteristics of a bureaucracy, such as departmentalization, vertical decision-making processes, and many formal rules and procedures, the characteristics are more pronounced in government organizations. A critical reason for this phenomenon is that government organizations are legislated into existence, giving the organization or agency life until it is legislated out of existence. As a result, the organization receives funding that sustains its existence regardless of performance. Although budgets at all levels of government are reviewed and adopted annually, the complete elimination of a public sector agency or organization is rare. The effect is that public sector organizations, despite their purpose, can be much less responsive to citizens and customers than private sector organizations because they aren't directly reliant on the customer for funding to sustain their existence.

The political nature of the legislative and representation process and the efficiency orientation of the administrative process produce important tensions in a public sector organization. OD practitioners must be aware of these tensions and the implications they have for OD practice. First, OD practitioners must understand that a public sector organization's primary mission, unlike private sector organizations, is set by law and can be changed only through additional legislative action. Even so, appointed officials and staff have much flexibility and discretion on how to implement government services and programs. The implication for OD is that many of the interventions used to help private sector organizations, such as business process reengineering, total quality management, large-group interventions, and team building, can be used successfully in the public sector.

Second, public sector interventions often require approval and funding from an elected board. This increases the probability that the design will be scrutinized and challenged to ensure its efficacy. OD practitioners need to be ready to provide evidence of success for particular interventions in public sector organizations.

Third, OD processes that support elected officials in enacting policy must consider the public environment in which they are being conducted. Public sector organizations have a much broader array of responsibilities and are subject to greater direct public access, media coverage, and more distributed power than are most private sector organizations. As a result, most policy-level OD applications will be conducted in public. OD practitioners must select processes that create a constructive environment on the one hand and allow for public participation and review on the other. In addition, OD interventions must account for the vulnerability which elected officials, and sometimes public administrators, experience. For example, the results of a community visioning process may serve as the political platform for candidates seeking the same public office that the incumbents leading the visioning process currently hold. OD practitioners need to be aware of this possibility as interventions are designed and implemented.

Fourth, the values of the political and legislative domains may differ from traditional OD values. The win–lose dynamics associated with passing legislation, mediating competing interests, and balancing scarce resources can conflict with OD values of collaboration, teamwork, and efficiency. Improving organization effectiveness is an OD value often at odds with the political process. Last, administrative values and OD values are more likely to be aligned. As such, the OD practitioner may find more affinity for the administrative domain than for the political domain. To be effective, an OD practitioner must appreciate the tensions found in these differences.

Multiplicity of Decision Makers

The public sector is webbed by multiple access to multiple authoritative decision makers, a phenomenon designed to ensure that "public business gets looked at from a variety of perspectives."[84] The norm in government is full and legitimate access to all decision makers at every level. As a result, decision making and accountability are more dispersed than in private sector organizations where such access is uncommon and responsibility is more clear-cut.[85] Further complicating the public sector decision-making process is that different organizations are responsible for different steps in the governmental process, often making it confusing and difficult for citizens, clients, customers, and even public officials and staff to understand who is responsible for what decision and accountable for what product.

In addition, Golembiewski noted that decision making by public officials, "tends to favor *patterns of delegation* that maximize their sources of information and minimize the control exercised by subordinates."[86] Specifically, the goal was to have all decisions brought to their level for action and review. While this may have been the case in the past, most public sector organizations today are just as embroiled as the private sector in the task of evolving from a command-and-control decision-making structure to one of empowered workers. Within the constraints of the regulations governing the organization, public officials can delegate decision-making responsibility and accountability to the public worker closest to the citizen and customer if they want to and if it is in alignment with their leadership philosophy. The implication is that OD values that seek to expand worker self-control and move decision making closest to the citizen and customer are consistent with many government transformation efforts currently underway.

This multiplicity of decision makers and accountability results in additional implications for OD interventions. First, multiple decision makers make it difficult to determine the identity of the client and the expected results. For example, a legislative body may adopt a policy, such as pay-for-performance, and direct staff to implement the program. In this example, both the legislative body and the staff are accountable and responsible for different parts of the intervention. Because of the interdependence of the policy and administrative decision-making process, the OD practitioner may be unable to gain the same level of clarity about client identities and responsibilities that is possible in the private sector.

Second, approval, support, and funding for OD interventions may be more difficult to obtain. Operating with multiple agencies or at multiple levels of the same organization adds a degree of difficulty relative to approval and support for OD interventions that is greater than private sector organizations. The implication for OD practitioners is most direct when entering and contracting. The project may require staff support for the intervention and legislative approval and funding for the project. As a result of the public approval process, OD practitioners must be able to explain the process and outcomes that will result and must expect that the public or politicians resisting the project may challenge the efficacy of the intervention(s).

Stakeholder Access

A stakeholder is any group or individual who is affected by or who can affect the policies and operations of the public sector organization—citizens, customers, political parties, corporations, employees, other governments, interest groups, critics, and so forth.[87] In contrast to private industry, the public sector conducts business in open public meetings and involves a "greater variety of individuals and groups with different and often mutually exclusive sets of interests, reward structures, and values."[88] In addition, citizens and interest groups have full access to documents, plans, and other background information via public records, public notices, and the Internet. OD practitioners must recognize that all stakeholders have legitimate entry into the public policy and administrative processes and bring different values, goals, or proposed solutions to public issues. For example, the values inherent in the Americans with Disabilities Act must compete for funding with the values inherent in the Endangered Species Act and its programs. Such diversity of interests and access create a broad array of challenges for OD. Foremost among the challenges is helping diverse groups of people with different and competing interests to publicly collaborate with each other in developing a common goal that may represent an unpopular compromise to any individual group.

All citizens have access to and may impact public policies. Such broad access may exist in the private sector with respect to certain types of information, but is much more restricted with respect to influence over decisions and activities. Thus, the role demands of an elected official are much broader than the role demands of a private sector board member. In addition, public sector administrators, who are responsible for enacting public policy, have a duty to respond to the citizens, elected officials, and the staff that work for them. Such access and responsibility complicate the roles of politicians and administrators and politicize their position. The implications of this web of roles and responsibilities for OD practitioners is that anybody can make a demand to be involved in the process at virtually any level of a public organization and the likelihood is that the individual or group will have legitimate standing to do so.

In addition, public sector employees are stakeholders as a result of their legal right to form unions to represent them on matters concerning wages, hours, and working conditions. Because collective bargaining laws are structured for managing disagreement, a challenge for OD practitioners, if involved, is to help facilitate the process in a way where all parties perceive their interests have been considered and they feel heard. A poor labor relations environment and poor employee morale will make it difficult, if not impossible, to implement OD interventions successfully. Importantly, OD practitioners must understand that, in contrast to the private sector, it is difficult to arrange stakeholder interests and expectations behind a common goal. Even so, practitioners must appreciate that "attention to stakeholder concerns is crucial because the key to success in public and nonprofit organizations is the satisfaction of key stakeholders."[89]

Intergovernmental Relations

Government comprises a latticework of interrelated government agencies and organizations providing different public services to the same citizens and customers. The result is an intergovernmental relations environment where federal, state, and local government share power, responsibility and, in some cases, resources.[90] These intergovernmental relationships raise several considerations for public sector OD applications.

First, issues of coordination and power may emerge out of the sharing of responsibility across public sector organizations in the provision of public services. Although the services may appear to be provided by "the government," the reality is that a number of public organizations often are responsible for different aspects of the same public service. For example, providing an integrated transportation system requires federal, state, special district, private developer, and local government participation. The federal government and special districts work together to provide train and bus service. The state works with federal and local governments to provide interstate and state highways. Local governments provide the local road system with financial assistance from development, federal, and state agencies. OD practitioners working on intergovernmental relations projects must adopt a transorganizational development process that results in agreement about purpose, responsibility, and shared resources.

Second, governments often work together on intergovernmental projects involving two or more public sector organizations. In such cases, it is common to find that a federal policy, such as the Clean Water Act or the Endangered Species Act, sets the goals and objectives for state and local government organizations working together to implement the law. The resulting debate and conflict over goals and purposes from each level of government have important OD implications. For example, a transorganization development intervention would help all agencies, each with a different degree of power, achieve reasonable agreement in addressing the legislation. As with the private sector, however, reaching agreement often involves differing positions and conflict. Since different levels of government have different degrees of power, the OD practitioner could facilitate a positive result to the process by getting early agreement between the organizations on how decision making and conflict will be managed. Such an intervention is complex, however, because of the tendency of governmental agencies to participate while limiting their financial and resource responsibility. Appreciation for the mission and power relationship among agencies is critical in designing an effective transorganizational intervention.

Clearly, there are important differences between public and private organizations, and in many instances, the public sector organization is more complex. In addition, one must appreciate the distinctions between the political domain and the administrative domain to consult or work in public organizations. With this understanding and an appreciation of the political arena in which public organizations operate, application of OD programs and techniques can be successful.

Recent Research and Innovations in Public Sector Organizational Development

The comparisons between the public and private sectors described above suggest that OD has a role in government and not-for-profit organizations. OD practitioners need to appreciate the inherent differences and understand that OD applications in the public sector are conducted in a complex political and organizational environment. Moreover, the unique features of public organizations—the values and structures, the multiplicity of decision makers, stakeholder diversity, and the intergovernmental relations environment—make OD applications challenging but not impossible.

Despite these challenges to OD practice in the public sector, there is growing evidence that OD interventions in government are successful, even when compared with change efforts in private industry. One review of 574 OD applications across the two sectors showed a similar pattern of predominantly positive results in both government and private industry.[91] Another study of 154 quality circle interventions in public and private organizations concluded that, although the highest levels of success occurred in private firms, overall success rates were substantial in both sectors.[92] A recent and particularly rigorous review of fifty-two OD interventions in government and industry confirmed these conclusions. The findings suggested that OD interventions were similarly successful in the two sectors, and led the researchers to conclude that the results "serve to contradict the common notion that planned change is likely to be less successful in the public sector."[93]

In addition to these promising findings, recent innovations in government point to the continued growth and success of OD in the public sector. At the federal level, for example, both Congress and the Clinton administration have enacted legislation and reforms to create a twenty-first-century government that will "get results Americans care about" with the overarching goal to "restore trust in America's government." In 1993, President Bill Clinton created the National Performance Review, which has been renamed as the National Partnership for Reinventing Government. To date, this initiative has produced impressive results, including the creation of more than four thousand customer service standards, the introduction of the Hammer Award for federal employees who reinvented their part of the government, and the passage of thirty-four laws enacting recommendations needing legislation. In addition, there have been over $136 billion in cost savings, more than sixteen thousand pages of reduced regulation, a reduction of 351,000 positions, and eighty-three laws enacting NPR recommendations.[94] These results have been achieved through interventions aimed at creating learning organizations (Chapter 20) and high-involvement organizations (Chapter 15), reengineering projects aimed at streamlining work flows and response times (Chapter 14), and, perhaps most difficult of all, efforts to change the civil service system so that the federal workforce is more flexible, development oriented, and performance driven.

These national reforms have their complement in state and local governments. Faced with similar pressures to reform, become more focused on citizens and customers, and operate in a more businesslike manner, state and local governments are introducing initiatives to become more productive and efficient while providing top-quality services. For example, a national survey of 987 state agencies found that 60 percent of them were using some type of strategic planning.[95] Another national survey found that all but three states have performance-based budgeting requirements,[96] and almost every state has enacted quality awards based on the Hammer Award and Malcolm Baldrige National Quality Award criteria.[97] In addition, local governments have conducted a variety of OD activities, such as team-building and total quality management programs, to become more effective.[98]

Finally, nongovernmental organizations are working to help improve government. The National Innovations in American Government Awards, cosponsored by the Ford Foundation, the John F. Kennedy School of Government at Harvard University, and the Council for Excellence in Government, recognize examples of creative problem solving in the public sector. The National Civic League's All-America City Award recognizes exemplary community problem solving and is given to communities that cooperatively tackle challenges and achieve results. The Alliance for Redesigning Government of the National Academy of Public Administration is a national network for all levels of government that advocate performance-based, results-driven governance. The Innovations Group is a national network and clearinghouse of local government organizations with the mission of innovation in the provision of public services, sustaining meaningful connections, and renewing passion for public service.

Conclusions

OD applications have proven to be effective in public sector organizations. Faced with many of the same pressures as private industry and some that are unique to government, public organizations will continue to use OD applications and interventions to transform themselves into citizen- and customer-driven, high-performance, results-oriented organizations. But to be effective, practitioners helping government must appreciate the differences incumbent in public sector values and organization structure; the differences in public and private organizations; and the mindsets of elected officials and government workers. OD practitioners need to understand public sector organizations and tailor interventions to fit highly diverse, politicized situations where elected officials and bureaucrats struggle with moving toward a new emphasis on continuous improvement, teamwork, customer focus, employee development, and learning. Although public sector OD is difficult and challenging, the successes cited in this chapter illustrate that OD is an invaluable tool in helping public sector organizations provide top-quality services.

SUMMARY

Traditionally, the published material in organization development has focused on applications in industrial organizations. This chapter presented broad applications of OD in nonindustrial organizations, such as hospitals, schools, and government agencies. The results of these change programs to date suggest that OD needs a greater range of diagnostic methods, interventions, and values when it is applied to nonindustrial settings.

Foster Mobley pointed out how dramatic changes in the health-care industry are affecting the practice of OD in that setting. He noted how changes in the nature of the health-care product, the way it is delivered, and how it is paid for are altering fundamentally the industry's structure and making it more difficult to identify the target of change. To be effective under these new conditions, OD practitioners will be under considerable pressure to demonstrate their competence in nontraditional areas, such as strategy, organization design, and mergers and acquisitions. Change projects likely will be focused on integrating a diverse set of previously uncoordinated stakeholders. They will be more reactive than proactive; more solution oriented than people oriented.

Paul Spittler pointed out that school systems are different from industrial firms because they are not subject to the same types of competitive pressures, are subject to close public scrutiny from multiple stakeholders, and are loosely structured at the horizontal level. Their vertical structures, however, are sophisticated and bureaucratic. As a result, recent interventions are aimed at developing structures to support better collegial problem solving. Programs such as high-involvement management and total quality management are producing important improvements in the quality of both educational outcomes and teachers' quality of work life.

Ray Patchett's section suggested that the public sector is more bureaucratic and adheres more strongly to bureaucratic norms than does the private sector. Thus, differences between the two sectors stem largely from differences in underlying value structures that encourage people to behave in different ways. He indicated that many of the differences between the public and private sectors may be a matter of degree, rather than kind. Further, the public sector has multiple access by multiple decision makers, which can make it difficult to know who really is at the top of the organization. Thus, OD interventions in the public sector focus more on technostructural interventions, such as work flow design and structure, than on process-oriented interventions, such as team building. Despite these differences, OD interventions in the public sector have an admirable track record of success, nearly equal to the success rate in industrial settings.

NOTES

1. F. Massarik, "Chaos and Change: Examining the Aesthetics of Organization Development," in *Advances in Organization Development*, vol. 1, ed. F. Massarik (Norwood, N.J.: Abelex, 1992).

2. D. Berwick, A. Godfrey, and J. Roessner, *Curing Health Care: New Strategies for Quality Improvement* (San Francisco: Jossey-Bass, 1991).

3. F. Mobley (unpublished study of health-care industry executives, November-December 1995).

4. "What Creates Health?" *Healthcare Forum Journal* (May-June 1994): 16–17.

5. D. Vickery, "Toward Appropriate Use of Medical Care," *Healthcare Forum Journal* (January-February 1996): 15–19.

6. Ibid.

7. R. Lamm, "The Coming Dislocation in the Health Professions," *Healthcare Forum Journal* (January-February 1996): 58–62.

8. C. Appleby, "Health Care's New Heavyweights," *Hospitals and Health Networks* 5 (May 1995): 26–34.

9. E. Neuborne, "Health Care Costs Slowing for Employers," *USA Today* (30 January 1996).

10. Massarik, "Chaos and Change."

11. Mobley, unpublished.

12. T. Cummings, "Transorganizational Development," in *Research in Organizational Behavior,* vol. 6, eds. B. Staw and L. Cummings (Greenwich, Conn.: JAI Press, 1984): 367–422.

13. M. Sashkin and W. Warner Burke, "Organization Development in the 1980's," in *Advances in Organization Development,* vol. 1, ed. F. Massarik (Norwood, N.J.: Abelex, 1992).

14. A. Nordhaus-Bike, "The Battle Against Burnout," *Hospitals and Health Networks* (20 May 1995): 36–40.

15. J. Moore Jr., "Morale Hits a New Low," *Modern Healthcare* (11 December 1995): 52–57.

16. E. Schein, "Back to the Future: Recapturing the OD Vision," in *Advances in Organization Development,* vol. 1, ed. F. Massarik (Norwood, N.J.: Abelex, 1992).

17. Ibid.

18. R. W. Boss and R. Golembiewski, "Do You Have to Start at the Top? The Chief Executive Officer's Role in Successful Organization Development Efforts," *Journal of Applied Behavioral Science* 31 (1995): 259–77.

19. F. Cerne, "Learning to Survive," *Hospitals and Health Networks* 5 (September 1995): 47–50.

20. Ibid.

21. N. Margulies and A. Raia, "The Significance of Core Values," in *Advances in Organization Development,* vol. 1, ed. F. Massarik (Norwood, N.J.: Abelex, 1992).

22. National Commission on Excellence in Education, *A Nation at Risk: The Imperative for Educational Reform* (Washington, D.C.: U.S. Government Printing Office, 1983); S. Mohrman and E. Lawler, "Motivation for School Reform" (working paper, Center for Effective Organizations, University of Southern California, Los Angeles, 1995).

23. R. Cooke, "Organization Development in Schools," in *Organization Development and Change,* 5th ed, eds. T. Cummings and C. Worley (St. Paul, Minn.: West, 1993).

24. L. Lezotte, (personal interview, Poway, Calif., April 1995); P. Spittler, "Total Quality Management: Applications in Public Education" (unpublished Master's thesis, Pepperdine University, 1995).

25. Cooke, "Organization Development in Schools."

26. Ibid.

27. C. Derr, "OD Won't Work in Schools," *Education and Urban Society* 8 (1976): 227–41.

28. Cooke, "Organization Development in Schools."

29. D. Lortie, *Schoolteacher: A Sociological Study* (Chicago: University of Chicago Press, 1975).

30. J. Savedoff, "The Distribution of Influence and Its Relationship to Relevance, Expertise and Interdependence in Educational Organizations" (Ph.D. diss., University of Michigan, 1978).

31. Cooke, "Organization Development in Schools."

32. C. Flynn, "Collaborative Decision Making in a Secondary School: An Experiment," *Education and Urban Society* 8 (1976): 172–92.

33. W. Hawley, "Dealing with Organizational Rudity in Public Schools" (undated manuscript, Yale University).

34. C. Bidwell, "The School as a Formal Organization," in *Handbook of Organizations,* ed. J. March (Chicago: Rand McNally, 1965).

35. K. Weick, "Educational Organizations as Loosely Coupled Systems," *Administrative Science Quarterly* 21 (1976): 1–79.

36. Cooke, "Organization Development in Schools."

37. Ibid.

38. Ibid.

39. Spittler, "Total Quality Management"; J. Kingsley, "Cause for Hope: A Strategic Change Case Study of Bowling Green Elementary School" (unpublished Master's thesis, Pepperdine University, 1994).

40. T. Cummings, "Designing Work for Productivity and Quality of Work Life," *Outlook* 6 (1982): 35–39; J. Gabarro, "Diagnosing Organization–Environment Fit: Implications for Organization Development," *Education and Urban Society* 3 (1974): 18–29.

41. Cooke, "Organization Development in Schools."

42. E. Lawler, *High-Involvement Management* (San Francisco: Jossey-Bass, 1986).

43. Mohrman and Lawler, "Motivation for School Reform."

44. Ibid.

45. B. Rowan, "Commitment and Control: Alternative Strategies for the Organizational Design of Schools," in

Review of Research in Education, ed. E. Cazden (Washington D.C.: American Educational Research Association, 1990); B. Rowan, S. Rauderbush, and Y. Cheong, "Teaching as a Non-Routine Task: Implications for Management of Schools," *Education Administration Quarterly* 29 (1993): 479–500.

46. S. Mohrman, E. Lawler, and A. Mohrman, "Applying Employee Involvement in Schools," *Educational Policy Analysis* 14 (1992): 31–57.

47. E. Lawler, S. Mohrman, and G. Ledford, *Creating High-Performance Organizations: Practices and Results of Employee Involvement and Total Quality Management in* Fortune *1000 Companies* (San Francisco: Jossey-Bass, 1995).

48. W. Glasser, *Control Theory in the Classroom* (New York: Perennial Library, 1986); A. Kohl, *No Contest—The Case Against Competition* (Boston: Houghton-Mifflin, 1986); W. Deming, "Foundation for Management of Quality in the Western World" (paper delivered at a meeting of the Institute of Management Sciences, Osaka, Japan, 1990).

49. W. Deming, *Out of the Crisis* (Cambridge: Massachusetts Institute of Technology, 1986).

50. J. Stampen, "Improving the Quality of Education: W. Edwards Deming and Effective Schools," *Contemporary Education Review* 3 (1987): 423–33.

51. M. Tribus, "The Application of Quality Management Principles in Education at Mt. Edgecumbe High School, Sitka, Alaska," in *An Introduction to Total Quality for Schools,* ed. American Association of School Administrators (Arlington, Va.: American Association of School Administrators, 1991): 30.

52. American Society for Quality Control, "Fourth Annual Quality in Education Listing," *Quality Progress* 27, 9 (1994): 27.

53. Spittler, "Total Quality Management."

54. Deming, "Foundation for Management."

55. American Association of School Administrators, ed., *An Introduction to Total Quality for Schools* (Arlington, Va.: American Association of School Administrators, 1991); Stampen, "Improving the Quality of Education."

56. Stampen, "Improving the Quality of Education."

57. Spittler, "Total Quality Management."

58. B. Malen, R. Ogawa, and J. Kranz, "What Do We Know about School-Based Management? A Case Study of the Literature—A Call for Research," in *Choice and Control in Education,* eds. W. Clune and J. Witte (Philadelphia: Falmer Press, 1990): 289–342.

59. J. David, "The Who, What, and Why of Site-Based Management," *Educational Leadership* 53 (1995): 4–9.

60. R. Ogawa and P. White, "School-Based Management: An Overview," in *School-Based Management—Organizing for High Performance,* eds. A. Mohrman and P. Wohlstetter (San Francisco: Jossey-Bass, 1994).

61. David, "Who, What, and Why."

62. R. Campbell, L. Cumnningham, R. Nystrand, and D. Usdan, *The Organization and Control of American Schools,* 5th ed. (Columbus, Ohio: Charles E. Merrill, 1985).

63. P. Hill and J. Bonan, *Decentralization and Accountability in Public Education* (Santa Monica, Calif.: Rand Corporation, 1991).

64. Malen, Ogawa, and Kranz, "What Do We Know?"

65. B. Bimber, *Decentralization Mirage: Comparing Decision Making Arrangements in Four High Schools* (Santa Monica, Calif.: Institute on Education and Training, Rand Corporation, 1994).

66. S. Sharan, ed., *Cooperative Learning Theory and Research* (New York: Praeger, 1990).

67. P. Wohlstetter and R. Smyer, "Models of High-Performance Schools," in *School-Based Management—Organizing for High Performance,* eds. A. Mohrman and P. Wohlstetter (San Francisco: Jossey-Bass, 1994).

68. J. Comer, *School Power* (New York: Free Press, 1980).

69. H. Levin, "Accelerated Schools for Disadvantaged Students," *Educational Leadership* 44 (6, 1987): 19–29.

70. T. Sizer, *Horace's School: Redesigning the American High School* (Boston: Houghton-Mifflin, 1984).

71. Spittler, "Total Quality Management."

72. P. Robertson, P. Wohlstetter, and S. Mohrman, "Generating Curriculum and Instructional Innovations Through School-Based Management," *Educational Administration Quarterly* 31 (1995): 257–76.

73. M. G. Popovich, *Creating High-Performance Government Organizations* (San Francisco: Jossey-Bass, 1998).

74. *From Red Tape to Results: Creating a Government That Works Better and Costs Less* (Washington D.C.: U.S. Government Printing Office, September 1993); *Common Sense Government Works Better and Costs Less* (Washington, D.C.: U.S. Government Printing Office, September 1995); *Reinvention's Next Steps: Governing in a Balanced Budget World* (Washington, D.C.: U.S. Government Printing Office, March, 1996). Much of this information can be found on the federal government Website http://www.npr.gov.

75. KPMG LLP, *Transforming State and Local Government: The Critical Role of Public Management* (Montvale, N.J.: 1999).

76. This information was found at http:www.hmco.com/college/polisci/psn/index.html, and was accessed in December 1999.

77. R. Dilger, R. Moffett, and L. Struyk, "Privatization of Municipal Services in America's Largest Cities," *Public Administration Review* 57 (1997): 21–26.

78. P. Robertson and S. Seneviratne, "Outcomes of Planned Organizational Change in the Public Sector: A Meta-Analytic Comparison to the Private Sector," *Public Administration Review* 55 (1995): 547–58.

79. J. Nalbandian, "City Council–City Manager Partnerships" (presentation to the California City Managers Conference, 1998).

80. H. G. Frederickson, *The Spirit of Public Administration* (San Francisco: Jossey-Bass, 1997).

81. Ibid., p. 164.

82. Frederickson, *Spirit of Public Administration;* W. Morris, *The American Heritage Dictionary of the English Language* (Boston: Houghton-Mifflin, 1981); P. Appleby, "Government Is Different," in *Classics of Public Administration,* eds. J. Shafritz and A. Hyde (Oak Park, Ill., Moore, 1978): 101–07.

83. Frederickson, *Spirit of Public Administration.*

84. R. Golembiewski, "Organization Development in Public Agencies: Perspectives on Theory and Practice," *Public Administration Review* 29 (July-August 1969): 370.

85. Popovich, *Creating High-Performance Government Organizations,* p. 29; Golembiewski, "Organization Development in Public Agencies."

86. Golembiewski, "Organization Development."

87. Bryson, *Strategic Planning;* T. Cummings and C. Worley, *Organization Development and Change,* 6th ed. (Cincinnati: South-Western College Publishing, 1997): 163; Golembiewski, "Organization Development," p. 370.

88. Golembiewski, "Organization Development," p. 370.

89. Bryson, *Strategic Planning.*

90. Ibid., p. 246.

91. R. Golembiewski, C. Proehl, and D. Sink, "Success of OD Applications in the Public Sector: Toting up the Score for a Decade, More or Less," *Public Administration Review* 41 (1981): 679–82; R. Golembiewski, C. Proehl, and D. Sink, "Estimating the Success of OD Applications," *Training and Development Journal* 72 (April 1982): 86–95.

92. S. Park, "Estimating Success Rates of Quality Circle Programs: Public and Private Experiences," *Public Administration Quarterly* 15 (1991): 133–46.

93. Robertson and Seneviratne, "Outcomes."

94. Information on the National Partnership for Reinventing Government (formerly the National Performance Review) can be found on the federal government Website, http://www.npr.gov.

95. F. Berry and B. Wechsler, "State Agencies' Experience with Strategic Planning: Findings from a National Survey," *Public Administration Review* 55 (1995): 159–68.

96. J. Melkers and K. Willoughby, "The State of the States: Performance-Based Budgeting Requirements in 47 out of 50," *Public Administration Review* 58 (1998): 66–73.

97. H. Hill and K. Shook, "Virginia's Results Manager," *New Public Innovator* (1998): 30–33.

98. Robertson and Seneviratne, "Outcomes"; E. M. Berman and J. P. West, "Municipal Commitment to Total Quality Management: A Survey of Recent Progress," *Public Administration Review* 55 (1995): 57–66.

23

Future Directions in Organization Development

The field of organization development continues to grow and mature. New theories and concepts are being developed, more complex and rigorous research is being conducted, new methods and interventions are being applied, and organizations from more diverse countries and cultures are becoming involved. Because so much change has occurred in a relatively brief period, predicting the future of OD is risky if not foolhardy. However, several trends can be identified at the turn of of the twenty-first century that provide clues about the larger context within which OD will operate. These may be used to speculate about where the field is heading. In this concluding chapter, we first describe these trends and then draw implications for future directions in OD.[1]

TRENDS IN THE CONTEXT OF ORGANIZATION DEVELOPMENT

As summarized in Figure 23.1, several interrelated trends are affecting the context within which OD will be applied in the near future. They concern various aspects of the economy, the workforce, technology, and organizations. In some cases, the trends will affect OD practice directly. Technology trends, such as groupware and Internet conferencing, surely will influence how OD practitioners facilitate teams and manage change. Other trends, such as the increasing concentration of wealth, represent important contextual forces that will affect OD indirectly through their interaction with other trends.

The Economy

Researchers have described a variety of alternative economic futures and there is substantial agreement that the world's economy is undergoing an important transition from the industrial age which characterized much of the twentieth century.[2] Those scenarios differ in their particulars, but many of the same trends are identified as drivers of economic change—globalization, the increasing concentration of wealth, and concerns for the ecosystem, among others. Trends such as technology and workforce changes also are mentioned and they will be discussed separately.

As noted in Chapter 1, the economy rapidly is becoming global. The shift in manufacturing from high- to low-labor-cost countries, the growth of international mergers and acquisitions, and the spread of worldwide service businesses suggest that the emergence of a global economy is well under way. Today, almost any product or service can be made, bought, and delivered anywhere in the world.

Globalization can help companies reduce costs, gain resources, expand markets, and develop new products and practices more quickly. In addition, because globalization and growth often work together, organization members are provided with opportunities for development and advancement. But globalization also can present difficulties. Managing a worldwide organization is a daunting task, as described in Chapter 21, and it can present difficult problems for national governments. Because

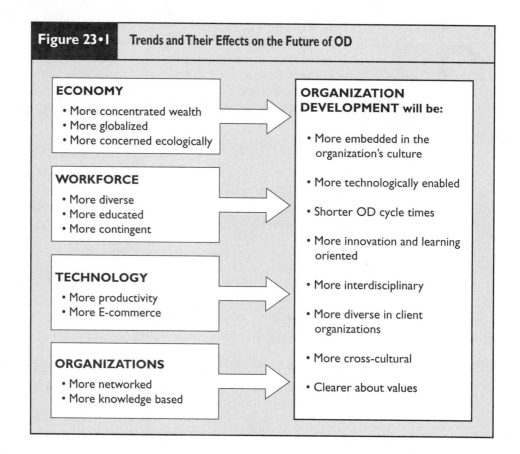

Figure 23•1 Trends and Their Effects on the Future of OD

ECONOMY
- More concentrated wealth
- More globalized
- More concerned ecologically

WORKFORCE
- More diverse
- More educated
- More contingent

TECHNOLOGY
- More productivity
- More E-commerce

ORGANIZATIONS
- More networked
- More knowledge based

ORGANIZATION DEVELOPMENT will be:
- More embedded in the organization's culture
- More technologically enabled
- Shorter OD cycle times
- More innovation and learning oriented
- More interdisciplinary
- More diverse in client organizations
- More cross-cultural
- Clearer about values

a global economy transcends national borders, it has evolved with relatively little order and organization.[3] This makes it difficult for governments to control how globalization develops and affects them. For example, China is trying diligently to preserve its cultural and communist underpinnings while facing a rapid influx of capitalist goods and services,[4] and many other developing nations face pressures to move to a western capitalism model despite questions about whether it is appropriate for their cultures.

A second trend in the economy is the increasingly concentrated wealth in relatively few individuals, corporations, and nations. Over the past two decades, for example, the ratio of CEO compensation to that of the average employee grew from 35:1 to 150:1 in large U.S. firms;[5] the number of billionaires in the world increased over fourteen-fold;[6] the world's five hundred largest corporations, which employ 0.05 of 1 percent of the world's population, produced about 25 percent of the world's economic output;[7] and fifty corporations achieved sufficient wealth to place them among the *world's* one-hundred largest economies. At the same time, 4.8 billion of the world's 6 billion people lived in developing countries, and 3 billion of them existed on less than $2 a day.[8]

The concentration of wealth may be a natural outcome of capitalism, but it also can contribute to misallocation of resources, environmental degradation, and short-term thinking.[9] For example, Wall Street's current focus on quarterly earnings can skew decision-making criteria to delay preventive maintenance or safety initiatives, to postpone implementation of necessary environmental protection equipment, or to forego important long-term capital investments. The concentration of wealth also can contribute to social conflict driven by fears that the wealthy will act in their own self-interest at the expense of those who are financially less fortunate. The bloody demonstrations that occurred at the December 1999 meeting of the World Trade Organization in Seattle derived in part from such fear and people's willingness to act on it.

Finally, our view of the natural environment as a consumable in economic success is being challenged. There are ever more clear warnings that the ecosystem no longer can be treated as a factor of production, and that success cannot be defined as the accumulation of wealth and material goods at the expense of the environment. These concerns arise in part from the proliferation of capitalism, but also from the growing realization that free and open markets can have negative unintended consequences for the global ecosystem. Recent studies suggest that industrialization is a controversial but probable cause of global warming,[10] and several traditional organizations, such as BP Amoco and Royal Dutch/Shell, are reversing long-held opinions about their contribution to environmental decay by setting aggressive goals to reduce greenhouse gases.[11] Unfortunately, many developing economies, including China, the Philippines, and Mexico, continue to operate with loose environmental controls. As a result, there are more calls for change in the values underlying capitalism—from consumption to investment,[12] from open to mindful markets,[13] and from wealth accumulation as an end in itself to an examination of the return on living capital.[14] Some observers note that such value shifts are already under way in many nations and organizations. For example, traditional business models which assume that labor is scarce and natural resources are abundant are being tempered by models that emphasize the abundance of knowledge and the scarcity of natural resources. IKEA, the Dutch furniture manufacturer, has altered its environmental policies and practices radically to reduce emissions, waste, and environmental degradation and increase sustainability, profits, and customer satisfaction.[15]

The Workforce

The workforce is becoming more diverse, educated, and contingent. Chapter 18 documented the diversity trend and suggested that organizations, whether they operate primarily in their home country or abroad, will need to develop policies and operating styles that embrace the changing cultural, ethnic, gender, and age diversity of the workforce.

The workforce is also becoming more educated. The 1998 U.S. Census data, for example, report that almost 83 percent of adults over twenty-five years of age have completed high school and that a little more than 24 percent have a bachelor's degree. Both of those numbers represent significant increases over 1997 data. A more educated workforce is likely to demand higher wages, more involvement in decision making, and continued investment in knowledge and skills. For example, the current half-life of information systems personnel is about two years and requires continual updating of their knowledge and skills to remain competent in these jobs. In response, organizations are increasing their training and management development budgets significantly.[16] They are investing far more in corporate universities and corporate–university partnerships, and many organizations, such as Motorola, 3M, and Xerox, have policies outlining the minimum hours of technical and managerial training that each employee will receive yearly.

Finally, the continued high rate of downsizings, reengineering efforts, and mergers and acquisitions described in Chapters 14 and 19 is forcing the workforce to become more contingent and less loyal. The implicit psychological contract that governs relationships between employers and employees is being rewritten with new assumptions about long-term employment and rewards in exchange for commitment and loyalty. For example, a study by the Conference Board of ninety-three multinational companies showed that more than 50 percent employ hourly, part-time workers; 87 percent use independent contractors and make regular use of temporary workers hired from agencies.[17] The study suggests that the size of the "contingent" workforce increased from 12 percent in 1990 to 21 percent in 1995, and was expected to reach 35 percent by 2000.

Technology

By almost any measure, information technology is becoming an increasingly important and common fact of life. For example, in 1998 there were an estimated 150.9 million Internet users worldwide, representing less than 1 percent of the population. That number is expected to grow to over 717 million by 2005, covering about 11 percent of the population.[18] In five years, the percentage of people in the United States connected to the Internet is estimated to grow from 27 percent to more than 71 percent.

Information technology is changing internal operations and increasing productivity. For years, economists were puzzled by a "productivity paradox." Despite a thirty-year, $2 trillion investment in computers and technology, productivity rose very slowly during the 1970s and 1980s. But in 1999, productivity rose 2.9 percent in the United States (and 5 percent in the last six months of 1999), nearly twice the 1.5 percent average annual gains seen since the early 1970s. The biggest gains were in manufacturing, but service businesses such as transportation, trade, and finance also have started to see the payoff from new technology investments. The productivity lag apparently resulted from the relatively long time it took for organizatons to adopt the new technology and learn how to apply it.[19] For example, Countrywide Home Loans, one of the largest mortgage lenders in the United States, has been experimenting with technology solutions since the late 1980s. But only recently have the benefits of technology paid off. The 1997 implementation of an automated information system in its customer service center has helped reduce the average cost per call from $4 to less than $0.60 on more than twenty thousand calls per day. The increased productivity has not cost jobs; Countrywide nearly doubled its workforce between 1996 and 1999.

Information technology is also fueling the growth of e-commerce, an economy that knows no boundaries.[20] E-commerce concerns the buying and selling of products and services over the Internet, and ranges from withdrawing cash from an automatic teller machine to more complex interactions such as purchasing products from a Website. In the United States, the value of e-commerce transactions has increased 700 percent over the past five years, and is expected to grow from $100 billion in 1999 to between $2 and $3 trillion by 2005.[21]

There are typically three types of e-commerce transactions: business-to-business, business-to-consumer, and consumer-to-consumer. eBay, a Web-based business that links consumers interested in purchasing items from each other in an auction-like format, is an example of the consumer-to-consumer form of e-commerce. Although consumer-to-consumer transactions are important elements of e-commerce, the first two forms provide the radically new context for OD.

The business-to-consumer market is the focus of much attention and awareness because it is how the public participates in e-commerce, and includes e-tailers such as Amazon.com and E-TRADE.com. This market is expected to grow to over $184 billion in revenues by 2004. The business creations and transformations fueled by information technology are likely to be the focus of OD attention in the future. Dell Computer, for instance, sells custom-made computers to consumers and businesses, but it started out as a mail-order company advertising in the back of magazines. Today, 25 percent of its computer sales comes through the Internet. The shift in organization structures, labor skill sets, work designs, and work processes in the transformation from a mail-order business to a leader in e-commerce represents the kind of change that many organizations will face and the challenges OD practitioners must meet.

The issues in the business-to-business market are even more complex. Estimates suggest that this form of e-commerce will grow to over $2.7 trillion by 2004. A good example of the implications and potential of this market is the online store being created by General Motors, Ford, and DaimlerChrysler. It represents the first major migration of an entire industry's supply chain onto the Internet, and will reengineer radically the way businesses interact with each other. This virtual marketplace will handle $250 billion in parts and supplies purchased from sixty thousand suppliers each year, automate routine transactions, and streamline the bidding process for everything from car windows to paper clips and paint. Web-based transactions will replace the inefficient phone, mail, and face-to-face sales call processes that dominated this industry for decades. Such business-to-business marketplaces are expected to be adopted by other auto makers as well as other industries, such as aerospace, construction, and office supplies.[22]

The Organization

The interventions described in this book represent the best practices in OD. They help organizations become more streamlined and flexible, and more capable of improving themselves continuously in response to trends in the economy, workforce, and technology. But many organizations are not aware of these practices and still others resist applying them.[23] For example, despite the attention to them in the business press, only a small percentage of organizations use self-managed work teams, are organized into networks, or successfully manage strategic alliances. But these are the organizations of the future, and they will invent entirely new, entrepreneurial structures capable of exploiting new ideas and technologies quickly. The "dot-coms" so prominent in the technology industry represent one vision of the future.

Organizations clearly will be more networked. As explained in Chapter 14, network or "fishnet" structures rely on strategic alliances, joint ventures, and other transorganization relationships.[24] These configurations enable single organizations to partner with other organizations to develop, manufacture, and distribute goods and services. Networks are highly adaptable and can disband and reform along different task or market lines as the circumstances demand. To succeed, organizations are learning how to assess quickly whether they are compatible with network partners and whether the joint product/service is successful. They are gaining competence to enter into and to breakup networks swiftly, thus enabling them to exploit product/market opportunities rapidly and to "fail quickly" when the network is unproductive.[25]

Network structures also are enabling organizations to gain many of the efficiencies traditionally reserved for large firms while remaining small and nimble. Organizations have tended to grow large to gain economies of scale in manufacturing, distribution, and marketing. Large size, however, can lead to rigid and slow responses that can be disastrous in today's rapidly changing environments. Network structures can help small organizations join together to produce goods and services efficiently. Small, focused firms that perform particular tasks with excellence can align with organizations that have complimentary resources and expertise. Thus, the network can gain economies of scale while each of the partner organizations can remain small and flexible.

As discussed in Chapter 20, knowledge is becoming a key source of organizational competence and competitive advantage. Organizations increasingly will structure themselves around knowledge processes rather than functions, products, or geography. Such structures typically transcend both internal and external organizational boundaries. They remove barriers to learning and facilitate how employees acquire, organize, and disseminate knowledge assets. For example, at HP Consulting, a five thousand–person global consulting organization within Hewlett-Packard, learning communities, project snapshots, and knowledge maps are used to give members access to all of the organization's knowledge and experience when they are consulting. Learning communities are informal groups composed of organization members who operate in different parts of the organization but whose success is dependent on each other's knowledge. Current and former clients also can be part of the learning community. They are encouraged to discuss best practices, issues, or skills that they want to learn about through whatever means possible, including face-to-face meetings, electronic chats, emails, or conference calls. More formally, project snapshots are organized meetings of team members who have collaborated on a project to discuss learnings that can be applied to future projects. Through this knowledge management process, the HP consulting organization is building a knowledge base that can be shared by all members and applied to their client's problems.[26]

IMPLICATIONS FOR OD'S FUTURE

The economic, workforce, technology, and organization trends outlined above have significant implications for how OD will be conceived and practiced in the coming years. Figure 23.1 summarizes them. A global economy populated with flexible, networked organizations and driven by information technology and a diverse workforce will require OD to be more embedded in the organization's operations, more technologically enabled, shorter in cycle time, more innovation and learning oriented, more interdisciplinary, applied to more diverse clients, more cross-cultural, and clearer about values.

OD Will Be More Embedded in the Organization's Operations

As the economic and technical demands facing organizations require faster, more flexible organizations, the ability to manage change continuously will become a key source of competitive advantage. This suggests that OD practices will become more embedded in the organization's normal operating routines. For example, Chapter 3 defined three types of OD practitioners, including line managers who applied OD principles to their work. OD activities such as diagnosis, intervention planning, and change management can and should become part of the daily work of managers and employees. When managers integrate OD knowledge into their role, change capabilities will be diffused throughout the organization rather than located in a special function or role. That would permit faster and more flexible reactions to challenges faced by the organization. In addition to embedding OD skills into managerial roles, OD interventions themselves will be integrated into core business processes, such as product development, strategic planning, and order fulfillment. This should provide a closer linkage between OD and business results.

This does not mean that the role of the professional OD practitioner will go away. Professionals will be needed to help organization members gain change management competencies. Small, entrepreneurial firms will need specialized assistance in bringing on new members rapidly and organizing their efforts. Organizations involved in strategic alliances and mergers and acquisitions will need professional help managing interorganizational interfaces and integrating diverse corporate cultures and business practices. OD professionals also will be needed to assist in the implementation of new technologies, particularly knowledge management practices. The demand for OD practitioners is likely to increase rather than decrease. For example, there is some anecdotal evidence to suggest that as line and senior managers learn more about the knowledge and skills associated with OD practice, their requests for assistance in formulating change processes increase. Managers will look more frequently for a partner and coach to help them lead and facilitate organization change.

OD Processes Will Be More Technologically Enabled

Information technology is pervasive; it will affect not only organizations, work, and the economy but will have a significant affect on OD practice. First, it will enable OD processes to be both synchronous and asynchronous (anytime, anywhere) as well as more virtual and less face-to-face. In global organizations, members work in a variety of locations, cultures, and time zones. OD interventions, such as team building, employee involvement, and integrated strategic change, will have to be planned and implemented in ways that encourage contributions from a variety of stakeholders at times that are convenient or at times when creative ideas emerge. Information technology, such as email, newsgroups, and bulletin boards, allow organization members to make these contributions at any time they are ready. In addition, groupware technologies allow members to discuss issues in chat rooms, in Web and video conferences, and on the more traditional telephone conference.

As a result, the process of OD is likely to change. For example, using these technologies to exchange ideas, discuss policies, or decide on change processes will produce different types of group dynamics from those found in face-to-face meetings. OD practitioners not only will need to be comfortable with this technology but also will need to develop virtual facilitation skills that recognize these dynamics. In many cases, a more structured and assertive approach will be necessary to ensure that all members have an opportunity to share their ideas. The effect of these technologically mediated exchanges on work satisfaction, productivity, and quality is not yet known. In addition, processes of visioning, diagnosis, data feedback, and action planning will have to be reengineered to leverage new technologies.

Second, information technology will provide much more information about the organization to a greater number of participants in a shorter period of time. OD processes will be adapted to recognize that members have more information at their fingertips. For example, organization intranets provide members with an information channel that is richer, more efficient, more interactive, and more dynamic than are such traditional channels as newsletters and memos. Thus, intranets can provide a timely method for collecting data on emerging issues, to provide performance feedback on key operational measures, and to involve members in key decisions.

OD Cycle Times Will Be Shorter

Trends in the economy and technology are shortening product, organization, and industry life cycles. Pressures to reduce the cycle time of OD activities are also likely to increase. To be seen as relevant, OD practitioners must be mindful of opportunities to quicken the pace of key processes, and contemporaneously remain aware of the practices and processes that cannot be hurried.

New information technologies and interventions will expedite certain steps in the change process. For example, a large-scale organization diagnosis involving member interviews and surveys used to take as long as six months. By the time the data were ready, many of the pressing issues had faded because of new developments in the marketplace, turnover in personnel, or proactive management. Today, with electronic surveys and large-group designs, organization diagnosis can be completed in as little as a few hours. In coming years, new technologies, such as groupware and video conferencing, increasingly will be used to bring more people together faster than ever before. In short, there is real potential to reduce dramatically the time required to perform many OD practices.

There are physical and psychological limits to reductions in the OD change cycle, however, and it is not realistic to expect change to be instantaneous.[27] For example, managers often are disturbed by estimates that major structural or cultural changes take two to five years. A new organization chart or a new vision and values statement hung on members' office walls often gives the illusion that change has occurred, but the working relationships, process improvements, and other aspects of fully implementing these large-scale changes often take longer than expected. Similarly, most organization members are not capable of dropping a well-known and understood set of behaviors one day and picking up a new set of behaviors the next with the same level of efficiency. There are clear minimums with respect to the speed of change in individual behavior, and members may face a steep learning curve when they are asked to change their routines.

OD Will Be More Innovation and Learning Oriented

Given the emerging context facing OD, change processes are more likely to be aimed at creating entirely new structures, processes, and behaviors than at fine-tuning the status quo. Christos Cotsakos, CEO of E-TRADE, has suggested that organizations that are "managing change" are behind; successful organizations in the future will be the ones *creating* change. This will require unprecedented amounts of innovation and learning. Multiple stakeholders representing a diversity of interests will come together to envision a shared future and to learn how to enact it. Because this process typically leads into uncharted waters, both organizational members and change agents will be joint learners, exploring new territory together. Implementing new organizational innovations will require significant amounts of experimentation as participants try out new ways of operating, assess progress, and make necessary adjustments. In essence, they will learn from their actions how to create a new strategy, organization, or service. A collaborative learning effort is capable of implementing radically new possibilities and ways of functioning that could not be envisioned beforehand. Thus, it is a process of innovation, not of detection and correction of errors. In turn, the new structures and systems increase feedback and information flow to the organization, thereby improving its capacity to learn and adapt in a rapidly changing technological and economic environment. OD interventions such as action science,[28] appreciative inquiry,[29] self-designing organizations,[30] and learning organizations[31] are forerunners of the innovation and learning that will evolve in the coming years.

OD Will Be More Interdisciplinary

Globalization, technology, diversity, and other trends rapidly are broadening the focus of OD and making other social sciences more relevant to planned change. This suggests that OD will continue to become more interdisciplinary and rely on a variety of perspectives and approaches to develop and change organizations. Historically, the focus of OD expanded from small groups and social process to organization structures and work design, and more recently, to strategic and global social change.[32] Along the way, different disciplines have been applied to OD practice, including organization theory, industrial engineering, labor relations, comparative management, and corporate strategy. In the future, OD will be called on to help organizations address issues related to global networks, e-commerce, ecological sustainability, temporary employment, entrepreneurial growth, and economic and workforce diversity. This enlarged sphere of practice will require new approaches to planned change informed by such fields as information systems, international relations, social ecology, entrepreneurship, and labor economics. Fortunately, many of these other disciplines are expanding their boundaries and becoming more aware of the contributions that OD can make. For example, strategic management, sociology, and economics, fields that traditionally focused on technology, product development, class structure, and economic performance, are integrating human resources, change, and other organizational processes into their models of profitability, corporate valuation, and social development.[33]

As OD becomes more interdisciplinary, the prospects for an integrated approach to planned change seem near. Recent developments in complexity science and chaos theory, for example, provide fascinating new conceptual frameworks and metaphors for OD practitioners and represent how other disciplines, such as mathematics and physics, might contribute to a unified theory of change.[34] Ideally, an integrated perspective will balance human fulfillment and economic performance, provide a fuller recognition of the systemic and dynamic nature of organizations, and develop improved techniques for managing large-scale, transformational change within and across national cultures. For OD practice, the benefit will be organizations where all employees think strategically, guided jointly by self-interest and organizational and ecological welfare.

OD Will Work with More Diverse Client Organizations

The changes occurring in OD's context suggest that in the future, planned change will be applied to a more diverse client base. Traditionally, OD was focused on large business organizations, but three other types of organizations increasingly will become targets of planned change: small entrepreneurial startups, government organizations, and global social change organizations. Small, entrepreneurial startups are an important and underserved market for OD. Many of these organizations are at the forefront of the technology trends cited earlier. Because they are operating on scarce and finite venture capital, time is their most valuable asset and the one most critical to their success. As a result, there is a clear action orientation, little perceived need to reflect and learn, and few structures and systems to guide behaviors and decisions.[35] This is a context that can be well served by fast, flexible change processes orienting new people quickly to the business strategy, integrating them rapidly into new work roles, increasing the efficiency of work processes, and helping founders and key managers think about how the market, competitors, and technology are changing. Entrepreneurs are not inclined to think about nor are they trained to examine these issues. OD can help them address such matters and gain needed competence.

Chapter 22 described the differences between public and private sector organizations and the implications of those differences for the practice of OD. The economic, workforce, technology, and organization trends also are pushing government organizations to become more efficient, flexible, and networked. As a result, government increasingly is applying OD interventions such as strategic planning, employee involvement, and performance management, and we expect that the demand for change management assistance in the public sector will grow. Moreover, in combination with the globalization trend, governments will become more proactive in managing the effects of economic development. Public–private partnerships, a form of transorganization development, also are likely to flourish and will require the assistance of OD practitioners sensitive to the differences between these two types of organizations and to the demands the partnerships will be under, such as environmental protection, employment, corporate citizenship, and taxation.

Similarly, Chapter 21 described the application of OD in global social change organizations. The increasing concentration of wealth and globalization of the economy will create a plethora of opportunities for OD to assist developing countries, disadvantaged citizens, and the ecology. In China, for example, as the government reduces bureaucracy and creates state-owned enterprises, the need for nongovernment organizations to take over the delivery of social services is great. In response, the Global Village of Beijing has begun practical campaigns to involve the Chinese people in pro-environment practices and to develop leaders for other nongovernment organizations. OD practices and processes can help these organizations achieve their objectives, manage their resources, and improve their functioning through team building, transorganization development, and strategic planning.

Similarly, limits to the world's ecosystem, including its capacity to absorb population growth, function with a depleted ozone layer, and operate with polluted waters, are causing a rethinking of the traditional business model. The revised model, in turn, will require a new organization that values different outcomes and processes. For example, the Natural Step model stresses the importance of organization strategies and designs that work within a sustainability framework, and the natural capitalism model argues that business strategies built around the productive use of natural resources can solve environmental problems at a profit.[36] Organizations, such as IKEA, Interface, and Motorola, are rethinking their business models to address these issues. For example, Interface, a manufacturer of carpet products, has pioneered the idea of "leasing" its carpets. Under its "Evergreen Lease," they accept responsibility for keeping the carpet clean and fresh in exchange for a monthly fee. By installing carpet tiles instead of large rolls, and because only a small fraction of carpeting actually gets used, they can replace the tiles and save approximately 80 percent of the cost of carpeting materials. OD practitioners will need to make themselves aware of these alternative models and can help organizations develop and implement practices that are more environmentally sustainable.

OD Will Become More Cross-Cultural

As organizations and the economy become more global, the recent growth of OD applications in international and cross-cultural situations is a harbinger of the future. Despite increased research and practice in this area, we know little about planned change processes in cross-cultural settings. Traditionally, OD has been practiced in organizations *within* specific cultures: British-trained OD practitioners helped British organizations in Great Britain; Mexican OD practitioners helped Latin American organizations; and so on. But the current trends clearly point to the need for OD applications that work *across* cultures. Team-building interventions need to be modified to help a team composed of Americans, Indians, Chinese, Koreans, and French Canadians who have never met face-to-face but are charged with developing a new product in a short period of time. The merger and acquisition process needs to be adapted to help a Japanese and U.S. firm implement a new organization structure that honors both cultures. Because the number of organizations operating in multiple countries is growing rapidly, opportunities for OD in these situations seem endless: interorganizational and transorganizational relationships between subsidiaries, operating units, and headquarters organizations; team building across cultural boundaries; working out global logistic and supply chain processes; implementing diversity-centric values in ethnocentric cultures; designing strategic planning exercises at multiple levels. Moreover, OD is likely to find increased opportunities in GSCO organizations that are often part of an international network. Transorganization development processes and network structure development interventions adapted for cross-cultural contexts have yet to be developed and will have important applications in the future.

OD Will Become More Clear About Values

The economic and technological trends suggest that OD practitioners are likely to face more value dilemmas in the coming years. For example, the increasing concentration of wealth conflicts with OD's traditional values of equality and egalitarianism, and OD practitioners will need to be clear about how they are helping to centralize or decentralize power. Similarly, technology can isolate people or bring them together. The choices OD practitioners make in incorporating technology into change management processes will have an important effect on feelings of inclusion, influence, and participation. Finally, despite OD's best efforts to embrace diversity, it is common to find practitioners frustrated by differences in cultural assumptions.

As discussed in Chapter 3, OD professionals initially promoted a coherent set of humanistic and democratic values for organizations. Over time, those values were supplemented with values favoring organizational effectiveness, thus creating potential conflicts in trying to jointly satisfy both humanistic and effectiveness outcomes. The field currently reflects that division. Many practitioners believe that OD has become too corporate and is in danger of colluding with powerful managers to concentrate wealth further. They argue that OD should return to its original values and focus on liberating the human potential inside organizations. Other practitioners argue that focusing on human potential exclusively will doom OD to irrelevance and limit its contribution to a better world. This is an important and ongoing debate within OD, and it is likely to become even more intense as additional values, such as ecological sustainability and economic equality, enter the field of planned change. OD practitioners will be called on more often to help organization members balance personal development and work demands, increase the organization's short-term profitability, and maximize its long-term environmental sustainability. Balancing these diverse values will be extremely difficult. OD will be able to influence the future of organizations if practitioners clearly recognize these value dilemmas and help clients develop strategies for resolving them.

■ SUMMARY

In this concluding chapter, we described four interrelated trends—the economy, the workforce, technology, and organizations—likely to affect the context within which organization development will be practiced. Each trend has been proposed as an important driver of the future. The chapter went on to propose several themes or directions that OD will be likely to take. If our speculations prove accurate, the practice of OD will be more embedded in the organization's key functions, more technologically enabled, expected to operate within shorter cycle times, more collaborative and oriented toward action learning, more interdisciplinary, more likely to serve a diverse client base, more cross-culturally oriented, and more confronted with values conflicts.

To be relevant, OD practitioners and the field as a whole must act together to influence the future they prefer or adjust to the future that is coming. Our hope is that this text was able to inform and equip the reader with the skills, knowledge, and value awareness necessary to shape the future.

■ NOTES

1. The authors wish to thank many people who responded to requests for their thoughts on the future of OD, including Stan Herman, Jay Hays, Vana Prewitt, Diane Hildebrand, Martin Nelson, Nancy Taylor, Herb Kessner, Lori Preston, Don Cole, Nancy Polend, Ann Kruse, Connie Fuller, and Ivy Gordon. The content of the chapter was greatly influenced by their thoughts and our hope is that it reflects their inputs as well as our own beliefs.

2. D. Bell, *The Coming of Post-Industrial Society: A Venture in Social Forecasting* (New York: Basic Books, 1973); A. Toffler, *The Third Wave* (New York: Morrow, 1980); D. Korten, *When Corporations Rule the World* (West Hartford, Conn.: Kumarian Press; San Francisco: Berrett-Koehler, 1995); L. Thurow, *The Future of Capitalism* (New York: William Morrow, 1996).

3. R. Wright, "The New Mantra of Globalization: Inclusion Conference," *Los Angeles Times* (8 February 2000): A-10; Thurow, *Future of Capitalism*.

4. T. Carrel, "Beijing: New Face for the Ancient Capital," *National Geographic* 197 (2000): 116–37.

5. L. Thurow, "Building Wealth," *Atlantic Monthly* (June 1999): 57–69; R. Senser, "Loaded at the Top: The Growing Inequalities in Wealth and Income in the United States," www.senser.com/loaded.htm, accessed on December 11, 1999. The article, in a slightly different form, first appeared in *Commonweal* (1 December 1995).

6. Thurow, "Building Wealth."

7. Korten, *When Corporations Rule.*

8. Wright, "New Mantra."

9. Thurow, *Future of Capitalism;* Korten, *When Corporations Rule;* N. Mankiw, *Principles of Economics* (Fort Worth, Tex.: Dryden Press, 1997).

10. U. McFarling, "Climate Is Warming at Steep Rate Study Says," *Los Angeles Times* (23 February 2000): A1.

11. J. Guyon, "A Big Oil Man Gets Religion," *Fortune* (6 March 2000): F87–F89.

12. Thurow, *Future of Capitalism.*

13. Korten, *When Corporations Rule.*

14. A. Lovins, L. Lovins, P. Hawken, "A Road Map for Natural Capitalism," *Harvard Business Review* (May-June, 1999): 145–58.

15. Information on IKEA's transformation can be found at http://www.naturalstep.org/event/cases.

16. L. Bassi and M. Van Buren, "The 1999 ASTD State of the Industry Report," *Training & Development,* supplement (January 1999).

17. K. Edelman, *Building the Case for Workplace Flexibility,* publication 1154 (New York: Conference Board, 1996).

18. Information gathered at http://cyberatlas.internet.com/big_picture/demographics/article/0,1323,5911_200001,00.html, December 4, 1999.

19. E. Sanders, "Tech-Driven Efficiency Spurs Economic Boom," *Los Angeles Times* (22 February 2000): A-1.

20. P. Drucker, "Beyond the Information Revolution," *Atlantic Monthly* (October 1999): 47–57.

21. D. Marshall and R. Morales, "FTAA-Joint Government-Private Sector Committee of Experts on Electronic

Commerce," www.ecommerce.gov/PressRelease/ecom-01.htm, accessed December 16, 1999.

22. A. Dunn and J. O'Dell, "Auto Makers Plan Behemoth E-Business," *Los Angeles Times* (26 February 2000): A-1.

23. G. Colvin, "Managing in the Info Era," *Fortune* (6 March 2000): F6–F9.

24. Institute for the Future, "21st Century Organizations: Reconciling Control and Empowerment," http://www.iftf.org, accessed December 4, 1999.

25. From remarks of Kirby Dyess, vice president for business development, Intel, in a speech at Pepperdine University's MSOD alumni conference, Watsonville, Calif., July 1999.

26. M. Martiny, "Knowledge Management at HP Consulting," *Organizational Dynamics* 27 (1998): 71–77.

27. C. Worley and R. Patchett, "Myth and Hope Meet Reality: The Fallacy of and Opportunities for Reducing Cycle Time in Strategic Change," in M. Anderson, *Fast-Cycle Organization Development* (Cincinnati, Ohio: South-Western College Publishing, 2000); C. Worley, T. Cummings, and P. Monge, "A Critique, Test, and Refinement of the Punctuated Equilibrium Model of Strategic Change" (working paper, Pepperdine University, 1999).

28. C. Argyris, R. Putnam, and D. Smith, *Action Science* (San Francisco: Jossey-Bass, 1985).

29. D. Cooperrider, P. Sorensen, D. Whitney, and T. Yaeger, *Appreciative Inquiry: Rethinking Human Organization Toward a Positive Theory of Change* (Champaign, IL: Stipes, 2000).

30. L. D. Brown and J. Covey, "Development Organizations and Organization Development: Toward an Expanding Paradigm for Organization Development," in *Research in Organizational Change and Development*, vol. 1, eds. R.

Woodman and W. Pasmore (Greenwich, Conn.: JAI Press, 1987): 59–87.

31. P. Senge, *The Fifth Discipline: The Art and Practice of the Learning Organization* (New York: Doubleday, 1990).

32. R. Jacobs, *Real Time Strategic Change* (San Francisco: Berrett-Koehler, 1994): C. Worley, D. Hitchin, and W. Ross, *Integrated Strategic Change* (Reading, Mass.: Addison-Wesley, 1996); J. Preston, L. DuToit, and I. Barber, "A Potential Model of Transformational Change Applied to South Africa" in *Research in Organizational Change and Development*, vol. 9, eds. R.Woodman and W. Pasmore (Greenwich, Conn.: JAI Press, 1998).

33. D. Hambrick, "Strategic Awareness Within Top Management Teams," *Strategic Management Journal* 2 (1981): 263–79; S. Finkelstein and D. Hambrick, "Top Management Team Tenure and Organizational Outcomes: The Moderating Role of Managerial Discretion" (working paper, Center for Effective Organizations, University of Southern California, Los Angeles, 1989); L. Greiner and A. Bhambri, "New CEO Intervention and Dynamics of Deliberate Strategic Change," *Strategic Management Review* 10 (Summer 1989): 67–86; Thurow, *Future of Capitalism;* R. Winter and S. Nelson, *An Evolutionary Theory of Economic Change* (Cambridge, Mass.: Belknap Press, 1982).

34. M. Wheatley, *Leadership and the New Science: Learning about Organization from an Orderly Universe* (San Francisco: Berrett-Koehler, 1992).

35. K. Chee, "Strategic and Organization Development Challenges Faced by High-Technology Startup Chief Executive Officers" (unpublished Master's thesis, Pepperdine University, 1999).

36. Lovins, Lovins, and Hawken, "Road Map"; information on the Natural Step can be found at http://www.naturalstep.org.

■ B. R. Richardson Timber Products Corporation

Jack Lawler returned to his desk with a fresh cup of coffee. In front of him was a file of his notes from his two visits to the B. R. Richardson Timber Products Corporation. As Lawler took a sip of coffee and opened the file, he was acutely aware that he had two tasks. In a week, he was to meet with the company president, B. R. Richardson, and the industrial relations officer, Richard Bowman, to present his findings with regard to the lamination plant and his recommendations for what might be done. Lawler knew he had a lot of preparation to do, starting with a diagnosis of the situation. It wouldn't be easy. He took another sip of coffee, leaned back in his chair, and recalled how this project had begun.

Making a Proposal

It was about 2:30 p.m. when the office intercom buzzed. His secretary said there was a Richard Bowman calling from Papoose, Oregon. Lawler knew that Papoose was a small community about a hundred and fifty miles south, a town with three or four lumber mills lying in the mountain range of western Oregon. When he picked up his telephone, Bowman introduced himself as being in charge of industrial relations for the B. R. Richardson Timber Products Corporation; he was calling because a friend of his in a regional professional training and development association had recommended Jack Lawler, and Bowman had heard of Lawler's management training and consulting reputation. Bowman said he was searching for someone to conduct a "motivation course" for the blue-collar employees of the lamination plant. Morale in the plant was very low, there had been a fatality in the plant a few months before, and the plant manager was a "bit authoritative." Given the gravity of the plant situation, Bowman wanted to conduct the course within the next few months. Lawler asked if the plant manager was supportive of the course idea. Bowman replied that he hadn't asked him but had gotten approval from B. R. Richardson, the founder and president of the firm. Lawler then said that he really didn't have enough information on which to design such a course nor enough information even to determine whether such a course was appropriate. He suggested a meeting with Bowman and Richardson the next week; he would be able to stop in Papoose in the late afternoon on his way home from another engagement. Bowman immediately accepted his proposal and gave Lawler directions.

Taking another sip of coffee, Jack Lawler continued to reminisce, visualizing the road winding past two very large lumber and plywood plants and over a small hill, and recalling his first sight of the B. R. Richardson Corporation. It was much smaller than its neighbors, consisting of a one-story office building; a medium-sized lumber mill; open storage yards; an oblong, hangarlike structure; dirt connecting roads; lumber and log piles scattered around; and cars and pickup trucks parked at random. The office building entryway was paneled with photographs showing the company buildings as they had changed over many years.

Bowman greeted Lawler, led him to a carpeted and paneled conference room, and introduced him to Ben Richardson. "BR" was a man in his late fifties, dressed in western apparel. The subsequent conversation was one in which the company as a whole was outlined; Lawler described his preferred ways of working (essentially, diagnosis before training or other action); BR and Bowman shared their concerns that the plant manager, Joe Bamford, was getting out the work but wasn't sensitive to the workers; information was presented about the plant workers; and Bowman then took Lawler on a tour of the lamination plant. The meeting ended cordially, with Lawler promising to write a letter in a few days in which he would outline his thoughts about going forward.

Jack Lawler opened the file in front of him on his desk and smiled as he found the copy of the letter he had sent:

Mr. Richard Bowman
B. R. Richardson Timber Corporation
P.O. Box 66
Papoose, Oregon

Dear Mr. Bowman:

When I departed from your office about a week ago, I promised a letter outlining my thoughts on some next steps regarding the laminating plant. Let me sketch some alternatives:

1. One is for me to put you in touch with someone in your immediate region who could design and/or present the "motivation" course for the laminating workers that you originally had in mind.

2. Second is for me to be engaged as a consultant. Recall the experience I described with the plywood plant in northern California in which I facilitated an approach called "action research." You'll remember that it basically involved a process wherein the concerned parties were helped to identify noncontrolled problems and plan to overcome them. This would begin with a diagnosis conducted by myself.

3. Third, you'll also recall that I teach part-time at State University. This relationship leads to two ways graduate students might become involved:

I believe I could get a colleague in personnel management training to create a student team to design and conduct the motivation course.

I can have a student team in my change seminar do a diagnosis of the laminating plant and provide you with their analyses and recommendations.

I believe I was clear during my visit that I think a diagnosis is needed first, regardless of next steps. When you and Mr. Richardson have thought about these alternatives, give me a call. I'll be prepared to outline what I see as the costs of alternatives 2 and 3.

Thanks for the opportunity to visit. I enjoyed meeting you and beginning to learn about your company.

Sincerely,

Jack Lawler
Partner
Oregon Consulting Associates

Visiting the Plant

Lawler remembered that six weeks went by before Bowman called. He had shown Lawler's letter to B. R. Richardson, and they agreed that a more adequate diagnosis probably was a useful first step. Bowman was quite clear that Richardson did not want to invest much money but also wanted Lawler's expertise. In the ensuing conversation, Bowman and Lawler worked out an initial plan in which Lawler would bring several of his graduate students for a one-day visit to the company to gather information. Lawler then would analyze the information collected and make a presentation to BR and Bowman. Using the graduate students would substantially reduce his time as well as provide the students with some useful experience. They agreed that he would bill for three days of his time plus the expenses incurred when he and the students visited.

The next week when Lawler went to campus to teach his evening seminar, called "The Management of Change," at the Graduate School of Business, he shared with the class the opportunity for some relevant fieldwork experience. He and four students could do the observing and interviewing in one day, leaving very early in the morning to drive to Papoose and arriving home by midevening. The information gained would be the focus of a subsequent class in which all seminar participants performed the diagnosis. When he asked his seminar who was interested in the information-gathering day, six students volunteered. When particular dates for the trip to Papoose were discussed, however, most of the six had conflicting schedules. Only Mitch and Mike, two second-year MBA students, were available on one of the days that Lawler's schedule permitted.

Having constituted the field team, Lawler suggested that the seminar invest some time that evening in two ways. He wanted to share with the class some information he had gained on his first visit to B. R. Richardson Timber and suggested that the class could help prepare Mitch and Mike for their experience in the field. Then he drew an organization chart on the blackboard to show the various segments of the corporation and the lamination business, including the personnel and main work groups. He further drew a layout of the laminating plant on the board. Exhibits 1 and 2 show these sketches. While doing this, Lawler spoke of his un-

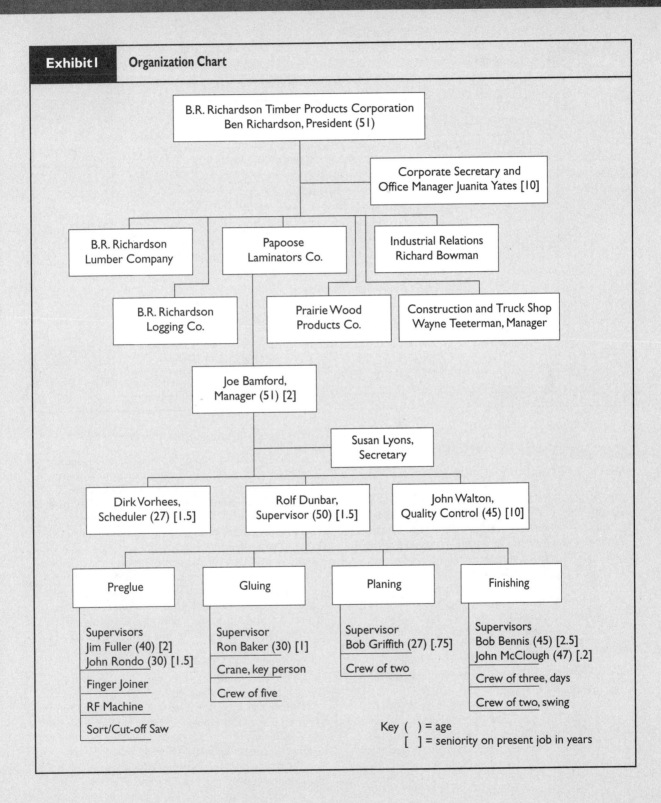

Exhibit 1 | **Organization Chart**

B.R. Richardson Timber Products Corporation
Ben Richardson, President (51)

Corporate Secretary and
Office Manager Juanita Yates [10]

B.R. Richardson
Lumber Company

Papoose
Laminators Co.

Industrial Relations
Richard Bowman

B.R. Richardson
Logging Co.

Prairie Wood
Products Co.

Construction and Truck Shop
Wayne Teeterman, Manager

Joe Bamford,
Manager (51) [2]

Susan Lyons,
Secretary

Dirk Vorhees,
Scheduler (27) [1.5]

Rolf Dunbar,
Supervisor (50) [1.5]

John Walton,
Quality Control (45) [10]

Preglue

Gluing

Planing

Finishing

Supervisors
Jim Fuller (40) [2]
John Rondo (30) [1.5]

Finger Joiner

RF Machine

Sort/Cut-off Saw

Supervisor
Ron Baker (30) [1]

Crane, key person

Crew of five

Supervisor
Bob Griffith (27) [.75]

Crew of two

Supervisors
Bob Bennis (45) [2.5]
John McClough (47) [.2]

Crew of three, days

Crew of two, swing

Key ( ) = age
[ ] = seniority on present job in years

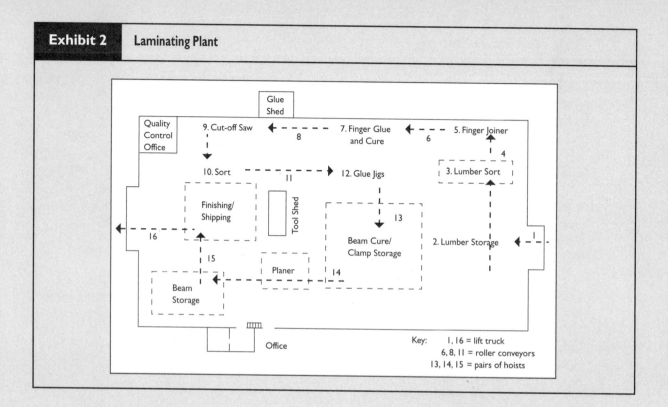

Exhibit 2   Laminating Plant

derstanding of the technology, work flow, and product of the laminating plant as follows:

It's a family-held corporation. It's composed of four small companies, divisions really, three in Papoose—a logging operation, a lumber mill, and the laminating plant—and a mill over in eastern Oregon. The head office, the mill, and the lam plant are on the edge of Papoose, which is a very small logging town about six or seven miles from the interstate highway. The lam plant looks like a long airplane hangar, the type with a curved roof. Rich Bowman took me on a tour, safety helmet on, and explained the activities as we went along.

Now, the end products are long, laminated wood roof trusses or beams like you sometimes see in supermarkets and arenas. These are built up out of many layers of two-by-fours, two-by-sixes, and two-by-eights glued together end to end and then side to side. So in one end of the plant come lift trucks of lumber, which is stacked up to a height of twelve to fifteen feet. According to orders—and all beams are made to customer order—the lumber is sorted and then hand placed on a machine that cuts deep notches in the ends of the lumber. These go along one wall of the plant where the notched ends, called fingers, are glued together to make really long pieces.

These then go on along the roller conveyor, to the other end of the plant almost, where they are cut to the correct length, and sets of these long pieces are grouped together—the right number of the right length to make up a beam. This set then goes to a work station where there is a metal jig. The pieces are put in the jig one at a time, the glue is applied, and they are tapped down by hand. When the beam is fully assembled, clamps are put on every little way. This rough, clamped beam, running anywhere from twenty to, say, seventy-eight feet in length and from one to three-plus feet high, obviously very, very heavy, is marked, then picked out of the jig by two small hoists and stacked up to cure (dry). The curing piles have cross sticks and must be fifteen to eighteen feet high in some places.

These beams cure and eventually are picked out of the stack with the hoists and maneuvered so that they are fed into the planer, which is set to plane the rough beam to exact thickness dimensions. After planing, the beam is stored until the finishing crew gets to it. This crew cuts the beam to length, patches minor surface blemishes, and wraps plastic around it for shipping. These beams then sometimes go directly onto a truck for shipment or into the yard until a load is ready.

The plant is noisy from saws, conveyors and hoists, and especially the planer. There are glue drippings, sawdust, and ends everywhere. The aisles tend to disappear in tools and piles. Above the plant offices of the manager, supervisor, and secretary is a lunchroom and another office for the scheduler. The company's head office is about fifty yards away in one direction and the mill about the same distance in another. The yard is graveled, with lumber of all kinds piled up and cars parked around the edges.

The class was encouraged to visualize the laminating plant and its working conditions. Lawler then divided the class into two groups around Mike and Mitch for the task of preparing for their visit to B. R. Richardson Timber. It was important to clarify what information it might be useful to seek and how informal interviewing on the work floor might be accomplished.

On the next Wednesday, the trio drove to Papoose. When they arrived at the Richardson head office, they were met by Richard Bowman. Lawler initially interviewed Juanita Yates while Bowman took Mike and Mitch to the lamination plant and introduced them to Joe Bamford, the manager. At lunch time, Lawler and his students drove into Papoose and ate at a cafe. They summarized what they had learned in the morning. Each of them had been jotting some notes, and Lawler encouraged even more. He reminded Mike and Mitch that they would dictate their information during the drive home but that notes were needed as cues. At 4:30 p.m., the three met at Bowman's office, turned in their safety helmets, thanked him, and left. The first hour of the drive was filled with the sharing of anecdotes from each other's day. After a dinner stop, they took turns in the back seat dictating their notes.

Reviewing the Notes

Jack Lawler's reverie was broken by the office intercom. His secretary announced a long-distance telephone call from a potential client. After the call, Jack turned his attention to the Richardson file. He realized that his forthcoming meeting with Ben Richardson and Richard Bowman would take place before his graduate seminar met to diagnose the laminating plant situation, and so he had best get to work himself. He decided to review the notes he and his students had created.

Jack's Notes

Current lam schedule Breakout crew 2:00 a.m. to 12:00 noon. Finish end 3:30 a.m. on. Joe typically works 7:00 a.m. to 6:00 p.m.

Ben Richardson (Juanita): "In the beginning he was very authoritarian, still is somewhat. Seen as a perfectionist." "Not quite a workaholic." "Has been, for several years, politically active—that is to say, locally." "When there is a cause, he throws his energies and resources behind it." Example, workers' compensation currently is a thorn in his side, and he has encouraged Rich to fight. "In the last few years, Ben has listened a little more and seems slightly more open." The last couple of years has had consultant Chuck Byron from Eugene, who has pushed the idea of a management team. Rich is the first real outsider hired as a professional. Ben has a "conservative philosophy." Will not have safety meetings on company time. Appreciates and rewards loyalty and dedication. Example, December 1978 Christmas party—a couple of twenty-year men were given $1,000 checks and plane tickets to Hawaii for themselves and families—it surprised everybody.

Who's influential (Rich): Juanita Yates, office manager and secretary, has been with Ben ten years. When Ben is away, he calls her once or twice a day. Second-most influential is Wayne Teeterman, also ten years with Richardson. Heads construction and truck shop. Formerly ran the sawmill. Ben's ear to the mill. Rich is a distant third in influence. Mostly via Nita. "Ben sees Joe, manager of lam plant, as an enigma—almost canned him a couple of times."

However, Joe is seen as dedicated, mostly because of the long hours put in.

Overall business pretty good (Rich): "Ben keeps thinking the other shoe will drop one of these days." "Ben used to be able to predict the lumber market. This is getting more difficult." Right now the economy is stable enough regarding lumber and lumber products. Richardson mill sales of clear-cut high grade are pretty much cutting to order. Laminating plant growing ever since it was started. It's very profitable, busy, and active—probably has the largest margin of all Richardson companies.

Laminating plant (Rich): Laminating plant has six- to seven-week delivery dates now.

Timber purchases (Rich): Timber purchases from Forest Service and BLM. One to two years' cutting is now available. Last year needed to cut only half of year's sales because of fortunate other purchases. Last year, half of timber requirements were from private ground. "Costs of cutting, however, go up, and it makes Ben nervous."

Laminating plant lumber (Rich): "Approximately 70 percent of laminating plant lumber purchased outside—30 percent from Richardson mill." This material is in the middle of the quality range. Outside purchases are primarily from Oregon companies—Weyerhaeuser, Bohemia, Georgia-Pacific, and smaller ones. Joe does the purchasing for lam plant. "He likes to do this."

Recent changes (Juanita): "Turnover has consistently been high and continues. For the company as a whole it is around 72–76 percent. In the lam plant there was 100 percent turnover last year" (among operators). "Right now this year it is down 50 percent."

Rolf (Juanita): Rolf was formerly industrial relations manager. A year ago April, he was appointed supervisor in the lam plant. Rolf's predecessor in lam plant was ineffectual; gone from company. Rolf did not do a good job with personnel. Fatality in lam plant happened two months before Rolf went

down there. It was in the breakdown area—several people quit at that time. There has been a constant concern for the height of stacking in the lam plant. "Joe has had a positive impact on morale—started a softball team in a community league."

Reward system (Juanita): "Nine paid holidays, hourly wage, liberal vacation plan, life insurance, no pension, no bonus except for those people who report directly to Ben (Nita, Wayne, Joe, and Rich). Joe has not had a bonus yet."

Incentives for safety: Joe and Rolf have introduced incentives for safety. Competition for groups about lost time. Joe gave a fishing outfit last month for the first time that a safety target was met.

Hiring (Rich): Hiring was traditionally done by division managers. At present, Rich has taken over that. He now goes into background more deeply.

Interaction with middle management (Rich): Normally when Ben is in Papoose, he and Joe interact a couple times a week, which is about the same as Ben interacts with other division or company managers.

Ben's style (Juanita): "He focuses on a problem. He will write a list and go over it with the manager item by item. Pretty much forcing his way. Later, he will pull out that list to check up with." He often wants Rich to play intermediary between top management and the lam plant. Rich tries to resist.

Rolf (Rich): "Fairly introverted, basically a nice guy. He finds it hard to be tough. Doesn't think he could do Joe's job." His folks were missionaries.

Dirk (Rich): "His goal is to get into sales. Ben has given okay, and he is supposed to look into local sales. Joe has agreed but has not given Dirk time to do any of this. Dirk probably has no long-run commitment to the company." He has a degree in forestry.

John Walton (Juanita): In charge of quality control. "Very loyal to the company. Very dedicated to quality. Member of national organization. Never gets very distressed. Seems well liked by crews. Not afraid to pitch in when they are a man short or behind."

Jim Fuller (Rich): "Ben doesn't like him." Had EMT training recently sponsored by the companies. Ben questions Jim's commitment. Jim gets into lots of community activities, has been a disc jockey on Sunday mornings, and is very active in community organizations with youth. "Not perceived as a real strong leadership type, but knowledgeable and pretty well liked in the lam plant."

John Rondo (Rich): "Dedicated, works hard. Pushes the men, too. Ben sees him as having future management promise." From an old logging family in the area. "Much more leadership oriented."

Ron Baker (Rich): Gluing supervisor. "Businesslike, could be sour. Likes to impress others."

John McClough (Rich): "Failing as a finishing supervisor. Originally from California. Worked in Roseburg area as carpenter; does excellent work by himself. He is a flop and probably won't last much longer."

Bob Bennis (Rich): Finishing supervisor. "Not really a pusher." "Time has made him knowledgeable about the work." "Willing to be directed." He has had a number of family conflicts and has been in financial trouble. "Overall, a nice guy."

Bob Griffith (Rich): Planer. Came to Richardson out of the service. Started in gluing, then in breakdown, then gluing. Finally, planer's job opened up, and he took it. "Still learning the job. Generally a good worker; some question about his leadership."

Supervisors summary (Rich): "In general, the supervisors all kind of plod along."

Jim Fuller (Juanita): Is lam plant safety committee representative.

General reputation in community (Rich): "Not good from employees' point of view. Matter of turnover, accidents, and the fatality. Seems to be turning around somewhat over the last year. The company, as a whole economically, has a successful image. It's made money, survived downturns, and so forth."

Summer: During summer, fill-ins are hired for vacationers—sometimes college or high school students. The supervisor spots are filled in by key men on the crew.

Communication: Bulletin board outside of lam office has safety information, vacation schedule, and production information. Blackboard in lunchroom has jokes, congratulations, etc.

Reports: Daily production is scheduled by Dirk. Daily report from lam plant to office is compared against that. Production and lam's information reported daily. Joe keeps records on productivity by lam plant area. This duplicates Susan's records. Quality control turns in three sheets a day: on finger-joint testing, glue spread and temperature, and finished product tests. Also Walton keeps cumulative information on block shear (where a core is drilled and stressed) and delamination tests made (where product is soaked and then stressed).

Records: A few years ago, 18,000 board feet was the high for preglue. May 9, daily was 16,406 board feet. Swing shift is consistently higher than the day shift preglue. Gluing, Ben expects 30,000 feet. On May 9, it was 27,815 feet.

Overtime (Juanita): "Is approximately 6 percent over the year. Right now lam plant is higher than that."

April (Juanita): Bids for the month were $8,166,000. Orders received for the month were $648,600. Shipped in April: $324,400. When $400,000 is shipped, that is an excellent month, according to Nita. Joe does all the bidding. Sue actually may do the calls, however. "The margin is significantly higher than the sawmill or planing mill."

History of lam plant (Juanita): "In 1968 Wayne Lauder started it. He had lots of prior experience." "The property that Richardson stands on had just been purchased. Wayne came to Joe with a proposition.

Ended up with Wayne having stock in the Papoose Laminators Company." Original crew was eight to ten men. "In fact Wayne taught Ben all Ben knows about the laminating plant." "Got into lamination business at a very good time." "In the early days, there were no accidents and no turnover." "Wayne had hired old friends, largely married family types." "Walton is the only one left from those days." In the spring of 1973, Wayne went to South Africa on a missionary call. Between then and Joe, there have been four managers and four or five supervisors. Ben has an image of Wayne that successive managers cannot live up to. Joe, in Ben's eyes, has done better than anyone since Wayne. The supervisor's job was started under Wayne; since then it is not clear what they do. At one time, there was an experiment to move the lam office up to the main office so that the supervisor was forced to see the manager up there. This did not work. With Joe, the office moved back to the plant.

Sue (Juanita): Secretary in lam plant. Now hand-extending the data. Could use a computer. It is programmed; she has computer skills. "Computer never used for lam bidding since Sue came two years ago." Phone coverage is awkward. To get copies of things means Sue has to come to the office.

Market conditions: Market conditions have been good since Joe became manager.

Joe's ability (Juanita): Highly questioned around planning. Example: "Sue away; he knew it beforehand; it was a day he wanted to be away. This left the head office trying to get someone to cover the phone." "Clearly sales is Joe's strong area. Get excellent reports back from customers. But Joe doesn't follow up, so payables are very weak. We still haven't got a ninety-day payment and are likely to ship the next load to the customer anyway."

Lack of communication (Juanita): "Lack of communication with us about cash flow is another weak spot of Joe's. Lack of supervision over key people like Sue and Rolf. Seems to just let them go. Certainly doesn't supervise them. Sue gets to set her own hours." Example offered by Nita of misbidding because Sue

didn't get the bid back to the customer. "Joe just wasn't aware of the timing—hadn't planned for it." Another example: "Sue runs out of invoice paper, which means we have to scurry around."

Sue's wages (Juanita): "At one time, Sue was all riled up about wages and upset the secretaries in the main office. She got no pay increase last year. Ben upset. Joe went to bat for her. Joe almost put his job on the line for her."

Sue's performance (Juanita): "Sue does sloppy work. Not very efficient. Poor letters; late; missing deadlines. Joe allows or accepts, or perhaps doesn't know." Nita is supposed to be responsible for Sue on quality matters. In general, to make sure that her backup is there. "Sue now works ten to fifteen hours a week overtime." Nita cannot see the reason for this.

Rolf's attitude (Rich/Juanita): Rolf's attitude is changing. Seems more cooperative to both Rich and Nita. Nita thinks Rolf is a very intelligent man. Neither are clear exactly about what Rolf does. Company policy is to send out invoices each workday and that invoices should be sent and dated on the day shipped. Sue doesn't send them.

After Wayne, a lot of lam workers were hippies, had long hair, etc. Part of that is the reason why Rich now hires. Why is Ben down on Jim Fuller? Nita says because of time lost with accidents. "Ben knows his family and all about the radio station. Doesn't think he is committed to the lumber company. There have been financial problems, too. There were garnishments in the past. He's quit or been laid off, or was fired about three years ago. Some things stick in Ben's throat. Now Jim is out of debt; they sold the home and moved; his wife works; they do an awful lot of volunteer work at the school. Ben sees this and wonders why he can't give that energy to the company."

John Rondo (Juanita): From a local logging family. He is a nephew of Butch (someone from a logging company). "Notorious redneck." Once called Ben from a bar when he was drunk and swore to Ben about his paycheck. "Ben doesn't forget those things."

Sue hired by Joe: Does all the paperwork in the lam plant. Doesn't really have to interact with any of the men except Joe. Takes care of the purchase orders, invoices, and daily records.

Glue used in lam plant: Twenty-two thousand pounds at sixty cents per pound; that's nearly $10,000 a month.

Maintenance man: Leon replacing rails and turning chair at preglue. "Had help until noon. Don't know where they took off to." It's really a two-person job. Also said that they're probably six to eight months overdue with this job.

Hoists: Planer and helper talking at break that it is awkward and sometimes have to wait either on the finish end or breakdown side of planing because of competition for hoists. Believe the roof could hold more hoists. Can't understand why Ben won't spring for a couple more hoists on each side. In the lunchroom, the planer was coaching a breakdown/finish helper on how to undo clamps efficiently. Says that the "whole operation has to be speeded up." 1:05 p.m.—lunchroom. The planer approaches Joe: "Can we get off a little early? We've been working lots of ten-hour days." Joe responds, "If you get that 57 job done, maybe we'll see." As Joe turns to leave, the other finish man, who helps the planer, says, "Hey, Joe, I want to talk to you later." Joe says, "Okay." The man turns to me and says, "He thinks we should be working harder. I want to tell him what's what."

Rolf put in lam plant by Ben: Probably consulted with Joe, but still he did it.

Goals for lam plant (Rich): Joe and Ben both have some goals in their heads, of course, and talk on occasion. "Probably not very systematically written down."

Jim Fuller, preglue supervisor: Swing shift now. Three men work directly under him. First work position is a lumber grading cut-off saw. A nineteen- to twenty-year-old tends to work here. "You need a big reach." Then there is a cut-off saw that feeds a finger joiner cut. Then the ends are glued. "Young men tend to be in this position, too. Need to have a lot of manual dexterity and a sense of rhythm." Then there is the radio frequency curing machine. It gives an eight- to ten-second jolt at 109; then the hardest job comes along. The lumber is stopped, set to length, and cut three inches longer than order and then put in stacks on rollers. "You need to check ahead visually, grade lumber, and everything else." This position has to be communicated back up to preglue line for amount.

Production scheduling (Rich/Jim): "Rolf is so-called production supervisor. However, if Joe has his druthers, he'd do that, too." Supposed to have orders from Joe to Dirk to Jim. Needs to be scheduling. This mostly happens, but sometimes he gets a message from Joe himself. Actually Jim says, "Both Rolf and Joe more or less equally give me orders." Jim confirms that the majority of materials come from external sources and suppliers. He thinks Joe is a "sharp bargainer." "If he can save $100 per thousand on eight- or ten-footers, he may buy them. Of course, this means they have to do a lot more cutting and gluing." Somehow it's known that thirty thousand feet a day per shift is what the lam plant is to produce. It takes two preglue shifts to get that. A few years ago, Jim reports, a production quota for the plant was eighteen to twenty thousand feet per day. "Joe is really production-minded, a real pusher."

Asking about problems (Jim): He quickly responds with "confusion" and elaborates that it has to do with scheduling. "Sometimes Dirk has to work on the line and get inaccurate figures, or we don't get them in time." Nonetheless, he thinks Dirk is a good man and tries hard. Another problem has to do with stacking. There is not enough room to handle items where beams are curing, particularly in the finishing area. He makes a big point about the difference between architectural and other grades. There are 15 percent of the former in general, but it takes more layout space in the finish end to handle it.

The most inexperienced crew, in Jim's opinion, is in the breakdown area (unclamping beams for planing). There seems to be a bottleneck around the planer. "The crew tries hard but is somewhat inexperienced. His helpers couldn't care a damn." Planing is to a tolerance of plus or minus $\frac{1}{16}$-inch. He gives an example of large beams for Los Angeles that were overplaned, and those beams now sit in the yard until they can be worked into some later order for someone.

Another problem, according to Fuller, has to do with Paul, an electrician who works under Wayne. Has strong sawmill preference. Can never find him. For example, the RF machine is only half rebuilt. "People who do this work for Wayne will probably never get it done."

Age of workers (Jim): Mostly young—"means that they don't really care about working, aren't very responsible. They take off when they feel like it; hence, there is a lot of personnel being shuffled around. Both Walton and Dirk, and even Joe, pitch in sometimes, not that this makes it really more efficient." "Personnel is shuffled too much." Fuller gives an example. He was hit by a beam and was off for seven weeks. Jay replaced him. There was stacking in the breakdown area on the main two. Jay tried to move a ceiling air hose; it came back; two top beams fell and "snuffed him out just like that." Maintenance men have to fill in on lines, too. This cuts into maintenance being done on time. The whole program is behind. It's sort of down to what Fuller calls "band-aid work." Also, major replacements are done poorly. Example: glue area where pipes come right down in the middle of the preglue line when they should have been run down the wall. Bruce did this.

Ben's approach (Jim): "Ben used to visit the laminating plant twice a week a few years ago. I haven't seen Ben through here for more than a month now. Ben likes to use a big stick approach." He gives example of Ben looking at maintenance work in gluing shop and insisting that the millwright come in on Saturday to get it done, "or else."

Those who report to Ben: Rich, industrial relations; Wayne, construction; Juanita, who is secretary and office manager; and managers of three companies. Richardson Lumber, which has 110 employees,

was founded in 1951. Papoose Laminators started in 1968, and Prairie Wood Products started in about 1976, with forty-five employees. There is a logging company, too, which is for buying.

Mitch's Notes

Jack, Mike, and I arrive at B. R. Richardson. We enter the office through the main building and are seated in a conference room located at the back of the main office, which is located up on a hill overlooking the rest of the plant.

Rich enters; after formal introductions, proceeds to talk about Joe, or I should say, describes Joe.

Describes Joe in the following way. Says that Joe is aware the training program was a possibility. Stated that Joe had had military experience, that he (Joe) believes he knows about management, that there are some possible resentful feelings toward our intrusion upon the plant, that he is aware of us and the fact that we are from State University.

Rich, Mike, and I leave the main office and go down to the plant to be introduced to Joe.

Rich introduces us to Joe by saying that we are with Jack and that we are down looking around at the plant, etc.—seemed awkward. Communication not straightforward. Not a lot of eye-to-eye contact. Rich is leaning up against the wall; he looks uncomfortable and leaves rather abruptly.

Joe immediately questions us as to what we are doing, why we are here, and what we are looking for. My perception is that he is resentful. In talking to Joe, I perceive that he felt the workers were good, that with the proper knowledge of the task they could lead themselves. He also stated they were "multicapacity"—that "they had many functions which they performed," and that it wasn't that specialized down on the floor. He mentioned that his functions were bidding, managing, and engineering. He made a comment toward work team functions ("work team crap"), and then he corrected himself. He also remarked that "theories come and theories go."

At one point, Joe stressed the use of communication as a tool in management. He showed Mike and me a little exercise and seemed to be impressed with it.

In looking at the walls of his office, he had approximately five awards or merits for leadership or worker participation.

His assistant Rolf had a desk right next to his, which was in an office off the side of the secretarial room serving as the entrance to his building.

Joe's background included working in many plants, primarily in forestry—that is my understanding. He said he preferred working at Richardson's mainly because it was a "small and nonpolitical plant." He likes leadership, and he enjoys working there. He stated, as we were walking through the plant, that he felt a high degree of frustration about the plant because the size was too small at times and the seasonal rush (which is beginning right now as of May) for summer building puts a crunch on things. He stated that production is up 10 percent from last year; that there have been scheduling problems—they received some wood in February, and it wasn't until May that they could use it and laminate it and get it out the other side, so it's been stacked taking up space. He stated that if they fall behind, they have no chance to catch up and that they are working at full capacity right now.

Later on that afternoon, I went back and talked to Joe. I asked him what his specific duties were. He replied in the following way: His duties were to take orders, to plan the shipping, to make bids on orders, and to manage the plant. His typical day was to arrive about 7:00–7:15 a.m., to look over the plant, to look at the new orders of the day, and to take care of any emergencies. Lately, he stated that he was making engineering drawings. When asked if this was common, he said it usually was done by the customers, but he felt it was a service he could render them. He stated, "It's foolishness because it takes too much time." However, he continued to work on that project. He stated that he liked the work, that he didn't mind long hours. When asked about the scheduling, he said that after he makes a bid and fills the order, it goes to Dirk, who schedules the work to be done, which goes to Ron, who is either in preglue or the gluing operation. I'm not sure, but I felt he was talking about the gluing operation. And he stated that Ron's job was very specific, that he had to coordinate the people to get the wood clamped up, to get the glue on, and to get it

organized in a rather specified manner. (I think it is interesting to check Ron's description, which I include later on.)

My personal comment on Joe is that he seemed very friendly with the workers, that it was a buddy–buddy relationship. At one time, we were in the lunchroom with Joe, and he was talking openly about the problems of the shop; it was kind of like "we all suffer through this, too, don't we?" He seemed to enjoy his work, he likes to work hard, he was proud of the fact that production was up, he was supportive of the men down there, and he was also apprehensive of Mike's and my presence. I think it is interesting to note the roles that Mike and I took. Mike took the role of a person interested in design, more or less, and I took the role, as I stated to Joe, that I was interested in seeing what it was like to be a manager in this situation and to learn any knowledge he might have to offer. Many times during our encounter, he asked me what my background was and also about what I wanted to do when I got through school. He seemed very interested in my studies and my goals.

Joe's secretary, while I did not talk to her, seemed to play an important role in the organization. At one point, I was talking to Joe when the secretary answered the phone and interrupted our conversation to tell Joe about a possible bid. Joe then made the bid based on the board footage, and the secretary questioned him on this bid, at which point Joe thought a minute and said, "Yeah, I want to keep the bid the way it is." The secretary then asked him, "Are you sure?" and Joe said, "Yes," at which point the secretary completed the preliminary parts of the bid over the phone.

At one point when we were walking through the plant with Joe, I made mental notes on safety aspects of the plant—this was something in question. Some of the things I noted are as follows.

There seemed to be many metal spacers or clamps by the glue section. This section wasn't in use, so I don't know if this was normal or not. It was very crowded and difficult to walk around. As we walked through the plant, I saw at least two different types of band saws with no guarding whatsoever—a very dangerous situation in my opinion. There were no safety signs around the plant—at least not outside the lunchroom. One worker did not have a safety helmet on. I also noticed that the safety helmets that they gave us were of very low quality. I base this on past experience in wearing them; they were the cheapest I have seen. I did see a safety insignia on one man's lunch box. (I wonder how they meet OSHA standards.) Also because of the crowdedness of the facility, it was very difficult to move around, and with things going on, I could see how it would be difficult not to get hurt. The workers at one point asked Joe about another worker (I think his name was Bob). It seems that Bob was going down the highway and was reaching for a speaker wire and hit the center rail on Highway I-5 and totaled his truck. He seemed to be okay with a mild concussion. The workers were very concerned. A group of about three of them asked Joe how Bob was doing.

I had a chance to talk to Ron, the team leader in gluing. His comment about his job was that there were long hours, that these were typically ten or more per day, and that he received overtime for the long hours provided that in total they were over forty hours per week. Each hour over the forty minimum would be paid at 1.5 times the normal rate. For Ron, the normal rate was about $8 an hour, $12 an hour overtime. His comments about his job and his attitude toward the plant were "sweatshop," "Richardson won't spend money," and "everyone's worked at BR's at one time or another before." "They have plans for expansion of the plant, but they don't want to spend the money on it." At one point, he said he didn't really know what he was doing in terms of how to be a supervisor, how to be a leader. When I questioned him some more, he really didn't know what the supervisor did, in this case Rolf. He had just finished his first year, as far as experience on the job.

Ron had a major complaint about his job in that the glue person also had to prepare the glue and was responsible for getting all the boards and clamps in the right direction. He seemed to think maybe an extra glue prepare person would help. It seems to be a major job for him. There seemed to be quite a bit of dissatisfaction about Rolf in his mind. He stated that when overtime or a certain amount of board footage was needed to meet a quota, this created work unrest, which led to accidents. He said that Rolf was always the one who initiated or told the workers that they had to work overtime. When asked about the death that had occurred, he stated that everybody was pretty upset about it, that it was bound to happen. I asked him what happened that day. He said that a guy got hurt, and yet management still wanted them to work even after the guy died. This seemed to upset Ron.

Ron mentioned that they (the workers) had a softball team; that he felt frustrated about it because he couldn't always play because the games were at six or seven o'clock and many times they were working until late in the evening trying to make a quota. He also said that accidents were very high around here, that it was not uncommon to get a finger smashed or something, and that management didn't seem to care too much. He stated that he liked Joe, the manager, that he was okay but that he was maybe more production-oriented than necessary. He stated that the work is very hard and the need for better methods is evident. He stated that most men had bad backs, hernias, and broken fingers or toes, and he seemed to be kind of embarrassed. He did say that they had medical insurance.

Ron stated that one of the biggest causes of unrest, he felt, was overtime, and his own personal frustration was that in a year he had obtained probably the highest vertical level on the management structure, that of supervisor. He said that the next job would probably be to take Joe's job. He said that wouldn't happen, so there seems to be a lack of job mobility in his eyes. He stated that workers do almost anything, any task at any time; that what needs to be done, needs to be done, and they do it. He also said that in the summertime, when it is warmer, the metal building that they work in gets really hot, and it's not uncommon for men to lose five or more pounds in one shift, which would be in an eight-hour period. When asked if it was possible to ventilate the building a little bit more, he said it would be hard, that even if they could, management wouldn't spend the money to do it.

Ron said he didn't have enough time for his home life. He also said that Rolf and Joe, who were the supervisor and manager, would come out and help when they had the time. He said they would actually end up losing a half-hour of production time that way and would be better off if they would just stay in their offices. Ron seemed to express a great amount of displeasure with Rolf, and he said most of the workers agreed that Rolf was a "thorn." When Rolf would give orders, men would get upset and throw things around, and this would cause accidents. When asked about new members, he said they don't last more than a couple of days, and very rarely do they last over a year. Ron stated that one of the jobs they gave new workers was to bang beams in the gluing job with a weight that was on a pole that is picked up and bounced up and down off the wood. It weighed anywhere from forty-five to one hundred pounds; very grueling work. He laughed a little bit and said that they usually hurt their back the first day, and it takes them a couple of weeks to learn how to do it, to learn the right technique, but he said "there is no other way to learn the job, other than just jumping up there and doing it."

My own personal opinion of Ron was that while somewhat upset at the conditions down there, he was dedicated, he did enjoy his role as a leader, and he was looked up to by fellow workers. He mentioned at one time that the record of total board footage was broken by his crew, and he seemed very proud of that fact. He did not seem to think that any of our suggestions would make any waves around there, that "I would not be listened to." He was enjoyable to talk to, and he was more than willing to help me obtain the information I needed.

Marty, who like Ron, has been there for over a year, was "key person" of the glue team. However, Ron acted as the leader. They seemed to be good friends and went home together that afternoon. Marty had been there the longest. He had stated that the work is hard, that there are long hours, and that he had been right next to the man who was killed. He stated that he was no more than three to six feet from his friend (I guess he was his friend) when it happened. He was the one to fill out the accident report for the police and insurance people. He stated that they wanted to stop work and that the plant, and he didn't say specifically who, didn't want to shut down but wanted to complete the

work that was started. It seemed that most of the workers there did not want to work that day. That was the extent of my talking to Marty.

When the workers were leaving, it seems they had set up a bet for a keg of beer if the planer Griffith could plane all the beams that were set out in front of him, which from the comments of the men, was quite a chore. But Griffith seemed pretty confident that he could get the work out. He did say that he was looking to go to pharmacy school as soon as he got his hernia fixed, and when asked about the hernia, he said he got it some time ago. He said he got it working while picking up some stuff in the plant. Again, this seemed to be common.

I had a chance to talk to a couple of the preglue people; there is a total of three. I believe Jack had talked to the leader, and I talked to the two workers. They pretty much agreed that a union would be nice; however, BR, the owner, would not allow one to come in. He said, "Work long hours, or you get fired." There seemed to be a lot of stress as far as meeting their quota, and they could not go home until they met the quota for the day. They stated that the job was okay, but that they didn't have much time for their families. One said, "I go home, I sleep, I get up, I go to work, and I go back home and go to sleep again." When asked about their salary, he said that they're paying, in his opinion, sixty cents per hour lower than the unions around here, and he said further, "The unions will get a sixty-five–cent-per-hour raise, and we'll get a forty-five–cent-per-hour raise."

I also had a chance to talk to some of the guys in the finish area. This seemed to be a typical eight-hour shift that consisted primarily of watching the beams run through the planer. They go back and clean up a beam so that it can be packaged and shipped out. One man's biggest complaint was that he was upset about the lunch break change, which he said was initiated by Rolf. It consisted of taking their one-hour lunch break and cutting it down to a half-hour. He stated that Rolf felt production would be increased by cutting down the lunch break. He seemed upset about this. I don't know his name. He lived five blocks away from the plant and didn't have time to go home to eat and then come back (on a half-hour break). He seemed to have a high degree of resentment toward Rolf, and he had no knowledge of what Rolf does.

I had an opportunity to meet with John, the quality-control man. He seemed like a very nice man. No real quotes. He was just there for a few minutes. He had had an eye operated on: I guess a new lens was put in. He seemed to talk with Joe very well. When I asked Joe about John, Joe stated John was officially to report to him; however, John reported to Rich, and that worked out for the best because quality control should really be removed from production somewhat. Joe seemed to see no conflict in that.

Mike's Notes

Mitch and I had a morning interview with Joe. Some of the quotes on management style were: "I don't know about this work team crap, oops, stuff," "Theories come and theories go," "I believe in giving my workers explicit instructions; perceptions differ, and you have to be sure they understand," and "I didn't like the politics of larger plants I've worked in." Also, Joe mentioned frustration over the lack of plant space. To a worker he said, "You are frustrated, aren't you, Bill?"

During our tour, Joe set a brisk pace. He seemed to have quite a competent manner.

When Rich approached Joe about taking Mitch and me under his wing for a tour, I think Rich was intimidated by Joe. Rich had his back against the wall sideways to Joe, and he shifted his eyes from Joe to Mitch and me during the conversation.

Joe was more than a bit curious in regard to our plant visit objective. I said it was for a class project. Joe replied, "Oh, then it's theory." I explained we covered all the theories equally. Another quote from Joe: "A day's production lost is a day lost," delivered with a hint of frustration and impatience.

Joe's office contained numerous good-worker awards. One prominent sign contained a message roughly to the effect that "I am right in the end." My impression of the plant—there were no safety glasses on the workers. One worker had no helmet; there were no band-saw safety devices. Seemed pretty lackadaisical. During our initial interview with Joe, Darrell, a truck driver, was in the office. He talked good naturedly with Joe, and he seemed

to like Joe in general. Later on in the day I had an interview alone with Dirk. Dirk is the scheduler. Dirk has a master's in forestry from the University of Washington. Dirk mentioned that he spends half his time filling in various positions. He says one of the major problems is the transition between shifts. This is in regard to mistakes. One of Dirk's quotes: "There is no communication between shifts. Mainly people don't want to take the blame for mistakes." During the course of the interview, Dirk's manner was fidgety; he moved around a bit, but he seemed fairly open. A quote from Dirk: "The men change jobs so much that it is hard to train them. Everyone has to know what is needed in beams." This implies that workers weren't really trained well enough to know what was needed in beams. "Production people go home after the quota." That was his perception of the amount of overtime worked. "Repairs after gluing are costly and difficult. Double checking is needed before they are glued together. Average beam is six thousand board feet, or approximately $840. I currently have seventy-five bastard beams I have to find a home for." Then Dirk went on to an example of mistakes made. A tapecloth shrunk two inches. They used this tape for quite some time before they finally found the mistake. He also mentioned there were frequent mix-ups between the $1^3/_{16}$-inch and $1^1/_4$-inch strips for laminated beams. Dirk's quote on the workers: "A few are incompetent; they just get soft warnings. Management should be harder on them."

Item on bidding or posting for jobs: seniority or ability (whoever they think will do best) decides who gets the job. On the workers: Morale is low. Safety and overtime are the main causes. On Rich, industrial relations: "The only contact I've had with him is when he came down and asked about people." I asked, "Who, what people?" and Dirk said, "I'd rather not say." On safety, he mentioned there are no physicals required. Later on in the interview, I asked why he didn't try to change things, seeing as he has a master's and seems to have his head together. Dirk mentioned, "Go up the line. Joe would listen." I said, "Listen?" and Dirk said, "Yeah, Joe would listen." At this point, Bruce, a bubbling and brassy guy who is a millwright in charge of special projects maintenance, came in. The interview with

Dirk was about thirty minutes under way; the next twenty minutes I spent with Dirk, he mentioned Ben Richardson, the president. I asked, "Do men like to see BR?" Dirk responded, "No, BR is bad news in the laminating plant." He also mentioned that in the year he has been there, BR had only been down to the laminating plant five times.

Item from Bruce: "I've had thirty projects in the year I've been here; I only finished one. Joe keeps jerking me around. As I get something operating but not all the kinks out, I'm on to something else." Bruce also mentioned that he is on emergency call every other week. He splits it with the other maintenance person.

The beam stacks before and after planing were mentioned as being in terrible disarray. Bruce mentioned that the Roseburg plants had a computer and a big yard with designated areas to organize their stacks. He said that this company should take a bulldozer and knock out the field to expand the outside stack area.

Item from Bruce: "Antiquated machinery. Maintenance is costly and time-consuming." Bruce commented on BR: "Joe thinks labor is cheap; we don't have that many benefits. An example of BR's attitude: one of his right-hand men got in a flap over the 3:30 a.m. shift parking down here instead of in the muddy, rutted parking lot an eighth of a mile up the road. Christ, they had a caterpillar running up there, and they didn't even smooth it out. Anyway, this guy tells Rolf, the super, if these guys are too lazy to walk down from the workers' parking lot, they can go work somewhere else." This was mentioned right in front of some of the men. Bruce went on to say, "It really makes us feel wanted." I then asked who was this guy, BR's right-hand man, and Bruce said, "I don't want to say. . . . What the hell, I'm quitting this heap in a while anyway. It was Wayne Teeterman, BR's special projects director." During most of Bruce's spiel, Dirk appeared to be quite happy with what Bruce was saying; I'm sure he was glad he didn't have to say it himself.

It was mentioned that the sawmill didn't have a lunchroom, so the laminating plant felt favored. Also, Rolf mentioned that the bathroom was one of the best in BR's operations.

Bruce on Rolf: "He, Rolf, is a nice guy. Nobody respects him, though."

Dirk and Bruce mentioned that there are only six or seven men who have made it ten years in all of BR's five companies.

Dirk on Joe: "Joe does too much. He keeps it all in his head. He is efficient. It would take two people to replace him. He's overworked, he doesn't like the hours, and he's just trying to keep his job." Bruce concurred on the above points.

Bruce: "Stacks of beams are too high. Two of them fell last week. Damned near got me and another guy." I noted that the accidental death last year and its details were repeated to me three times during the day.

Bruce mentioned that he recently organized a softball team. "The first thing this plant has ever had. It's hard practicing and playing games with all the overtime. We went to BR to ask him for $700 to start it up. He gave us $250. There's fourteen teams in our league, and the minimum anyone else has gotten is $700."

Dirk mentioned that the workers peak out at $8 an hour after one year. He seemed to think that money was a big motivating factor.

In response to my query why there was no union, Bruce and Dirk mentioned that hearsay has it that when union representatives came, BR said, "Fine, if you want a union, I'll just close the place down."

Dirk: "Communication is the main problem. Joe schedules some changes, and I never hear about them."

Bruce, on the foremen meetings with BR: "Hell, the foremen will have their say, and in the end BR will stand up and say, 'This is the way it's going to be because I pay the checks.' "

About five minutes before the session ended, Joe came in and with a friendly greeting said, "There you are," to Bruce and indirectly to Dirk. Dirk got up as if getting ready to go back to work. Bruce stalled. Bruce then said that he didn't know how BR made any money on the operation. Dirk giggled lightly and nodded his head.

In the afternoon, I spent an hour and a half to two hours with Rolf, the superintendent. About an hour of this talking was Rolf trying to prove his competence by divulging intricate, technical, and totally useless details of the plant. I got some tasty stuff anyway, and here it is:

Me: "What does Joe do?"

Rolf: "So doggone many things, I don't know." Then he went on to mention he is a general manager in charge of scheduling and raw materials procurement and to rattle off two or three more. I said, "What's your working relationship with Joe?" Rolf said, "I implement his schedules. Dirk, the head of the finishing and planing department, and I get Joe's schedules. Joe will skip me whenever he wants to make changes—goes right to planing and finishing. Then I have to go see what's going on." I asked him if he thought it would be more efficient if Joe went through him. Rolf said, "No, we get along well. Joe saves time by going directly to the workers. We spend a lot of time after the shift going over and discussing what happened and planning for the next day and weeks ahead."

Rolf mentioned that there are often schedule changes when customers' trucks pick up their orders. I wondered if maybe they could get tougher with the customers, and Rolf said, "No, we'd lose them."

Rolf mentioned that the company deals with brokers, not contractors. He said that customers sometimes cancel their orders.

On Bruce's idea of bulldozing a pasture to expand finish-beam storage, Rolf said that in the winter it was tough enough to keep the field clear with the current area.

Rolf on equipment: "BR gives us the junkiest stuff to work with." He went on to mention one particular piece of machinery that has four wheels and five feet of clearance (I don't know what it is called): "It has no brakes and no shut-off; you have to idle it to kill it."

On Joe: "Joe's good; he and I go to bat for the guys."

Me: "You must have a pretty little bat; I hear BR is a tough guy to get through to."

Rolf: "Yeah, he picks his battles."

On Dirk: "Effective, will improve with time; he doesn't always see the opportunities for utilizing stock beams. He has his master's degree in glue technology."

On John: "Quality control marginal." That's all he said.

On Nita, BR's secretary: "She doesn't always use her power right."

On Sue, Joe's secretary: "She does the work of two people. Has lots of customer respect; they often comment on her."

On Joe: "He's too intelligent for the job. I don't know why he does not get something better. I guess he likes to work."

On Rich: "Rich does his job well."

On the workforce: "There are three types of guys. One is eight to five and a paycheck—never volunteers or does anything extra—50 percent of the workforce. Second are the ones who use workers' compensation to get time off all the time; this is 20 percent. Workers' compensation is the biggest deterrent to an effective workforce," he went on to comment. "And third, the ones who try, 30 percent."

Rolf mentioned that 15–20 percent of the work hours were spent trying to unsort the beam piles, pre- and postplaner.

Rolf mentioned that architectural beams, 7–12 percent of the output, took three times as long to process as the plain beams.

On Joe again: "Joe does a good job of scheduling and customer relations."

On BR: "BR is secretive; he should keep the guys informed."

Rolf often has to juggle men around on their tasks and catches a lot of flack for this. I asked his criteria for deciding which men would go on which jobs. They were (1) how well the man will do the job and (2) how easy it is to replace him at his original task.

Rolf said overtime is a big problem. It's necessary to go through the jobs in order. Men never know how long they'll have to work. Lock-ups have to be finished. He mentioned that a good lock-up will take an hour, a bad one, one and a half to two hours. (A lock-up is essentially gluing and clamping the beam into a form.)

Rolf said he used to spend three hours a day on the glue crew. He doesn't do this anymore; he has a good crew. Eighty percent of the glue crew are good workers, in Rolf's opinion. He mentioned that two of the bad ones quit because they didn't want overtime. Also, Rolf noted that it was possible to avoid overtime by scheduling good or easy lock-ups. This was done when the glue crew had been putting in too much overtime.

Rolf stated that the overall problem with the operation was that everyone knows that "BR doesn't give a shit about them." I asked him if there was anything he liked about working for the company, and he said, "I like working for Joe." We ended the interview with Rolf saying, "Overall, it's not a bad place to work; the checks don't bounce."

Preparing the Diagnosis

Jack Lawler leaned back in his chair and stretched. It had all come back. Now he needed a plan for working. It seemed that the first step was to determine what ideas, models, or theories would be useful in ordering and understanding the information he had. Then he would have to do a diagnosis and, finally, think about what to say to Ben Richardson and Richard Bowman. Buzzing his secretary to say that he didn't want to be interrupted, Lawler rolled up his sleeves and began to work.

Questions

1. How would you assess Jack Lawler's entry and contracting process at B. R. Richardson? Would you have done anything differently?

2. What theories or models would you use to make sense out of the diagnostic data? How would you organize the information for feedback to Ben Richardson and Richard Bowman? How would you carry out the feedback process?

3. What additional information would you have liked Jack Lawler and his team to collect? Discuss.

Source: Reprinted by permission of Craig C. Lundberg, Cornell University. Events described are not intended to illustrate either effective or ineffective managerial behavior.

■ Qwik Paint and Body Centers, Inc.*

"Things got to a point where the company could no longer go on under the former president's leadership," began Ricardo de la Monte, chairman of the board of Qwik Paint and Body Centers, Inc. He had recently reassumed the post of president, as well. Visibly stiffening as he elaborated on the reasons for the March 1992 departure of Philemon Cordova, the former president, de la Monte explained:

> The main problem was that he never took the time to learn the business before making changes. I had hoped to withdraw from day-to-day involvement in the company in order to spend more time on my real estate investments. But, after Philemon proved to be completely ineffective, I was forced to step back in to try to save the business.

During this mid-April 1992 meeting with a long-time company consultant, de la Monte shared his analysis of the events of the previous two years and wondered aloud how he should proceed "in picking up the pieces" and restoring the company to a state of profitable growth.

"He's a very complex, very contradictory man," muttered Philemon Cordova, explaining *his* view of the problems that had led to his departure from the company. Asserting that de la Monte had never accepted that "change takes time, and also creates resentment among those obliged to change," Cordova declared, resignedly, "I was made the scapegoat for everything that happened."

Overview of Recent Operating Performance

While de la Monte and Cordova held opposing views of the reasons for Cordova's severance from the company, both agreed that the company's 1991 operating results had shown little improvement over the preceding year (see Exhibit 1). Indeed, 1991 sales of $26.8 million had been approximately

1 percent less than 1990 sales. Further, the 1991 net profit of slightly more than $1 million was the lowest since 1984—when the company had only about half its present total of 32 centers.

Equally disturbing had been the 1991 exodus of several top-producing center managers (despite a number of changes aimed at reducing turnover and improving morale) and of Brent McAvoy, the son-in-law of de la Monte, who had served as director of management training. Even Clayton Luneson, vice president–finance, who had been with the company for more than a decade, recently had let it be known that "unless things changed" he, too, might soon leave.

Against this backdrop of 1991 operating performance and managerial turnover, de la Monte and Cordova had, in February 1992, reached mutually acceptable terms for Cordova's March departure—leaving de la Monte, once again, as both chief executive and chief operating officer of the auto painting chain which he had founded some twenty years earlier.

Overview of Company History

Founded in 1972, Qwik Paint and Body had grown, via both internal development and acquisitions, from its lone initial center to its present total of 32 centers—located chiefly in southern California, but with shops in adjacent states. For years, the company had maintained an unbroken record of annual increases in both sales and profits. Beginning in 1989, however, stiffer competition in its southern California stronghold had combined with lower interest rates on new-car financing to precipitate dramatic performance declines (see Exhibit 1).

Beginning under de la Monte's guidance in late 1989, the company had undertaken a series of major personnel and structural realignments aimed at arresting the decline (see Exhibit 2). For the most part, however, these changes had succeeded

---

*This case, which is disguised to protect the anonymity of the focal firm, was prepared by Associate Professor Clifford E. Darden of Pepperdine University for classroom discussion. It is not intended to illustrate either effective or ineffective handling of a managerial situation. The case is published with the permission of the author and the North American Case Research Association, to whom all rights are reserved.

Exhibit 1	Qwik Paint and Body Centers, Inc. Comparative Income Statements for Fiscal Years 1987–1991 (All financial data rounded to 000s)				
	1991	**1990**	**1989**	**1988**	**1987**
Sales					
Wholesale	$ 9,395	$ 9,211	$ 9,669	$ 8,919	$ 7,338
Retail	17,446	17,879	19,631	19,851	12,842
Total sales	26,841	27,090	29,300	28,770	20,180
– Cost of Sales	14,754	14,870	15,476	14,443	10,313
Gross Margin	$12,087	$12,220	$13,824	$14,327	$ 9,867
– Center overhead	2,399	2,167	2,315	2,273	1,528
– Corporate overhead	5,624	5,851	5,714	5,466	3,612
– Selling expenses	2,919	2,790	3,018	2,935	2,038
Profit Before Tax	$ 1,145	$ 1,412	$ 2,777	$ 3,653	$2,689
Number of centers	32	27	27	27	20
Number of employees	587	545	564	579	427

Notes:

Sales: Margins on retail sales were 35–50 percent higher than wholesale margins. The above figures include parts and sublet revenues, but not the approximately $1.25–$1.5 million in annual sales of Regal Paint & Body Boutique, the company's sole custom paint shop, which operated under different performance standards than did the other thirty-two locations.

Gross Margin: On center manager profit-and-loss statements, gross margin was stated as a *percentage*, not in actual dollars. Regional and center managers were not held responsible for any profit-and-loss items below the gross margin line, and financial data below the gross margin line was not shared with them.

only in compounding a variety of internal inter-group and interpersonal difficulties, without having any appreciable effect on the company's deteriorating operating performance. Thus, in an October 1990 surprise announcement (shortly after his return to the helm after a six-month medical leave), de la Monte had relinquished his duties as president/chief operating officer to thirty-seven-year-old Philemon Cordova—a Harvard Business School graduate with a marketing and international business background, but with no previous experience in the paint and body business. (See Exhibit 3 for a list of the principal Qwik Paint executives.)

Assuming office in November 1990, Cordova immediately began a systematic analysis of Qwik Paint's competitive situation, organizational structure, and managerial systems (particularly, in the firm's vital operations area)—the latter analysis being assigned to an outside management consul-

tant. Prior to receipt of the consultant's report, Cordova began taking actions based on his own analysis to "stabilize the situation and lay the foundations for enhanced profitability."

Overview of Competitive Dynamics of the Business

The Competition

Although Qwik Paint's traditional competition had been the hundreds of small, owner-managed shops that populated the industry in southern California, in recent years several large companies—including two national chains—had emerged as major forces. Foremost among these were Day-Glo Paint & Body Shops (a franchise company that was especially strong in southern California); Karl Schwab Paint Shops (a publicly traded company with a chain of company-owned shops); and two smaller chains—

Exhibit 2	Qwik Paint and Body Centers, Inc. Structural and Personnel Changes Made by de la Monte During 1989–1990

DATE	ACTION TAKEN
October 1989	Assumes direct responsibility for operations by removing Jake Upshaw from post of vice president–operations (and making him quality control vice president, a new position in the hierarchy).
	Abolishes the regional manager structure (in which each of the three regional managers had wholesale and retail business supervisory responsibilities for centers within their assigned territories) and creates two new vice presidencies, which report directly to him. Emilio Bravo, one of the regional managers, is made vice president–wholesale; Victor Lazulli, another regional manager, is promoted to vice president–retail. Dismisses the third regional manager.
February 1990	Abolishes the wholesale/retail structure and reinstates the territorial structure. Although retaining their vice presidential titles, Bravo and Lazulli (whose feuding as vice presidents of wholesale and retail, respectively, had worsened the company's performance decline) are returned to regional manager positions. Also, two center managers are promoted to regional manager jobs.
April 1990	In aftermath of de la Monte's nervous breakdown (April 1990), an "office of the president" structure is created, comprising four of de la Monte's closest outside advisers and led by his principal financial advisor, Jacob Axelman, CPA. (During tenure of the office, Jim Vernon, a thirty-seven-year-old former entrepreneur with no previous experience in the paint business is hired [August 1990] to fill newly created position of director of marketing.)
September 1990	Jim Vernon, director of marketing, is promoted by the office of the president to the position of vice president–operations.
October 1990	De la Monte resumes executive control, disbanding office of the president. Several weeks later, he announces the imminent arrival of Philemon Cordova, to whom he has offered the position of president/chief operating officer.
November 1990	Cordova assumes office as president/chief operating officer of Qwik Paint.

Come 'n Go Paint Boutiques and Jiffy Paint & Body Shops. Of these firms, Day-Glo, Come 'n Go, and Jiffy were viewed as Qwik Paint's principal competitors, because they targeted the same market niche: the "medium-quality, moderate-price" segment of the market. Furthermore, in the mid-1980s, as the newer firms expanded aggressively, Qwik Paint found lost an increasing number of its experienced center managers to those same competitors.

Qwik Paint Competitive Strategy

The well-known and understood mechanics of vehicle body restoration and painting confined the bases for competitive advantage to four elements: locational convenience, quality workmanship, cus-tomer service, and price. With the low- and high-price ends of the market entailing intense competition from "production" and "custom" shops, respectively, Qwik Paint's strategy was to offer the "best value at a fair, competitive price." The company's steady rise to its mid-1980s position of dominance in southern California was evidence of the potency of this strategy, as were findings of a 1990 market study indicating that 40 percent of the firm's walk-in business was generated by "word-of-mouth" advertising from satisfied customers.

Key Operational Tasks

The preparation of accurate job estimates and the close control of labor and materials were critical

Exhibit 3	Qwik Paint and Body Centers, Inc. List of Principal Qwik Paint Executives as of January 1992

POSITION	APPOINTEE
Chairman/CEO	**Ricardo de la Monte,** 53, high school diploma, Texas. Formerly a regional manager with Schwab Paint Shops. [Founded company in 1972; he, his wife, and their children own all stock.]
President/COO	**Philemon Cordova,** 40, MBA, marketing, Harvard. Previously VP–International operations for large U.S. consumer goods manufacturer. [Hired in November 1990.]
VP–operations	**Jim Vernon,** 38, BA, economics, UCLA. Previously, founder/manager of small novelty products company (tee-shirt silkscreening). [Hired as marketing director in August 1990 and promoted to vice president in September 1990.]
VP–finance	**Clayton Luneson,** 62, BBA, accounting, Iowa State College. Previous experience as staff accountant in public accounting firms and as owner of small accounting firm. Avid Civil War history buff and collector of handguns. [Hired as chief accountant in 1980 and awarded title of vice president in 1982.]
VP–Quality	**Jake Upshaw,** 58, high school diploma, Chicago. Previously, a regional manager ("super salesman") with Schwab Paint Shops. [Joined company in mid-1973. Made VP–operations in 1987. Reassigned as V P–quality in October 1989.]
"Vice president"/ regional manager	**Emilio Bravo,** 50, high school diploma, Los Angeles. Prior to joining company, maitre d'hotel at local restaurant. [Hired as regional manager in 1975. Made VP–wholesale, October 1989. Back to regional manager in February 1990.]
"Vice president"/ regional manager	**Victor Lazulli,** 55, high school diploma, Brooklyn, New York. Previously, regional manager with Schwab Paint Shops. [Hired as regional manager in 1976. Promoted to VP–retail, October 1989. Back to regional manager in February 1990.]
Regional managers (two relatively recent appointees)	**Ted Ravine,** 43, high school diploma, Georgia. Previously, nearly two decades as master sergeant in U.S. Army. [Hired as center manager, June 1987. Promoted to regional manager in February 1990.] **Don Exeter,** 41, A A, business management, Orange Coast College. [Hired as center manager, March 1987. Promoted to regional manager in February 1990.]

aspects of the center manager's job. With direct labor and materials consuming approximately 45 percent of each sales dollar (excluding parts and sublet sales), a center's financial performance (see Exhibit 4) greatly depended on skillful diagnosis of vehicles and realistic estimates of the resources required to transform them into finished "products" of acceptably high quality. Furthermore, because ineffective operational controls within a center's production shop easily could strip the expected profit margin from even the most realistic of estimates, close monitoring of direct labor and materials costs was essential.

Organization and Management of Operations

Structure

Qwik Paint's thirty-two centers were grouped into four regions—each supervised by a regional manager responsible for assisting the centers in achieving financial targets and in ensuring their compliance with company policies. As of early 1992, there were seven classes of centers, grouped primarily by annual sales volume (see Exhibit 5). With classification determining the permissible number and type of

Exhibit 4	Qwik Paint and Body Centers, Inc. Profit and Loss Statement for Center 19: July 1–December 31, 1991		

	MONTH OF DECEMBER	**YEAR TO DATE**
Sales		
Auto painting	$71,479	$954,630
Body repairing	21,412	279,191
Materials	4,403	54,165
Parts and sublet	8,783	105,309
Total sales	**$106,007**	**$1,393,295**
Cost of Sales		
Materials costs		
Beginning inventory	6,351	19,053
+Purchases:		
Paint and supplies	20,353	230,393
−Ending inventory	6,351	19,053
Cost of materials	20,353	230,393
Direct labor costs		
Painting labor	16,143	219,222
Bodywork labor	7,882	108,609
Cost of direct labor	24,025	327,831
Total center overhead	10,776	158,195

(payroll taxes, parts and sublet expenses,
  rentals, telephone, utilities, vacation,
  payroll, maintenance)		

Total cost of sales	**−55,154**	**−716,419**
Gross Margin	**$50,923**	**$676,876**
Selling Expenses Management salaries and payroll taxes	**−11,362**	**−151,552**
Selling Margin	**$39,561**	**$525,324**

Notes:

Car cost consists of cost of materials plus direct labor cost for *painting* only. Bodywork direct labor was not included in car cost because bodymen worked on a 40 percent commission.

Beginning inventory and ending inventory figures were always estimates because physical inventories were taken only once each year.

personnel, the management teams at larger centers (e.g., class 7 shops) contained a larger number of people to whom center managers could delegate certain tasks.

Measurement Systems

Both center and regional managers were held accountable for attaining sales and gross margin tar-

gets. Independent of the goals set in the corporate planning process, these performance targets had long been deemed "fixed operating standards" by the senior executives.

The annual corporate planning and budgeting process had consisted traditionally of a meeting between de la Monte and Clayton Luneson, vice president–finance, in which Luneson reviewed the previous year's financial results; projected operating and corporate expenses for the upcoming year; and applied a "growth factor" to arrive at sales and profit targets. Subsequently broken down by individual center, these projections had not been shared with center managers until Cordova initiated changes in the planning process within a few months of assuming the presidency (see below).

Reward Systems

Center managers were compensated through a combination salary and triple-tiered incentive bonus.

Until Cordova's revisions, the approximate average salary for class 1 managers had been $30,000, and the average for class 7 managers had been about $45,000. Furthermore, prior to Cordova's changes, the quarterly bonuses—based on attainment of certain sales, gross margin, and parts and sublet targets—had contributed about 60 percent of managers' annual compensation.

Formerly, center managers were penalized whenever their usage of labor or supplies exceeded established standards (e.g., the paint standard of one gallon per vehicle). Prior to Cordova's changes,

Exhibit 5	Qwik Paint and Body Centers, Inc. Center Classification Scheme, with Associated Staffing and Salary Levels					
CLASS OF CENTER	BONUS (%) AND SALARY	SECRETARY From/To	3D ASSISTANT From/To	2D ASSISTANT From/To	1ST ASSISTANT From/To	MANAGER From/To
Class I: Startup to two years	Bonus				4.0/4.5	5.0/5.5
	Salary				$21.6K	$25.8K
Class II: $250,000– $900,000 annual sales	Bonus				4.0/4.5	5.0/5.5
	Salary				$21.6K	$25.8K
Class III: $901,000– $1,140,000 annual sales	Bonus	None	OR	0.5/1.0	3.5/4.0	4.5/5.0
	Salary	$12K/$14.4K		$21K	$24K	$28.8K
Class IV: $1,141,000– $1,490,000 annual sales	Bonus	None	AND	0.5/1.0	3.5/4.0	4.5/5.0
	Salary	$12K/$14.4K		$21K	$26.4K	$31.8K
Class V: $1,491,000– $1,650,000 annual sales	Bonus	None	0/0.5	0.5/1.0	3.5/4.0	4.5
	Salary	$14.4K/$16.8K	$21K	$22.8K	$31.2K	$38.4K
Class VI: $1,651,000– $1,840,000 annual sales	Bonus	None	0/0.5	0.5/1.0	3.5/4	4.5
	Salary	$16.8K/$19.2K	$21K	$22.8K	$31.2K	$38.4K
Class VII: $1,841,000+ annual sales	Bonus	None	0/0.5	0.5/1.0	3.5/4.0	5.0
	Salary	$19.2K/$21.5K	$24K	$26K	34.2K	$42.5K

"excess" labor or materials costs had been deducted directly from any bonuses otherwise payable.

Merit increases, the sole form of annual increments in salary, resulted from semiannual evaluations of managers' performance on dimensions of "shop cleanliness," "safety," and the like. Similarly, regional manager merit increases resulted from semiannual evaluations of their performance of the administrative aspects of their jobs.

Regional managers also could receive sizable bonuses—totalling as much as 35 to 40 percent of their annual compensation—if their assigned regions attained specified sales increases and gross margin targets. However, declining sales and gross margins had resulted in meager bonuses in 1989, followed by no bonuses at all in 1990 and 1991.

Selection and Development Systems

The company developed its own managers via a two-week period of classroom instruction, followed by on-the-job training. Brent McAvoy, the de la Monte son-in-law who, until late 1991, had served as director of the Qwik Paint Management Institute (earlier established by Cordova), had noted recent marked improvements in the caliber of trainees. He stated: "We were no longer getting what Clayton [Luneson] called 'truck drivers.' A lot of the recent recruits had two-year college degrees." Although traditionally it had taken about three years for the typical trainee to reach manager grade, high center manager turnover since 1990 had reduced this period to about two years for many trainees.

By mid-1991, two trends were causing alarm: increased resistance from outside salespeople to attempts to promote them to center manager positions, and increased discontent among veteran center managers over limited opportunities for further advancement. Although the first of a planned annual series of manager seminars (winter 1991) had scored some success in addressing these issues, it was generally believed that much remained to be done.

Prelude to a Termination: Cordova's 1991 Actions

Given his analysis of Qwik Paint's situation, Cordova had focused his initial attention on four areas: center management turnover and morale; corporate overhead expenses; corporate planning and budgeting systems; and strategic planning. Actions taken in these and related areas, as well as mediocre 1991 operating results, ultimately proved controversial and contributed to the events culminating in his resignation.

Actions Regarding Turnover and Morale

Weeks of listening to the views of center, regional, and corporate managers convinced Cordova that Qwik Paint's center manager compensation system had become an "albatross around the company's neck." Elaborating on the reasoning behind the actions he subsequently took to improve the situation, he stated:

> A high variable-to-fixed compensation system is okay when a company is experiencing year after year of record growth and profitability. But, when things begin to level off, such a system becomes a problem. And that's what was happening. Our managers were dependent on bonuses for 60 percent of their compensation! But, with the industry slump, they were finding it impossible just to stay even with the previous year's earnings, let alone obtain an increase. So, they were leaving to join the competition, which had compensation schemes which were just the opposite of ours: that is, high salary/low bonus, or in a couple of cases, *all* salary.

Cordova had sought de la Monte's approval of his proposed solution. "That's when I began to see the man in all his complexity," Cordova reminisced. "First, he hesitated. Then, he said 'ok.' Then, after checking with Luneson, he came back and said, 'I don't think it's a good idea.'"

Nevertheless, with the support of Jim Vernon (vice president–operations), Cordova forged ahead with a revised compensation system (effective April 1, 1991) in which bonus incentives were reduced and salaries were increased (by about 15 percent) so that salaries would thereafter average about 50 percent of managers' compensation. Simultaneously, in a bid to improve morale, Cordova removed the direct labor and materials usage penalties as part of an announced one-year experiment. "This was a calculated risk," he explained, "and I made it clear that if production costs increased, the penalties would return, *with a vengeance.*"

Actions Regarding Corporate Overhead

Having surmised from an analysis of the corporate financial statements that urgent action was required to halt the dramatic increase in overhead, which had grown from 16 percent of sales in 1986 to nearly 22 percent in 1990, Cordova imposed a hiring freeze in May, effective for the remainder of 1991. He explained his rationale:

> When I was finally able to wrestle enough data out of Luneson to do a reasonable analysis, I immediately saw that, more than any other single expense category, corporate overhead was out of control. But, when I tried to point this out to de la Monte, he seemed unconcerned. Only later did I discover that he doesn't really understand financial statements. Over the years, he has depended on Luneson to interpret the statements for him. Also, at the time, he was fixated on the decline in sales. I tried to convince him that until we could stop the hemorrhaging of sales, we had to get a grip on expenses. Frankly, I doubt that he ever understood what I was saying.

Actions Regarding Planning and Budgeting

Recalling his having been "appalled" at the manner in which the company's planning had been done, Cordova described his reactions to the first planning meeting that he had attended in November 1990:

> It was a complete charade. There you had Clayton Luneson and Ricardo de la Monte sitting around a table saying things like, "Well, next year center 27 ought to be able to increase sales by 7 percent." No input from even the regions, let alone the centers. I tried to point out the wisdom of planning *with*, not for, a manager. But, they had always done it that way, and they weren't about to be told that there was a better way of going about it. "What do these 'truck drivers' know about planning?" Luneson argued. "Let them concentrate on running their centers; we'll do the projections."

Despite Luneson and de la Monte's dim views of the advisability of a more participatory process, Cor-

dova had resolved to move toward a more "bottoms-up" approach to planning. His initial tack had been to persuade Jim Vernon of the value of such an approach. "That was not easy," Cordova recalled. "Vernon had limited experience in running a large, complex operation—having previously operated a small tee-shirt company. He didn't see anything wrong with 'top-down' planning." Eventually, however, Vernon joined Cordova in supporting an "experiment" in which regional managers submitted 1991 operating plans for their assigned territories. These plans were juxtaposed against those prepared by Luneson, and meetings were held to resolve the differences. Although the 1991 corporate plan was not finalized until March, Cordova had sought, throughout the process, to assure all concerned that "it was better to have a late, but realistic plan than a timely one that none of the operating managers really believed in."

Cordova's concurrent drive for operating budgets with which to monitor and control the plan had been less successful. Explaining that "Luneson managed to convince de la Monte that [the] business was much 'too unpredictable' to make budgets worth the trouble," Cordova was able to secure only de la Monte's commitment to "revisit" the issue at a later date.

Actions Regarding Strategic Planning

Early in his analysis of Qwik Paint, Cordova had become convinced that continual expansion in the number of outlets was the only way to ensure continued profitability. "A new center's dramatic annual increases in sales and profits eventually level off," he explained, "because it reaches a point of virtual market saturation in its particular locale."

With this analysis in hand, and with what he had taken to be de la Monte's concurrence, Cordova began in mid-1991 to involve several corporate managers in a rudimentary strategic planning process. In Cordova's judgment, this process—including the use of focus groups to gather customer perceptions of the company's products and advertising campaigns—had generated valuable data with which to begin to evaluate Qwik Paint's competitive thrusts.

Based on these strategic analyses, Cordova articulated the view that to remain competitive, Qwik Paint had to reach a $100-million sales level within five years. Further, because growth via internal expansion alone would likely be insufficient (because the company would be unable to generate internally the funds to finance the requisite number of company-owned centers), Cordova began to promote franchising as the primary route toward attaining the requisite sales level.

Neither de la Monte nor Luneson, however, could be convinced of the merits of the proposed growth-via-franchising strategy. Indeed, when Cordova broached the subject during a late-1991 planning meeting, de la Monte had proceeded to lambast him for having "wasted managers' time in endless meetings while the current business deteriorated."

Managerial Reactions to Cordova's Decisions

Reactions to Cordova's initiatives varied considerably both within and among the three main levels of management.

Center Manager Reactions

Center managers had split into three camps: those who welcomed the changes—particularly, the revised compensation system—and felt that Cordova was moving in the right direction; those who, for various reasons, disliked and (in some cases) were upset by the changes; and those who basically remained neutral, sometimes pointing out that "he's the boss, not me."

The following comments typify the reactions of the newer center managers to the revamped compensation system:

- "I think it's a fairer system because I don't think our income should depend so heavily on industry conditions. The bonuses are too hard to get—what with the competition building stores all around us. We don't have much control over the volume of business we get on a given day. It depends on so many other factors: competitor prices that week, the weather, you name it. And I'm glad, personally, that the penalties are gone. It's crazy to treat grown people like kids."

- "Now that we have a salary that we can actually live off of, we can relax a little and do a better job. Before, I think a lot of us were into a 'rip-off' mentality. It's not that we meant to antagonize our customers. It's just that if the customer was demanding something that was going to affect our bonuses that quarter, we dug in our heels: "No way!""

- "It's definitely an improvement over what we had before. I've always felt that the penalties were unfair—especially since we never got credit when we *beat* the labor and materials usage standards. The whole emphasis was always on the negatives. My complaint is that I don't think Cordova went far enough. For smaller stores like mine, the bonus is just 'pie in the sky' anyway. They create a real inequity between large and small shops. It's actually easier to run a big center because you have all those assistants helping you. Me and my outside salesperson work our butts off out here, and we haven't seen a bonus yet!"

A number of mostly veteran center managers held an opposing point of view, as indicated by the following comments:

- "Frankly, I grew up under the old system, where a guy could make a lot of money if he hit all his targets. With this new system, I get a whole lot less bonus if I hit the targets. So, as they say, 'where's the beef?'"

- "I'm sure that Cordova meant well when he changed the pay system. But, I wish he had let 'well enough' alone because it's hard as hell to motivate my assistants now that their salaries are enough to pay their rent and buy food. With some folk, you know, once the basics are taken care of, they could care less about working harder. Under the old system, if a guy didn't make his bonus, he might not eat!"

- "I don't care for the new plan: it ain't an even trade. What they've really done is give us *fifty cents more* in salary while *taking away a dollar in bonus*. I hope they'll bring back the old pay plan—soon."

Regional Manager Reactions

With the exception of Don Exeter, the regional managers had been opposed when Cordova had sought their input prior to revamping the compensation system. The majority now viewed the new plan as having had a negative impact on the motivation of center management teams. "The salaries are now way too high, relative to the bonus," asserted Lazulli. "Now there's no incentive for production managers to do a good job so they can become center managers. They're making enough salary as production managers!"

Pointing to the results-to-date of the suspension of the direct labor and materials usage penalties, Bravo commented, "We've gone through six months of this 'experiment' now, and when you look at the profit and loss statements, you can see that the managers are paying no attention to labor and materials control. That's why our gross margin bonuses for 1991 were zilch!"

Dissenting from his colleagues' opinions, Don Exeter saw Cordova's revised compensation plan as a "much-needed introduction of modern management practices." He observed:

> Personally, I see nothing wrong with providing our managers with a salary adequate for them to live on. Maybe there does need to be some adjustment in relative salaries of different members of the center management team. But, the overall thrust is appropriate, in my opinion. Same thing with the removal of the penalties. We should be able to *educate* our managers as to why labor and materials control is important.

Cordova's introduction of a more participatory planning process again bifurcated the regional management team—with Bravo and Lazulli deeming it unworkable (because they doubted de la Monte and Luneson's long-term willingness to abide such a "bottom-up" approach), but with Exeter and Ravine applauding it as "long overdue." Ravine was particularly enthusiastic, as he saw "bottoms-up" planning as an excellent way "to put a stop to [the] 'blue-sky' projections that the corporate office tends to come up with every year."

Senior Manager Reactions

Within senior management, Cordova's actions in the compensation, planning, and expense control areas had created much controversy. Generally, each member of senior management had found fault with one aspect or another of Cordova's actions in each of these areas.

Regarding the revised compensation plan, all senior executives, except Jim Vernon, took vigorous exception. De la Monte, describing it as "a big mistake," explained why:

> What Cordova did was to destroy the basis for motivation of our center managers. With this one move, he managed to demotivate the high performers and overcompensate the low performers. The really good managers decided to leave. Why? Because they would no longer see a connection between high performance and total compensation. And many of the managers who have stayed on are the very ones who *should* have been encouraged to leave.

Adding that labor and materials costs had climbed steadily since the removal of the penalties, Clayton Luneson observed, "Just as I predicted, costs have shot up. Mr. Cordova simply didn't understand the way you have to run this business. (And neither does Mr. Vernon, for that matter.)"

Cordova's push for increased operating manager involvement in the planning and budgeting processes had also engendered executive opposition, as Luneson's comments indicate:

> It's all fine and dandy to say that operating managers "should" be involved in forward planning. But, you have to look at what we've got to work with. Hell, I've tried for years to explain *basic* accounting to the regional managers. They've never been interested. And a couple of them simply don't have the native ability to understand these things, even if they were interested. So, for the life of me, I couldn't understand why [Cordova] would insist upon getting our center managers involved in financial analysis. For years, we had a system where we did the planning and let them focus on meeting the plan. And that system worked. Then in comes Mr. Cordova with the no-

tion that center managers should all become little MBAs.

It was perhaps his actions in the area of corporate overhead control that had most seriously eroded Cordova's credibility with de la Monte. Stating that he himself "probably would not have gone about it the way Cordova did," Vernon recalled Cordova's announcement to the staff:

In getting all the central office department heads together and announcing, out of the clear blue, that salaries were being frozen and that a hiring freeze was being imposed until business improved, Philemon scared the living daylights out of people. That one action cost him a lot of staff support. Some departments, like Accounting, were already short-staffed and overburdened with work. And what they were told was "expect no relief." Also, some people were right in the middle of their annual performance reviews. What they heard was "expect no raises." So, everybody started calling de la Monte and complaining. Ricardo had never had an office rebellion like that, and *he didn't like it one bit.*

De la Monte described himself as having been "outraged" that Cordova had, "in one meeting, 'shot himself in the foot' and called into question his own good judgment in selecting him as president in the first place." Calling Cordova's action "stupid" and "unauthorized," de la Monte continued:

What people heard in that meeting was, "The company is about to go down the tubes"; quite naturally, everybody panicked. After that, my most loyal and trusted associates, like Jake Upshaw, began to plead, "Ricardo, you've *got* to come back in. This guy is ruining the company." I had asked Cordova to concentrate on *sales* and *gross margin* problems out in the centers. Despite this, he decided in his typical "know-it-all" fashion, that *he* should worry about controlling overhead expenses.

Third-Party Conflict Resolution Processes

As the de la Monte–Cordova relationship had deteriorated, several related conflicts arose. Most no-

table was a split between Cordova and Vernon, as Vernon found himself increasingly "caught in the middle" between de la Monte and Cordova. Explained Vernon:

It got to a point where, literally, I would get two totally contradictory sets of instructions on almost every imaginable issue. And, no matter whose directive I followed, I'd always end up having to justify my actions to the *other* party, who would criticize me for not having followed *his* instructions. Ultimately, I had to decide who [sic] to listen to; and, since it's Ricardo's company, I decided to listen to him. This, of course, didn't exactly endear me to Philemon—who began to conclude that I was trying to undermine him. I got so 'stressed' that I was beginning to get severe headaches by the end of the day.

To assist in resolving these increasingly protracted conflicts, a team of outside consultants was engaged to conduct team-building sessions with de la Monte, Cordova, and Vernon. In the diagnostic phase of this process, each of the three executives was administered several instruments—that is, FIRO-B, the Strength Deployment Inventory, and the Hersey-Blanchard Situational Leadership Questionnaire—in an effort to increase their understandings of their individual leadership, personality, and managerial style profiles. Moreover, with their unanimous consent, the individual profiles were shared within the group in an attempt to sharpen their perceptions of those areas in which their styles and personalities collectively complimented or conflicted with each other.

Initially, this feedback, and the team-building sessions in which it was provided, went smoothly. However, despite the consultants' repeated caveats regarding inappropriate interpretations of, or reactions to, the style and personality dimensions drawn from the instruments, it soon became apparent that the participants were treating the data as additional ammunition in their ongoing intrateam battles. For example, in one session, de la Monte (addressing Cordova) exploded with, "It's just like that test said, you're too analytical and not action-oriented enough,"—to which Cordova responded, "As I recall, the instruments showed *me* to be an 'executive' and a 'developer' of people, whereas you, Ricardo, came out an 'autocrat.'"

By late January 1992, and despite several facilitated attempts to reconcile their differences, relations among the three of them had hit another low. This time, the conflict had been precipitated by de la Monte's accusation that Cordova had "mishandled" important negotiations for the acquisition of two paint shops in a neighboring state. Convinced that the relationship would never work, they met with two of the external consultants for a final time in early February—at which time they arrived at mutually acceptable terms for Cordova's departure from the company. On March 31, 1992, Cordova resigned, in consideration of the payment of nearly $250,000, which sum represented his salary for one of the two years remaining in his employment contract.

Aftermath of the Termination: "Where Do We Go from Here?"

Looking toward the future, de la Monte saw the need for action on several fronts. Most urgent were the problems of stagnating (and, in some centers, declining) sales and increasing production costs. With Cordova gone, Jim Vernon would have to take full responsibility for the performance of the four regions and their thirty-two centers. Yet, de la Monte was uncertain about Vernon's ability to provide the type of leadership required. He explained:

> He's begun to "over-identify" with his subordinates. Already I've had to tell him to stop trying to "love" the managers to death. At our monthly managers meetings, he gets up and talks about how much he "loves" them and how "great" they are, and how much they "love" him. Meanwhile, sales and margins continue to decline. So, what's all this talk about love doing for the company? We could "love" ourselves right into bankruptcy! It's more important to have the managers' *respect*: you get that by challenging them to do better, by insisting upon top performance—not by running a "mutual admiration society."

Jim Vernon had a different perspective on his management style. He explained:

Given all the changes and confusion of the past couple of years, who could blame the managers for being kind of "shell-shocked" and insecure? I'm trying to help them regain confidence in themselves and in us, as senior managers. I know that de la Monte is under a lot of personal pressure right now. He feels that he has to prove to everybody, himself included, that he can turn things around, that he made the right decision in letting Philemon go. And I want to help him in every way possible. But, more than anything right now, I need some space to run operations as I think appropriate.

A second major issue concerned the perceived "continuing ineffectiveness" of the regional managers—particularly Emilio Bravo and Victor Lazulli, with whom de la Monte continued to have very strained relationships. He stated:

> What Lazulli and Bravo have to understand is that the past is the past. They may have their regrets, as I may have mine. But, we cannot dwell on the past, and on what might have been. We have to focus on *now*—1992. We have a business to run. Either they get onboard, or they are free to go. I do not want people around me who constantly complain, criticize, and focus on the negative. As for their present situations: When they had the chance to prove what they could do (in 1989), they almost ruined the company. Now, they want to blame me. I could easily turn the tables and blame them for my nervous breakdown! And how true it would be! Because of their vicious infighting, they almost wrecked the company and caused my illness. But, I do not blame them. That's in the past, where it should stay.

For their part, Lazulli and Bravo continued to fret over what they viewed as their "predicament." Explained Lazulli:

> If I could, I'd quit right now. But, at my age, where can I go? That's what makes me so upset. It's like de la Monte knows that Emilio and me have no place else to go. So, he treats us like crap. And then he plays all these . . . games at the same time. Like, right after our last so-called "team-building" session with the professors, he says to me, "Victor, let's get together for lunch." I say, "Sure,

when?" "I'll call you," he says. *Three months later,* I haven't heard another word about getting together. So, the man don't wanna talk. He just wants *other* people to think he wants to talk.

Echoing Lazulli's views and feelings, Bravo said:

Victor and I are up a deep creek. No matter what de la Monte says, he's out to get rid of us. But, he won't come right out and say it. Myself, I try to roll with the punches. I've been around for a while—I know what to watch out for.

Finally, Luneson had begun to intimate that, barring some major changes (of an unspecified type), he might opt to retire before the end of the year. "He's trying to pull a 'power play,'" surmised Jake Upshaw, who (along with Jim Vernon) found working with Luneson exasperating. "He's basically threatening that unless we go back to the old way of doing things, he's out." Jim Vernon added:

I know for a fact that Clayton's unhappy with me in total control of operations, now that Philemon is gone. He's taken to ridiculing me—referring to me as the "tee-shirt man over in operations." I wish de la Monte would retire him so we could

get someone with a twentieth-century outlook in that job. But, Ricardo thinks of Clayton as a "genius," so you have to be careful.

Thus, in mid-April 1992, as he contemplated Qwik Paint's situation, de la Monte—although already beginning to feel the weighty burden of being in complete control of the company, again—voiced his determination to "get the company back on track." His immediate concern was that, given all that had transpired over the past year or so, he was not quite certain where to start or what actions to take.

Questions

1. Given your understanding of Qwik Paint's problems, when Cordova took over as president/CEO in late 1990, what is your assessment of his actions?

2. What could Cordova have done to avoid his conflict with de la Monte?

3. As de la Monte's principal outside consultant, how would you proceed with him as of mid-April 1992?

■ Gillette Metal Fabrication*

Walt Gillette

Walt Gillette took over Gillette Metal Fabrication from his father, William, in 1984. The company was founded in 1947 to do subcontracting work for firms supplying parts to the automobile industry. Durable goods sales boomed in the post-WWII period as consumers made up for the shortages of the war years, and Gillette Metal Fabrication grew significantly during that period. The company continued to prosper over the next two decades as automobile sales soared in direct proportion to the wealth of the American consumer. The company never grew beyond approximately two hundred employees, but the margins in the business were good. As a result, the Gillettes amassed enough of a fortune to be comfortable, but not ostentatious.

The company began to encounter difficulties with the first oil shock. As the automobile industry's fortunes waned under the combined effects of model downsizing and foreign automobile imports, Gillette Metal Fabrication fell on hard times. The company survived largely because William Gillette was willing to operate the company without drawing a salary. And he had long established relationships in the industry that kept sufficient work flowing his way to keep the company alive, although just barely.

By 1989, Walt had five hard years behind him and was beginning to wonder if there was any point keeping the company going. Japanese suppliers and subcontractors had become a significant presence in the industry, and it did not look like Gillette could compete with them. For reasons that were not apparent to Walt, Gillette's Japanese competitors were selling at prices well below Gillette's production costs. Walt did not see how they could make any money at the prices they were charging. They had the same basic labor costs that Gillette had, the same materials costs, and they bought their equipment from the same manufacturers. But they were beating Gillette's prices by a significant amount on every contract that came up for bid. Walt figured he could keep the company open for another year the way things were going. But if profits did not improve, he was going to close down. There were no other options.

The Project

Walt had gone to high school and college with Dennis Gordon. Dennis had continued his education right through to a Ph.D. in anthropology. He now worked as a professor at Midwestern University in Chicago. He and Walt were lifelong friends so no favor seemed too big. When Dennis asked if he could send one of his Ph.D. students—a young man named David Wade—down to do a year-long dissertation field study working inside Gillette's machine shop, Walt was not thrilled. But it was Dennis. After meeting Wade and finding out that he had prior experience as a machine operator, Walt okayed the project, figuring at worst he was getting a motivated employee for a year and was helping the university.

Wade had completed his year of work late last year, but Walt had heard nothing about the resulting dissertation. Walt and Dennis were talking one day on the phone, and Walt was bemoaning the fragile state of Gillette's finances. Dennis paused, then said "Walt, you need to take a look at Wade's dissertation. Things are not working the way you think they are in that plant of yours." Walt was shocked to hear Dennis express any opinion on a business matter. Dennis refused to discuss the matter over the phone, so the next day Walt was on his way to Chicago.

"Walt, you're not going to like what I'm about to show you, but you need to see it. Wade's dissertation research shows your workforce is not working half the time." Dennis was serious.

Walt was stunned by what he saw in David Wade's field notes. He knew that the people who

*Copyright © 1993 by Jack Brittain, School of Management, University of Texas at Dallas, Richardson, Texas 75083-0688. This case was inspired by Donald Roy's classic anthropological study, "Quota Restriction and Goldbricking in a Machine Shop."
The language at the plant was laced with expletives. The authors and editors have attempted to find a balance between an accurate reporting of the situation and offensiveness.

worked for him goofed off every now and then, but what Wade reported was systematic cheating. Workers were going off-premises for the afternoon and having their friends clock them out at their normal quitting time. Workers were finishing their work for the day by noon and spending their afternoon in the warehouse talking and hatching practical jokes. And a long coffeebreak was not five extra minutes, it was three extra hours. If Wade's estimates were right, the shop employees at Gillette Metal Fabrication spent much of their time not working. (Excepts from David Wade's field notes are shown in Appendix 1.)

The Compensation System

The employees in the machine shop where Wade had worked were paid a piece rate, a common practice in the industry. Every job had a per-piece compensation rate (for example, machining a transmission shaft paid $8 per shaft, so a machine operator who could finish two an hour was paid $16 per hour for the job). The rates were set by the firm's three industrial engineers. They based the rate on a timing study conducted the first time a job was run for a customer. Times were updated whenever material changes were requested, the part was modified by the customer, or industrial engineering came up with improved processing techniques. The engineers set the rate by watching a trained employee perform the job, then estimated the percent effort the employee was putting out during the timing period to arrive at the final "realistic" rate for the job, based on the company's compensation philosophy.

The piece-rate system was designed to provide an incentive for Gillette's employees to work harder. The system design called for a mean rate slightly higher than the average hourly rate for machine shop workers locally. In addition, Gillette had a guaranteed base rate of $12 per hour to protect workers from timing errors. This base rate was also the hourly rate used when workers were doing rework, conducting timing studies, and working on jobs that had not yet been timed or were one-time, special order work. The basic design of the compensation system is shown in Exhibit 1. Workers always were paid a minimum of $12 per hour, even when working on jobs where their actual production was less than $12 per hour on the piece rate.

The firm's cost accounting data indicated that the system worked as designed. Exhibit 2 shows the most recent numbers that Walt had on the distribution of hourly pay for the employees in the machine shop. As expected, the employees were working at the guaranteed rate less than half the time. The rest of the time, they were receiving a bonus based on superior output. The firm's average hourly cost of labor was $15.43, which was consistent with historical performance net inflation adjustments.

Bimodal Output Pattern

Although the accounting data were consistent with management's expectations, David Wade's study indicated the employees' actual output was distributed in a bimodal pattern, not the bell-shaped pattern of the expected normal distribution. The pattern observed by Wade is shown in Exhibit 3. Based on Wade's data, the employees were producing only at an average rate of $8.18 per hour, considerably below what was expected. Because labor costs were 50 percent of Gillette's cost of goods sold, this explained a great deal of the firm's cost disadvantage in recent years.

Wade's research indicated that the bimodal pattern of output reflected two distinct responses to the piece-rate system. First, the machine shop workers engaged in goldbricking (that is, they took it easy) when the piece rate was close to or below the guaranteed rate. Even if the worker could do the job for $11.50 per hour on the piece rate, the typical response was to work slowly and take the guaranteed $12 per hour. Based on Wade's data, the employees were only working at $5.22 per hour on jobs where they were earning $12 per hour. In addition, Wade's data indicated the machine shop employees even goldbricked on jobs where they could earn as much as $15 per hour. The logic of that completely escaped Walt.

The second response to the piece-rate system was a "quota restriction" norm developed and policed by the employees. According to Wade's observations, the employees enforced a maximum work rate of $20 per hour on the piece rate. Walt's cost

| Exhibit 1 | Piece-Rate System |

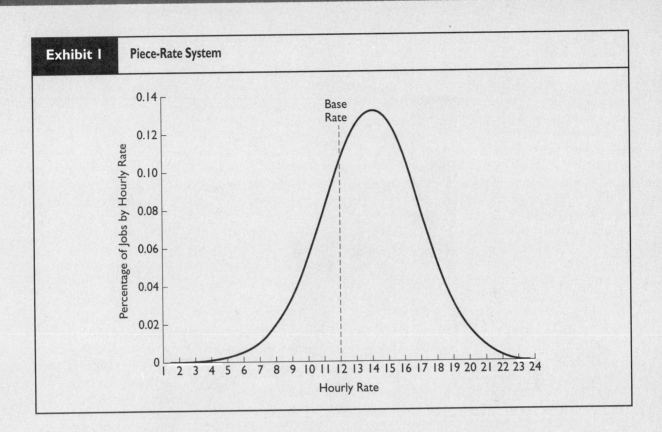

accounting information indicated that workers were turning in work in excess of the $20 quota, but only 3 percent of the jobs turned in were above quota, well below the 18 percent of the jobs completed at a rate above $20 per hour. According to Wade's description of the shop, more often than not, once the employees produced enough pieces to achieve $20 per hour for the day, they quit working for the rest of the day.

Given Wade's observations as graphed in Exhibit 3, workers were sacrificing an average of $21.65 a day in earnings on quota jobs. Walt found this especially baffling because in some cases the workers were giving up more than $32 a day—representing 20 percent additional earnings per day—just to do nothing. Why? Walt had no explanation.

The costs to the firm of lost productivity as a result of goldbricking were obvious. But the quota restriction was costing the firm as well. The firm bid jobs on a per-piece price, not on an hourly rate. So, for instance, a job with a piece rate of $16 per piece, a materials cost of $10 per piece, and $6 per hour fixed cost might be bid at $40 per piece. If an employee produced eight pieces in an eight-hour shift, the firm's earnings would be $64 per worker day on the job. If the employee produced ten pieces in an eight-hour shift, the firm's earnings would be $92 per worker day on the job, even though the employee's hourly earnings increased to $20 per hour. This was the beauty of the piece rate for the firm and its employees, both gained from increased productivity. The employee's gain was increased earnings per hour based on acquired skills. And the firm's earnings increased with workforce productivity because fixed costs per piece went down as productivity increased. So if the workers were producing at $24 per hour on a $16 job (twelve pieces per day)—a rate of production they were not claiming because of the quota restriction—the firm's earnings would be $120 per worker day, almost double the earnings from a 50 percent increase in productivity.

Exhibit 2	Cost Accounting Data on Rate Frequency for Machine Shop Employees

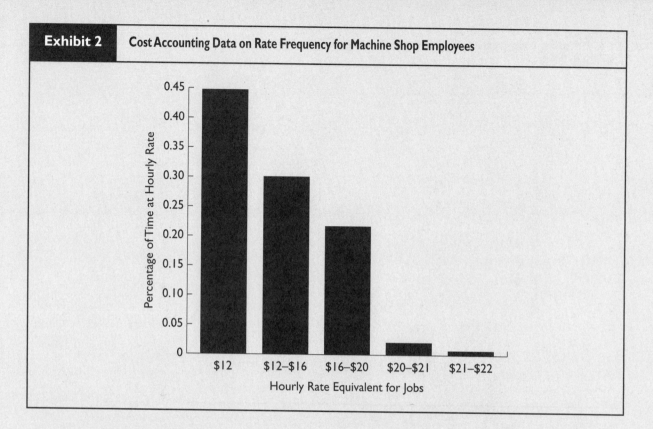

The same productivity logic applied to the jobs where the workers goldbricked, which made this behavior doubly distressing. The workers were not only drawing $12 per hour and working at a much lower rate; they also were eating up any earnings the firm might make by being unproductive.

Because Gillette was being hammered by foreign competition, an increase in productivity would allow the firm to bid lower and still make money. The firm was barely breaking even and steadily losing work. A 50 percent increase in productivity could make the firm competitive and profitable, the two conditions that Walt needed to meet to keep the firm in business. And Wade's data indicated a 50 percent productivity increase could be achieved if the employees just worked an eight-hour day.

Machine Shop Workforce

The pattern of work behavior uncovered by Wade was not apparent in the cost accounting data for two reasons. First, the accounting information only indicated what the workers were paid, so the lower hump was summed as work at the guaranteed rate. Second, Wade's analysis indicated the workers managed their turn-in rate to conform to the quota restriction, which resulted in a pattern of payment that appeared more in compliance with the expected pattern than was, in fact, the case. There was no way the cost accounting system could identify the bimodal pattern Wade had discovered because the system could only capture work turned in, not actual work behavior. Walt Gillette depended on his shop foremen to motivate and control his employees' work behavior.

The machine shop was the domain of Fred "Pappy" Mitchell. Pappy had worked for Gillette Metal Fabrication for over thirty years and had been machine shop foreman for eighteen years. Pappy assigned all the jobs, deciding who would work on what job on the basis of job difficulty, the employees' skills, and customer service considerations. Walt had always believed Pappy was a good man

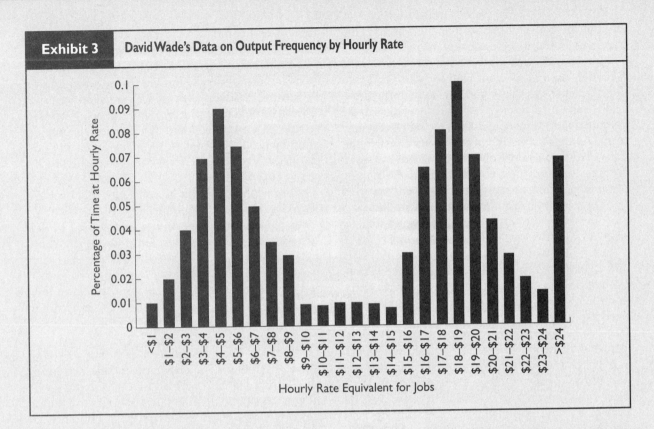

and could be trusted to run the shop in the best interests of the company. Sure he was a little coarse, sloppy in following company reporting rules, and not always completely cooperative with industrial engineering, but the men in the machine shop seemed to love him and would do anything he asked to get an emergency order out to a customer.

All of the employees in the machine shop were graduates of trade schools and had completed some kind of apprenticeship period before Gillette hired them. Times were too tough for Gillette to train anyone on the job. All the employees were highly qualified and had significant experience. They had the skills to be productive. The question that Walt had to wrestle with was, Why aren't they producing as expected? The incentives were in place, but the workers were working contrary to the rewards of the compensation system. It just did not make sense.

Walt was deeply disturbed by what he had seen in David Wade's field notes. If the information was correct, most of the firm's productivity disadvantages were due to goldbricking and quota restriction by the employees. Walt tossed and turned that night in bed, wondering what he was going to do next.

Jon Ball's Story

Jon Ball had worked for Gillette Metal Fabrication for eight years. He was thirty-four years old, had a wife, three kids, a mortgage, a car payment, and had feared losing his job for eight years. The company seemed constantly about to go under. Many of Gillette's competitors had already failed, developments all Gillette's employees followed closely. Everybody in the plant knew that if they lost their job at Gillette, it was very unlikely that they would ever find similar high-paying production work.

All things considered, Jon liked working at Gillette. The work was often challenging, he had the freedom to develop and use his own procedures for getting the job done, and he liked his coworkers. The downside was the insecurity of the job and the constant pressure of the Methods department looking over his shoulder.

Because Gillette's machine shop worked on the piece-rate system, you got paid for what you produced, which was sometimes fair, sometimes not. If a job was timed wrong, you had to work for the guaranteed day rate of $12 an hour, hardly enough to make ends meet. When a job was timed right, you could earn a bonus of up to $8 an hour without alerting Methods that you were actually making some money for a change. But if you went over $20 per hour, Methods would be on you like flies on a cowpile. And you would end up working for day rate.

All the workers in the shop were well trained and experienced hands, and Jon was no exception. He had trained as a machinist in a vocational program at Community College before joining Lockheed as a machinist. He had worked at Lockheed for four years, then made the move to Gillette. He was attracted to the job at Gillette because of the work variety, the opportunity to expand his skills, and the possibility of making more money working for a piece rate. He was a better machinist now than he ever could have become at Lockheed, and he was making better money. Not a lot better, but better.

There was a strict pecking order in the machine shop. Vern and Bud were the two most respected workers in the place. Both were in their late fifties and had been working at Gillette since the dawn of time, at least as far as Jon could tell. They had worked every machine and job in the place, and knew more about machining than anyone walking the planet. And as a result, the machine shop was their domain.

Pappy Mitchell was the shop foreman. Pappy had been around a long time, was a good friend with the Gillettes, and was in charge of job assignments. If you crossed Pappy, you would be working day rate for the rest of your life. So everyone gave Pappy a lot of room. He as a grouch, but lovable in his own way. If you did not make problems for Pappy, Pappy would not make trouble for you.

Gravy and Stinker Jobs

The jobs in the machine shop fell into two categories, gravy and stinker. A gravy job was any job where you could make a significant bonus above the $12-an-hour guaranteed rate. Most of the guys would not bust ass unless they could make at least $16 an hour on a job. Jon felt this was a good rule of thumb. Given the choice between cruising through the day at $12 an hour and being stressed out for $14 an hour, Jon preferred the $12 an hour. And by not killing himself for a measly $2 an hour, he had the energy he needed to crank when he hit a real gravy job.

Jon was to the point on some jobs that he could work at rates that approached $30 an hour. Of course, because of the quota maintained by the workers to avoid retiming by Methods, he could only turn in $20 an hour for the day. On days when he was finished early, Jon either worked on projects for the shop he had at home or left early. It seemed ridiculous to him that he was forced not to work a good portion of the time, but it was the way the shop ran.

The day rate was paid on jobs that were not timed, on rework, on jobs that were one-time work and would not be timed, and on jobs that were in the process of being timed by Methods. The timing process was a joke. Some young, green industrial engineer from Methods would come down and watch one of the guys run the job, then dream up a piece rate. It was all hocus-pocus guesstimation as far as Jon could tell. The guys doing the timing could not run the machines if their lives depended on it, and the guys being timed were dogging it to try to get a good time. If Methods wanted to know the right time, all they had to do was ask Vern. When Vern said a rate should be X, it should be X. You could count on it. And if a rate was below X, it was a stinker job.

Anything that did not pay a bonus was a stinker job. And there were more stinkers in this place than anybody liked. When you worked a stinker, you settled for the day rate. By working to the rules, you could run the job at an easy pace and take time to have some coffee, talk to the other guys, and maybe even catch an afternoon nap out in the warehouse. The warehouse stayed cool in the summer, and because so many workers went there it was sometimes hard to find an open spot to curl up on hot summer afternoons.

David Wade's Project

Jon had been good friends with David Wade, who had worked in the shop for a year some time back. It turned out that David had been doing a study of the behavior in the shop for a Ph.D. in anthropology at Midwestern University. Jon had thought David was quick, but he did not come across as a real brainy type. He was—all things considered—a pretty mediocre machinist. It was a good thing he had something else to fall back on.

David had finally told Jon about the project he was doing after he left. He apologized for the secrecy, but said he had to be one of the guys to get honest observations. Jon was a little miffed at first, but David was his friend and had been straight with him otherwise. They still got together for beers on occasion and were going on a fishing trip over the summer. And now that David was no longer undercover—at least not to Jon—Jon was getting some interesting information from David.

David had mapped the pattern of productivity in the machine shop. Jon found this pretty interesting. Judging from this data, there was a lot of wasted time in the shop. "How in the hell does this relate to the company's problems?" Jon wondered. If the company did not come down so hard on productivity, it seemed like output levels could go up. And Jon sure would like to know that he was going to have a job in a year.

Appendix 1: Excerpts from David Wade's Field Notes

Day 1

I started the day with an orientation session with Nick Whitman, director of personnel. As per the agreement between Dennis, Walt Gillette, and myself, no one is supposed to know I am studying the machine shop. Whitman did not seem to give me any special treatment. In fact, he was abrupt and hurried. I think my status as "employee" is secure.

Whitman indicated that I was hired because I had excellent experience. I asked him about pay. I know the shop is on piece rate, but with no experience, it is difficult to know how I will do. Whitman told me I should average about $20 per hour work-ing under the piece rate. Sounds pretty good, especially given my job last summer only paid $14 an hour.

After going over the company's health and benefits package, Whitman walked me down to the shop and introduced me to Pappy Mitchell, the shop foreman. Pappy is a piece of work. His office is an unbelievable mess of papers, tooling, bits, and scrapped parts. Whitman scurried back to his office after Pappy growled at him, "What the hell you hangin' around for?"

Pappy talked to me for about an hour after Whitman left, asking me questions about my previous experience, what jobs I had run at my last job, and all the training I had from high school on. Although he did not come out and say it, his line of questioning let me know that I was neither as experienced nor as trained as he would have liked. Our conversation ended with "You've got some things to learn" and my assignment was as a drill press operator, the lowest rung on the machine shop ladder.

Today was slow. I did not have any work assigned. I spent most of the day wandering around and getting acquainted, figuring out the procedures for checking tools out of the tool crib, for requisitioning materials, filling out job slips, and meeting the guys in the shop. Things must have been slow for everyone, because I spent two hours in the afternoon with Vern and Bud sitting in the warehouse, talking about the Skyhawks, and drinking coffee.

Day 2

I was assigned a housing with four holes at four different angles when I arrived this morning. Pappy told me to pick up the jig from the tool crib and get to work. The job looked simple enough and had a piece rate of $1.50. I was figuring I should be able to do a hole a minute, which would translate into $22.50 an hour. I was expecting a good day.

An hour into the job, I realized I was in Fantasyland when I calculated my potential earnings. I had only finished four pieces, was cursing the malevolent sinner that had designed the jig I was using, and had attracted the attention of several of my coworkers. Bud, who appears to be one of the "personalities" in the shop, decided to give a play-by-play of my work to those gathered around. I glared at him initially and made a remark about work piling up over on his bench, but my reaction only encouraged him. And not a lot of encouragement was needed, judging from the laughter that followed by repeated efforts to loosen the jig and remount it to drill the next hole. The group broke up when Pappy walked up and yelled at everyone to "Get the hell back to work!" Then he turned to me and offered the closest thing to encouragement I had heard yet: "Just don't turn all those parts into scrap. That's all I ask."

I got a lot of ribbing over lunch. Bud was still on me about my inability to handle "the sweetest of all gravy jobs." As best I can figure, the job I have has been performed at a rate generating tremendous bonuses by every man in the shop at some point in time. And they were all greatly amused by my inability to even make the guaranteed pay rate. I could feel myself getting angry, but I had to admit that I was not a productivity wizard. Even though I had experience, I had never had to crank out volume work with tight tolerances, and that was the name of the game in this shop.

After I got going again after lunch, Vern came over to take a look at what I was doing. After watching me run through a mounting cycle, he stepped up and said "Watch me run this." He drilled the first hole according to procedure, but then he took a small clamp out of his pocket and remounted the piece without adjusting the jig. He did the same thing after each of the next two holes, finishing the piece in three minutes maximum. He then handed me the clamp he had and said "Hang onto this. Be good to this job and it will be good to you."

I asked Vern why he did not use the jig as it was designed, and he gave the obvious answer: "I'll start using the jigs when the jigs are designed by someone that knows something about running these damn machines." It turns out that Vern had designed the clamp himself and used it for several years while he was still being given an occasional drill press job.

I was not a whiz, even with Vern's help. But I did do better this afternoon, producing at close to $15 per hour by the end of the day. I finished the job with an hour to work, but Pappy did not offer me anything else. "Just be thankful for day rate while you are learning the ropes," was all he said. I took this comment, plus his admonishment to "Get the hell out of my office," as an indicator that I was done for the day.

Day 7

Halfway through my second week and I have finally figured out what is "gravy" and what a "stinker" is. Gravy jobs are what I thought they were: jobs where it is easy to make a premium above "day rate," which is shop lingo for the $12 per hour guarantee. Stinker jobs—as in "this job stinks"—are jobs where no one can make a premium, even the very experienced guys like Vern.

Everybody dogs it on the stinker jobs. At first I thought it might be a good idea to try to get the stinker jobs over with so I could move onto something else, but Bud laid it out for me. "Why bust your hump for day rate? If you try to work through a stinker job, you are playing right into management's hands. Why do you think the rates on some of these jobs are so lousy? It is because management expects us to scurry around for the few crumbs they throw our way. Well, I am not willing to play their game and neither are the rest of the guys. If management wants us to work a job, they are going to have to raise the rate to make it worth our while."

The basic logic everybody follows on the stinker jobs is to punish management into changing the rate. Bud, for instance, went out to the warehouse for some material in the middle of his stinker job, returning two hours later looking like he had just gotten up. He assured me my perception was accurate. Bud only got his job half run by midafternoon, then he split at 2:00 p.m. to go to softball practice for his city league team. He said Ronny would punch him out.

Pappy came around looking for Bud about 3:30, but Vern covered for him. Pappy ranted and raved for about twenty seconds, then walked off cursing. It scared the hell out of me, but Vern was unconcerned. "It is okay to go home early if you finish up a gravy job early, but only Bud has the balls to leave with a stinker job in the queue. But that is because Pappy knows that he can count on Bud when there is rush work to be done. And the secret to getting along with Pappy is to make sure you always make him look good. Never, and I mean never, make Pappy look bad to a customer or management. If you do, you will find out just how many stinker jobs actually exist in this shop."

Day 18

There was an argument this morning between Vern and Bud over whether a valve body grinding job was a stinker or gravy. Bud said it was a stinker, and Vern said he thought it might be gravy. Vern was not as adamant as Bud and decided to put the part to a test. I asked Ronny about the argument, and he indicated that "if Vern says it's a stinker, it's a stinker. If Bud says it's a stinker, it probably is a stinker. Unless Vern proves that it is not. But then sometimes Vern is the only guy that can make gravy on it." It was clear to him.

The word came down on coffeebreak. The job was a stinker. Vern had tried it and could do no better than $14 per hour. I expressed the opinion that $14 sounded pretty good to me, but Vern sat me straight. "Do you mean to tell me that you are willing to bust your hump for an extra $16 a day?" Actually, at this point I was. But I could tell "yes" was not the right answer. "Kid, life is too short to kill yourself for $2 an hour when you can use the energy the next day to do a job that will get you $8 an hour gravy. You got a lot of years working in front of you. Put your effort into something with some returns. You cannot bust hump every day in here and stay human."

Day 43

Jon Ball and I went out last night after work and killed a few million gray cells. I am feeling it today. He and I are becoming pretty good friends. He is a stand-back guy, but he has been a big help the past two months. I have picked up a lot of pointers from him. If I make gravy anytime soon, it will be because of his help.

An interesting thing happened today. The timing men were down riding Vern on the valve body that he and Bud had the argument over awhile back. They were trying to persuade him that the milling operation could be done faster than he said it could be done. He told us about it later. "Those method guys got their heads up their ass. They do

not know what they are talking about. They want a rate of $15 to mill those valve bodies. They are out of their mind. It is going to take two hours minimum to run that job right. Every step on that thing is a stinker. Somebody bid the price on that thing too low a year ago and now Methods wants to take it out of my ass. Well, I can tell you right now that they are not getting any more than a piece every three hours out of me."

When Vern was doing the method study, there was little doubt that he was "doing it right." The job has very precise tolerances, and Vern is playing them for all they are worth, adjusting his machine after ever step and double checking every procedure. The methods guys knew he was dogging it, but what are they going to do? Vern is the only guy in the shop that can do this job with any kind of productivity at all.

Day 45

We got the rate on the valve body today, and we were floored. $18 a piece! Bud lit up the lunch room. "What do those Methods assholes think we are, a charity shop? They might as well ask us to work for free! Did you see Vern working on that job? Three hours per piece! If they are going to keep setting rates like this, we may as well pack it in. My kids are going to go hungry if this is what I am getting paid. What the hell do I care if the company folds if my family is going hungry because I am working here?"

I asked Jon about it later. "If Vern says it's a stinker, it's a stinker." I pointed out that Vern was really dogging it when they timed him, something the industrial engineers couldn't help but notice. "Yeah," Jon said, "but they should have listened to Vern in the first place. If it is a two-hour job, then the rate should be $30. It is the most complex piece in the shop. It has very precise tolerances and a lot of steps. They are lucky Vern can do it at all."

All the guys in the shop were bent out of shape over the valve body, even though most of us would never work the job. It was an interesting kind of anger, not really directed at anybody. One of the things that I have noticed here is that relations with the industrial engineers from Methods are pretty good. They are generally okay guys, willing to joke around, and helpful most of the time. But "Methods" is the enemy around the shop. The guys in the shop do not blame the individual engineers when they get screwed on a rate, but there is a lot of anger with the system here.

Day 68

I "made out" big for the first time today! I was cranking out pieces all morning, when Vern came over to see how I was doing. When I showed him, he became concerned. "Hey, you're doing great. But be careful. You are going to have to quit at noon at this rate. You might want to stretch it out a little. If you do this all day, we are going to have Methods down here tomorrow resetting the rate on this. Milk it a little. If you stretch it out until after lunch, Pappy will be too busy to notice you finished up with it. Then you can take your time cleaning your machine and get out of here. I will punch you out."

I wanted to crank parts all afternoon to build a kitty, but they are too big to store in my locker. Jon has a job he does all the time, and he can usually store up enough of a kitty that he does not have to work the job every third or fourth time. He uses the extra time to work on the bench he is building for his garage at home. It is a thing of beauty. He should have it finished in another month, then he can come in on Saturday when no ties are around and pick it up from the warehouse.

The quota really impacts what people do around here. But you have to respect it. If you don't, Methods will cut all the rates, and we'll all end up working for day rate. It sure would be nice to bring home $24 an hour for a change, however. But the company won't let it happen. Bud told me how Ronny and Vern got in a competition a couple of years back "to see who was champ on the milling machine. They had a big job that they worked on for a week, cranking out the pieces at $30 an hour by the end. Methods was down here the next week retiming that job so that we could not make more than $10 an hour on it. Now nobody will work it. We make Ronny and Vern deal with that stinker. It's their fault that we lost a gravy job. You got to respect the quota, because otherwise we will all be working day rate."

Day 74

I screwed up big time today. I was not watching my piece count very closely and ended up turning in $22 an hour for the day. Pappy seemed surprised but did not say anything. If the job gets retimed, the guys will be pissed. When Jon has the job, he can run it at $32 an hour. If it comes back with the rate halved, he is going to be pissed. And the job will be mine for life.

Day 92

Methods was back today, working on Vern and the valve body again. Vern and Ronny have been running the job at two to three hours per piece and are none too happy about it. Apparently methods is not either. All three engineers were down working with Vern, trying to get him to try some new procedures, and discussing tolerances. They spent the whole day on the part, and Vern was pissed. "A whole day on day rate because those Methods bastards got a problem. I will be running that stinker all day tomorrow because they screwed up the price to the customer. The only way they are getting any output on that job is if they set the rate at $30 a piece. It is a two-hour job! There is no getting around it."

Day 93

The job I busted quota on came back around again today. Thank heaven Methods did not retime it. I got lucky this time. I am going to be more careful. I cannot afford to screw things up for the rest of the guys.

Day 145

The saga of the valve body continues. They have retimed the job five times in the last six months. Vern finally got a $24 piece rate out of them two weeks ago. Then he got thirty pieces to do this week. "I am going to spend the rest of my life working this stinker" was his comment on Monday. Well, he finished the job today. After a day of dogging it, he got fed up and started working the job. By Thursday, he was doing a piece an hour.

I asked him about it when we were having afternoon coffee. He said, "I guess this is some real gravy after all. I am glad Methods finally set a reasonable rate. If they had set a decent rate in the first place, I would not have been working day rate a third of the time for the past three months."

Questions

1. From an ethics perspective, how do you evaluate David Wade's project?

2. How do you explain the discrepancies between Wade's data and the cost accounting data?

3. What interventions might be appropriate here? What are the pros and cons of these different approaches?

4. What would you do as Walt Gillette?

Glossary

This glossary was prepared to help the reader understand some of the more frequently used terms in OD. Not all the terms in the glossary appear in the text, but they are used frequently in the field. Conversely, the glossary does not try to define every term used in the text. In general, knowledge of the terms in the glossary can be useful in understanding what occasionally appears to be an overly specialized language.

Accountability Responsibility to produce a promised result within a specific time.

Achievement needs A phrase applied to an individual, referring to the desire to perform work successfully and to advance in one's career.

Acquisition The purchase of one organization by another. (See *merger*.)

Action learning A form of action research in which the focus is helping organizations learn from their actions how to create entirely new structures, processes, and behaviors. Also called action science, self-design, or appreciative inquiry, this process involves extensive trial-and-error learning as participants try out new ways of operating, assess progress, and make necessary adjustments. (See *action research*.)

Action research A cyclical process of diagnosis–change–research–diagnosis–change–research. The results of diagnosis produce ideas for changes; the changes are introduced into the same system, and their effects are noted through further research and diagnosis. The number of cycles may be infinite.

Active listening Reflecting back to the other person not only what the person has said but also the perceived emotional tone of the message.

Adaptive A term used to describe the behavior of many kinds of systems. Originally used mainly to describe individuals (e.g., adaptive behavior), it is now applied to groups and organizations vis-à-vis their environment.

Appreciative inquiry A contemporary approach to planned change. Contrary to typical approaches that assume organizations are like problems to be solved, appreciative inquiry works under the assumption that organizations are like mysteries to be understood. A focus on the "best of what is" in an organization provides the necessary vision for change.

Authenticity A term synonymous with the colloquial phrase to "be straight" with another person. It refers to one's openness and honesty.

Behavioral science A phrase for the various disciplines that study human behavior. As such, all of the traditional social sciences are included.

Body language An important part of nonverbal communications that involves the transmittal of thoughts, actions, and feelings through bodily movements and how other people interpret them.

Boundary A term used to describe systems or fields of interacting forces. Boundaries can be physical, such as a wall between two departments in an organization. More subtly, boundaries may be social processes, such as the boundaries between ethnic groups. Boundaries may be temporal: Things done at different times are said to be bounded from each other. Any set of forces or factors that differentiate parts of the system can be said to have a boundary effect.

Breakthrough A sudden and significant advance, especially in knowledge, technique, or results.

Career The sequence of behaviors and attitudes associated with past, present, and anticipated future work-related experiences and role activities. A career is work-related and may be lifelong.

Career development Activities directed at helping people attain career objectives. These may include skill training, performance feedback and coaching, job rotation, mentoring roles, and challenging and visible job assignments.

Career planning Activities aimed at helping people choose occupations, organizations, and jobs. It involves setting individual career goals.

Change agent A person who attempts to alter some aspect of an organization or an environment. (See *organization development practitioner*.)

Client system The person, group, or organization that is the object of diagnosis or change efforts. Often shortened to "the client." The client may be in the same organization as the consultant, as in the case of a line manager who is the client of a staff group, or the client and consultant may be in different organizations.

Closed system The tendency to disregard relations between a system and its environment. This is often an unwitting simplification and, as such, can lead to error.

Closure, need for A commonly felt need to see something finished or brought to a logical end point. Sometimes used in describing a person who is uncomfortable with ambiguity and uncertainty.

Coaching A new paradigm for management based on giving organization members committed support, feedback, new views of work, new visions of the organization, and new ways of relating to supervisors.

Collateral organization A parallel, coexisting structure that can be used to supplement the existing formal organization. It generally is used to solve ill-defined problems that do not fit neatly into the formal organizational structure.

Communication, one-way and two-way One-way communication describes an interaction in which one or both parties are paying little attention to what the other is saying or doing. In two-way communication, presumably both parties are engaging and responding to each other.

Conflict management Management's task is to manage conflict by reducing or stimulating it, depending on the situation, in order to develop the highest level of organizational performance.

Conformance The outputs produced as a part of work and passed on or delivered to the customer that will meet all the requirements to which the producer and the customer have agreed.

Confront The process by which one person attempts to make another person aware of aspects of behavior of which he or she seems unaware. It is used increasingly in the phrase *a confronting style* to describe a person who habitually gives such feedback to others.

Confrontation meeting A structured intervention that helps two (or more) groups resolve interdepartmental misunderstandings or conflict.

Consultant An individual (change agent) who is assisting an organization (client system) to become more effective. An external consultant is not a member of the system. An internal consultant is a member of the organization being assisted but may or may not have a representative job title.

Contingency approach This approach suggests that there is no universal best way to design an organization, that the design instead depends upon the situation.

Continuous improvement A philosophy of designing and managing all aspects of an organization in a never-ending quest for quality. The notion is that no matter how well things are going, there are always opportunities to make them better, and hundreds of small improvements can make a big difference in overall functioning. Also known as *kaizen.*

Contract A formal or informal agreement between the change agent and the client system to perform certain work. The contract typically identifies roles, expectations, resources, and other information required to carry out the consultation process successfully.

Core job dimensions These are the five basic dimensions of work, including skill variety, task identity, task significance, autonomy, and feedback.

Corporate culture This is the pattern of values, beliefs, and expectations shared by organization members. It represents the taken-for-granted and shared assumptions that people make about how work is to be done and evaluated and how employees relate to one another and to significant others, such as suppliers, customers, and government agencies.

Cost of quality The financial impact of poor quality. The cost of quality consists of the cost of conformance, nonconformance, and lost opportunity. The cost of conformance includes expenses associated with prevention measures, inspection, and appraisal. The cost of nonconformance is the dollar impact of not meeting customer expectations. The cost of lost opportunity is the revenue forgone when a customer leaves or does not renew a relationship with the organization.

Customer The person who receives the product of work. A customer may be either internal or external.

Data-based intervention A specific technique in action research. It follows some data collection phase and is an input into the system using the data that have been collected. Alternatively, it can be the act of presenting the data to members of the system, thus initiating a process of system self-analysis.

Defensive A term widely used to describe any kind of resistant behavior.

Diagnosis The process of collecting information about a client system and working collaboratively with the client to understand the system's current functioning. Diagnosis follows entry and contracting, and precedes action planning and implementation. Diagnosis is expected to point to possible interventions to address system effectiveness.

Differentiation The extent to which individual organizational units are different from each other along a variety of dimensions, such as time, technology, or formality. High uncertainty leads to the need for more differentiation, and low uncertainty leads to the need for less.

Dissonance A term reflecting the behavioral consequences of knowing two or more incompatible things at one time. Dissonance may be used to describe incompatibility in a person's point of view.

Diversity The mix of gender, age, disabilities, cultures, ethnic backgrounds, and lifestyles that characterize the organization's workforce and potential labor pool.

Dominant coalition That minimum group of cooperating employees who control the basic policy making and oversee the operation of the organization as a whole.

Double-loop learning Organizational behaviors directed at changing existing valued states or goals. This is concerned with radically transforming an organization's structure, culture, and operating procedures. (See *single-loop learning, organization transformation*.)

Downsizing Interventions aimed at reducing the size of the organization. Although typically associated with layoffs and reductions in force, downsizing also includes attrition, early retirement, selling businesses or divisions, outsourcing, and delayering.

Dyad Two people and their dynamic interrelations; more informally, two people. Its usage has been extended recently to triad, or three people.

Dysfunctional Those aspects of systems that work against the goals. The term is meant to be objective but is often used subjectively to refer to the bad parts of systems. (See *functional*.)

Empathic From *empathy:* to be able to project oneself into another's feelings and hence to understand the other person. It is used relatively interchangeably with "sensitive" and "understanding."

Employee involvement (EI) Any set of techno-structural interventions, such as quality circles, high-involvement organizations, or total quality management, that adjusts the power, information flows, rewards, and knowledge and skills in an organization. Also known as quality of work life.

Encounter An entire collection of interventions or techniques that aim to bring people into closer and more intimate relationships.

Entry The process that describes how an OD practitioner first encounters and establishes a relationship with a client system.

Environment The physical and social context within which any client system (a person, group, or organization) is functioning.

Ethics Standards of acceptable behavior for professionals practicing in a particular field, such as law, medicine, or OD. In OD, it concerns how practitioners perform their helping relationship with organization members.

Evaluation feedback Information about the overall effects of a change program. It generally is used for making decisions about whether resources should continue to be allocated to the program.

Expectancy The belief, expressed as a subjective estimate or odds, that a particular act will be successful.

Expectancy model A model of motivation suggesting that people are motivated to choose among different behaviors or intensities of effort by the degree to which they believe that their efforts will be meaningfully rewarded.

Experiential A kind of learning process in which the content is experienced as directly as possible, in contrast to being read or talked about. The term applies to a wide variety of training techniques. It is often used in the phrase *experiential level,* in contrast to *cognitive level*.

Expert power The power and influence that a person has in a situation by virtue of technical or professional expertise. (See *power*.)

External validity A research term concerned with assessing the general applicability of interventions. This helps to identify contingencies upon which the success of change programs depend. (See *internal validity*.)

Facilitate A process by which events are "helped to happen." Facilitating is a kind of influence role that is neither authoritarian nor abdicative.

Feedback Information regarding the actual performance or the results of the activities of a system. In communications, it concerns looking for and using helpful responses from others.

Filtering A barrier to communication that occurs when the sender intentionally shifts or modifies the message so that it will be seen more favorably by the receiver.

Fishbowl An experiential training technique in which some members of a group sit in a small inner circle and work the issue while other members sit in an outer circle and observe.

Formal (leader, organization, system) A term introduced originally in the Hawthorne studies to designate the set of organizational relationships that were explicitly established in policy and procedure (e.g., the formal organization). The term has been prefixed to many types of organizational phenomena.

Functional The term describes those parts of a system that promote the attainment of its goals. It comes from a mode of systems analysis that explains systems by describing the effects that parts of the system have on one another and the mutual effects between the system and its environment.

Gain-sharing Paying employees a bonus based on improvements in the operating results of an organization or department. It generally covers all employees working in a particular department, plant, or company and includes both a bonus scheme and a participative structure for eliciting employees' suggestions and improvements.

Gatekeeper A term from group dynamics that describes a person in a group who regulates interaction patterns by asking people for their ideas or suggesting to others that they should talk less.

Goal setting Activities involving managers and subordinates in jointly setting subordinates' goals, monitoring them, and providing counseling and support when necessary.

Group maintenance Those behaviors exhibited by members of a group that are functional for holding the group together, increasing members' liking for each other, and differentiating the group from its environment.

Group task activities Activities directed at helping the group accomplish its goals. Successful groups are more able to combine group maintenance and group task activities properly than are less successful groups.

Groupthink A form of decision making that occurs when the members' striving for unanimity and closeness overcomes their motivation to appraise alternative courses of action realistically.

Growth A term reflecting theorists' and practitioners' concern for improvement in personal, group, and organizational behavior. Identification of growth stages, rates, and directions is a major focus of contemporary theory and research.

Growth needs The desire for personal accomplishment, learning, and development. An important contingency affecting work design success (e.g., the greater people's growth needs, the more responsive they are to enriched forms of work).

Hawthorne effect When workers' behavior changes and productivity increases because the workers are aware that people important in their lives are taking an interest in them.

Hidden agenda An undisclosed motive for doing or failing to do something.

Human resources systems Mechanisms and procedures for selecting, training, and developing employees; these may include reward systems, goal setting, career planning and development, and stress management.

Ideal future state An articulated vision of the ideal state of the organization; the desired culture, infrastructure, and operation. What does it look like, sound like, feel like? What are people doing, with whom, and how? An ideal future state serves as the direction for present-day change efforts; it serves to bring the future into the present.

Implementation feedback Refers to information about whether an intervention is being implemented as intended. It is generally used to gain a clearer understanding of the behaviors and procedures required to implement a change program and to plan for the next implementation steps. (See *evaluation feedback*.)

Informal (leader, group, organization, system) A term introduced in the Hawthorne studies to designate the set of organizational relationships that emerge over time from the day-to-day experiences that people have with one another. Informal relationships are expressive of the needs that people actually feel in situations, in contrast to needs their leaders think they should feel.

Inputs Human or other resources, such as information, energy, and materials, coming into the system or subsystem. Also, more informally, used to describe people's contributions to a system, particularly their ideas.

Institutionalization Refers to making organizational changes a permanent part of the organization's normal functioning.

Integrated strategic change A model of large-scale organization change that integrates principles of strategic management with processes of planned change. It involves strategic analysis, strategic choice, strategic change plan design, and strategic change plan implementation.

Integration The state of collaboration that exists among departments that are required by their environment to achieve unity of effort. The term is used primarily for contingency approaches to organizational design. (See *differentiation*.)

Interaction Almost any behavior resulting from interpersonal relationships. In human relations, it includes all forms of communication, verbal and nonverbal, conscious and unconscious.

Internal validity A research term concerned with assessing whether an intervention is responsible for producing observed results, such as improvements in job satisfaction, productivity, and absenteeism. (See *external validity*.)

Intervention Any action on the part of a change agent. Intervention carries the implication that the action is planned, deliberate, and presumably functional. Many people suggest that an OD intervention requires valid information, free choice, and a high degree of ownership of the course of action by the client system.

Jargon Overly specialized or technical language.

Job diagnostic survey (JDS) A questionnaire designed to measure job characteristics on such core dimensions as skill variety, task identity, task significance, autonomy, and feedback.

Job enrichment A way of making jobs more satisfying by increasing the skill variety, task identity, significance of the task, autonomy, and feedback from the work itself.

Knowledge management (KM) A process that focuses on how knowledge can be organized and used to improve organization performance. KM focuses on the tools and techniques that enable organizations to collect, organize, and translate information into useful knowledge. Organizationally, KM applications often are located in the information systems function and may be under the direction of a chief technology officer. (See *organization learning*.)

Lab A shorthand term for a wide variety of programs that derive from the laboratory method of training, or T-group, an approach that is primarily experiential.

Large-group interventions Any of several techniques, such as search conferences and open space, designed to work with a whole system, including organization members, suppliers, customers, and other stakeholders.

Leadership A process of influence exercised when institutional, political, psychological, and other resources are used to arouse, engage, and satisfy the motives of followers.

Management by objectives (MBO) A process of periodic manager–subordinate or group meetings designed to accomplish organizational goals by mutual planning of the work, review of accomplishments, and mutual solving of problems that arise in the course of getting the job done.

Management development Training or other processes to increase managers' knowledge and skills in order to improve performance in present jobs or prepare managers for promotion. Increasingly tied to career planning and development.

Matrix organization An approach to integrating the activities of different specialists while maintaining specialized organizational units.

Mechanistic organization Highly bureaucratic organization in which tasks are specialized and clearly defined. This is suitable when markets and technology are well established and show little change over time.

Merger The formal and legal integration of two or more organizations into a single entity. (See *acquisition*.)

Microcosm group A small, representative group selected from the organization at large to address important organizational issues. The key feature of the group is that it is a microcosm or representation of the issue itself.

Model A simplification of some phenomenon for purposes of study and understanding. The concrete embodiment of a theory. To behave in an idealized way so that

others might learn or change their behavior by identifying with and adopting the behaviors displayed.

Motivation The conditions responsible for variation in the intensity, quality, and direction of ongoing behavior.

Motivation-hygiene model Originally developed by Frederick Herzberg and associates, the model describes factors in the workplace that dissatisfy people and factors that motivate them.

Need A central concept in psychology, referring to a biological or psychological requirement for the maintenance and growth of the human animal. It is used among practitioners chiefly to refer to a psychological demand not met in organizational life, with the emphasis on the search for ways in which more such wants can be satisfied.

Need hierarchy A particular theory about the operation of human needs introduced by Abraham Maslow. The model of motivation describes a hierarchy of needs existing within people. The five need levels are physiological, safety, social, ego, and self-actualization. The theory says that higher needs cannot be activated until lower needs are relatively satisfied. This particular theory also was the basis for McGregor's Theory X–Theory Y formulation.

Network organization A newly emerging organization structure that involves managing an interrelated set of organizations, each specializing in a particular business function or task. This structure extends beyond the boundaries of any single organization and involves linking different organizations to facilitate interorganizational exchange and task coordination. (See *transorganizational development*.)

Norms Rules regulating behavior in any social system. They are usually unwritten and are more specific and pointed than are values in that deviations from norms are followed by such punishments as kidding, silent disapproval, or in the extreme, banishment.

Off-site Away from the regular place of work, as an off-site lab or conference.

Openness Accepting the communications and confrontations of others and expressing oneself honestly, with authenticity.

Open-space meeting See *large-group intervention*.

Open system This concept in systems theory is borrowed from the biological sciences. It refers to the nature and functions of transactions that take place between a system and its environment.

Open-systems planning A method for helping organizations or groups to assess their task environment systematically and develop a strategic response to it.

Organic organization This type of organization is relatively flexible and relaxed. The organic style is most appropriate to unstable environmental conditions in which novel problems continually occur. (See *mechanistic organization*.)

Organization design Involves bringing about a coherence or fit among organizational choices about strategy, organizing mode, and mechanisms for integrating people into the organization. The greater the fit among these organizational dimensions, the greater will be the organizational effectiveness.

Organization development (OD) A systemwide application of behavioral science knowledge to the planned development, improvement, and reinforcement of the strategies, structures, and processes that lead to organization effectiveness.

Organization development practitioner A generic term for people practicing organization development. These individuals may include managers responsible for developing their organizations or departments, people specializing in OD as a profession, and people specializing in a field currently being integrated with OD (e.g., strategy or human resources management) who have gained some familiarity with and competence in OD.

Organization effectiveness An overall term that refers to the outputs of organization strategy and design. Typically includes financial performance, such as profits and costs; stakeholder satisfaction, such as employee and customer satisfaction; and measures of internal productivity, such as cycle times.

Organization learning (OL) A change process that enhances an organization's capability to acquire and develop new knowledge. It is aimed at helping organizations use knowledge and information to change and improve continuously. It involves discovery, invention, production, and generalization. In organizations, OL change processes typically are associated with the human resources function and may be assigned to a special leadership role, such as chief learning officer. (See *knowledge management*.)

Organization transformation A process of altering radically the organization's strategic direction, including fundamental changes in structures, processes, and behaviors. (See *double-loop learning*.)

Parallel learning structure (See *collateral organization*.)

Participative A term describing techniques used by a power figure that aim to involve subordinate, lower-power people in the decision-making process of an organization (e.g., participative management). One aim is to increase the sense of commitment to organizational goals.

Performance appraisal A human resources system designed to provide feedback to an individual or group about its performance and its developmental opportunities. The performance appraisal process may or may not be closely linked to the reward system.

Performance management A constellation of processes involving goal setting, performance appraisal, and reward systems that guide, develop, reinforce, and control member behavior toward desired organizational outcomes.

Planned change A generic phrase for all systematic efforts to improve the functioning of some human system. It is a change process in which power is roughly equal between consultants and clients and in which goals are mutually and deliberately set.

Power The ability to influence others so that one's values are satisfied. It may derive from several sources, including organizational position, expertise, access to important resources, and ability to reward and punish others.

Presenting problem The most salient reason the client system has asked for help from a change agent. For example, a conflict between two people can be a presenting problem or a symptom that is caused by structural problems. The presenting problem is often a symptom of the true underlying problem that diagnosis is expected to uncover.

Problem-solving process A systematic, disciplined approach to identifying and solving work-related problems.

Process The way any system is going about doing whatever it is doing. Social process is the way people relate to one another as they perform some activity. Organizational process is the way different elements of the organization interact or how different organizational functions are handled.

Process-based organizations A type of organization structure that uses teams focused on the accomplishment of core work processes.

Process consultation A set of activities on the part of the consultant that helps the client perceive, understand, and act upon the process events that occur in the client's environment.

Process observation A method of helping a group improve its functioning, usually by having an individual watch the group in action and then feeding back the results. Interviews also may be used. The group (or individuals) then use the data to improve functioning.

Production group A work group that is separated (by a boundary) from other work groups so that they can operate with relative independence.

Profit An accounting term that measures total revenues minus total costs.

Quality circles Small groups of workers who meet voluntarily to identify and solve productivity problems. These typically are associated with Japanese methods of participative management.

Quality of work life (QWL) A way of thinking about people, work, and organization involving a concern for employee well-being and organizational effectiveness. It generally results in employee participation in important work-related problems and decisions.

Quality (outcome) Meeting and exceeding the needs of internal and external customers.

Quality (process) The continuing commitment by everyone in the organization to understand, meet, and exceed the needs of its customers.

Quasi-experimental research designs These designs enable OD evaluators to rule out many rival explanations for OD results other than the intervention itself. They involve choices about what to measure and when to measure it. They are most powerful when they include longitudinal measurement, a comparison unit, and statistical analysis.

Reengineering An intervention that focuses on dramatically redesigning core business processes. Successful reengineering often is closely related to changes in an organization's information systems.

Refreezing The stabilization of change at a new state of equilibrium.

Return on assets An accounting measure formed by the ratio of profits to total assets.

Reward power The present or potential ability to award something for worthy behavior. (See *power.*)

Rewards, extrinsic Rewards given by the organization, such as pay, promotion, praise, tenure, and status symbols.

Rewards, intrinsic Rewards that must originate and be felt within the person. Intrinsic rewards include feelings of accomplishment, achievement, and self-esteem.

Role A set of systematically interrelated and observable behaviors that belong to an identifiable job or position. Role behavior may be either required or discretionary.

Role ambiguity A result of inadequate information regarding role-related expectation and understanding. This occurs when the individual does not understand clearly all the expectations of a particular role.

Role conflict A result of a conflict between managerial or individual expectations and managerial or individual experiences with regard to performance of the role.

Search conference A one- to three-day meeting involving as many organizational stakeholders as possible to reflect on the past, appreciate the present, and envision the future. The search conference specifically avoids a problem-solving approach in an effort to energize the organization toward a new way of working. (See also *large-group interventions.*)

Selective perception The tendency to perceive only a part of a message, to screen out other information.

Self-awareness A positive goal of most training techniques that aim at behavior changes. Self-awareness means becoming mindful of one's existing patterns of behavior in a way that permits a relatively nondefensive comparison of those patterns with potential new ones.

Self-designing organizations A change program aimed at helping organizations gain the ability to change themselves fundamentally. It is a highly participative process, involving multiple stakeholders in setting strategic direction, designing appropriate structures and processes, and implementing them. This process helps organizations learn how to design and implement their own strategic changes.

Self-regulating work group A work group with a clearly defined series of tasks and a clear boundary so that the group can be generally responsible for its own output, quality, and work space.

Self-serving activities Activities that satisfy individual needs at the expense of the group.

Sensitivity training A method of helping people develop greater self-awareness and become more sensitive to their effect on others. Individuals learn by interaction with other members of their group. (See *T-group.*)

Single-loop learning Organizational behaviors directed at detecting and correcting deviations from valued states or goals. This is concerned with fine-tuning how an organization currently functions. (See *double-loop learning.*)

Skill training Training that is more concerned with improving effectiveness on the job than with abstract learning concepts.

Smoothing Dealing with conflict by denying or avoiding it.

Social construction of reality An approach concerned with the processes by which people, their values, and common-sense and scientific knowledge produce meaning and reality.

Sociotechnical system A term that refers to considering both the social system (human) and the technical system simultaneously in order to match the technology and the people involved optimally.

Stakeholder A person or group having a vested interest in the organization's functioning and objectives.

Strategic change An approach to bringing about an alignment or congruence among an organization's strategy, structure, and human resources systems, as well as a fit between them and the larger environment. It includes attention to the technical, political, and cultural aspects of organizations.

Strategy A plan of action defining how an organization will use its resources to gain a competitive advantage in the larger environment. It typically includes choices about the functions an organization will perform, the products or services it will provide, and the markets and populations it will serve.

Stress management Activities aimed at coping with the dysfunctional consequences of work-related stress. These generally include diagnosing the causes and symptoms of stress and taking action to alleviate the causes and to improve one's ability to deal with stress.

Structure The structure of a system is the arrangement of its parts. Also, jargon for a change strategy that focuses on the formal organization. This is a particularly important class of interventions when the target for change is an entire organization.

Subsystem A part of a system. A change in any subsystem has an effect on the total system.

Survey feedback A type of data-based intervention that flows from surveys of the members of a system on some subject and reports the results of the surveys to the client system for whatever action appears appropriate.

System A set of interdependent parts that form a whole; each contributes something and receives something from the whole, which in turn is interdependent with the larger environment.

T-groups A method of helping people develop greater self-awareness and become more sensitive to their effect on others. Individuals learn by interaction with other members of their group. (See *sensitivity training*.)

Task control The degree to which employees can regulate their own behavior to convert incoming materials into finished (or semifinished) products or other outputs.

Task force A group established to solve a particular problem (it may be disbanded when its work is accomplished).

Team building The process of helping a work group become more effective in accomplishing its tasks and in satisfying the needs of group members.

Technology Consists of the major techniques (together with their underlying assumptions about cause and effect) that an organization's employees use while engaging in organizational processes or that are programmed into the machines and other equipment.

Theory X A management theory under which managers typically believe that people dislike work and will avoid it whenever possible. Such managers feel that they themselves are a small, elite group of individuals who want to lead and take responsibility but that the larger mass of people want to be directed and to avoid responsibility.

Theory Y A management theory under which managers usually assume that workers will accept responsibility, provided they can satisfy personal needs and organizational goals at the same time.

Third-party intervention Activities aimed at helping two or more people within the same organization resolve interpersonal conflicts.

Total quality management (TQM) A comprehensive and large-scale intervention that focuses all organization systems on the continuous improvement of quality.

Transition state A condition that exists when the organization is moving from its current state to a desired future state. During the transition state, the organization learns how to implement the conditions needed to reach the desired future; it typically requires special structures and activities to manage this process.

Transorganizational development (TD) An intervention concerned with helping organizations join into partnerships with other organizations to perform tasks or solve problems that are too complex and multifaceted for single organizations to resolve. Includes the following cyclical stages: identification, convention, organization, and evaluation.

Trust level The degree of mutual trust among a set of people. Raising the trust level usually is a major goal of team building.

Unfreezing A reduction in the strength of old values, attitudes, or behaviors.

Value judgment Statement or belief based on or reflecting an individual's personal or class values.

Values Relatively permanent ideals (or ideas) that influence and shape the general nature of people's behavior.

Visioning A process typically initiated by key executives to define the mission of the organization and to clarify desired values for the organization, including valued outcomes and valued organizational conditions.

Work design The arrangement of tasks, people, and technology to produce both psychological outcomes and work performance.

Note: Some of the terms used in this glossary were taken or adapted from *Reference Book: Organizational Effectiveness* (Fort Leavenworth, Kan.: U.S. Army Command and General Staff College, 1979).

Name Index

Numbers following *n* or *nn* indicate note numbers.

Svieby, K., 534*n*94
Svyantek, D., 196*n*14
Szilagyi, A., 369*nn*7,9

T

Taco, 520
Takeuchi, H., 526, 534*nn*86,90
Tang, A.P., 311*n*41
Tannenbaum, Robert, 13, 19*n*41,
49, 64*n*9, 65*n*32
Tapscott, D., 310*n*18, 311*n*49
Tavistock Institute of Human
Relations, 10, 353, 564
Taylor, A., 497*n*61
Taylor, Frederick, 343–344,
369*nn*1,2
Taylor, J., 18*n*23, 129*n*7, 196*n*13
Taylor, Nancy, 624*n*1
Taylor, R., 411*n*66
Taylor, W., 342*n*64
Teece, D., 533*n*61
Telkom, 562
Teplitz, C., 309*n*7
Terborg, J., 196*n*19
Terpstra, D., 409*n*24
Texaco, 431
Texas Instruments, 13, 45, 170, 301,
313, 345, 421, 530
Thachankary, T., 20*n*54,
586*nn*55,63
Thacker, J., 64*n*14
Thomas, G., 42*n*27, 454*n*77
Thomas, J., 454*n*75
Thomas, K., 268*n*28
Thomas, R., Jr., 452*n*43
Thompson, J., 97*n*14
Thomson Learning, 98
Thornton, G., 451*nn*18,19
Thorsrud, E., 17*n*20
3M, 45, 288, 313, 383, 429, 474,
510, 616
Thurm, S., 197*n*27
Thurow, L., 451*n*15, 495*n*14,
584*n*4, 624*nn*2,5,6,9,12,
625*n*33
Thushman, M., 97*n*4
Tichy, N., 18*n*31, 41*n*8, 172*nn*4,12,
173*n*21, 267*nn*3,4, 371*n*51,
531*n*15, 533*nn*48,51
Tierney, T., 534*nn*101,102,103
Tiger, 93
Time-Life, 527
Timex, 398
Tipton, D., 497*n*48
Tjosvold, D., 267*n*13, 341*n*38

Toffler, A., 495*n*25, 624*n*2
Torbert, W., 18*n*34
Tosi, W., Jr., 388, 409*n*23
Toyota, 479, 562
Travelers Insurance Companies, 350
Treece, J., 452*n*39
Treybig, Jim, 510
Tribus, Myron, 598, 611*n*51
Trist, Eric, 10, 17*n*20, 97*nn*8,10,
268*n*34, 370*n*29, 496*n*33,
585*n*32, 586*n*54
Trompenaars, F., 584*n*12
TRW Systems, 13, 35, 170, 253,
344, 401, 405
Tsui, A., 531*n*5
Tubbs, M., 408*nn*6,17
Tucker, L., 267*n*7
Tucker, R., 267*n*7
Tuecke, P., 586*n*53
Tully, S., 310*nn*13,16, 408*n*8,
410*n*47
Tung, R., 586*n*49
Turner, A., 369*n*7
Tushman, M., 18*n*32, 89, 97*n*7,
309*n*1, 495*nn*24,26, 499,
501, 531*nn*3,4,8,9,13,14,16
Tustin, C., 410*n*60
Tyson Foods, 329

U

UAW (Union of Automotive
Workers), 10, 11, 320
UCLA (University of California, Los
Angeles), 35, 56, 216, 218
UCLA's Extension Service, 45
Ulrich, D., 309*n*9
Unilever, 564
Union Bank, 429
United Auto Workers (UAW), 10,
11, 320
United Technologies, 353, 395, 424
University Associates, 45, 56
University of California, Irvine, 35,
333
University of California, Los Angeles
(UCLA), 35, 56, 216, 218
University of California, Santa
Barbara, 35
University of Michigan, 56, 116,
182, 325
University of Southern California
(USC), 35, 116, 134, 182,
428
Urwick, L., 309*n*3
U.S. Army, 517

U.S. Department of Defense, 445
U.S. Post Office, 427
USA Today, 333
USAir, 295
USC (University of Southern
California), 35, 116, 134,
182, 428
Usdan, D., 611*n*62
Uttal, B., 532*nn*25,26,42,43,44

V

Vaill, Peter, 13, 19*n*46, 586*n*67
Van Buren, M., 624*n*16
Van Cott, H., 311*nn*37,40, 312*n*65
Van de Ven, A., 196*n*5
Van de Voorde, M., 497*nn*46,50,54
van Eijnatten, F., 371*n*45
Van Fleet, D., 339*n*2
Van Mannen, J., 129*n*6
Vandenberg, J., 451*n*13
Varney, G., 18*n*36, 64*n*8
VF Corporation, 335
Viacom, 98, 487
Vickery, D., 609*nn*5,6
Virany, B., 531*n*14
Vlasic, B., 497*n*61
Vogt, J., 18*n*25, 341*n*33
Volvo, 334, 362, 367, 487, 564, 567
Von Werssowetz, R., 197*n*27
Vroom, V., 172*n*14

W

Wade, J., 312*n*66
Wagel, W., 410*n*54
Wagner, J., 340*n*10
Wahba, M., 584*n*21
Waldersee, R., 410*n*40, 451*n*17,
531*n*13
Wall, T., 369*n*16, 371*n*60
Wallace, J., 140*n*8
Walleck, S., 172*n*6
Wallin, J., 410*n*39, 451*n*17
Wal-Mart Stores, 161, 307, 329, 526
Walter, I., 496*n*43
Walters, R., 369*n*8
Walton, E., 63*n*4
Walton, M., 18*n*26
Walton, R., 65*n*34, 228, 229,
243*nn*27,28,29, 341*n*47,
370*n*39, 371*nn*40,47,48,
411*n*69
Wanous, J., 451*nn*11,12
Warner, K., 453*n*51
Warrick, D., 65*n*34, 153*n*3

Subject Index

Page numbers followed by an *f* or *t* indicate a figure or table, respectively.